TUTORIALS IN MOTOR BEHAVIOR II

ADVANCES IN PSYCHOLOGY

87

Editors:

G. E. STELMACH

P. A. VROON

NORTH-HOLLAND
AMSTERDAM • LONDON • NEW YORK • TOKYO

TUTORIALS IN MOTOR BEHAVIOR II

Edited by

George E. STELMACH

Exercise and Sport Science Institute
Psychobiology Section, Arizona State University
Tempe, Arizona, USA

and

Jean REQUIN

Cognitive Neuroscience Unit
Laboratory of Functional Neuroscience, C.N.R.S.
Marseille, France

1992

NORTH-HOLLAND
AMSTERDAM • LONDON • NEW YORK • TOKYO

NORTH-HOLLAND
ELSEVIER SCIENCE PUBLISHERS B.V.
Sara Burgerhartstraat 25
P.O. Box 211, 1000 AE Amsterdam, The Netherlands

Distributors for the United States and Canada:
ELSEVIER SCIENCE PUBLISHING COMPANY, INC.
655 Avenue of the Americas
New York, N.Y. 10010, U.S.A.

ISBN: 0 444 88801 2

Printed in The Netherlands

PREFACE

Eleven years have passed since we edited "Tutorials in Motor Behavior." For more than ten years, this volume was the most widely-cited book in the field of human movement. Most scientists knew the book as Volume I in the Advances in Psychology Series. The Volume's appeal was vested in the reputation of the contributing authors, in the attempt to bring some unity to a widely scattered literature, and in the vast size (673 pages).

Since the late 1970s, much has changed in the motor control and learning area. Today, the alliance with Experimental Psychology has diminished and in its place is an emerging federation with Cognitive-Neuroscience. This shift in orientation has been driven by the quest to describe movements in their entirety, complete dynamic and kinematic accounts of how a movement is executed. Similarly, technological improvements in the field of neurophysiology have provided opportunities for scientists to examine the neural events that precede and accompany purposeful movement. These two incidents have led to new and changing tropes: Closed- and open-loop control notions have been replaced by distributed control theories, and mass springs by oscillators and memory representations by neural networks. Furthermore, the methods of analysis have also changed; for the most part, reaction time and movement time methods have been replaced by dynamic and kinematic analyses.

We are now editing "Tutorials in Motor Behavior II". As was stated in our 1980 Preface, this volume is intended as a legacy of current theory and data in the field. We stated then, and repeat now, "By recording these contributions at this time we hope to direct the course of motor control and learning research, and perhaps reveal to later generations of scientists some of the pitfalls that should be avoided." It is our expectation that this text will provide some conceptual unification to an expanding and diverse literature on motor control and learning.

The theme of this volume is Motor Control. The book is organized into 8 sections and the topics covered include anatomical and physiological constraints, neural networks, movement kinematics and dynamics, sensorimotor integration, and cognitive and motor impairments in order to provide a comprehensive view of the main issues.

To produce a book like this is an enormous effort; thus, we are grateful to many individuals for their assistance. First, we are appreciative to Mr. Kees Michielsen at North-Holland for providing us with the opportunity to once again publish such an advanced level reference text. We hope this volume is as successful as the earlier book. Second, we want to thank all the contributors for their excellent manuscripts. Third, a very special thank you is due to Lynnette Winkelman for her superb typing and editing skills. Her extensive experience in desktop publishing was a valuable resource. She assisted in every aspect of the book: author correspondence, chapter organization, and the subject and author indexes. Finally, we are grateful to Professor Marc Jeannerod who allowed George Stelmach during his stay at the Vision and Motricite lab in the Fall and Spring of 1991/92 to send and receive what must have seemed like endless packages, fax messages, and telephone calls.

George E. Stelmach and Jean Requin
Tempe, Arizona
November 20, 1991

TABLE OF CONTENTS

SECTION 1
MODELS AND THEORIES OF MOTOR CONTROL

SECTION 2
REPRESENTATION AND CONTROL OF MOVEMENT

SECTION 3
CONTROL AND COORDINATION OF REACHING MOVEMENTS

SECTION 4
STRUCTURE AND FUNCTION RELATIONSHIPS

SECTION 5
INTERSEGMENTAL DYNAMICS OF MOVEMENT

SECTION 6
BIOELECTRICAL AND BIOMECHANICAL CORRELATES OF MOVEMENT

SECTION 7
FEATURE CODING AND SELECTIVE ACTIVATION

SECTION 8
ANATOMICAL AND BEHAVIOR CONTRIBUTION TO MOVEMENT

LIST OF CONTRIBUTORS

G.C. AGARWAL - Department of Electrical Engineering and Computer Sciences, University of Illinois at Chicago, Chicago, IL 60680, USA

M. AKAMATSU - Industrial Product Research Institute, A.I.S.T., 1-1-4 Hagashi, Tsukuba, Ibaraki 305, Japan

J. ARMAND - Centre National de la Recherche Scientifique, Laboratoire de Neurobiologie, B.P. 71, 13402 Marseilles Cedex 09, France

C. BARD - Université Laval, Laboratoire de performance motrice humaine, PEPS, Ste-Foy, Québec, Canada, G1K 7P4

A.G. BARTO - Department of Computer and Information Science, University of Massachusetts, Amherst, Massachusetts 01003 USA

P.J. BEEK - Department of Psychology, Faculty of Human Movement Sciences, Amsterdam, The Netherlands and Center for the Ecological Study of Perception and Action, Department of Psychology, University of Connecticut, Storrs CT, USA

KEREE BENNETT - Department of Anatomy, Cambridge, Downing Street, Cambridge CB2 DY England

A. BERTHOZ - Laboratoire de Physiologie Neurosensorielle, CNRS, 15 rue de l'Ecole de Médecine, 75270 PARIS Cedex 06, France

J.R. BLOEDEL - Division of Neurobiology, Barrow Neurological Institute, 350 West Thomas Road, Phoenix, Arizona 85013 USA

LAWRENCE E. CARLSON - Departments of Kinesiology and Mechanical Engineering, University of Colorado at Boulder, Boulder, Colorado 80309. USA

UMBERTO CASTIELLO - Istituto di Fisiologia Umana, Universita de Parma, Ospedale Maggiore, Via Gramsci 43100, Parma, Italy

M.G.H. COLES - Cognitive Psychophysiology Laboratory, University of Illinois, 603 E. Daniel, Champaign, Illinois 61820, USA

DANIELA CORBETTA - Department of Psychology, Indiana University, Bloomington, IN 47405 USA

D.M. CORCOS - College of Kinesiology, University of Illinois at Chicago, Chicago, IL 60680, USA

F. DADOUCHI - Université Laval, Laboratoire de performance motrice humaine, PEPS, Ste-Foy, Québec, Canada, G1K 7P4

A. DASZUTA - Neurochemistry Unit, Laboratory of Functional Neuroscience - CNRS 31, chemin Joseph Aiguier - 13402 Marseille cedex 9, France

G.C. DeGUZMAN -Program in Complex Systems and Brain Sciences, Center for Complex Systems, Florida Atlantic University, Boca Raton, FL 33431 USA

V. DIETZ - Department of Clinical Neurology and Neurophysiology, University of Freiburg, Hansastr. 9, D-7800 Freiburg, F.R.G.

E. DONCHIN - Cognitive Psychophysiology Laboratory, University of Illinois, 603 E. Daniel, Champaign, Illinois 61820, USA

MICHEL DUFOSSE - Laboratoire de Neurosciences Fonctionnelles, C.N.R.S. 31, chemin Joseph Aiguier, 13402 Marseille Cedex 9, France

M. FABRE-THORPE - Institut des Neurosciences (C.N.R.S.-U.P.M.C.), Département de Neurophysiologie Comparée. 9, Quai Saint Bernard, 75230 Paris Cedex 5. France

ANATOL G. FELDMAN - Institut de génie biomédical, Université de Montréal and Institut de réadaptation de Montréal, Centre de recherche, 6300 Darlington Ave., Montréal, Québec, Canada, H3S 2J4

DIDIER FLAMENT - Department of Anatomy, Cambridge, Downing Street, Cambridge CB2 DY England

J. RANDALL FLANAGAN - Department of Psychology, McGill University, 1205 Dr. Penfield Ave., Montréal, Québec, Canada, H3A 1B1

M. FLEURY - Université Laval, Laboratoire de performance motrice humaine, PEPS, Ste-Foy, Québec, Canada, G1K 7P4

H.L. GALIANA - Department of Biomedical Engineering, McGill University, 3775 University Street, Montreal, Quebec, Canada H3A 2B4

W.J. GEHRING - Cognitive Psychophysiology Laboratory, University of Illinois, 603 E. Daniel, Champaign, Illinois 61820, USA

G.L. GOTTLIEB - Department of Physiology, Rush Medical College, 1753 W. Congress Parkway, Chicago, IL 60612, USA

R. GOTTSDANKER - Psychology Department, University of California, Santa Barbara, CA 93106, USA

G. GRATTON - Cognitive Psychophysiology Laboratory, University of Illinois, 603 E. Daniel, Champaign, Illinois 61820, USA

D. GUITTON - Department of Neurophysiology, Montreal Neurological Institute and McGill University, 3801 University Street, Montreal, Quebec, Canada H3A 2B4

EMMA HALL - Department of Anatomy, Cambridge, Downing Street, Cambridge CB2 DY England

T. HASBROUCQ - Cognitive Neuroscience Unit, C.N.R.S., 31 chemin Joseph Aiguier, 13402 Marseille Cedex 9, France

A. HAYASHI - Department of Neurology, Juntendo University School of Medicine, 2-1-1 Hongo, Bunkyo-ku, Tokyo, 113, Japan and Department of Neurology and Speech Motor Control Lab, Waisman Center, University of Wisconsin, Madison, Wisconsin, USA

CLAES VON HOFSTEN - Department of Psychology, Umeå University, S-90187 Umeå, Sweden

J.C. HOUK - Department of Physiology, Northwestern University Medical Center, 303 E. Chicago Avenue, Chicago, Illinois 60611, USA

C.J. HUNKER - Department of Neurology and Speech Motor Control Lab, Waisman Center, University of Wisconsin, Madison, Wisconsin, USA

I. ISRAEL - Laboratoire de Physiologie Neurosensorielle, CNRS, 15 rue de l'Ecole de Médecine, 75270 PARIS Cedex 06, France

MARC JEANNEROD - Vision et Motricité, INSERM U94, 16 avenue du Doyen Lépine, F-69500 Bron, France.

JODY JENSEN - Department of Psychology, Indiana University, Bloomington, IN 47405 USA

B. KABLY - Centre National de la Recherche Scientifique, Laboratoire de Neurobiologie, B.P. 71, 13402 Marseilles Cedex 09, France

KATHI KAMM - Department of Psychology, Indiana University, Bloomington, IN 47405 USA

J.A.S. KELSO - Program in Complex Systems and Brain Sciences, Center for Complex Systems, Florida Atlantic University, P.O. Box 3091, Boca Raton, FL 33431 USA

L. KERKERIAN-Le GOFF - Neurochemistry Unit, Laboratory of Functional Neuroscience - CNRS 31, chemin Joseph Aiguier - 13402 Marseille cedex 9, France

R.A. KONOPACKI - Speech Motor Control Lab, Waisman Center, University of Wisconsin, Madison, Wisconsin, USA

SYLVAN KORNBLUM - Mental Health Research Institute, 205 Zina Pitcher Place, The University of Michigan, Ann Arbor, MI 48109-0720, USA

F. LACQUANITI - Istituto di Fisiologia dei Centri Nervosi, Consiglio Nazionale delle Ricerche, Via Mario Bianco 9, 20131 Milano, Italy

J. LARUE - Université Laval, Laboratoire de performance motrice humaine, PEPS, Ste-Foy, Québec, Canada, G1K 7P4

ROGER LEMON - Department of Anatomy, Cambridge, Downing Street, Cambridge CB2 DY England

WILLIAM A. MACKAY - Department of Physiology, University of Toronto, Toronto M5S 1A8, Canada

CHRISTINE L. MACKENZIE - School of Kinesiology, Simon Fraser University, Burnaby, British Columbia, Canada, V5A 1S6

C. MAIOLI - Istituto di Fisiologia dei Centri Nervosi, Consiglio Nazionale delle Ricerche, Via Mario Bianco 9, 20131 Milano, Italy

RONALD G. MARTENIUK - Department of Kinesiology, University of Waterloo, Waterloo, Ontario, Canada, N2L 3G1

OLIVIER MARTIN - Laboratoire RESACT UFR-APS Equipe Comportement Moteur Université Joseph Fourier BP 53X F-38041 Grenoble Cedex, France

JEAN MASSION - Laboratoire de Neurosciences Fonctionnelles, C.N.R.S. 31, chemin Joseph Aiguier, 13402 Marseille Cedex 9, France

P.V. MCDONALD -Department of Kinesiology, University of Illinois at Urbana-Champaign, 906 S. Goodwin Ave., Urbana, IL, 61801, USA

P.A. MCKINLEY - School of Physical and Occupational Therapy, McGill University, 3654 Rue Drummond, Montreal, Canada H3G 1Y5

PIETRO MORASSO - Department of Computer Science, University of Genoa, Via Opera Pia 11A, I-16145 Genoa, Italy

I. MOURET - Cognitive Neuroscience Unit, C.N.R.S., 31 chemin Joseph Aiguier, 13402 Marseille Cedex 9, France

F. MULLER - University Hospital Tübigen, Department of Neurology, Hoppe-Seyler-Str. 3, D7400 Tübingen, Germany

K.G. MUNHALL - Department of Psychology, Queen's University, Kingston, Canada

K. M. NEWELL - Department of Kinesiology, University of Illinois at Urbana-Champaign, 906 S. Goodwin Ave., Urbana, IL, 61801, USA

A. NIEOULLON - Neurochemistry Unit, Laboratory of Functional Neuroscience - CNRS 31, chemin Joseph Aiguier - 13402 Marseille cedex 9, France

DAVID J. OSTRY - Department of Psychology, McGill University, 1205 Dr. Penfield Ave., Montréal, Québec, Canada, H3A 1B1

C.E. PEPER - Department of Psychology, Faculty of Human Movement Sciences, Amsterdam, The Netherlands

R. PLAMONDON - Laboratoire Scribens, Département de Génie Électrique et Génie Informatique, École Polytechnique de Montréal, C.P. 6079, Succursale A, Montréal QC, H3C 3A7 Canada

CLAUDE PRABLANC - Vision et Motricité INSERM Unité 94 16 avenue du doyen Lépine F-69500 Bron, France

ROBERT W. PROCTOR - Psychology Department, Purdue University, 1364 Psychology Building, Room 3150, West Lafayette, IN 47907-1364 USA

T. GILMOUR REEVE - Motor Behavior Center, Auburn University, Auburn, AL 36849-5323, USA

JEAN REQUIN - Cognitive Neuroscience Unit, C.N.R.S. 31 Chemin Joseph Aiguier, 13402 Marseille cedex 9, France

ALEXA RIEHLE - Unité de Neurosciences Cognitives, C.N.R.S.-LNF1, 31 ch. Joseph-Aiguier, 13402 Marseille Cédex 9, France

A. ROUCOUX - Laboratoire de Neurophysiologie, University of Louvain, B-1200 Brussels, Belgium

VITTORIO SANGUINETI - Department of Computer Science, University of Genoa, Via Opera Pia 11A, I-16145 Genoa, Italy

G.J.P. SAVELSBERGH - Faculty of Human Movement Sciences, Free University, Amsterdam, Netherlands and Department of Psychology, University of York, York, England

R.A. SCHMIDT - Department of Psychology, University of California, Los Angeles, Los Angeles, CA 90024, USA

KLAUS SCHNEIDER - Department of Kinesiology, UCLA, Los Angeles, CA 90024-1568 USA

J. SEAL - Cognitive Neuroscience Unit, C.N.R.S., 31 chemin Joseph Aiguier, 13402 Marseille Cedex 9, France

A. SEMJEN - Unité de Neurosciences Cognitives, C.N.R.S., 31, chemin J. Aiguier, 13402 Marseille Cedex 9, France

L. HENRY SHAFFER - Department of Psychology, University of Exeter, Exeter, Devon, EX4 4QG, UK

GEORGE E. STELMACH - Exercise and Sport Research Institute, Department of Exercise Science and Physical Education and Psychology, Arizona State University, Tempe, Arizona 85287-0404 USA

NATALE STUCCHI - Department of Psychobiology, Faculty of Psychology and Educational Sciences, University of Geneva, 24 rue du Général Dufour CH-1211 Geneva, Switzerland

STEPHAN P. SWINNEN - Motor Control Laboratory, Dept. of Kinantropology, Group Biomedical Sciences, Catholic University of Leuven, Tervuurse Vest 101, 3001 Heverlee, Belgium

N. TEASDALE - Université Laval, Laboratoire de performance motrice humaine, PEPS, Ste-Foy, Québec, Canada, G1K 7P4

HANS-LEO TEULINGS - Nijmegen Institute for Cognition and Information (NICI), P.O. Box 9104, NL 6500 HE Nijmegen, The Netherlands

ESTHER THELEN - Department of Psychology, Indiana University, Bloomington, IN 47405 USA

ARNOLD J.W.M. THOMASSEN - Nijmegen Institute for Cognition Research and Information Technology (NICI), University of Nijmegen, P.O. Box 9104, 6500 HE Nijmegen, The Netherlands

S.I. HELMS TILLERY - Division of Neurobiology, Barrow Neurological Institute, 350 West Thomas Road, Phoenix, Arizona 85013 USA

PAOLO VIVIANI - Department of Psychobiology, Faculty of Psychology and Educational Sciences, University of Geneva, 24 rue du Général Dufour CH-1211 Geneva, Switzerland

STEPHEN A. WALLACE - Departments of Kinesiology and Mechanical Engineering, University of Colorado at Boulder, Boulder, Colorado 80309. USA

H.T.A. WHITING - Department of Psychology, University of York, Heslington, York YO1 5DD England

P.C.W. VAN WIERINGEN - Department of Psychology, Faculty of Human Movement Sciences, Amsterdam, The Netherlands

CHARLES J. WORRINGHAM - Department of Movement Science, The University of Michigan, 401 Washtenaw Avenue, Ann Arbor, MI 48109-2214, USA

D.E. YOUNG - Department of Physical Education, California State University, Long Beach, Long Beach, CA 90840, USA

TRISHA VAN ZANDT - Psychology Department, Purdue University, 1364 Psychology Building, Room 3150, West Lafayette, IN 47907-1364 USA

P.G. ZANONE - Program in Complex Systems and Brain Sciences, Center for Complex Systems, Florida Atlantic University, P.O. Box 3091, Boca Raton, FL 33431 USA

RONALD ZERNICKE - Department of Kinesiology, UCLA, Los Angeles, CA 90024-1568 USA

SECTION 1

MODELS AND THEORIES OF MOTOR CONTROL

Tutorials in Motor Behavior II
G.E. Stelmach and J. Requin (Editors)

Neural Models of Distributed Motor Control

Pietro Morasso and Vittorio Sanguineti

Department of Computer Science, University of Genoa,
Via Opera Pia 11A, I-16145 Genoa, Italy

Abstract

The basic idea of distributed processing is that any given function is performed by a large ensemble of processing elements and, at the same time, any processing element contributes to many different functions. In general, this has the advantage of robustness, because no processing element is crucial, although a distributed system is more difficult to study experimentally and to understand. In the case of motor control, distributed architectures can represent efficiently and flexibly constraints and mappings that characterize the co-ordination of multiple degrees of freedom, i.e. synergy formation. This paper reviews some of the trends in the field by comparing a few types of neural models which are representative of many of the relevant issues.

1. INTRODUCTION

There is no doubt that the traditional computer metaphor is increasingly being challenged in the research communities of artificial intelligence, cognitive science, and neurosciences and a conceptual framework is slowly emerging that re-evaluates the good old-fashioned cybernetic emphasis on analogic computation: parallelism, distributed representations, elimination of the software/hardware dualism, systems dynamics and adaptive control (learning), etc.

In the motor control area, in particular, this conceptual shift is a good motivation to re-evaluate the role of biomechanical constraints that can be seen as allies, not enemies, of the motor controller, a sort of mechanical analogic machinery to be exploited by a related neural analogic machinery in the brain. At the same time, the return to analogic computation is pushing backward the perceived influence domain of the symbolic approach, contrasting the tendency of AI advocates to express everything in terms of rules and symbolic problem-solving.

The purpose of this paper is to review some of the trends, with particular attention to the problem of co-ordination of multiple degrees of freedom, i.e. *synergy formation*. Several types of neural models are reviewed, without any claim of completeness as regards both the set of models and the brief account of each of them: (the only purpose is indeed to outline a few elements of convergence/divergence among different modelling approaches.)

- Multi-layer network models, including recurrent networks (Jordan, 1988, 1989a, 1989b);
- Networks based on optimization principles, with particular regard to the cascaded neural model with minimum torque change criterion (Kawato et al., 1990);
- Models of central pattern generators, i.e. the VITE model (Bullock and Grossberg, 1988, 1989), the adaptive sensorimotor network (Houk et al., 1990), and the M-Net model (Morasso et al., 1989, 1990, Morasso, 1990);
- Models of visuo-motor integration, i.e. INFANT (Kuperstein and Rubinstein, 1989), Darwin III (Reeke and Edelman, 1989), and a model of the visuo-motor transformations in the cerebral cortex (Burnod et al., 1990).

Before sketching the rationale of the different approaches and attempting a first-order comparative criticism, let us summarize a background topic, that is relevant for multi-joint, redundant motor control: the variety of motor spaces.

2. MOTOR SPACES

If we consider motor control problems that involve a large number of degrees of freedom, we must realize that different motor patterns co-vary in distinct descriptive frameworks, that we may call *motor spaces*: Muscle space, Joint space, and Task space. In each space, we can single out two main types of representation: patterns of *generalized motions* and patterns of *generalized forces* (figure 1). For example, generalized motions are angular rotation patterns in the joint space and muscular shortening/lengthening patterns in the muscles space; the task patterns, on the other hand, depend on the choice of an *end-effector* and the specification of its motion in 3D-6D space.

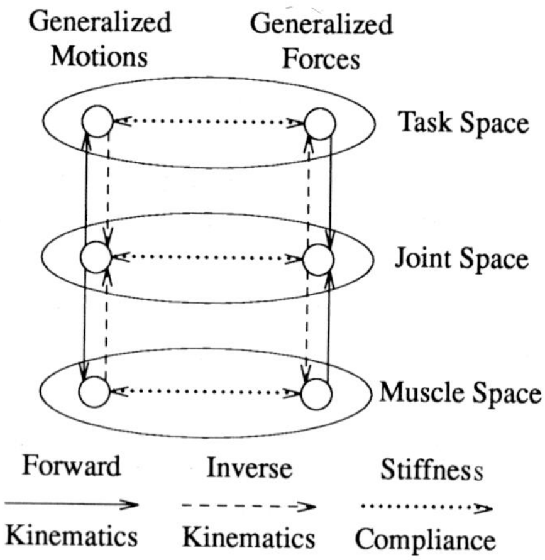

Figure 1. Motor Spaces. Continuous lines: forward kinematic mappings; dashed lines: inverse kinematic mappings; dotted lines: stiffness/compliance.

These patterns must satisfy kinematic constraints that correspond to the musculo-skeletal structure of the body and that determine well-posed mappings (forward kinematics) as well as ill-posed mappings (inverse kinematics). The latter, in particular, are due to the *redundancy* of the motor system, as regards task vs joints and joints vs muscles. Moreover, it is important to understand that if the controller focuses on motion representations it loses control of forces and vice versa. Keeping the middle way, between motion and force representations, means to focus on the stiffness/compliance of muscles that cross-connect the two kinds of representations.

Direct and inverse kinematic mappings are important modules for the theoretical study of motor controller architectures and in the following sections we shall examine some significant examples of neural models. However, it is important to realize that the same mappings are actually implemented by the musculo-skeletal system as real analogic computations: during active movements, input patterns in the muscle space are transformed into output patterns in the task space and during passive movements the opposite mappings are actually computed, in vivo. In other words, the musculo-skeletal system can be viewed by itself as a *kinematic computational engine* and we shall see in the following that this concept has been exploited by the M-Net model.

In summary, the consideration of motor spaces brings to our attention the fact that the motor controller must possess a *kinematic competence* (the ability to relate different motor spaces) as well as a *muscular competence* (the ability to relate position and force). To this we must add a *timing competence*, i.e. the capacity to constrain the motor mappings in the same time framework.

3. MULTI-LAYER NETWORK MODELS

Multi-layer networks (MLN's) are general purpose distributed architectures that can represent and learn complex mappings between input/output patterns. Let us summarize their equations (figure 2):

- Each layer L_i is an array of units and it has an input vector $\mathbf{I}_i$, an output vector $\mathbf{O}_i$, and a bias vector $\mathbf{B}_i$.
- There is no connection among units of the same layer and the input-output transformation is a smooth sigmoidal non-linear function, applied separately to all vector components: $\mathbf{O}_i = f\,(\mathbf{I}_i + \mathbf{B}_i)$.
- The transformation from the output vector $\mathbf{O}_i$ of one layer to the input vector of the next layer $\mathbf{I}_{i+1}$ is a linear combination with the weight matrix $\mathbf{W}_i$: $\mathbf{I}_{i+1} = \mathbf{W}_i\ \mathbf{O}_i$
- For a given topology and a given set of weight matrices and bias vectors, a MLN implements an input-output mapping that is obtained by means of a forward propagation of an input pattern, through the intermediate (hidden) layers, to an output pattern: $\mathbf{O} = MLN\,(\mathbf{I})$.

A MLN can be trained by a supervisor on the basis of a teaching set $((\mathbf{I}^*, \mathbf{O}^*), * = a, b, ...)$ and a learning technique, known as back propagation (LeCun, 1985, Rumelhart et al., 1986), that consists of three logical steps, repeated a large number of times:

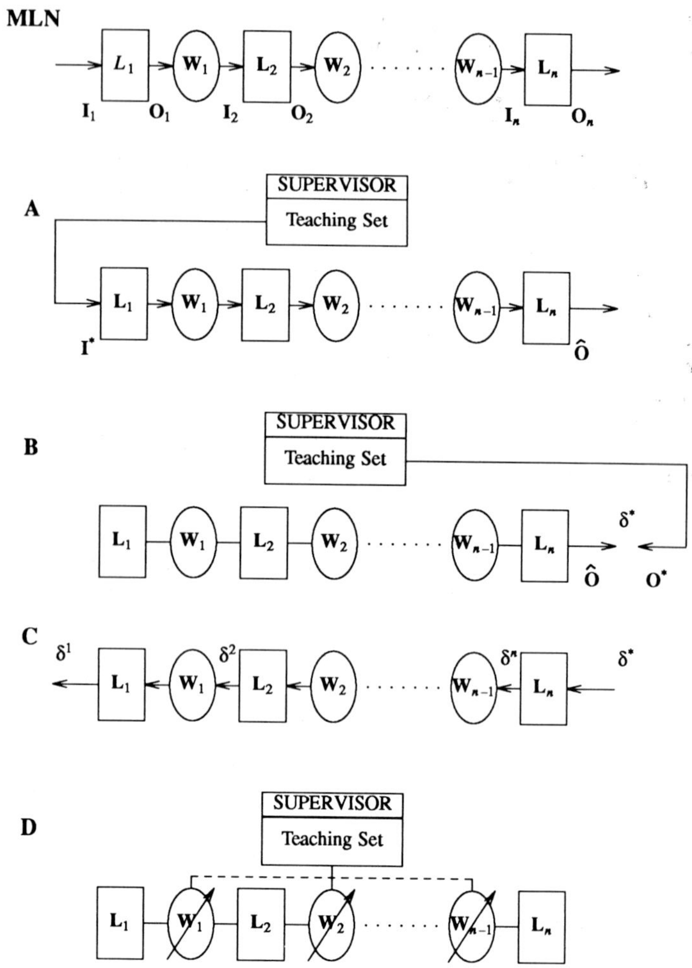

Figure 2. Multi-Layer Network (MLN). A: Forward propagation of teaching input. B: Computation of output error. C: Back-propagation of output error. D: Learning (adaptation of weights). $L_1, L_2, ..., L_n$ are the subsequent layers of units and $W_1, W_2, ..., W_{n-1}$ are the corresponding inter-layer connection weights.

[1] Forward propagation of the input pattern $\mathbf{I}^*$ into an output pattern $\hat{\mathbf{O}}$.

[2] Computation of the output error vector $\delta^* = \mathbf{O}^* - \hat{\mathbf{O}}$ and back propagation of the error to the input of the different layers:
$(\delta^* \rightarrow \delta_n^* \rightarrow \delta_{n-1}^* \;.... \rightarrow \delta_1^*)$.

[3] Adaptation of the weights via gradient descent, with the purpose of minimizing the output error; this can be carried out with a local computation that only requires the output vector from the previous layer and the error vector at the current layer.

If the input/output mapping is sufficiently "regular", the trained network will show "generalization" capabilities, i.e. it will be able to interpolate among the associations of the teaching set. Moreover, if the network is learning a one-to-many mapping, we can induce it to learn other constraints in addition to the requirement of reproducing as well as possible the associations of the training set: it is sufficient to add a term $\gamma\,\mathbf{C}$ to the output error vector δ^*, where $\mathbf{C}$ is the additional criterion, somehow linked to the input and the state of the network. γ is a scalar coefficient that is decreased smoothly to zero during the training and, at the completion of the learning phase, the network will be able to choose an output pattern that satisfies the input/output mapping while attempting to maximize the prescribed criterion.

3.1 MLN's for inverse kinematics

MLN's have been used for learning direct/inverse mappings between motor spaces. For example, learning direct kinematics is a rather straightforward application where the teaching input is a set of angular patterns and the teaching outputs are the corresponding position/orientation vectors of the end-effector. More interesting is learning an inverse mapping in the case of motor redundancy, because infinite output vectors can be associated with the same input pattern (Eckmiller, 1990). In this case, indeed, the supervisor has the big problem of providing a consistent training set. A technique which has been proposed (Jordan, 1988, 1989, Nguyen and Widrow, 1990) is to use a forward model as a *distant teacher* (figure 3). This technique uses the combination of two MLN's, a direct model (DK) and an inverse model (IK):

- DK is initially trained in order to learn the direct kinematic mapping from joint angular rotations Θ to end-effector motions $\mathbf{X}$.
- IK is then linked with DK, with the purpose of learning the global chain of transformations from desired end-effector motion $\hat{\mathbf{X}}$ to Θ and then to the predicted end-effector motion $\mathbf{X}$.

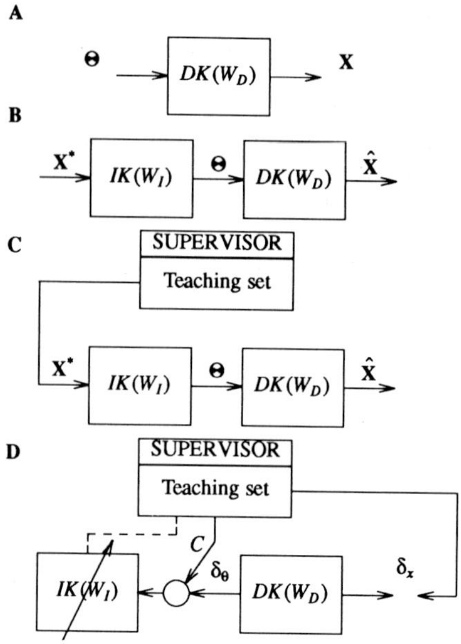

Figure 3. Learning Inverse Kinematics via a Forward Model. A: Trained Direct Kinematics MLN (DK, with weight matrix W_D). B: Linking DK with IK (Inverse Kinematics MLN with weight matrix W_I). C: Forward propagation of the desired motion ($\hat{\mathbf{X}}$: desired end-point motion, **X**: predicted end-point motion, Θ: joint motion). D: Back-propagation of the output error, formation of the composite error and learning (δ_x: end-point error, δ_θ: joint error, C: optimization criterion).

The teaching of IK is performed as follows:

[1] $\hat{\mathbf{X}}$ is propagated through the entire network and the output error $\hat{\mathbf{X}}$–**X** vector is computed.

[2] This vector is back-propagated through DK without changing the weights, with the only purpose of estimating the error vector at the joints, (the error at the output layer of the IK) which is then combined with an additional criterion, as mentioned above, yielding a composite error.

[3] The composite error is back-propagated through IK with adaptation of weights.

After training, the network can perform inverse kinematics in an optimal way, i.e. it is able to co-ordinate patterns of joint rotations that match the desired end-point positions and, at the same time, minimize a desired criterion such as smoothness.

3.2 Recurrent MLN's

Standard MLN's can learn non-linear and ill-posed mappings but are unable to generate time varying motor patterns, for example a trajectory as a response to a target stimulus. However, it is possible to overcome this limitation by means of recurrent MLN's, originally proposed by Jordan (1988, 1989). In the simplest case (shown in figure 4) the input layer, which is meant to represent the plan or target of the movement (*plan units*), is extended with another set of units (*state units*) that are fed recurrently from the output layer. For example, Massone & Bizzi (1989) implemented a recurrent MLN that can generate patterns of muscle activity for the arm muscles during reaching movements. The teaching set, in this case, consisted of a set of associated pairs: an input stimulus in a 2D domain and the corresponding complete trajectory.

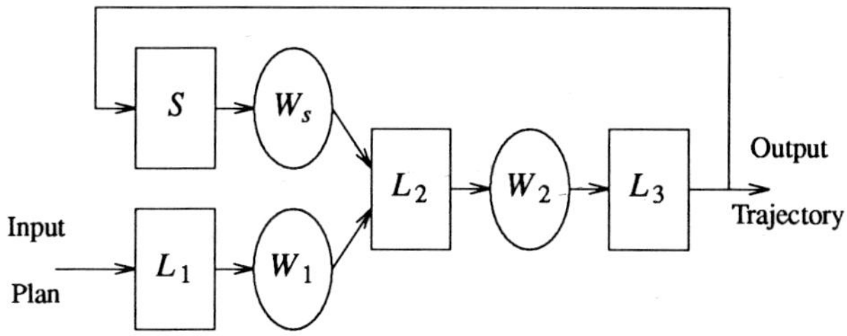

Figure 4. Recurrent multi-layer network. The network consists of a layer of input units (L_1), hidden units (L_2), output units (L_3), and state units (S).

3.3 Pros and Cons of MLN's

MLN's have been very successful because they are simple mechanisms for representing a wide variety of categorization/association problems, independently of the application domain. However, the price of this generality is that the knowledge that MLN's are able to encapsulate is totally dependent on the teaching set and therefore their generalization capability is intra-task but not inter-task. For example, direct and inverse kinematic mappings between task space and joint space are task-dependent, in the sense that the selection of the end-point is arbitrary and the kinematic mapping learned with one configuration is not easily generalizable to a different one. Therefore, the motor planner would need a very large number of MLN's and teach all of them separately. As regards timing structure, recurrent MLN's are very good at learning them. The point, however, is that they are too good because, again, the learned structure is totally embedded in the training data.

Summing up, although MLN's are not credible models for representing the mappings between motor spaces, they are still good candidates at a more abstract level, for representing the general motor ability of learning specific motor skills in a very focused way.

4. NETWORKS BASED ON OPTIMIZATION PRINCIPLES

A significant part of research in neural networks is devoted to the issue of optimization, i.e. to the configuration of networks that are capable to find optimal values of some decision variable. In motor control, the choice of a suitable criterion of optimality is an open question as well as the identification of the implementation mechanisms that are suitable for translating optimization into synergy formation. Among the different studies, we discuss a model developed by Kawato and coworkers (Kawato et al., 1990) that specifically addresses the implementation issue.

4.1 Cascaded Neural Networks with Minimum Torque Change Criterion

A cascaded neural network with minimum torque change criterion (CN-MT) is a composite network architecture (Kawato et al., 1990) that combines the paradigm of association (a set of MLN's for representing direct kinematics/dynamics) with the paradigm of relaxation, for representing motor optimization. This network is the result of three main motivations:

- A global view of ill-posed motor problems that implies the requirement for the neural network architecture to represent all of them at the same time.
- An integrated approach to motor spaces, i.e. the concept of designing an architecture in which it is possible to combine goal specifications in task space (target point, via points, obstacles) with movement optimization in muscle/joint space.
- The identification of the minimum torque-change criterion (Uno et al., 1989) as a global *smoothness constraint* that can reproduce the bell-shaped profiles of arm trajectories (Morasso, 1981) and better fits experimental data than purely kinematic criteria like the minimum jerk model (Flash and Hogan, 1985) or the 2/3 power law (Viviani and Terzuolo, 1982).

The function that the network is supposed to fulfill can be described as follows:

[1] For a pre-defined duration T_f of the movement, an outside planner provides, as input to the network, the target (i.e. the end-point position to be reached at the final time) as well as intermediate via points and obstacles, if necessary.

[2] A pattern of torques is produced (for all the joints and the total time span) that is compatible with the task-constraints and, at the same time, minimizes the integral of the squared torque derivatives, computed for the total movement duration and summed over all the joints.

In order to implement the stated function, the model needs to be unfolded in time, i.e. it is necessary to setup a *spatial representation of time* where system variables and system transformations are replicated for each time instant. The inner skeleton of the network (figure 5, top) is a cascaded network where FD and FK are two MLN's that were previously trained to implement forward dynamic and forward kinematic transformations, respectively. FD, in particular, receives in input the current torque vector and the current state vector (joint angles and joint rotation speeds) and produces in output the next state vector which is the input both to FK, for predicting the end-point movement, and to another copy of FD, in order to propagate the computation to the next time step.

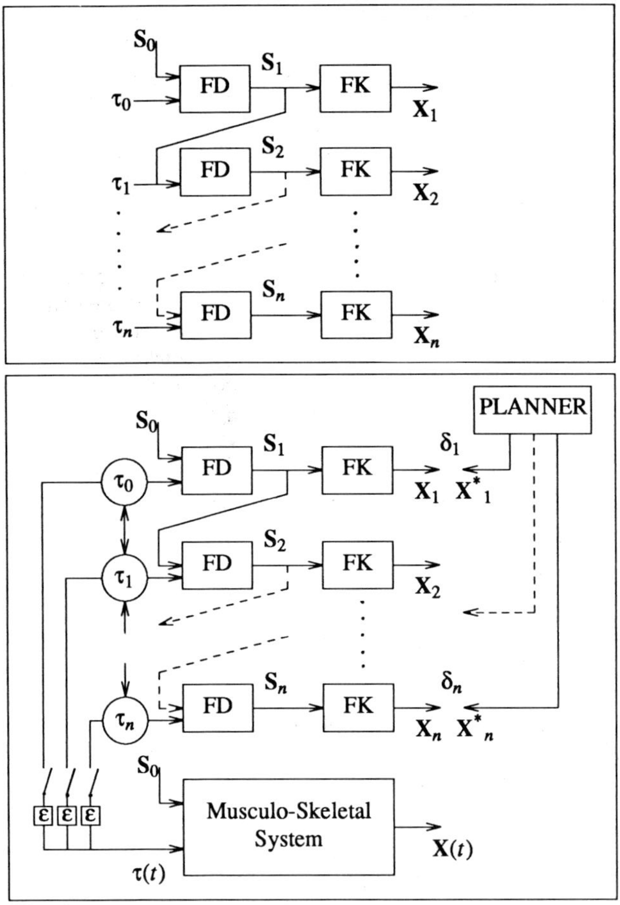

Figure 5. Cascaded neural network with minimum torque-change criterion. Top box: Structure of the network (FD: forward dynamics MLN; FK: forward kinematics MLN; τ_i: joint torque vector at time-step i; $\mathbf{S}_i$: state vector; $\mathbf{X}_i$: position of the end-effector). Bottom box: torque optimization via relaxation of the torque pattern (ε: delay elements).

All together, the network maps the global spatio-temporal torque pattern into the predicted trajectory of the end-effector. In actual operation, when the spatio-temporal torque pattern must be produced, the torque signals are generated by a relaxation network which has one unit for each element of the torque vector (figure 5, bottom). The torque units are cross-connected by means of symmetric synapses of constant weight that link each unit (identified by a joint and a time instant) with the two units that correspond to the same joint, one time step before and one step after. These cross-connections induce a relaxation dynamics, (Little and Shaw, 1975, Hopfield, 1982, Cohen and Grossberg, 1983, Hopfield, 1984), that automatically seeks maximally smooth patterns.

The optimal torque patterns are constrained by the task errors that are back propagated through the recurrent MLN's, similarly to the technique described in the previous section for the forward model technique. In other words, the errors detected at some of the units of the output layer are back propagated in order to estimate the corresponding torque input errors and these errors, in turn, are spread throughout the torque units via relaxation. The resulting torque variations are then propagated forward for updating the samples of the end-point trajectory and the three processes (forward and back propagation as well as relaxation) proceed until an equilibrium configuration is reached: in that situation, the whole torque pattern, localized on the torque units, can be transmitted through a delay line to the motor system that carries out the actual movement.

4.1.1 Pros and Cons of CN-MT. This model was applied to two-joint systems and was able to reproduce bell shaped velocity profiles as well as small but significant anomalies of trajectory formation in reaching, such as the slight deviations from straightness of the trajectories and the small asymmetries of the velocity profile that have been reported by several authors. The model has *temporal competence*, in the sense that the temporal structure is not exogenous (implicit in the training set) but is an emergent property of network dynamics, and it also has a *kinematic competence*, i.e. an explicit knowledge of the link among motor spaces.

However, the units of action that it can manage (whole movement patterns) are too big and there is no easy way to break them up into smaller chunks. This is a consequence, we believe, of two key points: the choice of the smoothness criterion and the lack of a *muscular competence*, i.e. the fact that the actuators are represented as pure torque generators, without considering the mechanical properties of muscles. As regards the former point, we wish to make the following observation: the fact that the minimum torque-change is a good predictor of actual movement smoothness does not necessarily imply that the motor planner/controller uses internally the same criterion because the global external smoothness is a complex function of the internal smoothness and the interaction of the motor system with the mechanical context. In particular, the motor controller might use a local smoothness criterion and this would not require an unfolding in time of the network.

As regards the lack of muscular competence, it means that the motor controller ignores the structural linkage between position & force, intrinsic in the motor spaces; the consequence is that an explicit model of limb dynamics is required. This is not a heavy computational burden for simple kinematic structures, but we are afraid that scaling up kinematic complexity can be seriously damaging.

Nevertheless, CN-MT pioneers two basic concepts that we deem very fruitful: the integration of different motor spaces in motor planning/programming and the attempt to build a composite neural architecture, i.e. a network of networks.

5. CENTRAL PATTERN GENERATORS

Some modelling approaches are focussed on the pattern generation function of the central nervous system. We discuss three models: the VITE model (Bullock and Grossberg, 1988, 1989), the cerebellar-like adaptive sensorimotor network (Houk et al., 1990), and the M-Net model (Morasso et al., 1989, 1990, Morasso, 1990).

5.1 VITE Model

The VITE model (Vector Integration To Endpoint) is motivated by its proponents (Bullock and Grossberg, 1988, 1989) on the basis of the concept that during the development of skills there appears to be a gradual strategic shift from low-compliance/low-speed to high-compliance/high-speed. Therefore, it is important that the neuro-motor system is capable to factor out trajectory and speed, on one hand, and posture and stiffness, on the other. We shall focus on the former factorization because it is closer to the topic of this article.

The basic idea, around which the model is built, is to use a multiplicative gating signal that controls the rate of change of all the elements of the motor array and is instrumental for factoring out trajectory and speed. Figure 6 shows a schematic diagram of the network:

- The input to the network is the Target Position Command (TPC), which is a representation of the target in muscle space (an array of desired muscle lengths). TPC, that might be located in the posterior parietal cortex, is produced hypothetically by an associative mapping from an input stimulus.
- The TPC vector is compared with the PPC vector (Present Position Command, a motor cortex representation that corresponds to the array of current muscle lengths); the difference is time-averaged through a bank of leaky integrators, producing the difference vector DV, in the pre-central motor cortex.
- The components of DV are gated by a common multiplicative GO signal (a scalar supposed to originate in the globus pallidus) and finally are processed by a bank of integrators that update the PPC.

Let us now consider the operation of the network. If we start with a given PPC and suddenly apply a new TPC, nothing happens as long as the GO signal is shut off. When this signal is activated with some kind of monotonically increasing profile, then the different components of the PPC vector start evolving toward their target values and eventually reach them, all at the same time. Simulation studies have shown that the exact shape of the profile is not critical and the behaviour of all the PPC components is generally characterized by a bell-shaped velocity. Moreover, modulation of the GO-profile with a gain coefficient is a direct method to affect the movement time; the velocity profile is slightly influenced, in a way which is compatible with the behavioral data.

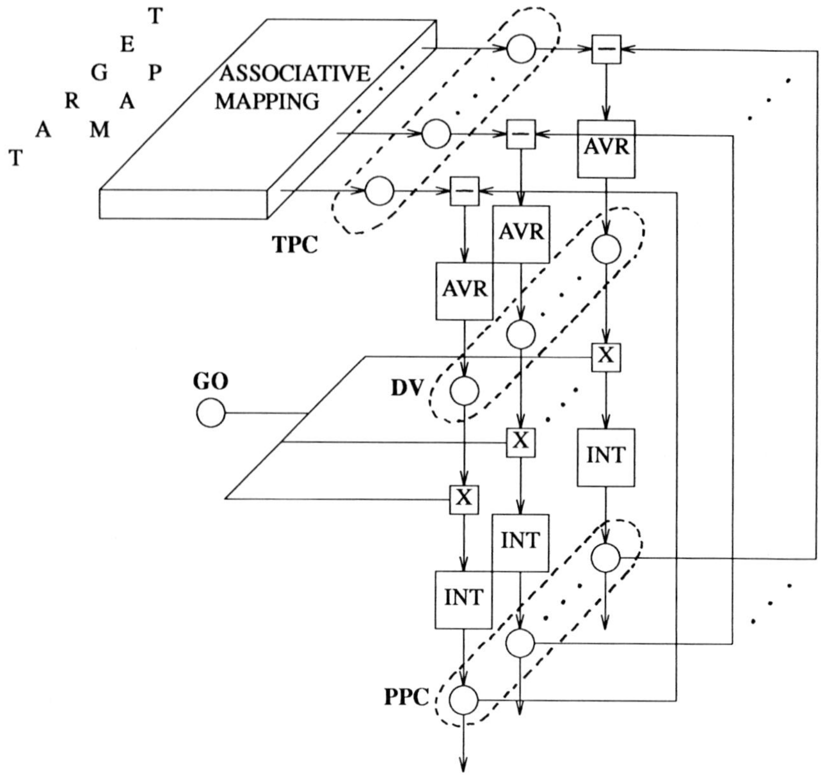

Figure 6. VITE model. An associative mapping transforms a target map into the TPC (Target Position Command) which is compared with PPC (Present Position Command) and the time averaged difference (AVR: bank of leaky integrators) produces DV (Difference Vector). This is gated by GO and integrated over time (INT: bank of integrators), thereby updating the PPC.

5.1.1 Pros and Cons of VITE. VITE has a *temporal competence* as well as the Kawato model does, but perhaps in a deeper sense. The idea of bringing a very large number of degrees of freedom under control of a single time function is a very powerful one, which also fits with a number of neurophysiological observations, as reported by the authors. On the other hand, VITE does not have a *muscular competence*, because a positional code is assumed for the central motor commands; this is a dual assumption with respect to Kawato, but in both cases the structural linkage between position and force is ignored.

Perhaps more questionable is the choice of the muscle space for the VITE mechanism. In fact, this mechanism can be considered as a sort of vectorial interpolator which is assumed to operate in muscle space. The point, however, is that muscle lengths are not independent variables and thence, even if PPC (at t=0) and TPC were valid representations, the intervening arrays might be kinematically wrong. Moreover, it is well known that interpolation in muscle and joint spaces generally produces implausible end-point trajectories (Morasso, 1981).

Nevertheless, the attractiveness of the non specific, scalable, speed control signal (GO) can well survive the problems of muscle space interpolation. One might indeed think of having GO operate in task space instead of muscle space. In this case, PPC can be thought of as the end-effector, to be compared with the task-defined target: the output of the GO-gating module would then have the meaning of a *moving target* in task space which is the input to some kind of motor programming network (This network carries out the function of the bank of integrators of the VITE model.) A significant advantage of bringing VITE to the task space is that multiple VITE-circuits can be instantiated at the same time, in accordance with the fact that, in many motor skills, multiple end-effectors are concurrently active. In other words, this implies the solution of another, more abstract, factorization problem: the factorization of task dynamics (motor planning) and neuromotor dynamics (motor programming) inside the same global synergy.

5.2 Adaptive Sensorimotor Network

This model is inspired by the anatomy and physiology of the cerebellum (Houk at al., 1990) which has repeatedly attracted the attention of theoreticists and modelers (Marr, 1969, Albus, 1971) and is based on the idea that the function of the cerebellum is to modulate a set of adjustable pattern generator (APG) modules and to learn the modulation functions through experience (Figure 7).

An APG is a neural circuit loop which has units in three nuclei (red nucleus (R), deep cerebellar nucleus (N), and lateral reticular nucleus (L)) and is controlled by an array of Purkinje cells (P: the Purkinje domain of the APG). The excitatory connections from R to L to N to R guarantee the self-sustained activity of the APG once it has been triggered on by an input coming from the sensorimotor cortex that excites R. The level of activity is modulated by the inhibitory influence of the P cells on N which is then the control site of the APG. The output is represented by the rubro-spinal fibers that convey to the spinal cord motor commands which are supposed to code movement velocity.

P cells are represented as bistable devices, i.e. binary elements with histeresis. The output variable generated by an APG is a positive quantity linearly related to the number of inactive neurons in its Purkinje domain. In summary, after an APG has been turned on by the cortical trigger signal, it establishes a steady level of activity which depends on a pre-selection of P-units performed by cerebellar cortical circuits and the activity proceeds until another input pattern to P turns on most of the P-units. The histeresis of the P cells is necessary in order to decouple the activity of the APG from fluctuations of the input signals to the cerebellar cortex. Therefore, APG's operate in a quasi feedforward manner, because movement related signals only are used to turn on and off the generators.

The P-arrays are the trainable elements. They receive input signals via parallel fibers and teaching signals via the climbing fibers. The input is a vast array of sensory-motor signals transmitted to granule cells (G cells) from different parts of the brain; they somehow code the "state" of the system. The synapses between the input lines and the P units (w_{ij}) are adjusted by means of signals coming from the inferior olive (O cells) and conveyed by the climbing fibers. The learning rule is:

$$\delta w_{ij} = \alpha\,(1-c_i)\,(1-y_i)\,\varepsilon_{ij} - \beta\, c_i\, y_i\, \varepsilon_{ij}$$

where w_{ij} is the connection weight between P cell i and parallel fiber j, y_i is the activity of the P cell, c_i is the activity of the climbing fiber, and ε_{ij} is the activity of the parallel fiber (the "elegibility" of the P cell). The learning rule is applied at the end of an actual movement, as a measure of its success or failure (dysmetria). For simple, mono-dimensional movements this rule was shown to converge to solution.

Globally, we can look at this kind of architecture as a two layer network (the input layer are the G cells and the output layer are the P cells) which fulfills two purposes:

- Mapping an initial input vector into a pattern of disactivation of the P-units of all the APG's, therefore selecting their levels of activity;
- Detecting an input pattern that signals termination and then turning on all the P cells that cutoff the corresponding APG's.

The output pattern conveyed by the rubro-spinal fibers is a set of rectangular pulses whose amplitude is pre-programmed and whose duration is modulated by sensorimotor feedback.

5.2.1 Pros and Cons of the Adaptive Sensorimotor Network. The strongest point of this model is its attempt to adhere as much as possible to known neurobiological facts. On the other hand, the global rationale is unclear, because, admittedly, the present model does not face the problem of coordinating a set of APG in order to produce composite motor programs. In fact, the representational power of a set of APG's has to be demonstrated in sufficiently complex configurations; in other words, is the set of signals generable by the network (an array of rectangular pulses) powerful enough to sustain the control of muscles?

A similar comment can be made as regards the teaching and input signals: the real complexity is how these signals are coded. This is the main problem of sensorimotor models: modularizing the pattern generation part is somehow easy but attempting the same for the sensory part, in a general situation, is hard. In the next section we consider a couple of examples in this direction.

In any case, the pattern generator posited by the model is simple, biologically sound and it is an idea that might be exploited in different frameworks.

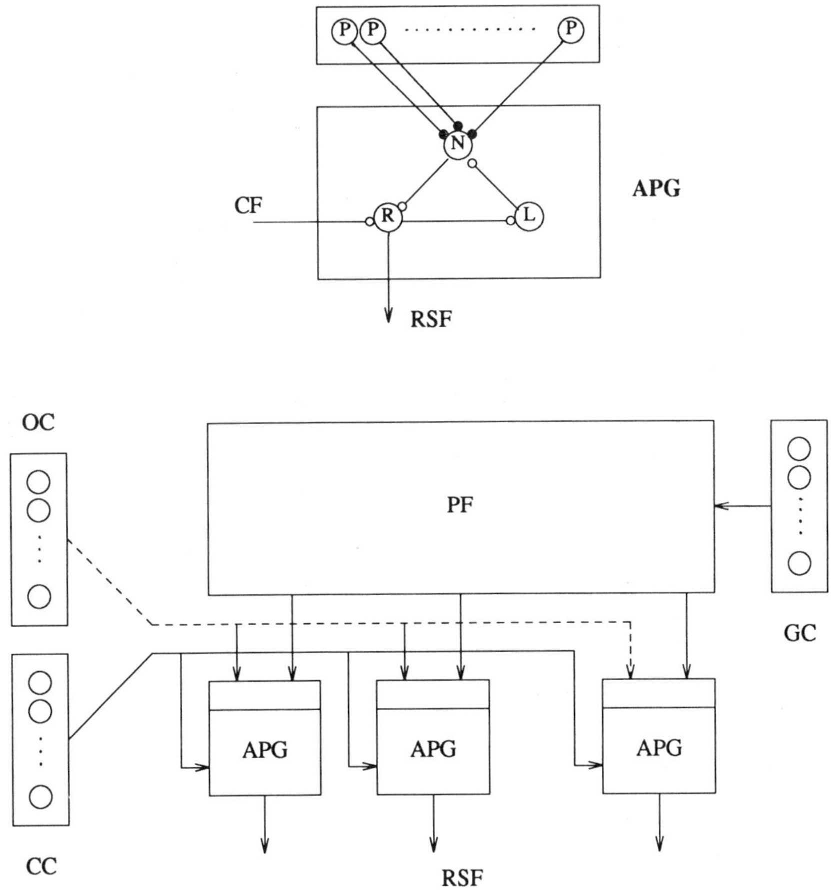

Figure 7. Adaptive Sensorimotor Network. APG: Adjustable Pattern Generator. (Open small circles: excitation; Filled small circles: inhibition.) P: Purkinje Cells. N: Nuclear Cells. R: Rubral Cells. OC: Olivary Cells. GC: Granule Cells. CC: Cortical Cells. CF: Cortical Fibers. PF: Parallel Fibers. RSF: Rubro-Spinal Fibers. Dashed lines: teaching signals.

5.3 M-Nets/P-Nets: a muscle-oriented synergy formation model

M-Nets (Motor relaxation Networks) attempt to bring *muscular competence* to the synergy formation process, in accordance with the concept that the elastic properties of muscles do not represent only a significant low-level feature of the motor system, but can also provide an organizing principle for the global computational architecture (Morasso et al., 1989, 1990, Morasso, 1990).

The main concept is that muscle elasticity provides a unified approach to posture and movement. Postures are determined by equilibrium configurations resulting from the balance of agonist and antagonist muscles, in the sense that these configurations act as points of attraction whenever external disturbances perturbe a posture. Such reference postures are associated with patterns of neural commands directed to each muscle and then, as the neural inputs to the muscles change in time, the reference posture shifts in space and acts as a moving center of attraction interacting with limb inertia and viscosity. In energetic terms one can define a global elastic potential function, tuned by the patterns of neuromuscular activity, whose equilibrium configurations determine posture and fuel action via a centrally induced modification of the shape of the potential field in the direction of the intended movement.

The origin of this concept can be traced back to the pioneering work of Astratyan and Feldman (Astratyan and Feldman, 1965, Feldman, 1966) and to the following development of so called *equilibrium-point models* (Bizzi et al., 1976, Bizzi et al., 1984, Hogan, 1984, Mussa Ivaldi et al., 1985, Feldman, 1986, Flash, 1987) which are based on different pieces of experimental evidence: several experiments on multi-joint coordination have shown that the spring-like behavior of the muscles is *tuned* by the central nervous system in order to generate a field of elastic forces which stabilize the hand in the intended posture; other experimental and simulation studies have shown that at all times during a trajectory the hand is attracted toward an equilibrium position defined by the elastic balance of muscular forces; recent neurophysiological experiments on the spinalized frog (Mussa Ivaldi et al., 1990) have shown that the electrical micro-stimulation of sites in the gray matter of the spinal cord induces a force field on the frog's ankle, whose equilibrium point is a function of the stimulation site.

However, these studies did not provide a computational model of the neural mechanisms that underly the selection and the continuous modification of equilibrium points, compatible with task constraints. In order to obtain this goal, a principle was formulated (Mussa Ivaldi, Morasso and Zaccaria, 1988), called *Passive Motion Paradigm* (PMP), according to which the continuous modification of equilibrium points is produced via a central neural mechanism that simulates *passive movements*, i.e. movements driven by *virtual force impulses* that correspond to the intended movement direction. The rationale of PMP is based on the following points:

- Passive motion occurs quite naturally in the interaction between the musculo-skeletal system and the environment;
- Passive motion has the remarkable property of selecting patterns of joint-rotation and muscle lengthening/shortening that solve the inverse kinematic problem, independently of the degree of redundancy and the kinematic degeneracy which occurs at the limits of the workspace;

- A central neural mechanism that is capable to simulate passive motion is the most natural way to incorporate musculo-skeletal competence in the central neural controller;
- This mechanism can be used directly for synergy formation in the sense that the muscular and articular variations that result from the simulation are an effective representation of the pattern of motor commands.

PMP can be viewed as a conceptual mechanism for establishing a well defined mapping between a high-dimensional neural-activation pattern and a lower-dimensional kinematic representation. M-Nets are parallel and distributed architectures that have been proposed as an implementation of the simulation mechanism discussed above (Morasso et al., 1989, Morasso, 1990, Morasso and Sanguineti, 1990). It is an analogic device in several senses: (i) it operates as a dynamic system (an analogic computer) and not as a symbolic system; (ii) it has a structural similarity with the neuromuscular system, i.e. it is somatotopically organized; (iii) its dynamics is a *neural relaxation* that strictly mirrors the corresponding mechanical relaxation of passive movements. M-Nets are driven by a computational energy analogous to the elastic potential energy of the muscles. The model is constructed as a network of units which correspond to the different constituent parts of the musculo-skeletal system: S-units (skeletal segments), M-units (mono- and multi-joint muscles), and L-units (mono- and multi-joint ligaments).

These units are defined by the local computations they perform: M-units and S-units behave as impedances, i.e. receive positional information and react feeding back force information; S-units, on the contrary, behave as admittances, i.e. they receive force information and react, modifying positional parameters. S-units model the different skeletal body segments, considered as rigid bodies to which complex sets of forces are applied: *internal forces*, applied by M&L units for taking into account the biomechanical constraints, and *external forces*, applied as sequences of impulses from the outside of the M-Net for expressing intended directions of movement. The activation function of S-units consists of the simulation of the passive motion of the body segment, thereby changing the current position vectors of the insertion points of all the forces impinging on the unit. M-units and L-units model the elastic elements of the system as cables passing through pulleys and fixed at their extremities onto two different bodies. The functions that they compute reflect the length-tension curves that characterize the corresponding real devices. These functions are obviously invariant for L-units but tunable for M-units.

With these units it is possible to build networks that can relax in a similar way to the underlying musculo-skeletal system. In this sense, an M-Net is a computational *body schema* that implements the pattern generator required by the equilibrium-point hypothesis. The inputs to an M-Net are sequences of virtual force impulses that express the intended direction of motion: we may call them *synergy vectors*. These vectors displace the equilibrium state of the network and the ensuing dynamics provides two streams of output data at the same time: a stream of *muscle activations* and a stream of *kinematic expectations*. From the network modelling point of view, M-Nets are dynamic systems with a well defined Ljapunov function and therefore are similar to the content addressable memories (CAM) initially investigated by Hopfield (Hopfield, 1982, 1984) and by Cohen and Grossberg (1983):

- The role of neurons in Hopfield nets is played by S-units; the difference is that inputs and outputs in M-Nets are vectors, not scalars, and the activation function is more complex.

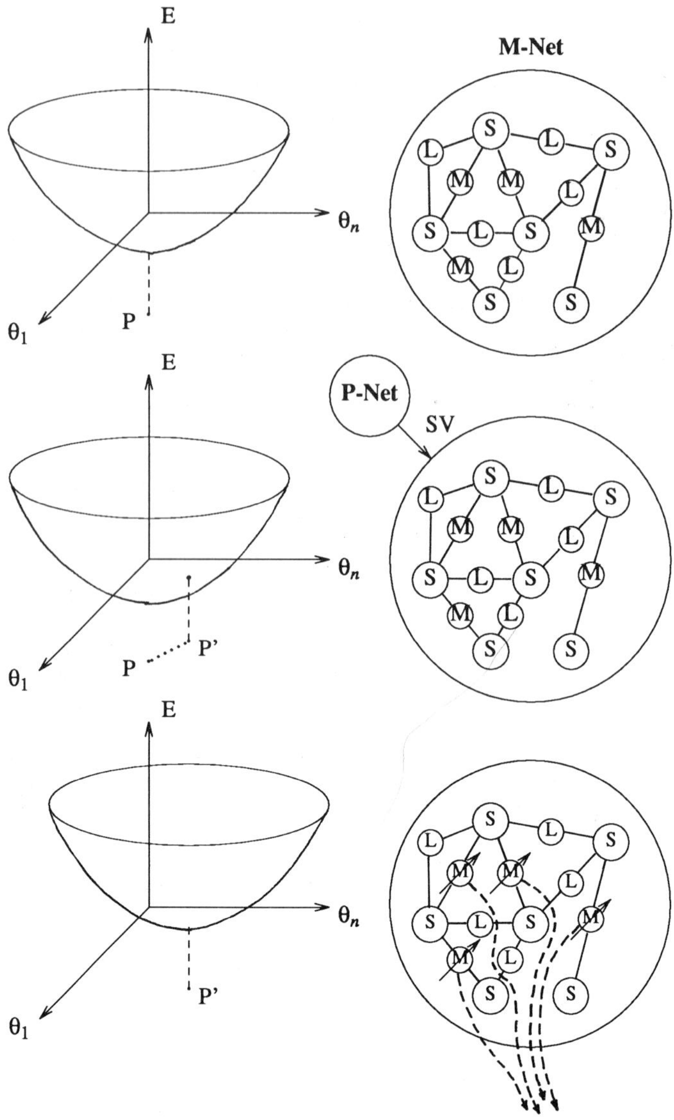

Figure 8. M-Net/P-Net Model. Top part: The M-Net is initially in equilibrium (point P in the potential energy landscape E). Middle part: The P-Net fires a synergy vector (SV) that displaces the equilibrium point of the M-Net from P to P'. Bottom part: The M-units of the M-net are updated in such a way to re-gain equilibrium (the updating pattern is the outflow synergy).

- The role of connections (which are linear functions in Hopfield nets) is played by M-units and L-units which are non linear functions. (An additional non-linearity is due to the connectivity of the musculature on the skeletal system.)
- The role of input signals is played by the synergy vectors.

In spite of significant differences, in both cases we have a similar relaxation behaviour which is driven by a potential energy function: in the Hopfield continuos model, this function is the total electrostatic energy stored in the membrane capacitances; in the M-Net model, it is the total mechanical elastic energy, stored in M-units and L-units. However, the purpose of the relaxation is quite different:

- A CAM can store multiple patterns as equilibrium configurations (points of minimum in the energy landscape) and the purpose of the relaxation is to recover a pattern from an initial representation which may be partial and/or corrupted.
- In an M-Net, there is only one significant equilibrium configuration (the current posture) and this is changed during the simulation process in accordance with the passive motion principle.

Therefore, the pseudo connection-weights represented by M-units must be adaptively changed during relaxation and this can be obtained by interleaving a *passive phase* and an *active phase*. In the passive phase, an M-Net reacts to the application of a synergy vector by relaxing to a new equilibrium state in an iso-electric way, i.e. without changing the control variables of M-units; at equilibrium, these variables are changed in order to shift the point of minimum of the energy landscape onto the current configuration: this is the active phase. In other words, the neural relaxation process operates in such a way that the point of minimum in the potential field *tracks* the sequence of equilibrium configurations determined by the sequence of synergy vectors. Symmetrically, the mechanical relaxation induced by the neural relaxation evolves the other way around: the potential field *leads* the current posture and attracts it. The units in an M-Net must be conceived as cell assemblies not as single neurons and we might represent them as small MLN's replicated in a great number of exemplars: their function is to compute the linear and non linear vector operations described above and this can be learned through training.

In the proposed synergy formation architecture (Morasso, 1990, Morasso et al., 1990), an M-Net is the task-independent part that incorporates the basic biomechanical constraints, but it has no competence as regards goal selection and timing. This requires another neural mechanism which is the second half of the synergy formation system and logically operates at a more abstract level: a planning network (P-Net). The function of P-Nets is to select one or more end-effectors and to generate, for each of them, a sequence of synergy vectors which are transmitted to the M-Net. In the present implementation, the pattern generation function of a P-Net is carried out by a relaxation circuit, similar to an M-Net (Morasso and Sanguineti, 1990). Summing up, the synergy formation architecture is composed as follows:

- A planning system that has an analogic and a symbolic component: the former one consists of a set of neural networks that behave as synergy vector generators and the latter is a set of rules for setting up the generators and connecting them with the underlying M-Net. The symbolic component has the semantic competence, whereas the analogic components has the timing and targeting competence.

- A motor programming system, an M-Net, which is a somatotopically organized relaxation network of local MLN's. It has the biomechanical competence: it is able to absorb the different sequences of virtual force impulses produced by the planning system and to integrate them in the overall motor pattern.

5.3.1 Pros and Cons of the P-Net/M-Net model. The P-Net/M-Net model is an attempt to integrate in a composite architecture the different types of motor competences that we discussed above. There are points of contact with CN-MT as regards the general framework. The pattern generation module posited by the P-Net can be modelled in a variety of ways and this can be a fruitful field of interaction with the other patterns generators considered above (VITE and APG). Moreover, a significant analogy can be drawn between the synergy vectors generated by the model and the same entities defined by Burnod, Caminiti and coworkers (Burnod et al., 1990, Caminiti et al., 1990): this would suggest, among other things, to incorporate the population coding concept in the synergy formation architecture. On the other hand, it is possible to observe that the unfocused nature of M-Nets and their relaxation dynamics make them general but slow mechanisms of synergy formation that are not ideal for perfectioning specific motor skills. It is then reasonable to hypothesize some kind of supra-structure that exploits the P-Net/M-Net model as a bootstrap of motor learning and later relinquishes control to some form of MLN for specific skills.

6. VISUO-MOTOR MODELS

Other neural models have been centered on the sensory-motor transformations that precede and underly the generation of motor patterns. We shall consider the INFANT model (Kuperstein and Rubinstein, 1989) and a model of the visuo-motor transformations in the cerebral cortex (Burnod et al., 1990). For lack of space we cannot summarize Darwin III (Reeke at al., 1989), which is based on the application of Darwinian selectionist principles to the development and adaptation of neurally controlled organisms, also because Darwin III is an integrated system for pattern recognition, exploration and motor control. The motor control part of Darwin III has some degree of similarity with INFANT, as regards the learning of visuo-motor transformations, and with the adaptive sensorimotor network, as regards the role attributed to cerebellar and olivary neurons.

6.1 INFANT: Adaptive neural controller for sensory-motor coordination

INFANT (Kuperstein and Rubinstein, 1989) is a neural motor controller that learns to use visual information, coming from a pair of TV cameras, for grasping objects. Learning is totally unsupervised in the sense that the teaching set is autonomously generated in a "babbling phase" and the neural controller is designed to learn self-consistency between sensory and motor signals. Figure 9 shows the block diagram of the global visuo-motor system, in which the neural controller is a small part, although it is the trainable one:

- The robot manipulator is controlled in joint coordinates by means of a motor command vector **MC**.
- During the training phase, *spontaneous movements* are driven by a pseudo-random generator which produces the command vectors and allows the robot to sample the working space; while moving, the manipulator holds an object (a cylinder) which is

looked at by a pair of TV cameras, therefore generating reafferent visual signals.

- A visual pre-processing system operates on the pair of images in order to separate the object from the background and to extract the essential features for the motor controller. The features are measured by 18 numbers: the x and y coordinates of the centroid of the object on each image (x_1, x_2, y_1, y_2) as well as the values of their disparity ($\Delta x, \Delta y$); measures of normalized orientations of the object obtained by means of convolution of the images with kernels oriented in four different directions, 45 degrees apart ($d_{1,\alpha}$, $d_{2,\alpha}$, $d_{1,\beta}$, $d_{2,\beta}$, $d_{1,\gamma}$, $d_{2,\gamma}$, $d_{1,\delta}$, $d_{2,\delta}$) as well as the values of their disparity (Δ_α, Δ_β, Δ_γ, Δ_δ).
- The 18 scalar features are transformed into 18 mono-dimensional maps by means of a spatial coding scheme: scanning a map is equivalent to addressing the range of values of the corresponding feature. The feature maps are activated with a bell-shaped distribution of activity, centered around the unit that codes the current value of the feature.
- A two layer neural network maps the ensemble of feature maps (logically, a single, long array of units) into an array of motor commands: **MC′**. It is very similar to a classical perceptron, with the only difference that the neurons have linear activation functions.
- The network is trained in order to generate a visually-induced motor command **MC′** which matches as closely as possible the actual training command **MC**. For this purpose an error vector is defined as the difference between the two motor vectors and its components are back propagated through the network, updating the weights according to a strategy of gradient descent.
- After training, the babbling generator is disconnected and the presentation of an object of roughly similar shape to the teaching object will trigger a "reaching reflex" that tends to superimpose the hand on the object. Conventional methods are then used to provide the grasping commands.

6.1.1 Pros and Cons of INFANT. INFANT teaches us about self-consistency between sensory and motor signals and it does so without any claim of neurophysiological realism. Moreover, it demonstrates that complex sensory motor coordination can be achieved by means of a rather simple method of self-teaching, where the essential link is played by the feedback through the real world. However, INFANT is a toy-model not so much for its lack of biological realism but for its computational structure at the two ends of the neural controller: the visual and motor layers. The visual layer assumes that conventional algorithms are perfectly able to extract from the input images (iconic representations) a limited number of visual features (localized representations) that are then transformed into feature maps (distributed representations) in order to feed the neural controller. The problem is that once a localized visual representation is available there is really no need of a neural model for the visuo-motor transformation. A neural controller, on the contrary, would be perfectly justifiable if distributed representations of visual features could be obtained directly from the pre-processed iconic representations. As regards the motor layer, it can be observed that the motor control problem is trivialized, reducing the motor command to a localized representation (one unit for each motor) and leaving out the real complexity: kinematic and muscular competence.

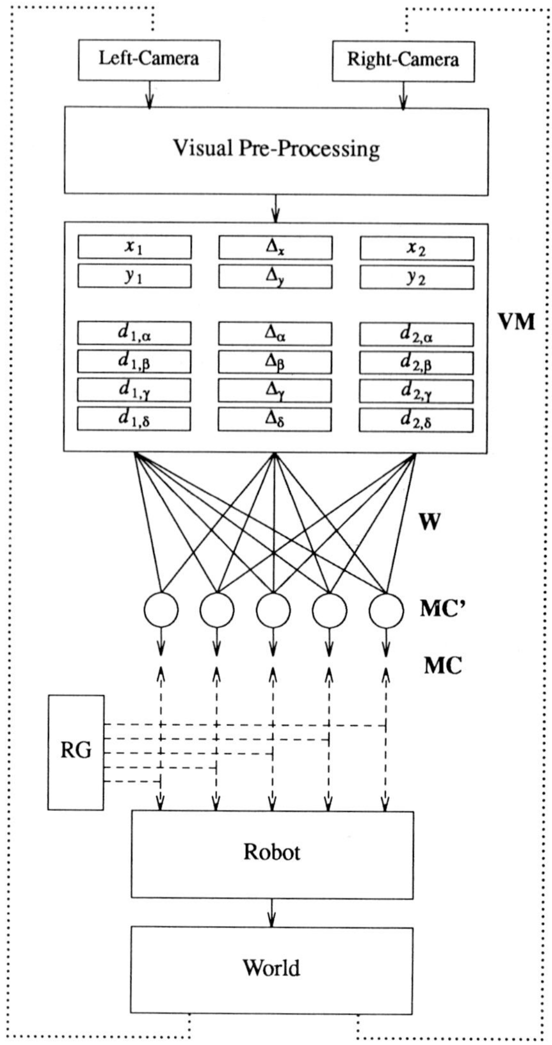

Figure 9. INFANT: Adaptive Neural Controller for Sensory-Motor Coordination. MC, MC': Motor Command Vectors. (The activation function of the motor command units is linear.) VM: Visual Maps. RG: Random Generator of spontaneous movements. W: connection weights. Dotted lines: reafferences. Dashed lines: spontaneous motor commands.

6.2 Visuo-motor transformations in the cerebral cortex

A model of the visuo-motor transformations performed by the cerebral cortex has been proposed by Burnod, Caminiti and coworkers (Burnod et al., 1990). The model is directly inspired by the recent investigations on the neuronal activity in the motor and pre-motor cortices (Georgopoulos et al., 1986, Georgopoulos, 1988, Caminiti et al., 1990) and is restricted to the initial ballistic phase of 3D arm reaching movements.

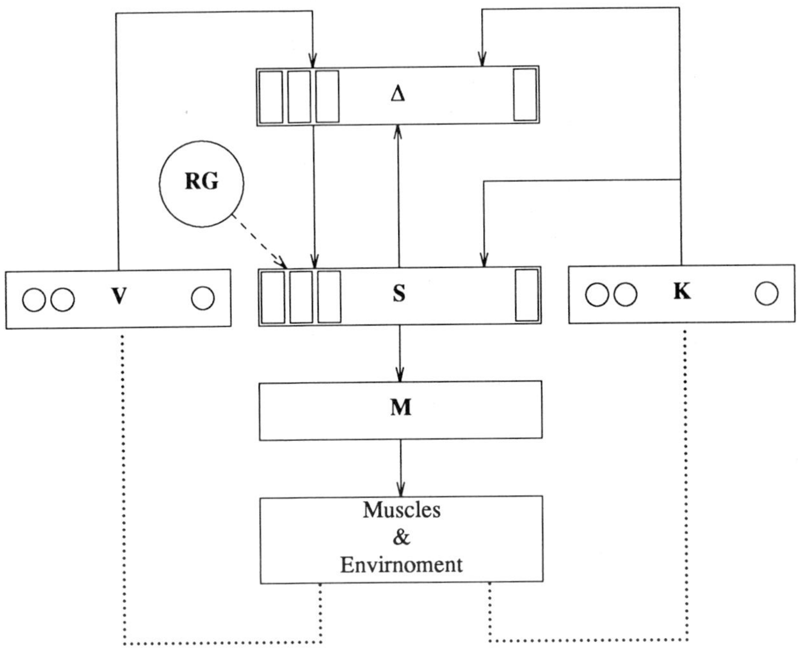

Figure 10. Synergy formation via cortical visuo-motor transformations. Δ: matching units. *S*: synergy units. *M*: motor units. *K*: kinesthetic units. *V*: visual units. RG: random generator of spontaneous movements (dashed lines: activation of synergy vectors during spontaneous movements). Dotted lines: visual and kinesthetic reafferences.

The central element of the model (figure 10) is a layer of *Synergy Units* that implement a *population coding scheme* of the initial movement direction. The scheme is defined by the following elements:

- The *Synergy Units* drive a set of *Motor Units* (a mapping one-to-many) according to pre-wired ("innate") connection patterns that guarantee, for each synergy unit, a fixed vectorial effect in an arm-centered coordinate system. In other words, synergy units are characterized by a *synergy vector* whose amplitude is modulated by the activity level of the unit.

- The distribution of synergy vectors, through the population of synergy units, is uniformly spread on a Gaussian sphere and this allows to synthesize any desired movement direction by means of a linear combination of synergy vectors, i.e. by means of a pattern of activity of the synergy units. A consequence of the population coding scheme is that each unit in the population is characterized by a broad tuning curve - an experimentally established fact.

The second part of the model is a layer of *Matching Units* that are intended to carry out the necessary visuo-motor transformations, i.e. mapping visual and kinesthetic patterns (conveyed by Visual Units and *Kinesthetic Units*, respectively) into a synergy pattern.

Matching and synergy units are modeled as schematized cortical columns, whose activation function is a variant of so called sigma-pi units (McClelland et al., 1986). This allows to take into account conjunctive as well as disjunctive interactions among the input signals to these units. Matching units receive three types of inputs: from visual, kinesthetic, and synergy units. Synergy units receive also three types of inputs: from kinesthetic, matching, and other synergy units. For all these input signals a distributed population code is assumed.

The sensory-motor transformation is learned in a way which is similar to the strategy adopted by INFANT: it uses the visual and kinesthetic reafferences which are produced during sequences of spontaneous movements. Differently from INFANT, which only needs visual reafference, the cortical model requires kinesthetic reafference as well because the synergy vectors are expressed in an arm-centered frame. During training, the network learns to associate synergy and kinesthetic vectors with the resulting visual patterns. This is obtained by means of a complex statistical adaptation of the different types of connection weights of matching and synergy units. After learning, visual patterns are capable to trigger the activation of synergy patterns that drive the initial part of the hand trajectory in the appropriate direction.

6.2.1 Pros and Cons of the motor cortical model. The cortical model shares with INFANT the same merit of emphasizing the self-organization of the visuo-motor mapping through spontaneous motor activity. It is perhaps worth noting that the importance of pseudo-random activity, as a morphogenetic entity, also has been recognized in early visual neuronal circuitry (Linsker, 1986a, 1986b). In any case, the distinctive feature of the cortical model is the population coding scheme. (INFANT, on the contrary, uses a spatial coding of a set of visual features.) An interesting and open question is the computational significance of this feature, i.e. the organizational advantage and the architectural consequences. On the other hand, the more questionable part of the model is the output part, i.e. the connection between synergy and motor units, which is assumed to implement a fixed mapping. Indeed, we think that a significant part of motor complexity is concentrated in this area because it is here that the mechanical properties of muscles must be taken into account. A natural complementarity exists between the cortical model, that practically terminates at the level of the synergy units, and the M-Net model, that begins from there: the meeting point is the concept of a synergy vector. However, in the cortical model the synergy vector has a purely kinematic meaning which does not fit with the sensitivity of motor cortical neurons to force (Evarts and Tanji, 1976); an M-Net, on the contrary, mixes force and movement, mirroring the elasticity of muscles.

7. CONCLUSIONS

At the end of this short excursus of the neural modelling community of the motor control system, there is no clear-cut conclusion to draw. The field is clearly in an early phase of development. Nevertheless, there is no doubt that motor neuroscience desperately needs a theory in order to give a meaning to the enormous body of experimental knowledge already available and in order to direct the future experimental activity. And there is little hope that a theory can emerge, self-evident, from the traditional bottom-up approach of the experimentalists.

We believe that neural modeling can be a useful tool of theory building in a field that does not lend itself to the well established paradigms of the physical sciences. The reason is that (actually implemented) neural models can allow to focus the attention (of both the experimentalist and the theorist) on organizational complexity, interaction dynamics, and self-consistency of the computational architecture. Usually, these aspects are completely overlooked by the experimentalists, who are obliged to isolate localized correlations among neural events. On the contrary, with the aid of powerful neural models, based on strong organizational principles and global self-consistency, it is possible to operate the other way around: to isolate key correlations that derive from the organizational structure of the model and then test them in vivo.

A significant consequence, we think, is that stressing biological realism in model building is not a sure guide per se and, in a sense, can be misleading. Modelling an intelligent system is a completely different matter from classical model building because the model itself must posses some degree of intelligence, organizational structure, and self-consistency. From this point of view, the state of the art of neural models of motor control is still primitive. Each model is essentially based on an idea, which emphasizes some aspect of the overall system, but the different ideas did not yet reach the level of integration which can "close the circle" and bootstrap self-consistency. In this process, we think that a necessary step, worth trying in the near future, is to perform integration exercises among the existing modelling approaches, in order to produce a new generation of modelling tools, more integrated, more intelligent, more useful for the experimenters.

8. REFERENCES

- Albus, J.S. (1971) A theory of cerebellar function. Mathematical Bioscience, 10, 25-61.
- Astratyan, D.G., and A.G. Feldman (1966). Functional tuning of the nervous system with control of movement or maintenance of a steady posture. I. Mechanographic analysis of the work of the joint on execution of a postural task. Biophysics, 10, 925-935.
- Atkeson, C.G. (1989) Learning arm kinematics and dynamics. Ann. Rev. Neuroscience, 12, 157-183.

- Bizzi, E., Accornero, N., Chapple, W., and N. Hogan (1984). Posture control and trajectory formation during arm movements. J. Neuroscience, 4, 2738-2744.
- Bullock D. and S. Grossberg (1988) Neural dynamics of planned arm movements: emergent invariants and speed-accuracy properties during trajectory formation. Psychological Review 95:49-90.
- Burnod, Y., Caminiti, R., Johnson, P., Granguillaume, P., and I. Otto (1990) Model of the visuo-motor transformations performed by the cerebral cortex to command arm movements at visual targets in the 3-D space. In "Advanced Neural Computers" (R. Eckmiller, Editor), North-Holland/Elsevier, Amsterdam, 33-41.

  Bullock D. and S. Grossberg (1989) VITE and FLETE: Neural modules for trajectory formation and postural control. In "Volitional Action" (W.A. Hershberger, Editor), North-Holland/Elsevier:Amsterdam, 253-297.
- Caminiti, R., Johnson, P.B., and A. Urbano (1990) Making arm movements within different parts of space. Dynamic aspects in the primate motor cortex. Journal of Neuroscience, 10, 2039-2058.
- Cohen, M.A., and S. Grossberg (1983) Absolute stability of global pattern formation and parallel memory storage by competitive neural networks. IEEE Trans. Systems, Man, and Cybernetics, SMC-13, 815-826.
- Eckmiller, R. (1990) Neural computers for motor control. In "Advanced Neural Computers" (R. Eckmiller, Editor), North-Holland/Elsevier, Amsterdam, 357-364.
- Evarts, E.V. and J. Tanji (1976) Reflex and intended responses in motor cortex pyramidal tract neurons of monkey. J. Neurophysiology, 39, 1069-1080.
- Feldman, A.G. (1966). Functional tuning of the nervous system with control of movement or maintenance of a steady posture. II. Controllable parameters of the muscle. Biophysics, 11, 565-578.
- Feldman, A.G. (1986). Once more on the equilibrium-point hypothesis (Lambda Model) for motor control. J. Motor Behavior, 18,17-54.
- Flash, T. and N. Hogan (1985) The coordination of arm movement: an experimentally confirmed mathematical model. J. Neuroscience 5:1688-1703.
- Flash, T. (1987) The control of hand equilibrium trajectories in multi-joint arm movements. Biological Cybernetics, 57, 257-274.
- Georgopoulos, A.P., Schwartz, A.B., and R.E. Kettner (1986) Neuronal population coding of a movement direction. Science 233:1416-1419.
- Georgopoulos, A.P. (1988) Neural integration of movement: role of motor cortex in reaching. Faseb Journal, 2, 2849-2857.
- Hogan, N. (1984). An organizing principle for a class of voluntary movements. J. Neuroscience, 4, 2745-2754.
- Hopfield, J.J. (1982). Neural networks and physical systems with emergent collective computational abilities. Proc. Nat. Acad. Sci. USA, 79, 2554-2558.

- Hopfield, J.J. (1984). Neurons with graded response have collective computational properties like those of two state neurons. Proc. Nat. Acad. Sci. USA, 81, 3088-3092.
- Houk, J.C., Singh, S.P., Fisher, C., and A.G. Barto (1990) An adaptive sensorimotor network inspired by the anatomy and physiology of the cerebellum. In "Neural Networks for Control" (W.T. Miller, R.S. Sutton, and P.J. Werbos, Editors), MIT Press, Cambridge (Mass., USA), chapter 14.
- Jordan, M. (1988) Supervised learning and systems with excess degrees of freedom. COINS 88-27, M.I.T.
- Jordan, M.I. (1989a) Indeterminate motor skill learning problems. In Attention and Performance XIII (M. Jeannerod, Editor), MIT Press:Cambridge Mass.
- Jordan, M.I. (1989a) Serial order: A parallel, distributed processing approach. In "Advances in Connectionist Theory: Speech" (J.L. Elman and D.E. Rumelhart, Editors), Lawrence Erlbaum Ass.:Hillsdale, NJ, 44-93.
- Kathib, O. (1986) Real-time obstacle avoidance for manipulators and mobile robots. The International Journal of Robotic Research, 5, 90-99.
- Kawato, M., Maeda, Y., Uno, Y., and R. Suzuki (1990) Trajectory formation of arm movement by cascade neural network model based on minimum torque-change criterion. Biological Cybernetics 62:275-288.
- Kuperstein, M. and J. Rubinstein (1989) Implementation of an adaptive neural controller for sensory-motor coordination. In "Connectionism in Perspective" (R. Pfeifer, Z. Schreter, F. Fogelman-Soulie, and L. Steels, Editors), Elsevier Science Publishers:Amsterdam, 49-61.
- LeCun, Y. (1985) A learning scheme for asymmetric threshold networks. Proceedings of Cognitiva 85, Paris, France.
- Linsker, R. (1986a) From basic network principles to neural architectures: emergence of spatial opponent cells. Proceedings of the National Academy of Sciences (USA), 83, 7508-7512.
- Linsker, R. (1986b) From basic network principles to neural architectures: emergence of orientation selective cells. Proceedings of the National Academy of Sciences (USA), 83, 8390-8394.
- Little, W.A. and G.L. Shaw (1975) A statistical theory of short and long term memory. Behavioral Biology, 14, 115-133.
- Marr, D. (1969) A theory of cerebellar cortex. J. Physiology, 202, 437-470.
- Massone, L. and E. Bizzi (1989) A neural network model for limb trajectory formation. Biological Cybernetics 61, 417-425.
- McClelland, J.L., Rumelhart, D.E., and G.E. Hinton (1986) The appeal of parallel distributed processing. In "Parallel Distributed Processing" (J.L. McClelland and D.E. Rumelhart, Editors), MIT Press, Cambridge, Massachusetts (USA), Chapter 1.

- Morasso, P. (1981) Spatial control of arm movements. Exp. Brain Res. 42:223-227.
- Morasso, P., Mussa Ivaldi, F.A., Vercelli, G., and R. Zaccaria (1989) A connectionist formulation of motor planning. In "Connectionism in Perspective" (R. Pfeifer, Z. Schreter, F. Fogelman-Soulie, and L. Steels, Editors), Elsevier Science Publishers:Amsterdam, 413-420.
- Morasso, P. and V. Sanguineti (1990) Neurocomputing concepts in motor control. In "Brain and Space" (J. Paillard, Editor), Oxford University Press, Oxford, Chapter 21.
- Morasso, P. (1990) Neural representation of motor synergies. In "Advanced Neural Computers" (R. Eckmiller, Editor), North-Holland:Amsterdam, 51-59.
- Mussa Ivaldi, F.A., Hogan, N., and E. Bizzi (1985). Neural, mechanical, and geometric factors subserving arm postures in humans. J. Neuroscience, 5, 2732-2743.
- Mussa Ivaldi, F.A., Morasso, P., and R. Zaccaria (1988). Kinematic networks - A distributed model for representing and regularizing motor redundancy. Biological Cybernetics, 60, 1-16.
- Mussa Ivaldi, F.A., Gistzer, S.F., and E. Bizzi (1990) Motor-space coding in the central nervous system. Proceedings 55th Cold Spring Harbor Symposium on Quantitative Biology: the Brain.
- Nguyen, D. and B. Widrow (1990) The truck backer-upper. In "Advanced Neural Computers" (R. Eckmiller, Editor), North-Holland:Amsterdam, 11-17.
- Reeke, G.N., Sporns, O., and G.M. Edelman (1989) Synthetic neural modelling. In "Connectionism in Perspective" (R. Pfeifer, Z. Schreter, F. Fogelman-Soulie, and L. Steels, Editors), Elsevier Science Publishers:Amsterdam, 113-139.
- Rumelhart, D.E., Hinton, G.E, and R.J. Williams (1986) Learning internal representations by error propagation. In "Parallel Distributed Processing. Vol. 1" (D.E. Rumelhart and J.L. McClelland, Editors), MIT Press, Cambridge, Massachusetts, USA, 318-363.
- Uno, Y., Kawato, M., and R. Suzuki (1989) Formation and control of optimal trajectory in human multijoint arm movement. Minimum torque-change model. Biological Cybernetics 61:89-101.
- Viviani, P. and C. Terzuolo (1982) Trajectory determines movement dynamics. Neuroscience 7:431-437.

Acknowledgments. This work was supported by the Esprit Projects FIRST and PAPYRUS, and by a National Programme on Bioengineering of the Italian Ministry of University & Research.

Tutorials in Motor Behavior II
G.E. Stelmach and J. Requin (Editors)

Distributed control of limb position and force

F. Lacquaniti and C. Maioli

Istituto di Fisiologia dei Centri Nervosi, Consiglio Nazionale delle Ricerche, Via Mario Bianco 9, 20131 Milano, Italy

Abstract

The problem of the control of the mechanical interaction with the environment is addressed here by considering experimental data on posture in cats and catching in man. Evidence is presented that argues in favour of a parallel, distributed control of limb position and force. In particular, stance appears to be governed by a hierarchical structure. Global geometrical variables describing the orientation and length of the limb axes in space are primarily controlled and dictate the values of the normal contact forces at the paws (or equivalently the projection of the body centre of mass). The tangential contact forces are partitioned among the limbs according to a fixed law. Joint torques are then specified in a subordinate manner. Neural mechanisms underlying the control of limb position and force during catching are discussed. Data are reviewed indicating that anticipatory muscle activity is scaled in proportion to the expected momentum of the falling ball. Reflex coactivation is elicited by the impact. It is preset within the CNS in preparation for impact by switching from the spinal pathways of reciprocal inhibition to those of coexcitation of antagonist motoneurones. The switching is aimed at dynamically tuning the value of hand compliance around impact time. Tuning of hand compliance requires an accurate model of the geometrical properties of the limb and object, model that is developed internally to the CNS.

1. THE PROBLEM OF THE MECHANICAL INTERACTION WITH THE ENVIRONMENT

The issue of whether the Central Nervous System (CNS) codes explicitly and controls either limb *kinematics* or *dynamics* is the subject of much current debate and controversy [1-3]. By *kinematics* is meant the position, velocity and acceleration of the limb segments. *Dynamics* is the set of forces and torques that result in a given motion of the limb.

Most experimental studies dealing with this problem have concentrated on unconstrained movements of a limb in space. Thus, numerous studies have been carried out on pointing, reaching and drawing movements [4-6]. Much less attention has been given to the problem of the controlled variable in the case in which the limb must interact mechanically with the external environment. For instance, mechanical interaction occurs at the upper limb during all manipulative task and at the lower limbs during locomotion and posture.

The distinction between unconstrained movements and movements constrained because of a mechanical interaction is essential, since the nature of the control problem differs markedly in these two cases.

Figure 1 illustrates schematically this point. When a limb is unconstrained, free to move in space (Fig. 1*A*), there always exists a unique relationship between the angular position α of each joint and the corresponding torque T (provided that the mass of the limb is constant). Thus, in line of principle, only one set of variables needs to be explicitly defined, the other set then being implicitly specified. For instance, if the system defines a set of desired torques at the joints, Newtonian mechanics determines uniquely the corresponding values of joint angles (so called *direct dynamics* transformation). By converse, if the system defines the desired angular positions of the joints, joint torques are specified by means of the transformations of *inverse dynamics*. Which transformations are actually performed and how they are implemented within the CNS are still open questions [1,2,7]. The point, however, is that a unique mapping exists between joint position and torque for unconstrained movements.

The case of a limb constrained in its motion by the environment, as during mechanical interaction, is illustrated in Fig. 1*B*. Here, the relationship between angular position and torque at each joint is no longer unique, but is mediated by the contact force F that develops at the interaction point. As a consequence, the same angular positions α of the limb joints are compatible with entirely different values of joint torques T. This is exemplified in the two panels of Fig. 1*B*. The joint angles α_1 and α_2 are the same in the two panels. Yet, while the torque T_1 is in extension and the torque T_2 is in flexion in the left panel, both torques T_1 and T_2 are in flexion in the right panel. Correspondigly, the tangential component F_T of the contact force that is exerted by the limb is opposite in the two cases.

Figure 1. Diagrams illustrating the relation between joint angular position *(α)* and torque *(T)* when the limb is free in space (panel *A*) and when it interacts with the environment (panel *B*). Underbars denote vector quantities. In panel *A*, torques are uniquely related to angles (and their time derivatives) by means of the nonlinear function *f*. In panel *B*, instead, the relationship is not unique but depends on the contact force *F* (the matrix *G(α)* corresponds to the transpose Jacobian).

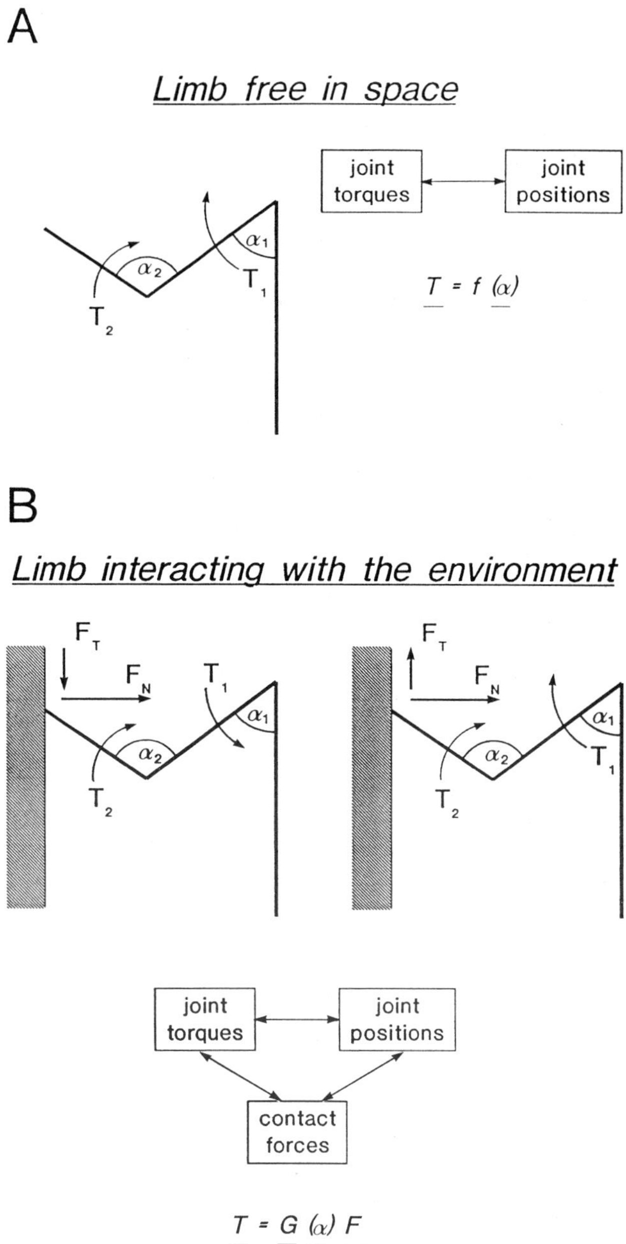
A
Limb free in space
joint torques
joint positions
α_1
α_2
T_1
T_2
$\underline{T} = f\,(\underline{\alpha})$
B
Limb interacting with the environment
F_T
F_N
T_1
T_2
α_1
α_2
joint torques
joint positions
contact forces
$\underline{T} = \underline{G}\,(\underline{\alpha})\,\underline{F}$

The contact forces are dictated, on the one hand, by the properties of the external surface (such as friction, elasticity and so on), and on the other hand by the way the limb acts on the surface. There is no *a priori* order or structure in the tripod relating contact forces, joint positions and torques. In other words, the CNS may choose to control primarily any one of these sets of variables. Only empirical evidence may provide *a posteriori* clues as to the type of control structure that is imposed by the CNS on the tripod mentioned above.

In the following we shall address the issue of separate control of limb position and force by considering two very different experimental conditions involving the mechanical interaction with the external environment: 1) Postural control of cats standing on a tilted platform, and 2) Catching a falling ball with the hand in man. We shall argue that the mechanical interaction generally requires a distributed control of limb position and force. According to this view, the transformations between the geometrical domain of limb positions and the kinetic domain of limb forces occur in several stages, along both hierarchical and heterarchical pathways.

Any lawful relation requires a specific reference frame to be defined and implemented. Since limb movement and mechanical interaction unfold simultaneously in the space extrinsic to the subject and in the intrinsic space of the joint angles and muscle activities, the brain must be able to represent the movement in both spaces and to map information from one space to the other [6]. We shall address the issue of the tranformation between extrinsic reference frames and intrinsic reference frames and we shall consider some of the neural mechanisms presumably involved in the control of mechanical interaction.

2. POSTURAL CONTROL IN CATS

Body posture is widely viewed as the result of a highly integrated, multisensory system of neural control that is hierarchically organized [8]. This control system incorporates several inner loops which use visual, vestibular and somatosensory informations. Thus, each of the inner loops has its own set of input and output variables to monitor and control. However, the coordinated action of the whole system is presumably aimed at the control of some global goal.

It is generally assumed that the global parameter being controlled during stance is the position of the centre of mass of the body. In fact, to stay in equilibrium, animals must keep the projection of their centre of mass (CMP) within safe bounds on the support surface. However, we present evidence in favour of an alternative hypothesis, namely that the CNS controls primarily the position of the limbs and body in space, the position of the centre of mass then being determined in a subordinate manner. As it will be shown, these two viewpoints are not at all equivalent as it would seem at a first glance, since they make divergent predictions under particular operating conditions of stance.

2.1. Primacy of the control of limb geometry

Balance can be equated to the outcome of the neural control processes which oppose the perturbing action of external forces. In the absence of forces other than gravity, an animal is statically balanced when the CMP falls within the support area. Thus, it has been widely hypothesized that the CMP is the variable regulated by the CNS during stance [9-11]. This amounts to postulating a neural control of the normal components of the contact forces at the paws ($d=[N_a-N_p]/2[N_a+N_p]$, where d is the distance of the CMP from the midpoint between fore- and hindpaws, and N_a, N_p are the sums of the normal contact forces at the fore- and hindpaws, respectively).

Indeed, the CMP and the normal contact forces are maintained approximately constant under a variety of conditions. Thus, CMP varies little when the support platform is tilted in the sagittal plane as in Fig. 2 [12-13]. However, also the geometrical configuration of the limbs in space vary little irrespective of platform inclination, as does the orientation of the trunk with respect to the orientation of the platform. Thus, under normal conditions, it cannot be established whether CMP or limb position are directly controlled by the CNS during stance.

These two hypotheses were tested experimentally by applying an external load to the cat forequarters [13]. Two different loads were used, equal to 10% or to 20% of the animal weight, respectively. In this way, a change of the weight distribution between fore- and hindlimbs was experimentally induced, namely CMP was shifted forwards. The hypothesis that CMP is the variable regulated in stance predicts that the CNS compensates for the applied perturbation by modifying postural geometry in such a way as to restore the desired CMP, for instance by rotating fore- and hindlimbs backwards.

This hypothesis, however, was falsified by the experimental results. In fact, the geometry of limb posture was maintained unmodified after the load application for all platform inclinations at the expenses of marked changes in the CMP. In particular, length and orientation of the main axis of the limbs did not change appreciably. This can be appreciated by comparing the stick diagrams of Fig. 2*A* with those of Fig. 2*B*. Mean values (+ 1 SD) of geometrical and force parameters were computed with the data obtained at all platform inclinations ($\pm$ 20°) and are plotted in *C-F*, using different patterns for the control, 10% or 20% loading conditions (inset in *F*).

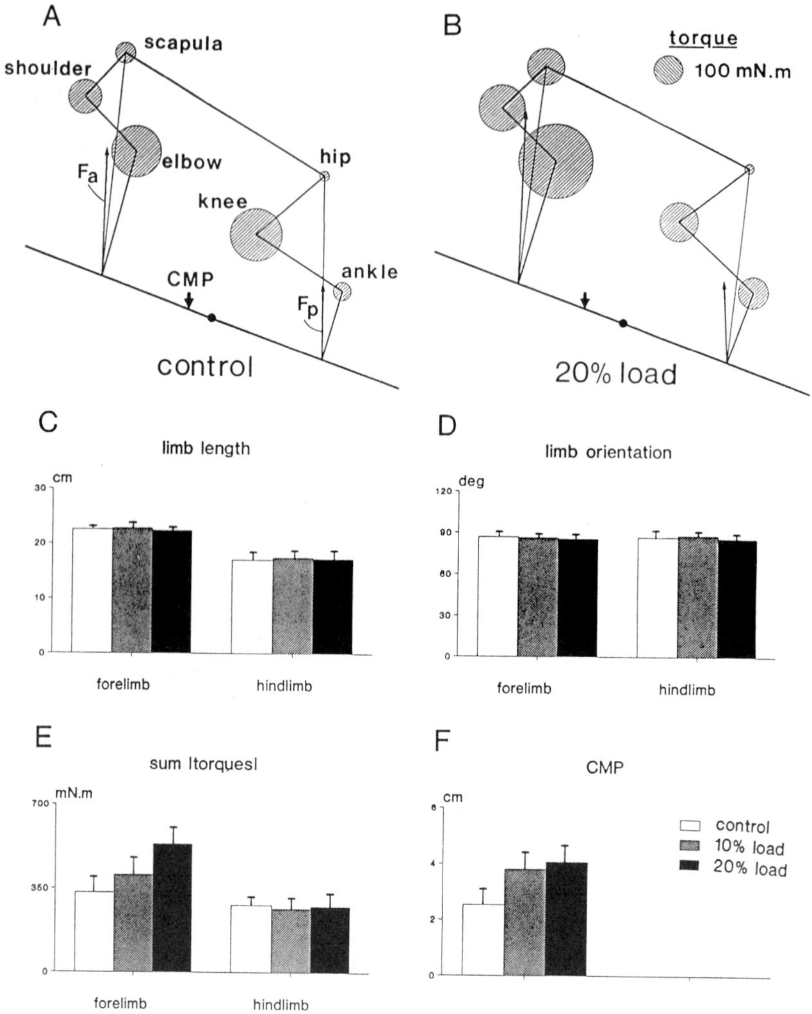

Figure 2. The stick diagrams depict the average posture (10 trials) of a cat on an inclined platform immediately before (*A*) and after (*B*) the application of a load (20% of the animal weight) under the pectoral girdle. CMP: projection of the centre of mass on the support surface. F_a, F_p: contact force vectors at the fore- and hindpaws. The thin lines indicate the main axes of the fore- and hindlimbs. The absolute magnitude of the joint torques is proportional to the radius of the shaded circles. *C-F*: mean values (+1 SD) computed from all results of one cat (± 20° platform tilt, 222 trials in 6 experiments) for each loading condition. *C*: length of the limb axis. *D*: limb axis orientation with respect to the horizontal. *E*: sum of absolute joint torques. *F*: CMP.

The load application also resulted in a substantial modification of the torques at the forelimb joints (joint torques are plotted in Figs. 2*A*-*B* as shaded circles whose radius is proportional to the absolute torque magnitude). Under static conditions, the torque at a joint is about equal to the vector product between the contact force and its moment arm about that joint. Thus, due to the increase in magnitude of the contact force, the magnitude of the joint torques generally increased at the forelimbs after load application. This abnormal effort was not redistributed between fore- and hindlimbs over a period of 24 h of continuous application of the load.

These results demonstrate that limb position is primarily controlled during stance in cats. In the hierarchy of control (see Fig. 5), the maintenance of a desired postural geometry takes precedence over the maintenance of desired normal contact forces and CMP.

At the higher levels of this hierarchical structure we find the global variables that describe the geometrical configuration of the main axis of the limbs in the external space, namely its length and angle of orientation with respect to the vertical. These two parameters are effectively controlled by the CNS, since they undergo very limited changes with both static [12] and dynamic [14] tilt of the platform, independent of external loading conditions [13].

Limb length and orientation define an egocentric polar reference frame with the origin at the limb endpoint. This reference frame is normally anchored to the environmental invariant of the vertical, as indicated by the general tendency shown by all cats to maintain the limb axis closely lined up with the vertical. The vertical is estimated using a complex combination of sensory informations: labyrinthine gravitoinertial cues, as well as visual and somatosensory cues [15]. In fact, a tilt of the visual surround inducing an illusory change of the vertical determines corresponding changes of limb orientation and a transient perturbation of the equilibrium [14].

2.2. Coordinate transformations involved in the control of joint angles

We have seen in the previous section that postural control in cats is organized in the extrinsic reference frame defined by the length and orientation of the main axis of the limbs. However, these two variables define an intended posture only in a global manner, since they specify the position of the limb endpoints in external space. In order to define completely the geometrical configuration of the limb, also the values of angular position at each limb joint must be specified. However, each limb has a redundant number of degrees of freedom with respect to the extrinsic space. Namely, there are 3 degrees of freedom of angular motion at each limb (e.g. hip, knee and ankle for the hindlimbs, see Fig. 2) but only 2 dimensions in the sagittal plane of movement. This means that while 3 coordinates are needed to define completely the geometrical configuration of all limb segments, only 2 coordinates are necessary to uniquely define the position of the limb endpoint in external space. Therefore, the coordinate transformation that must occur between an intended posture expressed in the 2-dimensional polar reference frame in the extrinsic space and the actual posture expressed in the 3-dimensional joint space is *a priori* indeterminate, that is it admits infinitely many different solutions.

However, we found experimentally that the CNS solves this indeterminacy problem by imposing a constraint on the values that the joint angles can take [16]. If we represent the limb configuration measured in each trial as a point in the 3-dimensional space of joint angles, we observe that all points lie close to a plane. For this analysis, the mean value of each angular coordinate was first subtracted, and the results from all experiments and cats were subsequently pooled together. The best-fitting plane and the 95% tolerance ellipsoid are plotted in Fig. 3 for the data of the forelimbs (*A,C*) and hindlimbs (*B,D*) in two different views.

Three points must be noted with regard to Fig. 3. First, while relative angles (i.e. anatomical angles of flexion-extension) are used for the distal joints (elbow and shoulder at the forelimbs, ankle and knee at the hindlimbs), absolute angles (with respect to the horizontal) are instead used for the most proximal joints (scapula and hip, see Fig. 2*A*). This particular choice of angles yields the best linear regression (as compared to that using either all absolute angles or all relative angles). Moreover, it is quite natural to utilize an absolute reference for the representation in joint space given our previous observation that cats keep the main axis of the limbs closely lined up with the absolute vertical.

The second point to be noted is that the data presented in Fig. 3 include all trials obtained at different platform inclinations ($\pm$ 20°) and a wide range of interfeet distances (up to $\pm$ 25% of the mean value) in order to increase the variability of postures considered. Thus, the range of values exhibited by individual joint angular positions spans a large fraction of the anatomical range for such joints. This clearly indicates that the planar covariation cannot derive from a biomechanical constraint.

The third and most important point is that the slope of the best-fitting plane for the forelimbs (Figs. 3*A,C*) is very similar to that of the hindlimbs (Figs. 3*B,D*). This similarity is all the most remarkable if one considers 1) the biomechanical differences in the individual segments of the fore- and hindlimbs, and 2) the very different postures that are usually adopted at the forelimbs and at the hindlimbs. While the forelimbs are relatively erect, the hindlimbs are kept more flexed. Therefore, the similarity of the planar covariation of the joint angles at fore- and hindlimbs further reinforces the argument that this constraint cannot depend on biomechanical factors but must arise from the neural laws mapping the extrinsic coordinates of the limb endpoints into the intrinsic coordinates of the joint angles.

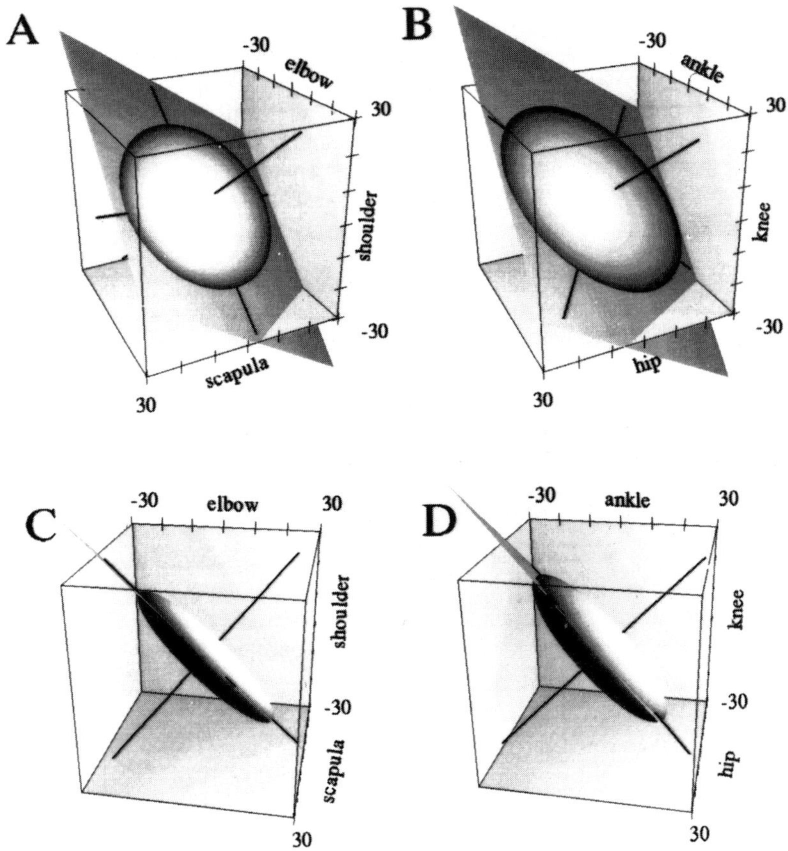

Figure 3. Limb configuration in joint space. The coordinates correspond to flexion-extension angles for the distal joints, and absolute angles (with respect to the horizontal) for the most proximal joints (scapula and hip). Best-fitting planes and 95% tolerance ellipsoids were computed from the results of 13 experiments in 4 cats (443 trials). The data of the forelimbs (*A,C*) and hindlimbs (*B,D*) are presented in two different views. The axes sticking out of the ellipsoids correspond to the eigenvectors of the covariance matrices of the data.

2.3. Control of the contact forces

We have seen that limb geometry is actively controlled by the CNS in stance. However, a given postural geometry is compatible with very different distributions of joint torques. We shall now demonstrate that torques are prescribed by the CNS using an accurate control of the tangential components of the contact forces at the paws.

Contact forces can be decomposed into normal and tangential components (see Fig. 1*B*). Their significance is different in stance. The normal forces simply reflect the weight distribution among the limbs and therefore they are entirely dictated by the assigned postural geometry. However, it is not so for the tangential forces. A tangential force produced by lever actions of proximal muscles is generally required for equilibrium [8,17]. This lever action can be distributed between forelimbs and hindlimbs in a very different manner, and yet the same stable posture will ensue.

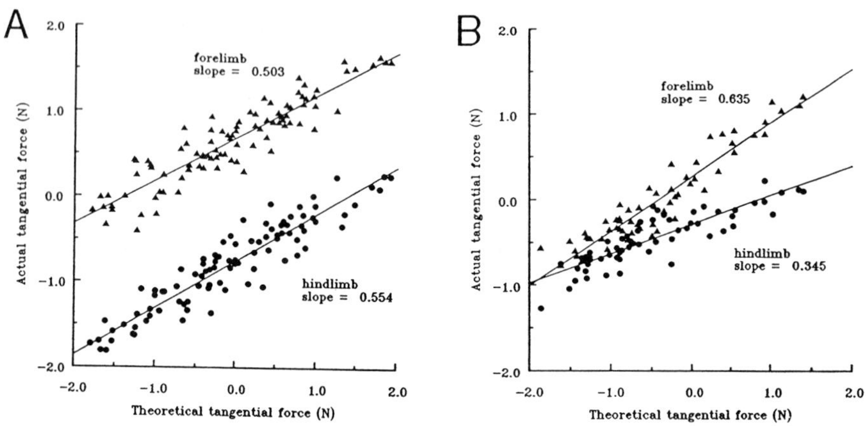

Figure 4. Contact forces at the paws under variable conditions of platform tilt ($\pm$ 20°) and interfeet distance (up to $\pm$ 25% of the mean value) in 2 cats (93 trials in *A* and 58 trials in *B*). In any given trial, the contact forces required for equilibrium were computed by means of free-body analysis of the measured postural geometry [17]. These contact forces can be decomposed in a "strut" component which is aligned with the main axis of the limb and does not require any lever action by the proximal muscles (zero net torque at the scapula and hip) and in a residual "lever" component which must be contributed by the proximal muscles. The abscissa values correspond to the net "lever" tangential force that is computed theoretically from the geometrical data. The ordinates correspond to the values of the "lever" tangential force that are derived from the experimental recordings performed at the forelimbs (triangles) and at the hindlimbs (dots) using force plates [13].

For instance, let us consider the case of an animal leaning forward. The required lever action can be produced by either the retractor muscles of the shoulder, or the retractor muscles of the hip, or a combination thereof. The choice of one particular solution lies entirely within the strategy adopted by the CNS during stance.

In order to determine whether or not the CNS actually controls the distribution of tangential forces among the limbs, we computed from the measured postural geometry the theoretical tangential force that must be produced by lever actions of the limbs [17]. This theoretical force was then compared with that measured in each trial using force plates. The results obtained in 2 animals under variable conditions of platform tilt ($\pm$ 20°) and interfeet distance (up to $\pm$ 25% of the mean value) are plotted in Figs. 4*A* and 4*B*. Each single trial yields a pair of points corresponding to the values for the forelimbs (triangles) and for the hindlimbs (dots). The only mechanical constraint for any given trial is that the sum of the two ordinate values corresponding to the fore- and to the hindlimbs is equal to the value given on the abscissa.

Despite the large variability of the force values resulting from the wide range of experimental conditions, there is an amazingly consistent law of control of the tangential contact forces: all data points lie very close to two straight lines, one for the forelimbs and one for the hindlimbs. Thus, we conclude that the active tangential forces are accurately partitioned between fore- and hindlimbs according to a fixed proportion.

Interestingly, if one compares the slopes of the regression lines in Figs. 4*A* and 4*B*, one can notice that the specific value of force partitioning is not constant in all cats, but is idiosyncratic to each animal. Thus, for a net tangential force of 2 N, the contribution by the forelimbs is about 2.5 as large as that by the hindlimbs in Fig. 4*A* and Fig. 4*B*. However, for a net force of -2 N, the contribution by the forelimbs is 0.4 that at the hindlimbs in Fig. 4*A*, but it is 1.5 in Fig. 4*B*.

2.4. A hierarchical model of postural control

A conceptual model of the distributed control of limb geometry and force based on the data reviewed above is depicted in Fig. 5. There are two main flow paths. A first path corresponds to a strictly hierarchical organization under the primacy of the control of limb geometry. The global variables describing the desired length and orientation of the limb axis are initially prescribed by the CNS and subsequently transformed in the values of the joint angles by means of a simple linear mapping. Desired limb geometry then determines uniquely the values of the normal contact forces and therefore also the projected centre of mass (CMP).

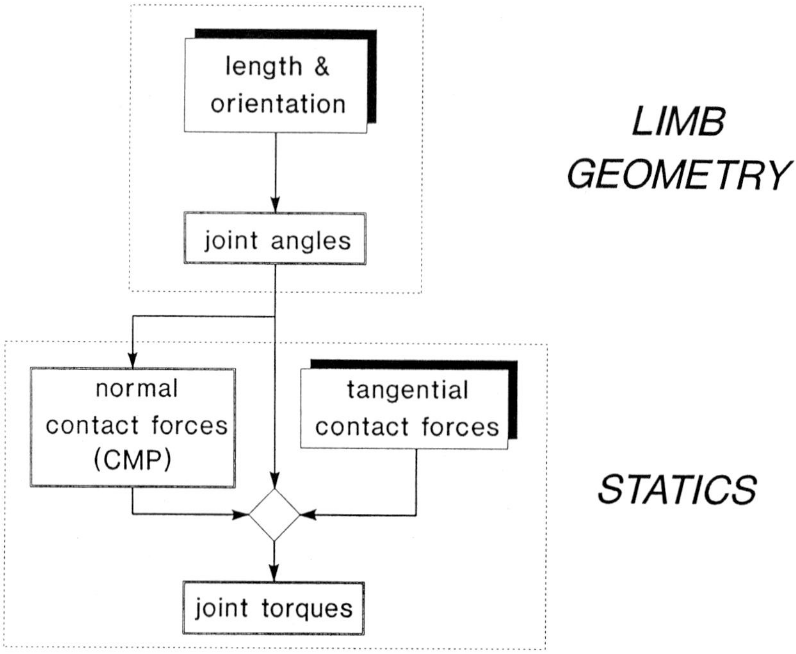

Figure 5. A hierarchical model of postural control. Two flow paths are illustrated: limb length and orientation are primarily controlled in the first, while tangential contact forces are controlled in the second. The two paths converge to determine joint torques.

One can equate the internal model of the geometrical state of the limbs in space to a *Body Scheme* (see also section 4) for posture. Thus, the problem of the maintenance of balance is solved by complying to the internal body scheme. Limited changes of the projected centre of mass and thus stability of the body are predicted outputs of the neural control endowed with this body scheme. This prediction is normally realized but can fail under altered conditions, as when an external load is applied. No correction of the postural geometry can occur unless the internal model of the body scheme is adapted to the new conditions. The absence of adaptation of cat posture over several hours of continuous application of the external load indicates that the body scheme can be surprisingly rigid.

The second path illustrated in Fig. 5 holds a separate, heterarchical position with respect to the first path. It refers to the experimentally demonstrated control of the tangential contact forces according to a fixed law, whose parameters are idiosyncratic to each animal. Note that an active neural control of the tangential forces has been independently proposed by Macpherson [18] using a different experimental paradigm (transient horizontal translations of the support surface).

Finally, the joint torques are determined by the confluence of the two separate paths (since they are the vector product of the contact force and the moment arm). Thus, although they represent the actual output of the control system, they are specified in a subordinate manner relative to both the geometrical variables and the tangential forces.

2.5. Significance of a hierarchical control of postural geometry

Posture is often considered to be synonimous of balance. Thus, posture is defined as the stabilization of the body against gravity in several textbooks. In fact, posture and balance are two distinct concepts. Balance is compatible with a wide range of entirely different postures, that is spatial configurations of the body segments. The well known existence of a standard (or preferred) posture for each subject indicates that the neural processes involved in postural control impose stronger constraints than the simple maintenance of balance, constraints that result in the reduction of the number of degrees of freedom of body motion. Thus, the planar covariation of the joint angles that we described in Fig. 3 effectively eliminates one degree of freedom at each limb.

The standard posture is a characteristic feature of each animal species. By comparing the characteristic posture adopted by different quadrupeds, we can appreciate once more the primacy of the control of postural geometry. First, we note that the conditions of stable equilibrium, as well as the requirements for least muscular effort are similar across different species [17]. Also, comparative studies demonstrate that terrestrial mammals are nearly geometrically similar over most of their size range (0.005 to 2000 kg, [19]), in other words bone shape remains constant and all linear dimensions scale proportional to body mass power one-third. Yet, postures differ markedly: small mammals (such as the ground squirrel) adopt a crouched posture at the hindlimbs, while larger mammals (such as the horse) adopt a more upright posture [20]. The former posture involves great maneuverability and accelerative capability. The latter posture aligns all limb joints with the ground contact force, thus substantially reducing the forces that the muscles must exert and hence the stress that the bones must resist.

Cat posture is intermediate between these two extremes. Cats usually tend to keep their hindlimbs slightly flexed and their forelimbs almost straight (see Fig. 2*A*-*B*). Since the length of the individual segments of the hindlimbs is greater than that of the forelimbs, this posture results in the alignment of the trunk with the support platform [12]. Since the proximal joints of both fore- and hindlimbs lie vertically above the paws, they experience small torques [13]. It is obvious, therefore, that the specific posture that has been selected by evolution for a given species depends on a complex weighed combination of different factors, including biomechanical and neural constraints. The latter are no less important than the former as determinants of the body posture. In this context, it is interesting to note that the rather different postures adopted at the forelimbs and at the hindlimbs by cats can be explained by the same planar covariation of joint angles (see Fig. 3).

Coming back to the two notions of posture and balance we contrasted at the beginning of this section, it should be clear from all we said that the CNS controls posture directly and not balance. The system has learnt that its preferred posture is stable under normal operating conditions. Such posture may not be stable, however, under unusual conditions and yet the system may choose to transiently sacrifice balance rather than posture.

On the other hand, not only has posture largely evolved to oppose gravity to maintain balance, but it is also organized in a reference frame that is anchored to the direction of gravity. Thus, cats align their limb axis with the vertical at all platform tilts. Furthermore, the planar covariation of limb joint angles holds in the absolute reference frame anchored to the vertical. Note that also human posture is organized around the gravity vector [21]. In man, interestingly, also the orientation in space of the head can be stabilized relative to the vertical under several operating conditions [22]. The direction of gravity is continuously monitored by the otolith organs. However, it is also interiorized to some extent during lifelong experience, as indicated by the observation that the posture adopted by blindfolded astronauts during exposure to microgravity does not differ markedly from normal erect posture, even though no measure of the reference vertical is available under such conditions [23].

Of course the standard posture that develops philogenetically and ontogenetically within all members of a given species carries subtle variations among the individuals, variations that are acquired during growth and experience. Being particularly tuned to the "shape" of human posture, we can easily recognize known people from behind, due to their characteristic posture. (Thomas defined the individual posture as "the signature with the body" [24].) The specific geometrical configuration of body posture then becomes a complex "Gestalt" whose significance is not only in the control of equilibrium but also in expressive and emotional behaviour.

3. CATCHING BEHAVIOUR IN MAN

The studies on posture reviewed above have indicated some general organizational principles of the neural control of the stable mechanical interaction between the limbs of a standing animal and the supporting ground. However, in other circumstances the mechanical interaction of a limb with the environment may not be sustained over prolonged epochs of time, but may be more transient, with the characteristics of an impulsive impact. Stepping or landing on the ground are examples of an impulsive impact of the lower limbs, as is catching of objects for the arm.

A preplanned transient mechanical interaction poses some special problems to the central controller. In fact, a successful mechanical interaction requires the correct specification of both target position and limb compliance. Limb compliance is defined as the dynamic relation between a given change in position and the corresponding change in force [25]. Let us refer to Fig. 1*B* and consider that the interaction between the limb endpoint and the external environment be dynamic (as in catching an object), rather than static as in the case of cat posture. It is intuitive that the smaller is the limb compliance, the greater the reactive force *F* for a given displacement.

Man has evolved to interact with objects and manipulate tools optimally. Conceivably, he is able to tune arm compliance according to the specific physical properties of the different objects; for instance, grasping an egg with the hand most likely involves a very different control of limb compliance as compared to grasping a bowl. Much thinking has been recently devoted to the problem of adaptive compliance control [26-28]. However the neural mechanisms that are actually involved in compliance control are still poorly understood.

Catching a falling ball represents an ideal paradigm for the study of preplanned mechanical interactions with objects. This task requires an accurate control of limb position to intercept the trajectory of the ball [29]. It also requires the control of limb compliance in order to absorb optimally ball momentum. Furthermore, subjects cannot self-pace the modulation in time of these variables (limb position and compliance), but must comply with the timing constraints imposed from outside. By changing the mass of the ball and/or the height of fall one can study the effect of cognitive set and expectation about the anticipated properties of the forthcoming impact. In the next sections we review some findings on the neural mechanisms involved in the control of limb position and compliance.

3.1. Control of limb position and compliance in catching

Figure 6 illustrates typical findings obtained when catching is performed in the presence of vision and prior information about both the mass of the ball and the height of fall [30-31]. The effect of varying the height of fall and mass of the ball is illustrated with the results from 2 different subjects (Figs. 6*A-C* and Figs. 6*D-F*).

The muscle activity (rectified electromyographic recording) associated with catching is organized in two main segments relative to the time of ball impact (indicated by the vertical lines in Fig. 6): anticipatory (voluntary) activity prior to the impact, and reflex activity after the impact.

Anticipatory activity is contingent on the presence of vision and comprises early and late components (first and second arrows in the Figure, respectively) [32]. Late components represent the major build-up of activity prior to impact. Their onset time is locked to the estimated time of impact independent of the height (and duration) of fall. Time-to-contact can be estimated using optical flow information (i.e. the field of the instantaneous positional velocities of the image on the retina, [29,33]). The mean amplitude of the late anticipatory activity is scaled in proportion to the magnitude of the expected momentum at impact. The prediction of ball momentum (mv) depends on a cognitive operation performed on the basis of heterogeneous informations. Instantaneous velocity (v) information is available through vision, but subjects must extrapolate from velocity measured at one instant to the final velocity some time later at impact. The expected mass (m) of the ball can be estimated based on an internal model of the ball's properties.

Anticipatory activity is generally accompanied by flexion of the limb to meet the incoming ball. This represents clear evidence for a control of limb position just prior to impact time.

Ball impact on the hand results in a sudden extension of the limb. According to the classical notions about stretch reflexes, one would expect that this extension evoked EMG responses organized reciprocally over antagonist muscles: flexor muscles that are stretched by the perturbation should be reflexly activated, while extensor muscles that are shortened should relax. Instead, the EMG responses that follow the impact at a short latency violate the law of reciprocal innervation, since both flexor and extensor muscles are coactivated [30]. Although these responses are reflexly triggered by the impact, their amplitude and direction are preset within the CNS *prior to impact* by using the available information on the forthcoming perturbation.

When subjects are provided with accurate information on the impending perturbation, the mean amplitude of the reflex responses generally increases proportional to the intensity of the perturbation, both in the stretched muscles and in the shortening muscles [31]. Once again this is not in

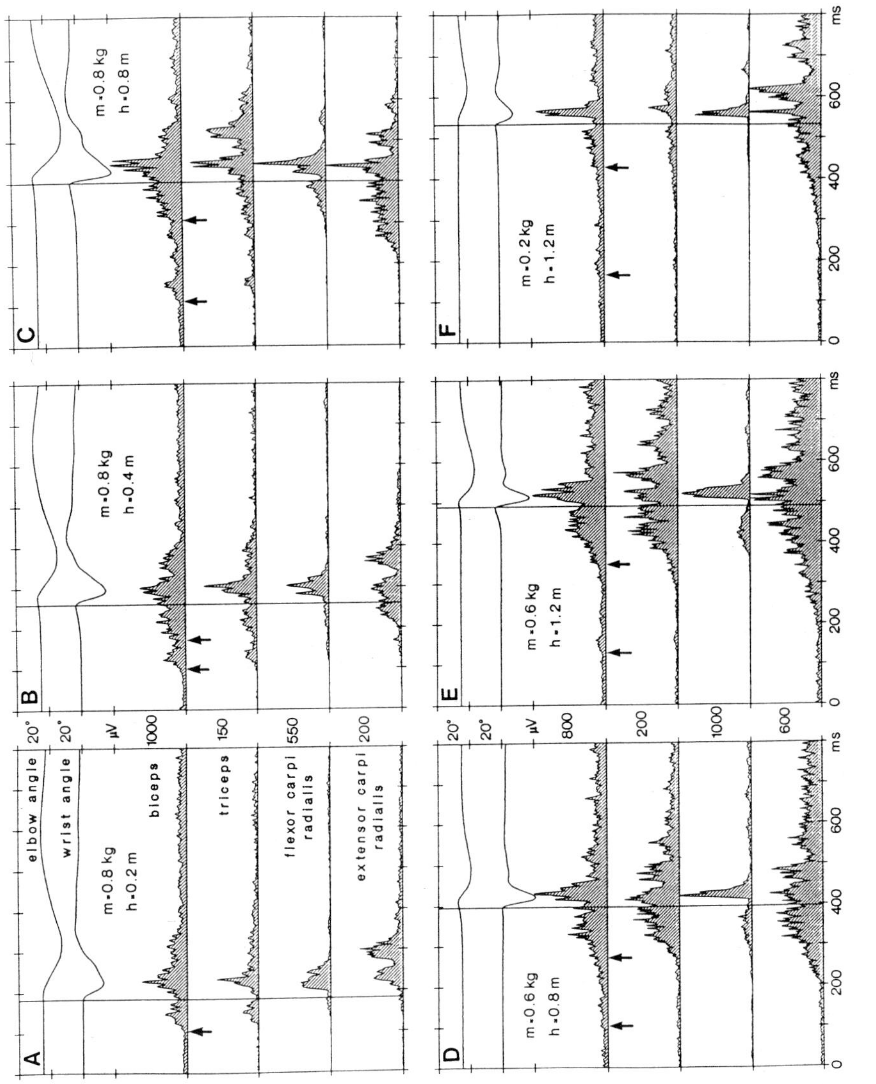

Figure 6. Ensemble averages (10 trials each) from 2 experiments (2 subjects) are plotted in *A-C* and *D-F*, respectively. The mass of the ball and the height of fall are indicated in each panel. The ball was released at 0 s and hit the hand at the time indicated by the vertical line. The times of onset of the early and late anticipatory EMG responses are indicated by the arrows. (Modified from ref. 31).

accordance with the behaviour of classical stretch reflexes: the amplitude of muscle activity in shortening muscles should decrease with increasing shortening velocities.

In the absence of visual information, however, the amplitude of the mechanical oscillations induced by the impact is much larger in the first trial than in the following trials, indicating fast adaptive calibration of the responses [32].

This adaptive calibration of the responses has been interpreted as resulting from the operation of a model reference system [32]. According to this hypothesis, the CNS would be endowed with an internal model of the dynamic interaction that is expected to occur at impact. The response of the model to the disturbance is compared with the actual mechanical response of the limb and generates an error signal. This error is then used to calibrate the parameters of the reflex controller and to update the internal model. Initially, the model does not accurately predict the desired performance, possibly because of an erroneous estimate of ball momentum in the absence of vision. However, kinesthetic and cutaneous informations obtained during the first trial are adequate to correct the estimate and achieve the desired performance in the subsequent trials.

As for the functional significance of the anticipatory and reflex coactivation, it should be noted that contraction of antagonist muscles results in joint torques with opposite signs, but in additive joint compliances. Thus, the observed scaling of the amplitude of both anticipatory and reflex responses proportional to the amplitude of the perturbation suggests that the compliance of the limb is tuned according to the expected properties of the impact [31]. This hypothesis has been demonstrated by further experiments (see next section).

3.2. Central gating of stretch reflex responses

Recent experiments have provided the conclusive evidence that reflex coactivation does not merely depend on the nature of the peripheral stimulus associated with ball impact, but is preset within the CNS [34]. In these experiments torque motor perturbations were randomly applied to the elbow joint at different times before and during catching. It was found that the pattern of the reflex responses evoked in elbow muscles was not constant, but depended on the time of application of the torque pulse. Reciprocal responses, consisting of an increase of activity in the stretched triceps and a decrease of activity in the shortening biceps, were consistently elicited when a flexor pulse was applied at any time in the course of a trial, except during a limited time interval centered on impact. During that interval (from about 60 ms prior to impact up to 60 ms after impact), the pattern of the reflex responses consisted in a coactivation of both stretched and shortening

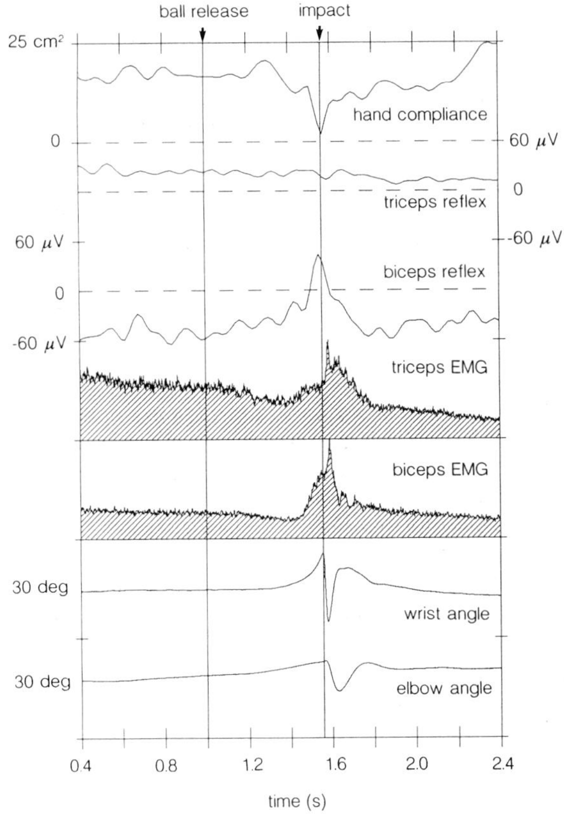

Figure 7. Time course of the changes of the indicated variables during catching. Pseudo-random perturbations were applied continuously to the elbow joint by a torque motor during each trial starting with time 0 s [34]. The ball was released 1 s later and hit the hand at 1.55 s. The pseudo-random sequence was shifted by one element from trial to trial until all elements were shifted. In the Figure, the bottom 4 traces are plotted from the ensemble average of all trials. In the average, the effect of the motor perturbations cancels out. The EMG traces have been scaled to their maximum. EMG and kinematic data of single trials were cross-correlated with the pseudo-random perturbations, thus eliminating the activity uncorrelated with these perturbations (such as the activity related to catching). The traces labelled *biceps reflex* and *triceps reflex* correspond to the mean amplitude (over the 20-60 ms interval) of the EMG responses obtained by cross-correlation. Note the reversal of the direction of the reflex response in biceps around impact time. The trace labelled *hand compliance* corresponds to the variance of the mechanical oscillations of the hand in the vertical direction induced by the torque pulses (the mechanical oscillations were obtained by cross-correlation with the measured changes in hand position). Note the minimum in hand compliance around impact.

muscles, due to a transient reversal of the direction of the short-latency response of biceps. The traces labelled *biceps reflex* and *triceps reflex* in Fig. 7 indicate the time course of the changes of the mean amplitude (over the 20-60 ms interval from pulse onset) of the reflex responses in the respective muscles. The reversal of biceps responses around impact can be clearly noted.

Since the reflex reversal begins prior to the time of impact, it does not depend on the peripheral stimuli elicited by the impact but it is generated within the CNS. Reflex coactivation is then part of a prospective control scheme that involves the central gating of stretch reflex responses from the spinal pathways of reciprocal inhibition (via lamina VII Ia interneurones) to the pathways of co-excitation of antagonist α-motoneurones (via lamina V-VI interneurones, [35]).

The key to understand the functional significance of this gating mechanism lies in the experimental finding that the compliance of the hand (top trace in Fig. 7) is transiently minimized during that same time interval in which the biceps reflex reverses direction. Since the torque motor pulses applied at different times during catching were constant, the amount of the mechanical oscillations of the hand induced by each such pulse provides a measure of the overall hand compliance [36]: the larger the oscillations, the larger the compliance and viceversa. The variance of the hand oscillations was then computed at different times during catching. The changes of this variance are plotted in the upper trace of Fig. 7 and correspond to the changes of hand compliance.

The time course of the changes in hand compliance is generally poorly correlated with that of the changes in overall EMG activity (traces labelled *biceps, triceps EMG*). (The maximum EMG lags behind the minimum compliance and therefore cannot be its cause.) By contrast, the timing of the minimum in hand compliance is well correlated with the reversal of biceps reflex.

One can therefore hypothesize that the reversal of stretch reflex responses prior to impact corresponds to a transition between two distinct control modes: from a position control, based on reciprocal innervation, to a compliance control, based on coactivation. The switching between these two operating modes could be implemented in a network that changes synaptic weights so as to dynamically optimize the performance criterion corresponding to hand compliance.

3.3. The role of the internal model of limb geometry for compliance control

The minimization of hand compliance suggests that the CNS is able to represent internally the intended hand compliance and to transform it into appropriate patterns of output muscle activities. However, hand compliance is a global variable that depends on both the pattern of muscle activities *and* the geometrical configuration of the limb [37]. In other words, the same pattern of muscle activity may result in a very different value of hand compliance depending on the values of joint angles. Therefore, the transformation of intended hand compliance into the appropriate muscle activities requires an internal model of limb geometry. The results obtained on catching can then be interpreted as indicative of the fact that the stretch reflex is gated based on the internal model of limb geometry.

This is a striking conclusion, because it leads to postulate a linkage between two different domains of neural control that are usually considered to be indepedent, remote from each other, namely the domain of the internal models and representations of limb geometry, on the one hand, and the domain of muscle reflex control, on the other hand. According to the prevailing views on the hierarchical organization of motor systems, the level of movement planning and the level of movement control represent two independent stages of processing, dealing with entirely different kinematic and dynamic variables. At the higher level of planning, limb movements are represented in the global terms describing the action of the end effector (e.g. the hand). By contrast, it is often assumed that the level of reflex control deals only with the local variables pertaining to a single muscle (e.g. muscle length, force or stiffness).

The picture that comes out from the series of studies on catching, instead, is one in which the operation of the reflex control does also deal with global variables, much of the same nature as those involved in the process of trajectory formation. Indeed, we showed that gating of the stretch reflex is involved in the minimization of one such global variable, the hand compliance, based on an internal model of limb geometry.

An old quotation appears pertinent here: "The nervous system reflects the external world by creating an internal model of its environment ..... The idea of the reflex as a manner in which the images of the environment are derived from the model internal to the nervous system leads us to conclude that the reflex is by its nature an active process" [38].

It is conceivable that, in the course of the ontogenesis of the brain processes involved in the construction of motor acts, an isomorphism emerges epigenetically between the internal models of the body and space, on the one hand, and limb movement and its perception, on the other hand. The existence of these internal models allows a virtual, simulated exploration of the external environment and an anticipatory adaptation of the motor behaviour to the demands posed by the environment before they actually occur.

4. CONCLUSIONS

We have reviewed data on cat posture and human catching that argue in favour of the existence of a parallel, distributed control of geometrical parameters, such as limb position, and kinetic parameters, such as limb force or compliance. Not only does a parallel control of limb position and force satisfy the requirements inherent in the mechanical interaction with the external environment, but it also affords a great flexibility of motor behaviour to the CNS. A modular structure in the organization of motor acts is particularly well suited for optimal or adaptive control.

We have presented evidence that the brain is endowed with fairly accurate internal models of the spatial relations of limb and body segments relative to each other and to the external environment [39]. The term *Body Scheme* has been used by the neurologists to identify this multidimensional spatial map of the body resident in the brain. The *Body Scheme* is largely inborn, but model parameters, such as the estimate of mass and length of the individual limb segments, can be recalibrated to compensate for body remodelling during growth in childhood.

However, once established, the body scheme is fairly robust, and can resist modifications. Thus, we showed that cats do not modify their posture in the presence of an external load applied to their body. Another example is given by the well known symptom of the *Phantom Limb* in amputees.

Given the availability of such elaborated internal models of the limb physical properties, a smart use of relatively simple automatic mechanisms, such as the reflexes, can afford optimal and adaptive behaviour under several operating conditions. We have discussed one such instance, namely the switching of the stretch reflex during catching.

The data on cat posture and human catching have also indicated that the internal models of limb geometry are shared by the paths of neural control of limb kinematics and by the paths of control of limb dynamics. Thus, in cat stance, both the control of the joint angular position and the control of torques are predicated on the model of the geometrical configuration of the limbs in space (see Fig. 5). A similar sharing occurs for the control of hand position and the control of hand compliance in catching. Therefore, the control of kinematics and the control of dynamics, though separate, are not independent.

As for the neural substrates of these paths of control, there is growing evidence on the existence of multiple, distributed representations of kinematics and dynamics in the brain. Thus, kinematic variables (such as the direction of movement) and dynamic variables (such the external load to counteract during movement or the pattern of muscle activities) appear to be coded by populations of neurones that are segregated in different cortical areas or within different layers of the same area, at the level of motor, premotor and parietal cortex [40-42].

Acknowledgements

This work was partially supported by grant n. 3149 ESPRIT II Basic Research awarded by the Commission of the European Communities, and by a grant awarded by the Human Frontier Science Program.

5. REFERENCES

1 Bizzi, E., Chapple, W., Hogan, N., Trends Neurosci. 5 (1982) 395.
2 Hildreth, E.C., Hollerbach, J.M., In: Handbook of Physiology, Sect. 1, Vol. 5, Part. 2 (J.M. Brookhart and V.B. Mountcastle, eds.) Am. Physiol. Soc. Bethesda, MD, pp. 605-642, 1987.
3 Soechting, J.F., Flanders, M., In: Motor Centrol: Concepts and Issues. (D.R. Humphrey and H.-J. Freund, eds.) Wiley, NY, pp. 293-306, 1991.
4 Georgopoulos, A.P., Ann. Rev. Neurosci. 9 (1986) 147.
5 Jeannerod, M., The Neural and Behavioural Organization of Goal-Directed Movements. Clarendon Press, Oxford, 1988.
6 Lacquaniti, F., Trends Neurosci. 12 (1989) 287.
7 Atkeson, C.G., Ann. Rev. Neurosci. 12 (1989) 157.
8 Roberts, T.D.M. Neurophysiology of postural mechanisms. Buttherworths, London, 1978.
9 Brookhart, J.M., Parmeggiani, P.L., Petersen, W.A., Stone, S.A., Am. J. Physiol. 208 (1965) 1047.
10 Massion, J., Gahery, Y., In: Reflex Control of Posture and Movement, Progress in Brain Research, Vol. 50:219-226 (R. Granit and O. Pompeiano, eds.) Elsevier, Amsterdam, 1979.
11 Horak, F.B., Nashner, L.M., J. Neurophysiol. 55 (1986) 1369.
12 Lacquaniti, F., Maioli, C., Fava, E. Exp. Brain Res. 57 (1984) 82.
13 Lacquaniti, F., LeTaillanter, M., Lopiano, L., Maioli, C., J. Physiol. (London) 426 (1990) 177.
14 Maioli, C., Poppele, R.E., Soc. Neurosci. Abstr. 15 (1989) 392.

15 Jeannerod, M., Biguer, B., In: Neurophysiological and Neuropsychological Aspects of Spatial Neglect. (M. Jeannerod, ed.) Elsevier, Amsterdam, pp.87-113, 1987.
16 Maioli, C., Lacquaniti, F. In: Posture and Gait: Development, Adaptation and Modulation. (B. Amblard, A. Berthoz, F. Clarac, eds.) Elsevier, Amsterdam, pp.371-379, 1988.
17 Gray, J., J. Exp. Biol. 20 (1944) 88.
18 Macpherson, J.M., J. Neurophysiol. 60 (1988) 204.
19 Biewener, A.A., Science 250 (1990) 1097.
20 Biewener, A.A., Science. 245 (1989) 45.
21 Lestienne, F.G., Gurfinkel, V.S., In: Prog. Brain Res. Vol. 76 (O. Pompeiano, J.H.J. Allum, eds.) Elsevier, Amsterdam, pp. 307-313, 1988.
22 Berthoz, A., Pozzo, T., In: Posture and Gait: Development, Adaptation and Modulation. (B. Amblard, A. Berthoz, F. Clarac, eds.) Elsevier, Amsterdam, pp.189-198, 1988.
23 Clement, G., Gurfinkel, V.S., Lestienne, F., Lipshits, M.I., Popov, K.E., Exp. Brain Res. 57 (1984) 61.
24 Thomas, A., Equilibre et Equilibration. Masson, Paris, 1940.
25 Agarwal, G.C., Gottlieb, G.L., CRC Crit. Revs. Biomed. Engrg. 12 (1984) 49.
26 Feldman, A.G., Neurosci. 5 (1980) 81.
27 Hogan, N., IEEE Trans. Autom. Contr. AC29 (1984) 681.
28 Houk, J.C., Ann. Rev. Physiol. 41 (1979) 99.
29 Sharp, R.H., Whiting, H.T.A, J. Motor Behav. 6 (1974) 139.
30 Lacquaniti, F., Maioli, C., Brain Res. 406 (1987) 373.
31 Lacquaniti, F., Maioli, C., J. Neurosci. 9 (1989) 134.
32 Lacquaniti, F., Maioli, C., J. Neurosci. 9 (1989) 149.
33 Lee, D.N., In: Tutorials in Motor Behavior (G.E. Stelmach and J. Requin, eds.) North-Holland Publishing, pp. 281-295, 1980.
34 Lacquaniti, F., Borghese, N.A., Carrozzo, M., Soc. Neurosci. Abstr. 16 (1990) 69.7.
35 Jankowska, E., McCrea, D., Mackel, R., J. Physiol. (London) 316 (1981) 411.
36 Kearney, R.E., Hunter, I.W., CRC Crit. Rev. Biomed. Engin. 18 (1990) 55.
37 Mussa-Ivaldi, F.A., Hogan, N., Bizzi, E., J. Neurosci. 5 (1985) 2732.
38 Bernstein, N., Anochin, P.K., Sokolov, E.N., Neurofisiologia e cibernetica (translated from Russian). Mecacci, Roma, 1973.
39 Gurfinkel, V.S., Levik, Yu., Human Physiol. 5 (1979) 269.
40 Crutcher, M.D., Alexander, G.E., J. Neurophysiol. 64 (1990) 151.
41 Georgopoulos, A.P., Caminiti, R., Kalaska, J.F., Exp. Brain Res. 54 (1984) 446.
42 Kalaska, J.F., Hyde, M.L., Exp. Brain Res. 59 (1985) 197.

Tutorials in Motor Behavior II
G.E. Stelmach and J. Requin (Editors)

A THEORY OF RAPID MOVEMENTS

R. Plamondon

Laboratoire Scribens, Département de Génie Électrique et Génie Informatique, École Polytechnique de Montréal, C.P. 6079, Succursale A, Montréal QC, H3C 3A7 Canada

Abstract

This paper provides a theoretical framework for the study of rapid movements in terms of velocity control. A sequential generation model is used to explain the origin of the asymmetric bell-shaped velocity profiles and to describe them with a log-normal function. Using the intrinsic properties of these curves, it is shown that a large part of the previously reported observations in the field are consequences of the power relationship that exists between the movement time and the relative spatial error. Among other things, this relationship predicts Fitts' data with a better accuracy than Fitts' law and gives a unified description of the speed accuracy trade-offs.

1. INTRODUCTION

One important class of human movements that has been extensively studied to understand basic laws in motor behavior is called rapid-aimed movement or target-directed movement. These movements are very simple and their study constitutes a cornerstone for any movement understanding theory. So far, no general and complete view has been proposed to describe these movements although several interesting phenomena have been consistently reported by many independent research groups over the last century, starting with Fullerton and Cattell (1892), and Woodworth (1899) experiments on movement control.

Amongs these basic facts, the most well known is probably the relationship between the average movement time and the logarithm of the relative spatial error, as described by the Fitts' law (1954). This relationship holds when subjects are asked to make accurate and fast movements to a target. Although not perfectly fitting the data at low difficulty index (Crossman and Goodeve 1963; Klapp 1975), the equation has been found successful under a variety of experimental conditions: reciprocal tapping, disk and pin transfer (Fitts 1954), movements performed under a low-power stereoscopic microscope (Langolf et al. 1976), rotary movements of a knob (Knight and Dagnall 1967), joystick movements, handle turning (Jagacinski et al. 1980), mouse movements (Card et al. 1978), underwater movements (Kerr 1978), one shot aiming movements (Fitts and Paterson 1964), peg transfer (Amet et al. 1958), throwing darts and tapping movements (Kerr and Langolf 1977). Similarly the Fitt's law has been found to apply to subjects of different ages (Welford et al. 1969; Wallace et al. 1978), for retarded persons as well as for normal (Wade et al. 1978), for people with Parkinsonian desease (Flowers 1976), for different anatomical units (Langolf et al. 1976). In all these cases, the slopes and intercepts of the Fitt's function might differ, but the general form of the equation seems to be a good description of the speed-accuracy trade-off.

Although, no consistent theories have been able to perfectly account for this phenomenon for the whole range of relative spatial error reported by Fitts, interesting models have been developed (see for example Fitts 1954; Crossman and Goodeve 1963, 1983; Keele 1968; Meyer et al. 1982; Meyer et al. 1988). Alternate views of the speed-accuracy trade-off have also been reported. When subjects have to move to a point target within certain specified movement times, so that timing and distance accuracies are both required, then a linear speed-accuracy trade-off is observed, between the standard deviation of the spatial error and the movement velocity (Schmidt et al. 1979). Some studies have also been cited for which the speed-accuracy trade-off appears not to hold. For example, in movement where emphasis is made on timing at the expense of spatial accuracy, the opposite is observed that is, the timing error is smaller the higher is the movement velocity, even when the movement time is held constant (Schmidt 1969; Newell et al. 1979). This speed-accuracy paradox (Newell 1980) has not been given a consistent explanation either, although a space-time approach has been proposed to reconcile partly the observations related to spatial and temporal movement errors functions, based on the error distributions for the first four moments of amplitude-time combination (Hancock and Newell 1985).

This paper describes, in a more formal way than its preliminary version (Plamondon 1991), a general model for the generation of rapid movements from a set of movement processors acting in such a way as to produce log-normal velocity profiles. The origin of these outputs is given an interpretation, in terms of the central-limit theorem applied to linear systems. The overall approach leads to a simple mathematical equation describing the movement time in terms of the properties of a velocity generator. Once analyzed in terms of the movement parameters (distance, duration, spatial and temporal errors...) the model predicts Fitts' data with a better accuracy than Fitt's law (particularly at low ID). It also explains why a linear speed- accuracy relationship was observed by Schmidt et al. (1979) and moreover, why a speed-accuracy paradox was also reported by Newell et al. (1979).

2. A VELOCITY MODEL

A general way to look at movement generation is to consider the overall sets of neural and muscle networks involved in the production of a single rapid movement as a linear system producing the proper velocity profile (Plamondon 1990a,b; Plamondon 1991) from an impulse command $U_0(t-\tau)$ of amplitude D. In this case, one can write:

$$v(t) = \int_0^t DU_0(t-\tau)H(\tau)d\tau \quad (1)$$

$$= D\ H(t) \qquad with\ t \geq 0 \quad (2)$$

Equation (2) shows that, in this context, the velocity profile directly reflects the impulse response $H(t)$ of the global system.

Many investigators have reported that the velocity profiles of rapid movements are approximately bell-shaped (Beggs and Howard 1972; Georgopoulos et al. 1981; Morasso 1981; Soechting and Laquantini 1981; Abend et al. 1982; Atkeson and Hollerbach 1985). Moreover the shapes of the bell, after appropriate rescaling, are approximately superimposable that is the general shape is almost preserved for movements that vary in duration, distance or peak velocity (Atkeson and Hollerbach 1985; Bullock and Grossberg 1987). These velocity profiles have also been observed in handwriting, for curvilinear velocity (Morasso and Mussa Ivaldi 1982; Plamondon et al. 1990) and for angular velocity as well (Plamondon 1989). They are also commonly observed in prehension movement (Jeannerod 1984; Marteniuk et al. 1987). This invariance in the shape of the velocity profiles is in accordance with equation (2) since the system has a unique impulse response. Many indirect evidences also support this view (Gibson et al. 1985; Houk 1989; Houk and Gibson 1987; Plamondon and Parizeau 1988; Plamondon and Maarse 1989; Plamondon 1990a,b; Weeks et al. 1987, 1989, etc.).

The mathematical description of H(t) can be specified if one considers that it reflects the density function of the response time T of the different subprocesses involved in the activation of the system. If one assumes that the global system is made up of a cascade of n linear subsystems acting in such a way that the response time T_j of the jth stage is related to the response time T_{j-1} of the (j-1)th stage by a law of proportional effects (Gibrat 1931):

$$T_j = (1 + \varepsilon_j)T_{j-1}, \quad (3)$$

where ϵ_j is a random variable,
then, for an n stage system,

$$T_n = (1+\epsilon_1)\ (1+\epsilon_2)\ (1+\epsilon_3)...\ (1+\epsilon_n)\ T_0 \quad (4)$$

where T_0 defines the time resolution of the global system.

Then, it can be shown (Plamondon, in preparation) that, if n is sufficiently large and if some general mathematical conditions are met by each of the subsystem impulse responses, the central-limit theorem applies and predicts that H(t) will tend toward a log-normal curve (Aitchison and Brown 1966).

Using this type of curve, we have repeated a previous analysis by synthesis experiment (Plamondon et al, 1990) using this new model. Experimental results show that, for the majority of the strokes analyzed, the velocity data could be fitted almost perfectly with a support bounded log-normal,

that is:

$$\mathbf{v(t) = D} \Lambda (\mu, \sigma^2, \mathbf{t}_0, \mathbf{t}_1) \tag{5}$$

where D = stroke displacement

$\Lambda (\mu, \sigma^2, t_0, t_1)$ = log-normal curve bounded in time between the minimum (t_0) and the maximum (t_1) response time.

The mean square error between the original and the reconstructed velocity profiles, for the 1000 strokes studied, was 0.357 cm^2/sec^2. A recent comparative study has also clearly demonstrated that this performance constitutes a very significant improvement over all the previous models that have been published on the subject. None of these 20 other approaches, as tested over the same database, really challenged the log-normal model.

3. MOVEMENT TIME

Movement time is physically defined, from a velocity profile by the time elapsed between two points of zero velocity. Since the velocity profile is proportional to the system impulse response (see equation 2 and 5), t_0 and t_1 can be directly linked to the starting and ending time of the movement by:

$$MT = t_1 - t_0 \tag{6}$$

Using equation (4), where we assume for simplicity that all ϵ_i are equal, one can write:

$$MT = (1 + \epsilon)^n (T_{01} - T_{00}) = (1 + \epsilon)^n MTmin \tag{7}$$

where T_{00} and T_{01} represents the time resolution of the fastest and the slowest subsystems respectively. The difference of these two terms represents the minimum movement time (MTmin). If one assumes that the displacement caused by the activity of one subsystem follows a relationship similar to equation (3):

$$D_j = (1 + \alpha_j)\, D_{j-1} \tag{8}$$

then the total displacement covered after the activity of the n th stage will be of the form:

$$D = (1 + \alpha)^n\, D_0 \tag{9}$$

where all the α_j have been assumed to be equal, here again, for mathematical simplicity and where D_0 represents the spatial resolution of the global system. If one assumes that there is a proportionality between the α_i and ϵ_i:

$$\alpha_i = K\epsilon_i \tag{10}$$

then one can write after appropriate substitution:

$$MT \simeq \left(\frac{D}{D_0}\right)^{1/K} (T_{10} - T_{00}) = \left(\frac{D}{D_0}\right)^{1/K} MTmin \tag{11}$$

If one assumes that the absolute spatial error directly reflects the spatial resolution of the system, this equation predicts a linear relationship between the natural logarithm of the relative spatial error and the natural logarithm of the movement time (instead of the movement time as used in Fitts'law). Figure 1 shows the Fitts' data for the 1-ounce stylus-tapping experiment (1a) and the 1-pound stylus-tapping experiment (1b), as plotted according to the format of equation (11) where the measured spatial error dD has been equated to the spatial resolution of the system (D_0). The best-fitting straight line, in terms of minimizing the root mean square error, is shown on each graph, that is: ln MT = -1.999 + 0.353 $\ln(D/D_0)$ (Figure 1a), and ln MT = -1.994 + 0.368 $\ln(D/D_0)$ (Figure 1b).

The dotted line represents the best Fitts' law predictions in each case.

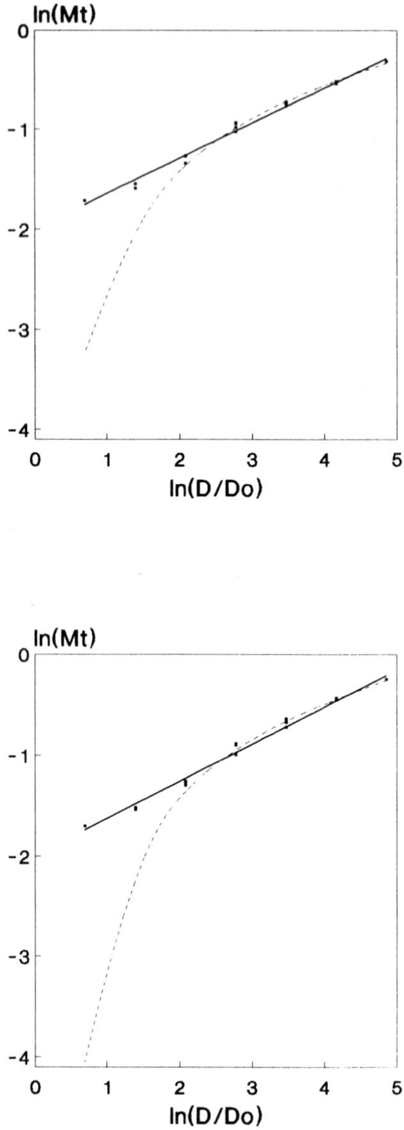

Figure 1 - Best fitting predictions from equation (11) on Fitts's data.
(a) 1 ounce stylus-tapping experiment
(b) 1 pound stylus-tapping experiment
The dotted lines show the best predictions according to Fitts'law.

As may be seen from this Figure, equation (11) makes better predictions than Fitts' law on Fitts' data. In terms of total mean square errors, it provides up to a three-fold improvement over Fitts' law. This effect is clearly apparent in the Figure for high D_0/D, where Fitts' equation can make up to a 40% error. In fact, it can be shown mathematically that Fitts' law constitutes a good approximation of the power relationship described above. If one expands equation (11) into series, Fitts' law constitutes the first two terms of this series. Moreover, the effect of the stylus weight on MTmin and K seems to be negligible in these experiments; both parameters are almost constant (MTmin ≃ 135 ms, K = 2.83 and 2.72).

Equation (11) can also be used to explain the linear relationship between the spatial error and the movement distance, as reported by (Schmidt et al., 1979). Indeed, when D_0 is taken as the dependent variable, the power equation (11) can be rewritten as:

$$D_0 \approx \frac{(MTmin)^K D}{MT^K} \tag{12}$$

If the minimum movement time is constant for a specific set of experiments, this equation predicts a proportional relationship between the absolute spatial error (reflecting D_0) and the displacement (D) and one which is inversely proportional to a power factor of MT. Such a proportionality relationship makes more sense physically than a linear relationship because it predicts a null error at null displacement. Why a linear relationship has been reported in the past then? The linear results described by Schmidt et al. (1979) concerns the effective target width as measured from the standard deviation of the spatial error along or perpendicular to the overall direction of movement, not the absolute error. However, since the relationship for the absolute error parallels that for the total error, one can write as a first approximation:

$$\tilde{D}_0^2 \approx E_{ex}^2 = W_{ex}^2 + CE_{ex}^2 \tag{13}$$

where:

$\tilde{D}_0$ = estimated value of the absolute error.

E_{ex} = total error along the overall direction of movement.

W_{ex} = standard deviation of the spatial error measured along the overall direction of movement (as reported by Schmidt et al. (1979)).

CE_{ex} = constant error along the same direction.

Combining (12) and (13), one predicts an approximate linear relationship between the square of the movement amplitude (D) and the variance of the parallel spatial error(W_{ex}^2) with CE_x^2 as the intercept. Although the exact and complete data from Schmidt et al. (1979) paper, were not available, we have roughly estimated the mean values directly from their graphs and plotted, in Figure 2a, the variance of the spatial error (W_{ex}^2) as a function of the square of the displacement (D^2) for two experiments. A linear relationship ($\rho > 0.95$) is observed in both cases ($W_{ex}^2 = 0.00058\ D^2 + 0.218$ for MT = 140 mS and $W_{ex}^2 = 0.00028\ D^2 + 0.116$ for MT = 200 mS). Using the intercept of this linear relationship to estimate CE_{ex}, one can then estimate $E_{ex} \simeq \widetilde{D}_0$ and plot it as a function of D, where the proportionality relationship described by (12) should become apparent. These results are plotted in Figure 2b ($\widetilde{D}_0 = 0.029\ D - 0.079$ for MT = 140 mS and $\widetilde{D}_0 = 0.025\ D - 0.088$ for MT = 200 mS). As one can see, this rough evaluation supports equation (12) in a sense that the relationship between the estimated absolute error ($\widetilde{D}_0$)and the movement amplitude (D) is almost proportional ($\rho > 0.95$) and moreover, the slope of the proportionality relationship decreases as MT increases.

Finally, the conditions for observing the speed-accuracy paradox, as reported by Newell (1980), can also be stated immediately if one differentiates equation (11), assuming MTmin and D_0 constant for these experiments, and expresses the absolute temporal error as a dependent variable:

$$dMT \simeq \frac{MT}{K}\frac{dD}{D} \tag{14}$$

Generally speaking, if the relative spatial error (dD/D) is a constant for one set of experiments, dMT will be proportional to MT, that is, the absolute timing error will be proportional to the movement time, when the emphasis is on timing accuracy. Moreover, equation (14) predicts that dMT will decrease with distance, as Newell et al. (1979) also reported between different set of experiments. Figure 3 reproduces the data from experiment 1 of Newell et al. (1979) (dMT = 0.104 MT for D = 5 cm and dMT = 0.070 MT for D = 15 cm; with $\rho > 0.99$ in both cases). Both the proportionality relationship and the distance effect clearly reflect the predictions of equation (14). A similar proportionality relationship was also reported by Schmidt et al. (1969).

4. DISCUSSION

The theory presented here is quite simple and parcimonious; it integrates within two basic equations (5 and 11) the majority of the observations that have been repeatedly observed in the past decades about rapid movements. The key idea of this approach is to consider the sets of neural and muscles networks involved in the production of a rapid movement as a set of dependent linear processes acting sequentially under the law of proportional effect (Gibrat 1931) and whose global behavior converges toward the generation of log-normal velocity profiles.

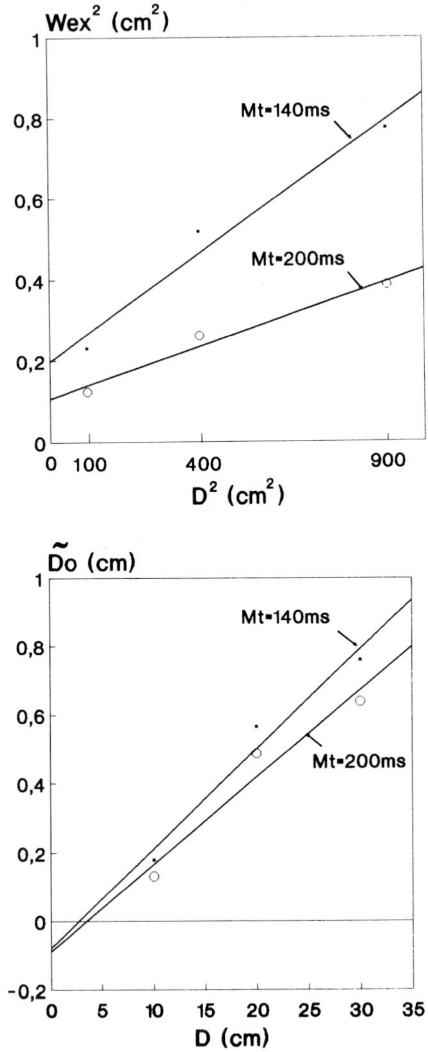

Figure 2 -

(a) Variance of the effective target width measured along the required direction of movement (as evaluated from Schmidt et al. (1979) as a function of the square of the distance.

(b) Absolute spatial error ($\widetilde{D}_0$) as roughly estimated from Schmidt et al. (1979) data, versus movement amplitude (D).

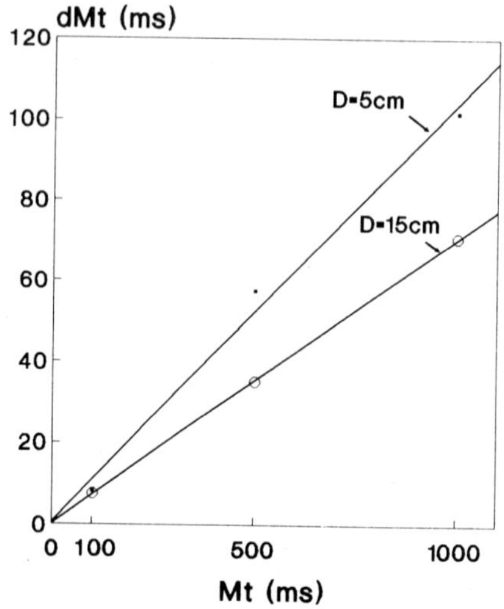

Figure 3 - Absolute timing error (dMT) as reported by Newell et al. (1979), (experiment 1, table 1), versus movement time (MT).

In this perspective, the model leads to a clear definition of a ballistic or a spontaneous movement: a movement whose velocity is made up of a single asymmetric bell-shaped profile that can be described in terms of the parameters of a log-normal curve. For this fundamental unit of rapid movement, depending on the experimental protocol, different relationship can be observed: a power relationship between the movement time and the relative spatial error, a proportionality relationship between the absolute spatial error and the movement amplitude and a proportionality relationship between the absolute timing error and movement time. It is not necessary to assume any feedback or correction hypothesis (Grossman and Goodeve 1963) nor any sequence of submovements (Meyer et al. 1988) to explain Fitts' law. According to our model, Fitts'law happens to be a good approximation of the more general power law that links the movement time and the spatial resolution of a movement. Equation (11) shows also the arbitrariness of defining the relative spatial error D_o/D in terms of a difficulty index, as proposed by Fitts (1954). Only the value of D_o/D is necessary to understand the underlying mechanism and its rescaling in a base 2 logarithm is completely artificial and unnecessary.

Moreover, the theory predicts that the fitting of the data with a power relationship may deteriorate if a rapid movement is made up of more than one fundamental unit. Indeed more complex rapid movements can be seen as a sum of fundamental units described by log-normal velocity profiles (equation 5). Depending on the timing between two consecutive units, the resulting velocity profile will be described in terms of a superimposition of log-normal curves (when the second unit starts before the end of the first one, that is $t_{02}<t_{11}$) or in terms of a sequence of independent units (when $t_{02}>t_{11}$). Generally speaking, it will be observed that for a movement composed of two units the total movement time (MT_{tot}) will be equal to:

$$MT_{tot} = MT_1 + MT_2 + (t_{02} - t_{11}) \tag{15}$$

In the superimposition condition ($t_{02}<t_{11}$), MT_{tot} will be smaller than the sum of the movement times of its two constituting units and longer than that sum, in the sequence condition ($t_{02}>t_{11}$).

Only when $t_{02}=t_{11}$, that is when the second unit starts immediately at the end of the first one that a power relationship will hold exactly, provided that the relative spatial errors of both units are proportional and that their power exponents are the same.

In all the other cases, the unsynchronized summation of submovement will be reflected by changes in the slope of the approximate power relationship. These changes of slope have been reported by many in the past. Similarly, for very slow movements or for movements where velocity profiles might not be log-normal, the power relationship will be a very rough equation to predict the data.

5. CONCLUSION

The theory developped in this paper shows that a large part of the observations reported on rapid movement can be seen as different views of a universal power relationship (11) that results from the converging behavior of the different processes involved in the control of the movement velocity.

Using a linear system approach, we have explained the origin of the asymmetric bell-shaped velocity profiles and described it in terms of a log-normal curve. We have also discussed the different relationships that result from this model, between different variables, particularly the spatial and temporal resolution vs the movement time and amplitude. From this point of view, it has been shown, among other things, that Fitts (1954), Schmidt et al. (1979), Newell et al. (1979) data were observations of the same unique process, studied under different experimental conditions that focus on different dependent variables.

This approach does not rely upon any internal description of the different neural and muscles networks involved in the production of rapid movements but focusses on the global behavior of the system. In that perspective, it is very general. It depicts the ideal behavior of the system. As long as movements are characterized by log-normal velocity profiles, the theory should hold. The better the approximation, the better the predictions will be. New experiments are under way to clarify some the concepts presented here and to determine the limit of application of this theory.

6. ACKNOWLEDGEMENTS

A part of this work was completed when Réjean Plamondon was a Fellow of the Netherlands Institute for Advanced Study. This work was also sponsored partly by CRSNG grant A0915 from Government of Canada and FCAR grant CRP2665 from Government of Québec. The author wants to thank Pierre Yergeau, engineer at Laboratoire Scribens for his kind assistance in the computer simulations, model verification and critical support throughout this work, and Yves de Ros, scientific analyst at NIAS for his kind help in computer simulations. The author also extend his grateful appreciation to Gilles Deslauriers and Marc Moore, both professors at the Department of Applied Mathematics, École Polytechnique de Montréal, for their fruitfull comments.

7. REFERENCES

1. Abend W., Bizzi E., Morasso P. (1982), Human arm trajectory formation, Brain 105, p. 331-348.
2. Aitchison J., Brown J.A.C. (1966). The lognormal distribution, Cambridge University Press, 176 p.
3. Amet J., Golby C.W., Kay H. (1958). The measurement of elements in an assembly task - the information output of the human motor system, Quaterly Journal of Experimental Psychology 10, p. 1-11.
4. Atkeson C.G., Hollerbach J.M. (1985). Kinematic features of unrestrained vertical arm movements, Journal of Neuroscience 5/9, p. 2318-2330.
5. Beggs W.D.A., Howarth C.I. (1972). The movement of the hand toward a target, Quaterly Journal of Experimental Psychology 24, p. 448-453.
6. Bullock D., Grossberg S. (1987). Neural dynamics of planned arm movements: emergent invariants and speed-accuracy properties during trajectory formation. In: Neural Networks and Natural Intelligence, S. Grossberg (Ed.) MIT Press, p. 553-622.
7. Card S.K., English W.K., Burr B.J. (1978). Evaluation of Mouse Rate-Controlled Isometric Joystick, Step Keys and Text Keys for Text Selection on a CRT. Ergonomics, Vol. 21, no. 8, p. 601-613.
8. Crossman E.R.F.W., Goodeve P.J. (1983). Feedback control of hand-movement and Fitts' Law, Quaterly Journal of Experimental Psychology 35A, p. 251-278.
9. Fitts P.M. (1954). The information capacity of the human motor system in controlling the amplitude of movement, Journal of Experimental Psychology 47/6, p. 381-391.
10. Fitts P.M., Peterson J.R. (1964). Information capacity of discrete motor responses, Journal of Experimental Psychology 67/2, p. 103-112.
11. Flowers K.A. (1976). Visual "closeloop" and "openloop" characteristics of voluntary movement in patients with Parkinsonism and intention tremor, Brain 99, p. 269-310.

12. Fullerton G.S., Cattell J. McK (1892). On the perception of small differences, University of Pensylvania Philosophical Series n°2.
13. Georgopoulos A.P., Kalaska J.F., Massey J.T. (1981). Spatial trajectories and reaction time of aimed movements: effects of practice, uncertainty, and change in target location, Journal of Neurophysiology 46/4, p. 725-743.
14. Gibrat R. (1931). Les Inegalités Economiques: Application d'une loi nouvelle: la loi de l'effet proportionnel. Thèse de doctorat, Université de Lyon, 296 p.
15. Gibson A.R., Houk J.C., Kohlerman N.J. (1985). Relation between red nucleus discarge and movement parameters in trained macaque monkeys, Journal of Physiology (London) 358, p. 551-570.
16. Hancock P.A., Newell K.M. (1985). The movement speed-accuracy relationship in space-time, In Motor Behavior: Programming, Control and Acquisition, H. Hewer, U. Kleinbeck, K.H. Schmidt (eds.), Springer-Verlag, p. 153-188.
17. Houk J.C., Gibson A.R. (1987). Sensorimotor processing through the cerebellum. In New Concepts in Cerebellar Neurobiology, Alan R. Liss Inc., p. 387-416.
18. Houk J.C. (1989). Burst of discharge recorded from the red nucleus may provide real measures of Gottlieb's excitation pulses. Behavioral and Brain Sciences 12, p. 224-225.
19. Jagacinski R.J., Repperger D.W., Moran M.S., Ward S.L., Glass B. (1980). Fitts' Law and the microstructure of rapid discrete movement, Journal of Experimental Psychology: Human and Perception and Performance 6/2, p. 309-320.
20. Jeannerod M. (1984). The timing of natural prehension movements. J. Motor Behavior 16, p. 235-254.
21. Klapp S.T. (1975). Feedback Versus Motor Programming in the Control of Aimed Movement. J. Experimental Psychology: Human Perception and Performance 104, p. 147-153.
22. Keele S.W. (1968). Movement control in skilled motor performance, Psychological Bulletin 70, p. 387-403.
23. Kerr B.A., Langolf G.D. (1977). Speed of aiming movements, Quaterly Journal of Experimental Psychology 29, p. 475-481.
24. Kerr R. (1978). Dividing adaptation and Fitts' Law, Journal of Motor Behavior 10/4, p. 255-260.
25. Knight A.A., Dagnall P.R. (1967). Precision in Movements Ergonomics 10/3, p. 321-330.
26. Langolf G.D., Chaffin D.B., Foulke J.A. (1976). An investigation of Fitts' Law using a wide range of movements amplitudes, Journal of Motor Behavior 8/2, p. 113-128.
27. Marteniuk R.G., Mackenzie C.L., Jeannerod, M., Athènes S. and Dugas (1987). Constraints on Human Arm Movement Trajectories, Canadian Journal of Psychology, 41(3), p. 365-378.
28. Meyer D.E., Smith J.E.K., Wright C.E. (1982). Models for the speed and accuracy of aimed limb movements, Psychological Review 89, p. 449-482.
29. Meyer D.E., Abrams R.A., Kornblum S., Wright C.E., Smith J.E.K. (1988). Optimality in human motor performance: ideal control of rapid aimed movement, Psychological Review 95, p. 340-370.

30. Morasso P. (1981). Spatial control of arm movements, Experimental Brain Research 42, p. 223-227.
31. Morasso P., Mussa Ivaldi F.A. (1982). Trajectory formation and handwriting: a computational model. Biological Cybernetics 45, p. 131-142.
32. Newell K.M., Hoshizaki L.E.F., Carlton M.J., Halbert J.A. (1979). Movement time and velocity as determinant of movement timing accuracy, Journal of Motor Behavior 11, p. 49-58.
33. Newell K.M. (1980). The speed-accuracy paradox in movement control: errors of time and space, in Tutorials in Motor Behavior, G.E. Stelmach and J. Requin (eds.), North-Holland, p. 501-510.
34. Plamondon R., Parizeau M. (1988). Signature verification from position, velocity and acceleration signals: a comparative study. Proc. 8th Int. Conf. on Pattern Recognition, Rome, p. 260-265.
35. Plamondon R. (1989). Handwriting control: a functional model. In: Models of Brain Functions. R. Cotterill (Ed.), Cambridge University Press, p. 563-574.
36. Plamondon R., Maarse F.J. (1989). An evaluation of motor models of handwriting, IEEE Trans. on System, Man and Cybernetics, p. 1060-1072.
37. Plamondon R., Yu L.D., Stelmach G.E., Clément B. (1990). On the automatic extraction of biomechanical information from handwriting signals, IEEE Trans. on Systems, Man and Cybernetics.
38. Plamondon R. (1990a). A fundamental law of human movement. NIAS Conference on Sequencing and Timing of Human Movement, p. 19-20.
39. Plamondon R. (1990b). A unified approach to the study of target directed movements. Nato Advanced Study Institute, Tutorials in Motor Neuroscience, Corsica, Sept. 15-24.
40. Plamondon R. (1991). On the origin of asymmetric bell-shaped velocity profiles. In: Tutorials in Motor Neuroscience, J. Requin, G.E. Stelmach (eds.), Kluwer Scientific Publ., 13 pages.
41. Schmidt R.A., Zelaznik H.N., Franck J.S. (1978). Sources of inaccuracy in rapid movement, in Information Processing in Motor Control and Learning, G.E. Stelmach (ed.), Academic Press, p. 183-203.
42. Schmidt R.A., Zelaznik H.N., Hawkins B., Frank J.S., Quinn J.T. (1979). Motor output variability: a theory for the accuracy of rapid motor acts, Psychological Review 86, p. 415-451.
43. Soechting J.F., Laquantini F. (1981). Invariant characteristics of a pointing movement in man, Journal of Neuroscience 1/7, p. 710-720.
44. Wade M.G., Newell K.M., Wallace S.A. (1978). Decision time and movement time as a function of response complexity in retarded persons, American Journal of Mental Deficiency 63, p. 135-144.
45. Wallace S.A., Newell K.M., Wade M.G. (1978). Decision and response time as a function of movement difficulty in preschool children, Child Development 49, p. 509-512.

46. Weeks D.L., Sherwood D.E. and Wallace S.A. (1987). The effect of spatio temporal constraints on EMG characteristics of a rapid reversal response. Proceedings of the 1987 Annual Conference of the North American Society for the Psychology of Sport and Physical Activity, p. 75.
47. Weeks D.L., Sherwood D.E. and Wallace S.A. (1989). Initial agonist burst structure in rapid discrete limb movements: an expansion-contraction phenomenon. Proceedings of the 1989 Annual Conference of the North American Society for the Psychology of Sport and Physical Activity, p. 65.
48. Welford A.T., Norris A.H., Shock N.W. (1969). Speed and accuracy of movement and their change with age. In: W.G. Koster (ed.), Attention and Performance II, Amsterdam; North-Holland.
49. Woodworth R.S. (1899). The accuracy of voluntary movements, Psychological Review, Monograph Supplement 3, Whole 13/3.

Tutorials in Motor Behavior II
G.E. Stelmach and J. Requin (Editors)

Distributed Sensorimotor Learning

J. C. Houk and A.G. Barto

Department of Physiology, Northwestern University Medical Center, 303 E. Chicago Avenue, Chicago, Illinois 60611

Department of Computer and Information Science, University of Massachusetts, Amherst, Massachusetts 01003

Abstract

This paper outlines a new theory of sensorimotor learning. The theory is constrained by the anatomy and physiology of neural pathways through the cerebellum, motor cortex, brainstem and spinal cord. It also draws upon recent knowledge regarding cellular and molecular properties and receives insight from the results of learning experiments with artificial neural networks. The zonal organization that aligns climbing fibers, Purkinje cells and nuclear cells in the cerebellum provides an ideal neuronal architecture for efficient learning. Climbing fibers are postulated to acquire properties that improve their ability to train longitudinal zones of Purkinje cells. The Purkinje cells then control movements by selectively inhibiting premotor networks. Repetition of this control establishes sensorimotor habits that are then carried out automatically by the premotor networks. Trophic mechanisms align the topography of the overall network thus improving its ability to adapt. These processes in combination are considered capable of explaining the salient features of sensorimotor learning.

1. INTRODUCTION

The long-range goal in this work is to develop a comprehensive theory of sensorimotor learning. We seek to understand how motor programs are represented in the nervous system, how these programs are adaptively controlled to accommodate novel and complex environments, and how the brain perfects its capabilities for adaptive control. While motor programs are executed on a time scale of milliseconds, adaptation occurs on a time scale of seconds to days, and the ability to adapt is perfected over a developmental time course of months or years. We seek a theory capable of relating to this spectrum of time scales.

The theory should also be comprehensive in the levels of knowledge that it addresses. The anatomy of the brain has been studied for over a century, and well-established neuroanatomical findings provide invaluable constraints for a theory of motor learning. Similarly, we know much about the physiology of the pathways, and we wish to consult this store of knowledge both for constraints and for inspiration. Recently there has been a major expansion of our knowledge about cellular and molecular properties of neurons, and some of this information would be valuable to include. We should likewise heed findings from biomechanics and motion studies. Work with artificial neural networks has advanced rapidly in recent years, and insights gained from these experiences would also be valuable in constructing a theory of motor learning. While we cannot possibly deal with every detail of this vast, multi-level body of knowledge, neither should we ignore any particular area. Rather, the theory should draw upon key findings in each area. These elements should then be integrated into a model that can be tested and explored.

The aim of this particular paper is to outline some ideas that could form the basis for a comprehensive theory of sensorimotor learning (also see Houk, 1991). While much is known about the relevant subsystems in sensorimotor learning, little progress has been made on the total problem. What seems required to foster some progress is a willingness to grapple with all aspects of the problem. Although this effort is bound to be speculative, it can be informed. The hope here is to identify some of the important elements that need to be included in a comprehensive theory. Considerable additional work will be required to develop a mechanistic model that is actually capable of explaining sensorimotor learning. Although some of the ideas that we incorporate in this synthesis have been proposed by others, for the sake of avoiding lengthy digressions into their history, we generally cite review articles rather than the original papers.

2. FOUNDATIONS FOR THE THEORY

2.1. Overview of Anatomical Pathways

Fig. 1 identifies the main anatomical structures to which this theory relates and shows how we envision information to flow along pathways connecting these structures. This schema is not unique to the present theory; rather it should be looked upon as an outline of fundamental anatomical and physiological knowledge that serves to provide constraints on plausible theories of motor learning. More information about the general anatomy of the motor system can be obtained from Brodal (1981). Most of this section reviews the basic operations and interactions envisioned to occur along the pathways shown in Fig. 1. At the end of the section a brief synopsis of the proposed learning mechanisms will be introduced within the framework of this organizational plan.

The bottom of Fig. 1 emphasizes somatomotor interactions with the environment. Motor units produce actions on the environment in response to motor programs generated by premotor networks, and somatosensory receptors monitor the consequences of these actions. The present theory places special emphasis on these tactile and proprioceptive sensors, whereas vision and other special senses are considered to influence higher-level mechanisms that become superimposed on basic somatomotor mechanisms.

The premotor networks in Fig. 1 range in complexity from simple spinal reflexes to motor cortical circuits controlling voluntary movement. Correspondingly, the eliciting events that trigger the premotor networks to generate motor programs range from simple somatosensory cues to multifarious events such as might be detected by the visual system. The motor programs produced by the premotor networks are regulated by output from the cerebellar cortex. These regulatory actions are especially important in controlling voluntary movements but are also involved in modulating reflexes. Premotor networks can function without regulation to mediate basic reflexes or to perform well-rehearsed, habitual actions.

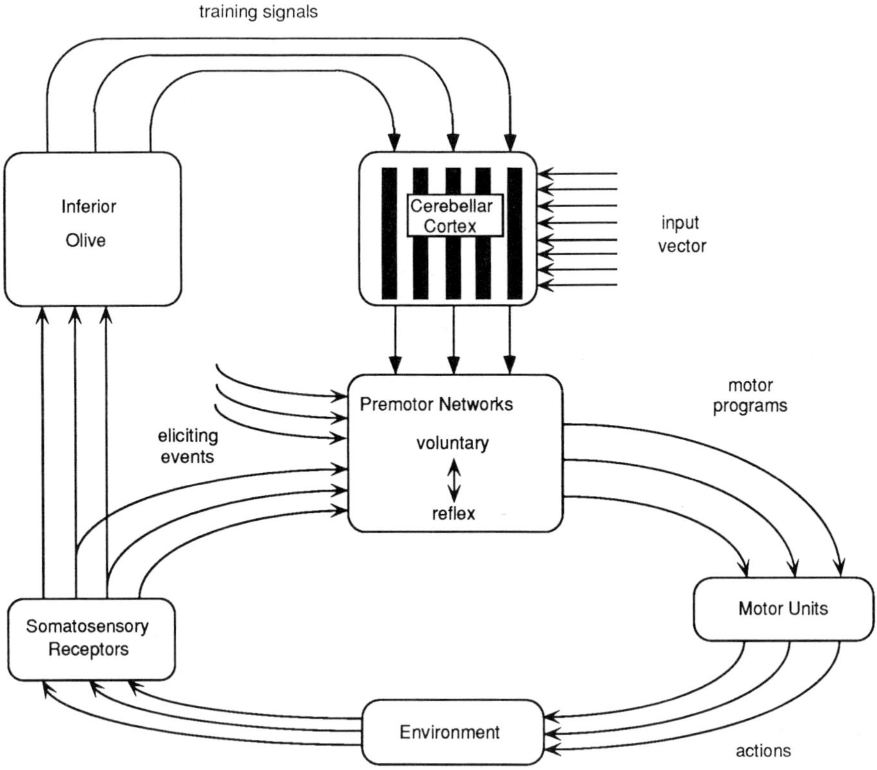

Figure 1: Anatomical organization and information flow in sensorimotor pathways. Learning is postulated to be distributed between the inferior olive, the cerebellar cortex and the premotor networks. The large input vector to the cerebellar cortex is comprised of diverse state and context information transmitted in mossy fiber pathways. Filled arrow heads indicate inhibitory (from cerebellar cortex to premotor networks) or decrementing (from inferior olive to cerebellar cortex) effects. The other arrow heads designate positive influences. These conventions are followed in all of the figures in this chapter.

We subscribe to the view that the cerebellar cortex is needed to control complex, precise and/or novel actions, and that it accomplishes these functions by regulating a relatively stereotyped set of habitual reactions and basic reflexes. The intricate regulatory actions postulated to occur in the cerebellar cortex require the assimilation of a large amount of information about the external environment and the internal state of the body. The unique neuronal architecture of the cerebellar cortex is considered ideal for this purpose. The output neurons, the Purkinje cells, are exposed to a large input vector comprised of context and state information and also receive training signals from the inferior olive.

According to our theory, sensorimotor learning occurs in all three CNS structures shown in Fig. 1: the inferior olive, the cerebellar cortex and premotor networks. The most rapid and versatile adaptive process is placed in the cerebellar cortex where longitudinal bands of Purkinje cells receive semiprivate training signals from small clusters of neurons in the inferior olive. The Purkinje cells learn how to utilize the diverse information supplied by the input vector to regulate premotor circuits in an intelligent fashion. A slower adaptive process is placed in the premotor networks. We assume that this process is use-dependent, allowing the network to learn new habits simply as a consequence of persistent regulatory actions sent from the cerebellar cortex. This frees up Purkinje cells for coordinating more complex and novel actions. A third adaptive process is placed in the inferior olive. According to our theory, adaptive mechanisms adjust the response properties of olivary neurons to make them provide more informative training signals. In this manner a climbing fiber progressively learns how to train Purkinje cells more effectively. Finally, we postulate that trophic influences, operating particularly during development but also during adulthood, may function to improve the functional alignment between training signals from the inferior olive and premotor circuits controlling elemental motor programs. These mechanisms in combination are considered capable of accounting for most of the organism's capacity for sensorimotor learning.

2.2. Information Processing Modules

The cerebellum is organized in a modular fashion, as summarized in Fig. 2 (cf. Ito, 1984; Houk, Singh, Fisher & Barto, 1990). Its main processing units are the millions of Purkinje cells present in the cerebellar cortex, five of which are shown in Fig. 2. Purkinje cells have fan-shaped dendritic trees which are ideal for receiving the large input vector discussed in the previous section. This vector is transmitted by parallel fibers, which receive their inputs from mossy fibers (not shown); the latter transmit a diversity of signals from many CNS sources. In contrast to the multiple inputs from parallel fibers, each Purkinje cell receives only a single climbing fiber input, from a neuron located in the inferior olive. Climbing fibers are believed to transmit training signals that adjust the weights of parallel fiber synapses onto Purkinje cells, via mechanisms that are discussed in the next section.

The inhibitory outputs from a longitudinal band of Purkinje cells converge upon a small cluster of cerebellar nucleus cells to form the information processing module contained within the shaded rectangle in Fig. 2. These nuclear cells receive a collateral input from the climbing fibers that belong to the same module. Section 3 discusses the organization and function of these olivo-cerebellar complexes in more detail.

The present theory assumes that the premotor network is also organized in a modular fashion. A premotor module (contained within the dashed rectangle in Fig. 2) consists of a cluster of cerebellar nuclear neurons that is reciprocally connected with a cluster of premotor neurons (note bidirectional flow of information between cerebellar nucleus and premotor neurons in Fig. 2). The driving force for the generation of a motor program is thought to depend on positive feedback transmitted through the reciprocal connections in premotor modules. Purkinje cells are thought to exert their controlling actions by guiding this regenerative process, thus shaping the spatiotemporal pattern of activity in the premotor network. In this manner, the neural activity transmitted from premotor neurons to motor units can be adjusted to control the accuracy of movement.

In contemplating the control of action, it is useful to consider a larger module comprised of a premotor module together with the band of Purkinje cells that control it. This type of module has been called an adjustable pattern generator (APG) and is considered to be a basic element in the generation of a motor program (Houk *et al.* 1990). The signal sent from one APG module to motor units can be considered an elemental motor program. The output from an array of APG modules then serves as a composite motor program for controlling action.

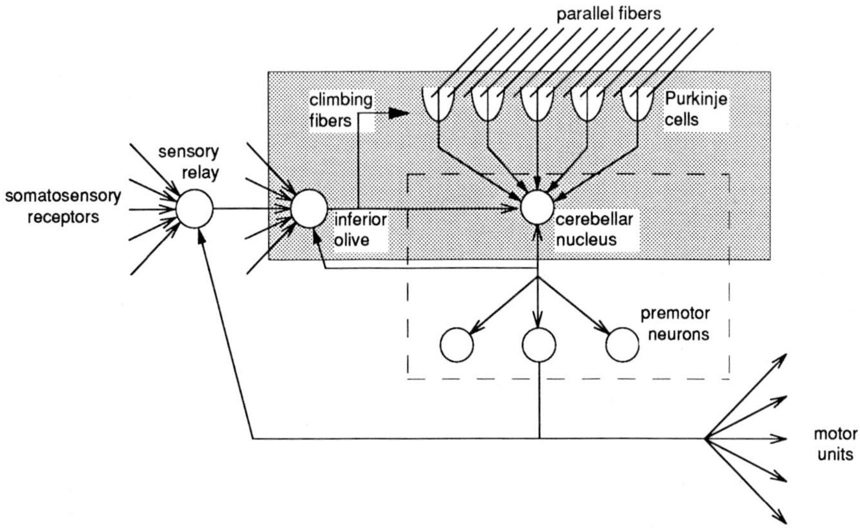

Figure 2: Information processing modules in the sensorimotor system. The stippled box contains an olivo-cerebellar complex and the dashed rectangle delineates a premotor module (Section 3.1). Adjustable pattern generator (APG) modules include both of these elements.

2.3. Synaptic Learning Rules

In this section we review recent results regarding cellular mechanisms that appear to be important in regulating the efficacy of synaptic transmission, and we describe two cellular-level models of synaptic weight modification, one proposed for Purkinje cells and the other for premotor and inferior olivary neurons.

The model illustrated in Fig. 3*A* shows the relations between several intracellular signals that are believed to be important in adjusting the synaptic weights of parallel fiber inputs to Purkinje cells. This model was developed by Houk *et al.* (1990) on the basis of cellular neurophysiological data (Crepel & Krupa, 1988; Ekerot, 1984; Ito, 1989). Protein kinases are a family of enzymes that regulate cellular functions by modifying other protein molecules. One of the kinases found in Purkinje cells (protein kinase C or cyclic GMP-dependent protein kinase have each been suggested) modifies the receptor molecules for glutamate, the excitatory neurotransmitter released by parallel fibers. When this kinase is activated, the receptors are desensitized, and this produces a decrement in the efficacy of parallel fiber synapses. Activation of the kinase requires an elevated concentration of calcium ions and also a cofactor (diacylglycerol) that is formed whenever a synapse is activated. Since the cofactor is membrane-bound, it serves as a local signal that identifies recently active synapses. Calcium, on the other hand, is a more global signal. It enters the dendrites of Purkinje cells via voltage-dependent calcium channels which can be opened in two ways: (i) by the summed input from many parallel fiber synapses culminating in the depolarization of one or more Purkinje cell dendrites or (ii) by a climbing fiber spike which starts at the cell body and spreads into all of the dendrites. These two effects potentiate each other, such that the maximal degree of calcium channel opening, and calcium entry, occurs if the climbing fiber fires while a dendrite is depolarized in response to parallel fiber input.

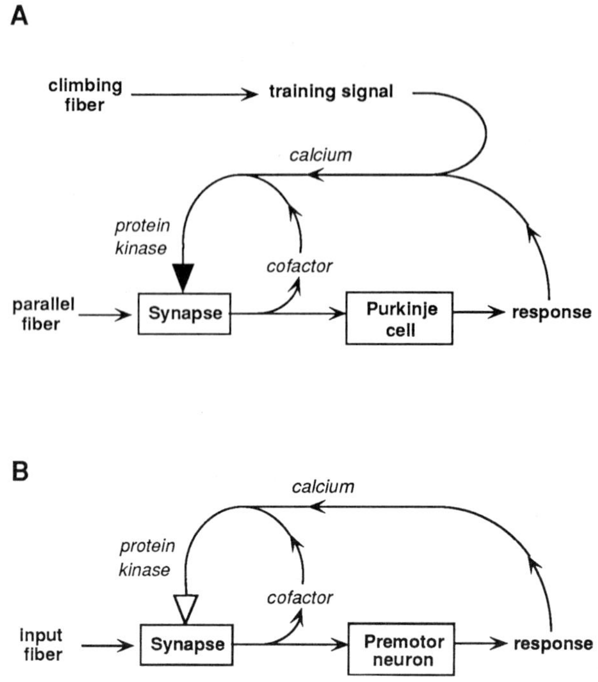

Figure 3: Flow diagram summarizing the postulated learning mechanisms that operate at (*A*) parallel fiber synapses in the cerebellar cortex and (*B*) excitatory synapses in premotor and inferior olive neurons.

In Section 3.2 we will suggest that the climbing fiber serves as a relatively pure training signal without producing much effect on the response transmitted by the Purkinje cell. What a climbing fiber actually produces is a large excitatory synaptic potential that leads to both an influx of calcium (the training signal) and a brief, high-frequency burst of discharge (a transmitted response). However, the high-frequency burst is always followed by a pause in Purkinje cell firing, and since these two effects occur in rapid succession, their influences on cerebellar nuclear cells tend to counteract each other. A third factor that one needs to consider is the excitation produced in nuclear cells by the climbing fiber collateral (Fig. 2). This also tends to counteract the inhibition produced by the high-frequency burst of Purkinje cell discharge. In line with the concept that these various effects tend to cancel each other, recording studies indicate that the immediate effects of climbing fiber activity on nuclear cells are quite minimal, although climbing fibers can produce brief modulations in sensitivity that alter the amplitudes of responses mediated via parallel fiber inputs (McDevitt, Ebner & Bloedel 1987). The latter modulatory features warrant further consideration, but are not incorporated in our present model. The basic inference that we make from these data is that a climbing fiber can produce a potent training signal without greatly affecting the transmitted response of the Purkinje cell.

The cellular findings reviewed in the previous paragraphs suggest the following learning rule for adjusting parallel fiber synapses. A decrement in synaptic weight is postulated to depend on the simultaneous presence of three factors: (1) the particular parallel fiber synapse is, or was recently, active (the cofactor for the kinase which is localized to the synapse), (2) the Purkinje cell is responding to the summed input from many parallel fibers (calcium entry into selected dendrites), and (3) the climbing fiber transmits a training signal (calcium entry into all dendrites). Calcium entry sufficient to activate the protein kinase seems to require the concurrence of factors 2 and 3. Although less is known about the cellular mechanisms that mediate weight increments at parallel fiber synapses, it appears that an increment in synaptic weight occurs when the parallel fiber is active (factor 1) but the climbing fiber is inactive (absence of factor 3). Current experimental data do not provide much guidance for deciding whether or not the weight increment rule should also depend on factor 2, the response status of the Purkinje cell. In our previous work we assumed that increments require a very low concentration of calcium, occurring when both the Purkinje cell and the climbing fiber are inactive. Table 1 summarizes how the contingencies of the postulated learning rule depend on the three factors identified earlier: (1) the activity state of the synapse, (2) the postsynaptic response of the Purkinje cell, and (3) the presence or absence of climbing fiber activity.

Premotor and olivary neurons appear not to receive any special training signal analogous to the climbing fiber input to Purkinje cells. This is reflected in Fig. 3*B*, which outlines a cellular-level model for synaptic weight adjustment in premotor and olivary neurons. Although this model is speculative, it builds upon parallels with the Purkinje cell model, and it also draws heavily from recent findings with hippocampal and visual cortical neurons, cell types in which plasticity has been extensively studied (Brown, Ganong, Kairiss, Keenan & Kelso, 1989; Collingridge & Singer, 1990; Jaffe & Johnston, 1990; Kennedy, 1988; Stanton & Sejnowski, 1989). There is evidence that similar mechanisms may operate in motor cortical and in other premotor neurons (Racine, Wilson, Gingell & Sunderland, 1986; Sakamoto, Porter & Asanuma, 1987).

In analogy with the Purkinje cell model, the weight adjustment model in Fig. 3*B* utilizes a protein kinase to modify the sensitivity of receptor molecules that respond to excitatory synaptic inputs. However, in this case it appears that activated kinase sensitizes the receptors rather than desensitizing them, thus producing a weight increment rather than a decrement. This increment is called long-term potentiation, or LTP. As in the model for Purkinje cells, we assume that activation of this kinase requires both an elevated calcium concentration and a local cofactor, and that the cofactor is formed whenever the synapse is active. In some of the cell types studied, the calcium requirement is met by voltage-gated channels similar to those present in Purkinje cells, whereas in other cell types calcium enters mainly via another category of channel, called an

NMDA-activated channel. NMDA channels have the unusual property of being controlled by a neurotransmitter (glutamate) in addition to being voltage dependent. This channel opens only when it is activated both by neurotransmitter and by depolarization, whereupon calcium can enter the cell.

Table 1: Purkinje cell model of learning contingencies

	postsynaptic response	***no response***
If climbing fiber fires		
active synapse	decrement	no change
inactive synapse	no change	no change
	postsynaptic response	***no response***
If no climbing fiber		
active synapse	no change	increment
inactive synapse	no change	no change

The usual definition of a Hebbian synapse is an adjustable synapse in which conjunctive presynaptic and postsynapic activity are required to produce a weight increment. The dual dependence of NMDA channels on neurotransmitter and depolarization has been invoked to explain the origin of this conjunctive requirement; presynaptic activity would supply the neurotransmitter and postsynaptic activity would provide the depolarization. However, an alternative hypothesis stems from the dual requirements for protein kinase activation; presynaptic transmitter release is needed to form the cofactor and postsynaptic depolarization is needed to open calcium channels. The kinase-based hypothesis has the advantage that it also explains the origin of a conjunctive requirement in those cell types that do not have NMDA channels.

The cellular mechanisms that regulate decreases in synaptic efficacy are not as well understood. However, empirical evidence suggests that decreases may occur under two conditions (Collingridge & Singer, 1990; Stanton & Sejnowski, 1989). Synapses that are active while the cell is rendered unresponsive (by a strong inhibitory input) are weakened. Also, synapses that are inactive while the cell is activated (through other inputs) are weakened. Inactive synapses in inactive cells are not altered. Table 2 summarizes the contingencies for the various cases.

Table 2: Premotor and olivary model of learning contingencies

	postsynaptic response	***no response***
active synapse	increment	decrement
inactive synapse	decrement	no change

We propose that this basic model applies to both premotor and olivary neurons, though the mechanism for controlling calcium would be different. NMDA channels are prevalent throughout premotor networks in spinal cord (Grillner, Wallén, Dale, Brodin, Buchanan & Hill, 1987), brainstem (Keifer & Houk, 1991) and motor cortex (Sakamoto *et al.* 1987). In contrast, inferior olivary neurons express prominent calcium currents of the purely voltage-dependent type (Llinás & Yarom, 1981).

Calcium influx is further modified by several chemical substances which modulate the relation between calcium channel opening and the voltage and/or transmitter concentration. For example, norepinephrine modulates the voltage-sensitivity of calcium channels, and these effects translate into an influence on the rate and degree of learning (Gray & Johnston, 1987; Neerven, Pompeiano, Collewijn & Steen, 1990). This is particularly interesting in view of evidence that norepinephrine is an important transmitter in the brain's reward system (Stein, 1978).

Both of the models shown in Fig. 3 place the weight-adjustment process in the postsynaptic membrane. Although mechanisms for modifying presynaptic terminals have also been described, they will not be discussed here. Rather than being comprehensive, our purpose is simply to provide a basic mechanistic framework for the subsequent discussion of learning tasks and strategies.

2.4. Computational Issues for Learning

The discussion of learning rules in the previous section was mechanistically, rather than functionally, oriented. We dealt with what theorists have called learning methods or rules, without reference to the the kinds of computational tasks these rules can perform (Barto, 1991). Learning tasks are usually divided into categories on the basis of the objectives of the task and the nature of the information available to the learning system. A learning task is *unsupervised* if no explicit training information is available to the neurons or synapses of the adaptive network. Unsupervised learning can result in useful recoding of a network's input as exemplified by models of the development of feature detectors in visual cortex (Linsker, 1988; Barlow, 1989), and it can explain the emergence of sensory maps during development (Willshaw & von der Malsburg, 1976).

A task is said to involve *supervised* learning if training information is available to instruct the learning mechanisms as to what changes they should make. Training signals can function as "forcing inputs" that activate the neuron to the appropriate level through established connections and thus teach by setting an example. According to our theory, Purkinje cells act as this kind of forcing input for premotor neurons. Alternatively, training signals can act by altering synapses without producing neuronal activity, as is postulated for climbing fibers. Learning rules of the latter type appear extensively in theoretical studies due to their attractive mathematical properties. Examples are the perceptron rule (Rosenblatt, 1962; Minsky & Papert, 1988), the Widrow-Hoff, or least mean square (LMS), rule (Widrow & Hoff, 1960) and the closely related "delta rule" (Rumelhart, Hinton & Williams, 1986). For these learning rules, a training signal is either a "target" signal, specifying desired neuronal activity, or an "error signal," giving the signed difference between the actual and the desired activity.

Reinforcement learning is another type of learning task studied by theorists. Because it also requires training information, it is sometimes viewed as a kind of supervised learning. However, the training information is less informative than it is in a supervised problem. Instead of telling the neuron what its activity should be, or how its activity should change, training information for reinforcement learning simply evaluates the neuron's behavior. This can be done by the generation of "reward" or "penalty" signals, or by the generation of graded evaluation signals. Unlike the target or error signals of supervised learning, evaluation signals do not directly specify the required activity or the direction in which activity should change. It is normally easier to generate evaluative signals than to generate the target or error signals used in supervised tasks because it is possible to evaluate the consequences of a neuron's activity without comparing it with a known target activity. However, rules for learning under the guidance of evaluation signals have to be somewhat more complex than rules for supervised learning. The directional information required for making changes has to be gathered during exploratory activity in which the consequences of alternative behaviors are observed (Barto, 1985).

A major issue in the study of learning systems is how the necessary training information is made available at the sites of learning. This is an aspect of what learning theorists call the "credit assignment" problem (Minsky, 1963). When overt behavior is generated by the interaction of many components, as is the case for motor behavior, it is difficult to determine how the behavior of individual components should be altered in order to change overt behavior in some useful way. This problem severely interferes with efficient learning when networks contain many components which are massively interconnected. Theorists sometimes distinguish between structural, or spatial, aspects of credit assignment, which pertain to assigning credit or blame to specific components of a complex system, and temporal aspects of credit assignment, which pertain to the problem of determining when the activity of these components was helpful or deleterious to overall behavior.

The error backpropagation method popularized recently by theorists (Rumelhart *et al.* 1986) is one kind of solution to structural aspects of the credit assignment problem. This method applies to supervised learning tasks in which target or error signals are assumed to be available for some "visible" neurons. The error backpropagation method effectively converts this information into training information for the other, "hidden" neurons that directly or indirectly influence the visible neurons. Although error backpropagation is a useful tool for theoretical studies of adaptive networks, it is hard to see how it might be implemented in a real neural network.

Learning rules designed to work with the evaluation signals of reinforcement learning tasks can be used to address the structural credit assignment problem in a different way. Because evaluation signals do not provide directional information, there does not have to be a separate evaluation signal for each adaptive neuron in the network. A signal that evaluates the collective behavior of a group of neurons can be broadcast to each neuron in the group. With appropriate learning rules working with exploratory neuronal activity, the neurons in the group can learn *as if* they were individually instructed (Barto, 1985; Barto & Jordan, 1987). Learning under these circumstances is not as efficient as learning with error backpropagation, but it is simpler and more plausible as a biological mechanism for learning by hidden units. Key facets of our theory address this problem of supplying appropriate training information to the adaptive sites within a complex network.

The temporal aspect of the credit assignment problem is also an important concern in our theory. Although the error backpropagation method has been adapted to address temporal credit assignment (Jordan & Jacobs, 1989; Nguyen & Widrow, 1991), the resulting learning systems appear to bear little relationship to neural mechanisms. Reinforcement learning methods have also been extended to address temporal issues through the idea of an "adaptive critic" (Barto, Sutton & Anderson, 1983; Sutton, 1988). An adaptive critic improves the temporal specificity of the evaluation signals available to a learning system by learning to predict primary reinforcing events. Our theory borrows some aspects of this idea but includes additional mechanisms for obtaining precisely timed training signals.

3. INFERIOR OLIVE

The inferior olive is, with minor exception, the origin of all of the climbing fiber input to APG modules in the cerebellum. The characteristic properties of this pathway are unique in several ways, and in this section we explore how the anatomy and physiology of climbing fibers may relate to the postulated role of the inferior olive in motor learning.

3.1. Zonal Organization and Structural Credit Assignment

While many areas of the brain are organized in a topographic fashion, one of the most striking examples occurs in the climbing fiber input to the cerebellar cortex. Anatomical (Gibson, Robinson, Alam & Houk, 1987; Jansen & Brodal, 1942; Voogd & Bigaré, 1980), physiological (Andersson, Ekerot, Oscarsson & Schouenborg, 1987; Oscarsson, 1980) and immunohistochemical (Scott, 1964; Doré, Jacobson & Hawkes, 1990; Gravel, Eisenman, Sasseville & Hawkes, 1987) studies of the cerebellar cortex have each demonstrated a highly organized system of longitudinal, parasagittal zones. These zones extend, albeit with some distortion, throughout the entire cerebellar cortex. While the ontogenetic origin of these zones remains incompletely understood, the fact that several different classes of intrinsic molecules are organized in longitudinal zones at an early stage of development suggests that some aspects of the zonal organizational plan are genetically prescribed, whereas others are probably shaped by developmental plasticity.

The zonal organization in the cerebellar cortex relates to the information processing modules discussed in Section 2.2. The set of five Purkinje cells in Fig. 2 serves to symbolize a longitudinal zone that would actually be comprised of about a hundred Purkinje cells and associated interneurons. This zone receives a focused band of climbing fiber input from a small cluster (symbolized by a circle in Fig. 2) of inferior olive neurons. The axons of the Purkinje cells in a given zone project a focus of inhibition to a small cluster of cerebellar nuclear cells. This cluster of nuclear cells receives collateral input from the climbing fibers that innervate the same zone. There is considerable specificity in these interconnections among the inferior olive, the cerebellar cortex and the cerebellar nuclei contained within the shaded rectangle in Fig. 2. Oscarsson (1980) discovered a precision in physiological properties that matches this precision in wiring and suggested that this circuit represents a fundamental computational unit of the cerebellum which he called an "olivo-cerebellar complex". Judging from the quantitative morphological data summarized in Ito (1984), the cerebellum in higher mammals is comprised of about a hundred thousand relatively discrete olivo-cerebellar complexes.

Projections from olivo-cerebellar complexes to premotor neurons and on to motor units are less precisely organized than are the connections within an olivo-cerebellar complex. Intra-axonal staining has demonstrated considerable branching in these pathways (Shinoda, Yamaguchi & Futami, 1986; Shinoda, Futami, Mitoma & Yokota, 1988), as illustrated by the divergent connections in Fig. 2. Because of this divergence, a given olivo-cerebellar complex contributes input to a large and relatively diverse set of motor units. There is also considerable convergence in the pathways from the cerebellum to motor units, such that any given motor unit receives input from large numbers of olivo-cerebellar complexes. Convergent pathways are not illustrated in Fig. 2 since this drawing emphasizes relations with a single olivo-cerebellar complex.

As mentioned in Section 2.2, APG modules are larger, but related, functional elements as contrasted with olivo-cerebellar complexes. The appreciable divergence and convergence present in the premotor network makes it difficult to conceptualize APG modules as discrete entities. Instead, they have overlapping borders, and they influence overlapping sets of motor units. This overlap complicates somewhat the definition of an APG module and an elemental motor program. In the Section 2.2 we defined an elemental program as the signal present in an individual premotor neuron. An alternative approach would be to define an elemental program as the output of an individual olivo-cerebellar complex. While the overlapping connections within the premotor network make it impractical to specify precise borders between APG modules, they have the beneficial consequence of providing a kind of "coarse coding" (Hinton, McClelland & Rumelhart, 1984) of APG influence on motor units: patterns of activity involving many APGs determine motor behavior. This is beneficial since similarities among these patterns, where patterns are similar to the extent that they share the same activity of the same APGs, should facilitate learning by enabling generalization to occur among experiences obtained with different movements.

The degree of topographic specificity along the sensory pathway to the inferior olive is also less striking than the precision of the zonal organization within olivo-cerebellar complexes. The clearest example of an organized representation within the inferior olive occurs in the rostral division of the dorsal accessory olive where there is a detailed cutaneous map of the contralateral body surface (Gellman, Houk & Gibson, 1983). Tracing this pathway backward to sensory relays in dorsal column nuclei, the somatotopic specificity becomes much more difficult to recognize (McCurdy, 1988). These and other findings indicate that there is considerable convergence along the input pathways to the inferior olive (Oscarsson, 1980; Andersson *et al.* 1987). This convergence may in fact provide the basis for some of the unique physiological properties of olivary neurons described in the next section.

In summary of this anatomy, there appears to be a gradient in topographic specificity to and from the cerebellum. Topographic specificity increases along the input pathway from somatosensory receptors through the inferior olive to the cerebellar cortex, but then decreases along the output pathway from the cerebellar cortex through premotor networks to motor units. The greatest precision of alignment occurs in the center of the network, in the cerebellar cortex, where climbing fibers, Purkinje cells and nuclear targets of Purkinje axons appear to be precisely aligned by molecular markers that are expressed at different stages of development.

Our interpretation of the zonal organization in the cerebellar cortex is that it may represent an evolutionary adaptation that helps to alleviate the structural credit assignment problem discussed in Section 2.4; this is the problem of transmitting appropriate training information to the particular sites where it is needed. The precise alignment of climbing fiber input to the cerebellum would be expected to provide semiprivate training signals for the longitudinal zones of Purkinje cells within individual APG modules. However, for this alignment to contribute to credit assignment, special mechanisms would be required for insuring that any given training signal has the correct spatial and temporal specificity for training the particular APG module that it innervates. In the next section we discuss aspects of inferior olive physiology that may contribute to achieving the requisite spatiotemporal specificity.

3.2. Training Information Based on the Somatosensory Modality

The electrical activity of olivary cells differs strikingly from that of most neurons (Eccles, Llinás & Sasaki, 1966; Llinás & Yarom, 1981). Their action potentials consist of an initial sodium spike followed by a calcium plateau and then a long refractory period. Three implications of this unusual electrical activity warrant consideration: (1) The long refractory period makes olivary neurons fire at very low frequencies, and they typically respond to sensory stimuli with just a single action potential. While this binary responsiveness is appropriate for signalling the occurrences of sensory events that may supply training information, it interferes with the transmission of parametric information about the intensity and duration of the stimulus as might be required for direct control functions. (2) The calcium plateau is interesting since this ion is implicated in synaptic plasticity (Section 2.3). (3) Olivary refractoriness limits the amount of excitation delivered to Purkinje cells. This may be another factor (in addition to those discussed in Section 2.3) that helps climbing fibers transmit training signals without greatly altering the transmitted response of the Purkinje cell.

The sensory properties of olivary neurons are intriguing. In studying receptive fields, one finds a strong emphasis on somatosensory modalities, and the cells appear to be specialized for detecting different types of somatic event (Gellman, Gibson & Houk, 1985). Many are sensitive to contact with a patch of skin or with hairs, and another large group is responsive to small displacements of a limb in particular directions. Yet others are sensitive to slip, vibration or to tugs on muscles. Even the group of cells receiving visual input seems more specialized for detecting motion of the body, a somatic event detected by retinal slip, rather than being sensitive to the motion or location of a visual target.

Detections of somatic events might seem to be unlikely signals for adaptively adjusting the metrics of movements. One typically thinks of calibrating movement based on spatial errors detected visually; however, a visual computation of error followed by coordinate transformation into the motor space regulated by the cerebellum represents an elaborate computation. We are attracted by the possibility that somatosensory signals from the olive might be used to calibrate our use of vision, rather than the other way around. This hypothesis could help explain the emergence of appreciable postural and locomotor skills prior to eye opening in neonatal rats (Altman & Sudarshan, 1975). Visual guidance of movement is present, though initially extremely rudimentary, in the human neonate (Hofsten, 1982), and the development of more precise visuomotor coordination appears to lag behind abilities to control limb movements on the basis of somatosensory input (Piaget, 1953). Although visual input is obviously essential for the calibration of motor systems with respect to goals defined in terms of visual space, many other essential adjustments can be made using only somatosensory information. For example, learning to achieve goals defined in terms of haptic properties need not involve precise calibration with respect to vision.

How could responsiveness to low-threshold somatic stimuli be useful in training the cerebellum to control motor programs? We postulate that the utility of light touch and proprioception for training would derive from an ability of these signals to predict more primal training signals originating from high-threshold receptors. High-threshold receptors, including nociceptors, are located in skin, muscle and joints, and they detect painful, or potentially painful, events. For example, when the moving limb bumps hard against an external object, high-threshold receptors with receptive fields at the site of contact are activated. The signals sent from these receptors could provide useful training information for adjusting motor programs. If adjustments were made in the context of visual input to the cerebellum providing information about an object's presence and location, associative links could be formed so that the probability of similar collisions in the future would be decreased. Similarly, high-threshold receptors located in muscle and joint are activated when uncoordinated movements are produced, clumsy movements that unduly stress the joint capsules, ligaments and muscles. If these high-threshold signals were available to appropriate pattern generators in the cerebellum, they could be used to produce adaptive adjustments in motor programs to avoid the stresses that result from poorly coordinated movements.

Motor learning would be most unpleasant if it had to rely solely on high-threshold, potentially painful, somatosensory responses as training signals. However, if olivary neurons acquired an ability to determine when the cerebellum produces movements that come close to causing pain, learning could occur without the occurrence of a painful outcome. Support for this concept comes from studies that compared high-threshold and low-threshold cutaneous receptive fields of individual olivary neurons (Ekerot, Oscarsson & Schouenborg, 1987). The location of the receptive field and the gradient in sensitivity was essentially identical for high-threshold noxious and low-threshold tactile modalities of stimuli. Given these properties, a light cutaneous response could become an excellent indication that an agonist muscle is being too strongly activated. A slightly stronger activation on a subsequent occasion could result in a painful collision.

A capacity of olivary neurons to predict stimulation via low-threshold afferents is probably not originally present but instead is acquired through experience. A simple associative mechanism would allow an olivary neuron to learn to respond to light cutaneous stimulation of the patch of skin overlying the high-threshold field, since any situation in which the cell's high-threshold input is activated by a strong cutaneous stimulation would be accompanied or preceded by an activation of overlying low-threshold cutaneous receptors. A low-threshold input that initially produces a synaptic potential too small to activate the cell would be strengthened until it becomes capable of producing a response in the absence of the high-threshold input. Similarly, input from an uncorrelated pathway would be weakened. The contingencies in Table 2 provide a suitable rule for implementing this learning. The learning task is a form of supervised learning, guided by training signals sent from high-threshold receptors via established connections with olivary neurons. This training signal is a type of forcing input that shows an olivary neuron how it should respond to its low-threshold inputs.

The acquisition of a low-threshold olivary response suggested above is analogous to Pavlovian conditioning in which high-threshold nociceptive input and low-threshold cutaneous input act respectively as unconditioned and conditioned stimuli. This learning process would contribute to resolving structural and temporal aspects of the credit assignment problem by providing signals that correctly predict where (via receptive field alignment) and when (via slightly anticipatory responding) stimulation from high-threshold afferents is about to occur. The hypothesis that high-threshold afferents act as primal training signals for endowing predictive lower-threshold signals with the ability to also act as training signals is similar to the idea of an adaptive critic mentioned in Section 2.4. The high degree of convergence in the somatosensory pathway to the inferior olive commented upon earlier, and shown in Fig. 2, fits well with the hypothesis that olivary neurons adaptively select the right mixture of complex sensory properties to fulfill their predictive roles.

3.3. Improvement of Training Information with Timed Inhibition

The spatial and temporal specificity of training signals may be additionally shaped by input from anatomical pathways that modulate sensory input to the olive. Two such pathways are shown in Fig. 2. One involves collateral fibers to sensory relays derived from the axons that transmit motor programs from premotor neurons to motor units. Another involves a special set of inhibitory neurons that are located in the cerebellar nuclei and project to the inferior olive (Andersson, Garwicz & Hesslow, 1988; Nelson & Mugnaini, 1989). Electrophysiological studies of the former pathway have revealed an inhibitory gating mechanism that modulates tactile input to the olive (Weiss, Houk & Gibson, 1990). The time course of the modulatory effect is unusual, and it appears to give rise to a simple, though elegant, mechanism for detecting when a motor program commands a movement with too large of an amplitude (i.e., an hypermetric movement). To explain this feature, we will describe an hypothetical example concerning human reaching movements that extrapolates from the results of neurophysiological studies in cats (Gellman *et al.* 1985; Weiss *et al.* 1990).

Consider an olivary neuron that is sensitive to light cutaneous stimulation of the palm of the hand. The subject now generates a motor program commanding the arm to reach for a door knob. Transmission of this program to motor units in the spinal cord produces corollary discharge to the sensory relays to the olive (Fig. 2). Extrapolating from the delayed time course of inhibition found in the physiological studies, this corollary mechanism would not inhibit sensory input during the movement, but rather would produce a rebound inhibition just as the motor program is terminated. Because of this timing, the olivary neuron would not fire if the planned movement were of a correct amplitude, in which case the doorknob would be touched appropriately at the movement's end, and not earlier. This is because a motor program generally ends just before a movement ends, and inertia carries the movement to completion. Thus, if the brain generates a correct command, inhibitory gating would prevent the olivary neuron from responding. However, if the brain commands too large a movement, the hand would contact the door knob before the motor program ends, and the olivary neuron would fire. This response would signify that the duration (or intensity) of the motor program's execution was too long (or too strong). One of the attractive properties of this mechanism is that it will obviously work, without further modification, for reaches to objects anywhere in the workspace, and it does not require elaborate coordinate transformations.

The previous example illustrates how a relatively unsophisticated mechanism for inhibitory gating can be combined with a simple tactile receptive field to produce an effective mechanism for detecting when a motor program runs too long or too intensely, and thus commands too large a movement. In effect, this mechanism opens a temporal window for sampling a simple event (touch) by inhibiting responsiveness of climbing fibers for times outside of this window. If touch occurs within this temporal window (when the olive is not inhibited), it signifies the likelihood that a specific type of error has occurred. If there is a correct match between the receptive field of a climbing fiber and the APG module to which it is connected, then its firing is also, in effect, filtered through an appropriate spatial window so that it should be capable of efficiently training that APG to assist in the production of an accurate movement. What is meant by a correct match and how such alignment might be achieved in development is considered in Section 4.1.

The previous discussion is directed toward olivary neurons with cutaneous receptive fields that are inhibited at the end of a movement. However, analogous principles may apply to other categories of olivary neurons. Some cells, particularly those with proprioceptive receptive fields, are inhibited during movement rather than at the end of a movement (Gellman *et al.* 1985). These neurons appear to resume their sensitivity just after the end of a normal movement, since they respond to perturbations that occur in that time window (Andersson & Armstrong, 1987). Elsewhere we have interpreted these data as revealing a mechanism for detecting when a motor program generates too small of a movement (Houk *et al.* 1990). In analogy with the cutaneous neurons discussed in the previous paragraph, the detection mechanism appears to function by opening a spatiotemporal window for sampling a simple somatosensory event. In this case the window occurs at the end of a movement, rather than during it, and leads to a mechanism for detecting when a movement's amplitude is too small, as opposed to too large. These signals might also derive from innate high-threshold inputs, in this case from receptors located in joint capsules and ligaments which are known to provide a strong input to the inferior olive (Miller & Oscarsson, 1970).

The detection mechanisms described in the previous paragraphs do not require a very sophisticated inhibitory gating process and are probably explicable in terms of the corollary pathway in Fig. 2 that inhibits sensory relays to the olive. This raises the question as to the function of the special pathway from inhibitory cerebellar nuclear cells to the inferior olive.

This pathway is directly controlled by zonal output from the cerebellar cortex, which raises the possibility of it being adaptively adjusted. This might permit an adaptive tuning of the temporal window during which a somatic event is detected and might lead to quite sophisticated training signals.

In summary, we have suggested that climbing fiber training signals may be initially specified by the pattern of high-threshold input to the inferior olive, and that these relatively crude training signals are progressively refined by two tuning processes. One refinement is provided by an associative mechanism that seeks out low-threshold somatosensory signals in a combination capable of predicting when movements come close to activating high threshold receptors causing tissue stress or pain. The evolving receptive field can be thought of as a kind of spatial window for evaluating performance. A second refinement is provided by an inhibitory gating process that superimposes a temporal window of evaluation. The two processes in combination provide a spatiotemporal window that ingeniously bases evaluation on the detection of simple somatic events, such as touch, that occur within this window. The resultant of these processes would be an improvement in the capacity of the inferior olive to provide training information to the cerebellum as to how it can generate better motor programs. However, before we discuss learning mechanisms in the cerebellum, it will be helpful to consider how the cerebellum interacts with premotor networks to regulate the motor units that control action.

4. PREMOTOR NETWORKS

Our use of the term premotor networks is meant to encompass all of the fundamental sensorimotor circuits for controlling action. In particular, we include spinal and brainstem reflex arcs, circuits through the sensorimotor cortex and the many pathways that interconnect these structures with themselves and with the deep cerebellar nuclei. Information flow through the cerebellar cortex is considered as a separate mechanism that provides rapid supervisory control over the neurodynamics that occur in premotor networks (Section 5). As pointed out in Section 2.3, many of the neurons in premotor networks are endowed with NMDA-activated channels, and may therefore be sites of use-dependent synaptic plasticity. In this section we explore how this adaptive feature, guided by regulatory input from the cerebellar cortex, might contribute to intermediate- and long-term aspects of sensorimotor learning.

4.1. Developmental Alignment of APG Modules

An important theme of the present work is credit assignment in adaptive neural networks controlling movement. Efficient learning in large networks requires getting appropriate training information to where it is needed, when it is needed. In Section 3.1 it was suggested that the zonal organization of the cerebellar cortex facilitates the resolution of structural credit assignment problems by aligning climbing fibers with narrow strips of Purkinje cells that in turn control small clusters of cerebellar nuclear cells. This neuronal architecture provides a good foundation for sensorimotor learning because it connects semiprivate training signals to individual APG modules. In Sections 3.2 and 3.3 we discussed some of the unique properties of the inferior olivary neurons that give rise to these training signals, and pointed out how they might detect when movements are of an incorrect amplitude. This type of informed evaluation by semiprivate training signals could create an effective learning situation in the cerebellar cortex, but only if each climbing fiber innervates an appropriate APG module.

According to our theory, an appropriate APG to be innervated by a given climbing fiber is one whose activity, if suitably adjusted through learning, can diminish the firing probability of that climbing fiber. Which APGs are appropriate in this sense therefore depends on the logic of both the learning rule and the mechanism by which APG activity influences climbing fiber activity. Because climbing fiber activity produces a long-term depression of the response of Purkinje cells to excitatory input from parallel fibers, and because Purkinje cell activity inhibits an APG's output by reducing premotor activity, an adaptive adjustment due to climbing fiber activity has the net effect of increasing the intensity of APG output (Purkinje cells are less active, and thus provide less restraint on on premotor activity). Therefore, in the case of cutaneous climbing fibers that detect when the amplitude of the movement is too large, the correct alignment would occur if the climbing fiber connected to an APG that controlled muscles opposing the movement that was responsible for stimulating the climbing fiber. In contrast, climbing fibers that detect when the movement amplitude is too small should connect to APGs that innervate agonist muscles.

The correct alignment might be provided if there were an adaptive mechanism for selecting the motor units controlled by a given APG module. As indicated earlier, our theory of distributed sensorimotor learning includes a use-dependent learning process operating at the level of premotor networks. In the present section we describe how this learning mechanism could guide an alignment process that would facilitate the resolution of the structural credit assignment problem. Fig. 4 illustrates how the process might work for APG modules innervated by cutaneous climbing fibers.

The diagram shows a stylized forearm and hand in profile, with a pair of antagonistic muscles to provide flexion and extension about the wrist. A high-threshold cutaneous receptor on the back side of the hand is shown connected appropriately to provide an innate withdrawal reflex that will move the hand away from a noxious stimulus. The flexor motor unit is excited and the extensor motor unit is inhibited. We further assume that during development connections are made from high-threshold cutaneous receptors to the inferior olivary nucleus such that different olivary cells receive input from different high-threshold receptors; no particular ordering of these connections is required. This together with the zonal organization in the cerebellum will insure that different APG modules are innervated by climbing fibers with different high-threshold cutaneous fields in some random arrangement. Similarly, APG modules need not connect in any specific manner to limb motor units; these connections could be random. Thus, the APG on the left in Fig. 4 might by chance receive input from the illustrated cutaneous receptor, whereas the one on the right receives input from another (undesignated) cutaneous receptor. We will be concerned with how the left module establishes its appropriate connections (shown solid) and eliminates the inappropriate ones (shown dashed).

Assume that stochastic neural activity activates both APG modules and that the one on the right produces contractions of the extensor muscle. Whenever a contraction causes the hand to bump into some object, a withdrawal reflex activating the flexor muscle and inhibiting the extensor muscle will be elicited. Although the APG module on the left is initially weakly connected to both the flexor and extensor motor units, use-dependent synaptic modification would strengthen the connection to the flexor motor unit since it is simultaneously activated by the withdrawal reflex. The connection to the extensor motor unit would be weakened since it is simultaneously inhibited by the withdrawal reflex. This is precisely what is needed to align the APG module so that it can perform as an adaptive controller.

After the alignment and tuning processes are completed, climbing fiber activity will signal instances in which the antagonist fails to brake a movement properly, thus permitting premature or unexpected contacts with an object in the environment. The resultant climbing fiber activity will lead to a reduction of excitatory parallel fiber input to the Purkinje cells. This will diminish the inhibitory restraint on the reciprocal loop the next time that the APG is used, and the augmented command sent to the flexor motor unit will brake the movement more intensely, thus reducing the likelihood of contact-induced firing of the climbing fiber.

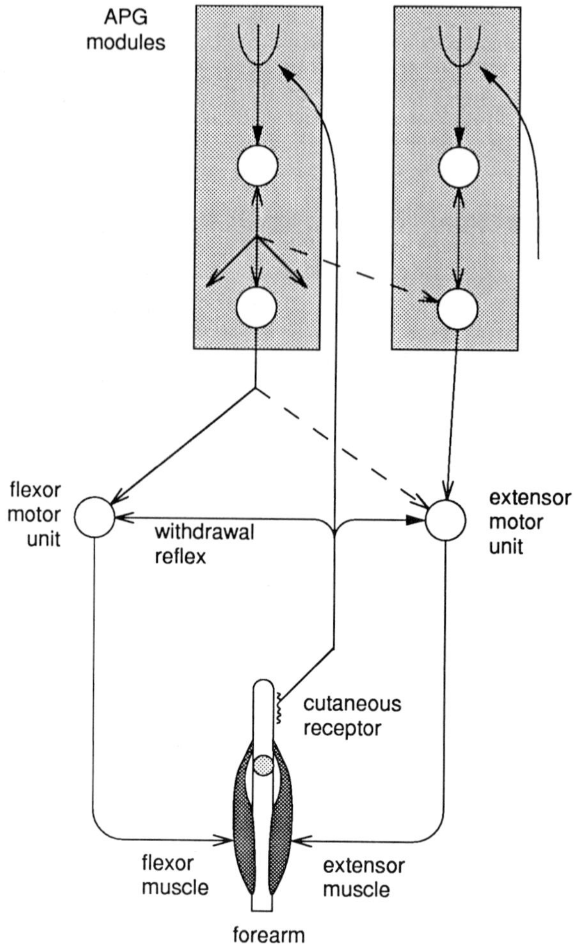

Figure 4: Alignment of APG modules. This diagram is used to illustrate how we envision APG modules may become aligned with motor units that are appropriate for efficient learning. Inappropriate connections that are thought to be eliminated during development are shown dashed. For simplicity, we consider only one pair of opposing muscles, and thus do not represent the coarse coding of movement direction that is actually present in premotor networks.

The use-dependent mechanism for the alignment of APG modules outlined above is assumed to operate on an intermediate time scale, slower than the climbing fiber induced adaptation postulated to occur in the cerebellar cortex but faster than the structural adaptations that remodel nerve endings and synapses. We postulate that this intermediate-speed alignment mechanism provides an important driving force that then guides adaptations in the physical connectivity of the network. Adaptations in connectivity have been postulated to be mediated by trophic processes that use chemical signals to regulate the development and maintenance of axonal terminal branches and their synaptic junctions (Cotman, 1985).

The trophic theory (Purves, 1988) builds upon the observation that nerve endings are continually eliminating old connections and sprouting new ones. While this process is particularly active during development, it continues in the adult at a reduced rate. Trophic interactions are thought to be guided by a two-way interaction between arrays of nerve endings and arrays of target cells. In one direction of interaction, the target cells release trophic substances that promote sprouting of new nerve terminals and synaptogenesis, and these mechanisms attract new inputs. In the other direction, functional synapses produce postsynaptic activity that attenuates the production of the trophic substance. When a cell is incompletely activated, the production of trophic substance may be sufficiently elevated to attract and maintain both weak and strong inputs, but when the activation is strong, only strong inputs would be stabilized whereas weak ones would become eliminated. The latter competition essentially extends to a longer time scale the use-dependent functional modifications discussed earlier. The main additional feature of the trophic mechanism is its capacity for attracting and stabilizing new anatomical connections, whereas the functional mechanism merely strengthens existing synapses.

In summary, trophic mechanisms stimulated by use-dependent functional alterations in synaptic efficacy might contribute importantly to the generation and stabilization of an appropriate alignment between the climbing fiber input and the motor unit outputs of an APG module. Modules aligned in this manner would resolve important credit assignment problems, and an array of aligned modules should provide a highly efficient system for the adaptive control of movement. These mechanisms operating in premotor networks would not replace, but rather would use to advantage, the genetically specified zonal organization in the cerebellar cortex discussed in Section 3.1.

4.2. Sensorimotor Habits

Reactions to sensory stimuli that are repeatedly performed in the same context start to adopt an automatic quality characterized by shorter reaction times and more consistent movement parameters. These features are similar to those characterizing innate reflexes, raising the possibility of similar neural mechanisms. In this section we suggest that the acquisition of highly automated responses, what we refer to as sensorimotor habits, is an adaptive process that occurs in premotor networks under the guidance of regulatory signals from the cerebellar cortex. The mechanism proposed for the acquisition of these habits is the use-dependent synaptic modification of functional connections, and possibly also the trophic modification of structural connections, as discussed in the previous section.

The neuronal architecture of premotor networks is well-suited for implementing sensorimotor reactions. Premotor networks are characterized by a meshwork of pathways that occur in a few basic patterns (Graybiel, 1979; Lorente de Nó, 1938). One pattern is that of an elementary reflex arc, typically involving only a few synaptic linkages between a sensory input and a motor output. While there are many elementary reflex arcs in premotor networks, these direct linkages may not be sufficiently powerful to represent the main functional units of the network. A second pattern involves multi-synaptic feedforward pathways that are in parallel with each elementary reflex arc. This complexly branching feedforward pattern effectively expands the number of neurons that can participate in a sensorimotor reaction. A third pattern involves reciprocal connections between the various neuronal stages of a sensorimotor pathway. Reciprocal connections constitute feedback loops, and a sensorimotor circuit typically includes several feedback loops. The multiplicity of feedforward and feedback pathways serves to amplify signals and create spatiotemporal patterns of neural activity. These patterns may then serve as composite motor programs commanding the execution of sensorimotor reactions.

The conversion of a sensorimotor reaction, guided by the cerebellar cortex, into a sensorimotor habit, capable of execution in the absence of the cerebellar cortex, is postulated to result from use-dependent enhancement of selective pathways through a premotor network. Fig. 5 illustrates how this might occur. The "a" and "b" circuits for information flow represent the neural substrates for two different sensorimotor reactions, implemented by interconnections between three nuclei in the illustrated premotor network. The elementary reflex arcs are organized in nucleus 1, providing direct pathways from sensory cues to motor programs. Nucleus 2 provides feedback loops through the cerebellum that are subject to regulation by inhibitory input from Purkinje cells in the cerebellar cortex. Nucleus 3 connects reciprocally with nucleus 1 and thus provides feedback loops that are not subject to direct regulation by Purkinje cells. This particular example relates well to the premotor circuits that interconnect the motor cortex (nucleus 1), thalamus (nucleus 3) and the cerebellum (nucleus 2), though essentially the same principles would apply to other premotor circuits.

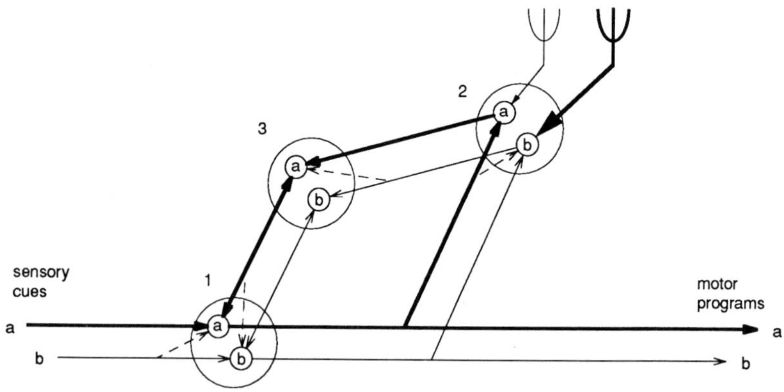

Figure 5: Sensorimotor circuits in a premotor network. Positive feedback through circuit b is inhibited by strong Purkinje cell input to nucleus 2, whereas feedback through circuit a is allowed to occur due to a low level of inhibition. Repetition of this pattern of sensorimotor responding is postulated to lead to the formation of a sensorimotor habit. After the habit is acquired, it would be triggered whenever sensory cue a provides sufficient input to the a1 neurons to initiate positive feedback in the bidirectional pathway between neurons a1 and a3.

The state of the premotor network portrayed in Fig. 5 is one of readiness to perform sensorimotor reaction a. We assume that the cerebellar cortex has already learned to control this sensorimotor reaction. The inhibitory input from Purkinje cells to the a2 neurons is set to a weak value whereas that to the b2 neurons is set strong. Correspondingly, the arrival of a sensory cue in either channel a or b would be expected to trigger regenerative neural activity in loop a, but not in loop b. The dashed arrows show some of the cross connections between loops a and b. We assume that, prior to the formation of the sensorimotor habit, there would be many such cross connections. The strong inhibition of the b2 neurons would minimize the spread of activity to loop b.

Now assume that the organism repeatedly uses this pattern of Purkinje cell activity to guide motor program a in response to sensory cue a. Given the presence of a use-dependent mechanism for modifying synaptic inputs, the connections in circuit a would become stronger, as symbolized by the heavy lines in Fig. 5, whereas the cross connections shown dashed would become weaker. The circuit b connections shown by light lines would not be altered. The suggested adaptive mechanisms conform to the learning contingencies summarized in Table 2. This sequence of events would comprise an initial stage in the formation of a sensorimotor habit.

A second stage in the formation of a sensorimotor habit might involve the streamlining of information flow through circuit a. The reciprocal connections between the a1 and a3 neurons would continue to be strengthened with continued use of the circuit. As this occurs, the inhibitory input to the a2 neurons would be increased in compensation for the greater strength of the a1-a3 loop, and this would reduce the degree of involvement of the longer loop from a1 to a2 to a3 back to a1. Eventually, differential Purkinje cell activity would not have to be used to control this sensorimotor reaction, and cerebellar cortical outflow could return to a uniform level of modest spontaneous activity. At this point expression of the sensorimotor habit would be controlled predominantly by reciprocal activity between a1 and a3 neurons. A third and final stage in the formation of this habit might involve actual structural modification of the connections in the premotor circuit, mediated by trophic mechanisms like the ones described in Section 4.1. At this stage the habit might become structurally embedded in a premotor network, and in this sense would be indistinguishable from an innate reflex.

The mechanisms suggested here for the formation of sensorimotor habits are analogous to those advanced to explain the role of the cerebellum in the plasticity of the vestibuloocular reflex (Galiana, 1986; Peterson, Baker & Houk, 1991). These mechanisms may also help to explain the controversy regarding the potential role of the cerebellum in conditioned reflexes (Bartha, Thompson & Gluck, 1991; Houk, 1990; Kelly, Zuo & Bloedel, 1990; Welsh & Harvey, 1989; Yeo, 1987). The acquisition of conditioned responding may generally depend both on the strengthening of a sensory input (a conditioned stimulus) to a premotor network and an adaptive adjustment of the motor program (a conditioned response) that is triggered by that sensory input. The strengthened sensory input would reside outside of the cerebellum (for example in nucleus 1 in Fig. 5), whereas adjustments in the motor program, if these are actually required, would occur initially in the cerebellum but could then migrate to the premotor network.

In summary, we have proposed that premotor networks are both controlled and supervised by the inputs they receive from Purkinje cells. These inputs seem to be clear examples of training signals that function by forcing their target neurons to behave in a desired manner. The APG alignment process proposed in Section 4.1 and the sensorimotor habit formation advanced in Section 4.2 are supervised learning tasks that could be readily implemented by the contingencies summarized in Table 2.

5. CEREBELLAR CORTEX

The cerebellar cortex has long been celebrated as a neuronal architecture ideally suited for learning to recognize complex patterns (Marr, 1969; Albus, 1971). One favorable feature is the enormous divergence in the mossy fiber/parallel fiber input to the cerebellum. This arrangement is ideally suited for distributing a given input to a maximal number of Purkinje cells across large areas of cerebellar cortex. A second favorable feature concerns the tremendous convergence of parallel fibers onto individual Purkinje cells. This arrangement exposes each Purkinje cell to approximately 200,000 potential inputs. The resultant of these divergent and convergent features is the high dimensional input vector comprised of context and state information that is distributed to a large number of Purkinje cells. A third favorable feature is the innervation of each Purkinje cell by a single climbing fiber. This input is presumed to function as a semiprivate training signal that instructs Purkinje cells how to respond to parallel fiber inputs (Section 2.3).

Successful learning would result in different Purkinje cells acquiring the ability to recognize different critical patterns of activity in the input vectors by markedly altering their states of activation in response to these critical patterns. However, translation of this activation state into a temporal pattern of activity that could serve as a motor program is not trivial. We begin this section by reviewing some of the past work on this problem of using a cerebellar architecture to generate temporal patterns.

5.1. Generation of Temporal Patterns

In the cerebellum models proposed by Marr (1969) and Albus (1971), the cerebellar cortex functions as an associative memory capable of learning complex transformations, though their theory is restricted to non-dynamical, memoryless transformations. The outputs of these transformations could serve as motor programs, but because the transformations are without dynamics, temporal features of the motor programs would have to be derived from time variations already present in the parallel fiber inputs to the cerebellum. This, we believe, is a severe limitation.

In contrast, our previous work on this topic (Houk, 1989; Houk *et al.* 1990; Sinkjær *et al.* 1990) proposed that APG modules are capable of generating temporal patterns of output independently of the time course of the input. This capacity, originally motivated by physiological studies of single unit discharge in behaving animals, was accounted for by including two nonlinear dynamical processes in our model.

Abstracting on the basis of intracellular recordings from dendrites (Ekerot, 1984; Llinás & Sugimori, 1980), we modeled Purkinje cells as multistable elements with hysteresis. We assumed that synaptic excitation has a small effect on membrane potential until it achieves a critical value designated the on-threshold; at this point the Purkinje dendrite flips to a depolarized state. It then remains in this depolarized state until synaptic inhibition exceeds an off-threshold, at which point the dendrite flips back to a hyperpolarized state. Individual dendrites were thus modeled as bistable devices with hysteresis. This gives rise to multistability at the level of the cell body where the effects of events in several dendrites are combined. The simplified case of a cell with just one dendrite (bistability instead of multistability) was assumed in the simulation studies of our model (Houk *et al.* 1990; Sinkjær *et al.* 1990).

We can now reinterpret the pattern recognition properties of Purkinje cells described earlier in light of the bistable or multistable properties discussed in the previous paragraph. In effect, each Purkinje cell dendrite can be trained to utilize the information present in the input vector to determine when to switch state. This switching is analogous to a state transition in a finite state automaton (e.g., Tomovic & McGhee, 1966). It comprises the recognition that a particular state of the automaton has just been achieved and marks this by producing a transition in the state of a Purkinje cell. State transitions in Purkinje cells are then used to control a second process.

The second nonlinear dynamical process was motivated by the reciprocal pathways in premotor networks discussed in Section 4.2. We postulate that the recurrent network displays stable equilibrium states similar to those described for symmetrically connected recurrent networks (Cohen & Grossberg, 1983; Hopfield, 1984), and we distinguish between relatively quiescent states and highly active states of the network. When the recurrent network is in a quiescent state, its activity is relatively insensitive to the inhibitory input from Purkinje cells: Purkinje cells can be turned on and off to prepare for anticipated movements. This is like recalling a motor program from memory, the memory being the synaptic weights of parallel fiber synapses. Once a motor program is recalled from memory, it can then be executed by injecting a trigger signal that causes the recurrent network to make a transition to a stable active state, the characteristics of which are determined by the preselected pattern of Purkinje cell inhibition, that is, by the recalled motor program.

A transition to an active state of the recurrent network is triggered by a transient input to loop neurons, as might be produced by the eliciting event inputs to the premotor networks in Fig. 1, or sensory cue a in Fig. 5. Once the network is triggered toward an active state, the intensity and spatial distribution of activity tends to build up in a regenerative fashion, due to positive feedback. (We have suggested that reaction times are caused by this progressive spread of recurrent activity.) Inhibitory inputs from Purkinje cells to the recurrent network determine the equilibrium state of the network and the trajectory toward this state over time, thus specifying the intensity of the movement command. It is noteworthy that the usual kind of sigmoid activation function studied by theorists is not appropriate for allowing modulatory inputs to have significant influence on the equilibrium states of a symmetrically connected network. However, another form of activation function, which has some physiological justification, could produce the desired modulatory effects (Eisenman, Keifer & Houk, 1991).

In addition to influencing characteristics of the active state, Purkinje cells are also believed to be responsible for terminating loop activity, thus stopping the motor program. We hypothesize that they utilize the variety of parallel fiber input they receive to detect when the endpoint for a movement is about to be achieved. At this point, a large enough number of Purkinje cells in relevant APGs flip to their on-states so that the resultant inhibition terminates positive feedback within the premotor network and, thus, terminates the motor program's execution.

In summary, positive feedback in the premotor network is postulated to serve as the driving force for generating a motor program, and preselected states of Purkinje cells guide the regenerative process to regulate the intensity and direction of the intended movement. As the movement proceeds, the pattern recognizing capabilities of Purkinje cells are used to detect when the desired endpoint is, or is about to be, reached. This fires the Purkinje cells which then terminates the motor program, thus bringing the movement to a coordinated conclusion. (Purkinje cells may also change their states during movement which would influence the trajectory, as when inflections occur at via points.)

5.2. Learning Task of the Cerebellum

The hysteretic properties of Purkinje cell dendrites implies that Purkinje cell activity depends in two ways on the past history of activity of the cerebellar cortex. As in other models, it depends on past history through synaptic changes produced as a result of learning, but it also depends on the state of dendritic activation as set by previous parallel fiber activity.

Consequently, the cerebellar cortex behaves more like an adjustable finite state automaton than an adjustable associative mapping. Instantaneous parallel fiber input modulates, rather than determines, Purkinje cell activity so that temporal patterns of output can be generated with time courses not locked to the time courses of the input. While these temporal properties are likely to be very useful for controlling movement, they can be expected to make learning more complicated. It is difficult to devise methods for learning how to produce correct temporal patterns that are not directly driven by external input, especially when training information comes from event detectors that are not continually active.

Models of the cerebellum as non-dynamical associative memories have utilized variants of the perceptron and LMS rules for adjusting the synaptic strengths of the parallel fiber inputs to Purkinje cells. The learning contingencies shown in Table 1 are, in fact, consistent with the basic error correction properties of the perceptron rule, as has been pointed out by Bartha, Thompson and Gluck (1991). The effectiveness of a perceptron rule in controlling a learning system depends on the training signal being capable of instructing the adaptive element as to the desired, or target, response at each time step. Utilizing the model of a Purkinje cell learning rule given in Table 1, the climbing fiber provides this instruction in the sense that the climbing fiber activity is the opposite of the target response of the Purkinje cell; that is, an active climbing fiber instructs the Purkinje cell to be inactive, and vice versa. However, if climbing fibers were to correctly instruct the moment-to-moment target responses required for movements, then the process generating climbing fiber activity would have to be more sophisticated than it appears to be. This would imply that the inferior olive is a kind of "oracle" already knowing how Purkinje cells should behave to correctly control movement. We discussed in Section 3 how the olive may be capable of providing useful training information, but the low firing frequencies and event-detecting character of olivary cells are not consistent with a role of moment-to-moment instruction of Purkinje cells. Instead, we view climbing fiber activity as instructing Purkinje cells about how and when to change state in a manner whose logic depends on details of the dynamics of APG modules and how they influence motor behavior.

We have explored the use of physiologically-based properties of climbing fiber activity in training a model of a single APG module to generate movements to several targets from arbitrary starting points (Houk *et al.* 1990). In this model, we dealt with climbing fibers that were assumed to fire at the end of each trial in which the movement fell short of the target. By simulating an asymmetric version of the learning rule, with each weight increment being much smaller than each weight decrement, the model was able to adjust movement amplitude in an appropriate manner. Small weight increments occurred at each time step of a trial when the climbing fiber was inactive, whereas a large weight decrement occurred when the climbing fiber fired at the end of the trial. The net effect was a weight decrement, Purkinje inhibition was decreased and the APG module produced a more intense and longer duration output in the next trial. This process occurred for each trial in a sequence until the endpoint of the movement went beyond the target. At this point, the climbing fiber ceased to fire, signifying that the movement's amplitude was correct. Performance then oscillated around this "zero error" point, as determined by the balance between net weight increments in trials when climbing fibers do not fire, and net weight decrements in trials when movement amplitude becomes too small and the climbing fibers do fire. Although the physiologically-based learning strategy worked well, this was a very simple example with a one degree-of-freedom task. Performance of the postulated learning rule needs to be explored in more complex tasks, work that is currently in progress (Barto *et al.* 1990).

Because this learning paradigm differs from those typically studied by theorists, the informational significance of the signals sent to the cerebellum by olivary neuron is not immediately clear. Are they best regarded as error signals, target responses (or, in this case, the opposites of target responses), evaluation signals, or do they have still other properties? Does the olive instruct or merely evaluate Purkinje cell activity? According to our current view of these issues, the cerebellum confronts the problem of learning how to avoid climbing fiber activity. Given that climbing fibers detect uncoordinated and inaccurate movements, the cerebellum can minimize this "punitive" climbing fiber activity by generating motor programs that produce coordinated and accurate movements. If we were to take this hypothesis at face value, climbing fiber activity would appear to be merely evaluative, signalling when errors are made but not providing the directional information required to correct them. One method for minimizing punishment in this reinforcement learning task would be to utilize exploratory activity of the network of Purkinje cells in order to discover appropriate parallel fiber weights.

A different view comes from the realization that climbing fiber activity implicitly contains directional information as a consequence of the anatomical alignment postulated to occur between an APG module and its climbing fiber input (Section 4.1). Each climbing fiber connects with an APG module that, when active, tends to reduce that particular climbing fiber's probability of being stimulated. Consequently, exploratory activity by a Purkinje cell is not needed to determine how it's activity influences the firing probability of the relevant climbing fiber, information necessary for determining the direction in which parallel fiber weights should be changed. The requisite exploration effectively took place during development, and this converted the problem into a supervised learning task. Thus, according to our theory, explicit exploration is not needed to solve the structural credit assignment problem arising from the size and complexity of the neural networks involved.

The view advanced in the previous paragraph is a simplification, however, since a composite motor program and the resultant movement will, in general, depend on other APGs in addition to the one to which a given climbing fiber is connected. Thus, although anatomical specificity and developmental alignment may connect the network such that increases in an APG's activity will tend to reduce the firing probability of its climbing fiber, what APGs do in controlling action will clearly depend on the context in which they are active. By this reasoning we conclude that some form of exploratory activity will probably be required for learning to coordinate cellular activity in the cerebellar cortex, but at the level of the APG module rather than at the level of individual Purkinje cells. In addition, it is important to point out that at a higher level of motor program selection, not dealt with in the present chapter, some form of overt exploratory motor behavior will be necessary for learning to perform with skill a rich repertory of motor behavior.

In summary of the various learning tasks confronted by this theory of distributed sensorimotor learning, it appears that all three stages included in our theory (Fig. 1) utilize one or another form of supervised learning. The ultimate driving forces for this learning derive from the high-threshold inputs to the inferior olive. These inputs teach olivary neurons to detect uncoordinated actions, olivary neurons teach Purkinje cells to recognize endpoints of movements, Purkinje cells force premotor neurons to terminate movements at these endpoints, and premotor neurons learn to automate this process when it is frequently repeated.

6. SUMMARY AND CONCLUSIONS

In this chapter we have attempted to provide a foundation upon which a comprehensive theory of sensorimotor learning might eventually be built. Our theory is clearly preliminary and speculative. In fact, most aspects have not yet been tested by simulation. Furthermore, some important aspects of sensorimotor integration, such as attention and selection, have not been touched upon. However, the proposed theory has the advantage that it is strongly based on the anatomy and physiology of the sensorimotor system, at both cellular and systems levels, and it also relates to theoretical work with adaptive neural networks. These features should permit appropriate modifications and additions to the theory to be implemented as future experimental and theoretical advancements are made.

Several facets of this theory address a particularly important problem addressed in theoretical studies of learning, the problem of supplying appropriate training information to adaptive sites within a complex neural network. Theorists call this the credit assignment problem. To recapitulate these facets as they apply to successive stages in the sensorimotor system (Fig. 1), we postulated that olivary neurons use high-threshold afferents to instruct the acquisition of responses to low-threshold afferents. These low-threshold responses, in combination with inhibitory gating mechanisms, become capable of detecting when movements are not well coordinated and are in danger of causing tissue damage or pain at particular locations on the body.

As a consequence of the zonal organization of the cerebellar cortex and a developmental alignment postulated to occur between olivary training signals and the APG modules they innervate, these training signals are transmitted specifically to where they can have appropriate effects. In this manner, Purkinje cells learn to detect when selected endpoints for movements are about to be reached. These cells then utilize their specific connections with premotor networks to shape regenerative premotor activity into motor programs that command accurate movements, or more precisely, movements that minimize the probability of occurrence of the events detected by olivary neurons. These mechanisms in combination provide a reasonable resolution of credit assignment for an olivo-cerebellar learning system that rapidly adjusts the coordination and accuracy of movements.

Purkinje cells, in turn, provide training information for learning sensorimotor habits. These cells serve both as controllers and as sources of training information by acting as forcing inputs to premotor circuits. When premotor neurons repeatedly control the same sensorimotor reaction, this reaction becomes engraved in the synapses of the premotor network by a relatively simple use-dependent learning rule. The ultimate result is a rapidly and automatically performed sensorimotor habit, still subject to modification by the more versatile control actions of the cerebellar cortex.

An important outcome of this analysis is the perspective it has provided regarding the value of devising a theory that deals with a diversity of time scales. The present theory is capable of dealing with the millisecond events of synaptic transmission; fractions of seconds during which single movements occur; rapid adaptation in the cerebellar cortex believed to occur over minutes and hours; the instigation of sensorimotor habits which may take hours, days or weeks; the developmental alignment of APG modules which might occur over weeks to years; and the evolution of cerebellar zones over the course of generations. We have found it illuminating to contemplate the overall effect of having learning processes operating on this diversity of time scales.

In the future it will be necessary to address attentional and selection mechanisms that could permit the discovery and refinement of a rich repertoire of motor acts, through overt exploratory behavior. We anticipate that some of these features can be appended to the present theory by introducing reward mechanisms, both as modulatory influences on the learning mechanisms described in this chapter, and as additional mechanisms present in anatomical structures that were not included in the present theory, namely higher areas of the cerebral cortex and the basal ganglia.

This work was supported by ONR contract N00014-88-K-0339 and by NIH grant R01-NS21015. The authors thank Wendy Fraser for editorial assistance and Damon LaPorte for help with the illustrations.

7. REFERENCES

Albus, J.S. (1971) A theory of cerebellar function. Math Biosci **10**: 25-61

Altman, J., Sudarshan, K. (1975) Postnatal development of locomotion in the laboratory rat. Animal Behav **23**: 896-920

Andersson, G., Armstrong, D.M. (1987) Complex spikes in Purkinje cells in the lateral vermis (b zone) of the cat cerebellum during locomotion. J. Physiol. London **385**: 107-134

Andersson, G., Ekerot, C.-R., Oscarsson, O., Schouenborg, J. (1987) Convergence of afferent paths to olivo-cerebellar complexes. In: Glickstein, M., Yeo, C., Stein, J. (eds) Cerebellum and Neuronal Plasticity. London, Plenum Press, pp 165-173

Andersson, G., Garwicz, M., Hesslow, G. (1988) Evidence for a GABA-mediated cerebellar inhibition of the inferior olive in the cat. Exp. Brain Res **72**: 450-456

Barlow, H.B. (1989) Unsupervised learning. Neural Computation **1**: 295-311

Bartha, G.T., Thompson, R.F., Gluck, M.A. (1991) Sensorimotor learning and the cerebellum. In: M. Arbib, J. Ewert (eds) Visual Structures and Integrated Functions. Berlin, Springer-Verlag, in press

Barto, A.G. (1985) Learning by statistical cooperation of self-interested neuron-like computing elements. Human Neurobiology **4**: 229-256

Barto, A.G. (1991) Some learning tasks from a control perspective. In: L. Nadel, D. Stein (eds) 1990 Lectures in Complex Systems. Addison-Wesley, in press

Barto, A., Berthier, N. , Singh, S., Houk, J.C. (1990) Network model of the cerebellum and motor cortex that learns to control planar limb movement. Soc. Neurosci. Abstr, vol 16, pt 2, p 1223

Barto, A.G., Jordan, M.I. (1987) Gradient following without back-propagation in layered networks. In: M. Caudill, C. Butler (eds) Proc. IEEE 1st Ann. Conf. Neural Networks. San Diego, CA, IEEE, part II, pp 629-636

Barto, A.G., Sutton, R.S., Anderson, C.W. (1983) Neuronlike elements that can solve difficult learning control problems. IEEE Transactions on Systems, Man, and Cybernetics **13**: 835-846

Brodal, A. (1981) Neurological Anatomy in Relation to Clinical Medicine, 3rd Ed. Oxford, Oxford Univ. Press

Brown, T.H., Ganong, A.H., Kairiss, E.W., Keenan, C.L., Kelso, S.R. (1989) Long-term potentiation in two synaptic systems of the hippocampal brain slice. In: Byrne, J.H., Berry, W.O. (eds) Neural Models of Plasticity, Ch. 14. San Diego, Academic Press, pp 266-306

Cohen, M.A., Grossberg, S. (1983) Absolute stability of global pattern formation and parallel memory storage by competitive neural networks. IEEE Trans. Syst. Man & Cybern **5**: 815-826

Collingridge, G.L., Singer, W. (1990) Excitatory amino acid receptors and synaptic plasticity. Trends in Pharmacological Sciences **11**: 290-296

Cotman, C.W. (1985) Synaptic Plasticity. New York, Guilford Press

Crepel, F.C., Krupa, M. (1988) Activation of protein kinase C induces a long-term depression of glutamate sensitivity of cerebellar Purkinje cells. An in vitro study. Brain Res **458**: 397-401

Doré, L., Jacobson, C.D., Hawkes, R. (1990) Organization and postnatal development of Zebrin II antigenic compartmentation in the cerebellar vermis of the grey opossum, Monodelphis domestica. J. Comp. Neurol **291**: 431-449

Eccles, J.C., Llinás, R., Sasaki, K. (1966) The excitatory synaptic action of climbing fibers on the Purkinje cells of the cerebellum. J. Physiol. London **182**: 268-296

Eisenman, L.N., Keifer, J., Houk, J.C. (1991) Positive feedback in the cerebro-cerebellar recurrent network may explain rotation of population vectors. In: Eeckman, F. (ed) Analysis and Modelling of Neural Systems, in press

Ekerot, C.-F. (1984) Climbing fibre actions of Purkinje cells -- plateau potentials and long-lasting depression of parallel fibre responses. In: Bloedel, J., et al. (eds) Cerebellar Functions. Berlin, Springer-Verlag, pp 268-274

Ekerot, C.-F., Oscarsson, O., Schouenborg, J. (1987) Stimulation of cat cutaneous nociceptive C fibres causing tonic and synchronous activity in climbing fibres. J. Physiol **386**: 539-546

Galiana, H.L. (1986) A new approach to understanding adaptive visual-vestibular interactions in the central nervous system. J. Neurophysiol **55**: 349-374

Gellman, R., Gibson, A.R., Houk, J.C. (1985) Inferior olivary neurons in the awake cat: Detection of contact and passive body displacement. J. Neurophysiol **54**: 40-60

Gellman, R., Houk, J.C., Gibson, A.R. (1983) Somatosensory properties of the inferior olive of the cat. J. Comp. Neurol **215**: 228-243

Gibson, A.R., Robinson, F.R., Alam, J., Houk, J.C. (1987) Somatotopic alignment between climbing fiber input and nuclear output of the intermediate cerebellum. J. Comp. Neurol **260**: 362-377

Gravel, C., Eisenman, L.M., Sasseville, R., Hawkes, R. (1987) Parasagittal organization of the rat cerebellar cortex: Direct correlation between antigenic Purkinje cell bands revealed by mabQ113 and the organization of the olivocerebellar projection. J. Comp. Neurol **265**: 294-310

Gray, R., Johnston, D. (1987) Noradrenaline and ß-adrenoceptor agonists increase activity of voltage-dependent calcium channels in hippocampal neurons. Nature **327**: 620-622

Graybiel, A.M. (1979) Some patterns of connectivity in the central nervous system: a tribute to Rafael Lorente de Nó. In: H. Asanuma, V.J. Wilson (eds) Integration in the Nervous System. Tokyo, Igaku-Shoin, pp 69-96

Grillner, S., Wallén, P., Dale, N., Brodin, L., Buchanan, J., Hill, R. (1987) Transmitters, membrane properties and network circuitry in the control of locomotion in lamprey. Trends in Neurosciences **10**: 34-41

Hinton, G.E., McClelland, J.L., Rumelhart, D.E. (1987) Distributed representations. In: Rumelhart, D.E., McClelland, J.L. (eds) Parallel Distributed Processing: Explorations in the Microstructure of Cognition, Volume 1: Foundations, Ch 3. Cambridge, Mass., Bradford Books/MIT Press, pp 77-109

Hofsten, C. von (1982) Eye-hand coordination in the newborn. Dev. Psychol **18**: 450-461

Hopfield, J.J. (1984) Neurons with graded response have collective computational properties like those of two-state neurons. Proc. Natl. Acad. Sci. USA **81**: 3088-3092

Houk, J.C. (1989) Cooperative control of limb movements by the motor cortex, brainstem and cerebellum. In: Cotterill, R.M.J. (ed) Models of Brain Function. Cambridge, Cambridge Univ Press, pp 309-325

Houk, J.C. (1990) Role of the cerebellum in classical conditioning. Soc. Neurosci. Abstr, vol 16, pt 1, p 474

Houk, J.C. (1991) Outline for a theory of motor learning. In: Stelmach, G.E., Requin, J. (eds) Tutorials in Motor Neuroscience, NATO ASI. Kluwer Acad. Publ., in press

Houk, J.C., Singh, S.P., Fisher, C., Barto, A.G. (1990) An adaptive sensorimotor network inspired by the anatomy and physiology of the cerebellum. In: Miller, W.T., Sutton, R.S., Werbos, P.J. (eds) Neural Networks for Control, Ch 13. Cambridge, Mass., MIT Press, pp 301-348

Ito, M. (1984) The Cerebellum and Neural Control. New York, Raven Press

Ito, M. (1989) Long-term depression. Ann. Rev. Neurosci **12**: 85-102

Jaffe, D., Johnston, D. (1990) Induction of long-term potentiation at hippocampal mossy-fiber synapses follows a Hebbian rule. J. Neurophysiol **64**: 948-960

Jansen, J., Brodal, A. (1942) Experimental studies on the intrinsic fibers of the cerebellum. The corticonuclear projection in the rabbit and in the monkey (Macacus rhesus.). Norske Vid. Akad., Oslo, Avh. I. Mat. Natury, Kl **3**: 1-50

Jordan, M.I., Jacobs, R.A. (1990) Learning to control an unstable system with forward modeling. In: Touretzky, D. (ed) Advances in Neural Information Processing Systems 2. San Mateo, CA, Morgan Kaufmann

Keifer, J., Houk, J.C. (1991) Role of excitatory amino acids in mediating burst discharge of red nucleus neurons in the in vitro turtle brainstem-cerebellum. J. Neurophysiol **65**: 454-467

Kelly, T.M., Zuo, C.-C., Bloedel, J.R. (1990) Classical conditioning of the eyeblink reflex in the decerebrate-decerebellate rabbit. Beh. Brain Res **38**: 7-18

Kennedy, M.B. (1988) Synaptic memory molecules. Nature **335**: 770-772

Linsker, R. (1988) Self-organization in a perceptual network. IEEE Computer, March, 1988: 105-117

Llinás, R., Sugimori, M. (1980) Electrophysiological properties of in vitro Purkinje cell dendrites in mammalian cerebellar slices. J. Physiol. London **305**: 197-213

Llinás, R., Yarom, Y. (1981) Electrophysiology of mammalian inferior olivary neurons in vitro. Different types of voltage-dependent ionic conductances. J. Physiol. London **315**: 549-567

Lorente de Nó, R. (1938) Analysis of the activity of the chains of internuncial neurons. J. Neurophysiol **1**: 207-244

Marr, D. (1969) A theory of cerebellar cortex. J. Physiol **202**: 437-470

McCurdy, M. (1988) Sensory input to the forelimb inferior olive and its relationships to motor pathways. Ph.D. Thesis, Northwestern U.

McDevitt, C.J., Ebner, T.J., Bloedel, J.R. (1987) Changes in the responses of cerebellar nuclear neurons associated with the climbing fiber response of Purkinje cells. Brain Res. **425**: 14-24

Miller, S., Oscarsson, O. (1970) Termination and functional organization of spino-olivocerebellar paths. In: W.S. Fields, W.D. Willis (eds) The Cerebellum in Health and Disease, Ch 6. St. Louis, Warren H. Green, pp 172-200

Minsky, M.L. (1963) Steps toward artificial intelligence. In: E. A. Feigenbaum, J. Feldman (eds) Computers and Thought. New York, McGraw-Hill, pp 406-450

Minsky, M.L., Papert, S.A. (1988) Perceptrons, 3rd ed.. Cambridge, Mass, MIT Press

Nelson, B.J., Mugnaini, E. (1989) Origins of GABAergic inputs to the inferior olive. In: Exp. Brain Res, Series 17. , pp 86-107

Neerven, J. van, Pompeiano, O., Collewijn, H., Steen, J. van der (1990) Injections of beta-noradrenergic substances in the flocculus of rabbits affect adaptation of VOR gain. Exp. Br. Res **79**: 249-260

Nguyen, D., Widrow, B. (1990) The truck backer-upper: an example of self-learning in neural networks. In: Miller, W.T., Sutton, R.S., Werbos, P.J. (eds) Neural Networks for Control. Cambridge, Mass., MIT Press, pp 287-299

Oscarsson, O. (1980) Functional Organization of Olivary Projection to the Cerebellar Anterior Lobe. In: J. Courville et al. (ed) The Inferior Olivary Nucleus: Anatomy and Physiology. New York, New York, Raven Press, pp 279-289

Peterson, B.W., Baker, J.F., Houk, J.C. (1991) A model of adaptive control of vestibuloocular reflex based on properties of cross-axis adaptation. Proc. N.Y. Acad. Sci, in press

Piaget, J. (1953) The Origins of Intelligence in Children. London, Routledge & Kegan Paul

Purves, D. (1988) Body and Brain: A Trophic Theory of Neural Connections. Cambridge, Mass., Harvard Univ. Press

Racine, R.J., Wilson, D.A., Gingell, R., Sunderland, D. (1986) Long-term potentiation in the interpositus and vestibular nuclei in the rat. Exp. Brain Res **63**: 158-162

Rosenblatt, F. (1962) Principles of Neurodynamics. New York, Spartan Books

Rumelhart, D.E., Hinton, G.E., Williams, R.J. (1986) Learning internal representations by error propagation. In: D.E. Rumelhart, J.L. McClelland (eds) Parallel Distributed Processing: Explorations in the Microstructure of Cognition, Vol 1. Cambridge, Mass., Bradford Books/MIT Press

Sakamoto, T., Porter, L.L., Asanuma, H. (1987) Long-lasting potentiation of synaptic potentials in the motor cortex produced by stimulation of the sensory cortex in the cat: a basis of motor learning. Brain Res **413**: 360-364

Scott, T.G. (1964) A unique pattern of localization within the cerebellum of the mouse. J. Comp. Neurol. **122**: 1-8

Shinoda, Y., Futami, T., Mitoma, H., Yokota, J. (1988) Morphology of single neurones in the cerebello-rubrospinal system. Beh. Brain Res **28**: 59-64

Shinoda, Y., Yamaguchi, T., Futami, T. (1986) Multiple axon collaterals of single corticospinal axons in the cat spinal cord. J. Neurophysiol **55**: 425-448

Sinkjær, T., Wu, C.H., Barto, A., Houk, J.C. (1990) Cerebellum control of endpoint position—a simulation model. IJCNN 90, San Diego, vol II, pp 705-710

Stanton, P.K., Sejnowski, T.J. (1989) Associative long-term depression in the hippocampus induced by hebbian covariance. Nature **339**: 215-218

Stein, L. (1978) Reward transmitters: catecholamines and opioid peptides. In: Lipton, M.A., DiMascio, A., Killam, K.F. (eds) Psychopharmacology: A Generation of Progress. New York, Raven Press, pp 569-581

Sutton, R.S. (1988) Learning to predict by the method of temporal differences. Machine Learning **3**: 9-44

Tomovic, R., McGhee, R.B. (1966) A finite state approach to the synthesis of bioengineering control systems. IEEE Trans **HFE-7**: 65-69

Voogd, J., Bigaré, F. (1980) Topographical distribution of olivary and corticonuclear fibers in the cerebellum. A review. In: Courville, J., Montigny, C. de, Lamarre, Y. (eds) The Inferior Olivary Nucleus. New York, Raven Press, pp 207-234

Weiss, C., Houk, J.C., Gibson, A.R. (1990) Inhibition of sensory responses of cat inferior olive neurons produced by stimulation of red nucleus. J. Neurophysiol **64**: 1170-1185

Welsh, J.P., Harvey, J.A. (1989) Cerebellar lesions and the nictitating membrane reflex: performance deficits of the conditioned and unconditioned response. J. Neurosci **9**: 299-311

Widrow, B., Hoff, M.E. (1960) Adaptive switching circuits. 1960 WESCON Convention Record Part IV, 96-104

Willshaw, D.J., Malsburg von der, C. (1976) How patterned neural connections can be set up by self-organization. Proc. R. Soc. Lond. B **194**: 431-445

Yeo, C.H. (1987) Cerebellum and classical conditioning. In: Glickstein, M., Yeo, C., Stein, J. (eds) Cerebellum and Neuronal Plasticity. London, Plenum Press, pp 321-338

Tutorials in Motor Behavior II
G.E. Stelmach and J. Requin (Editors)

Issues in Goal Directed Motor Learning: Feedforward Control, Motor Equivalence, Specificity, and Artificial Neural Networks

Ronald G. Marteniuk[1]

Department of Kinesiology[2], University of Waterloo, Waterloo, Ontario, Canada, N2L 3G1

INTRODUCTION

Research in human movement learning has a rich history, experimentally starting with S-R psychology (cf Adams, 1971) and carrying through to the more contemporary theories of closed-loop learning theory (Adams,1971), and schema theory (Arbib,1981, 1985; Schmidt,1975). Arbib's theory has attempted to incorporate multiple degrees of freedom movements into its treatment of learning while the earlier theories of Schmidt and Adams appear to have been formulated with single degree of freedom movements as their focus. However, while Arbib's theory deals with coordination of multiple component movements, the exact nature of how coordination is achieved is not explicit. Abbs, Gracco, and Cole (1984) have a relatively recent sensorimotor learning theory that is quite explicit on how planning and execution of multiple degrees of freedom movements are effected. Among other issues, their theory deals with the important concepts of feedforward control and motor equivalence.

Besides differing with respect to the issue of degrees of freedom, another contemporary issue unevenly dealt with by the above theories concerns the form of central representation that results from the learning process. Adams' theory is quite explicit in postulating perceptual and memory traces as the underlying form of representation. Schmidt's schema theory postulates the motor and recognition schemas as being the basis for learning and these are abstract, rule based memories that are used for generating movement parameters and recognizing just completed movements. However, both these theories have been criticized for being reliant on an executive that dictates how information is processed and stored for movement learning to occur. The executive models of performance and learning have as their general weakness an infinite regress problem in terms of the origin of the executive (Beek & Meijer, 1988).

On the other hand, the sensorimotor theory of Abbs et al. (1984) is much less reliant on an executive in that detailed planning of movements is not

1 Thanks to Reinoud Bootsma, Claude Dugas, and Heather Carnahan for giving valuable suggestions on an earlier draft of this chapter.

2 As of September 1, 1991, my new address is Department of Kinesiology, Simon Fraser University, Burnaby, British Columbia, Canada, V5A 1S6.

postulated to occur but rather sensory consequences of past, similar movements are thought to result in the generation of a ball-park movement which is then controlled through the use of feedback in conjunction with feedforward centers that have been formed through the integration of previous sensory and motor experiences. Considerable effort is made to base this theory on the physiological foundation of sensorimotor integration, thus somewhat alleviating the infinite regress problem. Finally, Arbib's schema theory is also quite physiologically based and at the same time has a computational framework. In particular, Arbib introduces the notion of artificial neural networks as the basis for his schema models and points out quite nicely how these computational models have some physiological validity as well as accounting for the representation of the motor learning process.

The final general issue for a contemporary theory of motor learning is the issue of goal directed learning. The above theories might be called goal directed theories in that after each movement attempt at the defined goal, feedback is used to assess the degree of the movement's success and thus the next attempt has the potential to be better attuned to the demands of the goal. However, the treatment of goal directed learning is uneven over these four theories. Goal directed learning concerns the learning of ways of altering the **current** movement to make it more successful in terms of the movement goal (Jordan, 1990). Closed-loop learning theory and Schmidt's schema theory are silent on this issue. Abbs et al. introduce the feedforward center that allows rapid translation between sensory information and motor commands to make the current movement more appropriate to the goal. Finally, Arbib's computational approach also incorporates feedforward controllers that, through past experience, allow adaptation of movements so that they more successfully accomplish the intended goal.

The purpose of the present paper will be to first outline, by reviewing the results of a series of experiments, some of the performance and learning characteristics that should be accounted for by a contemporary theory of motor learning. Second, Jordan's (1990) sequential, forward model, neural network will be presented as one way of conceptualizing a framework for a theory of motor learning.

CHARACTERISTICS OF MOTOR CONTROL AND LEARNING

A. MOTOR CONTROL: SPECIFICITY OF CONTROL, MOTOR EQUIVALENCE, AND RAPID ADAPTABILITY.

1. Specificity of control

The organization and control of movement have been investigated by observing the characteristics of movement trajectories over a variety of different tasks (Atkeson & Hollerbach, 1985; Flash & Hogan, 1985; Hollerbach and Atkeson, 1987; Munhall, Ostry & Parush, 1985; Soechting, 1984). Trajectory formation refers to the planning and control of the kinematics of movement and, more specifically, is concerned with the path the movement describes in space and with the speed of movement from the initial to the final position in space.

A general research strategy that we have pursued is to see the effects on movement trajectories of varying the number and extent of potential movement constraints. A movement constraint is defined as a variable that limits the way in which movement can be organized and controlled (MacKenzie & Marteniuk, 1985a; Marteniuk, MacKenzie, Jeannerod, Athenes, & Dugas, 1987). Marteniuk et al. (1987) suggested that various potential movement constraints, from different levels of analyses, might include: target size; instructions of speed and accuracy; specific task characteristics; the structure inherent in communicated information (e.g. music structure); anatomical structure; neurological structure; and, experience and intentions (goals) of the performer.

In an attempt to determine whether target size and movement amplitude were constraints on the planning and control of movement trajectories, MacKenzie, Marteniuk, Dugas, Liske and Eickmeier (1987) examined three dimensional movement trajectories over a broad range of movement difficulty, as measured by Fitts' index of difficulty (Fitts & Peterson, 1964). The three dimensional motion analyses consisted of analyzing the movement trajectory of the stylus for the various aiming movements. The kinematic variable selected to form the trajectory was the resultant velocity (a combination of the tangential velocities from each of the three planes of the movement) of the movement throughout its duration.

Our analysis of the salient trajectory characteristics showed that for a given index of difficulty, trajectories changed dramatically (even though movement time remained almost identical). In an attempt to understand this result we normalized the resultant velocity profiles and found that the profiles could be scaled to a common profile when dealing with trajectories to a specific target size over different movement amplitudes. With respect to target size the profiles differed by the proportion of time spent after peak resultant velocity. Smaller targets showed skewed velocity profiles with longer right hand tails or deceleration phases. Thus target size determined the shape of the trajectory in terms of time spent in acceleration and deceleration.

The above data are suggestive of a representation of a movement trajectory but it is not simply scalable in the time domain. Remember, our logic in examining the normalized resultant velocity profile was to look for scalability as a function of movement amplitude or target size. The results showed that for a given target size, the resultant speed could be scaled as a function of amplitude. However, movements could not be scaled over different target sizes. Thus, since invariance in relative time suggests a program with a scalable parameter, for the conditions of this experiment one might say that a base trajectory (program) exists for a given target width and this trajectory is scaled or parameterized according to the movement amplitude. In fact, of the many studies we have done on three dimensional analyses of motor control, this is the only data for which we have found support for a base trajectory. All other studies have found specificity of motor control in that trajectories have not scaled over the different values of various movement constraints.

An example of this is the recent work by Marteniuk, et al. (1987) where the goal of the first experiment was to investigate whether the fragility of an object could influence the form of the movement trajectory resulting from reaching and grasping objects. Subjects were required to reach and grasp either a tennis ball or the round end of a light bulb. Both objects had a diameter of approximately 6 cm and were placed on a table top 30 cm in front of the seated subject. No instructions as to speed of the reach and grasp were given. The results showed that movement trajectories to the two objects differed. In particular, movement to the light bulb took longer and peak velocity of the trajectory was reached proportionately sooner. This meant that subjects spent proportionately more of the time involved in reaching for the light bulb in a limb deceleration phase. This is similar to the precision effect noted in the Fitts' data presented above, under conditions where target size became smaller. However, in the present study, the index of difficulty of the movement was constant. Presumably the precision effect occurred for the light bulb condition as a result of the subject making sure the hand was travelling slow enough so that the bulb would not break when contact was made. No such caution was needed for grasping the tennis ball so subjects could spend proportionately more time in accelerating their limb to the object and proportionately less in decelerating.

In a second experiment from the above paper, we tried to structure the task in order to determine the effect of a person's intent on the movement planning and control processes. Here, subjects were asked to reach for and grasp a wooden disk (one cm thick and four cm in diameter) placed 30 cm in front of them. Two movement conditions were employed differing only in what the subject was asked to do after the disk had been grasped. In one, the disk was to be placed in a tight fitting well (4.1 cm in diameter) situated close to where the disk initially lay. In the other condition, the disk was to be thrown into s 20x40x15 cm cardboard box positioned 15 cm to the left of where the disk lay.

Results of this experiment showed that the movement trajectory of the wrist in picking up the disk was influenced by what the subject was going to do with the disk once it had been picked up. It was shown that proportionately more time was spent in the deceleration phase of the trajectory when subjects were planning to place the disk in the well. It was as if the precision required in placing the disk in the tight fitting well exerted an influence on the motor control processes responsible for guiding the limb to the object. Likely, however, it was the planning before the reach and grasp portion of the task that resulted in the movements being specifically designed for the unique demands of the two conditions.

In another study, (Marteniuk, Leavitt, MacKenzie & Athenes, 1990) we asked the question how people planned and executed movements when they were asked to reach and grasp objects of varying sizes. This experiment required subjects to reach for and grasp ten different sized disks (from one to ten cm in diameter and all were one cm thick) that were placed on a table top 30 cm in front of them. The instructions to subjects were to reach as quickly as possible but without so much speed that would result in fumbling the object during the grasp.

To determine how the trajectory kinematics were affected by increases in disk size, the resultant velocity function was calculated from the three dimensional coordinates of the wrist. Results showed that the acceleration portion of the velocity profile (from the start of the movement to zero acceleration at peak velocity) was constant while the deceleration portion of the movement became shorter with increases in disk size. In essence, the smaller the disk, the more time the subject took in decelerating the limb before contact with the disk. This "precision" effect on deceleration was very similar to the effect noted above and very consistent with the results of the experiment on Fitts' Law (MacKenzie, et al., 1987) where the index of difficulty correlated to a greater degree with time of the deceleration phase than with total movement time. In terms of theoretical significance, these results indicate that the planning and control processes are task specific in that each disk size resulted in a relatively unique movement trajectory being produced by the subject.

Other results from the Marteniuk et al. (1990) study were concerned with describing the hand aperture as the hand approached the disk. The aperture was defined as the distance between the index finger and thumb markers, calculated directly from the three dimensional data. The first analysis showed that the maximum grasp aperture (achieved in time approximately three-quarters of the way to the disk) correlated with the size of the disk, r=.998. While all subjects maximum aperture was larger than the disk to be grasped, the time based profile of the aperture was always the same. That is, during the first three-quarters of the movement the aperture opened to its maximum and then during the final quarter of the movement duration, it closed down to the size of the disk until contact with the disk was made. The fact that the above correlation was so high indicates that there is a highly integrated relationship between the physical demands of this task and the resulting fine motor control in response to those demands. Results from both the wrist (arm) trajectory and the grasp aperture indicate functionally specific responses of the motor system to task demands.

Collectively, the studies reviewed in this section speak to motor planning and control processes that result in movements that are relatively specific to the conditions of the task. The key term here appears to be "functional specificity" which underscores the apparent ability of the human motor system to produce movements that are ideally suited to the specific requirements of attaining the movement goal.

2. Motor Equivalence and Rapid Adaptability

One characteristic of a multiple degree of freedom movement is that it has the potential to solve the motor coordination problem in various ways. In general, an over-complete system (one where the degrees of freedom exceed the number required to solve the motor problem) has an infinite number of ways in which to organize itself for the attainment of a movement goal. The arm and hand, when reaching for and grasping objects is one such over-complete system and we (Paulignan, MacKenzie, Marteniuk, & Jeannerod, 1991) have used this task in an attempt to more fully understand the nature of the coordination involved in a highly learned skill.

In this study, subjects were requested to reach, grasp and lift as accurately as possible one of three dowels using the distal pads of the thumb and index finger. On certain trials, upon movement initiation towards the middle dowel, the dowel was made to instantaneously change its location to one of the two other dowel positions, requiring the subject to reorient the arm and hand to the new dowel. Data acquisition consisted of monitoring the arm (a marker on the wrist), the wrist angle (derived from markers on the elbow, wrist, and back of the hand) and grip aperture (markers on the index finger and thumb) through a two-dimensional optoelectric system.

Data analyses revealed several interesting characteristics of how this visual-motor system adapted to the changed location of the dowel. First, it was shown that on perturbed trials, the wrist began amending its movement to the location of the middle dowel in approximately 100 ms after the dowel had changed its location. This time was derived from the acceleration profile of the wrist and if EMGs of the appropriate muscles could have been monitored, the time of EMG change would likely have been 10 to 15 ms shorter than the acceleration change. This implies a very rapid visuomotor transformation and is certainly much shorter than typical reaction times reported to visual signals. Interestingly, these rapid modifications occurred in a non-stereotypical way. Analysis of the wrist angle, wrist spatial path, and the grip aperture showed that the configuration of the wrist and hand during movement execution and up to contact with the dowel were different for each dowel location. In essence there was a covariation of movement components that resulted in relatively unique inter-component configurations while still allowing the successful accomplishment of the task. This is a classic example of motor equivalence and demonstrates, at least for prehension, the flexibility of skilled motor control and its rapid adaptability to visual perturbations.

B. MOTOR LEARNING: SPECIFICITY OF LEARNING AND TRANSFER

1. The functional specificity of motor learning.

Proteau, Marteniuk, Girouard and Dugas (1987) have shown the functional specificity of motor learning and have attempted to provide a theoretical framework for understanding this phenomenon. They studied the learning of an aiming task where subjects were required to use their left (non-preferred) arm in an underswinging movement to attempt to hit a small target with a hand held stylus. The basic objective of the subjects in this task was to move the hand (there was a straight line distance of 90 cm between the starting position of the hand and the target) in 550 msec with as much accuracy as possible. After each attempt the experimenter gave feedback to the subject by orally giving the movement time and the spatial accuracy in the two axes of the target.

There were four different groups of subjects. Two groups were given 200 trials of practice while the other two were given 2000 trials. One group from each level of practice practiced the task in normal laboratory conditions while the other two groups practiced in total darkness. Thus, for the latter two groups, only the small target was visible to them; they could see neither the moving arm nor the hand as it hit the plate containing the target. After the last training trial all subjects were transferred to a condition that involved the same conditions as the groups who practiced in total darkness except that feedback for movement time and spatial accuracy was not given. This meant that subjects initially practicing under normal conditions were now in a condition where no visual information about the task or their movements was available.

The results indicated that all subjects improved their performance (both in the temporal and spatial domains) over practice. Furthermore, subjects who practiced with only the target visible were constantly worse than those groups who had the normal condition. The interesting results were what happened to performance during the transfer condition. After 200 trials of practice, both the normal and vision of target only groups showed a small increase in spatial errors due to the transfer task conditions. Statistically, the difference between the two groups at the end of the 200 trials of practice was maintained during the transfer condition except that both groups performance here was worse than at the end of the regular practice.

After 2000 trials of practice the transfer task conditions produced a different set of results. The target only group maintained their pre-transfer level of performance. The normal group, deprived of vision of everything except the target, showed a large increase in spatial error in their transfer performance. In fact, the spatial error of this group was about 400 times larger than their spatial error at the beginning of practice. Obviously taking away vision after 2000 trials of practice was detrimental to their ability to perform the task.

These results support the idea that learning a movement results in some change within the central nervous system that allows the performer to become more skilled at the task, and, at the same time (at least for the conditions of the present study), interferes with performance when the source of feedback is changed. Here, the inference is that some kind of internal structure develops that allows for efficient planning, execution, and movement correction processes necessary for skilled movement. Since this structure is rather specific to the task and the types of information received about the task-performer interaction, when relevant feedback channels are eliminated (as in the transfer condition of the normal practice group of the present study) performance declines dramatically, especially if the performer is skilled.

The above interpretation was confirmed with a different experimental design in a study by Proteau, Marteniuk and Levesque (In press). Instead of having one group of subjects practice with normal vision and the other practice with only vision of the target, both groups practiced under the latter condition for 1,200 trials with test trials after 200 and 1,200 trials. The test trials consisted or performance under normal visual conditions. Performance under the test trials was compared to performance under normal vision that were obtained before the 1,200 practice trials had begun.

Results showed quite convincingly that transfer from practice without normal vision to normal vision resulted in a deterioration of performance both after 200 and 1,200 trials of practice compared to the pre-test condition described above. Thus, although performance in the target only condition improved over the acquisition period, once the feedback condition changed, performance was immediately affected in a negative way. These results are not only confirmatory of a specificity of practice view, but demonstrate quite nicely that visual feedback must be integrated or calibrated with other sensorimotor processes before it can be used in an optimal manner.

2. Specificity of transfer

Bamford & Marteniuk (1988) studied the learning of two versions of the same task and asked what would happen when subjects were switched to the other version. The logic of the design was similar to the above studies in that our hypothesis was that when people learn a movement task, internal structures are developed to efficiently represent and process information about the task. We reasoned that one way of uncovering the nature of the internal structure was to have subjects learn two versions of the same task where the versions differed either by the type of information available for movement execution or by some other type of manipulation relevant to motor control and learning processes. In the present case we manipulated the information display-movement compatibility. We used a elbow rotation task where the subject was seated next to a horizontal arm rest that pivoted around one end. The arm of the subject was placed on the manipulandum so the elbow was directly over the point of rotation and the subject's hand held a handle attached at the other end. By flexing or extending the elbow the subjects could move the manipulandum in the horizontal plane. At the base of the manipulandum was a potentiometer that was used to record the amount of elbow rotation. This potentiometer was interfaced with a computer that performed an analog to digital conversion and then put this signal out to a graphics terminal. The result was a display on the graphics terminal in the form of a continuous line, with the amplitude above or below the starting level being proportional to the amount of elbow flexion or extension.

Subjects were required to learn a series of elbow flexions and extensions that were defined by a criterion wave form generated by the experimenter. This criterion "movement" (identical to the one used by Marteniuk & Romanow, 1983) was used to define the required movement to the subjects. The subjects then attempted to produce the criterion by moving the manipulandum in a manner that would produce a wave form identical to that of the criterion. After each attempt, the experimenter displayed the subject's waveform on the graphics terminal and then superimposed the criterion on it. The subject could then see the discrepancy between what was produced and what was required.

There were two groups of subjects that attempted to learn the criterion movement. One was the compatible group where the criterion and subject produced wave form moved in the same direction as the subject's arm. That is, when the subject extended the elbow (movement to the right) the line, coming down from the top of the graphics terminal, would move to the right. Similarly a movement to the left by the subject resulted in the line moving to the left. Thus the movement was described by the terminal in a compatible manner with the subject's movement. The orthogonal condition had the line coming from the left side of the terminal and when the subject's arm moved left the line would go down. Movements to the right caused the line to go up. Thus, the wave form was orthogonal to the movements of the arm.

Both groups of subjects had ninety learning trials where their produced wave form and the criterion were displayed after every trial. Discrepancies between these two wave forms was measured by Root Mean Square Error. Results showed that both groups of subjects reduced error over the 90 trials and they had identical performance at the end of practice. After this learning, the two groups were switched to the other condition. These results proved interesting. The orthogonal group, now performing under the compatible condition, showed a decrement in their performance of about 30% of their pre-switch level. The compatible group, now under the orthogonal condition, showed a much greater decrement (about 70% of the pre-switch level) in their performance. In fact this group's mean performance for the first five switch trials was at the same level as the mean of their first five trials under the compatible condition. In essence there was no transfer when switching from the compatible to the orthogonal condition.

These results indicated that the orthogonal group learned something that transferred to the compatible condition. On the other hand, the compatible group's initial switch performance indicated no transfer or benefit from their previous experience. As we explained, the former group had perhaps developed an information processing stage that deals with transforming the information from the display to body centered coordinates within a visual-spatial map. The compatible group was not concerned with this transformation since information from the display was already directly compatible with limb movement. When the two groups were switched to the opposite condition, transfer occurred for the group switched from the orthogonal condition because of the similarity of the two tasks. The other group, however, lacked the ability to transform display information into useable body information and as a result no transfer occurred. Thus, it would appear that what is learned in tasks like this is relatively specific to the conditions present during the practice of the task.

C. SUMMARY AND IMPLICATIONS

The first issue we addressed above was the apparent specificity of movement control. For the studies we reviewed, there did not appear to be much support for the existence of a generalized linear motor program. Some support was found in the Fitts' aiming experiment where for different movement amplitude requirements to the <u>same</u> target, the resulting resultant velocity profiles could be scaled to a base trajectory. As soon as the target size was changed however, unique trajectories resulted, primarily from a lengthening of the deceleration component of the trajectory. Similar precision effects were shown in the other two studies on reaching and grasping objects where trajectories were unique to the objects being grasped or to the intent of the use of the object. In this regard our overall results agree with those studies reviewed by Gentner (1987) which show only limited support for the idea of the generalized motor program.

The phenomenon of specificity was also seen in movement learning. Three studies showed that whatever is learned during the acquisition of a movement skill influences the performance on a second task that varies in the form of feedback available to the performer or in the compatibility of an information display and the direction of movement. In general, these studies suggest that learning results in some change within the central nervous system that optimizes performance in regard to the conditions that exist during acquisition and that when these conditions change performance deteriorates. It is as if changing the task conditions even slightly requires a recalibration of the senorimotor relationships established during the learning phase under the previous conditions.

Finally, the studies of prehension gave two more insights into the control characteristics of the movement system. First, for the highly practiced skill of grasping objects in near body space, it was shown that the grasp aperture was highly attuned to the size of the object. In essence, the motor system produced movement that was ideally suited to the demands of the task. This demonstrates the precise nature of the sensorimotor transformations that are possible in movement skills that have been practiced extensively. Second, in addition to this high level of skill, this movement system also demonstrates very rapid adaptability to visual perturbations of the to-be-grasped object. This indicates that the sensorimotor transformations underlying these movements must be rapid and, perhaps, dependent on feedforward processes.

Prehension is not the only movement skill that has demonstrated rapid modifications to unexpected perturbations. Abbs and Gracco (1986) reported latencies to perturbations of the lip during speech movements that ranged between 36 and 72 ms. Zelaznik, Hawkins and Kisselburg (1983) found evidence for visual corrections occurring under 100 ms for rapid aiming movements. More recently, Van Sonderon, Gielen, and Van der Gon (1989) have shown that for rapid arm movements to visually perturbed targets, trajectories deviated significantly from their original trajectories within 60 ms and, on occasion, within 30 ms. Finally, recent work by Patla, Beuter, and Prentice (1991) showed that in gait, when subjects were required to step over suddenly, and unexpectedly, appearing obstacles, the limb trajectory, as characterized by displacement profiles of the heel, was modified within 120 ms of the appearance of the obstacle. Given these times were derived from displacement data, had accelerations or EMG profiles been used, the reported modification times would have been lower.

The above times are considerably shorter than those reported for typical visual reaction times (usually greater than 200 ms) and for those studies which report latencies to visual target displacements before the movement begins. For example the work of Georgopoulos, Kalaska, and Massey (1981), and Van Sonderen, Van der Gon, and Gielen (1988), report movement reorganization times of 130 ms to 200 ms. As Paulignan, et al. (1991) point out, the difference between these situations and those where shorter modification times have been reported, is that perturbations arising during the movement create a discrepancy between the visual signals related to the new target position and the proprioceptive signals generated by the movement. When the visual perturbation occurs before movement begins, a complete reorganization would occur which would be around one visual reaction time. However, when the perturbations occur during the movement, the modification could arise directly from a feedforward center that has an existing map of the sensorimotor contingencies necessary to solve the problem. The presence of dynamic proprioceptive feedback presumably explains the faster use of this sensorimotor store as compared to the situation when the limb in not moving.

A composite model for goal directed learning. Figure 1 can be used to help conceptualize the role that feedback and feedforward may have on the control of a multiple degree of freedom movement. The feedforward controller would provide the controlled system with the best estimate of the signal required to achieve the goal of the movement. The feedback controller would be responsible for refining this estimate and assuring precise acquisition of the goal when the feedforward controller is not completely accurate or when unanticipated disturbances are encountered. The learning of the feedforward model is central to achieving fast, goal directed movements. Feedforward models are developed through experience at a given task where goal directed movements are attempted and feedback regarding their success is received. Feedback here would not only be about how, for example, the endpoint of an effector was approaching an object or target, but also about how the multiple degrees of freedom of the effector were being covaried to allow the end point to reach its goal. Through many such experiences sensorimotor relationships are established that allows the system to predict the result it expects, given the output it has produced. This in turn leads to an improvement in the speed of performance and to an effective use of multiple degrees of freedom.

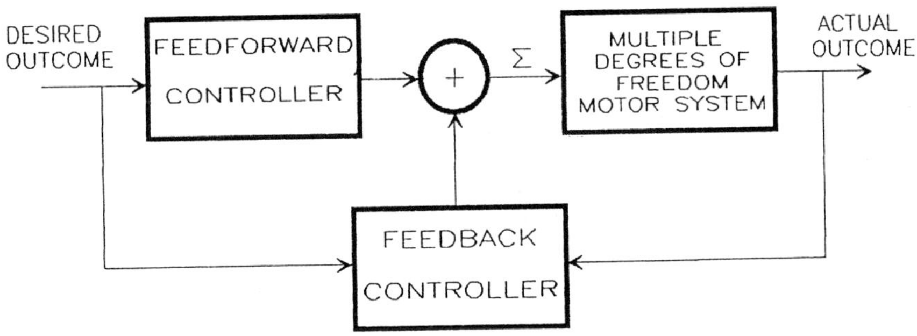

Figure 1. Schematic model showing the role of feedback and feedforward in the control of a multiple degree of freedom movement.

GOAL-DIRECTED LEARNING AND JORDAN'S (1990) NEURAL NETWORK

To this point I have reviewed relevant literature that speaks to motor control and learning characteristics that should be accounted for by movement learning theory. These characteristics are: goal directed learning; motor equivalence; rapid adjustments to unexpected perturbations, a characteristic of feedforward control; specificity of trajectory formation; and, specificity of learning. As well, since one of the aims of this type of research is to uncover those central nervous system processes that contribute to movement control and learning, one important question concerns the form of movement representation within the brain. This, then, with all its potential problems, must also be part of an account of movement control and learning.

The purpose of this section is to present Jordan's (1990) artificial neural network of motor control and learning as one way of conceptualizing how the central nervous system might be involved in movement learning and control. The model will be used to help understand how the above characteristics of learning and control might be accounted for within the central nervous system. As well, the model will be used to help delineate future directions for human movement research.

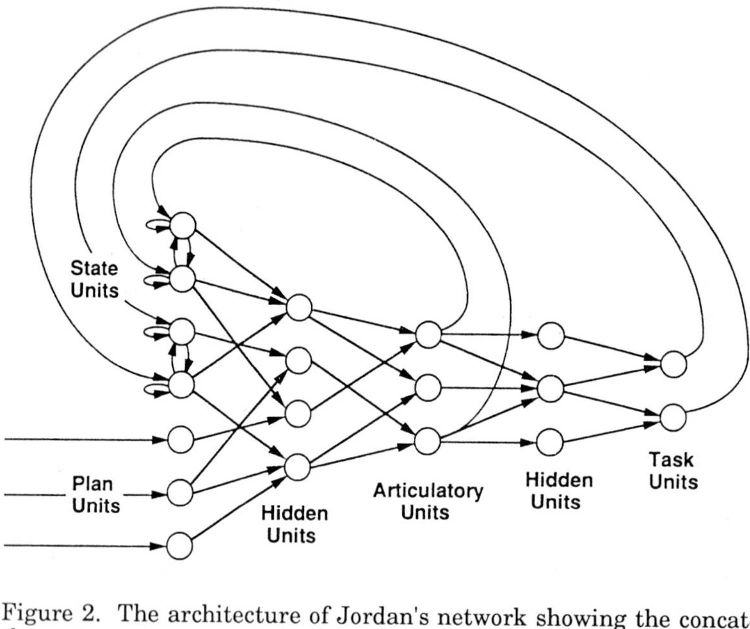

Figure 2. The architecture of Jordan's network showing the concatenation of the motor program and the forward model subnetworks. (From Jordan, 1990).

1. Jordan's neural network model

Figure 2 displays Jordan's (1990) neural network which is a concatenation of two subnetworks: what he terms a motor program network and a forward model network. The motor program network is a feedforward processing, sequential network where learning algorithms change the weights of the connections among the units so that the network will produce goal directed output. The network connects the plan units and the state units to the articulatory or output units which are,in turn, connected to the effectors. Intervening units, called hidden units, allows the network to learn non-linear functions. The input units receive activation from other sources and designate which particular motor program will be activated. The plan need not contain the detailed structure of the designated movement because the network, through learning, already has the details of the movement embedded in the weights of the connections of the network. In essence, in dynamical terms, the plan instantiates a particular vector field.

One role of the state units is to provide the ability of the network to produce a sequence of outputs such as a series of movements to a set of targets. The state units are activated by the first output pattern of the network being copied back to these units. For the next feedforward sweep through the network, the activation of each state unit is set equal to the activation of the corresponding output unit plus an amount of activation based on inputs from other units. This process allows the state units to capture the prior history of activation in the network. For each time step, the same process occurs until the movement sequence is complete. A second role of the state units is to estimate the state of the environment so that control of environmental dynamics by the network becomes possible.

The primary purpose for the forward model is to allow movement constraints expressed in distal coordinate systems to be transformed into internal or motoric coordinate systems (Jordan, 1990). It is a learned internal mapping of task space among the environmental state, a particular action, and the outcome of the movement. As Jordan (1990) indicates the forward model is analogous to a schema and in control system terminology is known as system identification.

Once the forward model has been learned over a particular task space, the weights of its connections are held fixed and the motor program subunit is then presented with learning a set of sequential movements. When the motor program provides an output to the articulatory units, an error is generated as the difference between the actual outcome and the desired outcome. During this learning phase, this error is transformed by a learning operator obtained by differentiating the forward model. The end result of this exercise is a transformation of errors in task space into errors in output or articulatory space. These errors are then used to change the weights of the connections within the motor program subnetwork so that the output of the motor program on the next attempt becomes more congruent with the goal of the task.

Jordan's (1990) model combines feedforward control with feedback control to allow the network to successfully accomplish the movement goal on the first attempt, even though it does so in an awkward, slow fashion. The network does this by the forward controller supplying, for the first movement in a sequence of movements, a control vector which is then passed to a feedback controller that iteratively updates the control vector so as to null the performance error between the desired result of the movement and the actual result. For the next movement in the sequence, control is passed back to the feedforward controller for the next control vector in the sequence and the process is repeated until the sequence is complete. Early in learning the feedforward controller is relatively inaccurate in its estimation of the control vector and thus many iterations through the feedback controller are necessary. However, through learning, the feedforward controller provides control vectors that are closer to the movement required to complete the movement and hence fewer feedback based corrections are necessary. Jordan (1990) makes the point that once the feedforward model is completely learned, no feedback iterations are necessary. This is indeed what happens in simulation experiments carried out by Jordan (1990) but whether this would hold for human movement is open to question. For example, one might expect that a feedforward controller developed for a complex movement would never be able to predict the exact outcome of a movement given the variability of the human movement system and, in many skills, the variability of the environment. Thus, it might be the case that a well learned feedforward controller would provide a control vector that was nearly correct, but all movements would have to have feedback control in order to successfully accomplish the movement goal. The control vector, in this case, would be similar to the "ball park" commands mentioned above with feedback serving to fine tune the movement.

2. The representation problem.

A continuing debate in the motor control and learning literature deals with the issue of how much the brain controls movement vs how much of the control is left to the biomechanics of the movement apparatus including the geometrical and mechanical properties of muscles. One answer is that since movement involves physical interaction with the environment, any planning and control mechanisms within the brain must take into account those mechanical principles that result from movement. However, some literature is especially critical, at least at the present time, of ascribing any role to brain mechanisms in motor control and learning because of the substantial "loans on intelligence" (Kugler & Turvey, 1987). As an example of this consider the rapid compensations alluded to in the studies reviewed above, which in the present framework are seen to be due to feedforward processes. Proponents of a physical/dynamical account of motor control, where central representations are not invoked, contend that such feedforward processes require a complete knowledge base of the dynamics of the effector systems. Given the notorious non-linearity of the movement system, the claim is that representation of such knowledge within the brain is seen to be improbable because of space and computational limitations. Another view, consistent with the idea that there are central representations of movement, is that there are undoubtedly biomechanical factors that constrain movement control processes and that can account for a substantial part of coordinated movement. However, there are also brain mechanisms, potentially complimentary to the biomechanical factors, that take part in planning and control processes, and that account also for a portion of the coordination process. Neglecting one approach at the expense of the other will not solve the complex problem of understanding how coordinated movement occurs.

Recently, the re-emergence of artificial neural networks has provided a means of bridging the gap between brain and mechanical processes in the theoretical and empirical investigation of motor control and learning. Churchland (1989, Chapter 9) describes how neural nets, with a layer of hidden units connecting input and output units, can indeed "represent knowledge" of very complex non-linear processes. Reviewing some of the literature, he describes one such network that was trained to discriminate submarine sonar signals returning from rocks vs mines. Another network takes vector codings for seven-letter segments as inputs and produces vector codings for phonemes as outputs. These outputs, after being fed through a speech synthesizer, allows the network to transform printed words into audible speech.

Churchland makes the point that what is interesting about neural nets that learn tasks like the above, is that the "knowledge" that the networks have acquired and represent consists of a set of connection weights, among the network's units, that were established during the "training up the network" phase. These connection weights, during training, essentially partition the abstract space represented by the possible activation levels of each of the hidden units into activation vectors so that novel inputs can be "recognized" as belonging to a particular subvolumn of this abstract space. Thus knowledge representation is seen as the configuration of weighted connections among a set of neuron like units. Once trained, these networks are very rapid in performing their task. As well, the amount of space that can be used to represent the countless tasks humans encounter in a lifetime is virtually limitless. If, as Churchland speculates, this view of knowledge representation is congruent with how the brain represents knowledge, then we can expect the brain to be able to be partitioned into billions of functionally relevant subdivisions of its internal vector spaces, each responsive to a broad but proprietary range of highly complex stimuli. This is based on the premise that a network the size of the human brain has approximately 10^{11} neurons, and 10^3 connections on each neuron, for a total of 10^{14} total connections, and at least 10 distinct layers of hidden units. The time to "process" or classify an input takes only tens or hundreds of ms because the parallel coded input only has to make its way through up to ten layers of the massively parallel network to the functionally relevant layer that will produce the appropriate information at the output units.

Another characteristic of neural networks that make them similar to the non-linear, self-organizing principles used to model human movement organization (e.g. Kugler & Turvey, 1987) is that these networks exhibit principals of attractor dynamics with relaxation being their main mode of computation. The brain might be best understood as a kind of relaxation system in which computations are performed which attempt to iteratively seek to satisfy a large number of weak constraints (Rumelhart & McClelland, 1986, Chap. 4). The system is thought of as settling into a solution rather than calculating a solution. An example of this is the recent work of Massone and Bizzi (1989) where, using Jordan's (1990) recurrent neural net, they showed that this neural net was capable of learning to control a redundant three-joint limb from an initial posture to several targets. During the testing of this network, it was shown to spontaneously exhibit attractor-dynamics properties with final end-point positions behaving like point attractors. Jordan (1990) has found the same for a network controlling a simulation of a six degree of freedom manipulator. The solution found by the network was stable and was a periodic attractor both in articulatory and endpoint coordinates.

What the above discussion implies, particularly in light of the details of Jordan's neural network given above, is that the brain, through interconnections of these neuron like units, can represent "knowledge" and has considerable "space" to do so. As well, very complex, non-linear "computations" are performed within these neural nets that exhibit the same properties as those computations performed to model movement as a non-linear dynamical system (Kugler & Turvey, 1987). Except in the former case, no formula exists upon which to base the calculations. The "calculations" are an inherent aspect of the system. However, this similarity brings up an interesting point. Action theorists like Kugler and Turvey focus on what can be explained in terms of the dynamical properties of interacting physical systems and tend to ignore the role of the brain in movement control. On the other hand motor theorists, with their emphasis on the functioning of the brain in the central control of movement, tend to ignore the role of the physical system. Neural networks would appear to be an approach to motor control and learning that eliminates much of the ideological disharmony between these two approaches. First, neural nets emphasize the physical basis of knowledge representation and as such eliminate the infinite regress problem. Second, since neural nets, like non-linear dynamical systems are self organizing, a common mechanism exists for explaining movement control and learning. Thus, rather than treating the two approaches as ideologically disparate, one can conceive of them as representing complimentary approaches to the study of motor control and learning: one concentrating more on brain mechanisms and the other more on biophysical mechanisms.

3. Goal Directed Learning and Motor Equivalence

As Jordan (1990) and Jordan and Rumelhart (1990) explain, forward modelling is basically goal-directed. After the forward model is learned and then composed with the inverse model (the motor program subnetwork) an identity mapping is learned across the composed network. In essence this implies that the inverse model converges to an inverse of the environment. When there is a many to one mapping problem (that is, there are more degrees of freedom available than is needed to solve a motor problem and as a result there are several joint configurations that will allow the end-point of an effector to achieve the desired end-point) the above composed network finds a particular inverse.

Also, as reviewed earlier, before an identity mapping is achieved between the forward model and the motor program subnetworks, the network is inherently goal directed because of its ability to combine feedforward control with feedback control. This allows the network to achieve the desired outcome on the first trial even though many iterations through the feedback loop may be required.

In terms of motor equivalence, Jordan's network achieves this phenomenon through introduction of a smoothness constraint on the network. This allows the same target position to be achieved in different ways by a multidegree of freedom effector depending on the temporal context. As one of Jordan's simulations shows, performance of a six degrees of freedom manipulator was variable in articulatory coordinates while invariantly achieving to goal of the task. Massone and Bizzi (1989) demonstrated motor equivalence in a different way through the use of Jordan's motor program subnetwork and a redundant three joint limb. After the network had been trained to move from an initial position to one of several targets in task space, the target was suddenly moved to a new location once the limb had begun movement towards it (not too dissimilar to the experiment described above by Paulignan et al. (1990)). When this happened, the network was still able to successfully accomplish the task even though the initial posture of the limb for the new target position was different from the initial position of the limb during network training.

4. Feedforward Control and Motor Programs

Feedforward control has always been implicated in highly skilled acts. The main reason is that highly skilled movement usually occurs very rapidly and is difficult to explain entirely through feedback control processes. Thus, the ability to predict what the results will be of a particular action on a given environment helps in being able to overcome unexpected perturbations that, if not responded to, will result in movement not achieving a successful goal. Feedforward control is the basis of Jordan's motor programme subnetwork and his simulations (Jordan, 1990) indicate that learning of the feedforward controller results in improvements in speed of performance. As mentioned above, this reduction in time is accomplished because of the decreasing use of feedback control and the increasing use of feedforward control as the motor programme subnetwork is learned.

Yet there may be a related basis for conceptualizing the rapidity of highly skilled people. This deals with the conceptual issue of parallel processing which artificial neural nets embody and for which the brain appears to be ideally suited. As Rumelhart and McClelland (1986) assert, given the relatively slow processing rate of neurons (10s of ms), the apparently fast speed of the brain in solving complex problems is due to the fact that single neurons only compute very simple functions and they proceed in massive parallelism. Since there might be as many as 10^{11} neurons with each neuron being an active processor, the parallelism is on a very large scale. Further, as Churchland (1989, Chapter 9) points out, there may be at least 10 distinct layers of hidden units in the human brain which means, given the total number of possible neuronal connections, that its internal vector spaces can be partitioned into many billions of of functionally relevant subdivisions. If an input is received that is relevant to one of these divisions, the network is capable of producing the appropriate activation vector in tens or hundreds of ms. The estimate is that for each layer of hidden units only a few tens of ms are necessary because of the parallel coded input. Thus, depending on where the functionally relevant layer of hidden units are, the massively parallel network literally needs only tens or hundreds of ms to traverse through the two to ten layers of hidden units. Finally, since the relevant information is stored as a set of connection weights, the information is automatically accessed by the coded input which means there is no additional time required to search for the information.

In essence, then, through feedforward control in a massively parallel system, one might envisage information about movement being accessed and implemented in relatively short time intervals. Certainly, the times to amend or modify movements that were reviewed above (under 100 ms) would appear to be entirely within the realm of the capacity of a massively parallel system like the brain.

Within this context, what might be the structure of the motor program? As mentioned previously in this chapter, the behavioral literature appears not to support the idea of a generalized linear motor program. However, within the context of neural network theory there appears to be a conceptual basis for retaining the idea that some aspects of movement may be stored within the internal vector spaces of the brain. This information, when accessed, may then be used in cooperation with the physical or mechanical properties of the human motor system to produce coordinated movement. What is most certain from this viewpoint, is the notion that what is represented in the brain about movement is not verbal descriptions or symbolic representations of past movement experiences. Rather, movement "knowledge" would be in the form of a configuration of connection weights that have been developed through learning and that when accessed by an appropriately coded input signal, interacts with other relevant aspects of the motor system to produce goal directed movement. As Jordan (1990) states, explicit in this notion of a motor program is the fact that the plan of action would not contain any details of the motor program. This latter information is embedded in the configuration of weights interconnecting the involved units.

5. Sensorimotor Integration and Specificity of Movement Control and Learning

We (MacKenzie & Marteniuk, 1985a,b) have argued that at the base of all coordinated movement is an integrated store of sensory and motor information that defines relations among body parts and near body space for the achievement of movement goals. The actual expression of coordinated movement, however, is modified by an interplay of motor and sensory information that fine tunes movement to the specific context of the situation. Prediction is a trademark of such a system and is derived from past experience where the learned relationship between afferent signals (interoceptive and exteroceptive) and efferent signals allows the prediction of the consequences of a particular action.

While the brain appears to abound in areas concerned with sensorimotor integration, artificial neural networks may be one way of studying the characteristics of this process. For example, Massone and Bizzi (1989) give an example of how visually based targets triggered a network to perform sensorimotor transformations to produce time trajectories of a limb to acquire the targets. In another case, Dean (1990) constructed a neural net that simulated walking in the stick insect. The simulation showed that walking occurred by directly associating the joint configurations in one leg with those of another, in this way demonstrating proprioceptive-motor transformations.

Given that sensorimotor transformations are an intrinsic aspect of motor control and learning, several issues about the nature of this process can be raised. One such research topic concerns the apparent specificity of learning and control. For example, the work reviewed earlier in this chapter suggested that motor control appears to be specific to the precision demands of the required movement in that movement trajectories were uniquely shaped for various tasks that varied precision demands. On the other hand, the movement learning studies that were reviewed suggested that learning is very dependent on the feedback conditions present during movement acquisition as well as on the work space-performer compatibility in terms of movement direction.

The issue now is whether a knowledge of how neural nets "represent" movement might help conceptualize the underlying mechanisms accounting for specificity of human motor control and learning. To discuss this issue, it is assumed that there are a sufficient number of neuronal interactions within the brain to accommodate the necessary representations of all movements that people require in their daily lives. Notice the representation does not need to contain all relevant movement information, leaving out for example, the mechanical and anatomical constraints involved in movement that make their own dynamical contributions to movement. Given this space (hidden unit vector space) it is not unrealistic to think that something like Jordan's forward model can be established for classes of movement like gait, prehension, throwing, jumping, etc. As Jordan points out (Jordan & Rosenbaum, 1989) his forward model is not unlike a schema in that it maps out relations between movements and their consequences taking into consideration the state of the environment. Once the forward model is accurate over a particular domain it can then be used in creating feedforward models (motor programs) for solving specific movement problems. To date simulation work by Jordan (1990) has shown that several stable movement trajectories can be learned together in one network. Thus, it is not inconceivable that for a skill like prehension, many hours of practice at prehension tasks result in a large number of relatively specific movement representations that can individually be accessed when the need arises.

In terms of specificity of learning, where the research reviewed earlier suggests movement is very dependent on the feedback conditions present during its acquisition, one might predict that the weights of the connections amongst the units of a network are not only relatively specific to the source of feedback regarding movement execution, but the weights are also biased by the type of feedback. For example, it might be that visual feedback, when both visual and proprioceptive feedback are available, is given a larger role in the activation function, thus accounting for its major influence in normal motor control. On the other hand, if a movement is learned without visual feedback, one might expect that when it became available the weights within the network would be inappropriate for optimum performance. Hence movements based on this feedback would be not be able to effectively accomplish a movement goal until further learning took place.

Finally, related to the specificity of movement control issue is the role that task constraints play in making movement specific to the objectives of the task. Jordan (1990) provides an ideal example of this when he used his network to simulate effectors playing an ascending scale on the piano. Humans are taught to cross the thumb under the index finger and the middle finger so that every third note is played by the thumb. In Jordan's simulation, a two effector manipulator learned a linear sequence where the finger assignments were alternated. The manipulator learned the task but did so by using its translational degrees of freedom rather than crossing one of its effectors over the other. Jordan noted, however, that his network constrained the smoothness of the articulators which in essence optimized their "energy" cost making the finger crossing task improbable. However, when the smoothness constraint was placed on the endpoint units of the network, making the potential speed of transitions paramount, the network readily learned to cross its effectors. Thus, constraints placed on movement by the demands of a movement goal (e.g. move efficiently or move as fast as possible) can change dramatically the nature of the coordination process for accomplishing physically similar outcomes (in this case pressing a series of keys).

6. Validity Of Using Neural Networks To Infer Brain Mechanisms

There has been (e.g. Roberts, 1989) and will continue to be controversy over whether neural nets tell us how the brain works. However, balanced accounts of their potential contributions to understanding brain mechanisms have been published (Churchland, 1989, Chapter 9; Rumelhart & McClelland, 1986) and if one is aware of their limitations, their use may lead to advances in several areas of research on human behavior. As Rumelhart and McClelland (1986) point out, artificial neural nets do not focus on neural modelling but rather on neurally inspired modelling of brain processes involved in behavior such as cognition and motor control. That is not to say, however, that they do not capture some known brain characteristics (see the Churchland and Rumelhart & McClelland references for a discussion of this). As such, these models represent a large step forward from the "black-box" or computer analogy approach to the study of human behavior.

Perhaps the biggest contribution that neural nets can make to the understanding of human behavior is their use in conjunction with human experimentation (see Iberall and MacKenzie, (In Press) for a extended discussion of this issue). It may be that neural nets can suggest novel ways of conceptualizing the central nervous system's role in movement control and thus lead to innovative ways of designing and analyzing behavioral experiments. Likewise, behavioral data may provide ways of validating neural nets or suggest ways in which they have to be altered to give them greater validity. In essence, neural net modelling and human experimentation may best be done in collaboration with one another rather than in isolation.

REFERENCES

Abbs, J.H. & Gracco, V.L. (1983). Sensorimotor actions in the control of multimovement speech gestures. *Trends in Neuroscience. 6,* 391-395.

Abbs, J.H., Gracco, V.L. & Cole, K.J. (1984). Control of multimovement coordination: sensorimotor mechanisms in speech motor programming. *Journal of Motor Behavior, 16*, 195-231.

Adams, J.A. (1971). A closed-loop theory of motor learning. *Journal of Motor Behavior, 3* , 111-149.

Arbib, M.A. (1981). Perceptual structures and distributed motor control. In Brooks, V.B. (Ed.), *Handbook of Physiology: Vol 2, Motor Control* (pp 1449-1480). Bethesda, Maryland: American Physiological Society.

Arbib, M.A. (1985). Schemas for the temporal organization of behavior. *Human Neurobiology, 4,* 63-72.

Atkeson, C.G. & Hollerbach, J.L. (1985). Kinematic features of unrestrained vertical arm movements. *Journal of Neuroscience, 5,* 2318-2330.

Bamford, R.B. & Marteniuk, R.G. (1988). Spatial ability and the early learning of a complex arm action. *Human Movement Science, 7,* 1-26.

Beek, P.G. & Meijer, O.G. (1988). On the nature of "the" motor-action controversy. In Meijer, O.G. & Roth, K. (Eds.),*Complex Movement Behaviour: "The" motor-action controversy.* Amsterdam: North Holland.

Churchland, P.M. (1989). *A Neurocomputational Perspective.* Cambridge: MIT Press.

Dean, J. (1990). Coding proprioceptive information to control movement to a target: Simulation with a simple neural network. *Biological Cybernetics, 63,* 115-120.

Fitts, P.M. & Peterson, J.R. (1964). Information capacity of discrete motor responses. *Journal of Experimental Psychology, 46,* 199-210.

Flash, T. & Hogan, N. (1985). The coordination of arm movements: an experimentally confirmed mathematical model. *Journal of Neuroscience, 5,* 1688-1703.

Georgopoulos, A.P., Kalaska, J.F., and Massey, J.T. (1981). Spatial trajectories and reaction times of aimed movements: effects of practice, uncertainty and changes in target location. *Journal of Neurophysiology, 46,* 725-743.

Gentner, D.R. Timing of skilled motor performance: Tests of the proportional duration model. *Psychological Review, 94,* 255-276.

Hollerbach, J.M. & Atkeson, C.G. (1987). Deducing planning variables from experimental arm trajectories: Pitfalls and possibilities. *Biological Cybernetics, 56,* 279-292.

Iberall, T. & MacKenzie, C.L. (In press). *The Grasping Hand.* New York: Springer-Verlag.

Jordan, M.I. (1990). Motor learning and the degrees of freedom problem. In M. Jeannerod (Ed.). *Attention and Performance XIII.* Hillsdale, N.J.: Erlbaum.

Jordan, M.I. & Rosenbaum, D.A. (1989). Action. In M.I. Posner (Ed.), *Foundations in Cognitive Science.* Cambridge: Bradford/MIT Press.

Jordan, M.I. & Rumelhart, D.E. (In press). Forward models: Supervised learning with a distal teacher. *Cognitive Science.*

Kugler, P.H. & Turvey, M.T. (1987). *Information, Natural Law, and the Self-Assembly of Rhythmic Movement.* Hillsdale, N.J.: Erlbaum.

MacKenzie, C.L. & Marteniuk, R.G. (1985a). Motor skill: Feedback, knowledge, and Structural Issues. *Canadian Journal of Psychology, 39,* 313-337.

MacKenzie, C.L. & Marteniuk, R.G. (1985b). Bimanual coordination. In Roy, E.A. (Ed.), *Neuropsychological Studies of Apraxia and Related Disorders.* Amsterdam: North-Holland.

MacKenzie, C.L., Marteniuk, R.G., Dugas, C., Liske, D. & Eickmeier, B. (1987). Three dimensional movement trajectories in Fitts' task: Implications for control. *Quarterly Journal of Experimental Psychology: Human Experimental Psychology, 39A,* 629-647.

Marteniuk, R.G., Leavitt, J.L., MacKenzie, C.L. & Athenes, S. (1990). Functional relationships between grasp and transport components in a prehension task. *Human Movement Science, 9,* 149-176.

Marteniuk, R.G. MacKenzie, C.L., Jeannerod, M., Athenes, S. & Dugas, C. (1987). Constraints on human arm movement trajectories. *Canadian Journal of Psychology, 41,* 365-378.

Marteniuk, R.G. & Romanow, S.K.E. (1983). Human movement organization and learning as revealed by variability of movement, use of kinematic information and Fourier analysis. In Magill, R. (Ed.), *Memory and Control of Action.* Amsterdam: North Holland.

Massone, L. & Bizzi, E. (1989). A neural network model for limb trajectory formation. *Biological Cybernetics, 61,* 417-425.

Munhall, K.G. Ostry, D.J. & Parush, A. (1985). Characteristics of velocity profiles of speech movements. *Journal of Experimental Psychology: Human Perception and Performance, 11,* 457-474.

Patla, A., Beuter, A. & Prentice, S. (1991). A two stage correction of limb trajectory to avoid obsticles during stepping. Submitted.

Paulignan, Y., MacKenzie, C.L., Marteniuk, R.G., & Jeannerod, M. (1991). Selective perturbation of visual input during prehension movements. 1. The effects of changing object position. *Experimental Brain Research, 83,* 502-512.

Proteau, L., Marteniuk, R.G., Girouard, Y. & Dugas, C. (1987). On the type of information used to control and learn an aiming movement after moderate and extensive training. *Canadian Journal of Psychology, 6,* 181-199.

Proteau, L., Marteniuk, R.G., & Levesque, L. (In press). A sensorimotor basis for motor learning: Evidence indicating specificity of practice. *Quarterly Journal of Experimental Psychology, Human Experimental Psychology.*

Roberts, L. (1989). Are neural nets like the human brain? *Science, 243,* 481-482.

Rumbelhart, D.E. & McClelland, J.L. (1986). PDP models and general issues in cognitive science. In: Rumelhart, D.E. & McClelland, J.L. (Eds.), *Parallel Distributed Processing. Volume 1: Foundations.* Cambridge: Bradford/MIT Press.

Schmidt, R.A. (1975). A schema theory of discrete motor skill learning. *Psychological Review, 82,* 225-260.

Soechting, J.F. (1984). Effect of target size on spatial and temporal characteristics of a pointing movement in man. *Experimental Brain Research, 54,* 121-132.

Soneren, van J.F., Denier van der Gon, J.J., Gielen, C.C.A.M. (1988). Conditions determining early modifications of motor programs in response to changes in target location. *Experimental Brain Research, 71,* 320-328.

Sonderen, van J.F., Gielen, C.C.A.M., & Denier van der Gon, J.J. (1989). Motor programmes for goal-directed movements are continuously adjusted according to changes in target location. *Experimental Brain Research, 78,* 139-146.

Zelaznik, H.N., Hawkins, B. & Kisselburg, K. (1983). Rapid visual feedback processing in single-aiming movements. *Journal of Motor Behavior, 15,* 217-236.

Tutorials in Motor Behavior II
G.E. Stelmach and J. Requin (Editors)

POSTURO-KINETIC INTERACTIONS : MODELING AND MODES OF CONTROL

Michel Dufossé and Jean Massion

Laboratoire de Neurosciences Fonctionnelles, C.N.R.S.
31, chemin Joseph Aiguier, 13402 MARSEILLE Cedex 9, France

Abstract

In the present paper, it is proposed to review two main aspects of the co-ordination between posture and movement. The first is more theoretical and involves a formal approach to posture as opposed to movement, an engineering approach of the cybernetic type and a neural network approach to the possible role of the motor cortex and cerebellum. In the second, more experimental part, the data from the literature are reviewed, illustrating why and how anticipatory postural adjustments are organized in relation with the movement to be performed, how the organization can be changed by learning and how it is modified after brain damage.

Part 1 : MODELLING THE CO-ORDINATION BETWEEN POSTURE AND MOVEMENT

1. FORMAL APPROACH

"Give me a resting point and I will lift up the world" : this claim made many centuries ago by Archimedes continues to be relevant. It is obvious to physicists that it is not possible to consider a movement unless the frame of reference is specified. In fact, theory of general relativity made it possible to do away with the absolute (Galilean) frame of reference. Likewise in brain theory, no absolute reference frame may exist unless strict invariants exist between the various perceptions based on the various sensory channels. As an example, the set of resting points between the body and its environment may constitute a unique reference frame, provided that the distances between the resting points are fixed with respect to each other in daily life. This point illustrates one of the many difficulties involved in understanding sensorimotor control, that is to say the absence of any single reference frame with respect to which a movement can be described.

1.1. Posture as a reference frame

The displacement of a given number of segments during goal directed movements requires the postural stabilization of other segments, despite the reactional forces exerted by the moving segments. The postural control exerted over several segments then makes it possible to build up a frame of reference with respect to which the body's position and its movements beyond the immediately surrounding space will be referred. More generally speaking, motor activities can be modelled as a sequential pattern of more elementary movements (BERTHOZ and POZZO, 1988), each of which is referred to an appropriate set of postural segments, selected on the basis of the task and the actual resting points.

A frame of reference can be roughly defined as a set of points at fixed distances from each other. The visual background of a moving target can be said to provide a frame of this kind. If one takes a seated subject writing at a desk, this frame would consist first of the set of contact points between the body and the ground, the desk and the chair unless the chair is swinging or falling, and secondly of the segments (head, body, arm, etc...) that are stabilized for a short moment during the task. Preventing the paper from slipping on the desk or generally stabilizing the sheet of paper relative to this set of contact points is essential during writing. The choice and the maintenance of an appropriate frame of reference for controlling a target position is an essential prerequisite for movement initiation in a living body or for a multijoint compliant robot moving in a complex environment. This choice depends upon the goal of the action and constitutes one of the main objectives of the sensorimotor control system.

A systemic study of autonomy has been worked out, according to which a given number of couplings exists between the living system and its environment (VARELA, 1978). These include the resting point on the ground, the visual anchorage on a target or rather on the target's background, the vestibular information about the vertical gravity, and the platform support during stance. At this level of analysis, the resting points of the body on a support, for example, are not inputs or outputs of the system but more simply a set of interaction points. These interactions obey the elementary physical principle of equality between action and reaction.

Learning the relationship between an event and its context can be said to build a link or interface between the perturbing outer sphere and the sensitive living system. In this respect, a movement corresponds to changing the couplings that exist between the autonomous system and its environment. Voluntary movements and passive movements resulting from a perturbation caused by the environment do not constitute two separate classes of movements, unless of course one obtains minute electrophysiological data on spinal activities demonstrating that one of the two mechanisms occurs before the other at the interface level, i.e. the muscle. By recording both the afferent proprioceptive signals and the motor and fusimotor commands, and comparing their lag times in various experimental paradigms, it is possible to make a distinction between active and passive forces. This distinction would be impossible in rational mechanics and thus no detailed comparisons is possible between the compliant properties of a muscle and those of a spring.

It is therefore no longer sufficient to take the classical approach according to which the nervous system is said to convey "information" between input channels and output channels through "black boxes", via feedback and feedforward pathways. The computational part of the nervous system is not comparable to a computer processing all kinds of information, whatever the code may be. It seems more likely that it may be an autopoietic system able to structure its internal state depending on the external perturbations caused by the environment (VARELA, 1979). According to this picture, there is no information processing in the brain but mainly interactions between many neuronal activities subscribing to various adaptive processes.

Within this formal approach, the various segments under postural control, including their resting point with external physical objects at a given time, can be globally considered as a single body reference frame for movement. In addition, more abstract frames may exist such as the body's momental ellipsoid for example. Such a frame would include the body's center of gravity, and the vertical direction of earth gravity together with egocentric axes such as the rostrocaudal and left/right axes. This system certainly contributes to implementing the body's postural scheme (GURFINKEL et al., 1988).

In order to maintain this frame, the nervous system adaptively corrects any change in body segment positions resulting from expected or unexpected perturbations, caused by either self-motion or an environmental event. Likewise, movement control in a flexible, multi-jointed robot must include two components : performing the action that is aimed towards a goal, and compensating for the internal disturbances transmitted as the result of this action via viscoelastic joints.

1.2. Relationship between the various reference frames

The goal of an action is never an abstract point in three dimensional space nor a moving point in four dimension space-time, but rather a structured set of actions within a complex context. Fast reaching movements directed towards visual targets with minimum postural perturbations (CORDO and NASHNER, 1982; FRIEDLI et al., 1988; BENVENUTI et al., 1990) or body equilibrium during various ground perturbations (NASHNER and McCOLLUM, 1985; MACPHERSON, 1988; GOLLHOFER et al., 1989) are possible examples. In addition to the external world, two reference frames at least must therefore coexist at each instant, the first of which relates to the autonomous system, and the other to the goal of the action, such as the three dimensional object to be reached (DUFOSSE, 1989). Thus, on the one hand, the postural control serves to maintain a preselected body reference frame whatever the goal reference frame. On the other hand, the movement control serves to ensure the smooth performance of a movement between an initial position where the body is the reference frame and a final position, where the reference frame is mainly based on visual information. As a result, the coordination between posture and movement is essential and involves a strictly controlling the relationships between the various reference frames.

These relationships should be taken into account when interpreting the results of the neuronal activity recordings. A mathematical transformation between posture-related activities and movement-related activities can be approximated at the neuronal level in the associative, premotor and primary motor areas of the cerebral cortex in a mathematical bilinear form (BURNOD et al., 1991). The resulting population unit activity is perfectly satisfactory provided that all the movement directions are uniformly encoded at the cerebral level (CAMINITI et al., 1991). Both the theoretical predictions and the experimental data have shown that parallel directions in the exo-centric world are coded by similar neuronal activities, which led to an elegant solution to the problem of coordinate transformations between visual and body reference frames.

When a subject is reading a book while walking, all the joints are independently fixed and stabilized in order to maintain the distance between the eyes and the book in the subject's hands, whatever his trunk movements. This rigid attitude results from a so-called conservative mode, whereas during a glass carrying task, a different, so-called projective mode is observed (DROULEZ and BERTHOZ, 1986). In this case, the relationship between the body reference frame and the goal reference frame is strictly controlled. Here the joint angles are not individually controlled and the subject's attitude frees the hands from the disturbances resulting from the trunk movements (DROULEZ, 1988). In cases such as these, the goal reference frame has to be related to the external world. Its stabilization is essential in order to counteract the disturbances resulting from the body movements.

Both movement and posture control involve sensorimotor actions on one or more couplings. A simple distinction between these two components can be made in terms of their respective finalities. Roughly speaking, the purpose of movements is to make a change of state, whereas the purpose of posture is to maintain a given state notwithstanding external or internal disturbances. Manual manipulations involve several postural tasks, such as holding the manipulated object with the contralateral hand during a bimanual task, fixation of the trunk and shoulder, etc. A bimanual task such as opening the screw-cap of a bottle with the one hand firmly holding the bottle and the other hand holding the cap, involves two symmetrical actions from the physical point of view. However a task of this kind is solved by the nervous system in terms of two dissymmetrical, specialized actions to be performed by the right and left hands. In a right handed person, the right hand is usually given a goal directed action, whereas the left hand has a postural action serving to stabilize the movement's reference frame.

1.3. Separate controls upon high and low frequencies

The distinction between posture-related and movement-related neuronal activities has been made by defining movement as a change of state and postural control as the means of maintaining or stabilizing a prior state. This clearcut dichotomy can be less rigidly defined. Instead of making a hard and fast distinction between the static and the dynamic aspects of the sensorimotor control, one can take into account the temporal frequencies of sensorimotor actions. This leads to a more general distinction between control of position and control of position changes, the latter of which includes velocity control (PAILLARD and AMBLARD, 1985).

In this context, the neuromuscular spindle is endowed with a mixed sensitivity to position and velocity. It has been demonstrated by computer simulation that a simple adaptive neural network with recurrent collaterals is able to separate these two components by orthogonalizing the input vectors (HERAULT et al., 1985). The static and dynamic sensitivities are controlled separately through the static and dynamic gamma fusimotor commands. During the co-ordination between posture and movement, central commands may favor either the static sensitivity of the joints involved in the goal directed movement in order to precisely define the final position, or the dynamic sensitivity of the postural segments in order to detect any position change. The biological need to provide high precision captors with a large focal depth was paralleled by similar bioengineering requirements. The neuromuscular spindle may be controlled in such a way that it is permanently in its zone of highest static or dynamic sensitivity depending upon the ongoing task.

Static and dynamic signals are not conveyed by separate channels in the central nervous system, since they continuously intermingle from the periphery to the cortex. At the peripheral level, the transformation between neuronal activities to power forces has to be servoregulated and servocontrolled. At the hardware level, the spinal mechanism require many cybernetic controls of this kind. At a more functional level, whatever the physical variables being servocontrolled at a given muscle motor unit, during a given moment in a given task, it is necessary to make a distinction between several parameters, such as the variable that has to be servocontrolled, the various (static and dynamic) variables that are used in this control, the functional role of the global muscle activity, etc.

The value of taking into account both static and dynamic parameters can be demonstrated by taking into account the computer systems based on the fuzzy set mathematical theory. Several methods have already been proposed for solving for example the "inverted-pendulum problem" that consists of maintaining the unstable equilibrium of a vertical stick by horizontally moving its support. The most classical method would consist of solving the differential equations leading to the problem's solution. More recently, a fuzzy logic chip was designed in order to implement a small number of fuzzy rules such as "do not move the horizontal support if the stick is in a more or less forward position with a more or less backward velocity" (YAMAKAWA, 1987; SANCHEZ, 1989).

Then, a general distinction between posture and movement can be made based upon both temporal and spatial frequencies. During writing for example, the right hand of a right handed person has a micrometric goal, rapidly and finely controlling the finger muscles, while the left hand has a macrometric action consisting of moving the sheet of paper from time to time, in order to keep the target portion of the paper near the tip of the pen held by the right hand. Broadly speaking, the one hand has a specialized action in the high spatial and temporal frequencies whereas the other hand performs low spatial and temporal frequencies (GUIARD, 1987). As a result of this distinction between micro and macrometric controls, the notes of a piano finger-board are always distributed from the left to the right in an order corresponding to increasing auditory frequencies. Higher frequencies devoted to the right hand generally correspond to high finger movement frequencies, since the low frequencies cannot be controlled so rapidly because they have larger time overlap. During skilled movements such as those performed when playing golf or handling a tool, the two arms also cooperate with a view to achieving optimal global action, each contributing a different specialization. Their two actions are built one upon the other, i.e. the right hand's action upon that of the left hand, like a hierarchical set of two motors placed in series (GUIARD, 1987).

2. ENGINEERING APPROACH

Despite the considerations developed in the previous paragraph on the formal approach to the co-ordination between posture and movement, it should be stressed that the cybernetic approach to postural control has already been very fruitful, for example as a means of studying the anticipatory postural adjustments. In the past, many models based on this approach have been developed.

2.1. A response to servomotor properties of the muscle

The muscle provides the body with a compliant interface with the environment. Together with the spinal reflexes, it may constitue a stiffness servoregulator (FELDMAN, 1974; 1987). This spring-like property of muscles has two main advantages. First, when the energy stored in the spring is utilized, fast ballistic movements can be performed which in turn have to be controlled in a feedforward manner. Secondly, any unwanted action caused either by the environment or by an inappropriate motor action can be partly absorbed due to the compliancy of this device.

The first disadvantage of interface results of this kind results however from the perturbations affecting the position of remote segments as the result of the forces involved in the movement. These perturbations are transmitted along a kinematic chain of joints. Their effects must be actively counterbalanced by anticipatory postural adjustments of the type described above, because they would otherwise cause the loss of both stability and equilibrium. The small gains observed in spinal servomechanisms may correspond to the biological need to smoothly and rapidly absorb any shock or impact (HOUK and RYMER, 1981). The compliant interface would then be comparable to the shock-absorbers in a car. In turn, supraspinal nervous structures such as the cerebral cortex, must rapidly send out the appropriate motor commands for the goal to be reached by triggering the appropriate spinal servomechanisms.

The second disadvantage of an interface of this kind is the complexity of the controls that must be exerted via focused commands on a great number of spinal circuits. This control not only includes setting and initiating the movement itself, but must also take into account the postural control on many body segments serving as a reference frame for the movement. As a result, two global controls are necessary. Central nervous structures must first stabilize this reference frame and secondly, must adaptively build up the co-ordination between the various descending actions through learning.

Happily, due to the recent progress in aeronautic engineering, new concepts have emerged for solving the problem of simultaneously controlling many degrees of freedom for an optimal coordination between the six degrees of freedom of modern aircraft under various conditions such as turbulence or the side effects of pilot's commands.

2.2. Stabilization versus co-ordination

In aircraft control, severe limitations resulting from the pilot's reaction time and his computational power had to be overcome in order to deal with the great number of controls available in modern aircrafts. Thanks to the electrical flight commands that now replace the mechanical transmissions between the pilot's joy-stick and the aircraft's controls, several computer systems have been designed in order to help the pilot. As a result, aircraft's lift has been improved by modifying the distribution of masses in order to place the center of gravity backward from the center of lift, leading to the unloading of the tail wings. This was achieved to the detriment of the aircraft's maneuverability, however. An appropriate set of computer systems was then designed because the aircraft's stabilization could no longer be worked out by the pilot himself.

Some experimental results on the basal ganglia might be interpreted within this context of improving stabilization (ITO, 1986). It has been suggested that the basal ganglia nuclei might deal here with body or segmental stabilization during disturbing actions resulting from voluntary movements. Secondly, it may ensure the necessary destabilization during the transition phases between successive sensorimotor activities. Neurological symptoms in parkinsonian patients such as difficulty in initiating a movement might reflect a deficit in the transition phase between standing immobile and walking, for example. Another related role that might be attributed to the cortical areas receiving signals from the basal ganglia is that of selecting the joints to be used in a given goal directed movement, or conversely, selecting the postural joints that are not to be used in the task but need to be stabilized. During hand-writing for example, the movements can involve very different joints and muscles according to the context : it may require either distal finger and wrist movements with simultaneous postural fixations of proximal shoulder and elbow joints when writing on a paper lying on a table, or movements of the shoulder and elbow joints together with simultaneous postural fixation of the wrist when writing on a vertical board. Nevertheless, somebody's signature and general style of hand writing remain the same in both cases. The kinematics of the trajectory are similar enough whatever the context to be able to identify the author of the text (VIVIANI and McCOLLUM, 1983).

Recent network models describe how cell populations might code general movement directions such as forward, backward, upward, downward, leftward and rightward, independently of the muscles involved (BURNOD, 1989). It is essential however, to know which structure will preselect the joints or muscles involved and how this is performed. In any case, this preselection is tightly coupled with the postural conditions associated with the movement. Even if perfect stability of the reference frame is achieved, the movement control necessitates the co-ordination of many muscles.

When a task is performed repeatedly, the cerebellum gradually intervenes, finely adjusting and automatizing the motor response (ITO, 1984). The cerebellum can thus help the cerebral cortex during goal directed tasks. Cybernetic models based upon experimental data have been proposed in order to explain the respective roles of the cerebral and cerebellar cortices (KAWATO et al., 1987; ITO, 1990). It can be assumed that the central nervous structures first learn an inverse dynamics model of the skeleto-muscular apparatus in order to translate a desired trajectory into the appropriate commands, the corrections being made through a feedback loop. A distinction should be made between the cerebral cortex level, which seems to take into account the arm's initial position (CAMINITI et al., 1991) and the sub-cortical structures that may control the final position by controlling the length-tension curves of the servo-regulated muscles (BIZZI et al., 1982; BERKENBLIT et al., 1986). Later, the cerebellar cortex builds a feedforward control which replaces this closed loop cerebral process and might produce anticipatory postural adjustments.

Two successive phases in the co-ordination learning can then be distinguished in this cerebellar take-over. First, the external feedback loop with which the movement may be corrected is replaced by a dynamics model of the skeleto-muscular apparatus which makes it possible to predict and anticipate the corrections. The functioning of this internal model imitates the functioning of the real skeleto-muscular postural and movement control apparatus. The internal model may be built up thanks to the adaptive mechanisms of the cerebellum. At the end of this learning phase, in addition to the inverse dynamics model already learnt by the cerebral cortex for commanding the movement, the cerebellum has learned the dynamics model (Fig. 1A). The learning phase may then make anticipatory postural corrections possible because the model implemented internally in the brain simulates the movement. At each step in the command, the cerebral cortex can predict the mechanical effects of a given command through this internal loop. Secondly, with practice, the command system performed by the cerebral cortex may be taken over by the cerebellum in a feedforward mode. In this case, the feedforward system may learn an inverse dynamics model of the skeleto-muscular apparatus, since the whole system is designed to make an actually performed trajectory equal to a desired trajectory. Numerical simulation and robotic applications have shown that this second phase produces a smooth, efficient trajectory (KAWATO et al., 1987). This is probably learned by the lateral cerebellum, which can progressively implement the inverse dynamics model previously learned by the cerebral cortex. The result will be a completely automatic control of the movement, which will free the computational capacity of the cerebral cortex for other tasks.

In the first case, a representation of the effects of a command, including the postural perturbations (direct dynamics) is learned. In the second case, a representation of the command itself, including the postural anticipations (inverse dynamics) is learned.

2.3. Solving the problem of motor redundancy

Among the various problems facing the robotics engineers as well as the neuroscientists involved in sensorimotor research, the motor redundancy is still puzzling. Two kinds of motor redundancy at least have to be solved. The first deals with the excess number of muscles (and moreover that of the number of motor units) as compared with the number of degrees of freedom of any part of the body, such as the seven degrees of freedom of an arm for example. The second arises from the excess number of degrees of freedom of an arm as compared with the three dimensions of a target location in a pointing task.

In fact, the first problem can be solved without any computation, thanks to the spring-like properties of the muscle servomotor. In a quadruped for example, the total body weight is equally distributed over the four support points, because of the compliant properties of the legs. The second problem involving an excess number of degrees of body freedom in a given task is quite different and may have been solved at the biological level, since a task may involve several spatial constraints. Three parameters are involved in locating a target to be reached point and six translation plus rotation parameters in designating an object to be caught. Thus the seven biological degrees of freedom of an arm are not so very excessive. It may be assumed that a selection of a minimal number of degrees of freedom is made at the basal ganglia and supplementary motor area level before movement initiation. The premotor and motor cortex may then only control the non-redundant joints selected. This movement control would be performed together with a collateral control aimed

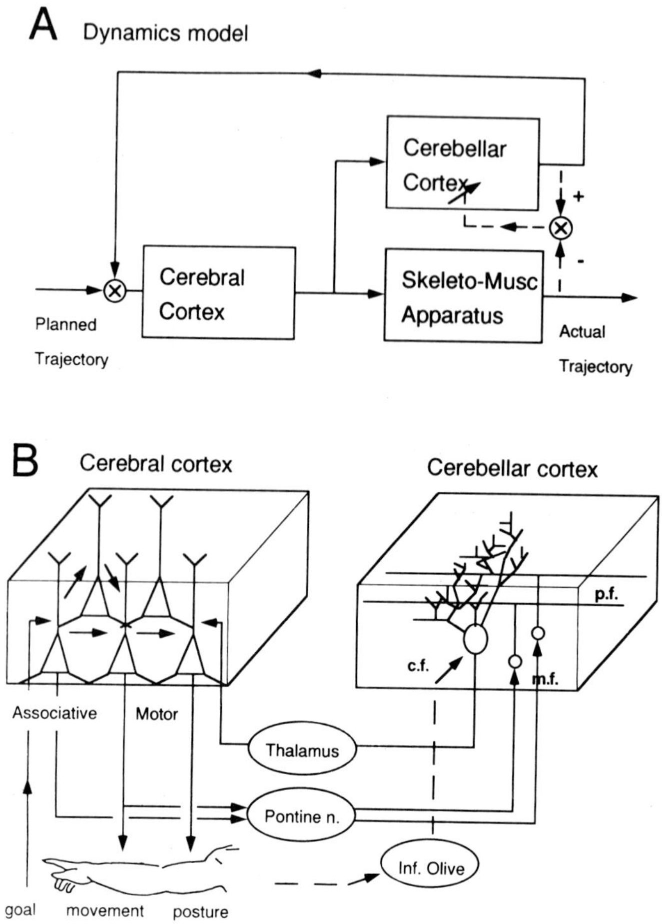

Figure 1 : Learning the dynamics model of the skeleto-muscular apparatus

A - An initial cerebral learning phase uses external feedback (not shown). Later, an error signal (dotted lines) originating from a comparison between the actual trajectory and a cerebellar microzone output can adaptively build a dynamic model of the arm. As a result, the effect of a command sent by the cerebral cortex to the skeleto-muscular apparatus will be predicted by this internal feedback (modified from ITO, 1990). **B** - Within the cerebral cortex, a goal may be signalled by a strong activity in microcolumns of an associative cortex. Cerebellar learning (left) will then consist of increasing the connective coefficients between the sets of microcolumns which commmand the appropriate muscular contraction. Postural disturbance in another body segment gives rise to an error message transmitted from the periphery to the inferior olive and then to a specific cerebellar microzone (right) which cooperates with the cerebral microcolumns of the motor cortex that are able to correct the error (c.f.: climbing fiber; m.f.: mossy fiber; p.f.: parallel fiber).

at stabilizing the joints not involved in the task but liable to be disturbed by the forecoming movement.

3. NEURAL NETWORK APPROACH

A voluntary movement includes several components. It generally consists of a combination of muscle actions which make it possible both to change the relative positions of body segments and the position of selected segments relative to the external world via a postural reference frame, in order to reach a goal. In addition, these displacements are accompanied by a set of postural adjustments serving to stabilize this reference frame. Learning the co-ordination between posture and movement is therefore essential for efficient motor performance to be possible.

As stressed by MARR (1982), the neural network approach is a question of connecting up the three levels at which the functionning of the brain can be understood : the computational or formal approach level, the algorithmic level involving information processing in elementary units such as the cerebral microcolumns or the cerebellar microzones, and the anatomical hardware. When studying the mechanisms underlying the co-ordination between posture and movement, it is necessary to keep in mind these three levels when defining the basic properties of the nervous structures to be simulated.

3.1. Need for adaptive processes

During computer implementation of the formal concepts described above, one major difficulty arises from the nature of the signals conveyed by the nervous system, which are quite different from those manipulated by engineers in robotics (KUPERSTEIN, 1988). Despite the fact that the external world is altogether Euclidean (metric) and Galilean (Newton's law), the nervous system can never code, propagate or process signals as pure as those dealt with in Physics, such as joint angles, muscle lengths and their derivatives, momentum or forces. The natural captors and effectors are not calibrated. Moreover their transfer functions are not known a priori by the central structures. Nevertheless the aim of a pointing task, such as reaching a target, is purely metric and will be executed by a finely adjusted control of muscular actions. A set of adaptive processes distributed over several central nervous structures is responsible for the learning of the physical laws and their consequences (ARBIB, 1981).

According to modern control theory, learning requires not only an adaptable system but also the possibility of changing the information processing rules (ITO, 1984). Nervous systems seem to perform learning by modifying the flows of signals transmitted between internal structures. In general, sensorimotor learning occurs in succesive steps. Each step has a given role and a time constant that depends upon the learning properties of the nervous structures involved.

3.2. Modelling the cortical neural networks

Many questions exist that can be solved by a neural network approach. Amongst them, the main problem might be first to understand how a given movement can be learned, and secondly to know what is learned during the co-ordination between posture and movement : how to perform a great variety of tasks or acquiring more abstract parameters, such as the body's center of gravity and inertial torque, or the direct and inverse dynamics model of any part of the body. This crucial question leads us to the learning rules and adaptive properties of the nervous structures invovled in the postural control.

A scheme of interactions between the main nervous structures has been proposed by ITO (1984). In a neural network approach, operations performed by the various neural structures are learned in parallel by basic units and their local interactions rules. The whole processing involves three components : local activation rules and learning rules applicable to the units, and cooperation rules defining the architecture of the network linking the units. The learning of the whole command is performed in parallel by both cerebral and cerebellar cortices and can be analyzed in terms of a dialogue between cerebral and cerebellar cortices. During this dialogue, each structure is guiding the processing and learning that is taking place in the other structure (BURNOD and DUFOSSE, 1990).

Within the cerebral cortex, a goal may be signalled by a strong activity in a subset of microcolumns in an associative cortex. Learning will then consist of increasing the connective coefficients between these microcolumns and the subsets of microcolumns in the motor or premotor cortex which command the appropriate muscular contraction. The movement may in turn produce several postural disturbances in other body segments. Displacement of a postural segment then gives rise to an error message transmitted from the periphery to the inferior olive and then to a specific cerebellar microzone which cooperates with the cerebral microcolumns of the motor cortex that are able to correct the error (Fig. 1B).

These cerebello-cerebral connections can then guide activities in the corresponding microcolumns and produce the appropriate cerebral commands for postural corrections to be made. At this step, the postural adjustment is made in a closed loop mode by means of an error signal.

At the end of this learning phase, the appropriate motor commands are adequately tuned but the cerebral cortex is still in charge of the task. Cerebral loading is not necessary here because it corresponds to a redundant control of the motor commands expressed by the whole set of cortico-cortical interactions which have contributed to the movement learning. The cerebellar learning can suffice to produce the general command and progressively replace the cortico-cortical influences on the microcolumns of the motor cortex. The output activities of these columns will therefore be due only to the cerebellar influences provided by the thalamic inputs.

The cortico-cortical processes are slower than the cerebellar ones, since the response of a column is a decision process elaborated through a progressive recruitment of neuronal activities within the column; whereas the input/output relations in the cerebellum are a more direct process with no recruitment lags. If the thalamic input to the motor cortex suffices for an appropriate command to occur, this command will inhibit the subsequently unnecessary cortical activities. The microcolumns influencing the motor cortex will this progressively decrease their influence, since they are no longer able to produce the appropriate motor commands.

The error signal disappears with the progressive decrease in the redundant cortical influences on the motor cortex. As a result, learning is completely automatized and stored in the cerebellar circuits. In this way, the cerebellum has learned a function which was previously performed by the cerebral cortex. This function corresponds to the inverse dynamics model of the skeleto-muscular apparatus formerly held to exist at the cerebral level.

Part 2 : ANTICIPATION AND REACTION : TWO MODES CONTROLLING POSTURE AND EQUILIBRIUM

Introduction

Motor actions can be subdivided into two categories, depending on the function they serve. The function of those belonging to the first category is to reach a goal, such as grasping a glass, which involves displacing the hand through a trajectory toward the target. The initial position is disrupted until the object is grasped and a new final position is built up.

The functions of the motor actions belonging to the second category is very different. It consists of stabilizing a reference value against external or internal disturbances. The reference value to be stabilized can be either the position or the orientation of a segment, such as the forearm, the head or the trunk, or that of the whole body. Another example of a reference value which needs to be stabilized is the center of gravity position in relation to the supporting surface : this stabilization is necessary to maintain equilibrium. Stabilizing all these reference values involves the use of error detecting sensors which induce appropriate corrections.

In most of our motor actions, functions of both categories are served at the same time. Raising a leg while standing is a good example of a motor action during which these two very different functions are controlled simultaneously. The performance of the movement is preceded by a displacement of the center of gravity onto the supporting leg which serves to maintain equilibrium. At the same time the head and/or trunk axis is maintained vertical by rotating the head with respect to the trunk or the trunk with respect to the leg (MOUCHNINO et al., 1990).

The coordination between the movements of one or several segments and the stabilization of other segments is a difficult task because performing the voluntary movement disturbs the posture and equilibrium.

First the movement changes the body geometry, causing the projection of the center of gravity onto the ground to shift, and thus disturbing the balance. Secondly, the internal forces associated with voluntary movements are accompanied by reaction forces acting on the supporting segments which also disturb posture and equilibrium. Feedforward postural adjustments minimizing the effects of these disturbances were first described in the pioneering study by BELENKIY et al. (1967), who observed that during arm raising while standing, a feedforward anticipatory activation of leg muscles involved in postural maintenance occurs shortly before the prime mover activation.

Since the latter finding was made, so called "anticipatory" postural adjustments have been found to accompany various limb, trunk and leg movements in both quadrupeds and humans as shown schematically in figure 2. The purpose of this review is to analyze various aspects of these anticipatory postural adjustments : their purpose, their central organization, their acquisition and their pathology.

1. PURPOSE OF THE ANTICIPATORY POSTURAL ADJUSTMENTS

1.1. Posture and equilibrium

Before beginning to analyse the goals of these anticipatory postural adjustments, it might be appropriate to first outline the main differences between posture and equilibrium.

Body posture is mainly built up against the force of gravity. Each species has a genetically predetermined reference posture, namely standing.

The human standing posture is not a rigid block oscillating like an inverted pendulum around the ankle joint, although it can behave in this way (GURFINKEL, 1973; NASHNER and McCOLLUM, 1985). It consists rather of a set of superimposed modules (legs, trunk, head) built up from the ground to the head, each linked to the

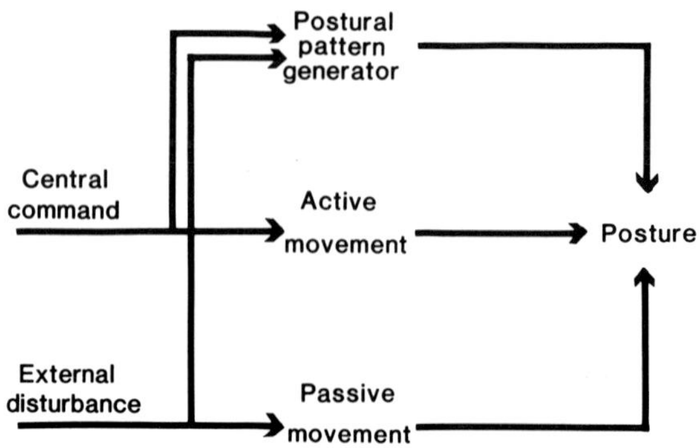

Figure 2 - Feedforward and feedback postural adjustments. Diagram showing the two mechanisms involved in the compensation for a postural perturbation. They operate either under the control of sensory inputs resulting from the postural disturbance or under that of internal feedforward signals originating from collaterals on the movement control pathway.

next by a set of muscles having its own central and peripheral control. Specific defects in the postural maintenance of some modules have been described in the literature. MARTIN (1967) has reported that postencephalitic patients can show a forward bending of the head while resting, but adopt a normal erect position when asked to perform a voluntary movement. This finding indicates that the automatic postural stabilization of the head can be dissociated from the voluntary control of the head muscles. The reference position of a module such as the head or trunk can vary depending on the context. The head for example is a module which involves three categories of sensors : the visual sensors, which collect information about the external world, the labyrinthine sensors, which detect the gravity vector, and the neck proprioceptors which specify on the head position with respect to the trunk. Depending on the context, the head position can be regulated with respect to either the external world (during gaze fixation), the gravity vector or the trunk position (BERTHOZ and POZZO, 1988; POZZO et al., 1989; NASHNER et al., 1989; AMBLARD et al., 1990; ASSAIANTE and AMBLARD, 1990 a and b). Postural control therefore involves multiple, parallel commands for regulating the position of each individual module depending on the instructions received and on the environmental requirements.

In addition to the modular control, there exists an overall postural control, as shown by the decerebrate rigidity which affects all the antigravity muscles. The central organization of this whole-body postural control, which has recently been analyzed in the cat by MORI (1987; 1989), takes place at the brain stem level.

Equilibrium control in fact constitutes a specific body postural constraint. The positions of the various body segments can vary considerably provided that the center of gravity projection onto the ground is located inside the supporting surface. This reference value is strictly regulated. LACQUANITI et al. (1984) have shown that in the standing cat, the center of gravity projection remains at the same place when the supporting surface is inclined forward or backward. The main reference value to be regulated in cat is the leg axis, however (LACQUANITI et al., 1990). In man, several lines of experimental evidences suggest that the center of gravity projection onto the ground undergoes strict regulation during oscillations of the supporting platform (GURFINKEL et al., 1981; DIETZ et al., 1989; GOLLHOFER et al., 1989) or during upper arm (MARTIN, 1967) or trunk (BABINSKI, 1899) movements.

1.2. Anticipatory postural adjustment

The anticipatory postural adjustments associated with voluntary movements are feedforward postural controls which occur before posture and equilibrium are disturbed by the movement and minimize these disturbances. Their purpose is two-fold : they contribute to maintaining equilibrium and to stabilizing body segments such as the head, trunk and arm.

1.2.1. Equilibrium maintenance

Equilibrium maintenance is one of the main functions of anticipatory postural adjustments. These adjustments help to maintain the center of gravity projection onto the ground inside the supporting surface during movement performance. BABINSKI (1899) was the first to observe that upper trunk movements are accompanied by hip and knee movements in the opposite direction which serve to maintain equilibrium. "Asynergia", in a cerebellar patient was characterized by the loss of these associated movements when bending the upper trunk, which resulted in falling. MARTIN (1967) also observed that when the arm was raised to the horizontal, a slight backward bending of the upper trunk occurred, which compensated for the forward center of gravity displacement associated with the arm lifting.

The anticipatory postural adjustments associated with upper trunk movements were recently analyzed by ODDSSON (1988; 1990), ODDSSON and THORSTENSSON (1986; 1987 a and b) and CRENNA et al. (1987; 1988) and PEDOTTI et al. (1989).

A characteristic muscle pattern is associated with each movement, direction. With forward movement a set of muscles in the front of the body is activated : Rectus abdominis (prime mover), Quadriceps and Tibialis anterior (Fig. 3). The sequence of muscle activation is distoproximal; whereas with backward upper trunk movements, the back (ErSp) muscles, thigh (Bi) and leg (GL) muscles are activated synchronously. The simulation of the muscle torques exerted during upper trunk movements indicates that in absence of thigh and leg muscle activation, the CG projection onto the ground would not be stabilized (RAMOS and STARK, 1990). Thus, the thigh and leg muscles early activation are anticipatory postural adjustments aimed at minimizing the CG displacement during upper trunk movement. This synchronous pattern of activation can be observed with most untrained subjects. Interestingly, it can be changed by training : in gymnasts, a distoproximal pattern occurs in the case of backward movements as well as forward upper trunk movements, and this new pattern is accompanied by an improved center of gravity control (PEDOTTI et al., 1989). This result suggests that the distoproximal pattern is more efficient as far as movement and equilibrium control are concerned, and that it can be acquired through long term training in backward upper trunk movements, while in the case of forward upper trunk movements, the distoproximal pattern can be observed without any special training, probably because forward upper trunk movements are part of the normal daily repertoire.

Do the postural adjustments associated with arm movements also serve to maintain the center of gravity position, as initially proposed by BELENKIY et al. (1967)? BOUISSET and ZATTARA (1987b) after a detailed dynamic analysis, have shown that the force and torque generated by the anticipatory postural adjustments were specific to each movement : the forces generated at the level of the center of gravity prior to the movement were opposite to those generated at the same level by the voluntary arm movement. These adjustments therefore probably stabilize the center of gravity position while the movement is being performed. They might, however, also stabilize the position of segments such as the trunk. It is worth noting that the displacement of the trunk occurring as the result of the reaction forces during arm raising, has been reported by RAMOS and STARK (1990) to amount to very little.

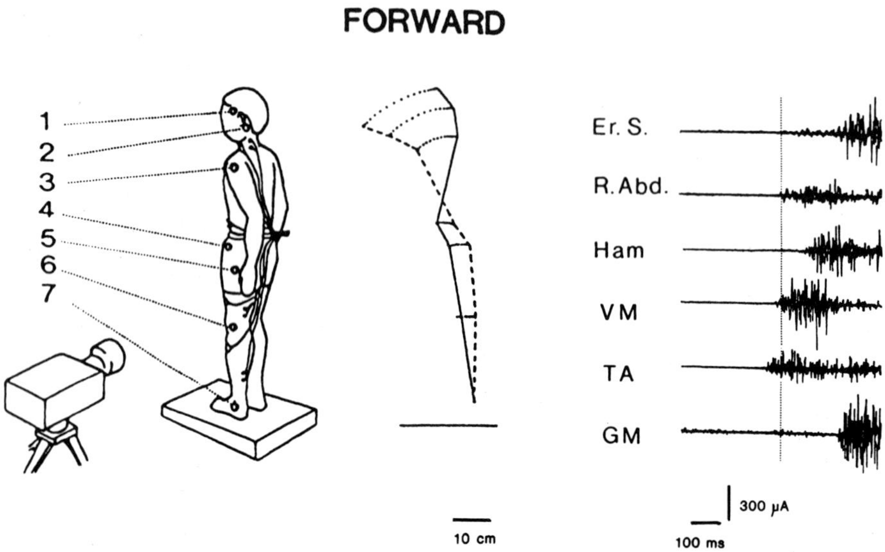

Figure 3 - Forward upper trunk movement. Stick diagram showing that the forward movement of the trunk was accompanied by a backward hip and knee displacement. Continuous line : initial position, striped line : final position. A set of muscles in the front of the trunk and leg (TA, VM, R Abd) is activated at an early stage after the "go" signal in a disto-proximal sequence. The antagonist muscles were activated during the braking phase. Er.S. (erector spinae), Ham (Hamstring), GM (gastrocnemius medius), R. Abd.: rectus abdominis, VM : vastus medialis, TA : tibialis anterior.

One interesting question raised by BOUISSET and ZATTARA (1986) and ZATTARA and BOUISSET (1986b) concerns the adaptation of the anticipatory postural adjustments to the force exerted by a movement. During arm raising, these authors compared the latency of the prime mover onset with that of the postural muscle activation depending on whether the arm being raised was unloaded or loaded. The main finding here was that the latency of the activation of the postural muscles was quite stable, whether the arm was loaded or unloaded. The duration of the postural adjustment increased however as a function of the load to be lifted, and the prime mover onset was delayed when a load was added. This interesting result should be taken into consideration when measuring reaction times, because it means that part of the reaction time depends on the duration of the anticipatory postural adjustments. Similar findings were recently made by LEE et al. (1990) in self paced movements consisting of pulling a lever while standing.

Another type of postural adjustment subserving equilibrium control is observed when the moving limb is also a supporting limb. Here the motor act is sequential and consists first of displacing the center of gravity toward a new position compatible with equilibrium maintenance during the leg movement, before performing the movement itself. This was first demonstrated in the cat when lifting a leg : the center of gravity is displaced inside the triangle formed by the three supporting legs (DUFOSSE et al., 1982; BIRJUKOVA et al., 1989). The same pattern occurs in humans when lifting one leg. When subjects are instructed to perform a fast movement, a thrust is first exerted by the moving leg, which initiates the displacement of the center of gravity toward the other leg(s) in both cats and humans (DUFOSSE et al., 1982; BIRJUKOVA et al., 1989); ROGERS and PAI, 1990; MOUCHNINO et al., 1990).

1.2.2. Stabilization of segments

The second goal of anticipatory postural adjustments is to maintain the reference position of segments such as the head, trunk or limbs. As shown by LACQUANITI et al. (1984; 1990), the orientation of body segments such as the limb axis is closely regulated by the central nervous system. One of the reasons why the position of segments is stabilized during movement performance is that their position is utilized as an egocentric reference frame to calculate the target position in peripersonal space as well as the limb trajectory necessary to reach the target. As shown by BIGUER et al. (1988), applying vibration to the neck muscles on one side mimicking the afferent Ia discharge occurring when that muscle is stretched induces an illusory displacement of a target seen in the dark and a misreaching because the movement is directed toward the illusory target. A change in the position or the orientation of segments which provide an egocentric reference frame for the movement to be performed would thus result in misreaching, and stabilizing these values during movement performance is therefore a priority task for the central nervous system.

One example of feedforward stabilization of the position of particular segments is that of a human subject during a bimanual load lifting task (Fig. 4) (HUGON et al., 1982; DUFOSSE et al., 1985; PAULIGNAN et al., 1989). Seated subjects keep their forearm loaded with a 1 kg weight in a horizontal position. When unloading is carried out by the subject himself, the forearm position is preserved although the disturbance caused by the unloading should have displaced the forearm position. This is due to a phasic decrease in the forearm flexor activity which occur prior to the unloading and can be variably time locked with the activation of the biceps of the "voluntary arm". An anticipatory postural adjustment therefore takes place here which very efficiently minimizes the disturbance of the forearm position due to the voluntary unloading movement. This type of coordination between posture and movement is an old habit acquired during childhood, which serves to stabilize the forearm position during manipulation of an object by the other hand.

Another category of anticipatory postural adjustments consists of those which minimize the reaction forces generated by the voluntary movement, as occurs for example during arm raising while standing (BELENKIY et al., 1967; LEE, 1980; BOUISSET and ZATTARA, 1981; 1986; 1987b; 1988; CORDO and NASHNER, 1982; FRIEDLI et al., 1984; 1988; HORAK et al., 1984; BROWN and FRANCK, 1987; LEE et al., 1987; BENVENUTI et al., 1990). Here the anticipatory adjustments probably fulfill two purposes at the same time, namely minimizing of the center of gravity displacement and stabilizing of segments such as the trunk; it is not easy to dissociate the respective contributions of the adjustments to position maintenance and to equilibrium control.

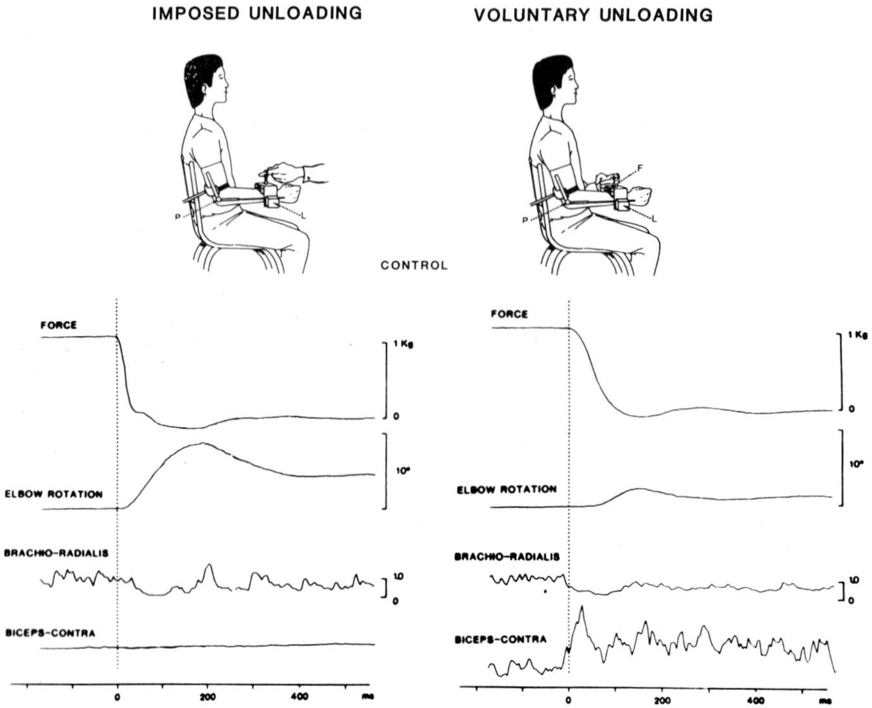

Figure 4 - Comparison between imposed unloading and voluntary unloading. The seated subject maintained a loaded forearm (1 kg) in a horizontal position. The load was lifted either by the experimenter (imposed unloading) or by the voluntary movement of the other hand (voluntary arm). The vertical dashed line shows the onset of unloading. On the left, imposed unloading : the experimenter lifted the weight supported by the postural forearm; on the right, voluntary unloading : the subject himself lifted the weight with his other hand. Note that during voluntary unloading, the position of the postural forearm was maintained and a deactivation of the postural forearm flexors occurred before the onset of unloading. Average of 20 trials.

1.2.3. Coordination between stabilization of segments and equilibrium control

Equilibrium control and stabilization of segments can be contradictory during movement performance because equilibrium control is achieved by moving segments which at the same time need to be stabilized. For example, during leg raising while standing, the body center of gravity is shifted toward the supporting leg by rotating the body externally around the ankle joint of the supporting leg. According to the inverted pendulum model, the trunk and head should also be inclined toward the same side, and, as a result, the vertical axis of these segments would be lost. Experimental data (MOUCHNINO et al., 1991) have shown that in dancers performing leg raising, the head and trunk axis remain vertical during the performance of the movement. This is due to the fact that they perform a counterotation of the trunk around the hip joint which is organized in a feedforward manner and compensate for the lateral inclination of the leg. Co-ordination is therefore necessary not only between movement and posture or movement and equilibrium, but also between the orientation of segments and the control of equilibrium.

2. ANTICIPATORY AND REACTIONAL POSTURAL ADJUSTMENTS : COMMON RULES AND DIFFERENCES

Anticipatory and reactional postural adjustments both involve stabilizing a reference value, such as the center of gravity projection onto the ground or the orientation of particular segments. Both are also controlled in an open loop way, at least during the early phase. The fast postural reactions "anticipate" the effects of the mechanical disturbance, because their onset takes place before when the external stimulus has actually started to displace the body segments (TRAUB et al., 1980). The main difference between the anticipatory and postural reactions is that the former are initiated centrally and the second by an external stimulus which is the origin of the postural disturbance.

The rules governing the anticipatory and reactional postural adjustments are largely similar. As an illustration, let us take the diagram in figure 5 showing the various elements involved in the organization of equilibrium control (Fig. 5).

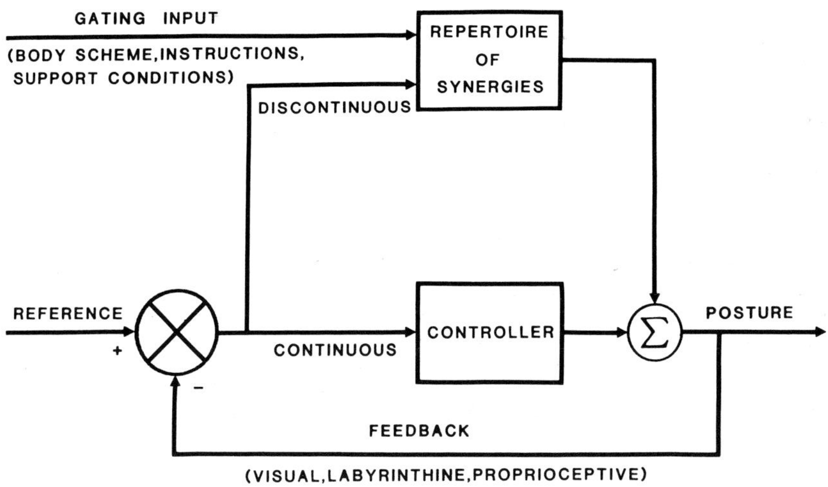

Figure 5 - Control of posture by continuous and discontinuous feedback. Note that three sources of input (visual, labyrinthine, and proprioceptive) contribute to the feedback regulation of whole body posture. The reference value for equilibrium control is usually the center of gravity position with respect to the ground, but it can change when explicit or implicit instructions are received, as for example when a subject is holding a glass full of liquid. The gated input preselects the appropriate set of synergies as a function of the body scheme, learning, and the support conditions.

2.1. The reference value to be stabilized is determined centrally. In the case of equilibrium control, this value is the center of gravity projection onto the ground. Other reference values, such as the position of a point in space can be stabilized by training ("cup of tea", MARSDEN et al., 1981); in the field of postural control, topological reference values such as combined fixation of head, trunk and arm when reading a paper can be regulated, as noted by DROULEZ (1988) and DROULEZ and BERTHOZ (1986). Here both the postural reactions and the anticipatory adjustments are organized on the basis of the reference value to be regulated.

2.2. Error detecting inputs : Three main groups of inputs involved in equilibrium control have been identified, namely the visual, vestibular, and proprioceptive inputs, to which the plantar cutaneous inputs, which are often neglected, should be added (BROOKHART et al., 1965; ASAI et al., 1990; MAGNUSSON et al., 1990). The fact that these serve as error detecting inputs was established from the fact that artificial stimulation of each of these types of input elicits a postural change which mimicks that which would occur if they were error messages triggered in a natural way. Examples of artificial error messages are muscle vibration (EKLUND, 1972), galvanic vestibular stimulation (LUND and BROBERG, 1983; GURFINKEL et al., 1988), and moving visual scenes (DICHGANS et al., 1972; LESTIENNE et al., 1977).

2.3. The internal representation of the body or **postural body scheme** (see CLEMENT et al., 1984; LESTIENNE and GURFINKEL, 1988). This representation, which is partly genetically determined and partly learned, involves a representation of verticality on the basis of labyrinthine, proprioceptive and visual inputs, and a representation of the body geometry and its dynamic characteristics. The representation of the body geometry is based on muscle proprioceptive afferents which provide information about the position of a given segment in relation to the others (ROLL and ROLL, 1988; ROLL et al., 1989). An example of the role of the proprioceptive inputs in the postural body scheme is provided by experiments involving triceps tendon vibrations (QUONIAM et al., 1990). The vibration artificially stimulates the Ia receptors of that muscle and mimicks the stretching of that muscle that would have occurred during elbow flexion. Normally, vibrating the triceps tendon when the subject is holding an elbow joint position induces an extension of that joint which compensates for the erroneous information that the joint is moving toward flexion. When the subject is asked to maintain the finger tip position in space while standing, the triceps proprioceptive inputs specify the position of the body in relation to the finger tip position in space and a backward body sway is produced to compensate for the erroneous proprioceptive information interpreted as a forward bending of the body around the elbow joint. The basis for representing the body dynamics has not yet been clearly identified; it seems to involve kinetic information about the support conditions and the weight and inertia of the various segments. The postural body scheme is very stable even under microgravity conditions (see CLEMENT et al., 1984) although the sensors normally activated directly or indirectly by gravity forces are operating here beyond their normal functional range. The concept of the postural body scheme is important because both the postural reactions and the anticipatory adjustments are being organized as a function of the body geometry and dynamics at the time of occurrence of the postural disturbance. For example, the postural reactions and the anticipatory postural adjustments are largely organized as a function of the support conditions (BELENKIY et al., 1967; CORDO and NASHNER, 1982; MARSDEN et al., 1981).

2.4. Postural adjustments : Two modes of postural adjustment have been found to exist (DIENER and DICHGANS, 1986; 1988) : slow continuous adjustments through a feedback loop, under the influence of error detecting inputs, and fast adjustments through an open loop mode under the influence of the sensory inputs elicited by the disturbance.

The anticipatory postural adjustments have been compared to the fast postural reactions. NASHNER (1977) and CORDO and NASHNER (1982) have suggested that in man, and GAHERY and MASSION (1981) that in cats reservoir of stereotyped spatiotemporal patterns or synergies may exist. These synergies may be brought into action by sensory as well as central inputs. This organization would reduce the number of degree of freedom and simplify the central control process. The concept of fixed synergies was questioned by MACPHERSON (1988; 1990) who expressed the idea that the synergies involved in postural reactions may not be fixed but flexible, because they have to deal with particular kinematic and dynamic constraints which can vary at each trial. The synergies may be organized on-line on the basis of computations made by the local networks. A third possibility would be that the synergies are organized on the basis of local networks build up or modified by learning. In the domain of the anticipatory postural adjustments, there exists evidence that the pattern of postural adjustments can be modified by long term training (PEDOTTI et al., 1989; MOUCHNINO et al., 1990). Also, short term adaptation to changes in the constraints can be seen to occur when subjects are performing fast upper trunk movements when standing on a narrow basis; under these conditions, gymnasts can suppress the distal muscles activation which is part of the postural synergy (PEDOTTI et al., 1989). It still remains to be established however whether the suppression of distal muscle activation results from on-line computation of the new support conditions or from short term learning.

A new concept, that of strategy, was introduced by NASHNER and McCOLLUM (1985) and HORAK and NASHNER (1986) in the domain of postural reactions. These authors proposed that two hierarchical levels should be considered. A higher level, the strategy level, where the general kinematic and dynamic parameters to be controlled in order to reach a goal (equilibrium maintenance) are defined. Examples are the "hip strategy" and "ankle strategy" used to control equilibrium after the disturbance of stance. At the lower level we have synergy, which means the implementation of the strategy by the spatio-temporal activation of muscles.

Do these concepts of strategy and synergy proposed in connection with postural reactions also apply to the anticipatory postural adjustments? This problem has been investigated by analyzing upper trunk movements under microgravity conditions (MASSION et al., 1991).

When a subject bends the upper trunk forward and backward, opposite movements of the hip and knee occur. This could be called a strategy aimed at maintaining the center of gravity position with respect to the foot area and can be compared with the hip strategy described by HORAK and NASHNER (1986) observed after stance disturbance.

Under microgravity conditions, with the feet attached to the floor, the same strategy is used. This finding was most surprising because there is no need to regulate the center of gravity position under microgravity. What does change is the muscle pattern or synergy. For example, the early SOL activation which is used to create ground reaction forces pushing the body backward is replaced by an early activation of the TA which is reponsible for knee flexion under microgravity. Interestingly the preflight pattern is not recovered immediately : the early TA activation is still present after 5 days on earth and only after 8 days does the early SOL activation reappears (Fig.6).

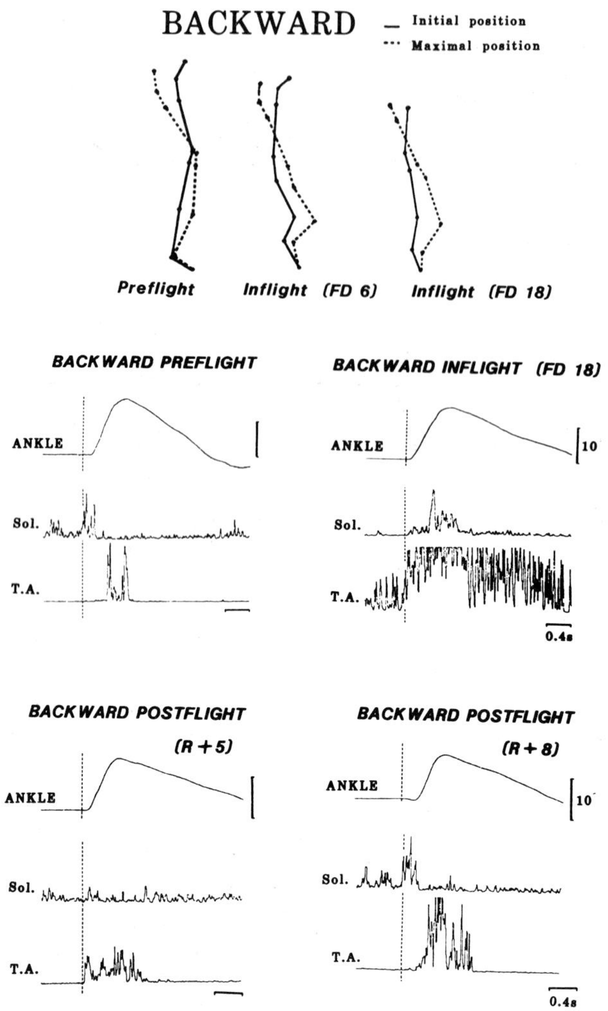

Figure 6 - Difference between strategy and synergy during upper trunk movements. Kinematic and electromyographic recordings under preflight, inflight and postflight conditions. The markers for kinematic recordings were placed at the following sites : head (2), shoulder, superior iliac crest, trochanter, tibia (above the ankle). Note the preservation of the kinematic strategy under microgravity. The EMG pattern (tibialis anterior and soleus recordings are shown) during backward upper trunk movement changed depending on the gravity conditions. The early Sol activation occurring on earth was replaced by early TA activation inflight. At the 5th postflight recording, the early TA activation was still present; it was replaced by an early Sol activation on the 8th day postflight.

This example shows the invariance of the strategy under the new constraints and the adaptation of the synergies to new environmental constraints.

To conclude, the concept of strategy may be applicable to the postural reactions and anticipatory postural adjustments. Inborn synergies do exist, giving rise to postural adjustments, mainly against increased vertical forces. Most of the patterns involved in equilibrium regulation are in fact learned patterns, triggered in an open loop mode; they are fairly fixed and can be modified by short term learning. The flexibility of these learned pattern may reflect the state of the interneuronal and motoneuronal pools, which depend on the afferent inputs relating to the body's kinematic and dynamic state at the time of the movement onset.

3. ACQUISITION

The anticipatory postural adjustments are feedforward controls, most but not all of which result from learning. Some of them, such as those associated with the control of the muscle force against the vertical gravity forces, might be genetically determined. The muscle control which characterizes the diagonal pattern of support described in quadrupeds in association with the limb movements induced by cortical stimulation (GAHERY and NIEOULLON, 1978; GAHERY and MASSION, 1981) appears to be comparable to the muscle pattern described by SHERRINGTON (1906) after cutaneous stimulation of a limb in the decerebrate animal. Generally speaking, however, the anticipatory postural adjustments are acquired by learning, and most of them are acquired during childhood. As a result of the acquisition process, the disturbance of posture and equilibrium due to the movement performance is progressively minimized as the anticipatory postural control is built up (PAULIGNAN et al., 1989). A general process which has been suggested to account for the acquisition of motor skills is the building up of an internal model first of the dynamics of the disturbance and then of its inverse dynamics (ITO, 1990). The same process might be involved in the acquisition of anticipatory postural adjustments.

The acquisition of anticipatory adjustments has been dealt with in very few investigations. IOFFE (1973) and IOFFE et al. (1988) have elicited the acquisition of new postural patterns in cats and dog. The role of the motor cortex and that of the pyramidal tract in both the acquisition process and its relationship with voluntary movement was demonstrated by these authors. The first question as to the mechanisms involved in the acquisition process concerns the role of the voluntary movement. Does the acquisition occur only when a voluntary movement is the source of the postural disturbance or is it also possible when an external disturbance can be predicted from a sensory cue triggered shortly before the disturbance? This question has been investigated during the acquisition of anticipatory adjustments of the forearm posture when the load supported by the forearm is briskly released by the switching off of an electromagnet (PAULIGNAN et al., 1989). No anticipatory adjustment of the posture was observed when a tone was delivered at a fixed interval prior to the load release, even after several training sessions where the tone and the disturbance were paired; whereas when the load release was triggered by a voluntary movement of the other arm, such as an isometric contraction of the biceps against a force platform, an anticipatory adjustment minimizing the forearm disturbance was built up within 30-60 trials. This experiment showed that no anticipatory adjustment acquisition took place in the absence of voluntary movements. However, all voluntary movements are not able to start the process. For example, when the load release is triggered by pressing a key with the finger of the other arm with low (100 g) or high (1 kg) forces, no anticipatory adjustments could be built up during a single training session, even with forces as high as 1 kg. Only well trained subjects could develop anticipatory adjustments after several training sessions. It was concluded that in a task such as bimanual load lifting, the acquisition of the anticipatory postural adjustments were specifically linked to the performance of voluntary movements and that the proximal movements (elbow joint) were much better suited than the distal ones to developing the acquisition process. This finding can be explained by the fact that during childhood, the bimanual lifting of the objects which cause forearm posture disturbance mainly involves proximal (elbow) movements, while their exploration is performed by finger movements. It is not surprising to observe that the voluntary movements which lend themselves best to building up the new coordination are similar to those used in the original learning process. This is in line with the data by KONORSKI (1948) indicating that a conditioned reflex of type II is more efficiently learned when the acquisition process involves the use of a natural reflex.

The role of the voluntary movement in the acquisition of anticipatory postural adjustments was not confirmed by LACQUANITI et al. (1984) who noted that anticipatory postural adjustments of forearm posture could be present in a task where a load was dropped onto the horizontally maintained forearm. In this task, the forearm disturbance was not synchronous with the load release but occurred after a time interval from which all the subjects estimated the kinetic energy of the load at the time of the impact. No such calculation takes place in the load lifting task paradigm.

The second question which arises concerns the respective roles of the anticipatory and reactional postural adjustments in minimizing the postural disturbance associated with voluntary movements. The postural reactions induced by the onset of the disturbance also contribute to minimizing the postural changes. The minimization is much less efficient here, however, because the onset of the correction is delayed with respect to the disturbance onset. The postural reactions become more efficient when a presetting of the gain of the circuits involved in the postural reactions takes place. This occurs, for example, when information about the occurrence of the disturbance or its timing is given prior to the disturbance onset (DUFOSSE et al., 1985; PAULIGNAN et al., 1989). The increased efficiency of the postural reactions also results from learning. For example, when an unloading of the forearm posture is triggered by switching off an electromagnet by pressing a key with the other hand, the forearm displacement is gradually decreases with the number of trials (PAULIGNAN et al., 1989). This finding indicates that the reflex action due to unloading becomes more efficient with repetition and that learning is taking place.

To conclude, two parallel and non mutually exclusive processes take place during the acquisition of the coordination between posture and movement : the first consists of improvements to the efficiency of the postural reactions, which can be observed both when the disturbance is caused by an external source and when it results from a voluntary movement; the second is the building up of an anticipatory postural adjustment when the voluntary movement is the cause of the disturbance. The latter process minimizes the postural disturbance more efficiently.

4. CENTRAL ORGANIZATION

The anticipatory postural adjustments are one aspect of a motor act, which also includes movement control. The postural aspects of the control involve first that a reference value, such as the CG projection onto the ground or the position of given segments, is regulated in a feedforward manner. The reference values to be regulated can be organized on different levels depending on their nature. For example, normal stance can be observed in thalamic animals and is based on networks located predominantly at the brain stem or spinal cord level; whereas other regulated reference values are under the control of higher levels : the position of given segments in space or in relation to the body is under the control of the motor, premotor and parietal cortex. The second aspect of the anticipatory postural adjustments concerns the localization of the postural networks responsible for the anticipatory control, which has not yet been definitely established. The third aspect concerns the link between postural adjustment and movement.

Two main questions will be discussed here : 1. Where are the networks responsible for the anticipatory postural adjustments? 2. How and where is the link between posture and movement organized?

4.1. Postural networks

Data from the literature suggest that the anticipatory postural adjustments might be organized at the brain stem-spinal cord level. First, it has been reported that in children with cerebral palsy, the anticipatory adjustments are either absent or impaired in the spastic leg (NASHNER et al., 1983). According to HORAK et al. (1984), the onset of anticipatory adjustments was delayed in the spastic leg of adult patients. In a bimanual load lifting task, it was furthermore observed that the inhibition of the postural forearm flexor, which is responsible for the maintenance of the forearm position during the voluntary unloading of that arm by the other arm, was absent (MASSION et al.,1989; VIALLET et al., 1991). As postural reaction defects have also been observed in spastic patients (TRAUB et al., 1980; NASHNER et al., 1983; HORAK et al., 1989), it has been suggested that the local networks responsible for the postural adjustments are located at the spinal cord level and that they cannot function properly in the absence of a central setting exerted by supraspinal structures.

Experimental data on quadrupeds also suggest that postural networks responsible for the anticipatory postural adjustments might be organized at the brain stem - spinal cord level. For example, cortical microstimulation in the standing cat co-activates the contralateral movement and the anticipatory postural adjustment in a feedforward manner (GAHERY and NIEOULLON, 1978; GAHERY and MASSION, 1981). More recently, ALSTERMARK et al. (1987 a, b, c; 1991 a, b) have provided evidence for the existence of long propriospinal neurones which might be involved in the simultaneous control of movement and posture through descending corticospinal pathways. LUCCARINI et al. (1990) have suggested that pontine and medullary reticulospinal pathways might be involved in the anticipatory postural control elicited by cortical stimulation.

4.2. Modes of coordination between posture and movement

Several authors have indicated that the time relationship between the onset of the anticipatory adjustment of posture and the movement onset are not fixed but show some flexibility. First, the time relationship between the postural adjustments and the movement onsets vary according to how the movement is initiated. The precession of the postural adjustment is larger when the voluntary movement is self-initiated, than when it is triggered by a sensory cue (HORAK et al., 1984; LEE et al., 1987; BENVENUTI et al., 1990). Secondly, the time interval between the anticipatory postural adjustment and the movement increases as a function of the inertia of the segment to be moved (ZATTARA et BOUISSET, 1986 a, b). Thirdly, during locomotion, the anticipatory postural adjustments are not necessarely linked to the movement but to given events in the locomotor cycle (NASHNER and FORSSBERG, 1986). All these data indicate that the control of postural adjustments is a parallel control which is coordinated in various ways with the movement control. Figure 7A illustrates this concept and also shows that there is a priority of postural control over movement control in such a way that in many cases, the movement onset is delayed until the postural adjustment has reached a given level (see CORDO and NASHNER, 1982). Contrasting with this parallel mode of control, the hierarchical mode of control is characterised by the fact that the postural adjustment is initiated by collaterals from the movement control pathway (Fig. 7B). Examples of the second mode are postural adjustments associated with movements induced by cortical stimulation in the standing cat, or anticipatory adjustments associated with movement in a load lifting task.

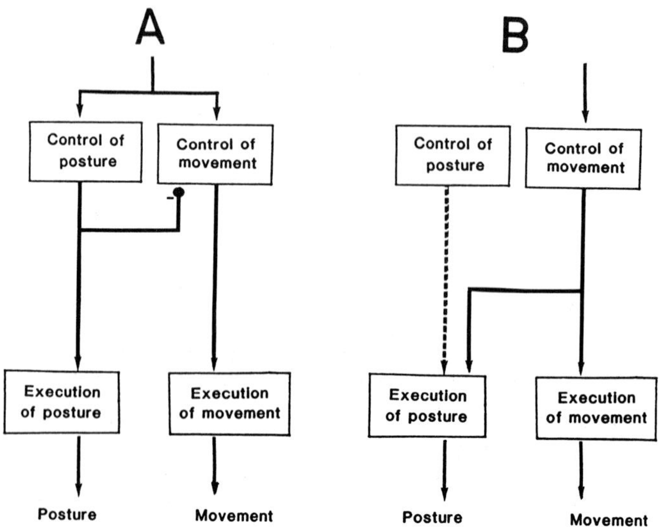

Figure 7 - Two modes of organization of the coordination between posture and movement. In A : parallel mode; in B : hierarchical mode. For further explanations see text.

The question as to the site of the coordination between posture and movement is still open. BABINSKI (1899) claimed that the cerebellum might be the site of the coordination, because asynergia was observed in cerebellar patients while performing upper trunk movements. Another putative coordination site was that proposed by GURFINKEL and ELNER (1988) at the level of the supplementary motor area (SMA) and the premotor area. Patients with defective coordination between posture and movement had lesions affecting these areas. SMA lesion was also accompanied by a defective coordination between posture and movement in a load lifting task when the lesion was contralateral to the postural arm (VIALLET et al., 1991). This suggests that the cortex contralateral to the postural arm is responsible for the organization of the coordination in this specific task. The role of the basal ganglia in this coordination has also been proposed, but controversial results have been obtained (BAZALGETTE et al., 1986; DICK et al., 1986; ROGERS et al., 1987; VIALLET et al., 1987; DIENER et al., 1989; 1990). Finally, no clear cut coordination defect has been reported in cerebellar patients apart from the fact that their timing of the onset of the various components of the motor act was not very accurate. It should be mentioned that the role of the cerebellum has not been tested with a paradigm including the acquisition of the task. It can be hypothesized that the cerebellum may be predominantly involved in the acquisition process, while the premotor and SMA areas might become predominant once the acquisition process has been compteded.

Acknowledgments - This work was supported by grants of Centre National d'Etudes Spatiales (CNES), Human Frontier Science Program (grant to Prof. C. Blakemore) and French Ministry of Research and Technology (grant "Sciences de la Cognition 89").

The authors wish to thank Dr. Jessica Blanc for correcting the English version of the manuscript.

REFERENCES

ALSTERMARK B, ISA T, TANTISIRA B (1991a) Integration in descending motor pathways controlling the forelimb in the cat. 18. Morphology, axonal projection and termination of collaterals from C3-C4 propriospinal neurones in the segment of origin. Exp Brain Res 84: 561-568

ALSTERMARK B, ISA T, TANTISIRA B (1991b) Pyramidal excitation in long propriospinal neurones in the cervical segments of the cat. Exp Brain Res 84: 569-582.

ALSTERMARK B, LUNDBERG A, PINTER M, SASAKI S (1987a) Long C3-C5 propriospinal neurones in the cat. Brain Res 404: 382-388.

ALSTERMARK B, LUNDBERG A, PINTER M, SASAKI S (1987b) Vestibular effects in long C3-C5 propriospinal neurones. Brain Res 404: 389-394.

ALSTERMARK B, LUNDBERG A, PINTER M, SASAKI S (1987c) Subpopulations and function of long C3-C5 propriospinal neurones. Brain Res 404: 395-400.

AMBLARD B, ASSAIANTE C, CREMIEUX J, MARCHAND AR (1990) From posture and gait : which sensory input for which function? In : Disorders of posture and gait. T. Brant, W. Paulus, W. Bles, M. Dieterich, S. Krafczyk & A. Straube (eds). Georg Thieme Verlag, Stuttgart-New York. Pp. 168-176.

ARBIB MA (1981) Perceptual structures and distributed motor control. In : Handbook of Physiology. VB Brooks (ed). Section 1, The Nervous System. Part 2. Amer Physiol Soc. Bethesda, Maryland, Pp. 1449-1480.

ASAI H, FUJIWARA K, TOYAMA H, YAMASHINA T, NARA I, TACHINO K (1990) The influence of foot soles coding on standing postural control. In : Disorders of posture and gait. T Brandt, W Paulus, W Bles, M Dieterich, S Kracfzyk, A Straube (eds). Georg Thieme Verlag, Stuttgart-New York. Pp. 198-201.

ASSAIANTE C, AMBLARD B (1990a) Head stabilization in space while walking : effect of visual deprivation in children and adults. In : Disorders of posture and gait. T. Brandt, W. Paulus, W. Bles, M. Dieterich, S. Krafczyk & A. Straube (eds). Georg Thieme Verlag, Stuttgart-New York. Pp. 229-232.

ASSAIANTE C, AMBLARD B (1990b) Head-trunk coordination and locomotor equilibrium in 3 to 8 year old children. In : The head-neck sensory-motor system. Vol. I: Evolution biomechanics and basic aspects. A. Berthoz, W. Graf & P.P. Vidal (eds). John Wiley & Sons, Chichester. In press.

BABINSKI J (1989) De l'asynergie cérébelleuse. Rev Neurol 7: 806-816.

BAZALGETTE F, ZATTARA M, BATHIEN N, BOUISSET S, RONDOT P (1986) Postural adjustments associated with rapid voluntary arm movements in patients with Parkinson's disease. In : MD Yahr & KJ Bergman (eds). Advances in Neurology. Vol. 45: 371-374. Raven Press, NeW York.

BELENKIY VE, GURFINKEL VS, PALTSEV EI (1967) On elements of control of voluntary movements (in Russian). Biofizica 12: 135-141.
BENVENUTI F, PANZER V, THOMAS S, HALLET M (1990) Kinematic and EMG analysis of postural adjustments associated with fast elbow flexion movements. In : Disorders of posture and gait. T Brandt, W Paulus, W Bles, M Dieterich, S Krafczyk, A Straube (eds). Georg Thieme Verlag, Stuttgart-New York. Pp 72-75.
BERKENBLIT MB, FELDMAN AG, FUKSON OI (1986) Adaptability of innate motor patterns and motor control mechanisms. Behav. Brain Sci. 9: 585-638.
BERTHOZ A, POZZO T (1988) Intermittent head stabilization during postural and locomotory tasks in humans. In : Posture and gait : development, adaptation and modulation. B. Amblard, A. Berthoz & F. Clarac (eds). Elsevier, Amsterdam-New York-Oxford. Pp. 189-198.
BIGUER B, DONALDSON IML, HEIN A, JEANNEROD M (1988) Neck muscle vibration modifies the representation of visual motion and direction in man. Brain 111: 1405-1424.
BIRJUKOVA EV, DUFOSSE M, FROLOV AA, IOFFE ME, MASSION J (1989) Role of the sensorimotor cortex in postural adjustments accompanying a conditioned paw lift in the standing cat. Exp Brain Res 78: 588-596.
BIZZI E, ACCORNO N, CHAPPLE W., HOGAN N (1982) Arm trajectory formation in monkeys. Exp Brain Res 46: 139-143.
BOUISSET S, ZATTARA M (1981) A sequence of postural movements precedes voluntary movement. Neurosci Lett 22: 263-270.
BOUISSET S, ZATTARA M (1986) Etude chronométrique de programme posturo-cinétique lié au mouvement volontaire. J Physiol (Paris) 81: 14-16.
BOUISSET S, ZATTARA M (1987a) Postural muscular activities and intentional movements. Medicine Sport Sci 26: 163-173.
BOUISSET S, ZATTARA M (1987b) Biomechanical study of the programming of anticipatory postural adjustments associated with voluntary movement. J Biomech 20: 735-742.
BOUISSET S, ZATTARA M (1988) Intermittent head stabilization during postural and locomotory tasks in humans. In : Posture and gait : development, adaptation and modulation. B Amblard, A Berthoz & F Clarac (eds). Elsevier, Amsterdam-New York-Oxford. Pp. 189-198.
BROOKHART JM, PARMEGGIANI PL, PETERSEN WA, STONE SA (1965) Postural stability in the dog. Am J Physiol 208: 1047-1057.
BROWN JE, FRANK JS (1987) Influence of event anticipation of postural actions accompanying voluntary movement. Exp Brain Res 67: 645-650.
BURNOD Y (1989) An adaptive neural network : the cerebral cortex. Masson, Paris.
BURNOD Y, DUFOSSE M (1991) A model for the co-operation between cerebral cortex and cerebellar cortex in movement learning. In : Brain and Space. J Paillard (ed). Oxford University Press. Pp. 446-458.
BURNOD Y, CAMINITI R, JOHNSON P, GRANGUILLAUME P, OTTO I (1991) Model of visuo-motor transformations performed by the cerebral cvortex to command arm movements at visual targets in the 3-D Space. J Neurosci. In press.
CAMINITI R, JOHNSON PB, GALLI C, FERRAINA S, BURNOD Y, URBANO A (1991) Making arm movements within different parts of space : the premotor and motor cortical representation of a coordinate system for reaching to visual targets. J Neurosci 10: 2039-2058.
CLEMENT G, GURFINKEL VS, LESTIENNE F, LIPSHITS MI, POPOV KE (1984) Adaptation of postural control to weightlessness. Exp Brain Res 57: 61-72.
CORDO PJ, NASHNER LM (1982) Properties of postural adjustments associated with rapid arm movements. J Neurophysiol 47: 287-302.

CRENNA P, FRIGO C, MASSION J, PEDOTTI A (1987) Forward and backward axial synergies in man. Exp Brain Res 65: 538-548.
CRENNA P, FRIGO C, MASSION J, PEDOTTI A, DEAT A (1988) Forward and backward axial movements : two modes of central control. In : Stance and motion, facts and concepts. VS Gurfinkel, M Ioffé, J Massion & JP Roll (eds). Plenum Press, Nes York. Pp. 195-201.
DICHGANS J, HELD R, YOUNG L, BRANDT T (1972) Moving visual scenes influence the apparent direction of gravity. Science 178: 1217-1219.
DICK JPR, ROTHWELL JC, BERARDELLI A, THOMPSON PD, GIOUX M, BENECKE R, DAY BL, MARSDEN CD (1986) Associated postural adjustments in Parkinson's disease. J Neurol Neurosurg Psych 49: 1378-1385.
DIENER HC, DICHGANS J(1986) Long loop reflexes and posture. In: Disorders of posture and gait. W Bles & Th Brandt (eds). Amsterdam, Elsevier. Pp. 41-51.
DIENER HC, DICHGANS J (1988) Pathophysiology of posture. In : Posture and gait : Development, adaptation and modulation. B Amblard, A Berthoz & F Clarac (eds). Excerpta Medica, Amsterdam. Pp. 229-235.
DIENER HC, DICHGANS J, GUSCHLBAUER B, BACHER M, LANGENBACH P (1989) Disturbances of motor preparation in basal ganglia and cerebellar disorers. In : Progress in Brain Research. Vol. 80. Pp. 481-488. JHJ Allum & M Hulliger (eds). Elsevier Science Publishers B.V.
DIENER HC, DICHGANS J, GUSCHLBAUER B, BACHER M, RAPP H, LANGENBACH P (1990) Associated opstural adjustments with body movement in normal subjects and patients with Parkinsonism and cerebellar disease. Rev Neurol 146: 555-563.
DIETZ V, HORSTMANN GA, TRIPPEL M, GOLLHOFER A (1989) Human postural reflexes and gravity-an under water stimulation. Neurosci Lett 106: 350-355.
DROULEZ J (1988) Topological aspects of sensori-motor control. In : Stance and motion : facts and concepts. VS Gurfinkel, ME Ioffé, J Massion & JP Roll (eds). Plenum Press, New York-London. Pp. 251-259.
DROULEZ J, BERTHOZ A (1986) Servo-controlled (conservative) versus topological (projective) mode of sensory motor control. In : Disorders of posture and gait. W Bles & TH Brandt (eds). Elsevier, Amsterdam-New York-Oxford. Pp. 83-97.
DUFOSSE M (1989) Formal approach and neural network simulation of the co-ordination between posture and movement. In : Neurocomputing : algorithms, architectures and applications. F Fogelman-Soulie & J Hérault (eds). Springer-Verlag. NATO ASI Series. Serie F : Computer and Systems Sciences. Vol 68: 389-394.
DUFOSSE M, HUGON M, MASSION J (1985) Postural forearm changes induced by predictable in time or voluntary triggered unloading in man. Exp Brain Res 60: 330-334.
DUFOSSE M, MACPHERSON J, MASSION J (1982) Biomechanical and electromyographical comparison of two postural supporting mechanisms in the cat. Exp Brain Res 45: 38-44.
EKLUND G (1972) Position sense and state of contraction : the effect of vibration. J Neurol Neurosurg Psych 41: 433-444.
FELDMAN AG (1974) Control of the length of the muscle. Biofizika 19: 749-753.
FELDMAN AG (1987) A model for one-joint motor control in man. In : Motor control. GN Gantchev, B Dimitrov & P Gatev (eds). Pp. 183-187.
FRIEDLI WG, COHEN L, HALLETT M, STANHOPE S, SIMON SR (1988) Postural adjustments associated with rapid voluntary arm movements. II. Biomechanical analysis. J Neurol Neurosurg Psych 51: 232-243.

FRIEDLI WG, HALLETT M, SIMON SR (1984) Postural adjustments associated with rapid voluntary arm movements. I. Electromyographic data. J Neurol Neurosurg Psych 47: 611-622.
GAHERY Y, MASSION J (1981) Coordination between posture and movement. TINS 4: 199-202.
GAHERY Y, NIEOULLON A (1978) Postural and kinetic coordination following cortical stimuli which induce flexion movements in the cat's limbs. Brain Res 155: 25-37.
GOLLHOFER A, HORSTMANN GA, BERGER W, DIETZ V (1989) Compensation of translational and rotational perturbations in human posture : stabilization of the centre of gravity. Neurosci Lett 105: 73-78.
GUIARD Y (1987) Asymmetric division of labor in human skilled bimanual action : the kinematic chain as a model. J Motor Behav 19: 486-517.
GURFINKEL EV (1973) Physical foundations of stabiligraphy. Agressologie 14, Suppl C: 9-13.
GURFINKEL VS, ELNER AM (1988) Participation of secondary motor area of the frontal lobe in organization of postural components of voluntary movements in man. Neurophysiology 20: 7-14.
GURFINKEL VS, LEVIK YuS, POPOV KE, SMETANIN BN, SHLIKOV VYu (1988) Body scheme in the control of postural activity. In : Stance and motion : facts and concepts. VS Gurfinkel, ME Ioffé, J Massion & JP Roll (eds). Plenum Press, New York. Pp. 185-193.
GURFINKEL V, LIPSHITS M, POPOV K (1981) Sabilization of body position as the main task of postural regulation (Translation). Fiziologiya Cheloveka 7: 400-410.
HERAULT J, JUTTEN C, ANS B (1985) Détection de grandeurs primitives dans un message composite par une architecture neuromimétique en apprentissage non supervisé. Xème Colloque GRETSI.
HORAK FB, ESSELMAN PE, ANDERSON ME, LYNCH MK (1984) The effects of movement velocity, mass displaced and task certainty on associated postural adjustments made by normal and hemiplegic individuals. J Neurol Neurosurg Psychiatr 47: 1020-1028.
HORAK FB, NASHNER LM (1986) Central programming of postural movements : adaptation to altered support surface configurations. J Neurophysiol 55: 1369-1381.
HORAK FB, SHUPERT CL, MIRKA A (1989) Components of postural dyscontrol in the elderly : a review. Neurobiology of Aging. 10: 727-738.
HOUK JC, RYMER WZ (1981) Neural control of muscle length and tension. In : Handbook of Physiology. VB Brooks (ed). Sect. I, Vol 2. Amer J Physiol. Bethesda, Maryland. Pp. 257-323.
HUGON M, MASSION J, WIESENDANGER M (1982) Anticipatory postural changes induced by active unloading and comparison with passive unloading in man. Pflüg Arch 393: 292-296.
ITO M (1984) The cerebellum and neural control. Raven Press, New York.
ITO M (1986) Neural systems controlling movement. TINS 9: 515-518.
ITO M (1990) A new physiological concept of cerebellum. Rev Neurol. In press.
IOFFE ME (1973) Pyramidal influences in establishment of new motor coordinations in dogs. Physiol Behav 11: 145-153.
IOFFE ME, IVANOVA NG, FROLOV AA, BIRJUKOVA EV, KISELJOVA NV (1988) On the role of motor cortex in the learned rearrangement of postural coordinations. In : Stance and motion : facts and concepts. VS Gurfinkel, ME Ioffé, J Massion & JP Roll (eds). Plenum Press, New York-London. Pp. 213-226.
KAWATO M, FURUKAWA K, SUZUKI R (1987) A hierarchical model for control and learning of voluntary movement. Biol Cybern 57: 169-185.

KONORSKI J (1948) Conditionned reflexes and neuron organization. Cambridge University Press.
KUPERSTEIN M (1988) Neural model of adaptive hand-eye co-ordination for single postures. Science 239: 1308-1311.
LACQUANITI F, MAIOLI C, FAVA E (1984) Cat posture on a tilted platform. Exp Brain Res 57: 8-88.
LACQUANITI F, Le TAILLANTER M, LOPIANO L, MAIOLI C (1990) The control of limb geometry in cat posture. J Physiol (Lond) 426: 177-192.
LEE WA (1980) Anticipatory control of postural and task muscles during rapid arm flexion. J Motor Behav 12: 185-196.
LEE W, BUCHANAN T, ROGERS M (1987) Effects of arm acceleration and behavioural conditions on the organization of postural adjustments during arm flexion. Exp Brain Res 66: 257-270.
LEE WA, MICHAELS CF, PAI YC (1990) The organization of torque and EMG activity during bilateral handle pulls by standing humans. Exp Brain Res. In press.
LESTIENNE F, GURFINKEL VS (1988) Postural control in weightlessness : dual process underlying adaptation to an unusual environment. TINS 11: 359-363.
LESTIENNE F, SOECHTING J, BERTHOZ A (1977) Postural readjustment induced by linear motion of visual scenes. Exp Brain Res 28: 363-384.
LUCCARINI P, GAHERY Y, POMPEIANO O (1990) Cholinoceptive pontine reticular structures modify the postural adjustments during the limb movements induced by cortical stimulation. Arch ital Biol 128: 19-45.
LUND S, BROBERG C (1983) Effects of different head positions on postural sway in man induced by a reproducible vestibular error signal. Acta Physiol Scand 117: 307-309.
MACPHERSON JM (1988) The neural organization of postural control. Do muscle synergies exist? In : Posture and gait : development, adaptation and modulation. B Amblard, A Berthoz & F Clarac (eds). Elsevier Science Publishers B.V. Pp. 381-390.
MACPHERSON JM (1990) How flexible are muscle synergies? In : Motor control : concepts and issues. Dahlem Konferenzen. DR Humphrey & HJ Freund (eds). Chichester, John Wiley & Sons Ltd. In press.
MAGNUSSON M, ENBOM H, JOHANSSON R, PYYKKO I (1990) The importance of somatosensory information from the feet in postural control in man. In : Disorders of posture and gait. T Brandt, W Paulus, W Bles, M Dieterich, S Krafczyk, A Straube (eds). Georg Thieme Verlag, Stuttgat-New York. Pp. 190-193.
MARR D (1982) Vision. Freeman.
MARSDEN CD, MERTON PA, MORTON HP (1981) Human postural responses. Brain 104: 513-534.
MARTIN JP (1967) The basal ganglia and posture. London, Pitman.
MASSION J, DEAT A, GURFINKEL VE, LIPSHITS M, POPOV K (1991) Axial synergies under microgravity conditions. Exp Brain Res. In press.
MASSION J, DUFOSSE M (1988) Co-ordination between posture and movement : why and how? NIPS 3: 88-93.
MASSION J, VIALLET F, MASSARINO R, KHALIL R (1989) La région de l'aire motrice supplémentaire est impliquée dans la coordination entre posture et mouvement chez l'homme. C R Acad Sci Paris 308: 417-423.
MATTHEWS PBC (1981) Evolving views in the internal operation and functional role of the muscle spindle. J Physiol (Lond) 320: 1-30.
MORI S (1987) Integration of posture and locomotion in acute decerebrate cats and in awake, freely moving cats. Progr Neurobiol 28: 161-195.

MORI S (1989) Contribution of postural muscle tone to full expression of posture and locomotor movements : multi-faceted analyses of its setting brainstem-spinal cord mechanisms in the cat. Jap J Physiol 39: 785-809.

MOUCHNINO L, AURENTY R, MASSION J, PEDOTTI A (1990) Coordinated control of posture and equilibrium during leg movement. In: Disorders of posture and gait. T. Brandt, W Paulus, W Bles, M Dieterich, S Krafczyk, A Straube (eds). Georg Thieme Verlag, Stuttgart-New York. Pp. 68-71.

MOUCHNINO L, AURENTY R, MASSION J, PEDOTTI A (1991) Stratégies de contrôle simultané de l'équilibre et de la position de la tête pendant l'élévation d'une jambe. C R Acad Sci Paris 312: 225-232.

NASHNER LM (1977) Fixed patterns of rapid postural responses among leg muscles during stance. Exp Brain Res 30: 13-24.

NASHNER LM, McCOLLUM G (1985) The organization of human postural movements : a formal basis and experimental synthesis. Behav Brain Sci 8: 135-150.

NASHNER LM, FORSSBERG H (1986) Phase-dependent organization of postural adjustments associate with arm movements while walking. J Neurophysiol 55: 1382-1394.

NASHNER LM, SHUMWAY-COOK A, MARIN O (1983) Stance posture control in select groups of children with cerebral palsy : deficits in sensory organization and muscular coordination. Exp Brain Res 49: 393-409.

NASHNER LM, SHUPERT CL, HORAK FB, BLACK FO (1989) Organization of posture controls : an analysis of sensory and mechanical constraints. In : Progress in Brain Research, Vol. 80: 411-423. J.H.J. Allum & M. Hulliger (eds). Elsevier Science Publishers B.V.

ODDSSON L (1988) Coordination of a simple voluntary multijoint movement with postural demands : trunk extension in standing man. Acta Physiol Scand 134: 109-119.

ODDSSON L (1990) Control of voluntary trunk movements in man. Mechanisms for postural equilibrium during standing (Thesis). Acta Physiol Scand 140, Suppl 595.

ODDSSON L, THORSTENSSON A (1986) Fast voluntary trunk flexion movements in standing : primary movements and associated postural adjustments. Acta Physiol Scand 128: 341-349.

ODDSSON L, THORSTENSSON A (1987a) Fast voluntary trunk flexion movements in standing : motor patterns. Acta Physiol Scand 129: 93-106.

ODDSSON L, THORSTENSSON A (1987b) Co-ordinative movements of the pelvis and trunk are controlled by task specific motor programmes in man. J Physiol (Lond) 390: 136P.

PAILLARD J, AMBLARD B (1985) Static versus kinetic visual cues for the processing of spatial relationships. In : Brain mechanisms and spatial vision. DJ Ingle, M Jeannerod & DN Lee (eds). Martinus Nijhoff Publ. Dordrecht. NATO ASI Series D, Behavioural and Social Sciences. Vol 2: 299-330

PAULIGNAN Y, DUFOSSE M, HUGON M, MASSION J (1989) Acquisition of co-ordination between posture and movement in a bimanual task. Exp Brain Res 77: 337-348.

PEDOTTI A, CRENNA P, DEAT A, FRIGO C, MASSION J (1989) Postural synergies in axial movements : short and long-term adaptation. Exp Brain Res 74: 3-10.

POZZO T, BERTHOZ A, LEFORT L (1989) Head kinematic during various motor tasks in humans. In : Progress in Brain Research. Vol 80: 377-383. J.H.H. Allum & M. Hulliger (eds). Elsevier Science Publishers B.V.

QUONIAM C, ROLL JP, DEAT A, MASSION J (1990) Proprioceptive induced interactions between segmental and whole body posture. In : Disorders of posture and gait. T Brandt, W Paulus, W Bles, M Dieterich, S Krafczyk, A Straube (eds). Georg Thieme Verlag, Stuttgart-New York. Pp 194-197.

SANCHEZ E (1989) Importance in knowledge systems. Information systems 14: 455-464.

RAMOS CF, STARK LW (1990) Simulation experiments can shed light on the functional aspects of postural adjustments related to voluntary movements. In : Multiple muscle systems : Biomechanics and movement organization. JM Winters & L-Y Woo (eds). Springer-Verlag, New York. Pp. 507-517.

ROGERS MW, KUKULKA CG, SODERBERG GL (1987) Postural adjustments preceding rapid arm movements in parkinsonian subjects. Neurosci Lett 75: 246-251.

ROGERS MW, PAI YC (1990) Dynamic transitions in stance support accompanying leg flexion movements in man. Exp Brain Res 81: 398-402.

ROLL JP, ROLL R (1988) Extraocular proprioception and body postural references. In: Stance and motion : facts and concepts. VS Gurfinkel, ME Ioffé, J Massion & JP Roll (eds). New York, Plenum Press. Pp. 23-26.

ROLL JP, VEDEL JP, ROLL R (1989) Eye, head and skeletal muscle spindle feedback in the elaboration of body references. In : Progress in Brain Research. Vol. 80: 113-123. JHJ Allum & M Hulliger (eds). Elsevier, Amsterdam.

SHERRINGTON CS (1906) The integrative action of the nervous system. Constable, London.

TRAUB MM, ROTHWELL JC, MARSDEN CD (1980) Anticipatory postural reflexes in Parkinson's disease and other akinetic-rigid syndromes and in cerebellar ataxia. Brain 103: 393-412.

VARELA FJ (1978) Describing the logic of the living : adequacies and limitations of the idea of autopoiesis. In : Autopoiesis, a theory of living organization. M Zeleny (ed). Elsevier, North-Holland.

VARELA F (1979) Principles of biological autonomy. G. Klir (ed). 2 volumes, North-Holland, General systems research.

VIALLET F, MASSION J, MASSARINO R, KHALIL R (1987) Performance of a bimanual load-lifting task by Parkinsonian patients. J Neurol Neurosurg Psych 50: 1274-1283.

VIALLET F, MASSION J, MASSARINO R, KHALIL R (1991) Coordination between posture and movement in a bimanual load lifting task : putative role of a mesial region including the supplementary motor area. Exp Brain Res. In press.

VIVIANI P, McCOLLUM G (1983) The relation between linear extent and velocity in drawing movements. Neurosci. 10: 211-218.

YAMAKAWA T (1987) A simple fuzzy computer hardware system employing min and max operations. A challenge to 6th generation computer. IFSA Congress, Tokyo, 827-830. July 20-25.

ZATTARA M, BOUISSET S (1986a) Etude chronométrique du programme posturo-cinétique lié au mouvement volontaire. J Physiol (Paris) 81: 14-16.

ZATTARA M, BOUISSET S (1986b) Chronometric analysis of the posturo-kinetic programming of voluntary movement. J Motor Behav 18: 215-223.

SECTION 2

REPRESENTATION AND CONTROL OF MOVEMENT

Tutorials in Motor Behavior II
G.E. Stelmach and J. Requin (Editors)

From action representation to movement control

Jean Requin

Cognitive Neuroscience Unit, C.N.R.S.
31 Chemin Joseph Aiguier, 13402 Marseille cedex 9, France

Abstract

For a decade, experimental data obtained by using single-neuron recording techniques in behaving monkeys supported models in which the cognitive processes involved in motor planning and control would result from the successive activation of three, hierarchically organized levels of representation: action goal, motor program and basic movement units or commands. However, these data appear at the same time, increasingly incompatible with the current conception in which, according to a one-to-one mapping between neural functions and neural structures, these three representation levels would be implemented in the associative, premotor and primary motor cortical areas, respectively. This is suggested by anatomical evidence for unidirectional pathways, serially interconnecting these structures. Such a conception must be now reconsidered, on the grounds of three emerging notions: the functional heterogeneity of the neocortical areas involved in motor control, the continuum of functionality of individual neurons and the functional cooperation of neuronal populations in coding operations. This suggests that the representational processes involved in action planning and control are implemented in widely distributed and flexibly interconnected neuronal networks which overlap throughout a large part of the neocortical tissue.

1. INTRODUCTION

Advances in our knowledge of both the cognitive processes and the neural mechanisms by which motor actions are planned have mainly been the results of the fast growing cognitive neuroscience approach to human cognition and its neural basis. In the field of motor control, this integrated approach to higher brain functions was opened by the convergent research strategies that both cognitive psychologists and neuroscientists have simultaneously developed. On one side, physiological measurements, as event-related potential (ERP) recordings (cf. Coles, 1989; Meyer, Osman, Irwin & Yantis, 1988) and measurements of the local changes in cerebral metabolism (cf. Roland, 1985) were introduced in the experimental paradigm designed in the field of human cognitive psychology. On the other side, these experimental paradigms were imported and adpated to non human primates on which invasive techniques of studying brain activity in behaving animals, such as single-neuron recording techniques, have been developed (cf. Evarts, Shinoda & Wise, 1984; Mountcastle, 1986; Requin, Brener & Ring, 1991).

The discovery and/or improvements of new methodological and technical tools during the last decade have thus played an important role in making the research strategy of cognitive neuroscience successful (cf. Mountcastle, 1986). However, a deeper reason for ensuring such a success was the structural isomorphism between the architectures of cognition, on one hand, and of brain organization, on the other, which have been developed independently by either cooperating discipline. For Sternberg (1969), cognitive psychologists have proposed models of human information processing in which sensorimotor information is transformed within, and transmitted between independant, functionnally specialized, serially and even hierarchically organized processing stages (cf. Meyer, Osman, Irwin & Yantis, 1988; Miller, 1988). For Allen and Tsukahara (1974), neuroscientists have developed models of brain processes involved in motor control in which sensorimotor information is processed within, and conveyed between functionally specialized, cytoarchitecturally identified neuronal ensembles, which are sequentially interconnected by unidirectional input-output pathways (cf. Requin, 1980; Requin, Riehle & Seal, 1988; Wiesendanger, 1990). Such an isomorphism between models of information processing and of brain functional organization formed an especially favorable theoretical ground for designing experiments, in which concepts and methods of functional neurophysiology and of cognitive psychology were combined (cf. Mountcastle, 1976; Requin, 1982), with the somewhat reductionistic objective of verifying a one-to-one mapping between neuronal structures and processing stages.

Data accumulated in studies on preparation for action, most of them having been either explicitely conducted within, or influenced by this conceptual framework, has led to the current views of motor planning. Disregarding a number of variations (e.g. Jeannerod, 1990; Keele, Cohen & Ivry, 1990; Paillard, 1982; Requin, 1985; Rosenbaum, 1987; Schmidt, 1988), the organization of motor activity is supposed to be based upon the utilization by the motor system of information stored in memory in the form of multiple, more or less abstract, hierarchically-organized "representations" of motor actions. These representations, which are elaborated and permanently updated during ontogenesis and learning, may be viewed as the "language" of the motor system.

HIERARCHICAL ORGANIZATION OF REPRESENTATION LEVELS OF ACTION	
I. SEMANTIC :	**Action goal** (→ response determination) - non motoric, holistic, context-independent, symbolic - frontal and parietal association cortex
II. SYNTACTIC :	**Motor program** (→ motor programming) - non motoric, parametric, context-dependent, subsymbolic ? - lateral and medial premotor cortex
III. PHONEMIC :	**Basic motor units** (→ motor output) - motoric, anatomical, biomecanically constrained, neuromuscular - primary motor cortex and corticospinal pathways

Table 1: See explanations in the text

Such a metaphoric reference to linguistics is recurrent in the domain of motor control, from Lashley (1951), when calling for a "syntax" of movement units (or words) determining the ordering of the movement sequence (or sentence) to Shaffer (1982), describing the structure of the motor program as a "set of grammatical representations of intended actions". Note that "multiple", "abstract" and "hierarchical", which define the main features of this representational conception of motor control, were not introduced by the cognitive revolution. They were already the key-words used, for example, by Von Monakow (1914) at the beginning of the century, for describing the brain mechanisms responsible for movement control.

Table 1 is an attempt to summarize the three representation levels of motor activity which have been most often identified in stage models of information processing, as well as in neurophysiological conceptions of movement organization. For each level, the main features and properties attributed to these representations as well as the neural structures currently considered as being involved in these processes have been specified. Such a one-to-one mapping between stages of information flow and anatomically connected cortical regions well illustrates the popular concept of the closed isomorphism between the macro structural and functional organizations of the brain.

2. NEURAL REPRESENTATION OF ACTION GOAL

At the highest level, which may be called "semantic", motor actions would be represented in a non-motoric, holistic and symbolic mode and could give rise to a conscious experience. Non-motoric means that this level of representation does not contain the spatio-temporal structure of the forthcoming motor action, i.e. the ordering and parameters of the elementary movement units. Holistic means that action is represented by a unique feature which conceptually defines the behavioral goal to be reached (i.e. "the change in the surrounding world that will result from acting", to quote W. James). Symbolic means that this representation of the action goal is stored in an abstract, or conceptual, form: by analogy to concept formation in linguistics, a symbol may be viewed here as some single code which results from extracting a common feature of several more elementary codes. The process by which this context-independent representation of action goal is retrieved from memory is what is called "response" selection or determination in the framework of information processing stage models of cognitive psychology.

First, empirical evidence for this highest level of action representation came from early neuropsychological studies identifying, among the different apraxic syndromes, disorders which seemed to specifically result from the inability either to intentionally initiate a well-anticipated action (ideomotor apraxia), which could, however, be automatically performed, or, even, to evoke the image of the forthcoming action (ideatory apraxia). The possible implication of the association cortex, especially the posterior parietal and prefrontal areas, in the setting up of action goal representation and its transmission downstream to the motor system was hypothetized on the basis of lesions studies (cf. Paillard, 1982). However, it is only recently that studies conducted in the cognitive neuroscience approach with single-neuron recording techniques have provided direct evidence for the neuronal substrate of action goal representation.

The starting point was undoubtedly the influencial work of Mountcastle and his colleagues (cf. Mountcastle, Lynch, Georgopoulos, Sacata & Acuna, 1975) who discovered in the posterior parietal areas 5 and 7 changes in neuronal activity which were triggered by an object, provided that this object was the target for limb reaching

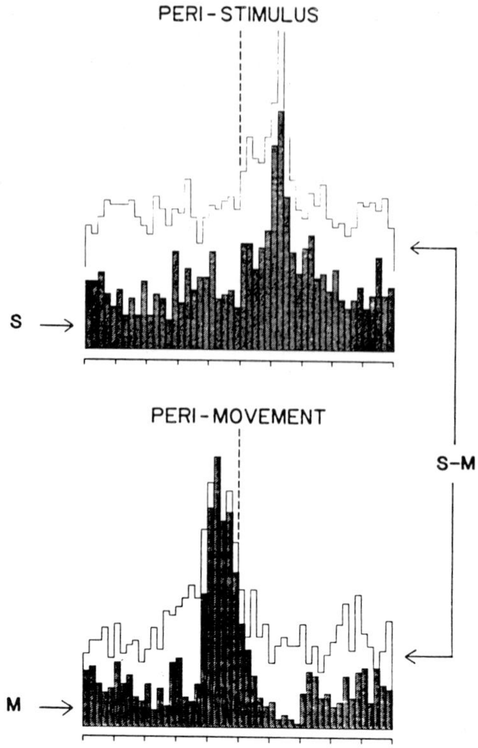

Figure 1: Peri-stimulus and peri-movement histograms of neuronal activity in a "sensorimotor" neuron in area 5. The activity recorded when the monkey performed the movement in response to the stimulus (black columns, S-M) is compared with that recorded during stimulus presentation only (hatched columns, S) and during movement performance only (hatched columns, M) (*from Requin et al., Biological Psychology, 1988*)

and/or grasping movements. The hypothesis that this brain region generated a "command" function for initiating motor activity, on the basis of a synthesis of multiple-sensory information, was subsequently challenged (for review, see Lynch, 1980). The debate focused on whether this increase in neuronal activity after the stimulus and before the movement was due to an attentional facilitation of sensory processes or a preparatory facilitation of motor processes. The impossibility to demonstrate unequivocally the "sensory" vs "motor" function of this "enhancement" phenomenon stressed the difficulty in delimiting the boundary between perception and action, which is exactly as one would expect for an interfacing neural system responsible for making connections between perceptual and action representations.

Studies conducted during the last 10 years with single neuron techniques have provided strong support for such a view. The central origin of the changes in activity of the population of parietal neurons - the so-called "early" cells - which are activated prior to the onset of a visually-cued movement and for which there was no apparent visual receptive field, was demonstrated. These changes were found when sensory feedback from the trained limbs had been suppressed (cf. Seal, Gross & Bioulac, 1982). Subsequently, "sensorimotor" neurons, i.e. which modified their activity in relation to both the stimulus presentation and motor response execution were found in area 5 (Seal, 1989; Seal & Requin, 1987). These neurons showed two components in their activation (cf. Figure 1). The first component was a change in activity time-locked to stimulus onset with a time-course similar to that of the change in activity observed when only the stimulus was presented. The second component was a change in activity time-locked to movement onset with a time course similar to that of the change in activity

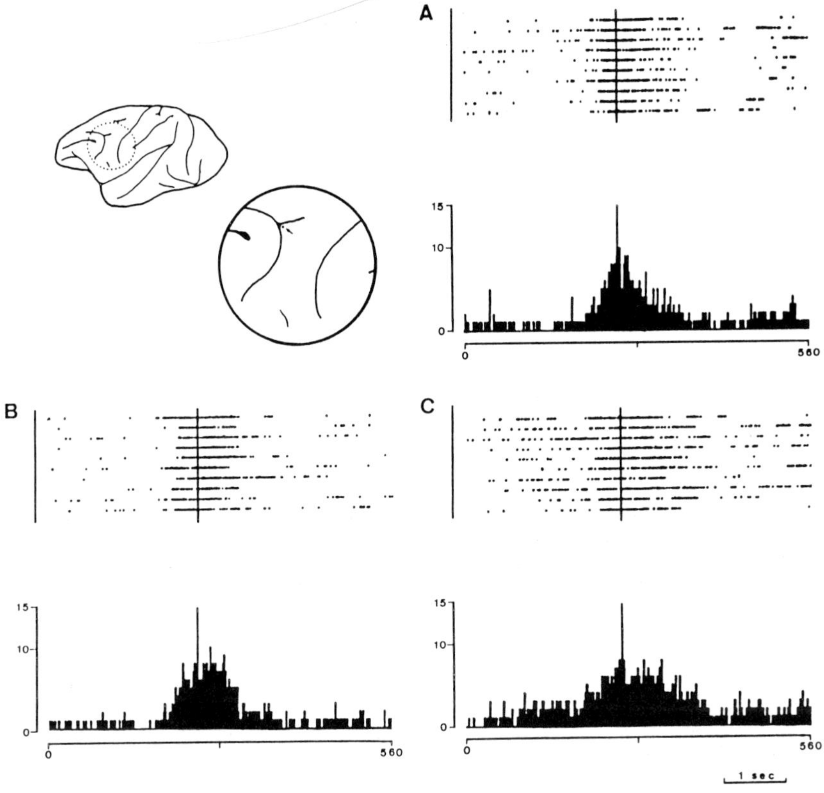

Figure 2: A "grasping-with-the-hand-and-with-the-mouth" neuron. Neuronal activity is shown when grasping with the mouth (A), with the contralateral hand (B) and with the ipsilateral hand (C). Histograms are aligned with the moment when the monkey touched the food (*from Rizzolatti et al., Experimental Brain Research, 1988*)

observed when only the movement was performed. It must be underlined that changes in activity of these two-component neurons, whose features did not depend upon the stimulus and movement physical parameters, have been observed only after monkeys were trained in a task associating arbitrary stimuli and responses. Thus one may infer that these neuronal changes appeared only when the stimulus has acquired a behavioral meaning, i.e. became able to evoke a representation of the forthcoming action. Very similar neurons have been found in area 7 by Andersen, Essick and Siegel (1987; see also Andersen, 1989), who stressed their possible role in sensorimotor integration and, more precisely, in the implementation of the process responsible for "the formulation of motor behaviors".

However, recent data suggest that the neural mechanisms associated with action goal representation are not restricted to the posterior parietal cortex but would extend to the frontal cortex. Sensorimotor neurons are also found in the premotor cortex and the timing of their changes in activity is quite similar to that observed for sensorimotor neurons of area 5 (cf. Requin, Riehle & Seal, 1988, in press). Moreover, Rizzolatti, Camarda, Fogassi, Gentilucci, Luppino and Matelli (1988) have shown in the inferior part of the premotor area 6, neurons which are specifically activated by the "holistic" meaning of action sequences in term of their behavioral goal, but not in terms of sequence elements or movement features. For instance, some neurons were activated before and during the action of grasping food with the hand, - but not when the hand, although shaped similarly as for grasping, performed a pointing-pushing movement - or before and during the action of grasping with the mouth - but not during mouth movements when feeding the monkey. Thus these neuronal activities seem to express the basic elements of some kind of "lexicon" of motor actions semantically defined. In such a perspective, the changes in activity of neurons associated with the action of grasping food, whenever the grasp was performed with either the hand or mouth, are even more suggestive (cf. Figure 2). They may be viewed as participating in the process by which symbolic representations - for example that of the "grasping action" - are built by extracting the common concept for a class of similarly goal-directed motor activities.

In some studies, the effects of manipulating the experimental factors known, in the field of cognitive psychology studies, as acting specifically on the response selection stage, i.e. response probability and S-R compatibility (cf. Kornblum, Hasbroucq & Osman, 1990; this volume), were examined by combining behavioral and physiological approaches. For example, in experiments designed in the framework of the Eriksen's noise-compatibility paradigm (cf. Eriksen & Eriksen, 1974; see also Eriksen, Coles, Morris & O'Hara, 1985), in which conflict between stimulus features results in a competition between responses, Coles, Gratton and Donchin (1988; cf. also Coles, 1989 and Osman, Bashore, Coles, Donchin & Meyer, in press) have demonstrated that the lateralized part of the readiness potential recorded over the motor cortical areas in human subjects is a good index of subthreshold activation of inappropriate responses. In the "incompatible" condition, the lateralized component of the readiness potential first developed over the motor cortex contralateral to the incorrect response before shifting over to the motor cortex contralateral to the correct response. One may argue, obviously, that this first activation of motor cortical areas does not index the processes by which the response is incorrectly selected but more likely results from the subthreshold activation of the processes by which the programming and execution of this incorrect response are controlled. In a recent study, however, Riehle, Miller and Requin (1991) have shown that in a go/no go task designed according to the same logic, the primary motor cortex neurons which were directly involved in controlling movement execution did not change their activity during the no/go trials, suggesting that the cortical activation found during inappropriate (i.e. either incompatible or no/go) responses expressed an earlier stage of motor control processes.

The effects of manipulating response probability were analyzed by Requin, Lecas and Vitton (1990; cf. also Lecas, Requin, Anger & Vitton, 1986) in monkeys trained to perform a visuo-manual pointing-task in a between-hands choice RT procedure (i.e. when the biomechanical features of the movement to be performed by either hand did not change). It was shown that changes in preparation-related neuronal activity were closely related to the changes induced experimentally with probabilities for either hand to perform the movement and, thus, to changes in RT. Although they were found more often in the posterior parietal association cortex than in the premotor cortex and more often in the latter than in the motor cortex (cf. Figure 3), these probability-related neurons cannot be considered as characterizing specifically one cortical region.

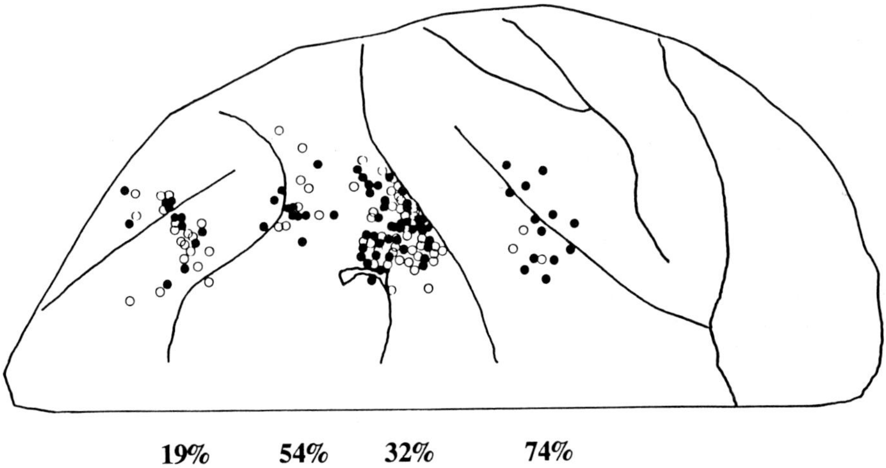

Figure 3: Anatomical location of neurons which showed preparation-related (black circles) and execution-related (open circles) changes in activity. Percentage of neurons of the first type is indicated for each of the 4 cortical areas explored (*adapted from Requin et al., Neuroscience Letters, 1990*)

For ten years, the development of methods to analyze neuronal activity in behaving monkeys has led to the discovery of an increasing number of brain processes which occur during the execution of sensorimotor tasks, but whose timing and features, being unrelated to any partition of the sensory inputs and motor outputs, are hardly explainable without refering to the notion of conceptual representations of action goals. At the same time, the traditional conception in which association cortical areas are mainly, even exclusively responsible for implementing this highest representational function is increasingly challenged by data which strongly suggest that such a function could be widely distributed in a neuronal network throughout a large set of neocortical structures, including the premotor and primary motor cortex.

3. NEURAL REPRESENTATION OF MOVEMENT FEATURES

At the intermediary level of representation, which may be called "syntactic", motor actions are represented in a non-motoric, parametric and subsymbolic mode, and do not give rise to conscious experience. Non-motoric means that the content of this representation, although structured in terms of the features specifying classes of motor activities rather than movements themselves, are not yet ready to be directly used by the neuromuscular system. Parametric means that these features have, however, some homomorphic relationships with either the physical and/or biomechanical parameters with which movements can be described. Subsymbolic is used - by analogy to the meaning of this word in the connectionist approach (cf. Smolensky, 1988) - to describe the form in which movement features are stored in memory: a subsymbolic mode of representation (or a subconcept) is intermediary between the symbolic mode of representation of cognitive architectures - in which the elementary codes from which the symbol is extracted are no longer retrievable - and an elementary code, which results from a simple translation, as, for example, the translation of one stimulus physical parameter into frequency of neural impulses at the level of peripheral sensory coding. Briefly, the main interesting property of a subsymbolic mode of representation would be to have a certain level of abstraction, although maintaining some relationships with the more elementary and specific codes from which it derives. This could provide the theoretical ground for solving the difficult problem of the translation of movement features, represented in some abstract, non motoric, language, into the language of the neuromuscular system, a criticism which was rightfully and recurrently addressed against the motor program concept. The processes by which these representations of motor features are selected in memory and, then, completed, specified and continuously updated according to the detailed requirements of the forthcoming movement are what is currently called "motor programming" in the information processing models (cf. Schmidt, 1982, 1988).

Before the beginning of the last decade, most of the physiological evidence for a stored representation of motor features from which the subroutines of the motor program are selected was mainly indirect (cf. Brooks, 1979). The notion that movement performance was controlled by a prestructured pattern of neural activities which prescribed movement parameters resulted indeed from an inferential reasoning based upon the analysis of the physiological mechanisms observed during the performance of the movement itself, but not of those which were supposed to be associated with the earlier motor programming process. Such indirect evidence was drawn from three kinds of experimental data. The oldest were probably those showing that electrical stimulations specifically localized in the midpart and lower part of the brain could evoke behaviorally significant sequences of movements. A second set of data were provided by studies showing that well-structured spatio-temporal patterns of electromyographic, spinal or more centrally recorded activities (cf. Grillner, 1975) were observed during the performance of rythmic behaviors, such as locomotion, even when motor outputs were artificially blocked at the peripheral level. The last, and well-known, line of indirect evidence was drawn from studies demonstrating that skilled and well-organized movements or, even, movement sequences, can be performed when sensory feedbacks are disrupted (cf. Bizzi, 1980; Evarts, Bizzi, Burke, Delong & Thach, 1971).

Although such kind of data may be viewed as strongly suggesting a central pattern generator or motor program interpretation, the lack of any direct experimental support for the neural mechanisms of the motor programming process itself left the door open for any likely alternative explanation of movement production. Such an alternative explanation was proposed by proponents of action view when they claimed that the motor program remained an assumption and that order, regularity and invariant features of motor outputs are shaped through the synergy of biological and environmental constraints in a continuous dynamical perspective.

This is the main reason for considering experimental findings collected by recording the activity of neural structures during tasks designed in the framework of the preparation paradigm as directly relevant for the motor programming concept. Here, the neural processes underlying the preparatory phase and the execution phase of movement performance can be dissociated in time and separately analyzed. Provided, first, that the neural processes occurring during the planning period can be modulated by experimentally manipulating prior information about the features of the forthcoming movement, and, second, that these modulations are found to correlate with movement performance speed or accuracy. The rationale of the preparation paradigm necessarily implies the notion of representation. The role of the first, preparatory event is to select in, and to extract from memory the representation of one or several movement features, which will be utilized, after the remaining movement features are selected when the second, imperative event occurs, to assembly the motor program. The greater the number of movement features so preselected and the most accurate this presection process, the faster the program assembling process and the shorter the time to initiate movement performance (cf. Rosenbaum, 1983; Lépine, Glencross & Requin, 1989).

In the framework of this preparation paradigm, the study of neuronal activity related to the programming of movement parameters was initiated by the work of Evarts and his colleagues (for reviews see Evarts, 1984 and Evarts, Shinoda & Wise, 1984). They developed a prototypic behavioral situation, similar to the RT protocols used with humans, in which monkeys were trained to push or pull a handle by either flexing or extending the forearm. The preparatory stimulus indicated to the animal whether a pull or push was required after the imperative stimulus. During the preparatory period a large number of pyramidal as well as non-pyramidal tract neurons of the motor cortex (area 4) exhibited changes in their resting discharge frequency, which depended upon advance information provided to the animal about the direction, i.e. flexion vs extension, of the forthcoming movement. The neurons that controlled the muscles to be activated exhibited an increase in their activity, while a decrease in activity was found for neurons that controlled the muscles to be relaxed during movement performance. Similar data were subsequently found, by using not only monoarticular but also polyarticular movements, in the premotor cortex, i.e. the lateral part of area 6 (Godschalk & Lemon, 1983; Wise, 1984; Wise & Mauritz, 1985; Wise, Weinrich & Mauritz, 1986), as well as in the supplementary motor area, i.e. the medial part of area 6 (Tanji, Taniguchi & Saga, 1980; Kurata & Tanji, 1985; Tanji & Kurata, 1982).

Such an implication of motor and premotor cortical areas in the programming of movement direction has been confirmed indirectly by using transcortical reflex techniques in human subjects. Changes in the amplitude of the late components of the EMG response to muscle stretch were analyzed during the preparatory period in a procedure requiring the performance of a wrist movement. It was shown that the late components of the long-loop reflex were differently modulated when movement direction was precued, being consistently larger when the stretched muscle was precued as an agonist than as an antagonist in performing the forthcoming movement (Bonnet, 1983; Bonnet, Requin & Stelmach, 1991). Note that when movement extent was precued, no such a differential effect was found.

While evidencing the possibility to evoke in a large set of cortical structures some representation of the movement parameters which could be then incorporated into the motor program, this ensemble of data suffered from various weakness with regard to the constraints of the preparation paradigm. First, although changes in neuronal activity were observed before movement execution and were found to be sensitive to one parameter of the forthcoming movement, there was no direct evidence for their predictive value for performance speed and/or accuracy. Second, advance information about only movement direction, i.e. a kinematic parameter, was shown to result in changes in neuronal activity, and moreover, most often when movement direction was a dimension confounded with the reciprocal activation of antagonistic muscles.

By adapting to monkeys the movement dimension precuing technique used in human subjects (cf. Rosenbaum, 1983; Lépine, Glencross & Requin, 1989), preparation-related changes in the neuronal activity of the motor and premotor cortex have been examined in detail by Riehle and Requin (1989). Reaction times (RT), as well as changes in neuronal activity of the premotor cortex were analyzed as a function of information provided by the preparatory signal on the parameters of the forthcoming movement. As shown in Figure 4, two patterns of results were found. For one monkey,

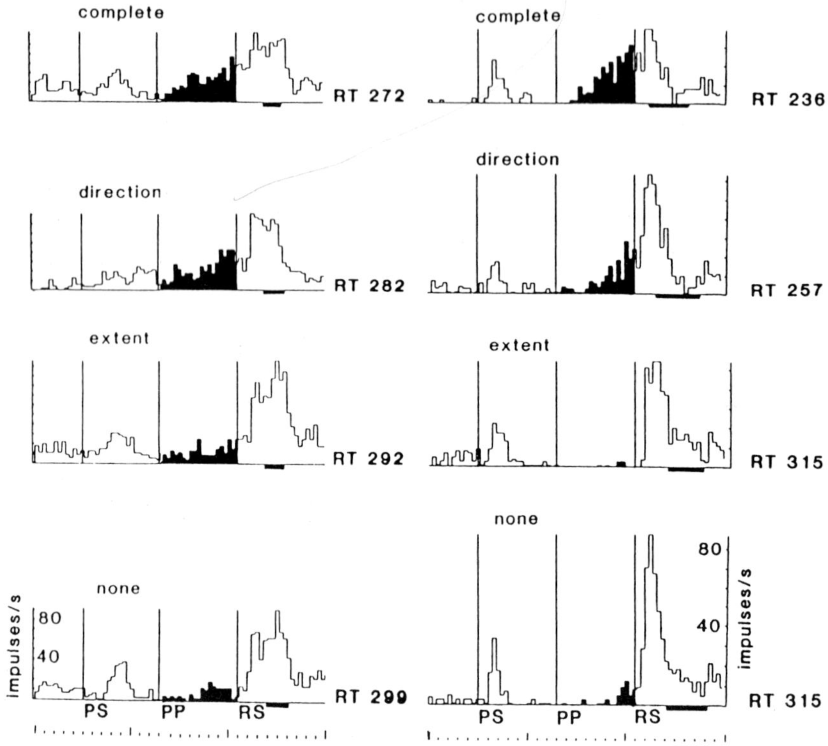

Figure 4: Changes in activity of two directionally selective, preparation-related neurons in area 6 during four conditions of advance information when the same movement was performed. Averaged reaction time (RT) in each condition is indicated. Data on the left fits a serial, non ordered model of the programming process. Data on the right fits a serial, hierarchical model of programming process, in which the extent cannot be specified before direction. Horizontal black bars indicate movement duration; time base: 100 ms; PS: preparatory signal; RS: response signal (*adapted from Requin et al., in D.E. Meyer & S. Kornblum (eds.), Attention and Performance XIV, Hillsdale: Lawrence Erlbaum, in press*)

data were compatible with a serial model of motor programming: refered to RT when no dimensional information was provided, RT slightly decreased when extent was precued and markedly decreased when direction was precued. These RT shortenings were additive, that is the sum of changes in RT for either parameter approximated the reduction of RT when both parameters were precued together. One can see that changes in neuronal activity during the preparatory period were in agreement with these behavioral data. For the two other monkeys, while the precuing of movement direction resulted in a large decrease in RT associated with significant changes in neuronal activity during the preparatory period, the precuing of movement extent did not reduce RT and, accordingly, no preparation-related changes in neuronal activity were found. However, when only direction was precued, RT was longer than when both parameters were precued - that is RT shortenings were underadditive - a result which is compatible with a hierarchical model of movement programming in which movement extent could not be specified before movement direction. Accordingly, preparation-related changes in activity when both parameters were precued were of greater amplitude than when only movement direction was precued.

Although Alexander and Crutcher (1990) did not find any neuron in the primary motor as well as in the supplementary motor cortex whose preparatory changes in activity were clearly related to a change in the loading conditions in which an elbow movement was performed, these data nevertheless suggest that the representation of a dynamic movement parameter may be evoked by an adequate manipulation of prior information and could be used to build the motor program. They are in agreement with the data collected by Kutas and Donchin ten years ago (1980) who showed in human subjects that the amplitude of the readiness potential recorded before the execution of a limb movement is related to the force to be exerted. Such an effect of the anticipated force to perform the movement on slow brain potentials was recently confirmed by Bonnet and MacKay (1989). Note, along the same lines, it has also been found that precuing the duration of isometric movements was associated with specific changes in the late component of the Contingent Negative Variation (cf. Vidal, Bonnet & Macar, in press).

Moreover, by using trial-by-trial correlation analyses, changes in neuronal activity during the preparatory period were found to be highly predictive for RT, suggesting that these changes are closely associated with the process which participates in movement planning (cf. Riehle & Requin, 1991). The strength of these relationships between the preparatory neuronal activity and performance level depended upon prior information provided about the forthcoming movement. Stronger correlations were found when movement direction was cued contrasted with movement extent. Also, for precued directionally selective neurons, correlations were stronger for the neuron's prefered direction contrasted with the opposite direction. Correlations were of negative sign, i.e. the higher the neuronal activity, the shorter the RT, when neuronal activity increased during the preparatory period and were of positive sign when neuronal activity decreased during the same period. This rule also applied for some neurons that showed an increase in preparatory activity for one direction and a decrease of this activity for the other direction.

By showing that it is possible to evoke and to experimentally manipulate patterns of neuronal activities which have homomorphic relationships with some of the dimensions with which motor outputs can be described, data collected in the frame of the preparation paradigm therefore provide strong support for the motor programming concept. These data also suggest that not only the kinematic but the dynamic parameters of a movement are represented in the motor program. This answers one of the current criticisms against the motor control view, i.e. that only the brain processes associated with the planning of the movement dimensions which would be centrally coded in terms of the topological distribution of the peripheral effectors, could be evidenced.

The possible participation of the prefrontal cortex in implementing the representation of the action goal is suggested by recent data collected during delayed-response tasks designed in the frame of the paradigm assuming that this cortical region is primarily involved in memory processes (cf. Fuster, 1984). Sustained changes in prefrontal neuron activity during the delay between the sensory cue and the response were most often viewed as an index of the storage of the physical features of the stimulus, before it was found to be related to information provided by this stimulus on the features of the delayed response (cf. Boch & Goldberg, 1989; Dehaene & Changeux, 1989; Goldman-Rakic, 1987; Okono & Tanji, 1987; Sawagushi, Matsumara & Kubota, 1989; Yajeya, Quintana & Fuster, 1988; Watanabe, 1986). Even more suggestive of such a participation of the prefrontal cortex in movement planning were the data provided by Barone and Joseph (1989) who have described in the frontal eye field neuronal processes that seem to be closely involved in the control of a sequence of reaching movements to visual targets. After monkeys have learnt the temporal order in the illumination of three differently located targets, they have to perform the sequence of corresponding reaching movements in the correct order. Changes in activity of the so-called "context" neurons were found to depend upon the rank of the illuminated/to

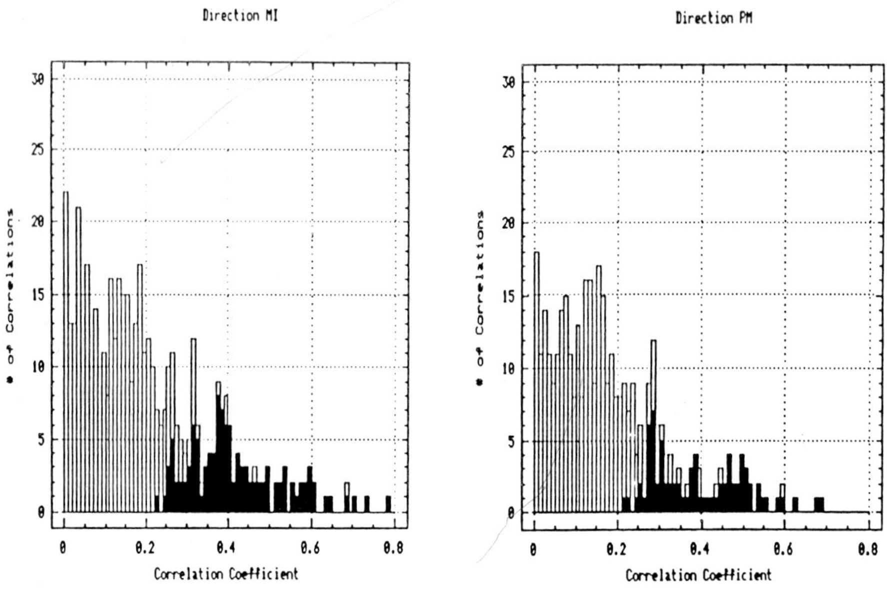

Figure 5: Histograms of trial-by-trial product-moment correlations between neuronal activity during the preparatory period and RT, calculated for 250 neurons in the primary motor cortex (left: MI) and 250 neurons in the premotor cortex (right: PM) in condition of advance information on movement direction. Black columns: statistically significant (p<.05) correlation coefficients; white columns: statistically non significant correlation coefficients (*from Requin et al., in D.E. Meyer & S. Kornblum (eds.), Attention and Performance XIV, Hillsdale: Lawrence Erlbaum, in press*)

be reached target in the sequence, i.e. upon the movements which were already performed and those which remained to be performed. Such neurons therefore appear as good candidates for insuring the mechanism by which the spatio-temporal features of motor planning are up-dated during execution.

To summarize, recent neurophysiological studies suggest, once again, that the representational function implied by the motor program concept is not implemented in a precisely localized anatomical region of the brain, for example the premotor cortex, as currently proposed. Riehle and Requin (1989) have recently compared the roles played in movement preparation by the motor and premotor cortex respectively and concluded that there are quantitative but not qualitative differences between the two structures. Movement-related neurons, preparation-related neurons, as well as neurons sharing both these properties were found to be closely intermixed in both areas, with the proportion of the first class decreasing and the proportion of the second class increasing from the central sulcus to the arcuate sulcus. Moreover, when the predictive value for RT of the preparation-related changes in neuronal activity induced by precuing movement parameters was considered, the number, distribution and strength of correlations were found to differ slightly between the two cortical regions (cf. Figure 5). MacKay and Riehle (this volume) have recently shown that such a conclusion must probably be extended to the posterior parietal areas, thus suggesting that the intermediary level of movement feature representation must also be viewed as distributed in a widely extending neuronal network, which could include not only the premotor and primary motor cortex but also parietal association cortical areas.

4. NEURAL REPRESENTATION OF MOVEMENT COMMANDS

At the lower level of representation, which may be called "phonemic", would be represented the basic movement units, or movement "commands" - in the same sense as that used when saying cortico-spinal commands - which, after being selected according to program instructions, result in the pattern of neuromuscular activations. This process underlies what is called movement execution or motor output. Although the precise relationships of these basic movement units with peripheral effectors, such as controlling muscles, muscle synergies, coordinative structures or, even, pre-structured elementary movements, was and remains controversial, some of their features are logically necessary. Motoric means that the activation of movement commands has mechanical consequences at the periphery. Anatomical means that there is some homomorphic relationships between the distribution of movement units in the central nervous system and the spatial organization of the muscular effectors. Biomechanically-constrained means that the activation of some of the possible patterns of movement units is unlikely because the activation of the corresponding patterns of muscular effectors is excluded by, at least, the biomechanical limitations of the musculo-articulatory system. Neuromuscular refers to the type of language in which movement commands are represented and operate. In contrast to the problems raised by the language in which representations at the higher levels are stored and used, the coding processes by which movement units are activated and communicate with the neuromuscular system, uses obviously the current language of the nervous system, i.e. frequency of neuronal impulses.

Recent neurophysiological studies of the mechanisms by which movement features are controlled during execution (cf. Hepp-Reymond, 1988; Humphrey, 1986) emphasize what is probably one of the major findings of the last decade: the control of movement parameters during execution would result from the cooperative action of large populations of neurons, rather than from the collection of the independent activations of individual neurons, each of them being connected to peripheral effectors in a one-to-one mapping mode. The work of Georgopoulos and his colleagues (Georgopoulos, Kettner & Schwartz, 1988; cf. also Georgopoulos, 1990) is especially relevant in this way (cf. Figure 6).

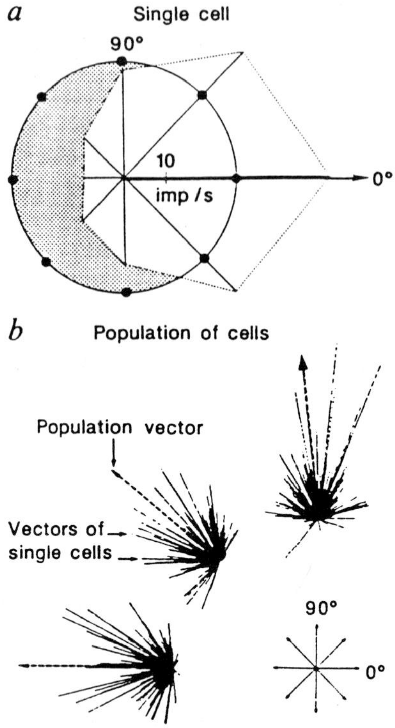

Figure 6: Neuronal activity in the monkey motor cortex when pointing with the hand at one of 8 targets located around the starting position. a: a single neuron is activated for reaches in all 8 directions, but is more active for one (0°) preferred direction (the length of lines from the center is proportional with the neuronal discharge frequency during the movement performed in the corresponding direction). b: when a population of neurons is considered, the "population vector" (dotted line) is the weighted sum of the contributions (i.e. discharge frequencies) of all the neurons when the movement is performed in one direction: the population vector points in this direction (*adapted from Lemon, Nature, 1989)*

Neuronal activity of the motor cortex was recorded when monkeys had to move a handle from a central position to one of different targets located around at the same distance. When the activity of individual neurons in the motor cortex was considered, each neuron was activated for the differently oriented reaching movements, but showed a maximum of activity for a prefered direction. This first finding suggested that one neuron is not fully specialized in controlling movements performed in a particular direction and, conversely, that one neuron could partly be involved in the control of differently oriented movements. Now, if one considers a population of neurons, in which the amount of activation during the execution of a movement in a particular direction differs from one neuron to another, the sum of the contributions of this neuronal population may be represented by a population vector which precisely points in the direction of the movement. These data suggest that movement trajectory is controlled due to the cooperation of a large number of neurons, including neurons whose prefered direction is not that of the movement actually performed.

Although initially demonstrated in the motor cortex, this mode of control of movement trajectory cannot be considered, however, as only characterizing the motor cortex . Very similar data were found in the premotor cortex (cf. Caminiti, Johnson & Urbano, 1990; Caminiti, Johnson, Galli, Ferraina & Burnod, in press), as well as in the posterior parietal area 5 by Kalaska (1988). Together, these data suggest, once again, that even the representation of movement commands is not the privileged function of a highly specialized cortical region - as initially proposed for the primary motor cortex - but widely extends over the neocortex.

5. RECONSIDERING THE FUNCTIONAL ORGANIZATION OF MOTOR CORTICAL AREAS

Not only data provided by studies of the neuronal correlates of action and movement representations support a hierarchical conception of the cognitive processes involved in motor control but, more importantly, they add to the current reconsideration of the classical views on the anatomical separation of these cognitive functions. This applies to the macroanatomical level of cortical structures and microanatomical level of neuronal units. These classical views about the link between neural structures and behavioral functions are being seriously reconsidered because of the pressure of three emerging concepts.

One is the functional heterogeneity of neural structures that is being found at the macroanatomical level of large areas: neurons involved in the implementation of the same behavioral function are found in several different areas, although in varying proportions. Conversely, functionally different populations of neurons can be found within the same cortical area. For example, the recent discovery in area 4 (cf. Kwan, MacKay, Murphy & Wong, 1985; Riehle, 1991; Wannier, Maier & Hepp-Reymond, 1989) of neurons which are selectively activated by the presentation of a visual stimulus, provided that their stimulus is a relevant one for executing a movement, confirms that the motor cortex is far from beeing the "keyboard" which is activated for producing corticospinal commands, but is undoubtedly involved in the translating function between perceptual and motor processing. Thus, the notion of a rigid functional specialization of cortical areas appears to be suspect, not only when the complex cortical association areas are considered, but even in the primary sensory and motor areas: functional differences between cortical regions must be viewed as more quantitative than qualitative (Goldman-Rakic, 1988; Requin, Riehle & Seal, 1988).

The second concept that is emerging is the continuum of function for neuronal populations: the notion that each neuron is highly specialized for contributing to the implementation of a particular function, and, thus, that neurons can be classified into discrete functional categories, must be abandoned: functional differences between neurons must similarly be viewed as more quantitative than qualitative, i.e. a neuron may be more or less involved in implementing different functions (cf. Bruce & Goldberg, 1985; Requin, Riehle & Seal, 1988).

Closely related to such a low functional specification of neuronal units, is the third concept of functional cooperation of neuronal populations in the implementation of the same function. The resulting idea that the activation of one neuron makes sense only when considered in relation to the activation of other neurons suggests two possible mechanisms by which a sensory or motor event could be coded within a neuronal population. In a first concept, this coding would result in the sum of the activations of individuals neurons. In such case, differences in activation between neurons, as well as temporal variability in the activation level of each neuron, could thus express some trade-off function between neurons in order to maintain the amount of activation of the whole neuronal population constant: a decrease in activation of one neuron would be compensated by an increase in activation of another neuron. In a second concept, the coding process would result in the spatio-temporal pattern of the activation of the neuronal population, so that the activation level of each neuron would express the specific participation of this particular neuron in the functional cooperation between the elements of the whole neuronal population.

For some years, revised views of the correlation between the structural and functional aspects of the brain have been stimulated mainly by the influential conception of a modular organization of the neocortex (Mountcastle, 1978; but see Swindale, 1990 and Douglas & Martin, 1991). In the modular concept, all cortical areas are formed by aggregates of similar units or modules with the same neuronal circuitry and performing the same basic operation. Networks of modules, which are delimited by the extent of the extramodular input and output connections, are distributed throughout the cortex, or at least a large part of it, and the functions implemented in different networks would depend upon the relative weighting of these extramodular connections. Of course, this does not imply that the whole cerebral cortex is an entirely homogenous structure, nor that each neuron is totally unspecific in its functional involvement. Quantitatively different functions between neurons, resulting in variations in the statistical parameters of neuronal populations (cf. Requin, Riehle & Seal, 1988, in press), make the existence of topographical differences in function between cortical regions compatible with the distributive parallel network concept (cf. Goldman-Rakic, 1988).

Such a view of cortical organization appears to be particularly appropriate for integrating the two main aspects of neurophysiological data on movement representations. First, the continuum of function for individual neurons implies that each representational function is necessarily implemented in a large neuronal population. Second, the distribution of each representational function over different cortical areas implies that different representational functions overlap in the same cortical area. In order to develop this conception further, we need to understand how the cognitive processes underlying the planning of motor actions are brought into play, either continuously or in a hierarchical sequence - as suggested above - by the network organization of the neocortex. One may suggest that, now, the key step to take towards this understanding is to be looked for in the microstructural organization of the cortical tissue - i.e. the functional cooperation between neurons at the modular level - rather than in the interrelationships between macroanatomically defined cortical regions. In this perspective, recent technological improvements making possible to record simultaneously the activities of a small neuronal population within a cortical area of size comparable to that of a cortical column (cf. Mountcastle, Reitboeck, Poggio & Steinmetz, 1991) provide a powerful tool to get a deeper insight into the functional micro organization of the cerebral cortex.

5. ACKNOWLEDGEMENT

This work was supported by grant N 00014-89-J-1557 from the Office of Naval Research

6. REFERENCES

Alexander, G.E. & Crutcher, M.D. (1990). Preparation for movement: neural representations of intended direction in three motor areas of the monkey. **Journal of Neurophysiology, 64**, 133-150.

Allen, G.I. & Tsukahara, N. (1974). Cerebro-cerebellar communication systems. **Physiological Reviews, 54**, 957-1006.

Andersen, R.A. (1989). Visual and eye movement functions of the posterior parietal cortex. **Annual Review of Neuroscience, 12**, 377-403.

Andersen, R.A., Essick, G.K., & Siegel, R.M. (1987). Neurons of area 7 activated by both visual stimuli and oculomotor behavior. **Experimental Brain Research, 67**, 316-322.

Barone, P. & Joseph, J.P. (1989). Prefrontal cortex and spatial sequencing in Macaque monkey. **Experimental Brain Research, 78**, 447-464.

Bizzi, E. (1980) Central and peripheral mechanisms in motor control. In G.E. Stelmach & J. Requin (Eds.), **Tutorials in Motor Behavior**, North-Holland: Amsterdam, pp. 131-143.

Boch, R.A., & Goldberg, M.E. (1989). Participation of prefrontal neurons in the preparation of visually guided eye movements in the Rhesus monkey. **Journal of Neurophysiology, 61**, 1064-1084.

Bonnet, M. (1983). Anticipatory changes of long latency stretch responses during preparation for directional hand movements, **Brain Research, 280**, 51-62.

Bonnet, M. & MacKay, W.A. (1989). Changes in CNV and reaction time related to precueing of direction and force of a forearm movement, **Brain, Behavior and Evolution, 33**, 147-152.

Bonnet, M., Requin, J. & Stelmach, G.E. (1991). Changes in electromyographic responses to muscle stretch, related to the programming of movement spatial parameters. **EEG and Clinical Neurophysiology, 81**, 135-151.

Brooks, V.B. (1979). Motor programs revisited. In R.E. Talbott & D.R. Humphrey (Eds.), **Posture and Movement**. Raven Press: New York, pp. 13-49.

Bruce, C.J. & Goldberg, M.E. (1985). Primate frontal eye fields. I. Single neurons discharging before saccades. **Journal of Neurophysiology, 53**, 603-635.

Caminiti, R., Johnson, P.B. & Urbano, A. (1990). Making arm movements within different parts of space: dynamic aspects in the primate motor cortex. **Journal of Neuroscience, 10**, 2039-2058.

Caminiti, R., Johnson, P.B., Galli, C., Ferraina, S. & Burnod, Y. Making arm movements within different parts of space: the premotor and motor cortical representation of a coordinate system for reaching two visual targets. **Journal of Neuroscience**, in press.

Coles, M.G.H. (1989). Modern mind-brain reading: psychophysiology, physiology, and cognition. **Psychophysiology, 26**, 251-269.

Coles, M.G.H., Gratton, C. & Donchin, E. (1988). Detecting early communication: using measures of movement-related potentials to illuminate human information processing, **Biological Psychology, 26**, 69-89.

Dehaene, S. & Changeux, J.P. (1989). A simple model of prefrontal cortex function in delayed-response tasks. **Journal of Cognitive Neuroscience, 1**, 244-261.

Douglas, R.J. & Martin, K.A.C. (1991). Opening the grey box. **Trends in Neuroscience, 14**, 286-293.

Eriksen, B.A. & Eriksen, C.W. (1974). Effects of noise letters upon the identification of target letter in visual search, **Perception and Psychophysics, 16**, 143-149.

Eriksen, C.W., Coles, M.G.H., Morris, L.R. & O'Hara, W.P. (1985). An electromyographic examination of response competition, **Bulletin of the Psychonomic Society, 23**, 165-168.

Evarts, E.V. (1984). Neurophysiological approaches to brain mechanisms for preparatory set. In S. Kornblum & J. Requin (Eds.), **Preparatory States and Processes**. Hillsdale: Lawrence Erlbaum, pp. 137-153.

Evarts, E.V., Shinoda, Y., & Wise, S.P. (1984). **Neurophysiological approaches to higher brain functions**. New-York: Wiley and Sons.

Evarts, E.V., Bizzi, E., Burke, R.E., Delong, M., & Thach, W.T. (1971). Central control of movement. **Neurosciences Research Program Bulletin, 9**, n° 1.

Fuster, J.M. (1984). Behavioral electrophysiology of the prefrontal cortex. **Trends in Neuroscience, 7**, 408-414.

Georgopoulos, A.P. (1990). Neurophysiology of reaching. In M. Jeannerod (Ed.), **Attention and Performance XIII**. Hillsdale: Lawrence Erlbaum, pp. 227-263.

Georgopoulos, A.P., Kettner, R.E. & Schwartz, A.B. (1988). Primate motor cortex and free arm movements to visual targets in three-dimensional space. II. Coding of the direction of movement by a neuronal population. **Journal of Neuroscience, 8**, 2928-2937.

Godschalk, M., & Lemon, R.N. (1983). Involvement of monkey premotor cortex in the preparation of arm movements. **Experimental Brain Research , suppl. 7**, 114-119.

Goldman-Rakic, P.S. (1987). Motor control function of the prefrontal cortex. In **Motor areas of the cerebral cortex**. New-York: Wiley and Sons, pp. 187-200.

Goldman-Rakic, P.S. (1988). Topography of cognition: parallel distributed networks in primate associative cortex. **Annual Review of Neuroscience, 11**, 137-156.

Grillner, S. (1975). Locomotion in vertebrates: central mechanisms and reflex interactions, **Physiological Reviews, 55**, 247-304.

Hepp-Reymond, M.C. (1988). Functional organization of motor cortex and its participation in voluntary movements. In H.D. Steklis & J. Erwin (Eds.), **Comparative primate biology**, vol. 4. New-York: Alan R. Liss, pp. 501-624.

Humphrey, D.R. (1986). Representation of movements and muscles within the primate precentral motor cortex: historical and current perspectives. **Federation Proceedings, 45**, 2687-2699.

Jeannerod, M. (1990). A neurophysiological model for the directional coding of reaching movements. In J. Paillard (Ed.), **Brain and Space**. Oxford University Press, pp. 49-69.

Kalaska, J.F. (1988). The representation of arm movements in postcentral and parietal cortex. **Canadian Journal of Physiology and Pharmacology, 66**, 455-463.

Keele, S.W., Cohen, A., & Ivry, R. (1990). Motor programs: concepts and issues. In M. Jeannerod (Ed.), **Attention and Performance XIII**. Hillsdale: Lawrence Erlbaum Associates, pp. 77-110.

Kornblum, S., Hasbroucq, T., & Osman, A. (1990). Dimensional overlap: cognitive basis for stimulus-response compatibility: a model and taxonomy. **Psychological Review, 97**, 253-270.

Kurata, K., & Tanji, J. (1985). Contrasting neuronal activity in supplementary and precentral motor cortex of monkeys. II. Responses to movement triggering vs nontriggering sensory signals. **Journal of Neurophysiology, 53**, 142-152.

Kutas, M. & Donchin, E. (1980). Preparation to respond as manifested by movement-related brain potentials, **Brain Research, 202**, 95-115.

Kwan, H.C., MacKay, W.A., Murphy, J.T., & Wong, Y.C. (1985). Properties of visual cues responses in primate precentral cortex. **Brain Research, 343**, 24-35.

Lashley, K.S. (1951) The problem of serial order in behavior. In L.A. Jeffress (Ed.), **Central mechanisms in behavior**. New-York: Wiley.

Lecas, J.C., Requin, J., Anger, C. & Vitton, N. (1986). Changes in neuronal activity of the monkey precentral cortex during preparation for movement. **Journal of Neurophysiology, 56**, 1680-1702.

Lemon, R. (1989). Cognitive control of movement, **Nature, 337**, 410-411.

Lépine, D., Glencross, D. & Requin, J. (1989). Some experimental evidence for and against a parametric conception of movement programming. **Journal of Experimental Psychology: HPP, 15**, 347-362.

Lynch, J.C. (1980). The functional organization of posterior parietal association cortex. **Behavioral and Brain Sciences, 3**, 485-534.

Meyer, D.E., Osman, A.M., Irwin, D.E. & Yantis, S. (1988). Modern mental chronometry. In B. Renault, M. Kutas, M.G.M. Coles & A.W.K. Gaillard (Eds.), **Event related potential investigations of cognition**. Amsterdam: North-Holland, pp. 3-67

Miller, J.O. (1988). Discrete and continuous models of human information processing: theoretical distinctions and empirical results. **Acta Psychologica, 67**, 191-257.

Mountcastle, V.B. (1976). The world around us: Neural command functions for selective attention. **Neuroscience Research Progress Bulletin, 14**, suppl. 1, 1-47.

Mountcastle, V.B. (1978). An organizing principle for cerebral function: the unit module and the distributed system. In F.O. Schmitt & F.G. Worden (Eds.), **The Neurosciences. Fourth Study Program**. Cambridge: MIT Press, pp. 21-42..

Mountcastle, V.B. (1986). The neural mechanisms of cognitive functions can now be studied directly. **Trends in Neurosciences, 9**, 505-508.

Mountcastle, V.B., Reitboeck, H.J., Poggio, G.F. & Steinmetz, M.A. (1991). Adaptation of the Reitboeck method of multiple microelectrode recording to the neocortex of the waking monkey. **Journal of Neuroscience Methods, 36**, 77-84.

Mountcastle, V.B., Lynch, J.C., Georgopoulos, A., Sakata, H. & Acuna, C. (1975). Posterior parietal association cortex of the monkey: command functions for operations within extrapersonal space. **Journal of Neurophysiology, 38**, 871-908.

Okono, K. & Tanji, J. (1987). Neuronal activities in the primate motor fields of the agranular frontal cortex preceding visually triggered and self-paced movements. **Experimental Brain Research, 66**, 155-166.

Osman, A.M., Bashore, T.R., Coles, M.G.H., Donchin, E. & Meyer, D.E. On the transmission of partial information: inferences from movement-related brain potentials. **Journal of Experimental Psychology:HPP, 16**, in press.

Paillard, J. (1982). Apraxia and neurophysiology of motor control. **Philosophical Transactions, Royal Society of London. B 298**, 111-134.

Requin, J. (1980). Toward a psychobiology of preparation for action. In G.E. Stelmach & J. Requin (Eds.), **Tutorials in motor behavior**. Amsterdam: North-Holland, pp. 373-398.

Requin, J. (1982). The meaning of an experiment combining cognitive and neurobiological approaches. In J. Mehler, S. Walker & A. Garrett (Eds.), **Perspectives on Mental Representation.** Hillsdale: Lawrence Erlbaum.

Requin, J. (1985). Looking forward to moving soon. Ante factum selective processes in motor control. In M. Posner O. Marin (Eds.), **Attention and Performance XI.** Hillsdale: Lawrence Erlbaum, pp. 147-167.

Requin, J., Brener, J. & Ring, C. (1991). Preparation for action. In J.R. Jennings & M.G.H. Coles (Eds.), **Handbook of Cognitive Psychophysiology: Central and Autonomic Nervous System Approaches**. New-York: Wiley, pp. 357-448.

Requin, J., Lecas, J.C. & Vitton, N. (1990). A comparison of preparation-related neuronal activity changes in the prefrontal, premotor, primary motor and

posterior parietal areas of the monkey cortex: preliminary results. **Neuroscience Letters, 111**, 151-156.
Requin, J., Riehle, A. & Seal, J. (1988). Neuronal activity and information processing in motor control: from stages to continuous flow. **Biological Psychology, 26**, 179-198.
Requin, J., Riehle, A. & Seal, J. Neuronal networks for movement preparation. In D.E. Meyer and S. Kornblum (Eds.), **Attention and Performace XIV**. Hillsdale: Lawrence Erlbaum, in press.
Riehle, A. (1991). Visually-induced signal-locked neuronal activity changes in precentral motor areas of the monkey: hierarchical progression of signal processing. **Brain Research, 540**, 131-137.
Riehle, A. & Requin, J. (1989). Monkey primary motor and premotor cortex: single-cell activity related to prior information about direction and extent of an intended movement. **Journal of Neurophysiology, 61** (3), 534-549.
Riehle, A. & Requin, J. (1991). Correlation between neuronal preparatory activity and reaction time. **European Journal of Neuroscience**, suppl. 4, 312.
Riehle, A., Miller, J. & Requin, J., 1991. Partial transmission of sensorimotor information in the cerebral cortex. **European Journal of Neuroscience**, suppl. 4, 311.
Rizzolatti, G., Camarda, R., Fogassi, L., Gentilucci, M., Luppino, G & Matelli, M. (1988). Functional organization of inferior area 6 in the macaque monkey. **Experimental Brain Research, 71**, 491-507.
Roland, P.E. (1985). Cortical organization of voluntary behavior in man. **Human Neurobiology, 4**, 155-167.
Rosenbaum, D.A. (1983). The movement precuing technique; assumptions, applications and extensions. In R.A. Magill (Ed.), **Memory and control in motor behavior**. Amsterdam: North-Holland, pp. 231-274.
Rosenbaum, D.A. (1987). Successive approximations to a model of human movement programming. In G. Bower (Ed.), **The psychology of learning and motivation**. New-York: Academic Press, pp. 153-182.
Sawaguchi, T., Matsumara, M. & Kubota, K. (1989). Depth distribution of neuronal activity related to a visual reaction time task with monkey prefrontal cortex. **Journal of Neurophysiology, 61**, 435-446.
Schmidt, R.A. (1982). **Motor control and learning. A behavioral emphasis,** Champaign: Human Kinetics Press.
Schmidt, R.A. (1988). Motor and action perspectives in motor behaviour. In O.G. Meijer & K. Roth (Eds.), **Complex movement behavior; the motor-action controversy**. Amsterdam: North-Holland, pp. 3-44.
Seal, J. (1989). Sensory and motor functions of the superior parietal cortex of the monkey as revealed by single neuron recordings. **Brain, Behavior and Evolution, 33**, 113-117.
Seal, J. & Requin, J. (1987). Sensory to motor transformation within area 5 of the posterior parietal cortex in the monkey. **Society for Neuroscience Abstracts 13**, part 1, p. 673.
Seal, J., Gross, C. & Bioulac, B. (1982). Activity of neurons in area 5 during a single arm movement in monkeys before and after deafferentation of the trained limb. **Brain Research, 280**, 229-243.
Shaffer, L.H. (1982). Rhythm and timing in skill. **Psychological Review, 89**, 102-122.
Smolensky, P. (1988). On the proper treatment of connectionism. **Behavioral and Brain Sciences, 11**, 1-74.
Sternberg, S. (1969). The discovery of processing stages: extensions of Donder's method. **Acta Psychologica, 30**, 276-315.
Swindale, N.V. (1990). Is the cerebral cortex modular ? **Trends in Neuroscience, 13**, 487-492.

Tanji, J. & Kurata, K. (1982). Comparison of movement-related activity in two cortical motor areas of primates. **Journal of Neurophysiology, 48**, 633-653.

Tanji, J., Taniguchi, J.& Saga, T. (1980). Supplementary motor area: neuronal responses to motor instructions. **Journal of Neurophysiology, 44**, 60-68.

Vidal, F., Bonnet, M. & Macar, F. Programming response duration in a precueing reaction time paradigm, **Journal of Motor Behavior**, in press.

Von Monakow, C. (1914). **Die Lokalisation im Grosshirn und der Abbau der Funktion durch kortikale Herde**. Wiesbaden: Bergman.

Wannier, T.M.J., Maier, M.A. & Hepp-Reymond, M.C. (1989). Responses of motor cortex neurons to visual stimulation in the alert monkey. **Neuroscience Letters, 98**, 63-68.

Watanabe, M. (1986). Prefrontal unit activity during delayed conditional go/no go discrimination in the monkey. II. Relation to go and no go responses. **Brain Research, 382**, 15-27.

Wiesendanger, M. (1990). The motor cortical areas and the problem of hierarchies. In M. Jeannerod (Ed.), **Attention and Performance XIII**. Hillsdale: Lawrence Erlbaum, pp. 59-75.

Wise, S.P. (1984). The non-primary motor cortex and its role in the cerebral control of movement. In G. Edelman, W. Cowan & E. Gall (Eds.), **Dynamic aspects of cortical function**. New-York: Wiley, pp. 525-555.

Wise, S.P. & Mauritz, K.H. (1985). Set-related neuronal activity in the premotor cortex of rhesus monkey:effects of changes in motor set. **Proceedings of the Royal Society of London, B 223**, 331-354.

Wise, S.P., Weinrich, M. & Mauritz, K.H. (1986). Movement-related activity in the premotor cortex of rhesus macaques. In H.J. Freund, U. Buttner, B. Cohen & J. Noth (Eds.), **Progress in Brain Research 4**. Amsterdam: Elsevier, pp. 117-131.

Yajeya, J., Quintana, J. & Fuster, J.M. (1988). Prefrontal representation of stimulus attributes. II. The role of behavioral significance. **Brain Research, 474**, 222-230.

Tutorials in Motor Behavior II
G.E. Stelmach and J. Requin (Editors)

MOTOR PROGRAMMING AND CONTROL

L Henry Shaffer

Department of Psychology, University of Exeter,
Exeter, Devon, EX4 4QG, UK

Abstract

A concept of motor programming is discussed from first principles. The discussion takes speech as a paradigm skill exhibiting the major properties of programming, and thus providing a perspective from which to consider alternative ideas of programming. A basic analysis of speech requires us to consider two levels in its organization: a cognitive level organizing linguistic structures and a motor level implementing speech sequences through movements in the vocal tract. Speech programming is described as a dynamic cognitive process deriving structured seqences of motor goals from a semantic intention. In keeping with current theory of motor control, the motor system in speech is assumed to be able to compute autonomously the details of movements from an abstract specification of their phonetic goals. The concept of motor programming enables us to give a systematic account of speech errors, and the analysis of these errors in turn reveals a hierarchic structure in speech programs.

1. MOTOR PROGRAMMING

The term motor programming is nowadays used so loosely it is in danger of losing its meaning. There is basic agreement that motor programming plays a role in organizing skilled action, but the questions of what is this role, and whether programming occurs in all skilled action may be answered very differently by different theorists. It has even been suggested that motor programming is a redundant concept distracting attention from the dynamic interactions of an organism with its environment (Michaels and Carello, 1981). It would be a tedious exercise trying to tease out the strands of argument that have led to this state, and it seems more productive in the time available to consider the concept fundamentally, starting with the phenomena that gave rise to it in the first place. As soon as one attempts this it becomes apparent that the concept has to be defined in relation to a theory of the motor system. As it happens, current theory allows us to distinguish between programming of action and computation of movement, and assign the latter fully to the motor system.

Much of the initial impetus for a theory of motor programming arose from studying speech (Fromkin, 1971; Lashley, 1951). In saying "I regard your question as imprecise", it appears that the speaker formulates a semantic intention and communicates it as a sound pattern. To get from intention to sound the brain must form a symbolic representation, with appropriate syntax, of the semantic entity and translate this into a pattern of movement involving the respiratory system and vocal tract. The muscles effecting movement know nothing about natural language or its meaning and must be instructed what to do in a muscle language. Stated in general terms, this is the problem of getting a robot to perform a motor task. The logical order of translating a linguistic intention into a motor language implies a temporally ordered process. Motor programming is understood here as this process of formulating an intended action in an appropriate motor language.

To say that an action is intended does not explain it, it only provides a theoretical marker indicating that the action is not fully determined by its context. In general, skilled action is almost never fully constrained by the environment and is often created under conditions of almost limitless choice. Similarly, saying that an action is preceded in the brain by its symbolic representation has no explanatory force, but it can acquire this if we specify the symbol structure. For instance, the above sentence was actually spoken in conversation as "I disregard your question as precise" (Fromkin, 1973). The intention and the nature of its corruption in the speech process are clear. We can see that in forming the utterance an element of negation has shifted from the concept "precise" to the concept "regard", and has been realized as a different affix from the one appropriate to the target word, "dis-" instead of "im-". This implies that in a speech program negation is represented abstractly at one level, and acquires a phonological form in a derived level. We are led to understand through such examples that speech programming unfolds according to linguistic rules in successive levels of decreasing abstraction.

Taking this idea to its extreme, motor programming might be conceived as a process deriving muscle commands from an intention. Such a theory for speech production was adumbrated by certain linguists in the 1960s (Liberman, Cooper, Shankweiler and Studdert-Kennedy, 1967). They were primarily concerned with a motor theory of speech perception and only indirectly with speech production. They simply took a then current linguistic theory of generative grammar to its logical conclusion and allowed an utterance to unpack by rule through successive levels of linguistic, phonological and muscular detail to produce speech sound. It is not difficult to fault such a theory: it takes no account of the dynamics of movement or of its adaptiveness to environmental contingencies. We know, for instance, that the sound output of speech is little affected by ongoing changes in head and trunk posture, or by unusual loads or obstacles in the vocal tract (MacNeilage, 1980). The rules needed to allow such adaptiveness would proliferate endlessly. Kugler and Turvey (1987) and others have exposed the inadequacy of such theories, but this is largely a straw-man exercise since no serious motor-control theorist holds them.

Considering speech as a system translating language into sound, we are led to postulate two distinct systems organizing it in the brain, a cognitive system organizing symbolic representations of linguistic goals and a motor system organizing movements in the vocal tract to realize these goals. In general, we suppose that flexibility in planning the structure of an action arises solely in the cognitive system, and the flexibility of its motor execution arises solely in the motor system. Modern theories of motor skill often assume this broad division of responsibility though they may differ in the details of its allocation. Where the boundary of allocation is placed depends on what one assumes to be specified in the representation of a motor goal. For instance, in discussing the organization of speech MacNeilage (1970) suggested that a goal in a motor program describes a configuration of the vocal tract. In the light of later evidence he was led to suppose that it describes the motorically more abstract event of a speech sound in an equivalence class (MacNeilage, 1980). Note that in either case the goal is far removed from specifying details of muscle action.

In principle, if an organism has to be able to improvise action in a wide variety of tasks, it is desirable that the planning of action should be unencumbered by the need to consider details of its execution (Sacerdoti, 1974). Thus, for any motor skill, a goal described in a motor program should be sufficiently abstract that it can be realized in all likely physical contexts. This requires that the motor system has the capacity to compute appropriate movements in all such contexts, and the recent theory of motor systems shows this to be feasible (Bullock and Grossberg, 1988; Hinton, 1984; Kugler and Turvey, 1987; Morasso, this volume; Morasso and Tagliasco,1986; Saltzman and Kelso, 1987).

Taking the abstract conception of a goal as the starting point, we can define motor programming as the cognitive (ie symbolic) processing involved in organizing and representing the goal structure of an intended action, and a motor program as the manifold representation of this goal structure.

To get some idea of what is now assumed of the motor system, consider an example from speech. It is observable that speakers can spontaneously adapt the clarity of their articulation to the ambient noise. On the present assumption this adaptation is achieved by the motor system. It is supposed that the motor system knows the acoustic consequences of articulatory gestures, and can modify the latter given feedback of the signal-to-noise ratio of its speech output. It is also observable that speakers tend to articulate more clearly when speaking to foreigners, children and the hard of hearing. Here adaptation seems based on a cognitive appraisal of the listener. We are led to different accounts of similar phenomena, but this is needed for a complete theory of skill. A motor system can compute a default motor solution for a given task and context, but can compute other solutions on instruction from a motor program. The importance of this assumption will be seen when we consider more generally the shaping of skilled movement.

Given the centrality of speech among human skills, it is convenient to take it as a paradigm skill and consider motor programming from this perspective. The following points, relevant to any skill that involves motor programming, arise from and expand the definition of a motor program:

(a) The definition takes sides in the issue of whether a motor program is a declaration or a procedure. Motor programs have at different times been identified with two distinct metaphors. One is that of a theatre program, which is a declaration of intent; the other is that of a computer program, which contains the procedures for realizing an intent. The latter was used, for instance, by Rumelhart and Norman (1982) in their simulation modelling of typing performance. There are several reasons, however, for preferring the former. The most obvious is that we have already allocated the implementation of action to the motor system, and thus suppose that it contains much of the procedural knowledge required. Another reason is that a major productive use of programming theory is in constructing an epistemology of action, which focusses interest on the information in representations, rather than the processes that construct them. A fully computational theory of motor programming, of course, has to consider both, sometimes at the expense of having to commit itself to arbitrary process assumptions to make the theory work.

(b) In defining a motor program as the total manifold representation of an intended action, we abandon any attempt to partition information in the head into what is latently relevant to a current action and what is currently being used to control ongoing movement. The criterion of context dependency that has been used to try to determine the scope of the current "program" (eg Hulstijn and van Galen, 1983) is an elusive one. It depends on a perspective of action. Thus the exact sound of a phoneme in a speech sequence can be a function of the syllable in which it occurs, of the stress pattern and intonation contour over the phrase, and on whether one is speaking to another adult or reading to a child. Speech has a hierarchic structure and there are different perspectives corresponding to the different levels in which it can be represented. Significant information affecting the shape of motor output can be introduced at each of these.

(c) Speech is typically improvised. We have to suppose that the programming of speech is a dynamic process continually constructing a renewing representation of a sound output out of the linguistic material of lexical knowledge together with rules of grammar and phonology. This is in marked contrast to the concept of a program representing a fixed action pattern, stored in memory and called up when required. That conception arose in considering such things as invariant birdsong (Keele, 1968): in human action it is more relevant to habits than to skilled action. Note that an invariant motor sequence does not need symbolic representation, since there is no need to form an abstraction of motor information. In principle it can be organized by an associative process in the motor system. We can regard a habit as a degenerate skill, in which a once programmed action has been frozen into a fixed motor sequence.

Sometimes we memorize a text and give repeat performances on that text on different occasions. The text becomes a fixed part of the intention and hence of the program, but it is important to note that it leaves the expressive part of the program unspecified. Thus, a concert pianist has the option, having memorized a score, of improvising the details of expression on each occasion of performance.

It might be argued that though discourse is improvised, the words that form it have fixed action patterns, and that speech programs are assembled from these elementary programs. This argument does not stand up to evidence. The sound pattern of a spoken word is heavily determined by its context. Consider the following facts: (i) The rhythm of a word depends on whether it occurs early in a clause or ends it. (Cutler and Isard, 1980). (ii) Its stress pattern depends on the stress locations in the words that precede or follow it. Thus maximum stress in "Tennessee" falls on the last syllable in "The State of Tennessee", but on the first syllable in "Tennessee valley". There is a tendency in spoken English to alternate stressed and unstressed syllables (Liberman and Prince, 1977), and so "Tennessee" concedes stress location to the first syllable in "valley". (iii) The pitch contour of the word depends on its position in an intonation group and the overall shape of the intonation contour. (iv) A word can be spoken, whispered or sung, markedly affecting the patterning of the vocal tract. Thus we have to regard a word as having an abstract invariance, capable of being spoken in quite different ways.

(d) Speech has a syntax and a prosody, and these confer respectively a serial ordering and an overall shape to a sound sequence. We need a concept of motor programming in order to understand the composition of both order and shape. The concept is sometimes applied to simple as well as serial action, simple in the sense that movement is directed to a single goal, such as catching a ball. This seems unnecessary if it is supposed that a motor system can autonomously compute a coordinated movement to a goal: saying that the movement is programmed does little more than assert that the action is intentional. However, if a simple action is intentionally given a gestural shape beyond its functional requirement, as in mime, dance, calligraphy, speech, and playing music (Morasso and Tagliasco, 1986), then we have to suppose that the shape is part of the motor goal and consider its programming. It is thus important to distinguish a default movement, computed as perhaps the functionally optimal movement by the motor system, from a designed movement, specified by a motor program and computed accordingly by the motor system.

(e) The shape of movement can be designed in time as well as space. The ability to perform definite rhythms of movement is an aspect of motor fluency, which is the hallmark of skilled action. Movements flow into one another without abrupt changes in direction and acceleration (Shaffer, 1982). A motor sequence can be analysed as a composition of simple ballistic movements, and it can be shown that its fluent shaping requires a temporal overlap of control of the production of individual movements (Morasso, 1986). This requires not only that the separate goals of movement must be programmed, but also that programming should occur sufficiently ahead of execution to allow the motor system time to organize a motor sequence and arrange to overcome inertial constraints on movement.

In summary, motor programming is described as a dynamic symbolic process composing a structured sequence of motor goals in the performance of a given task. It is a process translating a motorically abstract intention into a language that can be interpreted by a motor system. It becomes fully effective in skilled performance when the motor program is composed sufficiently ahead of its execution to allow the action to be fluent and expressive.

The theory makes a clear division in the organization of action between motor programming, a cognitive process which creates a goal structure of action, and motor computation, a process which arranges the details of movement. This distinction between programming and computation is sometimes made elsewhere as a distinction between planning and programming. The labelling of concepts is, of course, relatively unimportant: what is important is that different workers should agree on the labelling. The argument for the present usage is partly on historical grounds, but perhaps more importantly on the grounds that a motor system computes in a way better described as constraint satisfaction than programming. Let us now consider how a motor system can be capable of organizing movement from abstract goal specifications.

2. MOTOR COMPUTATION

Some 60 years ago Bernstein (1967) conjectured that a neuromotor system can solve motor problems, set by a given task, more or less autonomously on the principles of its own internal dynamics. He was led to this by observing that an action can be stably reproducible from one occasion to another though it involves coordinating muscles acting over many joints of the body; and conversely that a given motor goal can be reliably attained on different occasions, regardless of starting position and external conditions, and even if it involves different sets of muscles. Under the impetus of recent research on robotics, there have been many attempts to exploit this insight and develop a theory of self-organizing motor systems. Such a system can be flexibly configured to perform a given task, and can be adaptive to the physical conditions in which the task is performed, but it is solely responsible for organizing movement.

The recent attempts at modelling a motor system share a common principle: in one way or another they make use of a network of mutually interacting elements, which collaborate in achieving stable states of the network. An input to the network perturbs the current stable state, and activity among the elements will continue until a new stable state is reached. This process of convergence to a stable state is described mathematically as relaxation, and we have referred to it here as a computation, though not all theorists would wish to use this term. The term is often associated with symbol manipulation, but the general concept is much broader than this, and in most of the network theories the computation is nonsymbolic (Morasso, this volume). (There is no essential difference between a symbol and an analogue: it is a matter of how transparently a symbol represents information about its referent.)

Different theorists have characterized the elements of the network as oscillators (Kugler and Turvey, 1987) or information processors (Hinton, 1984; Morasso and Tagliasco, 1986), and the interaction among them, accordingly, as entrainment or the transmission of activation or information. What is important is that because the elements act in parallel, a network can solve problems in a large number of variables, defined by the task and by the environment.

In quite general terms we can consider the input to a network as a pattern of activity and the output of the network as another pattern. In these terms problem solving by the network is a mapping of input patterns into output patterns. The motor system can be regarded as such a network. Its input is a task description and an environment; its output is movement. In a given state of the network a repeated input will produce the same output. It is also possible to arrange that inputs that belong in an equivalence class converge on a common output. Thus in principle such networks can exhibit the properties of reproducibility and adaptiveness that Bernstein observed in human action.

There is a long way to go from a general theory of motor systems to an adequate theory of an actual motor skill. Nevertheless it is a major step forward to understand how a motor system can function autonomously and without recourse to symbol manipulation, even though its input from a motor program is symbolic. The ability to interpret symbols is a matter of pattern recognition, and we can suppose that the input elements in the network are specialized in this. A central issue for a theory of motor systems, and for network theory generally, is to be able to show how a network can learn to map input patterns into desired output patterns, or of tasks into actions. The theory of skill acquisition is still in its infancy, but powerful learning algorithms already exist for certain classes of connectionist network (Grossberg, 1982; Rumelhart, Hinton and Williams, 1986).

Modern theories characterize the networks in terms of information, activation or oscillation. It is not yet clear whether the theoretical differences are fundamentally significant. Some of the recent models that treat the lumped properties of networks mathematically seem indifferent to the distinction (Bullock and Grossberg, 1988; Saltzman and Kelso, 1987). Theories that focus on information tend to model the spatial properties of movement, whereas those that focus on oscillation tend to model its temporal properties. Oscillation is essentially a temporal process, and so it is not surprising that theories based on this are primarily concerned with rhythm and temporal coordination in movement. Nor is it surprising that these theories obtain empirical support mainly from studies of cyclic action. It is worth noting, however, that information-based theories, making simple assumptions about the kinematics and dynamics of motor trajectories, can also provide accounts of cyclic action and timing (Morasso and Tagliasco, 1986).

Some tasks constrain the action towards temporal periodicity. Given the pendular movement of the limbs in walking and running, or the flight trajectories of balls in juggling, it is clear on physical grounds that the stability of action would be jeopardized by departing far from periodicity. The real theoretical interest, then, is not on rhythmic regularity as such but in the way in which the motor system converges on this solution.

The descriptive potential of oscillatory theory, and particularly of limit-cycle oscillators, has been exploited by Beek (1989) in a study of cascade juggling. This is one of the most subtle analyses of a motor skill yet conducted. It reveals that professional juggling conforms closely to what one would expect of a system of coupled nonlinear oscillators. Nevertheless, for many jugglers their movement cycles exhibit occasional discontinuities that cannot be accounted for within the theory.

Beek is reluctant to go outside nonlinear dynamic theory, for reasons of theoretical economy and explanatory power. In particular he is reluctant to admit cognitive intervention in the performance. Yet it becomes apparent, when we consider jugglers like W C Fields, that the skill can go beyond the domain of juggling, turning it into comedy and introducing a cognitive dimension. By exploiting the alternative solutions of ball trajectory and phase relationship that leave the action stable, the juggler can, for instance, give the appearance of fumbling, making the skill seem fallible. Thus motor programming can take on a nontrivial role in the action, making it expressive. One needs to understand the cognitive intervention in terms of how it affects the biomechanical system, but such a description remains incomplete if we do not take account of the cognitive goals.

It is quite common in human action that once full mastery of control is achieved, it acquires the potential to go beyond an autonomous patterning of movement and become expressive. Thus, for example, walking acquires the potential to extend into mime and dance. The ultimate stage in skill acquisition, then, is to cognitively exploit the degrees of freedom in the biomechanical system for expressive purposes.

3. SPEECH ERRORS

The concept of motor programming makes explicable how language can be spoken fluently at speeds up to 200 words a minute, how articulatory gestures producing the speech sounds can complexly overlap in time, and how rhythm, stress and intonation can be patterned over large stretches of the sound sequence. Describing any one of these kinds of phenomena could occupy a full paper, but in the remaining space we shall concentrate on what appears to be a side-effect of programming, the occurrence of certain errors, sometimes called slips of the tongue, in otherwise fluent speech. These show systematic patterns that are explicable only in terms of motor programming, and do much to reveal the hierarchic organization of programs. Many of them affect the ordering of speech sounds.

If someone says "We need a laboratory in our computer", when it is clear that what was intended was "We need a computer in our laboratory", then an error has crept into a mental process deriving the utterance from the intention. We can also infer that much of the utterance was represented in the head before starting to speak the sentence, otherwise the word "computer" could not have been anticipated. Comparing it with other errors we find common features which suggest that there are important constraints on their occurrence in fluent speech (Fromkin, 1971), which have important implications for their etiology. These features have been known intuitively for centuries, and were exploited, for instance, in the comic inventions of Rabelais. In the last two decades they have come to be seen as a major source of data for studying the organization of speech.

If we consider fundamentally how a speech system can get from meaning to sound, it becomes obvious that it must construct one or more intermediate representations. The candidates for these are structured sequences of phrases, words, morphemes, syllables and phonemes. Before going further we need a brief description of morphemes and phonemes.

A morpheme is the smallest meaning-bearing unit in language, and many words can be decomposed into a root morpheme and one or more affixes. Thus "scold", "new" and "cat" are root morphemes which can become "scolded", "renew" and "cats" with the addition of affixes that modify the sense of the word by changing tense, number, and so on. We can think of the root as being modifiable by operators, marked in a semantic level of representation, to produce a complex word. (This blurs a distinction linguists sometimes make between roots and stems, but the effect seems benign.) Thus a tense operator, for instance, sometimes merely adds to the root, as in "scolded", and sometimes alters its form, for example changing "is" to "was" and "go" to "went". It seems likely that a word is often represented in the mental lexicon both as a modification of a root and in its modified form (Cutler and Isard, 1980).

Phonemes define the basic alphabet of sounds from which word forms are constructed. They are abstract descriptions of sounds in the sense that each phoneme can be realised by different sounds, or allophones, depending on the phonemic context. An adult speaker has a vocabulary of some tens of thousands of words or morphemes, composed of some thousands of syllables, reducing to some tens of phonemes. Although a motor system could in principle learn the mapping relations into sound for any of these units, the collapse in scale between the phoneme and the other units makes it the most likely unit of input to the motor system, involving the least knowledge stored in that system.

The error data suggest that phonemes and words, or modified morphemes, may be sufficient intermediary units in composing the speech sequence. The large body of error data can be seen to consist of corruptions occurring in one or other of these levels of unit.

By assumption, errors occur when an ambiguity arises in deriving an output from a superordinate representation. The "noise" can arise in many ways in the context of the utterance, but whatever its source it tends to affect points in the speech sequence made vulnerable by the availability of alternative, similar constructions. This is illustrated in the sets of examples that follow.

Let us consider first three kinds of error that arise in forming a syntactically ordered word sequence from an underlying semantics. They affect in turn the syntax itself, the choice of words and the placing of word forms within an abstract syntactic structure.

The first kind of error arises from the possibility of alternative syntaxes for a semantic entity. The ambiguity can affect the whole sentence or be confined to a lexical choice, and the system failing to choose between the possibilities forms a blend from both (Fay, 1982; Fromkin 1973). Thus:

It doesn't make any matter
    It doesn't make any difference / It doesn't matter
You'll be another Bud Powell when you get up
    ..when you get older / ..when you grow up
four to ten years of old
    four to ten years of age / four to ten years old
work with severely profound children
    ..severely retarded children / ..profoundly retarded children
if I don't get the ball on the show
    ..get the ball rolling/ ..get the show on the road
momentaneous
    momentary / instantaneous
grastly
    grisly / ghastly
herrible
    terrible / horrible.

Fay (1982) provides a subtle analysis of how the alternative syntaxes can combine to produce the blend.

In the second kind, the malapropism (after Sheridan's Mrs Malaprop), ambiguity arises from the phonetic similarity of words that can be semantically dissimilar. The error words and their targets tend to have some phoneme agreement, or to agree in the number of syllables and their stress pattern. They indicate that words are often accessed in the mental lexicon by means of their phonetic properties, and hence that these properties are fairly central in lexical descriptions. In the case of the malapropism an ambiguous description leads to access of a lexical neighbor of the intended word. Thus:

ERROR	TARGET	
easy	early	
determination	denomination	
equivocal	equivalent	
accurate	adequate	
analyse	advertise	(Fay and Cutler, 1977)

Similarly, in the tip-of-the-tongue phenomenon the attempt to recall a word from its semantic description may lead by association to a phonetic neighborhood and the accessing of a series of near-miss candidate words.

The third kind, spoonerisms (after Rev. Spooner), involve an interchange of units. When they are at the word level of unit they tend to involve words from the same syntactic class, as in

threw the window through the clock	..clock through the window
used the door to open the key	..key to open the door
dinner is being served at wine	..wine is being served at dinner
a laboratory in our own computer	..computer in our own laboratory

Another feature of these errors is that they tend to involve the words that receive stress in the utterance. Furthermore the exchange typically leaves the intonation contour of the utterance unaffected. Thus in the last example, tonic stress was placed on "laboratory" instead of on the intended "computer". The above examples could be considered as either word or morpheme exchanges, but the following examples make it clear that the errors have arisen in deriving words from their more abstract morphemes:

A hole full of floors	..floor full of holes
Fancy getting your model renosed	..nose remodeled
Where are the living chickens?	..chicken livers
It is careful to measure with reason	..reasonable to measure with care
I disregard this as precise	..regard this as imprecise
I'd hear one if I knew it	..know one if I heard it

The first two examples demonstrate an exchange of root morphemes, leaving their affixes in correct syntactic position. The next example shows an exchange of roots in an adjective-noun sequence, turning "liver", now in the adjectival position, into "living". This example shows that roots from different syntactic classes may transpose if they are adjacent. The roots "care" and "reason" are both nouns that can take adjectival forms, but they require different suffixes, and the error shows that an abstract syntactic marker triggers these. Similarly, when a negation marker shifts from "precise" to "regard" it triggers "dis-" rather than "im-". Finally, inherited tense markers alter the forms of the exchanging verbs, "hear" and "know".

Looking back over these kinds of error we see the need to postulate the derivation of an explicit syntactic representation from a semantic representation, in which syntax is only implicit. The error, by assumption, occurs in the process of derivation. We glimpse the semantic representation as a set of morphemic roots embedded in a network of syntactic and semantic relationships. This network contains markers that control variables like tense, number, gender, grammatical category and logical status.

The perhaps more common kinds of speech error involve the movement or exchange of phonemes, usually singly but sometimes in clusters. Some examples attributed to the Reverend Spooner are

You have hissed my mystery lectures	..missed my history..
You have tasted the whole worm	..wasted the whole term

These have been selected for their literary effect, but they are otherwise typical of the more commonly observed errors, which however lead to real words only about half the time. Examples are

heft lemisphere	left hemisphere
poppy of my caper	copy of my paper
caked a bake	baked a cake
karpsihord	harpsichord
cuff of coffee	cup of coffee
steep dructure	deep structure
pope smiker	pipe smoker
salt and shecker papers	..pepper shakers
plotoprasm	protoplasm
coursety	courtesy

Such errors tend to occur within a short phrase or within a word. Phonemes typically move to comparable positions in another syllable, and the movement or exchange usually involves stressed syllables, though the last example in fact shows an exchange between two unstressed syllables. To make the phenomenon clear we need to say a little bit about syllable structure.

The syllables of English can be analysed into an onset and a rime, in which the onset contains one or more consonants or a null element, and the rime contains a nuclear vowel perhaps followed by a coda of one or more consonants. Consonant clusters in an onset or coda take only a limited variety of orderings, and these differ between the onset and the coda (Levelt,1989). Restating the above generalization, movements seldom occur between an onset and a coda. It is also true that phoneme movements do not violate the rules of admissible sequence in the language. What is less obvious from the examples but is statistically true is that (a) the phonemes that move tend to share phonetic features with the phonemes they displace, and (b) their target and host environments tend to be phonetically similar (Shattock-Hufnagel and Klatt, 1980; van den Broecke and Goldstein, 1980). Consonants in clusters may move singly or together, constrained only by their phonetic compatibility in the host position.

By assumption, these errors arise in deriving phoneme sequences from a sequence of abstract word symbols. They can be seen as the result of an ambiguity of addressing, locating phonemes in sequence within a syntactic frame (Shattuck-Hufnagel, 1979). The ambiguity can arise if phonemes in different parts of the sequence share similar descriptions. This indicates that a phoneme location is specified in relation to both the location and sound shape of its syllable.

When phonemes move they take allophones appropriate to their new environments, leaving the speech phonetically fluent. It also sometimes happens that the environment alters to accommodate its guest, as in:

at a pearly period	at an early period

in which the intrusion of the "p" has had the effect of changing "an" to "a". This suggests that the a/an distinction is determined quite late in construction, possibly by the motor system, to promote fluency in the utterance.

A phoneme may itself be represented as a set of phonetic features, specifying broadly such things as its place and manner of articulation and whether or not it is immediately voiced. It is possible for features themselves to move if, in a neighborhood of similar sounds, location becomes ambiguous. Thus:

capsy tag	taxi cab	
medication darden	meditation garden	
glear plue sky	clear blue	
pig and vat	big and fat	(Fromkin, 1973)

The first two are examples of place exchange (ie the place at which tongue action occurs) and the other two are examples of voicing exchange (ie voicing or nonvoicing of the nuclear vowel during the consonant). Thus the place sequence, middle-back, in "taxi" has transposed with the sequence, back-front, in "cab"; the voicing in "blue" has transposed with the nonvoicing in "clear"; and so on. Again, such errors can arise if phoneme location is specified by the location and sound pattern of its host syllable.

In short, in order to understand how the brain can get from abstract semantics to symbols that can be interpreted by the motor system, we have been led to consider the decomposition of the semantic entity first into word (or modified morpheme) symbols and then into phoneme symbols within a syntactic frame. Phoneme symbols provide the basic instructions needed by the motor system. Slips of the tongue occur as failures in their derivation from more abstract symbols. It is also suggested that phoneme symbols or the syllables they compose carry fairly direct information about the intended speech sound, which can be conveyed to the motor system.

One further kind of error is best understood as a failure of the motor system to pick up information from the motor program. This is the telescopic error, collapsing part of the utterance, as in

shrig souffle	shrimp and egg souffle
I have a spart for him	I have a spot in my heart for him
extinguish your seat belts	extinguish your cigarettes and fasten your seat belts

If the motor system has to extract information from a continually renewing motor program, it is important to keep a pointer on where it currently is in the program. These errors can be seen as failures of this pointer, which however remains sensitive to the proper syllabic continuation of its current output. If a pointer loses its position, we should expect it occasionally to jump backward as well as forward, leading to a repetition of material. It is likely, however, that these would be seen as stutters rather than slips of the tongue.

Prosodic features of speech, such as stress, rhythm and intonation, have to be specified at the semantic level and mapped by the syntax onto the phonetic level. They provide parameters of expression to the motor system. It is likely that the stored representation of a word includes its typical stress pattern (Cutler and Isard, 1980), but this may be modified by a metrical patterning of stress assigned to the overall utterance (Selkirk, 1984). For example, the typical stress pattern of "sixTEEN" changes in contexts like "SIXteen tons". The temporal rhythm of an utterance seems jointly determined by stress pattern and sentence syntax. In particular, slowing and pausing tend to occur at syntactic boundaries (Klatt, 1976). Intonation, the patterning of voice pitch over an utterance, can be shaped to convey aspects of meaning. For instance, the sentence "This is his dog" can be spoken as an assertion or a question depending on whether voice pitch falls or rises at the end of the utterance. The placing of tonic stress can be used to imply a semantic contrast, as in: "THIS is his dog", "This IS his dog", "This is HIS dog", or "This is his DOG" (Cutler and Isard, 1980).

With certain exceptions (Cutler, 1980), the prosodic patterns of the intended utterance are unaffected by errors of morpheme or phoneme movement. This is to be expected if they are mapped relative to the syntactic frame rather than to the surface details of the programmed utterance.

Prosodic patterns can range over large segments of speech, perhaps the length of a sentence and sometimes beyond. Since some of these patterns, such as intonation, are continuous in time, the motor system implementing them must have the capacity to scan the motor program sufficiently far ahead to be able to compute this continuity.

Motor programming in speech can thus be seen as an exercise in synthesis by analysis: a motor program analyses a semantic intention into a sequence of motor goals that can be easily specified to the motor system, but provides that system with sufficient information to resynthesize patterns that range over the sequence.

4. REFERENCES

Beek, P J. Juggling Dynamics. Amsterdam: Free University Press, 1989.

Bernstein, N A. The Control and Regulation of Movements. London: Pergamon, 1967.

Bullock, D and Grossberg, S. Neural dynamics of planned arm movements. Psychological Review, 1988, 95, 49-90.

Cutler, A. Errors of stress and intonation. In V A Fromkin (ed), Errors in Linguistic Performance. New York: Academic Press, 1980.

Cutler, A and Isard, S D. The production of prosody. In B Butterworth (ed), Language Production I. New York: Academic Press, 1980.

Fay, D. Substitutions and splices: a study of sentence blends. In A Cutler (ed), Slips of the Tongue. Amsterdam: Mouton, 1982.

Fay, D and Cutler, A. Malapropisms and the structure of the mental lexicon. Linguistic Inquiry, 1977, 8, 505-520.

Fromkin, V A. The non-anomalous nature of anomalous utterances. Language, 1971, 47, 27-52.

Fromkin, V A (ed). Speech Errors as Linguistic Evidence. The Hague: Mouton, 1973.

Grossberg, S. Studies of Mind and Brain. Boston: Reidel/Kluwer, 1982.

Hinton, G E. Parallel computations for controlling an arm. Journal of Motor Behavior, 1984, 16, 171-194.

Hulstijn, W and van Galen, G P. Programming in handwriting: reaction time and movement time as a function of sequence length. Acta Psychologica, 1983, 54, 23-49.

Keele, S W. Movement control in skilled motor performance. Psychological Bulletin, 1968, 70, 387-403.

Klatt, D H. Linguistic uses of segmental duration in English. Journal of the Acoustical Society of America, 1976, 59, 1208-1221.

Kugler, P N and Turvey, M T. Information, Natural Law, and the Self-Assembly of Rhythmic Movement. Hillsdale: Lawrence Erlbaum, 1987.

Lashley, K S. The problem of serial order in behavior. In L A Jeffress (ed), Cerebral Mechanisms in Behavior. New York: Wiley, 1951.

Levelt, W J M. Speaking: From Intention to Articulation. Cambridge, Mass: MIT Press, 1989.

Liberman, A M, Cooper, F S, Shankweiler, D P and Studdert-Kennedy, M. Perception of the speech code. Psychological Review, 1967, 74, 431-461.

Liberman, M and Prince, A. On stress and linguistic rhythm. Linguistic Inquiry, 1977, 8, 249-336.

MacNeilage, P F. Motor control of serial ordering of speech. Psychological Review, 1970, 77, 182-196.

MacNeilage, P F. Distinctive properties of speech motor control. In G E Stelmach and J Requin (eds), Tutorials in Motor Behavior. Amsterdam: North-Holland, 1980.

Michaels, C F and Carello, C. Direct Perception. Englewood Cliffs, NJ: Prentice Hall, 1981.

Morasso, P. Analogic and symbolic aspects in distributed motor control. (This volume).

Morasso, P. Trajectory formation. In P Morasso and V Tagliasco (eds), Human Movement Understanding. Amsterdam: North-Holland, 1987.

Morasso, P and Tagliasco, V (eds). Human Movement Understanding. Amsterdam: North-Holland, 1987.

Rumelhart, D E and Norman, D A. Simulating a skilled typist: a study of skilled cognitive-motor performance. Cognitive Science, 1982, 6, 1-36.

Rumelhart, D, Hinton, G and Williams, R. Learning internal representations by error propagation. In D Rumelhart and J McClelland (eds), Parallel Distributed Processing I. Cambridge, Mass: MIT Press, 1986.

Sacerdoti, E D. Planning in a hierarchy of abstraction spaces. Artificial Intelligence, 1974, 5, 115-135.

Saltzman, E and Kelso, J A S. Skilled actions: a task dynamic approach. Psychological Review, 1987, 94, 84-106.

Selkirk, E O. Phonology and Syntax: the Relation Between Sound and Structure. Cambridge, Mass: MIT Press, 1984.

Shaffer, L H. Rhythm and timing in skill. Psychological Review, 1982, 89, 109-122.

Shattuck-Hufnagel, S. Speech errors as evidence for a serial order mechanism in sentence production. In W Cooper and E Walker (eds), Sentence Processing. Hillsdale, NJ: Lawrence Erlbaum, 1979.

Shattuck-Hufnagel, S and Klatt, D H. How single phoneme error data rule out two models of error generation. In V A Fromkin (ed), Errors in Linguistic Performance. New York: Academic Press, 1980.

van den Broecke, M P R and Goldstein, L. Consonant features in speech errors. In V A Fromkin (ed), Errors in Linguistic Performance. New York: Academic Press, 1980.

Tutorials in Motor Behavior II
G.E. Stelmach and J. Requin (Editors)

REPRESENTATION OF SPACE AND MOTION IN MAN

I. Israël & A. Berthoz

Laboratoire de Physiologie Neurosensorielle, CNRS, 15 rue de l'Ecole de Médecine, 75270 PARIS Cedex 06, FRANCE

1. INTRODUCTION

This paper will deal with the question of the mechanisms underlying the ability to remember a path which has been followed with active or passive motion in space.

The ability to retrace a path along which a subject has been transported blindfolded, or to orient toward a hidden goal after a passive displacement, has been demonstrated in various species : geese (Mittelstaedt & Mittelstaedt, 1982), hamsters (Etienne et al., 1986), rats (Morris, 1981 ; Abraham et al., 1983), gerbils (Mittelstaedt & Mittelstaedt, 1980), and humans (Beritoff, 1965). Performances in this paradigm, currently labelled "return from passive transport" (Miller et al., 1983 ; Abraham et al., 1983) have been shown to be due to the vestibular system, which registers head displacements in space (Beritoff, 1965 ; Miller et al., 1983). The ability of humans to assess the amplitude of angular whole-body displacements is actually well known, since it is one of the methods used for measuring the detection threshold of passive angular motion in man (Guedry, 1974).

H. Mittelstaedt (Mittelstaedt & Mittelstaedt, 1980) has coined the expression of *"path integration"* for homing and goal-oriented navigation, and described its theoretical mechanism. With continuous integration of the proprioceptive signals generated during the displacement, an animal should always know its position with respect to the starting point, even if it does not access any external reference. For this author, "path integration" belongs to "inertial navigation", because the use of inertial sensors, whether the vestibular system or any part of the whole body,is probably the best way for most animals to navigate, without man-made devices like the compass (although Baker, 1989, suggested that humans can oriente to earth magnetic fields).

Mittelstaedt also proposed the term of "idiothetic orientation", which designates spatial orientation behavior based on self-generated signals, like for instance the vestibular signals. Although another source of self-generated spatial cues is provided by the spatial memory, according to his definition stored orientation derived from exogenous cues is not idiothetic (Mittelstaedt & Mittelstaedt, 1973).

Rats have been shown to be able to return to a memorized location. This orientational behavior is due either to path integration (Potegal, 1982), or to the stored *positions* of precedingly seen cues (radial maze : O'Keefe et Conway, 1978), or to the memorized *relations* between the now hidden goal and the environment (water maze : Morris, 1981).

Paillard (1987) has suggested that spatial behavior is based on two processing modes : the *sensorimotor and cognitive modes*, which probably operate in parallel. The cognitive mode would be based on *mental representations of the physical world*, which can proceed from memory of this world. When the representational mode only is used for spatial behavior, then navigation is at play.

2. RETURN FROM PASSIVE TRANSPORT

In the first part of this paper, we shall present some results about the internal representation of whole body displacements. We have used a particular paradigm which consists in submitting subjects to passive transport and then test the ability of the subject to evaluate the displacement by asking him to perform, in darkness, an eye movement to a previously seen earth fixed target (Bloomberg et al., 1988 ; Israël & Berthoz, 1989).

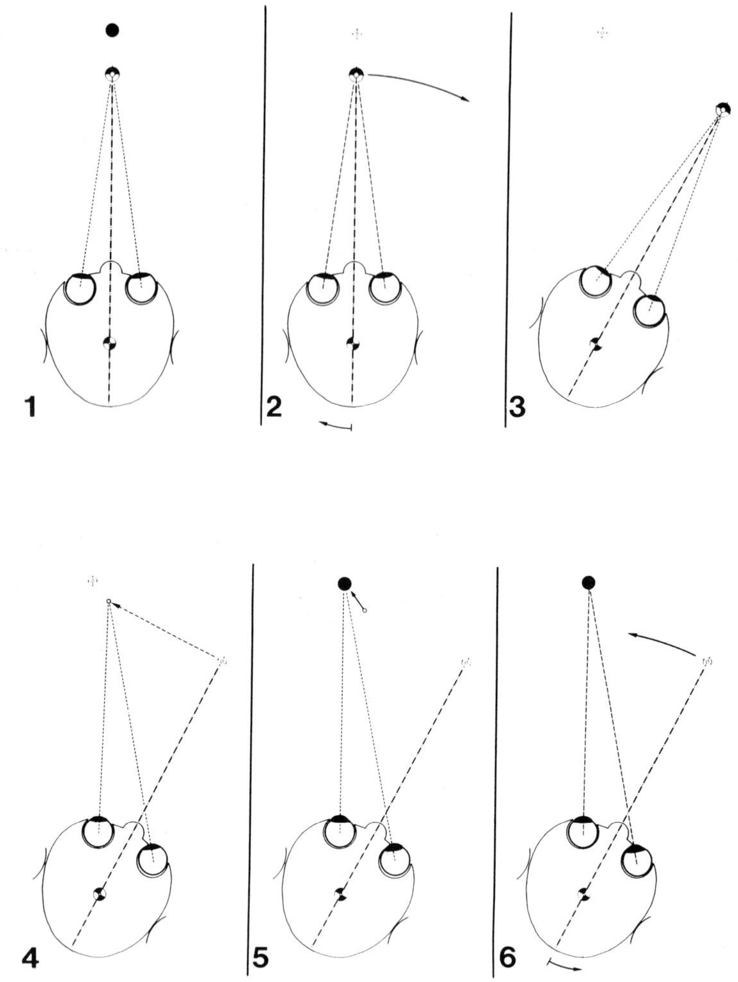

Figure 1 : Protocol of the oculomotor return from passive transport task, for angular displacement.

2.1. Methods

Eight healthy subjects aged 25-40 took part to each of the two experiments (angular and linear transport) presented here, but they were not the same subjects for both experiments.

The whole experiments were performed in complete darkness.

For the linear displacements test, the subject was seating in chair inside a linear accelerator, rolling on a rail-track 6 meters long. Its electromagnetic motor with velocity feedback was driven by a microcomputer (PC). The accelerator displacements were damped position steps, i.e. single displacements with a sine-wave velocity profile of 0.2 Hz.

For the angular displacements experiments, the subject was seating in a chair fixed on the floor, which could be manually rotated about the vertical axis. In order to control rotation amplitude, a fluorescent angular scale of 5 deg resolution had been drawn on the floor, at the base of the rotating chair, and a fluorescent was fixed to its pivoting axis.

Subject's head was firmly maintained to the chair. Horizontal eye position was measured by the Electro-Oculographic (EOG) technique. An Earth-Fixed Target (EFT) was 63 cm in front of the subject's initial position for linear displacements, and at 80 cm for angular displacements. A Chair-Fixed Target (CFT) was also used in order to suppress the Vestibulo-Ocular Reflex (VOR) generated during angular displacements. This was not required for linear displacements, as the Otolith-Ocular Reflex (OOR) is about inexistent for the frequency used in this experiment : 0.2 Hz (Tokita et al., 1981 ; Paige, 1989).

The experimental protocol for testing vestibular memory and path integration was as follows (Fig.1) :

(1) The visual EFT was presented straight ahead to the subject during about 5 sec. The subject was required to fixate it.

(2) The EFT was turned off (and replaced by the CFT, at the same location, for angular displacements). Then, the chair or the cart was displaced with a non-predictible amplitude and direction. During the rotation, the subject was required to keep his eyes on the CFT (VOR suppression), and during the translation, he was simply asked to keep looking straight-ahead, with his eyes in the primary position.

(3) After the displacement cessation, the subject was asked to keep maintaining his eyes straight ahead during a varying retention or memorization delay (D), still fixating the CFT for angular displacements.

(4) After this delay, the CFT was turned off, or a verbal signal was given for linear displacements tests. The subject had then to move his eyes to the memorized EFT location previously shown, i.e., to the starting point of the displacement, and to keep his eyes on that position in complete darkness.

(5) The EFT was turned on again, about 1 to 2 sec after the oculomotor return. The subject made, if necessary, a corrective saccade to foveate the visual EFT.

(6) The chair or the cart was then moved back to its initial position, with the subject still foveating the visual EFT, by the combination of smooth-pursuit and the VOR produced by the displacement (Fig.2).

For angular displacements tests, three different classes of retention durations were used : D lower or equal to 20 sec, D equal to 1 min, and D about 5 min. For linear displacements, only durations up to 40 sec were tested.

Eye position and chair (i.e. head) position signals were recorded on tape during the experiments, for their off-line analysis. When the data had been digitized onto the PC, the oculomotor return amplitude (E), i.e., the eye movement angle from straight-ahead up to the memorized EFT, was quantified, as well as the corresponding transport, i.e. the head displacement amplitude (H).

For linear displacements, E was evaluated in cm. This measure corresponds to the projection of the eye movement angle on a horizontal line, parallel to body displacement and crossing the EFT. An eye movement E of 1 cm represents the angle 0 (deg) of the eye rotation which displaces its view point of 1 cm, on a line 63 cm in front of the eye. Thus 0 = Arctang(1/63) = 0.91 deg, since the EFT is 63 cm away from the subject. This is in accordance with Paige & Tomko (1991), who suggested that the OOR should be quantified by *fonctional* measurements, as for VOR. This quantification allowed the amplitude ratio : E/H to be computed for both linear and angular displacements tests and thus allowed their comparison.

2.2. Results

In angular displacement tests, all subjects experienced a strong illusion of persistent target rotation when looking at the CFT, during 1 to 2 sec after the end of chair rotation. The same phenomenon was also perceived by the operators when they tracked the rotating CFT with the head and the eyes, but not when they tracked it without moving the head. This apparent target motion is probably a manifestation of the *oculogyral illusion* (Graybiel and Hupp, 1946). Since there was no CFT during subject's translation, the corresponding *oculogravic illusion* (Graybiel, 1952) could not be perceived.

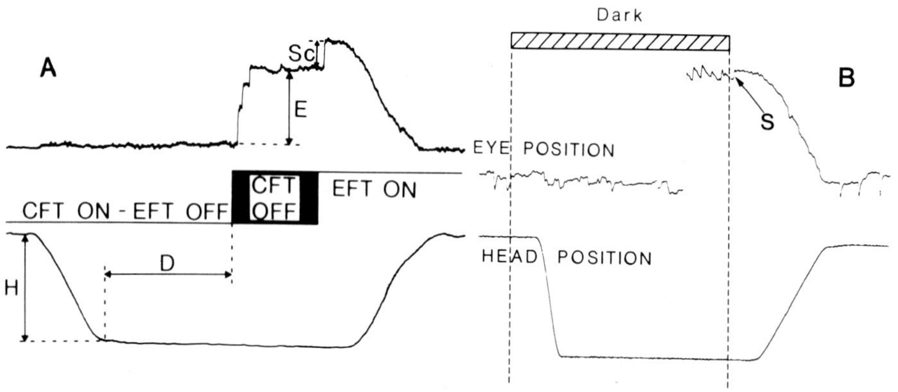

Figure 2 : Examples of the oculomotor return from passive transport tasks. A : Angular displacement. B : Linear displacement. Upper trace : Eye position. Lower trace : Head position. The middle trace on the angular displacement example (A) is the CFT-EFT ON/OFF status.

It can be seen in Fig.2 that subjects used saccades in order to "return" to the starting point, i.e., to the EFT, after angular as well as linear displacements. They most often used more than one saccade ; this primary saccade was followed by several secondary or corrective ones, of smaller amplitude than the primary saccade, and always with the same direction.

An drift of the eye position can be seen between those saccades, when the subject was still in complete darkness. Although this drift amplitude and duration varied among the subjects and the trials, it was always centripetal, thus identical to the direction of this drift in darkness most often observed by Hess et al. (1985).

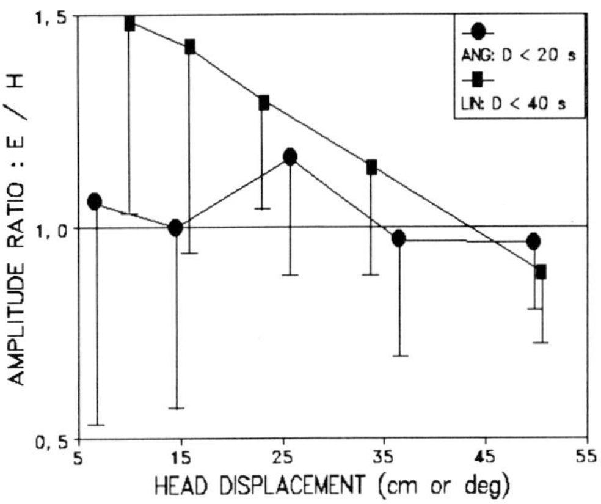

Figure 3 : Amplitude ratio (Eye movement / Head displacement) with respect to head displacement amplitude (H). Average - 1 SD.
Circles : Angular displacement.
Squares : Linear displacement.

In Fig.3 is plotted the amplitude ratio or gain E/H against the preceding head displacement amplitude (H), for both rotation and translation experiments, when D is shorter than 20 sec for angular displacement, and shorter than 40 sec for linear displacement. Although qualitatively, both graphics do exhibit about the same trend, i.e., a *decrease of E/H when H increases*, this trend is much stronger for linear than for angular displacements : when D increases, the amplitude ratio goes from 1.06 ± 0.52 to 0.96 ± 0.16 (n = 30) for angular displacements, and from 1.49 ± 0.45 to 0.89 ± 0.17 (n = 19) for linear displacements. This overshoot of the EFT for small values of H and the undershoot for larger values of H, observed with both angular as well as linear displacements, could be a manifestation of the *range effect*, a cognitive non-intentional process of approximation of all values belonging to a known or experienced range, which has been shown to occur also in the saccadic system (Kapoula, 1985). It is actually the only common result which was obtained in different psychological experiments about distance evaluation (Bartram & Smith, 1984). We can observe here the sensorimotor manifestation of this phenomenon.

For angular displacements, the amplitude ratio E/H was actually fairly close to the ideal amplitude ratio, i.e., unity, over the whole range of head rotation amplitudes used in this experiment : E/H = 1.03 ± 0.36 (n = 150), whereas for linear displacements, the average gain is larger than unity : 1.26 ± 0.41 (n = 93).

Figure 4 shows the amplitude ratio E/H with respect to the retention duration D up to 60 sec for angular displacements and up to 40 sec for linear ones. *For angular displacements*, a continuous *increase of E/H* can be seen *with increasing D*. The amplitude ratio actually keeps increasing also for D larger than 1 min : it is 1.12 ± 0.43 for D = 1 min, and 1.31 ± 0.57 for D = 5 min (n = 40). *For linear displacements*, on the other hand, the trend is reversed : *E/H decreases when D increases*. However in both cases, it can be seen that the standard deviation increases when D increases.

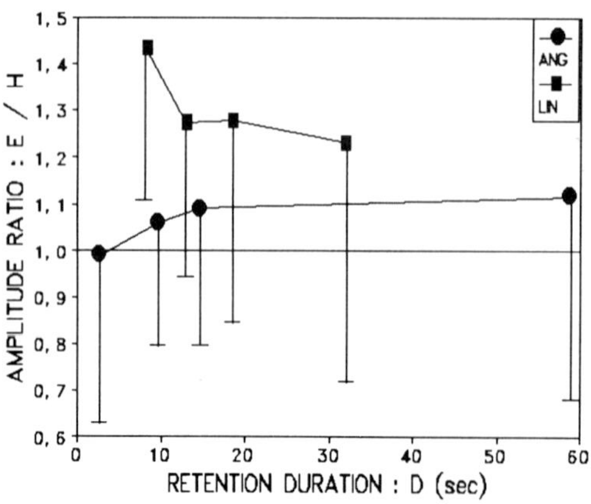

Figure 4 : Amplitude ratio (E/H) with respect to the retention duration (D : sec). Average - 1 SD.
Circles : Angular displacement.
Squares : Linear displacement.

Because subjects' responses seemed to vary with the retention duration D (Fig.4), all data have been separated into two classes, corresponding to D smaller or larger than the mediane value of all delay values used, 11 sec for the lower D < 20 sec class of angular displacements (see Methods) and 13 sec for linear displacements. The parameters of regression lines between E and H have then been computed, and the correlation between the stimulus and the - delayed - response was found significant in all cases ($p < 0.01$). In both angular and linear displacements regression lines, *the slope increased when D increased*. Besides, *the intercept increased for angular displacements, and decreased for linear ones*. Furthermore, whereas the correlation coefficient slightly decreased when D increased in angular displacements : $r^2 = 0.81$ to $r^2 = 0.78$, it increased from $r^2 = 0.58$ to $r^2 = 0.70$ for linear displacements, when D increased. This correlation coefficient criterion, taken together with the amplitude ratio (Fig.4), suggests that this *internal representation of passive linear displacement*, allowing the oculomotor return to the starting point, *becomes more accurate with time*, in decreasing...

3. REPRODUCTION OF DISPLACEMENT

The two previous path integration tasks have assessed the memory of the displacement by saccades executed in complete darkness. We therefore considered that it was necessary to obtain control measurements of the characteristics of memory-guided saccades. The main reason for testing the reproduction of visual target displacement was to obtain a control data base about those memory-guided saccades in darkness, and the effect of the retention duration, in order to be able to discuss the preceding results.

Furthermore, in the return from passive transport tests, it has been seen that the subjects' responses accuracy did vary with the retention duration (Fig.4). As the subjects had been presented with a visual anchoring target before they were displaced, *the question is whether the reference target position (visuospatial memory) or the displacement amplitude (vestibular memory) been altered with time.*

The experiments described in the second part of this paper were performed in order to study this question.

3.1. Methods

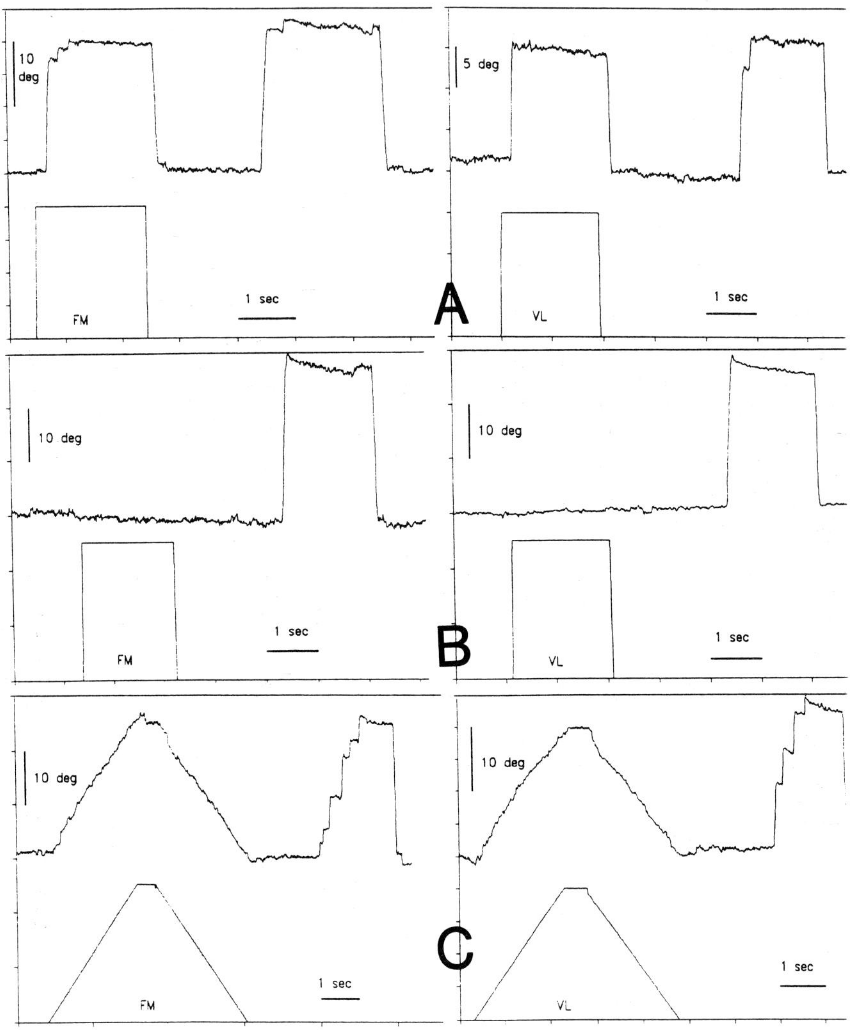

Figure 5 : Reproduction of displacement paradigm.
Upper traces : eye position. Lower traces : visual target position.

Two subjects took part to this experiment, which was again performed in complete darkness. The subject was seating in front of a tranlucent screen on which the beam of a laser driven by two galvanometric mirrors was projected. All target positions were on the left hemifield. Three different paradigms, i.e. different location acquisition conditions were used (Fig.5).

"Saccade" (SA) condition : The visual target jumped from straight-ahead to an eccentric position on the horizontal axis, stayed there for 2 sec, then jumped back to the center. The subject was required to track and fixate the target. After a retention duration D (2 or 12 sec) at the center, the target disppeared, and the subject had to make a saccade toward the memorized eccentric target position previously shown, i.e. to reproduce the preceding visually-guided saccade in complete darkness (Fig.5A).

"Fixation" (FI) condition : Target displacements were the same as described above, but the subject did not track it. He fixated a stationnary central target, which disappeared simultaneously to the moving target, after the same retention durations D as above. Thereafter, the subject was also required to make a saccade to the memorized target eccentric position, in complete darkness (Fig.5B).

"Pursuit" (PU) condition : The visual target moved slowly (10 deg/sec) from the center up to an eccentric position, where it stayed during 1 sec, and then moved slowly back to the center. The subject had to pursue and fixate it. Like in the other conditions, the target disappeared after D sec, and the subject had to make a saccade to the memorized peripheral final visual target position (Fig.5C).

Eye position was measured with EOG. Eye and target positions were recorded on tape during the experiments, then digitized onto a PC-microcomputer for off-line analysis. Memory-guided eye movement amplitude (E) was compared to the visual target displacement amplitude (T) in order to assess the accuracy of location memory.

3.2. Results

Although the subjects always used saccades in order to reach the memorized target location, they made much more numerous (Fig.5) secondary, or corrective saccades in complete darkness, in the PU condition than in the two other ones. Although the instruction given to the subjects was exactly the same for all conditions, i.e. to make a saccade to a memorized position, it seems that they tried to *reproduce target movement* in order to reach its final position, in PU condition. However, it is the final eye position which we used in order to assess target position memory, and not the primary saccade.

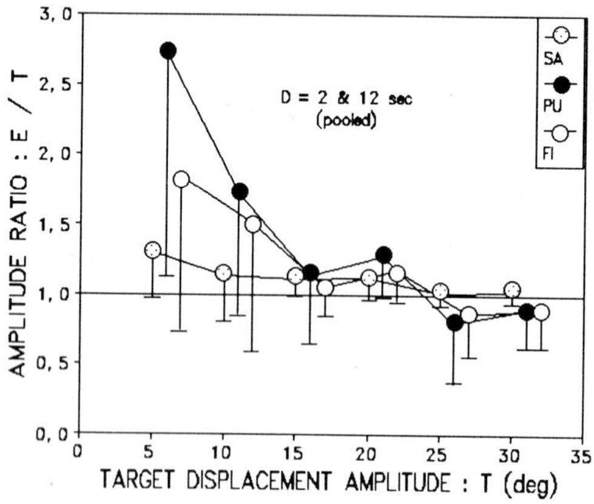

Figure 6 : Amplitude ratio (Eye displacement / Target displacement) with respect to target displacement amplitude, for all conditions, with both retention durations (D) averaged. Average - 1 SD. White Circles : Fixation. Black Circles : Pursuit. Dotted Circles : Saccade.

Figure 6 shows the amplitude ratio or oculomotor gain E/T with respect to target displacement amplitude, for each of the three conditions, with both retention durations pooled. The same tendency as had been observed for return from passive transport (Fig.3), i.e. *hypermetry of the lower target displacements and hypometry of the larger ones* (range effect), is again exhibited in all cases. However, the hypermetry is far larger than what had been found for angular as well as linear displacements (Fig.3), in all conditions but SA, where the amplitude ratio is quite close to unity over the whole range of target displacements. It should be reminded that in SA, the subjects had access to both target *position* and eye *displacement* informations, and this was also the case in the return from passive transport tasks, where the subject had been presented with a reference visual target before to be passively displaced in complete darkness. Lastly, it can be noted in Fig.6 that the hypermetry at lower target displacements is the largest in PU condition.

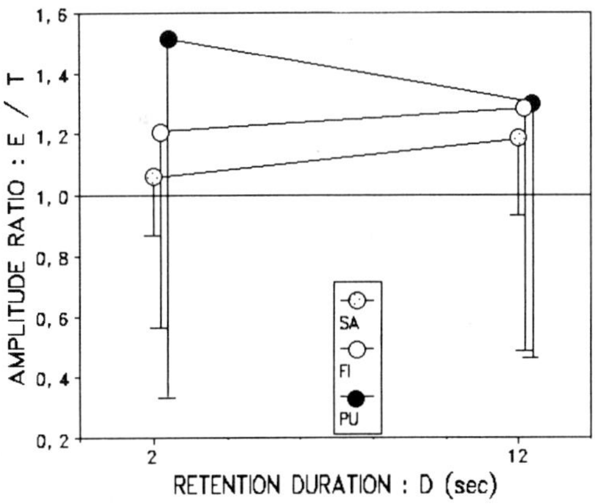

Figure 7 : Amplitude ratio (E/T) with respect to the retention duration (D : sec). Same symbols as in Fig.6.

It can be further seen, in Fig.7, that the final eye position in complete darkness is closer to the desired position (visual target eccentric position) in the SA than in both other conditions, for both retention durations. The amplitude ratio E/T is closer to unity, and the standard deviation is smaller.

The amplitude ratio slightly increases when D increases from 2 sec to 12 sec, together with its standard deviation, for SA and FI conditions, whereas this ratio decreases in PU condition. The effect of the retention duration on the performance, i.e. spatial accuracy, is thus opposite in the conditions FI and SA from in PU : the final eye position in darkness goes further from the desired position in SA and FI, whereas it becomes closer to that position in PU, when D increases. The hypermetry in PU, however, remains larger than in FI and SA, even when it decreases for 12 sec retention duration.

The relative difference of the amplitude ratio between the two retention durations is weakest in FI : 5.78%, where it is 11,32% in SA and 14,47% in PU. SA is then half-way between FI and PU, from the point of view of the effect of D on the memory-guided saccades hypermetry, although this hypermetry is always lower in SA than in both other conditions.

Lastly, we computed the parameters of the regression lines between target displacement and delayed saccade, for all conditions and both retention durations, as it had been done for the path integration tasks. The correlation was found significant ($p < 0.01$) in all conditions but PU. Also in both SA and FI conditions, but not in PU, *the slope of the regression line increases with D and the intercept decreases*. Actually, it seems that when D is 2 sec, the subjects in the PU condition always made about the same eye movement amplitude for all target displacements, whereas when D is at 12 sec, the correlation stimulus-response is quite better (from $p > 0.1$ when D is 2 sec to $p < 0.02$ when D is 12 sec). Thus, the same *tendency of mental representation improvement with time* which had been noted for linear displacements is also observed in PU condition, although it is much clearer in this PU condition.

4. DISCUSSION

In the different paradigms presented in this paper, the behavioral performance has been assessed through saccadic eye movements in complete darkness, and the performance criterion was saccadic final position accuracy with respect to a desired position, a spatial location which should have been memorized. Although in all cases, some hypermetry or overshoot has been observed, differences appeared with the strategy for location acquisition, and with the duration of retention. This hypermetry is actually not surprising, since it has been shown by Becker & Fuchs (1969) that saccadic eye movements in complete darknes are hypermetric. Therefore, the evaluation and memorization of the displacement and/or position could actually have been more precise than what is suggested by the results.

4.1. Position and/or displacement representation

In our "control" experiments with displacement reproduction, subjects had to return to a location they had discovered before, either by purely visuospatial information (FI), or by the information brought about by eye movement (PU), or by the combination of both types of information (SA). This was to be compared to the return from passive angular displacement (AD) and linear displacement (LD), after a visuospatial reference information had been acquired.

The fact that the memory-guided saccades accuracy is better in SA than in both other conditions confirms the hypothesis that subjects have utilized both available informations, and each of those information types does contribute to location memory.

It can be seen in Fig.8 that this accuracy (amplitude ratio) is also better in AD than in FI and PU, but that in LD the accuracy is close to FI, suggesting a different use of the internal/external informations in each of those whole body displacements tests. However, the standard deviation of both AD and LD average amplitude ratio is smaller than in FI and PU, and actually also smaller than in SA for the longer retention durations, whereby suggesting a differential effect of time on actively and passively acquired displacement representation.

The retention duration D has a qualitatively similar effect on the responses in SA and FI conditions, as well as in AD condition (Fig.8). This suggests that subjects did rely, in SA like in AD tests, mostly on visuospatial rather than on displacement or movement information, since such motion representation (PU) leads to an opposite effect of D.

For LD, however, the amplitude ratio reveals a qualitatively similar effect of D as in PU, i.e. a decrease of this ratio, thus accuracy improvement with time, as it had been shown with the regression lines parameters. This suggests that in LD, subjects relied mostly on displacement information, like they had to do in PU. This "positive" effect of the retention duration in PU condition is in accordance with Stelmach's results (1982) on arm movements short-term memory : memorized arm movement amplitude does *shrink* with time. It is possible that in this experiment, the shrinking with time of the memorized movement did compensate for the hypermetry of saccades in darkness. That could also explain the fact that the relative amplitude of the retention duration effect in the SA condition is precisely half-way between FI and PU conditions.

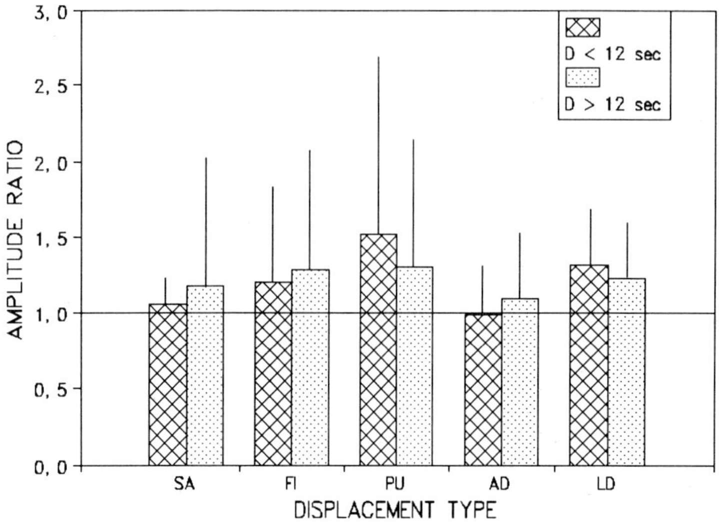

Figure 8 : Amplitude ratio (E/H or E/T) in each condition of return from passive transport with angular displacement (AD) and linear displacement (LD), as well as displacement reproduction. Average + 1 SD.

In summary, in order to answer to our question, i.e. the representation and memory of position or of displacement when returning from passive transport, we would be tentated to say that since exactly the same paradigm was used in angular and linear displacements tests, and since a different effect of the retention duration has been observed between those two exercises, memory was about displacement rather than about position : *the only difference was the type of displacement*. However, we then revealed through quantitative global amplitude ratios computation, that *the "weight" of external position and of body displacement in the internal representation depends upon the type of displacement* : *external position is predominant for body rotations* whereas *body displacement representation seems more important for body translations*.

It should be recalled, however, that the effect of D on the slope of the regression lines between stimulus and response is similar in PU, AD and LD, similar in SA and FI, but different between those two groups of tests. This suggests that saccadic eye movement does not bring the same movement information as smooth pursuit, so that the main information stored in SA was probably visuospatial. Furthermore, this points out that displacement is also considered in body rotation representation, since according to this criterion AD and LD conditions are together.

4.2. Angular versus linear displacement representation

We have shown that the mental representation of angular and linear body displacements is fundamentaly different. In other experiments, some differences between those two types of displacement have already been noted.

A striking difference was already observed, with the same kind of path integration paradigm, by Mittelstaedt & Mittelstaedt (1982) and by Etienne et al. (1988). In both experiments, small mammals could not return home after linear displacement, although they could accurately return home after angular transport, in the same conditions.

Benson & Brown (1989) studied the influence of a visual target, fixed relative to the subject, on thresholds for detection of linear and of angular movements. Thresholds for the detection of the linear motion in darkness were not different from those obtained when a LED was illuminated. None of the subjects reported apparent movement of the visual display. In contrast, the presence of a visual display lowered angular motion thresholds from that obtained in darkness, and all subjects reported apparent movement of the visual display, an oculogyral illusion. These findings, according to the authors, imply that otolithic afferents, unlike those from the semicircular canals, do not interact with neural centres mediating visual localization.

Although this conclusion seems to support our hypothesis about external position and displacement weight in motion representation, there was no interaction in our case, but rather the addition of two successive informations. We would like to suggest another interpretation of this phenomenon. It is well known that otoliths have an effect on the oculomotor system mainly, if not only, when in cooperation with another sensory system, like acoustic (Buizza et al., 1979), optokinetic (Buizza et al., 1980), or rotational stimulation about off-vertical axis (Darlot et al., 1988) or off-centered (Gresty et al., 1987). We suggest that in the presence of a visual stimulus, the otolith-oculomotor system becomes merely *dependent* on this external cue. The oculogyral illusion has been attributed to a conflict between visual and vestibular systems : pursuit and VOR (Graybiel, 1952). During linear displacement, there is no conflict with the visual stimulus but gating of the otolithic information. The increase of this dependence in microgravity (see e.g. Young & Shelhamer, 1990) could then be seen like parametric adjustment of a pre-existing mechanism.

In our paradigm, however, there is another important difference between those two types of displacement. Actually, the distance of the earth-fixed target from the subject at the initial position, i.e. its position on the X axis, is less crucial for the return eye movements after rotation than after translation. We could then infere that the predominance of displacement representation for translation is a smart mechanism allowing to *reduce from one degree of freedom* the displacement representation. The same *"economy principle"* does justify the predominance of position information for angular displacement, in this return paradigm : in this case, it is easier to remember the shortest, i.e. *straight line* to the starting point than the angular displacement itself. This linear distance can be computed with only the visuospatial information.

The next remarks are more speculative : translation implies *furthering away* from the starting point, and not rotation. It might be that this furthering is associated to a movement, which could then be memorized like a motor movement, i.e. with shrinking (Stelmach 1982). Rotation does not suggest such distancing movement, but rather position adjusting...

4.3. The need for an external reference

The path integration theory states that through continuous integration of proprioceptive signals, here vestibular, the subject should know his position with respect to a starting point. This is why we presented the subject with a visual anchoring point. But is this external reference point really necessary ?

The poor performance in PU condition when D was 2 sec could be attributed to the fact that the subjects could not access an image of the aim location. It might be that the improved performance observed in the same condition after 12 sec delay is due to the time needed for the subject to "construct" a mental image of this location. In Viviani &

Velay's (1987) experiment, subjects made two successive eye movements, with one path in PU condition, but the way back to the center was a visually-guided saccade. It is thus possible that the information provided by this visual cue destroyed the effect expected by the smooth movement, thus leading the authors to suggest that both informations are equivalent.

With active arm movement memory tasks, Laabs (1973) has found that a movement is better reproduced when the subject defines himself the pattern to reproduce, than when this movement is assigned. This "preselection effect" could be due, according to Stelmach (1982), to the fact that a mental image of the movement is in this case available to the subject.

Finally, whereas the mental representation of the anchoring point is crucial for the initialization of the integration process, the relevance of the different perceptual modalities remains to be established.

5. REFERENCES

Abraham L, Potegal M, Miller S (1983) Evidence for caudate nucleus involvement in an egocentric spatial task: return from passive transport. *Physiol Psychol* 11(1): 11-17

Baker RR (1989) Human navigation and magnetoreception. Manchester University Press, Manchester, New-York

Bartram D, Smith P (1984) Everyday memory for everyday places. In: Harris JE, Morris PE (eds) Everyday memory, actions and absent-mindedness. Academic Press, London, pp 35-52

Becker W, Fuchs AF (1969) Further properties of the human saccadic system: eye movements and correction saccades with and without visual fixation point. *Vision Res* 9: 1247-1257

Benson AJ, Brown SF (1989) Visual display lowers detection threshold of angular, but not linear, whole-body motion stimuli. *Aviat Space Envir Med* 60: 629-633

Beritoff JS (1965) Character and origin of spatial orientation. In: Liberson WT (ed) Neural mechanisms of higher vertebrate behavior. Little, Brown and Comp., Boston, pp 107-123

Bloomberg J, Melvill Jones G, Segal BN, McFarlane S, Soul J (1988) Vestibular-contingent voluntary saccades based on cognitive estimates of remembered vestibular information. *Adv Oto Rhino Laryngol* 40: 71-75

Buizza A, Leger A, Berthoz A, Schmid R (1979) Otolithic-acoustic interaction in the control of eye movement. *Exp Brain Res* 36: 509-522

Buizza A, Leger A, Droulez J, Berthoz A, Schmid R (1980) Influence of otolithic stimulation by horizontal linear acceleration on optokinetic nystagmus and visual motion perception. *Exp Brain Res* 39: 167-176

Darlot C, Denise P, Droulez J, Cohen B, Berthoz A (1988) Eye movements induced by off-vertical axis rotation (OVAR) at small angles of tilt. *Exp Brain Res* 73: 91-105

Etienne AS, Maurer R, Saucy F, Teroni E (1986) Short-distance homing in the golden hamster after a passive outward journey. *Anim Behav* 34: 696-715

Etienne AS, Maurer R, Saucy F (1988) Limitations in the assessment of path dependent information. *Behaviour* 106: 81-111

Graybiel A (1952) The oculogravic illusion. *Arch Ophthalm* 48: 605-615

Graybiel A, Hupp DL (1946) The oculogyral illusion: a form of apparent motion which may be observed following stimulation of the semicircular canals. *J Aviat Med* 3: 1-12

Gresty MA, Bronstein AM, Barratt H (1987) Eye movement responses to combined linear and angular head movement. *Exp Brain Res* 65: 377-384

Guedry FE (1974) Psychophysics of vestibular sensation. In: Kornhuber HH (ed) Handbook of Sensory Physiology, Vol. VI/2 : Vestibular system, Part 2 : Psychophysics, applied aspects and general interpretations. Springer, Berlin. Heidelberg. New York, pp 3-154

Hess K, Reisine H, Dürsteler M (1985) Normal eye drift and saccadic drift correction in darkness. *Neuro-ophtalmology* 5(4): 247-252

Israël I, Berthoz A (1989) Contribution of the otoliths to the calculation of linear displacement. *J Neurophysiol* 62(1): 247-263

Kapoula Z (1985) Evidence for a range effect in the saccadic system. *Vision Res* 25(8): 1155-1157

Laabs GJ (1973) Retention characteristics of different reproduction cues in motor short-term memory. *J Exp Psychol* 100: 168-177

Miller S, Potegal M, Abraham L (1983) Vestibular involvement in a passive transport and return task. *Physiol Psychol* 11(1): 1-10

Mittelstaedt H, Mittelstaedt ML (1973) Mechanismen der Orientierung ohne richtende Außenreize. *Fortschr Zool* 21: 46-58

Mittelstaedt H, Mittelstaedt ML (1982) Homing by path integration. In: Papi F, Wallraff HG (eds) Avian navigation. Springer Verlag, Berlin, Heidelberg, pp 290-297

Mittelstaedt ML, Mittelstaedt H (1980) Homing by path integration in a mammal. *Naturwiss* 67: 566-567

Morris RGM (1981) Spatial localization does not require the presence of local cues. *Learn & Mot* 12: 239-260

O'Keefe J, Conway DH (1978) Hippocampal place units in the freely moving rat: why they fire where they fire. *Exp Brain Res* 31: 573-590

Paige GD (1989) The influence of target distance on eye movement responses during vertical linear motion. *Exp Brain Res* 77: 585-593

Paige GD, Tomko DL (1991) Eye movements and visual-vestibular interactions during linear head motion. In: Berthoz A, Vidal PP, Graf W (eds) Head-neck sensorimotor system. , ,

Paillard J (1987) Cognitive versus sensorimotor encoding of spatial information. In: Ellen P, Thinus-Blanc C (eds) Cognitive processes and spatial orientation in animal and man. Martinus Nijhoff Publishers BV, Dordrecht, The Netherlands, pp 43-77

Potegal M (1982) Vestibular and neostriatal contributions to spatial orientation. In: Potegal M (ed) Spatial abilities. Development and physiological foundations. Academic Press, New York, pp 361-387

Stelmach GE (1982) Memory for movement with emphasis on short-term aspects. In: Kelso JAS (ed) Human motor behavior. Lawrence Erlbaum Associates, Hillsdale, New Jersey, London, pp 117-139

Tokita T, Miyata H, Masaki M, Ikeda S (1981) Dynamic characteristics of the otolithic oculomotor system. *Ann NY Acad Sci* 374: 56-68

Viviani P, Velay JL (1987) Spatial coding of voluntary saccades in man. In: O'Regan JK, Levy-Schoen A (eds) Eye movements: from physiology to cognition. Elsevier, North-Holland, pp 69-78

Young LR, Shelhamer M (1990) Microgravity enhances the relative contribution of visually-induced motion sensation. *Aviat Space Envir Med* 61: 525-530

Tutorials in Motor Behavior II
G.E. Stelmach and J. Requin (Editors)
1992 Elsevier Science Publishers B.V.

Plans and programs for short movement sequences

A. Semjen[a] and R. Gottsdanker[b]

[a]Unité de Neurosciences Cognitives, C.N.R.S.,
31, chemin J.Aiguier, 13402 Marseille Cedex 9, France

[b]Psychology Department, University of California,
Santa Barbara, CA 93106, USA.

Abstract

The principle of multi-level organization and the generative concept of motor programming were examined in the production of short sequences of movements. The sequences consisted of combinations of normal and accented finger taps. Serial patterning was introduced, most often, by varying the sequential location of a single accented element. Subjects were required to produce such sequences in a choice reaction time paradigm, i.e., under conditions of initial uncertainty regarding the serial organization of the elements. Results showed that a) sequential uncertainty is resolved before execution begins, whenever rapid execution is required; b) motor programming of a series of responses is preceded by construction of a sequence plan that is uncommitted to a particular effector realization; and c) motor programming may benefit from advance knowledge about the abstract serial pattern of the intended movement sequence. It is concluded that even simple serial actions are organized on several levels, with higher-order abstract representation contributing to the generation of executable programs of the serial movements.

1. INTRODUCTION

The execution of rapid, skilled movements is thought to be contingent upon some prior organization frequently termed "planning" or "programming" by which is meant that, before acting, a person generates a representation of the ultimate goal of his (her) action along with the specification of the way in which the action will unfold. The thinking about which aspects of the action are represented in the plan or program has undergone some rather profound changes over the past two decades. These changes seem to have been characterized by an increasing shift of interest from relatively simple motor acts towards highly complex motor activities, and can conveniently be described as an evolution from a "muscle specific command assumption" towards an "abstract program" assumption (MacKay, 1982). At the end of the sixties, the motor program was conceived of as a prestructured set of muscle commands which, once initiated, runs off until completion of the preselected movement without need for peripheral feed-back (Keele, 1968). The origin of such a conception can be traced back at least to Lashley's demonstration that voluntary flexion and extension movements may be executed quite accurately in the absence of any signals from the moving organ (Lashley, 1917). Subsequently, electro-myographic analysis of simple flexion and extension movements allowed Wachholder to suggest that the primary central command determines the form and timing of activity not only in the agonist muscle, but in the antagonist and the synergist muscles as well (Wachholder, 1932). Such a proposal had obvious relevance to a programming notion, much in the same way as the subsequently introduced concept of "ballistic" movement, which was intended to designate the fast, initial portion of simple aiming movements that was supposed to be executed without on-line sensory control (e.g., Craik, 1948). Keele's definition (1968) of the motor program appeared thus on the background of sustained interest in simple, single, spatially-oriented arm or hand movements in humans.

The limitations of a prestructured command view of motor programming soon became apparent. Because such a view has difficulties in dealing with generalization and transfer of learned movements, it cannot easily be integrated into a learning theory (Pew, 1974; Schmidt, 1975). In addition, it assumes a single level of organization of the motor output though meaningful, complex skills always appear to be organized on several levels (Lashley, 1951). For instance, the motor control of speech can hardly be understood if one ignores the "non-motoric" aspects of speech production such as establishment of a syntactic and semantic structure suitable for conveying a message, choice of the lexical items, and serial organization of the to-be-pronounced phonemic segments (MacNeilage, 1980). In an integrated account of speech production (or of the production of any other complex skill) programming becomes thus synonymous with multi-level, hierarchic, advance organization of the intended performance. One important question concerns the relationship between the different levels of organization. As Shaffer (1980, 1984) pointed out, a distinction can be introduced between the "plan" level that provides the serial structure of the action over a relatively large time-span, and the "program" level where the "logistic details" of the movements are determined. Between the most abstract initial plan, and the most concrete "motor" program, there may be intermediate levels of representation of the output where various aspects of the intended action are specified to various degree. The communication between levels is not viewed as a one-to-one mapping of higher-level codes onto lower-level instructions. Instead, lower level programs are thought to be derived from, or generated on the basis of, the initial serial plan (Newell, 1978; Ostry, 1980; Shaffer, 1980, 1984).

The principle of multi-level organization, and the generative concept of motor programming have been proposed as a theoretical framework for the understanding of complex, deeply structured skills such as speaking, writing, typing, or playing the piano. The purpose of the present paper is to show that experimental evidence supports the notion that these basic principles also hold for the production of relatively short bursts of movements such as sequences of accented and nonaccented finger-taps. First we will review some earlier findings that show that in such sequences the serial order of movements must be organized prior to execution. In addition, we will report data suggesting that the serial organization is a constructive process rather than simple retrieval of a particular order from among a number of pre-selected alternatives. In the subsequent sections, experiments will be presented that address the question of whether a serial order may be planned without knowing a) the required effector realization of the movement sequence or b) the type of movement required at each sequential position. The conclusion will be advanced that content-free, generative representations may intervene in program construction for short bursts of rapid serial movements.

2. THE BASIC PARADIGM

2.1. Task

In the following experiments subjects were required to produce sequences of finger taps on a response key. Typically, a tapping sequence consisted of a fixed number of "normal" taps, and a single accented tap the location of which could vary either between blocks of sequences or randomly from sequence to sequence within a block of sequences. The subject's task consisted thus of producing different movement sequences by arranging the same elements (i.e., the accented and nonaccented taps) in different orders. The required order was indicated to the subject by a digit that was visually presented on a 7-segment display. The digit specified the serial position of the accented tap, i.e., it indicated which of the taps (first, second, third...) was to be tapped more strongly than the others. Subjects were instructed to *begin tapping as soon as possible* after the presentation of the visual digit. The digit thus had the status of a reaction stimulus (RS) in an ordinary reaction time (RT) experiment. The tapping frequency, i.e., *rate of execution* was specified by a string of isochronous, equal-intensity, auditory clicks delivered at the beginning of each trial. The number of clicks was generally the same as the number of required taps, and tapping frequency was constant within a trial block.

2.2. Measurements

Any contact between the finger and the response key triggered an electronic circuit whose output indicated the onset of a tap. The following data were recorded for each response sequence: (a) the RT, that is the delay between the digit onset and the onset of the first tap; (b) the intertap intervals measured from tap-onset to successive tap-onset; and (c) the force of each tap as the peak output voltage of a strain gauge or a piezoelectric sensor attached to the response key. Time was measured to the nearest millisecond, and force in arbitrary units. No particular force values were required; the measures were used in a relative way to ascertain that the location of the accented and nonaccented taps was correct.

3. SERIAL ORGANIZATION AS A CONSTRUCTIVE PROCESS

3.1. The effects of number of alternative organizations

If the serial order of the constituents of a short motor sequence must be decided in advance of execution, then the choice RT to initiate such a sequence should display the well-established relationship between the RT and the number of response alternatives (e.g., Hick, 1952): the greater the number of alternative serial organizations, the longer the RT should be. This has been confirmed (Semjen, Garcia-Colera and Requin, 1984; Semjen and Garcia-Colera, 1986) and is illustrated in Figure 1 (after Semjen and Garcia-Colera, 1986, Experiment 4). In this experiment subjects produced 5-tap sequences at either a fast (150-msec intertap interval) or a slow (600 msec) rate. The rate of execution was manipulated because it was assumed that, unlike fast movement sequences that must be programmed before execution begins, slow sequences may be organized step-by-step, as execution unfolds. The number of alternative accent locations in a block of trials was varied from one to five. In the 1-alternative (simple RT) condition the same accent location was required throughout a block and this location was known by the subject. In the choice RT conditions a different set of accent locations was used in each block of trials. In one series of blocks (called "first tap included"), four sets of locations were used: 1-2, 1-2-3, 1-2-3-4, and 1-2-3-4-5. In the other series (called "first tap excluded"), three sets of locations were used: 4-5, 3-4-5, and 2-3-4-5. Each accent location of a set was required the same number of times, at random. When the first tap was excluded from among the possible locations for the accent, the subject knew that every tapping sequence would begin with a nonaccented tap. This initial tap was thus predictable, whereas the over-all sequence organization was not. When the first tap was a possible location for the accent, the over-all organization of the sequence as well as the identity of the initial tap both were uncertain. Figure 1 shows the mean RT to initiate the tapping sequence as a function of the number of alternative accent locations and tapping speed. It can be seen that for *fast* sequences, the RT was an increasing function of the number of alternatives both when the first tap of the sequence was nonpredictable ("first tap included") or predictable ("first tap excluded"). This result supports the notion that at the fast tapping rate response uncertainty was introduced at the level of the over-all sequence organization. In contrast, *slow* sequences had their RT influenced by changes in the number of alternatives only to the extent this manipulation affected the predictability of the first tap. When the first tap was excluded from the set of alternative locations, the choice RT barely differed from the simple RT (i.e., the 1-alternative case). When the first tap was included in the set, a single step-like change occurred between the 1-alternative and 2-alternative conditions, with no further increase thereafter. These results indicate that slow sequences may be initiated with a program for the initial tap.

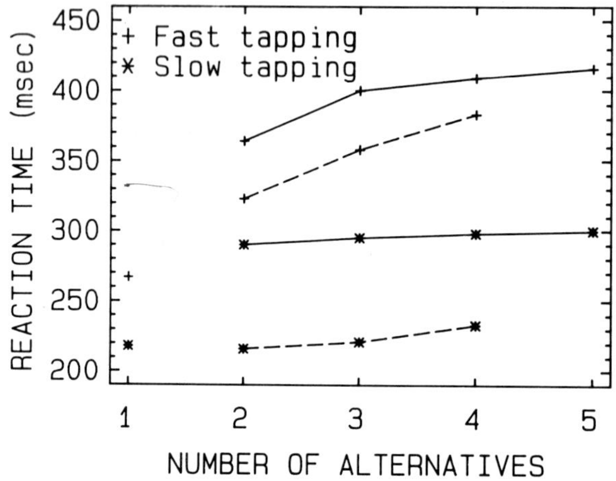

Figure 1. Reaction Time as a function of number of alternatives at two tapping rates. Continuous lines: First tap included. Broken lines: First tap excluded. (After Semjen and Garcia-Colera, 1986)

What kind of process would account for the effects of the number of alternatives in the case of fast sequences? One possibility is that the subject prepares and stores several alternate serial organizations and begins *searching* for the required one when the RS is presented. Under this "retrieval" hypothesis, the lengthened RT would reflect longer search time among a greater number of ready-made programs. Alternatively, one may think of the subject preparing a common memory representation for the alternative sequences, with "blanks" for the unspecified constituents and, upon presentation of the RS, working on this representation until all blanks were replaced by the required values. The sequence is then executed. Under this hypothesis, the choice RT would lengthen because more time is needed for specifying a greater number of uncertain constituents. Such a "constructive" conception of sequence planning was first proposed by Cooper and Ehrlich (1981). These authors had subjects memorize pairs of visually presented phrases that differed in 0, 1, 2, or 3 constituents (e.g., "A casino with a gift shop in the city" vs. "A casino with a snack bar in the city"). Both the memorization time and, in subsequent testing, the choice RT to produce one of the two sequences upon presentation of a cue, increased as a function of the number of contrasting words. An additional finding was that the lengthening of the choice RT occurred even when the initial word of the phrase was held constant. The fact that the choice time between the alternative sequences increased as a function of the number of contrasting words suggests that the subjects did not prepare the sequences for execution as separate entities but, as Cooper and Ehrlich pointed out, they specified the uncertain constituents of a "carrier phrase" after the cue was presented.

3.2. Context effects on sequence choice time

3.2.1. A two-choice experiment. If sequence selection consists merely of recovering one of several serial organizations from a temporary store, choice RT should vary only with the number of alternatives, not with the context of choice. For example, the time to choose a particular movement sequence should not depend on the identity of the alternative sequences and their interrelation. If, however, the serial program is constructed on the basis of an initial, relatively undifferentiated representation of the sequence which is specified according to the stimulus information (as was suggested in the previous paragraph), the choice RT could depend not only on the number of constituents that need to be specified, but also on their interrelations in the alternative sequences. Consider the process of choosing between two tapping sequences that differ in the location of a single element, e.g., an accented tap. A context effect would be demonstrated if one could show, for example, that the time to choose a sequence is longer when the possible accent locations are adjacent (e.g., tap 1 in one sequence, tap 2 in the other), rather than nonadjacent (e.g., tap 1 in one sequence, tap 3 in the other). Confusability of, or competition between, adjacent locations might account for such an effect. The time to program might also depend on whether the uncertain taps are located toward the beginning, or the end, of the sequence. When both uncertain locations are late in the sequence (e.g., the next-to-last and last taps), the program for the known, initial sequence part may be prepared prior to the RS occurrence. Members of such sequence pairs could be initiated with shorter choice RT than sequences in which the uncertain locations occur earlier. Such a result has been reported in several studies (Rosenbaum, Hindorff, and Munro, 1987; Garcia-Colera and Semjen, 1988). In sum, context-dependency of the sequence choice time would favor the constructive view, rather than the retrieval account, of the sequence-selection process.

An experiment was run in which the subjects (2 men and 3 women) were required to produce sequences of five finger-taps with one accented element and 180 msec intertap intervals. The subjects were trained and instructed on the task during a practice session in which they produced 32 sequences with each possible accent location. Data were collected in two further sessions. Ten blocks of 16 trials were recorded during each session. The first five blocks in each session consisted of simple RT trials in which the same accent location was required on each trial. The required accent location (1, 2, 3, 4, or 5) was varied over trial blocks. The last five blocks consisted of choice RT trials in which one of two equiprobable accent locations was presented, at random. All possible pairings of the five different accent locations were used and presented to the subjects in a variable order. The main experimental question was whether the particular pairs used in the choice condition would significantly affect the RT.

Sequences in which more or fewer than five taps were produced or in which the accent location was incorrect, were classified as errors. Error rate was 10.8% in the simple RT condition, and 9% in the choice RT condition. Roughly half the errors in the simple RT condition occurred when the accent was required on the second tap. In the choice RT condition, the 1-2, 1-5, 2-5, and 3-5 pairings showed fewer errors than other pairings.

The simple RT for accent locations 1 to 5 was, respectively, 272, 283, 266, 271, and 271 msec, a variation that did not reach the significance level, $F(4,16)=1.46$. The longer RT for location 2, along with the high error score for this same location suggests, however, that the program for this sequence was more difficult to activate and/or to execute than the programs for other sequences.

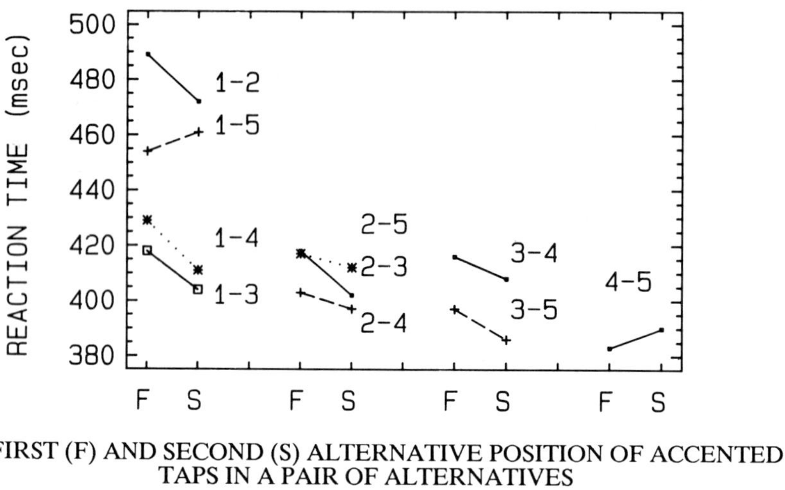

Figure 2. Reaction Time as a function of accent pairing.

Figure 2 shows the choice RT as a function of particular accent pairings and the order of the accent (first or second) within the pair. Note that the pairings are grouped according to the location in the sequence of the first member of the pair. The figure shows that lengthened RTs occurred when the accent was either on the first or on the second tap (1-2), and when it was on the first or the last tap (1-5). A 10 x 2 Analysis of Variance (ANOVA) tested the effects of Pairing and Place of the accent in the pair. The former effect was significant, $F(9,36)=4.56$, $p < .01$, the latter was not, $F(1,4)=1.18$. No significant interaction appeared. Removal of the 1-2 and 1-5 pairings from the analysis eliminated the effect of Pairing, $F(7,28)=0.68$. Separate analysis of the 1-2, 1-3, 1-4, and 1-5 pairings yielded a significant effect for Pairing, $F(3,12)=6.18$, $p < .01$.

3.2.2. Discussion. Two pairings of accent locations, first and second and first and last, induced longer RTs than other pairings. A previous experiment (Semjen et al., 1984) with a 4-tap sequence yielded similar results. The fact that particular pairs, i.e., choice context, may significantly affect the RT argues in favor of a constructive view of sequence selection. It would appear, however, that choosing between adjacent locations is difficult only if the *beginning* of the sequence needs to be organized; adjacent locations in the middle of the sequence present no such difficulties. The difficulty in choosing between sequences with one initial and one terminal accent may appear surprising unless we suppose that these accents organize the sequence in a functionally similar way. Such a proposal follows from the observation that, when tapping short sequences without required voluntary accent, subjects spontaneously accent either the first or the last element, and when a *voluntary* accent is required in initial or terminal position, they produce *non-voluntary* secondary accents on the last or first tap (Semjen and Garcia-Colera, 1986).

Several studies (Rosenbaum et al., 1984, 1987; Garcia-Colera and Semjen, 1988) have shown that members of a pair of sequences are initiated with longer choice RT if the first uncertain element in the pair occurs at, or close to, the beginning of the sequence than if it occurs towards the end of the sequence. The shifting of the first uncertain element towards the end of the sequence shortens the choice RT, presumably because the initial elements that are common to the alternatives may be programmed before the RS is presented. In the present experiment, this effect was not observed. When the 1-2 and 1-5 pairs were discarded from analysis, the remaining pairs did not show significant variations in RT despite the fact that in some pairs (1-3, 1-4, 2-3, 2-4, 2-5) the first uncertain location occurred early and in other pairs (3-4, 3-5, 4-5) both uncertain locations occurred late in the sequence. However, according to previous results (Garcia-Colera and Semjen, 1988) the effect of shifting the first uncertain element depends both on the amount of the shift (in terms of ordinal positions) and the overall length of the sequence. In very short sequences, like those used in this experiment, the effect tends to be weak.

4. PLANNING WITHOUT COMMITMENT TO PARTICULAR RESPONSES

Thus far we have reported results which indicate that short finger-tapping sequences with one accented element are organized before execution begins. We have also suggested that the program for such sequences is constructed after the RS was presented, based on some representation of the general features of the required movement sequences. In the present section we will argue that between the broadest, categoric representation of the action, and the detailed program for the serial movements, there is an intermediate, planning, level where the serial pattern of the sequence may be selected without commitment to particular responses.

4.1. Effector-independent plan selection

The idea that the organizational aspects of serial skills are represented in an effector-independent manner stems largely from experimental and theoretical work on skill learning and transfer (e.g., Pew, 1974; Schmidt, 1975; Cohen, Ivry and Keele, 1990). Effector-independence appeared, prima facie, characteristic of long-term memory codes. It remained to be shown that in the course of short-term program construction for serial movements, information about sequential organization is processed independently of information about effector implementation. The next experiments were designed to examine this conception, using the brief precue-to-stimulus (PSIs) procedure (Gottsdanker and Shragg, 1985). In this procedure an informative precue is presented shortly before the RS. For example, a signal identifying the position in the sequence of the accented tap is followed by the stimulus which indicates the effector hand. It was reasoned that if the planning of the sequential order is a processing stage that may be carried out prior to, and independently of, the stage of effector selection, then providing information about sequence with a short PSI should reduce RT by exactly the same amount, by allowing a head-start in planning. In general a -1 slope between RT and PSI would hold over PSIs that are shorter than the shortest duration of the planning process. Thus, direct evidence is provided that the operations dependent on the precue information are immediately triggered, and go to completion, before other operations are initiated. Moreover, the inference may be drawn that there is the same seriality in the choice reaction performed in the ordinary way, without a precue (Gottsdanker, 1989).

4.1.1. Task. In one experiment (called "Planning"), four-tap sequences were used with an accent being required at any of the four locations, equiprobably. The precue stimulus was a digit presented on a 7-segment display; it indicated the serial position (1, 2, 3, or 4) of the accented tap. The RS identifying the effector was presented 0, 30, 60, 90, 120, or 2100 msec after the onset of the precue, and consisted of the illumination of one of two light emitting diodes (LEDs) that were located on the left or right side of the 7-segment display. Illumination of the right or left LED assigned sequence execution to the right or left hand with equal probability, at random. In this experiment the hypothesis was tested that the precue allows for a head-start in planning, which would be indicated by a -1 slope between RT and the PSIs.

In a second experiment (called "Control"), the same stimuli were used and delivered with the same PSIs; however, the rules that governed sequence production were changed. On trials where the digit was followed by illumination of the right LED, subjects were required to produce a four-tap sequence with the right hand, with an accent on the tap indicated by the digit. Thus, the right-hand responses were the same as in the original experiment. On trials where the digit was followed by illumination of the left LED, subjects were required to produce rapidly alternating left-right taps (doublets). The number of *doublets* was to be equal to the digit presented. In this experiment, then, the digit precue did not identify a unique sequential organization; it reduced only, from eight to two, the number of alternative sequences among which the subject had to choose when the RS was presented. It is known that the choice RT decreases when a precue stimulus indicates momentary reduction of the size of the set of responses (Leonard, 1958). However, such a decrease in RT does not result from a single processing stage being carried out in advance and, therefore, no basis exists in this case for predicting a slope as steep as - 1 between RT and PSI (Gottsdanker, 1989). Predictions concerned the absolute RT level in producing the right-hand sequences; this was expected on the average to be longer in the Control than in the Planning experiment, because of the added operation, on each trial, of determining which of the sequence-production rules applied. In addition, the difference was predicted to increase as PSI lengthened. This is because in the Planning experiment, the processing initiated by the precue could progress until the stage of sequence planning was completed, whereas in the Control experiment, this stage could be initiated only after the RS had indicated the production rule.

4.1.2. Procedure and Subjects. A trial began with the presentation of 4 clicks of equal intensity separated by 150-msec intervals. The last click initiated a countdown interval intended to reduce time uncertainty. This interval consisted of three epoches of 1050 msec duration each. The end of the first and the second epoch was marked by a 10-msec illumination of two horizontal bars on the digital display. The RS was presented at the end of the third epoch and was preceded 0, 30, 60, 90, or 120 msec by the precue. PSI was constant within each trial block. On control-trial blocks the precue stimulus was presented for 30 msec at the end of the first and second epoches. The PSI on control blocks was thus 2100 msec. Each block consisted of 64 trials. A trial was considered terminated when the RT or any interval between successive taps was over 600 msec. The intertrial interval was about 6 s.

Six subjects, two women and four men, participated in the experiments. All received several hundreds of trials in the 4-tap production task before entering the Planning experiment. Three subjects were tested for six sessions, with all six PSIs used once in each session according to a latin square design. The other subjects were tested in four sessions and received the PSIs in a counterbalanced, ascending and descending order. There was one practice session for the Control experiment. Subject were tested subsequently in four sessions; they performed one block per PSI and session. Again the PSIs were presented in a counterbalanced, ascending-descending order.

4.1.3. Results. Regression of the RT on PSI was calculated subject-by-subject for the three shortest PSIs (0, 30, 60 msec), the next four (0, 30, 60, 90 msec), and all five PSIs (0, 30, 60, 90, 120 msec). Table 1 shows the individual slope constants and their means for three and four PSIs. The results for five PSIs were not included because the RT ceased to change in several subjects beyond a PSI of 90 msec.

Table 1.
Estimated slope constants for individual subjects and means

Experiment	Subject	Right Hand		Left Hand	
		3 PSIs	4 PSIs	3 PSIs	4 PSIs
Planning	1	-.99	-.88	-.97	-.88
	2	-.80	-.71	-.62	-.50
	3	-.84	-.87	-.80	-.83
	4	-.91	-.80	-.84	-.66
	5	-.89	-.71	-.58	-.66
	6	-.85	-.76	-.70	-.61
	Mean	**-.88**	**-.79**	**-.75**	**-.69**
Control	1	-.63	-.59	-.46	-.50
	2	-.83	-.66	-.74	-.64
	3	-.55	-.48	-.33	-.34
	4	-.60	-.45	-.42	-.38
	5	-.48	-.50	-.67	-.66
	6	-.55	-.46	-.63	-.59
	Mean	**-.60**	**-.52**	**-.54**	**-.51**

The slope constants were all negative indicating that the RT decreased as PSI increased. Moreover, they were higher, approaching in some instances -1, in the Planning experiment than in the Control experiment. Finally, the slopes were somewhat steeper for the right hand than for the left hand, especially in the Planning experiment.

Additional analyses were carried out on the individual mean RTs. First, the RTs from the Planning experiment were subjected to a 5 x 2 ANOVA that tested the effects of PSI (0, 30, 60, 90, 120 msec) and Hand. The effect of PSI was significant, $F(4,20)=125.2$, $p < .001$, that of Hand was not, $F(1,5)=1.04$. A significant interaction between these factors ($F(4,20)=3.50$, $p < .05$) confirmed the difference between hands, seen in Table 1. A second, identical ANOVA was done on the data stemming from the Control experiment. Here again, the effect of PSI was significant, $F(4,20)=87.7$, $p < .001$ and that of Hand was not. There was no significant interaction between PSI and Hand, $F(4,20)=1.85$. Finally, a third, and crucial analysis was done on the data of right hand in both experiments. This ANOVA tested the effects of PSI and Condition (i.e., Planning vs. Control). The means of individual means are shown in Figure 3. The effect of PSI was, of course, significant. In addition, this ANOVA confirmed two of our major predictions: a) that choice RT would be longer in the Control experiment than in the Planning experiment and b) that this difference would increase over lengthening PSIs. In accordance with these predictions, the effect of Condition was significant, $F(1,5)=33.64$, $p < .01$, as was the interaction between PSI and Condition, $F(4,20)=5.69$, $p < .01$. Subsequent trend analysis revealed that the linear trend of the RT was significantly different between Conditions.

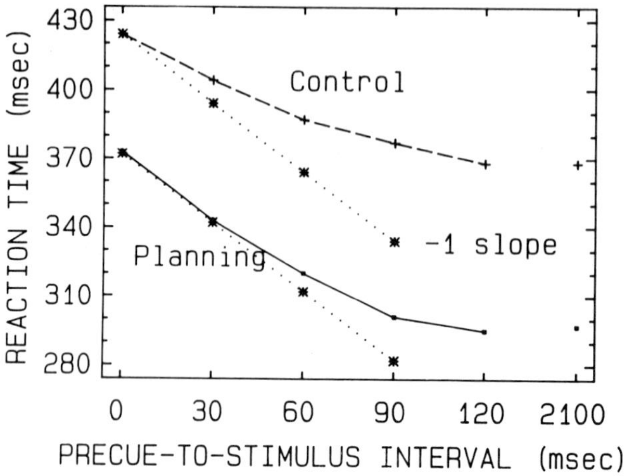

Figure 3. Reaction Time to initiate 4-tap sequences with one accent in the Planning and Control experiments, as a function of precue-to-stimulus interval.

The errors in these experiments were classified as *production errors*, i.e., incorrect number of taps or incorrect accent; *wrong-hand errors*, i.e., tapping any element with the hand that was not required, or *omissions*, i.e., failure to respond within 600 msec after the RS.

In the Planning experiment, there were 1261 errors, i.e., 10.9% of the total number of trials. The overall percentage of production errors, wrong-hand errors and omissions was 9.6%, 1%, and 0.3% respectively. There were fewer overall errors with the right hand than with the left hand: 426 against 835. However, this difference was due entirely to production errors; wrong-hand errors and omissions occurred with the same frequency for both hands. From among the three categories of errors, only wrong-hand errors were linked with PSI; their proportion systematically increased with PSI: 0.1%, 0.4%, 0.6%, 1.5%, 1.8%. At a PSI of 2100 msec the percentage was 0.4%.

In the Control experiment there were 876 errors, i.e., 9.5%. The number of erroneous trials differed only slightly between 4-tap sequences with one accent and series of left-right doublets. In the case of 4-tap sequences, executed with the right hand, the production errors (6%), wrong-hand errors (1.1%) and omissions (1.1%) closely reproduced the pattern found in the "Planning" experiment. Here again, the proportion of wrong-hand responses tended to increase over brief PSIs: 0.8%, 0.6%, 1.2%, 1.7%, 2.2%; at a PSI of 2100 msec the proportion was 0.4% .

4.1.4. Discussion. The purpose of the present experiments was to show that in the course of short-term program construction for serial movements, information about serial organization is processed prior to, and independently of, information about effector implementation. We have argued that if the planning of the serial order is a single, separate processing stage, then providing information which identifies a particular organization should allow for a head-start in planning, and this would be indicated by an RT - PSI function with a slope of -1 (Planning experiment). In contrast, less effect was expected from giving precue information which merely restricts the set of alternative responses without allowing for selection of a particular plan (Control experiment). Both expectations were supported by the results in Figure 3. While the RT-slope in the Control experiment was far shallower than -1, in the Planning experiment it was very close to -1 over the range of PSIs and exactly -1 between 0 and 30 msec. Hence we conclude that the serial order is planned prior to, and independently of, the selection of the effector.

This conclusion raises two issues that need to be discussed. One concerns the fact that in the Planning experiment the RT-slope was slightly, but consistently steeper for right-hand responses than left-hand responses. At first glance, such a difference might appear harmful to the notion that the sequence plan was not committed to a particular effector, and might suggest some bias in favor of responding with the right hand. However, a response-bias interpretation is inconsistent with the finding that the proportion of wrong-hand errors was the same for both hands. A more plausible explanation would be that the sequence plan can be implemented more readily for the right hand than for the left hand, because the left hemisphere, which has specific competence in generating sequential plans (e.g., Webster, 1990) also controls the right-hand movements. In contrast, left-hand implementation of the sequence plan requires interhemispheric communication and this process could occasionally introduce some noise in the process of programming, thereby reducing the slope of the RT-function.

The second issue concerns the discrepancy between the present results and our previous failure to show a head-start in sequence plan selection (Semjen and Gottsdanker, 1990). In one of the experiments of an earlier study, subjects produced 8-tap sequences with one of two possible accent locations (first or second tap), with either the right or the left hand. When the precue identified accent location and the RS identified the required hand (as in the "Planning" experiment), RT decreased as a function of PSI with a slope shallower than -1. However, the two experiments differ in two important ways. First, there possibly was no real particularizing of an abstract plan in the previous task. Instead, there may have been a decision on how to initiate an otherwise long, uniform tapping sequence. This operation would be less distinct from that of choosing a response unit and the processes could overlap. Second, the subjects of the previous experiment were tested on a much smaller number of trials per PSIs, which did not permit separate examination of the right-hand and left-hand RTs. The possible role of each of these factors deserves further experimental work.

4.2. Structural facilitation of movement sequence planning

The evidence presented thus far supports the notion that a sequence of movements may be planned without commitment to a particular *effector*. The question arises, however, as to whether a sequence of movements may be planned without commitment to particular *responses*. Consider, for example, a sequential pattern denoted "OXOOX". Two finger-tapping sequences, consisting of strong (S) and weak (W) taps, may implement this pattern: "S W S S W" and "W S W W S". Although these sequences differ at each serial position, they share the same serial pattern in terms of repetition of, or transitions between, dichotomous events. If planning a sequence of movements may occur in such *relational* terms, then receiving advance information about the pattern -- even without receiving concomitant information about the concrete events that must fill in the pattern -- should facilitate subsequent programming of the sequence. An extension of the hypothesis is that execution of a sequence of movements should facilitate subsequent programming of another sequence of movements, if both share the same serial pattern. Evidence was found that supports both expectations (Semjen and Gottsdanker, in press). The next sections briefly summarize the most relevant results.

4.2.1. Choosing between pairs of sequences. Subjects were instructed to produce eight-tap sequences that consisted of combinations of strong (i.e., stressed) and weak (nonstressed) taps. The imposed intertap interval was 160 msec. The taps were made with the same finger (index or middle) of the preferred hand. There were two serial patterns (A and B) each of which gave rise to two finger-tapping sequences by interchanging the assignment of strong and weak taps (see Table 2). Sequences that started with a weak tap, and involved more weak taps than strong ones, will be referred to as "normal stress"; sequences that started with a strong tap, and involved more strong taps than weak taps, will be called "inverted stress".

Table 2.
Sequences used by Semjen and Gottsdanker (in press)

PATTERN	STRESS	SEQUENCES
A: 0 X 0 X 0 0 0 X	Normal	W S W S W W W S (1)
	Inverted	S W S W S S S W (2)
B: 0 0 0 X 0 X 0 X	Normal	W W W S W S W S (3)
	Inverted	S S S W S W S W (4)

Note: W: weak tap S: strong tap

Subjects received several practice sessions during which they learned to produce the sequences according to the requirements of an RT paradigm. The visual codes serving as RS consisted of two horizontal bars presented on the 7-segment display for sequence 1, and two vertical bars for sequence 3. These codes were supplemented by simultaneous illumination of a LED located close to the 7-segment display, to call for production of these sequences with inverted stress (i.e., sequences 2 and 4).

At the end of the practice period, subjects were tested in a single session during which they produced the sequences under four-choice and two-choice conditions. In the four-choice condition all four sequences were presented in a block with the same probability ($p = 0.25$), at random. In the two-choice condition subjects were told which sequences constituted the alternatives ($p = 0.50$) in a block. Such information may be viewed as a global precue that allows the subject to preselect a higher-order sequential plan if, and only if, the alternative sequences implement the same serial pattern. (By "higher-order" is meant that the plan is structural only, and is uncommitted with regard to concrete events, such as strong or weak taps, that must fill in the serial order.) Preselection of a sequential plan could thus occur when sequences 1 and 2, or 3 and 4, constituted the alternatives in a block. Since in the case of these pairings subjects had to choose -- after the RS was presented -- between stress assignments, this choice condition is referred to as "stress-choice". When sequences 1 and 3, or 2 and 4, constituted the alternatives in a block, subjects had to choose between sequences of different pattern but identical initial stress assignment. This condition is called "pattern-choice". Finally, when sequences 1 and 4, or 2 and 3, constituted the alternatives, subjects had to choose between sequences of different pattern and stress assignment;

this condition is called "mixed choice". The main hypothesis tested in this experiment was that programming a sequence takes less time (as indexed by shorter choice RT) if preselection of a sequential plan is possible, than if it is not.

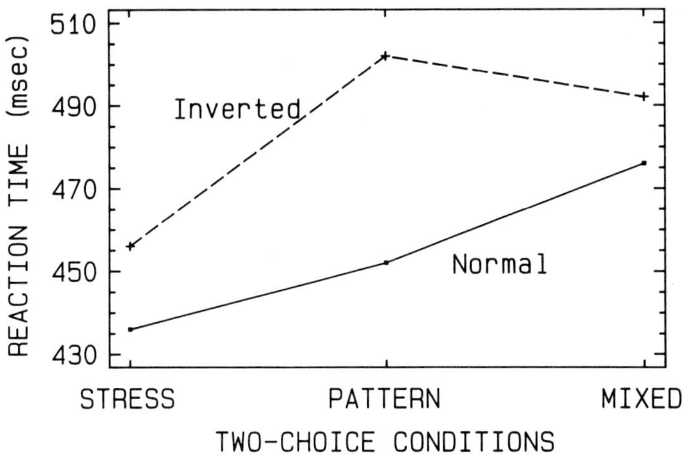

Figure 4. Reaction Time to initiate tapping sequences with "normal" and "inverted" stress assignment in the two-choice conditions.

The means of individual median reaction times were calculated, based on correct responses only, and averaged over subjects. Four-choice RT was significantly longer than average two-choice RT: 584 msec vs. 454 msec with "normal" stress assignment; 673 msec vs. 483 msec with "inverted" stress assignment. However, our chief interest was in determining whether the two-choice conditions would be different from one another. Two-choice RTs are presented in Figure 4 as a function of choice conditions (i.e., stress-choice, pattern-choice and mixed choice) and stress assignment. The prediction that preselection of the serial plan allows for responding with shorter choice RT was clearly supported by the significant difference between the stress-choice and mixed choice conditions. There was a suggestion of similar difference between the stress-choice and pattern-choice conditions. However, the difference might have been reduced (namely in normal stress sequences) because the initial stress was known in advance in the pattern-choice condition. As we have already mentioned, the time to choose between alternative sequences often decreases as the first nonpredictable element recedes from the beginning of the sequence towards its end.

4.2.2. Priming a sequential structure. Further experiments were aimed at examining whether a higher-order plan for sequential organization could subserve different motor domains such as, for example, verbal and manual responses. If the same higher-order plan may subserve a spoken sequence consisting of binary syllables, and a tapping sequence consisting of strong and weak taps, and if that plan were to remain activated for some time after the verbal sequence has been pronounced, then generating a tapping sequence with the same pattern should take less time than generating a tapping sequence with a different pattern. The effect we hypothesize here is reminiscent of the repetition effect, well-known from the literature on sequential choice RT, that is, a shortening of the choice RT on trial n if the stimulus presented and/or the response required on that trial are the same as on the preceding trial n-1 (e.g., Kornblum, 1973; Holender, 1980; Soetens, Boer and Hueting, 1985). However, in the foregoing example there are two successive tasks rather than a single task, and that which may be repeated in performing these tasks is neither a stimulus, nor a response, but the serial pattern of the sequence of responses called for in each of them.

In one experiment reported by Semjen and Gottsdanker (in press), subjects (N=6) were required to read aloud, at the beginning of each trial, one of four verbal sequences presented as equally likely alternatives. The sequences were printed on a card, one sequence per row. The reading was directed by the illumination of one of four LEDs, each located on a different row. The illumination of the LED was followed, 1.2 sec later, by the presentation of a string of auditory clicks, paced at 160 msec. This model indicated to the subject the required rate of tapping. Finally, the required tapping sequence was identified by one of four learned visual codes (similar to those described in the previous section), presented 700 msec after the last click of the string. The verbal sequences as well as the tapping sequences implemented one of two serial patterns (A and B), as Table 3 shows. Each verbal sequence was followed by one of the tapping sequences with the same probability. Therefore, the verbal sequence and the subsequent tapping sequence implemented the same pattern on half of the trials, and a different pattern on the other half, at random. The former case will be referred to as "congruent priming", and the latter case as "noncongruent priming".

Table 3.
Verbal and tapping sequences used by Semjen and Gottsdanker (in press)

PATTERN	Verbal sequences	Tapping sequences
A: 0 X 0 X	Ba Bi Ba Bi	W S W S (N)
	Bi Ba Bi Ba	S W S W (I)
B: 0 0 0 X	Ba Ba Ba Bi	W W W S (N)
	Bi Bi Bi Ba	S S S W (I)

Note: W: weak tap N: normal stress
S: strong tap I: inverted stress

Subjects performed three blocks of 64 trials. Individual data were pooled over trial blocks (correct sequences only), median RTs were determined and averaged over subjects. The mean RT of sequences with normal stress assignment was 582 msec when priming was congruent, and 610 msec when priming was noncongruent. The mean RT of sequences with inverted stress assignment was 630 msec when priming was congruent, and 641 msec when priming was noncongruent. Over-all, the effect of type of priming (i.e., Congruent vs. Noncongruent) was significant, $F(1,5)=24.86$, $p < .01$, with no significant interaction between stress assignment and type of priming. It thus appears established that providing subjects with a model of sequential organization in one motor domain may benefit, or interact with, subsequent programming of a sequence of movements in a different motor domain. An extension of this notion is that there are higher-order plans for serial organization that may be interfaced with different production systems.

5. GENERAL DISCUSSION

The present series of experiments investigated how short motor sequences are prepared for execution under conditions of initial uncertainty regarding the serial organization of the elements of the sequence. The motor sequences consisted of combinations of normal and accented finger taps and, for the most part, serial patterning was introduced by varying the location of a single accented element. This paradigm is unusual in that it assigns sequential organization to the "response intensity" domain, while studies in discrete-serial actions have most often concentrated on the sequencing of different *effectors*. Thus, any convergence between the conclusions drawn from investigations made with such different paradigms would highlight the generality of the processes underlying the sequential control of motor actions.

One of the first conclusions we arrived at was that, even in such simple sequences, uncertainties regarding the successive responses are resolved before execution begins, whenever *rapid* execution is required. Put in another way, rapid execution supposes some program for the sequential order. The second suggestion we proposed was that, in a choice situation, the alternative programs may not be prepared in advance as separate entities. Rather, programming appears as a constructive process whereby a "protoprogram" is specified in details according to actual constraints, either external (e.g., stimulus information) or internal. This suggestion was mainly based on comparisons between results from Cooper and Ehrlich's (1981) sentence production task and our finger-tapping task, as well as on the context effects found in our 2-choice experiment (3.2.1). The notion that programs for movement sequences are differentiated from an initial representation, common to the sequence alternatives, has received impressive support from theoretical and empirical work on *effector* sequences, pursued for a number years by Rosenbaum and his associates (Rosenbaum et al., 1984; Rosenbaum, 1987).

How tightly is a serial plan for a pattern of normal and accented taps coupled with specifications regarding the actual effector of the sequence (e.g., right or left hand)? Before summarizing our conclusions on this point, let us recall that effector independence has long been regarded as one of the supportive arguments for generalized "motor" programs (see Cohen et al., 1990). However, Wright (1990) has recently pointed out the critical importance of knowing the *level of representation* that is common or generalized across the same movement made with different effectors. "Presumably, he wrote, all *nominally* identical movements -- for example 'Press the button' -- are related at the highest, intentional level of representation. But if this is the lowest level of representation common to two instances of that nominal movement task, I would not wish to label this an effector-independent, generalized motor program" (Wright, 1990, p. 298).

The results from our brief-precue experiments provided evidence that information about sequential organization of normal and accented responses may fully be utilized without commitment to a particular effector realization. Hence, the level of representation which was common across movement sequences made with different hands may be considered higher than the "motor" program level, and certainly lower than the level of "nominal identity." The existence of an effector-independent, serial-plan level of representation does not involve, however, equal quality of motor execution when the plan is implemented for different effectors. In line with Wright's (1990) demonstration of considerable differences between the quality of writing with the right and left hands, we also observed more production errors in left-hand tapping than in right-hand tapping. Obviously, certain effector systems or sub-systems (such as the nondominant hand) have only moderate "procedural knowledge" (Shaffer, 1984) about how the serial plan may be implemented to give fluent and error-free motor performance.

The last issue we addressed in this series of experiments concerned the possibility that planning of the serial order may occur, in some instances, at a higher level of abstractness than that involved in effector independence. In effector independence, there is a "surface" description of the sequence elements that is common to the alternative motor implementations. At a higher level of abstractness, which would be still below the level of "nominal identity," all that would matter would be the relationship between sequences of events, rather than the nature of the events themselves. The existence of such a level of planning received support from the advantage of knowing in advance, in a sequence-choice task, the abstract sequential pattern of the to-be-programmed series of movements.

We started this review with an outline of recent evolutions of the motor program concept. The shift from a "muscle specific command" view toward an abstract programming view appeared to be linked with the displacement of interest from relatively simple movements toward the cognitive control of serially organized, deeply structured, complex skills. The present studies suggest, however, that the principle of multi-level organization including motor programs and increasingly abstract sequential plans, and the principle of generative relationship between those plans and the final motor program, apply even for short burst of serial movements.

6. ACKNOWLEDGEMENTS

The authors thank Sylvan Kornblum for his helpful comments on the initial manuscript.

7. REFERENCES

Cohen A., Ivry, R., & Keele, S.W. (1990). Attention and structure in sequence learning. Journal of Experimental Psychology : Learning, Memory and Cognition, 16, 17-30.

Cooper, W.E. & Ehrlich, S.F. (1981). Planning speech: Studies in choice reaction time. In J. Long and A. Baddeley (Eds), Attention and Performance IX. Hillsdale, NJ.: Erlbaum, pp. 537-552.

Craik, K.J.W. (1948). Man as an element in a control system. British Journal of psychology, 38, 142-148.

Garcia-Colera, A. & Semjen, A. (1988). Distributed planning of movements sequences. Journal of Motor Behavior, 20, 341-367.

Gottsdanker, R. (1989). Subtractive decomposition of perceptual-motor reactions after Donders. In: D. Vickers and P.L. Smith (Eds.), Human Information Processing: Measures, Mechanisms, and Models. Amsterdam: North Holland.

Gottsdanker, R. & Shragg, G.P. (1985). Verification of Donders' subtraction method. Journal of Experimental Psychology: Human Perception and Performance, 11, 765-776.

Hick, W.E. (1952). On the rate of gain of information. Quarterly Journal of Experimental Psychology, 4, 11-26.

Holender, D. (1980). L'effet de répétition dans les tâches de réaction de choix: préparation volontaire ou activation automatique? In: J. Requin (Ed.), Anticipation et comportement. Paris: Edition du CNRS, pp. 523-542.

Keele, S.W. (1968). Movement control in skilled motor performance. Psychological Bulletin, 70, 387-403.

Kornblum, S.(1973). Sequential effects in choice reaction time. In S. Kornblum (Ed.): Attention and Performance IV. New York: Academic Press, pp. 259-288.

Lashley, K.S. (1917). The accuracy of movements in the absence of excitation from the moving organ. American Journal of Physiology, 43, 169-194.

Lashley, K.S. (1951). The problem of serial order in behavior. In L. A. Jeffress (Ed.), Cerebral mechanisms in behavior. New York: Wiley, pp. 112-136.

MacKay, D.G. (1982). The problems of flexibility, fluency, and speed-accuracy trade-off in skilled behavior. Psychological Review, 89, 483-506.

MacNeilage, P.F. (1980). Distinctive properties of speech motor control. In G.E. Stelmach and J. Requin (Eds), Tutorials in motor behavior. Amsterdam: North Holland, pp. 607-621.

Newell, K.M. (1978). Some issues on action plans. In G.E. Stelmach (Ed), Information processing in motor control and learning. New York: Academic Press, pp. 41-54.

Ostry, D.J. (1980). Execution-time movement control. In G.E. Stelmach and J. Requin (Eds), Tutorials in motor behavior. Amsterdam: North Holland, pp. 457-468.

Pew, R.W. (1974). Levels of analysis in motor control. Brain Research, 71, 393-400.

Rosenbaum, D.A. (1987). Successive approximations to a model of human motor programming. In: G.H. Bower (Ed.), The psychology of learning and motivation. Vol. 21. New York: Academic Press, pp.153-182.

Rosenbaum, D.A., Inhoff, A.W., & Gordon, A.M. (1984). Choosing between movement sequences: A hierarchical editor model. Journal of Experimental Psychology: General, 113, 372-393.

Rosenbaum, D.A., Hindorff, V, & Munro, E.M. (1987). Scheduling and programming of rapid finger sequences: Tests and elaborations of the Hierarchical Editor Model. Journal of Experimental Psychology: Human Perception and Performance, 13, 193-200.

Schmidt, R.A. (1975). A schema theory of discrete motor skill learning. Psychological Review, 82, 225-260.

Semjen, A. & Garcia-Colera, A. (1986). Planning and timing of finger-tapping sequences with a stressed element. Journal of Motor Behavior, 18, 287-322.

Semjen, A., Garcia-Colera, A, & Requin, J. (1984). On controlling force and time in rhythmic movements sequences: the effect of stress location. Annals of the New York Academy of Sciences, 423, pp. 168-182.

Semjen, A. & Gottsdanker, R. (1989). Rapid serial movements: Relation between the planning of sequential structure and effector selection. In: M. Jeannerod (Ed.), Attention and Performance XIII. Hillsdale, N.J.: Lawrence Erlbaum Associates, pp. 409-427.

Semjen A. & Gottsdanker, R. (in press). Structural facilitation of movement sequence planning. In: J. Requin and G. Stelmach (Eds), Tutorials in motor neuroscience. Dordrecht: Kluwer Academic Publishers.

Shaffer, L.H. (1980). Analysing piano performance: a study of concert pianists. In G.E. Stelmach and J. Requin (Eds), Tutorials in motor behavior. Amsterdam: North Holland, pp. 443-455.

Shaffer, L.H. (1984). Motor programming in language production. In: H. Bouma and Don G. Bouwhuis (Eds), Attention and Performance X. Control of language processes. London: Lawrence Erlbaum Associates, pp. 17-41.

Soetens, E., Boer, L.C., & Hueting, J.E. (1985). Expectancy or automatic facilitation? Separating sequential effects in two-choice reaction time. Journal of Experimental Psychology: Human Perception and Performance, 11, 598-616.

Wachholder, K. (1932). Willkürliche Haltung und Bewegung. Ergebnisse der Physiologie, 26, 559-775.

Webster, W.G., (1990). Motor performance of stutterers: A search for mechanisms. Journal of Motor Behavior, 22, 553-571.

Wright, C.E. (1990). Generalized motor programs: reexamining claims of effector independence in writing. In: M. Jeannerod (Ed.), Attention and Performance XIII. Hillsdale, N.J.: Lawrence Erlbaum Associates, pp. 294-320.

Preparation of this chapter was supported in part by a grant for international collaboration in research from the NATO Scientific Affairs Division (reference 0135/87) to Robert Gottsdanker.

Tutorials in Motor Behavior II
G.E. Stelmach and J. Requin (Editors)

Motor-perceptual interactions

Paolo Viviani and Natale Stucchi

Department of Psychobiology, Faculty of Psychology and Educational Sciences, University of Geneva, 24 rue du Général Dufour CH-1211 Geneva, Switzerland

1. Introduction

When Carlo Terzuolo and one of us (P.V.) were invited to participate to the Sénanque ASI in the summer of 1979, we had just begun to explore some structural properties of drawing and handwriting movements. Our story was far from complete, but we opined that preliminary results were intriguing enough to be worth reporting (Viviani & Terzuolo, 1980). Ten years after the Sénanque event, we believe that the basic findings presented there are still valid. Many important details have changed, however, and many new elements have been added to the original picture. So, when Jean Requin and George Stelmach confronted some of the original participants with the question "What have you done since ?", we first thought we would present an outline of the revised and broader picture. Then, however, we felt it would have been more appropriate to keep in touch with the spirit of Sénanque, and do again what we had already done ten years before, namely to present work in progress. Ultimately, the direction that we are heading to at the moment may turn out to be a dead end (by the time the third ASI is held, in year 2000, we shall know). Be as it may, we have been tempted once again to submit some intriguing preliminary findings to the attention of our neuroscience colleagues.

Over and above this common spirit, there is a substantive connection between the work reported in Sénanque and the work reported here. In Sénanque it was shown that the kinematics of two-dimensional human movements is jointly modulated by local (differential), and global (metric) properties of the trajectory, and we suggested some non-trivial implications that this modulation might have for movement planning. Here, it is suggested that the fact that form and kinematics are related has implications beyond the domain of motor control. Indeed, evidence will be produced that also visual perception of dynamic stimuli takes into account the presence of such a relation in many human movements. Since the evidence is directly relevant to the ongoing debate on the status of the so-called "Motor theories of perception", and will be discussed within this framework, it is appropriate to begin with a brief overview of these theories.

2. Motor theories of perception

Motor theories of perception concern themselves with modalities and conditions under which motor processes enter into the genesis of percepts. In recent years this general notion has been discussed primarily within the context of speech perception. Specifically, Liberman and his coworkers (Liberman, 1982; Liberman, Cooper, Shankweiler & Studdert-Kennedy, 1967; Liberman & Mattingly, 1985; Liberman & Studdert-Kennedy, 1978) have presented a comprehensive theory of the role of articulatory commands in auditory perception. The theory is based on the following tenets (Liberman & Mattingly, 1985): 1) "The objects of speech perception are the *intended phonetic gestures of the speaker*, represented in the brain as invariant motor commands that call for movements of the articulators through certain linguistically significant configurations" (p. 2, our emphasis). 2) "[since] speech perception and speech production share the same set of invariants, they must be intimately linked. ... The link *is not a learned association .... [it] is innately specified.*" (p. 3, our emphasis). It is beyond the scope of the chapter to discuss the evidence marshalled in support of these views (for an independent assessment, see Jusczyk (1986) who also discusses such related issues as phonetic categorization and the existence of specialized phonetic detectors; Kluender & Greenberg (1989) epitomize the skepticism with which the theory has been received in some quarters). For our purposes it will be sufficient to stress that Liberman's theory is, in many respects, prototypic. The quotes that have just been emphasized capture the two main features common to several other motor theories of perception, namely the role of implicit motor competencies, and the fact that the motor-perceptual link is held to be innate. Indeed - bold as it may appear - the view expressed by the quotes is in fact the last embodiment of a general idea that has a venerable history (cf Scheerer, 1984, 1987; Viviani, 1990). To place our own work in perspective, it may be useful to highlight a few antecedents.

2.1 Levels of interaction

Already a century ago Mach wrote "That space sensation is connected with motor processes has long since ceased to be disputed. Opinions differ only as to how this connection is to be represented" (Mach, 1885). Opinions still differ at the moment of this writing. Nonetheless, most would agree, perhaps, that motor-perceptual interactions may occur at different levels of generality. Three such levels are relatively well established:

1) *The ecological level.* Since all sensory system display some amount of spatial selectivity, any movement of the body - active or passive, aimed or random - results in some change in the perceptual input array. Moreover, for both physical and biological reasons, the pattern of change features necessarily a number of principled covariations. The main contribution by J.J. Gibson (1950, 1979) and his followers has been to recognize the possibility for the organism to access directly the whole bundle of covariations arising from movements, and use this information for establishing and maintaining a stable representation of the world. At the ecological level motor-perceptual interactions are ubiquitous.

2) *Active exploration.* This the earliest acknowledged form of interaction between movement and perception. Ever since Berkeley (1709/1969) and Condillac (1754/1982), in the Eighteenth Century, the hypothesis has been advanced many times over and in

many forms that active exploratory movements provide a necessary complement to vision. Specifically, veridical representation of external objects is supposed to be mediated by the reflexive consciousness that individuals have of these exploratory movements. Recent formulations of the hypothesis tend to establish a link between this level of interaction and the ecological level described above. In particular, Gibson (1962) in his analysis of visuo-tactile exploration emphasizes the role of action for turning affordances into meaningful information: "Active touch is an exploratory rather than a merely receptive sense. When a person touches something with his fingers, he *produces* the stimulation, as it were. (p. 477, our emphasis). "[...] vision and touch have nothing in common *only when they are conceived as channels for pure and meaningless sensory data.* When they are conceived instead as channel for information pick-up [...] they have much in common" (p. 490, Gibson's emphasis).

3) *The generation of expectations.* There are many ways of knowing whether a movement has been successful, that is, whether it has changed our relationship with the environment in the desired way. However, when a failure is detected, it is generally too late to attempt on-line modifications of the motor plan; subsequent and time-consuming corrective actions must be taken. The inconvenience would be circumvented if one could predict beforehand the state of affairs resulting from the execution of the movement. Provided that sufficient information is available about the motor plant in charge of execution, and the external forces that will be met, Helmholtz's (1867) *outflow hypothesis* describes a way in which this can be achieved. As it is well known, Helmholtz's idea was that a copy of the motor commands issued to the muscles is also used to generate the desired set of expectations by running a fast simulation of the impending action (Grüsser, 1986a; von Holst & Mittelstaedt, 1950).

In addition to providing the basis for early corrections, this predictive mechanism may also be instrumental for maintaining perceptual stability. For example, it has been suggested that retinal spatial coordinates during ocular saccades are recalibrated by anticipating size and direction of the eye's movements (Grüsser, 1986b). More generally, the view has been expressed that "The unity and stability of our perceptions might [...] be more understandable if we were to trace the information flow in the central nervous system not only in traditional fashion, from sensory to motor regions, but in the reverse direction as well, so that *intended and potential movements* are seen to enter into the structure of our perception" (Teuber, 1977, our emphasis). It is worth stressing that, unlike interactions arising in conjunction with exploratory movements, those envisaged here are not contingent upon actual execution of motor actions.

2.2 A more abstract level

The fact that Liberman's theory of speech perception posits direct accessibility of movement *intentions* may lead one to view the theory has an exemplar development of the general idea that Teuber was adverting to. In fact - and here we touch upon the main theme of the chapter - the theory points to a fourth and more abstract level at which the intrinsic properties of the motor control system may come to interact with the structure of perception. The three scenarios that have been considered so far involve either actual movement, or, at least, the planning stage that precedes the execution of movement. By contrast, the idea that in perceiving speech individuals may in effect be perceiving some abstract invariant correlate of articulatory gestures amounts to postulate that perceptual processes tap into motor information that is available quite independently from any intention on the part of the perceiver to perform a movement.

At this hypothetical fourth level, motor information relevant to the perceiver does not concern some actual specific gesture, but rather procedural knowledge about his own *entire repertoire of potential gestures*. This information does more than simply interact with sensory inputs: it provides the key to making sense of those inputs. Such a "neo-Kantian" characterization of the fourth level may seem a bit far-fetched. In actual facts, however, it represents a continuous conceptual thread connecting current theorizing to some early motor theories of perception. A few examples from different scientific quarters are offered to substantiate this claim.

Shortly before Mach wrote the statement quoted above, the eminent russian physiologist Sechenov had argued that movements with an intrinsic rhythmicity are instrumental for segmenting the continuous flow of information into perceptual units. Thus, for instance, considering the problem of how humans gauge durations of silent intervals between sounds, he stated "... the capacity to assess the brief time intervals is engendered by the primary periodic movements of the body and chiefly by the act of walking. Developing here, it subsequently *inculcated* the sense of hearing" (Sechenov, 1878/1956, p. 386, our emphasis). Twenty-five years later Poincaré reaffirmed the connection between motor processes and perception in more abstract terms "[Motor space] may have as many dimensions as we have muscles. [Thus, to localize an object in space] simply means that we represent to ourselves the movements that we have to make to reach this object" (Poincaré, 1905, p. 75, our translation).

Finally, after three more decades, the psychologist Piaget made a further step in the same direction. Not only the perception of objects, but indeed their ontological reality, was related to an even more abstract aspect of movements, namely the fact that they constitute a commutative group: "It is clear, in effect, that the reversibility inherent in the [displacement] group presupposes the notion of object and conversely. This is because, in order to recapture an object, one must have the possibility of a reversal (either by a displacement of the object, or by a displacement of his own body): *the object is nothing but the invariant originating from the reversible composition of the group*" (Piaget, 1947, p. 137, our translation and emphasis). Cutting across epistemological boundaries - from empiricism and "muscular sense", to constructivism and groups - the same general idea has been running through scientific thinking for over a century.

2.3 How real is the fourth level ?

By itself, the remarkable pedigree of the alleged fourth level does not guarantee much; clearly, more solid arguments must be adduced before lending credibility to this concept. The experimental support to Liberman's theory - convincing as it may be in the case of speech - does not automatically extend to other perceptual modes. Indeed, as pointed out by the same Liberman, speech is quite special in that the motor competencies which are called into play for decoding input sounds are the very same ones used for production. Moreover, speech sounds have always been produced exclusively by using these specialized competencies.

In spite of this note of caution, it may still be plausible to attempt an extension from speech perception to other perceptual modes whenever similar conditions apply. A case in point is visual perception of biological motion. Admittedly, visual patterns corresponding to biological motion are not as highly characteristic as are sound patterns in speech: the probability that some physical event be visually mistaken for a wing's beat is much higher than the probability that the noise of some physical event be perceived as a word. Yet, certain complex types of motor behavior, such as running or dancing, do seem to partake some of the uniqueness of speech sounds. If a visual pattern can only correspond to a specific motor behavior, and if humans are genetically equipped to produce that behavior, one can speculate that specialized motor competencies are called upon in the perception of the pattern. The question is, then, whether such a tentative generalization is supported by experimental facts.

3. Visual perception of biological motion

There is plenty of evidence that the human visual system is finely attuned to certain forms of biological motion. Indeed, gait (Beardworth & Bukner, 1981; Cutting, 1981; Cutting & Proffitt, 1981; Cutting, Proffitt & Kozlowski, 1978; Johansson, 1973) and dancing (Johansson, 1973, 1977), and other salient body movements can be recognized easily even when they are described visually in an extremely impoverished form, by a few light spots placed at the articulations of the body segments. Gender of a moving person can also be reliably discriminated from these patch-light displays (Kozlowski & Cutting, 1977; Runeson & Frykholm, 1983). The basis for such a peculiar perceptual competence is already present before 5 months of age (Bertenthal, Proffitt & Cutting, 1984; Bertenthal, Proffitt & Kramer, 1987; Bertenthal, Proffitt, Kramer & Spetner, 1987; Fox & McDaniel, 1982). Thus, it is unlikely that perceptual learning plays a major role in establishing this basis. Rather, the hypothesis can be entertained that competence results from the operation of dedicated functional modules which, like the equally specialized modules for parsing speech sounds, and for recognizing facial expressions (Bruce, 1988; Bruyer, 1986), are integral part of the genetic endowment.

Much as this selective attuning is important for the nature/nurture debate, it still does not provide the sought-for evidence in favor of a motor theory of perception of biological motion. In fact, the data referenced above are compatible with the more parsimonious hypothesis that selectiveness results from purely visual processes (Runeson & Frykholm, 1983). One specific piece of evidence, however, points to the desired direction.

Beardworth and Bukner (1981) performed a visual recognition experiment on a group of college students who shared the same quarters and were thoroughly acquainted to each other. Subjects were shown a schematic dynamic record of the walking movements of each member of the group - including themselves - and were asked to guess the name of the walker. Although subjects obviously had much more visual experience with the gait of their fellows students than with their own, the probability of correct self-recognition was higher than all other probabilities. This result not only de-emphasizes further the importance of perceptual learning, but, more importantly, suggests a link between the perceptual competence involved in the task and the availability of some specific motor information about what makes the gait of a given individual idiosyncratically different from that of others.

4. Functional properties of biological motion

Clearly, the conclusions of Beardworth and Bukner's study cannot be extended safely to other motor tasks. Pending further research, the existence in general of a link between perception and performance of *specific gestures* is best considered for the moment as a working hypothesis. Nevertheless, the recognition of what we have termed the fourth level can be pursued further by adopting a somewhat broader perspective. The direction that is explored in the remaining part of the chapter is introduced in the next section.

4.1 Constraints and parameters

Whatever system of description one chooses to adopt, instances of a given class of movements are characterized uniquely by some set of parameter values. At the same time, however, each and every instance shares with all the others a certain number of organizing principles. Even within a class as large as that of hand movements, there are common rules that are respected by any one member of the class. Thus, at the very least, hand movements must be solutions of the dynamic equations of motion; in addition, they must respect very strict biomechanical constraints. The situation bears some analogy with the behavior of certain physical systems. It is well known, for instance, that clamped metal plates display a great variety of oscillatory modes. Yet, all these modes derive from a limited set of physical principles embodied in a single system of differential constraints.

The analogy should not be taken literally because dynamic and biomechanical "rules" in biological movements overlap and interact with other principles of organization that are still poorly understood. Nevertheless, to the extent that behavioral and physiological studies provide increasingly detailed descriptions of these principles, the ground begins to exist for addressing some basic questions. In the next two sections a few selected studies are presented that suggest the possibility that perceptual organization is influenced not only by information concerning specific movements, but also by information concerning the general procedures followed for generating any movement within a given class.

4.2 Dynamic representations

In order to conceive of the possibility that implicit motor competencies interact with perceptual ones, the two must share some common framework (for an extensive discussion of this point, see Prinz (1987)). Thus, the preliminary question to be considered is the extent to which motor and perceptual representations may be said to have similar qualifying attributes. In particular, a necessary condition for bridging the gap between motor and perceptual domains seems to be the identity of the respective coding schemes. Following Palmer (1978), we shall distinguish only two possibilities, *intrinsic* and *extrinsic* representations. In the former case spatio-temporal (dynamic) relationships among physical events are represented isomorphically (i.e. preserving their original topological structure). In the latter case the relationships are represented by abstract codes.

The nature of perception-driven representations is still hotly debated, mostly in reference to mental imagery (see, Pylyshyn, 1981; Kosslyn, 1980; Shepard & Cooper, 1982; Shepard & Podgorny, 1978). However, reviewing a considerable body of experimental evidence, Freyd (1987, 1991) has argued convincingly that visual dynamic representations must necessarily by intrinsic. In particular, the fact that the final position of an abruptly halted object is displaced in the direction of the represented motion (the so-called *representational momentum* phenomenon) appears incompatible with a purely symbolic (extrinsic) coding of spatio-temporal variables.

The nature of implicit motor competencies is far more ambiguous. However, at least two lines of evidence can be cited in support of the contention that also implicit motor information is represented intrinsically. The first one derives from experiments suggesting that recognition of handwriting involves knowledge of the actual movements used to trace the letters (Babcock & Freyd, 1988; Freyd, 1983; Zimmer, 1982). On the other hand, behavioral data indicate that orienting a movement with respect to some pre-cued reference involve a mental rotation of the imagined movement vector (Georgopoulos & Massey, 1987). Furthermore, electrophysiological experiments (Georgopoulos, Crutcher, & Schwartz, 1989) have shown that this rotation is supported by nervous processes that satisfy the continuity condition expected from intrinsic representations. In summary, while the question raised at the beginning of this section cannot yet be answered unambiguously, a certain degree of commonality between motor and perceptual representations is at least compatible with the available evidence.

4.3 Perceiving biomechanical constraints

We turn now to the more substantive question of what proof ia available (if any) that motor regularities and constraints do indeed bias perception. Inasmuch as they are truly inflexible, biomechanical constraints are the most likely candidates for originating these biases. In fact, anecdotical evidence exists that any violation of these constraints - such as the unnatural twisting of the limbs following a serious accident - are immediately perceived as being "impossible". Moreover, a recent experiment has demonstrated a perceptual effect that is likely to result from implicit knowledge that humans have of their bodily structure.

The experiment is based upon a well documented bias present in the phenomenon of apparent motion: whenever two alternate routes exist from initial to final stimulus position, illusory motion tends to follow the shortest path (Kolers, 1972). Shiffrar and Freyd (1990) used as stimuli photographs of the human body in which only one body segment changed position. At the pictorial level, the final position could be reached in two different ways (e.g. clockwise and counterclockwise rotations of the forearm); in human bodies, instead, only one solution is compatible with anatomical constraints. The results showed that, when stimulus onset asynchronies are in the range of biological timings, illusory motion tends to follow the compatible solution, even though the incompatible route is far shorter. Somehow, implicit knowledge that the shorter route would lead to a broken elbow overrides the purely perceptual bias.

A skeptic could object that before imputing the results to some implicit knowledge about admissible body movements one should verify that bias reversal does not occur if the image represents some mechanical contraption in which the impossibility of the shorter route is signified explicitly by pictorial means. In fact, there is some evidence that under certain conditions occlusions deflect apparent movement from the shortest path (Kolers, 1972). Moreover, Shepard and Zare (1983) have shown that the usual straight-line movement between alternately flashing dots may also be deflected by suggesting with purely pictorial means an alternate curved route. We do not believe, however, that Shiffrar and Freyd's elegant demonstration is seriously weakened by such an argument. We agree with these authors that paths of apparent motion may be constrained by structural information about real objects, that is by information that is not visual. However, we also agree that their results leave open important questions such as "How life-like do stimuli need to be in order to tap object-specific knowledge? Does the perceptual system have knowledge of other object-appropriate transformations or is biological motion 'special'?"(p. 264). More decisive evidence for answering these questions would accrue from considering constraints that, unlike biomechanical ones, are specifically characteristic of the motor control system. In the next section one such constraint introduced, and reasons are discussed why it can be used to gather the desired evidence.

4.4 Relational constraints and biological force fields

The research program outlined in Sénanque ten years ago led to the formulation of a functional relation - known as *Two-thirds power law* - between velocity and radius of curvature in two-dimensional hand movements. Empirical demonstrations of the relation, as well as a number of speculations concerning its functional significance, have been presented in several papers (Lacquaniti, Terzuolo & Viviani, 1983,1984; Viviani & McCollum, 1983; Viviani & Schneider, 1991; Viviani & Terzuolo, 1982,1983), and need not to be reviewed here in any detail. For the present purpose it will be sufficient to state the law in its most recent formulation.

Two-dimensional hand movements can always be described by a pair of parametric equations x = x(t), y = y(t). The so-called *Law of Motion* of the movement is the function L = L(t) describing how the length of trajectory L covered from movement onset increases with time. The law of motion specifies entirely the kinematics of the movement. In particular, tangential velocity is the time derivative of L(t). In many cases it is possible to eliminate the time variable between the parametric equations and specify the form of the trajectory by an explicit function y = y(x), quite independently from kinematics. Let V(t) be the instantaneous tangential velocity of the movement, and R(t) the corresponding radius of curvature of the trajectory. It was found that the empirical relation:

$$V(t) = K \cdot \left(\frac{R(t)}{1 + \alpha \cdot R(t)} \right)^{\beta} \qquad \alpha \geq 0, \; K(t) \geq 0 \tag{1}$$

is satisfied with good approximation by many types of hand movements. The parameter K in this formula is constant over relatively long segments of trajectory. Its value is proportional to a power function of the segment length. Typically, the endpoints of the segments - where K changes - coincide with the points of inflection of the trajectory. For dimensional reasons, K is called velocity gain factor (Viviani, 1986; Viviani & Cenzato, 1985). In adults, the exponent ß takes values very close to 1/3; the parameter α ranges between 0 and 0.1.

Of course, any given trajectory can be traced with infinitely many different laws of motions. However, for fixed α, ß and K, only one of these laws is compatible with equation 1. Thus, the equation represents a specific constraint delimiting a subset of all possible two-dimensional movements. Before describing how this constraint is exploited for our purposes, a short digression is in order to clarify an important point.

Trajectory and kinematics of a moving mass are jointly specified by Lagrangian principles, boundary conditions, and the external force field that is applied to the mass. Therefore, once mass and boundary conditions are fixed, any functional relation between tangential velocity V and radius of curvature R identifies in fact a narrow subset of all possible force fields. In particular, the Two-thirds power law identifies a class of force fields that we suggest to characterize as "biological". Such a characterization requires some justification. In principle, for any triple of reasonably well-behaved functions $V=V(t)$, $R=R(t)$ and $K=K(t)$, one can always solve the inverse dynamic problem and find the (generally, time-varying) force field that, when applied to the mass, results into the assigned velocity and trajectory. Moreover, it is also always possible to envisage a scenario wherein this particular force field derives from non-biological principles, such as gravitation or electromagnetism. Qualifying any force field as biological on the sole basis of kinematic evidence seems therefore unwarranted.

The objection is logically well-taken. One must consider, however, that there is a kind of trade-off between the complexity of the relation that is assumed to exist between V and R, and the complexity of the force field required to generate such relation. For instance, whereas the solar gravitational field is both simple and (relatively) constant, the relation between velocity and radius of curvature of planetary motions is vastly more complex than equation 1 (cf. Goldstein, 1980 p. 98). Conversely, this relatively simple equation is satisfied by random scribbling movements of the hand which involve complex and time-varying force fields. In order to obtain such fields from gravitational or electromagnetic sources would require an extravagantly contrived scenario. There are exceptions to this trade-off. For example, a simple mechanical model exists (the so-called *Lissajous model,* Viviani and Schneider, 1991) which produces elliptic motions satisfying equation 1. These exceptions notwithstanding, it remains true in general that the *simplest* interpretation that one can give of a movement satisfying equation 1 is to assume that the movement is biological. With this proviso, the notion of biological force field introduced above becomes meaningful. We hope to be able to show that it also has heuristic value.

5. Experimental strategies

Having justified the characterization of equation 1 as a kind of biological signature for movements, we proceed now to show how this provides the basis for testing the hypothesis that implicit motor competencies interact with perception. The general idea is to measure the perceptual effects of tampering with this signature: how is movement perception affected by introducing controlled discrepancies in the relation between velocity and shape ? There are two complementary strategies for controlling the discrepancy. Starting from a stimulus movement in which R (i.e. the form of the trajectory) and V (i.e. the kinematics) covary as prescribed by the biological rule, one can either maintain the law of motion unchanged and modify progressively the form, or do the other way around. Both possibilities have been explored experimentally.

5.1 Geometric illusions

In a first series of experiments (Viviani & Stucchi, 1989), following the first strategy, we demonstrated the possibility of modifying both the constant error (CE) and the differential limen (JND) in the perception of circularity. A light spot traced continuously an ellipse on a computer screen (period = 0.6 sec). The orientation of the major axis of the figure could be either vertical or horizontal; the subjects' task was to indicate this orientation. For each correct answer the eccentricity of the ellipse was progressively reduced till, eventually, the trajectory appeared subjectively as a circle and subjects were forced to guess. The trial was terminated after a fixed number of response alternations. Means and standard deviations of the eccentricity of the figure perceived as a circle were then used to estimate CE and JND. The key factor in the experiment was the instantaneous velocity of the spot. In one series of trials the velocity was always modulated as prescribed by equation 1 (with $\beta = 1/3$ and $\alpha = 0$) in the case of an ellipse with a vertical orientation and an eccentricity of 0.9. In another series the velocity was again modulated in the same fashion, but for an ellipse oriented horizontally. Finally, in a third series the velocity was kept constant ($\beta = 0$).

The third (control) condition showed that the mere presence of movement induces a subjective stretching of the horizontal dimension: what is perceived as a circle is in fact an ellipse that is elongated in the vertical direction. The distortion is quite large and would be clearly detected in a static stimulus. It is remarkable that, under static conditions, the classic "hat illusion" would in fact stretch the opposite direction. Even more remarkable, however, are the differential effects observed in the first two conditions. When the velocity varies as it would be appropriate for an horizontal ellipse, all subjects experienced a large stretching of the horizontal dimension. In the second condition, the bias of the CE disappears but the JND increases considerably.

In order to interpret these results it must be remembered that, according to equation 1, circles are drawn by hand at constant velocity (since R is constant). Thus, as the eccentricity decreased toward the point of objective circularity, stimuli became more and more incompatible with the "biological" model. Perceptual distortions of the geometry can be explained with the same line of reasoning followed to explain many size illusions. It is known, for example, that two objectively equal objects in a picture appear different in size if the context suggests a different distance from the observer. The illusion is generally credited to an irrepressible tendency to perceive visual displays in a 3-D framework, and to expect therefore that the laws of perspective apply to all elements in the picture. In similar fashion, it is assumed that subjects implicitly adopted a biological model for the target, and that illusory stretching represents an unconscious effort to reduce the discrepancy between such model and what is actually presented. In short, the experiments indicate that motor competencies provide cognitive frameworks for processing visual information. Such a contribution to the process of interpretation of sensory data is precisely the kind of contribution that is supposed to characterize the fourth level of motor-perceptual interaction discussed in section 2.2.

5.2 Kinematic illusions

Further support to our general hypothesis has been obtained recently by following the second strategy described above. A series of experiments investigated the perception of uniform velocity using both regular (elliptical), and complex (pseudo-random) dynamic stimuli (Viviani & Stucchi, 1991). The details of the experiments are rather complex. However, a simplified account will be sufficient for our present purposes. Stimuli consisted of a light spot tracing continuously a fixed trajectory on a computer screen. In all cases the kinematics of the stimuli covaried with curvature as indicated by equation 1. The experiments were based on the fact that within this general constraint, and for any given trajectory, different values of the parameter ß result into different profiles of tangential velocity. For $ß < 0$ the velocity increases in the regions of high curvature and decreases in the flatter regions. The contrary occurs when $ß > 0$. The velocity is constant throughout the movement only when $ß = 0$. We recall that for $ß = 1/3$ the velocity modulation of the stimulus mimic the one that would be observed if the trajectory were traced by a hand movement.

Subjects were told that during a trial they could modify step by step the kinematics of the stimuli using two keys. The task in each trial was to adjust the velocity profile of the spot until it appeared constant throughout the movement. The trial terminated when this condition was satisfied. The effect of the keys was described to the subjects in the same qualitative terms used above, without specifying the real action of the keys. In reality, one key reduced the current value of ß by a small constant amount, the other increased it by the same amount. Average velocity was kept invariant by compensating the effect of changing ß with appropriate changes of the velocity gain factor K. Different trajectories were displayed in successive trials. At the beginning of a trial ß could take initial values ranging between -0.25 and 0.75.

Thirteen subjects were tested using five random trajectories and seven elliptic trajectories with eccentricity ranging between 0.52 and 0.96. The results were extremely clear. In all cases the velocity profiles that subjects perceived as constant were in fact highly variable (relative variations between maxima and minima exceeded 200%). Conversely, true constant-velocity stimuli were always perceived as accelerating and decelerating. On average, ß values corresponding to selected profiles ranged between 0.17 and 0.22 for ellipses, and between 0.33 and 0.37 for random trajectories. In both cases the variability of the final ß estimates was very small. A control experiment ruled out the possibility that subjects had adopted implicitly a definition of constant velocity different from the physical one. A modified version of the basic paradigm was used in another control to rule out the possibility that the observed dynamic illusions resulted from a 3-D interpretation of the stimuli.

The experiments illustrate the exquisite attuning of the visual system to dynamic stimuli that possess qualifying attributes of biological movements (see above). The significance of the results, however, goes beyond the simple confirmation of this well established phenomenon. Experiments on perception of biological motion have shown that highly schematic - albeit veridical - representations of real human movements can be *interpreted* correctly. In addition, we have also been able to show that it is possible to *discriminate* very accurately veridical representations from distorted ones. It is conceivable that correct interpretation be the achieved via purely visual processing of the proximal stimuli. By contrast, discrimination seems to involve two logically distinct processing components. On the one side, an internal model must exist in which, for some (unknown) reason, the large modulations of velocity that occur in biological movement are adopted as a standard of uniformity (Runeson, 1974, 1975). On the other side, a metrics must be available to gauge the fit of the stimuli to the internal model.

It seems highly unlikely that such a metrics be based exclusively on visual information. Remember in fact that, for a given trajectory, equation 1 maps the simple one-dimensional ß-space into a vector space of high dimensionality: laws of motion that differ only in the value of a scalar quantity (ß) can be entirely different time functions (cf figure 4 in Viviani & Stucchi, 1991). Thus, fitting the stimuli to the internal model can be realistically achieved only in the ß-space. Indeed, the characteristic signature shared by many natural movements corresponds to a narrow region (interval) in ß-space centered around the point ß = 1/3. Since ß-space is defined by motor and not by visual variables, the ultimate significance of the results of these experiments is to support our claim that motor competencies enter into the structure of visual perception.

5.3 Perceiving whole-body movements

The dynamic stimuli considered so far were much simpler than those typically used for studying perception of biological motion; our single moving dots could not possibly describe or evoke complex bodily movements. This important difference could be cited against the possibility to relate our work to previous studies on bio-motion. The last experiment to be described here demonstrates that such a connection is in fact legitimate.

Using the ELITE system (Ferrigno & Pedotti, 1985), we recorded movements of the whole body during the execution of a physical exercise (throwing the ball in the *pétanque* game). Following the technique pioneered by Johansson (1973), movements were characterized by the trajectories of 13 reference points placed at the major articulations of the body (ankle, knee, hip, etc). The left upper panel in Figure 1 illustrates a typical recording (duration of the recording: 5 sec). As expected, when movement samples are displayed dynamically the real underlying movement "pops out" vividly. The stick-diagram version of the same recording (right upper panel) suggests graphically the perceived dynamic event.

In throwing the ball the hand follows a complex trajectory with large variations of curvature. Analysis shows that the velocity of this point covaries with the curvature in accordance with equation 1. This fact was used to design a perceptual experiment in which subjects had to judge the naturalness of the movement as described by the whole set of 13 moving points. It was specified to the subjects that within a block of trials the trajectory of the points was kept constant, and that attention had to focus only on velocities. Before reaching a decision, subjects could play back the entire motor sequence as many times as desired. They were told that, if the movement looked in any way different from what they would expect from a real event, the distribution of velocities along the trajectory could be modified by pressing on two keys. The action of the keys was described as complementary, but we did not specify what was the actual effect of keypresses

All the stimuli within a block of trials were graded modifications of one original recording. As indicated to the subjects, the modifications did not concern the trajectory of the 13 body landmarks, but only their kinematics. Specifically, for each of 25 equispaced values of ß in the range [-0.583,1.500], the landmark representing the more distal point of the upper limb (hand) was provided with a law of motion such that velocity and radius of curvature would covary as predicted by inserting this value of the exponent in equation 1. The law of motion of the other 12 points was derived from that

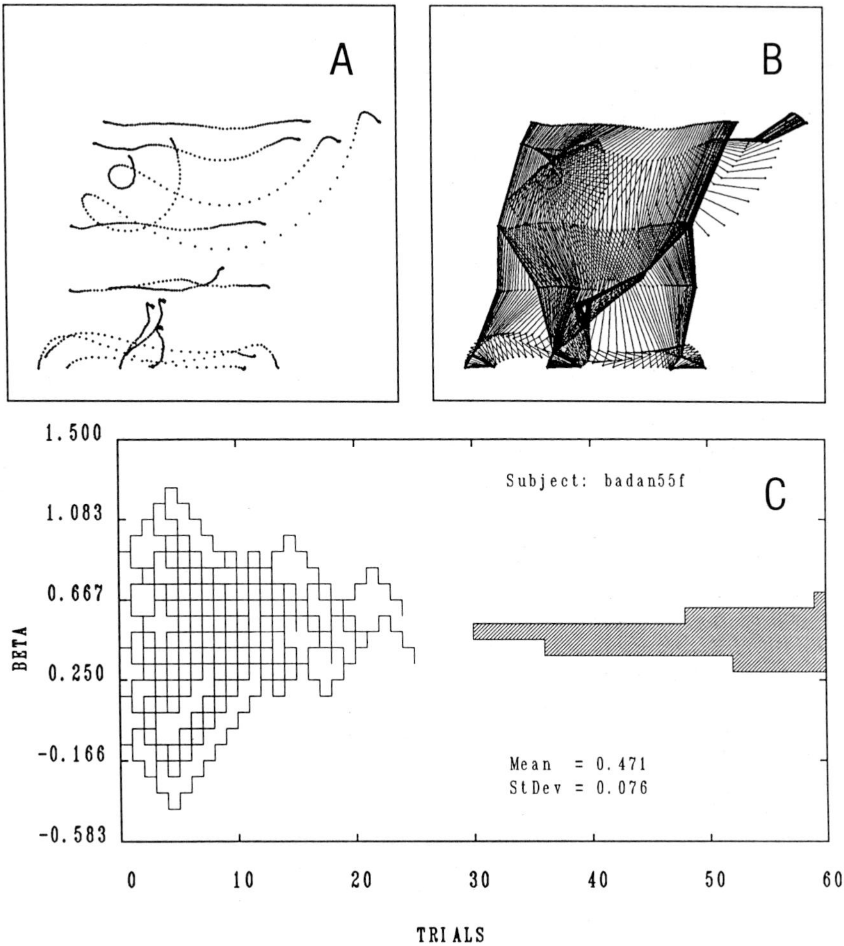

Figure 1. Perceiving the naturalness of whole-body movements. A: Space trajectory of thirteen landmarks placed at the major articulations of the body during the throwing of the ball in the *pétanque* game. B: Stick diagram corresponding to the same recording as in A. C: Complete history of an experimental session in one subject. A session comprised 75 independent sequences of perceptual judgments [(3 different recordings of the same movement) x (5 starting values of ß) x (5 repetitions)]. In successive trials within a sequence the subject adjusted progressively the initial value of the exponent ß until the corresponding dynamic display was judged a realistic representation of the actual movement. The staircase curves on the left side of the panel show the converging sequences of ß values (many curves are superimposed). On the right the distribution of the 75 final estimates of ß. Both median and mean of the distribution are close to the value of ß observed in real movements.

of the upper limb by imposing the constancy of the trajectories and the constancy of the length of the limbs. The greater the difference between the selected value of ß and the "natural" value 1/3, the larger was the violation of the biological constraint. Notice that, although we controlled directly only the kinematics of one point, the kinematics of all the others was also affected by this procedure. As in the previous experiments, the actual result of pressing the two keys was to increase and decrease the ß value by a small constant amount. The initial ß in each trial was chosen at random within the range indicated in the figure.

Also in this case the results were fairly clear. For all subjects the stimuli that were perceived as the most realistic representation of a real event corresponded to values of ß close to the biological 1/3 value. The lower panel in Figure 1 illustrates the data in a typical subject. Each staircase trace in this panel describes the complete sequence of adjustments that the subject went through in a trial from the initial ß value to the one corresponding to a perceptually satisfactory stimulus. On the right edge of the panel is shown the histogram of the final sequence values.

Again, the demonstration that humans are very good at interpreting schematic representations of natural movements is but a confirmation of classical results. The specific contribution from this last experiment is rather the suggestion that dynamic naturalness of whole-body movements, *qua* perceptual quality, can be captured adequately by the exponent ß in the Two-thirds Power Law. Of course, differences in the value of ß translated in corresponding differences in all visual parameters of the stimulus. However, it should be clear that the dimensional argument raised in the last section is even more cogent in the present case; the hypothesis that the whole set of 13 velocity profiles provides directly the basis for judging naturalness is in fact even less plausible than the hypothesis that just one profile is sufficient to single out constant velocity stimuli. Irrespective of whether stimuli are simple or complex, the most parsimonious interpretation of the data is again one that posits an important role of motor competencies.

6. Conclusions

We have developed the hypothesis that implicit motor competencies enter into the structure of visual perception even in those cases when no movement is being executed, planned or intended. The idea, of course, bears more than an occasional resemblance with at least one contemporary motor theory of perception, Liberman's theory of speech perception. In building our case, however, we have attempted to broaden the perspective, by showing that the notion of implicit motor competence is actually deeply rooted in the physiological and psychological tradition of perceptual studies.

Motor-perceptual interactions that are not contingent on actual delivery of motor commands, but only on the general rules that these commands obey when they are delivered, pertain to a more abstract level than the class of interactions with which the literature is mostly concerned. This does not preclude, however, the possibility to subsume all these phenomena under a common conceptual framework. Indeed, the reason for evoking in some detail other, better-known, instances of motor-perceptual interactions has been precisely to stress the existence of a common denominator.

Although rather abstract interactions of the kind discussed here have already been envisaged by several classical authors, intuition and speculation have played perhaps a bigger role in the past than it is deemed acceptable nowadays. The few recent experiments that we have described - both ours and by other investigators - suggest that those intuitions and speculations were not too much off the mark, after all. We believe that the progress made toward confirming earlier claims is mainly the result of the better insight that we are gaining into the structural properties of movements. In fact the most convincing evidence in favor of these claims is in the fact that perception of dynamic stimuli bear the imprint of specific quantitative rules obeyed by the motor control system. To be sure, much work remains to be done. In particular, we are aware that data and arguments brought up against an interpretation of the observed phenomena in purely visual terms are not watertight yet. Nevertheless, they are sufficient to shift the burden of the proof. A visual theory for explaining all the perceptual phenomena described in this chapter, without invoking the intervention of motor competencies, is bound to be considerably contrived. Until convincing evidence is produced that the visual system is indeed capable of affording the necessary information, the hypothesis that part of the information derives from the motor system remains the simplest, and therefore the best one. "Perceiving is acting" runs a well-known dictum. "Perceiving is knowing how to act" might be a fitting paraphrase for describing the position that have advertised in this chapter.

Acknowledgments: The preparation of this chapter has been partly supported by FNRS Research Grant 31.25265.88 (MUCOM ESPRIT Project). We are grateful to Gérard Laissard for discussing with us many of the issues discussed here.

References

Babcock, M.K. & Freyd, J.J. (1988). The perception of dynamic information in static handwritten forms. *American Journal of Psychology, 101*, 111-130.

Beardworth, T., & Bukner, T. (1981). The ability to recognize one self from a video recording of one's movement without seeing one's body. *Bulletin of the Psychonomic Society, 18*, 19-22.

Berkeley, G. (1709). *An essay towards a new theory of vision*. Dublin. [reprinted: London: J.M. Dent & Sons, (1969).]

Bertenthal, B.I., Proffitt, D.R., & Cutting, J. (1984). Infant sensitivity to figural coherence in biomechanical motions. *Journal of Experimental Child Psychology, 37*, 213-230.

Bertenthal, B.I., Proffitt, D.R., & Kramer, S.J. (1987). Perception of biomechanical motion by infants: Implementation of various processing constraints. *Journal of Experimental Psychology: Human Perception and Performance, 13*, 577-585.

Bertenthal, B.I., Proffitt, D.R., Kramer, S.J., & Spetner, N.B. (1987). Infants' encoding of kinetic displays varying in relative coherence. *Developmental Psychology, 23*, 171-178.

Bruce, V. (1988). *Recognizing faces*. Hillsdale, NJ: Lawrence Erlbaum Associates.

Bruyer, R. (1986). *The neuropsychology of face perception and facial expression*. Hillsdale, NJ: Lawrence Erlbaum Associates.

Condillac, E.B. de (1982). *Philosophical writings of Etienne Bonnot, Abbé de Condillac*. Edited and Translated by F. Philip and H. Lane. Hillsdale, NJ: Lawrence Erlbaum Associates. [first edition: Paris, 1754]

Cutting, J.E. (1981). Coding theory adapted to gait perception. *Journal of Experimental Psychology : Human Perception and Performance, 7*, 71-87.

Cutting, J.E., Proffitt, D.R., & Kozlowski L.T. (1978). A biomechanical invariant for gait perception. *Journal of Experimental Psychology : Human Perception and Performance, 4*, 357-372.

Cutting, J.E., & Proffitt, D.R. (1981). Gait perception as an example of how we may perceive events. In R. Walk and H.L. Pick (Eds.) *Intersensory perception and sensory integration*. New York, NY: Plenum, pp. 249-273.

Ferrigno, G., & Pedotti, A. (1985). ELITE: A digital dedicated hardware system for movement analysis via real-time TV signal processing. *IEEE Transactions on Biomedical Engineering, 11*, 443-950.

Fox, R., & McDaniel, C. (1982). The perception of biological motion by human infants. *Science, 218*, 486-487.

Freyd, J.J. (1983). Representing the dynamics of a static form. *Memory & Cognition, 11*, 342-346.

Freyd, J.J. (1987). Dynamic mental representations. *Psychological Review, 94*, 427-438.

Freyd, J.J. (1991). Five hunches about perceptual processes and dynamic representations. In D.E. Meyer and S. Kornblum (Eds.) *Attention and Performance XIV*, Cambridge, MA: MIT Press (in press).

Georgopoulos, A.P., & Massey, J.T. (1987). Cognitive spatial-motor processes, 1. The making of movements at various angles from stimulus directions. *Experimental Brain Research, 65*, 361-370.

Georgopoulos, A.P., Crutcher, M.D., & Schwartz, A.B. (1989). Cognitive spatial-motor processes, 3. Motor cortical predictions of movement direction during an instructed delay period. *Experimental Brain Research, 75*, 183-194.

Gibson, J.J. (1950). *The perception of the visual world*. Boston, MA: Houghton Mifflin.

Gibson, J.J. (1962). Observations on active touch. *Psychological Review, 69*, 477-491.

Gibson, J.J. (1979). *The ecological approach to visual perception*. Boston, MA : Houghton Mifflin.

Goldstein. H. (1980). *Classical mechanics*. Reading, MA: Addison-Wesley.

Grüsser, O.-J. (1986a). Interaction of efferent and afferent signals in visual perception. A history of ideas and experimental paradigms. *Acta Psychologica, 63*, 3-21.

Grüsser, O.-J. (1986b). Some recent studies on the quantitative analysis of efference copy mechanisms in visual perception. *Acta Psychologica, 63*, 49-62.

Helmholtz, H. van (1867). *Handbuch der Physiologischen Optik*. Leipzig : Voss. [english translation : J.P.C. Southall (Ed. and trans.) *A treatise on physiological optics*. New York, NY: Dover, 1962]

Holst, E. von & Mittelstaedt, H. (1950). Das Reafferenzprinzip. *Naturwissenschaften, 37*, 464-476. [english translation in : R. Martin (Ed. and trans.) *Selected papers of Eric von Holst: The behavioral physiology of animals and man*. (Vol 1) London: Methuen, 1973]

Johansson, G. (1973). Visual perception of biological motion and a model for its analysis. *Perception & Psychophysics, 14*, 201-211.

Johansson, G. (1977). Studies on visual perception of locomotion. *Perception, 6*, 365-376.

Jusczyk, P. (1986). Speech Perception. In K.R. Boff, L. Kaufmann, & J.P. Thomas (Eds.) *Handbook of perception and performance. Vol. II, Cognitive processes and performance*. New York, NY: Wiley, pp. 27.1-27.57.

Kluender, K.R., & Greenberg, S. (1989). A specialization for speech perception? *Science, 244*, 1530.

Kolers, P. (1972). *Aspects of motion perception*. Oxford: Pergamon Press.

Kosslyn, S.M. (1980). *Image and mind*. Cambridge, MA: Harvard University Press.

Kozlowski, L.T., & Cutting, J.E., (1977). Recognizing the sex of a walker from a dynamic point-light display. *Perception & Psychophysics, 21*, 575-580.

Lacquaniti, F., Terzuolo, C.A., & Viviani, P. (1983). The law relating kinematic and figural aspects of drawing movements. *Acta Psychologica, 54*, 115-130.

Lacquaniti, F., Terzuolo, C.A., & Viviani, P. (1984). Global metric properties and preparatory processes in drawing movements. In S. Kornblum and J. Requin (Eds.) *Preparatory states and processes*. Hillsdale, NJ: Lawrence Erlbaum Associates, pp. 357-370.

Liberman, A.M. (1982). On finding that speech is special. *American Psychologist, 37*, 148-167.

Liberman, A.M., Cooper, F.S., Shankweiler, D.P., & Studdert-Kennedy, M. (1967). Perception of speech code. *Psychological Review, 74*, 431-461.

Liberman, A.M., & Studdert-Kennedy, M. (1978). Phonetic perception. In R. Held, H.W. Leibowitz, and H.-L. Teuber (Eds.) *Handbook of sensory physiology. Vol. 8: Perception.* New York, NY: Springer Verlag

Liberman, A.M. & Mattingly, I.G. (1985). The motor theory of speech perception revisited. *Perception, 21*, 1-36.

Mach, E. (1885). *Beiträge zur Analyse der Empfindungen.* [english translation : *Contributions to the analysis of the sensations*. La Salle, IL.: Open Court Publishing Co., 1897]

Palmer, S.E. (1978). Fundamental aspects of cognitive representation. In E. Rosch and B.B Lloyd (Eds.) *Cognition and categorization*. Hillsdale, NJ: Lawrence Erlbaum Associates, pp. 259-303.

Piaget, J. (1947). *La psychologie de l'intellegence*. Paris: A. Colin. [english translation : *The psychology of intelligence*. London: Rutledge & Kegan, 1950]

Poincaré, H. (1905). *La science et l'hypothèse*. Paris: Flammarion. [english translation : *Science and hypothesis*. New York, NY: Dover, 1952]

Prinz, W. (1987). Ideo-motor action. In H. Heuer and A.F. Sanders (Eds.) *Perspectives on perception and action*. Hillsdale, NJ: Lawrence Erlbaum Associates, pp. 47-76.

Pylyshyn, Y.W. (1981). The imagery debate: Analogue media versus tacit knowledge. *Psychological Review, 87*, 16-45.

Runeson S. (1974). Constant velocity - Not perceived as such. *Psychological Research, 37*, 3-23.

Runeson S. (1975). Visual prediction of collision with natural and nonnatural motion functions. *Perception and Psychophysics, 18*, 261-266.

Runeson, S., & Frykholm, G. (1983). Kinematic specification of dynamics as an informational basis for Person-and-action perception: Expectation, gender, recognition, and deceptive intention. *Journal of Experimental Psychology: General, 112*, 585-615.

Scheerer E. (1984). Motor theories of cognitive structure : A historical review. In W. Prinz and A.F. Sanders (Eds.) *Cognition and motor processes*. Berlin, Heidelberg: Springer Verlag, pp. 77-97.

Scheerer E. (1987). Muscle sense and innervation feelings : A chapter in the history of perception and action. In H. Heuer and A.F. Sanders (Eds.) *Perspectives in perception and action*. Hillsdale, NJ: Erlbaum, pp. 171-194.

Sechenov, I. (1878). *The elements of thought*. [english translation in: *Selected physiological and psychological works*. Moscow: Foreign Languages Publishing House, 1956, pp. 265-401]

Shepard, R.N., & Podgorny, P. (1978). Cognitive processes that resemble perceptual processes. In W.K. Estes (Ed.) *Handbook of learning and cognitive processes*. Hillsdale, NJ: Lawrence Erlbaum Associates, pp. 409-430.

Shepard, R.N., & Cooper, L.A. (1982). *Mental images and their transformations*. Cambridge, MA: MIT Press/Bradford Books.

Shepard, R.N., & Zare, S.L. (1983) Path-guided apparent motion. *Science, 220*, 63-634.

Shiffrar, M., & Freyd, J.J. (1990). Apparent motion of the human body. *Psychological Science, 1*, 257-264.

Teuber, H.-L. (1977). *James R. Killian, Jr. Award Lecture*.

Viviani, P. (1986). Do units of motor action really exist? In H. Heuer and C. Fromm (Eds.) *Generation and modulation of action patterns*. Berlin: Springer Verlag, pp. 201-216.

Viviani, P. (1990). Motor-perceptual interactions: The evolution of an idea. In M. Piattelli Palmarini (Ed.) *Cognitive science in Europe: Issues and trends*. Golem Monograph Series, 1, pp. 11-39.

Viviani, P., & Cenzato, M. (1985). Segmentation and coupling in complex movements. *Journal of Experimental Psychology: Human Perception and Performance, 11*, 828-845.

Viviani, P., & McCollum, G. (1983). The relation between linear extent and velocity in drawing movements. *Neuroscience, 10*, 211-218.

Viviani, P., & Schneider, R. (1991). A developmental study of the relation between geometry and kinematics in drawing movements. *Journal of Experimental Psychology: Human Perception and Performance, 17*, 198-218.

Viviani, P., & Stucchi, N. (1989). The effect of movement velocity on form perception: Geometric illusions in dynamic displays. *Perception & Psychophysics, 46*, 266-274.

Viviani, P., & Stucchi, N. (1991). Biological movements look uniform: evidence of motor-perceptual interactions. (submitted)

Viviani, P., & Terzuolo, C.A. (1980). Space-Time invariance in learned motor patterns. In G.A. Stelmach and J. Requin (Eds.) *Tutorials in Motor Behavior*. Amsterdam: North-Holland, pp. 525-533.

Viviani, P., & Terzuolo, C.A. (1982). Trajectory determines movement dynamics. *Neuroscience, 7*, 431-437.

Viviani, P., & Terzuolo, C.A. (1983). The organization of movement in handwriting and typing. In B. Butterworth (Ed.) *Language production : vol II. Development, writing and other language processes*. New York, NY: Academic Press, pp. 103-146.

Zimmer, A. (1982). Do we see what makes our script characteristic or do we only feel it? Modes of sensory control in handwriting. *Psychological Research, 44*, 165-174.

Tutorials in Motor Behavior II
G.E. Stelmach and J. Requin (Editors)

Interaction of cognitive and biomechanical factors in the organization of graphic movements

Arnold J.W.M. Thomassen

Nijmegen Institute for Cognition Research and Information Technology (NICI), University of Nijmegen, P.O. Box 9104, 6500 HE Nijmegen, The Netherlands

Abstract

The paper reviews three experiments in which the stroke sequences adopted in the copying of simple geometrical patterns are studied as a function of higher-order and lower-order variables. Among the higher-order variables are the symbol class of the context in which the target stimuli are presented, and the option to execute the same motor program repeatedly. The lower-order variables are concerned with the biomechanical features of the effector system. It is shown that there is a strong interaction in the sense that the effects of the biomechanical constraints are modulated by higher-order constraints and that the effects of the symbolic context and of program repetition are influenced by the mapping of the biomechanical system upon the geometry of the model patterns. A model outline is proposed in which a global mechanism percieves and parses a visual pattern, and prepares its copying sequence. This mechanism is sensitive to higher-order context and it sets speed and precision requirements; it is aware of the cost involved in each possible movement direction; and it takes into account the cost of computing new starting points and stroke parameters.

1. INTRODUCTION

In movement research the major focus has been on small-scale and detailed features of motor control and performance. The organization of the global features of whole movement sequences in complex action has received far less attention. This paper is concerned with such features as they become apparent in the selection of the order and movement direction of the successive graphic strokes when performing the perceptual-motor task of copying geometrical patterns. In a sense, the selection of such an action sequence may be seen as a specific way of solving a degrees-of-freedom problem, because there are usually many ways in which a graphic action can be organized. For example, in a pattern of only four segments, such as the capital letter E, there are 24 orders of dealing with the four segments. Moreover, each segment can be started at one of its two extremes, which implies 16 combinations. This results in 24x16=384 different productions of any four-segment pattern. Similarly, for a six-segment pattern, there are 46,080 possibilities, and for an eight-stroke pattern more than 10 million to choose from. As it appears, the draughtsman's job is greatly facilitated by a number of constraints. Over a group of subjects, and over large numbers of trials, we see that only a few of the many possible stroke sequences are actually selected. The leading research questions are: Which exactly are these constraints, how do they operate, and to what extent do they interact with each other?

Recently, a series of intriguing studies of macroscopic aspects of movement selection have started to appear (Rosenbaum & Jorgensen, 1991; Rosenbaum, Marchak, Barnes, Vaughan, Slotta & Jorgensen, 1990). These experiments study the selection of hand posture, or grip, in transport tasks. However, practically all the earlier studies concerned with global aspects of movement selection, which were carried out over the past two decades, deal with the selection of graphic movement sequences. They follow in the footsteps of the pilot article by Goodnow and Levine (1973). Seen from a movement-planning point of view, most of these studies, however, were not systematically designed: they were performed in frameworks related to child development, to cultural determinants, and to educational implications. Nevertheless, they did evidence the existence of strong biases or constraints. These were labeled 'rules'; collectively they have been called a 'grammar of action'. Incidentally, these earlier studies also demonstrated the fruitfulness of graphic action as a field for investigation. Extensions to this work have been made by Van Sommers (1984, 1989) who applied a cognitive, neuropsychological framework to his many interesting findings.

Without going into great detail, the constraints or 'rules' which have been demonstrated in righthanded adults can be distinguished in starting rules and progression rules. Starting rules are concerned with the place where the copying movement (on paper, i.e., pen-down) tends to begin: At the top, at the left extreme, at a vertical stroke, and - following a pen lift - at a point on a stroke produced earlier ('anchoring'). Progression rules describe the directions and the order in which the strokes are generally produced: Downwards, rightwards, parallels in the same direction, a subsequent stroke joined - without a penlift - onto the preceding stroke ('threading'), and closed contours in a counter-clockwise fashion. Evidently, these rules are not independent. Indeed, amongst themselves, some of the rules may show overlap whereas others may be in conflict, depending on the structure of the patterns to be copied. Also, some rules may have greater strength and dominate over weaker ones.

In our laboratory, we have been studying graphic action with the aim to establish dominance or hierarchical relationships between the different rules, which are seen as movement constraints with widely varying origins. In our experiments we took care to define the sets of patterns to be copied precisely, because the 'strength' of a certain rule may depend on the opportunity provided by the stimulus materials to apply it. A simple example is the preference in righthanders to start drawing an inverted V at the top and to draw the left diagonal first: This tendency may increase if the material includes many patterns with an apex.

The present paper presents a review of three recent experiments of which the main data are presented in different places (Thomassen, Meulenbroek & Hoofs, 1991a; Thomassen, Meulenbroek & Tibosch, 1991b; Thomassen & Tibosch, 1991; Thomassen, Tibosch & Maarse, 1989). Here we will view these studies from a different perspective and highlight those aspects (also involving new data and new analyses) that reveal interactions between constraining factors which operate at higher and lower levels in the motor system. The presumed factors at higher, cognitive levels are associated with symbol context, motor programming, organization, planning and anticipation. The factors at lower levels of the motor system are concerned with the biomechanics of the effector system and with the preferred movement directions presumably associated with these biomechanics (see Meulenbroek & Thomassen, 1990; 1991).

In general, the subjects were seated individually at a table on which a digitizer was placed, and they copied geometrical patterns with a special pressure-sensing pen which was connected to the far end of the digitizer by a flexible wire. The model patterns were presented either one by one on a screen or in a row on the response sheet immediately above the place where their copies were to be produced. The patterns contained mostly three or four straight line segments and orthogonal or oblique angles. In Experiment 1, some of these patterns were capital letters. In Experiments 1 and 3, the patterns were presented at different rotation angles; their copies had to be produced at these angles. The model patterns were always surrounded by an orthogonal square, and the response sheets contained similar squares to indicate to the subject the required size of the copy, and to provide a frame of reference for rotated patterns. All subjects were righthanded naive students, either paid or receiving credits. Although the timing of the copying task was strict, there was no time pressure. Experimental trials were preceded by a sufficient amount of training. The specific methodological details concerning the three separate experiments follow below.

2. EXPERIMENTS

We will now consider the three experiments, concentrating on the interaction between the 'higher' and 'lower' levels involved in the organization of the graphic stroke sequences. For righthanders, the lower-order variables may be defined in a straightforward way: They are concerned with the biomechanically determined stroke-direction preferences. These result in a strong bias to draw strokes downwards and rightwards (see, e.g., Meulenbroek & Thomassen, 1991). In contrast, higher-order variables may be of widely varying kinds and, in fact, the experimental manipulations were of a different type in the three experiments. They will be summed up separately for each of the experiments.

2.1. Experiment 1: Programs vs rules in movement control

2.1.1. Rationale of Experiment 1

Two groups of subjects copied the same target patterns (familiar printed capital letters) in 29.4 percent of the trials. This they did in different higher-order contexts, which were present in the remaining 70.6 percent of the trials. One of these was the letter context (LC). The other was the non-letter context (NC). The patterns were presented randomly at varying clockwise rotations, ranging from a near-vertical (80-degrees) to a very slanted (40-degrees) orientation. The dependent variable with which we are concerned in the present study are the probabilities of habitual, *program-driven* stroke sequences. These we define as any production sequence starting at the top of the 'vertical' segment (cf. Suen, 1983). It is assumed that subjects have generalized motor programs available for the execution of these habitual sequences. It is to be expected that under increased rotation these sequences will give way to a *rule-driven* production sequence (starting at the bottom-left) due to the tendency to draw rightwards rather than leftwards. It is, moreover, an empirical question whether the latter tendency is counteracted under the LC context, since this context might generally favor the implementation of the motor programs for characters. This experiment thus provides a suitable test of the sensitivity of the stroke-selection mechanism to the highest-order variable 'symbol-class context'.

2.1.2. Method of Experiment 1

Twenty-four subjects were equally divided over two groups, the Letter Context (LC) group, and the Non-letter Context (NC) group. The model patterns included a set of seven capital letters (B, D, E, F, K, P, R) for both groups. These were the target patterns. They were copied in 35 out of 119 experimental trials. The remaining 84 trials involved the copying of seven other model patterns. These served as context patterns which were copied twelve times each. For the LC group the context patterns were seven other letters from the alphabet; for the NC group these were seven arbitrary non-letter characters (see Figure 1). Each of the model patterns was copied once in each of five rotation conditions, namely with their normally vertical segment rotated rightwards over different angles (-10, -20, -30, -40, -50 degrees). The height of the copied patterns was approximately 10 mm. The time available for copying was 4.5 s per trial. For more details, see Thomassen et al. (1989).

Figure 1. Stimulus materials used in Experiment 1. The top row contains the target patterns, the second row the non-letter context (NC) patterns, and the bottom row the letter context (LC) patterns. The patterns are reproduced here at their 'mean' orientation, viz., at minus 25 degrees rotation from their normal vertical orientation.

2.1.3. Results of Experiment 1

The results as presented in Table 1 show that there is a very strong tendency for the program-based stroke sequence to be reduced under increased rotation of the pattern. Apparently, lower-order constraints overrule the higher-order program-based production mode. In an analysis of variance involving contrasts, the linear and cubic trends for angle of rotation were highly significant ($t=7.68; p<.01$ and $t=2.68; p=.014$). This tendency, moreover, is under the influence of the main variable of this experiment, namely the symbol-class context in which the patterns are copied. Under the LC context the program-based stroke sequence is maintained significantly longer than under the NC context. The analysis of variance yielded highly reliable interaction effects for both the linear and the cubic trend ($t=3.71; p<.01$ and $t=3.09; p<.01$). This is evidence for higher-order effects being capable of moderating lower-order effects in graphic production. The LC context enhanced the strength of the tendency to stick to the motor program under increased pressure to abandon this tendency in favor of lower-order stroke-direction preference.

Table 1
Probability of program-based copying as a function of pattern orientation (Data from Experiment 1).

Pattern context	Pattern orientation (degrees) 80	70	60	50	40
Letter context (LC)	.930	.882	.786	.616	.382
Non-letter context (NC)	.948	.846	.606	.246	.144

The orientations correspond to rightward rotations of -10, -20, -30, -40, and -50 degrees compared to the normal vertical orientation.

2.2. Experiment 2: Hierarchy in movement organization

2.2.1. Rationale of Experiment 2

This experiment addresses the hierarchical approach of the patterns by studying the reaction times and kinematics of copying performance as a function of stimulus characteristics on the one hand, and of specific response sequences on the other. The *stimulus* characteristics involve the structural and geometrical features of a pattern which may or may not allow it to be copied entirely in correspondence with (some of) the graphic production rules. In a number of patterns this characteristic was present; we refer to these as non-conflicting (NC) patterns. In contrast, a number of matched patterns could be copied only if some rules are violated; these we call conflicting (C) patterns.

We expect the copying sequence of NC patterns to be organized more rapidly because of the availability of rules which unambiguously facilitate their graphic production. Since the global organization and planning of an entire stroke sequence must be assumed to take place early in the planning phase, this should be reflected by the reaction times in the sense that NC patterns will have shorter RTs as compared to C patterns. This assumption is accounted for in the model by Van Galen (see Van Galen, 1991; Van Galen, Meulenbroek & Hylkema, 1986; Thomassen & Van Galen, 1991). To the extent that the movement sequence needs to be specified further following the start of the first copying stroke, there will subsequently be more 'intermittent activity' in between successive strokes of C patterns than of NC patterns since, following Van Galen's model, such activity (during pen-up movements) reflects the preparation of the next stroke.

The specific *response* sequences studied are concerned with the anchoring rule, a rule which is associated with precision. Anchoring is the start of a later segment, following a pen-up movement, from a point on an earlier segment (such as in the lower horizontal of the printed capital F). Although anchoring has the drawback of requiring the replacement of the pen onto the writing surface, it takes advantage of reduced spatial uncertainty: One dimension of the location is fully determined by the earlier stroke from which the start is made. In a large proportion of the patterns allowing an anchored production mode, the anchoring rule was actually followed. For the purpose of the present analysis, however, we only consider those 39 sequences where an individual subject adopted the anchoring (A) mode in one of the two productions of a specific pattern and the non-anchoring (NA) mode in the other production.

The present analysis of Experiment 2 is subsidiary to the main study in which the weights of the various graphic production rules were determined (see Thomassen & Tibosch, 1991). This was done in an approximative, though highly promising fashion which disregarded segment length. For the purpose of the present study, we wished to see whether the *relative* length of the segments in a pattern has an effect on the selected stroke sequence. In the positive case, this might mean that not only the next stroke but also the subsequent ones determine the locus where and the direction in which the copying sequence starts, the planning of such a sequence thus being of a hierarchical nature. These relationships were investigated in detail for one type of two-segment patterns, viz., for reversed L-shapes. The results will be reported at the end of the next section.

2.2.2. Method of Experiment 2

Fifteen subjects were requested to copy 4 one-segment, 25 two-segment, and 120 three-segment patterns, presented randomly, twice each, so that a total of 298 patterns were copied. These patterns were all the designs containing up to three connected strokes that could fit in a virtual 3x3 dot matrix. The segments of the 145 multi-segment patterns were interconnected by right angles or they contained orthogonally touching segments or segments crossing in the center of the matrix (see Figure 2 for some examples). The maximum height and width of a copy were 9 mm. There were no time constraints. Every next presentation followed 1.5 s after the completion of the previous pattern. Incorrect or inaccurate trials were signalled to the subject and were repeated at the end of the session. For more details, see Thomassen et al. (1991b) and Thomassen and Tibosch (1991).

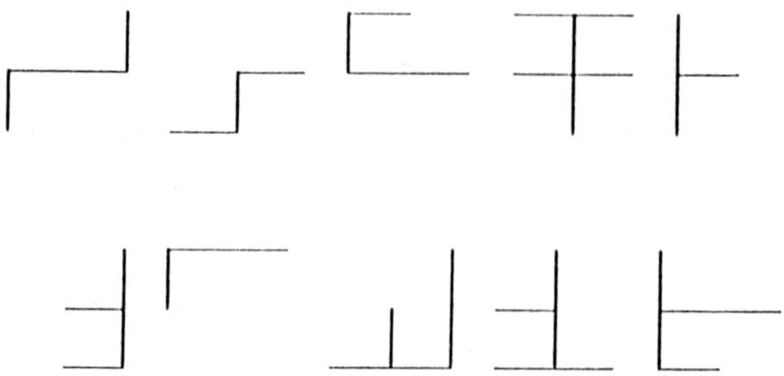

Figure 2. Some of the 129 stimuli presented in Experiment 2. Each structure could occur in four different orthogonal orientations to form four different model patterns.

2.2.3. Results of Experiment 2

The copying sequences of the NC patterns showed only one-third of the structural variability of those of the C patterns (1.69 vs 5.10; $p<.01$). From Table 2 it appears that both RT and the intermittent activity (pen-up movement duration = MTup; and pen-up distance covered by the pen tip in between strokes = DCup) are significantly lower for NC than for C patterns. These results are in agreement with our interpretation that the *preparation* of stroke sequences and of individual strokes is facilitated by the availability of non-conflicting rules. If also the execution of the strokes were facilitated in the NC patterns, there would have been significant effects of pen-down MT, and of velocity measures of stroke performance, which appeared not to be the case: None of these differences between NC and C patterns were significant at the $p=.05$ level. This, again, is evidence for a facilitation by 'rules' of early, hierarchical organization and planning of stroke sequences.

Anchored copies were significantly more accurate than non-anchored copies ($p<.02$). The anchoring results of Table 3 show that there is a (non-significant) tendency for anchored sequences to have slightly longer latencies and intermittent pen-up movement durations. In contrast to the above findings with the other rules, it thus appears that anchored sequences are not easier to prepare than non-anchored sequences. In contrast, velocities during anchored performance are significantly decreased, both on paper and above paper. This indicates that anchoring, with its inherently greater precision, is associated not with effects on high-level preparation but, instead, with increased control at the lowest hierarchical level of the actual on-line performance of individual strokes.

With respect to the segment-length analysis, it appeared that for two equal-length segments there was no difference in the frequencies with which various stroke sequences were adopted whether the segments were both short or long (Chi-square=1.01;df=3;$p>.70$). However, if one of the segments was long, there were large differences (Chi-sqare =13.27;df=3;$p<.01$). The subjects showed a tendency to start with the longer segment and the avoid drawing the longer segment in a non-preferred direction. This difference between unequal-legged and equal-legged L-shapes irrespective of the absolute length of the segments is evidence for a higher-order, hierarchical mechanism which takes the proportions of the entire pattern into account before a start is made with the execution of the first stroke. In a pattern with the same global structure, segments of the same absolute length are copied in different directions depending on the length of the adjacent segment.

Table 2
Latency and intermittent activity in the copying of matched non-conflicting (NC) and conflicting (C) patterns (Data from Experiment 2).

	NC	C	(C1, C2, C3)	F	p
Reaction time (RT;ms)	924	978	(1015, 955, 965)	3.79	.018 *
Pen-up movement duration (MTup;ms)	353	439	(468, 454, 396)	9.90	.001 **
Pen-up distance covered (DCup;mm)	712	923	(976, 961, 832)	6.24	.002 **

The C-values in brackets are for the three different matched controls upon which the statistical analysis is based.

Table 3
Latency, intermittent activity and performance speed of anchored and non-anchored copying sequences (Data from Experiment 2).

	Anchored sequences	Non-anchored sequences	p
Reaction time (RT;ms)	962	912	.174
Pen-up movement duration (MTup;ms)	333	395	.068
Pen-up tangential velocity (MVup;cm/s)	2.193	2.546	.040 *
Pen-down tangential velocity (MVdo;cm/s)	2.170	2.502	.021 *

* Difference significant at the 5-percent level.

2.3. Experiment 3: Anticipation in movement planning

2.3.1. Rationale of Experiment 3

In the third experiment, we again study the hierarchical organization of stroke sequences in copying. This time, we concentrate on making early stroke selections in anticipation of certain execution features later in the sequence. One of these anticipations involves stroke directions preceding and following an obtuse as compared to an acute angle; the second involves the completion of the stroke sequence in such a way that the final stroke is drawn in a preferred direction (rightwards, downwards). These two form examples of lower-order constraints as defined above, i.e., reflecting stroke-direction preferences. An example of a higher-order constraint, also studied in the present experiment, involves the option to execute the same motor program twice in immediate succession. In all cases in this experiment, we study stroke-sequence frequencies as a function of stimulus features. Orientation of pattern segments appears to be a strong determinant of the former two dependent variables. The presence of parallel lines induces the adoption of the repeated motor-program execution. Moreover, we will consider one kinematic variable, namely, pausing at the transition between two segments as a function of the size of the angle joining the segments.

2.3.2. Method of Experiment 3

Fifteen subjects were asked to copy 256 different variations of a basic pattern containing four segments. One segment was the 'main axis'. To one extreme was attached a second segment under an acute angle of 45 degrees; a third segment was attached to the other extreme under an obtuse angle of 135 degrees. The fourth segment was also attached to the main axis, not to one of its extremes, but close to and parallel to either the second or the third segment. The 256 variations also comprised mirror images and eight orientations of the entire pattern (see Figure 3 for a few examples). The size of a copy was approximately 12 x 10 mm. Subjects had 3 s to complete the copy of each pattern. A new pattern was presented every 5 s. For more details, see Thomassen et al. (1991a).

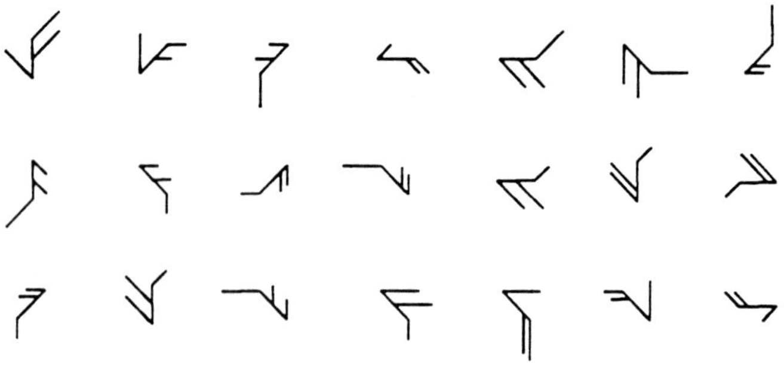

Figure 3. Some of the 256 stimuli presented in Experiment 3. Each structure could occur in eight different orientations to form eight different model patterns.

2.3.3. Results of Experiment 3

We will concentrate here on a few specific findings in this third experiment. First, it appeared that there was a very strong tendency for the patterns to be drawn under the following constraints: (1) a considerable amount of 'threading', in which at least two, but mostly three strokes are joined continuously; (2) 'anchoring' of the fourth stroke to an earlier stroke; and (3) parallel performance, in which the two parallel segments are copied by two successive strokes in the same direction. Table 4 presents these probabilities for three parsing modes, i.e., for three degrees of 'threading'. A characteristic feature of these findings is that the entire stroke sequence was often organized such that the three above constraints were all met, which implied that copying was started at the extreme with a single segment and continued in the direction of the two parallel segments. Moreover, (4) the second parallel was generally copied as the last stroke and following a preferred direction, possibly in response to 'postural attractors' (Morasso, 1991). Over and above these effects, there was a predominant effect of pattern orientation. The major determinant here appears to be the mapping of the latter orientation onto the biomechanical effector system with its preferred downward and rightward movement directions. All these effects were shown to be significant at the .01 level or better in analyses of variance and in t-tests for contrasts (see Thomassen et al., 1991a).

Table 4
Probabilities of stroke sequences involving parallel performance and anchoring (Data from Experiment 3).

Parsing mode	Parallel performance		Non-parallel performance	
	Anchored	Non-anch.	Anchored	Non-anchored
3 + 1	.410	.002	.141	.283
2 + 2	.062	.070	.008	.004
1 + 1 + 1	.008	.013	.000	.000
Totals	.480	.084	.148	.288

Table 5
Probability of drawing acute and obtuse angles with and without pauses and pen lifts (Data from Experiment 3).

Production mode	Acute angle (45 degrees)	Obtuse angle (135 degrees)
Without pause or pen lift	.565	.391
With pause	.300	.524
With pen lift	.011	.022

A second finding not reported earlier is concerned with the copying of segments joined by angles of different size. It appears from Table 5 that there is a strong preference for acute angles to be drawn in a continuous fashion, whereas obtuse angles more frequently have pauses and pen lifts. This difference is highly significant ($p<.01$). Looking closer at this relationship in two-stroke sequences involving one stroke in a preferred direction and one stroke in a non-preferred direction (Figure 4), we see that the continuous drawing of an acute angle is most likely when a stroke in a preferred direction follows the angle, while in the case of an obtuse angle the continuous join is made more frequently when the preferred-direction stroke precedes the angle.

Taking these two findings together, we conclude that the anticipation of a 'reversal' of the end effector (which occurs at acute angles) often leads to the planning of a two-stroke sequence in which the preferred direction is postponed until after the completion of the first stroke. This generally leads to fluent copying. Obtuse angles, however, result in only small direction changes, so that at the effector level a flexed (or extended) joint often needs to be flexed (or extended) even further in approximately the same direction. In many instances, this is incompatible with the efficient movement of that joint. As a consequence, two-stroke sequences are not so often planned as such when obtuse angles are involved. In general terms, this contrast between graphic sequences surrounding acute and obtuse angles contradicts the geometric view held by Van Sommers (1984) on this point, which sees a small direction change as more continuous and therefore easier to perform graphically. More importantly in the present context, it provides strong evidence for an interaction of lower-level (effector state) variables affecting higher-order (planning) variables in graphic production.

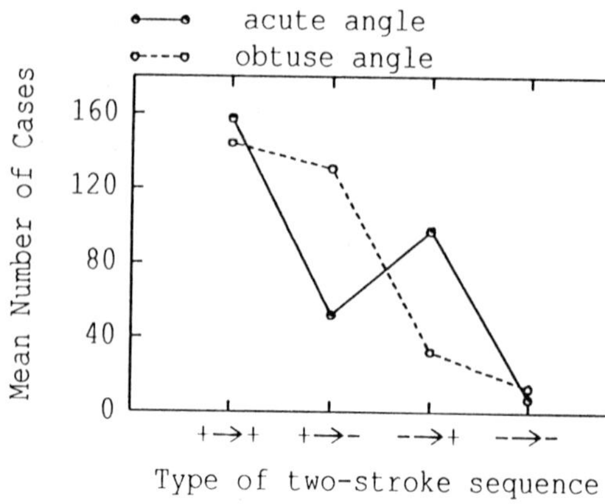

Figure 4. Occurrence of continuation across acute and obtuse angles in two-stroke sequences in Experiment 3. The data represent means to correct for a priori opportunities. Plus and minus signs indicate strokes in preferred and non-preferred directions, respectively. Signs to the left and to the right of an arrow represent the first stroke and second stroke, respectively.

3. DISCUSSION

In Experiment 1, physical constraints were manipulated by varying the orientation of highly familiar characters. This was done to such an extent that the available generalized (and therefore somewhat orientation independent) motor programs could no longer be executed efficiently by the effector system, and a novel, rule-based production mode was gradually adopted. Lower-order biomechanics apparently override higher-order (program-based) stroke-organization. The main point that we wished to make in the experiment, however, is that this shift is under the influence of higher-order context. The same familiar characters are performed differently depending on the performance of the surrounding characters. If stable programs are not available for the context characters (the NC context), their execution is considerably more sensitive to orientation, and the directions followed spontaneously in the adopted stroke sequences in these context characters appear to generalize to those of the target characters for which generalized motor programs are available.

Thus, in this experiment we saw that the highest-order context (which could also be called 'semantic' or 'cognitive'; see the contributions by Jean Requin and by Henry Shaffer in the present volume), i.e., the symbolic class of the context patterns, determines the rotation angle at which the lowest-order constraints ('phonemic' or 'motor' in the terminology of these authors), i.e., the biomechanically preferred directions, start to exert their influence, and at which rule-based production overrides habitual, program-based production. This appears to be an important implication from the first experiment.

It should be noted that it is unlikely that the observed interaction in this experiment is simply due to the frequent repetition of similar stroke sequences. The target characters were selected on the basis of their vertical bar at the left (see Figure 1), the criterion for their program-based production being the start of this segment at its top. Only two of the LC-context patterns (L, N) had such a bar at the left, whereas the five others (C, G, J, S, Z) did not. Similarly, exactly two of the NC-context letters had such a vertical bar at the left. The interaction we obtained must thus be seen as the result of the abstract symbol class of the context items and not of their concrete pattern structure.

In Experiment 2 it was shown that stroke sequences are planned hierarchically, and that where constraints like starting and progression rules can be applied unambiguously, such higher-order planning is more efficient. If accuracy is to be achieved, there appears to be less advance planning of the entire sequence, but more local planning and on-line control at the stroke level. We also saw that cost is taken into account, specifically the cost involved in non-preferred stroke directions: There is a selective avoidance of relatively long strokes in these directions, a strategy which determines the organization of whole stroke sequences.

In general terms, Van Galen's model (see Van Galen, 1991; Van Galen et al., 1986; Thomassen & Van Galen, 1991) specifies that larger units in graphic behavior are prepared earlier (i.e., farther ahead of their real-time performance) than smaller units. It could be deduced from this model that the advance preparation of an entire stroke sequence will result in prolonged RTs, whereas the preparation of a single stroke after the copying task has started will lead to increased pen-up movements preceding the next stroke. Finally, preparation at the lowest levels could be assumed to be reflected by reduced velocity of the current stroke. Applying these relationships in the reversed order allows the derivation of the level of organization (and the unit of preparation) from the locus of the observed retardation effects. The fact that this logic has again led to consistent results in the present study may be taken as further evidence of the model's power.

Experiment 3 demonstrated that the entire stroke sequence is organized such that the various constraints of very different kinds are met: (1) the 'threading' rule reflects economy with respect to repositioning the pen; (2) the 'anchoring' rule is evidence of economy with respect to determining the next starting point; (3) the 'parallel' rule reflects economy with respect to specifying and implementing a motor program; and (4) the 'terminal relaxation' rule displays economy with respect to the biomechanics of executing especially the final stroke, possibly in anticipation of further motor activity for which 'neutral' initial conditions are generally optimal. Moreover, the analysis of direction changes in angular sequences revealed that (5) the direction of subsequent strokes is taken into account in the selection of the current stroke. It may be that advantage is taken of simple agonist-antagonist relationships or of elastic properties of the effector system which favor reversed movement sequences at acute angles (see Morasso, 1991). At any rate, the basis of this differential effect must be sought in the periphery of the motor system.

If we attempt to reconcile the present findings in a conceptual model of graphic behavior, we would first of all require a global mechanism for implementing the task context and the task requirements such as those pertaining to speed and accuracy. More specifically, it should percieve and parse the pattern into manageable stroke sequences. It might be difficult to decide whether this mechanism is of a 'perceptual' or 'motor' type. As a result of a long history of graphic production, it is probably of a mixed kind. On the motor side, it should have access to rules on the one hand and to programs on the other. On the basis of either or both of these, it would specify a global stroke sequence for the parsed pattern. The anticipated execution of this sequence would have consequences in terms of imagined (partial) products. Together, these further specify the strokes with their starting points and other parameters. The cost involved in each of these is taken into account in this specification. For the ultimate performance of the individual strokes, motor programs are invoked, irrespective of whether the entire sequence is program driven or rule driven. Their execution leads to specific effector states and to visual feedback which have their effect on the current stroke as well as on the further planning and execution of the stroke sequence.

If a program for the entire pattern is not available, if it is not applicable in the context, or if the necessary experimental conditions are lacking (see e.g., Smyth (1989) for the case where visual feedback is witheld), graphic production will be guided by 'rules'. If these are conflicting or ambiguous, or if accuracy is a special requirement, the initial preparation will probably not involve the entire sequence, but only its first part; further planning will be done 'on-line', at least at a shorter temporal distance from real-time performance. The mapping of the geometry of the model patterns onto that of the anatomy and biomechanics of the effector system is of primordial importance so that the cost of the different movement directions is accounted for in the organization of the sequence. It is essential that these lower- order constraints are flexible in the sense that they will interact with the higher-order constraints imposed by the context (e.g., symbol context), by priorities (e.g., 'threading'), and specific decisions (e.g., 'anchoring'), and by economy considerations (e.g., repeated execution of a single motor program). The reality of precisely this interaction has been demonstrated in the present paper.

We are still far removed from answering the question of how the different constraints are represented in the brain. Most likely, they have entirely different central representations, depending on their origin and on the level of organization where they exert their primary influence. As we have shown in the above review, the primary effects of a constraint are likely to interact with those of other constraints. This implies that at some higher level of representation even the lowest-level constraints are 'known' so that they may be accounted for in the organization, preparation and execution of action sequences.

Note

The research reviewed in the present chapter was in part conducted while the author was a Fellow at the Netherlands Institute for Advanced Study (NIAS) at Wassenaar.

4. REFERENCES

Goodnow, J.J., & Levine, R.A. (1973). The grammar of action: Sequence and syntax in children's copying. *Cognitive Psychology, 4,* 82-98.

Meulenbroek, R.G.J., & Thomassen, A.J.W.M. (1990). Stroke-direction preferences as a function of arm position, handednedd, and hand posture.*Technical Report,* NICI, University of Nijmegen.

Meulenbroek, R.G.J., & Thomassen, A.J.W.M. (1991). Stroke-direction preferences in drawing and handwriting. *Human Movement Science, 10,* xxx-xxx.

Morasso, P. (1991). Neural mechanisms of synergy formation, *Human Movement Science, 11,* xxx-xxx.

Rosenbaum, D.A., & Jorgensen, M.J. (1991). Planning macroscopic aspects of manual control. *Human Movement Science, 11,* xxx-xxx.

Rosenbaum, D.A., Marchak, F., Barnes, H.J., Vaughan, J., Slotta, J.D., & Jorgensen, M.J. (1990). Constraints for action selection: Overhand versus underhand grips. In M. Jeannerod (Ed.), *Attention and performance XIII* (pp. 321-342). Hillsdale, N.J.: Erlbaum.

Rosenbaum, D.A., Weber, R.J., Hazelett, W.M., & Hindorff, V. (1986). The parameter resetting effect in human performance: Evidence from tongue twisters and finger fumblers. *Journal of Memory and Language, 25,* 710-725.

Smyth, M.M. (1989). Visual control of movement patterns and ther grammar of action. *Acta Psychologica, 70,* 253-265.

Suen, C.Y. (1983). Handwriting generation, perception and recognition. *Acta Psychologica, 54,* 295-312.

Teulings, H.-L., & Maarse, F.J. (1984). Digital recording and processing of handwriting movements. *Human Movement Science, 3,* 193-217.

Thomassen, A.J.W.M., Meulenbroek, R.G.J., & Hoofs, M.P.E. (1991a). Economy and anticipation in graphic production sequences. *Human Movement Science, 11,* xxx-xxx.

Thomassen, A.J.W.M., Meulenbroek, R.G.J., & Tibosch, H.J.C.M. (1991b). Latencies and kinematics reflect graphic production rules. *Human Movement Science, 10,* xxx-xxx.

Thomassen, A.J.W.M., & Teulings, H.-L. (1979).The development of directional preference in writing movements. *Visible Language, 13,* 218-231.

Thomassen, A.J.W.M., & Tibosch, H.J.C.M. (1991). A quantitative model of graphic production. In J. Requin & G.E. Stelmach (Eds.),*Tutorials in motor neuroscience: Proceedings of the NATO ASI*. Dordrecht: Kluwer.

Thomassen, A.J.W.M., Tibosch, H.J.C.M., & Maarse, F.J. (1989). The effect of context on stroke direction and stroke order in handwriting. In R. Plamondon, C.Y. Suen, & M.L. Simner (Eds.), *Computer recognition and human production of handwriting* (pp. 213-230). Singapore: World Scientific.

Thomassen, A.J.W.M., & Van Galen, G.P. (1991). Handwriting as a motor task: Experimentation, modelling and simulation. In J.J. Summers (Ed.), *Approaches to the styudy of motor control and learning* (pp. xxx-xxx). Amsterdam: North-Holland.

Van Galen, G.P. (1991). Handwriting: Issues for a psychomotor theory. *Human Movement Science, 10,* xxx-xxx.

Van Galen, G.P., Meulenbroek, R.G.J., & Hylkema, H. (1986). On the simultaneous processing of words, letters and strokes in handwriting: Evidence for a mixed linear and parallel model of handwriting. In H.S.R. Kao, G.P. van Galen & R. Hoosain (Eds.), *Graphonomics: Contemporary research in handwriting* (pp. 5-20). Amsterdam: North-Holland.

Van Sommers, P. (1984). *Drawing and cognition: Descriptive and experimental studies of graphic production processes*. Cambridge: Cambridge University Press.

Van Sommers, P. (1989). A system for drawing and drawing-related neuropsychology. *Cognitive Neuropsychology, 6,* 117-164.

SECTION 3

CONTROL AND COORDINATION OF REACHING MOVEMENTS

Tutorials in Motor Behavior II
G.E. Stelmach and J. Requin (Editors)

COORDINATION MECHANISMS IN PREHENSION MOVEMENTS

Marc Jeannerod

Vision et Motricité, INSERM U94, 16 avenue du Doyen Lépine, F-69500 Bron, France.

1. INTRODUCTION

The control of actions involving several segments of the same limb must involve two main levels of organization. First, the specification of joint positions implies selection of the proper muscles and calibration of the force of contractions applied to those muscles. Second, the timing of the muscular contractions implies a mechanism subserving coordination of the joint positions. In this paper, I will propose a description of these two levels by using the action of prehension as an example.

During prehension movements (unlike during pointing, where the hand is merely transported at the target as a whole by rotation of the sole proximal joints), the different segments that compose the arm simultaneously subserve different parts of the same action. The hand, which ultimately achieves grasping and manipulation of an object, assumes movements and postures that are apparently unrelated to those assumed by the more proximal segments of the limb. Indeed, the shape and orientation of the hand in anticipation to the grasp are largely independent of where the object is located in the working space : they are better defined with reference to an opposition space (e.g., 24) which, for a given task over a given object, describes the relative positions of the thumb, the other fingers and the object. Table 1 gives an idea of how the various attributes of an object could be separately encoded by the visual system and how the resulting outputs could combine for producing the appropriate motor pattern of the hand (see 4, 28). This pattern will also determine the subsequent haptic exploration of the object by the hand and the fingers.

The working hypothesis in this paper will be twofold. I will postulate first, that transport and grasp each pertain to an identifiable input-output system for extracting the relevant information from the visual world and specifying the commands to the appropriate muscles; and second, that the coordination between these input-output systems is achieved by a common kinematic plan.

Table 1.

Object attributes		**Motor output**	
SIZE	small	FINGERS	Thumb opposed to index finger
	large		Thumb opposed to all fingers
ORIENTATION	horizontal	HAND	Full pronation
	vertical		Semi pronation
WEIGHT	light	WRIST	No dorsiflexion
	heavy		Dorsiflexion

2. EVIDENCE FOR PARALLEL SPECIFICATION OF COMPONENTS OF PREHENSION

In this section, the neurophysiological evidence for separate mechanisms, each one specifying one of the submovements of prehension, will be reviewed. Neurophysiological experiments performed in behaving monkeys provide a wealth of data showing neuronal activation in relation to discrete aspects of visuomotor behaviour, such as target-oriented arm movements and precsion grip.

2.1. Mechanisms underlying directional coding of reaching movements.

Neurons coding for the direction of reaching arm movements were first found in the posterior part of monkey parietal cortex, where they belong to a broader category of neurons involved in visuomotor function. Other neurons from the same region are selectively activated during different aspects of visuomotor behavior, such as manipulation, visual fixation or eye movement. Neurons related to reaching or manipulation were described by Hyvarinen and Poranen (23) and by Mountcastle, Lynch, Georgopoulos, Sakata and Acuna (48) in the superior and inferior parietal lobules, more specifically within areas 5 and 7. The cells described by Mountcastle et al in both areas have no receptive field or other sensory properties in the visual or somatosensory modalities : instead, they discharge during active reach of objects of motivational interest (a piece of food for example), or during active manipulation of these objects. Hence the terminology of "projection neurons" and "command functions" used by these authors to designate an unspecified reaching system. By contrast, Hyvarinen and Poranen (23) considered that the cells responding to arm movement in area 7 had directional properties related to reaching in a given direction of extrapersonal space. In their experiments, activation of such neurons required association of a visual stimulus and a movement toward it. Neither presentation of the visual stimulus, nor execution of the movement alone were found sufficient conditions for firing these neurons. A population of neurons coding for movement direction was also found in parietal area 5 (32).

Thus, both Hyvarinen and Poranen (23) and Mountcastle et al (48) tended to assign the parietal cortex a role in generation of neural commands for movements directed at extrapersonal space. Other authors (e.g., 61), however, considered that properties of the visuomotor neurons (specially a category of eye movement-related cells, the visual-fixation cells) could well be explained by "passive" responses to visual stimuli. Accordingly, they proposed that area 7 is specialized in high-order sensory (visual) processing and has a predominant role in visual and visuospatial functions. In order to account for the fact that discharges of inferior parietal lobule neurons do increase when movements are actively produced by the animal during presentation of the stimuli, they proposed the intervention of an additional "attentional" mechanism. The cells fulfilling these criteria are concentrated in subarea 7a. It remains, as Lynch (41) argued, that the fact that a given cell receives a sensory input does not preclude its participation to sensorimotor or even motor processes. Indeed, according to the conception of cooperating visual and proprioceptive mechanisms (see Jeannerod, 27), it is critical that these parietal "reaching neurons" receive the relevant inputs (visual, tactile, kinesthetic) for elaborating the representation of the movement and controlling its execution. Finally, new experiments by Andersen, Essik and Siegel (3) have disclosed in area LIP (an area buried into the intraparietal sulcus), a population of cells responding directionnally to saccadic eye movements.

Other arguments as to visuomotor function of parietal cortex can be drawn from lesion experiments. One problem raised by posterior parietal lesions is to distinguish between impairments affecting spatial processes involved in goal-directed actions, from impairments in visual processes related to the perception of spatial relationships between objects. It has been clearly established that large posterior parietal lesions do not affect complex visual discriminations (e.g., 7). According to Pohl (58) the location of lesions producing impairments in spatial orienting (in the parietal cortex) is clearly different from the location of those that produce impairment in non-spatial visual discrimination (in the inferotemporal cortex). More recently, Mishkin and Ungerleider (45) and Mishkin, Lewis and Ungerleider (46) showed that visual modality-specific spatial abilities are subserved by the inferotemporal zone, although the inferior parietal lobule would subserve a supramodal spatial ability to which the visual modality (among others) would contribute. The effects of simultaneous ablation of the two areas cumulate in producing spatial disorientation (44, 46). The validity of this dichotomy has been recently confirmed (5), in spite of abundant interconnections between the two cortical systems (47).

Studies focusing on the effects of inferior parietal lobule lesions on visuomotor behavior in monkey have revealed highly specific impairments, including a reaching deficit first mentionned by Peele (55). Reaching impairment following this lesion is characterized by the fact that the animals misreach with their arm contralateral to the lesion in either part of the visual field (the so-called "hand effect") (13, 14, 22, 36). Their ipsilesional arm is usually not affected, though a "visual field effect" (involving also misreaching with the ipsilesional arm within the contralesional field) has been observed by Stein (65). Misreaching following parietal lesion consistently involves a systematic bias of reaches toward the side of the lesion, a fact which was reported by all the above mentioned authors. Finally, the reaching deficit is more severe in the absence of visual feedback from the limb (e.g., in darkness) than under visual guidance.

Neurons coding for the direction of movements were also found in the monkey cortical premotor and motor areas. Concerning the premotor areas, Gentilucci, Fogassi, Luppino, Matelli, Camarda and Rizzolatti (16) described a population of neurons located in the lower part of area 6 (subarea F4) that fired in relation to movements affecting the proximal joints, particularly during reaching at visual objects. These neurons can be passively activated by visual stimuli located within reaching distance and also fire during arm movements directed to a particular space sector, congruent with the location of the visual receptive field. The authors have suggested that F4 neurons play a role in specifying the end-point area for reaching movements. Another population of neurons related to hand and finger movements was found in a distinct subarea (see below).

In the primary motor area itself, Georgopoulos, Kalaska, Caminiti and Massey (17) found that the activity of single neurons changed in an orderly fashion with the direction of arm movements. Each of these neurons discharged preferentially prior to movements in a given direction and was therefore characterized by a preferred vector along which its discharge was maximum. Assuming that a movement in a particular direction involves the activation of a whole population of neurons, Georgopoulos, Schwartz and Kettner (18) summated a large number of individual vectors measured during a reaching task. They found that the resulting population vector was a good predictor of the direction of movements.

Parietal (areas 5 and 7) and motor (areas 4 and 6) cortical mechanisms combine for selecting the proper movement direction as a function of the visual goal. The timing of movement-related neuronal discharges in the two cortical locations suggests that premotor and motor cortex neurons relate to movement initiation, whereas parietal neurons relate to its monitoring during execution.

2.2. Mechanisms involved in the control of isolated finger movements.

Finger movements are controlled by highly specific mechanisms which seem to depend exclusively on cortical function. The cortical network involved in finger movements includes not only motor cortex, but also areas within premotor and parietal cortex.

2.2.1. Motor cortex. In primary motor cortex, experiments in behaving monkeys performing a grip task have revealed the existence of a population of neurons, the firing of which is directly related to activation of individual hand and finger muscles. First, these neurons only fire during execution of a precision grip, and not of a power grip, which demonstrates their connection with intrinsic hand muscles rather than with forearm muscles (49). Second, they burst with a short latency (about 11 ms) prior to muscle activation, which indicates monosynaptic connection (40). Finally, each of these neurons has a relatively large "motor field", in that it seems to be connected to several hand muscles. The muscles facilitated by one given cortical neuron usually behave as synergists in the precision grip task (9). These data are thus indicative of a relatively large divergence of corticomotoneuronal (CM) connections (for a review, see 64). In addition, electromyographic results in man show that gating mechanisms may come into play to produce highly specific activations. Normal subjects are able to control voluntarily the discharge of motor units of an intrinsic hand muscle and may eventually be able to select the discharge of only one unit, that is, of one of the motoneurons connected with that muscle (e.g., 33). According to Phillips (57), such a remarkable ability to select single motoneurons argues for a "subtle routing of activity in the thick synaptic neuropil of Area 4 to pick up, in appropriate functional groupings, the required CM neurones..." (pp 112-113). Indeed, recent mapping studies based on intracortical microstimulation showed that fingers are multiply represented within the upper arm primary motor subarea. This redundancy might be the anatomical basis for synergies between fingers or between fingers and other segments of the upper limb (63).

The effects of lesion of motor cortex and pyramidal tract in the monkey also contribute to establishing the critical importance of the corticospinal tract in the control of discrete finger movements. This notion was first introduced by Tower (67) and later confirmed by Lawrence and Kuypers (38) and Woolsey, Gorska, Wetzel, Erickson, Earls and Allman (70), who all showed that section of the pyramidal tract produces a long-lasting, if not permanent, inability to perform independent finger movements. The classical observations made by Tower (67) following unilateral pyramidotomy illustrate this point. Tower had noted that "all discrete usage of the digits is utterly and permanently abolished", specially in those actions where "the digits are used separately as in the opposition of thumb and index to pick up small objects, or in fine manipulation of objects, or in separation of one digit from the others..." (p. 55). This specific deficit was well illustrated by impossibility for the animals to execute grooming or by their awkward attempts to grasping food. "Instead of the normal movement which culminates in the opposition of thumb and index to pick up small objects, ... the residual movement of the paretic arm is a highly stereotyped reaching-grasping act involving the entire body half, similar to the reaching-grasping act of the newborn monkey". "The hand is brought down on the object in half pronation and scoops it into the ulnar side of the hand, unless, as frequently happens, the fist closes before reaching the object" (p. 56).

The degree of recovery from this deficit has been quantified in monkeys by Chapman and Wiesendanger (10) following unilateral section of the pyramidal tract at the pontine level and by Passingham, Perry and Wilkinson (50) and Passingham, Perry and Wilkinson (51) following unilateral lesion of primary motor cortex. In the Chapman and Wiesendanger experiment, the animals' performance was scored in a Kluver board task, i.e., the number of pellets of food extracted from holes of different sizes and the time needed for clearing the board, were measured for each hand. The strategy utilized by the animals for grasping the pellets was found to be changed after pyramidotomy when the hand contralateral to the lesion was tested. Animals first used all four fingers for extracting the food, a strategy that was efficient only for the larger holes. At a later stage (30 to 40 days after surgery), monkeys regained the ability to pry out the pellets from the smaller holes by using either the thumb or the index finger. Once extracted, the pellets could be grasped between the opposed thumb and index finger, but this precision grip remained weak and clumsy and the food was eventually dropped before reaching the mouth. Passingham et al obtained very similar results, except that recovery was limited to reaching the board, and that the animals never recovered the normal use of wrist and fingers. Partial recovery of grip formation observed by Chapman and Wiesendanger might be explained by incompleteness of the pyramidal tract lesions.

Neonatal lesion of the cortico-spinal system corresponding to the hand area results in lack of development of the distal component of prehension. Lawrence and Hopkins (37) and Passingham et al (50, 51) have shown that monkeys with complete unilateral ablation of area 4 performed during infancy never acquire a precision grip when tested later in adulthood. Precision grip in monkeys normally develops around the 8th postnatal month, i.e., by the time when maturation of the corticospinal tract is completed, as judged from the formation of corticomotoneuronal synapses (35) and the level of excitability of motoneurons by motor cortex stimulation (15).

Premotor cortical areas also contribute in controlling finger movements. In area 6 a specific population of neurons (in subarea F5) was found to be related to execution of distal movements of either hand. The discharge of many of these neurons was influenced by the way in which the hand was shaped during the action : precision grip neurons, finger prehension neurons, whole hand prehension neurons, could be identified (60). These neurons, however, are poorly sensitive to "passive" visual stimuli, as opposed to the neighbouring population of cells related to proximal joint movements (see above).

2.2.2. Parietal cortex. Recently, posterior parietal areas have been shown to be involved in the control of finger movement. As shown by Sakata, Shibutani, Kawano and Harrington (62), neurons in monkey area 7 (in the posterior bank of the intraparietal sulcus) respond to complex visual stimuli, including moving stimuli of different sizes and orientations. More recently, the same group found within the same part of area 7 (subarea 7a) a population of neurons which are selectively activated during manipulation by the animal of objects of a given configuration (e.g., a push-button, a handle, etc). Neurons showed differential changes in activity with different objects. Some of them were "motor dominant" : they dicharged during hand manipulation of one given object in the light and in the dark, and were not influenced by mere visual fixation of the object by the animal. Other neurons were more active during manipulation in the light ("visual and motor" neurons). Finally, another category of neurons were "visual dominant" : they were not activated during manipulation in the dark, and were as much inflenced by visual fixation of the object as by its manipulation (66). The authors suggestion was that these neurons are able to integrate visual and motor signals related to object-oriented action, and might therefore represent the link between object properties and the corresponding motor commands. It is thus not surprising that lesions of posterior parietal areas also affect the ability to shape the hand according to object size or configuration. Monkeys with such lesions are impaired in grasping and manipulating small objects. The hand remains open and the fingers remain stretched until palmar contact occurs with the object. Tactile cues then trigger an inadequate grasp where the object is seized between the palmar surface of the hand and the palmar surface of the finger (8, 13, 20). Similar observations have been reported from human subjects (26).

The available data in the neurophysiological literature in animals thus provide a strong evidence for separate (parallel) processing of discrete elements of visuomotor behaviour. Separation of the anatomical pathways devoted to each type of processing can be found, not only at the level of motor areas, but also upstream, at the levels of parietal and premotor cortices. Other possible modes of organization of movements have been proposed. It has been suggested, for example, that the represented variable could be the final goal to be reached by the limb. This would imply that a single attractor (the target object) could determine the whole pattern of the movement. In that case, identification of separate components would only have a descriptive value, and would not allow inferences on mechanisms. At present, however, neurophysiological evidence for this mode of neural coding of movements is lacking. Such an evidence would require specific neuronal activation for a movement directed at a given object (as characterized by its size, shape, orientation, etc), and located at a given spatial position.

3. COORDINATION MECHANISMS

The existence of an independent neural coding for grip size and arm transport, for which we have presented some evidence in the previous section, does not preclude that these components have to be linked or coordinated in some way, so that the time course of the finger movements matches that of the transport of the hand at the spatial location of the object. This is critical for anticipatory closure of the finger grip to occur in tight synchrony with approach of the object by the fingertips. Early or late closure will both result in inaccurate grasps, with the consequence of bumping and eventually breaking fragile objects. Indeed, behavioural studies of prehension in man demonstrate both independence and covariation of segmental components during the integrated movement.

3.1. Arguments in favor of parallelism.

Observation of normal, unperturbed prehension provides first arguments in favor of the independence of the individual components. The main argument is that the pattern of grip formation is affected by changes in object size, whereas the other aspects of prehension remain relatively uninfluenced. The main effect of object size on grip formation is the well-known increase in maximum grip size with object size (25, 43, 68). The subjects may use two different strategies for achieving this pattern : either the grip size increases at the same rate for both small and large objects, with the consequence that maximum grip size is reached earlier in movement time for a small object than for a large object; or the rate of increase is faster for a large than for a small object, with the consequence that grip size peaks at the same time for both large and small objects. For each given strategy, however, these objet size related changes in grip formation occur without affecting movement time or transport kinematics, which is suggestive of an independance of the visuomotor control systems for finger movements and for arm movements.

Other arguments can be considered as well. They arise from a series of experiments where unexpected changes were made at the onset of the prehension movements. These changes will be referred to as "perturbations". Perturbing the input of a sensorimotor system is a commonly used paradigm for probing the various functional levels of control of that system (see 27). In this section, the effects of unexpected changes in position or in size of the object prior to or during a prehension movement are examined (for experimental details, see 52, 54). Change in position of the object can be considered as a way of perturbing specifically the transportation component of the movement, whereas a change in size of the object can be considered as perturbing the grip component. Other types of perturbations could be produced as well, like, for example, perturbation of object orientation : this would affect pronation/supination, another component of arm movements during prehension. The problem is thus to determine to what extent a perturbation theoretically limited to one of the components will exert its effects on that component only, or whether it will also affect the others.

The first aspect to be considered in these perturbation experiments is the time needed for each given system to process visuomotor information, i.e., to react to the change and to achieve the correction. The Paulignan et al's results showed that this processing time was consistently shorter in the case of perturbation of object position than in the case of perturbation of object size. Figure 1 displays the kinematic analysis of a trial where object position was changed, compared to that of a control trial, where no perturbation occurred. In the perturbed trial, the object was shifted by 10° to the right of the initial target at the onset of the movement. A corrective movement was produced by the subject, such that the hand accurately reached the displaced target. This correction is visible on the figure as double peaks of acceleration and velocity. The important point is that the process of correction was achieved in a rather limited amount of time.

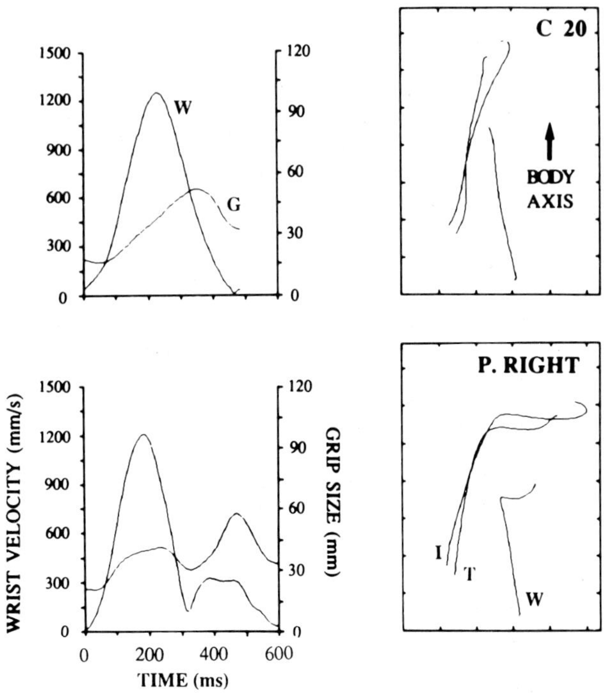

Figure 1. Effects of perturbation of object position on prehension movements. Left: Kinematic recordings of wrist (W) velocity and changes in grip size (G) as a function of time. Upper left, control trial. Lower left, perturbed trial. Note fast deceleration of the wrist after the first submovements and occurrence of a second submovement. Also note apparent coupling of finger movements with those of the wrist: two peaks are observed on the grip size profile, in temporal correspondence with the peaks in wrist velocity. Finally, note increase in movement time. Right: two dimensional reconstruction of the spatial paths of the wrist (W), tips of the thumb (T) and index finger (I). Upper right: control trial directed at target C20, located 20° from midline. Note curvature of index spatial path for enclosing the object. Lower right: perturbed trial. The movement was initially directed at target C20 and was redirected to another target located 10 degrees further on the right.

Movement time increased only by an average of 100 ms; the first peaks of acceleration and velocity (corresponding to the submovement directed at the initial target, before the perturbation) occurred earlier (by about 20 ms) than in control trials; the duration of the final deceleration phase after the second velocity peak was shorter (it lasted only 235 ms on average instead of more than 300 ms in control trials). All this suggests that the first submovement was interrupted early after the perturbation and that the second submovement was executed more rapidly than a normal movement directed at the same target. The fact that the first detectable difference between perturbed and non perturbed movements was seen some 100 ms after the perturbation (at the time of the first acceleration peak) desserves particular attention. A duration of 100 ms corresponds to the minimum delay needed for visual and/or proprioceptive reafferents to influence an ongoing movement. In the visual modality, evidence for fast processing exists in the context of reaching for targets. Zelaznik, Schmidt, Gielen and Milich (71) found that presence of visual feedback during the movement had a positive effect on accuracy, as compared to absence of visual feedback, even for movements of a duration as short as 70 ms (see also 12). In the proprioceptive modality, the time for processing kinaesthetic reafferent signals was estimated at 70 to 100 ms (e.g., 31, 39).

This early correction of perturbations of position sharply contrasts with the effects of perturbations of object size. Brisk changes in the size or shape of a graspable object are not easily produced. Paulignan et al (52) used concentric objects made of a central dowel (diameter, 1.5 cm) surrounded by a larger cylinder (6 cm). These objects were made of translucent material and were illuminated from below (Fig 2). The light illuminating the dowel could be shifted below the cylinder, so that the cylinder now appeared to be illuminated. This created the impression of a sudden expansion of the dowel, without change in spatial location. The reverse effect (light shifted from cylinder to dowel), thus giving the impression of a shrinking of the cylinder, could also be produced. As shown by Figure 2, perturbing object size at the onset of the movement clearly affected the grip component. Paulignan et al's results demonstrate that the earliest change produced in prehension movements by this perturbation occurred after about 330 ms, when the closure of the grip was interrupted and the sign of grip velocity began to revert. No change could be detected before this time on the acceleration or velocity profiles of the wrist. The latest considered landmark on the wrist trajectory (time to peak deceleration) was unchanged with respect to control unperturbed trials (see below).

The parallelist hypothesis would thus be a likely one for explaining the timing differences in responses to position and size perturbations. In neurophysiological terms, it could be speculated that the slower response to size perturbations relates to the higher degree of complexity of the visuomotor pathway for controlling distal movements. This pathway would involve processing, at the cortical level, of visual attributes of objects which relate to object identification and

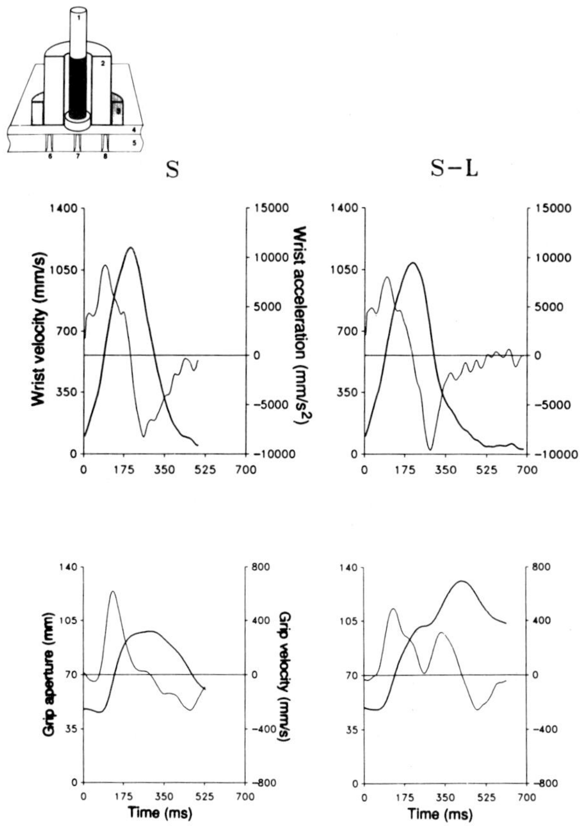

Figure 2. Effects of perturbation of object size on prehension movements. Perturbations were produced with the apparatus shown at the extreme upper left. LEDs were used to illuminate from below either the central dowel (1) or the surrounding cylinder (2). Shifting the light from 1 to 2 or 2 to 1 produced changes in apparent size of target-object. Left: control trial directed at the small object (the central dowel). Upper Left: kinematic recordings of wrist movement (velocity, thick line, acceleration, thin line). Lower Left: recording of change in finger grip size (thick line) and velocity of change ("grip velocity", thin line).

Right: perturbed trial from the small to the large object (from dowel to cylinder). Upper right: Note increased duration of the low velocity phase of the wrist movement following peak deceleration.

Lower right: Note correction in grip size. The time between the two grip velocity peaks represents the earliest sign of correction following size perturbation.

recognition. Such a processing would be likely to be time consuming and would be compatible with the observed delay of 330 ms for correcting perturbations at this level. By contrast, the pathway for processing spatial localization and controlling proximal movements would be simpler and have a shorter time constant.

3.2. Arguments in favor of integrated movements.

Other results obtained in studying prehension movements, however, can lead to a different interpretation of the organization of prehension, in showing kinematic coupling between the two components. This should not be a surprise, because the fact that the individual components have to be coordinated with each other will necessarily create apparent covariations. Such a covariation was demonstrated by Wing, Turton and Fraser (69). Their subjects were requested to perform reaching movements at different speeds. Duration of movements performed at a 'normal' speed averaged 735 ms, that of movements performed at 'fast' speed, 376 ms. Measurement of finger grip size as a function of speed of the movement revealed that maximum grip size associated with fast movements was on average 13 mm larger than with normal movements. In addition, in movements performed at normal speed, but without vision of the hand, maximum grip size was on average 35 mm larger than in the same movements performed under visual control. Wing et al's interpretation of these results was that exaggerated grip aperture occurred in conditions which degraded accuracy of the transportation component (e.g., fast speed, lack of visual control), whith the function of increasing tolerance for terminal errors of the hand. This interpretation (based on Fitts law) has important implications, in suggesting that the manipulation component is determined, not only by the physical dimensions of the object, but also by the dynamic aspects and the accuracy constraints of the whole action of prehension. Another possible interpretation of these results is that, due to coordination between the two components, the total movement duration was in fact too short to allow full expression of the grasp. The faster the movement, the larger the grip, because there was no time available for anticipatory closure of the fingers. Wallace and Weeks (68) confirmed experimentally both the independence and the covariation of the two components. They showed that varying object size did not affect the duration of the transport component, whereas grip size tended to become larger when the duration of movements was decreased.

Other covariations appear during perturbation experiments. As mentioned above, perturbations affecting the position of the object at the onset of the movement produce rapid corrections of the wrist trajectory, such that the object is correctly grasped with only little increase in movement time (53, 54). A more complete analysis of these results, however, showed that the effects of object displacement were not limited to corrections affecting the transport component. As shown by Figure 1, the grip aperture was also affected, so that, in most perturbed trials, the two components of prehension became kinematically coupled during corrective responses. The alteration of the wrist trajectory for reorienting the movement to the new target position was immediately followed (within about 50 ms) by a brief interuption of grip aperture, unrequired by the situation since object shape and size remained unchanged (53, 54). This finding was subsequently replicated by Haggard and Wing (21). In their situation, the subject's arm was suddenly pulled back by a mechanical device during approach to the object. This perturbation triggered a rapid correction of the transport component, such that the arm was reaccelerated in order to reach for object position. In about 70% of perturbed trials, the perturbation applied to the arm also provoked a reversal of grip aperture. As the change in grip formation occurred some 70 ms later than the change in transport, Haggard and Wing interpreted this coupling of the two components as an effect of a coordination mechanism. They proposed that (proprioceptive) information generated by the arm movement was used for stopping grip formation during the correction for the transport. By this way, the temporal coordination between the two components would be restored during the final phase of the movement. This explanation will be reexamined later in this paper.

A similar coupling between components could also be demonstrated by perturbations affecting object size. If the perturbation consisted in increasing object size (from dowel to cylinder), the grip formation initially sized to the small object was interrupted and the grip aperture was reincreased in order to accomodate the large object. As seen above, this correction in grip size began a relatively long time (330 ms) after the perturbation. Response to the perturbation in object size, however, was not limited to the grip component. Total movement time was increased by over 170 ms in the small to large perturbation, and by about 85 ms in the large to small case. Because no change could be seen in the timing of kinematic landmarks of the transport component, at least during the first 300 ms, this means that the additional movement time was spent in the later part of the movement. Indeed, as clearly seen in Figure 2, a long-lasting low velocity phase was present in the transport component, so that the hand virtually stopped at the vicinity of the object before the fingers adopted the correct grip size and came in contact with it.

Taken together, these results, including those of perturbation experiments showing covariation of movements of the wrist and the fingers during corrections, create the impression of a synergy of the two components of prehension. Perturbation of object location, which should, in principle, affect the transport component only, also affects grip formation; Similarly, perturbation of object size affects not only grip formation, but also transport. A synergy, however, would imply a strict temporal correlation of the components, which was not confirmed by statistical analysis of the data. Instead, the two submovements that compose prehension appeared to be only losely time-coupled (53).

Several interpretations can be proposed for explaining the observed covariations of the two components. One of these interpretations relates to the idea of a central coding of the "desired" final position of an effector system, as proposed by several authors for the control of various kinds of movements (e.g., speech movements, 1, 42; arm movements, 6; finger movements, 11). This hypothesis postulates that joint rotations, although they may be specified separately for each of the involved joints (in accordance with the parallel hypothesis), are subordinate to the resultant goal of the action. In the case of prehension, the central representation of the desired final hand configuration would be used as a reference for guiding the movement. This pattern of coordination is remindful of the coordinative-structure concept, whereby independent musculoskeletal elements can become functionnally linked for the execution of a common task, without implying structural relationships between them (e.g., 34).

A more plausible variant to this interpretation is that coordination of the two components would rely on a comparison between informations generated by each segmental movements, and the represented action. When a perturbation occurs during execution of the movement, a mismatch would arise between the updated represented action and the incoming kinesthetic signals generated by each segment. The segmental motor commands would thus have to be modulated in order to preserve coordination between components (see 27, 59). The rate at which the reorganization and corrections can be generated following perturbations would depend mostly on the amount and the rate of visual processing needed for detecting and analysing changes occurring in object attributes and for updating the representation. The above experimental results of Paulignan et al suggest that the rate of processing differs according to whether object spatial or iconic attributes are modified by the perturbation.

Finally, some suggestions can be made about possible neural structures involved in this coordination mechanism. It can be first suggested that the C3-C4 propriospinal neurons could play a role. These neurons are likely to receive proprioceptive signals generated by several segments of the same limb and to control the activity of the corresponding motoneuron pools. In addition, they receive visual input via a tectospinal route (2, in cat), which would ensure rapid corrections. To be entirely valid, however, this suggestion should account, not only for the data of perturbation of object position during prehension, where coupling between components has been shown to occur during fast corrections, but also for those of perturbation of object size where the duration of the movements is increased and the velocity of the arm during the final phase of transport is decreased by the slow correction in grip size. In other words, signals generated by the distal component should be able to influence the proximal component to the same extent as signals generated by the proximal component are postulated (by Haggard and Wing) to influence the distal component. In addition, there is a specific prediction arising from this hypothetical mechanism. This prediction is that peripherally deafferented subjects should loose the temporal coordination between transport and grasp and, in addition, would be unable to correct their prehension movements in response to perturbations of either object position or size. Although this prediction, to our present knowledge, has never been tested directly, there are a few indirect arguments against the "spinal" hypothesis. Prehension movements were examined by Jeannerod, Michel and Prablanc (30) in one patient with a complete anaesthesia (including loss of position sense) of one hand and forearm, due to a lesion of parietal cortex. While in this patient, the proprioceptive mechanisms were spared at the spinal level, her prehension movements were deeply disorganized, and coordination between components was lost. This result indicates that mechanisms for temporal coordination between motor components during prehension should lie upstream with respect to spinal cord, possibly at the cortical level.

A more likely suggestion can be made for this mechanism of comparison between the represented goal and the incoming signals. This suggestion attributes an important role to parietal cortex. Lesions of posterior parietal cortex produce a profound disorganization of prehension. First, the accuracy of reaching toward the object is impaired (13, in monkey, 56, in man). The kinematics of the transport component is altered, with increase in movement duration due to lengthening of the deceleration phase, decrease in peak velocity, occurrence of several secondary velocity peaks during deceleration (26, in man). Finally, grip formation is impaired, with exaggerated grip opening, incomplete or absent grip closure, inaccurate posturing of the fingers (13, in monkey, 26, 56 in man). This massive impairement in object-oriented action suggests that posterior parietal cortex might be involved in building the representation of the desired final configuration of opposition space during prehension.

This role of posterior parietal cortex in organizing object-oriented action must be dissociated from the role of other cortical structures in object identification and recognition. A recent observation by Goodale, Milner, Jacobson and Carey (19) gives some substance to this dissociation. These authors reported the case of a patient who, following a bilateral lesion of occipito-temporal cortex, was unable to recognize objects. The patient was also unable to purposively size his fingers according to the size of visually inspected target objects (an easy task for normal subjects, 29). In contrast, when instructed to take these target objects by performing prehension movements, the patient was quite accurate and her maximum grip size correlated normally with object size. This observation suggests that the object attributes which are used for controlling the movement are represented separately from the iconic attributes which are used for object recognition.

REFERENCES

1. Abbs, J.H. and Gracco, V.L. Control of complex motor gestures: Orofacial muscle responses to load perturbations of lip during speech. J. Neurophysiol., 1984, 51:705-723.

2. Alstermark, B., Gorska, T., Lundberg, A. and Petterson, L.C. Integration in descending motor pathways controlling the forelimb in the cat. 16. Visually guided switching of target-reaching. Exp. Brain Res., 1990, 80:1-11.

3. Andersen, R.A., Essik, G.K. and Siegel, R.M. Encoding of spatial location by posterior parietal neurons. Science, 1985, 230:456-458.

4. Arbib, M.A. Perceptual structures and distributed motor control. In: V.B. Brooks (Ed), Motor Control, Handbook of Physiology, vol. II, Part 2, Williams and Wilkins, 1981, pp. 1449-1480.

5. Baizer, J.S., Ungerleider, L.G. and Desimone, R. Organization of visual inputs to the inferior temporal and posterior parietal cortex in macaques. J. Neurosci., 1991, 11:168-190.

6. Bizzi, E., Accorneo, N., Chapple, W. and Hogan, N. Posture control and trajectory formation during arm movement. J. Neurosci., 1984, 4:2738-2744.

7. Blum, J.S., Chow, K.L. and Pribram, K.H. A behavioural analysis of the organizsation of the parieto-preoccipital cortex. J. Comp. Neurol., 1950, 93:53-100.

8. Brinkman, J. and Kuypers, H.G.J.M. Cerebral control of contralateral and ipsilateral arm, hand and finger movements in the split-brain rhesus monkey. Brain, 1973, 96:653-674.

9. Buys, E.J., Lemon, R.N., Mantel, G.W.H. and Muir, R.B. Selective facilitation of different hand muscles by single corticospinal neurons in the conscious monkey. J. Physiol., 1986, 381:529-549.

10. Chapman, E. and Wiesendanger, M. Recovery of function following unilateral lesions of the bulbar pyramid in the monkey. Electroenceph. Clin. Neurophysiol., 1982, 53:374-387.

11. Cole, K.J. and Abbs, J.H. Kinematic and electromyographic responses to perturbation of a rapid grasp. J. Neurophysiol., 1987, 57:1498-1510.

12. Elliott, D. and Allard, F. The utilisation of visual feedback information during rapid pointing movements. Quart. J. Exp. Psychol., 1985, 37A:407-425.

13. Faugier-Grimaud, S., Frenois, C. and Stein, D.G. Effects of posterior parietal lesions on visually guided behavior in monkeys. Neuropsychologia, 1978, 16:151-168.

14. Faugier-Grimaud, S., Frenois, C. and Peronnet, F. Effects of posterior parietal lesions on visually guided movements in monkeys. Exp. Brain Res., 1985, 59:125-138.

15. Felix, D. and Wiesendanger, M. Pyramidal and nonpyramidal motor cortical effects on distal forelimb muscles of monkeys. Exp. Brain Res., 1971, 12:81-91.

16. Gentilucci, M., Fogassi, L., Luppino, G., Matelli, M., Camarda, R. and Rizzolatti, G. Functional organization of inferior area 6 in the macaque monkey. I. Somatotopy and the control of proximal movements. Exp. Brain Res., 1988, 71:475-490.

17. Georgopoulos, A.P., Kalaska, J.F., Caminiti, R. and Massey, J.T. On the relations between the direction of two-dimensional arm movements and cell discharge in primate motor cortex. J. Neurosci., 1982, 2:1527-1537.

18. Georgopoulos, A.P., Schwartz, A.B. and Kettner, R.E. Neuronal population coding of movement direction. Science, 1986, 233:1416-1419.

19. Goodale, M.A., Milner, A.D., Jakobson, L.S. and Carey, D.P. Perceiving the world and grasping it. A neurological dissociation. Nature, 1991, 349:154-156.

20. Haaxma, H. and Kuypers, H.G.J.M. Intrahemispheric cortical connections and visual guidance of hand and finger movements in the rhesus monkey. Brain, 1975, 98:239-260.

21. Haggard, P. and Wing, A.M. Remote responses to perturbation in human prehension. Neurosci. Letters, 1991 (in press).

22. Hartje, W. and Ettlinger, G. Reaching in light and dark after unilateral posterior parietal ablations in the monkey. Cortex, 1973, 9:346-354.

23. Hyvärinen, J. and Poranen, A. Function of the parietal associative area 7 as revealed from cellular discharges in alert monkey. Brain, 1974, 97:673-692.

24. Iberall, T., Bingham, G. and Arbib, M.A. Opposition space as a structuring concept for the analysis of skilled hand movements. In: H. Heuer and C. Fromm (Eds), Generation and modulation of action pattern, Exp. Brain Res. Series 15, 1986, pp. 158-173.

25. Jeannerod, M. Intersegmental coordination during reaching at natural visual objects. In: J. Long and A. Baddeley (Eds), Attention and Performance IX, Erlbaum, Hillsdale, 1981, pp. 153-168.

26. Jeannerod, M. The formation of finger grip during prehension. A cortically mediated visuomotor pattern. Behav. Brain Res., 1986, 19:99-116.

27. Jeannerod, M. The interaction of visual and proprioceptive cues in controlling reaching movements. In: D.R. Humphrey and H.J. Freund (Eds), Motor Control: Concepts and Issues, J. Wiley, New York, 1990, pp. 277-291.

28. Jeannerod, M. and Biguer, B. Visuomotor mechanisms in reaching within extrapersonal space. In: D. Ingle, M. Goodale and R. Mansfield (Eds), Advances in the analysis of visual behaviour, MIT Press, Boston, 1982, pp. 387-409.

29. Jeannerod, M. and Decety, J. The accuracy of visuomotor transformation. An investigation into the mechanisms of visual recognition of objects. In: M. Goodale (Ed), Vision and Action. The control of grasping, Ablex, Norwood, 1990, pp. 33-48.

30. Jeannerod, M., Michel, F. and Prablanc, C. The control of hand movements in a case of hemianaesthesia following a parietal lesion. Brain, 1984, 107:899-920.

31. Johansson, R.S. and Westling, G. Signals in tactile afferents from the fingers eliciting adaptive motor responses during precision grip. Exp. Brain Res., 1987, 66:141-154.

32. Kalaska, J.F., Caminiti, R. and Georgopoulos, A.P. Cortical mechanisms related to the direction of two dimensional arm movements. Relations in parietal area 5 and comparison with motor cortex. Exp. Brain Res., 1983, 51:247-260.

33. Kato, M. and Tanji, J. Conscious control of motor units of human finger muscles. In: G.G. Samjen (Ed), Neurophysiology studied in man, Excerpta Medica, Amsterdam, 1972.

34. Kelso, J.A.S., Holt, K.G., Kugler, P.N. and Turvey, M.T. On the concept of coordinative structures as dissipative structures. I. Empirical lines of convergence. In: G.E. Stelmach and J. Requin (Eds), Tutorials in motor behavior, North Holland, Amsterdam, 1980, pp. 49-70.

35. Kuypers, H.G.J.M. Corticospinal connections: postnatal development in rhesus monkey. Science, 1962, 138:678-680.

36. Lamotte, R.H. and Acuna, C. Defects in accuracy of reaching after removal of posterior parietal cortex in monkeys. Brain Res., 1978, 139:309-326.

37. Lawrence, D.G. and Hopkins, D.A. Development aspects of pyramidal control in the rhesus monkey. Brain Res., 1972, 40:117-118.

38. Lawrence, D.G. and Kuypers, H.G.J.M. The functional organization of the motor system in the monkey. I. The effects of bilateral pyramidal lesions. Brain, 1968, 91:1-14.

39. Lee, R.G. and Tatton, W.G. Motor response to sudden limb displacements in primates with specific CNS lesions and in human patients with motor system disorders. Can. J. Neurol. Sci., 1975, 2:285-293.

40. Lemon, R.N., Mantel, G.W.H. and Muir, R.B. Corticospinal facilitation of hand muscles during voluntary movements in the conscious monkey. J. Physiol., 1986, 381:497-527.

41. Lynch, J.C. The functional organization of posterior parietal association cortex. Behav. Brain Sci., 1980, 3:485-498.

42. Mac Neilage, P.F. Motor control of serial ordering of speech. Psychol. Rev., 1970, 77:182-196.

43. Marteniuk, R.G., Leavitt, J.L., MacKenzie, C.L. and Athenes, S. Functional relationships between grasp and transport components in a prehension task. Hum. Mov. Sci., 1990, 9:149-176.

44. Milner, A.D., Ockelford, E.M. and Dewar, W. Visuospatial performance following posterior parietal and lateral frontal lesions in stumptail macaques. Cortex, 1977, 13:350-360.

45. Mishkin, M. and Ungerleider, L.G. Contribution of striate inputs to the visuospatial functions of parieto-preoccipital cortex in monkeys. Behav. Brain Res., 1982, 6:57-77.

46. Mishkin, M., Lewis, M.E. and Ungerleider, L.L. Equivalence of parieto-preoccipital subareas for visuospatial ability in monkeys. Behav. Brain Res., 1982, 6:41-56.

47. Morel, A. and Bullier, J. Anatomical segregation of two cortical visual pathways in the macaque monkey. Visual Neuroscience, 1990, 4:555-578.

48. Mountcastle, V.B., Lynch, J.C., Georgopoulos, A., Sakata, H. and Acuna, C. Posterior parietal association cortex of the monkey: command functions for operations within extra-personal space. J.

Neurophysiol., 1975, 38:871-908.

49. Muir, R.B. and Lemon, R.N. Corticospinal neurons with a special role in precision grip. Brain Res., 1983, 261:312-316.

50. Passingham, R.E., Perry, H. and Wilkinson, F. Failure to develop a precision grip in monkeys with unilateral neocortical lesions made in infancy. Brain Res., 1978, 145:410-414.

51. Passingham, R.E., Perry, V.H. and Wilkinson, F. The long-term effects of removal of sensorimotor cortex in infant and adult Rhesus monkeys. Brain, 1983, 106:675-705.

52. Paulignan, Y., Jeannerod, M., MacKenzie, C. and Marteniuk, R. Selective perturbation of visual input during prehension movements. 2. The effects of changing object size.

53. Paulignan, Y., McKenzie, C., Marteniuk, R. and Jeannerod, M. The coupling of arm and finger movements during prehension. Exp. Brain Res., 1990, 79:431-436.

54. Paulignan, Y., McKenzie, C., Marteniuk, R. and Jeannerod, M. Selective perturbation of visual input during prehension movements. I. The effects of changing object position. Exp. Brain Res., 1991, 83:502-512.

55. Peele, T.L. Acute and chronic parietal lobe ablations in monkeys. J. Neurophysiol., 1944, 7:269-286.

56. Perenin, M.T. and Vighetto, A. Optic ataxia: a specific disruption in visuomotor mechanisms. I. Different aspects of the deficit in reaching for objects. Brain, 1988, 111:643-674.

57. Phillips, C.G. Movements of the hand. Liverpool University Press, Liverpool, 1986.

58. Pohl, W. Dissociation of spatial discrimination deficits following frontal and parietal lesions in monkeys. J. Comp. Physiol. Psychol., 1973, 82:227-239.

59. Prablanc, C., Echallier, J.F., Jeannerod, M. and Komilis, E. Optimal response of eye and hand motor systems in pointing at a visual target. II. Static and dynamic visual cues in the control of hand movements. Biol. Cybernetics, 1979, 35:183-187.

60. Rizzolatti, C., Camarda, R., Fogassi, L., Gentilucci, M., Luppino, G. and Matelli, M. Functional organization of area 6 in the macaque monkey. II. Area F5 and the control of distal movements. Exp. Brain Res., 1988, 71:491-507.

61. Robinson, D.L., Goldberg, M.E. and Stanton, G.B. Parietal association cortex in the primate. Sensory mechanisms and behavioral modulations. J. Neurophysiol., 1978, 41:910-932.

62. Sakata, H., Shibutani, H., Kawano, K. and Harrington, T.L. Neural mechanisms of space vision in the parietal association cortex of the monkey. Vision Res., 1985, 25:453-463.

63. Sanes, J.N. Static and dynamic organization of motor cortical representation patterns, paper presented at Symposium on Control of arm movement in Space, Spoleto, 14-16 September 1990.

64. Schieber, M.H. How might the motor cortex individuate movements? TINS, 1990, 13:440-445.

65. Stein, J. Long-loop motor control in monkeys. The effects of transient cooling of parietal cortex and of cerebellar nuclei during tracking tasks. In: J. Desmedt (Ed), Cerebral motor control in man: long-loop mechanisms, Karger, Basel, 1978, pp. 107-122.

66. Taira, M., Mine, S., Georgopoulos, A.P., Murata, A. and Sakata, H. Parietal cortex neurons of the monkey related to the visual guidance of hand movements. Exp. Brain Res., 1990, 83:29-36.

67. Tower, S.S. Pyramidal lesion in the monkey. Brain, 1940, 63:36-90.

68. Wallace, S.A. and Weeks, D.L. Temporal constraints in the control of prehensive movements. J. Mot. Behav., 1988, 20:81-105.

69. Wing, A.M., Turton, A. and Fraser, C. Grasp size and accuracy of approach in reaching. J. Mot. Behav., 1986, 18:245-260.

70. Woolsey, C.N., Gorska, T., Wetzel, A., Erickson, T.C., Earls, F.J. and Allman, J.M. Complete unilateral section of the pyramidal tract at the medullary level in Macaca Mulatta. Brain Res., 1972, 40:119-123.

71. Zelaznik, H.N., Schmidt, R.A., Gielen, S.C.A.M. and Milich, M. Kinematic properties of rapid aimed hand movements. J. Mot. Behav., 1983, 15:217-236.

Tutorials in Motor Behavior II
G.E. Stelmach and J. Requin (Editors)

The gearing of early reaching to the environment

Claes von Hofsten[1]

Department of Psychology
Umeå University

Abstract

How actions gets geared to the environment in early development is discussed in the context of reaching and grasping. It is argued that the gearing of actions to the environment has to do with foreseeing the consequences of ones movements and of the external events with which one is interacting. Research is reported which shows that infants have a remarkable ability to be predictive in these respects. The origins of these abilities and the processes by which they develop are discussed.

1. INTRODUCTION

To enable smooth coordination, every action has to be adjusted to the environment in many different ways. These adjustments rarely appear as ready made procedures. They are typically developed. In fact, gearing action to the environment is all what ontogeny is about. On the other hand, no organism is "tabula rasa". Phylogeny has prepared for the solution of basic action problems by setting the organism off on the right track. Developmental studies are crucial in finding out how the organism is prepared for gearing its action to the environment, the strategies employed, and how mastery comes about.

One of the most basic aspects of gearing actions to the environment has to do with foreseeing the consequences of the action itself and the consequences of external events. The most basic consequences are the forces and momentums induced by every movement, however small, which have to be counteracted before they upset the flow of action and the balance of the body. The encounter with the environment has to be prepared and controlled. The hand has to prepare the encounter with the target in reaching and the foot has to foresee the encounter with the ground in stepping. Finally,

[1] This article was made possible by fonds supplied to the author from the Swedish Council for Research in the Humanities and the Social Sciences and the Tricentennial Fond of the Bank of Sweden. Correspondence should be addressed to Claes von Hofsten, Department of Psychology, Umeå University, S-90187 Umeå, Sweden.

in dealing with external events, whether it is the deck of a boat in open sea, a tennis ball in play, or a partner in dance, the consequences of these events have to be accurately predicted and monitored if coordination is going to be successful and the action mastered.

I will exemplify, in the context of reaching and grasping, how action gets geared to the environment. The development of reaching skills is one of the most remarkable motor achievements of the human child during the first year of life. At around four months of age infants start to reach for and grasp objects in the surrounding (1,2). To begin with, the reaches are rather awkward and circuitous, but within just a few months they straighten out and turn into smooth and well coordinated actions (1,2,3).

First of all it is important to point out that the gearing of reaching movements to the environment does not begin with the first successful reaches, but much earlier. The arm movements of neonates may indeed be aimed toward objects in the surrounding (4). However, the rich opportunities of practising reaching after the problems of getting the hand to the target have been overcome provide for an extraordinary interesting and dynamic developmental period.

2. POSTURAL PREPARATIONS FOR REACHING

In order to maintain balance during reaching, anticipatory postural adjustments needs to be performed to counteract the upcoming forces created by the forward extension of the arm. These adjustments cannot just be confined to the moving limb itself. The motor system has to be recruited in a more global way. How is this done?

A traditional view of the postural system says that it has a different mode of control than the voluntary movement system. Instead of foreseeing and counteracting the specific upcoming forces created by the movement, it is said to function according to a set of fast stretch reflexes that maintains posture (5). The work by Belen'kii et.al. (6), Cordo & Nashner (7) and others has shown that this is, at least, not the only mode of postural control in adults. They showed that the muscles of the legs were activated immediately prior to the prime mover muscle of the arm in such a way as to counteract the forces created by the upcoming movement. However, is it possible that this is just a higher level control that increases the stability of the body in order to increase the accuracy and smoothness of fine manipulatory skills but to a degree that is beyond what is necessary for maintaining stance. If that is so, then the young child might start off with a more primitive reflex mode and eventually add the more sophisticated and efficient prospective element to it. After studying running in children of various ages, Bernstein (8) concluded that children start off controlling their walking by "*post-factum*" control and only gradually turn over to a more efficient "*ante-factum*" control. Kelso (9) has also suggested that young children are characterized by a general inability to use "feedforward control".

There is however a possibility that foreseeing and counteracting the specific upcoming forces created by the movements is a basic requirement for maintaining balance and stability at any age. In other words, only when a child can negotiate the upcoming forces created by his or her own action in an anticipatory way, coordinated movements are possible. If this is true, anticipatory postural control should emerge much before preschool age. It should indeed emerge together with the ability to sit and stand unsupported.

Hofsten and Woollacott (10) studied anticipatory adjustments of the trunk in 9-month-old infants reaching for an object in front of them while balancing the trunk. The infants were seated astride on one of the knees of the accompanying parent who was supporting the child by the hips. The movement itself was monitored through an optoelectronic technique. Muscle responses were recorded from the abdominal and trunk extensor muscles as well as from the deltoid muscle of the reaching arm. The deltoid muscle was chosen as a representative of the muscles extending the arm forward in the reach.

The results showed clearly that trunk muscles participated in the reaching actions of 9-month-old infants. It seemed to be the trunk extensors that primarily prepare the posture for reaching. In a large majority of the recorded reaches, the trunk extensors were activated before the deltoid muscle. An example of this is shown in Figure 1. The role of the abdominal muscles in preparing the infant for reaching seems to be less clear cut. The data suggested that the abdominal muscles participate in the reach but maybe less in the preparation for it and more as part of the reaching movement itself. For instance, a major role of the abdominal muscles seems to be to bend the body forward toward the end of the reach (see Figure 1).

Postural preparations are not something separate and independent from the reach itself. Rather it should be regarded as an integrated part of the action. Reaching for an object does not only involve the upper limb. The whole body is engaged in accomplishing the reaching act and trunk adjustments both before the arm is extended and after it has reached its goal are important parts of that process. Figure 1 shows that reaching in 9-month-olds is embedded in an envelope of trunk adjustments.

There are at least two important differences between the postural preparations for reaching in infants observed by Hofsten and Woollacott (10) and in adults as observed by Cordo and Nashner (7). First, the average time difference between the onset of the trunk extensors and the onset of the deltoid muscle is much larger in our subjects than the one found in adults. The time difference found in adults is in the order of 50 msec (7) while the time differences measured in the present study were much larger. Secondly, the preparatory action was found to be much more variable in infants than in adults.

The larger time difference between trunk and arm action and the greater variance makes it appropriate to characterize the trunk action of 9-month-olds as more of a general preparation for reaching than as a pure anticipatory stabilizing action. The greater variability in timing the trunk response indicates that preparatory part of the reach is only crudely mapped to the reach itself. Variability is an important aspect of early coordination (11) which opens up possibilities for constraining the action, as a function of experience, in a number of different task-related ways into the finely tuned and efficient synergies found in adults.

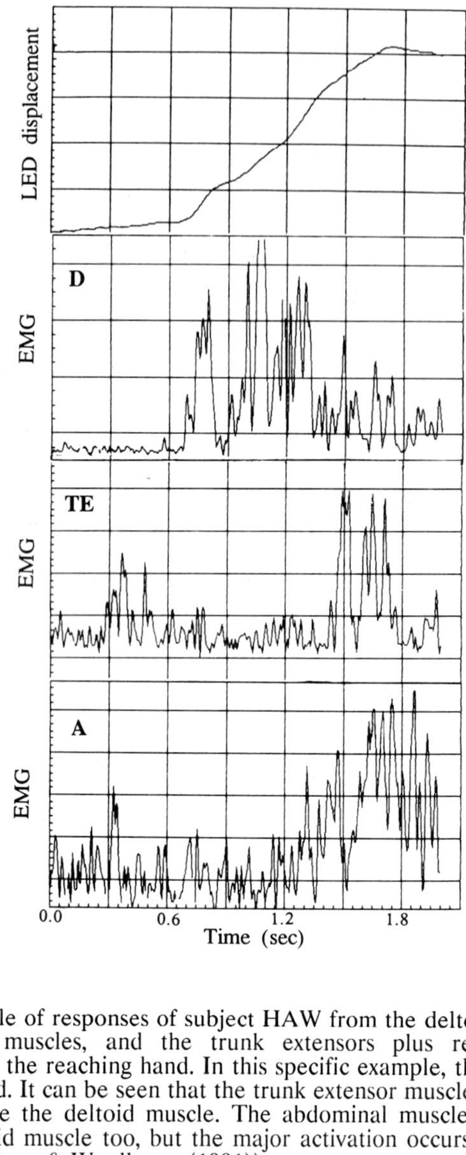

Figure 1. Example of responses of subject HAW from the deltoid of the reaching arm, the abdominal muscles, and the trunk extensors plus records of the relative displacements of the reaching hand. In this specific example, the reach was performed with the left hand. It can be seen that the trunk extensor muscles (TE) starts increasing firing well before the deltoid muscle. The abdominal muscles have some activation before the deltoid muscle too, but the major activation occurs toward the end of the reach. (from Hofsten & Woollacott (1991))

3. THE REACHING TRAJECTORY

Reaching movements geared to the environment need to be planned in terms of space coordinates. However, this is not the level of representation closest to implementation, as Abend, Bizzi, and Morazzo (12) have pointed out. The spatial representation of the movement need to be converted into joint coordinates before being implemented through appropriate muscle activities. Therefore, there is no reason why the implementation of a curved trajectory should differ from that of a straight one. However, Abend, Bizzi, and Morazzo (12) found that even when they asked adults to produce curved trajectories toward a stationary target they found that the path typically had a segmented appearance as if the subject had tried to approximate a curve with low curvature elements. Velocity profiles associated with these movements contained speed valleys or inflections which were associated with curvature peaks. This speed-curvature coupling has also been observed in adults for such well practiced movements as cursive handwriting (13).

From a principle of "equal simplicity", Bernstein (8) has argued that the structure of the central complex which governs the production of movements is much more closely related to spatial form than to joint and muscle schemes. Bernstein took the example of cursive writing. The handwriting of a person is very similar whether he or she, for instance, rests the forearm on the tabletop or is letting the arm support its own weight. In terms of joint or muscle schemes, these two situations are very different but not in terms of spatial schemes.

Therefore, there is no surprise that adults movements seem to divide up into spatially defined units. What is less clear, is when in development this mode of structuring emerges. If joint space is closer to the implementation of the movement, it is not unreasonable to believe that development proceeds from joint space to euclidian space. What are the principles of trajectory formation of arm movements in infants.

Hofsten (2) found it warranted to divide up infant reaching movements into units each consisting of an acceleration and a deceleration phase. These principles had earlier been applied by Brooks (14) and seemed to make sense from a functional point of view. At every acceleration, new energy is invested into the movement. Thus, there is a possibility that this investment of new energy at reaccelerations is coupled to the control of the movement. If that is so, then any abrupt changes in the direction of the movement should occur between units rather than within units. In other words, curvature peaks should be coupled to speed valleys.

Fetters and Todd (15) analyzed speed and curvature profiles of reaches performed by 5 and 9 month old infants and found a that the curvature-speed relationship in these movements were tightly coupled. Almost all curvature peaks coincided with speed valleys.

I have recently analyzed reaches of infants followed from 19 weeks of age, every third week, to 31 weeks of age (3). The reaches were recorded with an optoelectronic technique (SELSPOT) at 300 Hz and subsequently filtered at 50 Hz. Altogether 723 speed valleys were identified, of which 631 (87%) were associated with

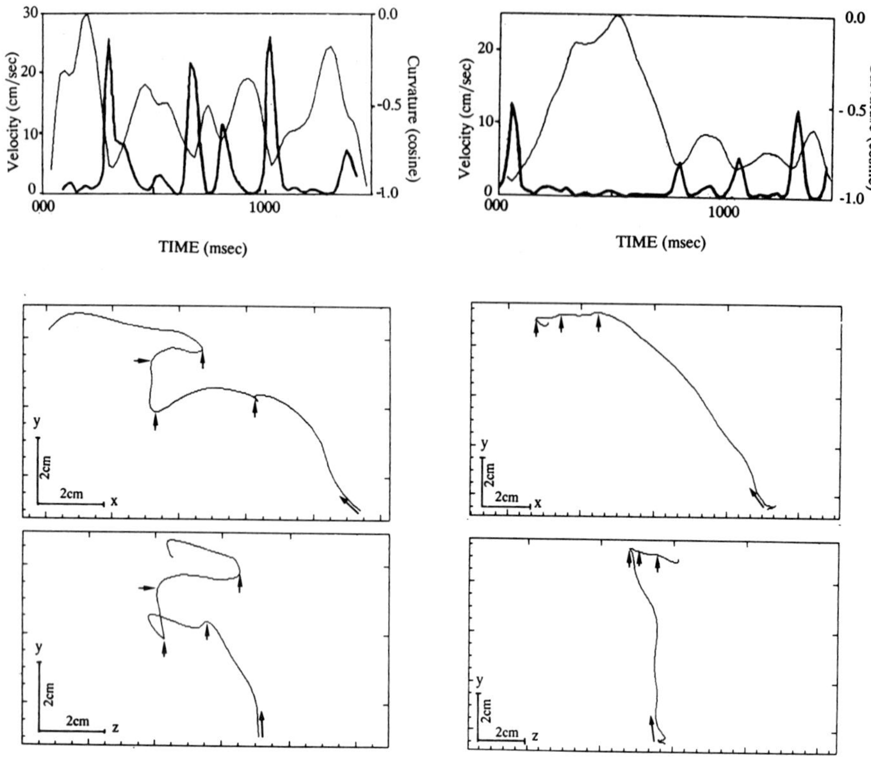

Figure 2. Two reaches showing the relation between velocity and curvature. The upper figures show velocity (thin line) and curature (thick line) as a function of time. Curvature is measured in cosine of the angle. Thus -1 equals 180 deg. (no curvature) and 0.0 equals 90 deg. The middle figures are front views of the reaches and the bottom figures side views of the reaches. The arrows indicate the borderlines between action units. (LEFT) A reach by LIB at 19 weeks of age. Duration is 1.45 sec. The movement consists of 5 action units.(RIGHT) A reach by LIB at 31 weeks of age. Duration is 1.47 sec. The movement consists of 4 action units. (From Hofsten (1991) with permission)

a curvature peak more pointed than 165 deg. and occurring within 20 msec of the velocity minimum. Two examples of couplings between speed and curvature can be seen in Figure 2.

In a recent study on neonatal arm movements, Hofsten and Rönnqvist (16) analyzed speed-curvature coupling. Trajectory formation of spontaneous arm movements were recorded during 10 second periods in eight alert newborns. The same optoelectronic device was used as above (SELSPOT). Recording frequency was 100 Hz. Altogether, 86 10-second periods were documented. The parts of these periods containing very slow movements or unreliable recordings were excluded from further analysis. The remaining parts were divided up into units according to their acceleration-deceleration pattern, i.e. speed valleys constituted the borderlines between units. This procedure resulted in altogether 1757 movement units. Curvature peaks coincided with 1138 of them. Long sequences of movements had perfect coupling between curvature and speed while other parts were only loosely associated. Even during periods when the coupling was not perfect, the curvature peaks were always greater when they occurred at speed valleys. An example of perfect coupling between curvature and speed is shown in Figure 3.

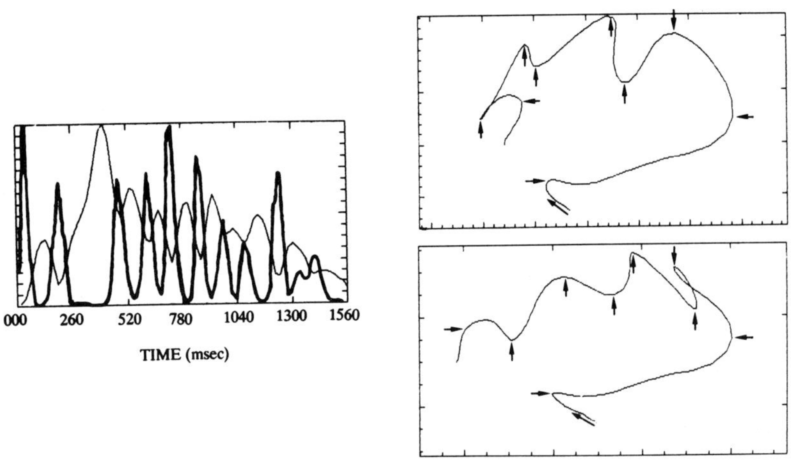

Figure 3. A reach showing the relation between velocity and curvature in neonate reaching. The infant is two days old. The movement consists of 10 action units. The left figure shows velocity (thin line) and curature (thick line) as a function of time. Curvature is measured in cosine of the angle. Thus -1 equals 180 deg. (no curvature) and 0.0 equals 90 deg. The upper right figure is a front view of the reach and the lower right figure a side view of the reach. The arrows indicate the borderlines between action units. (from Hofsten & Rönnqvist, 1991)

In summary, spatial mapping of arm movements occur very early in development. Even though it may be rather imperfect at birth, data suggest that it is well underway. If development proceeds from joint space to euclidian space as suggested above, the process must start prenatally. That is perfectly reasonable. The fetus moves very much in the womb. DeVries, Visser, and Prechtl (17) have shown that the incidence of isolated armmovements in the 13-19 week old fetus may be close to 100 per hour. One function of these movements could be to calibrate reaching space. Reaching space is also coupled to visual space at birth, at least directionally, as shown by Hofsten (4). He found that infants, 4 to 9 days old, directed their armmovements crudely toward a seen object in front of them. This is more intriguing. That kind of coupling cannot have emerged from experience, as opportunities for visually directed reaching are absent in the womb.

4. APPROACHING THE TARGET

Mature reaching consists of two movement units with different functions, structured differently and ordered in a specific way (18,19). The discontinuity is not simply an effect of visual correction for undershooting. Reaccelerations also occurred in the absence of visual feedback from the reaching hand (20). The first unit is by far the largest unit. Jeannerod found that the time at which the discontinuity occurred in the reach invariably corresponded to 70-80 % of the total movement time. The function of it is to transport the hand to the vicinity of the target while the second unit is more geared toward merging on the target in order to grasp it. At the same time as the reacceleration occurred, the hand was found to have its peak aperture after which it started to close (18).

Hofsten (2,3) found evidence that the transitions in infant reaching, the months after successful reaching and grasping of objects had been acquired, were aimed toward such an adult organization. This is not to say that differentiation of action units was absent at 4-5 months of age. One of the units was generally larger than the rest, carrying the hand a longer distance. However, the position of this unit in the action sequence varied. With age, the structuring of the reach changed in, at least, four important ways.

First, Hofsten (3) found that the order between the units became more systematic. At the youngest age, the transport unit was positioned at the beginning of the movement in only half the reaches, while at the oldest age level, 31 weeks of age, 84% of the reaches started with the transport unit. This kind of transition has earlier been discussed by Bruner (21) in the context of development of reaching and grasping. In prereaching infants, he observed that an attractive object presented to an infant might arouse many of the constituent parts of the appropriate action sequence but not in the correct order for successful object capture.

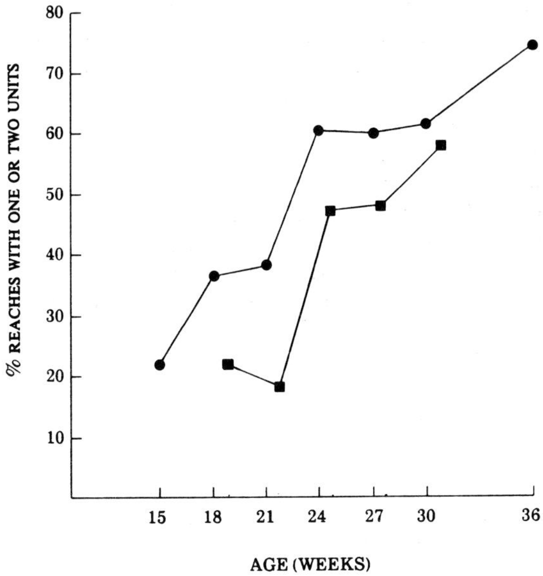

Figure 4. Proportion of reaches consisting of one or two action units as a function of age of the subjects. CIRCLES = data from Hofsten (1979). SQUARES = data from Hofsten (1991).

The second kind of development observed concerned the properties of the transport unit. Hofsten (2,3) found that the duration of it became greater and it covered a larger proportion of the approach with age. This is illustrated in Figure 2. Hofsten (3) found that at 31 weeks of age, 69% of the approach was allocated to the transport unit compared to 46 % at 19 weeks. At the same age, the transport unit was the largest approach unit in 94% of the reaches compared to 635 at 19 weeks. The duration it the transport unit doubled during the same period. In summary, the transport unit became increasingly efficient as an approach unit. The remaining units changed comparably little during the same period.

The third kind of development observed, was a decreasing number of units in a reach. This is shown in Figure 5. An increasing proportion of the reaches consisted of no more than two units. At 19 weeks of age, this was true for 22 % of the reaches while it was true for 58 % of the reaches at 31 weeks. As shown in Figure 5, this replicates the finding by Hofsten (2).

The fourth kind of development observed was a straightening of reaching trajectories. This effect is partly coupled to the observed decrease in number of action units per reach. Better spatial planning may lead to fewer units. However, units of action do not seem to be just a consequence of spatial planning. With age, there were an increasing proportion of speed valleys not associated with directional change of the reach. The straightening of reaching trajectories was also be observed in the within-unit curvatures. The result suggests that the formation of reaching trajectories improves at least two levels. First, aiming precision improves. The first action unit gets the hand increasingly closer to the target. Secondly, the process of getting the hand from one position to another becomes more efficient and more finely geared to a spatial frame of reference. Fewer action units are needed to get the hand to the target.

The increasing proportion of speed valleys not associated with directional change of the reach suggests that there are other aspects of action units than spatial correction. There could be preset constraints on the structure of the reach and the magnitudes of the component units. This is in accordance with Jeannerod & Biguer's (20) finding in adult reaching that reaccelerations also occurred in the absence of visual feedback from the reaching hand. Furthermore , apart from correcting the direction of approach to the target, modulating the rate of approach to the target may be another functional reason for dividing up movements into units. In the case of reaching movements, it is a good strategy to make a gross movement to the vicinity of the target and then home in on it.

5. PREPARING THE GRASP

One of the most important aspects of grasping skill is to what degree the grasp is prepared before the target is encountered. All these preparations are visually controlled. In mature reaching, preparations for grasping the target can be observed throughout the approach. They may be of two kinds. First, there are spatial adjustments of the reaching hand to the orientation, form, and size of the object. Secondly, the securing of the target should be timed in such a way that the hand starts to close around the target in anticipation of and not as a reaction to the encounter with the object.

Young infants will adjust the orientation of the hand to the orientation of the object before it is encountered (22,23,24). These adjustments need to be performed if the hand is going to close around the object in an adequate way. Hofsten and Fazel-Zandy (23) and Morrongiello and Rocca (24) found that infants as young as five months made such preparatory adjustments of hand orientation. At this age, the preparation was found to be rather crude and mainly done close to the start of the reach or even before. After six months of age, the adjustments improved greatly and were often performed during the later part of the approach. However, strategies varied between individuals and also some 5-month-olds showed clear tendencies to adjust the orientation of the hand during the final approach (23).

Adults will alter the opening of the hand as a function of the size of the object to be reached for (18). The hand opens up during the transport phase of the approach and closes during the second phase. Adjustments occur during both these phases. The hand will open up more for a larger target than a smaller one . Preparatory adjustments to object size are less crucial than preparatory adjustments to object orientation. Instead of adjusting the opening of the hand to the size of the object it would also be possible to always open the hand fully during the approach. The disadvantage of that strategy is the additional time it takes to close a fully opened hand relative to a semi-opened hand. The advantage of opening the hand more fully is that less endpoint accuracy is needed. Therefore, adults will use this strategy when having to make a fast reach (25).

The opening of the hand during the transport phase is present already in neonatal reaching. The very fact that the hand opens up constitutes a preparation for grasping the target although the opening may also be regarded as a part of an extension synergy. The question is when the amount of opening gets geared to the size of the target. Hofsten and Rönnqvist (26) monitored the distance between thumb and index finger with an optoelectronic technique (SELSPOT) in reaches performed by 5-6-month-olds, 9-month-olds, and 13-month-olds. Spherical targets of three different sizes were used. They were 15 mm, 25 mm, and 35 mm in diameter. It was found that, at least, the infants in the two older age groups adjusted the opening of the hand to the size of the target reached for.

A smooth reaching action requires that the grasp is adequately timed relative to the encounter with the object. This is especially true if the object to be grasped is moving. If the hand closes too late, the object will just bounce on the palm and be lost. If it closes too early, it will hit the knuckles. Alderson, Sully and Sully (27) found that the time precision in grasping a lightly thrown ball had to be around 14 msec. As most adults master this task with ease it can be concluded that precise timing is a prominent feature of adult grasping.

Precise timing requires the grasp to be planned for and initiated in anticipation of the encounter with the target. Such planning can only occur under visual control. Tactual control of the grasping act implies that the grasp is initiated after the target has been touched which will be too late for securing the target if it is moving for instance. As tactually controlled grasping is initiated after contact it will by necessity also induce an interruption in the reach-and-grasp act. Thus, the emergence of visually controlled, well timed grasping is crucial for the development of manual skill. It is well known that grasping also can be tactually controlled in the prereaching infant (28) but little is known when visual control of grasping starts to be effective. When, during development does the child start to use visual information for controlling grasping in an anticipatory way?

Hofsten and Rönnqvist (26) studied the question of timing of the grasp in infant reaching. They monitored the distance between thumb and index finger as the infant approached the target and determined precisely when this distance started to diminish. They also monitored the position of the target. When the hand encountered the target it was immediately displaced and the time of this event could be precisely determined too. An example of this is shown in Figure 5. At all three age levels, the

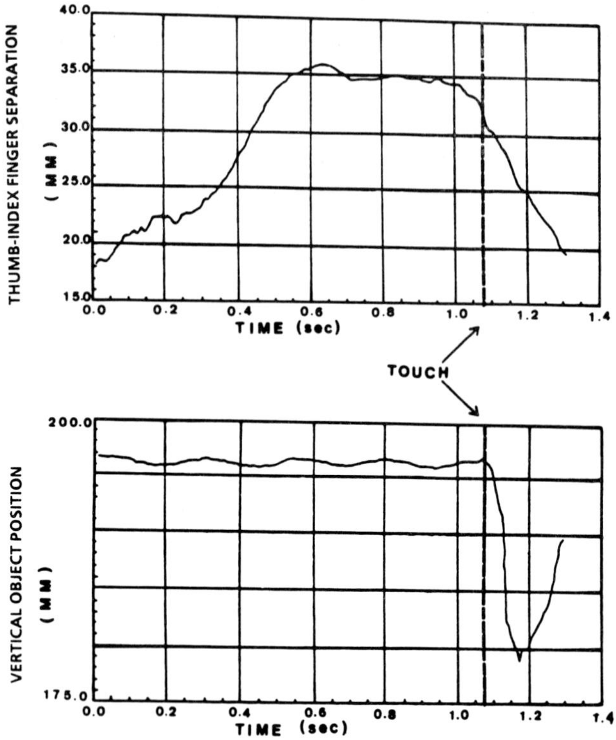

Figure 5. An example of a reach performed by a 5-month-old infant. The target size was 15 mm in diameter. The upper graph shows the distance between the thumb and indexfinger as a function of time. The lower graph shows the position of the target as a function of time and how it is displaced when contacted. Note that the hand starts to close before contact.

closing of the hand was well timed in relation to the encounter with the object. In the two younger age groups the distribution of timing centers around touch. For the 5-6 month-olds, 57% of the grasps started before the encounter with the target and for the 9 month-olds, 51 % did. However, for the 13 month-olds, the distribution of timing did not center around touch anymore. At this age the grasping action started before touch in 84 % of the cases.

A majority of grasps were visually controlled. To determine whether a grasp has to be visually controlled or could be tactually controlled, the contact time itself is not the appropriate comparison time. Rather it should be a delay corresponding to what could be considered as s minimum response latency of the hand to tactile stimuli. Johansson and Westling (29) found that the minimum response latency in the distal hand muscles in the adult were in the order of 60 ms. If that comparison time is used the percentage of grasps starting within that time limit was 83, 73, and 87 for the 5-6, 9, and 13 month-olds, respectively.

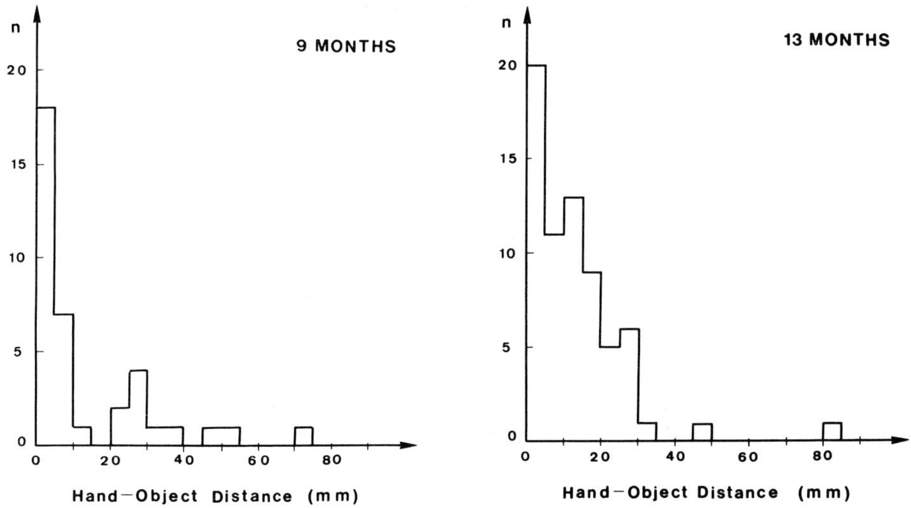

Figure 6. Distributions of distances between hand and target at the time when the hand started to close for the 9-month-old infants and the 13-month-old infants. (from Hofsten & Rönnqvist (1988) with permission)

The capacity for planning and initiating the grasp in anticipation of the encounter with the object is a necessary but not a sufficient requirement for the emergence of integrated reach-and-grasp action. Even if both the approach and the grasp are well controlled, there might very well be a discontinuity between these two subactions. Jeannerod & Biguer (20) have shown that approach and grasp are well integrated and synchronized in the adult subject. The beginning of the second, visually guided part of the approach also marks the beginning of the closing of the hand. How well integrated are approach and grasp when infants start to reach for and grasp objects successfully at 4-5 months of age? Is the target first approached and then grasped or is the grasping action initiated during the approach as in the adult. Hofsten and Rönnqvist

(26) found that their two younger age groups (5-6 and 9 months of age) would most often start closing the hand in the very close vicinity of the target. However, the 13-month-olds started to close the hand further away from the target during the actual approach, thus indicating that the reaching and grasping acts, at this age, are getting integrated. This is illustrated in Figure 7.

6. CATCHING

The mastering of reaching and grasping provides a foundation for the establishment of other more specific perception-action systems that relies on these capacities. Catching is such a case. It is also the nicest and most striking example of anticipation in infants' manual action. To be able to catch a moving object, the subject not only needs to perceive the position of the object at an instant but also where the

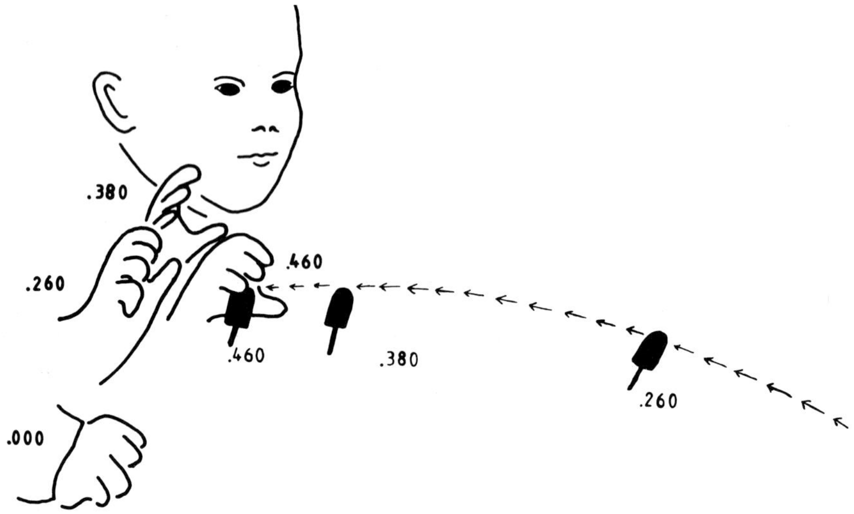

Figure 7. An infant catching an object moving in front of her at 120 cm/sec. The duration of the reach was 460 msec.; the object was encountered at 430msec. The picture shows the hand and the object at different time intervals from the start of the reach. Note tha during the reach, the hand opens and the closes in anticipation of the encounter with the object. (from Hofsten (1983) with permission)

object is going and how fast. A successful catch has to aimed for some point ahead of the object where the hand and the object would meet and as the hand gets there it should close around the object at the right time. Obviously, timing has to be extremely precise.

In a series of studies, I have found that infants possess a remarkable capacity to catch objects (30,31,32). Hofsten and Lindhagen (32) found that from the very age an infant starts to master reaching for stationary objects, he or she will also reach successfully for fast moving ones. Eighteen-week-old infants caught the object as it moved at 30 cm/sec. Hofsten (31), studying 8-month-old infants, found that they would successfully catch objects moving at 120 cm/sec. The initial aiming of these reaches were within a few degrees of the meeting point with the target and the variable timing error was between 50 and 60 msec. An example of a reach for an object moving at 120 cm/sec is shown in Figure 7.

7. THE DEVELOPMENTAL PROCESS

Gearing reaching actions to the environment is a complex process. As shown above, a number of problems have to be solved before reaching and grasping can be skillfully performed. The solution of each of these problems requires that certain kinds of information about the world are available to the action system. Thus, the development of action is very much a story about the development of perception. Reaching skills are based on vision as well as proprioception. Vision is needed to define the position of the target to be reached for, its form, orientation, and substance, and if appropriate its speed and direction of motion. Vision may also be needed to define the position of the hand relative to the position of the target during the last part of the approach. Proprioception is needed to define the position of the hand relative to the body during the first part of the approach. The results presented above suggest that the mapping of a proprioceptively defined reaching space onto joint and muscle schemes is well underway at birth. Furthermore, the results by Hofsten (4) suggest that visual space is at least directionally mapped, in a course way, onto proprioceptive space. These are basic requirements for the emergence of reaching actions.

Mapping perception to action and gearing actions to the environment requires new connections to be formed in the brain. Studies of the developing brain seem to point to two basic strategies for the construction of neural systems. First, there is a stage of coarse mapping connected with an overproduction of cells, axons or synapses followed by a second stage of focused, activity dependent mapping through the elimination of less useful parts or connections (33). The first stage sets the organism off on the right track. However crude, it seems to be a necessity. Computer simulations have shown that if separate regions of a network independently become organized, the resulting maps may be out of register along their boundaries or may have conflicting orientations (34). This is avoided if a coarse map is given at the outset that is subsequently refined by local processes.

In the second stage, systems may organize themselves through spontaneous activity in the circuits themselves and through interactions with the outer world. The latter kind of process can, for instance, be observed in the formation of ocular columns in layer IV of the visual cortex (35,36). These columns are only finally formed after birth, and the structuring of them is a function of the input to the two eyes. Organizing neural systems through interactions with the outer world is directly addressing the problem of gearing actions to the environment. It implies that actions are geared to the environment through actions.

In the development of reaching and grasping, we find firm evidence for the importance of the principle of gearing actions to the environment through actions. The dramatic improvement of reaching skills during the first months of practicing reaching is a good example.

However, at the first time an infant performs a reaching and grasping action, there are sign of prospective control of that action. At the onset of successful reaching and grasping, the orientation of the hand is adjusted to the orientation of the target and the timing of the grasp is adjusted to the encounter with the target. When the infant starts to be able to balance and reach at the same time, the posture gets geared to prepare for the forward extension of the arm. All of that indicate that prospective control does not emerge out of some trial and error, but is there when the action is there.

This does not mean that all the prospective abilities that we find in the emerging manual skills of the infant are phylogenetically given. With respect to some of them, we may be able to trace them back to some more fundamental prospective ability at an earlier age. Catching may be an example of that. As indicated above, infants are quite sophisticated catchers at the onset of successful reaching and grasping. To catch an object seems to require an ability to track it in an anticipatory way. There are evidence that anticipatory smooth eye tracking is starting to emerge a couple of months before the onset of functional reaching (37). If catching ability can be traced back to an underlying ability of smooth eye tracking, we have to ask how that ability gets established and, furthermore, how it gets mapped onto reaching skills. Somewhere at the bottom we are bound to step into some, phylogenetically given, crude prospective mappings.

However, as stated in the beginning of this paper, the function of phylogenetically given mappings are not to create ready made action patterns. Rather, it is to set the subject off on the right track of gearing actions to the environment. Development is a highly complex and nonlinear process. One great challenge for the future is to find out exactly what "being set off on the right track" implies in terms of prestructuring and what it's role is in assembling a system. Another great challenge is to determine how the system assembles and organizes itself through it's interaction with the environment, and how the interaction with the environment determines the developmental process.

8. REFERENCES

1. Halverson,H.M. Study of prehension in infants. **Genetic Psychological Monographs, 10**, (1931), 107-285.
2. Hofsten,C.von Development of visually directed reaching: The approach phase. **Journal of Human Movement Studies, 5**, (1979), 160-168.
3. Hofsten, C. von, Structuring of early reaching movements: A longitudinal study. **Journal of Motor Behavior**, in press.
4. Hofsten, C. von, Eye-hand coordination in newborns. **Developmental Psychology , 18**, (1982), 450-461.
5. Nashner, L.M. Fixed patterns of rapid postural responses among leg muscles during stance. **Experimental Brain Research, 30**, (1977), 13-24.
6. Belen'kii,V.E., Gurfinkel,V.S., and Pal'tsev,Yl. On elements of voluntary movement control. **Biofizika, 12**, (1967), 135-141.
7. Cordo,P.J. and Nashner, L.M. Properties of postural adjustments associated with rapid arm movements. **Journal of Neurophysiology, 47**, (1982), 287-302
8. Bernstein, N.A. The coordination and regulation of movements. London: Pergamon Press, 1967.
9. Kelso, J.A.S. The process approach to understanding human motor behavior: An introduction. In J.A.S. Kelso (Ed.) **Human motor behavior.An Introduction**. Hillsdale, N.J.: Erlbaum, 1982.
10 Hofsten, C. von and Woollacott, M. Postural preparations for reaching in 9-month-old infants. Manuscript. (1990)
11. Touwen, B. Variability and stereotypity in normal and deviant development. **Clinics in Developmental Medicine**, 67, (1978), 99-110.
12. Abend,W., Bizzi,E., and Morasso,P. Human arm trajectory formation. **Brain, 105**, (1982), 331-348.
13. Viviani, P. and Terzuolo, C. Space-time invariance in learned motor skills. In G.E. Stelmach and J. Requin (Eds.) **Tutorials in Motor Behavior.** Amsterdam: North Holland, 1980.
14. Brooks, V.B. Some examples of programmed limb movements. **Brain research, 71**, (1974), 299-308.
15. Fetters,L. and Todd,J. Quantitative assessment of infant reaching movements. **Journal of Motor Behavior, 19**, (1987), 147-166.
16. Hofsten, C. von and Rönnqvist, L. Structuring of neonatal arm movements. Manuscript, 1991.
17. deVries, J.I.P., Visser, G.H.A. and Prechtl, H.F.R. The emergence of fetal behavior. II. Quantitative aspects. **Early Human Development**, 12, (1985), 99-120.

18. Jeannerod, M. Intersegmental coordination during reaching at natural visual objects. In J. Long & A. Baddeley (Eds.) **Attention and Performance IX** , Hillsdale: Earlbaum, 1981, pp. 153 -168.

19. Jeannerod,M. The timing of natural prehension movements. Journal of Motor Behavior, 16, (1984), 235-254.

20. Jeannerod, M., and Biguer, B. Visuomotor mechanisms in reaching within extrapersonal space. In D.J. Ingle, M.A. Goodale and R.J.W. Mansfield (Eds.) **Analysis of Visual Behavior**. Cambridge: MIT Press, 1982.

21. Bruner,J.S. Organization of early skilled action. **Child Development, 44**, (1973), 1-11.

22. Lockman, J.J., Ashmead, D.H. and Bushnell, E.W. The development of anticipatory hand orientation during infancy. **Journal of Experimental Child Psychology, 37**, (1984) 176 -186.

23. Hofsten, C. von, and Fazel-Zandy, S. Development of visually guided hand orientation in reaching. **Journal of Experimental Child Psychology, 38**, (1984), 208-219.

24. Morrongiello, B. and Rocca, P. Age-related changes in reaching behavior. Paper presented at ICIS, Los Angeles, april, 1986.

25. Wing, A.M., Turton, A. and Fraser, C. Grasp size and accuracy of approach in reaching. **Journal of Motor Behavior, 18**, (1986), 245-261.

26. Hofsten, C. von and Rönnqvist, L. Preparation for grasping an object: A developmental study. **Journal of Experimental Psychology: Human Perception and Performance, 14**, (1988), 610-621.

27. Alderson, G.J.K., Sully, D.J., and Sully, H.G. An operational analysis of a one-handed catching task using high speed photography. **Journal of Motor Behavior, 6**, (1974), 217-226.

28. Twitchell, T.E. Reflex mechanisms and the development of prehension. In K. Connolly (Ed.) **Mechanisms of Motor Skill Development**. London: Academic Press, 1970. pp. 25-37.

29. Johansson, R. and Westling, G. Signals in tactile afferents from the fingers eliciting adaptive motor responses during precision grip. **Experimental Brain Research, 66**, (1987), 141-154.

30. Hofsten, C. von. Predictive reaching for moving objects by human infants. **Journal of Experimental Child Psychology, 30**, (1980), 369-382.

31. Hofsten, C. von. Catching skills in infancy. Journal of **Experimental Psychology: Human Perception and Performance, 9**, (1983), 75-85.

32. Hofsten, C. von., & Lindhagen, K. Observations on the development of reaching for moving objects. **Journal of Experimental Child Psychology, 28**, 1979, 158-173.

33. Sretavan,D.W., Shatz,C.J. and Stryker,M.P. Modification of retinal ganglion cell axon morphology by prenatal infusion of tetodotoxin. **Nature, 336**, 468-471.

34. Linsker, R. Perceptual neural organization: Some approaches based on network models and information theory. **Annual review of Neuroscience, 13**, (1990), 257-281.

35. Gilbert,C.D., and Wiesel,T.N. Clustered intrinsic connections in cat visual cortex. **Journal of Neuroscience, 3**, (1983), 1116-1133
36. Hubel,D.H., Wiesel,T.N., and LeVay,S. Plasticity of ocular dominance columns in monkey striate cortex. **Philosophical Transactions of the Royal Society,(Biological Sciences). London. 278**, (1977), 377-409.
37. Aslin, R.N. (1981) Development of smooth pursuit in human infants. In D.F.Fisher, R.A.Monty, & J.W.Senders (Eds.) **Eye Movements: Cognition and Visual Perception.** Hillsdale N.J.: Erlbaum, 1988.

Tutorials in Motor Behavior II
G.E. Stelmach and J. Requin (Editors)

PREHENSION MOVEMENTS IN PARKINSON'S DISEASE

F. Müller[a] and G.E. Stelmach[b]

[a]University Hospital Tübingen, Department of Neurology, Hoppe-Seyler-Str. 3, D7400 Tübingen, Germany

[b]Exercise and Sport Research Institute, Department of Exercise Science and Physical Education, Arizona State University, Tempe, AZ 85287, USA

ABSTRACT

Prehension movements to wooden dowels have been studied in healthy elderly adults and Parkinson's disease patients, using a three camera WATSMART system. Patients were slower overall and showed an additional impairment in the deceleration period when they were instructed to move fast or to grasp without vision of the target. Proportion of time to peak velocity was smaller, but coordination between transport and manipulation components of the movement was not differentially impaired. While PD patients could vary tangential velocity of the wrist within subnormal limits, they were unable to pick up the objects very fast when they were instructed to do so. They use a reduced safety margin of grip aperture for movements in which errors in spatial accuracy have to be taken into account and need significantly more time to establish a firm grip when they have no vision of the objects and must rely on somatosensory information for grip control. These impairments may contribute to clinically well known handicaps in fine motor control and the impression of PD patients' movements as being clumsy.

INTRODUCTION

Arm movements in Parkinson's disease (PD) patients show reduced movement velocity, prolonged movement duration (Sheridan, Flowers and Hurrell, 1987; Hallett and Khoshbin, 1980) and a deterioration of performance when task difficulty is increased (Sanes, 1985). PD patients have been thought not to be able to speed up their movements intentionally for complex trajectories, especially when a sequence of arm movements is required (Berardelli, Accornero, Argenta, Meco and Manfredi, 1986). PD patients show an additional increase of the prolonged movement time, when they have to combine a flexing movement of the elbow with a finger squeeze. This has been interpreted as a deficit in superimposing two motor programs (Benecke, Rothwell, Dick, Day and Marsden, 1986). In addition, Flowers has theorized (1976), that patients perform movements towards targets in a closed loop mode, indicating an inability to program the movement in one sequence. However, those studies in PD have looked at pointing movements or rather artificial combinations of other movements. Since impairments of fine motor control are obvious in everyday life of PD patients, it seems worthwhile to study movements more similar to what is required in daily life.

Prehension movements towards visual targets have been thought as composed of at least two elements, a transportation component and a manipulation component. Jeannerod (1984) suggested, that the movement components are controlled by two independent visuomotor channels, which are independently organized but share a common time course. Marteniuk, MacKenzie, Jeannerod, Athènes and Dugas (1987) looked at different reaching movements, i.e. grasping, pointing, throwing, fitting. Their results show, that shapes of arm trajectories vary considerably in young healthy adults, depending on the type of movement. When greater precision is required, the main deceleration phase is prolonged. Similar results have been obtained by Wing, Turton and Fraser (1986), when comparing movements towards different sizes of targets and with different instructions. They have also shown, that subjects adjust grasp aperture for different conditions of movement. In spatially less accurate movements, for movements with eyes closed or for faster than normal movements, subjects use a wider grasp aperture.

Our study investigated the ability of PD patients to perform prehension movements towards a cylindric target. Since control of prehension movements has to account for spatially less accurate movements, e.g. movements in a faster mode and without vision of the target, the experiment focused on studying PD patients' ability to adapt prehension movements to different task demands.

METHODS

Subjects: 4 PD patients and 4 age matched control subjects were studied. Patients were in mild and moderate stages, according to Hoehn and Yahr (1967); a detailed description is given in table 1. Subjects had been selected to suffer from bradykinesia as a predominant symptom and show as little tremor as possible. All subjects were screened to be free of other neurological diseases. They were tested while on their normal medication.

Table 1. Age, medication and ratings of primary symptoms of PD patients

Subj	Age	Medication	Bradykinesia	Tremor	Rigidity
WD	69	Sinemet, Amantadine, Bromocriptine, Trihexyphenidyl	++	+	++
GN	59	Eldepryl	+	+	-
WE	68	Eldepryl, Sinemet	+	-	-
CS	63	Sinemet, Amantadine	++	+	+

Apparatus: Movements were recorded with a WATSMART system of three cameras, allowing to record movements in three dimensions. Infrared light emitting diodes were attached to the radial bone at the wrist, the tips of thumb and index finger as well as on top of the target object. Wooden dowels of 18 and 55 mm diameter, which were brought to same weight by a filling of lead inside the small one, were used as objects. The starting position of the hand and the position of the grasped object were indicated by small aluminum plates, which were connected to a force transducer (Interface Super Sealed Mini Beam) thus allowing to register precisely lift-off of the hand and first touch at the object. Signals of the force transducers were sampled simultaneously using a WATSCOPE. An IBM AT-PC was used to record all data with a sampling frequency of 300 Hz and perform the data processing and analysis at a later stage.

Procedure: Subjects sat in front of a table with their hand resting on the start plate, with tips of thumb and index finger being closed. The sitting position was selected as to have subjects bend their upper arm ten degrees backward and to allow reaching movements without varying trunk position. Upon a beep subjects had to reach for the wooden dowel, grasp it with the finger pads of thumb and index finger using a precision grip and lift it. Setting it back and return movement of the hand were recorded but not analyzed. In a blocked order with random sequence, movements had to be performed across two movement amplitudes (15 cm vs. 30 cm). Accuracy requirements were varied by using the two dowels of different diameter. which had to be grasped. After performing ten prehension movements with normal speed, subjects were instructed to carry out the same number of movements as fast as possible. Finally, after another series of trials in normal speed that were not analyzed, 10 movements were recorded with eyes closed. Trials in which the object was displaced without being grasped were repeated.

Analysis: Trajectorial velocity was computed off-line by the x-y-z coordinates of the marker on the radial bone at the wrist joint. For the analysis of handshaping we computed the three-dimensional distance between the tips of thumb and index finger. Since the IREDs were placed at the edges of the fingernails to not interfere with the grip itself, complete finger closure is indicated by a finger distance of 10 to 15 mm, the exact value for each individual subject being easily determined during the baseline period. First touch was indicated by a ground reaction force, which was signalled by a peak in the signal of the force transducer underneath the target plate. After being processed with a second order butterworth filter with a cutoff frequency of 10 Hz, data were analyzed via interactive graphics using additional algorithms where appropriate for marking breaks of the baseline, peaks and regional lows. ANOVAs were computed with group, instruction, distance and diameter as independent factors.

RESULTS:

Normal controls and PD patients could perform the task without obvious problems; only when vision was excluded, some movements by PD patients and rarely by controls had to be repeated because the subjects missed the object. Figure 1 gives representative samples of single movement recordings for a PD and a control subject. The velocity profile approximates a bell-shaped trajectory, while the manipulation component shows a gradually increasing grip aperture, which decreases only during the final approach to the target. A small peak in the ground reaction force signal indicates the first touch, which is followed by a decline in the force signal, until gravity is overcome and the dowel is lifted.

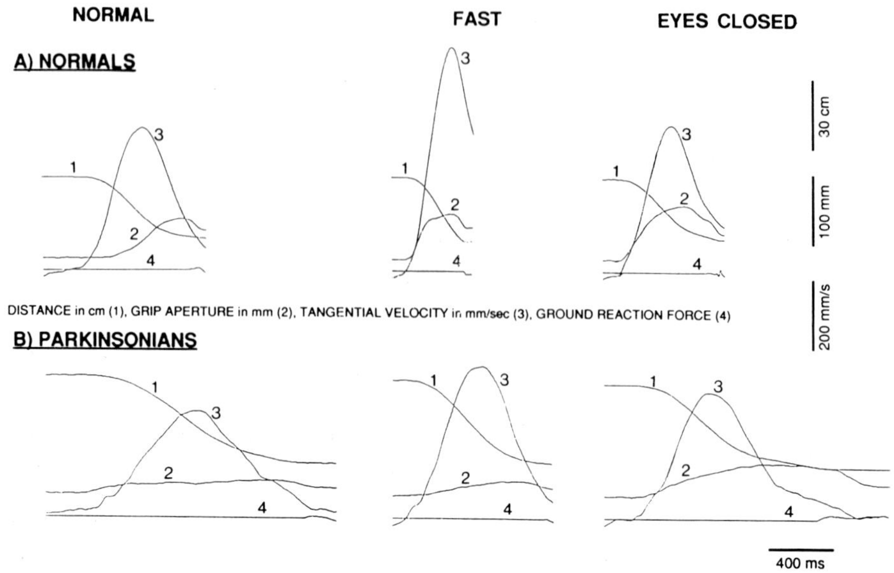

Figure 1. Representative single trials of prehension movements with the instructions to move "normal," "fast" or with "eyes closed," as performed by a healthy control and a PD patient.

Transportation Component

Data confirmed longer movement times ($F(1,70)=146, p<0.001$) and slower peak resultant velocities ($F(1,70)=42.4, p<0.001$) for PD patients overall, compared to normals. Controls and patients were able to modulate peak velocity and movement time with movement amplitude and instruction. Mean movement time increased significantly by 160 msecs when distance was doubled. When instructed to move as fast as possible controls could cut their movement time into half, while PD patients could reduce it to two thirds. Closing the eyes did not affect movement time in normals, however increased it in patients by 160 msecs (instruction by group interaction, $F(2,70)=3{,}68, p<0.05$). Since the difference of 50 msecs in shorter movement time for the smaller dowel did not reach significance, we collapsed the movement times for the different object diameters in table 2, which gives a summary of total MT and its components. Similar results were found for the amplitude of peak velocity. Peak velocity was faster in controls, however for normal movement speed there was only a difference of 70 mm/sec in group means, while this difference increased to 175 mm/sec, when subjects were asked to move as fast as possible. Without vision PD patients again did not reach a similar peak velocity as normals. The biggest difference is caused by movement amplitude: peak velocity was twice as high for double the distance in normals and in patients. Diameter of the dowel did not influence peak velocity significantly.

Table 2. Group means and standard deviations (SD) for movement time (MT), time to peak velocity (TPV) and deceleration time (DET) for PD patients and normal controls.

	SHORT DISTANCE						LONG DISTANCE					
	NORMAL		FAST		EYES CLOSED		NORMAL		FAST		EYES CLOSED	
	PD	N	PD	N	PD	N	PD	N	PD	N	PD	N
MT	1145	837	742	450	1299	799	1342	1009	889	535	1536	1030
(SD)	251	131	69	42	113	105	152	111	150	53	136	241
TPV	491	387	357	274	430	338	545	455	422	297	497	366
(SD)	80	37	15	25	36	18	44	63	18	26	26	39
DET	653	450	384	175	869	461	797	553	466	237	1038	664
(SD)	194	102	80	32	131	93	140	69	143	42	142	209

Velocity Profiles

Despite this ability to scale velocity, PD patients showed different velocity profiles. We divided total movement time in time to peak velocity (TPV) and the remaining deceleration time. Deceleration time was defined as latency from time of peak velocity to time of the end of the movement. Absolute and relative duration of TPV as well as deceleration time was significantly different for the different groups, instructions and distances ($p<0.001$). Diameter of dowel did not influence total MT or TPV. However, when performing movements to the small dowel, deceleration time is approximately 70 msecs longer in both groups. From figure 2, which gives relative proportion of movement time spent in acceleration phase, it becomes obvious, that PD patients spent relatively more time during deceleration, $F(1,70)=35.3$, $p<0.001$. Mean deceleration time increased considerably for PD patients without vision, while controls increased deceleration time only marginally, group by instruction effect, $F(1,70)=4.4$, $p<0.05$. The degree of movement symmetry was calculated by the ratio of acceleration duration divided by deceleration duration. Normal movements were characterized by a symmetry ratio of 0.8 in both groups. Fast movements were again performed in a symmetric profile by PDs (ratio of 1.01), while normals displayed shorter deceleration phases, yielding a ratio of 1.5. With eyes closed the ratio changed only slightly in normals (0.69), whereas patients' movements were more asymmetric, the ratio being 0.54. Movement amplitude and diameter of the target object influenced the shape of the velocity profile as well, i.e. a longer distance and a smaller object caused an increase of the proportion of the deceleration phase.

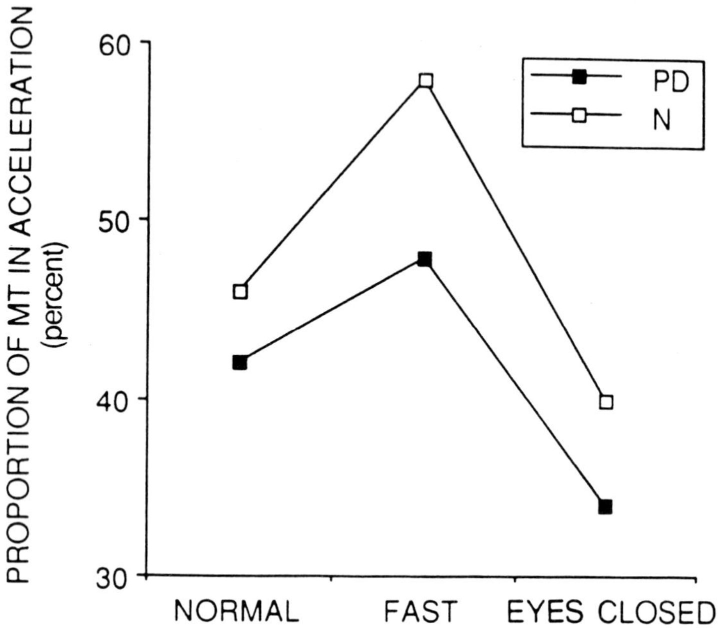

Figure 2. Proportion of total movement time (MT) spent in acceleration period.

Approach to the Target

Since subjects were instructed to pick up the dowel, they were not required to stop the transport movement at target position. Rather, they had to perform the manipulation while being engaged in the transport movement. Tangential velocity did not drop to zero when the dowel was grasped, but did show a regional low. Velocities at the very moment when the object was touched were significantly different between groups, $F(1,70)=92.3$, $p<0.001$ and for different instructions, $F(1,70)=113.4$, $p<0.001$. While velocity at touch is similar for PDs (96 mm/sec) as for controls (130 mm/sec) in normal movements, healthy subjects pick up the object much faster (485 mm/sec compared to 194 mm/sec for PDs) when instructed to do so. As shown in figure 3, without vision PDs are considerably slower than normals (group by instruction $F(1,70)=33.1$, $p<0.001$.

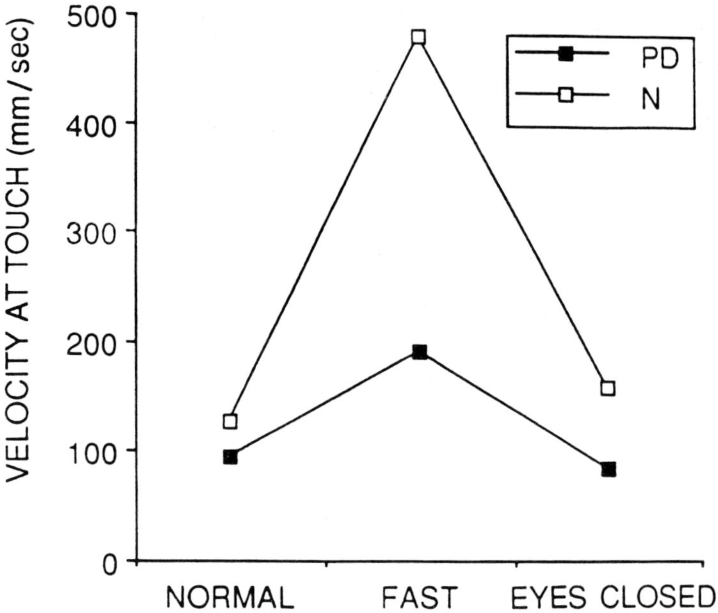

Figure 3. Tangential velocity at moment of contact between finger and dowel.

Manipulation Component

It is known that during a prehension movement grip aperture increases systematically to a maximum, then decreases again as the hand approaches the target object. This pattern was consistent for normals and patients. By dividing the time of the handshaping movement of the two fingertips relative to each other into an opening and a closing phase, we find that normally about 67% of the whole movement time is spent for opening without group differences. However, when subjects perform the movements with eyes closed, controls and patients reach peak opening already at midflight. Distance does not influence relative timing, but the larger dowel leads to a short closure duration (relative proportion for opening being 58% and 66% respectively.)

Grip aperture is always opened wider than absolutely necessary to allow a safety margin for minor spatial errors in transport trajectories, before closing onto the object. Because precise position of IRED markers on the fingertips differed slightly between patients, the distance between fingertips when subjects were actually holding the objects was subtracted from maximum grip aperture to analyze the safety margin of the grasp aperture (figure 4). PD patients do significantly open their grip aperture less wide in all conditions, main group effect, $F(1,70)=41.1$, $p<0.001$. This group difference increases in fast movements and in movements without vision, where accuracy of approach is even more important (group by instruction, $F(2,70)=5.6$, $p<0.01$).

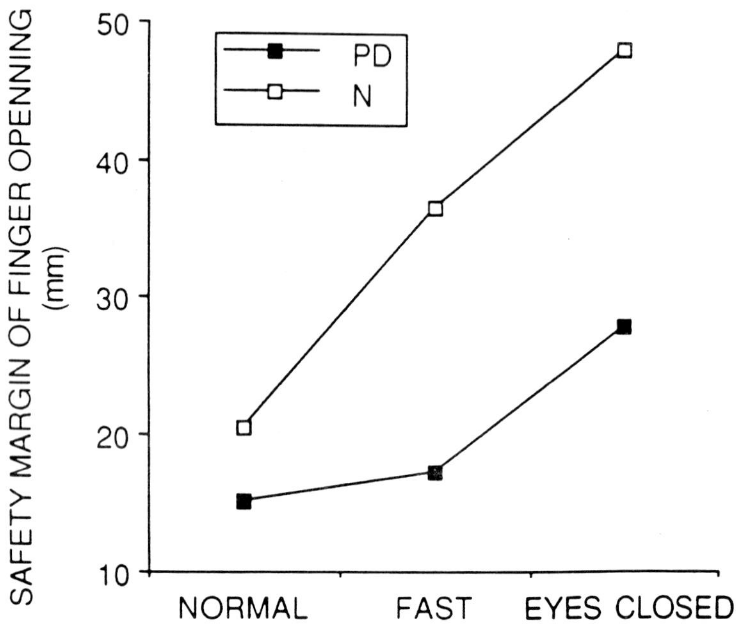

Figure 4. Safety margin of grip aperture, defined as maximum aperture minus distance between fingertips during firm grip.

Coordination of Movement Components

Transport movement and manipulation are two components of one ongoing movement. Transport begins on the average 70 msec before the handshaping movement is started in both groups (controls 80 msec, PDs 60 msec, not significant). However difficult movement conditions (fast and without vision) cause normals to cut that latency to 10 msec (fast) or 20 msec (without vision), while patients can modulate this latency only marginally (fast movements 30 msec, no vision 60 msec) (group by instruction $F(2,70)=3.6$, $p<0.05$).

Although the relative timing of handshaping is well preserved in PD patients, because of a relatively longer deceleration duration of the transport component, maximum hand opening occurs at a different point in flight for fast movements and no vision condition than in normals. Figure 5 shows the remaining distance to move at point of maximum hand opening. Thus, normals have prepared for the grasp of the object spatially more in advance before final approach takes place.

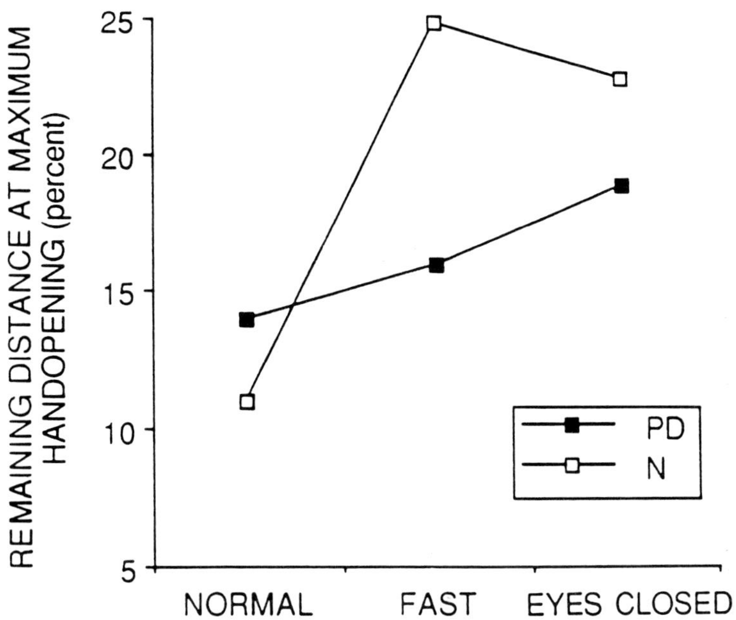

Figure 5. Remaining distance of the hand movement towards target position at time of maximum hand opening.

When the dowel has been reached and a first touch has occurred, subjects have to establish a firm grip and lift the object. Time from first touch to actual start of the lifting movement is indicated by the ground reaction force from the first peak to a drop to zero. This latency differed significantly between patients and controls, $F(1,70)=135.3$, $p<0.001$, and increased dramatically in patients when movement was performed without vision, group by instruction, $F(2,70)=19.7$, $p<0.001$, while controls were still faster with eyes closed than PDs in a normal movement with vision.

Discussion

PD subjects and healthy controls performed prehension movements. While there are considerable differences in the time domain, patients with Parkinson's disease are able to accomplish the task. It is noteworthy, that patients with mild and moderate PD can speed up their movement velocity when they have to move a longer distance and when they are instructed to move faster. However, the range of patients' ability to scale tangential velocity and (reciprocally) movement time is limited. While time to peak velocity (acceleration period) is longer in PD patients than in controls, it is not differentially affected by different instructions. In all conditions proportion of time to peak velocity is smaller in PDs due to an even more prolonged deceleration period.

Spatial coordinates of the major part of a movement can be programmed in advance. For grasping a target integrating visual or sensory information about the position of the hand into the ongoing movement is essential for the final stage of the movement. Thus our result of a prolonged deceleration period in PD corresponds well to a similar finding by Inzelberg, Flash and Korczyn (1990) in pointing movements on a digitizing tablet. A relatively longer deceleration duration has also been reported in patients with mild cerebellar dysfunction, when performing uniaxial flexion movements (Brown, Hefter, Mertens and Freund, 1990). However, Hore, Wild and Diener (1990) found in a comparable paradigm a different movement asymmetry with smaller acceleration amplitudes and higher deceleration amplitudes in more severely affected cerebellar patients, that produced considerably hypermetric movements. While there is enough evidence to conclude, that PD results in a longer deceleration phase, when accuracy at the target is important, this seems to be specific for PD and not a general finding in movement disorders. When no visual information is available, the subject has to rely on somatosensory information for movement control. The significant increase of deceleration time under this condition is still more pronounced in PD patients.

The velocity at which subjects are able to pick up a dowel differs strikingly between patients and controls. During fast movements controls can pick up objects with high speed, while PD patients reduce tangential velocity for the grasp of the target. Without vision PD patients' final speed becomes still slower. Since our study used a non-balanced design, which allowed for considerable practice with vision before performing the movements with eyes closed, the effect of the no vision condition might have been underestimated. Marteniuk et al. (1987) have shown, that velocity profiles can drastically be modulated by normals depending on different task demands. In PD, modification is possible in terms of movement time and peak velocity, but critical phases of the prehension movements, i.e., reaching at the target and grasping the target are impaired.

While there may be a deficit in superimposing two separate motor programs (Benecke et al., 1986), coordinating the initiation of transport and manipulation component of a prehension task is intact in PD patients. Shaping grip aperture in advance and starting to close the hand in anticipation of object touch is an ability that is acquired during motor development of the first year (von Hofsten and Rönnqvist, 1988). It is well preserved in Parkinson's disease. Transport and handshaping are interlocked in a way, that perturbations by mechanically pulling back the moving arm produce a parallel reversal of the handshaping movement (Haggard and Wing,

1991) in normals. Proportion of hand opening phase as percentage of total handshaping period is identical in patients and in normals and differs only as a function of instruction in both groups. Because of the relatively longer deceleration duration in PD this leads to a point of maximum hand opening, which is closer to the target.

Grip aperture is opened wider for larger targets by normals (Wing, Turton and Fraser, 1986; Gentilucci, Castiello, Corradini, Scarpa, Umilta and Rizzolatti, 1991) and PD patients. However, on the average PD patients do not open grip as much as healthy controls. For movements, where spatial accuracy is compromised, controls increase grip aperture significantly. While the decrease of final accuracy without vision is known in PD (Inzelberg et al., 1990), it is striking that patients use the same maximum grip aperture in fast movements and increase aperture only marginally when moving without vision. This reduction in handshaping reduces tolerance for spatial errors at target prehension and adds to the patients behaving more clumsy.

Hand closure starts roughly after two thirds of movement time. The process of closure is ideally coming to an end at time of contact with the target, when a firm grip has to be established and the lifting movement starts. Studies in precision grip have shown a short latency for the coordination of grip and lift force, which is increased in PD patients from 115 msec to roughly 175 msec (Müller and Abbs, 1990). Duration from first touch to final pickup shows comparable latencies in this experiment for controls, however a dramatic increase in PD patients when attempting prehension movements without vision. When eyes are closed, sensory input from the mechanoreceptors has to trigger the final closure movements of the finger joints and the production of pinch force. In PD patients this uncertainty about when to really grip causes a delay of approximately 500 msecs. Switching motor programs from transport to lift is accomplished during normal movement and fast movement as well, but the integration of sensory information into motor functions is critical without vision. While usual clinical tests of sensory functions do not show a disability in PD, our results add to the mounting evidence, that sensorimotor integration is impaired in Parkinson's disease (Schneider, Diamond and Markham, 1986; Schneider, Diamond and Markham, 1987).

REFERENCES

R. Benecke, J.C. Rothwell, J.P. Dick, B.L. Day and C.D. Marsden: Performance of simultaneous movements in patients with Parkinson's disease. Brain. 109 (1986) 739-757.

A. Berardelli, N. Accornero, M. Argenta, G. Meco and M. Manfredi: Fast complex arm movements in Parkinson's disease. J Neurol Neurosurg Psychiatry. 49 (1986) 1146-1149.

S.H. Brown, H. Hefter, M. Mertens and H.-J. Freund: Disturbances in human arm movement trajectory due to mild cerebellar dysfunction. J Neurol Neurosurg Psychiatry. 53 (1990) 306-313.

K.A. Flowers: Visual 'closed-loop' and 'open-loop' characteristics of voluntary movement in patients with Parkinsonism and intention tremor. Brain. 99 (1976) 269-310.

M. Gentilucci, U. Castiello, M.L. Corradini, M. Scarpa, C. Umilta and G. Rizzolatti: Influence of different types of grasping on the transport component of prehension movements. Neuropsychologia.

P. Haggard and A.M. Wing: Remote responses to perturbation in human prehension. Neurosci Lett. (in press).

M. Hallett and S. Khosbin. A physiological mechanism of bradykinesia. Brain. 103 (1980) 301-314.

M.M. Hoehn and M.D. Yahr: Parkinsonism: onset, progression, and mortality. Neurology. 17 (1967) 427-442.

C. von Hofsten and L. Rönnqvist: Preparation for grasping an object: a developmental study. J Exp Psychol Hum Percept. 14 (1988) 610-621.

J. Hore, B. Wild and H.-C. Diener: Cerebellar dysmetria at the elbow, wrist, and fingers. J Neurophysiol. 65 (1990) 563-571.

R. Inzelberg, T. Flash and A.D. Korczyn: Kinematic properties of upper-limb trajectories in Parkinson's disease and idiopathic torsion dystonia. Adv Neurol. 53 (1990) 183-189.

M. Jeannerod: The timing of natural prehension movements. J Mot Behav. 16 (1984) 235-254.

R.G. Marteniuk, C.L. MacKenzie, M. Jeannerod, S. Athènes and C. Dugas: Constraints on human arm movement trajectories. Can J Psychol. 41 (1987) 365-378.

F. Müller and J.H. Abbs: Precision grip in Parkinsonian patients. Adv Neurol. 53 (1990) 191-195.

J.N. Sanes: Information processing deficits in Parkinson's disease during movement. Neuropsychologia. 23 (1985) 381-392.

J.S. Schneider, S.G. Diamond and C.H. Markham: Deficits in orofacial sensorimotor function in Parkinson's disease. Ann Neurol. 19 (1986) 275-282.

J.S. Schneider, S.G. Diamond and C.H. Markham: Parkinson's disease: Sensory and motor problems in arms and hands. Neurology. 37 (1987) 951-956.

M.R. Sheridan, K.A. Flowers and J. Hurrell: Programming and execution of movements in Parkinson's disease. Brain. 110 (1987) 1247-1271.

A.M. Wing, A. Turton and C. Fraser: Grasp size and accuracy of approach in reaching. J Mot Behav. 18 (1986) 245-260.

Tutorials in Motor Behavior II
G.E. Stelmach and J. Requin (Editors)

Critical variables in the coordination of prosthetic and normal limbs

Stephen A. Wallace and Lawrence E. Carlson*

Departments of Kinesiology and Mechanical Engineering*
University of Colorado at Boulder. Boulder, Colorado 80309.

Abstract

This paper provides a critical review of studies on the reaching of grasping of objects with anatomical and prosthetic (artificial) hands. The emphasis of this analysis is on the characterization of the patterns of motion among the co-articulators and whether significant changes in these patterns emerge as task parameters are manipulated.

1. INTRODUCTION

Given the myriad of muscles, joints and nerves of the body that subserve goal-directed movement, what are the appropriate variables to measure at a given level of analysis? At the behavioral level, sophisticated motion analysis systems are commonplace today making it relatively easy to calculate a host of kinematic measures of most joint motions of interest. Armed with these tools, one would think it would therefore be easy to characterize the coordination that appears self-evident in most motor skills requiring both spatial and temporal precision. While these sophisticated motion analysis systems can assist in characterizing the spatial-temporal coordination among the various components, the research strategy of the researcher is equally, if not more important. Measurement, for the sake of measurement, will generally not take us very far, but measurement, which accompanies the right questions and methodology, will. The problem then becomes primarily one of asking the right questions and using the appropriate methodology.

Our view is that since individual joints rarely move in complete isolation, the important variables to measure are ones which attempt to describe the collaboration among the joints, often termed synergies (e.g. Bernstein, 1967; Lee, 1984; Kelso & Schoner, 1988) and to determine how this collaboration or organization changes across different task demands. Identifying these type of variables is difficult because one rarely knows a priori, what they will be, a point emphasized by Jeka & Kelso (1989). Identifying these critical variables is only the first, albeit important, step. Because of the dynamic nature of human motion, it is also critical to eventually describe the dynamics of these variables. If a number of observable relationships among the joints can be identified, it is important to determine 1) their relative stability, 2) the preferred relationships or patterns as task demands change and 3) the dynamics of pattern change. This type of strategy, better known as the "Dynamic Pattern" perspective (see Schoner & Kelso, 1988; Jeka & Kelso, 1989) has been applied to the coordination of bimanual behavior (e.g. Kelso, Scholz & Schoner, 1986; 1988; Scholz & Kelso, 1989), to the synchronization of one's actions to a perceptual event (Kelso, Delcolle & Schoner, 1989), to single limb, multi-joint behavior (Kelso, Buchanan & Wallace, in press) and also to between-people coordination (Turvey, 1990). Can this approach, which has been primarily used to characterize the dynamics of rhythmic behavior among two or more articulators, be applied to discrete behavior, such as reaching and grasping for an object? The present paper provides a summary of past research in normal reaching and grasping behavior and attempts to identify the critical variable(s) which may characterize the collaboration or coordination among the articulators in this type of task. After describing evidence for what we think is a critical variable in normal reaching and grasping, we then turn to our recent and preliminary attempts to uncover the critical variables in prosthetic (artificial) limbs engaged in reaching and grasping behavior. The final part of the paper will discuss a number of limitations of this work and will emphasize the need for further research in terms of extensions of the Dynamic Pattern Strategy to different tasks such as reaching and grasping.

1.1 Critical Variables in Reaching and Grasping

The human hand is truly a remarkably versatile and complex organ. To some extent, the hand could be thought of as a "microcosm" of the body itself in the sense that it is composed of many muscles, joints and nerves (see Tubiani, 1981) and is capable of a seemingly endless variety of postures and movements. This flexibility is due to the large number of degrees of freedom (N = 27) contained in the hand, wrist, elbow and shoulder joints in a given arm. An appropriate, and certainly not novel (see Bernstein, 1967; Turvey, 1977) question to ask, is how are the degrees of freedom of the hand and arm organized and coordinated in tasks such as reaching and grasping which demand both spatial and temporal precision? Due to the vast complexity of the hand and arm, the motor control researcher must first choose not only a given level of analysis (e.g. cellular, muscular, behavioral) but also choose the degrees of freedom of interest. Most of the recent work on reaching and grasping has tended to focus on the behavioral level at the kinematic changes seen in the index finger and thumb in grasping an object and in the arm which transports the hand to the object. A summary of these kinematic changes seen in the gripping motions of the finger and thumb and in transport of the arm is presented below. At this level of analysis, can critical variables be identified which characterize the patterns among the articulators involved in reaching and grasping?

1.2 The Kinematics of Reaching and Grasping

The first detailed description of the kinematic changes in mature, adult reaching and grasping was provided by Jeannerod (1981) and later by a number of researchers (Frazer & Wing, 1981; Jeannerod, 1984; Marteniuk, MacKensie, Jeannerod, Athenes & Dugas, 1987; Marteniuk, Leavitt, MacKensie & Athenes, 1990; Von Hofsten & Ronnqvist, 1988; Wallace & Weeks, 1988; Wallace, Weeks & Kelso, 1990a; Wing & Fraser, 1983; Wing, Turton & Fraser, 1986). In all of these studies, subjects were required to reach out and grasp or pick up an object, such as a ball or wooden dowel, using only the index finger and thumb. The distance between the finger and thumb (aperture) has been taken as a measure of the grip or manipulation component and changes in arm motion, a measure of the transport component, have been determined by the monitoring of a fixed position on the distal portion of the forearm. Typically, the subject starts with the finger and thumb together so that aperture is minimal at the beginning of the movement. A major finding by Jeannerod (1981) was that the maximum aperture reached during the movement was dependent on the size or diameter of the object - the larger the object, the greater the aperture. Wing et al. later found that the size of maximum aperture increased as transport speed increased, although Wallace & Weeks (1988) showed that this effect may be due to transport movement time and not transport velocity. Wallace & Weeks (1988) and Wallace et al. (1990a) further illustrated that the opening and closing velocities of the fingers were scaled to transport speed - as transport speed increased, the initial opening and the final closing velocity of the fingers also increased. Finally, Marteniuk et al. (1987; 1990) determined that the size of the object can affect the shape of the velocity profile of transport. Many of these findings point to some functional linkage between the fingers of the hand and the arm. To accurately reach and grasp an object clearly requires coordination between the hand and arm. But what is the critical variable that best captures or characterizes this coordination?

1.3 Temporal Relations Between Manipulation and Transport

One way to investigate this question is to observe cases where the coordination between manipulation and transport is clearly abnormal. One example will be discussed here involving infant reaching (Von Hofsten & Ronnqvist, 1988) Spanning over a decade of work in this area, Von Hofsten has shown that infants as young as 13 months can reach and grasp an object with similarities to mature adult behavior. Infants have been shown to open the hand in anticipation of the object prior to closing down on the object. However, before this developmental period, infants show a lack of coordination, usually in a rather specific way - the timing of final hand closure is typically delayed in transport. Oftentimes, the final closure of hand occurs very late in transport and sometimes not until after contact with the object. Clearly, in these cases, the coordination between the hand and arm is lacking.

The finding of underdeveloped reaching and grasping suggests, to a first approximation, that the temporal coordination of the hand and arm may be associated with the relative timing (or phasing) of hand closure with respect to arm transport. If this variable truly represents a temporal constraint on the degrees of freedom we would expect this constraint to be preserved across several dimensions of the same task. This type of temporal constraint could be likened to an "attractor" in the synergic sense (e.g. Haken, 1983; Schoner & Kelso, 1988; Jeka & Kelso, 1989). The essential idea is that even though there are potentially many ways that the hand can move with respect to the arm, during prehensile tasks, the hand-arm system move together in a preferred way or pattern. We would expect this pattern to naturally have some variability across trials that may reflect its stability, in a non-linear dynamic sense (e.g. see Haken, 1983 and Kelso, Scholz & Schoner, 1986 for empirical evidence) yet its mean state should be preserved across changes in certain "control" parameters imposed on the system. Thus, the preferred pattern could be related to the relative timing of final hand closure (which can be quantitatively measured) while various control parameters (which can be manipulated) may be identified such as the transport speed or movement time, the size of the object and perhaps other parameters yet to be explored.

Before the synergetic or dynamic pattern strategy can be applied to the coordination of prehensile movements, it is necessary to obtain evidence for some type of pattern(s) that is preserved across changes in task demands. The early work by Jeannerod (1981; 1984) and later work by Wallace & Weeks (1988) provided a starting point for the identification of this pattern. Jeannerod found that while the maximum aperture increased in anticipation of larger objects, its time occurrence remained a relatively fixed percentage of transport (approximately 70%). Wallace & Weeks (1988) showed further that the temporal occurrence of the maximum aperture remained relatively constant across changes in object size, transport distance, and speed (or movement time). Hence, we have the first evidence for some type of recognizable, temporal pattern that may be at the heart of prehensile movement and may quantitatively express the coordination between the hand and arm. But how confident can we be that the relative time to maximum aperture is the relevant kinematic event? Wallace et al. (1990a) explored this issue and their logic went as follows. In most instances, the time to maximum aperture and the time to final closure of the hand (best measured from changes in aperture velocity) are nearly synchronous. However, in some cases it can be observed that the two events are disassociated in time, usually with maximum aperture occurring first, leveling off for a time before final closing. Normally, as we have previously described, subjects start with their index finger and thumb close together. As the arm is transported towards the target, aperture increases to a peak and then reduces as the subject begins the final closing down on the object. But what would happen if subjects started with a large aperture, with their finger and thumb spread apart at the beginning of the movement? Maximum aperture would be, under these conditions, at the <u>start</u> of the movement, making it difficult to use this kinematic feature as a critical variable defining the coordination of the hand and arm. However, it might be possible to notice changes in aperture velocity near the end of the movement which would indicate when final closing occurs. Wallace et al. required subjects to adopt two initial hand postures, either open (near 75% of physical maximum) or closed (finger and thumb pinched together). The subjects were trained to reach and grasp a small dowel in either 300 or 800 msec. Wallace et al. found that the relative time to maximum aperture in the closed grip conditions was not significantly different than the relative time to final closing in the open grip condition. In both conditions, relative timing was preserved across the two movement times. Because the time to maximum aperture could not be used in the open grip condition, Wallace et al. argued that the relative time to final closing may be a more accurate and robust measure of the temporal coordination between the hand and arm.

Some reservations about using either the relative time to maximum aperture or to final closing must be mentioned. Both Marteniuk et al. (1990) and Von Hofsten and Ronnqvist (1988) have shown what appears to be different relative timing when the size of the target to be grasped is manipulated. In particular, relative timing in these kinematic events is smaller with smaller objects. Marteniuk et al. manipulated target sizes from 1 to 10 cm in increments of 1 cm. Relative timing to maximum aperture varied from 66 to 92%. With three object sizes, Von Hofsten and Ronnqvist (1988) found relative times to closure of 72, 81 and 84%. What are we to make of these seemingly discrepant data? It may be possible that there is no relatively fixed temporal pattern between the hand and the arm as object size is manipulated. However, it appears in Marteniuk et al's. (1990) data (see Figure 5) that between object sizes from 2 to 8 cm, the relative time to maximum aperture only changed from approximately 78 to 85%. Most of the slope in the relationship between the relative time to maximum aperture and object size may have been attributed to the extreme object sizes. Also, in Von Hofsten and Ronnqvist's (1988) data the range of relative timing changes was 12% on the average. The point here is that relative timing in these studies appeared to be preserved across a rather wide range of object sizes. The regions of the object size parameter space, where different relative timing may be observed, should not be overlooked. These regions may, in fact, indicate areas where different temporal patterns between the hand and the arm may exist.

We conclude this section with the speculation that relative timing measures may be one way to characterize the coordination between the hand and arm in prehensile tasks which include both reach and grip components. Some evidence was presented which suggests that the relative time to hand closure is the more relevant variable capturing this coordination. In the following section, we summarize our recent and preliminary work which has attempted to apply this type of analysis to the control of body-powered upper limbprosthetic devices.

1.4 The Coordination of Prosthetic Reaching and Grasping Behavior

Whereas normal motion of the upper limb may be characterized by coordinated control of multiple degrees-of-freedom, prosthetic motion generally consists of sequential control of far fewer degrees-of-freedom. A typical below-elbow prosthesis replaces only 1 degree of freedom distal to the elbow. Therefore, amputees generally move their prostheses in more limited ways, using their limb more as a holding device than for active transport. Additional joint motions are usually provided only passively, if at all. However, in active reaching, the type of prosthesis, the direction moved in the physical workspace and the orientation of the object to be grasped relative to the user's body can affect which joints control the opening and closing of the mechanical prehensor. We shall see that the speed of motion can also influence the temporal coordination of prosthetic movement (Grammens, Wallace & Carlson, in press).

There has been very little published research on how amputees control body powered, upper limb prostheses. Keller, Taylor and Zahm (1947) photographed normal subjects performing various activities of daily living in order to measure the ranges of motion of normal individuals and made recommendations regarding the ranges of prosthetic motion that should be provided in an arm prosthesis. They did not attempt, however, to provide a detailed kinematic analysis of prehensor motion. While they searched for evidence of coupling between joint motions, they did not have the computational power to do so systematically.

Engen and Spencer (1969) also performed kinematic studies of normal individuals in selected daily living activities, both with and without arm orthoses, to determine the degree of impairment represented by orthotic devices. They also sought information relevant to prosthetic joint prescription. The manual reduction of three-dimensional photographic data precluded detailed quantitative analysis, but they found joint measurements to be "finely synchronized by hand-eye coordination." They also found minimal active elbow flexion in the motions studied, forming the basis for the recommendation that greater effort should be directed toward providing active wrist movement.

Wing and colleagues (Fraser & Wing, 1981; Wing & Fraser, 1983) focussed their research on movements of the prehensor (end effector for gripping) in reaching and grasping a stationary object. Fraser and Wing (1981) found some similarity in the motions of the artificial hand of one amputee compared with her opposite, anatomical hand. In both hands, maximum aperture was reached in advance of contact with the object and was similarly affected by the diameter of the object. Interestingly, while maximum aperture in the artificial hand was reached somewhat earlier and showed a plateau rather than a peak as in the normal, anatomical hand, it appeared as though the relative time to closing for both hands was similar (roughly 75% of transport time). Wing and Fraser (1983) confirmed these results in a different study with the same subject. It was difficult to discern from the study whether relative time to closure was the same in both hands even though absolute timing was clearly later in the prosthetic hand.

In a recent study, we (Grammens, Wallace & Carlson, in press) attempted to determine whether the relative timing patterns in the normal anatomical hand and those in the prosthetic hand were similar across different transport speeds. Is it the case that the coordination of prosthetic reaching and grasping involves, as may be the case in the normal hand, only one temporal pattern between the hand and arm? To investigate this question, we conducted a detailed case study with an amputee who has been an experienced prosthetic user for over 12 years. The subject wore a left below-elbow body-powered prosthesis of the voluntary closing type. The prehensor is operated by a cable attached to a harness which is anchored to the contralateral shoulder. Since the cable traverses the ipsilateral elbow and shoulder, upper torso (posterior side) and attaches to the contralateral shoulder, a wide variety of muscular actions can be used to control the tension on the cable and therefore the opening and closing of the prehensor. With the voluntary closing device, the prosthetic (fixed) finger and the moveable "thumb" are spread apart in a relaxed starting position when the ipsilateral elbow is close to the body. A simple reach forward increases the tension on the cable and causes the prehensor to close. However, we asked the subject to start with the finger and thumb closed (small aperture). He accomplished this requirement by moving his ipsilateral elbow laterally away from the body which effectively increased the cable tension and closed the prehensor at the start of the movement. One interesting question was, from this position, how would the subject open the prehensor during the reach forward. If the ipsilateral elbow remained in the initial lateral position, a reach forward would actually increase the tension in the cable preventing the opening of the prehensor. The answer to how the subject overcame this problem is shown in Figure 1.

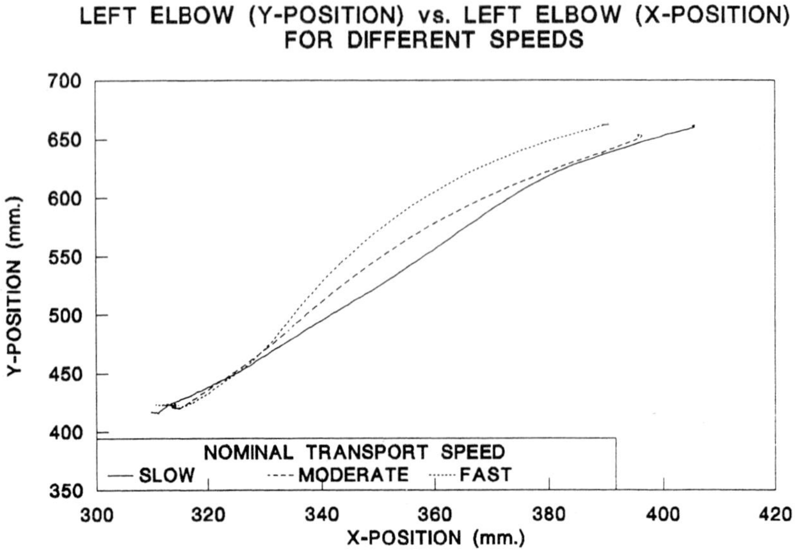

Figure 1. Left elbow (y-position) vs. left elbow (x-position) across three transport speeds in prosthetic reaching and grasping.

The subject was trained to reach and grasp a small cylinder (18 mm in diameter and 100 mm in height) resting on a table top (distance = 50 cm) at three transport movement times (1.3, .90 and .6 sec). Regardless of transport speed (or movement time), there was a strong coupling between the elbow transport toward the object (y-direction) and lateral elbow movement inwardly towards the body (x-direction). Thus, as the subject reached forward, a coordinated inward, lateral motion of elbow occurred allowing for a release of cable tension and an opening of the prehensor.

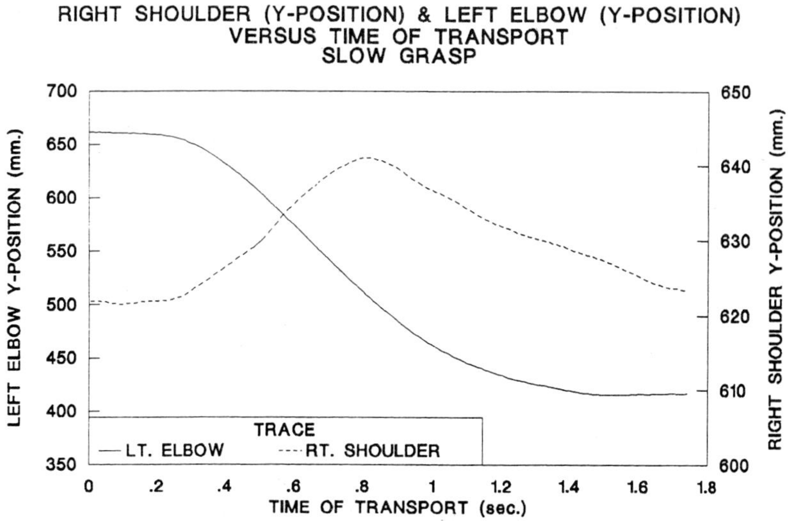

Figure 2. Right shoulder (y-position) and left elbow (y-position) across transport time in slow, prosthetic grasp.

But the story is not quite that simple. Figures 2, 3 and 4 also show the motion of the right contralateral shoulder plotted along with the transport of the left elbow in the y-direction as it moved toward the subject. As the elbow of the prosthetic hand (solid lines) was transported forward (downward), the contralateral right shoulder (dashed lines), which anchors the harness, was first retracted (upward on the graph) and then protracted (downward on the graph). What is apparent is that the magnitude of the contralateral right shoulder displacement (from baseline to peak) is dependent on the transport speed, ranging from approximately 2 cm to 3.5 cm. While these values are small, we speculate that in addition to inward lateral motion of the prosthetic elbow during transport, the subject also initially retracted the contralateral right

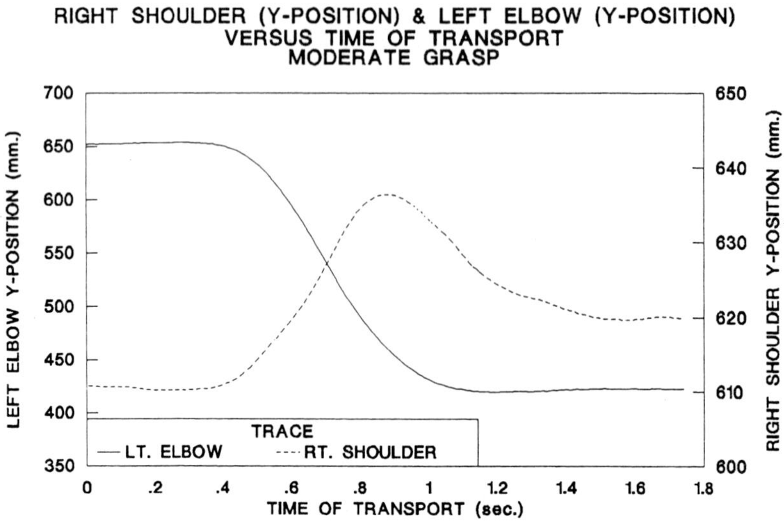

Figure 3. Right shoulder (y-position) and left elbow (y-position) across transport time in moderate, prosthetic grasp.

shoulder to reduce the cable tension which allowed for the opening of the prehensor. But what of the closing of the prehensor? Is the relative timing of closing of the prehensor perserved across transport speeds and is it the same as in the anatomical hand? Finally, how is the actual closing of the prehensor perserved across transport speeds and is it the same as in the anatomical hand? Finally, how is the actual closing of the prehensor accomplished? Figure 5 provides some cluses. Illustrated in this figure are the composite trajectories (N = 15 trials each) of the prosthetic aperture at each transport speed in normalized time. What is clearly apparent is that aperture closing occurs much earlier in relative time for the fast transport speed. However, Figure 6 shows similar closing characteristics of the anatomical (natural) hand. A clearer picture of these results can be observed in Figures 7 and 8. Plotted in these figures are the points of final aperture closing (as a percentage of total transport time) against total time of transport for all 15 trials in each transport velocity condition. For the natural arm (Figure 7), relative time of closure was similar across all three transport speeds, supporting our

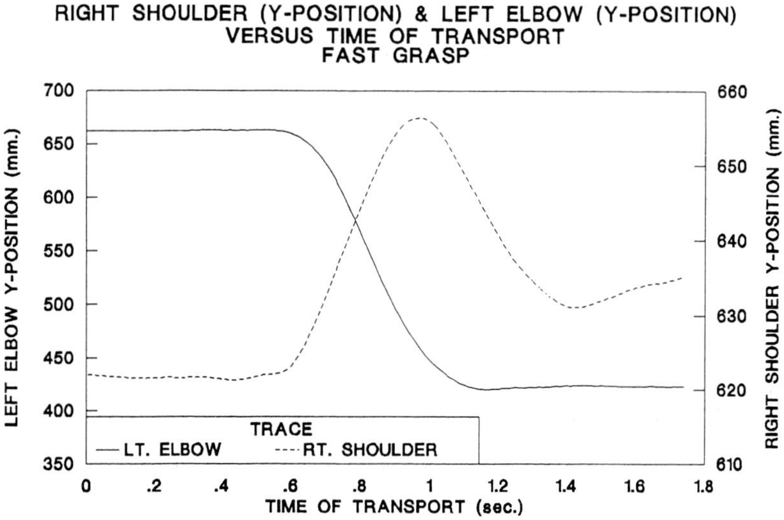

Figure 4. Right shoulder (y-position) and left elbow (y-position) across transport time in fast, prosthetic grasp.

relative timing patterns is of interest. On average, the relative timing variability of the natural hand was much greater than that of the previous work (Wallace & Weeks, 1988; Wallace et al. 1990a). In the prosthetic arm however, two distinct temporal patterns were observed (Figure 8). One pattern was preserved across the slow and moderate transport speeds and another emerged at the fast transport speed. Also of interest was the small number of trials of overlap between the two patterns around the .8 sec transport time. The variability (or spread) of the prosthetic hand. Thus, the closing characteristics of the prehensor were different in two important ways: 1) there were two patterns of closing in the prehensor and only one in the anatomical hand and 2) the variability of the prosthetic hand closing was less than the anatomical hand.

How is the closing of the prosthetic hand accomplished? Again, let us turn to Figures 2, 3 and 4. It can be seen that following right, contralateral shoulder retraction, which allowed for the reduction of cable tension and prehensor opening, the right shoulder was finally protracted.

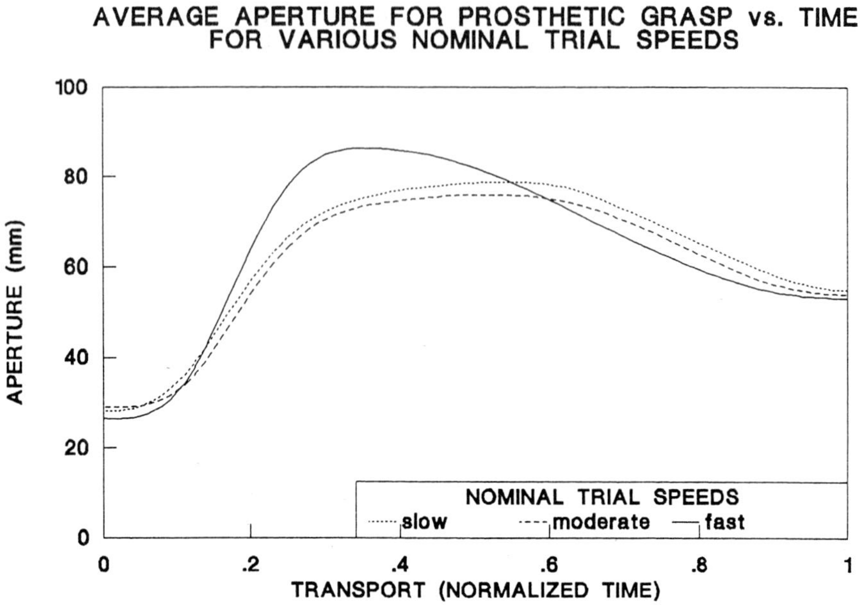

Figure 5. Composite (N = 15) aperture trajectories of three transport speeds across normalized transport time in prosthetic movements.

This protraction, which was scaled in speed to transport velocity, presumably caused an increase in cable tension and contributed to prehensor closing. If this were true, we would expect the relative timing of initial shoulder protraction to be similar to relative timing of aperture closing. In Figure 9, we correlated these two variables to determine the association during transport. The correlation between these variables was .78 with an $r^2 = 61\%$. Thus, there was a moderately high relationship between these two kinematic events but other motions, not identified in this study, may also have contributed to prosthetic aperture closing.

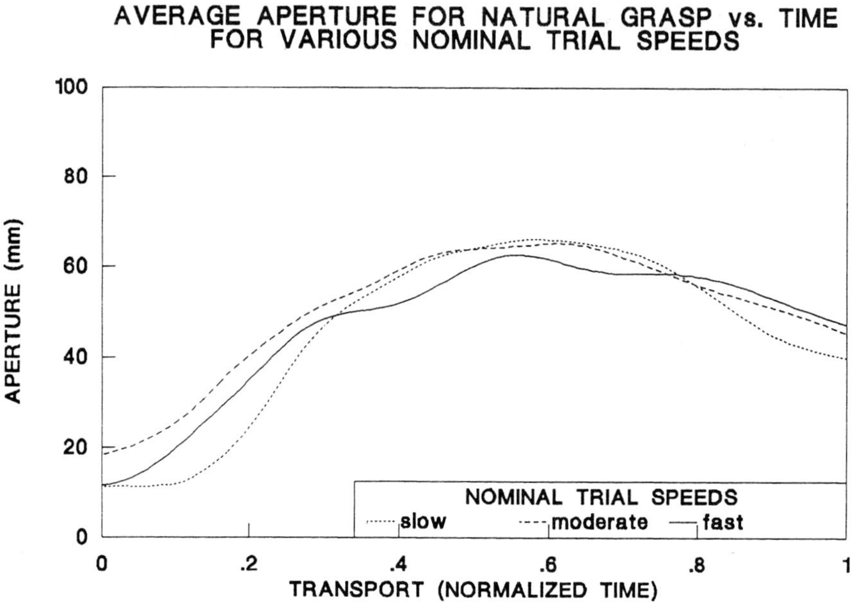

Figure 6. Composite (N = 15) aperture trajectories of three transport speeds across normalized transport time in natural movements.

2. SUMMARY

Our preliminary work has uncovered, at least in one case study, evidence for two temporal patterns of coordination in the control of a voluntary closing, body powered prosthesis. Should the same types of patterns be expected with a voluntary opening device? In this case, increase tension on the cable causes the prehensor to open from its normally closed position. Preliminary tests with the same subject and similar methodology has revealed only one relative timing pattern. Also, no detectable motion in the right shoulder was observed and it appeared as though the subject was using a peculiar set of motions in the upper torso to help close the prehensor. However, we were not able to measure these motions due to the camera angles used. Another limitation of this preliminary work was that the subject, being rather inexperienced with

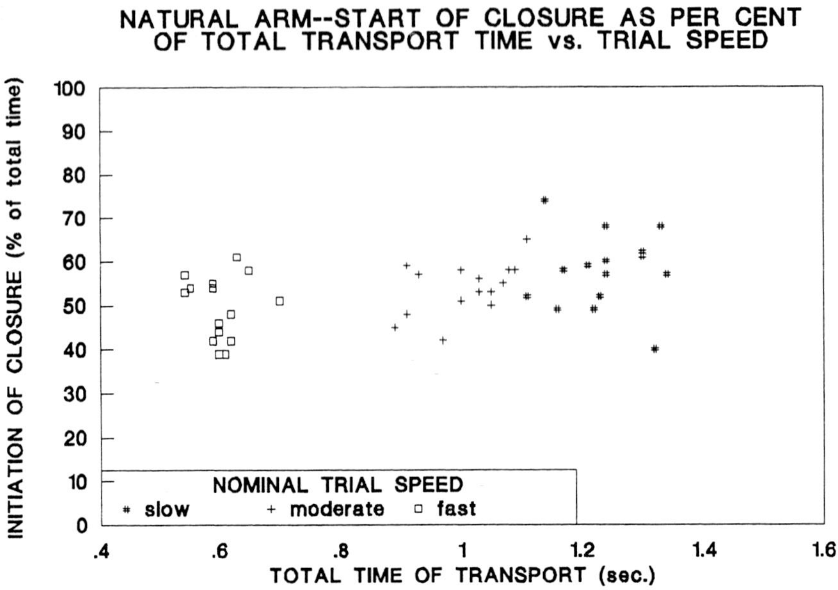

Figure 7. Initiation of closure as a percentage of transport time in the three transports speeds using the natural arm.

the voluntary open prosthesis, found it difficult to achieve the same, fast transport speeds as was possible with voluntary closing device, which he was more accustomed to. If a different temporal pattern existed, it may have been obscured by the lack of attainment of the faster transport speed. It may be possible to show two temporal grasping patterns if the subject is given more practice; we are currently exploring this possibility. Also, it would be interesting to demonstrate that relative timing patterns in the voluntary closing prosthesis are produced by different combinations of joint motion compared to the voluntary open device. This type of result would implicate mechanical constraints on the various joint motions due to the type of prosthesis.

In addition to temporal and mechanical constraints, we believe that spatial constraints also have an effect on joint patterns used in prosthetic reaching. For example, as in our voluntary closing study, the initial position (either open or closed) of the prehensor requires the user to adopt

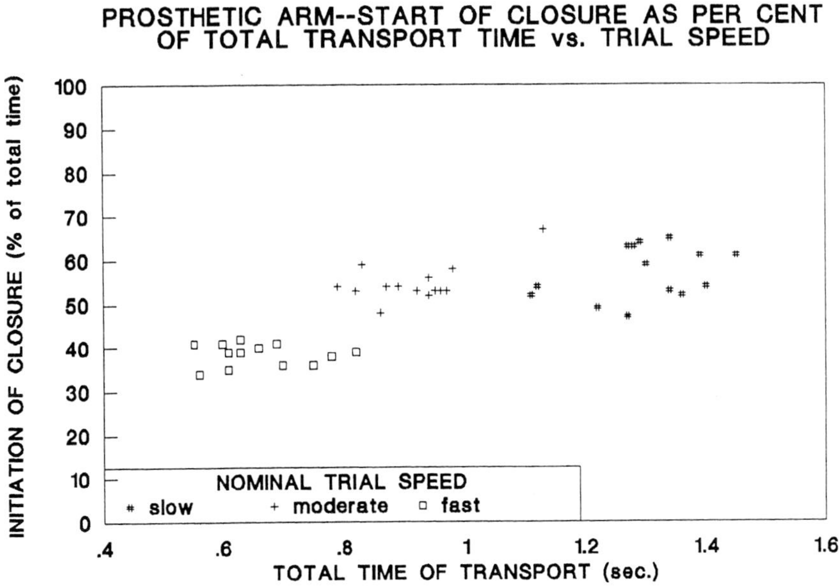

Figure 8. Initiation of closure as a percentage of transport time in the three transport speeds using the prosthetic arm.

different postures in order to develop the appropriate cable tension during transport. The direction of transport is certainly another major variable effecting proper opening and closure of the prehensor. For example, suppose we require the user of a voluntary closing device to reach forward, pick up a coffee mug from the table and place the cup on the table closer to his/her body. To maintain enough pressure on the cup after it is picked up, the user must develop some type of body motion which will increase cable tension as the cup is repositioned closer to the body. Here, the direction of transport provides a spatial constraint on the recruitment of the degrees of freedom (Bernstein, 1967; Turvey, 1990) available to the user. How this spatial constraint would affect the recruitment of the available degrees of freedom is, of course, an empirical question. It is certainly unclear, a priori, what patterns of motion would be adopted.

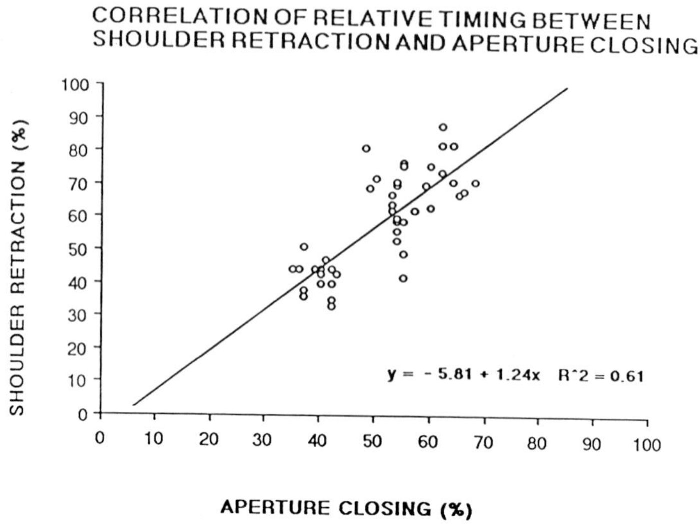

Figure 9. Correlation of relative timing between right contralateral shoulder protraction and aperture closing.

However, we believe that uncovering the temporal, spatial and mechanical constraints of prosthetic use is a necessary and important line of furture research.

3. CONCLUSIONS

The identification of what we have termed "critical variables" which capture or characterize multi-joint coordination in reaching and grasping behavior has been the major focus of this paper. While similar arguments for different tasks have been made before in the likes of topological features (Newell, 1985), invariant features (Schmidt, 1985) and synergies (Bernstein, 1967; Lee, 1984), we believe it is the dynamics of these critical variables that ultimately will best characterize the motor system which is itself, dynamic (see Kelso & Schoner, 1988). It is one thing to identify these critical variables, but quite another to map out and explore their dynamics. The premise of this approach, best known as the Dynamic

Pattern perspective (e.g. Schoner & Kelso, 1988) is based upon synergetic concepts originally applied to complex physical systems (Haken, 1975) but later to chemical and biological systems consisting of many components and degrees of freedom (Haken, 1983).

At the heart of synergetics is the concept of self-organization - the ability of a complex system far from equilibrium to self-organize. As certain control parameters are imposed on the system, patterns among the components spontaneously emerge from the intrinsic system dynamics which effectively "constrain" the many degrees of freedom. What we have termed "critical" variables are nothing more than what Haken (1983) has termed "order parameters" or collective variables which describe the emerging patterns. Every complex system, whether it be physical, chemical or biological will take on characteristics of self-organization, but the order parameters which characterize the patterns will be specific to the system and to the level of analyses (i.e. molecular, cellular, or behavioral as in the case of biological systems). Understanding the dynamics of a <u>given</u> component of the system will not reveal the cooperation among the components, which is where the patterns 'live'. It is only by exploring the <u>relationships</u> among the components, that insights to the pattern dynamics can be found.

Returning to reaching and grasping behavior, aperture velocity, for example, provides information about only one component of prehensile action. Aperture velocity, in and of itself, tells us nothing about relationships among the articulators of the hand and arm. Any interesting patterns of behavior will not be found in this singular kinematic variable. However, relative timing of final closure may be a candidate critical variable or order parameter because 1) it describes a relationship among the major components in reaching and grasping, and 2) appears to be preserved across changes in task demands. But how confident can we be that this variable is truly an order parameter in the synergetic sense (Haken, 1983; Schoner & Kelso, 1988)? The answer is, not very, and for a number of specific reasons. One, while it has been shown that relative timing has been preserved across changes in certain task demands (i.e. movement time, object size, initial hand posture), the range of task demand manipulation has, in most cases, been limited. For example, in the Wallace et al. (1990a) study, movement time was varied from only 300 to 800 msec. To identify potential patterns, the range of the manipulated task variable should be as wide as possible. Two, to explore pattern dynamics, the task variable should be manipulated in a continuous fashion, (see Kelso, 1984), not randomly, as has been the case in past studies. A continuous manipulation in discrete steps over time allows for the stability of the patterns to be observed at each level of the task variable and also allows for dynamic changes from one pattern to another to be observed, if more than one pattern exists. The stability of the patterns can be assessed by requiring many replications of the pattern at each level of the task variable and determining the resulting variability. Thus, until experiments are conducted which incorporate these procedures, we cannot be completely sure that relative timing of final closure is a candidate critical variable or order parameter. Another consideration is whether synergetic theoretical concepts can be applied to discrete, rather than continuous behavior. It may be that discrete behavior is just a special case of continuous behavior and therefore the non-linear dynamic principles of synergetic theory may be applicable to both. This, of course, would be desirable, but until the mathematics can be worked out (see Schoner, 1990 for recent attempts), we must exert caution in applying synergetic concepts to discrete behavior.

We have argued that the relative timing of final closure may signify the temporal coordination between the hand and arm. But is this the relevant relationship to observe in reaching and grasping for an object? Consider a recent experiment by Wallace, Weeks and Kelso (1990b) in which we asked subjects to "catch" an object mounted on a small treadmill which could transport the object towards them at different speeds. The subjects rested their hand at the end of the treadmill, and with just their index finger and thumb, were required to grasp the object when it arrived and lift the object from the treadmill. Object speed was continuously manipulated in the manner described above. Because the arm was stationary, we asked whether a pattern between the final closing of the hand and the object could be identified. We showed that the timing of hand closure relative to the object was preserved across five of the six object velocities. In the reaching case, the arm is in motion and the object is stationary. In the catching case, the object is in motion and the arm is stationary. In both cases, final closing of the hand can be temporally related to the moving component. Are these two cases that fundamentally dissimilar to warrant different relative timing measures? Perhaps they are, but it would be more parsimonious to have only one measure which captures the coordinative patterns regardless of whether the object or the arm is moving.

The Dynamic Pattern perspective offers an interesting methodology in the study of prosthetic reaching and grasping. The opening and closing of the mechanical prehensor is the result of the coordination of many joints and muscles. If the synergetic concept is correct, we would expect that even though there are potentially many combinations of joint and muscle action possible, only a few preferred patterns are used. As in normal reaching and grasping, one major challenge is the identification of critical variables (or order parameters) which describe these patterns. Moving the system through these patterns are the so-called control parameters (or task requirements). We have suggested that spatial, temporal and mechanical factors can serve to constrain the many degrees of freedom available to the user. But, as opposed to focussing on the kinematic analysis of individual components, a better characterization of both normal and prosthetic limb coordination can be achieved by identifying the patterns among the articulators and by eventually discovering factors which contribute to pattern formation and their loss of stability.

4. REFERENCES

Bernstein, N. (1967). The coordination and regulation of movement. Oxford: Pergamon.

Engen, T.J. & Spencer, W.A. (1969). Development of externally powered upper extremity orthotics. Final Report. SR5 RD 1564, Texas Institute for Rehabilitation and Research.

Fraser, C. & Wing, A.M. (1981). A case study of reaching by a user of a manually-operated artificial hand. Prosthetic and Orthotics International, 5, 151-156.

Grammens, G.M., Wallace, S.A. & Carlson, L.E. (in press). Coordination of reaching and grasping in prosthetic and normal limbs. In G.E. Stelmach (Ed.), Tutorials in Motor Neuroscience, Kluwer Academic Publishers.

Haken, H. (1975). Cooperative phenomena in systems far from thermal equilibrium and in non-physical systems. Review of Modern Physics, 47, 67-121.

Haken, H. (1983). Synergetics: an introduction: Non-equilibrium phase transitions and self-organization in physics, chemistry and biology. Berlin: Springer.

Jeannerod, M. (1981). Intersegmental coordination during reaching at natural visual objects. In J. Long & A. Baddeley (Eds.). Attention and Performance IX (pp. 153-168). Hillsdale: Earlbaum.

Jeannerod, M. (1984). The timing of natural prehension movements. Journal of Motor Behavior, 16, 235-254.

Jeka, J.J. & Kelso, J.A.S. (1989). The dynamic pattern approach to coordination behavior: A tutorial review. In S.A. Wallace (Ed.). Perspectives on the Coordination of Movement. Elsevier: North-Holland.

Keller, A.D., Taylor, C.L. & Zahm, V. (1947). Studies to determine the functional requirements for hand and arm prosthesis. Final Report, Dept. of Engineering, UCLA.

Kelso, J.A.S. (1984). Phase transitions and critical behavior in human bimanual coordination. American Journal of Physiology: Regulatory, Integrative and Comparative Physiology, 15, R1000-R1004.

Kelso, S.A.S., Buchanan, J.J. & Wallace, S.A. (In press). Order parameters for the neural organization of single, multi-joint limb movement patterns. Experimental Brain Research.

Kelso, J.A.S. Delcolle, J.D., & Schoner, G. (1989). Action-perception as a pattern formation process. In M. Jeannerod (Ed.), Attention and Performance XIII, Hillsdale: NJ, Erlbaum.

Kelso, J.A.S. Scholz, J.P. & Schoner, G. (1986). Non-equilibrium phase transitions in coordinated biological motion: Critical fluctuations. Physics Letters, A118, 279-284.

Kelso, J.A.S., Scholz, J.P. & Schoner, G. (1988). Dynamics governs switching among patterns of coordination in biological movement. Physics Letters, A, 134, 8-12.

Kelso, J.A.S. & Schoner, G. (1988). Self-organization of coordinative movement patterns. Human Movement Science, 7, 27-46.

Lee, W.A. (1984). Neuromotor synergies as a basis for coordinated intentional action. Journal of Motor Behavior, 16, 135-170.

Marteniuk, G.G., Leavitt, Mackenzie, C.L. & Athenes, S. (1990). Functional relationships between grasp and transport components in a prehension task. Human Movement Science, 4, 149-176.

Marteniuk, G.G., Mackenzie, C.L., Jeannerod, M., Athenes, S. & Dugas, C. (1987). Constraints on human arm trajectories. Canadian Journal of Psychology, 41, 365-378.

Newell, K.M. (1985). Coordination, control and skill. In D.Goodman, R.B. Wilberg, & I.M. Franks (Eds.), Differing perspectives in motor learning, memory, and control. Amsterdam: North-Holland.

Schmidt, R.A. (1985). The search for invariance in skilled movement behavior. Research Quarterly for Exercise and Sport, 56, 188-200.

Scholz, J.P. & Kelso, J.A.S. (1989). A quantitative approach to understanding the formation and change of coordinated movement patterns. Journal of Motor Behavior, 21, 122-144.

Schoner, G. (1990). A dynamic theory of coordination of discrete movement. Biological Cybernetics, 63, 257-270.

Schoner, G. & Kelso, J.A.S. (1988). Dynamic pattern generation in behavioral and neural systems. Science, 239, 1513-1520.

Tubiana, R. (1981). Architecture and functions of the hand. In R. Tubiani (Ed.), The Hand, 1, Philadelphia: W.B. Saunders, 19-93.

Turvey, M.T. (1977). Preliminaries to a theory of action with reference to vision. In R.E. Shaw & J. Bransford (Eds.). Perceiving, acting, and knowing. Hillsdale, NJ: Erlbaum.

Turvey, M.T. (1990). Coordination. American Psychologist, 45, 938-953.

Von Hofsten, C. & Ronnqvist, L. (1988). Preparation for grasping an object: A developmental study. Journal of Experimental Psychology: Human Perception and Performance, 14, 610-621.

Wallace, S.A. & Weeks, D.L. (1988). Temporal constraints in the control of prehensile movements. Journal of Motor Behavior, 20, 81-105.

Wallace, S.A., Weeks, D.L., & Kelso, J.A.S. (1990a). Temporal constraints in reaching and grasping behavior. Human Movement Science, 9, 69-93.

Wallace, S.A., Weeks, D.L. & Kelso, J.A.S. (1990b). Perceptual-motor relations in the coordination of catching behavior. ICS Technical Report. #90-16.

Wing, A.M. & Fraser, C. (1983). The contribution of the thumb to reaching movements. Quarterly Journal of Experimental Psychology, 35A, 297-309.

Wing, A.M., Turton, A. & Fraser, C. (1986). Grasp size and accuracy of approach in reaching. Journal of Motor Behavior, 18, 245-260.

Author Notes

We would like to thank Babak Baharlo, Gerry Grammens and Alison Speer for their help in the preparation of this manuscript.

Tutorials in Motor Behavior II
G.E. Stelmach and J. Requin (Editors)

ONLINE CONTROL OF HAND REACHING AT UNDETECTED TARGET DISPLACEMENTS

Olivier MARTIN[1] and Claude PRABLANC [2]

Introduction

The purpose of this paper was a reinvestigation of the main factors influencing the control of multi-joint responses aimed at a goal in the prehension space such as pointing at a small visual target. A current view on hand motor control is the existence of preset commands, whose accuracy is limited, and on which are superimposed corrections provided by the visual feedback from the moving hand together with the goal. We will bring evidence that, in addition to some raw command presetting, an "eye to hand" loop controls most of the so-called open loop pointing, in the absence of vision of the hand.

A considerable amount of knowledge on the role of the visual external loop, allowing a retinal comparison between the goal and the ongoing movement, has been accumulated since Fitts (1951) found a mathematical link between the speed and accuracy of a goal directed movement. The minimum time to implement the necessary corrections of a finely guided movement was expressed as a function of a simple formula called the index of difficulty. This index was homogeneous to a quantity of information in the sense of the Theory of Information (for instance for hitting a disk the index of difficulty was equal to a function of the ratio of distance to move over the diameter of the disk). These observations were seen as the expression of a limited processing capacity of the sensorimotor channel per unit of time. The more complex the task to be carried out, the longer the time to transmit and process the corresponding information without distortion. If some minor changes have been brought to what has been then called Fitts' law, the basic assumptions underlying this law have never been questioned. A series of hypotheses within this framework have been elaborated, proposing either an iterative process of discrete subcorrections along the path of a response (Crossman and Goodeve, 1983), or a correction in the final part of the trajectory when the hand enters the central visual field, where both the foveated target and the moving hand are analyzed by a retinal area of high acuity (Paillard, 1982).

What has received a late interest is the source of inaccuracy of the initial motor response, considered as the expression of the limits of the learning capabilities. The notion of a motor program has been advanced by reference to the early computer science terminology, to describe the processes of selection of a series of preset muscle activities. Though many interpretations of a motor program have been given, most of them have considered the motor program as an "open loop" process, which once initiated is carried out in a rigid way, in the absence of visual feedback. Schmidt (1975) gave a first formulation of this notion by proposing that a motor program responsible for the execution of a movement of a given extent was characterized by an initial impulse which amplitude determined the level of noise in the neural recruitment and thus the corresponding level of motor error, when hand visual feedback reafferences were prevented.

The following preliminary study tried to show that within a physiological range, aimed movements are not exclusively composed of a preprogrammed component and of an external visual feedback allowing corrections of the first component when it departs from the goal, but that another source of error correction is modifying online the contents of the motor response, in a very automatic way, without need for any external feedback. As a consequence this study led to a reevaluation of the notion of motor programming in the execution of normal movements.

---

[1]Laboratoire RESACT UFR-APS Equipe Comportement Moteur Université Joseph Fourier BP 53X F-38041 Grenoble Cedex, France

[2]Vision et Motricité INSERM Unité 94 16 avenue du doyen Lépine F-69500 Bron, France

The early attempts to see whether a motor program was something rigidly organized (i.e. once initiated was uninfluencable by the occurrence of a new stimulus), have been performed in the oculomotor system (Wheeless et al.,1966, Becker and Jurgens, 1975) and then in the hand motor system (Megaw, 1974; Georgopoulos et al., 1981; Soechting and Lacquaniti, 1983). A common technique was used, called the double-step stimulus paradigm. It consisted in presenting a first stimulus as a goal for the motor response followed or not by a second stimulus either away or ahead of the initial stimulus, in a random sequence. For interstimuli intervals properly selected, it was shown on both systems that the ongoing motor program in response to the first stimulus could be altered: either be replaced by a new one or be modulated by the occurrence of the second step stimulus. The above double-step paradigms have been used mainly to show that ongoing motor responses could be intentionally altered in a quasi continuous way, just by changing the previous visual goal.

In a previous study, Goodale et al. (1986), Pélisson et al. (1986) used this double-step technique as a tool for understanding unintentional corrections to an ongoing movement.They proposed that a eye to hand coupling allowed adjustments of goal directed movements, without any need for a vision of the hand. In their paradigm a pointing response was elicited by a stimulus which further stepped a few degrees ahead or away around the onset of the hand movement; in addition through an artificial technique, the second step of the stimulus was made undetectable by the subject. By contrast with classical double-step experiments, in Goodale et al's experiment, subjects perceived the stimulus as unique; thus the second step stimulus produced an effect which could be considered as similar to the selection of a very inacurate motor program towards a stationary target. The observation of a complete compensation of the perturbation (introduced during the early part of the response), suggested this corrective action to be a low level process and not to interfere with higher levels such as intentional reprogramming. However the perturbation lied along the line joining the initial to the final point of the movement. Though random in time and direction the applied perturbations never produced a change of the direction of the initial response, nor a change of the orientation of the movement which always lied along a frontoparallel line: only its extent could be reduced or increased. If, as suggested earlier by previous studies (Vicario and Ghez, 1984), an aimed motor response was composed of two components, one specifying the orientation and the other the extent of the movement, Goodale et al.'s results could be interpreted in a restrictive way and considered not as a general phenomenon, but only as an automatic adjustment of movement extent.

Rationale

This paper intended to generalize Goodale et al.'s findings (1986) and tried to extend the notion of automatic correction from movement amplitude to both movement amplitude and orientation when undetected errors were introduced. The baseline idea was that the so-called "motor program" was under the permanent control of a loop acting at a low level (well below intention) in which the goal or its internal spatial representation guided the movement all throughout. We hypothesized that once the higher processes such as the decision to perform a given type of movement had been taken, the basic features of the execution level included an internal feedback control of the trajectory with respect to inner loops (Whether such a control was exerted via a visuo-kinaesthetic feedback loop comparing vision of the target and felt position of the hand, or whether it was exerted via a loop comparing the vision of the target and the efference copy of the initiated response, could not be answered by this type of experiment, though some indirect arguments could favor one of the two alternatives).

The following questions were asked: Are online unintended corrections of path observed when not only the amplitude of the goal is modified in flight but also its spatial direction ? Are the corrections for changes in orientation more time consuming than those for changes in amplitude ? When the direction of the second step is such that the general structure of the movement at the joint level may be altered, are the corrections still possible ? For instance if the initial part of the trajectory, up to its peak velocity, is directed towards the initial target, the correction needed to deviate the trajectory towards the final target location may imply joint reversal: is such a drastic change in muscular synergy possible during the execution of the response ? What is the earliest spatio-temporal cue indicating a departure of the perturbed paths from the unperturbed paths ?

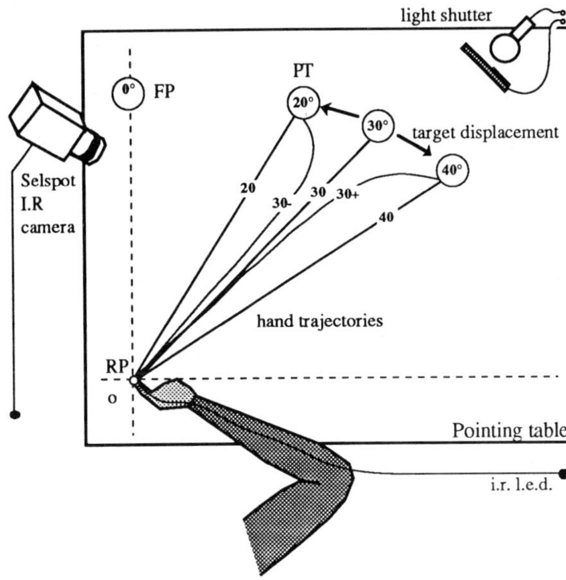

FIGURE 1 : Experimental display. The subject had to point with his forefinger tip to visual targets which randomly appeared in his right hemivisual field. Three types of targets were presented: the unperturbed single-step targets at 20, 30, 40 degrees of eccentricity, the perturbed double-target "30-", in which after an initial step from 0 to 30 degrees, the target jumped to 20 degrees, and the perturbed double-step targets "30+", in which after the same first step from 0 to 30 degrees, the target jumped to 40 degrees. A fast light electronic shutter (3 to 5 ms response time) was used to cut off all subjects visual reafferences from his limbs and body, while maintaining vision of the target. An infra-red light emiting diode (l.e.d) was stuck on the fingertip and allowed a recording of the movement in the horizontal plane by a Selspot camera operating at 333 hz.

Methods and procedure

Hand movements were performed on a horizontal 1.50 depth by 2.00 m wide flat isotropic surface on which no detail could be perceived, with practically no visual frame of reference. Underneath the surface, a matrix of red light emitting diodes (l.e.d.s.) was disposed in polar coordinates with a 65cm radius angles (ranging from 0 to 20, 30, 40 degrees on the right subject's hemispace). The subject's head was at 40cm above the center of this polar coordinate system. The hand pointing started initially from a resting position RP located in the sagittal plane 30 cm behind the 0 degrees FP fixation point (see fig. 1). Subject had a chin and forehead rest and was instructed not to move his head when orienting both his eyes and hand towards a peripheral target. An EOG method using disposable Ag-AgCl electrodes of low impedance (100 ohms), disposed near the outer canthi of the eyes, and giving the orientation of an equivalent cyclopean eye, allowed to monitor eye movements. The task of the subject was "to look and point with his fingertip as quickly and accurately as possible" onto the lit target. The sequence was always the following: The room was initially illuminated, the subject was fixating FP with his finger on RP; after one second in this rest position, FP was turned off and a randomly selected PT was turned on. The subject's task was to look and point at PT. The saccadic eye movement triggered an electronic shutter which cut-off the illumination of the room, the only remaining lit point beeing PT; simultaneously the whole limb body parts became unvisible (see fig 2). The saccadic eye movement towards PT could randomly have no effect (single-step stimulus), or move PT 10 degrees left (noticed (30-)) or 10 degrees right (noticed (30+))along the arc of circle of peripheral targets. A simple or composite PT lasted for two seconds; then the stimulus went back on FP. At the onset of the hand movement back to FP, the room was illuminated allowing a perfect coincidence between the proprioceptive and the visual cues for the next trial. The return hand movement was performed slowly to allow an accurate repositioning of the fingertip on RP and of the eye on FP.

Central and peripheral targets lied along a circle centered on the subject's head. Resting hand position RP was chosen at a different location from fixation point FP in order to maximize the change of movement orientation required by the perturbation (see fig 1). Target perturbations were applied in the following way: the presentation of a PT elicited an ocular saccade with a latency of 250 to 350 msec; during the saccade an electronic device generated a pulse, which could instantaneously shift the PT 10 degrees left or right or let it stationnary.

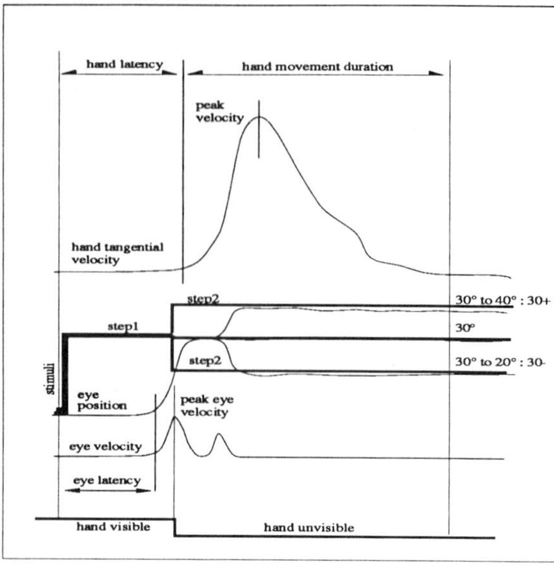

FIGURE 2 : Diagram of spatio-temporal organization of eye and hand movement in the three different tasks of target pointing. The single step stimulation (step 1, "30") corresponds to the target jumping from its sagittal reference position to a randomly determined stationary peripheral position (20° or 40°). The double step stimulation is obtained by making the target to jump once more after the first step (step 1) either to a more eccentric position (step 2, "30+") or to a less eccentric position (step 2, "30-"). The double-step stimulation is triggered by the signal of the peak eye velocity, while the vision of the hand is simultaneously cut off, only the target remaining visible. The upper curve represents the hand tangential velocity; the hand movement onset occurs nearly at the same time as the peak eye velocity. Only the main parts of movement parameters analyzed are displayed on the figure.

Recording techniques and control of real time feedback piloting of the experiments

An online program running on a PDP 11/73 controlled the whole experiment. Eye and hand movement data were collected at 333 Hz (every 3msec). Eye movements were recorded as mentioned above by a DC EOG technique, with a low-pass Butterworth analog filter with a -12db/octave cut-off frequency of 30 Hz; they were sampled through a 12 bit A/D converter; a 20 min rest in the apparatus allowed a stabilization of both EOG gain and drift; however as drift could not be perfectly nullified, a special electronic device produced a zeroing of the EOG offset at peripheral target onset (Prablanc et al., 1978). Electronic Butterworth derivative filters computed both velocity and acceleration. After the eye velocity had reached a threshold twice over its maximum noise, the test of zero-crossing of the acceleration (i.e. the time of peak eye velocity) began; as this peak eye velocity was reached, a logical pulse triggered an electronic shutter which cut-off the illumination of the room (see figs 1 and 2), preventing any visual reafferences from subject's movement (the absence of those reafferences being called "open loop"). The logical pulse triggering the electronic shutter 3 to 5 msec long, was also sent to the computer for an on line feedback control of the target stimuli.

The x-y horizontal components of the hand pointing were recorded through a small l.e.d. (emitting in the infra-red spectrum) 3x2 mm, stuck on the nail of the fingertip and coupled with a Selspot II system. The Selspot camera, two meters above the working surface, recorded the x-y displacements of the fingertip (with an accuracy of +/-2 mm). At every 3 msec clock-tick, the x-y coordinates were compared with the coordinates of the resting point RP's

An experimental session was composed of an equal number of unperturbed targets, perturbed targets left and perturbed targets right, the 5 different types of stimulations were 20 deg stationary, 30 to 20 deg (30-); 30 deg stationary, 30 to 40 deg (30+) and 40 deg stationary. All types of stimulations were randomized and equiprobable; however after a given type of stimulus had occured twice consecutively, the third occurence of the same stimulus type was forbidden to prevent a predictive effect. For instance for a 30 degrees eccentricity peripheral target, the target could either remain stationary, jump to 20 degrees, or jump to 40 degrees with an equal probability. Each type of stimulation was repeated 5 times every session. One session included thus 5x5=25 stored trials.

Two naive male and female subjects, 21 and 25 years old, with a normal vision, underwent the experiment; each subject was submitted twice to every experimental session. There was thus a number of 2 (repeated sessions) x2 (subjects) =4 experimental sessions, each one including 5 types of stimulation x 5 repetitions, i. e. 100 trials. For each subject and condition the two (identical) sessions were grouped for the analysis, allowing to average 10 repetitions for each type of stimulation. For each parameter measured, a one-way analysis of variance was performed: perturbation left (30-), no perturbation, perturbation right (30+) for each subject with a 10 repeated measures average. For all parameters, means, standard deviations were computed. Intra-subjects correlations among possibly coupled variables were performed: correlations between hand latency versus eye latency, peak hand acceleration versus delay between perturbation and hand movement onset, absolute error versus hand movement duration, distance error versus hand duration, angular error (re-head) versus hand duration, absolute error versus deceleration time, distance error versus deceleration time, angular error (re-head) versus deceleration time, absolute error versus peak tangential velocity and distance error versus peak tangential velocity.

Computational methods

The x-y hand position data were filtered with a zero phase Finite Impulse Response (FIR) filter using 24 coefficients with a frequency cut-off set at 20 Hz. The same type of filter was used for the eye but with a 30 hz frequency cut-off, this choice being a compromise between the real power spectrum of a normal saccade (Bahill et al 1981) and the noise present with our EOG method. A 20 Hz cut-off frequency was chosen for the hand to detect fast changes on an ongoing motor response. Eye and x,y hand velocities were computed from the filtered positions by a least square second order polynomial method using a window of +/- 3 points. The same method was then applied to compute the x,y and the tangential acceleration (colinear with the tangential velocity) from the tangential velocity. Tangential velocity was computed from its vectorial x,y components. It was defined by its modulus and phase (or spatial angular orientation).

The main parameters analyzed are represented on figs. 2 and 3: eye latency, hand latency, hand movement duration, acceleration phase or time to peak velocity, peak velocity, modulus and orientation of the tangential velocity vector in space, absolute error, i.e. the distance between final target and endpoint hand pointing, angular error of the hand pointing in a head coordinate system and distance error, i.e. the difference between the distance from initial to final hand pointing and the distance between initial hand pointing and final target. The above parameters were computed automatically by an algorithm with the following thresholds: eye velocity = 20°/sec, eye acceleration = 200°/sec2, hand velocity = 8cm/sec, hand acceleration = 200°/sec2. The hand thresholds corresponded statistically to the values obtained by comparison with a hand pointing contact sensitive method.

Position, velocity and acceleration traces were averaged by synchronizing them at the onset of eye movement (for eye) and at the onset of hand movement (for hand). Statistical analyzes were performed to detect the earliest point where the trajectories to perturbed targets began to deviate from the trajectories

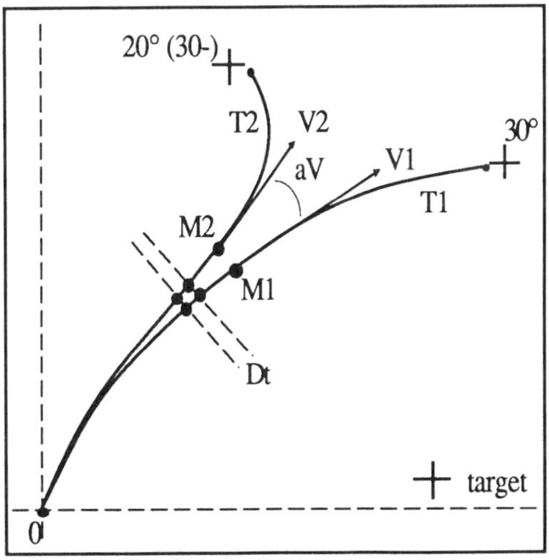

FIGURE 3 : Symbolic diagram of comparative kinematic parameters of hand paths to perturbed and unperturbed target. Only the perturbation left (target jump from 30 to 20 degrees) has been represented. Both paths are synchronized in time and the dotted lines represent slices of equal times for each path. 0 : initial hand position; T1 : unperturbed hand path; T2 : perturbed left path; M1V1, M2V2 : tangential velocity vectors of T1 and T2; aV : divergence angle between tangential velocity vectors M1V1 and M2V2 of T1 and T2 (Dt=9 msec: time interval between two divergence angle frame analysis); frequency filtering for all hand parameters: 20 Hz. The computation of velocity vectors allows to build a function of velocity angle divergence aV=f(t).

TABLE 1. Means and standard deviations of movement parameters in open loop condition.

subjects	GC				MG			
targets	30-	30	30+		30-	30	30+	
time to double step (msec.)	280	-	258		235	-	229	
	27	-	34		20	-	22	
eye latency (msec.)	255	251	234		211	198	214	
	28	35	37		26	18	38	
hand latency (msec.)	265	266	259		256	257	244	
	19	66	34		23	43	35	
hand duration (msec.)	456	413	496	**	450	398	501	**
	42	39	77		47	60	30	
peak hand tangential veloc. (cm/sec)	170	170	188		157	193	206	**
	19	19	21		28	42	31	
acceleration phase (msec.)	171	185	176	*	164	193	194	
	13	16	14		28	38	41	
absolute error (mm)	18	17	22		17	17	22	
	8	8	17		13	9	10	
angular error re-head (deg.)	1.4	0.5	-1		0.5	0.6	-0.2	
	0.8	1	1.7		1.7	0.8	1.4	

** : $p \leq 0.01$; * : $p \leq 0.05$.

table 1 : Means, standard deviations and levels of signification (one-way Anova) of movement parameters for perturbed (30-, 30+) and unperturbed (30) target; Subject G.C and M.G; (n=10).

to stationary targets. Perturbations left: the synchronized curves obtained with the normal responses to 30 degrees were taken as a reference; the perturbed left synchronized curves (eye and hand) were shifted as to align their hand acceleration profiles on those of the normal responses; then by increasing steps of time every 9 msec a t test was performed to determine the time of significant differences (at $p<0.05$) in angles between the tangential velocity vectors of the normal responses and those of the perturbed left responses. Perturbations right: the same 30 degrees synchronized curves for the normal responses were taken as a reference; the perturbed right synchronized curves were shifted in the same way as for the perturbed left curves by aligning their hand acceleration profiles on those of the normal responses; however as for those perturbations left, most of the initial pathes were common to the unperturbed responses, we used as an index of the earliest change of the responses the time at which the modulus of the tangential velocity vectors were diverging.

The measure of the reaction time to the perturbation was taken as the difference between the time of divergence minus the time of peak saccadic eye velocity (corresponding to the occurrence of the perturbation). The real delay in the processing of the perturbation is in fact likely to be lower than the above reaction time; indeed during the saccade the retinal signals are blurred, and omitted (Campbell and Wurtz, 1978); it is only towards the end of the saccade that they begin to be interpretable (Prablanc et al, 1978), when the eye velocity is low enough (<100 deg/sec, corresponding approximately to 40 msec after peak velocity for a 30 deg eccentricity target). If this estimation is taken as the instant of visual recovering from the saccade, the real reaction becomes thus 40 msec. shorter than the measured one.

Results

After the end of the last session, the two subjects, questioned about their sensations, could not report any detection of double-step stimuli. Their unperturbed two-dimensional spatial paths (projection of the movement on the plane of pointings) exhibited a curvature which increased with the eccentricity of the target. The perturbations right produced paths with the same general pattern as those of the unperturbed trials, but with an increased curvature towards the end the movement. The paths corresponding to the perturbations left exhibited an inversion of curvature. On the average, corrections were nearly complete whatever the direction of the perturbation (see hand fig.6 upper part).

For each movement parameters analyzed, table 1 shows the mean and standard deviations. The eye latency did not depend on the perturbation factor, neither did the hand latency. The instant of the perturbation (called time to double-step on table 1) was delayed on the average by 7 msec from the hand latency. The time from hand movement onset to peak velocity (or acceleration phase), was significantly affected by the perturbation factor ($p<0.05$) only for subject GC, the acceleration phase being decreased by 14 msec for the perturbation left (30-) ;The perturbation factor had a significant effect on the modulus of the peak hand tangential velocity only for subject M.G., the (30-) condition producing a decrease of 36 deg/sec with respect to the unperturbed conditions. The angular error referenced in a eye (or head) coordinate sytem (deg.) with respect to the final target position did not depend on the perturbation factor, which meant that the compensation was nearly complete (see fig 4 and 6). The angular error ranged from -0.2 to 1.4 deg as can be seen on table 1. The distance error was not affected by the perturbation factor; its values ranged from 7 to 15 mm. If we compare the distance error and the angular error, expressed not in degrees but in equivalent linear displacements in mm, they apppear to be in the same range (7,15 against -2, 14). The absolute error was the distance between the pointing position at the time of impact and the final target position; it did not depend significantly on the perturbation factor; with an error raising from 17 mm in unperturbed trials to 22 mm in perturbed ones; as the target perturbation was 10 degrees (i.e. an equivalent distance of about 100 mm), the error was compensated for about 80 %.

The hand movement duration was the most massively affected parameter by the perturbation factor; for both right and left perturbations ($p<0.01$). The average duration was increased by 44 msec for the perturbations left (30-) and by 98 msec for the perturbations right (30+) (see fig 5). The durations of unperturbed movements at 20 or 40 degrees target were respectively 362 and 412 msec; if we normalize the durations of the perturbed trials relatively to their theoretical path length, we obtain normalized increases of hand movement duration which are equal to (453-362) i.e. 91 msec for the perturbations left (30-) and (499-412) i.e. 87 msec for the perturbations right (30+).

The overall mean correlation between hand latency and eye latency was 0.56 indicating a loose coupling between the onsets of hand movement and saccade. All types of pointing errors: angular, distance or absolute, were insensitive to the total duration of the movement, to the peak hand velocity or to any of its deceleration components, the highest correlation coefficient being 0.38.

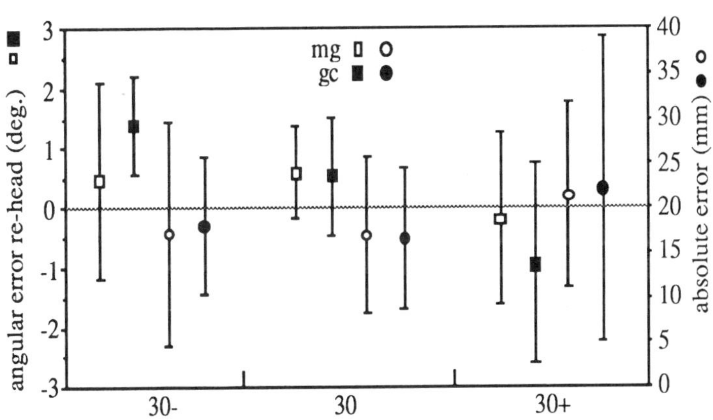

FIGURE 4 : Relationship between absolute error pointing means (circle; in mm), angular pointing error re-head means (square; in deg.) for the different types of unperturbed (30) and perturbed (30- or 30+) responses, for subjects G.C and M.G. Vertical lines indicate standard deviations; (n=10).

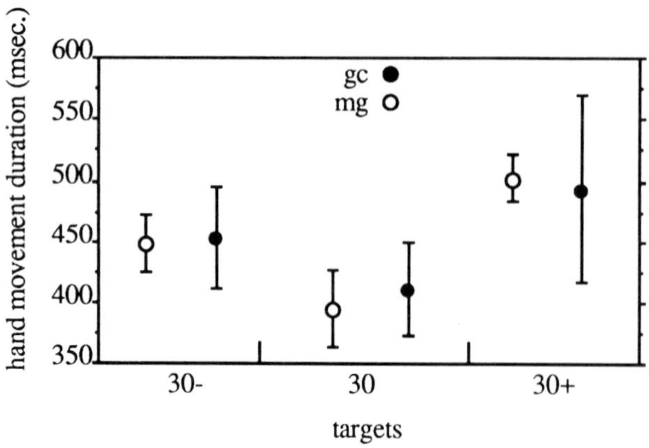

FIGURE 5 : Relationship between mean hand movement durations and the different types of unperturbed (30) and perturbed (30- or 30+) targets. Vertical lines indicate standard deviations; Subject G.C and M.G; (n=10).

Reaction time of the sensorimotor system to the perturbation.

This reaction time has been defined in the methods section as the time from the perturbation to the earliest detectable signs of corrections. It was measured from the angles of the tangential velocity vectors of the perturbed and the unperturbed family of curves (see fig. 3). We have mentioned above that the measured reaction times in this experiment are an overevaluation of the processing time, as the retinal information is known not to be available during the early phase of the saccade and that for a 30 deg eccentricity target the processing delay (or real reaction time) has to be diminished by 40 msec.

For the perturbations left (30-) the reaction times were on the average 149 msec (see table 2 and fig 6), the real reaction time being evaluated at 109 msec. The hand movement durations analyzed above have shown averaged measures of 406 msec for stationary targets and 453 msec for perturbations left (30-), (i.e. a normalized increase in hand movement duration of 91 msec). Thus both the real reaction time to the perturbation and the corresponding increase in normalized hand movement duration were in the same range (109-91 msec)

For the perturbations right (30+), the reaction times measured from the divergence between modulus tangential velocities gave much higher values: 404 msec (or a real reaction time of 364 msec). However the normalized increases in hand movement durations (87 msec) were much lower than the real reaction times.

Thus for both types of perturbations, it is worthnoting that though estimated real reaction times were quite different (104 and 364 msec) the normalized increases of hand movement duration were both much shorter than the corresponding real reaction times, and of the same amount around 90 msec.

TABLE 2. Reaction time to target perturbations (msec).

perturbations	30-/30	30+/30
subject G.C	105	417
subject M.G	192	390
means	149	404

Table 2 : Reaction time of corrected movement to perturbed targets measured from significant variation of tangential velocity vector when comparing perturbed to unperturbed trajectories (30-/30; 30+/30); Subject G.C and M.G; (in msec; n=10).

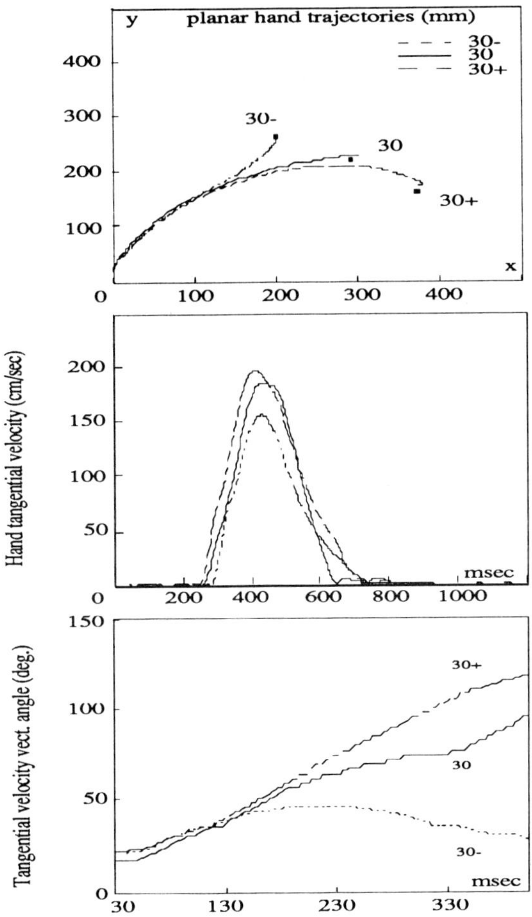

FIGURE 6 : Upper part : mean spatial paths of normal, perturbed left and perturbed right pointings; middle part: corresponding variation of synchronised hand tangential velocites; observe that for the perturbation left (30-) the peak tangential velocity has been substantially decreased, indicating that the perturbation has been already taken into account at that time; lower part: tangential velocity vector angles, for hand movements directed to unperturbed (30) and perturbed targets (30- or 30+); the evolution of the tangential velocity vector angle indicates for the perturbation left (30-) a more early departure from normal than for the perturbation right (30+). Subject M.G.; (curves averaged over 10 trials).

Discussion

The essential feature of the above experiment is the generalization of the automatic corrective process observed by Goodale et al (1986), Pélisson et al (1986) when an unconsciously detected artificial error was introduced; this corrective process was independent from the visual feedback of the hand, which was removed near the onset of the movement. It basically shows that the hand followed a path deviated towards the actual target position like if a spring attached in between the hand and target had pulled the former to the latter. In the Goodale et al.'s experiment the perturbation was such that the necessary corrections to be performed resulted, at the level of the hand, in a modulation of the amplitude of the movement (lengthening or shortening according to the type of perturbation), not of its general orientation. Conversely in the present experiment, with the same paradigm, the perturbation involved mainly a modification of the orientation of the movement and to a lesser extent of its amplitude. The possible generalization of the automatic correction process from amplitude to orientation was so much more important to establish as an evidence of independent programming of amplitude and direction has been shown (Vicario and Ghez, 1984). However by applying to our experimental data independent analysis on errors in distance and errors in orientation (or angular error re-head), we did not find important differences between distance errors and equivalent orientation errors expressed in mm. Basically our perturbations, considered in a head centered coordinate system, were perturbations in orientation and had no distance component viewed from the head (or eye), as they occured at a nearly constant distance from the head. However the movement of the hand had its origin 30 cm ahead of the head center. Thus movements to 20, 30 and 40 degrees stationary targets were of unequal amplitude. Would orientation and distance be coded by independent channels, the above results would suggest the same type of flexibility for the amendment of either orientation or distance, so far accuracy is concerned. The absence of correlation between the above aspects of pointing accuracy and the duration of the movement or the deceleration parameters seem to indicate that there is no speed accuracy trade-off in this kind of corrections. The moderate speed at which the movements were performed (around 400 msec) could explain it; nevertheless the fastest corrections detectable by the analysis were implemented within relatively short reaction times, around 149 msec from the perturbation (i. e. around 109 msec from the reupdating of the retinal signals at the end of the saccade), which is suggestive of an automatic operating mode of these basic mechanisms. In Goodale et al.'s experiment no additional processing time was found for the corrections to a perturbed target: durations of perturbed responses lied along the same duration vs amplitude curve as normal trials. In the present experiments a normalized increase in hand movement duration of about 90 msec was found for both perturbations left (30-) and right (30+), which would suggest that the complexity of the required correction could lengthen slightly its duration. Moreover the fact that, despite large changes in reaction times between perturbations left (30-) and perturbations right (30+), the normalized increase in hand movement duration did not change, suggests that the (30+) reaction times were close to the (30-) ones, but were in fact difficult to detect by the analysis, as both unperturbed and perturbed right (30+) hand movements followed very close paths.

In this experiment, a crude modelling of the two joint systems (shoulder and elbow) using our kinematic data and the geometry of the subjects anatomy, allowed to reconstruct the joint angles under the perturbation left; the angle of the shoulder was shown to extend first to approximately the value corresponding to the 30 degrees stationary target and then to reverse by about 30% its movement, while the elbow angle practically did not change its flexion extension pattern. Thus the fact that the modifications to the trajectories perturbed left involved not only an inverted radius of curvature of the path but also deep structural changes in the flexion-extension patterns at the level of the shoulder and elbow, is an indirect argument suggesting that the possible modifications to an ongoing movement without vision of the hand, not only apply to amplitude modulation but that they control the whole trajectory of the finger end point. In the Goodale et al (1986) and Pélisson et al (1986) experiments, the corrections required by the perturbations involved only a modulation of movement amplitude and practically no reversal of the initial joints pattern. In the present experiment, the complexity of the corrections likely explains why the duration of the movement was lenghthened by as much as 91 msec for the perturbed left trials; why the perturbed right trials, which did not involve reversal of joint angles with respect to the original joint pattern, were lengthened as much as the perturbed left trials remain unclear. To summarize the comparison of the present results with Goodale et al's, the flexibility of the response appears as easy for distance as for orientation of the movement so far accuracy is concerned, but changing the orientation seems to take an extra 90 msec. for the hand pointing.

Another interesting point to note is the similarity between the shortest reaction times we obtained with unvoluntary corrections to undetected artificial errors, and the reaction times obtained by all classical double step experiments. Those latter ones involved voluntary changes to ongoing motor responses, like in Soechting and Lacquaniti's experiment (1983), where the orientation of a two joints hand pointing was intentionally changed 110 msec after perturbation, or like in Van Sonderen et al.'s experiments (1989), where a manipulation of the movement orientation, rather than its of its extent, produced very early modifications of the initial response. Our reaction times were also similar to Alstermark et al.'s (1990) who found that cats could switch the direction of an ongoing target-reaching forelimb movement, within 83 to 118 msec., or to Paulignan et al. 's (1990), who found reaction times as low as 100 msec, with perturbations in the location of objects to be grapsed.

Thus our experiments of unvoluntary pointing corrections to a perturbed location give orders of magnitude in error processing time similar to those of voluntary corrections in the range of 100-150 msec. In addition the corrections implied both changes in orientation and extent of the movement; interesting implications may derive from: both types of intentional and unintentional corrections could well share common processes after the visual detection (conscious or not) of the discrepancy between the ongoing response and the goal. Those corrections suggest the image of a spring attached in between the fingertip and the target, like if the goal of the corrections was to bring the end point effector to the target. It favors the hypothesis of a main inner loop, which would compare the current hand position with the spatial representation of the target location,either obtained centrally from an efference copy of the initial response or peripherally from the kinaesthetic signal of the hand. This idea of an internal control system has already been proposed for the coordination of oculomotor and head orientation (Laurutis and Robinson, 1986; Guitton et al., 1987; Pélisson et al., 1988), in speech control (Abbs and Gracco,1984) and for multi-joint hand motor control (Prablanc et al., 1990). Our results are consistent with this top down approach view where intermediate variables such as joint angles, torques and muscle forces are devoted to meet the goal of the endpoint effector, which role is to bring the motor error down to zero. This view is now more than hypothetical: it has received recently an electrophysiological confirmation, for the orienting eye-head motor systems, in the superior colliculus of the cat (Munoz et al., 1989, 1991) where population cells have been found to encode the gaze motor error, i.e. a variable including the sum of the two eye and head elementary variables. The equivalent of this motor error in hand pointing could be the different between the spatial encoding of the target and the fingertip in space, itself composed of shoulder and elbow angular variables.

Conclusion

This study has shown the generalization of an automatic on-line control of complex movements involving several joints in a pointing task, regulating not only the extent of the movement but also the orientation of its spatial path. The modification of the initial path did not require the conscious detection of the perturbation (introduced during the orienting saccade and around the onset of the hand movement). However the latencies of the earliest corrections were approximately in the same range as in experiments where the possible occurrence of a perturbation was a priori known, and consciously detected. Thus both intentional and unintentional changes to an ongoing movement could share a common mechanism. It could be that once the decision process to perform a given motor act has been engaged, the necessary adjustments or modifications to achieve the goal are automatically initiated at lower levels. It is reminiscent of the notion of motor equivalence proposed by Abbs and Gracco (1984), in which a given goal may be carried out by several ways whenever the initial planning encounters obstacles. But mostly the present results suggest that such a correcting mechanism acts as well in natural conditions, when the initiation of the response is inaccurate and when an error is detected betwen the efferent or afferent signals related to the movement and the goal.

Acknowledgements
We thank M. Soulier for typing the manuscript and P. Giroud for the illustrations. This study has been supported by grant BRAIN SCI 0029C from the Commission of the European Communities.

References

ABBS, J.H., AND GRACCO, V.L. Control of complex gesture: oro-facial muscle responses to load perturbations of lip during speech. J. Neurophysiol., 51, 705-723, 1984.

ADAMS, J.A. A closed loop theory of motor learning. J. Mot. Behav., 3, 111-149, 1971.

ALSTERMARK, B., GORSKA, T., LUNDBERG, A., AND PETTERSON, L. G. Integration in descending motor pathways controlling the forelimb in cat. 16. Visually guided switching of target reaching. Exp. Brain Res., 80, 1-11,1990.

BAHILL, A.T., ROCKENBROUGH, R.A. AND TROOST, B.T. Variablity and development of a normative data base for saccadic eye movements . Investig. Ophtalmol. and Visual Sci.,21,116-125,1981.

BECKER, W., AND JURGENS, R. Saccadic reactions to double-step stimuli: evidence for model feedback and continuous information uptake. In Basic mecanism of ocular mobility and their clinical implications. G. Lennerstrand and P. Bach-y-Rita (Eds) Pergamon Press Oxford and New-York.,1975, pp 519-524.

CAMPBELL, F.W. and WURTZ, R.H. Saccadic omission: why we do not see a grey-out during a saccadic movement? Vision Res. 18, 1297-1303, 1978.

CROSSMAN , E.R.F.W. AND GOODEVE, P.J. Feedback control of hand movement and Fitts' law. Paper presented at the Meeting of Exp. Soc., Cambridge, 1963: Reprinted in Q. J. Exp. Psychol.,35A, 251-278, 1983.

GEORGOPOULOS, A. P., KALASKA, J. F., AND MASSEY, J. T. Spatial trajectories and reaction times of aimed movements: effects of practice, uncertainty, and change in target location. J. Neurophysiol., 46, 725-743, 1981.

GOODALE, M. A., PELISSON, D., AND PRABLANC, C. Large adjustements in visually guided reaching do not depend on vision of the hand or perception of target displacement. Nature, 320, 748-750, 1986.

GUITTON, D., AND VOLLE, M. Gaze control in human: Eye-head coordination during orienting movements to targets within and beyond the oculomotor range. J. Neurophysiol., 58, 427-459, 1987.

LAURUTIS, V. P., AND ROBINSON, D. A. The vestibulo-ocular reflex during human saccadic eye movements. J. Physiol (London), 373, 209-233, 1986.

MEGAW, E.D Possible modification to a rapid on-going programmed manual response. Brain Res., 71, 425-441, 1974.

MUNOZ, D.P., GUITTON, D. AND PELISSON, D. Gaze control in the head-free cat. II. Spatio-temporal variations in the discharge of superior colliculus output neurons. Soc. Neurosci. Abstr.,15, 807, 1989.

MUNOZ, D.P., PELISSON, D. and GUITTON, D. Sites of neural activity moves on superior colliculus motor map during gaze shifts. Science, 1991, in press.

PAILLARD, J. The contribution of peripheral and central vision to visually guided reaching. In: Analysis of visual behavior, D.J. Ingle, M.A. Goodale and R.J.W. Mansfield (Eds.), MIT Press, Cambridge, Mass., 1982, pp 367-385.

PELISSON, D., PRABLANC, C., GOODALE, M. A., AND JEANNEROD, M. Visual control of reaching movements without vision of the limb : II Evidence for a fast unconscious process correcting the trajectory of the hand to the final position of a target step. Exp. Brain Res.,62, 303-311,1986.

PELISSON, D., PRABLANC, C., AND URQUIZAR, C. Vestibulo-ocular reflex inhibition and gaze saccade control characteristics during eye-head orientations in humans. J. Neurophysiol., 59, 997-1013, 1988.

PRABLANC, C., PELISSON, D. AND GOODALE, M. A. Visual control of reaching movements without vision of the limb.I. Role of retinal feedback of target position in guiding the hand. Exp. Brain Res. 62,293-302, 1986.

PRABLANC, C., ECHALLIER, J. F., AND MASSE, D. Error correcting mechanisms in large saccades. Vision Res. 18, 557-560, 1978.

PRABLANC, C., PELISSON, D., AND GOODALE, M. A. Visual control of reaching movements without vision of limb. I. Role of retinal feedback of target position in guiding the hand. Exp. Brain Res., 62, 293-302, 1986.

PRABLANC, C., AND PELISSON, D. Gaze saccade orienting and hand pointing are locked to their goal by quick internal loops. In Attention and Performance XIII, Motor representation and control, M. Jeannerod. (Ed.), Laurence Erlbaum, Hillsdale, New Jersey, 1990, p. 653-676.
SCHMIDT, R.A. A schema theory of discrete motor skill learning. Psycho. Rev., 82, 225-260, 1975.
SOECHTING, J.F., AND LACQUANITI, F. Modification of trajectory of a pointing movement in response to a change in target location. J. Neurophysiol. 49, 548-564, 1983.
SONDEREN, J. F. van, DENIER van der GON, J. J., AND GIELEN, C. C. A M Conditions determining early modification of motor programmes in responses to changes in target location. Exp. Brain Res. 71, 320-328, 1988.
VICARIO, D. S., AND GHEZ, C. The control of the rapid limb movement in the cat. IV. Updating of ongoing isometric responses. Experimental Brain Res., 55, 134-144, 1984.
WHEELESS, L., Jr., BOYNTON, R., AND COHEN, G. Eye movement responses to step and pulse step stimuli. J. Optical Soc. America 56: 956-960, 1966.

Tutorials in Motor Behavior II
G.E. Stelmach and J. Requin (Editors)

Effects of practice on reaching movements made to moving targets

J.R. Bloedel and S.I. Helms Tillery

Division of Neurobiology, Barrow Neurological Institute, 350 West Thomas Road, Phoenix, Arizona 85013

Abstract

These experiments were performed to examine the kinematics of trajectories characterizing the reaching movements used by human subjects to contact a moving target and to determine whether these trajectories are modified with practice. Each subject was asked to reach for a target accelerated to a specific velocity along a horizontal track on each of twenty consecutive trials. Three different target speeds were used, and movements made by both the right and left hand were examined. The kinematics of the movements were evaluated by determining the changes in the location of infrared-emitting diodes located on the shoulder, elbow, wrist and index finger. The data show the movements made to this type of moving target consist of several successive curved components and that these components do not vary qualitatively as the movement is practiced. However as movements were made to faster targets and in some cases as movements were practiced, the trajectory's curvature and the tangential velocity of the distal extremity increased.

1. INTRODUCTION

Most previous studies examining the characteristics of reaching movements focused on movements to stationary targets and usually employed paradigms in which the task was well practiced [5]. Furthermore, although exceptions have been reported (see Discussion), in most of these experiments the trajectories of movements made by the distal extremity between the starting point and the target were straight. Other reports indicate that the degree of curvature of the trajectory may be task and/or direction dependent [3,8]. Together these findings open the possibility that the trajectory of a given movement may vary as the strategy under which it is performed varies. The purpose of this study was to assess whether any changes occurred in the strategy characterizing arm movements to moving targets as human subjects attempted to improve their accuracy with practice. The experiments are based on the assumption that changes in strategy as the task is practiced will be reflected in modifications of the kinematics describing the trajectory of the limb's movement over successive trials.

Specifically these experiments were designed to test the hypothesis that the trajectories of limb movements directed towards moving targets are relatively invariant over several successive trials in which the movement is practiced. Based on this view, improvements in performance resulting from practice would not likely be accompanied by substantial changes in the movement strategy across trials, at least as characterized by the kinematics of the movement. The data in this study will indicate that the trajectories characterizing the movements of a given subject consist of several curved components which qualitatively remain unchanged despite alterations in target speed and/or practice. However, increases in the magnitude of the curvature covaried with increases in tangential velocity that occurred as movements were practiced and as movements were made to more rapidly moving targets.

2. METHODS

In these experiments each of thirteen young adult human subjects were seated in front of the apparatus on a chair. The subjects were not instructed how to orient the chair relative to the manipulandum and were told to seat themselves in as comfortable a manner as possible. Four infrared-emitting diodes (IREDs) were attached to the extremity using tape to secure them to the skin. One diode each was attached over the shoulder, elbow and wrist joints as well as near the tip of the index finger. These emitters were used together with a Watscope/Watsmart System to analyze several kinematic features of the limb's trajectory.

The subjects were instructed to make a movement to a moving target from a start position in response to a light signal. The moving target consisted of a circle 26 mm in diameter moving along a fixed horizontal track. The origin switch was located 7.5 cm in front of and 15.5 cm below the target track. Once the subject was in contact with the origin switch for at least two seconds, a "ready" light was lit, and the movement of the target was initiated. The target moved slowly until it arrived at a point along the track initially unknown to the subject. When it reached this point the target was accelerated to one of three predetermined target velocities. As the target passed a specified point, a blue "go" lamp was lit, indicating to the subject that a movement to the target could be made. Usually the blue "go" lamp was lit simultaneously with the initial acceleration of the target. Both the velocity and size of the target were selected so that the successful execution of the reaching movement was challenging to each subject. The subject was instructed to contact the target before it reached the end of the track, and no instruction was given concerning the speed of the movement nor the manner in which the movement should be executed.

Each experiment consisted of three sequences of twenty consecutive trials, each sequence at one of three specified terminal target velocities. Reaching movements made to targets moving to the right and to the left were assessed in the same sitting. Data were analyzed initially by examining the stick figures representing the movements of the extremity to the target across all trials. In order to compare the features of the trajectories characterizing movements made in different trials, graphic methods were developed to compare two or more normalized trajectories generated by an individual subject. For this comparison the trajectories were normalized to the average length of all the trajectories being compared. The characteristics of the trajectories of each joint were then compared qualitatively based on visual inspection of the plots.

In addition tangential velocity was calculated for the movement of the most distal IRED mounted on the index finger based on changes in its position on successive data frames, which were read usually at a frequency of 100 Hz. The changes in this measurement were then compared over the succession of trials performed by each subject.

3. RESULTS

3.1. Curved Nature of the Trajectories

A consistent observation across all subjects was the curved nature of the trajectories characterizing the movements of the distal extremity in this paradigm. The characteristics of an arm movement to a target moving at 75 cm/sec are illustrated in Figure 1. The stick figure in A shows the characteristics of the movement as viewed from above the subject's head with the target located at the top of the figure. In B and C two successive components of the same movement are shown in views from the side with the target located on the right. In the first part of the movement (B) the subject moved upward from the start position (S) with a movement consisting of at least two curved components. As the finger left the start position there was an initial curved movement almost in the vertical plane (compare A and B). The curvature then reversed as the finger moved rapidly to the highest position. In the second component of the movement (C) the hand moved rapidly toward the target (T) once maximum height was achieved. The successive changes in movement velocity can be ascertained qualitatively because the spacing between each stick figure is inversely proportional to the velocity of the limb, since data points were collected every 10 msec. It is apparent that the velocity of the movement increased substantially as the limb moved horizontally, again along a curved path. As the target was approached the limb decelerated.

In general the succession of curvatures characterizing the trajectory provided a "signature" for the reaching movements performed by any given subject. The characteristic differences in these "signatures" across subjects were not studied systematically in these experiments. The trajectories of some subjects were quite different from those shown in Figure 1. Others generated movements with sequences of curved components similar to those in this example.

The effect of practice on the trajectories of movements made towards targets moving at various speeds is illustrated in Figure 2. A-B and C-D show reaches during the first and last trial to a target (T) moving at 75 and 90 cm/sec, respectively. In all thirteen subjects participating in this study the curvature of the trajectory near its midpoint increased as the movement was practiced. Furthermore as shown clearly in C and D, the curvature near the

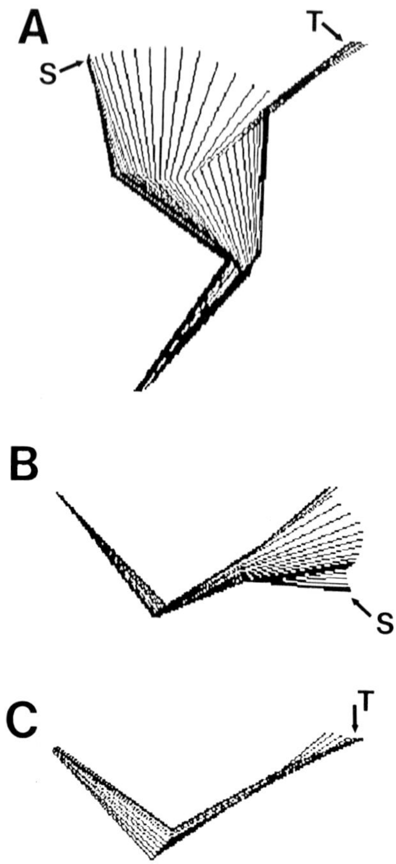

Figure 1. Basic characteristics of arm movements to moving targets. Detailed descriptions for this and subsequent figures are provided in the text.

midpoint of the movement was greatest for practiced movements toward targets moving at the fastest speeds.

Changes in temporal characteristics of the movements such as movement time and reaction time did not consistently change with practice across all subjects. Very likely this was due to the fact that no instructions regarding movement speed or speed with which the movement should be initiated were given. Figure 2 provides an example in which the subject decreased movement time as the movement was practiced at the faster speed and contacted the target after it moved a shorter distance horizontally (C and D).

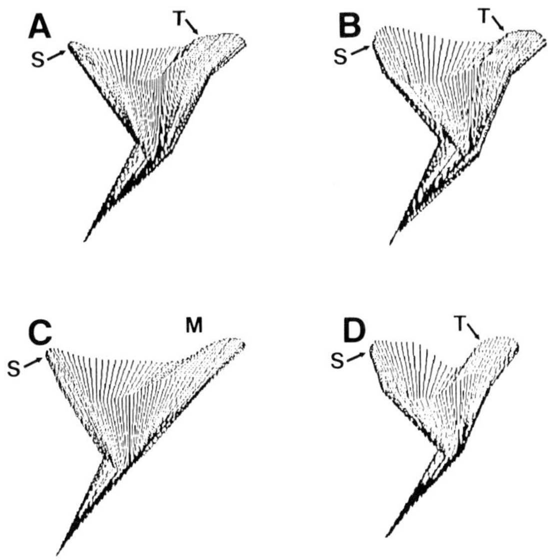

Figure 2. Effects of practice on movements to targets moving at different speeds.

In addition no differences have been observed to date between trajectories made in successful and unsuccessful trials. Note that in C the subject missed the target in the first of twenty trials.

The effects of practice on the velocity with which the movement was performed is shown more clearly in the plots of Figure 3. These data illustrate the relationship between tangential velocity and the absolute movement time for the IRED located on the index finger during movement execution. Zero on the abscissa is the time at which the movement was initiated. Characteristic of the findings in most subjects, the peak tangential velocity increased as the movement was practiced (compare trial 1 and trial 20). Furthermore the maximum tangential velocity occurred near the midpoint of the movement time. Note also that the velocity of the finger at the time of target contact also increased with practice. The contours of these tangential velocity plots as well as the comparative durations of the movements made in the first and twentieth trials were strikingly similar despite the intervening practice.

3.2. Characteristics of Normalized Trajectories

To further examine whether the basic features of a trajectory are progressively modified during practice or whether a rather consistent

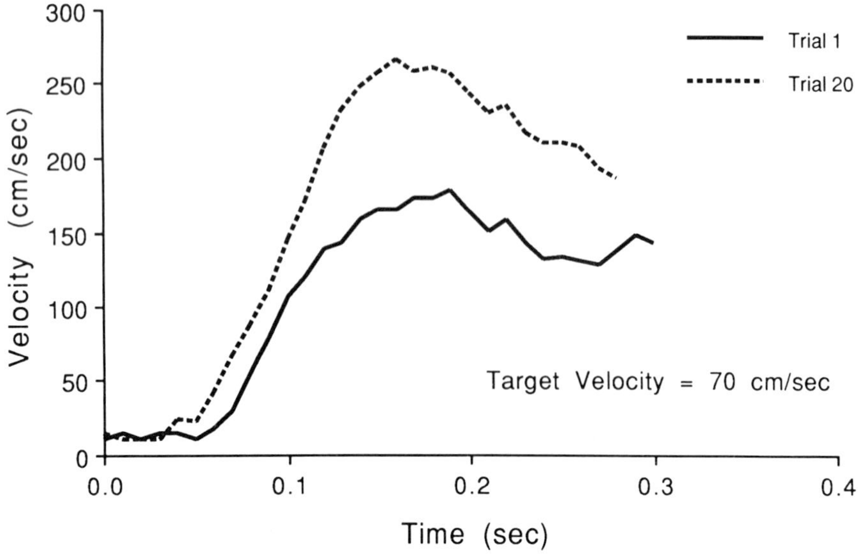

Figure 3. Effects of practice on movement velocity.

envelope can be used to describe the kinematics of the movements, the trajectories made by each subject over each twenty-trial session were spatially normalized on the basis of trajectory length and subsequently compared graphically. Figure 4 compares the trajectories of the movement of the index finger during the first and twentieth trials to a target moving at 90 cm/sec. The stick figures characterizing the same two movements are shown in Figure 2, C and D. Both the three-dimensional plots as well as their projection on the X, Y and Z planes illustrate the decrease in the radius of curvature in at least two regions of the trajectory as the movement was practiced over the twenty trials. Due to the fact that the target was missed on the first trial, there is a clear difference in the end point of the trajectories on the Z axis. As pointed out above, despite the fact that the subject failed to contact the target, the contour of the movement trajectory was very similar to that observed for movements in which the target was contacted.

Across all thirteen subjects the only variation from this principle was observed for movements made by some subjects to targets moving at the slowest velocity. Figure 5 shows the movements in the first and last trial to a target moving at 70 cm/sec for the same subject whose movements were shown in Figure 4. Note that there is a much greater difference in the structure of these two trajectories than for those in Figure 4 characterizing the movements in the first and twentieth trial to targets moving at a higher velocity. At the slower velocity (Figure 5) the movement in trial 1 clearly employed a much straighter trajectory over approximately the first 75% of the hand path.

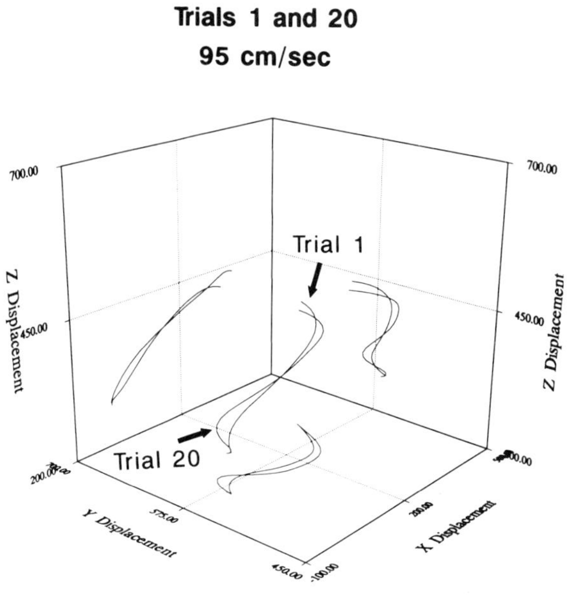

Figure 4. Three-dimensional plots of normalized trajectories illustrating the effects of practice.

3.3. Comparison of Movements to Stationary and Moving Targets

To determine whether the curved nature of the trajectories observed in these experiments is due to the fact that the movements are performed to a moving target or whether this characteristic is dependent only on the spatial relationship between the start point and the target used in this paradigm, trajectories generated by movements performed by each of two subjects were compared under two conditions: (1) movements to a moving target using the paradigm described above and (2) movements to a stationary target located at the position it was contacted during trials employing moving targets. If the curved trajectories reflected the fact that the movements were made to moving targets, the properties of the trajectories should be quite different under these two conditions. However if the curved trajectories were dependent only upon the characteristics of the target and start point and the distance and direction between them, the limb's trajectories should be fairly comparable under these conditions.

Figure 6 illustrates the stick figures characterizing movements of one subject to a stationary target (A) and to a moving target contacted very close to the same location in two different trials (B and C). In this experiment five

IREDs were placed on the subject's extremity. In addition to the location of the IREDs described in Methods, an IRED was placed directly over the knuckle located just below the index finger. Notice the similarities in the curvature describing the hand paths of the movements made under these two conditions. Interestingly there are modest differences in the trajectories of the wrist, elbow, and shoulder joints despite the similarities in the hand paths.

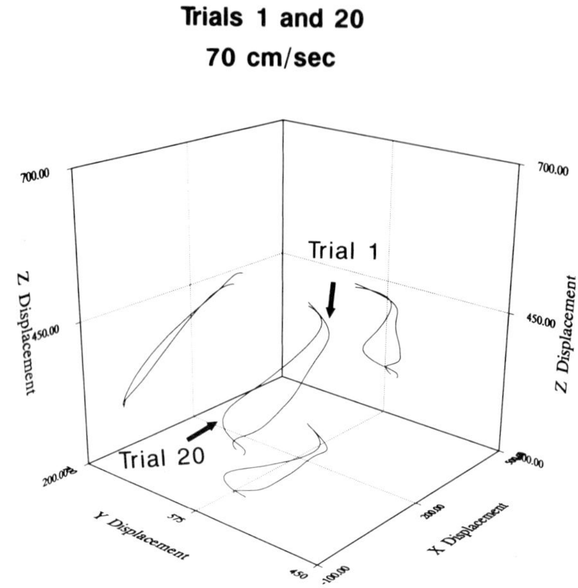

Figure 5. Normalized trajectories of movements made by the same subject to a slower moving target.

3.4. An Anecdote

Several anecdotal observations obtained in a few subjects further emphasize the fact that reaching movements of the type executed in this paradigm are inherently curved. In the movements shown in Figure 7, the subject was told to contact the target as quickly as possible after the "go" light was lit. Under these circumstances the speed-accuracy tradeoff was clearly changed in the direction of increased movement speed. In the trials shown in Figure 7, the subject's first attempt to hit the target failed. The subject then made a second movement toward the target in an attempt to contact it before it reached the end of the track. On the second attempt the subject successfully contacted the target (T). Notice that in both instances the trajectory was dramatically curved. This observation is consistent with those described above in which the curvature increased as the subject practiced reaching movements to the faster moving targets. Interestingly this strategy required that the distal extremity move a greater distance in pursuing the missed target than would have been the case if the hand had moved along the board in a relatively straight line. Although observations such as the one shown in Figure 7 were not a systematic inclusion in these experiments, they further emphasize the inherently curved nature of the trajectories which characterize movements of the distal extremities in this paradigm.

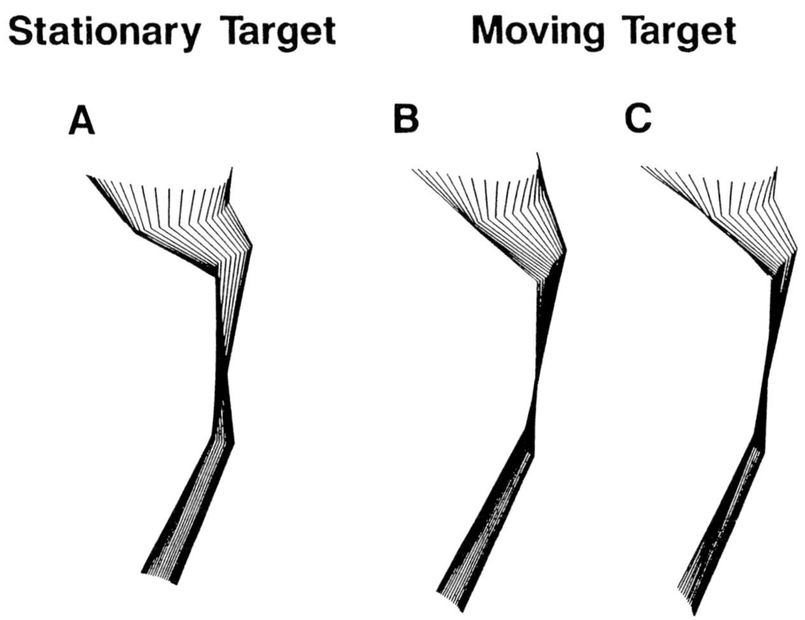

Figure 6. Comparison of movements to stationary and moving targets.

4. DISCUSSION

The two principal findings in this study were: (1) that the trajectories characterizing the reaching movements performed in this paradigm were predominantly curved and (2) that there were only minimal modifications in the characteristics of these trajectories as the movement was practiced. The predominance of curved trajectories in the reaching movements performed in this study were initially somewhat surprising because of the predominance of straight trajectories in much of the related literature [5].

However, curved trajectories have been reported in several studies performed under a variety of experimental and behavioral conditions. Curved trajectories characterizing movements to moving targets have been reported recently by Bairstow [1] as well as by von Hofsten [14] and by Forsstrom and von Hofsten [7]. In a recent study examining the relationship between the discharge of motor cortical units and reaching movements made in three-

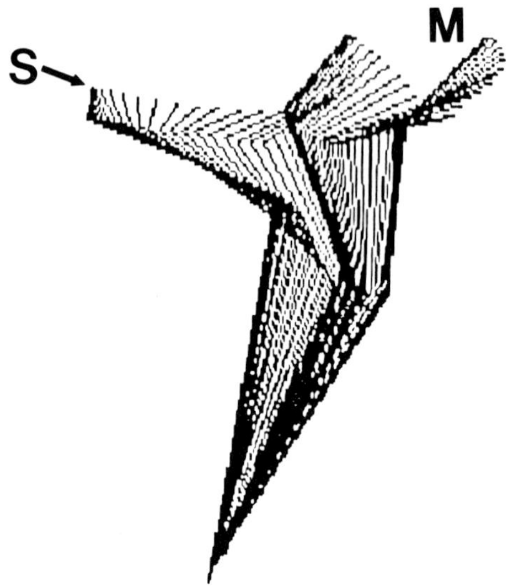

Figure 7. Curved trajectories while "chasing" a target.

dimensional space by trained monkeys, curved trajectories were also found [3]. Even in studies reporting predominantly straight trajectories, curved trajectories also were observed, particularly when movements were performed in specific directions [6,8,11].

The basis for the curvature in the trajectories observed in our study has not yet been systematically addressed. The data in Figure 6 clearly indicate that the curved trajectories were not due to the fact that the subjects were reaching for moving targets. The hand paths characterizing movements to the same points in space were the same independent of whether or not the target was moving.

Several postulates have been proposed to explain the occurrence of curved trajectories. Flash [6], in detailing the equilibrium trajectory hypothesis, argued that curved trajectories may be dependent upon the relation between the movement's direction and the characteristics of the stiffness fields measured at the hand at various limb positions. A strategy minimizing torque change in the generation of reaching movements has also been proposed as a basis for curved trajectories [11]. Applications of tensor theory to the generation of limb movements also provide a rationale for movements of this type [2,10]. Specifically they may be dependent on the characteristics of the coordinate transformation required to execute an intended goal-directed movement and the extent to which the metric is updated during the course of the movement.

The curved characteristics of the trajectories in reaching movements also may be related to differences in the experimental paradigms used to study the reaching movements. Interestingly many of the studies reporting straight trajectories used paradigms that either provided support for the distal extremity using devices such as a draftsman's arm or restricted movements to a two-dimensional plane (see [5] for review). In contrast, the paradigm employed in our studies as well as the others reporting curved trajectories assess movements made in free space with no support of the distal extremity.

Several studies in the literature suggest that the curved trajectories may result from the fact that the reaching movements made across a substantial work space may consist of multiple segments. The observations of Viviani and Terzuolo [13]; Lacquaniti et al. [9]; and Bairstow [1], as well as those from von Hofsten's laboratory [14,7] all provide illustrations of the segmentation of complex reaching movements. These data also illustrate that segmentation need not be dependent upon the fact that the movements are made in free space. The extent of the segmentation may be related to several factors. Clearly the complexity of the movement is important [13,9]. Bairstow [1] argued that segmentation may reflect changes in movement direction due to succession of improved estimates of movement velocity. Movement speed also appears to affect the extent to which a movement is segmented [4].

Based on characteristics of the movements performed by subjects in our paradigm and the related findings in the literature, our working hypothesis is that the curved trajectories are task- and target-dependent. In this paradigm the target consists of a disk protruding from the board in which the track is located. Interestingly the increased curvature of trajectories occurring with practice resulted in the terminal portion of the hand path becoming progressively more perpendicular to the target surface. This characteristic may reflect an implicit strategy that optimizes the force applied to the switch when it is initially contacted. The curvature may also reflect a strategy that minimizes the complexity of torques and patterns of muscle activation required to generate the movement [8]. Additional studies will be required to delineate the specific basis for this observation.

Interestingly the effects of practice on the movements performed by these subjects were minimal, producing principally quantitative changes characterized by increases in curvature rather than qualitative changes that could reflect a change in movement strategy. The changes in curvature typically observed were comparable to those shown in Figure 4. Only when movements were performed at the slowest speed were trajectories observed that could be considered qualitatively different from those characterizing movements to targets moving at faster speeds (Figure 5). This finding may imply that the consistent properties of trajectories are maintained for movements performed above certain velocities. Additional studies will be required to determine if this is true.

The absence of substantial modifications in movement parameters with practice is consistent with the observations of Viviani et al. [12]. These investigators required human subjects to trace on a planar surface scribbles that had been generated previously by a different individual. By following a backlit target, subjects were required to retrace the movements using either the same tangential velocities employed by the person making the original scribble or a constant tangential velocity throughout the trial. In these studies in which the movement path was specified, practice produced very little modification in the characteristics of a given subject's movement. Each subject developed a specifiable and somewhat individualistic strategy for performing the task. This was most often characterized by a specific temporal lag in the pursuit tracing movement relative to the movement of the target.

Taken together these studies imply that subjects tend to adapt strategies for performing goal-directed arm movements which are relatively fixed. In these experiments the principal characteristics of the trajectory, namely its regions of curvature, remained qualitatively the same with practice. As emphasized above, only modifications in trajectory which could be construed as a tendency to approach the target with the hand path more perpendicular to the target surface were observed. Furthermore the anecdotal finding reported in Figure 7 emphasizes the dramatically curved trajectory that is specified even when the subject is attempting to contact the target as rapidly as possible. In this example a dramatically curved trajectory occurs despite the fact that the extremity must move over a substantially greater distance than if a straight line trajectory were selected.

In summary these experiments demonstrate that the spatial characteristics of a trajectory characterizing the arm movements made by human subjects to moving targets do not vary substantially over the trials in which the subject optimizes the performance of the movement. The observed trajectory is substantially curved, and the envelope of the trajectory is not substantially modified with practice despite the fact that increases in curvature and tangential velocity do occur. These inherent characteristics of the hand path associated with the trajectory are dependent only upon the start point and target location and are not a consequence of the fact that the movement is made to a moving target.

5. ACKNOWLEDGEMENT

This research was supported by NIH Grant No. NS21958. Mr. Tillery was supported by a Barrow Neurological Institute Undergraduate Student Fellowship during the conduct of these experiments and is presently enrolled in the Neuroscience Training Program at the University of Minnesota.

6. REFERENCES

1 P.J. Bairstow, Human Movement Science, 6 (1987) 205.
2 J.R. Bloedel, S.I. Tillery and A.J. Pellionisz, Neurosci. Abstr., 14 (1988) 952.
3 R. Caminiti, P.B. Johnson and A. Urbano, J. Neurosci., 10 (1990) 2039.
4 W.G. Darling, K.J. Cole and J.H. Abbs, Exp.Brain Res., 73 (1988) 225.
5 A.P. Georgopoulos, Ann. Rev. Neurosci., 9 (1986) 147.
6 T. Flash, Brain Behav. Evol., 33 (1989) 63.
7 A. Forsstrom and C. von Hofsten, Develop. Med. and Child Neurol., 24 (1982) 653.
8 F. Lacquaniti, J.F. Soechting and C.A. Terzuolo, Neurosci., 17 (1986) 313.
9 F. Lacquaniti, C. Terzuolo and P. Viviani, Acta Psychol., 54 (1983) 115.
10 A.J. Pellionisz in J. R. Bloedel, J. Dichgans and W. Precht (eds.), Cerebellar Functions, Springer-Verlag, Berlin, 1985.
11 Y. Uno, M. Kawato and R. Suzuki, Biol. Cybern.,61 (1989) 89.
12 P. Viviani, P. Campadelli and P. Mounoud, J. Exp. Psych., 13 (1987) 62.
13 P. Viviani and C. Terzuolo, Neurosci., 7 (1982) 431.
14 C. Von Hofsten, J. Human Movement Studies, 5 (1979) 160.

Tutorials in Motor Behavior II
G.E. Stelmach and J. Requin (Editors)

Constraints, phases and sensorimotor processing in prehension

Christine L. MacKenzie[1]

School of Kinesiology, Simon Fraser University, Burnaby, British Columbia, Canada V5A 1S6

Abstract

The dextrous and versatile performance of human prehension can be viewed as emerging from a large multidimensional constraint space that includes: high level constraints such as goals of movements, and knowledge based on past experiences; physical constraints such as frictional and gravitational forces, object properties and environmental characteristics; and sensorimotor constraints relating to the performer's anatomy and physiology. Reaching and grasping are controlled through parallel, distributed computations by the nervous system, given these constraints. Jeannerod (1981, 1984) distinguished 2 parallel visuomotor channels, one for transporting the hand to the location of an object and one for shaping the hand appropriately to grasp the object. These are captured by Arbib (1981, 1985) and Paillard (1982) in control models for grasping. Experiments are reported that deal with the relative contributions of central and peripheral vision, proprioceptive, tactile and haptic information when manipulating the object characteristics of size and weight. Results indicate that central vision is critical for distinguishing object size for grip calibration; without central vision, grasp aperture and limb transport are both affected and subjects adopt a tactile strategy. In contrast, peripheral vision is important for calibrating object distance; without peripheral vision, subjects consistently undershoot the object. An important distinction is found between object properties which can be visually determined (e.g., size), and those which may be visually inferred, but must be haptically determined (e.g., weight). Further, evidence is provided for unique control processes prior to and after contact with the object. We consider the differential contributions of the senses in providing information during the various phases of prehension.

Grasping objects is a fundamental human skill, used in eating, grooming, dressing and other activities of daily living. Grasping tools and objects also provides a mode for work, communication, creative, and generative expression, as in writing, painting, sculpting, woodworking, keyboarding, and playing musical instruments. The goal of this chapter is to examine the constraints on prehension, the role of vision, proprioception and haptics, the

---

[1] Thanks to Thea Iberall, Barbara Sivak, and Patricia Weir for discussions. The experiments, supported by NSERC Grant #A8303, were conducted at U. of Waterloo.

effects of object characteristics and task requirements and to identify unique phases in prehension through combined analyses of the kinematics of prehensile motions, and the forces applied during grasping.

1. CONSTRAINTS ON HUMAN PREHENSION

We define prehension as the application of functionally effective forces to an object for a given task, consonant with numerous constraints (Iberall & MacKenzie, 1990). The dextrous and versatile performance of human prehension can be viewed as emerging from a large multidimensional constraint space. Roboticists, computer modellers, theorists and experimentalists seem to be at odds currently in terms of the important variables examined in the quantification of motor control. It has been argued (Nelson, 1983; MacKenzie, 1985; MacKenzie & Marteniuk, 1985; Marteniuk, MacKenzie, Jeannerod, Dugas & Athenes, 1987; Newell, 1986, this volume) that interactions are occurring among multiple performance constraints. Nelson (1983) suggested that dynamic models, such as that of Hollerbach (1980), are inadequate for explaining human movement unless they also include both the performance constraints and the objectives affecting the neural and neuromuscular inputs.

MacKenzie and Marteniuk (1985) described two types of constraints: those variables that constrain the use of feedback and those due to structural limitations that affect the preparation and execution of goal directed movement. These are not limitations in a negative sense. Rather, they limit the possible solutions available in constraint space for movement organization. MacKenzie and Marteniuk (1985) emphasized the interaction between knowledge constraints (which includes a person's experience and movement objectives) and the constraints of biological structure. Marteniuk, et al. (1987) make even more explicit the notions of task constraints and conditions of speed and accuracy. Taking a task-specific view of movement planning and control, a task is defined as the interaction of the performer with the environment under given movement goals. This view predicts that movement is optimized and specific to the unique requirements that arise from an individual interacting with the environment.

In order to study the complex interaction between movement goals, object properties, environmental characteristics, and the performer's biological structure and experience, it can be argued that there are different levels of analysis within this constraint space (after Marr, 1981). We have grouped these constraints, or levels of analyses, into three broad categories, as seen in Table 1. This list expands and reorganizes the constraints listed in MacKenzie and Marteniuk (1985) and Marteniuk et al. (1987). Note that higher level goals and functional objectives work together with harder constraints. For example, when one studies the constitution of a stable grasp, she is detailing the constraints imposed by an implicit functional goal 'not to drop the object.' Instructions such as, 'move as quickly and accurately as possible', impose constraints on how to plan and effect the movement, given the person's biomechanics and sensorimotor constraints. Even physicians and therapists, when evaluating impairment of hand function, make distinctions between physical and functional evaluations (Jones, 1989; Swanson, Hagert & Scanson,

1983). Having the multiple constraint influences acting on prehensile systems, provides a more complete approach to prehension, and builds bridges among those studying at different levels of analysis. For example, roboticists can develop higher level control of dextrous robot hands, animators can develop algorithms constraining possible configurations, therapists can explore different techniques and kinesiologists can refine further their models of human performance.

Table 1
Sources of constraints on grasping. Movement constraints and goals act to limit the ways in which the human hand is controlled in prehension (from Iberall & MacKenzie, 1990, 1991).

Group	Level of Analysis	Examples
High Level	Social/Cultural	don't stick out elbows; stick out little finger
	Motivational	thirst; anger
	Informational	convey affection, anger
	Functional	don't drop object; manipulate object; 'move as quickly and as accurately as possible'
Physical	Object Properties	intrinsic (texture, surface length, weight, etc); extrinsic (location, distance, environment, etc)
	Biomechanical/ Mechanical	kinematics; dynamics; limitations on force generation due to bones, muscles, tendons, ligaments, skin; effect and use of pads
Sensori-motor	Neural	temporal and spatial limitations on CNS; pyramidal tract needed for fractionated finger movements; sensory info needed to sustain movement; sensory information needed to preshape hand; tonic vibration reflex
	Perceptual	types, locations, and response characteristics of receptors; numerous tactile receptors in pulps with small receptive fields
	Anatomical/ Physiological	structural limitations on movements, directions, and extents; length of phalanges; additional muscles in index and little finger; pads; anatomical couplings
	Evolutionary/ Developmental	evolutionary pressures; five fingers; pyramidal tract develops in about eighth month

1.1. High level constraints

At the highest level, four classes of constraints in living systems can be grouped together. These constraints are imposed for a variety of reasons. There are probably large individual differences. The constraints are labeled as follows: semiotic/informational, motivational, social/cultural, and functional/intentional.

Semiotic, symbolic, or emotional information may be conveyed in the way an object is grasped (Nespoulous & Lecours, 1986). For example, one might hold a cigarette in a suggestive manner. Anxiety or anger may be communicated by gripping an object tightly. Motivations, such as needs being satiated, may add an urgency to the movement. As well, sociocultural constraints create boundaries on acceptable behavior. Refined behavioral interactions with objects in one culture might be taboo in another. For example, sticking out the little finger as one grasps a teacup may be a sign of good upbringing in a culture. On the other hand, sticking out one's elbow while reaching might be an invasion of someone else's extrapersonal space.

While this is merely anecdotal evidence for such effects on prehension, kinesiologists and psychologists have begun to explore the functional, goal related issues. Movement constraints act within and around the intentions of the performer, which delineate goals for a movement. An example would be the 'sherry-glass response' (Traub, Rothwell & Marsden, 1980). Subjects were asked to maintain their thumb and index finger a few millimeters from the rim of a full sherry glass. A perturbation was made to the wrist sufficient to cause the hand to hit the glass and knock it over. A short-latency grab response (50 msec) occurred in the thumb muscle in response to the perturbation, thereby saving the glass from being knocked over. However, the response was observed only when the subject's intent was to prevent the glass from falling over. Traub et al. argued that this suggests the presence of a grab reflex, where the digits respond within a time too short to be voluntary, flexing in order to maintain contact but only if contact is the person's intent. Related results were reported by Winstein, Abbs and Patashnik (1991) who found that the grasping forces prior to and in response to perturbations of object weight were a function of instructions 'to hold' or 'to let go' of the object.

Intent can emerge from the experimenter's request to the subject to perform a certain task. In grasping and aiming tasks, Marteniuk et al. (1987) showed how intention, context, and object properties affect the timing of kinematic parameters of prehensile movements. The first experiment varied the task (pointing to a target or grasping a disk); the second one varied object properties (grasping a compliant tennis ball or a fragile light bulb); the third one varied movement intent or task goal (grasping to place or grasping to throw). Note that in all cases, movement was measured from start of movement just to completion of the grasp. Using Fitts' Law (Fitts, 1954) to equate the index of difficulty, it was observed that the grasping took longer than pointing. The percentage of time spent in the deceleration phase (after peak velocity) was longer for grasping than pointing, for grasping the light bulb than grasping the tennis ball, and for grasping when placing than when throwing the grasped objects. They argued that this relative lengthening of the deceleration phase of the movement could be due to the requirement for "precision". Less variability between conditions was seen in the early or acceleration phase of the movement, and more variability during the deceleration phase. They suggested that the early part of the movement is more likely to be directly influenced by stereotyped movement planning or programming, while the latter part of the movement, during the deceleration phase, uses more sensorimotor adjustments for controlling the movement, giving rise to more variability. Increasing precision requirements of a task may induce subjects to use more sensory information, particularly in the 'homing in' part of the task.

In summary, people grasp objects to achieve some functional goal, to convey some information, or to satisfy some internal motivations, and the movement is carried out within a socio-cultural context. While goals in the strictest sense are not hard constraints (people do drop objects), their effect on human prehensile behavior can be seen in the choice of prehensile postures and the selection of movement parameters. Because multiple grasping solutions are possible, the controller is faced with the question of how best to achieve the goals of the task, given biological structure, and physical constraints.

1.2. Physical constraints

The laws of physics, captured in a variety of equations, create limitations on the planning and control of prehension. Whether or not the central nervous system solves these equations directly, they detail the meaning of movement within inertial reference frames. As well, they express the forces in making contact with objects in the environment. In the example where the implicit functional constraint is to 'not drop the object', a posture must be chosen that effects a stable grasp. The three requirements for a stable grasp are (Fearing, 1986): 1) the object must be in equilibrium (no net forces and torques); 2) the direction of the applied forces must be within the cone of friction, which is twice the angle between the arc-tangent of the coefficient of static friction and a normal to the surface; and 3) it should be possible to increase the magnitude of the grasping force to prevent any displacement due to an arbitrary applied force. Creating a stable grasp means taking into account active forces and torques as well as passive ones caused by the frictional components of the skin contacting the object surface. In addition, counteracting forces must be separated into their grasping and manipulation components (Yoshikawa & Nagai, 1990). If the applied force is too powerful, there is both unnecessary expenditure of energy and the possibility of crushing/breaking the object. What is being optimized in human systems is a question (Nelson, 1983).

Hand postures afford different ways to apply forces. Biomaterials such as bones, muscles, tendons, ligaments, and skin create limitations on static and dynamic force generation. For example, skin has viscoelastic and lubricious properties that affect the frictional component of force generation (Bowden & Tabor, 1967; Moore, 1972). The coefficient of static friction, measured by various researchers (Comaish & Bottoms, 1971; Dinc, Ettles, Calabrese & Scarton, 1990; Johansson & Westling, 1984; Buchholz et al., 1988), is a function of the properties of both the skin surface and object surface, thus constraining the grasping forces for establishing a stable grasp. Johansson and Westling (1984) looked at precision grasping of objects with different textures and different weights. If the object's surface texture is sandpaper, then there is a higher frictional component to the interactive forces than if the surface texture is suede or silk. They looked at the ratio between the grip force (force normal to the object's surface) and the load force (force tangential to the object surface, in line with gravitational force). The value of this ratio below which the object will slip out of the fingers is called the slip ratio. Johansson and Westling found evidence that subjects maintain a safety margin above this ratio, and even use one of two strategies for maintaining a safety margin: either the safety margin is a constant fraction or else a constant absolute value of the grip force. While the slip ratio is a physical constraint, maintaining a safety margin above it is a functional constraint, imposed by some goal of the performer (in fact, for Johansson and Westling to measure the slip ratio, they had to request that their subjects slowly separate the thumb and index finger until the object drops, which is a difficult task to perform).

Object properties and the object's spatial relationship to the individual can affect the chosen posture and applied forces. In his discussion of visuomotor channels, Jeannerod (1981, 1984) made a distinction between intrinsic and extrinsic properties of objects. Extrinsic properties are those spatially related to the person (i.e., location, distance, angle, etc.) and would include support constraints, such as a table supporting a surface, and other obstacle constraints (forcing one to reach around another object). Intrinsic properties of the object include size, shape and other visible characteristics. Lederman and Klatzky (1987) have shown how, through stereotypic hand motions called exploratory procedures, subjects can extract perceptual information about object properties relevant to the task. These include surface properties (texture, hardness, and temperature), structural properties (shape, volume, weight), and functional properties (part motion, specific function). In terms of the constraints that object properties impose on prehension, examples are numerous: object shape can delimit grasp postures and the number of fingers potentially contacting a surface; the weight of the object can determine the type and strength of grip; and the availability of object surfaces will constrain the orientation of the reach and potential contact locations.

With respect to object size, Jeannerod and Decety (1990) examined the role of object related retinal information by having subjects match with hand and finger movements those object properties relevant to grasping. In one experiment subjects had to match the diameter of a target object by extending the fingers (increasing the aperture between thumb and index finger) as if they were going to grasp the object. They saw neither the hand, nor any visual surround, only the target object. The size of this matching aperture correlated highly with the diameter of the object, although there were individual differences in the size of variable and constant errors of the matching aperture from the aperture actually used for grasping. Similarly, when subjects are actually grasping objects, there is a reliable linear increase in maximum aperture prior to closure as object diameter increases, at least for cylindrical objects, and to the biomechanical limit of handspan (Jeannerod, 1984, Marteniuk, this volume, Marteniuk, Leavitt, MacKenzie & Athenes, 1990; von Hofsten & Ronnqvist, 1989).

Other object properties have an effect on force generation also. Cochran and Riley (1986) found that handle shape affects the force exerted: higher forces were seen with irregularly shaped handles (rectangular and triangular) than with uniformly shaped ones (circular). For a given flat surface, the surface area available for grasping has been shown to affect the grasping forces (Weir, 1991).

In summary, prehensile behaviors are subject to the constraints imposed by the laws of physics. Given high level goals, and physical laws, grasping is constrained by the anatomical and physiological characteristics of the body, including cutaneous, soft tissue, musculoskeletal, and neural aspects. We now consider some of these constraints explicitly.

1.3. Sensorimotor constraints

The hand of *Homo sapiens sapiens* represents millions of years of evolutionary pressures, changing it from a tool of tree-dwellers into what it is today. Holder (1983) noted, from studying 145 limb skeletons of amphibians, reptiles, birds, and mammals, that the overall skeletal (and muscular) pattern has varied little in 350 million years, even though the limbs have become adapted for different functions. LeGros-Clark (1959) noted the development of the pentadactyl (five-fingered) hand, the replacement of claws by nails, and the specialization of the finger pads. Other signs of refined functionality have been noted as in the remodeling of joints (Lewis, 1977; Marzke, 1983), and intradigital proportions between phalanges (Musgrave, 1971). These, and other characteristics of hand structure, such as the obvious presence of five fingers, are evolutionary constraints in the sense that they have modified the organization of prehension over the eons (see LeGros-Clark, 1959 and Napier, 1962 for further reading). Today, as one moment in time, they have left the human hand with a variety of highly asymmetrical, anatomical and physiological features and constraints.

The anatomy and physiology of the hand and arm create structural limitations on possible joint configurations, movements, directions and extents. In the robotics literature, the directions and extents of movements are referred to as the 'workspace'. In the human literature, the region of extrapersonal space where prehension may occur has been termed 'grasping space' (Grusser, 1986). Grasping space is a function of motions about the shoulder, the elbow and wrist joints of the arm, given that the body is stationary.

Although the hand has over 25 degrees of freedom, many are coupled by the nature of the ligamentous structure and location of tendon insertions (Kapandji, 1982). For example, although each finger has four degrees of freedom, they are not individually controllable. The flexors tend to work together (Tubiana, 1981): when the index finger begins to close in toward the thumb in a precision grip, the flexion of the proximal interphalangeal joint releases tension on the retinacular ligament, allowing flexion of the distal interphalangeal joint. Flexion of the proximal interphalangeal joint puts the intrinsic muscles under tension, initiating flexion of the metacarpo-phalangeal joint. In another example, the intrinsic lumbrical muscle runs from the extrinsic flexor tendon to the extensor tendon and plays multiple roles in flexion and extension (Ranney & Wells, 1988). It is primarily responsible for interphalangeal joint extension, by decreasing the flexor force. Because of its attachment to tendons moving in opposite directions and the great number of muscle spindles (sensors), Ranney and Wells suggested that the lumbrical muscle may be monitoring the rate of hand closing during grasp.

A final feature of the hand's anatomy is the skin and the underlying fatty pads. Skin consists of multiple layers and tissues, notably the outer epidermis and inner dermis (Thomine, 1981). Palmar skin, which is thick, tough, resistant to pressure, and good for complying with objects, can be contrasted with dorsal skin, which is fine, supple, and does not impede mobility in flexion. The palmar skin, unlike the dorsal skin, is covered with epidermal ridges and exocrine sweat glands, and contains malleable 'fat pads'. At the distal ends of the fingers and thumb are the specialized pulps (Glicenstein & Dardour, 1981). Shearing forces at the pulps are resisted by strong interdigitating folds between the epidermis and dermis, where interpapillary ridges prevent the epidermis from sliding over the dermis (Quilliam, 1978). It is particularly noteworthy that the trajectory followed by the fingers during thumb opposition brings the finger pulps into the same plane as the thumb pulp (Kapandji, 1982). In perturbation studies of rapid pinch movements, Cole and Abbs (1987) observed that subjects consistently brought the finger pulps into contact although this was not part of the task instructions. To do this in response to the thumb perturbation required the reciprocal adjustments at two index finger joints, an adjustment more complex than a single joint one. The reason for this could be due to a higher level goal.

In terms of the nervous system, its anatomy and physiology create temporal and spatial physical limitations. The types of receptors (photoreceptors, cutaneous and proprioceptors), and their spatial and temporal response characteristics, serve as constraints in the control process. There are differential numbers of cell types in central and peripheral regions of the retina (Davson, 1980). Numerous tactile receptors are found in the finger pulps, more so than most other parts of the body, thus giving the CNS much information about the objects with which the fingers come into contact (Johansson & Vallbo, 1983; Vallbo & Johansson, 1984). Receptors having small and well-defined receptive fields are especially dense in the finger pulps. Westling and Johansson (1987) observed that at higher grip forces (when the skin is less compliant) these receptors are less responsive. In terms of proprioception, receptors in the muscles, tendons, and joint capsules signal the CNS about the current state of the limb (McCloskey, 1978). An interesting result relevant to prehension shows altered muscle spindle sensitivity (i.e., dynamic changes in 1a afferent firing patterns) with flexion and extension of the hand (Edin, 1988). This could possibly play an important role in hand preshaping. Georgopoulos (1990) and colleagues have shown how the CNS may code the direction of arm movement.

Constraints exist also on the speed/timing of sensorimotor integration processes. Sensory information appears to adjust ongoing movements in less time than previous estimates of visual reaction time, estimates in the range of 190-260 ms (Keele & Posner, 1968) or 120-200 ms (see Schmidt, 1982; MacKenzie & Marteniuk, 1985). In studies of visual perturbations to object location, Paulignan and colleagues (Paulignan, MacKenzie, Marteniuk & Jeannerod, 1990, 1991; Marteniuk, this volume) found kinematic evidence for on line, visually based adjustments to the hand trajectory about 100 ms after perturbation onset. With respect to proprioceptive information, Cole and Abbs (1988) and Johansson and Westling (1988, 1990) have shown responses in grip force of the index and thumb having a latency of 60-90 msec after onset of an unexpected increase or decrease in load force. The changes were dependent on the size and velocity of the perturbation force and independent of the original grip force level. These latencies are longer than a monosynaptic reflex but shorter than a reaction time, reflecting some rapid, automatic sensorimotor integration process responding specifically to unexpected changes in order to achieve the functional goal of the task.

Johansson and Westling (1987) have shown that as human subjects pick up objects, microslips occur beneath the conscious awareness of the subject; that is, the object slips slightly in the grasp as the object is lifted. Recording from the median nerve, Johansson and Westling demonstrate that sensory information about the object's state is being transmitted into the nervous system. The microslips are reduced to zero as the force level is adjusted and balanced to the frictional conditions, stabilizing the object in the grip. These data suggest physiological limitations on prehensile movements, specifically in the underlying sensory and motor pathways.

In summary, human prehensile behavior is further constrained by anatomical and physiological aspects of the body, just as robot manipulators and their computer controllers are constrained by their construction and interfaces. Human and robot manipulators share physical constraints and some functional constraints; in contrast, they have unique high level and sensorimotor (implementation) constraints. High level, physical, and sensorimotor constraints are all operating in the selection and parameterization of prehensile movements.

2. SENSORIMOTOR INTEGRATION: GRASPING OBJECTS OF VARIOUS SIZES AND WEIGHTS

Emerging from computations in multidimensional constraint space, we may consider the sensorimotor integration processes relating the coordination of grasping to information obtained through vision and proprioception. Experiments are reviewed on visual processing of intrinsic and extrinsic object properties, focusing on the roles of central and peripheral vision, especially for processing information about object size. Then results from grasping experiments manipulating object weight are discussed, and phases of movement identified, with implications for the role of various senses in extracting information about object properties relevant to the grasping objectives in each phase.

2.1. Central and peripheral vision: grasping objects of varying sizes

Typically when we grasp an object, we first turn the head and fixate the eyes on the object, to "foveate" the object. The motor control process of foveation, whereby the head and eyes are moved to control the direction of gaze so that the light reflected from the object is projected onto the fovea of the retina, may itself contribute important information for the limb control system (but see Carnahan & Marteniuk, 1991; Prablanc, this volume; Prablanc, Echallier, Komilis and Jeannerod, 1979). The sensory/visual information obtained from projections onto the central and peripheral regions of the retina also are providing input to the visuomotor channels in prehension. There are known anatomical and functional differences between central and peripheral retina (Davson, 1980). Central vision is functionally specialized to responding to spatial patterning of a stimulus. In contrast, peripheral vision is functionally specialized for responding to location and movement stimuli (Paillard, 1982). Observations of an individual reaching to grasp an object suggest the following for peripheral and central vision. Before the start of the grasping movement, both the hand and arm are in the peripheral visual field (hereafter referred to as peripheral vision) while the object is in the central visual field (hereafter referred to as central vision). During the reach, the hand and arm remain in peripheral vision, while the object to be grasped is in central vision. Near the end of the movement, the hand comes into central vision, along with the object, while the arm remains in peripheral vision. At the time of contact with the object, usually both the hand and object are seen in central vision while the arm remains in peripheral vision. Because visual information is provided in parallel by central and peripheral regions of the retina during prehension, it is important to understand the relative contributions of central and peripheral vision. Paillard (1982; Paillard & Amblard, 1985) has explicitly suggested that central vision is responsible for processing object shape and size information and that peripheral vision is responsible for processing information about object location.

Experiments were conducted to examine how the system behaved when visual information was provided through only peripheral vision or only central vision, compared to grasping under normal, complete vision conditions. These binocular viewing conditions were created by physical optical techniques, using either contact lenses or goggles (Sivak, 1989). In order to restrict information to only peripheral vision, we used a piggyback contact lens design in which a partially painted hard lens was positioned on top of a soft carrier lens (Sivak, Sivak & MacKenzie, 1985; Sivak & MacKenzie, 1990). The hard lenses were painted black in the centre so that when lenses were inserted in both eyes, visual field testing with static perimetry revealed that no visual information was available through the centre 10 degrees of the visual field. (Note we needed several pairs of painted lenses to achieve this due to individual differences in ocular and facial anatomy. Approximately 10 degrees of the central field remained as a scotoma and therefore could not be used to provide visual information, even when the eyes or head moved.

In contrast, to restrict information to only central vision, a goggle system was developed that allowed for binocular viewing of the central 10 degrees of the visual field (Sivak, 1989; Sivak & MacKenzie, 1990). Swimming goggles were painted black on the sides to eliminate light. The front of the goggles contained circular black opaque disks. Each disk had a 0.5 mm aperture that was displaced medially 4 mm from the centre of the disk. With the goggles on, only the central 10 degrees of visual field could be seen, confirmed by static perimetry tests. The remainder of the visual field remained as a scotoma.

Under these various binocular visual conditions, subjects used pad opposition (the pads of the index finger and the thumb) to grasp and lift a wooden dowel (11.5 cm high; 2.5 cm in diameter), positioned on a table 30 cm in front of a start position in the midline plane. Dowels of 1.0, 2.5, and 5.5 cm diameter were used. We collected three dimensional kinematic data, sampling at 200 Hz, using the WATSMART (Waterloo Spatial Motion Analysis and Recording Technique, Northern Digital Inc.) system. For the transport component, an infra-red emitting diode marker (IRED) was placed on the wrist, and for the grasp component (aperture), we used the distance between markers placed on the thumb and index fingernails.

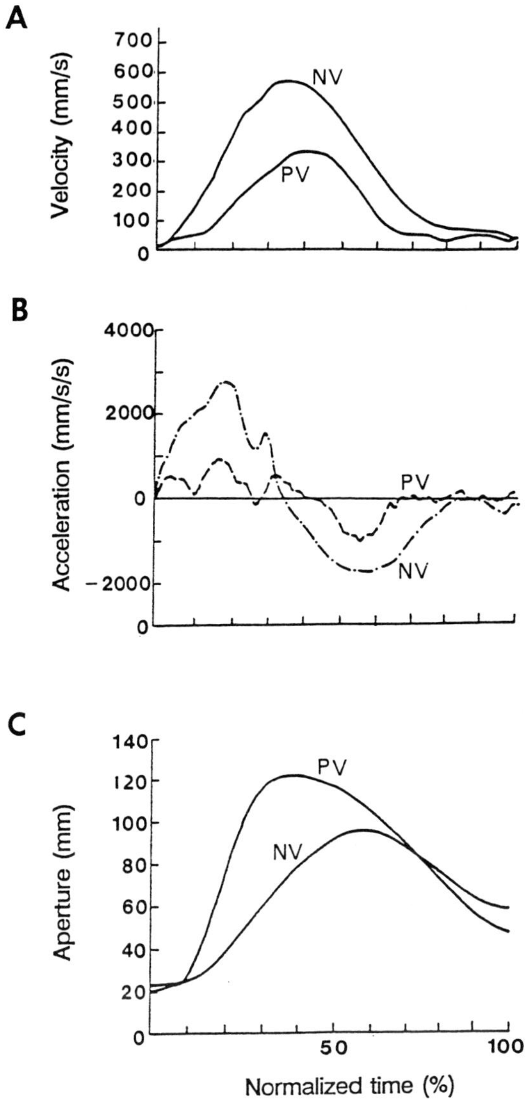

Figure 1. Kinematic profiles (means for one subject) when reaching to grasp a 2.5 cm diameter dowel with peripheral vision (PV) and normal vision (NV), showing (A) wrist resultant velocity, (B) wrist acceleration (differentiated resultant velocity) and (C) aperture between index finger and thumb. Note that the aperture is larger for peripheral vision, compared to normal vision.

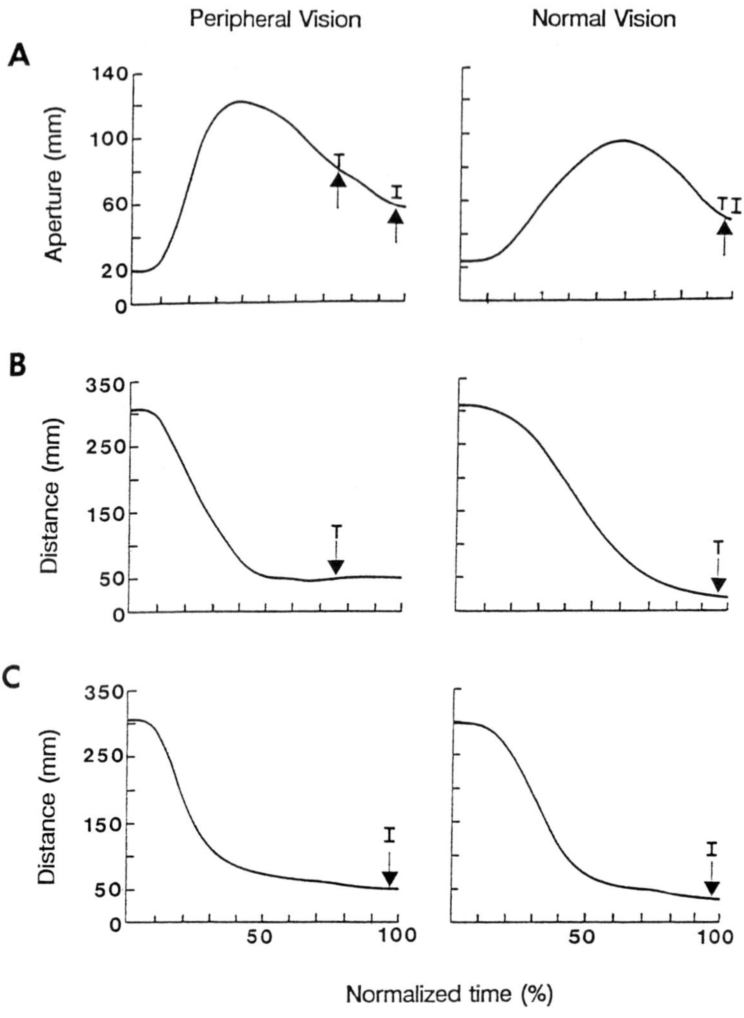

Figure 2. Mean profiles for one subject for (A) aperture, (B) distance between thumb IRED and dowel IRED, and (C) distance between index finger IRED and dowel IRED. T and I represent when the distance to the dowel IRED was unchanging for the thumb and index IREDS, respectively, and were used as an estimate of when the thumb and index finger made contact with the dowel. Note that subjects used a tactile control strategy whereby either the thumb or the index finger contacted the dowel first with peripheral vision, compared to both digits contacting at the same time with normal vision. Note also the larger aperture at first contact with peripheral vision (from Sivak & MacKenzie, 1991).

Analyses included examination of the trajectories, and ANOVAs of the timing and peak kinematic values, including peak velocity and deceleration of the wrist IRED and the maximum aperture between the thumb and index IREDs, for the transport and grasp components, respectively. Systematic variations and invariance in these profiles were used to infer processes subserving motor planning and control (Atkeson & Hollerbach, 1985; Jeannerod, 1981; MacKenzie et al, 1987; Marteniuk et al., 1987; Soechting & Lacquiniti, 1983).

The restriction of visual information to only the peripheral visual field (i.e., eliminating high resolution vision) had an important effect on the grasp and transport components, compared to normal vision. With the head stabilized in straight ahead position, subjects needed to turn their eyes to see the dowel with the remaining peripheral visual field. Results for the 2.5 cm dowel, shown in Figure 1, indicated that individuals moved much slower with peripheral than normal vision. The acceleration profiles were notably different in the two conditions; with peripheral vision, subjects decelerated, then appeared to maintain a near 0 acceleration. Subsequent analyses revealed that, with peripheral vision, the forward movement of the arm toward the dowel stopped when approximately 72% of the movement duration was completed, in contrast to 91% for normal vision. When the wrist stopped moving forward, the aperture was larger for peripheral than normal vision. From Figure 1, the maximum aperture was much larger with only peripheral vision (116 mm) than with normal vision (86 mm). Figure 2 shows the size of the aperture when the thumb and the index finger made contact with the object, demonstrating that, with peripheral vision, subjects adopted a tactile control strategy whereby either the thumb or index finger made initial contact, perhaps to trigger the continued closing of the aperture. Johansson and Westling (1987) found that the minimum response latencies of the distal hand muscles to tactile stimuli was approximately 60-80 ms. As the time from initial contact with the dowel to the dowel lift exceeded 80 ms, the tactile triggering strategy for grasp completion in the peripheral vision condition is a plausible explanation. In contrast, with normal vision, Figure 2 shows that the thumb and index finger made contact at about the same time, shortly before dowel lift. These findings were robust and reliable, consistently seen for every subject we tested (Sivak & MacKenzie, 1990).

In a second experiment, we manipulated the diameter of dowels to be grasped with normal or peripheral vision. The transport kinematics for the wrist, and larger aperture effects with peripheral vision were replicated. Figure 3 shows that under normal vision, the size of the maximum aperture increased monotonically with increasing dowel size. This agrees with Marteniuk et al (1990), Jeannerod and Decety (1990) and von Hofsten and Ronnqvist (1989). The results suggest that peripheral vision was not as sensitive to object size as normal vision. Although the hand opened wider for all sizes of dowels with peripheral vision compared to normal vision, the increase in aperture was not calibrated to object size in the same way; only the differences in aperture between the 1.0 and 5.5 cm dowels were significant with peripheral vision. An alternative explanation we considered but ruled out was that the results reflected a biomechanical constraint of maximum span between the index finger and thumb. If this were so, then one would have expected a ceiling in maximum aperture for the 2.5 cm dowel. Thus peripheral vision is less sensitive than normal vision in providing size information for calibrating grasp aperture.

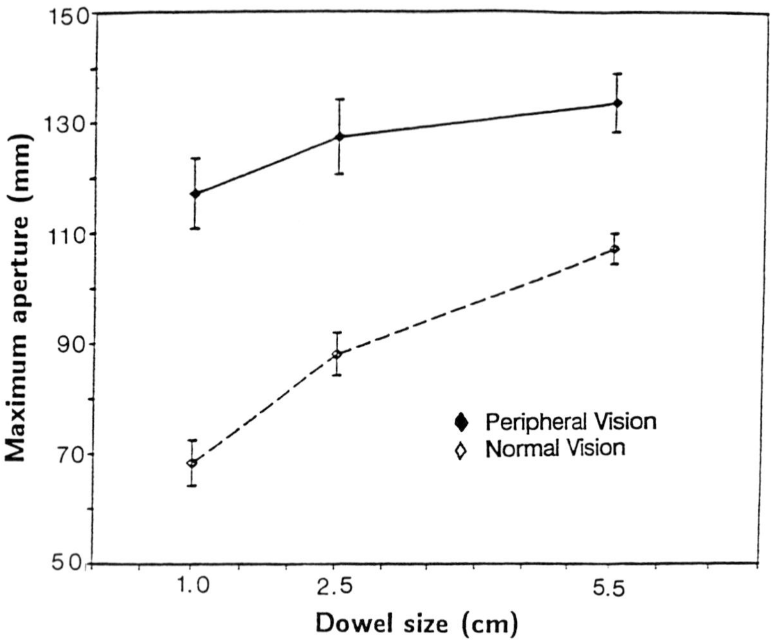

Figure 3. The effect of dowel size on maximum aperture achieved at the end of preshaping. Maximum aperture was always larger with peripheral vision only than with normal vision. Note the increased sensitivity of normal vision to dowel size.

The obvious difference between the peripheral and normal visual conditions is the lack of visual acuity or high resolution vision with peripheral vision. Without high resolution information about intrinsic object characteristics (normally provided by central regions of the retina under natural viewing conditions), the aperture is much larger, and subjects adopt a tactile control strategy to acquire intrinsic object information, complete the aperture closure and actually grasp the object. Thus central visual information about object size obtained before and during the movement is critical for the planning and control of the grasp component. We suggested that the transport component was modified along with the grasp component as part of this control strategy, that is, there is a communication link between the visuomotor channels controlling grip formation and transport of the hand (Sivak & MacKenzie, 1990).

Two experiments compared grasping using only central vision with normal vision. With the goggles on, the dowel was always visible; the arm and hand were visible neither at the start nor during the reach. The hand came into view as it approached the object at the end of the movement.

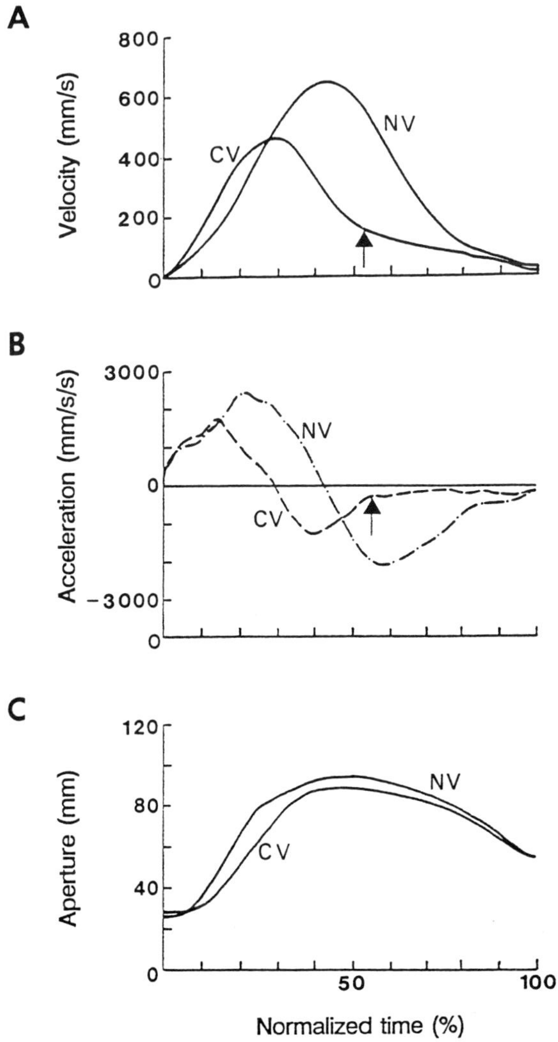

Figure 4. Profiles for one subject with central vision (CV) and normal vision (PV) for (A) wrist velocity, (B) acceleration and (C) aperture. Note no aperture differences. With only central vision, there appear to be two distinct phases of deceleration; the beginning of the second is indicated by the arrow.

Under conditions of central vision, the parameters of the transport component were organized based on information that suggested a nearer target than in reality. Figure 4 shows that subjects spent a greater proportion of time after peak deceleration with only central vision (52%) compared to normal vision (39%). Without the wide field of view provided by peripheral vision subjects did not estimate the distance to the dowel accurately. Figure 4 shows two distinct phases in the deceleration of the limb with only central vision.These suggested to us that subjects planned to end the movement earlier than they actually did. That is, when subjects did not reach the dowel when they expected to, they continued to decelerate at a constant rate until tactile contact was made with the dowel. It is important to note that these were not submovements indicated by changes in acceleration and deceleration, but rather a constant deceleration. This suggested to us that subjects were moving forward anticipating tactile contact, rather than making a series of corrections. The underestimation of the distance was confirmed by subjective reports that the target appeared closer than it was, and by pilot observations of subjects who revealed a consistent undershooting when reaching for the dowels as quickly as possible (Sivak, 1989; Sivak & MacKenzie, 1990). Proprioceptive information from the moving limb provided inadequate information as to where the limb was in relationship to the target. Perhaps proprioceptive information is decalibrated when visual information is disturbed (Soechting & Flanders, 1989).

The maximum aperture and relative time spent in preshaping and enclosing, from the normalized aperture profiles for central vision were similar to those for normal vision. With only central vision, there was no visual information of the position of the fingers both before and during movement as is the case in normal vision situations. This suggests that visual information for hand and finger posturing for grip formation is sufficient when acquired only from the object. On-line visual feedback information of finger position, during preshape and enclose while the hand is approaching the dowel, does not appear to be necessary for planning and control of the grasp component (Sivak & MacKenzie, 1990).

In a followup experiment, we compared central vision with normal vision for grasping dowels of diameters 1.0. 2.5, and 5.5 cm. In all cases with central vision, subjects continued to make the two-phase deceleration in transporting the limb, as if they underestimated the distance to the target. Further there were no differences in the aperture data between central and normal vision conditions, suggesting that central vision is sufficient for calibrating the aperture to the diameter of the dowel. Peripheral vision thus appears to be unnecessary for the planning and control of the grasp component.

The major difference between the central and normal visual conditions was the small field of view with only central vision. The small field size reduced the amount or quality of dowel location information, and on line visual feedback information about the moving limb. Although it has been suggested that peripheral vision is used to provide information necessary for directing the limb to the proper location of an object (Bard, Hay & Fleury, 1985; Paillard, 1982; Paillard & Amblard, 1985), subjects in the present experiment had no difficulty with the direction, only the distance of the movement in the absence of peripheral vision. Since the present experiment required only one direction to move, i.e., in the midline plane, it is not clear whether peripheral vision was necessary to assess the direction of movement. In the absence of peripheral vision, eye and head position (and the motor control process of foveation) may provide sufficient information about the direction of an object to be grasped. The results from this study suggest that direction and distance are separable entities for location of an object (Sivak, 1989; Sivak & MacKenzie 1990).

In considering the roles of central and peripheral vision in visuomotor integration processes, we suggest the following for grasping under normal viewing conditions. Peripheral vision provides important information about the distance of an object (Sivak & MacKenzie, 1990), direction (Bard et al, 1985), and information about object or limb motion (Bard et al, 1985; Paillard, 1982). As suggested by Paillard (1982),this information appears to selectively contribute to the planning and control of transport of the hand to the object, not to the formation of the grip. Under natural viewing, central vision provides important information about object size (and possibly other intrinsic object characteristics), for accurate grip calibration. This objective object size information contributes to the organization and control of both the grasp and transport components. Without the high resolution provided by central vision, subjects adopt a tactile control strategy, increasing the length of time they are in contact with the object, in order to successfully complete the grasp. We now consider from a converging perspective this time spent in contact with the object before stable grasp is achieved.

2.2. During contact: grasping objects of varying weights

We obtain information about visible, intrinsic object properties in order to plan hand posturing, and to calibrate the grip aperture appropriate for the object's diameter (this corresponds to the opposition vector, for pad opposition, see Iberall, Bingham & Arbib, 1986). Information about other object properties like shape and texture may also be obtained through vision. The object property of weight is not always veridically assessable by vision, although our everyday interactions with objects lead us to predict the weight of seen, familiar objects. Given a constant density of material, larger objects are heavier. However, with unfamiliar objects, vision does not always provide veridical information about object weight, as for example, when we lift a plastic beer pitcher for the first time.

In the last decade, investigations of invisible object properties such as weight in prehension have focused on the grasping forces (Cole & Abbs, 1988; Gordon, Forssberg, Johansson & Westling, 1991 a,b,c; Johansson & Westling, 1984, 1988, 1990) and proceeded independently of the research on visuomotor channels which has focused on the three dimensional kinematics prior to actually grasping the object. In recent experiments, the movement kinematics were examined when subjects grasped objects of different weight (Weir, MacKenzie, Marteniuk, Cargoe & Frazer, 1991) and combined kinematic and grasping force measures for a more complete picture of the effects of object characteristics and task requirements (Weir, 1991; Weir & MacKenzie, 1991).

Our initial experiments were motivated by the natural covariation of object size and object weight. In earlier studies of object size (Jeannerod, 1984; von Hofsten & Ronnqvist, 1989; Marteniuk et al, 1990), the larger objects were always heavier. In experiments in our lab at Waterloo with similar methodologies, the results for grasping (with pad opposition) taller dowels for a range of diameters (Sivak & MacKenzie, 1991) did not replicate those for grasping shorter disks of the same diameters (Marteniuk et al., 1990). Thus the systematic variation in movement kinematics with the diameter of the disks to be grasped may have been due to the weight (or height or volume) of the disks as well as the diameter of the object (or length of the opposition vector). A series of experiments were therefore designed to examine the effects of object weight uncontaminated by covariations in size, by using visibly similar cylindrical dowels of constant size (10.3 cm high and 2.5 cm in diameter), but varying in weight (from 20 to 410 grams).

From a fixed starting position, and relaxed hand posture, with the thumb and index finger in contact over the table top, the task was to grasp and lift a dowel placed 30 cm in front of the body midline. Subjects grasped the dowels under blocked (weight known, since a group of trials had all the same dowel weight) and random conditions (weight unknown, with random variation of the different weighted dowels over trials). Markers were placed on the wrist, index finger and thumb. Using the WATSMART system (sampling at 200 Hz, reconstruction error of about 2.1 mm, filtering at 4 Hz using a second order Butterworth filter with dual pass), kinematics of the grasp aperture and the transport of the wrist were analyzed from the time of hand lift to dowel lift.

Results revealed that, as expected, maximum aperture did not vary across the conditions, since the dowels were all of the same diameter. However, subjects spent a longer time after peak aperture and peak deceleration for the 410 gram dowel than the lighter dowels. Further, more time was spent in the latter (deceleration) portion of the movement on trials when the weight was unknown than when the weight was known. Visual examination of the wrist velocity and the aperture profiles suggested this longer time reflected "tails" or unchanging velocity/aperture values at the end of movement, during the time when the subject was in contact with the dowel prior to lift (see Weir et al., 1991 for details).

In a second experiment therefore, the time in contact with the dowel prior to lift was measured directly. A contact breaking system defined the times of hand lift, contact of the thumb and index finger with the dowel, and dowel lift. The results confirmed that the timing and kinematics of the movement **prior to** contacting the dowel were unaffected by the dowel weight or weight uncertainty. We were surprised to discover that even for blocked trials, when subjects knew the weight of the dowel, there were no anticipatory changes in the kinematics prior to contacting the dowel. Since the dowels were visibly similar, this emphasizes the dominance of visual information prior to contacting the object, and the influence of tactile and kinesthetic information once contact is made. All the timing and kinematic effects occurred **after** contacting the dowel, prior to lift off. Figure 5 shows how the time spent in contact with the dowel prior to lift increases systematically with dowel weight, and that more time is spent in contact with the dowel prior to lift when the weight is unknown than when the weight is predictable based on previous trials. This increased time spent in contact with the dowel is consistent with research showing that the functions for grip and load force application over time had an increased slope and longer duration prior to lift for heavier objects (Johansson & Westling, 1984, 1988) and that subjects are able to anticipate the forces required when weight perturbations are expected (Johansson & Westling, 1988; Cole & Abbs, 1988; Winstein, Abbs & Petashnik, 1991). The increased time after contact is reflecting two aspects of the sensorimotor control process: the production of functionally effective forces to acquire the object in a stable grasp, **and** the acquisition of proprioceptive (cutaneous, kinesthetic, haptic) information about the status of grasping and the weight of the object.

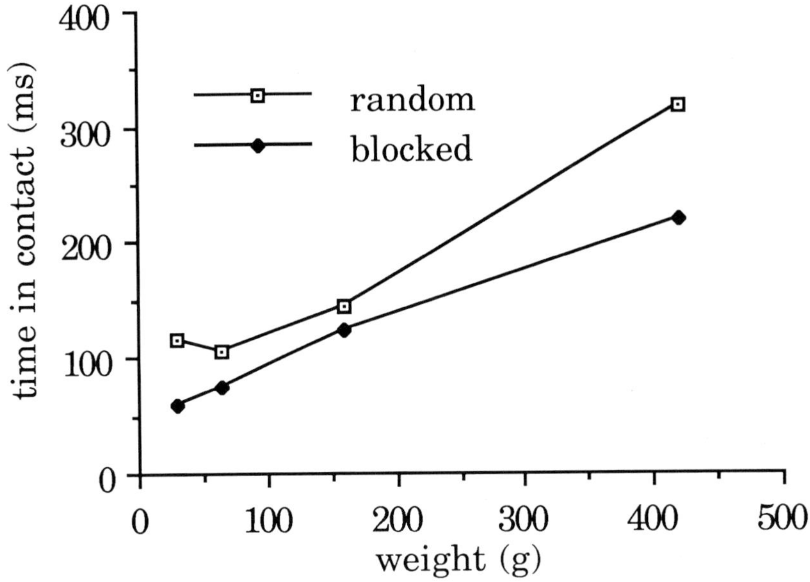

Figure 5. Time spent in contact with the dowel, prior to lift, as a function of dowel weight. Note that this time increased monotonically with object weight, and the time spent in contact with the dowel was greater when the weight was unknown (random order) than when the weight was known (when trials were blocked for each weight). These findings suggest that the time is spent both effecting the forces and acquiring the relevant information (from Weir, MacKenzie, Marteniuk, Cargoe & Frazer, 1991).

The results suggested also that indeed there were **two distinct phases** of grasping: a free motion phase and a compliant motion phase. In the **free motion phase**, prior to contacting the object (with accelerative and decelerative subphases), the hand is oriented, and the grip aperture calibrated to dowel diameter as the hand and contacting digits are transported to the appropriate locations (Arbib, 1981, 1985; Iberall & MacKenzie, 1991; Jeannerod, 1984; Weir et al, 1991), and subjects rely primarily on vision. In the **compliant motion phase**, kinesthetic, tactile and haptic information contributes to the generation of functionally effective forces so that stable grasp is achieved (c.f., Iberall &

MacKenzie, 1991; Johansson & Westling, 1984, 1988, who subdivided this contacting time into several subphases based on grip and load force analyses).

These findings led us to combine the kinematic measures (Weir et al, 1991; after Jeannerod, 1981) with the grip and load force measures (Cole & Abbs, 1988; Johansson & Westling, 1984; after Westling, 1986), for assessing object weight in a variety of tasks. A force transducing dowel was designed (after Westling, 1986 and Johansson & Westling, 1990), with a hollow, cylindrical base (3.8 cm in diameter and 11.5 cm high, weighing 66 grams), and strain gauges mounted above to measure load and grip forces. Weighted buckshot with foam inserts increased the weight of the dowel to either 155 or 423 grams. The grip and load forces channels were synchronized with channels recording contact breaks and WATSMART three dimensional position data so that the kinematics, forces and contact breaks denoting physical events could be examined simultaneously and through interactive graphics programs (Weir, 1991; Weir & MacKenzie, 1991).

These combined kinematic and force data are presented in Figure 6 for a single trial in which a subject reached for a 155 gram dowel placed 20 cm in front of the midline start position, grasped it with pad opposition, lifted it to match the height of a 4 cm block, replaced it on the contact plate and returned to the starting position. The dowel position as it is lifted to maximum height then replaced is shown in Figure 6E, and Figure 6D shows the peaks in the velocity profiles associated with wrist transport and the up and down motions of the lift and replace. The aperture profile in 6C shows the typical opening to a maximum aperture, and its closure can be related to the grip and load forces in Figures 6A and B. A priori, we identified the following unique phases of the movement: a **free motion phase**, from the time of hand lift to dowel contact; a **dowel acquisition phase**, from the time of dowel contact to dowel lift, a **dowel transport phase**, from dowel lift to dowel (re)place, and a **dowel release phase**, from the time of dowel replace to let go (Iberall & MacKenzie, 1991; Weir, 1991; Weir & MacKenzie, 1991). For the kinematic and force data in each phase, we analyzed peak values, associated timing, and the interrelationship of kinematic and force measures on a trial-by-trial basis.

In one experiment, we used these measures, and manipulated dowel weight (66, 155, 423 g) and task goal (grasp to lift or grasp to place), in an attempt to replicate the earlier object weight effects on grasping forces, task effects on kinematics, and to see how the task requirements might affect the grasping forces as well as the kinematics (Atkeson & Hollerbach, 1985; Johansson & Westling, 1984, 1988; Marteniuk et al., 1987; Weir et al, 1991). Results replicated our earlier findings that dowel weight had no effect on the kinematics prior to contact. Consistent with Weir et al. (1991) and Johansson and Westling (1988), dowel weight affected the time spent in contact with the dowel prior to lift; in addition, the values for rate of grip force increased with dowel weight for the lift task and corresponded well with those values reported by Johansson and Westling (1988). Dowel weight also affected the kinematics of the dowel transport phase (once the object had been grasped) for the place task only: for the heavier dowel, peak velocity of the dowel and wrist was lower than for the lighter dowels (Weir, 1991). Consistent with Atkeson and Hollerbach (1985), the time normalized velocity profiles showed shape invariance for transporting the loaded hand 30 cm during the dowel transport phase compared to the 30 cm transport during the free motion phase.

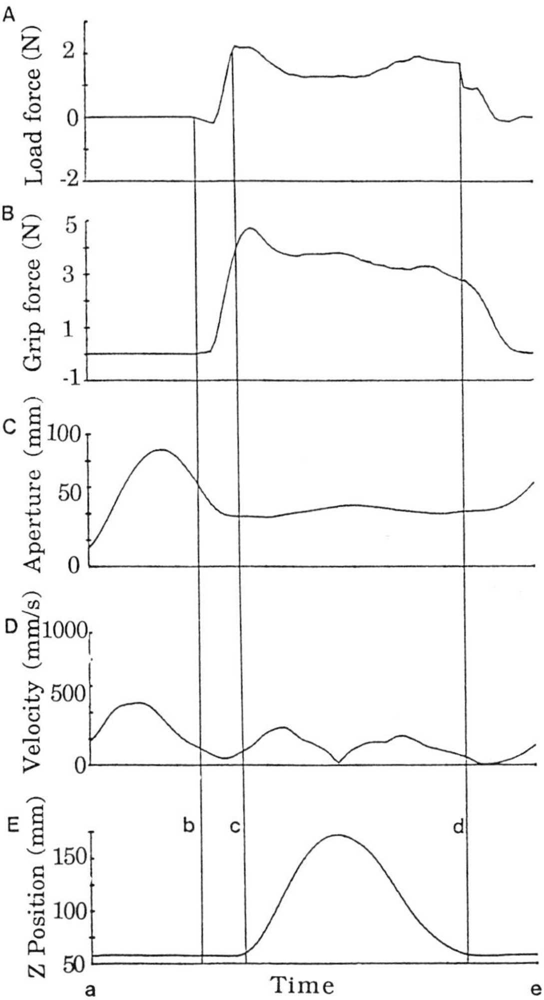

Figure 6. Representative force and kinematic profiles for a single trial of the lift task: (A) load force, (B) grip force, (C) aperture, (D) wrist velocity, and (E) vertical dowel position. Lower case letters represent the times of: (a) hand lift, (b) dowel contact, (c) dowel lift, (d) dowel replace and (e) let-go of the dowel. The average time taken to complete a lift trial was 2399 ms. Kinematic and force parameters were examined also in normalized time for each of the phases (from Weir, 1991).

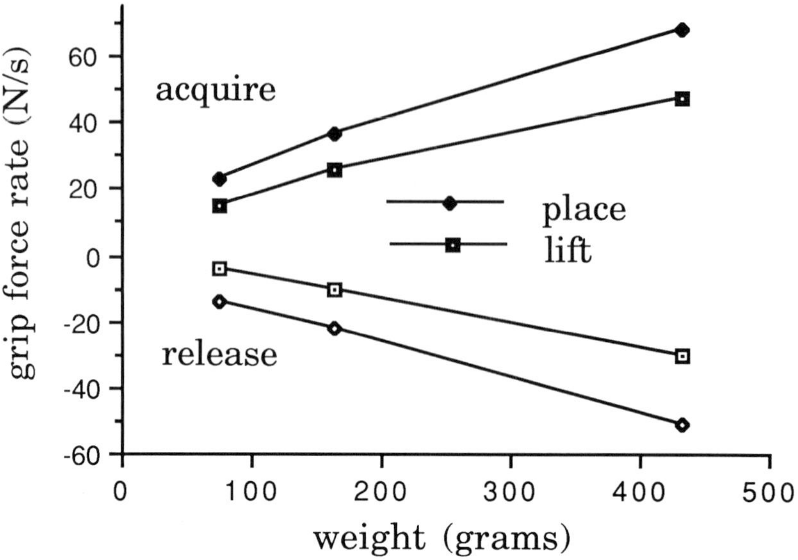

Figure 7. Grip force rate as function of dowel weight and task goal. The values plotted are averaged over 6 subjects. Positive values (filled symbols) represent the maximum rate during the dowel acquisition phase of grasping and negative values (open symbols) represent the maximum rate of decrease during the dowel release phase for the place and lift tasks. Note the rates were higher for the place than the lift task, and that this effect was most pronounced for the heaviest dowel (Adapted from Weir, 1991).

The rate of grip force increase during dowel acquisition and the rate of force decrease during dowel release changed sytematically with dowel weight, as shown in Figure 7, and was modified by task. Overall, the rate of force application was greater for the place task than the lift task, and this difference was most pronounced when grasping/releasing the heavier dowel. This new finding, that the grasping task goal (to lift or to place) affects the forces exerted during grasping, is important because it shows that the high level goal is interacting with the physical constraint of object weight in the application of functionally effective forces. That is, the forces applied during the acquisition of the object show anticipatory planning for the upcoming manipulation or transport of the object. Maximum forces and force rates were greater when the dowel was to be transported forward and placed on a target (place task) than when the dowel was to be lifted, then replaced (lift task). Combined analyses of kinematics and grasping forces in prehension are likely to be more revealing about the interactions between high level constraints and the physical constraints during the various phases of movement.

3. PHASES OF PREHENSION: SENSORIMOTOR INTEGRATION

The goal of this chapter has been to discuss constraints, identify unique phases of movement, and to highlight evidence for the differential contributions of sensory modalities in providing information relevant to the goal of the task and the objectives within each phase. Arbib (1985) considered how parallel computations in the schemas of the coordinated control program might give rise to the systematic unfolding of the serial order in prehension. In addition to the parallel unfolding of arm and hand movements, these computations included the parallel transfer of both visual and tactile information from perceptual schemata to the reaching and grasping schemata (Arbib, 1981, 1985; Arbib, Iberall & Lyons, 1987). Vision provides object size, orientation and location (both direction and distance) information. The only explicit mention of tactile information is that "[T]he 'actual' grasping movement shapes the hand on the basis of a spatial pattern of tactile feedback." (Arbib, Iberall & Lyons, 1987, p. 492). Proprioception (including its tactile, kinesthetic and haptic aspects) provides information during contact for assessing the weight of an object, in order to lift it.

Unique phases of prehension were identified. Some constraints are time varying (e.g. frictional forces become relevant during contact) while other constraints are not (e.g., the task goal usually persists until goal attainment). Before movement begins, high level constraints are operating, for example, motivations and task goals. There is task specific (or action oriented) perception of the relevant object properties, based primarily on vision, with central vision providing information about intrinsic properties like cylinder diameter, and peripheral vision providing information about extrinsic object properties like distance. This information, and past experience is used for planning and preparation of the upcoming movement. The task specific **planning phase** includes selection of: the type of grasp, the contacting locations on the object, and the appropriate motor set. During a **free motion phase**, from the time of hand lift to dowel contact, the hand is transported, oriented and postured to contact the object in the desired locations. In addition to the visual information above, proprioceptors provide information about the hand's location and orientation, and the arm and hand configuration. In the deceleration subphase of gettting the hand to the object (what roboticists term guarded motion), tactile contact is anticipated. Tactile contact occurs. This represents a major transition from a vision-dominated to a touch-dominated mode of control. The same hand muscles which before flexed the fingers now serve to apply forces to an object, i.e., compliant motion. During the **dowel acquisition phase**, from the time of dowel contact to dowel lift, touch and proprioception are providing information about contact with the object, other intrinsic object characteristics (shape, texture, weight, distribution of mass, etc), and the stability of the object in grasp. During this time, stable grasp is established, and we should consider the system being controlled as changing from the hand to the hand plus object. Vision is again working to plan for a **dowel transport phase**, from dowel lift to dowel (re)place, with peripheral vision providing information about the location for placement and central vision providing the high resolution detail concerning the task and working environment. Throughout dowel transport, cutaneous and kinesthetic receptors are providing information about the maintenance of stable grasp as well as the configuration of the limb. Finally, during a **dowel release phase**, from the time of dowel replace to let go, touch and proprioception are providing information about the hand configuration, contact with the object and with supporting surfaces, and where necessary, central vision is providing the resolution to determine correct placement. After release, the object and hand are to be considered again as separate systems (Iberall & MacKenzie, 1991; Weir, 1991; Weir & MacKenzie, 1991).

4. REFERENCES

Arbib, M.A. (1981). Perceptual structures and distributed motor control. In V.B. Brooks (Ed.) Handbook of Physiology-The Nervous System, II. Motor Control, Bethesda, MD: American Physiology Society, 1449-1480.

Arbib, M.A. (1985). Schemas for the temporal control of behavior. Human Neurobiology, 4, 63-72.

Arbib, M.A., Iberall, T. and Lyons, D. (1985). Coordinated control programs for movements of the hand. In A.W. Goodwin and I. Darian-Smith (Eds.), Hand Function and the Neocortex. Berlin: Springer-Verlag, 111-129.

Atkeson, C.G. and Hollerbach, J.M. (1985). Kinematic features of unrestrained vertical arm movements. Journal of Neuroscience, 5, 2318-2330.

Bard, C., Hay, L., & Fleury, M. (1985). Role of peripheral vision in the directional control of rapid aiming movements. Canadian Journal of Psychology, 39, 151-161.

Bowden, F.P. and Tabor, D. (1967). Friction and Lubrication. London: Methuen & Co. Ltd.

Buchholz, B., Frederick, L. J., and Armstrong, T. J. (1988). An investigation of human palmar skin friction and the effects of materials, pinch force, and moisture, Ergonomics, 31(3): 317-325.

Carnahan, H. and Marteniuk, R.G. (1991). The temporal organization of hand eye and head movements during reaching and pointing. Journal of Motor Behavior, 23,109-119.

Cochran, D.J. and Riley, M.W. (1986). The effects of handle shape and size on exerted force. Human Factors, 28(3), 253-265.

Cole, K.J. and Abbs, J.H. (1987). Kinematic and electromyographic responses to perturbation of a rapid grasp, J Neurophysiology, 57(5): 1407-1423.

Cole, K. J. and Abbs, J. H. (1988). Grip force adjustments evoked by load force perturbations of a grasped object, J Neurophysiology, 60(4): 1513-1522.

Comaish, S. and Bottoms, E. (1971). The skin and friction: Deviations from Amonton's Laws, and the effects of hydration and lubrication, Br J Derm, 84: 37-43.

Davson, H. (1980). Physiology of the Eye. New York: Academic Press.

Dinc, O.S., Ettles, C.M., Calabrese, S.J. and Scarton, H.A. (1990). Some parameters affecting tactile friction. Transactions of ASME: Journal of Tribology, 28, 1-6.

Edin,B.B. (1988). Muscle spindles influence not only the planning but also the execution of antagonist muscle activity in humans, Society for Neuroscience Abstracts, 14 (1): 468.

Fearing, R.S. (1986). Simplified grasping and manipulation with dextrous robot hands, IEEE Journal of Robotics and Automation, RA-2(4), 188-195.
Fitts, P. M. (1954). The information capacity of the human motor system in controlling the amplitude of movement, Journal of Experimental Psychology, 47, 381-391.
Georgopoulos, A.P. (1990). Neurophysiology of reaching. In M. Jeannerod (Ed.), Attention and Performance XIII, Hillsdale, NJ: Lawrence Erlbaum Associates, 227-264.
Glicenstein, J. and Dardour, J. C. (1981). The pulp: Anatomy and physiology. In R. Tubiana (Ed.), The Hand. Vol 1. Philadelphia: W.B. Saunders, 116-120.
Gordon, A.M., Forssberg, H., Johansson, R.S., and Westling, G. (1991a).Visual size cues in the programming of manipulative forces during precision grip. Experimental Brain Research, 83, 477-482.
Gordon, A.M., Forssberg, H., Johansson, R.S., and Westling, G. (1991b).The integration of haptically acquired size information in the programming of precision grip.. Experimental Brain Research, 83, 483-488.
Gordon, A.M., Forssberg, H., Johansson, R.S., and Westling, G. (1991c). Integration of sensory information during the programming of precision grip: comments on the contributions of size cues. Experimental Brain Research, 85, 226-229.
Grusser, M. (1986). The multimodal structure of extrapersonal space. In A. Hein and M. Jeannerod (Eds.), Spatially Oriented Behavior, NY: Springer-Verlag.
Hofsten, C. von and Ronnqvist, L. (1989). Preparation for grasping: A developmental study. Journal of Experimental Psychology: Human Perception and Performance, 14, 610-621.
Holder, H. (1983). Developmental constraints and the evolution of vertebrate digit patterns, Journal of Theoretical Biology, 104, 451-471.
Hollerbach, J. M. (1980). A recursive Lagrangian formulation of manipulator dynamics and a comparative study of dynamics formulation complexity, IEEE Tran System, Man, and Cybernetics, SMC-10(11): 730-736.
Hollerbach, J. M. and Atkeson, C.G. (1987). Deducing planning variables from experimental arm trajectories: Pitfalls and possibilities, Biological Cybernetics, 56, 279-292.
Iberall, T., Bingham, G. and Arbib, M.A. (1986). Opposition space as a structuring concept for the analysis of skilled hand movements. In H. Heuer and C. Fromm (Eds.), Generation and Modulation of Action Patterns, Berlin: Springer-Verlag, 158-173.
Iberall, T. and MacKenzie, C. L. (1990). Opposition Space and Human Prehension. In: S. T. Venkataraman and T. Iberall (Eds.), Dextrous Robot Hands, NY: Springer-Verlag.
Iberall, T. and MacKenzie, C. L. (1991). The Grasping Hand, in preparation.
Jeannerod, M. (1981). Intersegmental coordination during reaching at natural visual objects. In: J. Long and A. Baddeley (Eds.) Attention and Performance IX, Hills., NJ: Erlbaum, 153-169.
Jeannerod, M. (1984). The timing of natural prehension movements. Journal of Motor Behavior, 16, 235-254.
Jeannerod, M. and Decety, J. (1990). The accuracy of visuomotor transformation. An investigation into the mechanisms of visual

recognition of objects. In M. Goodale (Ed), Vision and Action: The Control of Grasping, NJ: Ablex.
Johansson, R. S. and Vallbo, Å. B. (1983). Tactile sensory coding in the glabrousskin of the human hand, Trends in Neuroscience, 6(1): 27-37.
Johansson R.S. and Westling, G. (1984). Roles of glabrous skin receptors and sensorimotor memory in automatic control of precision grip when lifting rougher or more slippery objects. Experimental Brain Research, 56, 550-564.
Johansson, R.S. and Westling, G. (1987). Signals in Tactile Afferents from the Fingers Eliciting Adaptive Motor Responses During Precision Grip, Exp Brain Res , 66: 141-154.
Johansson, R.S. and Westling, G. (1988). Programmed and triggered actions to rapid load changes during precision grip., Exp Brain Res , 71, 72-86.
Johansson, R.S. and Westling, G. (1990).Tactile afferent signals in the control of precision grip. In M. Jeannerod (Ed.), Attention and Performance XIII, Hillsdale, NJ: Lawrence Erlbaum Associates, 677-736.
Jones, L. (1989). The assessment of hand function: A critical review of techniques. The Journal of Hand Surgery, 14A: 221-228.
Kapandji, I. A. (1982): The Physiology of the Joints. Volume One. Upper Limb. Fifth Edition, Edinburgh: Churchill Livingstone.
Keele, S. W. and Posner, M.I. (1968). Processing of visual feedback in rapid movements, J Exp. Psychology, 77, 155-158.
Lederman, S.J. and Klatzky, R.L. (1987). Hand movements: A window into haptic object recognition. Cognitive Psychology, 19, 342-368.
LeGros-Clark, W.E. (1959). The Antecedents of Man, Edinburgh University Press, Edinburgh.
Lewis, O.J. (1977). Joint remodelling and the evolution of the human hand, J Anatomy, 123(1): 157-201.
MacKenzie, C.L., (1985). Structural constraints on timing of human finger movements. In D. Goodman, R. B Wilberg, and I.M. Franks (Eds.), Differing Perspectives in Motor Learning, Memory and Control. Amsterdam: North-Holland.
MacKenzie, C.L. and Marteniuk, R.G. (1985). Motor skill: Feedback, knowledge and structural issues. Canadian Journal of Psychology, 39, 313-327.
MacKenzie, C.L., Marteniuk, R.G., Dugas, C., Liske, D. and Eickmeier, B. (1987). Three dimensional movement trajectories in Fitts' task: Implications for control. Quarterly Journal of Experimental Psychology, 39A, 629-647.
Marr, D. (1981): Vision. W. H. Freeman, San Francisco.
Marteniuk, R.G, Leavitt, J.L., MacKenzie, C.L. and Athenes, S. (1990). Functional relationships between grasp and transport components in a prehension task. Human Movement Science, 9, 149-176.
Marteniuk, R. G. and MacKenzie, C.L. (1990). Invariance and variability in human prehension: implications for theory development. In M. Goodale (Ed), Vision and Action: The Control of Grasping, Norwood, NJ: Ablex, 49-64.
Marteniuk, R.G., MacKenzie, C.L., Jeannerod, M., Athenes, S. and Dugas, C. (1987). Constraints on human arm movement trajectories. Canadian Journal of Psychology, 41, 365-378.

Marzke, M.W. (1983). Joint Functions and Grips of the *Australopithecus afarensis* Hand, with Special Reference to the Region of the Capitate, J Human Evolution, 12: 197-211.
McCloskey, D.I. (1978). Kinesthetic sensibility, Physiological Reviews, 58, 763-820.
Moore, D. F. (1972). The Friction and Lubrication of Elastomers, NY: Pergamon Press.
Musgrave, J.H. (1971). How dextrous was Neanderthal Man?, Nature, 233, October 22, 538-541.
Napier, J.R. (1962). The evolution of the hand. Scientific American, 207, 56-62.
Nelson, W. L. (1983): Physical principles for economies of skilled movements, Biological Cybernetics, 46, 135-147.
Nespoulous, J. and Lecours, A.R. (1986). Gestures: Nature and function. In: J. Nespoulous, P.Perron, and A.R. Lecours (Eds.), The Biological Foundations of Gestures: Motor and Semiotic Aspects. Hillsdale, N.J.: Lawrence Erlbaum Associates.
Newell, K.M. (1986). Constraints on the development of coordination. IN M. G. Wade and H.T.A. Whiting (Eds.), Motor development in children: Aspects of coordination and control. Boston: Martinus Nijhoff, 341-360.
Paillard, J. (1982). The contribution of peripheral and central vision to visually guided reaching. In D.J. Ingle, M.A. Goodale, and R.J.W. Mansfield (Eds.), Visually Oriented Behavior. Cambridge: MIT Press, 367-385.
Paillard, J. and Amblard, B. (1985). Static versus kinetic visual cues for the processing of spatial relationships. In D.J. Ingle, M. Jeannerod and D.N. Lee (Eds.) Brain mechanisms and spatial vision. La Haye: Martinus Nijhof.
Paulignan, Y., MacKenzie, C., Marteniuk, R. and Jeannerod, M. (1990). The coupling of arm and finger movements during prehension. Exp Brain Research, 79, 431-435.
Paulignan, Y., MacKenzie, C., Marteniuk, R. and Jeannerod, M. (1991). Selective perturbation of visual input during prehension movements. 1. The effects of changing object position, Exp. Brain Research, 83, 502-512.
Prablanc, C., Echallier, J.F., Komilis, E. and Jeannerod, M. (1979). Optimal response of eye and hand motor systems in pointing at a visual target. Biological Cybernetics, 35, 113-124.
Pryce, J.C. (1980). The wrist position between neutral and ulnar deviation that facilitates the maximumpower grip strength, J Biomechanics, 13: 505-511.
Quilliam, T. A. (1978). The structure of fingerprint skin. In: G. Gordon (Ed.), Active Touch, Oxford: Pergamon Press Ltd, 1-18.
Ranney, D. and Wells, R. (1988). Lumbrical muscle function as revealed by a new and physiological approach, Anatomical Record, 222, 110-114.
Rothwell, J. C., Traub, M. M., Day, B. L., Obeso, J. A., Thomas, P. K., and Marsden, C. D. (1982): Manual motor performance in a deafferented man, Brain, 105, 515-542.
Schmidt, R. A. (1982): Motor Control and Learning: a Behavioral Emphasis, Human Kinetics, Champaign, Ill.
Sivak, B. (1989) Visual and motor control processes in reaching and grasping. Doctoral dissertation, Department of Kinesiology, University of Waterloo, Waterloo.

Sivak, B. and MacKenzie, C.L. (1990).The integration of visual information and motor output: the contributions of central and peripheral vision, Neuropsychologia, 28,1095-1116.
Sivak, B., and MacKenzie, C.L. (1991). The effects of object size on the organization of prehension: Sensitivity of central and peripheral vision, submitted.
Sivak, B., Sivak, J. and MacKenzie, C.L. (1985). Contact lens design for lateralizing visual input. Neuropsychologia, 28, 1095-1116.
Soechting, J.F. and Flanders, M. (1989). Errors in pointing are due to approximations in sensorimotor transformations. J. Neurophysiology, 62, 594-608.
Soechting, J.F. and Lacquiniti, F. (1983). Modification of trajectory of a pointing movment in response to a change in target location. J. Neurophysiology, 49, 548-564.
Swanson, A.B., Hagert, C. G. and Scanson, G. D. (1983). Evaluation of impairment of hand function, Journal of Hand Surgery, 8(5), 709-723.
Thomine, J. (1981): The Skin of the Hand. In R. Tubiana (Ed.), The Hand. Vol 1. Philadelphia: W.B. Saunders, 107-115.
Traub, M. M., Rothwell, J.C., and Marsden, C.D. (1980). A grab Rreflex in the human Hhand, Brain, 103: 869-884.
Tubiana, R.(1981). The Hand. Vol 1. Philadelphia: W.B. Saunders.
Vallbo, Å. B. and Johansson, R. S. (1984). Properties of cutaneous mechanoreceptors in the human hand related to touch sensation, Human Neurobiol, 3: 3-14.
Weir, P. L. (1991). The effects of object properties and task requirements on the planning and control of prehension. Doctoral dissertation, Department of Kinesiology, University of Waterloo, Waterloo.
Weir, P.L. and MacKenzie, C.L. (1991). Phases of prehension: Effects of dowel weight, dowel shape and task intent, submitted.
Weir, P.L., MacKenzie, C.L., Marteniuk, R.G., Cargoe, S. L. and Frazer, M.B. (1991). The effects of object weigh on the kinematics of prehension. Journal of Motor Behavior, 23, 192-204.
Westling, G. (1986). Sensorimotor mechanisms during precision grip in man. Umea University Medical Dissertations, University of Umea, Sweden.
Westling, G. and Johansson, R.S. (1984). Factors influencing the force control during precision grip. Experimental Brain Research, 53, 277-284.
Westling, G. and Johansson, R.S. (1987). Responses in glabrous skin mechanoreceptors during precision grip in humans. Experimental Brain Research, 66, 128-140.
Wilkes, G. L., Brown, I. A., and Wildnauer, R. H. (1973). The biomechanical properties of skin, CRC Crit Reviews in Bioengineering, 1(4): 453-495.
Winstein, C.J., Abbs, J.H., and Petashnick, D. (1991). Influences of object weight and instruction on grip force adjustments. Exp. Br. Res, in press.
Yoshikawa , T. and Nagai, K. (1990). Analysis of grasping and manipulation by multi-fingered robot hands, In: S. T. Venkataraman and T. Iberall (Eds.), Dextrous Robot Hands, NY: Springer-Verlag.

SECTION 4

STRUCTURE AND FUNCTION RELATIONSHIPS

Tutorials in Motor Behavior II
G.E. Stelmach and J. Requin (Editors)

FUNCTIONAL FORCE CONTROL IN PARKINSON'S DISEASE PATIENTS

George E. Stelmach and Umberto Castiello

Departments of Exercise Science and Physical Education and Psychology, Arizona State University, Tempe, Arizona 85287-0404

Abstract

Research on Parkinson's disease can inform cognitive neuroscience by describing the effect of a given pathology on the perception-action cycle, by identifying structural-functional relationships, and by localizing processing impairments. This chapter reviews some of the recent work on basal ganglia dysfunction and how it is manifested in movement control. The initial part of the chapter describes the pathology of the disease and its primary symptoms and is followed by an inspection of recent neuroanatomical findings. Data from Parkinson's patient studies are reviewed and grouped under general force control headings. This review documents how the various aspects of force are executed by patients in several categories: accuracy, simultaneous activation and sequential activation. Since impairments are frequently observed and because muscular force must have an appropriate amplitude and duration, the case is made that if movements disorders research is to achieve a veridical understanding of basal ganglia functioning more complex skills should be studied. In the final part of the article, two seminal research areas are described which show promise in unraveling some of the mysteries of basal ganglia function. The first area uses handwriting to demonstrate that the Parkinson's patients have difficulty in initiating and regulating force during movement sequencing. A second emerging area that uses the task of prehension suggests that basal ganglia dysfunction may also produce selective impairments in motor programming.

INTRODUCTION

Parkinson's disease (PD) is a neurodegenerative disease with predominant neuro-pathology of the basal ganglia. The main components of the basal ganglia are three large subcortical nuclei: the caudate, the putamen, and the globus pallidus. They are interconnected with two other subcortical nuclei; the subthalamic nucleus, and the substantia nigra. These five nuclei participate in the control of movement together with the cerebellum, the corticospinal system, and the brainstem (Cote and Crutcher, 1985). The damage associated with PD is primarily localized pharmacologically, and appears to affect more than one neurotransmitter system; however, it most specifically interferes with dopaminergic functioning (i.e., a loss of the dopaminergic cells in the substantia nigra (Forno, 1982; Hornykiewicz, 1982). The dopamine levels are reduced in both the substantia nigra and the ventral tegmentum (Javoy-Agid, Ruberg, Taquet, Bohobza, Agid, Gasper, Berger, N'Guyen-Legros, Alvarez, Esourelle, Scatton & Rouguier, 1984).

In its advanced form, this disease is quite specific with four predominant symptoms: (1) akinesia, a general slowness in movement, (2) bradykinesia, a slowness in the execution of voluntary movement, (3) rigidity of the musculature and (4) resting tremor of the limbs (Phillips, Mueller & Stelmach, 1989). It is generally considered that the motor abnormalities indicative of basal ganglia dysfunction are akinesia and bradykinesia (Marsden, 1984; Wing and Miller, 1984).

The previously mentioned symptoms occur early in the illness and progress often as a function of the duration of the disease. These symptoms can be, however, significantly reduced following the introduction of drug therapy. This observation has led some (Marsden, 1984; Stelmach, Worringham & Strand, 1986; Phillips et al., 1989a; Wing, 1989) to postulate that the study of loss of motor function in PD patients is perhaps the best way to learn of basal ganglia motor function, the primary pathology in humans. The task then, for research on movement disorders, is to not only identify structural disturbances associated with the disease but to show how these disturbances influence the organization and control of movement. The implication of these inferences is that the observed motor impairments in PD patients, the negative symptoms, may provide information about the role that the basal ganglia play in movement control.

RECENT NEUROANATOMICAL STUDIES

Studying the negative symptoms of Parkinson's Disease and making inferences about basal ganglia function is not without problems as the basal ganglia are connected to many other brain structures (Delong, Crutcher and Georgopoulos, 1985). The motor areas of the cerebral cortex receive major subcortical inputs from the peripheral sensory apparatus, the cerebellum and the basal ganglia. From the standpoint of understanding basal ganglia function, it is not clear, however, what the nature of their input is to the motor cortical areas for higher order of organization movement control parameters.

Basal ganglia do not project directly to the primary motor cortex; a major portion of their output from the globus pallidus and substantia nigra zona reticulata is directed via the thalamus to the supplementary motor area (SMA) and the lateral premotor cortical region (Jones, 1987). Thus the motor system is influenced via direct corticospinal projections (Wiesendanger, Hummelsheim, Bianchetti, Chen, Hyland, Mayer and Wiesendanger, 1987), as well as by projections to motor cortex itself. These findings in themselves suggest that the basal ganglia output is thus likely to be involved in the organization of movement. Moreover, other parallel basal ganglia pathways are directed, via other thalamic relay nuclei, to prefrontal cortex. To what extent these basal ganglia output are concerned with cognitive rather than movement processing is not known. The projections from basal ganglia to Area 46 seem to be involved with higher order control of movement (Goldman-RaKic and Porrino, 1985; Ilinsky, Jouandet and Goldman-Rakic, 1985). Some investigators have speculated that basal ganglia may have an important influence on supramotor areas of the cerebral cortex.

On this issue, evidence has been obtained from lesion experiments and single unit recordings in behaving animals (Alexander, DeLong and Strick, 1986; DeLong, Crutcher, 1983; DeLong, Georgopoulos, Crutcher, Mitchell, Richardson and Alexander, 1984; DeLong, Alexander, Miller and Crutcher, 1987). In order to evaluate the relationship of neural activity in basal ganglia neurons to the direction of arm movements (DeLong, 1971) and to the speed of movement (DeLong & Strick, 1974), neuronal discharge to movement parameters were examined in animals trained to perform a step-tracking task in which the amplitude, speed and direction of movement were varied (DeLong & Georgopoulos, 1979; Georgopoulos, DeLong and Crutcher, 1983). Neuronal activity in external and internal globus pallidus (GPe and GPi respectively), subthalamic nucleus and substantia nigra was recorded. It was found that significant neuronal activity for both direction and amplitude of movement were observed in GPe and GPi, and subthalamic nucleus during both the movement time and the initial premovement time. The frequency of cell discharge was a linear function of the movement amplitude. Moreover, the incidence of the amplitude finding was most prominent during movement time; some discharge effects were also present in the initial premovement time. When a wide range of movement amplitudes was used, the effect for movement amplitude became most apparent. The relationship between cell discharge and peak velocity of movement in the step-tracking task were similar to those previously described for the amplitude of movement.

The finding of significant directional activities in the globus pallidus may be explained (DeLong et al., 1984), by the observation that neurons in the putamen (Crutcher & DeLong, 1984b) and the subthalamic nucleus (Georgopoulos et al., 1983), which both project to globus pallidus, are strongly connected to the direction of movement. Since both precentral and parietal cortical cells show significant relations to the directions of movement, the relationship in the putamen and subthalamic nucleus can be accounted for by the inputs to these structures from the cerebral cortex (Evarts, 1966; Schmidt, Jost and Davis, 1975; Georgopoulos, Kalaska, Caminiti and Massey, 1982; Kalaska, Caminiti and Georgopoulos, 1983).

In 1984, Crutcher & DeLong trained monkeys to perform a visuomotor task which required elbow flexion/extension movements with assisting and opposing loads to determine whether the activity of neurons in the basal ganglia was related to the direction of movement per se, or to the activity of muscles. This task used dissociated the direction of arm movement from the pattern of muscular activity. A greater percentage (50%) of neurons related to direction of arm movement in the putamen were found, whereas only few (13%) showed pattern of muscular activity. This indicated that neurons in the putamen are more related to the direction of arm movement rather than to the activity of individuals muscles. These results, together with those for amplitude of movement (Georgopoulos et al., 1983), indicated that the basal ganglia may be involved in the control of movement parameters, rather than muscles. Moreover, since the observed neuronal relations in the putamen may reflect the nature of the inputs to this structure from the motor, premotor and somatosensory cortices, these data may have implications for the broader issue of cerebral control of movement, (DeLong et al.,1984). In addition to the observed relationship for movement amplitude and direction, it has been shown that discharge patterns are tied to steady state and dynamic loads (see Crutcher & DeLong, 1984b for a review; DeLong, 1972). On the basis of these findings, DeLong & Georgopoulos (1981), claimed that the basal ganglia serve as a "funnel" from association areas to the motor cortex (also see Evarts & Thach, 1969, Kemp & Powell, 1970).

MUSCLE ACTIVATION PATTERNS

In normal subjects, it has been shown that discrete movements are typically made with single biphasic or triphasic patterns of EMG activation in agonist and antagonist muscles. For example, Brown and Cooke (1984), have shown that movements of greater amplitude are normally accomplished by increasing the size and duration of the EMG activation. In contrast to these findings, Hallett and Khosbin (1980) have postulated that PD patients do not activate their musculature in the typically observed biphasic or triphasic patterns. They have reported data which show that PD patients are unable to generate the appropriate amount of agonist EMG activation in producing a rapid elbow flexion movement. As reported, PD patients exhibited more EMG bursts in order to accomplish the requested movement. Draper and Johns (1964) reported that in contrast to normal elderly, who show an increase in their peak velocity with increased movement amplitude, PD patients exhibited a nearly constant peak velocity across movements of different amplitude. Moreover, Hallet, Shahani & Young (1977) observed that in bradykinetic patients, additional cycles of alternating EMG bursts in the agonist and antagonist muscles are common.

These observations led Hallett and Khosbin (1980) to conclude that multiple EMG bursting is required because the amount of EMG activity that can be put into the initial burst is severely limited in PD patients. That is, PD patients fail to properly energize the agonist muscle. Subsequently Berardelli, Dick, Rothwell, Day & Marsden (1986) have shown that the first agonist burst may not completely saturate, and they suggested that in PD there is a breakdown of limb control between "perceptual appreciation" of the task goal and "delivery of the appropriate instruction" to the motor cortex.

In these previous experiments, movement amplitude covaried with movement duration such that movements of longer amplitudes were also of longer durations. Thus it is not known whether the additional cycles of EMG activity previously observed in PD patients were the result of the larger movement amplitudes or of the longer durations associated with movements of larger amplitudes. Teasdale, Phillips & Stelmach (1990) performed a study which examined the degree to which PD patients can vary the duration of their movements, and whether the increased cycles of EMG, previously observed, are associated with either slow or fast movements. EMG patterns and movement execution speed in PD patients were examined using a discrete arm task. Subjects were required to make a discrete movement through a fixed twenty-degree target barrier. Unlike previous experiments, there were no spatial accuracy constraints on the movement. In the baseline condition, subjects were instructed to produce ten self-selected maximum speed movements. In subsequent conditions, subjects were instructed to produce movements of varying speeds; ten percent faster, ten percent slower, thirty percent slower, and sixty percent slower.

The data obtained revealed that while the PD patients were slower, they were able to vary their movement speed. PD patients were able to vary their movement time when requested (191, 225, 272 and 309 ms was observed for the four speed conditions, respectively). The temporal variability revealed that the PD patients were more variable than the elderly. For both groups, the variability increased with an increase in movement time (from 16 to 31 ms) for the elderly and (from 25 to 58 ms) for the PD patients.

To examine the Hallett and Khoshbin (1980) hypothesis, the integrated agonist EMG activity for the ten percent faster and the 60 percent slower movement time conditions were compared. The results showed that PD patients did not exhibit a saturation problem. As did the elderly, PD patients modulated the amount of EMG activity produced so that faster movements were produced with much larger initial EMG activation. However, despite that the PD patients could produce more EMG activity when required, they surprisingly showed multiple bursts of EMG. Further inspection showed that the multiple bursts of EMG were not observed in the faster conditions but were produced with the slower movements. The elderly generated a constant number of bursts across differing durations whereas PD patients needed more bursts and exhibited more bursting over longer durations. These data demonstrate that rather than producing movements of longer durations by increasing the length of their first agonist burst, seven of eight PD patients required additional cycles of EMG activity. Further there was no indication that PD patients had problems appropriately activating the agonist muscle. This latter finding may be the result of reducing the need for terminal control via antagonist muscle activity. Waters and Strick (1981) found that the antagonist burst was considerably reduced and even abolished when ballistic responses were terminated by a mechanical stop.

Some support for this hypothesis is offered by Stelmach, Teasdale and Phillips (in press). They examined EMG burst activity in PD and elderly subjects during an isometric force control task. For the majority of the contractions in the elderly subjects, there was a single burst of agonist (biceps) followed by a single burst of antagonist (triceps) activity. However, the EMG patterns of PD patients were often different and were characterized by multiple EMG bursts. Furthermore, PD patients also showed inappropriate activation of the agonist muscle. For example, in Figure 1 there is shown representative force-time curves and EMG activity for the biceps and triceps muscles for two PD patients. A strong antagonist burst (triceps) was always present prior to or near the onset of force production. It is possible that this irregularity is due to an inability to inhibit antagonist muscle or an improper timing of agonists' and antagonists' muscles.

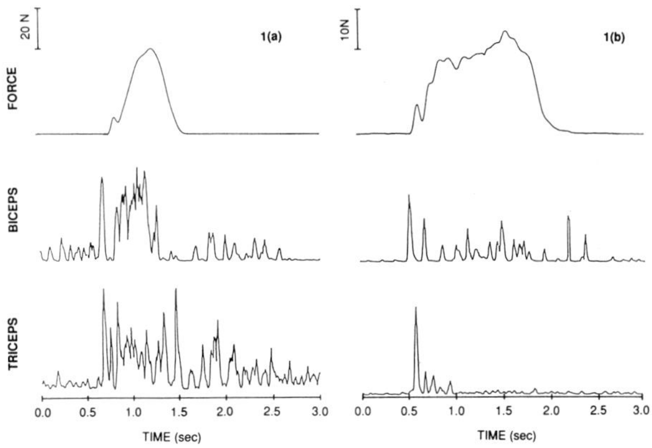

Figure 1. Representative force-time curves and their associated biceps and triceps EMG activity for two patients with Parkinson's disease. In Figure 1.(a), a strong burst of triceps activity was observed near the onset of the force production. The patient showed similar force-time curves and associated EMG in more than 60% of the trials. In Figure 1.(b), irregular triceps activity was seen throughout the force production in every trial [From Stelmach, Teasdale and Phillips, (in press)].

Milner-Brown, Fisher & Wiener (1979) have provided some insight into perhaps why PD patients have difficulties with force and velocity control. They reported that even when PD patients made an effort to maintain voluntary force control, some motor units stopped firing for prolonged periods; some of the units also fired at abnormally low frequencies (2-3 per second). Their data also agree with the Teasdale et al. (1990) data, in that they found more EMG abnormalities for slower movements. PD patients had difficulty in the recruitment of motor units at lower thresholds. Moreover, neurophysiological studies by Petajan (1983) and Dengler, Wolf, Schubert & Struppler (1986) indicate that PD patients have difficulty activating single motor units, and when activated, show an irregular firing pattern. Teulings and Stelmach (1991a) use these findings to suggest that motor unit activation may be the cause of handwriting problems in Parkinsonians. Collectively, these data suggest that in PD patients the relationship between EMG activation and force control may be somewhat impaired due to the inability to recruit and regulate motor unit activity. These findings when coupled with the observation that there is a relationship between neural activation and the amplitude of movement (DeLong et al.,1983; 1984a), may explain the observation that PD patients frequently have difficultly in controlling the amplitude of their limb movements.

FORCE CONTROL

Accuracy. Stelmach & Worringham (1988a) examined force production in PD patients in a study of isometric contractions of the elbow flexors. Using force levels of 25, 50 and 75 percent of their maximum, they found PD patients to be as accurate as controls in achieving requested force levels; however, the patients took longer to reach peak force and to complete the isometric aiming task. Slower rates of force development and irregular force-time patterns were also observed, suggesting that PD patients are deficient in producing the desired force-time pattern rather than the desired force level. There was no evidence that the PD patients did not have an accurate "internal representation" of the requested force values.

Force production was considered in more detail in a subsequent experiment by Stelmach, Teasdale, Phillips and Worringham (1989) in which patients were asked to produce similar isometric force levels. The experiment focused on examining the relationship between the peak force produced and its variability; and determining, for a given force level, how it varied in PD patients. As previously reported, patients took longer to reach their peak forces; although they produced forces as accurately as controls. Patients exhibited more irregular force-time curves, characterized by jerkiness in force production. By examining the force-time curves, it was revealed that increased force production was associated with a negatively accelerating increase in variability, which was similar to that of controls. A similar pattern was found with representative point-to-point force variability.

In executing the force aiming task, PD patients showed a much slower rate of force development (an average of 62 vs 213 n/s) and needed nearly twice as much time to achieve peak force as did the elderly controls. In a related experiment, using oral facial muscles, and showing similar trends, Abbs, Hartman & Vishwanst (1987) have shown that when asked to sustain a given force level, PD patients exhibit greater variability. Moreover, Sheridan, Flowers, Hurrel (1987) suggest that the increased variability of movement (both in time and space) exhibited by PD patients is related to their inherent variability in force production. They identify three potential sources of increased force variability: 1) an incorrect computation of the required force; 2) a defective memory for computed forces and 3) a noisy output system. While these statements are not all equally supported empirically, they do reflect trends observed in some data. Parkinsonians appear to be able to produce force levels required, but the manner in which they do it is somewhat atypical; the rate of force development is slow and the force-time curve is irregular.

Simultaneous activation. Simultaneous activation and cessation of force is an essential aspect of skilled behavior since it is necessary to control the body's many degrees of freedom for even the simplest skill (Bernstein, 1935). There have been many clinical reports that PD patients have difficulty in simultaneous actions; yet until only recently, there have been little data which have examined this ability. Benecke, Rothwell, Dick & Day (1986) examined performance of simultaneous movements in PD patients. Movements consisted of different combinations of (1) unilateral and bilateral flex and squeeze and (2) unilateral flex and cut. They found that unilateral squeeze and flex movements were significantly longer when performed together compared to the movement time of each movement performed alone. A different pattern was observed, however for the bilateral tasks, simultaneous movements showed only slight increases in movement time compared to when they were executed separately, while no change was observed in the controls. Benecke et al. interpreted these data as evidence that PD patients have an inability to carry out simultaneous movements.

Using a bimanual task which allows comparisons of initiation and termination synchrony, Stelmach and Worringham (1988b) compared PD and controls. Since bimanual arm movements to different targets have been shown to be often constrained by a temporal coupling, this task provides an excellent vehicle to examine simultaneous force control. Stelmach & Worringham (1988b) report that both control and PD patients took longer to initiate and execute asymmetrical movement compared to corresponding unimanual movements. PD patients were only shown to be slower. Unexpectedly, PD exhibited a pattern of reducing the movement durations of large amplitude movements when paired with smaller amplitude movements in the bilateral arm. The cumulative findings of Benecke et al. and Stelmach and Worringham suggest that PD does not impair the patient's ability to coordinate bimanual movement despite some reference to this in the PD literature.

Using discrete tasks designed to eliminate the temporal linkage between the limbs, as in the previous experiments, Lazarus and Stelmach (in press) utilized tasks which relied on force control in homologous muscle groups during simultaneous limb movement. At issue was whether this type of bimanual activity would bring more motor units closer to firing (Davis 1942; Wolff, Gunnoe & Cohen 1983; Todor and Lazarus 1986). Subjects performed an isometric contraction with one limb to a pre-specified submaximal force level and then initiated an isotonic movement with the other limb.

The attraction of this paradigm is that it avoids linkage via a temporal component and focuses on the potential for utilizing bilateral outflow to symmetrical muscle groups. The subjects performed three tasks: a) an isotonic elbow flexion as rapidly as possible through an angle of 30 degrees, b) an isometric contraction of the flexor muscles at the elbow joint to 40 and 60 percent of maximal volitional force for a 5 second period, and c) an isometric contraction task for 2.5 seconds with one limb while initiating the isotonic flexion task with the contralateral limb. Differential performance was observed in PD and control subjects.

The control subjects performed the isotonic movement faster and reached higher peak velocities when the movement was combined with an isometric contraction of the other limb as opposed to when it was performed alone. Conversely, PD patients performed the isotonic movement more slowly and some PD patients exhibited lower peak velocities when the movement was combined with an isometric contraction of the other limb. PD patients did not take advantage of the fact that they were using similar muscle groups (as did controls) and not only failed to enhance the isotonic movement, but demonstrated a differential slowing of the isotonic movements when executed in conjunction with the isometric contraction. As such, the patients exhibited an uncoupling or disengaging of the limbs from each other, requiring independent regulation, consequently the tasks appeared to be more difficult for the PD patients than controls.

This finding suggests that decrements in bimanual force control may be limited to tasks which have few inherent temporal components; even when using homologous muscle groups. Benecke et al. (1986); Schwab, Chafetz and Walker (1954); and Talland and Schwab (1964) using repetitive bimanual tasks have found slight impairments while using a discrete task which is known to exhibit temporal coupling. The exact nature of the decoupling observed by Lazarus and Stelmach must be further explored to determine whether the Parkinsonian difficulty can be attributed to the inability to time-share or shift attention between the bimanual tasks (Schwab et al., 1954; Talland and Schwab, 1964).

Sequential activation. It has been known for sometime that PD patients have difficulties in executing movement sequences (see Phillips et al., 1989a for review). Most of the available data suggest that PD causes a gradual deterioration in movement as the length and complexity of a movement-sequence increases. In a study which showed striking irregularities in movement-sequencing, Stelmach, Worringham and Strand (1986) found that PD patients did not organize a movement sequence as a total unit. That is, when asked to make a series of finger taps, PD patients did not exhibit a consistent couple inter-tap intervals across the movement sequence. The task employed consisted of making a series of 1, 2, 3, 4 or 5 taps as fast as possible when given an imperative response-signal. PD patients showed a striking dissociation between the first and second inter-tap interval regardless of sequence length. These findings were interpreted to suggest that PD patients may have difficulties releasing the force required to make the initial tap.

Subsequently, Stelmach, Garcia-Colera & Martin (1989) examined this issue further by requiring PD patients to make a series of 5 taps at either a slow or fast rate (200 or 600 ms inter-tap interval). Furthermore, the subjects were required to make a more forceful tap at each of the five tap locations, one through five. The subjects were either precued as to which tap was to be made more forceful or they were informed at the time of the imperative signal. This created a simple and choice RT situation. The data revealed that the production of a more forceful tap in the sequence created a dissociation in the inter-tap intervals that immediately followed the execution of force tap. This was observed for both tap rate (200 or 600 ms) conditions and for all force tap locations. This part of the data suggests that when an additional force must be layered into a movement sequence the structure of the tap sequencing breaks at the point of where the additional force is to be introduced. In other words, it appears that the CNS breaks the sequence into before and after segments regardless of the location of the additional force application in the tap sequence.

When mean reaction times were compared for the tap conditions, there was additional evidence that PD patients have trouble initiating the sequence when a force transition was added to the movement sequence. For the slow tap rate (600 ms) a RT difference was seen only for choice reaction situation. However, for the fast tapping rate (200 ms), where motor programming is required, both simple RT (precued) and choice RT rose in parallel while the no stress condition remained unchanged. These data suggest that having to make a more forceful tap in the programmed condition produced substantial delays in response latencies regardless of advance information.

Others have reported that PD patients have difficulties in making sequential responses. For example, Stern, Mayeux, Rosen and Ilson (1983) found that using a tracing task, patients had difficulty linking parts of a movement sequence without exact guidelines. Furthermore, in a series of experimental conditions, Benecke et al. (1986) required PD patients to simultaneously flex their arm and squeeze a manipulandum with the same limb. Patients with PD had a problem of superimposing and sequencing movements. For patients, unilateral squeeze and flex movements performed simultaneously were significantly longer when performed together compared to the movement times when performed alone. The data were interpreted by Benecke et al. as evidence that Parkinsonians are deficient in their ability to carry out simultaneous movements.

Tremor has been suggested as one of the causes of jerkiness and irregularity in movement sequences. For example, Nakamura, Nagasaki and Narabayashi (1978) observed that sequential movements were intrained by a characteristic rhythm, approximately at the frequency of Parkinsonian tremor. Nakamura et al. had patients perform finger taps in synchrony with a periodic stimulus. Patients exhibited difficulties at certain frequencies: between 2.5 and 5 Hz, control of tapping deteriorated and between roughly 5 and 6 Hz, hastening of movement developed, independent of the stimulus. Such data suggest that tremor may be associated with the consistently observed problems on movement sequencing in Parkinsonians.

The observed finding of force control impairments in PD patients points to the need to study complex skills related to daily life. More specifically, the data suggest that the basal ganglia in humans are concerned with the accurate execution of complex movements requiring simultaneous and sequential force activations.

HANDWRITING EXPERIMENTS

If a muscular force is to be effective in skilled movement, it must have an appropriate amplitude and duration. One area that has exploited these relationships is handwriting analyses. The analysis of stroke size and duration have proven to be an insightful way to examine force control in PD patients. Using such methods, Margolin and Wing (1983) performed handwriting analyses of micrographic patients to explore whether micrographia was caused by a primary change in applied force (measured by changes in the height of letter strokes) and/or reductions in the duration of individual letter strokes. Patients exhibited decreases in letter height with progressive decreases as a function of the number of strokes executed. Over consecutive letters, PD patients exhibited declining movement velocity and increased stroke duration. These data are supportive of the hypotheses that PD patients do not regulate or adjust force levels over sequence length.

Further evidence that demonstrates force control problems in handwriting is offered by Stelmach, Phillips and Teulings (in preparation) who examined the ability of PD and elderly to make a series of cursive e's and l's in a sequence. It was assumed that the execution of such handwriting sequences required subjects to specifically alter and execute differing amplitudes and durations of the letter strokes in a proportional manner if spatial consistency is to be maintained. These alterations require precise control of the amplitude and duration of the applied force. In normal handwriting, stroke amplitude and duration remain quite proportional for given letter sizes. This can be seen in Figure 2. These data from a typical elderly subject (upper scattergram) are plotted as a function of stroke length and duration while executing a sequence of e's and l's. As can be seen in the figure, the elderly were able to keep the stroke components (duration and length) nicely clustered when plotted against each other. This was not the case for the PD patient who exhibited a widely scattered profile. These data suggest that when PD patients are required to alter force control for the cursive e's and l's, the resultant changes are not clustered for length and duration. That is, the changes in stroke size do not appear to be modulated by changes in movement speed. These data are themselves impugn deficits in force control for PD patients but unfortunately they do not provide much insight into whether the control of amplitude or duration is the locus of the deficit.

In a similar study which used a digitizer to record the handwriting trajectories produced while executing a series of e's and l's arranged in a sequence, Phillips, Teasdale, Stelmach & Meeuwsen (1991) found that PD patients had problems modulating their movement velocities and had difficulties initiating sequences where more force alterations were required. These data were discussed in two ways: an impaired force control for individual strokes and an impaired force control between strokes when force levels are altered. On a relative basis, it appeared as though the most pronounced impairment was localized when switching from a small letter (e) to a larger letter (l) and the reverse. These data support the emerging picture that PD patients have a problem in dealing with changes in force amplitude.

In one of the seminal studies that attempted to gain insight into whether PD patients had a problem controlling force duration and/or force amplitude, Phillips, Stelmach & Teasdale (1989) required subjects to modulate their spatial or temporal aspects of handwriting. Subjects performed basic zig-zag writing strokes and were asked either to keep stroke length and duration constant, modulate the length of alternate strokes and keep stroke duration constant, or modulate duration of alternate strokes and keep amplitude constant. Phillips et al. found that PD patients were able to modulate stroke length while holding stroke duration constant. Both the control group and the PD patients had difficulty demonstrating control over their stroke durations compared to stroke length. These data are supportive of the earlier work of Teulings, Thomassen & van Galen (1986) who found that signal-to-noise ratios (SNR) for stroke size were always higher than those of stroke duration of peak acceleration. This result was interpreted as evidence that stroke size is organized at a higher level in the control hierarchy than stroke information which is thought to be derived from movement information.

Phillips et al. (1989b) also observed that PD patients had slower stroke velocities and that it was difficult to train them to execute faster. These data suggest that PD patients may be able to accurately control force, but that they take longer to prepare and execute these forces. Problems with the production of force could impose limitations on the PD patient's ability to alter movement velocities, in as much as variable and irregular force pulses pose difficulties for the CNS to predict movement outcomes. An impairment of this nature could in turn have consequences for subsequent movements causing the often observed reduction in writing velocity and compensatory change in letter size.

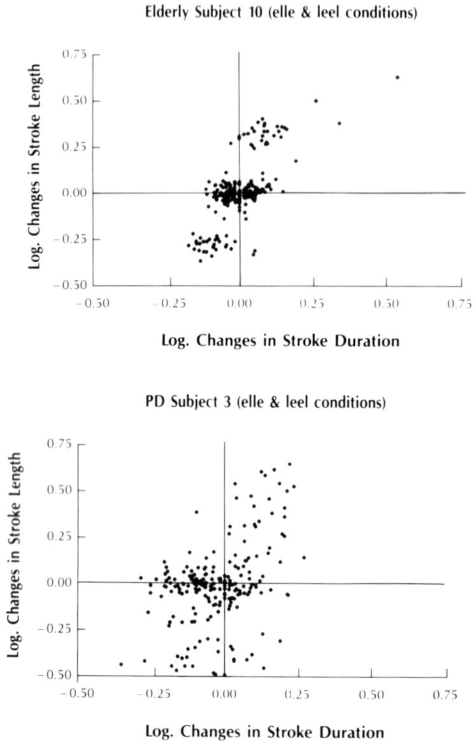

Figure 2. The scattergrams contain plots of two representative subjects making cursive e's and l's in a sequence. The top curve is for an elderly subject and the bottom one for a PD patient. The data are plotted as log changes in stroke length versus log changes in stroke duration. A scattered plot indicates that a subject is having difficulty modulating the length changes with the duration changes [from Stelmach, Phillips and Teulings (in preparation)].

When the length of the starting stroke and the number of stroke length alterations were varied, Phillips, Teasdale, Stelmach and Meeuwsen (1991) examined the handwriting of PD subjects during the performance of cursive e's and l's (2 e's and 2 l's). In normal elderly subjects, the initial writing stroke served to define the subsequent writing space by determining the size of the remaining letters in the handwriting sequence. As can be seen in Figure 3, when a sequence was initiated with a large stroke movement, normal subjects produced faster writing strokes. The elderly also had a lower average peak tangential velocity when they started with a short stroke and exhibited a much faster velocity for the large stroke. In contrast, patients had a relatively lower average peak tangential velocity when they started a movement sequence with a larger stroke and smaller peak velocity with large stroke. This finding suggests that the patients are not scaling the applied forces in a normal fashion.

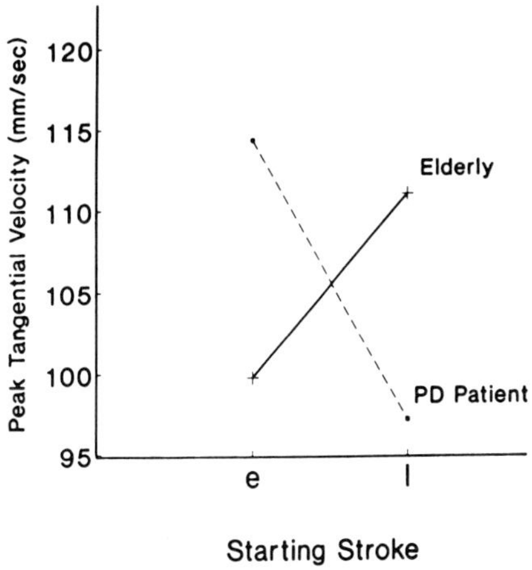

Figure 3. Average peak tangential velocity for elderly and PD patients when asked to produce either an "e" or "l" as a starting stroke. The elderly subjects produce fast velocities for larger strokes. This type profile is well established in the sensorimotor area [Phillips, Teasdale, Stelmach, Meeuwsen, 1991].

Problems in the fast initiation of movement may also create difficulties for the remainder of the handwriting sequence. For example, patients had difficulty maintaining their momentum within a movement sequence which were noted in the effects of starting stroke upon stroke length. Starting with a larger stroke created a larger writing space in normal subjects (33mm), while starting with a larger stroke had little effect upon the letter size of the PD patients. Similarly, starting with a larger stroke caused an increase in the duration of the writing strokes of elderly subjects but not in the duration of writing strokes of PD patients.

Deficits in the proper specification of initiation stroke velocities and in modulating the subsequent movement velocities have implications for the control of movement length and duration throughout a handwriting sequence. As can be seen in Figure 4, the writing strokes decrease as the PD patients progress through the sequence. A similar effect was observed for the duration of each stroke. This typical micrographic pattern suggests that the PD patients have difficulty maintaining the activated forces throughout the length of the sequence. These data are supportive of those of Margolin and Wing (1983) who have shown that letter height decreases as a function of the number of strokes executed in a sequence. Collectively, these handwriting data suggest that the PD patient cannot adjust the required force to maintain letter size over sequence length.

Teulings and Stelmach (1991a) further examined Parkinsonian handwriting and attempted to determine whether the control of stroke size or duration per stroke was substantially impaired in PD handwriting. The patient's task was to perform a specific writing pattern which contained long, short, up and down letter strokes. Besides the trajectory profiles of acceleration, velocity, and duration, the primary analysis was the use of signal-to-noise ratios (SNR) of the writing pattern. The SNR expresses the ratio between the amount of modulation due to the invariant, programmed component (signal), and the amount of modulation due to the impairment (noise). Thus, the SNR is high if a movement pattern is reproduced accurately, and low if the pattern is variable due to motor impairments (Teulings et al., 1986).

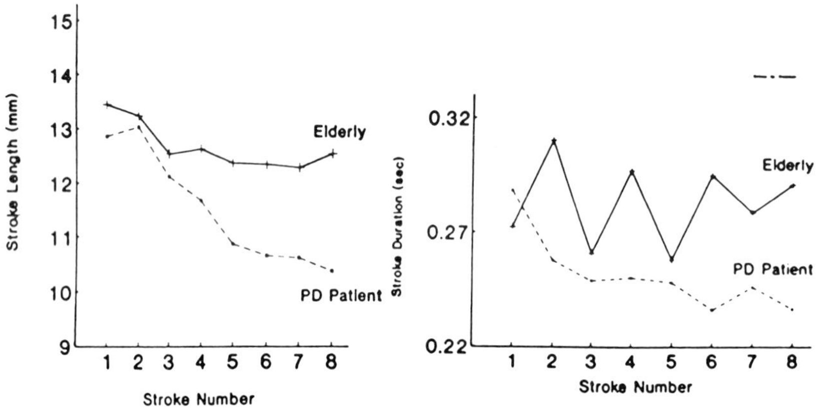

Figure 4. Average stroke length and stroke duration plotted as a function of stroke number for elderly and PD patients. The PD patients produce a typical micrographic pattern [Phillips, Teasdale, Stelmach, Meeuwsen, 1991].

The results from Teulings and Stelmach (1991a) showed that Parkinsonians, as well as normals, generally were able to modify stroke size, peak acceleration, force amplitude, and stroke duration. On the average, the PD subjects, wrote smaller and slower and did not exhibit any evidence of being influenced by the availability of feedback.

The signal-to-noise ratio analyses produced quite a different picture. For stroke size, the SNR was less in the PD patients than controls. In addition, the SNR for peak acceleration was also somewhat lower. In contrast to SNR's for stroke size and peak acceleration, the SNR for stroke duration yielded neither a significant subject group effect or a condition effect. These results offer no evidence that under conditions of reduced sensory feedback, PD patients produce their movement less accurately than do controls. Most importantly, stroke size and peak acceleration were impaired in PD patients, relative to controls, but stroke duration was not. Thus, the cumulative results suggest that during handwriting, PD patients are relatively more impaired in force amplitude, rather than in duration. Teulings and Stelmach draw upon neurophysiological studies by Petajan, 1983; Petajan and Jarcho, 1975; and Dengler, et al. 1986, to suggest that the observed handwriting impairments in Parkinsonians may be attributed to irregularities in motor unit activation patterns.

In order to produce legible handwriting, stroke shape and relative stroke size must be properly executed. These shapes and sizes are the result of net forces of appropriate amplitudes and durations at exact movements along two axes of movement. Using these concepts as a guide, Teulings and Stelmach (this volume) attempted to extend their previous findings by simulating distortions in horizontal and vertical force components of handwriting. In one simulation, force amplitude along the vertical axis of movement was lessened which created a stroke that was less than planned, which also displaced all the following strokes in the handwriting sequence. As a consequence, it was noticed that the baseline, which is normally straight, became now more varied. In the second simulation, force duration was distorted in such a way that the vertical acceleration at the beginning of a stroke was delayed relative to the horizontal component. When this was done, the sharp movement reversals required for such letters as i or u became rounded loops.

Based on the above simulations, it was possible to make predictions about the handwriting of PD patients. If the patient's primary force impairment was in amplitude, PD patients should have more irregular baselines; while if they have more loops in their letters, they would have more impairment in force duration. Of course, both force amplitude and force time could also be equally impaired.

These predictions were tested in PD patients and age-sex matched controls, where the subjects were required to perform a writing pattern repeatedly at normal speed and size, or larger or faster. The writing task was to execute a specific pattern containing upstrokes and downstrokes which were long and short and required sharp movement reversals as well as loops.

The results showed that the baseline in Parkinsonian handwriting was more irregular than that of control subjects. In contrast, relative to controls, PD patients did not make larger loops in their handwriting when letters with sharp movement reversals had to be performed (see Teulings and Stelmach for details). These observations are seen as supporting the notion that PD patients have precise control of force duration, but not force amplitude. Thus, these findings support their previous results (Teulings and Stelmach, 1991a) which suggested that force amplitude control in handwriting was impaired by Parkinson's disease. These experiments demonstrate that complex psychomotor skills such as handwriting may play a significant role in understanding how an impaired basal ganglia alters movement control.

PREHENSION EXPERIMENTS

The foregoing handwriting results point to the importance of studying more complex skills related to daily life demands. A second area that shows much promise is the study of the initiation and control of goal-directed arm movements during the act of reaching and grasping. This action combines two different type of motor behaviors. Reaching "is a primitively developed behavior for interacting with the external milieu; grasping, on the other hand, is a highly skilled type of behavior, which resulted from the unique features of the hand in primates and man" (Jeannerod, 1991).

The coupling of the two distinct behaviors in most everyday life actions make their study potentially interesting. Their quantitative analysis addresses how neural subsystems with different biological functions can be synchronized and coordinated. The level of both coordination and synchronization may be an index of how and whether Parkinsonians can couple different neural sets to perform a complex act like prehension.

Kinematic studies of prehension movements (Jeannerod, 1981; 1984; 1986) have proposed that two distinct visuo-motor channels work in a co-ordinated way to program spatial positioning of the hand (transport component) and its anticipatory posturing (grip component). The visuo-motor channel for the transport component appears to process the extrinsic properties of the object, such as spatial location, to produce appropriate movement of the arm. The channel for grip, codes for the intrinsic properties of the object, such as its size and shape, in order to program appropriate finger and hand shaping.

The concept of a two-channeled visuo-motor system is supported by both neuroanatomical and neurophysiological evidence from studies on monkeys. It is assumed that each system employs separate efferent pathways for the execution of appropriate motor responses. The crossed component of the corticospinal tract in primates has a predominant role in the control of independent finger movements. Finger control is thought to be achieved by mono-synaptic connections to the motoneurones projecting to distal forelimb musculature (e.g. Lawrence & Hopkins, 1972; Lemon, Mantel & Muir, 1986; Muir, 1985; Muir & Lemon, 1983; Passingham, Perry & Wilkinson, 1978). Such a motor pathway could be recruited during the grip component of prehension. In contrast, more proximal muscles are needed during the reaching or transport phase of prehension. These muscles may receive both ipsilateral and contralateral imput from the corticospinal and brainstem motor pathways. Such pathways could mediate neural information via polysynaptic pathways (Brinkman & Kuypers, 1973).

For each prehension component, specific linkage between the visual processing and motor pathways has been suggested by studying the behavior of single cortical cells in the inferior zone of area 6 (Gentilucci, Fogassi, Luppino, Matelli, Camarda & Rizzolatti, 1988; Rizzolatti, Camarda, Fogassi, Gentilucci, Luppino & Matelli, 1988). The activity of each set of neurons appears to code for a motor output that is relevant to the corresponding visual input. Neurons related to the transport component respond to the location of an object within a limited three-dimensional receptive field. They are active when the arm moves towards a specific sector of space. Another set of neurons are thought (Rizzolatti, et al., 1988) to be involved in the manipulation component of prehension. They are active during the performance of different types of grasps and frequently respond to visual objects, provided the object size is congruent with the type of grasp that activates the neuron.

Further evidence for a dissociation between the neural substrate for the grip and transport components comes from lesion studies. Damage to the parieto-occipital junction (area 7) of the monkey disturbs the control of grip formation. If the lesion is extended to involve the superior parietal lobule (areas 5 and 7) clear deficits in both reaching and grasping result (Denny-Brown, Yanagisawa & Kirk, 1975; Faugier-Grimaud, Frenois & Peronnet, 1985; Haaxma and Kuypers, 1975). Similar findings have been observed in human patients who suffered from damage to these independent cortical networks. With surgical resection of area 4 (Hecaen and Ajuriaguerra, 1948) contralateral recovery occurred primarily in the proximal upper limb while isolated finger movements were permanently lost. Extensive damage to the left primary parietal region (Jeannerod, Michel & Prablanc, 1984) produced deficits in preshaping and grip formation. Additionally, lesions more specifically located in the posterior parietal cortex led to spatial disorientation and misreaching which resembled that seen in monkeys with restricted lesions of Brodmann's area 7 (Jeannerod, 1986; Perenin & Vighetto, 1988).

Despite the apparent independence of these two systems, some degree of interplay must exist for the performance of accurate prehensile movements. The ability of primates to perform functional grasps which range from fine precision to more gross power grips (Napier, 1956) implies that the relationship between the two systems adjusts according to the requirements of the task. Prehension guided by the two channel systems provides an opportunity to examine how PD patients couple distinctly different movement components into a functional act.

In a seminal human study of prehension movement in patients affected by Parkinson's disease, Zackon (1989) analyzed the kinematic parameters of prehension movements under varying conditions of movement amplitude, speed and object size in parkinsonians and age-matched controls. Although parkinsonians were slower overall than controls, patients and controls similarly adjusted the spatial and temporal characteristics of their limb movement and grasping response to changes in task demands. All groups showed increases in the speed of limb transport, the speed of hand opening and began hand opening proportionately earlier at faster movement speeds and similarly increased hand opening velocity and initiated grasp earlier for smaller amplitude movements. Likewise, grasp was initiated earlier when reaching for wider objects. However, in contrast to controls, the onset time of hand opening during limb transport was delayed in these patients and was found to be more closely coupled with the timing of limb transport than in controls. Thus, the differences between patients and controls in the temporal sequencing of the transport and manipulation components may reflect an impairment caused by basal ganglia dysfunctions.

Similar results were found by Müller & Stelmach (see this volume). In this study patients were also slower than controls. Of interest, was that PD patients showed an impairment in the deceleration period when they were instructed to move fast or to grasp an object with their eyes closed. PD patients could vary their tangential velocity of the transport component, but they were unable to pick up the object very fast when they were instructed to do so. Of major interest are the results related to the manipulation component and the type of strategy patients used. The safety margin of grip aperture for movements in which errors in spatial accuracy occurred have to be taken into account. Furthermore, PD patients needed significantly more time to establish a firm grip when their eyes were closed.

Perturbation studies provide additional means of probing the temporal coupling between the two visuo-motor channels. The reorganization which occurs following the introduction of a visual perturbation during the movement may further clarify the basal ganglia's role in guiding the movement to its goal. Alterations to the movement kinematics and trajectory, and the temporal characteristics of such reorganization should reflect the activity of the neural structures involved in the goal-directed action.

A visual perturbation paradigm was used by Jeannerod and coworkers (Castiello, Paulignan & Jeannerod, in press; Paulignan, MacKenzie, Marteniuk and Jeannerod, 1990; Paulignan, MacKenzie, Marteniuk and Jeannerod, 1991) to examine the effects of introducing unanticipated changes in the position of a target object immediately prior to or during a prehension movement. Though, in principle, perturbation of object position should only affect the transport component, change was also observed in the formation of the grip. The targets were graspable dowels located on a concentric array at a fixed distance from the hand. The movement was started by the illumination of the central dowel, but sometimes (20 percent) the light shifted from that dowel to another, just at the onset of the reaching movement. When the perturbation took place, a complex rearrangement of the wrist and finger trajectories was observed, with a relatively small increase of movement duration (100 msec). Inspection of the wrist kinematic (transport component) showed that, following the perturbation, the initial acceleration was aborted and a secondary acceleration took place in order to direct the hand to the final target. The first acceleration peak occurred earlier in the perturbed trials than in non-perturbed trials. A more complete analysis of these results showed that the effects of object displacement were not limited to corrections affecting the transport component. The grip aperture was also affected. On most perturbed trials, the two components of prehension became kinematically coupled during corrective responses. The alterations of the wrist trajectory for reorienting the movement to the new target position was immediately followed by a brief interruption of grip aperture, unrequired by the situation since object size and shape remained unchanged.

A further study to verify if the kinematic events of transport and manipulation are temporally coupled was designed by Gentilucci, Chieffi, Scarpa & Castiello (in press). They used a visual perturbation paradigm similar to that employed by Paulignan et al.(1990; 1991). The only difference was that visual perturbation did affect movement amplitude instead of movement direction. The targets consisted of three spheric objects on the mid-sagittal plane located at 150, 270 and 40 cm from the resting position. In the first session, the subjects performed 10 experimental trials. The subjects were told which of the targets they were asked to grasp (blocked trials). In the second session the trial started by illuminating the nearest sphere. In 20% of cases (Perturbed trials) the light shifted to one of the two far spheres at the onset of arm movement. In order to verify if different processing times were required to reorganize the transport and manipulation components, the temporal course of both components after visual perturbation was examined. The results revealed that a temporal coupling between events of the two components was nonexistent. In addition, evidence was found that the time course of manipulation component is planned according to the time required to reach the object to be grasped.

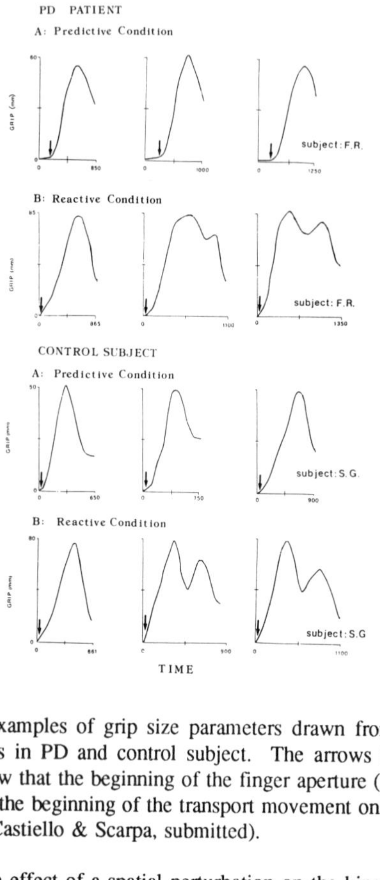

Figure 5. Representative examples of grip size parameters drawn from kinematic analysis for predictive and reactive trials in PD and control subject. The arrows indicate the onset of the transport movement and show that the beginning of the finger aperture (manipulation component) was delayed with respect to the beginning of the transport movement onset (transport component) in predictive trials for PD (Castiello & Scarpa, submitted).

In order to study the effect of a spatial perturbation on the kinematic characteristics of a prehension movement, an identical experiment was performed on elderly and PD subjects (Castiello & Scarpa, submitted). The authors postulated that the blocked trials condition related to a predictive behavior based on input from the visuo-motor channels prior to movement. The perturbed trials utilized a reactive behavior due to the displacement of the target during the reaching movement. This displacement produced a reorganization of both the transport and manipulation components. It was suggested by the authors that finding abnormal kinematics in the predictive condition and normal kinematics in the reactive condition would point to a selective disruption of open-loop, predictive motor control. Moreover, if a different pattern of acceleration curves is found in the two groups, it could underlie a different response strategy to the change in target location. Therefore, a impaired ability in superimposing or adjusting motor programs could be inferred. The problems of whether predictive motor behavior is damaged in PD (Flowers, 1975; 1976; 1978; Cooke, Brown & Brooks, 1978; Baroni, Benvenuti, Fantini, Pantaleo and Urbani, 1984; Sheridan et al. 1987; Stelmach et al., 1986; Frith, Bloxham and Carpenter, 1986) has produced mixed results. There has also been much debate about whether simultaneous movements control are impaired (Schwab, Chafetz and Walker, 1954; Talland, 1963; Talland and Schwab, 1964; Horne, 1953; Benecke et al., 1985; 1986; 1987).

Castiello and Scarpa found that PD patients are able to pre-program prehension movements, as well as control subjects. Also it was observed that during the transport or the manipulation component of the first movement, spatial perturbations caused an anticipation of all recorded kinematic components. The main difference between Parkinsonians and controls, besides an increase of all time intervals, was found in the delay in the onset of the manipulation with respect to the transport component (80 msec). This delay was significantly reduced by the introduction of a visual perturbation, indicating that PD patients, when using a reactive mode of control, can re-couple the two motor components. The delayed pattern in the PD patients was interpreted as a lack of coordination between two components, and their reorganization as an attempt at re-coupling. This observation, leads to the hypothesis that the reaching-grasping movement is directed by two distinct motor programs, and these motor programs are not tightly coupled in PD patients. This observation suggests that the basal ganglia may be involved in coupling these motor behaviors.

In their conclusion, Castiello and Scarpa suggested that, as stated previously, if reaching-grasping movement requires the activation of two motor programs, it may be concluded that Parkinsonians show a deficit in coupling two distinct motor programs within the same limb segment, and that the basal ganglia may play a role not only regulating movement execution but also in motor programming. As with the handwriting research, the work of prehension show promise in providing insight into how an impaired basal ganglia may alter dynamic skilled behavior.

CONCLUDING COMMENT

The data reviewed in this chapter suggest that basal ganglia impairment, caused by Parkinson's disease, impairs the ability to program muscular forces. This loss of force control is seen in slower reaction times when an accurate force is required, in slower and more irregular force time curves, and in movement sequences where force alterations are necessary. Furthermore, the study of complex skills such as handwriting and prehension suggest that the observed movement impairments may be selective and manifested in specific ways. Recent handwriting data suggest that when applied force is decomposed into amplitude and duration components, both appear to be impaired; however, on a relative basis, force amplitude may be slightly more affected. Additionally, prehension experiments further suggest that the programming of forces that regulate the transport and manipulation components of reaching may be altered in situations where the controlling forces are assembled from anticipatory information.

Cognitive-neuroscience has the task of elucidating the role(s) of the basal ganglia in motor control. Because Parkinson's disease is related to disturbances in the basal ganglia, research on PD patients provide some insight into basal ganglia function. When information is transmitted from and through an impaired brain structure, research must carefully document how and which motor functions are disturbed. In the case of Parkinson's disease, this is best accomplished by combining graphic accounts, in terms of the brain function involved, in terms of the motor processing operations utilized, and in terms of the pathology which propagated the perdition in the nervous system.

REFERENCES

Abbs, J.H., Hartman, D.E. and Vishwanst, B. (1987). "Orofacial motor control impairment in Parkinson's Disease," *Neurology, 37*, 394-398.

Alexander, G.E., DeLong, M.R. and Strick, P.L. (1986). "Parallel organization of functionally segregated circuits linking basal ganglia and cortex." *Annual Review of Neuroscience, 9*, 357-381.

Baroni, A., Benvenuti, F., Fantini, L., Pantaleo, T. and Urbani, F. (1984). "Human ballistic arm abduction movements: effects of L-dopa treatment in Parkinson's disease," *Neurology, 34*, 868-876.

Benecke, R., Day, B.L., Dick, J.P.R., Marsden, C.D., Rothwell, J.C. (1985). "Performance of various types of simultaneous movements in patients with Parkinson's disease," *Journal of Physiology, 369*, 30P.

Benecke, R., Rothwell, J.C., Dick, J.P.R., Day, B.L. and Marsden, C.D. (1986). "Performance of simultaneous movements in patients with Parkinson's disease," *Brain, 109*, 739-757.

Benecke, R., Rothwell, J.C., Dick, J.P.R., Day, B.L. and Marsden, C.D. (1987). "Simple and complex movements off and on treatment in patients with Parkinson's disease," *Journal of Neurology, Neurosurgery, and Psychiatry, 50*, 296-303.

Berardelli, A., Accornero, N., Argenta, M., Meco, G. and Manfredi, M. (1986). "Scaling of the size of the first agonist EMG burst during rapid wrist movements in patients with Parkinson's disease," *Journal of Neurology, Neurosurgery and Psychiatry, 49*, 1273-1279.

Berardelli, A., Dick, J.P.R., Rothwell, J.C., Day, B.L. and Marsden, C.D. (1986). "Scaling of the size of the first agonist EMG burst during rapid wrist movements in patients with Parkinson's disease," *Journal of Neurology, Neurosurgery, and Psychiatry, 50*, 1178-1183.

Bernstein, N. (1935). "The problem of the interrelation of coordination and localization," Arch. Biol., 38, 15-59. Reprinted in Bernstein, N. (1967). *The coordination and regulation of movements*. Oxford: Pergamon Press.

Brinkman, J. and Kuypers, H.G.J.M. (1973). "Cerebral control of contralateral and ipsilateral arm, hand and finger movements in the split-brain rhesus monkey," *Brain, 96*, 653-674.

Brown, S.H. and Cooke, J.D. (1981) "Amplitude and instruction dependent modulations of movement-related electromyogram activity in humans," *Journal of Physiology, 316*, 97-107.

Castiello, U., Paulignan, Y. and Jeannerod, M. "Temporal dissociation of motor responses and subjective awareness: a study in normal subjects," *Brain*, in press.

Castiello, U. and Scarpa, M. "Perturbation of a prehension movement in Parkinson's disease," submitted.

Cooke, J.D., Brown, J.D., Brooks V.B. (1978). "Increased dependence on visual information for movement control in patients with parkinson's disease," *Le Journal Canadien des Sciences Neurologiques, 5*, 413-415.

Cote, L. and Crutcher, M.D. (1985). "Motor functions of the basal ganglia and diseases of transmitter metabolism." In E. Kandel and J. Schwartz (Eds), *Principles of Neural Science*. Amsterdam, Elsevier, pp. 524-535.

Crutcher, M.D. and DeLong, M.R. (1984b). "Single cells studies the primate putamen. II. Relation to direction of movements and pattern of muscular activity," *Experimental Brain Research, 53*, 244-258.

Davis, R.C. (1942). "The pattern of muscular action in simple voluntary movement," *Journal of Experimental Psychology, 315*, 347-366.

DeLong, M.R. (1972). "Activity of basal ganglia neurons during movement," *Brain Research, 40*, 127-135.

DeLong, M.R. and Georgopoulos, A.P. (1979). "Motor functions of the basal ganglia as revealed by studies of single cell activity in the behaving primates," *Advances in Neurology, 24,* 131-140.

DeLong, M.R. and Georgopoulos, A.P. (1981). "Motor functions of the basal ganglia," In Brookhart J.M. et al. (eds). *The nervous system.* American Physiological Society, Bethesda, MD (Handb Physiol) pp. 1017-1061.

DeLong, M.R., Georgopoulos, A.P., Crutcher, M.D., Mitchell, S.J. and Richardson, R.T. (1984a). "Role of basal ganglia in limb movement," *Human Neurobiology, 2,* 235-244.

DeLong, M.R., Georgopoulos, A.P., Crutcher, M.D., Mitchell, S.J., Richardson, R.T. and Alexander, G.E. (1984b). *In functions of the basal ganglia.* London, Pitman, (Ciba Foundation Symposium 107) pp. 64-82.

DeLong, M.R., Crutcher, M.D. and Georgopoulos A.P. (1985). "Primate globus pallidus and subthalamic nucleus: functional organization," *Journal of Neurophysiology, 53,* 530-543.

DeLong, M.R., Crutcher, M.D. and Georgopoulos, A.P. (1983). "Relation between movement and single cell discharge in the substantia nigra of the behaving monkey," *Journal of Neuroscience, 3,* 1599-1606.

DeLong, M.R., Alexander, G.E., Miller, W.C. and Crutcher, M.D. (1987). "Anatomical and functional aspects of basal ganglia - thalamocortical circuits," *Motor areas of the cerebral cortex.* Chichester, Wiley, (Ciba Foundation Symposium 132) pp. 21-39.

DeLong, M.R. (1971). "Activity of pallidal neurons during movement," *Journal of Neurophysiology, 34,* 414-427.

DeLong, M.R. and Strick, P.L. (1974), "Relation of basal ganglia, cerebellum, and motor cortex units to ramp and ballistic limb movements," *Brain Research, 71,* 327-335.

DeLong, M.R. and Georgopoulos, A.P. (1979). "Motor functions of the basal ganglia," In Brookhart J.M. et al. (eds), *The Nervous system.* American Physiological Society, Bethesda, MD (Handb Physiol) pp 1017-1061.

Dengler, R.W., Wolf, M., Schubert, M. and Struppler, A. (1986). "Discharge pattern of single motor units in basal ganglia disorders," *Neurology, 36,* 1061-1068.

Denny-Brown, D., Yanagisawa, N., and Kirk, E.J. (1975). "The localization of hemispheric mechanisms of visually directed reaching and grasping," In K.J. Zulch, O. Creutzfeldt and G.C. Galbraith (Eds.), *Cerebral Localization,* New York, Springer-Verlag.

Draper, I.T. and Johns, R.S. (1964). "The disorders of movement in Parkinsonism and the effect of drug treatment," *Bulletin of the John Hopkins Hospital, 115,* 465-480.

Evarts, E.V. (1966). "Pyramidal tractactivity associated with a conditioned hand movement in the monkey," *Journal of Neurophysiology, 29,* 1011-1027.

Evarts, E.V. and Thach W.T. (1969). "Motor mechanisms of the CNS: cerebrocerebellar interrelations," *Annual Review of Physiology, 31,* 451-498.

Faugier-Grimaud, S., Frenois, C. and Peronnet, F. (1985). "Effects of posterior parietal lesions on visually guided movements in monkeys," *Experimental Brain Research, 59,* 125-138.

Flowers, K.A. (1975). "Ballistic and corrective movements on an aiming task," *Neurology, 25,* 413-421.

Flowers, K.A. (1976). "Visual 'closed-loop' and 'open-loop' characteristics of voluntary movement in patient with Parkinson's disease," *Brain, 99,* 269-310.

Flowers, K.A. (1978). "Lack of prediction in the motor behavior of Parkinsonism," *Brain, 101,* 35-52.

Forno, L.S. (1982). "Pathology of Parkinson's disease." In C.D. Marsden and Fahn (Eds.), *Movement disorders.* Butterworths, London, pp. 25-40.

Frith, C.D., Bloxham, C.A., Carpenter, K.N. (1986). "Impairments in the learning and performance of a new manual skill in patients with Parkinson's disease," *Journal of Neurology, Neurosurgery and Psychiatry, 49,* 661-668.

Gentilucci, M., Chieffi, S., Scarpa, M. and Castiello, U. (in press) "Temporal coupling between transport and manipulation components during prehension movements: effect of visual perturbation," *Behavioral Brain Research* (in press).

Gentilucci, M., Fogassi, L., Luppino, G., Matelli, M., Camarda, R. and Rizzolatti, G. (1988). "Functional organization of inferior area 6 in the macaque monkey. I. Somatotopy and the control of proximal movements," *Experimental Brain Research, 71*, 475-490.

Georgopoulos, A.P., Kalaska, J.F., Caminiti, R., Massey, J.T. (1982). "On the relation between the direction of two-dimensional arm movements and cell discharge in primate motor cortex,". *Journal of Neuroscience, 2,* 1527-1537.

Georgopoulos, A.P., DeLong, M.R. and Crutcher, M.D. (1983). "Relation between parameters of step-tracking movements and single cell discharge in the globus pallidus and subthalamic nucleus of the behaving monkey,". *Journal of Neuroscience, 3,* 1586-1598.

Goldman-Rakic, P.S., Porrino L.J. (1985). "The primate mediodorsal (MD) nucleus and its projections to the frontal lobe," *Journal of Comparative Neurology, 242,* 535-560.

Haaxma, H. and Kuypers, H.G.J.M. (1975). "Intrahemispheric cortical connections and visual guidance of hand and finger movements in the rhesus monkey," *Brain, 98,* 239-260.

Hallett, M. and Khosbin, S. (1980). "A physiological mechanism of bradykinesia," *Brain, 103,* 301-314.

Hallett, M., Shahani, B.T. and Young, R.R. (1977). "Analysis of stereotyped voluntary movements at the elbow in patients with Parkinson's disease," *Journal of Neurology, Neurosurgery and Psychiatry, 40,* 1129-1135.

Hecaen, H. and Ajuriaguerra, J. (1948). "Etude de troubles toniques, moteurs et vegetatifs et de leur recuperation apres ablation limitee du cortex moteur et premoteur," *Congres de Medecins Alienistes et Neurologistes,* pp. 249-274.

Hefter, J., Homberg, V., Lange, H.W. and Freund, H.J. (1987). "Impairment of rapid movement in Huntington's disease," *Brain, 110,* 585-612.

Horne D.J. De L (1953). "Sensorimotor control in Parkinson's disease," *Journal of Neurology, Neurosurgery and Psychiatry, 49,* 661-668.

Hornykiewicz, O. (1982). "Brain neurotransmitter changes in Parkinson's disease." In C.D. Marsden and S. Fahn (Eds.), *Movement disorders,* Butterworths, London, pp. 41-58.

Ilinsky, I.A., Jouandet, M.L., Goldman-Rakic, P.S. (1985). "Organization of the nigrothalamo-cortical system in the reshus monkeys," *Journal of Comparative Neurology, 236,* 315-330.

Javoy-Agid, F., Ruberg, M., Taquet, H., Bokobza, B., Agid, Y., Gaspar, P., Berger, B., N'Guyen-Legros, J., Alvarez, C., Gray, F., Esourelle, R., Scatton, B. and Rouquier, L. (1984). "Biomechanical neuropathology of Parkinson's disease." In G. Hassler and J.F. Chirst (Eds.), *Advances in Neurology.* Raven Press, New York, Volume 40, pp. 189-198.

Jeannerod, M. (1981). "Intersegmental coordination during reaching at natural visual objects," In J. Long and A. Baddeley (Eds.), *Attention and Performance IX,* Hillsdale, Erlbaum, pp. 153-168.

Jeannerod, M.(1984). "The timing of natural prehension movements," *Journal of Motor Behav., 16,* 235-254.

Jeannerod, M. (1986). "Mechanisms of visuomotor coordination. A study in normal and brain-damaged subjects," *Neuropsychologia, 24,* 41-78.

Jeannerod, M., Michel, F. and Prablanc, C. (1984). "The control of hand movements in a case of hemianesthesia following a parietal lesion," *Brain, 107,* 899-920.

Jeannerod, M. (in press) "Reaching and grasping: Parallel specification of visuomotor channels," In H. Heuer and S.W. Keele (Eds), *Motor Skills, Volume 3* of Enzyklopaedie der Psychologie. Goettingen: Hogrefe.

Jones, E.G. (1987). "Ascending inputs to, and internal organization of, cortical motor areas," In *Motor areas of the cerebral cortex*. Wiley, Chichester. (Ciba Foundation Symposium 132), pp.21-39.

Kalaska, J.F., Caminiti, R., Georgopoulos, A.P. (1983). "Cortical mechanisms related to the direction of two-dimensional arm movements: relations in parietal area 5 and comparison with motor cortex," *Experimental Brain Research, 51*, 247-260.

Kemp, J.M. and Powell, T.P.S. (1970). "The corticostriate projection in the monkey," *Brain, 93*, 525-546.

Lawrence, D.G. and Hopkins, D.A. (1972). "Development aspects of pyramidal control in the rhesus monkey," *Brain Research, 40*, 117-118.

Lazarus, J.C. and Stelmach, G.E. "Interlimb Coordination in Parkinson's Disease," *Journal of Movement Disorders*. In press.

Lemon, R.N., Mantel, G.W.H. and Muir, R.B. (1986). "Corticospinal facilitation of hand muscles during voluntary movements in the conscious monkey," *Journal of Physiology, 381*, 497-527.

Margolin, D.I. and Wing, A.M. (1983). "Agraphia and Micrographia: Clinical manifestations of motor programming and performance disorders," *Acta Psychologia, 54*, 263-283.

Marsden, C.D. (1984). "Function of the basal ganglia as revealed by cognitive and motor disorders in Parkinson's disease," *Canadian Journal of Neurological Science, 11*, 129-135.

Milner-Brown, H.S., Fisher, M.A., and Wierner, J. (1979). "Electrical properties in motor units in Parkinsonian and a possible relationship with bradykinesia," *Journal of Neurology, Neurosurgery, and Psychiatry, 42*, 35-41.

Muir, R.B. (1985). "Small hand muscles in precision grip: a corticospinal pregorative?," *Experimental Brain Research Supplement, 10*, 155-174.

Muir, R.B. and Lemon, R.N. (1983). "Corticospinal neurons with a special role in precision grip," *Brain Research, 261*, 312-316.

Müller, F. and Stelmach, G.E. (1991). "Prehension Movements in Parkinson's Disease," In *Motor Behavior II*, G.E. Stelmach and Jean Requin (Eds.). North-Holland, Amsterdam.

Nakamura, R., Nagasaki, H. and Narabayashi, H. (1978). "Disturbances of rhythm formation in patients with Parkinson's disease: Part I. Characteristics of tapping responses to the periodic signals," *Perceptual and Motor Skills, 46*, 63-75.

Napier, J.R. (1956). "The prehensile movement of the human hand," *Journal of Bone and Joint Surgery, 38B*, 902-913.

Passingham, R. E., Perry, V. H. and Wilkinson, F. (1978). "Failure to develop a precision grip in monkeys with unilateral neocortical lesion made in infancy," *Brain Research, 145*, 410-414.

Paulignan, Y., MacKenzie, C.L., Marteniuk, R.G. and Jeannerod, M. (1990). "The coupling of arm and finger movements during prehension," *Experimental Brain Research, 79*, 431-436.

Paulignan, Y., MacKenzie, C.L., Marteniuk, R.G. and Jeannerod M. (1991). "Selective perturbation of visual input during prehension movements. I. The effects of changing object position," *Experimental Brain Research, 83*, 502-512.

Perenin, M.T. and Vighetto, A. (1988). "Optic ataxia: a specific disruption in visuomotor mechanisms. I. Different aspects of the deficit in reaching for objects, *Brain, 111*, 643-674.

Petajan, J.H. (1983). "Motor unit control in movement disorders." In E. Desmedt (Ed.), *Motor Control Mechanisms in Health Disease*. Raven Press, New York.

Petajan, J.H. and Jarcho, L.W. (1975). "Motor unit control and Parkinson's disease and the influence of levodopa," *Neurology, 25*, 866-869.

Phillips, J.G., Mueller, F. and Stelmach, G.E. (1989a). "Movement disorders and the neural basis of motor control." In S. Wallace (Ed.), *Perspectives on the Coordination of Movement*. North-Holland, Amsterdam, pp. 367-417.

Phillips, J. and Stelmach, G.E. (1991). "The contribution of movement disorders research to theories of motor control and learning." In J. Summers (Ed.), *Approaches to the Study of Motor Control and Learning*. North-Holland Publishing, Amsterdam.

Phillips, J., Stelmach, G.E. and Teasdale, N. (1989b). "Preliminary assessment of spatio-temporal control of handwriting in Parkinsonians." In R. Plamondon, C.Y. Suen and M.L. Simner (Eds.), *Computer Recognition and Human Production of Handwriting*. World Scientific Publishing Company, Singapore, pp. 317-331.

Phillips, J.G., Stelmach, G.E. and Teasdale, N. (1991). "What can indices of handwriting quality tell us about Parkinson's disease handwriting?", *Journal of Human Movement Science, 10*, 301-314.

Phillips, J.G., Teasdale, N., Stelmach, G.E. and Meeuwsen, H. (1991). "Movement sequencing in the handwriting of patients with Parkinson's disease," (in preparation).

Phillips, J.G., Teasdale, N. and Stelmach, G.E. (1991). "Spatio-temporal control of handwriting in patients with Parkinson's disease," (in preparation).

Rizzolatti, G., Camarda, R., Fogassi, L., Gentilucci, M., Luppino G. and Matelli, M. (1988). "Functional organization of inferior area 6 in the macaque monkey. II. Area F5 and the control of distal movements," *Experimental Brain Research, 71*, 491-507.

Schmidt, E.M., Jost, R.G. and Davis, K.K. (1975). "Reexamination of the force relationship of cortical cell discharge pattern with conditioned wrist movement," *Brain Research, 83*, 213-223.

Schwab, R.S., Chafetz, M.E., Walker, R.N. (1954). "Control of two simultaneous voluntary motor acts in normal and parkinsonism," *Archives of Neurology and Psychiatry, 75*, 591-598.

Sheridan, M.R., Flowers, K.A. and Hurrell, J. (1987). "Programming and execution of movements in Parkinson's disease," *Brain, 110*, 1247-1271.

Stelmach, G.E., Garcia-Colera, A. and Martin, Z. (1989). "Force transition control with a movement sequence in Parkinson's disease patients," *Journal of Neurology, 236*, 406-410.

Stelmach, G.E. and Phillips, J.G. (1990). "Movement disorders: Limb movements and the basal ganglia," *Journal of Physical Therapy, 21*, 60-68.

Stelmach, G.E., Phillips, J. and Chau, A.W. (1989). "Visuo-spatial information processing in Parkinsonians," *Neuropsychologia, 27*, 485-493.

Stelmach, G.E., Phillips, J.G. and Teulings, H.L. "Force control irregularities during cursive handwriting. (in preparation).

Stelmach, G.E. and Teasdale, N. (1991). "Force control in Parkinson's disease patients," *Journal of Human Movement Science*, (in press).

Stelmach, G.E., Teasdale, N., Phillips, J. and Worringham, C.J. (1989). "Force production characteristics in Parkinson's disease," *Experimental Brain Research, 76*, 165-172.

Stelmach, G.E., Teasdale, N. and Phillips, J. (1990). "Initiation and accuracy of force production in Parkinson's disease." In *Advances in Parkinson's Disease Research*, Raven Press (in press). Also in M. Streifler (Ed.), Proceedings of the 9th International Symposium on Parkinson's Disease, Jerusalem, Israel, June 5-9, 1988 (in press).

Stelmach, G.E. and Worringham, C.J. (1988a). "The control of bimanual aiming movements in Parkinson's disease," *Journal of Neurology, Neurosurgery & Psychiatry, 51*, 223-231.

Stelmach, G.E. and Worringham, C.J. (1988b). "The preparation and production of isometric force in Parkinson's disease," *Neuropsychologia, 26*, 93-103.

Stelmach, G.E., Worringham, C.J. and Peters, H.H. (1989). "Preparatory processes in a case of hemi-parkinsonism," *Journal of Neurology, 236*, 174-178.

Stelmach, G.E., Worringham, C.J. and Strand, E.A. (1986). "Movement preparation in Parkinson's disease: The use of advanced information," *Brain, 109*, 1179-1194.

Stelmach, G.E., Worringham, C.J. and Strand, E.A. (1987). "The programming and execution of movement sequences in Parkinson's disease," *International Journal of Neuroscience, 36,* 55-65.

Stern, Y., Mayeux, R., Rosen, J. and Ilson, J. (1983). "Perceptual motor dysfunction in Parkinson's Disease: A Deficit in Sequential and Predictive Voluntary Movement," *Journal of Neurology, Neurosurgery and Psychiatry,* 46, 145-151.

Stern, Y. and Mayeux, R. (1986). "Intellectual impairment in Parkinson's disease." In M.D. Yahr and K.J. Bergmann (Eds.), *Advances in Neurology, Vol. 45,* Parkinson's disease. Raven Press, New York, pp. 405-408.

Talland, G.A. (1963). "Manual skill in Parkinson's disease," *Geriatrics, 18,* 613-620.

Talland, G.A. and Schwab, R.S. (1964). "Performance with multiple tests in Parkinson's disease," *Neuropsychologia, 2,* 45-53.

Teasdale, N., Phillips, J. and Stelmach, G.E. (1990). "Temporal movement control in patients with Parkinson's disease," *Journal of Neurology, Neurosurgery, and Psychiatry, 53,* 862-868.

Teasdale, N. and Stelmach, G.E. (1988). "Movement disorders: The importance of the movement context," *Journal of Motor Behavior, 20,* 186-191.

Teulings, J.L., Thomassen, A.J.W.M., and van Galen, G.P. (1986). "Invariances in handwriting: the information contained in a motor program." In H.S.R. Kao, G.P. van Galen and R. Hoosain (Eds.), *Graphonomics: Contemporary Research in Handwriting.* North-Holland, Amsterdam, pp. 305-315.

Teulings, J.H. and Stelmach, G.E. (1991a). "Force amplitude and force timing in Parkinsonian handwriting." In J. Requin and G.E. Stelmach (Eds.), *Tutorials in Motor Neuroscience.* Kluwer, Amsterdam, this volume.

Teulings, J.H. and Stelmach, G.E. (1991b). "Control of stroke size, peak acceleration, and stroke duration in parkinsonian handwriting," *Journal of Human Movement Science, 10,* 315-333.

Todor, J.I. and Lazarus, J.C. (1986). "Execution level and the intensity of associated movements," *Developmental Medicine and Child Neurology, 28,* 205-212.

Waters, P. and Strick, P.L. (1981). "Influence of strategy on muscle activity during ballistic movements," *Brain Research, 207,* 189-194.

Wiesendanger, M., Hummelsheim, H., Bianchetti, M., Chen, D.F., Hyland, B., Maier, V. and Wiesendanger, R. (1987). "Input and output organization of the supplementary motor area," In *Motor area of the cerebral cortex.* Wiley, Chichester (Ciba Foundation Symposium 132), pp. 40-62.

Wing, A.M. (1989). "A comparison of the rate of pinch grip force increases and decreases in Parkinsonian bradykinesia," *Neuropsychologia, 26,* 479-482.

Wing, A.M. and Miller, E. (1984). "Basal ganglia lesions and the psychological analyses of the control of voluntary movement," Ciba Foundation Symposium 107, Functions of the Basal Ganglia. Pitman, London, pp. 242-257.

Wolff, P.H., Gunnoe, C.E. and Cohen, C. (1983). "Associated movements in man." In P.J. Vinken and G.W. Bruyn (Eds.), *Handbook of Clinical Neurology.* North Holland, Amsterdam, pp. 404-426.

Zackon, T.W. "Reaching movements and pursuit tracking performance in patients with Parkinson's disease," Unpublished doctoral thesis, McGill University.

Tutorials in Motor Behavior II
G.E. Stelmach and J. Requin (Editors)

Simulation of impairment of force amplitude and force timing in Parkinsonian handwriting

Hans-Leo Teulings (a) and George E. Stelmach (b)

(a) Nijmegen Institute for Cognition and Information (NICI), P.O. Box 9104, NL 6500 HE Nijmegen, The Netherlands. E-mail: hlt@nici.kun.nl; Fax: +31-80-615938.

(b) Exercise and Sport Science Institute, Psychobiology Section, Arizona State University, Tempe AZ 85287, USA. E-mail: george=stelmach@espe1.la.asu.edu; Fax: +1-602-965-8108.

Abstract

Previous research gave rise to the hypothesis that Parkinsonian handwriting is impaired more in terms of force amplitude than force timing. We simulated the type of impairment found in Parkinsonian handwriting. The simulations demonstrated that impairment of force amplitude and of force duration produce distinct handwriting distortions. Force-amplitude impairment causes an altered baseline within a word whereas a force-timing impairment causes loops at the sharp movement reversals required for specific allographs, e.g., cursive-script "u". In comparison to age-matched controls, it was found that Parkinsonians exhibit substantial problems in maintaining a straight baseline but few problems with sharp movement reversals. The source of the force impairment may be located at the level of motor-unit recruitment. It seems that Parkinsonians show even sharper movement reversals than controls. The explanation is probably not that Parkinsonians write slower, but that they lack the capability to produce round shapes by coactivating different muscle sets.

INTRODUCTION

Previous research has suggested that Parkinsonian handwriting, in comparison to age-matched controls, is impaired in terms of the control of force amplitude rather than the control of its duration (Teulings and Stelmach, 1991a). Force amplitude refers to the magnitude of the force while force timing refers to the initiation and cessation of the applied force. The impairment was quantified by the signal-to-noise ratios of the patterns of force amplitude versus those of stroke duration (Teulings et al., 1986). Teulings and Stelmach (1991b) suggest that the increased force variabilities become manifest as distinct distortions of the handwriting patterns. Impairment of force amplitude causes a less straight baseline and impairment of force duration causes loops at sharp movement reversals, e.g., in cursive-script "u" (Schomaker et al., 1989). The present paper attempts to find support for these suggestions by simulating these impairments in recorded handwriting patterns. In the introduction, sources of impairment of force amplitude and force timing are discussed. An appropriate model is then presented and is used to simulate impairments in force amplitude and of force timing.

Force Amplitude

PD patients can produce, isometrically, a target force as accurately as normals (Stelmach and Worringham, 1988b; Stelmach et al., 1989b). In long force bursts, irregularities of force production may indeed be low-pass filtered due to muscle stiffness (van Galen & Schomaker, 1991). However, in short force bursts, like in handwriting, impairment of force amplitudes may become apparent because smoothing over time cannot take place. Indeed, short force pulses in PDs are more irregular than in control subjects and are not well sustained (Stelmach and Worringham, 1988b; Margolin and Wing, 1983; Stelmach et al., 1989b; Flowers and Sheridan, 1987).

The source of these short-term force fluctuations may be the inappropriate discharges of motor units in PD patients (Dengler et al., 1986; 1988; 1989). Normally, motor units discharge at regular intervals; however, in PDs they discharge in pairs and the number of paired discharges increases with the amplitude of the tremor. Neurophysiological studies by Petajan (1983) indicate that PD subjects also have difficulty activating single motor units. Elderly subjects show similar characteristics, but to a much lesser extent (Petajan and Jarcho, 1975). Therefore, force amplitude in short force bursts may be relatively irregular in PD subjects, due to the poorly controlled firing frequency of motor units.

The order of recruitment of motor units with increasing force output appears normal in PD subjects; however, the "primary motor unit" with the lowest threshold may fire at the tremor frequency during periods of rest or of increased effort (Petajan, 1983; Dengler et al., 1986; Petajan and Jarcho, 1975). Indeed, according to Margolin and Wing (1983), disturbances in Parkinsonian handwriting are primarily due to changes in force amplitude and secondarily due to changes in timing, and in some subjects, due to tremor.

Force Timing

Inappropriate variation of force production introduces timing problems. For example, PD subjects initiate their muscle contractions slower than normals (Stelmach and Worringham, 1988b) and they release muscle force even more slowly (Angel and Lewitt, 1978; Wing, 1988; Viallet et al., 1987). This may cause PD patients to write with less speed. According to Phillips et al. (1989), the slowness of PD handwriting movements may be explained partially by the temporal characteristics of the muscle-force changes and, to a lesser degree, by a low force amplitude. Margolin and Wing (1983) suggested that PD subjects write slow to achieve an acceptable writing size in spite of their low force amplitude. However, this is probably not the main reason because writing size did not increase if pen-to-paper friction was reduced and because Parkinsonians were able to increase writing sizes deliberately to some extent (Teulings and Stelmach, 1991a). Furthermore, low force output seems unlikely to be compensated deliberately by writing slower because neither PD patients nor elderly controls were able to modify their stroke durations as proficiently as their stroke lengths (Phillips et al., 1989). In considering movement sequences, Stelmach et al. (1989a) have shown that Parkinsonians have difficulty producing alterations of force levels within a movement sequence. Therefore, there are indications that a variation in force amplitude may introduce timing problems.

An example of a timing problem in PD patients is the "hastening phenomenon" (Nagasaki and Nakamura, 1982). PD subjects exhibited a hastening of movement when tapping at frequencies of 2.5 or 5 Hz. Such a hastening effect could cause writing problems in PD patients trying to write at a normal speed, yielding predominant frequencies that approximate 5 Hz (Teulings and Maarse, 1984). However, as PD patients write slow, this type of timing problem may not become readily apparent. There are still a number of other mechanisms which may cause force-timing problems in Parkinsonians: tremor and sequences of parallel component movements.

Tremor-Induced Timing Problems

Various kinds of tremor exist in Parkinsonians (Young, 1985; Findley, Gresty and Halmagyi, 1981). Enhanced physiological tremor comprises the noise remaining after the lowpass-filtering effects of the muscle (Freund, 1989). Writing tremor is only visible during the act of writing (Young, 1985). Findley and Gresty (1989) suggest that the cogwheel phenomenon (i.e., tremor in passive movements) has similar frequencies and wave forms as action tremor and postural tremor. Regular tapping sequences may interfere or synchronize with tremor (Frischer, 1989). Freund (1989) found that serial hand movements faster than 2 Hz are only possible in PD patients if they are synchronized with the tremor. Such an impairment may underlie the aforementioned "hastening" phenomenon and may lead to a timing problem in handwriting. Moreover, handwriting is probably not programmed as a rhythmic sequence as stroke duration is probably derived from the stroke size ratios (Teulings et al., 1986).

Timing of Sequences of Parallel Component Movements

Timing is also involved in the temporal organization of movement sequences. Benecke et al. (1987) and Goldenberg et al. (1986) found that in PD patients movements are executed more slowly in sequence than in isolation. Particularly, in the second part of a sequence, movement speed is reduced and the latency between the first and second parts of the movement is increased. When executing two separate motor programs or movement components in parallel, PD patients experience even more difficulty (Benecke et al., 1986; Shimizu et al., 1987; Horstink et al., 1990). In large-size writing and drawing patterns both shoulder and elbow joints are involved (Lacquaniti et al., 1987; Van Emmerik & Newell, 1990). Therefore, larger-size movements may be considered as superimposed movement components. Berardelli et al. (1986) found that PD patients execute straight lines well but the time necessary to trace the geometric figures and the pauses at the vertices were prolonged relative to controls. They concluded that Parkinsonians have a difficulty in generating two-joint ballistic movements which run component motor programs in parallel. Therefore, PD subjects preferably produce small writing sizes in sequential order to prevent parallel activation of various movement components.

Timing and Micrographia

A characteristic handwriting disturbance in PD patients is micrographia: PD patients write smaller than they did several years before their disease was diagnosed. In addition, writing size diminishes further as the writing progresses through the sentence (McLennan et al., 1972; Margolin and Wing, 1983; Lewitt, 1983). As writing size did not increase if pen-to-paper friction was reduced, and as Parkinsonians were able to increase writing size (Teulings and Stelmach, 1991a), it was suggested that a low force output was probably not responsible for micrographia A challenging explanation for micrographia is that Parkinsonians have trouble employing several muscle and joint systems in parallel. For acceptable writing sizes, fingers as well as wrist, arm and shoulder need to be activated in parallel (Lacquaniti et al., 1987). However, if the Parkinsonian tends to employ a minimum number of joints in parallel (e.g., only fingers and wrist), writing sizes will become smaller indeed. The wrist and the fingers produce different movement components which are both necessary to produce handwriting shapes (e.g., Teulings et al., 1989). Round shapes can only be produced by the independent timing of both component movements.

Model of Handwriting

Various models of handwriting production exist. Some models describe the movements at a higher, more abstract level (e.g., Schomaker et al., 1989), and some at a more peripheral level (e.g., Edelman and Flash, 1987), assuming predetermined, orientation-free stroke shapes (e.g., Morasso et al., 1983; Plamondon, 1989), or specific axes of movement (e.g., Denier van der Gon et al., 1962; Wing, 1978; Plamondon and Maarse, 1989). The peripheral type of model is best suited for the simulations to be presented for three reasons: it is based on force and time, it permits consideration of the movement as a sequence of action units, e.g., strokes, and it decomposes the movement into two components, e.g., a horizontal and a vertical component.

Force and Acceleration

Muscle-force amplitude appears to be impaired in Parkinsonian handwriting (Teulings and Stelmach, 1991a, b). Unfortunately, muscle force during handwriting cannot be measured directly. Only the muscle force resulting in acceleration of the pen point can be estimated. Under the assumption of friction and viscous forces, being much smaller than inertial forces (Denier van de Gon and Thuring, 1965), it may be assumed that force is proportional with, or at least, a monotonous function of the acceleration time function. The acceleration time function appears to be the best available approximation in small and fast handwriting under open-loop control. However, in the simulations the frictionless approximation yields unrealistic drifts so that specific measures are required to take friction into account.

Main Axes of Movement

Specific antagonistic muscle systems control movements along specific directions (Soechting and Ross, 1984). If the locus of handwriting impairment in Parkinsonians is at the level of muscle force amplitude (Teulings and Stelmach, 1991a, b), a deterioration may be simulated by multiplying the acceleration amplitude of one movement axis during a stroke. Various movement axes have been proposed (Teulings et al., 1989), e.g., defined by the biomechanical degrees of freedom of flexions and extensions of the fingers and wrist, or defined by the graphical axes of movement which are parallel to the baseline (horizontal) and perpendicular to it (vertical). However, the results of the handwriting simulation disruptions do not depend upon any specific choice of movement axes. For the simulation, it is sufficient to assume only two arbitrary, independent movement axes.

Strokes

Fluent handwriting consists of a sequence of ballistic movements which have such a short duration (typically 100 ms) that on-line feedback may not affect them. Therefore, each unimodal absolute-velocity versus time curve is defined as a stroke. Consequently, impairment of force timing can be simulated by delaying some of the strokes along one main axis.

In fluent handwriting the segmentation points between the strokes are mostly at the bottoms and tops of the cursive-script characters where the curvature is high and the pen changes movement direction sharply (Thomassen and Teulings, 1985). However, in handwriting of Parkinsonian and elderly subjects, pen movement is not always fluent and/or ballistic (e.g., Maarse et al., 1987) and a more extended definition of a stroke was employed. The absolute velocity-versus-time curve of a straight stroke may show more than one peak. Therefore, a stroke will be redefined as the segment between sharp changes of direction from up to down or vice versa. These points of sharp change of direction are referred to as 'segmentation points'. Furthermore, in order to facilitate detection of the segmentation points, the vertical component, was weighted 10 times relative to the horizontal component (Teulings et al., 1987) where horizontal is parallel to the baseline.

SIMULATIONS

Specific effects upon the shape of handwriting patterns due to impairment of force amplitude and due to impairment of force timing have been postulated (Teulings and Stelmach, 1991b). In extended simulations reported in this article, we tried to verify our conclusion more precisely. For that purpose the data reported in Teulings and Stelmach (1991b) was used.

Method

Impaired Force Amplitude

Impaired force amplitude can be simulated by manipulating the acceleration per stroke. Each stroke consists of an acceleration phase and a deceleration phase. However, manipulating only the acceleration phase at the beginning of a pattern would cause a constant, additional velocity during the rest of the writing pattern as friction has been neglected. Friction can be partially accounted for by manipulating the deceleration phase similarly. Therefore, both the acceleration and deceleration phase during each complete stroke is manipulated in the simulations by multiplying the acceleration with random factors per stroke. The random factors had uniform probability densities. The simulations were done in 5 series with density distributions ranging between plus and minus 0%, 5%, 10%, 15%, and 20% of the amplitude, respectively.

After multiplying the acceleration of a whole stroke, the average acceleration may be altered slightly causing still some drift in the frictionless component. This was corrected by adding a small amount to the acceleration pattern during the stroke (see Figure .1). In fact, only the vertical component of the acceleration needs to be manipulated because the horizontal component has no effect upon baseline or any other measured parameter. If another set of main axes would have been chosen, only the vertical component would have affected the baseline.

Impaired Force Timing

It appeared nontrivial to manipulate force timing while leaving force amplitude intact. For example, when force timing was manipulated by simply expanding and shrinking, respectively, without correcting force amplitude would yield huge effects on stroke lengths. Therefore, the vertical acceleration is primarily delayed at random where velocity is zero. The simulations were done in 5 series with delays of 0, 5, 10, 15, and 20 ms. corresponding to 0, 1, 2, 3, and 4 samples of the writing data. For that purpose, the data sampled at 100 Hz was resampled at 200 Hz (Teulings & Maarse, 1984).

A sample where the velocity is exactly zero does not exist thus the acceleration of the first sample of the delay was corrected to produce a hesitation. Also the first sample after the delay was corrected (in opposite direction) so that the net force correction was zero. This pair of corrections may introduce some peaks at places where movement delays were inserted. These peaks may very well resemble the acceleration peaks observed at momentary stops where static friction causes high pen-to-paper resistance (McDonald, 1966; Yasuhara, 1975).

A cumulation of delays in the vertical axis relative to the horizontal axis causes increasing distortions towards the end of the pattern. As this is not realistic, the horizontal component was delayed to the same extent after some strokes. The rationale for this procedure is that delays occur only in one muscle system at a time while the second muscle system, corresponding to the other main axis, is only weakly phase locked. Therefore, in the simulations, the vertical acceleration pattern was delayed, and 4 strokes later, the horizontal acceleration pattern was delayed, or, the reverse (See Figure 2). Four strokes were chosen in order to create some movement synchronies at stroke endpoints. Furthermore, the probability that a stroke pair was selected was only 1/8 so that delays did not mutually correct each other. Other choices of the number of strokes between x and y delays and the selection probability showed qualitatively similar but smaller effects.

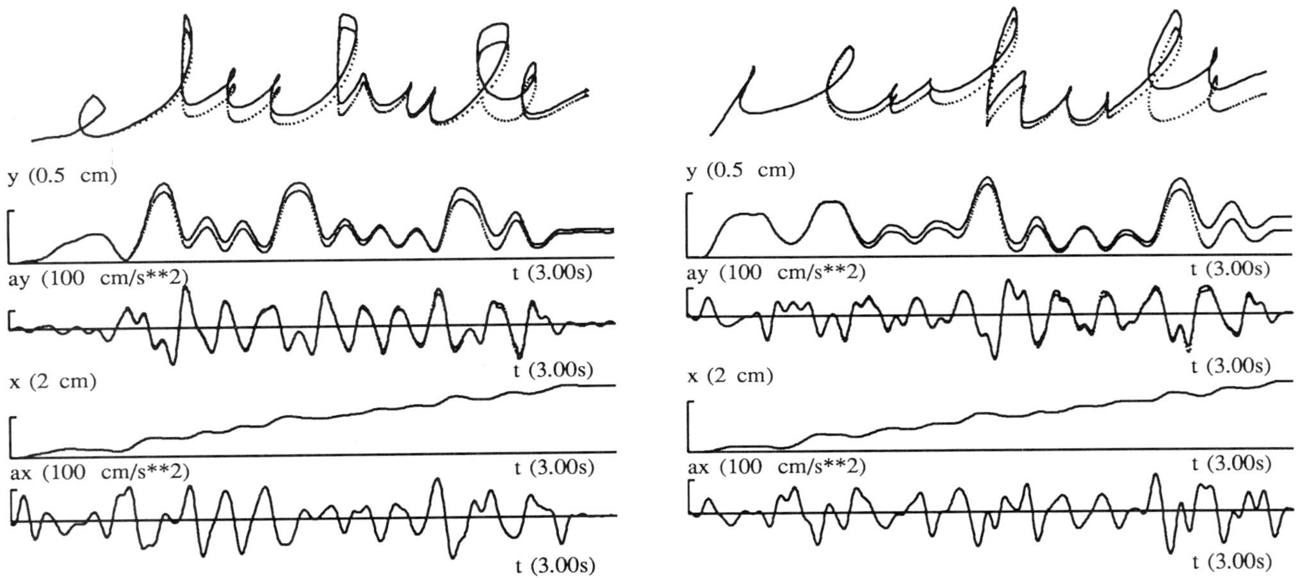

Figure 1. A recorded handwriting pattern (dotted) and the pattern with simulated, additional, impaired force amplitude (solid) by a control subject (left) and by a Parkinsonian (right). (The curves represent the vertical and horizontal position (y and x) and acceleration (ay and ax) time functions, respectively. In this simulation, force-amplitude variation is randomly chosen for each stroke and maximal 20% of its peak force. Due to the force-amplitude variation, the baseline inaccuracy increases but the loop areas do not change.)

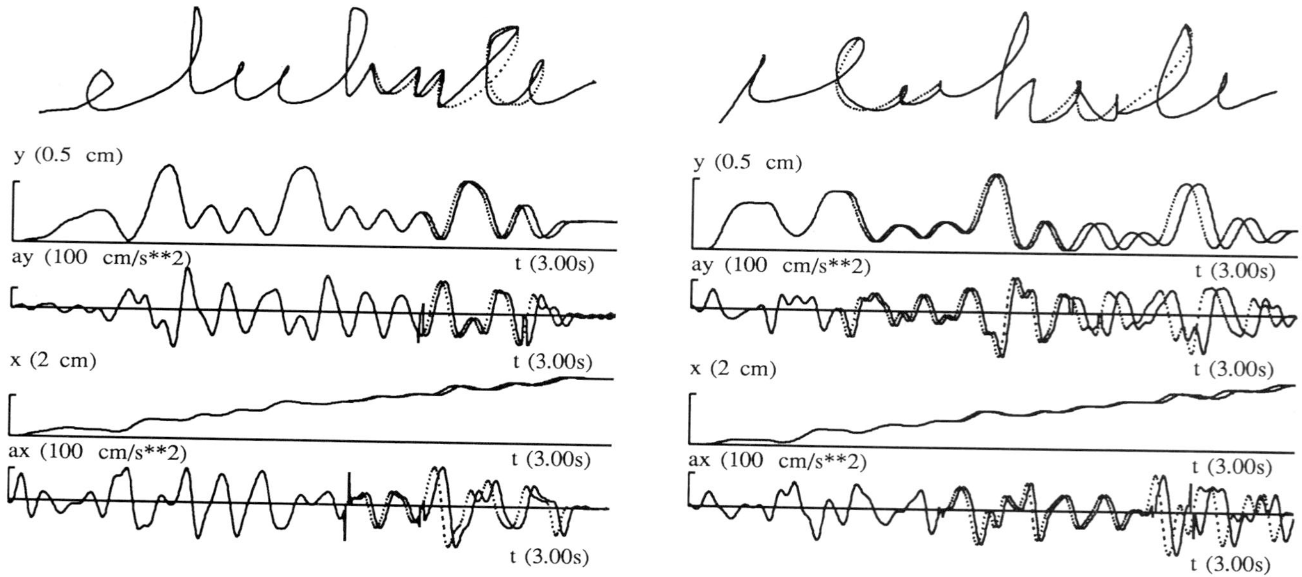

Figure 2. A recorded handwriting pattern (dotted) and the pattern with simulated, additional, impaired force timing (solid) by a control subject (left) and by a Parkinsonian (right). (The curves represent the vertical and horizontal position (y and x) and acceleration (ay and ax) time functions, respectively. In this simulation, force-timing variation consists of delays of 20 ms at random in 1/8 of the segmentation points of the x or y component and each delay is balanced 4 strokes later by the same delay of the other component. Due to the force-timing variation, the loop areas change, or increase where they should be zero, but the baseline inaccuracy does not change.

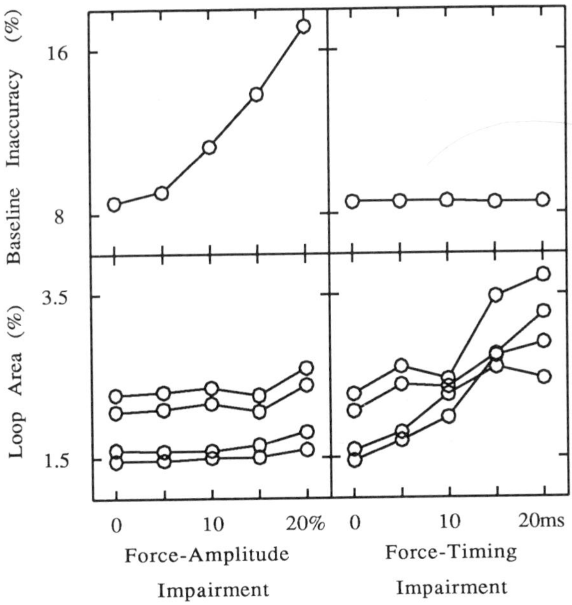

Figure 3. Relative measures of baseline inaccuracy and loop area as a function of simulated force-amplitude and force-timing impairment in the normal series in all subjects.

Results

Baseline

The baseline in cursive script is normally straight. The baseline can be controlled by the vertical component irrespective of the main axes of movement. The extent of the baseline inaccuracy can be expressed by measuring the standard deviation of the vertical positions of the low segmentation points. As the standard deviation is proportional to the overall size of the handwriting pattern, the ratio of this standard deviation and the pattern's average stroke height forms a dimensionless measure of the inaccuracy of the baseline. Figure 3 shows that the inaccuracy of the baseline is progressively affected by increasing force-amplitude impairments while it is virtually not affected by the simulated force-timing impairment.

Loop Area

The tops of a well-formed cursive-script "u" are sharp. A sharp movement reversal can only be produced if both horizontal and vertical velocity components change sign simultaneously, no matter which pair of main axes is chosen. Any timing asynchrony can be estimated independently of the choice of main axes by measuring the loop area at these points of sharp movement reversal. The area of the loop is defined by the enclosed surface between two subsequent strokes. As loop area increases with the square of the height of the entire pattern, the area of the loop divided by the heights of the two strokes forming the loop is a dimensionless measure for loop area. Figure 3 shows that loop area is progressively affected by increasing force-timing impairment while it is virtually not affected by the simulated force-amplitude impairment.

Conclusion

Two measures of handwriting distortion have been proposed: (1) distortion of the baseline which is a key measure of force-amplitude impairment, and (2) average loop area, at places where sharp movement reversals were to be performed (e.g., at the tops of cursive-script "u"), which is a key measure for force-timing impairment. Teulings and Stelmach (1991a) found that Parkinsonians have more problems with force amplitude than with force timing, so that it may be postulated that Parkinsonian handwriting shows a less accurate baseline in comparison to controls but not larger relative loop areas. This result was already predicted on the basis of empirical data by Teulings and Stelmach (1991b).

A secondary finding of this simulation is, in fact, the subtle interplay that seems to exist between force-amplitude impairment and force-timing impairment. Although impairments have been simulated as realistically as possible, it may be questioned whether the present simulation is sufficiently realistic. Although many variations were tried, they yield qualitatively the same result.

EXPERIMENT

In order to verify that Parkinsonian handwriting exhibits a more variable baseline than normal but no difference in average loop area, PD and age-matched control subjects performed a writing pattern, under various conditions. The experiment reported here used the same data as Teulings and Stelmach (1991b) but the data analysis is now compatible with those of the present simulations. The subjects' task was to execute a specific writing pattern containing long and short up- and down-strokes with sharp movement reversals or loops as in cursive-script "u" and "e", respectively.

Method

Subjects

Six subjects with idiopathic Parkinson's disease (5 males and 1 female; See Table 1) and six age-matched control subjects (1 male and 5 females) took part in the experiment. PD subjects were between 49.5 and 79.8 years of age. Control subjects' ages ranged from 1.0 to 4.2 years younger than the PD patients they were selected to match. The controls reported having no signs of neurological disease. The only screening criteria were willingness and ability to perform the handwriting tasks. All subjects were proficient in cursive handwriting and were right-handed, except for one PD subject, who was left-handed. The PD patients had a precise medication schedule, ranging from 2 to 4 Sinemet doses per day. Although gender is not matched well between both groups of subjects, it was not expected that this variable would affect the baseline inaccuracy and loop area at sharp movement reversals significantly. In general, female writers show less force, more backward slant and more rounded loops than male writers (e.g., Young, 1931).

Table 1

Parkinson's Disease Subjects (- means symptom absent).

Subject	Age (y)	Gender	Handedness	Impaired side	Diagnosed onset (y)	Movement bandwidth (Hz)	Action tremor (Hz)	Tremor at rest	Micrographia	Rigidity	Bradykinesia
1JP	64.2	Female	Right	Bilateral	4	6.0	-	T	M	R	-
3RC	75.3	Male	Right	Left	4	4.4	-	T	-	R	B
4WF	79.8	Male	Right	Right	7	4.0	-	T	M	R	B
6JH	72.8	Male	Right	Right	5	2.2	5.6	T	M	R	B
7JR	53.0	Male	Left	Both	2	4.2	-	-	M	-	B
8PB	49.5	Male	Right	Both	1	4.5	-	T	M	R	-

Apparatus

The subjects wrote on a large, height-adjustable digitizer with its standard blunt-barreled pen (CalComp 91240). The digitizer provided horizontal and vertical coordinates of the pen tip with a frequency of 100 Hz, and an RMS accuracy of 0.2 mm. The digitizer sampled the horizontal and vertical coordinates non-simultaneously but this will have little effect in small and slow handwriting. The subjects were asked to adopt their most comfortable writing posture. A sheet of paper with a 28-cm guide line was fixed upon the digitizer accordingly. This sheet was covered by a blank sheet transparent enough to see the guide line underneath. After each trial the covering paper was shifted by the subject such that they were able to write on this guide line while maintaining a constant writing posture. The forearm rested on the digitizer to minimize body movements and to dampen any tremor in the writing arm.

Design and Conditions

An experimental session consisted of the following tasks: (1) Write the sentence "They wrote eluhule." for 2 trials. (2) Write the pseudo word "eluhule" at normal size and speed, for 10 trials. (3) Write "eluhule" but alternate it with writing eludule" (yielding 20 trials). (4) Write "eluhule" but alternate with the same word written larger than normal.

(5) Write "eluhule" but alternate it with the same word written faster than normal. (The order of Tasks 3-5 was random). (6) Repeat Task 2. (7) Repeat Task 1. The purpose of Task 1 at the beginning and end of the experimental session was to estimate an individual's movement-frequency bandwidth and its constancy throughout the session. Task 2 was repeated at the end of a session in order to verify that the dependent variables did not change during the experimental session.

In Tasks 1 and 7 only the first 20.48 s per trial were recorded. In the other tasks the recording period was 4, 5, or 6 s per trial, depending upon the speed of writing of the subject. However, in the slowest Parkinsonian the recording period was 8 or 10 s per trial and only 5 trials per condition could be done. The total duration of an experimental session was approximately 60 minutes. The trials of the pseudo word can be divided into 8 conditions: Task 2 (1 condition), Task 6 (1 condition), Task 3 (2 conditions), Task 4 (2 conditions), and Task 5 (2 conditions).

Procedure

Subjects were instructed to use their normal style, size, and speed of writing. At the beginning of each trial, the subject placed the pen on the paper at the starting position. When the subject was ready, the experimenter signaled the start of the recording with a beep, after which the subject was free to initiate writing without time pressure. None of the subjects exhibited difficulties in initiating writing. The experimenter checked whether the correct letter sequence was written. For example, interchanging cursive-script "u" and "el" was not accepted. Non-accepted trials could be repeated.

Analysis

Frequency Bandwidth

Each subject's movement-frequency bandwidth was estimated in order to choose the appropriate lowpass cut-off frequency for calculating the velocity time function. The bandwidth was assumed to be equal to the frequency where the frequency spectrum dropped sharply. In order to estimate the frequency spectrum, each record of 2048 samples was multiplied by a Hamming window. Next, a Fast Fourier Transform was applied to obtain the spectrum for position, a first time derivative taken by multiplication with angular frequency, and the absolute value taken, to obtain the amplitude spectrum for velocity. This spectrum was subsequently averaged across segments. The transition band of the lowpass filter was a half raised-cosine wave which extended to 3.7 times the frequency where the lowpass filter started suppressing (Teulings and Maarse, 1984).

The bandwidths of the writing apparatus in the control subjects were 5.4 to 6.3 Hz, and in the PD subjects, 2.2 to 6.0 Hz. The lowpass filtering frequencies (frequencies were the half-raised cosine started) were 5.1 Hz for most subjects and 3.4 or 1.7 for the slower and the slowest Parkinsonian subjects, respectively. Interesting to note was that the latter Parkinsonian subject showed also considerable action tremor with an average frequency of 5.6 Hz, which was much higher than the movement bandwidth. Therefore, lowpass filtering with a transition band ranging from 1.7 to 6.3 Hz was capable of suppressing the action tremor entirely and yielded smooth movement curves.

Preprocessing

The writing patterns were first rotated to a horizontal baseline according to the orientation of the guide line, chosen by the subject. Subsequently, the data were lowpass filtered and differentiated. In order to obtain a more fine-grained time definition the movement patterns, sampled at 100 Hz, were resampled at 200 Hz by adding zero high-frequency components in the Fourier transform (Teulings & Maarse, 1984).

Segmentation

Subsequently, the absolute velocity was estimated. Actually the absolute velocity was the weighted sum of the squared horizontal and vertical velocity components with weights 0.1 and 1.0, respectively. Then, the writing patterns were segmented into strokes. This was done by detecting all local minima of the absolute velocity (i.e., the lowest minimum within an interval of -50 and +50 ms).

Initial and trailing strokes shorter than 0.3 mm were omitted. Ideally, the patterns of "eluhule" and "eludule" contain 21 strokes but the first two and the last three strokes were omitted, thus yielding 16 short and long up- and down-strokes. Four of the 12 subjects wrote "d" with an extra down and up stroke at the top of the c-shaped stroke. In order to enable comparison between subjects, these two strokes were discarded.

Movement Stops

Only those minima were selected where a downward stroke, if not the first stroke, is followed by a significant upward movement (i.e., beyond 0.03 cm in vertical direction) and where an upward stroke is followed by a significant downward movement. The vertical positions of these skipped movement stops were cumulated in 5 equally sized bins where bin 1 is at the beginning of the actual stroke and bin 5 at the end. Controls and Parkinsonians showed about equal probabilities of movement stops (0.032 versus 0.046, respectively). The stops were on average equally distributed during the stroke (0.006, 0.007, 0.010, 0.004, and 0.006, for the 5 bins, respectively).

Number of Accepted Trials

Only those trials were accepted for continued analysis which showed the required pattern of short and long vertical strokes: The height of the longest short stroke should be less than the height of the shortest long stroke. Thus, 6 to 10 trials per condition per subject (average 8.9) remained for the controls, and, 2 to 10 (average 7.1) for the PD subjects.

Results

Stroke Size and Duration

The vertical size and duration for each stroke was estimated. In order to minimize effects of outlyers, medians of the size and duration estimates across the accepted replications were taken per series, which were then averaged across the strokes of the average trial. Table 2 summarizes means across subjects of vertical stroke size, stroke duration averaged across all tasks. Analyses of variance were performed for 2-groups x 6-subjects x 8-tasks. The results per task have been presented in Teulings & Stelmach (1991b). That study showed that differences between first and last normal series were only minor, indicating that learning nor fatiguing took place during the experimental session. PD subjects were found to write marginally smaller than controls ($F(1,10)=3.83$, $p=0.08$), which may be a sign of micrographia (McLennan et al., 1972; Margolin and Wing, 1983; Lewitt, 1983). PD subjects write only marginally slower than the controls ($F(1,10) = 3.44$, $p = 0.09$).

Table 2

The mean vertical stroke size, mean stroke duration, relative inaccuracy of the baseline, and the mean relative loop areas of the tops of cursive-script "u", in the controls and the PD subjects.

	Controls	Parkinsonians
Size (cm)	0.33	0.27
Time (s)	0.128	0.185
Relative Baseline Inaccuracy	0.073	0.098 ($p<0.01$)
Mean Relative Loop Area of Tops of "u"	0.77	0.42

Baseline

The baseline was determined more precisely by the least-square error line through all adopted low segmentation points and the individual pattern was adjusted to horizontal orientation. A size-independent measure for the inaccuracy of the baseline was the standard deviation of these distances divided by the average stroke height. In order to minimize effects of outlyers, medians were taken across the accepted replications per series. An important result is that PD subjects show greater relative inaccuracy of the baseline ($F(1,10) = 16.25$, $p<0.01$).

Loop Area

Finally, per stroke the loop area, enclosed by the very stroke and the previous one, was estimated. A size-independent measure for the loop area is the area of the loop divided by the vertical sizes of the two crossing strokes. Loop area may be positive or zero (negative surfaces do not exist), so that averages across replications are taken in order to obtain a measure of their magnitude and frequency. The important result is that PD subjects do not produce significantly larger relative loop areas than controls ($F(1,10)=2.86$, $p>0.1$). They even seem to show a tendency to produce smaller loops.

DISCUSSION

PD patients and age-matched controls performed handwriting patterns under various natural conditions. These data were first used for simulating impairments of force amplitude and of force timing. The simulations showed that impairment of force amplitude affects baseline and impairment of force timing affects loop area of sharp movement reversals. The experiment showed that the baseline is more irregular in Parkinsonian handwriting than in control subjects. However, relative to the controls, PD patients did not show larger relative loop areas in sharp movement reversals. These results support earlier findings (Teulings and Stelmach, 1991a; 1991b) suggesting that PD patients show impaired control of force amplitude but have an intact control of their force timing. Also when examining the probability of movement stops, Parkinsonians do not differ from controls.

An alternative explanation for the high degree of inaccuracy of the baseline in Parkinsonian handwriting is that Parkinsonians shifted their baseline back to the guide line only at casual moments when they processed visual feedback of the ongoing pattern. This is unlikely as it was found in previous research (Teulings and Stelmach, 1991a) that both Parkinsonians and controls do not alter their handwriting in the absence of visual feedback.

PD subjects show a tendency to produce even smaller relative loop areas at sharp movement reversals than controls. Since they simply write faster, the larger average loop area in control subjects could be an artifact. However, this can be rejected as no marked change in loop area was found in conditions with the speed instruction (Teulings and Stelmach, 1991b). An interesting explanation of the smaller relative loop areas in Parkinsonian handwriting could follow from the recent findings by Flash (1990) that Parkinsonians do not tend to superimpose elementary motor programs in multi-joint movements, but rather finish one movement before starting the next. A disjunct sequence of movements, which could in principle be partly superimposed, may cause the very sharp movement reversals in characters such as the "u" observed in Parkinsonian handwriting. The lack of ability to superimpose elementary movement components is in line with similar observations by Berardelli et al. (1986), Benecke et al. (1986), Shimizu et al. (1987), and Horstink et al. (1990).

Finally, the lack of superimposing elementary movements by PD patients forms an interesting explanation for micrographia, which often is a precursor of the disease (McLennan et al., 1972; Margolin and Wing, 1983; Lewitt, 1983). In order to realize normal writing sizes, fingers, wrist, arm and shoulder have to cooperate (Lacquaniti et al., 1987). If the ability to coactivate various muscle systems is lacking, the PD patient will tend to limit the number of muscle systems involved. Most obviously, the PD patient will only use fingers, or fingers and wrist, resulting in smaller handwriting, possibly related to micrographia.

REFERENCES

Angel, R. & Lewitt, P.A. (1978). Unloading and shortening in Parkinson's disease. *Journal of Neurology, Neurosurgery, and Psychiatry, 41*, 919-923.

Benecke, R., Rothwell, J.C., Dick, J.P., Day, B.L., & Marsden, C.D. (1986). Performance of simultaneous movements in patients with Parkinson's disease. *Brain, 109*, 739-757.

Benecke, R., Rothwell, J.C., Dick, J.P., Day, B.L., & Marsden, C.D. (1987). Disturbance of sequential movements in patients with Parkinson's disease. *Brain, 110*, 361-379.

Berardelli, A., Accornero, N., Argenta, M., Meco, G., & Manfredi, M. (1986). Fast complex arm movements in Parkinson's disease. *Journal of Neurology, Neurosurgery, and Psychiatry, 49*, 1146-1149.

Dengler, R., Elek, J., Hermans, R., & Wolf, W. (1988). [Double discharges of motor units and tremor strength]. *EEG EMG, 19*, 77-80.

Dengler, R., Gillespie, J., Argenta, M., Elek, J., Wolf., & Struppler, A. (1989). The impact of paired motor unit discharges on tremor. *Electromyography and Clinical Neurophysiology, 29,* 113-117.

Dengler, R., Wolf, W., Schubert, M., & Struppler, A. (1986). Discharge pattern of single motor units in basal ganglia disorders. *Neurology, 36,* 1061-1066.

Denier van der Gon, J.J., & Thuring, J.Ph. (1965). The guiding of human writing movements. *Kybernetik, 2,* 145-148.

Denier van der Gon, J.J., Thuring, J.Ph., & Strackee, J. (1962). A handwriting simulator. *Physics in Medical Biology, 6,* 407-414.

Edelman, S., & Flash, T. (1987). A model of handwriting. *Biological Cybernetics, 57,* 257-36.

Findley, L.J., Gresty, M.A. (1989). Tremor and rhythmical involuntary movements in Parkinson's disease, In *Movement disorders: Tremors.* L.J. Findley & R. Capildeo (Eds.) New York: Oxford University Press, 295-404.

Findley, L.J., Gresty, M.A., & Halmagyi, G.M. (1981). Tremor, the cogwheel phenomenon and clonus in Parkinson's disease. *Journal of Neurology, Neurosurgery, and Psychiatry, 44,* 534-546.

Flash, T. (1990). *Studies into the timing, sequencing, and modification of hand trajectories in healthy subjects and patients with basal ganglia disorders.* Paper presented at the NIAS Conference: Sequencing and timing of human movement. Wassenaar, The Netherlands, June.

Flowers, K.A., & Sheridan, M.R. (1987). *Movement variability and bradykinesia in Parkinson's disease.* E.S.P. Symposium on Motor Skills, Oxford, July.

Freund, H.J. (1989). Motor dysfunctions in Parkinson's disease and premotor lesions. *European Neurology, 29,* 33-37.

Frischer, M. (1989). Voluntary versus autonomous control of repetitive finger tapping. *Neuropsychologia, 27,* 1261-1266.

Goldenberg, G., Wimmer, A., Auff, E., & Schnaberth, G. (1986). Impairment of motor planning in patients with Parkinson's disease: evidence from idiomotor apraxia testing. *Journal of Neurology, Neurosurgery, and Psychiatry, 49,* 1266-1272.

Horstink, M.W.I.M., Berger, H.J., Van Spaendonck, H.J.C., & Van den Bercken, J.H.L. (1990). Bimanual simultaneous motor performance and impaired ability to shift attention in Parkinson's disease. *Journal of Neurology, Neurosurgery, and Psychiatry, 53,* 685-690.

Lacquaniti, F., Ferrigno, G., Pedotti, A., Soechting, J.F., & Terzuolo, C. (1987). Changes in spatial scale in drawing and handwriting: Kinematic contributions by proximal and distal joints. *Journal of Neuroscience, 7,* 819-828.

Lewitt, P.A. (1983). Micrographia as a focal sign of neurologic disease. *Journal of Neurology, Neurosurgery, and Psychiatry, 46,* 1152-1153.

Maarse, F.J., Meulenbroek, R.G.J., Teulings, H.L., & Thomassen, A.J.W.M. (1987). Computational measures for ballisticity in handwriting. In R. Plamondon, C.Y. Suen, J.-G. Deschenes and G. Poulin (Eds.), *Proceedings of the Third International Symposium on Handwriting and Computer Applications* (pp. 16-18), Montreal: Ecole Polytechnique.

Margolin, D.I., & Wing, A.M. (1983). Agraphia and micrographia: Clinical manifestations of motor programming and performance disorders. *Acta Psychologica, 54,* 263-284.

McDonald, J.S. (1966). *Experimental studies of handwriting signals.* RLE Technical Report 443, Cambridge, MA: MIT Press.

McLennan, J.E., Nakoma, K., Tyler, H.R., & Schwab, R.S. (1972). Micrographia in Parkinson's disease. *Journal of Neurological Sciences, 15,* 141-152.

Morasso, P., Mussa Ivaldi, F.A., & Ruggiero, C. (1983). How a discontinuous mechanism can produce continuous patterns in trajectory formation and handwriting. *Acta Psychologica, 54,* 83-98.

Nagasaki, H., & Nakamura, R. (1982). Rhythm formation and its disturbance: A study based upon periodic response of the motor output system. *Journal of Human Ergology, 11,* 127-142.

Petajan, J.H. (1983). Motor unit control in movement disorders. In E. Desmedt (Ed.), *Motor control mechanisms in health disease.* New York: Raven Press.

Petajan, J.H., & Jarcho, L.W. (1975). Motor unit control in Parkinson's disease and the influence of Levodopa, *Neurology, 25,* 866-869.

Phillips, J.G., Stelmach, G.E., & Teasdale, N. (1989). Preliminary assessment of spatio-temporal control of handwriting. In R. Plamondon, C.Y. Suen and M.L. Simner (Eds.), *Computer and human recognition of handwriting*, (pp. 317-332), Singapore: World Scientific.

Plamondon, R. (1989). Handwriting Control: A functional model. In R.M.J. Cotterill (Ed.), *Models of brain function* (pp. 563-574). London: Cambridge University Press.

Plamondon, R., & Maarse, F.J. (1989). An evaluation of motor models of handwriting. *IEEE Transactions on Systems, Man, and Cybernetics, 19*, 1060-1072.

Schomaker, L.R.B., Thomassen, A.J.W.M., & Teulings, H.L. (1989). A computational model of cursive handwriting. In R. Plamondon, C.Y. Suen and M. Simner (Eds.), *Computer recognition and human production of handwriting* (pp. 153-177), Singapore: World Scientific.

Shimizu, N., Yoshida, M., & Nagatsuka, Y. (1987). Disturbance of two simultaneous motor acts in patients with Parkinsonism and cerebellar ataxia. *Advances in Neurology, 45*, 367-370.

Soechting, J.F., Ross, B. (1984). Psychophysical determination of coordinate representations of human arm orientation, *Neuroscience, 13*, 595-604.

Stelmach, G.E., Garcia-Colera, A., & Martin, Z.E. (1989a). Force transition control within a movement sequence in Parkinson's Disease, *Journal of Neurology, 236*, 406-410.

Stelmach, G.E., Teasdale, N., Phillips, J.G., & Worringham, C.J. (1989b). Force production characteristics in Parkinson's disease. *Experimental Brain Research, 76*, 165-172.

Stelmach, G.E., & Worringham, C.J. (1988b). The preparation and production of isometric force in Parkinson's disease. *Neuropsychologia, 26*, 93-103.

Teulings, H.L., & Maarse, F.J. (1984). Digital recording and processing of handwriting movements, *Human Movement Science, 3*, 193-217.

Teulings, H.L., Schomaker, L.R.B., Morasso, P., & Thomassen, A.J.W.M. (1987). Handwriting-analysis system. In R. Plamondon, C.Y.Suen, J.G. Deschenes, & G. Poulin (Eds.), *Proceedings of the 3rd International Symposium on Handwriting and Computer Applications* (pp. 181-183). Montreal: Ecole Polytechnique (ISBN 2-553-00197-5).

Teulings, H.L., & Stelmach, G.E. (1991a). Control of stroke size, peak acceleration, and stroke duration in Parkinsonian handwriting, *Human Movement Sciences, 10*, 315-333.

Teulings, H.L., & Stelmach, G.E. (1991b). Force amplitude and force duration in Parkinsonian handwriting. In J. Requin and G.E. Stelmach (Eds.), *Tutorials in Motor Neuroscience.* (pp. 149-160). Amsterdam: Kluwer.

Teulings, H.L., Thomassen, A.J.W.M., & Maarse, F.J. (1989). A description of handwriting in terms of main axes. In R. Plamondon, C.Y. Suen, and M. Simner (Eds.), *Computer recognition and human production of handwriting* (pp. 193-211). Singapore: World Scientific.

Teulings, H.L., Thomassen, A.J.W.M., & van Galen, G.P. (1986). Invariances in handwriting: The information contained in a motor program. In H.S.R. Kao, G.P. van Galen, and R. Hoosain (Eds.), *Graphonomics, contemporary research in handwriting.* (pp. 305-315). Amsterdam: North-Holland Press.

Thomassen, A.J.W.M., & Teulings, H.L. (1985). Time, size and shape in handwriting, exploring spatio-temporal relationships at different levels. In J.A. Michon and J.B. Jackson (Eds.), *Time, mind and behavior* (pp. 253-263). Heidelberg: Springer-Verlag.

Van Emmerik, R.E.A., & Newell, K.M. (1990). The influence of task and organismic constraints on intralimb and pen-point kinematics in a drawing task. *Acta Psychologica, 73*, 171-190.

Van Galen, G.P., & Schomaker, L.R.B. (1991). Fitts' law as a low-pass filter effect on muscle stiffness. *Human Movement Science* (in press).

Viallet, F., Massion, J., Massarino, R., & Khalil, R. (1987). Performance of a bimanual load-lifting task by Parkinsonian patients. *Journal of Neurology, Neurosurgery and Psychiatry, 50*, 1274-1283.

Yanagisawa, N., Fujimoto, S., & Tamaru, F. (1989). Bradykinesia in Parkinson's disease: Disorders of onset and execution of fast movement. *European Neurology, 29*, 19-28.

Yasuhara, M. (1975). *Experimental studies of handwriting process.* Rep. Univ. Electro-Comm., 25-2 (Sci. and Tech. Sect.), 233-254.

Young, P.T. (1931). Sex differences in handwriting. *Journal of Applied Psychology, 15*, 486-498.

Young, R.R. (1985). Tremor in Parkinson's Disease. In P.J. Delwaide and A. Agnoli (Eds.), *Clinical neurophysiology in Parkinsonism* (pp. 139-162). Amsterdam: Elsevier.

Wing, A.M. (1978). Response timing in handwriting. In G.E. Stelmach (Ed.), *Information processing in motor control and learning* (pp. 153-172). New York: Academic Press.

Wing, A.M. (1988). A comparison of the rate of pinch grip force increases and decreases in Parkinsonian bradykinesia. *Neuropsychology, 26*, 479-482.

Acknowledgements

This research was supported by grants from the USA National Institute of Neurological Diseases and Stroke (NS 17421) and American Parkinson's Disease Association awarded to George E. Stelmach, and the Nijmegen University Research Pool (SW4/88). The researchers wish to thank the subjects from the Madison Area Parkinson Support Group for their motivated cooperation.

Tutorials in Motor Behavior II
G.E. Stelmach and J. Requin (Editors)

Cooperative control of gaze by the superior colliculus, brainstem and cerebellum

J.C. Houk[a], H.L. Galiana[b] and D. Guitton[c]

[a]Department of Physiology, Northwestern University Medical Center, 303 E. Chicago Avenue, Chicago, Illinois 60611, USA

[b]Department of Biomedical Engineering, McGill University, 3775 University Street, Montreal, Quebec, Canada H3A 2B4

[c]Department of Neurophysiology, Montreal Neurological Institute and McGill University, 3801 University Street, Montreal, Quebec, Canada H3A 2B4

Abstract

This paper proposes a schema for the dynamic control of gaze by circuits involving the superior colliculus, brainstem and cerebellum. It is also used to illustrate a distributed theory of motor learning. The intent is twofold. First, we will indicate that the gaze control system contains many hierarchical levels which could interact in the manner postulated in a previous chapter, to both develop sensorimotor maps and dynamically monitor performance. Second, the degree of interconnectivity in such control systems provides robustness in that after learning, even lower level circuits can provide adequate responses in isolation. Both aspects are discussed with reference to known anatomy, neurophysiology and recent modelling techniques. This interpretation of the gaze control system can explain several experimental observations previously difficult to interpret.

1. INTRODUCTION

It is well known that the superior colliculus, the brainstem and the cerebellum are each important structures in the neural control of eye and head movements. However, relatively little effort has gone into exploring how these structures might work together in a cooperative manner. Recently one of us dealt with a similar problem regarding limb movement control, and this work led to the proposal of a cooperative control model to explain how the motor cortex, brainstem and cerebellum may cooperate in the control of goal–directed movements of the arm [Houk, 1989; Houk et al, 1990]. Here we explore the possibility that the superior colliculus, brainstem and cerebellum may interact in a similar manner to control gaze.

The cooperative control model for limb movement was motivated by a desire to incorporate diverse anatomical, physiological and behavioural data, a bottom–up rather than a top–down approach. Anatomical data indicated that the motor cortex and the cerebellum are interconnected, by way of recurrent pathways through brainstem nuclei, forming a premotor network. The recurrent pathways in this premotor network were postulated to function as positive feedback loops which bind together separate processing stages provided by the motor cortex and the cerebellum. Regarding the cortical processing stage, single unit data suggested that the motor cortex might be a major site where sensory triggers are processed to decide when to initiate movement. In contrast, the unique neuronal architecture of the cerebellar cortex, coupled with single unit data on the signals that enter and leave this structure, suggested that the cerebellum might be a major site for the storage and processing of motor programs that specify limb movements. Positive feedback between the motor cortex and the cerebellar nuclei was thought to serve as a basic driving force for generating sustained activity in a large population of cells in the premotor network. Inhibitory input to the premotor network from cerebellar Purkinje cells was postulated to regulate this positive feedback, thus shaping premotor population activity into multidimensional motor programs for commanding limb movements.

The cooperative control model for gaze movements presented here is similarly based on a desire to incorporate diverse anatomical, physiological and behavioural data. The anatomical data reviewed in the next section indicates that the superior colliculus and the cerebellum are interconnected by way of recurrent pathways through brainstem nuclei, thus forming a premotor network analoguous to the one interconnecting the motor cortex and cerebellum. This similarity leads us to suggest that the motor cortex and superior colliculus might be looked upon as analoguous structures, in that both may be sites where sensory triggers are processed to decide when to initiate movement. Positive feedback within the premotor network could serve as the driving force for generating motor commands for eye and head movements, and inhibition from Purkinje cells in the cerebellar cortex could serve to shape premotor population activity into a multidimensional motor program for controlling gaze.

In another chapter in this present volume [Houk & Barto, this volume], the cooperative control model is used as a basis for developing a theory of distributed sensorimotor learning. In correspondence with this theory, we will propose that visuomotor learning is similarly distributed. The cerebellar cortex is thought to be the initial site where motor programs are learned, but when these programs are repeatedly performed, they become adopted as visuomotor habits by premotor networks in the superior colliculus or brainstem. An analoguous two–stage process was proposed earlier for the adaptive control of the vestibulo–ocular reflex [Galiana 1986; Peterson et al, 1991].

2. BACKGROUND

Gaze refers to the orientation of the visual axis in space. Since the eyes are mounted on the head, and the head on the body, the direction of gaze is a composite variable determined by the summed effects of eye, head and body movements. In neurophysiological experiments the head is often held fixed, in which case eye movements alone determine the direction of gaze. Under conditions in which the head and eyes are allowed to move together, single unit, EMG and kinematic data all indicate that there is a great deal of coordination and interdependence between the eye and head control systems [Guitton et al 1980, 1984, 1990; Munoz & Guitton 1989; Roucoux et al 1980; Tomlinson, 1990; Tomlinson & Bahra, 1986a,b; Vidal et al 1982, 1983]. In the present paper we make the simplifying assumptions that brain activity associated with eye movements in head–fixed animals is qualitatively similar to activity associated with coordinated transitions in gaze that occur when the head is free to move, and we will use the term gaze to refer to both.

2.1 Anatomical Organization of the Gaze Control System

The control of gaze engages widespread regions of the central nervous system [Büttner–Ennever, 1988; Wurtz & Goldberg, 1989]. As shown diagrammatically in Fig. 1, there is a basic gaze control network in the brainstem which interconnects extensively with other brain regions – the superior colliculus (or tectum), the cerebellum and the cerebrum (engaging both the cerebral cortex and the basal ganglia). Furthermore, those areas of the cerebellum and cerebrum that are specifically involved in gaze control also interconnect with the superior colliculus and with each other. Thus all of the regions that participate in orienting the eyes and head in space are reciprocally interconnected with each other. Some of the interconnections are direct whereas others involve multisynaptic linkages via the thalamus, brainstem and other relays.

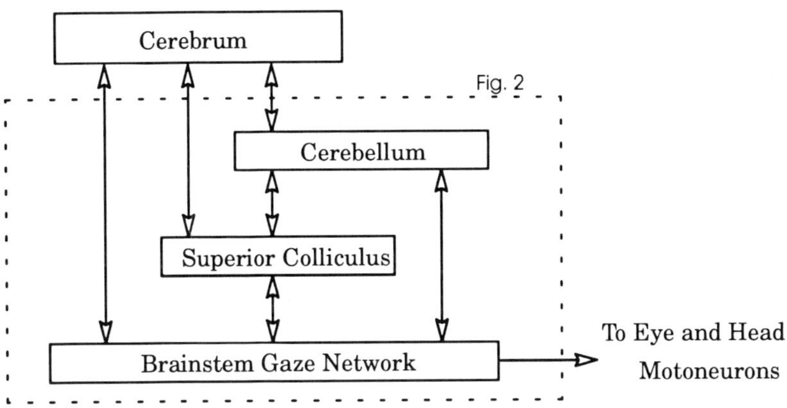

Figure 1. Regions of the central nervous system involved in gaze control.

This global pattern of anatomical interconnection and reciprocity promotes the concept that gaze control operates in a highly distributed manner, and lesion studies support this idea (see below). A large body of evidence indicates that the brainstem gaze network is the only region of the central nervous system that is absolutely required to produce the rapid eye–head movements called saccades. Lesions of other areas may cause severe initial impairments, but after a transient phase there is usually considerable recovery of function. For example, lesions of the superior colliculus or frontal eye fields at first abolish, or severely degrade the ability to initiate gaze saccades, but appreciable recovery of function is observed over a time course of several days. While lesions of the cerebellum do not have much effect on the ability to initiate gaze shifts, they severely impair the accuracy and coordination of the movements; again the initial deficit may be significantly compensated over time. One concludes that a crude ability to execute gaze commands resides in the brainstem, whereas the ability to control these movements in a more sophisticated manner is distributed among several higher centers in the brain.

The fact that the higher centers are capable of compensating for each other to a considerable degree suggests that they have some overlapping functions. However, there is also evidence that each area has different specialized functions. The cerebrum may be particularly important in high–level functions such as the selection of potential targets for attracting visual attention and the planning of strategies for visually scanning an object or an environment. The superior colliculus seems especially important for organizing the transfer between "fixation" and "orienting" modes of behavior and for commanding a gaze shift, though gaze saccades can also be commanded by directly accessing the brainstem gaze network. The cerebellum's special role seems to be that of regulating the accuracy of the various processes already mentioned, as contrasted with uniquely controlling a single process. While these statements highlight the special capabilities of the different brain regions, because of the distributed organization of the system, there is considerable overlap in function. Any given operation is normally the result of cooperative computation by the entire system.

The cooperative nature of computations in the gaze control system makes it difficult to study any one portion in isolation, without considering all the other regions. However, it can become very confusing to deal with all parts of the system simultaneously. The compromise adopted in this chapter is to focus on certain of the low–level features of gaze control, using this as justification for essentially ignoring the cerebrum. Our goal is to outline a theory that could explain how the superior colliculus, brainstem and cerebellum function in a cooperative manner to control fundamental features of gaze (dashed box in Fig. 1).

Fig. 2 provides a more detailed view of the main anatomical connections between the superior colliculus, brainstem and cerebellum [reviewed in Büttner–Ennever 1988; Grantyn 1988; Huerta & Harting 1984]. The superior colliculus shown on the left, is a layered structure with superficial (sSC), intermediate (iSC) and deep (dSC) lamina. Visual projections to the sSC are topographically organized to form a map of the visual field. Through precisely organized retinal and cortical projections, half of the visual field maps upon each colliculus,with the centrally located foveal region being represented in both rostral zones of the colliculi. Auditory and somatosensory inputs to the dSC are also topographically organized, and these maps are in spatial register with the visual map [Meredith & Stein, 1986]. The iSC contains a motor map, and it is also in basic register with the visual map as explained more fully in the following section. Cells in the iSC discharge in relation to rapid eye or eye–head movements, called gaze saccades, that serve to redirect the visual axis [Grantyn & Berthoz 1985; Guitton 1991; Munoz & Guitton 1985, 1986, 1989; Munoz et al 1991; Sparks 1986; Sparks & Mays, 1990; Wurtz & Goldberg, 1989].

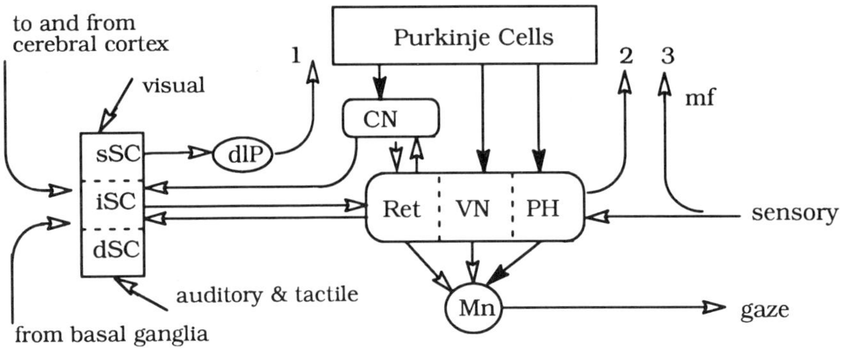

Figure 2. Schematic of anatomical pathways between collicular, brainstem and cerebellar centers: CN– cerebellar nuclei; mf– mossy fibers; sSC, iSC, dSC– superficial, intermediate and deep layers of the superior colliculi, respectively; Ret, VN, PH– reticular, vestibular and prepositus hypoglossi nuclei in the brainstem; Mn– motor nuclei; dlP– dorsolateral pontine nucleus. Filled arrows here and in subsequent figures represent inhibition.

Signals from iSC are sent via tecto–reticular (TRN) and tecto–reticulospinal (TRSN) neurons (together called TR(S)Ns), directly and indirectly to motoneurons (MNs) innervating eye and neck muscles. (After being processed by several brainstem nuclei in the latter case). This brainstem group is divided into three major subgroups in Fig. 2, (1) a collection of reticular nuclei (Ret); (2) the several divisions of the vestibular nuclei (VN); and (3) the prepositus hypoglossi nucleus (PH). The Ret subgroup includes the paramedian region of the pontine reticular formation, the reticularis tegmenti pontis, the raphe pontis, and several nuclei in the mesencephalic reticular formation (MRF): these contain important premotor cell–types, the best–known referred to as long–lead (LLBN) and short–lead (SLBN) burst neurons and omnipause neurons (OPN), as shown in more detail in Fig. 3 [Crandall & Keller 1985; Henn & Cohen 1976; Hepp & Henn, 1983; Hepp et al 1989; Keller, 1974; Raybourn & Keller, 1977; Robinson, 1975; Van Gisbergen et al, 1981], and summarized in separate chapters of Wurtz & Goldberg [1989].

Excitatory SLBNs are thought to provide the burst signal needed by motoneurons that drive saccades. Inhibitory SLBNs (known as inhibitory burst neurons) deactivate antagonist ocular motoneurons. OPNs gate saccades. Their tonic inhibitory activity silences SLBNs except during saccades, when OPN activity pauses. LLBNs are thought to constitute an intermediate processing stage between the SC and the SLBN–OPN complex. The TR(S)N input to excitatory and inhibitory LLBNs assures burst activation of SLBNs and concomitent silencing of OPNs, respectively. The Ret, VN and PH subgroups interconnect extensively with each other, to form a brainstem gaze network that has some capacity for autonomous function (discussed later), as shown in a recent model study [Galiana, 1991].

There are prominent reciprocal connections between the brainstem gaze network, the deep cerebellar nuclei (CN) and the iSC. Purkinje cells (PJ) in the posterior lobe and the flocculus portions of the cerebellar cortex send powerful inhibitory connections to the deep cerebellar nuclei (CN) and to the VN and PH subgroups of the brainstem network [Kawamura et al, 1982; Rolodán & Reinoso–Suárez, 1981; Stein et al, 1984; May et al, 1990]. Mossy fibre inputs to the cerebellar cortex provide Purkinje cells with a variety of information that could be useful in controlling gaze, as exemplified by the mossy fibre inputs labelled 1–3 in Fig. 2 [Blanks, 1988; Keller, 1989]. Visual, auditory and tactile information about events in the external world enters the cerebellum by way of the dorsolateral pontine nucleus (dlP); for simplicity, only one visual pathway from sSC to dlP is explicitly shown. Efference copy mossy fibres (inputs labelled 2 in Fig. 2) transmit the current firing patterns of Ret, VN and PH neurons, which provides Purkinje cells with diverse information about intended eye–head movements. Signals from various sensory sources (labelled 3) such as vestibular receptors in the labyrinth, tactile receptors and muscle proprioceptors provide a variety of information about the state of the body and the progress of movements as they are implemented. This diversity of information could be very useful for controlling the selection and regulation of motor programs for gaze.

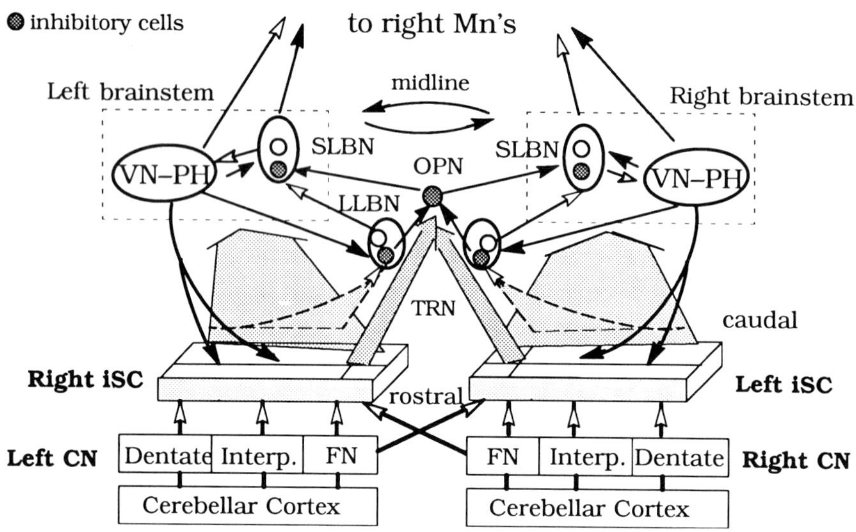

Figure 3. Recurrent connections between collicular and brainstem nuclei: only downward projections of Figure 1 are shown, from cerebellar cortex and CN. FN– fastigial nuclei; Interp.– interpositus; OPN– omnipausers; SLBN– short–lead and LLBN, long–lead bursters; TRN– tecto–reticular neurons with spatial projections represented as broad shaded arrows. (other symbols as in Figure 1, see text for details). Signs of brainstem output projections are compatible with the activation pattern in rightward–acting motoneurons, independent of saccade direction. Sensory afferents to all levels, as well as crossed interconnections between contralateral brainstem and CN–cerebellar system have been left out for clarity.

In addition, the iSC receives projections back from the brainstem network, especially the contralateral PH and MRF [Grantyn, 1988; Stechison et al, 1985; Moschovakis et al 1988a,b; McCrea & Baker, 1985], to complete an iSC–brainstem loop. The Ret subgroup of premotor neurons in particular, but also the other two brainstem subgroups, are reciprocally connected with the CN [Blanks, 1988]. The CN further send prominent projections to iSC to form additional loops. These multiple recurrent connections between iSC, CN and brainstem centers form a larger gaze control network with many levels. It is worth noting here that the iSC–CN networks provide spatio–temporal aspects to the system. Whereas the brainstem circuits contain mainly temporally coded premotor signals, the SC has a spatially coded signal. According to the theory proposed here, positive feedback in these loops provides the main driving force responsible for producing the premotor signals that are known to converge upon eye and neck MNs to control gaze. Further, the presence of such multiple levels provides robustness, since lesions at any one site cannot remove all available positive feedback loops. For example, the iSC receives feedback independently via brainstem or cerebellar routes (Fig. 3).

2.2 Neural Signals in the Superior Colliculus

The spatiotemporal patterns of single unit discharge in the superior colliculus have been extensively studied in behaving animals [reviewed in Guitton, 1991; Sparks, 1986; Sparks & Mays, 1990; Wurtz & Goldberg, 1989]. The results of these studies have provided a wealth of information about the functional organization of the SC, key elements of which are summarized in Fig. 4 (adapted from Mays & Sparks, 1980). The traces on the left are time plots of eye movement (horizontal H and vertical V components) in relation to the presentation of visual targets (O is a fixation spot and B is a briefly presented target to the right of fixation) and a set of single unit recordings from cells located in different parts of the left and right SC (records 1–8). The drawings on the right represent horizontal views of the two SC on which are shown the locations of the single cell recordings.

Let us begin with the response properties of visual cells located in the superficial lamina (in sSC, Fig. 2). Visual cells have broadly tuned receptive fields centered about a specific point in the visual field (also a point on the retina). For example, the cell at site 2 in Fig. 4 responds maximally to visual spots 20^0 to the right of fixation located along the horizontal meridian, and the response drops off progressively as the spot is moved away from its optimal point. Recording 2 shows the neuron's response to target B, a delayed burst of discharge that slightly outlasts the duration of the stimulus. These visual cells are basically unrelated to eye or eye–head movement except for an interesting modulatory feature. Response can be enhanced when the stimulus actually serves as a target for an upcoming saccade (called visual enhancement).

In contrast, cells in the iSC have a range of properties suggesting that they are imbedded within the network that transforms sensory stimuli into motor commands. Many of these cells show burst discharges that appear to reflect motor commands, since their timing and intensity is highly correlated with the onset, duration and speed of subsequent saccadic movements. Recordings 7 and 8 (Fig. 4) show examples of pure collicular burst cells; cell 7 is related to rightward horizontal saccades, and cell 8 is related to leftward horizontal saccades. These neurons show movement fields that are analoguous to the sensory fields of the visual neurons in the superficial lamina. The cells discharge maximally for a certain amplitude and direction of saccade (optimal vector), and discharge drops off progressively as these parameters depart from the optimal ones. Cells at different locations on the colliculus have different optimal vectors, and the spatial distribution of these optimal vectors on a plan view of the colliculus defines a unique motor map to which cells throughout the iSC comply. In the vicinity of the optimal site, a large population of collicular burst neurons fires simultaneously in association with a given saccadic movement [Guitton, 1991; McIlwain, 1986a; Van Gisbergen et al, 1987]. The centroid of this population activity is thought to be a major factor in the ultimate control of saccadic movement.

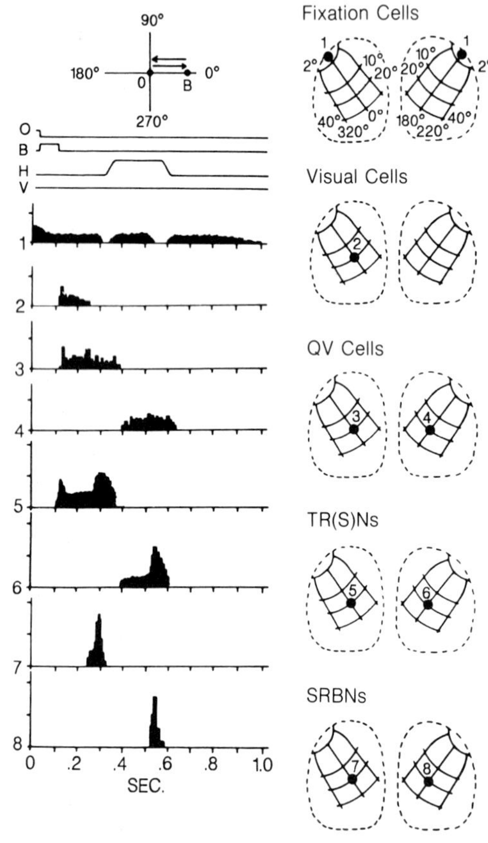

Figure 4. Schematic representation of the discharge of specific cell types in SC during the double saccade paradigm shown at top left. Monkey or cat fixates point 0 while target B flashes. Subject in the dark makes saccade first to B and then back to 0. On the right, dorsal views of the SC are shown with the location, on the map, of different cell types indicated by numbered dark circles. Correspondingly numbered traces on the left show discharges of these cells. Fixation neurons (1) in monkey and cat ("fixation TR(S)Ns") are active during fixation at points 0 and B even in the dark, provided these points have behavioral significance. With the eyes at 0, target B's onset will evoke: a burst in visual cells (2) in the superficial layers, and in TR(S)Ns (5) that will control the movement 0–B; sustained discharges in QV cells (3) and TR(S)Ns (5). About 20–40 ms prior to saccade 0–B, a high frequency burst of activity is seen in TR(S)Ns (5) and SRBNs (7). At the end of saccade 0–B, QV cells (4) and TR(S)Ns (6), both at the correct site to generate saccade B–0, show a sustained discharge. These TR(S)Ns (6) and SRBNs (8) will burst before saccade B–0. Adapted from Mays & Sparks (1980).

It is extremely interesting that the motor map in the iSC is in close register with the sensory visual map in sSC [Schiller & Koerner, 1971]. What we mean by being in register is the following. The sensory map describes the location of a visual target as a vector distance, and the site immediately below it on the motor map describes the amplitude and direction of a saccade that, if activated, would move the eye appropriately to orient the fovea to that visual target. The finding of this alignment between sensory and motor maps gave rise to the foveation hypothesis of collicular function [Schiller & Koerner 1971] . According to this hypothesis, cells in the superficial lamina of the SC project directly downward to the corresponding coordinate in the intermediate lamina, and this activation then commands an appropriate shift in gaze. One concern with this idea is whether the downward projection is sufficiently powerful to activate the relatively large population of iSC neurons believed responsible for commanding a saccade. A potentially more difficult problem is that of explaining why it takes approximately 100 ms for visual activity in sSC to become transformed into burst activity in iSC, which implicates a long, multisynaptic pathway. A third problem concerns the ability of the gaze system to keep track of the location of a target long after it has disappeared (called a remembered target) or after it has been displaced on the retina by an eye movement (called a transposed target). In this last case, motor activity in the iSC and dSC need not be linked to visual activity directly above in the sSC [Mays & Sparks, 1980].

Cells in iSC show differing combinations of four component types of discharge: (1) sensory evoked bursts, (2) low frequency activity that follows a sensory burst, (3) low frequency preamble to a motor burst, and (4) motor bursts [cf Guitton, 1991]. Cells with pure sensory bursts (found only in sSC), or pure motor bursts were already discussed; a sensory burst was illustrated in trace 2 of Fig. 4 and motor bursts in traces 7 and 8. As an example of a cell with complex features, the cat's TR(S)N (see Munoz & Guitton 1989; Guitton 1991 for details) illustrated by traces 5 and 6 in Fig. 4, has all four of these components, namely a sensory burst, low frequency activity that follows the burst which merges with a low frequency preamble to the motor burst, and finally a motor burst. Other cells show sensory and motor bursts but no low frequency activity in between (not illustrated). Yet another type found in primate, called a quasivisual (QV) cell, is particularly interesting for the insight it provides on the ability of the gaze system to keep track of remembered and transposed targets.

Quasivisual cells discharge like cat TR(S)Ns, but without motor bursts. They have visual receptive fields similar to purely visual cells in the sSC. In addition, they continue their discharge to indicate the locations of remembered targets. This is shown by extinguishing the target and making the animal wait during a delay period before responding with a saccade to the remembered location of the target. Quasivisual cells show an initial visual response and then continue their discharge throughout the delay period. This is shown in trace 3 of Fig. 4 where discharge continues for several hundred ms after the target was extinguished. Quasivisual cell discharge changes its site on the surface of the colliculus to compensate for intervening eye movements. These properties are illustrated in Fig. 4 by the offset of discharge in cell 3 and by the onset of discharge in cell 4. The offset of cell 3 activity following the rightward horizontal eye movement signifies that target B has shifted to a new location (a foveal location). In contrast, the onset of activity in cell 4 signifies that the remembered location of the target relative to the fixation point just shifted to this new location on the collicular map. The new location corresponds, on the motor map, to the amplitude and direction of an eye movement that would bring target O back to the fixation point. It is interesting that the discharge of cell

4 did not require the presentation of a visual target in its visual receptive field as required by the foveation hypothesis. Instead the discharge reflected movement of a remembered target to this location.

Fixation neurons represent another important category of iSC neuron [Munoz & Guitton 1989; Munoz et al 1990, 1991b]. These cells are concentrated in the foveal region of the collicular map, they discharge tonically whenever the animal fixates a target, and the frequency of discharge correlates with the motivational significance of the target. Many of their physiological properties can be understood by considering them to be quasivisual cells with foveal receptive fields. The example shown by cell 1 in Fig. 4 illustrates a sensory response to the fixation point, low frequency activity to the remembered position of the fixation target after the light is extinguished, and the disappearance of this activity during the rightward eye movement. (After the eye movement, the remembered fixation target activity moves to point 4 on the collicular map.) There is reemergence of activity in cell 1 after the eye movement is made to the remembered location of target B, and this activity disappears during the eye movement back to the location of the fixation point. (Actually there is some anticipation of the eye movement, which represents a motor component of this cell's discharge.) The third phase of tonic activity in cell 1 represents the remembered location of the fixation point. The tonic discharge of fixation cells is thought to be important in suppressing burst activity in other regions of the collicular map during periods of active fixation, and in suppressing brainstem burst cells via excitation of (inhibitory) OPNs (see Fig. 3 projections from rostral iSC) [Munoz & Guitton 1989].

2.3 Signals at Brainstem and Cerebellar Sites

The results summarized in the preceding section indicate that a variety of sensorimotor properties are present in the superior colliculus. This variety is present also at the other sites in the gaze control system, summarized in Fig. 3. There is close similarity between some tectal, brainstem and cerebellar neuronal properties. For example, the discharge of LLBNs resembles the QV–type–preamble–plus–burst seen on TR(S)Ns. The discharge of SLBNs can resemble that of saccade–related burst neurons present in the iSC, notably in their velocity coding [Munoz & Guitton, 1989; Waitzman et al, 1991]. Eye velocity components are also particularly prominent in VN neurons during saccades; while eye position components are more prominent in PH neurons. However the distinctions are in the weighting of components only. The cerebellum contains mixed examples of all of the components seen in the brainstem network [Gardner & Fuchs, 1975; Hepp et al, 1982; Kase et al, 1980; Keller, 1989; Ohtsuka & Noda, 1990].

To summarize, it is clear that a diverse mixture of sensorimotor properties is found in individual cells, and this variety is dispersed throughout the different stages of the gaze control system. This contrasts with earlier expectations of many investigators, who had imagined an orderly sequencing from sensory to motor properties at successive stages in the network. In retrospect, however, this distributed representation of properties is to be expected, based on the anatomy of the system. Multiple recurrent pathways provide ready conduits for distributing a property that arises at one site or level, to sites dispersed throughout the network. The challenge now is to understand the significance of this distributed, recurrent architecture.

3. FUNCTIONS FOR THE CEREBELLUM IN GAZE CONTROL

In the previous section, we reviewed the general anatomical layout of the gaze control system, emphasizing the existence of prominent recurrent pathways between the cerebellum, the superior colliculus and a group of brainstem areas that are premotor to gaze motor neurons. We called the latter group the brainstem gaze network, and this together with the iSC and CN were designated the gaze premotor network. We postulated that positive feedback in these neural networks drives or sustains neural activity, and that this activity is shaped into gaze motor programs by inhibitory input to the network from Purkinje cells in the cerebellar cortex. In this section, we develop these ideas concerning the functions of the cerebellar cortex in gaze control. We postpone to a later section a discussion of how the premotor network might learn to operate in the absence of cerebellar cortical control.

3.1 Architecture of the Tecto–cerebellar Network

As a first step, we will outline a network architecture suitable for exploring interactions between the SC and the cerebellum. A three–dimensional architecture is necessary to capture the salient spatiotemporal properties of SC neurons. Two dimensions are needed to represent the spatial coordinates of the sensory and motor maps corresponding to a plan projection on the surface of the colliculus (Fig. 5A), and a third dimension (dorso–ventral) is needed to represent the diverse sensorimotor properties encountered in the group of iSC cells at each map coordinate (Fig. 5B). This 3–D array of iSC neurons must then connect reciprocally with a 3–D array of CN neurons via a 3–D array of Ret neurons. Ret neurons with adequate spatial properties can be found among saccadic LLBNs [Hepp & Henn, 1983]. The array of CNs needs also to receive an organized inhibitory input from a large set of Purkinje cells.

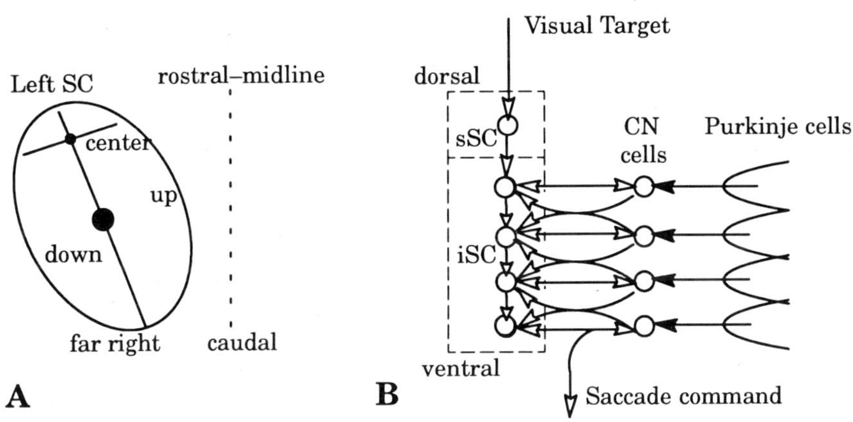

Figure 5. A– Projection of the right visual field onto the surface of the left superior colliculus (SC). B– Propagation of visual signals through layers of the SC, and cerebellar influence via interconnections with cerebellar nuclei (CN).

The overall network architecture is sufficiently complex to warrant approaching it a single dimension at a time. Fig. 5B emphasizes the organization that relates to the dorsal–ventral dimension in the SC [Grantyn 1988; Moschovakis 1988a,b]. The dashed rectangle encloses a group of collicular cells that are all located at a single coordinate on the collicular map, for example, the site marked by the filled circle in Fig. 5A. This 'column' is comprised of one sSC neuron and four iSC neurons (The numbers were chosen for convenience of discussion; in fact, each neuron could be considered as a cluster.) The four iSC neurons are each hypothesized to have strong reciprocal connections with corresponding CN neurons, by way of brainstem Ret neurons. For simplicity, the Ret neurons are not explicitly shown. Topographically organized projections from a parasagittal strip of Purkinje cells provide a powerful inhibitory input to each CN neuron [Ito, 1984], though only one projection per neuron is shown for simplicity.

Each reciprocal iSC–CN pair together with the associated Purkinje input forms an element, or basic building block, of the network. Cross–over connections between iSC–CN pairs provide one mode of communication between these network elements (Fig. 5B). An example will help to illustrate the utility of the cross–over connections. (While recognizing that the iSC can be activated independently of sSC [Mays & Sparks, 1980], we explore here the potential link between these layers). Assume that a visual input comes to the sSC at the top of the column. This cell would be expected to project out of the colliculus to the dlP [Mower et al, 1979; Fig. 2], but via its collaterals [Moschovakis 1988a,b], the visual activation can be passed on to the first iSC cell in the column, which we postulate is a quasivisual neuron. The iSC–CN reciprocal connection, together with interconnections in the iSC itself, would provide positive feedback which could give rise to activity that persists after the target is extinguished. This could explain the ability of quasivisual cells to remember the locations of visual targets beyond the time of their disappearance. Quasivisual activity would tend to spread to neighbouring computational units. One route for this spread would be through the ventrally directed projections of iSC collaterals within the colliculus [Moschovakis et al 1988a,b], but a potentially more important route would be through divergence in loop connections. Activity would progressively spread through these cross–over connections to recruit more network elements. We further postulate that there would be a population threshold for this spreading activation, such that the achievement of the population threshold would lead to an abrupt enhancement of positive feedback and cause the onset of an, intense, saccade–driving burst in many cells of the network.

In this manner, the hundred ms delay between visual responses in sSC and burst responses in iSC might result from a progressive build–up of positive feedback in reciprocally connected neurons, the low frequency preamble to the motor burst being an indication of this build–up. The collicular burst activity (TR(S)Ns) would transmit the saccadic command, principally via brainstem circuits to motoneurons (Fig. 3). A corollary of this command would be sent to PH and other brainstem centers where we postulate that an efference copy of the motor response is computed [Galiana et al, 1992; Guitton et al, 1990]. Due to the high interconnectivity in the premotor and iSC centers, the saccade command arising from the iSC carries both gaze velocity and gaze error signals.

Let us now consider the organization of the network in the map plane of the superior colliculus (Fig. 4 and 5A). The two main levels of feedback to iSC are evident in Fig. 3. This emphasizes the spatio–temporal transformations which link the iSC to other gaze control centers and the strong contralateral projection from PH to iSC [McCrea & Baker 1985] which could interact and reinforce the previously described cerebellar controls. Hence, spatial shifts in iSC activity could evolve under either or both CN and brainstem influences. Two aspects of gaze control will now be considered in this dimension: the initiation of a movement and the shaping of motor signals during a movement.

3.2 Initiating a Gaze Saccade

The manner in which the visual field is laid out on the SC surface is not particularly conducive to the conceptualization of bilateral collicular activity, as it evolves before and during a gaze shift. Conceptualization can be facilitated by transposing the collicular maps. In Fig. 6A, the left colliculus was rotated counter clockwise and moved to the right, while the right colliculus was rotated clockwise and moved to the left. The centers of the foveal regions were overlapped and aligned so as to provide a single map of the visual field. After this manipulation, the horizontal meridian of the visual field falls along the horizontal line of the map.

For simplicity, we are focussing on one layer at a time in the dorso–ventral dimension of the colliculus network, corresponding to a particular depth in the iSC. Furthermore, we will restrict ourselves to a single dimension corresponding to the horizontal dimension in the collicular map (rostral–caudal). This results in the row of iSC neurons enclosed in the dashed rectangle of Fig. 6B. Since the reciprocal network discussed earlier is organized in 3 dimensions, each of the iSC neurons in this row will be reciprocally connected with a corresponding CN neuron, and, as before, this iSC–CN pair together with its associated Purkinje input will comprise a network element. In this case, however, the cross–over connections between network elements will provide a mechanism for facilitating the spread of activity in the map plane of the colliculus. This spread thus relates to the spatial coordination of gaze as contrasted with the earlier discussion of temporal coordination of sensory–to–motor properties.

The cross–connections between network elements in Fig. 6B provide a ready explanation for the broad distribution of population activity in SC burst neurons that was described in Section 2.2. For example, consider that the row of iSC neurons in Fig. 6B represents either TR(S)Ns or saccade–related burst neurons (Fig. 4). If a neuron towards the left end of this row (mimicking cell 7 of Fig. 4) were actively generating a burst, this activity would tend to spread to adjacent neurons in the manner depicted by the concentric circles in Fig. 6A. In this way, the cross–connections would facilitate the firing of a large population of SC burst neurons, and this ensemble of neural activity could then serve as a command to *initiate* a movement.

Note that brainstem pause cells (OPNs) receive inhibition from reticular bursters (LLBNs) and excitation mainly from the rostral zone of the SC [Munoz et al, 1991a], while brainstem burst cells receive simultaneously excitation from the caudal areas of the SC (Fig. 3). Since initiation of a saccade requires the silencing of OPNs, the release of a saccade could occur from either loss of rostral iSC–to–OPN excitation, or an increase in LLBN–to–OPN inhibition associated with the appearance of caudal activity on the iSC. During normal movements, both mechanisms play a role since iSC fixation cells are silenced before the start of a gaze shift.

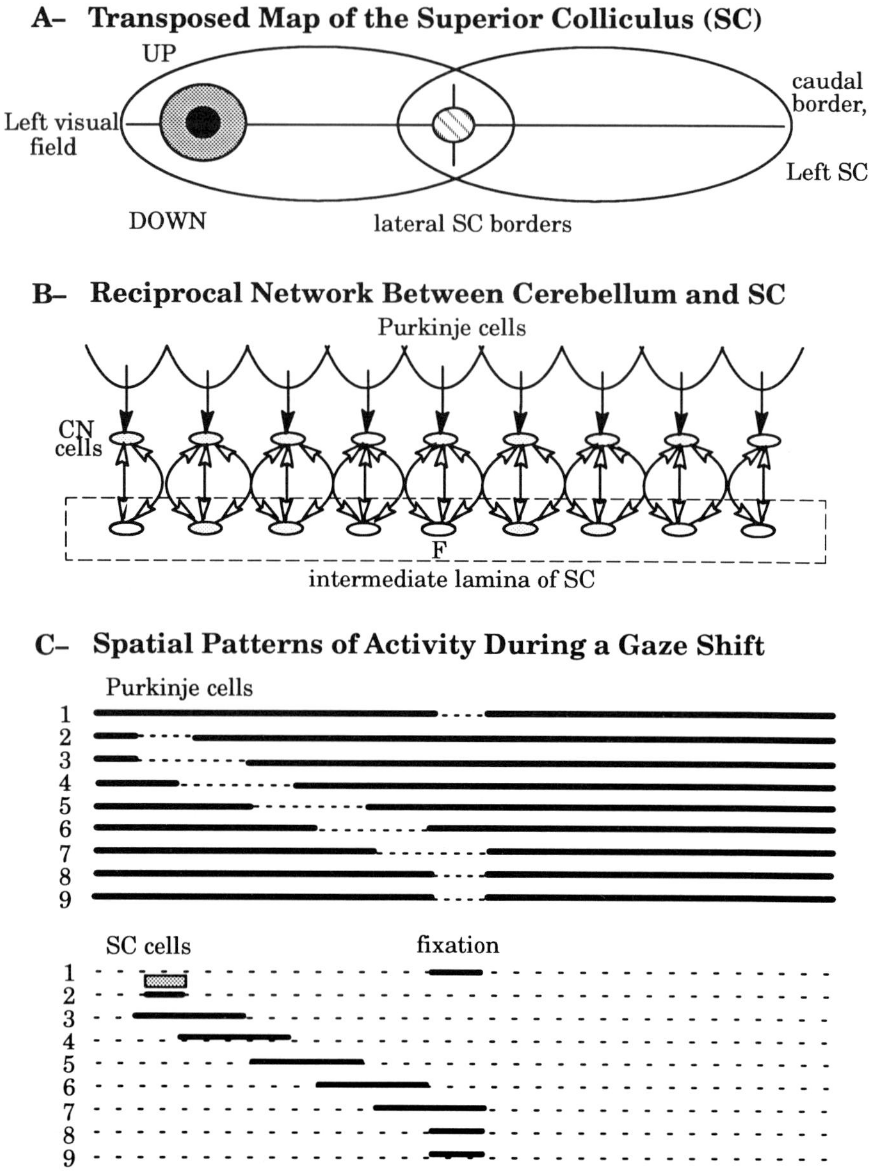

Figure 6. Postulated moving patterns of activity (heavy bars) or inactivity (dashed lines) on the collicular and cerebellar networks, from initial site (filled circle) to foveation area (hatched circle). See text.

3.3 Shaping Loop Activity into Gaze Motor Commands

Here we will discuss potential mechanisms to cause spatial shifts in iSC population activity, under cerebellar influences. Once a gaze command is initiated, mechanisms are needed to regulate collicular activity and to shape it into spatiotemporal patterns appropriate for the direction, velocity and duration of the ongoing saccade. Fig. 6C is presented to illustrate how spatial patterns of Purkinje cell discharge might regulate population activity in the intermediate lamina of the superior colliculus, by inhibiting activity in the the reciprocal network. The thick horizontal lines are used to represent the postulated spatial distribution of neural activity in Purkinje cells and in iSC neurons at nine different instants in time during the movement. The spatial coordinate depicted from left to right in Fig. 6C is the same as in parts A and B above. In the sequence shown in the lower panel of Fig. 6C, iSC activity at time step 1 is restricted to the fixation zone in the center of the transposed colliculus map, which represents an initial state of gaze fixation. This activity tends to spread laterally to left–of–center and right–of–center positions, due to the cross–connections of the reciprocal network in Fig. 6B. However, lateral spread is inhibited by the pattern of Purkinje cell activity in cells aligned with the lateral zones of the colliculus, as illustrated at time step 1 in the upper panel of Fig. 6C. The only inactive zone of Purkinje cells is in the center of the map where it permits the persistence of collicular fixation activity, mediated by feedback in the corresponding reciprocal loops.

Time steps 2–9 show the hypothetical responses to a visual target presented in the left visual field, symbolized by the small, stippled box above trace 2 in the lower panel of Fig. 6C. Responses of visual cortical neurons and sSC neurons to the visual target would be sent as a focal input to those iSC cells lying immediately below the stippled box and also, by way of the dlP and mossy fiber pathway (labelled 1 in Fig. 2), to widespread regions of the cerebellar cortex. We postulate that the focal input to iSC cells would initiate a progressive buildup of loop activity starting from this coordinate in the reciprocal network, as illustrated by the progression from steps 2 to 3. The buildup of loop activity would be controlled by the spatial pattern of Purkinje cell activity. At time step 2, we suppose that Purkinje cells on the left turn off, permitting the buildup of collicular activity under the stippled target box. At the same time, Purkinje cells in the center zone turn on, causing collicular fixation activity to die out.

The transition in the cerebellar cortex from pattern 1 to pattern 2 of PJ activity corresponds, in essence, to the recall of a motor program from its postulated storage site in parallel fiber synapses. We suppose that the turning off of PJ cells on the left is caused by the firing of basket cells, or other inhibitory interneurons, in response to their parallel fiber inputs from visual mossy fibers. The turning on of PJ cells in the center (fixation zone) is attributed to the same visual input exciting these particular PJ cells. The specificity of connections from mossy fibers to PJ and basket cells is attributed to an adaptive process that adjusts parallel fiber synapses: this learning mechanism provides for the 'storage' of a motor program, as elaborated in Section 4.3. At this point, however, we assume that motor programs have already been learned or stored, and we return to the problem of understanding how a gaze motor program, as specified by the spatiotemporal patterns of collicular activity, might be controlled by the cerebellum.

The spatiotemporal pattern of SC activity illustrated in Fig. 6C is the one observed during gaze shifts produced by coordinated eye and head movements in the cat whose head is unrestrained [Munoz et al, 1991a,b]. Under these natural conditions, collicular activity in iSC first builds up at a lateral site appropriate for the visual target location (e.g. TR(S)Ns, Fig.4), and then spreads as a travelling zone of activity toward the fixation zone in the center of the map (Fig 6C). We suppose that this travelling zone of collicular activity is controlled by the spatiotemporal pattern of PJ *inactivity* (disinhibition), which effectively drags behind it the zone of SC activity. Fixation activity resumes once gaze has acquired the selected visual target.

Assuming that these patterns of PJ cell activity control the gaze motor program, we should then attempt to explain what controls the PJ cells. Due to the great variety of mossy fiber inputs to the cerebellar cortex, there are various alternative explanations for this control, only one of which will be discussed in this chapter. We start by postulating that the leading edge of the wave of PJ cell inactivity is controlled by basket cell inhibition, and that the basket cells are excited by efference copy mossy fibers from Ret LLBNs. These mossy fibers would fire promptly at the onset of iSC burst activity, and thus would be ideally suited for facilitating the moving field of PJ cell inactivity. In contrast, we suggest that the turning on of PJ cells that defines the trailing edge of the inactive zone is controlled by a constellation of efference copy and sensory mossy fiber inputs, included in groups labelled 2 and 3 of Fig. 1, and in Fig. 2. On functional grounds, we believe that the particular constellation should depend on the laterality of the network element, related to the fact that elements far from the fixation zone are specialized for controlling large–amplitude gaze shifts, whereas those centrally located near the fixation zone are specialized for small gaze shifts. (The central elements also participate in controlling the terminal phases of large amplitude saccades, as shown in Fig. 6C, though this does not represent their unique function.) Since the eyes may be used alone for small saccades, vestibular and neck proprioceptive inputs giving information on head motion would not be useful in this case. Furthermore, since small saccades have short durations, proprioceptive feedback from eye muscles would arrive too late to be very useful in their control. This suggests that, by default, efference copy mossy fibers would be particularly important in controlling network elements near the fixation zone.

However, network elements more remote from the fixation zone could profit greatly from the vestibular and proprioceptive information supplied by sensory mossy fibers, since the large gaze shifts that they control include head movements and are of sufficiently long duration to permit the transmission of afferent information to the cerebellum. In fact, when considering brainstem projections directly to the iSC, this would explain the apparent predominance of intercalatus projections to the caudal part of the iSC, whereas Ph projections are more central and rostral [Stechison et al, 1985]. Vestibular and proprioceptive inputs inform the cerebellum about how the gaze shift is actually proceeding, and thus should be very valuable in helping to time the termination of a gaze motor program. These predictions on functional grounds are consistent with specializations in the organization of anatomical pathways from the cerebellar nuclei to the superior colliculus [May et al 1990]. For example, fastigial nuclei project mainly to the rostral zone of the SC (Fig. 2), which is known to be involved in the release and termination of saccades: saccades are halted upon stimulation of this SC zone in both cat (Munoz & Guitton 1989) and monkey (Munoz et al, 1990; Waitzman et al 1990), leading to the proposal that it plays a 'fixation' role.

3.4 Registering and Storing Potential Targets on QV–type Discharges

Recall from Section 2.2 that tonic activity in quasivisual cells and TR(S)Ns in the iSC effectively 'remembers' the locations of potential visual targets due to two unique properties. First, there is a persistence of low–level neural activity beyond the duration of target presentation; effectively a short–term memory on the collicular map of the target's location. It is likely that several potential targets can be registered in this manner. Second, during eye movements to one of these targets, the activity related to the others gets shifted across the surface of the iSC in such a manner as to retain information about the locations of these alternate targets with respect to the new, current, gaze position. The new coordinates are therefore appropriate and immediately available to redirect gaze, should the need to do so arise. In the present section, we discuss how extensions of the concepts proposed above are capable of explaining these quasivisual properties of the iSC neurons.

As discussed earlier, the stippled box in Fig. 6C marks the site of burst activity that would direct gaze to the indicated visual target; it also marks the location where quasivisual activity would originate to register the visual input as a potential target. Now let us consider how this quasivisual activity might be controlled, to maintain an appropriate zone of activity on the map irrespective of gaze position relative to the target. First, let us consider delaying the gaze shift to the potential target. A transition in PJ cell activity, similar to that shown between steps 1 and 2 in Fig. 6C, could result in quasivisual activity, provided the PJ pattern were modified in two ways. The central site of inactivity at time step 1 should continue through time step 2, in order to maintain activity in the fixation region of the iSC, and the lateral site of PJ cell inactivity should be reduced in magnitude. In other words, instead of these PJ cells turning completely off, they should simply reduce their discharge rate, or a smaller fraction of PJ cells should be turned off. In this manner, an intermediate level of inhibition at the lateral site would occur, and this would result in a low level of activity in the reciprocal loops at this map coordinate. If the subject decided to shift gaze to this target, PJ activity in the fixation zone would have to increase to shut down iSC fixation activity, and PJ activity at the lateral site would have to decrease further to permit the quasivisual activity to grow into burst activity.

Now let us consider what might happen if the subject were to shift gaze spontaneously to the right, which establishes a new error vector between the visual axis and the target. In Fig. 6C, the site of initial quasivisual cell activity (stippled box) should be shifted to the left. We will not be concerned with the activity at the site on the right map controlling the spontaneous rightward gaze shift, but instead will focus on activity on the left side of the map where the new error vector must be registered in quasivisual neurons. We know from single unit data (Section 2.2) that the site of quasivisual and sustained TR(S)N activity will shift further to the left on the tectal map. According to our theory, the mechanisms that cause this shift are quite analoguous to the mechanisms that were postulated to produce the rightward shift of burst activity controlling the gaze shift shown in Fig. 6. In Section 3.3, we postulated that the shift in burst activity is produced by a rightward wave of inactivity in PJ cells, created by a rightward wave of basket cell activity, and that the latter is controlled by efference copy mossy fiber input to the cerebellar cortex.

In analogy with this explanation, we propose that the required leftward shift of quasivisual activity, on the map of Fig. 6C, would be produced by a leftward directed wave of basket cell activity in the cerebellar cortex, during a rightward gaze shift to another target.

The tecto–cerebellar model proposed here accounts for a variety of properties of tectal neurons. It accounts for the registration of visual targets in quasivisual neurons, for gaze–related shifts in the sites of quasivisual activity, and for the growth of quasivisual activity into burst activity which then shifts to the fixation zone during the gaze shift. It should be noted that there is little difference between shifting burst activity for the selected target to the fixation zone, and shifting quasivisual activity for non–selected targets to other sites on the tectal map. The main difference is in the greater intensity of burst, as opposed to quasivisual, activity.

The above discussion deals with cat data (section 3.3) where activity on the SC map has been shown to shift in a dynamic manner *during* a gaze shift. Monkey data to date has been interpreted to support a fixed centroid for the population of cells on the map: they suggest that burst activity in monkey grows and then shrinks at lateral tectal sites, rather than shift as a wave to the central fixation zone as discussed here [Guitton, 1991; Sparks & Mays, 1990; Waitzman et al, 1991; Wurtz & Goldberg, 1989]. One possible explanation for this alternate interpretation of population activity is that only a low–intensity wave of quasivisual activity, as opposed to intense burst activity, moves from the site of burst initiation to the fixation zone; this has only recently been confirmed in alert monkey: this recent evidence shows translation of low–level activity across the monkey's SC map during a saccadic eye movement (Munoz and Wurtz, private communication). If, however, it turns out that there is no functionally important movement of activity in monkey, this could be explained by a temporal reversal of the spatial pattern of PJ cell activity shown in steps 1–3 of Fig. 6C. A sequence of PJ activity from step 2 to step 9 (equal to 1) could give rise to an activity that jumps from the peripheral site of burst activity to the central fixation zone, without an apparent intervening spatial wave. Alternatively, given spatially graded interconnections in a layer of the iSC, a radial spread of 'weakening' PJ cell disinhibition, centered on the site of initial collicular activation, could allow a threshold to be exceeded at the fixation site, thereby allowing the sudden appearance of a jump in rostral activity coincident with the end of the gaze shift [Lefevre & Galiana 1991].

4. CONTROL AND ADAPTATION IN A MULTI–LEVEL GAZE SYSTEM

4.1 Autonomous Capabilities of the Premotor Networks

In the previous section we considered the computational capabilities of the tecto–cerebellar network as if it operated in relative isolation from other parts of the gaze control system. This was a useful simplification that permitted us to focus on cerebellar mechanisms. In fact, model simulations have already shown that the tecto–reticular system in isolation can perform much of the required motor control during gaze shifts [Lefevre & Galiana, 1990, 1991]. Despite the omission of several other centers (e.g. at cortical levels), the gaze control system may enjoy a high degree of distributed processing which would contribute to its robustness.

It is clear from Fig. 2 that pathways are available whereby visual targets could trigger gaze saccades in the complete absence of information flow through the cerebellar cortex. Visual information could pass from the superficial to the intermediate lamina of the superior colliculus without going through the dorsolateral pons. In fact, this route could be important in the production of 'express' saccades [reviewed in Guitton 1991]. Activity initiated in the iSC could be sustained and controlled by the reciprocal pathways to and from the brainstem gaze network, as elaborated in Fig.s 3 and 7, and also by intrinsic collicular mechanisms as suggested in two previous models [Droulez & Berthoz, 1988, 1991; Guitton et al, 1990; Lefevre & Galiana, 1990, 1991]. An example of a pathway that might be particularly important in controlling iSC firing patterns is the one conveying eye position and/or eye velocity information (efference copies) from PH to contralateral iSC [Stechison et al 1985; McCrea & Baker, 1985]. Preliminary simulation studies indicate that both types of feedback would work equally well in controlling the gaze saccade duration, so long as the iSC is placed inside a premotor feedback loop [Lefevre & Galiana, 1990, 1991].

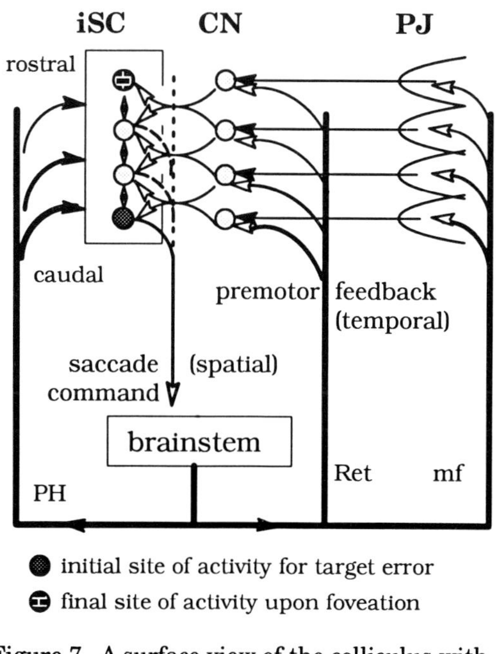

Figure 7. A surface view of the colliculus with premotor feedback pathways which could shape spatial activities during a gaze shift. (symbols as in Figure 2)

Given the anatomical relations, one would anticipate that the premotor networks and the iSC should have significant autonomous capabilities. For example, the extensive interconnections in the layers of the SC provide circuits for signal reverberation which could in themselves provide the potential to store visual (remembered) targets, even in isolation from the brainstem circuits. Also, given known feedback circuits from say PH to the iSC, several modelling approaches have illustrated how stored or remembered targets could be shifted on the collicular map in order to reflect updated motor conditions [Droulez & Berthoz, 1988, 1991; Lefevre & Galiana, 1990, 1991; Lefevre et al, 1991]. Now, the 2–D position of burst activity on the map of the SC codes the amplitude and direction of a gaze saccade that will bring a visual target to the central, or foveal, portion of the retina. In contrast, the eye and neck muscles that are used to implement the gaze saccade are organized in a different, and complex, coordinate system. In a sense each pool of motoneurons has its own coordinate system, since each muscle moves the eyes or head in a direction related to the origin and insertion of that particular muscle. Mechanisms are needed to perform spatial coordinate transformations. Formerly it was believed that a spatio–temporal transformation was also required, but recent evidence suggests that appreciable temporal coding is already present at the level of the tectum: TR(S)N firing frequency affects eye and head movement velocity and acceleration [Berthoz, Grantyn & Droulez, 1986; reviewed in Guitton 1991; Munoz & Guitton, 1989; Munoz et al, 1991; Waitzman et al 1991]. This is no longer surprising, given the strong iSC–brainstem interconnectivity.

Several models have been proposed to explain the change in spatial coordinate systems between the superior colliculus and motor neurons [van Gisbergen et al, 1985, 1987; Scudder 1988; Tweed & Vilis, 1990; see Guitton, 1991, for review]. The basic idea in each of these models is that different sites on the tectum should project with different weighting functions to each of the motor pools. For example, tectal neurons that code large, right–directed saccades would have strong connections with the motor neurons that cause right–directed movements, and weak connections with other motor neurons. Tectal neurons that code small, right–directed saccades would have weaker connections with the same motor pools. Similarly, tectal cells in caudal areas are expected to have stronger connections with head motor neurons, than tectal cells near the fixation zone, since small saccades often rely on eye movements alone. If these effects were combined by a relatively linear summation process in the pathway to the motor neurons, population activity in the iSC should provide a movement coded by the 'center of gravity' of the map's activity profile.

A use–dependent rule, guided by PJ cell activity, could drive the selection of connections during learning pre and post–birth. Thereafter, both sensory–motor and coordinate transformations would be imbedded at the level of the premotor network, at least sufficiently to perform stylized movements. Mechanisms to guide learning at this brainstem level are discussed in the next section.

4.2 Storing a Rudimentary Control Law in the Tecto–Reticular Network

Although gaze saccades can be made after extensive lesions of the cerebellum, these movements typically lack accuracy, and there is a failure to reduce inaccuracies due to deficits in adaptive processing [Keller 1989; Optican et al, 1986]. It is natural to attribute such inaccuracies to the absence of the tecto–cerebellar network discussed in section 3.

We assume that the tecto–reticular network utilizes a simple control law to generate approximate stereotyped gaze commands through iSC neurons. It is expected to be a rapid process, subserving standard 'express' saccades, for example. We then assume that the tecto–cerebellar circuit would provide a corrective component that would combine with the stereotyped tectal component to produce an accurate context–sensitive gaze command. In this manner, the cerebellum would implement more complex control laws as corrections to the simple control that is always automatically generated in the tectum–brainstem.

Support for a cerebellar 'teaching' role in shaping both sensory–motor and spatial coordinate transformations is also found in the literature concerning the adaptation of saccadic or vestibular ocular reflexes (as opposed to initial learning) [e.g. Lisberger, 1988]. In addition, if an adaptive sensory stimulus is sustained long enough, cerebellar activity apparently returns to its 'normal' monitoring levels once learning is well established, at least as documented in the adaptation of the vestibulo–ocular reflex. Several neurophysiological experiments suggest that in such cases, synaptic changes are offloaded from cerebellar down to brainstem or SC levels [Fitzgibbon & Goldberg, 1988; Lisberger & Pavelko, 1988; Miles & Lisberger 1981; Peterson et al, 1991; Robinson & Optican, 1981]. In fact, theoretical studies have shown that the sites of cerebellar projections and synaptic adaptation in the brainstem could well be identical [Galiana, 1986], simplifying the initial Miles–Lisberger [1981] postulate which required different sites for cerebellar control of movement and its guidance of parametric change. As a result, the iSC–brainstem premotor system can produce adequate 'adapted' responses, even in isolation. However, without the influence of cerebellar circuits, further adaptation in the gaze system would be much more difficult.

Cellular mechanisms capable of synaptic plasticity appear to be present in the superior colliculus [Llínas & Lopez–Barneo, 1988; Udin & Scherer, 1990] and at other sites in the premotor networks [Houk & Barto, this volume]. Assuming that plasticity in tecto–reticular neurons has properties analoguous to plasticity in hippocampal and visual cortical neurons [Collingridge & Singer, 1990], increments in synaptic weight would occur when presynaptic and postsynaptic activity are positively correlated, and decrements would occur with negative correlations. This type of local learning rule is capable of supporting both unsupervised learning tasks and a use–dependent form of supervised learning. Unsupervised learning may be responsible for the maintenance of the visual map in iSC [Wilshaw & von der Malsburg, 1976], whereas we hypothesize that use–dependent supervised learning guides adaptation in the tecto–reticular network.

More specifically, we postulate that Purkinje cells force the premotor network to perform in a manner that results in accurate gaze control. This forcing action in effect controls postsynaptic activity throughout the tecto–reticular network, thus guiding the learning process while simultaneously controlling performance. After repeated performances of a control law, the tecto–reticular network would learn how to use its sensory and efference copy inputs to execute the same law. The cerebellum would no longer be needed, unless, of course, the commanded saccade needed to overcome unusual nonlinearities, or unless the context changed and called for a different control law.

Assuming that the cerebellum is capable of executing sophisticated control laws that depend on complex non–linearities and on contextual differences, what law would the tecto–reticular network store in its synapses? We suppose that it would store a compromise law representing a weighted average of past performance. In this probabilistic manner, the adaptive mechanism would essentially compute expected values of control coefficients. These values would fix the parameters of a rudimentary control law that could be executed rapidly and automatically by the tecto–reticular gaze network.

4.3 Storing Complex Laws in the Cerebellar Cortex

According to the distributed theory espoused here, Purkinje cells teach by setting an example. They control gaze signals in the premotor network and consequently guide the learning process that occurs there. In order to do this, they must have already learned to implement complex control laws. This necessitates a learning mechanism in the cerebellar cortex that is considerably more sophisticated than the one postulated for the premotor network.

Several anatomic and physiologic features enhance the learning potential in the cerebellar cortex [Houk & Barto, this volume]. One enhancement stems from the unique architecture of the cerebellar cortex, which exposes Purkinje cells to a very large assortment of potential parallel fiber inputs [Albus, 1971]. The architecture of the tectum and reticular formation is less suitable for supporting such a large number and variety of potential inputs onto individual neurons.

A second enhancement also derives from the neuronal architecture, there being several hundred Purkinje cells for each nuclear cell [Ito, 1984]. This makes it possible for different Purkinje cells to become specialized and learn completely different control laws, such that different control strategies might be selected on the basis of different contexts. The potential utility of this feature in VOR plasticity is discussed elsewhere [Peterson et al 1991]. Processing in the tectum is likely to be more stereotypic and less adapted to context. Essentially the whole population of iSC neurons participates in the generation of any given gaze command, making it likely that afferent inputs to the tecto–reticular network serve only to modulate a relatively standard pattern of discharge rather than radically altering that pattern on the basis of some new context.

A third enhancement is a more powerful learning rule for adjusting synaptic inputs to Purkinje cells. Long–term potentiation in premotor neurons is thought to depend mainly on the concurrence of just two factors: presynaptic input and postsynaptic activity, as a local rule. In contrast, long–term depression of parallel fiber synapses appears to depend on three factors, a presynaptic and postsynaptic factor as before, but also the occurence of climbing fiber discharge [Ito, 1989; Houk & Barto this volume]. Climbing fibers provide channels for transmitting signals that can be specifically adapted for effective supervision of the learning process.

A fourth enhancement derives from the input–output organization of the cerebellar cortex into narrow parasagittal zones [Oscarsson 1980]. These zones align climbing fibers, Purkinje cells and nuclear cells into functional units that are considered to be capable of highly efficient learning, provided climbing fibers transmit useful information [Houk & Barto, this volume].

The climbing fiber inputs to saccade–related regions of the cerebellar cortex remain somewhat of a mystery. Although prominent input from eye muscle proprioceptors has been reported [Baker et al, 1972; Fuchs & Kornhuber, 1969], a study in awake animals reported that climbing fibers do not fire in association with saccades [Kase et al 1980]. Climbing fiber input to to other regions of the cerebellum is known to be inhibited during certain phases of movement [Gellman et al 1985], but is quite prominent during corrective movements [Gilbert & Thach, 1977]. On this basis, we predict that climbing fiber activity would be seen during corrective saccades and would have tuning curves deriving from their proprioceptive inputs. The training signals for adaptation might then come from responses to the corrective saccades that are made when the initial saccade fails to acquire the target. On entirely functional grounds, Optican [1981] suggested that corrective saccades would be a good error signal for the adaptive control of saccadic movements. Understanding the training information carried by climbing fibers is a crucial issue that will require careful experimental attention in the future.

5. DISCUSSION

5.1 Adaptation of Gaze Commands

Saccadic movements are subject to adaptive modification, and the cerebellum is implicated in this process of sensorimotor learning [Deubel 1987; Keller 1989; Miles & Lisberger 1981; Optican & Robinson 1980]. One example of adaptation occurs when eye muscles are surgically weakened. Saccades to a visual target are too small initially, and corrective saccades are made until the target is acquired. Over the time course of a few hours, the size of the initial saccade is progressively increased, until it achieves an amplitude sufficient to acquire the target without any corrections [Optican & Robinson 1980; Optican et al 1985]. Saccadic adaptation is also induced if the experimenter repeatedly shifts the position of a visual target to a displaced location while the eye is still in motion [Deubel 1987; Optican et al 1986]. Initially, the eye makes a corrective saccade to the displaced target, but after a few hundred trials the control system learns a new calibration between the position of the target and the amplitude and direction of the saccade that the target elicits, in this case a saccade which moves the eye to the displaced location.

Recent experiments by M.E. Goldberg and colleagues have shed light on some of the mechanisms of this adaptive process. They found that the visually–evoked activity on the map of adapted monkeys is left unaffected, in terms of its spatial registration with the visual field [M. Goldberg, personal communication]. Furthermore, saccades evoked by stimulation at the site corresponding to the position of the adapted error vector *remain identical* to those evoked before the adaptation [Fitzgibbon & Goldberg 1988]. These data are not consistent with changes in the visual mapping onto the colliculus. They are compatible with adaptive changes on afferent connections to the iSC, either direct or via the cerebellum/brainstem.

Once saccadic amplitude is adapted to the target shifts, the effect generalizes to different amplitudes of movement along the same direction, which is consistent with a simple modification in system gain. However, other findings are less consistent with the gain modification concept. For example, the adaptation does not generalize to movements in the opposite direction. In fact, the tuning curve of the generalization of adaptation is rather narrow. The fact that similar tuning curves apply to oblique as well as to vertical or horizontal saccades suggests that the adaptive changes occur along a radial vector in a polar coordinate system. This interesting finding seems to fit well with the model of saccade command generation discussed in Section 3.3. According to this model, the production of a saccade command would exercise a broad row of network elements extending from the position at which the target is represented, to the fixation region in the center of the tectal map. The adaptation protocol would repeatedly expose this radially directed row of elements to activity paired with the error condition, and this always in the same colliculus; no such training would occur on the contralateral colliculus. One might therefore expect that parallel fiber inputs to all of the PJ and basket cells that are aligned, via the reciprocal network, with this row of collicular neurons might be favoured sites of adaptive modification. This could explain why adaptation generalizes to different amplitude saccades in the same direction, but not to different directions.

5.2 Motor Efference Copies and Error Maps

The accurate control of occular saccades has long been known to rely on the presence of internal estimates of the peripheral response [Sparks & Mays, 1983. An example is the so–called oculomotor 'neural integrator' whose function is to provide a central estimate of eye position as an efference copy of the peripheral response; when intact, it also provides the capability to hold gaze at some desired angle with slow decay back to the resting position reflecting time constants above 15 s. This integrator is particularly sensitive to the integrity of the PH–VN complex [Cannon & Robinson, 1987, Chéron & Godaux 1987], while it is only degraded to a time constant of 1–2s with cerebellectomy. The normal integrator performance relies on all recurrent pathways distributed throughout the gaze control system. However, time constants of an integrator or motor response are a measure of the *dynamics* of motor trajectories, and these in principle can be dissociated from valid efference copies. A degraded integrator, for example, does not necessarily imply that associated efference copies become mismatched with motor response. All models of the gaze control system rely on the processing of premotor signals in order to generate the estimate of the concurrent peripheral eye, or gaze, position. Hence, if premotor signals are degraded, one can still expect the efference copy to accurately reflect the change, so long as its processing received a faithful corollary of the motor drive. The results of lesion experiments would suggest that the dynamics of motor responses reflect interactions between premotor circuits at all levels, while efference copy would be generated at sites more restricted to the premotor brainstem.

If this is true, it should be possible to control motor dynamics independently from the generation of efference copies, but experiments to verify this remain to be done. The characteristics of control dynamics would rely on learning and adaptation in distributed multi–level connections, whereas efference copies could be maintained and corrected in a more localized network, imbedded in the larger system. This is one advantage to the use of distributed processes. Another implication concerns the interpretation of signals in such a highly interconnected system. We should not be surprised to find activities even in SC efferents (TR(S)Ns) exhibiting both sensory–motor integration of signals, and correlations with motor *responses* (efference copies say).

Finally, we should comment on the functional advantages of dynamically updating a sensory–motor error map, like the superior colliculus. Originally, it was believed that activity on the map provided a constant error signal during a saccade to a selected target. In this case, any non–linear mapping of sensory space (visual or auditory, say) in the SC would have to be compensated by an effective inverse non–linearity when projecting onto motor coordinates. This problem is greatly simplified if one now considers that the error map be updated dynamically, *during* the movement (as clearly supported by recent experiments). Adequate registration of sensory and motor coordinates is still required, but now movement through the map is controlled in closed–loop fashion. Target acquisition will automatically be detected when SC activities move into the foveation zone, irrespective of the non–linear aspects of the map coordinates with respect to motor coordinates.

5.3 Responses to Electrical Stimulation and Local Inactivation of the SC

Eye movements are readily evoked by electrical stimulation of the superior colliculus, the threshold being lowest when the electrode is in the intermediate lamina. Some properties of the evoked movements are easy to explain, whereas others have been difficult to interpret [reviewed in Guitton 1991]. One feature that seems, at least initially, readily explicable is that the vectors of electrically evoked movements agree closely with the vectors of the preferred movements, as judged by the intensity of unit activity at the same site during natural saccades. This correspondence has been attributed to the postulated projection patterns from colliculus gaze neurons, through the reticular formation, onto the pools of motoneurons, discussed in Section 4.1. This projection scheme should account for the fact that simultaneous stimulation at multiple sites produces an 'average', not a vector sum, of the saccades expected from the individual sites. In our theory, stimulation at individual sites recruits positive feedback loops appropriate for a given saccade, while multiple stimulation sites would cause these positive loops to interact spatially on the iSC map, and hence produce an average response. Combined stimulation and recording studies have demonstrated that more than half of the colliculus is activated by near threshold stimulation at just one site [McIlwain 1986b]. Again, this supports the contention that cells in SC lamina are interconnected by reciprocal loops. Hence a robust projection scheme must process activation patterns over the whole colliculus, in order to consistently produce accurate, repeatable, saccades.

The above relates to short pulses of stimulation on the SC map. A different picture arises during long trains of stimulation. Here, sustained stimulation can cause staircase responses -- a repeated sequence of eye saccades in the head–fixed monkey and gaze saccades in the head–free cat, each one with a movement vector that is characteristic of the site being stimulated on the collicular map. These observations are more difficult to reconcile with current concepts of gaze control, and two interpretations are presented below in the context of the multi–level, cooperative model of gaze control.

First, it is useful to consider the possibility that the electrical stimulus does not directly drive the motor response, as typically assumed. Aided by local and lower level recurrent loops, it might instead function as a trigger for movement *enabling,* while movement *control and termination* could still rely on cerebellar and brainstem mechanisms. With direct SC stimulation, positive feedback could reach a critical level, and signals would grow in intensity without additional stimulation (iSC burst). The motor process released by this burst might then go to completion, and after a refractory period, be ready to start all over again. To be more specific, the motor program could be released by the effect of iSC bursts on brainstem saccadic neurons (OPN and SLBN cells, see Fig. 3). Via mossy fiber inputs to the cerebellum, the resulting modulation in brainstem bursters could activate basket cells, thus inactivating PJ cells, at a location corresponding to the site of stimulation on the SC. This would be in line with the gaze control sequence advanced in Section 3.3 and Fig. 6C. Having received both a trigger and the registration of a gaze program, the network could then go through an entire cycle of producing a gaze command, culminating in activity in the fixation region. Fixation activity is known to inhibit the production of gaze commands [cat: Guitton & Munoz, 1991; Munoz, 1988; Munoz & Guitton, 1991; monkey: Munoz, personal communication], thus accounting for the refractory period. However, since the train of electrical impulses continues, a new trigger and a new program would soon initiate a new gaze command.

These mechanisms may explain a staircase sequence, provided a spatial shift of activity is preserved in the PJ map; a spatial shift on the iSC map superimposed on the stimulation profile may also be present, but is not essential, so long as fixation activity appears at the appropriate point in the gaze shift. On the other hand, it is known that quick phases elicited by vestibular stimuli can still occur, even after ablation of the SC or the cerebellum [Robinson, 1974; Schiller et al, 1980; Klaus Hepp, personal communication]. For this reason, an alternate hypothesis has been proposed for the initiation and termination of rapid eye movements: In a recent model of the VOR [Galiana & Outerbridge 1984; Galiana 1991], recurrent connections in the premotor circuits linking VN–PH and saccadic cells (OPN–LLBN) could provide a final mechanism for the generation of repeated saccades. In this case, mutual inhibition and refractory periods in pause and burst cells would generate a sequence of saccades due to a constant stimulus from the iSC site; in essence OPN cells would act as pseudo–fixation cells, while the decaying bursts on premotor cells would be the temporal equivalent of the spatial shifts in activity mentioned above. Of course, motor programs would be expected to be degraded in such a case, in terms of the achieved saccadic goals and dynamics.

The injection of small volumes of anaesthetic or inhibitory compounds has been used to inactivate localized regions on the superior colliculus [Hikosaka & Wurtz, 1985; Lee et al 1988]. This causes a profound decrease in the velocity of saccades associated with the injected site, but has remarkably little effect on saccade amplitude. These findings are consistent with the weighted projection model from iSC to premotor centers, provided feedback to iSC is used to regulate the termination of a gaze command. With a reduced set of active cells on the iSC, fewer cells in the premotor circuits would be recruited for the movement, but their coordinate transformation would be unaffected. Hence, the observation of a slower saccade to the same goal. With this hypothesis, we should expect larger saccades (triggered by activity on the iSC more caudal to the lesion) to exhibit a slowing in their velocity as the collicular activity shifts through and around the inactivated zone. An appropriate extension of saccade duration is guaranteed by the feedback mechanisms using efference copies near the fixation zone, and proprioception at more lateral sites of the transposed map.

5.4 Conclusions

We have described anatomy and function supporting a gaze control system with many hierarchical layers, all of which are tightly nested and interconnected via positive and negative feedback loops. Such an architecture has important implications concerning the nature of signals to be expected at different levels: efference copy, motor and sensory signals would appear mixed at all levels while only their weighting on a given cell's activity would vary with its position along the sensory–motor pathway. For example, the signal arising from TR(S)N cells in the iSC would not be expected to consistently represent a pure gaze velocity signal, despite a strong correlation with movement dynamics; correlations with efference copies at the beginning of a movement, with subject alertness, or sensory modalities (e.g. visual vs remembered targets) are to be expected. This does not conflict with the observation that cell activity, for example, decreases with dynamic gaze error or velocity: it only proposes that the correlation would ride on a multi–faceted background activity.

The extensive connectivity of the gaze control system has also been shown to provide a powerful substrate for distributed learning, providing for both rapid reflex responses, and context–dependent strategies. The mechanisms proposed for this are compatible with anatomical and neurophysiological data, and provide ready explanations for unusual responses obtained during electrical stimulation of the central gaze networks. However, the theory espoused here goes well beyond the available data, and considerable experimental work motivated by conceptual models will be needed to test and refine this cooperative theory of gaze control.

Acknowledgements: This work was supported by ONR contract N00014–88–K–0339 and by NIH Grant R01–NS21015 to JH, by the Fonds de la Recherche en Santé du Québec and MRC (Canada) to HLG and DG.

6. REFERENCES

Albus J.S. (1971). A theory of cerebellar function. *Math. Bio. Sci. 10*: 25–61

Baker R., Precht W., Llinás R. (1972). Mossy and climbing fiber projections of extraocular muscle afferents to the cerebellum. *Brain Res 38*: 440–445

Blanks, R.H.I. (1988) Cerebellum In: Büttner–Ennever J.A (ed.) *Neuroanatomy of the Oculomotor System*. Chapter 7, Amsterdam/Elsevier Press, pp. 225–272

Berthoz A., Grantyn A., Droulez J. (1986). Collicular efferent neurons code saccadic eye velocity. *Neurosci. Lett 72*: 289–294

Büttner–Ennever J.A. (1988). *Neuroanatomy of the Oculomotor System*. Amsterdam, Elsevier Press

Cannon S.C., Robinson D.A. (1987). Loss of the neural integrator of the oculomotor system from brainstem lesions in monkey. *J. Neurophysiol. 57*: 1383–1409

Chéron G., Godaux E. (1987). Disabling of the oculomotor neural integrator by kainic acid injections in the prepositus–vestibular complex of the cat. *J. Physiol. 394*: 267–290

Collingridge G.L., Singer W. (1990). Excitatory amino–acid receptors and synaptic plasticity. *Trends in Pharmacol. Sci. 11*: 290–296

Crandall W.F., Keller E.L. (1985). Visual and oculomotor signals in nucleus reticularis tegmenti pontis in alert monkey. *J. Neurophysiol 54*: 1326–1345

Deubel H. (1987). Adaptivity of gain and direction in oblique saccades. In: O'Regan, J.K., Levy–Schoen, A. (eds) *Eye Movements: From Physiology to Cognition*. Amsterdam, Elsevier, pp 181–190

Droulez J. , Berthoz A. (1988). Spatial and temporal transformations in visuo–motor coordination. In: R. Eckmiller and C. Malsburg (eds) *Neural Computers*, Springer–Verlag/Berlin, pp. 345–358

Droulez J., Berthoz A. (1991). The concept of dynamic memory in sensorimotor control. In: D.R. Humphrey & H.J. Freund (eds) *Motor Control: Concepts and Issues*, John Wiley & Sons, pp. 137–161

FitzGibbon E.J., Goldberg M.E. (1988). Long term saccadic adaptation does not affect the saccades evoked by electrical stimulation of the superor colliculus. *Neurosci. Abstr 14*: 613

Fuchs A.F., Kornhuber H.H. (1969). Extraocular muscle afferents to the cerebellum of the cat. *J. Physiol. London 200*: 713–722

Galiana H.L., Outerbridge J.S. (1984). A bilateral model for central neural pathways in the vestibuloocular reflex. *J. Neurophysiol. 51*: 210–241

Galiana H.L. (1986). A new approach to understanding visual–vestibular interactions in the CNS. *J. Neurophysiol. 55*: 349–374

Galiana H.L. (1991). A nystagmus strategy to linearize the vestibulo–ocular reflex. *IEEE Trans. Biomed. Eng. 38(6)*, 532–543.

Galiana H.L., Guitton D., Munoz D.P. (1992). Modelling head–free gaze control in the cat. In: Berthoz, Vidal & Graf (eds.) *The Head–Neck Sensory–Motor System*, Oxford University Press, 520–525

Gardner E.P., Fuchs A.F. (1975). Single–unit responses to natural vestibular stimuli and eye movement in deep cerebellar nuclei of the alert Rhesus monkey. *J. Neurophysiol 38*: 627–649

Gellman R., Gibson A.R., Houk J.C. (1985). Inferior olivary neurons in the awake cat: Detection of contact and passive body displacement. *J. Neurophysiol. 54*: 40–60

Gielen C.C.A.M., van Gisbergen J.A.M. (1990). The visual guidance of saccades and fast aiming movements. *News in Physiol. Sci 5*: 58–63

Gilbert P.F.C., Thach W.T. (1977). Purkinje cell activity during motor learning. *Brain Res. 128*: 309–328

Grantyn R. (1988). Gaze control through superior colliculus: structure and function. In: Büttner–Ennever (ed) *Neuroanatomy of the Oculomotor System*, Elsevier Science Publishers, pp. 273–333

Grantyn A., Berthoz. A. (1985). Burst activity of identified tecto–reticulo–spinal neurons in the alert cat. *Exp. Brain Res. 57*: 417–421

Guitton D. (1991). Control of saccadic eye and gaze movements by the superior colliculus and basal ganglia. In: Carpenter, R.H.S. (ed) *Vision and Visual Dysfunction: Eye Movements*, Vol 8. Macmillan, in press

Guitton D., Crommelinck M., Roucoux A. (1980). Stimulation of the superior colliculus in the alert cat. I Eye movement and and neck EMG activity evoked when the cat is restrained. *Exp. Brain Res. 39*: 63–73

Guitton D., Douglas R.M., Volle M. (1984). Eye–head coordination in cat. *J. Neurophysiol. 52*: 1030–1050

Guitton D., Munoz D.P., Galiana H.L. (1990). Gaze control in the cat: studies and modeling of the coupling between orienting eye and head movements in different behavioral tasks. *J. Neurophysiol 64*: 509–531

Guitton D., Munoz D.P. (1991). Control of ortienting gaze shifts by the tecto–reticulo–spinal system in the head–free cat I. Identification, localization and effects of behavior on sensory responses. *J. Neurophysiol.* 66, in press (November)

Henn V., Cohen B. (1976). Coding of information about rapid eye movements in the pontine reticular formation of alert monkeys. *Brain Res. 108*: 307–325

Hepp K., Henn V. (1983). Spatial–temporal recoding of rapid eye movement signals in the monkey paramedian pontine reticular formation (PPRF). *Exp. Brain Res. 52*: 105–120

Hepp K., Henn V., Jaeger J. (1982). Eye movement related neurons in the cerebellar nuclei of the alert monkey. *Exp. Brain Res. 45*: 253–264

Hepp K., Henn V., Vilis T., Cohen B. (1989). Brainstem regions related to saccade generation. In: R. Wurtz and M. Goldberg (eds) *The Neurobiology of Saccadic Eye Movements*, Ch 4. Elsevier, pp. 105–212

Hikosaka O., Wurtz R.H. (1985). Modification of saccadic eye movements by GABA–related substances. I The effect of muscimol and bicuculine in monkey superior colliculus. *J. Neurophysiol. 53*: 266–291

Houk J.C. (1989). Cooperative control of limb movements by the motor cortex, brainstem and cerebellum. In: Cotterill R.M.J. (ed.) *Models of Brain Function*, Cambridge University Press/Cambridge, pp. 309–325

Houk J.C., Singh S.P., Fisher C., Barto A.G. (1990). An adaptive sensorimotor network inspired by the anatomy and physiology of the cerebellum. In: Miller W.T., Sutton R.S., Werbos P.J. (eds) *Neural Networks for Control*, Chapter 13, MIT Press/Cambridge, Mass, pp. 301–348

Huerta, M.F., Harting, J.K. (1984). The mammalian superior colliculus: studies of its morphology and connections. In: Vanegas, H. (ed) The Comparative Neurology of the Optic Tectum. New York, Plenum, pp 687–773

Ito M. (1984). *The Cerebellum and Neural Control*. New York, Raven Press

Ito M. (1989). Long–term depression. *Ann. Rev. Neurosci. 12*: 85–102

Kase M., Miller D.C., Noda H. (1980). Discharges of Purkinje cells and mossy fibres in the cerebellar vermis of the monkey during saccadic eye movements and fixation. *J. Physiol. London 300*: 539–555

Kawamura S., Hattori S., Higo S., Matsuyama T. (1982). The cerebellar projections to the superior colliculus and pretectum in the cat: an autoradiographic and horseradish peroxidase study. *Neurosci. 7*: 1673–1689

Keller E.L. (1974). Participation of medial pontine reticular formation in eye movement generation in monkey. *J. Neurophysiol. 37*: 316–332

Keller E.L. (1989). The cerebellum. In: Wurtz, R.H., Goldberg, M.E. (eds) *Neurobiology of Sacccadic Eye Movements*, Ch 11. Amsterdam, Elsevier, pp. 391–411

Lee C., Rohrer W.H., Sparks D.L. (1988). Population coding of saccadic eye movements by neurons in the superior colliculus. *Nature 332*: 357–360

Lefevre P., Galiana H.L. (1990). Velocity versus position feedback to the superior colliculus in gaze control modelling, *Soc. Neurosci. Abstr. Vol. 16*, Part 2, pp. 1084.

Lefevre P., Galiana H.L., Roucoux A. (1991) Dynamic feedback neural networks in the superior colliculus, *Proc. European Conf. on Eye Movements*, Louvain, Belgium, September 1991.

Lefevre P., Galiana H.L. (1991). Dynamic feedback to the superior colliculus in a neural network model of the gaze control system. submitted to *Neural Networks*.

Llinás R., Lopez–Barneo J. (1988). Electrophysiology of mammalian tectal neurons in vitro. II. Long term adaptation. *J. Neurophysiol 60*: 869–878

Lisberger S.G. (1988). The neural basis for learning of simple motor skills. *Science 242*: 728–735

Lisberger S.G., Pavelko T.A. (1988). Brain stem neurons in modified pathways for motor learning in the primate vestibulo–ocular reflex. *Science 242*: 771–773

May P.J., Hartwich–Young R., Nelson J., Sparks D.L., Porter J.D. (1990). Cerebellotectal pathways in the macaque: implications for collicular generation of saccades. *Neuroscience 36*: 305–324

Mays L.E., Sparks D.L. (1980). Diassociation of visual and saccade–related responses in superior colliculus neurons. *J. Neurophysiol. 43*: 207–232

McCrea R.A., Baker R. (1985). Anatomical connections of the nucleus prepositus of the cat. *J. Comp. Neurol. 237*: 377–407

McIlwain J.T. (1986a). Point images in the visual system: New interest in an old idea. *Trends Neurosci. 9:* 354–358

McIlwain, J. (1986b). Effects of eye position on saccades evoked electrically from superior colliculus of alert cats. *J. Neurophysiol. 55*: 97–112

Meredith M.A. , Stein B.E. (1986). Visual–auditory and somatosensory convergence on cells in superior colliculus results in multi–sensory convergence. *J. Neurophysiol. 56*: 640–662

Miles F.A., Lisberger S.G. (1981). Plasticity in the vestibulo–ocular reflex: a new hypothesis. *Annu. Rev. Neurosci. 4*: 273–299

Moschovakis A.K., Karabelas A.B., Highstein S.M. (1988a). Structure– function relationships in the primate superior colliculus. I. Morphological classification of efferent neurons. *J. Neurophysiol. 60*: 232–262

Moschovakis A.K., Karabelas A.B., Highstein S.M. (1988b). Structure– function relationships in the primate superior colliculus. II. Morphological identify of presaccadic neurons. *J. Neurophysiol. 60*: 263–302

Mower G., Gibson A., Glickstein M. (1979). Tectopontine pathways in the cat: laminar distribution of cells of origin and visual proprerties of target cells in dorsolateral pontine nucleus. *J. Neurophysiol. 42*: 1–15

Munoz D.P. (1988). On the role of the tecto–reticulo–spinal system in gaze control. McGill University, Montreal: Ph.D. Thesis, Department of Neurology and Neurosurgery

Munoz D.P., Guitton D. (1985). Tectospinal neurons in the cat have discharges coding gaze position error. *Brain Res. 341*: 184–188

Munoz D.P., Guitton D. (1986). Presaccadic burst discharges of tecto–reticulo–spinal neurons in the alert head–free cat. *Brain Res. 398*: 185–190

Munoz D.P., Guitton D. (1989). Fixation and orientation control by the tecto–reticulo–spinal system in the cat whose head is unrestrained. *Rev. Neurol. (Paris) 145*: 567–579

Munoz D.P., Guitton D. (1991). Control of orienting gaze shifts by the tecto–reticulo–spinal system in the head–free cat II. Sustained discharges related to motor preparation and fixation. *J. Neurophysiol.66*: in press (November)

Munoz D.P., Guitton D., Pélisson D. (1991a). Control of orienting gaze shifts by the tecto–reticulo–spinal system in the head–free cat III Spatio–temporal characteristics of phasic motor discharges *J. Neurophysiol. 66*: in press (November)

Munoz D.P., Pélisson D., Guitton D. (1991b). Movement of neural activity on the superior colliculus motor map during gaze shifts. *Science 251*: 1358–1360

Munoz D.P., Waitzman D.M., Wurtz R.H. (1990). Evidence for a fixation zone in the rostral superior colliculus of the monkey. *Soc. Neurosci. Abstr. Vol. 16*, pp. 1084

Ohtsuka K., Noda H. (1990). Direction–selective saccadic–burst neurons in the fastigial oculomotor region of the macaque. *Exp. Brain. Res. 81*: 659–662

Optican L. (1981). Saccadic dysmetria. In: G. Lennerstrand, E.L. Keller, D.S. Zee (eds) *Functional Basis of Ocular Motility Disorders.* Oxford, New York, Toronto, Etc., Pergamon Press, pp 441–451

Optican L.M., Robinson D.A. (1980). Cerebellar–dependent adaptive control of primate saccadic system. *J. Neurophysiol. 44*: 1058– 1076

Optican L.M., Zee D.S., Chu F .C. (1985). Adaptive response to ocular muscle weakness in human pursuit and saccadic eye movements. *J. Neurophysiol. 54*: 110–122.

Optican L.M., Zee D.S., Miles F. (1986). Floccular lesions abolish adaptive control of post–saccadic ocular drift in primates. *J. Neurophysiol. 64*: 596–598.

Oscarsson, O. (1980). Fnctional organization of olivary projection to the cerebellar interior lobe. In: J. Courville et al (eds.) *The inferior olivary nucleus: anatomy and physiology*. New York. Raven Press, pp. 279–289

Pélisson D., Guitton D., Munoz D.P. (1989). Compensatory eye and head movements generated by the cat following stimulation–induced perturbations in head position. *Exp. Brains Res. 78*: 654–658

Peterson B.W., Baker J.F., Houk J.C. (1991). A model of adaptive control of vestibulo–ocular reflex based on properties of cross–axis adaptation. *Ann. New York Acad. Sci.*, in press

Raybourn M.S., Keller E.L. (1977). Colliculoreticular organization in primate oculomotor system. *J. Neurophysiol. 40*: 861–878

Robinson D.A. (1974). The effect of cerebellectomy on the cat's vestibulo–ocular integrator. *Brain Res. 71*: 195–207

Robinson D.A. (1975). Oculomotor control signals. In: Lennerstrand G., Bach–y–rita P. (eds) *Basic Mechanisms of Ocular Motility and their Clinical Implications*. Oxford, Pergamon Press, pp 337–374

Robinson D.A., Optican L.M. (1981). Adaptive plasticity in the oculomotor system. In: Flohr H., Precht W. (eds) *Lesion Induced Neuronal Plasticity in Sensorimotor Systems*. Berlin, Springer–Verlag, pp 295–304

Rolodán M., Reinoso–Suárez F. (1981). Cerebellar projections to the superior colliculus in the cat. *J. Neurosci. 1*: 827–834

Roucoux A., Guitton D., Crommelinck M. (1980). Stimulation of the superior colliculus in the alert cat. II Eye and head movements evoked when the head is unrestrained. *Exp. Brain. Res. 39*: 75–85

Schiller P., Koerner F. (1971) Discharge characteristics of single units in the superior colliculus of the alert monkey. *J. Neurophysiol 34*: 920–936

Schiller P.H., True S.D., Conway J.L. (1980). Deficits in eye movements following frontal eye–field and superior colliculus ablations. *J. Neurophysiol. 44*: 1175–1189

Scudder C.S. (1988). A new local feedback model of the saccadic burst generator. *J. Neurophysiol. 59*: 1455–1475

Sparks D. (1986). Translation of sensory signals into command for control of saccadic eye movements: Role of primate superior colliculus. *Physiol. Rev. 66*: 118–170

Sparks D.L. (1988). Neural cartography: sensory and motor maps in the superior colliculus. *Brain Behav. Evol. 31*: 49–56

Sparks D.L., Mays L.E. (1983). Spatial localization of saccade targets I. Compensation for stimulation–induced perturbations in eye position. *J. Neurophysiol. 49*: 45–62

Sparks D.L., Mays L.E. (1990). Signal transformations required for the generation of saccadic eye movements. *Ann. Rev. Neurosci. 13*: 309–336

Stechison M.T., Saint–Cyr J.A., Spence S.J. (1985) Projections from the nuclei prepositus hypoglossi and intercalatus to the superior colliculus in the cat: an anatomical study. *Exp. Brain Res. 59*: 139– 150

Stein B.E., Spencer R.F., Edwards S.B. (1984). Efferent projections of the neonatal cat superior colliculus: facial and cerebellum– related brainstem structures. *J. Comp. Neurol. 230*: 47–54

Tomlinson R.D. (1990). Combined eye–head gaze shifts in the primate III. Contributions to the accuracy of gaze saccades. *J. Neurophysiol. 64*:1873–1891

Tomlinson R.D., Bahra P.S. (1986a) Combined eye–head gaze shifts in the primate I. Metrics *J. Neurophysiol. 56*: 1542–1557

Tomlinson R.D., Bahra P.S. (1986b) Combined eye–head gaze shifts in the primate II. Interactions between saccades and the vestibulo–ocular reflex. *J. Neurophysiol. 56*: 1558–1570

Tweed D., Vilis T. (1990). The superior colliculus and spatiotemporal translation in the saccadic system. *Neural Networks 3*: 75–86

Udin S.B., Scherer W.J. (1990). Restoration of the plasticity of binocular maps by NMDA after the critical period in Xenopus. *Science 249*: 669–672

Van Gisbergen J.A.M., Robinson D.A., Gielen S. (1981). A quantitative analysis of saccadic eye movements by burst neurons. *J. Neurophysiol. 45*: 417–442

Van Gisbergen J.A.M., Van Opstal A.J., Schoenmakers J.J.M. (1985). Experimental test of two models for the generation of oblique saccades. *Exp. Brain Res. 57*: 321–336

Van Gisbergen J.A.M., Van Opstal A.J., Tax A.A.M. (1987) Collicular ensemble coding of saccades based on vector summation. *Neurosci. 21*: 541–555

Vidal P.P., Corvisier J., Berthoz A. (1983). Eye and neck motor signals in periabducens reticular neurons of the alert cat. *Exp. Brain Res. 53*: 16–28.

Vidal P.P., Roucoux A., Berthoz A. (1982). Horizontal eye position–related activity in neck muscles of the alert cat. *Exp. Brain. Res. 46*: 448–453.

Waitzman D.M., Ma T.P., Optican L.M., Wirtz R.H. (1991). Superior colliculus neurons mediate the dynamic characteristics of saccades. *J. Neurophysiol.*, in press

Willshaw D.J., Malsburg von der C. (1976). How patterned neural connections can be set up by self–organization. *Proc. R. Soc. Lond. B 194*: 431–445

Wurtz R.H., Goldberg M.E. (eds) (1989). *The Neurobiology of Saccadic Eye Movements*. Amsterdam, Elsevier

Tutorials in Motor Behavior II
G.E. Stelmach and J. Requin (Editors)
1992 Elsevier Science Publishers B.V.

Remote facilitation of H-reflex during voluntary contraction of orofacial and limb muscles

A. Hayashi[a,b,c] R.A. Konopacki[c] and C.J. Hunker[b,c]

[a]Department of Neurology, Juntendo University School of Medicine, 2-1-1 Hongo, Bunkyo-ku, Tokyo, 113, Japan

[b]Department of Neurology and [c]Speech Motor Control Lab, Waisman Center, University of Wisconsin, Madison, Wisconsin, USA

Abstract

Remote facilitation of the soleus motoneurons during the voluntary contraction of orofacial and limb muscles was investigated in five healthy subjects. The H-reflex and a visually guided step tracking method were respectively used for testing motoneuron excitability and for controlling the timing of movement initiation. Five muscle groups were used for the conditioning voluntary muscle contractions (i.e., muscles of the fingers, jaw, tongue, lips, and eyelids). There were significant differences in the force levels achieved by the various muscle groups, but no statistically significant differences in their contraction times. Remote facilitation of the soleus H-reflex was recognized during contraction of the finger, jaw, and tongue muscles, which have numerous muscle spindles, with the extent of facilitation and the time-course being similar in each case. On the other hand, there was no significant facilitation during lip or eyelid muscle contraction. These findings suggest that the extent of remote facilitation may be related to the number of muscle spindles rather than the strength of the muscle contraction.

Key words; H-reflex, orofacial muscles, muscle spindle, remote facilitation Jendrassik maneuver

1. INTRODUCTION

The facilitating effect of the Jendrassik maneuver on monosynaptic reflexes has been known ever since 1883 when Jendrassik originally reported that a sustained voluntary muscular contraction in the upper limb produced facilitation of the knee jerk, but the neuronal mechanism is not yet clear. Gassel et al. (1964) and Landau et al. (1964) have demonstrated that the Jendrassik maneuver affected the H-reflex as well as the ankle jerk. Recently, Delwaide et al. (1980) reported that an isolated muscle contraction could also enhance the amplitude of monosynaptic reflexes (i.e., tendon reflexes and H-reflex), and they (1981) suggested that facilitation of the H-reflex would be related to proprioceptive afferent impulses originating from muscle spindles. However, it has not reported before whether or not remote facilitation of the soleus H-reflex occurs during voluntary contraction of the orofacial muscles, some of which have numerous muscle spindles and some of which have few muscle spindles.

Accordingly, we investigated remote facilitation of the soleus H-reflex during voluntary contraction of the orofacial muscles, and compared muscle groups with few spindles to those containing numerous spindles, such as masseter and the lingual muscles.

2. METHODS

This investigation was performed in five healthy adult volunteers aged 31-39 years (4 males and 1 female).

The experimental procedure used was almost same as that for the previous study (Hayashi et al., 1988), except for conditioning muscle contractions. Each subject was seated in a reclining armchair and the test leg was fixed to an immobile foot pedal so that the knee and ankle joints were held at an angle of approximately 120 and 100 degrees, respectively. Surface electrodes were used for both stimulation and recording. Paired electrodes were placed over the bellies of the soleus and the agonist of the conditioning movements. The tibial nerve was stimulated (1 ms duration) in the popliteal fossa to elicit the soleus H-reflex.

An oscilloscope was used to control the subject's movement. The oscilloscope was placed approximately 1 m in front of the subject and displayed a target and force cursor. The target moved up to the center of the screen from the baseline by stepwise increases in voltage, while the force cursor moved in proportion to the strain gauge applied to the transducers on the fingers, jaw, tongue, and lips (Barlow et al., 1983). Following the emission of an acoustic tone (pre-cue) with a random foreperiod (1.5-2.5 s), the target moved to a new position. The subject's task was make the force cursor quickly match the target's new position by using each of the conditioning muscle contractions (Table 1). Special attention was paid to keeping the conditioning muscle contractions as isolated as possible. Each subject was instructed not to make any other movements during performance the conditioning movement. In addition, we monitored the activity of the masseter by EMG during tongue and lip movements and eliminated the data if the EMG showed any activity of the masseter. The stimulator was triggered with a variable delay after the target movement, so as to evoke the H-reflex at varying intervals relative to the onset of voluntary contraction in the agonist. The procedure was repeated at intervals about 10 s. The tested contraction force was set at about 50 % of the force of the maximum voluntary contraction, while the tested H-reflex size was set at about half of the maximum H-reflex or 30 % of the maximum M response. Five different groups of orofacial and limb muscles were used for the conditioning movements and muscle contractions were maintained as isometrically as possible, except in the case of eyelid closing where no transducer was used.

2.1. Table 1

STRUCTURE	RECORDING MUSCLE	TASK
finger	thenar	pinch transducer between thumb and index finger
jaw	masseter	bite and squeeze transducer between upper and lower teeth
tongue	not recorded	elevate tongue tip against transducer
lip	orbicularis oris inferior	close lips against transducer
eye lid	orbicularis oculi	close and squeeze eyelid (force not measured)

2.2. Parameters measured

Figure 1 shows the parameters measured on a sample record from a tracking trial; (1) the time interval between the H-reflex and the onset of the EMG (mechanical onset was used for the tongue), (2) the amplitude of the H-reflex (peak to peak), (3) the EMG reaction time, (4) the mechanical reaction time, (5) the contraction time, (6) the force level, and (7) the peak velocity of force.

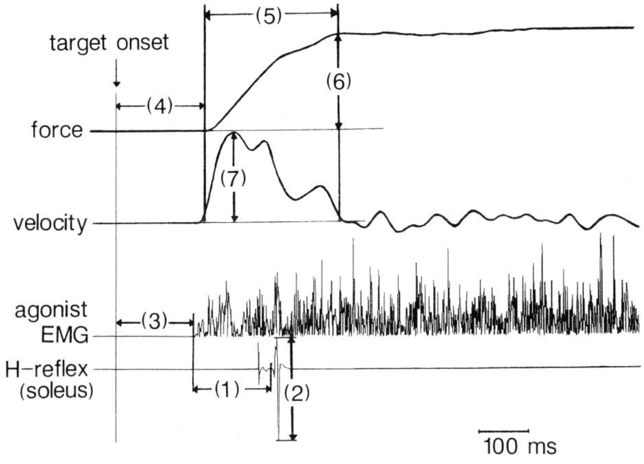

Figure 1.

3. RESULTS

3.1. Force trajectory, Reaction time, and Contraction time

Figure 2A demonstrates the force trajectories of 50 sample trials from the same subject that were superimposed and averaged for each task, and the curves for the five subjects are shown in Figure 2B. In the preliminary study, some subjects were instructed to perform at three different force levels; 25, 50, and 100 % of their maximum achievable force. It was found that it was sometimes difficult to maintain the force levels for orofacial muscle contraction at 25 or 100 % of the maximum when over 100 trials were performed. However, at the 50 % level, there was neither much difficulty in performing each task nor any abnormal findings such as tremor. Table 2 summarizes the means across the subjects for each conditioning movement with respect to the reaction time, contraction time, force level, and peak velocity. There were no statistically significant differences in reaction times and contraction times among the various conditioning movements, but the reaction time for eyelid closing (no transducer) was shorter than for the other tasks. On the other hand, there were significant differences in the force levels and the peak velocities of the some of the tested muscle groups, while the force levels for tongue and lip were similar to each other (Table 2).

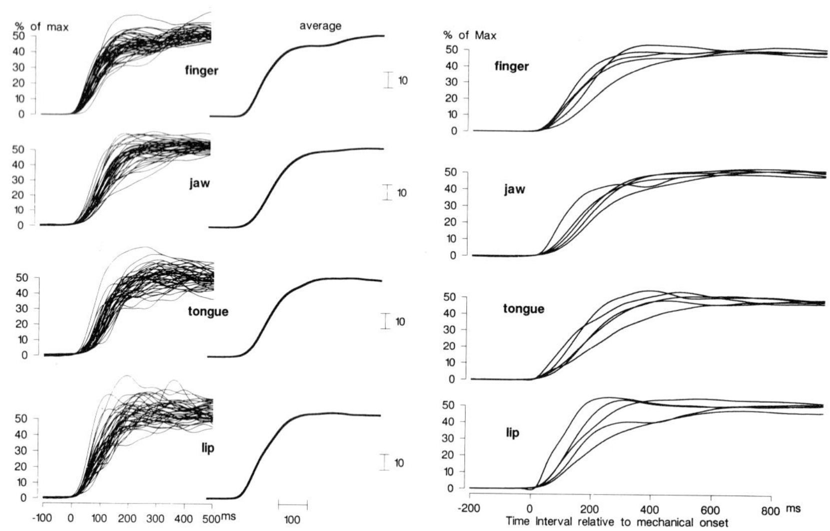

Figure 2 A&B.
A. Force trajectories of 50 trials from the same subject, superimposed (left side) and averaged (right) for each task. The abscissa shows the time interval relative to the mechanical onset of force and the ordinate shows the force as a % of the maximum achieved.
B. Force trajectory curves of for the fingers, jaw, tongue, and lips in the five subjects.

Table 2

	Contraction (Rise) Time (msec)	Reaction (EMG) Time (msec)	Force Level [Max/2] (N)	Peak Velocity of Force (N/sec)
FINGER	228±57	224±42	34.9±10.7	306±11
JAW	265±19	270±53	59.8±24.0	525±19
TONGUE	214±41	296±65**	3.92±.69	40.2±9.1
LIP	240±42	247±41	3.43±.43	35.5±8.6
EYE LID	*	203±14	(max)*	*

* Eye lid force was not transduced
** Reaction time for tongue was mechanical

3.2. Remote facilitation of the soleus H-reflex

Figure 3 shows changes in the excitability of the soleus motoneurons at the onset of orofacial and limb movements (fingers, jaw, tongue, lips and eyelids). Remote facilitation of the soleus H-reflex was recognized during the contraction of jaw and tongue muscles as well as during finger movements, and the time-courses were similar after taking account of the delay of a few milliseconds from the EMG onset to the mechanical onset. The peak remote facilitation ranged from about 100 to 300 ms after the EMG onset. Table 3 shows the mean of the amounts of remote facilitation from 100 to 300 ms after EMG onset (mechanical onset for the tongue) across the five subjects. Remote facilitation showed a statistically significant increase during finger, jaw, and tongue movements and the degree of the increase was similar in each case. In contrast, there was no significant facilitation during lip and eyelid movements (Table 3).

Table 3.

Structure	Muscle Group	Spindle Density	Amount of remote facilitation (%, 100 to 300 ms)
FINGER	thenar	numerous	Δ23.7±12.0*
JAW	masseter	numerous	Δ26.0±13.1*
TONGUE	intrinsic and extrinsic	numerous	Δ22.8±15.9**
LIP	orbicularis oris inferior	sparse	Δ3.3±3.9
EYE LID[1]	orbicularis oculi		Δ3.9±4.9

*significant increase ($p<0.02$) **($p<0.05$)
[1]three subjects

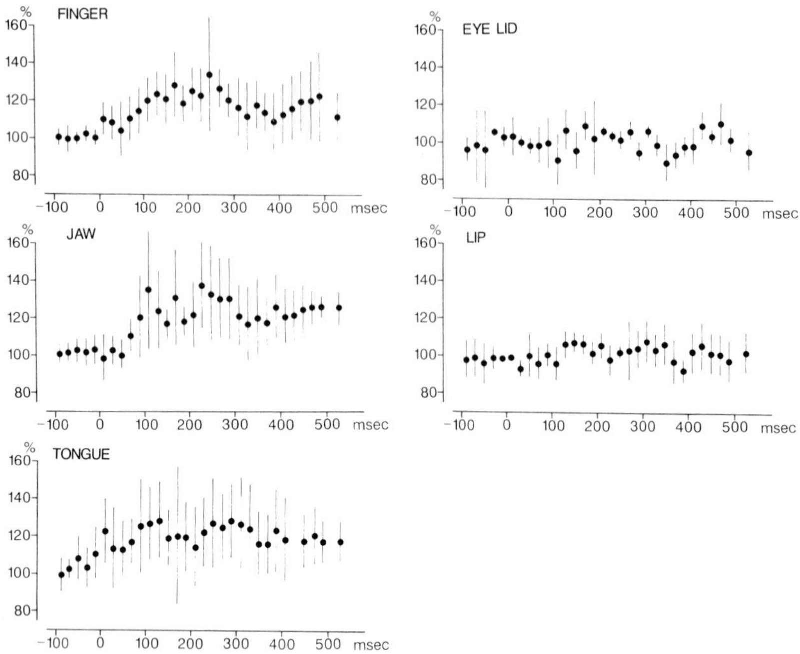

Figure 3. Changes in excitability of the soleus motoneurons at the onset of orofacial and limb movements (fingers, jaw, tongue, lips, and eyelids). The abscissa shows the time intervals between each H-reflex and the onset of the voluntary agonist EMG (mechanical onset for the tongue), with negative values indicating H-reflexes preceding the EMG onset). The ordinate shows the size of the H-reflex as a % of the reflex obtained at rest. The means of the five subjects are shown for responses evoked between ± 10 ms of the indicated times.

4. DISCUSSION

Isolated voluntary muscle contractions of the jaw and tongue as well as fingers under isometric conditions enhanced the amplitude of the soleus H-reflex. The time-course of the enhancement was very similar in each case and the maximum enhancement occurred from 100 to 300 ms after the EMG onset. These results were the same as those of previous studies performed during wrist extension (Delwaide et al.; 1980, Hayashi et al., in preparation). As Kawamura et al. (1975) have reported previously, these findings indicate that timing is a very important factor in determining the remote effect of the Jendrassik maneuver. In the present study, the amount of facilitation was also similar between the three types of movement, although there were significant differences in the force levels. On the other hand, there was no significant facilitation during lip and eyelid movements. In humans, different muscles contain different numbers of muscle spindles and the muscles from various part of the body can be classified as spindle-rich or spindle-poor (Table 3; Cooper, 1960; and Olkowski et al., 1973). The number of muscle spindles in humans has also been reported for the limb muscles (Voss, 1936), masseter (Freimann, 1954; Smith et al., 1967), the tongue muscles (Dubner et al., 1978), and orbicularis oris (Kadanoff, 1956). According to these reports, the muscles of the jaw and tongue as well as fingers have numerous spindles, while lip muscles contain few spindles. Delwaide et al. (1981) found no remote facilitation of the H-reflex when the conditioning muscle contraction did not appear, despite maximum voluntary effort, in case of nerve block by anesthesia or radial paralysis. Therefore, they suggested that this remote facilitation would be related to proprioceptive afferent impulses set off by the muscle contraction and transmitted by group Ia or II afferent fibers from muscle spindles. In our study, the force levels achieved by contraction of tongue and lip muscles were very similar, but there was only remote facilitation during tongue movements. These findings suggest that the extent of facilitation may be related to the number of muscle spindles rather than the strength of the muscle contraction.

Acknowledgment

This research was supported by a grant from the Visiting Associate Scientist Program of the Department of Neurology at the University of Wisconsin to Dr. Hayashi.

5. REFERENCES

Barlow, S.M. and Abbs, J.H. (1983). Force transducers for the evaluation of labial, lingual, and mandibular motor impairments. Journal of Speech and Hearing Research, 26, 616-621.

Cooper, S. (1960). Muscle spindle and other muscle receptor in The structure and function of muscle. ed. Bourne, G.H., 1, pp381-420.

Delwaide, P.J. and Toulouse, P. (1980). Jendrassik maneuver vs controlled contractions conditioning the excitability of soleus monosynaptic reflexes. Archives of Physical Medicine and Rehabilitation, 61, 505-510.

Delwaide, P.J. and Toulouse, P. (1981). Facilitation of monosynaptic reflexes by voluntary contraction of muscle in remote parts of the body: Mechanisms involved in the Jendrassik maneuver. Brain, 104, 701-719.

Dubner, B. Sessle, B.J. and Storey, A.T. (1978). The neural basis of oral and facial function. New York, Plenum, pp222-233.

Freimann, R. (1954). Untersuchungen über Zahl und Anordnund der Muskelspindeln in den Kaumuskeln des Menschen. Anatomischer Anzeiger, 100, 258-264.

Gassel, M.M. and Diamantopoulos, E. (1964). The Jendrassik maneuver; I. The pattern of reinforcement of monosynaptic reflexes in normal subjects and patients with spasticity or rigidity. Neurology, 14, 555-560.

Hayashi, A. Kagamihara, Y. Nakajima,Y. Narabayashi, H. Okuma, Y. and Tanaka, R. (1988). Disorder in reciprocal innervation upon initiation of voluntary movement in patients with Parkinson's disease. Experimental Brain Research, 70, 437-440.

Jendrássik, E. (1883). Beiträge zur Lehre von den Sehnenreflexen. Deutsche Archiv fur klinisch Medizin, 33, 177-199.

Kadanoff, D. (1956). Die sensiblen Nervendigungen in der minischen Muskulatur des Menschen. Zeitschrift Mikroskopisch-Anatomische Forschung, 62, 1-15.

Kawamura, T. and Watanabe, S. (1975). Timing as a prominent factor of the Jendrassik maneuver on the H reflex. Journal of Neurology, Neurosurgery, and Psychiatry, 38, 508-516.

Landau, W.M. and Clare, M.H. (1964). Fusimotor function. Part 4. Reinforcement of the H reflex in normal subjects. Archives of Neurology, 10, 117-122.

Olkowski, Z.L. and Manocha, S. (1973). Muscle spindle in the structure and function of muscle. 2nd ed. Bourne, G.H., 2, 366-474.

Smith, D.R. and Marcarian, H.Q. (1967). The neuromuscular spindles of the lateral pterygoid muscle. Anatomischer Anzeiger, 120, 47-53.

Voss, H. (1936). Ein besonders reichliches Vorkommen von Muskelspindeln in der tiefen Portion des M. masseter des Menschen und der Anthropoiden, Anatomischer Anzeiger, 81, 290-292.

Tutorials in Motor Behavior II
G.E. Stelmach and J. Requin (Editors)
1992 Elsevier Science Publishers B.V.

NEURONAL CONTROL OF STANCE AND GAIT

V. Dietz

Department of Clinical Neurology and Neurophysiology, University of Freiburg, Hansastr. 9, D-7800 Freiburg, F.R.G.

INTRODUCTION

Why do we investigate the neuronal control of human stance and gait? The more usual approach used to study human motor control is to stretch a muscle and to analyse the reflex activity, or the explore central neuronal mechanisms during ballistic movements of a single limb. In the latter experimental approaches we obtain little information about the function of reflexes and central mechanisms as well as their interaction during a natural complex movement. This is not only important in respect to the motor control in healthy subjects, but also in patients with a dysfunction of the motor system. For example, to what extent are exaggerated tendon reflexes responsible for the movement disorder in a patient with spasticity? The latter impairment is the problem for the patient, while the reflexes represent a

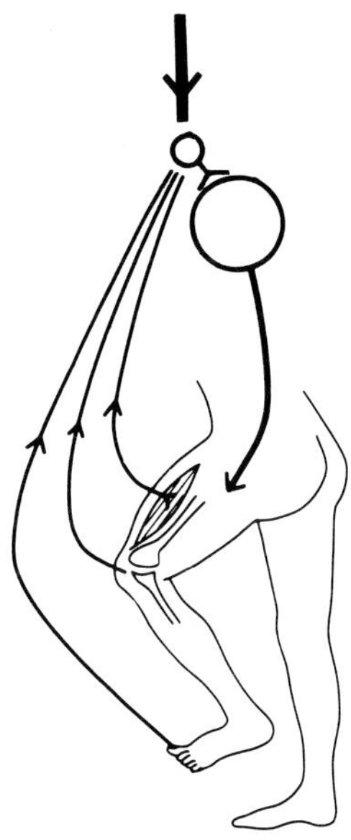

Figure 1: Schematic illustration of the mechanisms involved in the regulation of gait: the rhythmic activity of leg muscles, generated by interneuronal circuits, is modulated by a multisensory afferent input to adapt the pattern to the actual needs. Central (spinal)

programming as well as proprioceptive reflexes are under supraspinal control (from Jankovska & Lundberg, 1989).

useful physical sign for the doctor to diagnose spasticity. This has, of course, further consequences for the treatment of these patients. To reduce reflex activity by antispastic drugs may be comparable to the approach to treat the fever resulting from a pneumonia or the elevated pulse rate resulting from hyperthyreodism (cf. Landau, 1974).

We can answer the question about the significance of reflexes and central mechanisms only by the analysis of functional movements. The analysis of stance and gait performance represents a favorable experimental approach because of the reproducibility of such movements, their automatic performance and their comparability in gait disorders. Figure 1 shows schematically the mechanisms which are suggested to be involved in the regulation of stance and gait. The leg muscles are rhythmically activated by spinal interneuronal circuits. The latter activity is modulated and shaped by multisensory input. The spinal interneuronal circuits as well as the reflexes are under supraspinal control, a fact which explains the typical gait disorders in spastic paresis and cerebellar or extrapyramidal diseases. In the first part of this review, the behavior of reflexes and central mechanisms in healthy subjects will be described and, in a second part, the changes of these mechanisms in patients with spastic paresis will be discussed.

Function of postural reflexes and central mechanisms

The activity of spinal interneuronal circuits can best be studied during newborn stepping. These movements are initiated spontaneously or when a newborn is put on the ground. The rhythmical leg muscle activation begins before ground contact and is unlikely, therefore, to be due to a reflex activity (Forssberg & Wallberg, 1980). This activity pattern is also present in unencephalic newborns. Consequently, it is reasonable to assume that it is, as is the case for the cat, generated by spinal locomotor centers (Forssberg, 1986). A similar EMG pattern is

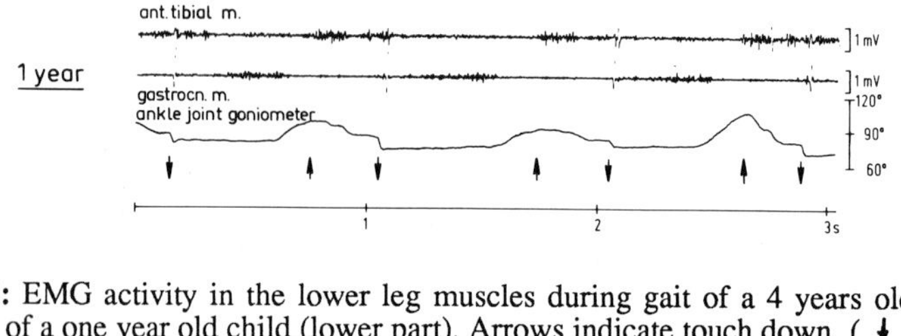

Figure 2: EMG activity in the lower leg muscles during gait of a 4 years old child (upper part) and of a one year old child (lower part). Arrows indicate touch down (↓) and lift off (↑) of the foot (from Berger et al., 1984a).

still seen in children around one year of age (Berger et al., 1984a; Forssberg, 1985). The leg muscle activity is little modulated at this age, and single EMG potentials appear in the gastrocnemius connected with muscle stretch. They most probably represent monosynaptic stretch reflex potentials (figure 2). Children at this age are not able to maintain body equilibrium. With the maturation of postural reflexes, which modulates the centrally programmed pattern according to actual needs, unsupported bipedal posture and gait become established. This is achieved at an age around 1 1/2 years (Berger et al., 1984a). The developmental changes are accomplished at an age of around 4 years (figure 2; Berger et al., 1984a).

The origin and behavior of postural reflexes which modulate the basic pattern of leg muscle activation has been further investigated by the introduction of perturbatory impulses during stance and gait. The compensatory EMG responses induced by these perturbations were then analysed. Figure 3 shows the gastrocnemius EMG responses to three different modes of stretches applied to the gastrocnemius muscle. In figure 3 A the gastrocnemius was stretched in a passive condition. The rapid dorsiflexion movement was followed by a single

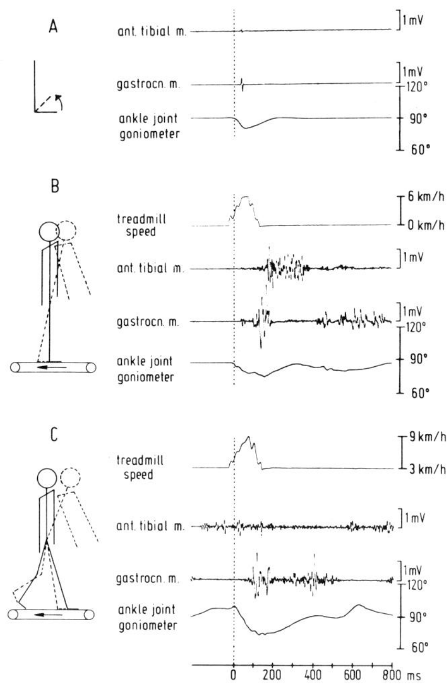

Figure 3: Raw records of leg muscle EMG responses following different types of displacement (foot dorsiflexion) in one subject, together with the ankle joint movements. A: passive foot dorsiflexion of the relaxed leg; B: positive acceleration impulse of the treadmill applied during stance and; C: during gait (3 km/h) (from Dietz et al., 1984).

monosynaptic reflex response. In figure 3 B, the subject was standing on a treadmill and a short, powerful, backwards directed translational impulse was induced. This perturbation was followed by a small monosynaptic reflex response and, with a latency of about 65 ms, a strong polysynaptic (or long-latency-) gastrocnemius EMG response. In figure 3 C the same pertubation was induced during gait, at the beginning of the stance phase. In this condition the monosynaptic response was absent (most probably due to presynaptic inhibition of group I afferents in this condition (cf. Capaday & Stein, 1986; for review see Stein & Capaday, 1988)), and only a functionally essential polysynaptic gastrocnemius response appeared. Further studies, using ischaemic blockade of group I afferents (Berger et al., 1984b) have revealed that these afferents do not contribute significantly to this late response. In addition, vestibulo-spinal reflexes have been shown to be little involved in the generation of this response (Horstmann & Dietz, 1988). It has, therefore, been argued that this response is mainly mediated by group II (and probably III) afferents (Berger et al., 1984b).

The question arising from these observations is, to what extent is the polysynaptic gastrocnemius response influenced by the parameters of a perturbation, i.e. the displacement velocity and amplitude applied during stance and gait? To answer this question, different treadmill acceleration rates and amplitudes were applied during perturbations of gait. Figure 4 shows the compensatory reactions following different acceleration impulses. Increasing displacement velocities were achieved at the ankle joints by these accelerations (from a to d).

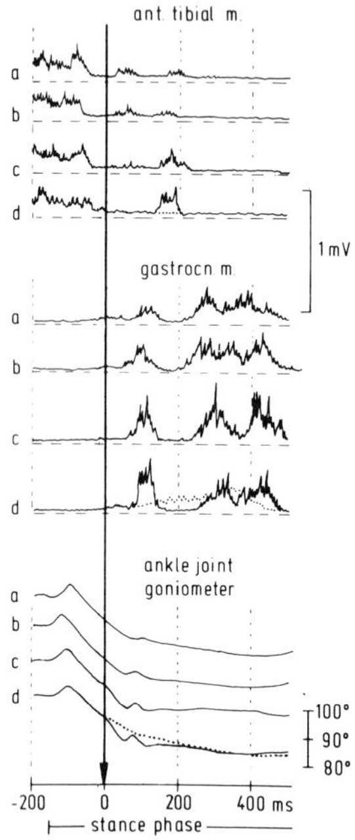

Figure 4: Leg muscle EMG responses following different acceleration impulses of a treadmill moving at a speed of 3 km/h. The EMG was rectified and averaged (n = 10), as were the movements of the ankle joint. Dotted lines (d) represent the normal walking pattern at 3 km/h. The impulse was released at the beginning of the stance phase and was used for triggering the recording of the different parameters. Different accelerations were applied: (a) 2.5; (b) 4.6; (c) 12; and (d) 14 m/s^2; the impulse amplitude was set at 6 deg. (from Dietz et al., 1987).

The dotted lines indicate the ankle joint movement and EMG activity during undisturbed gait. With increasing displacement velocity there was a steeper slope and increase in strength of the compensatory gastrocnemius EMG response. The gastrocnemius responses were followed by a tibialis anterior activation and, for the stronger impulses, by a second gastrocnemius EMG peak. This pattern is reminiscent of the triphasic pattern observed during ballistic finger and hand movements, which is thought to be centrally programmed. In analogy, we would suggest that the compensatory gastrocnemius EMG response is mediated by spinal reflex mechanisms and is incorporated in a centrally programmed pattern. The configuration of the compensatory gastrocnemius responses depended not only on the displacement velocity, but their amplitude and duration was also closely correlated with the impulse duration (Dietz et al., 1987; Diener et al., 1988). It can be concluded, therefore, that this compensatory response behaves like a stretch reflex response. This is schematically represented in figure 5. As indicated in this diagram not only the gastrocnemius response behaves like a stretch reflex response but, similarly, also the tibialis anterior m. to forward directed displacements of the feet (Dietz et al., 1989a). As will be shown in the following section this reflex mechanism

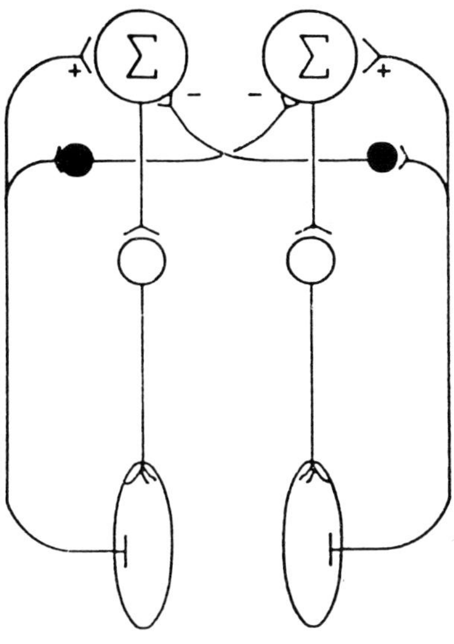

Figure 5: Schematic diagram showing the suggested generation and pathway of the polysynaptic leg muscle EMG response.

does not, however, behave like simple stretch reflexes but is directed to keep the body's centre of gravity over the support area i.e., the feet. This will be demonstrated by two experimental approaches: one concerns the bilateral coordination of leg muscle activation as a basis for the coordination of stance and gait; the second one concerns the influence of gravity on these reflexes as the basic reason for the need for postural reflexes.

Interlimb coordination

Figure 6 shows the gastrocnemius (A) and tibialis ant. (B) EMG responses of the right leg to uni- and bilateral displacements of the feet. In figure 6 A, the gastrocnemius EMG response to a bilateral backward displacement is much larger compared to a unilateral displacement and the latter response is still larger compared to a bilateral displacement of the feet in opposite directions. This was the case even though the displacement velocity of the right leg was the same in all three conditions. A similar observation was made for the tibialis anterior when comparable forward displacements of the feet were applied (fig. 6 B).

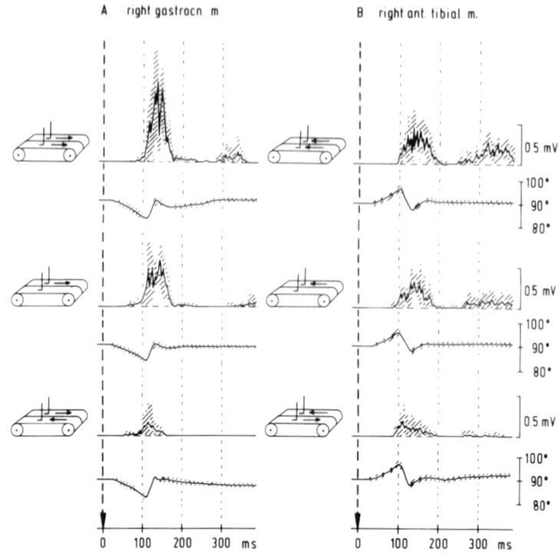

Figure 6: Mean values (with S.D.) of the rectified and averaged (n = 10) gastrocnemius (A) and tibialis anterior (B) responses of the right leg, together with the movement of the right ankle joint, after backwards (A) and forwards (B) directed acceleration of the treadmill (impulse acceleration: 12.4 $m/^2$) in one subject. Top to bottom: bilateral, unilateral, and opposing perturbations. Arrow indicates the onset of displacement at the ankle joint (velocity signal) (from Dietz et al., 1989a).

These differences between the EMG responses are meaningful in a functional sense: the strongest response is required if both legs are displaced in one direction, in order to restore body equilibrium; when the legs are displaced in opposite directions, the centre of gravity falls between the two legs and, therefore, there is little need for compensation. Figure 7 indicates the way in which spinal interneuronal circuits mediate this interlimb reflex behavior. During a unilateral backward translation not only the gastrocnemius of the displaced leg is activated but also that of the contralateral non-displaced leg (fig. 7 A).
Therefore, a linear summation of the EMG activity occurs when both legs are displaced in the same direction, which is shown in figure 7 B. The inverse is true when the legs are displaced in opposite directions: a reciprocal inhibition of the respective antagonistic muscle leads to a linear subtraction of the EMG activity in the antagonistic leg muscles (Dietz et al., 1989a). These results are summarized for the gastrocnemius EMG responses following the three different modes of displacements (fig. 8). For all four impulses (different treadmill accelerations) studied, there are significant differences in the amplitude of the EMG responses between the different modes of displacement: bilateral unidirectional displacements compared with the unilateral displacements and the latter again, compared with the bilateral displacements in opposite directions. The mechanism underlying this functionally useful behavior of the spinal reflexes is schematically represented in figure 9. The reflex mechanism shown for one leg (figure 5) is now extended to the spinal coordination of the two legs. The observations made during the investigation of bilateral coordination underlines the significance of the body's centre of gravity as the controlled variable during stance and gait. Because this variable depends on the influence of gravity, further experiments were directed to investigate this factor.

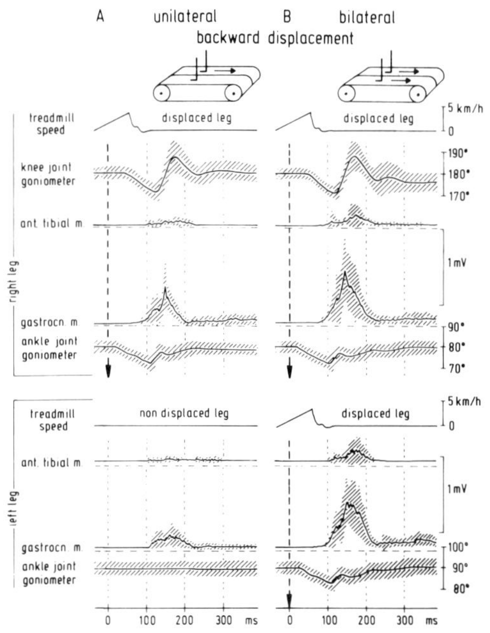

Figure 7: Mean values (with S.D.) of the rectified and averaged (n = 10) bilateral EMG responses of the legs, together with the corresponding joint movements, after a unilateral (A) and bilateral (B) backwards directed acceleration of the treadmill (same impulse as in fig. 6) in 32 subjects. Arrow indicates the release of the impulse (from Dietz et al., 1989a).

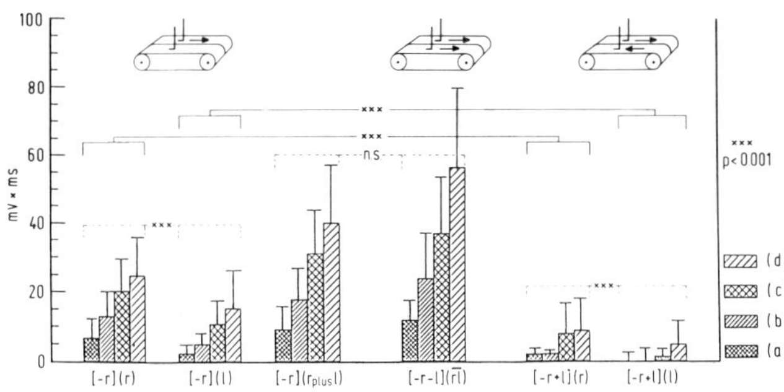

Figure 8: Mean values (with S.D.) of the integrated gastrocnemius EMG responses (minus background activity) of both legs after unilateral (right leg), bilateral, and opposing acceleration of the treadmill (4 different acceleration impulses were applied in each condition). Absolute values of the EMG responses are displayed (from Dietz et al., 1989a).

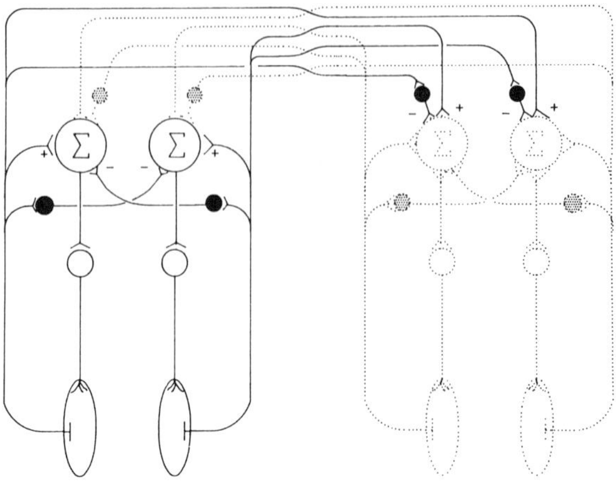

Figure 9: Schematic drawing of the expanded neuronal control of leg muscle activation, including the bilateral coordination of the leg muscles.

Influence of gravity on postural reflexes

It is already known from spacelab experiments (Clément et al., 1984, 1985; Young et al., 1986) that postural reactions in weightlessness are preserved in their basic structure but much reduced in amplitude. During weightlessness there is not only a change of input from proprioceptive reflexes but also of labyrinthine function and a separation between the effects of the two mechanisms cannot be made. In order to study the influence of gravity only on proprioceptive reflexes, postural experiments were performed in a water filled pool (Dietz et al., 1989b). Such an experimental approach has the advantage that the actual body weight can be changed by lead vests attached to the subject. The displacements during standing on a platform were induced by a pneumatic device (figure 10). Figure 11 shows the EMG responses of one subject following a backward displacement of the feet under water. The subject was loaded with 10 kg (left side of figure 11 A) or 60 kg (right side). The ankle and knee joint movements and head acceleration were similar in the two conditions. When the subject was loaded with 60 kg, the compensatory gastrocnemius and biceps femoris EMG responses were considerably larger than during loading with 10 kg. The coactivation of the tibialis anterior was not visibly changed. Corresponding observations were made for the compensatory tibialis anterior EMG responses following forward displacements (fig. 11 B). In figure 12 the EMG responses of all 10 subjects are displayed for backward (figure 12 A) and forward (figure 12 B) displacement. EMG responses and body weight were normalized to the EMG response and body weight unloaded out of water. During immersion in water there was a roughly linear relationship between the strength of the compensatory EMG response and the actual body weight. This was true for both the gastrocnemius response following backward displacement and the tibialis anterior response following forward displacement. No further increase in the amplitude of the EMG responses occurred when the subjects were loaded out of water. Functionally this behavior may be useful, in order to prevent a possible rupture of the muscle or tendon.

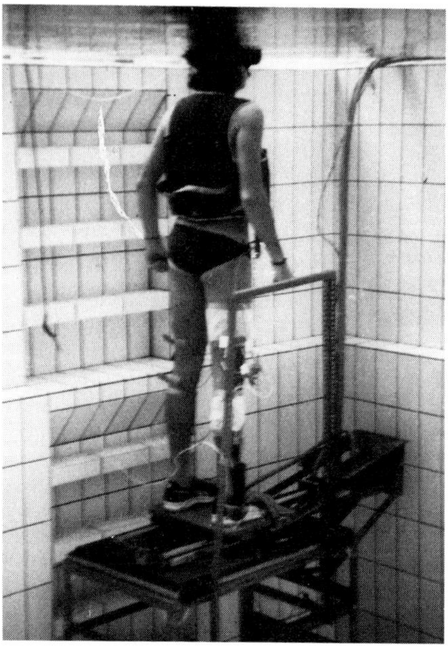

Figure 10: Equipment, showing the platform used to induce backwards and forwards displacement during water immersion (from Dietz et al., 1989b).

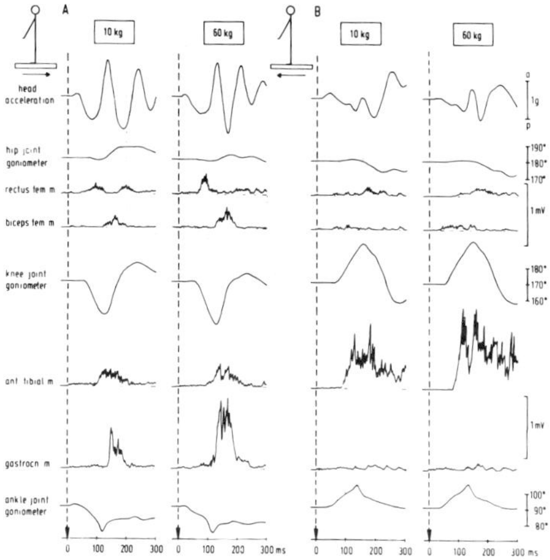

Figure 11: Leg and thigh muscle EMG activity, head acceleration signal and hip, knee and ankle joint movements following backwards (A) and forwards (B) displacement during stance under water, loaded with 10 kg or 60 kg. The rectified EMG and averaged (n = 10)

parameters of one subject are shown. The arrow indicates the release of the impulse (from Dietz et al., 1989b).

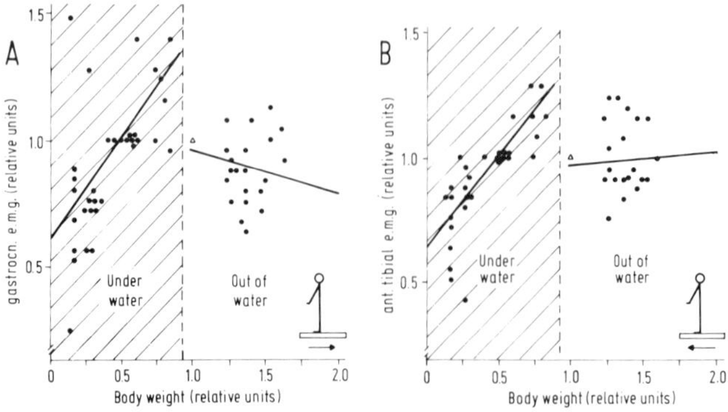

Figure 12: Correlative functions between body weight (abscissa) and integrated EMG responses (ordinate) following backwards (A, gastrocnemius m.) and forwards (B, tibialis anterior m.) displacement. The data of all subjects were normalized with respect to the integrated EMG activity and the body weight during displacement induced unloaded out of water (Δ) and are displayed as scatter diagrams and regression lines for both conditions (from Dietz et al., 1989b).

The immersion experiments indicate that the function of postural reflexes depends on contact forces, i.e. the activity of pressure receptors within the body (Dietz et al., 1989b). The following mechanisms may be considered: 1. the strength of background activity in the leg muscles might change with the body weight during stance, leading to a gain modulation of the postural reflexes. This is rather unlikely as the quantified leg muscle activity preceding the responses did not systematically change with loading; 2. pressure receptors within the sole of the foot might signal the actual force exerted on the supporting surface. This possibility is also improbable, as the compensatory responses are preserved after ischaemic blockade of the skin afferents of the foot (Berger et al., 1984b); 3. impulses from pressure receptors distributed over the whole body (within joints and the vertebral column) may converge with other reflex pathways on spinal interneuronal circuits (cf. Lundberg et al., 1987) and affect the generation of the response. There is some evidence to support this idea: when a subject is partially unloaded at the shoulders and a load is attached over the hips or the knees, the EMG response to a displacement is larger when the load is over the hips, and in both cases it is larger than in the pure unloading condition (Horstmann & Dietz 1990). The latter observation indicates that pressure receptors within the body axis are involved in the gain modulation of postural reflexes. Slowly adapting receptors within the knee joints, sensitive to externally applied pressure, have been found in the cat (Clark, 1975). Similarly, knee articular receptors in man have been shown to contribute little to the signaling of joint position, but rather, contribute to deep pressure sensation (Burgess et al., 1982). These receptors could supply the information about contact forces. These receptors may also indicate changes of body weight and, connected with this, the position of the centre of mass over the feet. The function of the otolith system has already been suggested to depend on the presence of contact forces opposing gravity (von Baumgarten, 1987; Roberts, 1973; Roberts, 1979).

Further investigations are necessary to define more precisely the location and distribution of these pressure receptors. The under-water observations make it neceassary to further expand the schematically drawn neuronal mechanisms involved in the regulation of stance and gait (figure 13). In the next section, the supraspinal control of the spinal reflexes and central mechanisms will be exemplified on the basis of experimental findings made in patients with spastic paresis.

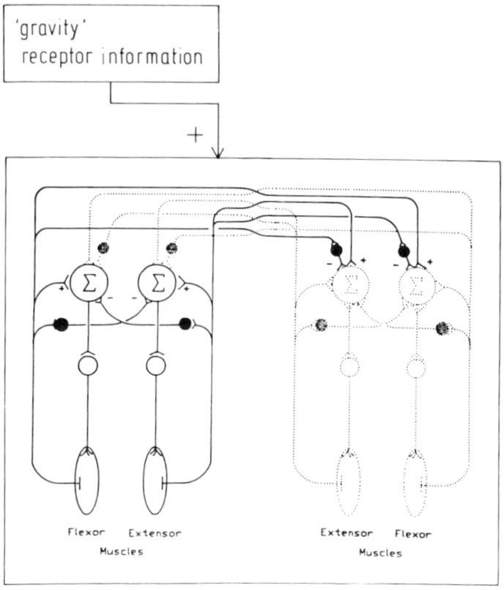

Figure 13: Schematic illustration of the neuronal regulation of stance and gait. The figure is now supplemented by the information of contact forces which are suggested to activate postural reflexes.

Supraspinal control mechanisms

The extent of the supraspinal control of spinal reflexes and central mechanisms during stance and gait is indicated by the characteristic gait impairment seen in patients with spastic paresis, as well as cerebellar and extrapyramidal disorders. In this section the changes seen in spastic paresis will be described (for extrapyramidal disorders see Dietz et al., 1988 and for cerebellar diseases see Mauritz et al., 1979). Usually, patients with spastic hemiparesis are investigated during stance and gait in order to compare the spastic side with the unaffected one of the same subject (Berger et al., 1984c). Figure 14 shows the compensatory gastrocnemius responses following a backward displacement of the feet during stance of a patient with spastic hemiparesis. The EMG responses in the unaffected leg (above) and those in the spastic leg (below) are displayed. In the unaffected leg the perturbation is followed, as in healthy subjects, by a small monosynaptic response and by a strong compensatory EMG response which appears with longer latency. In the spastic leg the monosynaptic response is a little larger in amplitude, as would clinically be expected. The polysynaptic EMG response is, however, absent. This is the case despite the fact that care was taken to distribute the body weight equally over the two legs. Figure 15 shows the EMG responses following displacement of the feet during gait. As in healthy subjects, a monosynaptic response is absent in the unaffected leg and only a polysynaptic response is present. When the same perturbation is applied at the beginning of the stance phase of the spastic leg, a monosynaptic response appears, i.e. it is not inhibited (as in normal subjects), the polysynaptic response is, however, much reduced.

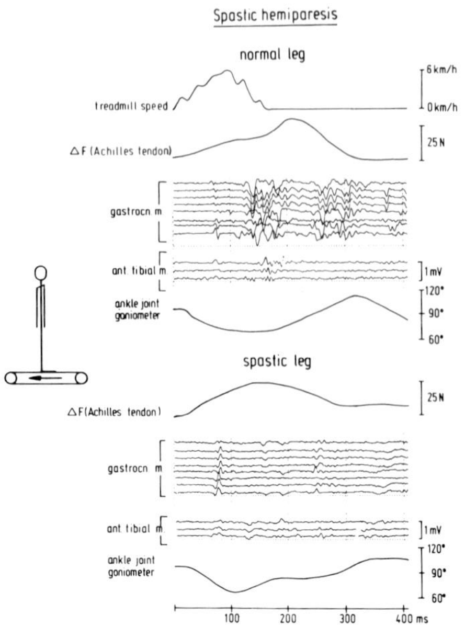

Figure 14: Leg muscle EMG responses in the unaffected (upper traces) and spastic (lower traces) leg following treadmill acceleration impulses during stance of a patient with spastic hemiparesis. Single gastrocnemius raw EMG responses are displayed, together with the treadmill speed and the averaged (n = 8) joint movements (from Berger et al., 1984c).

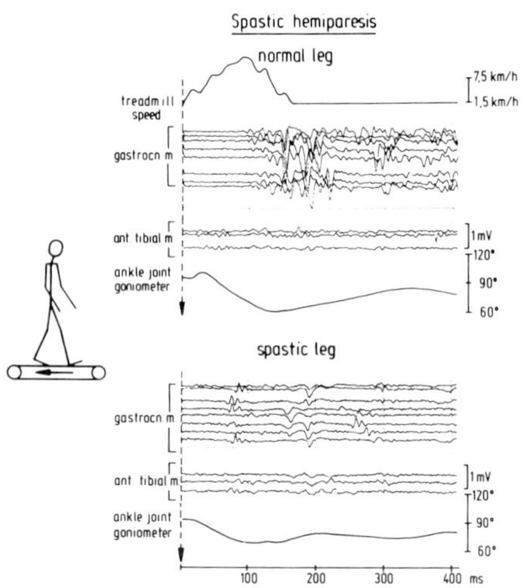

Figure 15: Leg muscle EMG responses in the unaffected (upper traces) and spastic (lower traces) leg following treadmill acceleration impulses during gait of a patient with spastic

paresis. The perturbation was induced randomly at heel contact of, respectively, the unaffected and the spastic leg. Single gastrocnemius raw EMG responses are displayed together with the treadmill speed and the averaged (n = 8) ankle joint movements. Arrows ( ) indicate ground contact (from Berger et al., 1984c).

The impaired function of the polysynaptic reflex response in spasticity is also apparent in the leg muscle activity occurring during gait. Figure 16 shows the gait pattern of a patient with spastic paraparesis and, for comparison, the pattern of a healthy subject. In the healthy subject the gastrocnemius activity during the stance phase is modulated. In the patient with spasticity a tonic EMG activity of low amplitude is present in the gastrocnemius muscle.

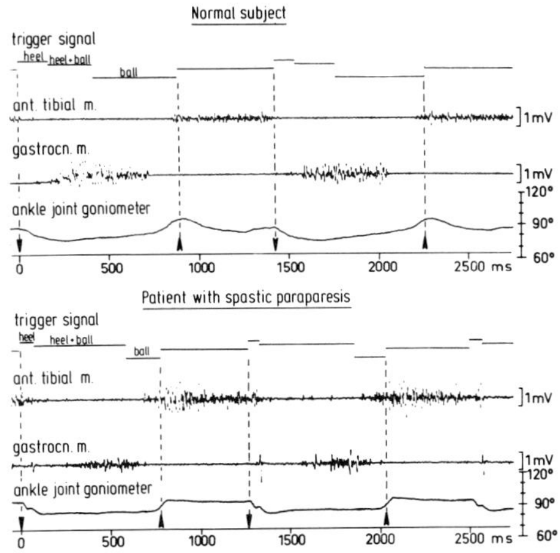

Figure 16: Original recordings from a normal subject (above) and a spastic patient (below). The raw EMG's from tibialis anterior und gastrocnemius muscles, together with the trigger and goniometer records of ankle joint angle are shown for both subjects. The different phases of the gait cycle are indicated by the trigger signal and the vertical lines. Vertical lines indicate touch down (↓) and lift off (↑) of the foot (from Dietz et al., 1981).

Single monosynaptic reflex potentials appear connected with stretch at the beginning of the stance phase. The reciprocal mode of leg muscle activation during the stance and the swing phase is preserved in the patient. This leads to the conclusion, that the poorly modulated gastrocnemius activity is due to the impaired function of polysynaptic reflexes; the centrally programmed pattern, with a reciprocal activation of the antagonistic muscles, however, is preserved in these patients (Dietz et al., 1981).

During both gait and during the displacement experiments, the overall EMG activity in the leg muscles is reduced compared to the healthy subjects. Therefore, the question arises, how can the spastic muscle tone be explained despite a reduced EMG activity? To answer this question, the changes of tension development at the Achilles tendon were investigated during gait in patients with spastic hemiparesis. Figure 17 shows a typical example of such recordings. In the lower part of the figure the tension development in the unaffected leg is displayed. The tension development is closely correlated with the gastrocnemius activity. At the onset of the first stance phase, the dorsiflexion movement of the foot starts without EMG activity in the gastrocnemius muscle. During this time period there is no increase in tension. During the later stance phase, the tension develops in parallel with the EMG activity. In the next stance phase, the EMG activity appears earlier and, connected with this, the tension increases earlier. In contrast to this, there is no modulation of gastrocnemius EMG

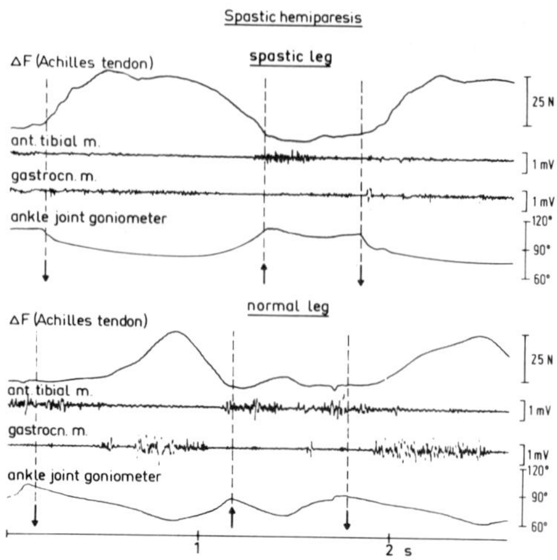

Figure 17: Gait recordings of a step cycle during slow gait of a patient with spastic hemiparesis; the spastic leg is shown above and the normal one below. From top to bottom in each recording: changes in tension recorded from the Achilles tendon, tibialis anterior, and gastrocnemius EMG's, potentiometer signal of the ankle joint. Vertical lines indicate touch down (↓) and lift off (↑) of the foot (from Dietz & Berger, 1983).

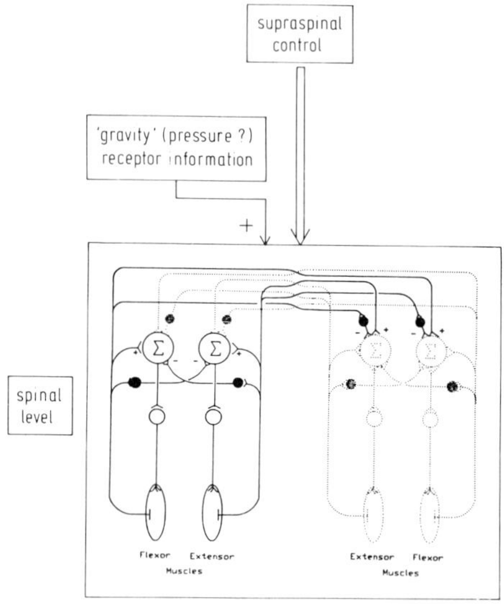

Figure 18: Schematic illustration of the neuronal control of stance and gait. The illustration is now supplemented by the supraspinal control of spinal reflex and central mechanisms.

in the spastic leg. The tension develops during the dorsiflexion phase of the foot, i.e. during the stretching period of the tonically activated gastrocnemius muscle. Single monosynaptic reflex potentials appear at the beginning of the stance phase which do not significantly contribute to the tension. This tension development is thought to be due to altered mechanical properties of muscle fibres (Berger et al., 1984c): after an acute supraspinal motor lesion, it takes time (about 3 to 4 weeks) until spastic muscle tone develops. During this time the changes of muscle fibre properties may occur (cf. Dietz et al., 1986). By the associated changes in tension development the patient is able to support the body weight during gait, although the performance of quick movements becomes impossible. Tension develops at a lower level of regulation, with the advantage, however, that the patient becomes mobile. Again, exaggerated monosynaptic stretch reflexes contribute little to this tension development during locomotion. One can, therefore, conclude with Landau (1974) "... to use activity of the ankle jerk as a measure of therapeutic success .... is to mistake the moss on a tree for the forest". The schematic diagram demonstrating the different parts of the neuronal control of stance and gait have to be supplemented by the supraspinal control of the spinal mechanisms involved in this control (figure 18).

REFERENCES

R.J. von Baumgarten, General remarks on the role of the vestibular system in weightlessness. Arch. Otorhinolaryngol. 244 (1987) 135.

W. Berger, E. Altenmüller and V. Dietz, Normal and impaired development of children's gait. Hum. Neurobiol. 3 (1984a) 160.

W. Berger, V. Dietz and J. Quintern, Corrective reactions to stumbling in man: neuronal coordination of bilateral leg muscle activity during gait. J. Physiol. (Lond.) 357 (1984b) 109.

W. Berger, G. Horstmann and V. Dietz, Tension development and muscle activation in the leg during gait in spastic hemiparesis: the independence of muscle hypertonia and exaggerated stretch reflexes. J. Neurol. Neurosurg. Psychiat. 47 (1984c) 1029.

P.R. Burgess, J. Y. Wei, F.J. Clark and J. Simon, Signaling of kinesthetic information by peripheral sensory receptors. Ann. Rev. Neurosci. 5 (1982) 171.

C. Capaday and R.B. Stein, Amplitude modulation of the soleus H-reflex in the human during walking and standing. J. Neurosci. 6 (1986) 1308.

F.J. Clark, Information signaled by sensory fibres in medial articular nerve. J. Neurophysiol. 38 (1975) 1464.

G. Clément, V.S. Gurfinkel, F. Lestienne, M.I. Lipshits and K.E. Popov, Adaptation of postural control to weightlessness. Exp. Brain Res. 57 (1984) 61.

G. Clément, V.S. Gurfinkel, F. Lestienne, M.I. Lipshits and K.E. Popov, Changes of posture during transient perturbations in microgravity. Aviat. Space Environ Med. 56 (1985) 666.

H. C. Diener, F.B. Horak and L.M. Nashner, Influence of stimulus parameters on human postural responses. J. Neurophysiol. 59 (1988) 1888.

V. Dietz, W. Berger and G.A. Horstmann, Posture in Parkinson's Disease: impairment of reflexes and programming. Ann. Neurol. 24 (1988) 660.

V. Dietz, G.A. Horstmann and W. Berger, Interlimb co-ordination of leg muscle activation during perturbation of stance in humans. J. Neurophysiol. 62 (1989a) 680.

V. Dietz, G.A. Horstmann, M. Trippel and A. Gollhofer, Human postural reflexes and gravity - an under water simulation. Neurosci. Lett. 106 (1989b) 350.

V. Dietz, U.P. Ketelsen, W. Berger and J. Quintern, Motor unit involvement in spastic paresis: relationship between leg muscle activation and histochemistry. J. Neurol. Sci. 75 (1986) 89.

V. Dietz, J. Quintern and W. Berger, Electrophysiological studies of gait in spasticity and rigidity. Evidence that altered mechanical properties of muscle contribute to hypertonia. Brain 104 (1981) 431.

V. Dietz, J. Quintern and M. Sillem, Stumbling reactions in man: significance of proprioceptive and pre-programmed mechanisms. J. Physiol. (Lond.) 286 (1987) 149.

H. Forssberg, Ontogeny of human locomotor control. I. Infant stepping, supported locomotion and transition to independent locomotion. Exp. Brain Res. 57 (1985) 480.

H. Forssberg, A developmental model of human locomotion. In: Grillner S, Stein PSG, Stuart DG, Forssberg H, Herman RM (eds) Wenner-Gren International Symposium Series. Neurobiology of Vertebrate Locomotion. Vol. 10, Macmillan, London, pp 485 - 501, 1986.

H. Forssberg and H.Wallberg, Infant locomotion: a preliminary movement and electroymographic study. In: Berg K, Eriksson BD (eds) Children and Exercise, IX. International Series on Sport Sciences. Vol. 10, University Press, Baltimore, Md, pp 32 - 49, 1980.

G. A. Horstmann and V. Dietz, The contribution of vestibular input to the stabilization of human posture: a new experimental approach. Neurosci. Lett. 95 (1988) 179.

G. A. Horstmann and V. Dietz, A basic posture control mechanism: the stabilization of the centre of gravity. Electroencephal. Clin. Neurophysiol. 76 (1990) 165.

E. Jankowska and A. Lundberg, Interneurones in the spinal cord. TINS 4 (1981) 230.

W. M. Landau, Spasticity: the fable of a neurological demon and the emperor's new therapy. Arch. Neurol. 31 (1974) 217.

K.H. Mauritz, J. Dichgans and A. Hufschmidt, Quantitative analysis of stance in late cortical cerebellar atrophy of the anterior lobe and other forms of cerebellar ataxia. Brain 102 (1979) 461.

T.D.M. Roberts, Reflex balance. Nature 244 (1973) 156.

T.D.M. Roberts, Otoliths and uprightness. In: Granit R, Pompeiano O (eds) Progress in Brain Research. Reflex control of Posture and Movement. Vol. 50, Elsevier, Amsterdam, pp 493 - 499, 1979.

R.B. Stein and C. Capaday,C The modulation of human reflexes during functional motor tasks. TINS 11 (1988) 328.

L.R. Young, C.M. Oman, D.G. Watt, K.E. Money, B.K. Lichtenberg and R.V. Kenyon, Canadian vestibular experiments on the Spacelab-1 mission: 1. sensory adaptation to weightlessness and readaptation to one-g: an overview. Exp. Brain Res. 64 (1986) 291.

Tutorials in Motor Behavior II
G.E. Stelmach and J. Requin (Editors)

Planning a reach: spatial analysis by area 7a neurons

William A. MacKay[a] and Alexa Riehle[b]

[a]Department of Physiology, University of Toronto, Toronto M5S 1A8, Canada

[b]Unité de Neurosciences Cognitives, C.N.R.S.-LNF1, 31 ch. Joseph-Aiguier, 13402 Marseille Cédex 9, France

Abstract

Single neurons in area 7a of monkey parietal cortex were found to discriminate specific spatial parameters pertaining to a planned reach. The position of a visual target on a videomonitor was distinguished, as was the direction and sometimes relative distance of a target from the hand. Thus area 7a may relate target positions to relevant body parts.

1. REACH PLANNING

In order to specify the trajectory of a reach into extrapersonal space, it is necessary to code both the initial position of the reaching limb and the position of the target relative to that limb. In theory that is sufficient information, but in practice the initial estimates of movement amplitude are generally inaccurate. Thus terminal adjustments are required under visual and non-visual control (Goodale et al. 1985; Prablanc et al. 1986; Soechting & Flanders 1989). The initial position of the reaching arm is probably represented by the somatosensory system. For example, neurons in area 5 are capable of coding limb position (Kalaska et al 1990; MacKay et al 1978; Sakata et al. 1973). Target position, however, is cued via the visual system and requires considerable transformation in order to become motorically useful.

Visual information is initially projected onto the retina, and it is possible that retinotopic coordinates are adequate to guide most eye/head movement (see chapters by Berthoz, and Roucoux in this volume). For visually-guided arm movements, however, it is assumed necessary to transform a retinally-coded target position into some body-centered reference frame. Soechting and coworkers (1990) have shown that humans pointing to targets without visual feedback are equally adept at using a head or "shoulder" reference, the latter actually centered about midway from the neck to the shoulder. Perhaps yet another reference point would appear if the hand was visible when the target locus was defined.

In order to determine the direction of an intended arm movement, the target position in space must be refered to the current position of the arm. Thus a head-centered reference or shoulder reference may not be generally useful. Local modulation of a head-centered representation according to current arm position could implement a distributed hand-centered frame in pertinent cortical networks. A major feature of the cerebral cortex as a parallel network processor appears to be the modulatory interactions between functional zones such that sensory (or behavioral) discriminations are increasingly context-specified (see White 1989).

An estimate of movement extent or amplitude relies on computations based on initial arm position and target position relative to the arm. In effect, a movement vector must be specified combining position, direction and extent information. This immediately poses the question of whether the brain ever separates abstracted parameters of direction and extent or always treats them as a vector. In motor and premotor cortex, there is now considerable evidence that the direction parameter is represented without extent information in many neurons (Riehle & Requin 1989). Extent information, on the other hand, is never coded in areas 4 and 6 independently of direction (ibid.). It would appear then that in the precentral gyrus, direction is represented and extent information is used to modulate it. The possibility remains, however, that an abstracted extent parameter is coded elsewhere and subsequently serves to modulate the directional representation.

Area 7 of the parietal lobe is a site of integration of somatosensory and visual information (Fig. 1). Area 7a (and 7ip inside the intraparietal sulcus) receives predominantly visual input (Andersen et al. 1990; Cavada & Goldman-Rakic 1989), much of it from the region of the superior temporal sulcus (STS). Area 7b, on the other hand, is the target of somatosensory input from the rostral bank of the intraparietal sulcus and from the second somatosensory cortex within the Sylvian sulcus (SS). Since area 7b projects into area 7a (ibid.), the latter is a logical place to search for the coding of visually-cued parameters pertaining to an intended movement.

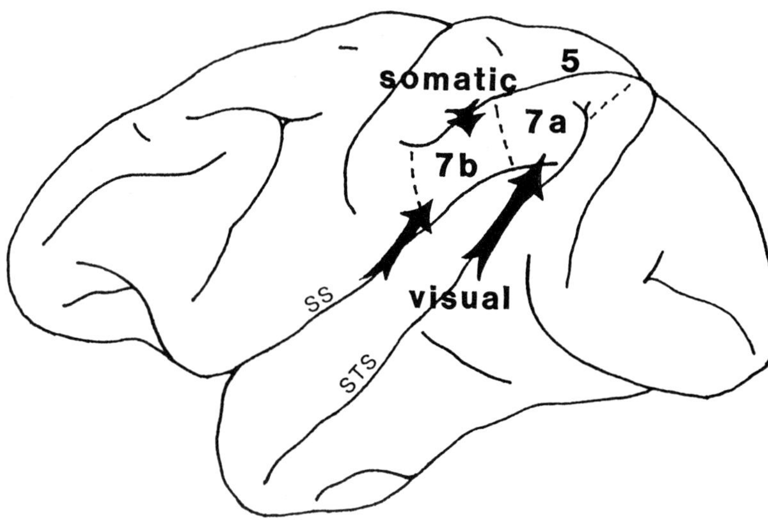

Figure 1. Schematic outline of the left hemisphere of the monkey cerebral cortex, showing the location of area 7 and some major inputs. SS Sylvian sulcus; STS superior temporal sulcus.

2. POSTERIOR PARIETAL LOBE

Visual guidance of the arm is known to require parts of the posterior parietal cortex. In particular, ablation of area 7a results in systematic misreaching to visual targets predominantly in the contralateral hemifield (Faugier-Grimaud et al. 1984, LaMotte & Acuña 1978). Neurophysiological studies of area 7a unitary activity in monkeys have demonstrated the existence of populations of neurons discharging during arm projection or hand manipulation in space (Hyvärinen & Poranen 1974, Mountcastle et al 1975). Furthermore, many area 7a neurons respond to visual signals (Robinson et al 1978) especially if they serve as targets for intended eye or arm movements. In other words, light-sensitive area 7a cells are not passive discriminators of specific characteristics of visual stimuli, but active (programmable) filters of visual cues, selecting features according to their behavioral relevance. Receptive fields of area 7a cells can be very large (Robinson et al. 1978; Motter & Mountcastle 1981), even covering parts of both hemifields. But in high-level association cortex, the concept of receptive field is so plastic that it has little meaning outside of the context in which it is measured. Thus it is essential to gather information about the properties of neurons in area 7 during performance of the specific behavior of interest.

Area 7ip, confined to the caudal bank of the intraparietal sulcus, projects to the frontal eye fields and is probably concerned mainly with the guidance of eye/head movements (Andersen et al. 1990; Goldman-Rakic 1988). Area 7a, on the other hand, projects to prefrontal zones (Cavada & Goldman-Rakic 1989) which ultimately influence premotor and motor cortex. Thus area 7a can be postulated to be involved with the guidance of limb movements (Goldman-Rakic 1988).

At the cognitive level, area 7a may contribute to the formulation of spatial *concepts* independently of immediate motor intention. One of the most striking symptoms of posterior parietal lesions in humans is the deficit in formulating spatial relationships between the external environment and the body in the contralateral field (Bisiach & Luzzatti 1978). In addition, Bisiach and colleagues (1979) have established that this process of spatial reconstruction does not rely on retinotopic ordering of input information, but rather on organizational criteria from an internal model of the information source. When that model is made inaccessible by a posterior parietal lesion, then the *expectations* necessary to organize sensory input into a body-environmental schema are lacking. Area 7a has strong reciprocal connections with the parahippocampal cortex (Cavada & Goldman-Rakic 1989). Perhaps the limbic connections are necessary for the generation of parietal expectancy.

3. TARGET POSITION

The responsiveness of area 7a neurons to the spatial position of visual targets for an arm reach was examined in two macaque monkeys, one trained to press buttons with the right hand as soon as they illuminated, and the other to touch pre-cued target positions on a videomonitor at the time of a GO signal (delay period of 1 s). In the latter protocol the arm to be used was specified by a color code (violet for right arm, blue for left) given before the target position cue. In both cases the arms rested on plates at the animal's side prior to a trial and no constraints were imposed on eye fixation. In the second paradigm, the head was also free to rotate to the left or right.

All neuronal recordings were made in the left hemisphere.

Depending on the monkey, 10-28% of the recorded population of area 7a cells responded to presentation of the target (Table 1). It may be a significant observation that far more target responsive cells (indeed task-related cells in general) were found in Rubah, who had a delay period and hence more cues to distinguish. About half of these showed a preference for specific spatial locations, usually on the contralateral (right) side. With the second protocol it was clear that responses occured only to initial target specification. GO signals elicited no response. Examples of position-dependent responses are shown in Fig. 2 and 3 for the two protocols, respectively.

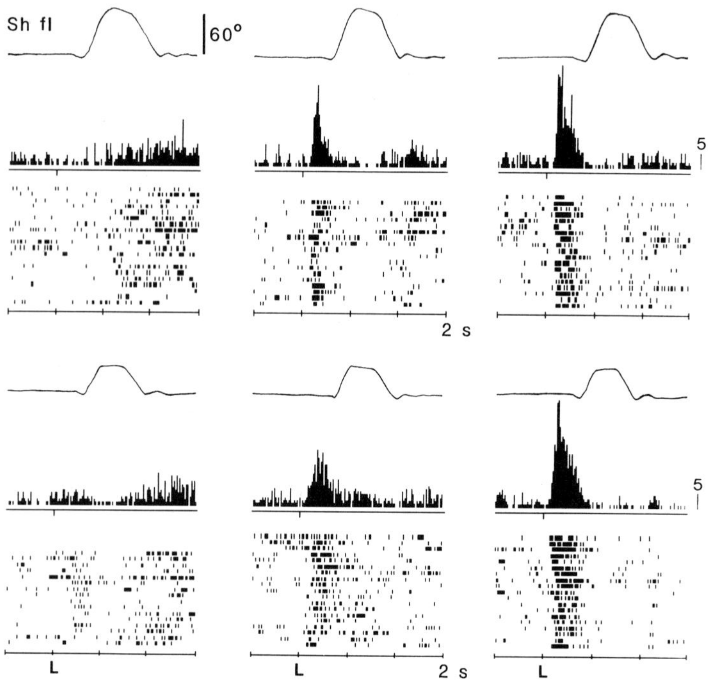

Figure 2. Spatially selective target responses in an area 7a neuron, tested with a panel of 6 pushbuttons. Individual data sets are arranged in the relative order of the buttons. Bin width of peristimulus time histograms is 4 ms. L, time of button illumination. Sh fl, record of shoulder flexion derived from SELSPOT measurements.

Table 1
Area 7a position-related responses

Monkey	No. of Cells tested	Target cells	Preferred Target Zone			
			Left	Center	Right	All
Leonid (pushbuttons)	389	40	3	6	10	21
Rubah (videomonitor)	212	59	2	7	13	37

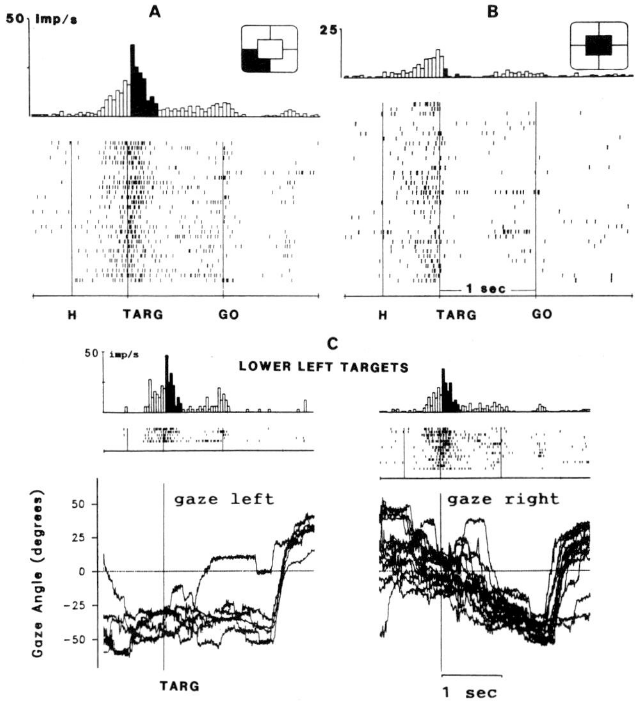

Figure 3. Spatially selective target response of an area 7a neuron. **A**: targets appeared in lower left section of videoscreen as indicated. Peristimulus time histograms and rasters are aligned on the time of the target cue (TARG). H, hand cue (colored background). Bin width is 40 ms. **B**: targets appeared in central part of screen. **C**: responses to lower left targets segregated according to whether the gaze angle was to the left or right of the target when it appeared.

The neuron illustrated in Fig. 3 responded best to targets displayed within the lower left portion of the videomonitor (Fig. 3A), and not at all to targets appearing in the center (Fig. 3B). Note that the neuron started discharging in anticipation of target appearance. The discharge continued for lower left targets but stopped for central targets. Target anticipation was found to be quite common among area 7a neurons (cf. MacKay & Crammond 1987). Gaze location at the time of target appearance was extremely variable. (This was not true during reach performance.) For each target group, individual trials were classified into one of 3 sets according to whether gaze was centered on the target (± 10°), to the left of the target or to the right. For the lower left target positions, the latter two gaze sets are shown in Fig. 3C: there was no observable difference in responsiveness attributable to gaze location. No conclusions can yet be drawn on how common such gaze-independent mechanisms may be, since too few cells have been tested with concomitant EOG recording and head angle monitoring to determine gaze position at the time of target presentation. Furthermore, it has not been shown that such responses code target position relative to the body, although that is a possibility. Position coding could also be relative to an external cue such as the frame of the videomonitor.

Target responses (both position-dependent and not) were sometimes modulated by the prior selection of the hand to be used. An example is shown in Fig. 4. This cell preferred center targets. Preparation of the left hand (blue background) resulted in a target response twice the magnitude of that when the right arm was prepared (violet background). The difference was significant ($t_{.005,26}=2.896$). In total, 10 neurons (Rubah only) had hand-dependent target responses: 4 were left-hand dominant and 6 right-hand.

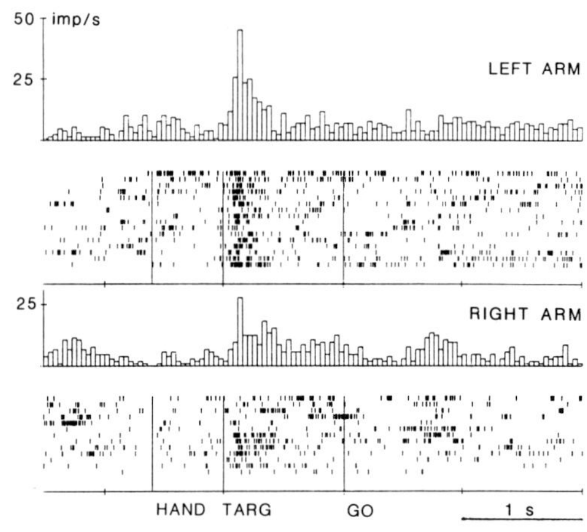

Figure 4. Peristimulus time histograms and rasters of responses in a single neuron to targets displayed in the central part of the screen. Top: left hand was cued to reach. Bottom: right hand was cued to reach. Bin width is 40 ms.

4. DIRECTION SELECTIVITY

A second task was designed to test the discrimination of target direction relative to the hand independently of spatial position. This has been done only in the second monkey trained to reach to targets on the videomonitor. Four target loci were used, equally spaced across the screen in the horizontal axis (Fig. 5C). When an initial target was correctly touched (only the right arm was used in this task), then a second target was indicated as an open square either to the left or right of the hand (which remained at the location of the first target). Note that the second target could be at a small (11 cm) or large distance (22 cm) from the first. The ensuing reach could not be initiated, however, until a GO signal appeared 1 s later (open square replaced by solid square). The set of tested reach trajectories is depicted in Fig. 5C.

Neuronal discrimination of the intended reach direction was manifested either by the relative magnitude of the visual response to target presentation, or by the relative firing rate during the last half of the preparatory period (PP). Directional selectivity was commonly seen in phasic responses to the second target but much more rarely in tonic PP activity. When the latter was observed, the pattern of neuronal activity was very similar to that described by Crammond and Kalaska (1989) for area 5 cells. We can only add that in both area 5 and 7a, PP activity significantly discriminated the intended direction of a reach only when the reach amplitude was relatively large (at least greater than 11 cm).

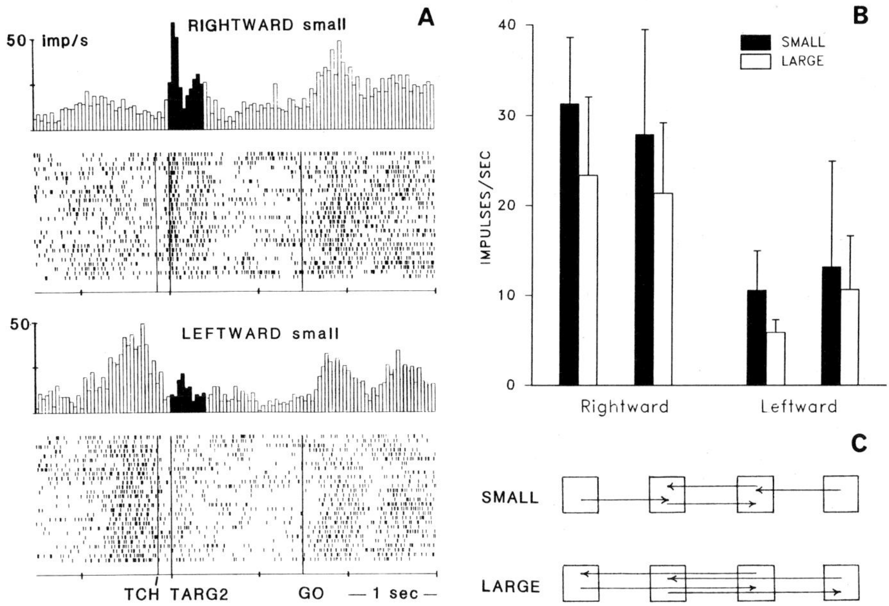

Figure 5. Directional preference of target responses relative to the position of the hand for an area 7a neuron. **A**: PSTHs and rasters for small extent targets to the right and to the left of the hand. TCH, time when the hand touches the screen at the first target; TARG2, time when the second target appears. Bin width is 40 ms. **B**: bar graph of mean responses to second target calculated over the interval marked by solid shading in **A**. Relative placement of each black and white pair marks hand position at the time of second target cue. Error bars are standard deviation. **C**: all of the tested reach trajectories between the first and second target positions. Small extent targets were 11 cm apart, large extent 22 cm.

The phasic target response shown in Fig. 5 readily distinguished rightward from leftward targets, regardless of the exact screen position. Although there was also a tendency for small target displacements to give bigger responses than large, this was not significant. Note that this cell also discharged during reach performance especially in the rightward direction.

Many neurons in area 7a were encountered which did not respond to the target cues, but did show activity changes during reach performance, often with a directional preference as noted above. An example is given in Fig. 6. Such cells were found in clusters scattered within area 7a and interspersed with clusters showing target responses.

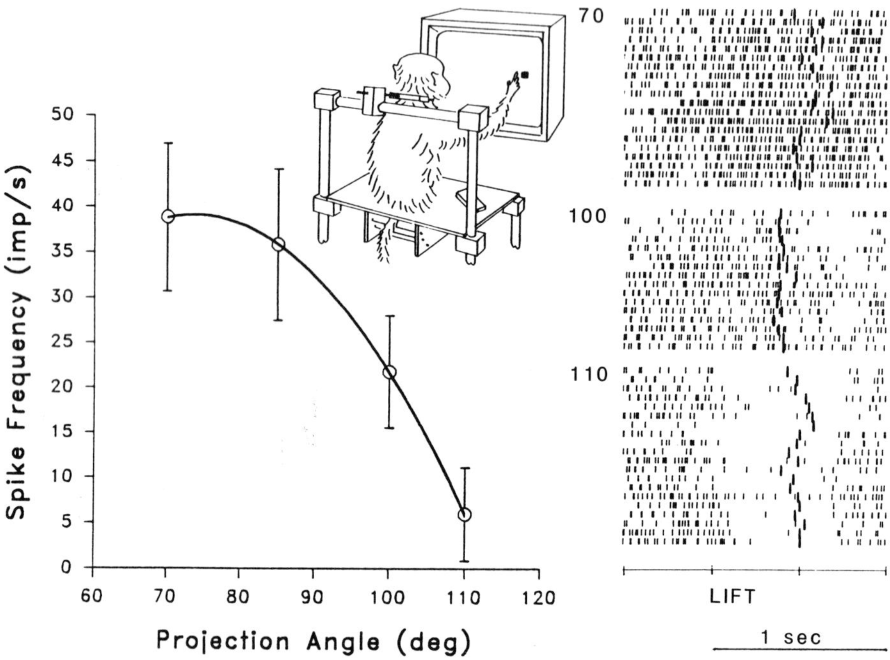

Figure 6. Example of an area 7a reach cell which was preferentially responsive to leftward trajectories. The rasters on the right are aligned to restplate release: the heavy strokes mark time of target contact. Mean reach activity was calculated over the release-contact interval and is graphed on the left for the 4 target positions. Error bars are standard deviation.

The juxtaposition of reach cells and visual target cells, to the point that single neurons often combined both features (Fig. 5), hints very strongly that they are functionally linked. The reach cells of area 7a are far from unique: they are more characteristic of area 5 (Kalaska et al. 1990) and area 7b. Usually such cells have demonstrable proprioceptive input from the right arm. Their re-appearance in area 7a may serve as a means of modulating target responses, i.e. proprioceptive modulation of the visual modality. Support for this hypothesis comes from a comparison of visual responses to the same targets when the arm is held at different locations. Such a comparison is made in Fig. 7 for the neuron illustrated in Fig. 5. (In Fig. 7 the target responses were calculated over a shorter interval [150 ms] than in Fig. 5 to avoid inclusion of the reach activity which followed initial targets, when no delay period was given.)

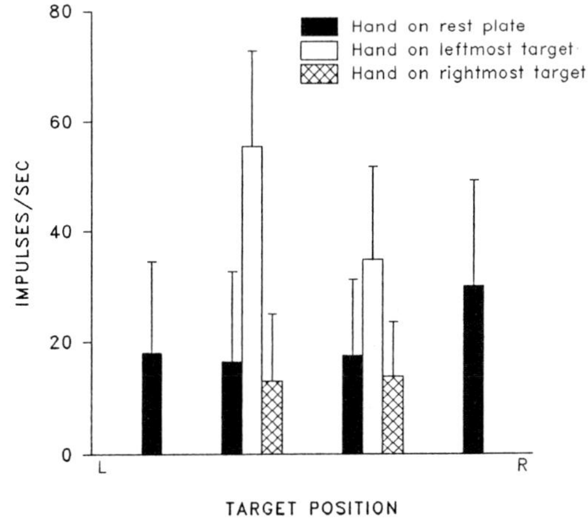

Figure 7. Comparison of target responses when right hand was in varying positions. Targets were always in same standard loci as indicated by the relative positions of the bar clusters. (Note that in Fig. 5 & 9, bars are positioned where the *hand* was located at the time of target appearance: here they occur where the *target* appeared.) When the hand was on the restplate, it lay 24 cm from the rightmost target position (in front and below). Error bars are standard deviation.

Alternative explanations are equally likely, however. Mean head position, for example, changed with hand position. Thus the retinal eccentricity of a given target stimulus altered with hand position as shown in Fig. 8. In principle, therefore, the response properties of the cell depicted in Fig. 6 could be due to a receptive field displaced 20° right of center. Further study is required to determine if these directionally selective target responses are more related to retinal receptive-field properties, arm position, head angle, or motor intention.

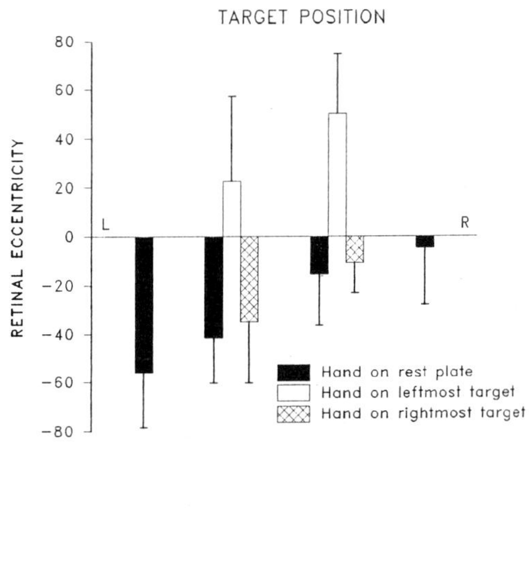

Figure 8. Retinal eccentricity (in degrees) of the target cue when it first appears, according to current hand position. Representation of target position same as in Fig. 7. Positive eccentricity is in the right hemifield, negative in the left. Error bars are standard deviation.

5. EXTENT DISCRIMINATION

In the task described above, two movement amplitudes were made (small and large) for each of the rightward and leftward directions. As with direction, extent discrimination could potentially be coded in two ways, phasically as a response to the target location cue or more tonically as sustained firing frequency during the PP. Few neurons were found which coded extent (15/212), and of those which did, ten discriminated extent by the phasic target response.

Furthermore, most cells (12/15) preferred small extents. Ten were heavily influenced by the intended direction: extent differences were only manifested for the rightward (contralateral) direction, or were greater in the rightward direction. Five neurons, however, maintained a consistent preference for small extents regardless of position or direction. An example of such a cell is given in Fig. 9.

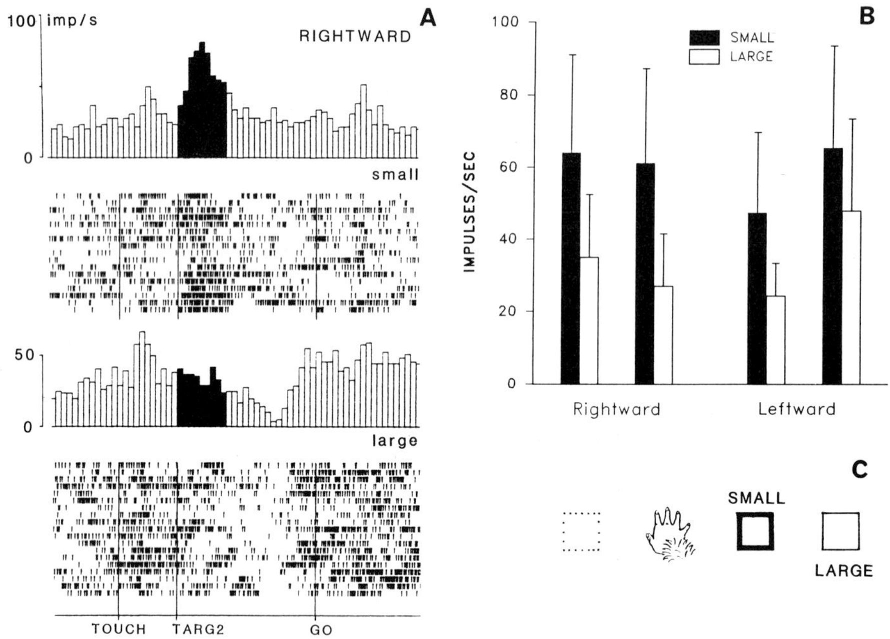

Figure 9. Target response of area 7a neuron showing preference for a small extent movement. A: histograms and rasters for small and large displacements of second target (TARG2) from hand, in the rightward direction. Bin width is 40 ms. B: mean discharge rates in response to small or large target displacements, plotted according to concurrent hand position. Discharge rates were calculated over the interval solidly shaded in A. Error bars are standard deviation. C: schematic outline of actual small and large extent target locations for one position of the hand.

For the 5 neurons preferring small extent targets in either direction, an explanation in terms of retinal receptive fields did not fit the data. Thus these neurons appeared to discriminate the relative distance of targets from the hand, regardless of the spatial position of the hand or target. In Fig. 9, it is interesting that there was quite a consistent increase in firing 150-200 ms after the hand arrived at the first target on the videoscreen, and the second target was awaited. This activity may reflect a modulatory influence involved in setting the cell's responsiveness to particular target ranges. Such firing patterns (and that shown in Fig. 3) may be manifestations of the parietal expectancy which Bisiach and colleagues (1979) have postulated is essential for transforming sensory inputs into a spatial schema.

6. FRAME OF REFERENCE

Both extent and spatial position discrimination by area 7a neurons could be variants of the same generic process, the recognition of object relationships. Detection of the directional and distance relationships between the hand and target is similar to recognition of the relationship of a target location relative to a frame or border. Indeed, Sakata and coworkers (1978) have shown that area 7a neurons responsive to moving visual stimuli are equally sensitive to movement of a frame in the opposite direction. Hence the motion which is discriminated is really relative figure-ground translation. Extensive testing of light-sensitive area 7 cells has been done in dark conditions, thereby eliminating all frames and background references for target lights. Only a fixation spot is foveated. Light responses under such conditions fail to show spatial coding although they are modulated by gaze angle (Andersen et al. 1990b). It is known, however, that peripheral vision provides a major input to area 7 (Baizer et al. 1991; Motter & Mountcastle 1981). One might speculate, therefore, that it shapes the response properties of parietal light-sensitive cells in an important manner. For example, the neuron shown in Fig. 3, which responded preferentially to lower left targets, may have been detecting the proximity of the target to part of the screen frame rather than a spatial position with respect to the body. This is likely because targets near the right upper and lower corners also gave quite clear responses: targets in the center did not elicit activity. The exact reference for such responses, however, remains to be determined.

In a study of patients suffering from hemispatial neglect produced by right parietal lobe damage, Ladavas (1987) showed that the deficit was as much related to the gravitational reference frame as to retinal coordinates. Given the existence of vestibular input to area 7a (Kawano et al. 1980), it may be hypothesized that visual responses are modulated by head tilts. Indeed gravity provides a very useful absolute spatial reference when head angle is rapidly changing. In human postural control, it is the vestibular system which provides the pivotal inertial-gravitational reference frame against which other modalities are checked and weighted (Nashner et al. 1982).

The question then arises, does visual input require complete translation into craniotopic coordinates in order to extract spatial information? From an extensive analysis of neuronal activity in the frontal eye fields, Goldberg and Bruce (1990) have concluded that spatial accuracy is attained for eye saccades without recourse to computation of craniotopic coordinates. Furthermore, Pozzo and colleagues (1990) have shown that in locomotory movements, the head is strategically stabilized with respect to gravity over specific time intervals. Sometimes the entire head-trunk axis is stabilized to provide a reference for limb movement. Such a strategy obviates the need for complex transformations between coordinate systems. Similarly, in our task, the head position tended to bear a relationship with the current hand position, (although the monkey did not stare at his hands). Since head position is the major determinant of gaze angle when the head is not fixed, and retinal receptive fields of area 7 neurons are very large, it follows that strategic head placement allows use of retinotopically mapped responses for coding spatial targets relative to the body. Thus simple motor habit can render retinotopically defined response properties very pertinent to the guidance of the arm. Nevertheless, we have found evidence for non-retinotopic coding of relative spatial position by single area 7a neurons (Fig. 3). Such neurons are probably uncommon, but their existence ensures reliable spatial guidance when gaze is wandering beyond its habitual range.

Andersen and colleagues (1990b) have shown that area 7a retinotopic responses are modulated by gaze angle, suggesting the possibility that proprioceptive input is modifying responsiveness in the visual modality. Furthermore, they have demonstrated the adequacy of this processing to effectively define targets in space relative to the head (Zipser & Andersen 1988). For reaching movements, however, arm position is an additional factor with which to reckon. The significance of visual stimuli as targets for arm movements will vary with the position of the arm. As relative positions change, the movement trajectory must change. Thus any visually-responsive cortical zone implicated in the guidance of movement should also show modulation with changing body positions. Area 7a appears to grossly satisfy this property. The modulated target responses which we have observed in area 7a, could in theory help to prepare the trajectory computation of the intended reach, both the direction and the extent.

The variability, however, of single cell activity would not allow any precise trajectory guidance, but it is possible that population vectors (Georgopoulos et al. 1983) would provide greater reliability. In addition, the cerebellum and frontal cortex would adjust and further process any signals coming out of the parietal lobe before they accessed motor areas.

Vision of both the hand and target, even if only at the time of target presentation before movement begins, improves reach accuracy (Prablanc et al. 1979). It probably aids in defining target positions relative to the hand. On the basis of our results, sight of the hand together with the target would probably make a great difference in area 7a only if the target was close to the hand.

We cannot conclude that area 7a ultimately creates a body-centered mapping of the external environment. It does appear to go part way, however, by discriminating specific spatial relationships between targets and the body. Moreover, a small subset of neurons distinguishes movement extent (or target proximity) as an independent entity.

7. ACKNOWLEDGEMENTS

This work was greatly facilitated in all respects by the able assistance of Antonio Mendonça. A number of the data collection and analysis programs were written by Alex Palimaka. Financial support was provided by MRC of Canada: AR was funded by

ONR grant N00014-89-J1557.

8. REFERENCES

Andersen, R.A., Asanuma, C., Essick, G. & Siegel, R.M. (1990a). Corticocortical connections of anatomically and physiologically defined subdivisions within the inferior parietal lobule. *Journal of Comparative Neurology 296*, 65-113.

Andersen, R.A., Bracewell, R.M., Barash, S., Gnadt, J.W. & Fogassi, L. (1990b). Eye position effects on visual, memory, and saccade-related activity in areas LIP and 7a of macaque. *Journal of Neuroscience 10*, 1176-1196.

Andersen, R.A., Essick, G.K. & Siegel, R.M. (1985). Encoding of spatial location by posterior parietal neurons. *Science 230*, 456-458.

Baizer, J.S., Ungerleider, L.G. & Desimone, R. (1991). Organization of visual inputs to the inferior temporal and posterior parietal cortex in macaques. *Journal of Neuroscience 11*, 168-190.

Bisiach, E. & Luzzatti, C. (1978). Unilateral neglect of representational space. *Cortex 14*, 129-133.

Bisiach, E., Luzzatti, C. & Perani, D. (1979). Unilateral neglect, representational schema and consciousness. *Brain 102*, 609-618.

Cavada, C. & Goldman-Rakic, P.S. (1989). Posterior parietal cortex in rhesus monkey: I. Parcellation of areas based on distinctive limbic and sensory corticocortical connections. *Journal of Comparative Neurology 287*, 393-421.

Crammond, D.J. & Kalaska, J.F. (1989). Neuronal activity in primate parietal cortex area 5 varies with intended movement direction during an instructed-delay period. *Experimental Brain Research 76*, 458-462.

Faugier-Grimaud, S., Frenois, C. & Peronnet, F. (1985). Effects of posterior parietal lesions on visually guided movements in monkeys. *Experimental Brain Research 59*, 125-138.

Georgopoulos, A.P., Caminiti,R., Kalaska, J.F., & Massey, J.T. (1983). Spatial coding of movement: a hypothesis concerning the coding of movement direction by motor cortical populations. *Experimental Brain Research (Suppl.) 7*, 327-336.

Goldberg, M.E. & Bruce, C.J. (1990). Primate frontal eye fields. III. Maintenance of a spatially accurate saccade signal. *Journal of Neurophysiology 64*, 489-508.

Goldman-Rakic, P.S. (1988). Topography of cognition: parallel distributed networks in primate association cortex. *Annual Review of Neuroscience 11*, 137-156.

Goodale, M.A., Pélisson, D. & Prablanc, C. (1986). Large adjustments in visually guided reaching do not depend on vision of the hand or perception of target displacement. *Nature 320*, 748-750.

Hyvärinen, J. & Poranen, A. (1974). Function of the parietal associative area 7 as revealed from cellular discharges in alert monkeys. *Brain 97*, 673-692.

Kawano, K., Sasaki, M. & Yamashita, M. (1980). Vestibular input to visual tracking neurons in the posterior parietal association cortex of the monkey. *Neuroscience Letters 17*, 55-60.

Ladavas, E. (1987). Is the hemispatial deficit produced by right parietal lobe damage associated with retinal or gravitational coordinates? *Brain 110*, 167-180.

LaMotte, R.H. & Acuña, C. (1978). Defects in accuracy of reaching after removal of posterior parietal cortex in monkeys. *Brain Research 139*, 309-326.

MacKay, W.A. & Crammond, D.J. (1987). Neural correlates in posterior parietal lobe of the expectation of events. *Behavioral Brain Research 24*, 167-179.

MacKay, W.A., Kwan, H.C., Murphy, J.T. & Wong, Y.C. (1978). Responses to active and passive wrist rotation in area 5 of awake monkeys. *Neuroscience Letters 10*, 235-239.

Motter, B.C. & Mountcastle, V.B. (1981). The functional properties of the light-sensitive neurons of the posterior parietal cortex studied in waking monkeys: foveal sparing and opponent vector organization. *Journal of Neuroscience 1*, 3-26.

Mountcastle, V.B., Lynch, J.C., Georgopoulos, A., Sakata, H. & Acuña, C. (1975). Posterior parietal association cortex of the monkey: command function for operations within extrapersonal space. *Journal of Neurophysiology 38*, 871-908.

Nashner, L.M., Black, F.O. & Wall, C. (1982). Adaptation to altered support and visual conditions during stance: patients with vestibular deficits. *Journal of Neurophysiology 2*, 536-544.

Pozzo, T., Berthoz, A. & Lefort, L. (1990). Head stabilization during various locomotor tasks in humans. I. Normal subjects. *Experimental Brain Research 82*, 97-106.

Prablanc, C., Echallier, J.F., Komilis, E. & Jeannerod, M. (1979). Optimal response of eye and hand motor systems in pointing at a visual target. I. Spatio-temporal characteristics of eye and hand movements and their relationships when varying the amount of visual information. *Biological Cybernetics 35*, 113-124.

Prablanc, C., Pélisson, D. & Goodale, M.A. (1986). Visual control of reaching movements without vision of the limb. I. Role of retinal feedback of target position in guiding the hand. *Experimental Brain Research 62*, 293-302.

Riehle, A. & Requin, J. (1989). Monkey primary motor and premotor cortex: single-cell activity related to prior information about direction and extent of an intended movement. *Journal of Neurophysiology 41*, 910-932.

Robinson, D.L., Goldberg, M.E. & Stanton, G.B. (1978). Parietal association cortex in the primate: sensory mechanisms and behavioral modulations. *Journal of Neurophysiology 41*, 910-932.

Sakata, H., Shibutani, H. & Kawano, K. (1978). Parietal neurons with dual sensitivity to real and induced movements of visual target. *Neuroscience Letters 9*, 165-169.

Sakata, H., Takaoka, A., Kawarasaki, A. & Shibutani, H. (1973). Somatosensory properties of neurons in the superior parietal cortex (area 5) of the rhesus monkey. *Brain Research 64*, 85-102.

Soechting, J.F. & Flanders, M. (1989). Sensorimotor representations for pointing to targets in three-dimensional space. *Journal of Neurophysiology 62*, 582-594.

Soechting, J.F., Tillery, S.I.H. & Flanders, M. (1990). Transformation from head- to shoulder-centered representation of target direction in arm movements. *Journal of Cognitive Neuroscience 2*, 32-43.

White, E.L. (1989). *Cortical Circuits*. Boston: Birkhäuser.

Zipser, D. & Andersen, R.A. (1988). A back propagation programmed network that simulates response properties of a subset of posterior parietal neurons. *Nature 331*, 679-684.

SECTION 5

INTERSEGMENTAL DYNAMICS OF MOVEMENT

Tutorials in Motor Behavior II
G.E. Stelmach and J. Requin (Editors)

Searching for solutions to the coordination function: Learning as exploratory behavior

K. M. Newell and P. V. McDonald

Department of Kinesiology, University of Illinois at Urbana-Champaign, 906 S. Goodwin Ave, Urbana, IL, 61801, USA.

Abstract

The process of learning a new coordination pattern is examined as a form of exploratory behavior in which search strategies are utilized in identifying and assembling the new movement pattern. The description and identification of search strategies is considered in light of a perceptual-motor workspace which emerges from the confluence of task, environmental, and organismic constraints. Some data from a two-limb coordination task are presented that pertain to key theoretical issues of learning as a search strategy embedded in a perceptual-motor workspace.

1. INTRODUCTION

An approach to motor skill acquisition that has search strategies, a form of exploratory behavior, as a central concept of both practice and learning is the focus of this paper. Although practice is an essential component of skill acquisition it is conspicuous by virtue of its absence in most theoretical accounts of motor learning. Furthermore, where practice is included in theory, such as in schema accounts of skill learning, the emphasis is on learning as the product of practice. The process of practice is rarely addressed directly, in spite of the centrality of this concept to motor learning.

The process of acquiring a skill may be viewed as a search for a task solution in a perceptual-motor workspace that continuously evolves from the confluence of constraints on behavior that arise from the learner, the environment, and the task (Fowler & Turvey, 1978; Newell, Kugler, van Emmerik, & McDonald, 1989). There are at least three interrelated components to developing a theory of motor skill acquisition from this perspective. The first is a characterization of the perceptual-motor workspace (Kugler & Turvey, 1987; Newell, McDonald, & Kugler, in press) and the way in which perception and action are mapped into a task solution (Shaw & Alley, 1985). The second is a characterization of the search strategies employed naturally by learners in exploring the perceptual-motor workspace for task solutions. The third is the instructional constraints that change agents, such as teachers and coaches, might employ to draw the learner's attention to the perceptual-motor workspace and/or guide the search through this workspace for task solutions (Newell, in press). In this paper we address the second component of this evolving framework for motor skill acquisition, namely search strategies and their relation to the *change* in the coordination and control of movement which accompanies practice and the acquisition of skill.

1.1. Examining exploratory behavior

The general concept of exploratory behavior can be found in many different domains of research, and in order to clarify our interest in such it is worth briefly highlighting some of the existing literature. One may read of exploratory activity in accounts of animal homing behavior, food foraging, human visual search, cognitive problem solving, and problems of optimization in artificial intelligence (AI) to name but a few domains. Each of the above instances of exploration possess some similarities, but at the same time some important differences, especially in terms of the constraints which impact the search. In homing, food foraging, visual search, and AI the exploring agent is usually considered to possess the necessary attributes for successful search. However, in each of these instances, the goals of the exploratory behavior may be defined with significantly differing degrees of clarity. Similarly the informational support for the guidance of the exploratory behavior can also vary in its nature.

Our interest lies in the exploratory process we usually call practice, and more particularly the learning of movement patterns. Movement skill learning considered as a particular instance of exploratory behavior possesses some similarities to the above behavior domains but at the same time has several unique elements. Perhaps most striking is that the learner of a coordination pattern needs to assemble something *new*. Thus the exploration that evolves is limited in that not all the possible exploratory routes are initially available to the learner. This feature sets movement learning apart from activities such as homing, food foraging, visual search, and AI where usually the whole problem space is considered accessible (although with the obvious temporal and sometimes memorial limitations). Search strategies in the acquisition of coordinated movement patterns are distinguished by the discovery and assembly of a functionally appropriate movement pattern[1].

Search strategies have been broached previously in the study of action, but they have never gained prominence in theoretical notions about motor skill learning. For example, E. J. Gibson's (1969) account of children's perceptual learning gives a strong emphasis to exploratory behavior as a means to pick-up information, but this apparent search behavior employed by infants in the development of action has rarely been formalized. Similarly, a few motor learning studies (that are briefly reviewed below) have examined the trial to trial or within trial relations of the ongoing movement sequence, but by and large, the attention given to these relations, which reflect the search strategies of the learner, has been brief. One reason that the concept of search strategies has not been developed, even as an empirical venture, is that analysis of variance approaches to characterizing trial to trial motor performance fail to provide information about the process of practice. Traditional analysis procedures focus on the amount of change on some performance metric rather than *how* the change in that metric occurred over time. Consequently the search strategies utilized by the learner during practice have been consistently overlooked.

2. PREVIOUS WORK ON STRATEGIES IN MOTOR SKILL ACQUISITION

There have been a number of previous accounts of the strategies employed by learners in the acquisition of motor skills. None of these accounts have advanced the theoretical orientation to motor skill learning proposed here but they are all consistent with a methodological orientation that includes examination of the trial to trial or within trial relations of certain properties of

---

[1]Some may argue that AI procedures such as genetic algorithms fall into the same class, however the genetic algorithm is essentially a parallel search with many explorations being performed at the same time. In addition the human learning analogies of mutation, reproduction, and crossover still need to be resolved.

movement dynamics and/or the movement outcome. The following is not intended as an exhaustive review of this strategy work in motor skills, but rather an illustration of the issues that have been addressed heretofore.

Fuchs (1962) suggested that with practice learners increasingly utilize higher order derivatives of the error signal in a tracking task. For example, performers initially exert control via the positional properties of motion, but with practice they switch to control via the velocity, and eventually the acceleration components of the error signal. This learning strategy, which was dubbed the progression hypothesis, corresponded to the complementary proposal that learners regress to a lower order derivative of the error signal when they are subjected to performance stress. These findings are consistent with the notion that learners regulate different variables of movement control as a function of practice, and this general principle was labeled the progression-regression hypothesis. Fuchs (1962) did not examine *how* subjects changed control of one movement derivative to another as a function of practice or stress, but this hypothesis proposed strategic behavior on the part of the learner that included the utilization of different informational cues. Several tracking studies subsequently have been published within this framework. Franks and Wilberg (1982) and Marteniuk and Romanow (1983) also found a systematic acquisition of higher order frequency control over practice in a discrete arm movement . However, a more recent study by Stanley and Franks (1990) on a similar task failed to support these findings, suggesting an interaction with task features as reason for the anomaly.

Ellis and Wade (1968) examined the trial to trial strategy of subjects in minimizing error in a discrete timing task. They found that over trials subjects predominantly adopted what they labeled a creeping strategy, whereby error was successively minimized by approaching the target time without changes in the sign of error. A bracketing strategy, whereby subjects reduced error by also changing the sign of error from trial to trial, was rarely adopted. A similar pattern of trial to trial strategies has been shown in the developmentally disabled while performing a timing task (Wade & Craig, 1970).

Krinskii and Shik (1964) examined the search strategies used by adult subjects to identify the particular configuration of the two elbow joint angles which corresponded to the global minimum of a mapping of the form, $E = f(x,y)$, where x and y were the joint angles and E was an error value which was equal to zero at the global minimum. The value of E was presented continuously to the performer throughout the search for the minimum of the function. They found that subjects employed both global and local searches of the task space. The global searches were characterized by two limb coordination whereas the local searches near the target were characterized by one limb control. This was a preliminary study that subsequently has not been pursued systematically and the basis for, and generality of, these search relations is not well established.

Spray and Newell (1986) used time series analysis to determine the trial to trial relations of timing error under knowledge of results and no knowledge of results conditions. It was shown that the data fitted a white noise model whereby error was randomly distributed about a stationary or nonstationary mean, depending on the knowledge of results condition. Blackwell, Simmons and Spray (1991) have adopted a similar approach to the analysis of the outcome scores of a knock-down barrier task and shown that some structure (i.e., nonrandomness) exists in the trial to trial outcome scores. Moreover, this trial to trial relational structure is influenced by the nature of the practice schedule in terms of the blocked or random presentation of the varying task constraints.

The above analyses of motor learning data have all provided suggestions of strategies used by subjects in seeking a task solution. A common feature of these studies is that they all go beyond the mere analysis of the amount of performance change over time to some attempt at understanding *how* change in performance occurs. The study of strategies in motor skill acquisition has been linked a variety of theoretical interpretations of which the concept of search strategies as we elaborate here is only one approach.

3. THE NATURE OF SEARCH STRATEGIES

Before we consider what a search strategy is, it may be informative to address what might be considered the *purpose* of exploratory behavior. Gibson (1966, 1979) has emphasized that it is the invariant features of the perceptual field that provide the informational support for action. In Gibson's view this information is movement relevant in that it affords certain actions or predisposes certain effectivities. For a learner who is naive with respect to accomplishing the task at hand many invariant features of the perceptual space remain undiscovered. And, following the same line of reasoning, the naive actor has still to assemble many of the movement configurations available to a system of many degrees of freedom. Exploratory behavior, which is guided by invariants recognized by the learner, is utilized to generate additional information which in turn channels the motor sequence. As a result, the mapping of perception and action in relation to the task goal begins to be established, and with continuing practice becomes increasingly better defined. Of course this is not to say that *all* practice is *appropriate* practice (where *appropriate* is seen to distinguish practice which aids in completing the task requirements effectively), but it certainly is the case that every moment of perceiving and acting causes the mapping of the perceptual-motor workspace to become more completely elucidated.

Exploratory behavior can be manifested in many different ways, and therefore the range of strategies one may observe in the acquisition of a seemingly similar movement pattern can be qualitatively different. For example, if a learner was informed that accurate performance is imperative one would surely observe different learning strategies compared to someone who had been informed to maximize speed of performance. Similarly, emphasis on maximization of performance while at an early stage of proficiency may impair learning by influencing the form of exploratory behavior utilized by the performer (see Hanssen & Løvborg, 1990, for evidence of this in a video game task). Of course one may argue that in such situations the learners are faced with different tasks; that is, the constraints on learning are different. However, the general point is that subtle and perhaps unforeseen quantitative features of a learning situation can change qualitatively the strategies employed to explore the task space.

What then is a learner attempting to gain through this process of exploration? We stated earlier that the acquisition of a coordination pattern entails the assembly of something new. To be more precise, actions are learned to be executed with specific contextual relevance such that the relationship between action and information in that specific task context becomes a one to one mapping. An example of the exploitation of this perception-action coupling is found in the discussion of knowing by wielding (Turvey, Solomon, & Burton, 1989). As adults we are remarkably adept at knowing about parts of, and whole, *unseen* objects by wielding them. The trick is to perform the appropriate exploratory behavior in order to reveal the specific information which enables one to determine the nature of the object. As Turvey et al. identify, the person wielding the object "must effect the right transformations in order to reveal the right invariant" (p. 389). This requires the wielder be capable of assembling the appropriate "device" which exploits a learned relationship between action and tissue deformation.

Search strategies as we use the term here reflect the way in which the perceptual-motor workspace is explored to solve a particular motor problem or task goal. A search strategy is identified by some qualitative feature of the pathway taken through the perceptual-motor workspace. In essence it characterizes the search (choice of path) through a multidimensional state space that maps perception to action consistent with the constraints of the task goal (Shaw & Alley, 1985). Search strategies in biological systems are also conducted in a nonstationary workspace. This is because the perceptual-motor workspace is continually evolving even in the predictable external environment of what Poulton (1957) termed closed skills. Indeed, not only is the workspace nonstationary, but as we will subsequently justify, location and trajectory in the space determines what is perceived by the organism. Information is, therefore, specific to the ongoing interaction of the organism and environment. Thus, the study of search strategies in biological systems presents some unique problems, many of which, are manifest in the study of movement control and skill acquisition (Gel'fand & Tsetlin, 1962, 1971). Before discussing in more detail the identification of search strategies in motor skill acquisition we briefly outline the notion of the perceptual-motor workspace and its link to search strategies.

4. SEARCH IN THE PERCEPTUAL-MOTOR WORKSPACE

The perceptual-motor workspace concept is an integral part of the ecological approach to perception and action (Gibson, 1979; Kugler & Turvey, 1987; Turvey & Kugler, 1984). It is the dynamic interface between the informational flows arising from perception and the kinetic flows arising from action. These perceptual and action flow fields are viewed as complementary in that informational flows can channel forces, and force flows can channel the information that arises from kinematics. It is the increased task relevant mapping of the perception and action flow fields that reflects learning (Shaw & Alley, 1985).

Information in the perceptual field specifies action properties such as throwable, graspable and walkable, in addition to ordinal modifiers of action such as 'closer to', 'further away', and 'time to contact'. Thus, a significant element of motor skill acquisition is perceptual learning, that is learning to pick-up the task relevant information that is available in the perceptual environment. In a complementary fashion, the learner organizes through practice a coordination mode that satisfies the task demands. Coordination modes reflect the organization of the many degrees of freedom over the variety of levels of analysis of the system. It is the invariant properties of the coordination mode that, to varying degrees according to the local task constraints, define the action (Newell, 1985).

Bernstein (1967) proposed that motor learning is a reflection of the gradual release of the ban on the degrees of freedom of the system. This intuition is operationalized within the ecological approach to motor learning by learners on the one hand gradually picking up more information from the environment relative to the kinematic flows of the perceptual field, and on the other hand, incorporating more degrees of freedom of the force field into the coordination mode. Motor learning is the perceptual-motor act of learning to coordinate (map) the perceptual invariants with the action invariants (Fowler & Turvey, 1978; Shaw & Alley, 1985).

Practice is a central feature of motor skill acquisition. In effect, practice is the operationalization of the ongoing search through the perceptual-motor work space to map the informational flow field with the force flow field consistent with the task demands. The flow fields are nonlinear nonstationary manifolds that are organized by the equilibrium and gradient regions of attractor spaces. Motor learning, therefore, can be characterized as a search through the attractor regions that constrain the perceptual and action flow fields (Newell et al., 1989). As the resultant coordination mode is an emergent property of the functional (function of functions) that constrains both the perceptual and action functions (Shaw & Alley, 1985) it is difficult a priori to give priority to either information or dynamics in the search process.

Twenty years ago Gel'fand and Tsetlin (1972) classified exploratory behavior according to its *global* or *local* nature. These terms are familiar in assessment of AI search procedures, where the aim often is to create a search procedure which is global enough such that the global minimum (if the algorithm is one for minimization) can be located, but oftentimes with optimal speed. Many search procedures fail by being trapped by local minima, and as a state space grows in dimensions, the likelihood of failure in realizing the task criteria grows. Human performers are not immune to this localization problem. If we accept the idea that there is an optimal solution to the movement problem at hand (albeit context dependent), then we can draw the analogy that many performers achieve a certain level of expertise only to fail at making the next progression. We would argue that part of the problem is a reflection of the limitations of that performer's search strategy, in that the performer becomes stuck in a local solution, and the search proceeds only within that locale. Whereas, in fact, a global change in their location in the perceptual-motor workspace is required to further enhance performance.

The perceptual-motor workspace itself is continually changing throughout due to the influence of learning, fatigue, development and many other factors. It should also be understood that with the evolution of the space it may be necessary for the performer to invoke a change in search strategies. Thus search strategies through the workspace cannot be considered independent of the layout of the workspace. These elements lead to a number of intriguing theoretical and practical questions. For example should an instructor/coach/teacher be teaching search strategies as well as the problem solution? Are there times (or locations in the workspace) when global exploration is more appropriate than local (and vice versa)? Doing is by its nature exploration, but is it always beneficial? As ones level of proficiency changes are there new search strategies that become more appropriate? While these questions remain unanswered the theoretical and empirical orientation we are advocating in this chapter would seem to provide a basis for a principled approach to realizing their solution. We now turn to a general consideration of search procedures as they have been identified in biological and artificial systems.

5. IDENTIFICATION OF BEHAVIORAL SEARCH STRATEGIES

When identifying and/or classifying search strategies in either biological or artificial systems a major challenge is to distinguish the appropriate dimension, or dimensions, along which to characterize the search. Before presenting the approach we are pursuing it is worth briefly examining existing attempts at the categorization of search behavior from a number of domains. Again, the emphasis of the synthesis of each category is representative rather than exhaustive of the respective approaches taken to date.

5.1. Homing behavior and food foraging

Descriptions of homing behavior and food foraging strategies often utilize geometrical forms such as spirals, and distributional accounts of both the directional changes and distance covered prior to a direction change. Implicit in this approach is an in depth knowledge of the topology of the work space. However, even then the description may be incomplete due to undiscovered informational properties which the animals may utilize to guide the search. Nevertheless, descriptions of the search behavior often are in terms of systematic (geometrical) progressions interspersed with random changes. Considerable effort has been directed at determining optimal search patterns for animals, and many natural observations appear close to this ideal (Hoffmann, 1983a,b). A number of the optimization models appear peculiar to the constraints present in the foraging and homing context. However, an interesting feature with more general appeal is the way homing insects will consistently return to the starting point - a point of reference perhaps, which serves as an origin for the search space geometry?

5.2. Cognitive problem solving

When considering search strategies in the domain of cognitive problem solving a foundational effort is the work of Newell and Simon (1972). Rather than attempt a brief summary of their extensive work, we note one interesting issue they discuss is that of isomorphic problem spaces. Their conception of a problem space is similar to what we describe as a task space, and they express a similar sensitivity to the problem of the performer's interpretation of this problem space. Quite often a performer will assess a task problem in a way contrary to the experimenter's description of the space that appears to define the problem. This disparity creates considerable difficulty when attempting to describe search behavior in terms of the task space! While Newell and Simon make the argument that more often than not a performer's understanding precedes search, we would argue that this relation is reflective of a circular process. As the task space becomes more complex in terms of the number of dimensions and variations in the attractor type, the more the performer's understanding will change as a function of search behavior.

Rasmussen (1986) proposed two forms of search utilized in diagnostic problem solving. The first was described as a topographic search in which diagnosis would proceed via serial testing of components compared to a reference of correctness which the individual had formulated a priori. The second form described as a symptomatic search would proceed by testing of hypotheses created using a modified model relative to the symptoms and the measurements performed. While the former strategy can very often rapidly identify the solution to the problem, in the long term the latter strategy proves to be more robust for realizing a given performance outcome.

Norman (1983) addressed the development of search strategies in cognitive problem solving in terms of a hill-climbing strategy. The performers were asked to search for the X,Y location which corresponded to a Z value of 10 000 arbitrary units, where Z = f(X,Y). After each change in X and/or Y the new value of Z was presented to the performer. The functions determining the relation of Z to X and Y were inverted elliptical parabaloids of the form,

$$\frac{Z}{c} = \left(\frac{X}{a}\right)^2 + \left(\frac{Y}{b}\right)^2$$

where a and b were constants determining the lengths of the axes and c was a scaling constant. Although Norman claimed many strategies could be utilized in solving this task he identified four which were typically used, namely, alternating univariate optimization, alternating step optimization, simultaneous multivariate optimization, and pattern search. These 4 strategies incorporate both the actions of the performer and the relation of the actions to the information that is generated. Norman's classification procedure was greatly facilitated due to explicitly knowing the function mapping X and Y to Z. In other words the topology of the workspace was explicitly defined a priori, a strategy that we have utilized in our approach to considering the acquisition of motor skills.

These examples of search behavior in human cognitive solving problems are sufficient to point up some of the key issues in characterizing effective and efficient search strategies. We close this section with a list of some of these issues: (1) what is the relation between the workspace that bounds the search and the strategy of search itself; (2) what factors contribute to an ambiguity between an extrinsic experimenter description of the space and an intrinsic subject based perception of the space; (3) is there a generic definable set of search strategies used by humans in searching biological workspaces; (4) is the search strategy used dependent on the layout of the workspace; (5) does the type of search strategy used vary with the amount of practice on the task and the level of expertise of the performer. These issues are germane to search behavior in all knowledge domains and tasks of human endeavor.

5.3. Perception-action

Norman (1983) had a priori knowledge of the workspace layout in his cognitive problem solving task. This experimental strategy is also useful in identifying search strategies in the acquisition of coordination and consequently turns our attention back to the formulation of the perceptual-motor workspace. As we have suggested previously (Newell et al., 1989) "...the description of exploratory behavior through the perceptual-motor workspace must be complementary to the description of the workspace" (p. 103). But how might we go about operationalizing this proposal?

Given that we have, at best, only a partial description of a performer's action space, and similarly limited knowledge with respect to those informational properties which a performer will utilize, the description of search behavior during the acquisition of coordination movement patterns poses quite a challenge. The investigations of Turvey et al. (1989) on knowing by wielding provide an excellent example of the form of perception-action mappings utilized by competent performers. In particular the event characterizing the identification of a wielded object's features is defined over the relation of a particular action (transformation) giving rise to the appropriate informational invariant. However, is it the case that the performer learning the mapping of transformations and invariants is always operating on the same dimensions which will be used for successful performance? Perhaps the problem can be realized more clearly when one considers learning to juggle, ride a bicycle, or walk. In the case of juggling, one would only be considered to be juggling when at least one (and preferably several) complete cycles of juggling were attained. Presumably, if the true novice (who can only pass and catch one or two balls) is not juggling part of the problem lies in an inappropriate mapping of information and action. What is the mapping, or along what dimension of the perceptual-motor workspace is the activity of the beginner organized? This issue is certainly not new and suggests the inappropriateness of carte blanche use of expert models for learners of perceptual-motor skills.

Gel'fand and Tsetlin (1962, 1971) described three general classes of search behavior which were blind search (requiring no memory), local search (continuous) and nonlocal search (discontinuous). Each of these three methods have certain advantages and disadvantages for locating a function minimum. In a blind search only a single value of the function is evaluated at a time with reference to the most recent previous evaluation. The lower of the two is maintained and matched to the next evaluation which is picked either at random or through a serial order move. Thus the intrinsic organization of the function is not exploited at all, and the search is often time intensive. In contrast, the various methods of local search are locally continuous and evaluate small regions of the workspace. However, a solely local method can easily fail to identify the global solution in a workspace which has many local solutions. Finally, the nonlocal search methods are characterized by discontinuous or intermittent searches which permit considerably more of the workspace to be explored in a given amount of time. Nevertheless, the discontinuous nature of the nonlocal search leaves open the possibility of bypassing an attractor region, which is why this search method is often combined with a local search method. Essential to classifying behavioral search in the terms described by Gel'fand and Tsetlin is a description of the work (state) space in which the search will proceed, and also (if possible) the gradient layout of the state space (Newell et al., 1989). This demands that the impact of the inherent nonlinearities of the perception-action system be determined, and only then will continous and discontinuous regions of the workspace be differentiated.

Having formulated the problem of describing the learning process in terms of search strategies we will briefly describe our approach to investigating such. In order to reduce the complexity of the problem somewhat we initially elected to pursue the method of Krinskii and Shik (1964) described above. This approach facilitates the description of the workspace by allowing an a priori definition of a mapping of the error information dynamic to the action dynamic. Of course this does not specify the complete perceptual-motor workspace, but through a careful choice of tasks, and the utilization of existing knowledge on action dynamics, we expect to be in a position to develop an operational description of the search process. In attempting to identify general search behavior we are pursuing analyses of action states, informational states, and the interaction of the two with each other in relation to the intrinsic features of the workspace. For the analysis of the action states we have developed a scheme to categorize coordination modes based on the investigations of Kelso and colleagues on stable modes of coordination in bimanual activity (see Kelso 1990 for a summary of this work). In the simple error reduction tasks that we have constructed, the informational states of importance more than likely include points of inflexion in the error history. Fowler and Turvey (1978) proposed the rate of error change as salient information, and that perhaps some threshold value of this rate would determine the point at which the coordination mode should be changed. Finally, by relating the error information to action via a known mapping we can add or remove implicit features of the mapping, permitting an assessment of their influence on exploratory behavior. Up to now, these features include the joint displacement--error gain, symmetry of the gradient layout, and the number of partial local minima in the mapping of joint space motion and error information.

6. SEARCHING FOR SOLUTIONS IN MOVEMENT COORDINATION FUNCTIONS

In this section we briefly report some data drawn from a series of experiments based on the Krinskii and Shik (1964) protocol. We chose to extend the Krinskii and Shik protocol because it provided a convenient method of addressing several issues emerging from the perceptual-motor workspace based consideration of motor learning. The basis of each experiment was a function of the form E = f(x,y), where x and y represented a measured joint angle and E scaled to the distance away from the global minimum of the function. The performers were instructed to minimize E as quickly as possible by manipulating the joint angles being monitored. In the first series of experiments performers were required to solve the problem using the elbow joints only (see McDonald & Newell, 1991, for a complete account of these data). In a subsequent investigation we had performers use either the two wrists (motion in the flexion-extension axis), the elbow joint and the wrist joint of the dominant limb, or the two axes of the wrist joint in the dominant limb, to search for the function minimum (see McDonald, Oliver, & Newell, 1991 for a complete account of these data).

Briefly, the performers were placed in a starting limb configuration (usually one combination of flexion and/or extension across the two anatomical search axes) which caused E to be at a maximum. E was continuously displayed to the performers via a VDT in the form of a vertically fluctuating error bar which would disappear when zero error (the function minimum) was attained. The goal was to identify the appropriate anatomical configuration (in the two appropriate axes) which corresponded to zero error. Figure 1 illustrates the experimental setup.

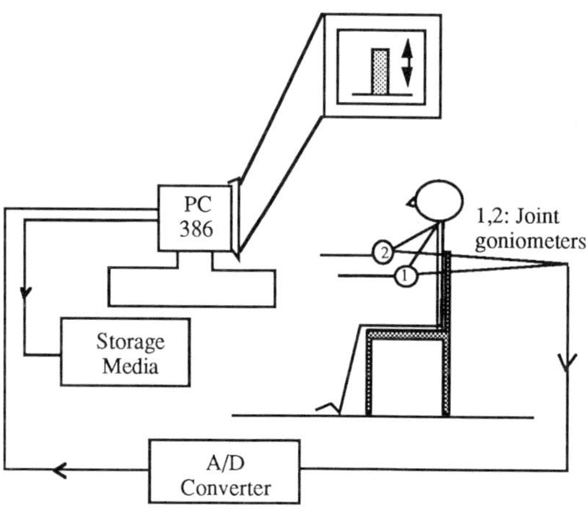

Figure 1. Joint angle displacement was monitored using goniometers interfaced to a PC386 computer. Changes in joint angles were monitored in real time in order to present on line error information in the form a vertically fluctuating error bar.

The solution to this task was a static joint configuration defined over two axes, which may appear at first pass to be a trivial exercise for the learner. However, to attain this static configuration it was necessary to coordinate movement in the two joint axes in order to minimize E. The advantage provided by the Krinskii and Shik protocol was that the mapping of action to information was explicitly defined a priori. Thus, a gradient field was defined via the function f(x,y), and while this was known to the experimenter, it was only revealed to the performer through movement based exploration.

Our analysis of learning and performance in this task is guided by our attempt to understand three functions of the behavior. The first is the nature of the error or information function over the trial duration. A particular question is whether there is a generic set of rules that subjects operate on in the information signal? The second is the nature of the joint space coordination function over the trial duration. Again, a particular question is whether there is a generic set of coordination and control rules that subjects use to solve the motor problem. The third is the mapping of the perceptual (information) function and the action (joint space) function over the trial duration. In general, as an analysis tactic, we convert the quantitative error and joint space information into qualitative events. It is the relation of these perception-action events over the practice trials that will reveal the nature of the search through the perceptual-motor workspace. Figures 2, 3, 4, and 5 illustrate examples of the trajectory generated by the joint angle changes, and the associated error time history, for each of the anatomical combinations we examined.

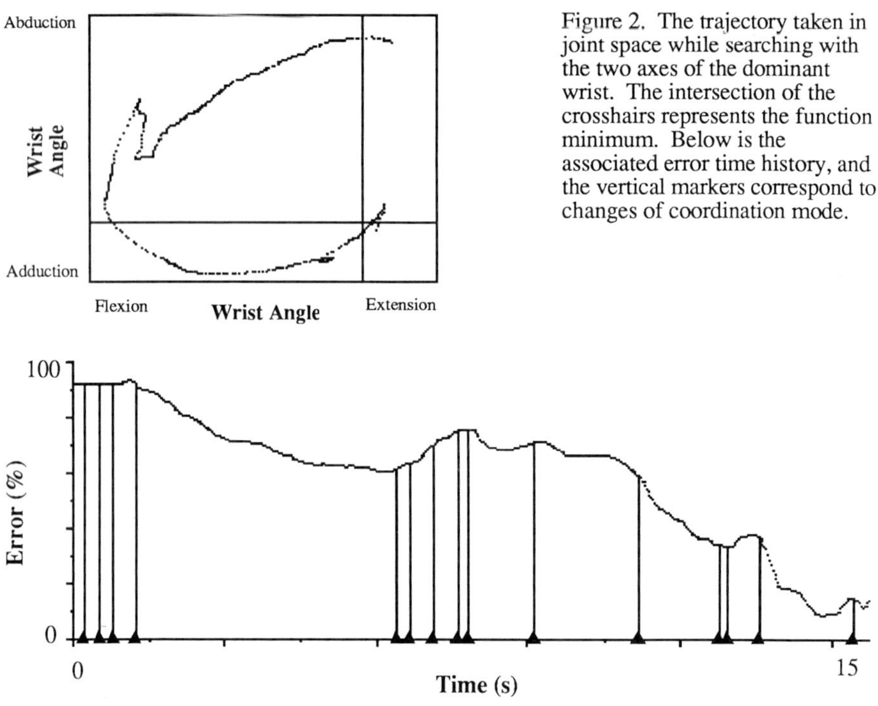

Figure 2. The trajectory taken in joint space while searching with the two axes of the dominant wrist. The intersection of the crosshairs represents the function minimum. Below is the associated error time history, and the vertical markers correspond to changes of coordination mode.

6.1. Joint space analyses

An important element in describing movement learning is the form of the limb assemblies. In the experimental situation we have described there was no redundancy in the relation of joint configuration to task solution. Nevertheless, the process of attaining the configuration could proceed in many different ways (recall the four methods Norman, 1983, described in hill climbing search). One element of our analysis is therefore directed at examining the distribution of coordination modes and transitions between coordination modes in single limb and dual limb motion. In fact we assessed joint coordination in terms of 9 possible categories (modes), which are flexion or extension in one or the other of the axes in question, and combinations of flexion and/or extension when both joints are moving together. These coordination mode categories are not determined as precise phase relationships, rather they are based on whether one or both joint angles are changing, and in which direction. Based on the differential stability of certain coordination modes (cf. Kelso, 1990), we anticipated that even though the extrinsic timing demands on coordination are not explicit, the intrinsic action constraints would impinge on the choice of coordination mode, as well as determining the distribution of mode transitions.

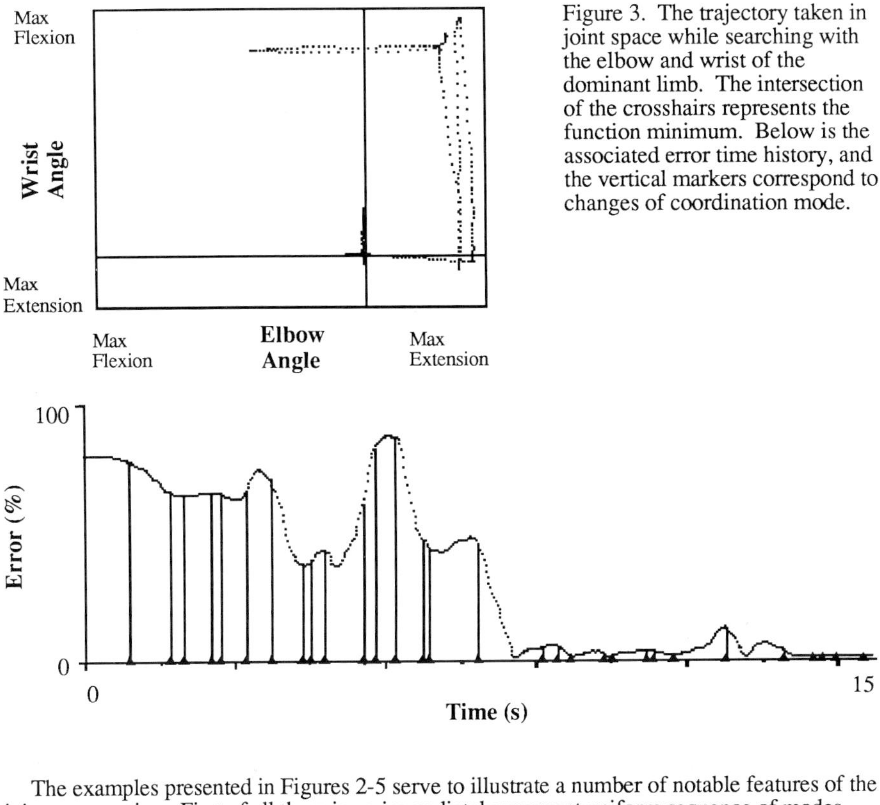

Figure 3. The trajectory taken in joint space while searching with the elbow and wrist of the dominant limb. The intersection of the crosshairs represents the function minimum. Below is the associated error time history, and the vertical markers correspond to changes of coordination mode.

The examples presented in Figures 2-5 serve to illustrate a number of notable features of the joint space action. First of all there is no immediately apparent uniform sequence of modes which performers use to locate the task solution. There are cases of both dual limb (indicated by diagonal portions of the trajectory) and single limb motion (indicated by trajectory segments parallel to the axes), both at the beginning and the end of the search. However, it does appear that the anatomical combination has some impact on the form of the trajectory through the workspace. This is noticed particularly when contrasting the dual-axis search using one joint (wrist, seen in Figure 2) to the two joint elbow-wrist search (Figure 3). The curved nature of the dual-axis wrist search suggests relatively sophisticated coordination in this joint complex, whereas the orthogonal nature of the elbow-wrist search indicates a series of single joint movements. While the dual wrist trajectory seen in Figure 4 demonstrates both single and dual limb motion, it should be noted that occasional curved and orthogonal search trajectories were exhibited in all the anatomical combinations.

These data suggest that anatomical factors, such as the nature of the particular biomechanical degrees of freedom to be coordinated, channel the search behavior by providing constraints on the joint space output. This feature occurs even though the task space defined across the conditions is consistent and the actual number of biomechanical degrees of freedom to be regulated is the same. On the error time history shown in Figures 2-5 we have indicated the points in time at which a change in coordination mode occurred. This analysis procedure provides us with an event series of the coordination modes, and mode changes, over each trial. We are seeking ways to determine the structure of this coordination mode event series and how it links to the structure in the changes of error magnitude.

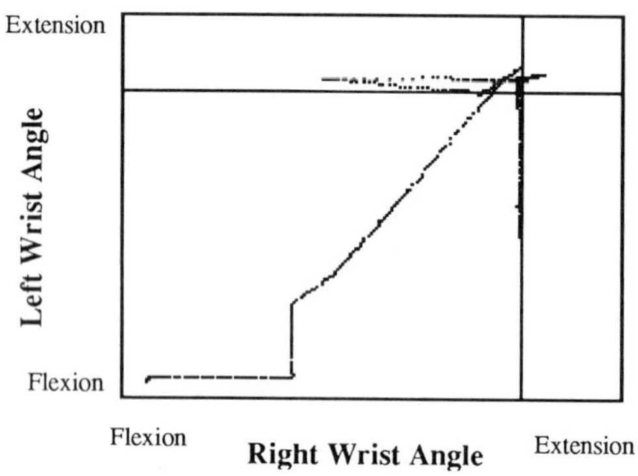

Figure 4. The trajectory taken in joint space while searching with the wrists of both the dominant and nondominant limbs. The crosshairs represents the function minimum. Below is the associated error time history, and the vertical markers correspond to changes of coordination mode.

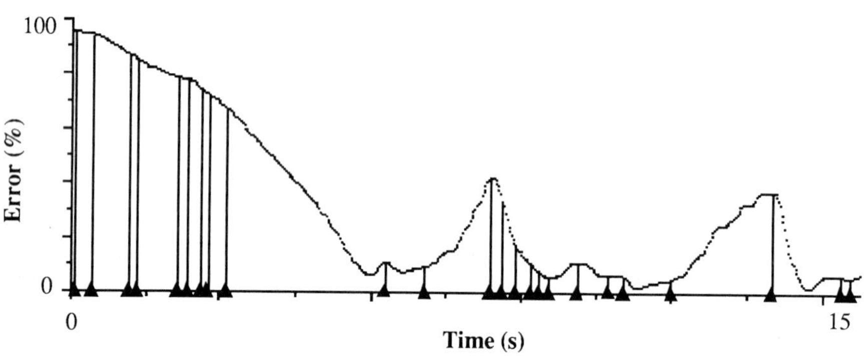

The metric we have chosen to describe the actions of the performer is by no means appropriate for all tasks. One factor that should be apparent from the discussion in this paper is that the appropriate metric for the description of search strategies is task dependent and will therefore be identifiable with the functional requirements of the task expressed in performer based terms. The use of the joint space analysis in this instance is expedient in that the task solution is directly expressible in this space.

6.2. Error information analyses

In order to approach an understanding of the search process which is expressed over the perception-action cycle we need also to examine the *form* of the information utilized by performers. Of particular interest is whether the structure of the informational space influences the search through the workspace and subsequently the resultant motor performance. As we acknowledged earlier we are not in the position of being able to completely describe the perception-action workspace, yet by constructing a known mapping of action and error information (the task space) an important part of the workspace is elucidated. In the companion paper, Newell et al. (in press), we provided some examples of how the nature of the task space, in terms of symmetry, gradient and number of local partial minima influenced performance in predictable ways. Here we broach the question of whether learners directly use the information drawn from the layout of the workspace to structure the search through the space.

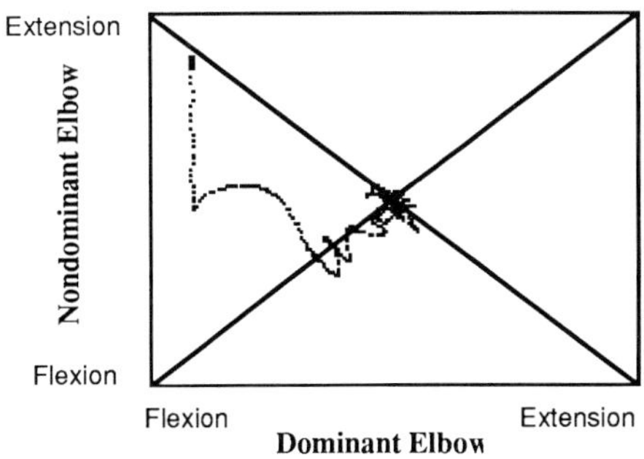

Figure 5. The trajectory taken in joint space while searching with the two elbow joints. The intersection of the crosshairs represents the function minimum. Below is the associated error time history. The vertical markers correspond to changes of coordination mode, and the crosses with dotted lines identify local minima crossings.

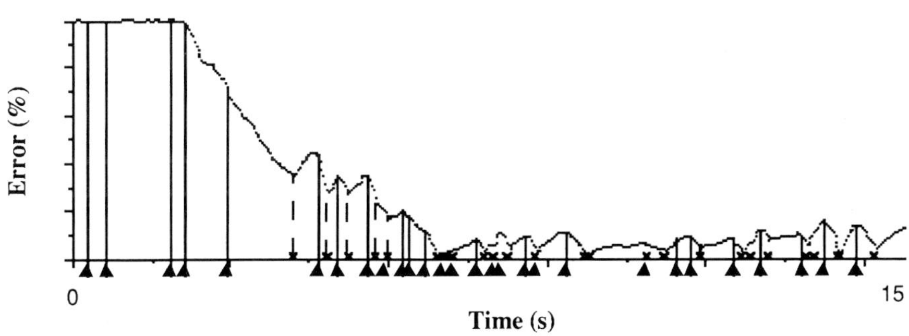

In Figure 5 an example is provided of a search through a function which could be described as an inverted pyramid, in that there are 4 partial local minima that provide discontinuities to the relation between change in joint relations and error. In this example, once the search trajectory of the subject makes contact with the partial local minima, the subject uses this intrinsic feature of the function as a guide to the global minimum. This is an illustration of a subject using a qualitative property of the environment to guide action as suggested by Gibson (1966, 1979). Not all subjects use this search strategy, and those who demonstrate this search pattern do not always repeat the strategy from trial to trial, or condition to condition.

The error profile over time can also be qualitatively analyzed in terms of events, in a fashion similar to that outlined above for the joint activity. Again, the motivation for adopting this description is to attempt to approach an expression of the continuous error history in terms of *informative* features. A well known example of an informational quality is the variable tau. Tau emerges from the flow pattern of the visual field and is an extremely informative feature of the optic array. By describing the error information in a manner similar to the action space description one establishes the foundation for an integrative analysis of information and action.

6.3. Perception-action analyses

The error time history illustrated in the lower portion of Figures 2-5 include temporal indications of the coordination mode changes. Figure 5 also contains indications of when the trajectory crossed a partial local minimum in the workspace. One might expect few mode changes while error continues to decrease at a suitable rate, and a high number of mode changes while error is increasing. In fact Figure 5 illustrates a reasonably strong correlation of error maxima to mode changes, and a similar correlation of error minima and partial local minima crossings. We are currently investigating this relationship of action and information in terms of an evolving series of events.

As a performer becomes more familiar with the action-information mapping one would expect a more orderly sequence to this series. In effect we would have a behavioral indication of the perception-action cycle being established over time. We suspect this cycle will also be modulated by the constraints brought to bear through the particular biomechanical degrees of freedom used, as we alluded to in section 6.1. In addition, Scholz and Kelso (1990) have presented evidence for differential switching times when changing coordination modes, hence we anticipate certain preferred mode transitions. This factor will impact on the evolution of the search trajectory by making certain directional changes more likely than others.

In section 6.2 we discussed the form of the information history which is generated directly by the imposed mapping f(x,y). The different mappings we used had the effect of changing the relation of joint angle change to error fluctuation. With certain mappings, some forms of joint coordination became equivalent to a trajectory along an isocontour line, with the consequence that at certain locations of the space adopting a certain coordination mode would result in no change in error. Thus, features of the action-information mapping act to constrain certain perceptual and action relations for the realization of a specific task goal.

7. Summary

The method of investigation we have advocated in this paper is intimately bound to the determination of an appropriate frame of reference for characterizing the perceptual-motor workspace. By attaining such a determination of the workspace the structure in exploratory behavior should become apparent. In the context of the acquisition of coordination the search strategy is the operationalization of the search for the solution to the perception-action coordination function. In essence, search strategies characterize the process of practice in motor skill acquisition.

8. REFERENCES

Bernstein, N. (1967). *The coordination and regulation of movements*. New York: Pergamon.

Blackwell, J. R., Simmons, R. W., & Spray, J. A. (1991). Time series analysis of knowledge of results effects during motor skill acquisition. *Research Quarterly for Exercise and Sport, 62*, 10-17.

Ellis, M. J., & Wade, M. G. (1968). Inter-trial response strategy in operative time estimation. *Psychonomic Science, 11*, 203.

Fowler, C. A., & Turvey, M. T. (1978). Skill acquisition: An event approach with special reference to searching for the optimum of a function of several variables. In G. E. Stelmach (Eds.), *Information processing and motor control* (pp. 1-40). New York: Academic Press.

Franks, I. M., & Wilberg, R. B. (1982). The generation of movement patterns during the acquisition of a pursuit tracking task. *Human Movement Science, 1*, 251-272.

Fuchs, A. H. (1962). The progression-regression hypothesis in perceptual-motor skill learning. *Journal of Experimental Psychology, 63*, 177-182.

Gel'fand, I. M., & Tsetlin, M. L. (1962). Some methods of control for complex systems. *Russian Mathematical Surveys, 17*, 95-116.

Gel'fand, I. M., & Tsetlin, M. L. (1971). Mathematical modelling of mechanisms of the central nervous system. In I. M. Gel'fand, V. S. Gurfinkel, S. V. Fomin, & M. L. Tsetlin (Eds.), *Models of the structural-functional organization of certain biological systems* (pp. 346-360). Cambridge, MA: MIT Press.

Gibson, E. J. (1969). *Principles of perceptual learning and development*. New York: Appleton Century and Crofts.

Gibson, J. J. (1966). *The senses considered as perceptual systems*. Boston, MA: Houghton Mifflin.

Gibson, J. J. (1979). *The ecological approach to visual perception*. Boston, MA: Houghton Mifflin.

Hanssen, J. P., & Løvborg, L. (1990). Hints for cognitive modelling of skill learning. *9th European Annual Conference on Human Decision Making and Manual Control*. Ispra, Italy: CEC, JRC, Inst. for Eng. and Informatics.

Hoffmann, G. (1983a). The random elements in the systematic search behavior of the desert isopod Hemilepistus reaumuri. *Behavioral Ecology and Sociobiology, 13*, 81-92.

Hoffmann, G. (1983b). The search behavior of the desert isopod Hemilepistus reaumuri as compared with a systematic search. *Behavioral Ecology and Sociobiology, 13*, 93-106.

Kelso, J. A. S. (1990). Phase transitions: Foundations of behavior. In H. Haken & M. Stadler (Eds.), Synergetics of Cognition, (pp. 249-268). Heidelberg: Springer-Verlag.

Krinskii, V. I., & Shik, M. L. (1964). A simple motor task. *Biophysics, 9*, 661-666.

Kugler, P. N., & Turvey, M. T. (1987). *Information, natural law, and the self assembly of rhythmical movement: Theoretical and experimental investigations*. Hillsdale, NJ: Erlbaum.

Marteniuk, R. G., & Romanow, S. K. E. (1983). Human movement organization and learning as revealed by variability of movement, use of kinematic information, and fourier analysis. In R. A. Magill (Eds.), *Memory and control of action* (pp. 167-197). Amsterdam: North Holland.

McDonald, P.V., & Newell, K.M. (1991). Search strategies in perceptual-motor workspaces. *Manuscript in preparation.*

McDonald, P.V., Oliver, S. K., & Newell, K.M. (1991). Anatomical constraints and perceptual-motor exploration. *Manuscript in preparation.*

Newell, A., & Simon, H. A. (1972). *Human problem solving*. Englewood Cliffs, NJ: Prentice-Hall.

Newell, K. M. (1985). Coordination, control, and skill. In D. Goodman, R. B. Wilberg, & I. M. Franks (Eds.), *Differing perspectives in motor learning, memory, and control* (pp. 295-317). Amsterdam: North Holland.

Newell, K. M. (in press). Augmented information and motor skill acquisition. In R. Daugs & K. Blischke (Eds.), *Motor learning and training*. Shornmdorf: Hofmann.
Newell, K. M., Kugler, P. N., Emmerik, R. E. A. van., & McDonald, P. V. (1989). Search strategies and the acquisition of coordination. In S. A. Wallace (Eds.), *Perspectives on the coordination of movement*, (pp. 85-122). Amsterdam: North Holland.
Newell, K. M., McDonald, P. V., & Kugler, P. N. (in press). The perceptual-motor workspace and the acquisition of skill. In J. Requin & G. E. Stelmach (Eds.), *Tutorials in Motor Neuroscience*. Boston, MA: Martinus Nijhoff.
Norman, K. L. (1983). Development of direct-search strategies in hill climbing problems. *Bulletin of the Psychonomic Society*, *21*, 469-472.
Poulton, E. C. (1957). On prediction in skilled movements. *Psychological Bulletin*, *54*, 467-478.
Rasmussen, J. (1986). *Information processing and human-machine interaction: An approach to cognitive engineering*. New York: North Holland.
Scholz, J. P., & Kelso, J. A. S. (1990). Intentional switching between patterns of bimanual coordination is dependent on the intrinsic dynamics of the patterns. *Journal of Motor Behavior*, *22*, 98-124.
Shaw, R. E., & Alley, J. R. (1985). How to draw learning curves: their use and justification. In T. D. Johnston & A. T. Pietrewicz (Eds.), *Issues in the ecological study of learning* (pp. 275-304). Hillsdale, NJ: Erlbaum.
Spray, J. A., & Newell, K. M. (1986). Time series analysis of motor learning. *Human Movement Science*, *5*, 59-74.
Stanley M. L., & Franks, I. M. (1990). Learning to organize the frequency components of a perceptual motor skill. *Human Movement Science*, *9*, 291-323.
Turvey, M. T., & Kugler, P. N. (1984). An ecological approach to perception and action. In H. T. A. Whiting (Eds.), *Human motor actions: Bernstein reassessed* (pp. 373-412). Amsterdam: North Holland.
Turvey, M. T., Solomon, H. Y., & Burton, G. (1989). An ecological analysis of knowing by wielding. *Journal of the Experimental Analysis of Behavior*, *52*, 387-407.
Wade, M. G., & Craig, T. (1970). Inter-trial response strategy of educable mentally handicapped children in learning time estimation. In G. S. Kenyon (Eds.), *Contemporary psychology of sport* (pp. 507-510). Chicago: Athletic Institute.

Tutorials in Motor Behavior II
G.E. Stelmach and J. Requin (Editors)

The role of intersegmental dynamics in infant neuromotor development

Esther Thelen[a], Ronald Zernicke[b], Klaus Schneider[b], Jody Jensen[a], Kathi Kamm[a], and Daniela Corbetta[a]

Department of Psychology, Indiana University, Bloomington, IN 47405 USA

Department of Kinesiology, UCLA, Los Angeles, CA 90024-1568 USA

Abstract

The resurgent interest in infant motor development is being fueled by theories and experimental data that emphasize the potent interactive relationships between the infant and the environment. Quantifying the complex and changing dynamics of infant movement behavior can provide a window for observing the elemental states of the sensorimotor system and how they change, the emergence of new forms of action, and the processes that engender change. We are engaged in a multidisciplinary research program that is probing the details of infant's limb movements through the combined use of kinematical, dynamical, and electromyographical analyses. Here, we highlight movement dynamics of spontaneous kicks of infants to reveal the self-organizing qualities of the developing neuromotor system, and we examine the movement dynamics in the transition from spontaneous arm waving to reaching behavior to show how intention can be mapped onto these self-organizing qualities. We summarize by commenting on the richness of infant motor development studies for providing new insights into our understanding about the complex processes of skill acquisition.

1. INTRODUCTION

In motor control and neuroscience, there is a burgeoning interest in infant and child motor development as a rich area for exploring the complex issues associated with motor coordination and control from a variety of theoretical and disciplinary perspectives (*e.g.*, Bloch & Bertenthal, 1990; Kelso & Clark, 1982; Wade & Whiting, 1986; Woollacott & Shumway-Cook, 1989). Pick (1989) suggested that this interest emanates, in part, from the growing emphases in motor development on the *control of action* and *origins of functional behavior* as postulated in the seminal works of Gibson (1979) and Bernstein (1967). Rather than focusing on an information-processing or cognitive theoretical framework for controlling behavior (*e.g.*, Piaget, 1954), the Gibsonian and Bernsteinian approaches espouse that the "... exquisite control of action by biological organisms is solved much more by a symbiotic relationship between organism and environment than by the problem-solving ability of the organism by itself" (Pick, 1989, p. 868). Reed (1982) theorized that early behavior is related to *action systems* with specific functions (*e.g.*, communication or exploration)—much as Helmholtz (1962) and others have noted that infants are intrinsically driven to experience their environment and that an infant's perceptual and motor behaviors are inextricably linked (*e.g.*, Gibson & Spelke, 1983; Hofsten, 1989; Rochat, 1989; Rochat, Blass & Hoffmeyer, 1988; Thelen & Fogel, 1986).

Human infants and children acquire motor skills over an extended period of time, and analyzing their motor behavior over these years can contribute to our understanding of motor behavior in several ways. First, we can describe the elemental state of the perception-action system that generates the early spontaneous and uncoordinated movements of infants. To the infant, such spontaneous and unskilled movements are significant because they form the neuromuscular substrate for eventual skilled movements such as reaching and locomotion. Second, by knowing the base-line status of the perception-action system, we can quantify the motor-behavioral parameters that change during infancy and the first years of childhood. And, third, we can determine the processes that engender such dramatic changes in motor behavior. In contrast to adults, with their relatively stable and well-learned movement repertoire, infants acquire motor skills in a protracted and accretional fashion which provides an informative window on the construction of novel movement forms.

These tripartite goals can, perhaps, be best realized by focusing on the period of infancy. Within the first year of life, there are enormous changes in motor coordination and control; newborns struggle simply to overcome gravity, but as toddlers, they are mobile and skillful in many functional activities. But movement studies with infants present formidable behavioral and technical problems over-and-above those encountered with adult subjects. Infants are easily fatigued, sometimes uncooperative, and must be presented with simple, age-appropriate tasks. Their behaviors are less constrained than adult subjects and, typically, are more variable and, frequently, unpredictable. Nonetheless, advances in movement analysis technology over the past decade have allowed us to begin to produce the kinematical and dynamical analyses of early-infant movements comparable to the resolution achieved in studies using adult subjects.

We are engaged in multidisciplinary research that is probing the details of infant's limb movements, through the combined use of kinematical, dynamical, and electromyographical analyses (Thelen *et al.*, in press). In this chapter, we use the dynamics of spontaneous kicks of infants to illustrate the self-organizing qualities of the developing neuromotor system, and we examine the transition from spontaneous arm waving to reaching behavior to show how intention can be mapped onto these self-organizing qualities. We finish with comments on the richness of infant motor development studies for providing new understanding about the complex processes of skill acquisition and on the implications of this work for adult motor behavior.

2. BERNSTEIN'S LEGACY

Views of motor development, traditionally, were dominated by the notion of the primacy of central nervous system (CNS) maturation in the emergence of movement patterns; changes in CNS were correlated to changes in motor function. Without question, substantial growth and dramatic changes in organization occur in the CNS during the first year of life, when basic motor skills are acquired (Goldman-Rakic, Isseroff, Schwartz, & Bugbee, 1983). But, our goal is to transcend the correlational approach to the more dynamic and interactionist perspective, first ascribed to Bernstein (1967).

Among Bernstein's many insights about the dynamics and control of motor behavior was that movement forms were not imposed on the organism by an autonomously maturing brain, but were forged into the neuromuscular system in an interactive manner with the periphery. Bernstein reasoned that the brain does not directly map functional movement forms because of the indeterminancy between the brain and the effectors. This indeterminancy arises because of: (1) anatomy (multiple degrees of freedom in multilinked limbs, numerous modes of action in the muscles, and context-dependent agonist-antagonist relations), (2) mechanically complex limb kinematics that arise from varying interactive forces during normal movements, and (3) common variance in effector nerve impulses (Edelman, 1987). How the CNS effectively controls movements—despite this indeterminancy—is one of the great puzzles facing neuroscience. Although the solution to this puzzle remains incompletely understood, generally, there is consensus that the formation of movement synergies or coordinative structures is involved.

Bernstein stated that the one of the primary problems in development is for the CNS to form stable, yet adaptive and functional movement categories in the face of such indeterminancy. Movements develop interactively and are further modulated during their execution. During various developmental stages, the CNS must adapt to new movement demands that emerge coevally with changes during growth. For example, as infants initially try to stand, they must learn to integrate the complex sensory information from muscle and tendon receptors with visual, tactile, and vestibular fields to produce the requisite muscle contractions to remain erect. These ensemble responses—in Bernstein's view—could not have been anticipated by the CNS, but must evolve with the periphery as a symbiotic and dynamic process.

3. Coordinative Synergies

Movement synergies, therefore, must be developed using the confluent information and forces in the environment, and by exploiting the motion-dependent forces that arise naturally from movements of the linked body segments (*e.g.*, Schneider, Zernicke, Schmidt, & Hart, 1989). Probing the construction of these movement synergies in adults is confounded by the learned and intentional features of adult movements, but infants lack experience in the gravitational world and must deal with gravity and the passive forces generated by their own movements long before they have effective voluntary control or can guide their movements by vision. Thus, what are the features of the adaptive dynamics that the newborn CNS possesses to deal with this complex world of forces? As infants acquire goal-directed, goal-corrected, and skilled movements, how are they able to take advantage of the intrinsic properties of the system to optimize forces and movements? Seeking answers to these questions drives our research program, and, here, we contrast spontaneous kicking, spontaneous arm waving, and early intentional reaches to show how quantitative analyses of movement dynamics can shed light on mechanisms of infant neuromotor development.

4. Dynamics of Spontaneous Infant Kicking

To characterize infants' movements, we not only collected traditional kinematical and electromyographical (EMG) data, but we also have adapted and extended techniques to quantify the dynamics of the movements. Using the inverse dynamics approach, equations of motion can be formulated in several ways, but the form we used allowed us to quantify not only how muscles and gravity influenced limb motion but also how the motion of the segments within the moving, multisegmented limb affected each other; we conducted an analysis of limb *intersegmental* dynamics. We partitioned the net torques acting at joints into torque components related to the muscular (MUS), gravitational (GRA), and inertial and centripetal forces (motion-dependent torques, MDT) acting on the moving segments (*e.g.*, Hoy & Zernicke, 1986; Schneider *et al.*, 1989; Wisleder, Zernicke, & Smith, 1990). When the passive torque components (GRA and MDT) were subtracted from the net torque, a generalized muscle torque (active and passive muscle forces and passive viscoelastic forces from the periarticular connective tissues) could be calculated—this is the torque actively controlled by the CNS.

For our dynamical analysis, we derived accelerations from spatial joint-coordinate data of freely moving limb segments. Limb kinematical data were recorded by a four-camera, optoelectronic motion analysis system (WATSMART, Northern Digital, Waterloo, ON). To provide estimates of segmental masses, centers of mass, and segmental moments of inertia, we validated a computational 17-segment model of the human infant based on detailed anthropometric measurements of each subject. These procedures are reported in detail in Schneider, Zernicke, Ulrich, Jensen, and Thelen (1990) and Schneider and Zernicke (in press).

We first examined the spontaneous kicks of three-month old infants in the supine posture. The dynamics of spontaneous kicking movements of young infants have given us some interesting, initial answers to our questions. Infant kicks, typically, consist of simple, but coordinated flexion-extension cycles of the hip, knee, and ankle joints. When behaviorally aroused, every normal infant can perform these movements, and, yet, during the first several months of life, the kicks do not appear to be goal-directed (Thelen & Fisher, 1983). Nonetheless, these kicks are commonly quite forceful and rapid (*e.g.*, cycle durations of 600-800 ms).

During the kicks, the rapid movements of the segments of the infants' lower extremities generate interactive forces between and among the thigh, leg, and foot segments. Furthermore, they must resist the pull of gravity—with its magnitude depending on the orientation of the limb. How do these potentially formidable forces influence an infant's ability to control the kicking movement? How does the CNS modulate muscle contractions in the context of these rapidly changing interactive forces? By focusing on infants, we are able to investigate the intrinsic features of the neuromotor system—before the acquisition of significant voluntary control.

The angular displacements of the hip, knee, and ankle joints of a single, representative kick are shown in Figure 1A. In this kick, the hip and knee flex and extend essentially in unison, while the ankle lags behind. This relatively simple movement, however, is produced by relatively complex dynamics (Fig. 1B). To facilitate our explanation of those complex dynamics, here (Fig. 1B), we combined the separate motion-dependent torque components that affect motion at the hip (*i.e.*, foot, leg, and thigh inertial and centripetal forces) into a summed, motion-dependent torque (MDT). On the same time scale as the accompanying kinematics (Fig. 1A), we illustrate three torque components (MUS, GRA, MDT) that interact to produce the net joint torque (NET) that causes first hip flexion and then hip extension.

Throughout the kick, the gravitational torque tends to produce hip extension (extensor torques are shown as positive values in Fig. 1B). At the beginning of the kick, the MDT is an extensor torque—changing to a flexor (see ≈ 0.2 s, Fig. 1B), an extensor (≈ 0.4 s), a flexor (≈ 0.5 s), an extensor torque (≈ 0.6 s). Muscle torque (MUS), which is controllable by the nervous system, is modulated in response to the passive torques (GRA, MDT). The MUS torque tends to flex (negative torque in Fig. 1B) the hip at the start of the kick and, thus, counteracts the hip-extensor influence of GRA and MDT. When the MDT torque becomes flexor (≈ 0.2 s) it combines with MUS—just prior to the reversal of hip motion (see ≈ 0.25 s, Fig. 1A)—to counterbalance the extensor effect of GRA. During the latter part of the kick (≈ 0.6 s), the MDT returns to an extensor torque to combine with GRA—counteracted by the MUS flexor torque. Thus, MUS torque is modulated to *resist* the hip-extensor effect of gravity and to *adjust* to the changing dynamics of the summed motion-dependent torques.

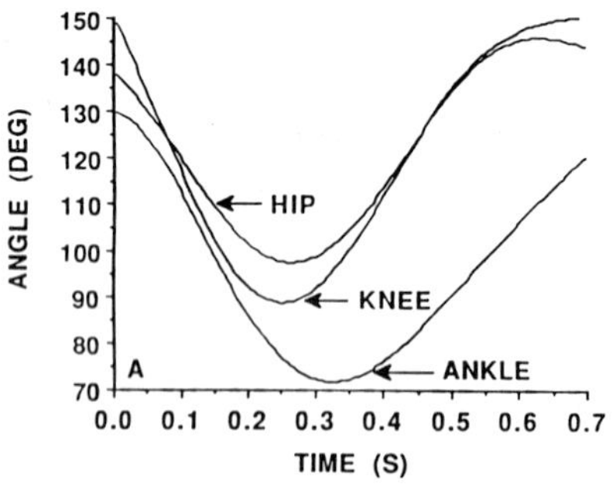

Figure 1A.

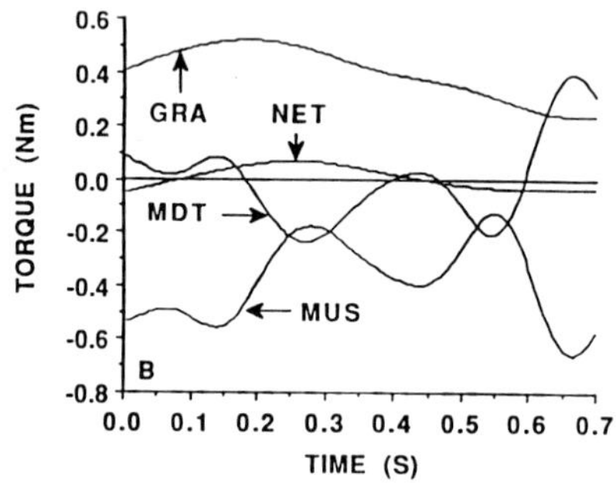

Figure 1B.

The movement trajectory of the foot is qualitatively smooth as these forces interact to produce the kick. The greatest muscular torques are needed at the start and end of the kicking motion; first to overcome the inertia of the limb and combat gravity and later to slow and stop the downward motion of the limb at the end of the kick. Minimal MUS flexor torque, however, is needed as the hip reverses from flexion to extension (see ≈ 0.25 s, Fig. 1B), as the MUS torque is modulated to permit GRA to start the extension phase of the kick. The overall picture is one of context-sensitive control of muscular torques.

To probe the context-sensitivity of these dynamics, we examined a population of kicks from 3-month old infants (Jensen, Ulrich, Thelen, Schneider, & Zernicke, submitted; Schneider *et al.*, 1990). These kicks were recorded with the infants in different torso orientations—supine, 45 degrees, or vertical. At each of the three orientations, infants readily performed kicks across wide ranges of motion and intensity (vigor). Some kicks were single events, while others were grouped as cyclic kicking movements.

Regardless of movement intensity and torso inclination, all kicks displayed a decisive hip reversal; hip flexion stopped, and extension began. But how did the infants accomplish this reversal in the context of varying kick vigor (Schneider *et al.*, 1990) and different gravitational environments (Jensen *et al.*, submitted)? To answer this, we examined the active and passive torques (peak torques, extensor impulses) just prior to hip reversal. We found, not unexpectedly, that the combinations of torques that reversed the leg were specifically dependent on context. In the supine posture, the vigor of the kick altered the forces that produced hip reversal. In supine nonvigorous kicks as in the other postures, hip reversal was principally a function of GRA. But when the infant kicked vigorously while in the supine posture, the lower limb typically was drawn so far toward the chest that the torque component related to gravity tended to cause hip *flexion*. The MDT was also flexor and comparatively large in magnitude. In the angled or vertical posture, the lower limb was pulled downward by gravity—whether or not the kick was vigorous—and hip MUS torque tended to flex the hip, even though the hip was actually extending. In these types of kicks, the MUS contribution was appropriately flexor or extensor—depending on the combination of vigor and limb position.

These results suggested that the trajectories of infant kicks may, in part, be related to the intrinsic elastic properties of the limb muscles. Because an elastic spring is position sensitive, when it is stretched the tension or stiffness in the spring will determine the resistance offered to the stretch. If muscle stiffness is set by the CNS, the mechanical properties of muscles could give the lower limb this self-organizing quality, which we observed in the covariation of "spring force" and joint angle in the phase-plane diagrams of infant kicks (Jensen, *et al.*, submitted). Modulations in the muscle torque during a particular kick may reflect—at times—these self-adjustments.

Qualitatively, infants appear to produce these smooth and rapid kicking movements relatively easily. But how do they do it? Previously, Thelen and Fisher (1983) revealed that infants initiate kicks by strong cocontraction of flexor and extensor muscles, thus altering the stiffness of the muscles around the joints. Out of this cocontraction contest, an imbalance of forces developed to produce the initial hip flexion. No comparable phasic bursts occurred as the hip stopped flexing and started extending—consistent with our present data that portray joint reversal as typically a "passive" event produced primarily by the gravity-induced loss of momentum with concurrent modulations of the muscle torque. A simple spring-model explanation of control of these movements, however, is likely too simple an explanation, as Jensen *et al.* (submitted) also described kicks in which the spring force did not vary smoothly with the excursion of the limb, suggesting an active intervention of the CNS to change stiffness.

In summary, we learned that nonintentional kicking movements in infants could be rapid, smooth, and coordinated from a tightly modulation combination of active and passive forces in a relatively self-organizing manner that exploited the spring-like characteristics of muscles and their consequent sensitivity to a force-environment. Taking advantage of the elastic qualities of the musculo-tendinous units can an important component in the control of voluntary behavior as well (Schneider *et al.*, 1989), but these muscle qualities must also be actively tuned to task demands. In the next section, we give a preliminary account of how these movement dynamics may be tuned or modulated as the transition from a relatively non-goal-directed to goal-directed movement occurs during neuromotor development.

5. TRANSITION FROM SPONTANEOUS TO VOLUNTARY ARM MOVEMENTS

As infants acquire dexterity in reaching and grasping, they are able to rein in their uncoordinated arm waving and eventually extend their hand toward the desired object. Although directed arm extensions can be seen even in newborns under special postural and attentional conditions (Hofsten, 1982), usually it is between 3 and 4 months that voluntary directed reaches can be consistently elicited (Hofsten, 1984). We are observing the development of reaching in an intensive longitudinal study of four infants. We have tested these infants every week from the age of 3 wk in multiple situations, including toys presented by the parents, toys presented by an overhead apparatus (without the social dimension) and in social interaction with the parent (without an object present). It is this latter situation that we used to generate non-goal-directed movements. In each session, we examined the spatial kinematics of both upper extremities by simultaneously recording the three-dimensional coordinates of the two shoulders, elbows, wrists, and hands. Synchronously, we collected surface EMG data from the biceps, triceps, deltoid, trapezius, and lower back muscles. When the overall quality of the kinematical data met our established criteria, we also calculated intersegmental dynamics of the arm, forearm, and hand. For all trials, infants were seated in an armless, inclined (75°) infant-seat, with their torso snugly but comfortably secured to the backrest with a broad soft band.

The transition from spontaneous to voluntary movements is patently illustrated by trials in which the infants alternate between apparently undirected waving or "flapping" movements and actual directed—sometimes successful—attempts to touch the toy. Here, we illustrate a representative trial from a 15-wk-old boy to trace the emergence of directed reaches. In this 14-s trial, the parent presented the toy at midline, the infant flapped his arms several times, reached forward and up toward the toy, and then leaned down. Figure 2 depicts the trajectory of his right wrist (projected onto the frontal plane), with the movement starting at the lower right-hand corner of the plot (time = 9.9 s of the 14-s trial, elapsed time between successive points is 6.7 ms), starting with an initial "flap" that ends at 10.6 s, followed by movement up and to the left—with the illustrated trajectory ending at 11.4 s.

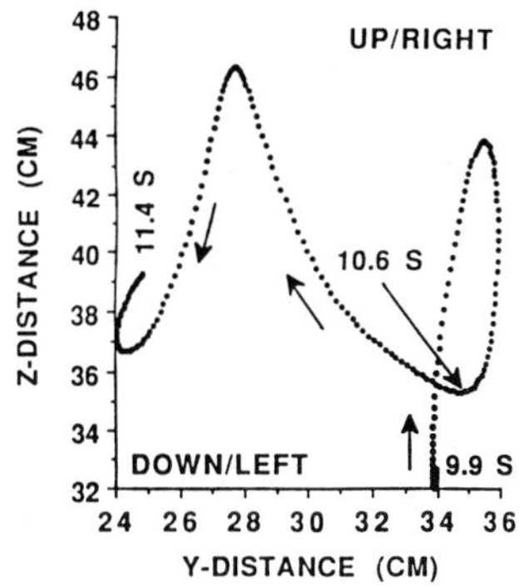

Figure 2.

Figure 3A shows the time-correlated changes in spatial angle of the elbow and shoulder (decreasing angles indicate flexion; shoulder flexion raises the limb). Again, the flap, reach, and leftward movements are apparent. At this age, infants reach by flexing and horizontally adducting the shoulder (with a relatively rigid elbow) to bring the hand up and into midline. For this movement trial, the elbow and shoulder angular velocities (Fig. 3B) are of comparable magnitudes for the flap and the reach.

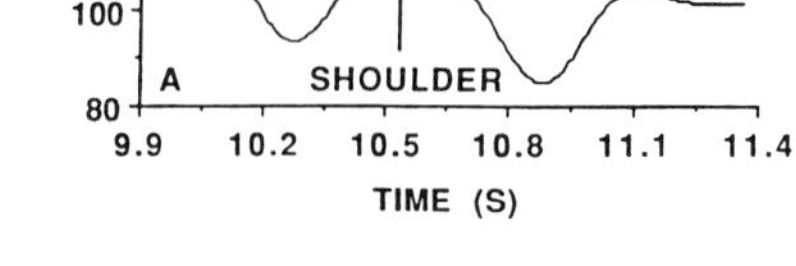

Figure 3A.

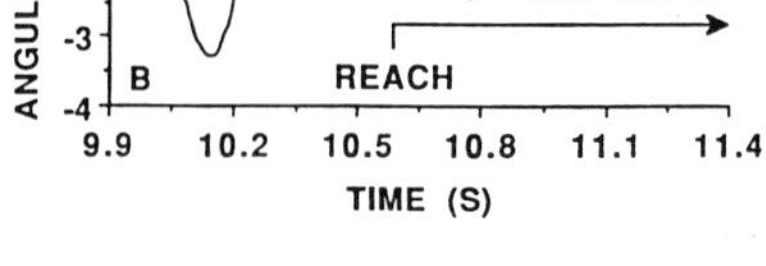

Figure 3B.

Although some of the kinematical features of the spontaneous and directed movements appear to be similar, the torque profiles were markedly different (see Fig. 4; same time base as in Figs. 2 & 3; flexor torques are positive). During the spontaneous flap, high MDT counterbalanced high MUS torques, but both torque components were damped considerably in the goal-directed reach, as was the resulting NET torque. During both activities, the gravitational component mainly tended to extend the limb.

The underlying EMG clarified some of these differences. In Figure 5—over the same time frame as the kinematical and dynamical records (9.9–11.4 s)—we present the raw EMG records from the arm, shoulder, and low-back muscle groups. Cocontraction of trapezius and deltoid initiated the reach, and triceps were activated when the limb was fully extended. Phasic reciprocal bursts of EMG were more typical of the spontaneous movements. Lower back muscles were relatively quiescent throughout this trial.

The uncontrolled flap of the limb was, undoubtedly, not directed toward a specific target. Our preliminary evidence suggests, however, that infants make the transition to goal-directed reaching early in development by several strategies. In some instances, infants tried to reach using velocities much slower than in their spontaneous movements, thus producing smaller inertial forces to control. The slower movements also increased the time available for error corrections. But most routinely we observed the marked cocontractions (Fig. 5) that stiffened or stabilized the shoulder joint against the motion-dependent torques generated by the distal segments of the upper limb.

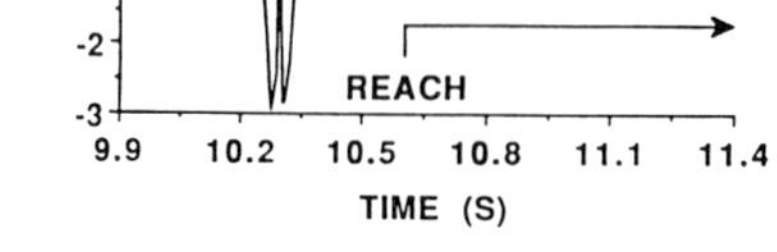

Figure 4.

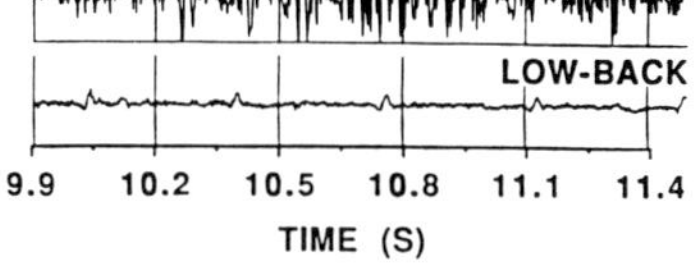

Figure 5.

In this way, the arm could be directed toward the target with a substantial velocity and with greater accuracy than if the shoulder were more compliant. Support for this hypothesis requires quantitative estimates of joint stiffness, which remain to be completed. Nevertheless, because we are only comparing spontaneous and goal-directed movements for the same infant at the same age (as flapping is transformed into reaching), we have begun to think about the requisite processes for early skill acquisition.

6. Processes of Early Skill Acquisition

An infant's neuromuscular system already displays a relatively complex dynamic organization. Proprioceptive information from sensory receptors in skin, joints, and musculo-tendinous units conveys a panoply of information to all levels of the infant's CNS. Even with spontaneous, unaimed limb movements, infants can gain a wealth of information about the properties and state of their limbs—for example, the physical-anatomical linkages, anisotropic inertial properties (Hogan, 1985); viscoelastic properties of muscles and tendons, and stretch reflexes. Before infants crawl or walk, they kick; before infants reach, they wave and flap their arms. These spontaneous movements emerge as infants become behaviorally excited, and the forms of these limb movements reflect their intrinsic organization. With such spontaneous movements, infants generate the neuromotor substrate on which control, accuracy, and intention are mapped. Obtaining precise information about the state and properties of a limb is vital for the fine control of movements (Ghez, Gordon, Ghilardi, Christakos & Cooper, in press; Hasan & Stuart, 1988; Polit & Bizzi, 1979). Accurate multijoint movements require the CNS to transform three-dimensional coordinates of a target or goal (represented in retinotopic or extrinsic coordinates) into an intricate set of commands (represented in terms of internal coordinates) that relate to the biomechanical variables of the limb (Atkeson, 1989; Ghez, *et al.*, in press; Soechting, 1989). Certainly, the excited movements of infants do not require accuracy or steadiness, but these spontaneous movements are an information-gathering bonanza for the infant.

Since Bernstein, many theorists have also proposed that exploration of the task through multimodal feedback is a process whereby reliable and efficient movements are established or selected from a larger universe of possibilities (*e.g.*, Edelman, 1987; Grossberg & Kuperstein, 1989; Kugler & Turvey, 1977). If this is true, then the infant (or adult) needs to experience success through all the perceptual modalities. It is likely that the first step in such exploration is to be able to do the task at all, which for infants, means breaking out of the cyclic waving movements of the arms or kicking of the legs. In a sense, they must interrupt the natural oscillatory dynamics by slowing or stiffening, and our early evidence suggests that they do.

As infants attempt to reach from different postures and starting positions, at different levels of energy, with their targets at different distances, sometimes moving and sometimes stationary, they are continually mapping these large perceptual spaces onto the movements they generate. By this manner they self-discover the task-specific dynamics. Studies documenting this self-discovery through multimodal exploration are a logical next step in our quest for understanding the acquisition of skill.

The dynamics data that we have and are continuing to collect on the acquisition of goal-directed movements in infants have already revealed putative mechanisms that infants may use for gaining control of their limb trajectories. At the sight of a toy, infants learn to convert their flapping movements into goal-directed reaching. Our data show that one significant first step in achieving this new level of control and accuracy is to minimize extraneous passive or motion-dependent torques in order to better guide the arm. They can achieve this minimization, for example, by increasing muscular cocontractions, decreasing velocities, or both.

These results are consistent with neural models that posit separate control of joint movement and stiffness (*e. g.*, Humphrey & Reed, 1983; Bullock & Grossberg, 1990). Bullock and Grossberg note that the form of a movement can be varied independently of the energy used to perform it; the position of a limb can be held steady despite tremendous differences in the inherent muscle tensions. Although infants' early movements may be undirected, they can vary markedly in vigor—depending on the level of behavioral excitation. Thus, even excited newborns are experiencing modulation of their limb stiffness, long before they have success with directed movements. Perhaps this modulation of limb stiffness through cocontraction is an early strategy to be recruited for voluntary control. In general, unskilled movements are performed stiffly, with considerable cocontraction. Certainly, this is obvious in new walkers (Okamoto & Goto, 1985). By interactively modulating compliance and velocity, infants can gain steadiness and accuracy, depending on the demands of the task.

Finally, we predict that after reasonable accuracy is achieved and movement categories are stable and reliable, infants will rescale their speed and compliance to become more time and energy efficient (Bullock & Grossberg, 1990). That is, they will implement the Bernsteinian-proposed strategy of exploiting—rather than fighting—the passive dynamics of the limb. Adults can be adept at using gravity, inertia, and the viscoelastic properties of the musculoskeletal system. Schneider *et al.* (1989) demonstrated the more efficient use of passive dynamics with skill by documenting these changes after adults practiced novel, rapid-arm movements. In infants, we expect that skilled reaches will use more passive dynamics and less muscle torque and cocontraction—with faster and smoother trajectories—after infants attain a reliable degree of accuracy. At what stage in the development of reaching this transition occurs remains unknown.

The integrated use of dynamical information, in combination with kinematics and EMG, is allowing us to explore processes of skill acquisition that were previously inaccessible. Developmental studies are an important complement to studies of control and coordination of practiced movements, because developmental studies are natural experiments in the processes of change. For continuing advances in infant neuromotor development, it will be essential for researchers to go beyond cursory correlations between anatomy and behavior to address both what the infant has and what the infant does to become a skilled and graceful mover in a complex world.

ACKNOWLEDGEMENTS

This research was supported by a grant from the National Institutes of Health (HD 22830) and a Research Scientist Development Award to Esther Thelen from the National Institutes of Mental Health. We thank Michael Schoeny, Dexter Gormley, Deanna Berkoben, and Jürgen Konczak for their assistance with data collection and analysis.

Address correspondence to Esther Thelen, Department of Psychology, Indiana University, Bloomington, IN 47405 USA.

REFERENCES

Atkeson, C. G. (1989). Learning arm kinematics and dynamics. *Annual Reviews of Neuroscience*, **12**, 157-183.

Bernstein, N. (1967). *Coordination and regulation of movements.* New York: Pergamon Press.

Bloch, H., & Bertenthal, B. I. (1990). *Sensory-motor organizations and development in infancy and early childhood.* Dordrecht, Netherlands: Kluwer Academic Publishers.

Bullock, D., & Grossberg, S. (1990). Motor skill development and neural networks for position code invariance under speed and compliance rescaling. In H. Bloch, & B. I. Bertenthal (Eds.), *Sensory-motor organizations and development in infancy and early childhood* (pp. 1-22). Dordrecht, Netherlands: Kluwer Academic Publishers.

Edelman, G. M. (1987). *Neural Darwinism.* New York: Basic Books.

Ghez, C., Gordon, J., Ghilardi, M. F., Christakos, C. N., & Cooper, S. E. (in press). Roles of proprioceptive input in the programming of arm trajectories. *Cold Spring Harbor Symposia in Quantitative Biology*, Vol. 55.

Gibson, E. J., & Spelke, E. S. (1983). The development of perception. In P. H. Mussen (Series ed.), *Handbook of child psychology* (Vol. 3, pp. 1-76). New York: Wiley.

Gibson, J. J. (1979). *The ecological approach to perception.* Boston: Houghton-Mifflin.

Goldman-Rakic, P. S., Isseroff, A., Schwartz, M. L., & Bugbee, N. M. (1983). The neurobiology of cognitive development. In P. H. Mussen, M. M. Haith & J. J. Campos (Eds.), *Handbook of child psychology*, 4th Ed., Volume II: Infancy and developmental psychobiology (pp. 281-344). New York: John Wiley.

Grossberg, S., & Kuperstein, M. (1989). *Neural dynamics of adaptive sensory-motor control: Expanded edition.* New York: Pergamon Press.

Hassan, Z., & Stuart, D. G. (1988). Animal solutions to problems of movement control: The role of proprioceptors. *Annual Reviews of Neuroscience,* **11**, 199-223.

Helmholtz, H. von. (1962). *Handbook of physiological optics* (Rev. ed.) New York: Optical Society of America. (Original work published 1925).

Hofsten, C. von (1982). Eye-hand coordination in newborns. *Developmental Psychology,* **18**, 450-461.

Hofsten, C. von (1984). Developmental changes in the organization of prereaching movements. *Developmental Psychology,* **20**, 378-388.

Hofsten, C. von (1989). Motor development as the development of systems: Comments on the special section. *Developmental Psychology,* **25**, 950-953.

Hogan, N. (1985). The mechanics of multi-joint posture and movement control. *Biological Cybernetics,* **52**, 315-331.

Hoy, M. G., & Zernicke, R. F.(1986). The role of intersegmental dynamics during rapid limb oscillations. *Journal of Biomechanics,* **19**, 867-877.

Humphrey, D. R., & Reed, D. J. (1983). Separate cortical systems for control of joint movement and joint stiffness: Reciprocal activation and coactivation of antagonist muscles. In J. E. Desmedt (Ed.), *Motor control mechanisms in health and disease* (pp. 347-372). New York: Raven Press.

Jensen, J. L., Ulrich, B. D., Thelen, E., Schneider, K., & Zernicke, R. F. (submitted). Posture-related limb dynamics in spontaneous infant kicking.

Kelso, J. A. S., & Clark, J. (1982). *The development of movement control and coordination.* New York: John Wiley.

Kugler, P. N., Kelso, J. A. S., & Turvey, M. T. (1982). On the control and coordination of naturally developing systems. In J. A. S. Kelso & J. E. Clark (Eds.), *The development of movement control and coordination* (pp. 5-78). New York: Wiley.

Kugler, P. N., & Turvey, M. T. (1987). *Information, natural law, and the self-assembly of rhythmic movement.* Hillsdale, NJ: Erlbaum.

Okamoto, T., & Goto, Y. (1985). Human infant pre-independent and independent walking. In S. Kondo (Ed.), *Primate morphophysiology, locomotor analyses and human bipedalism* (pp. 25-45). Tokyo, Japan: University of Tokyo Press.

Piaget, J. (1954). *The construction of reality in the child.* New York: Basic Books.

Pick, H.L. (1989). Motor development: The control of action. *Developmental Psychology,* **25**, 867-870.

Polit, A., & Bizzi, E. (1979). Characteristics of motor programs underlying arm movements in monkey. *Journal of Neurophysiology,* **42**, 183-194.

Reed, E. S. (1982). An outline of a theory of action systems. *Journal of Motor Behavior,* **14**, 98-134.

Rochat, P. (1989). Object manipulation and exploration in 2- to 5-month-old infants. *Developmental Psychology,* **25**, 871-884.

Rochat, P., Blass, E. M., & Hoffmeyer, L. B. (1988). Oropharyngeal control of hand-mouth coordination in newborn infants. *Developmental Psychology,* **24**, 459-463.

Schneider, K., & Zernicke, R. F. (in press). Mass, center of mass, and moment of inertia estimates for infant limb segments. *Journal of Biomechanics.*

Schneider, K., Zernicke, R. A., Schmidt, R. A., & Hart, T. J. (1989). Changes in limb dynamics during practice of rapid arm movements. *Journal of Biomechanics,* **22**, 805-817.

Schneider, K., Zernicke, R. F., Ulrich, B. D., Jensen, J. L., & Thelen, E. (1990). Understanding movement control in infants through the analysis of limb intersegmental dynamics. *Journal of Motor Behavior*, **22**, 493-520.

Soechting, J. F. (1989). Elements of coordinated arm movements in three-dimensional space. In S. A. Wallace (Ed.), *Perspectives on the coordination of movement* (pp.47-83). New York: North-Holland.

Thelen, E. (1989). The (re)discovery of motor development: Learning new things from an old field. *Developmental Psychology,* **25**, 946-949.

Thelen, E., & Fisher, D. M. (1983). The organization of spontaneous leg movements in newborn infants. *Journal of Motor Behavior,* **15**, 353-377.

Thelen, E., & Fogel, A. (1989). Toward an action-based theory of infant development. In J. J. Lockman & N. L. Hazen (Eds.), *Action in social context: Perspectives on early development* (pp. 23-63). New York: Plenum.

Thelen, E., Jensen, J. L., Kamm, K., Corbetta, D., Schneider, K., & Zernicke, R. F. (in press). Infant motor development: Implications for motor neuroscience. In G. Stelmach & J. Requin (Eds.), *Tutorials in motor neuroscience.* Dordrecht, Netherlands: Kluwer Academic Publishers.

Wade, M. G. & Whiting H. T. A. (1986). *Motor skills acquisition.* Dordrecht, Netherlands: Martinus Nijhoff Publishers.

Wisleder, D., Zernicke, R. F., & Smith, J. L. (1990). Speed-related changes in cat hindlimb interactive and muscular torques during the swing phase of locomotion. *Experimental Brain Research,* **79**, 651-660.

Woollacott, M., & Shumway-Cook, A. (1989). *The development of posture and gait across the lifespan.* Columbia, S. C.: University of South Carolina Press.

Tutorials in Motor Behavior II
G.E. Stelmach and J. Requin (Editors)

The Intermittent Dynamics of Coordination

J.A.S. Kelso & G.C. DeGuzman

Program in Complex Systems and Brain Sciences, Center for Complex Systems, Florida Atlantic University, Boca Raton, FL 33431

Abstract

The tendency toward phase and frequency synchronization is ubiquitous in natural and artificial systems, representing a primitive form of self-organization. But complex biological systems must balance the universal tendency to phase and frequency synchronize with the requirement to flexibly explore other coordinative states. We identify, through an experiment-theory relation , an intermittency mechanism which provides this vital mix of coherent yet flexible function. Intermittency accommodates the facts of both absolute and relative coordination in a unified way. A novel consequence of intermittent dynamics is that near critical points, the system is endowed with a 'predictive' or 'anticipatory' property.

1. Introduction

The tendency toward synchronization is common to material objects of very different natures and represents a primitive form of self-organization in nature. In biology, this tendency to phase- and frequency-synchronize is ubiquitous, appearing on many distinct levels. As a few examples, we cite the spontaneous electrical activity of motorneurons in embryo (Hamburger, 1970), cellular pattern generating circuits in vertebrates and invertebrates (Cohen, Rossignol & Grillner, 1988), chick embryo heart cells (Guevara, Glass & Shrier, 1981) and even cells in mammalian visual cortex (e.g. Eckhorn, et al. 1981; Gray et al. 1989). Phase and frequency synchronization appears to be one, maybe the chief way for complex biological systems to coordinate themselves for different functions.

The behavioral physiologist, Erich von Holst (1939/73) coined the term *absolute coordination* to describe when two or more components oscillate at the same frequency and maintain a fixed phase relation. Elsewhere, it has been possible to show that absolute coordination can be understood in detail using the concepts of synergetics and the mathematical tools of nonlinear dynamical systems (e.g. Beek, 1989; Haken, Kelso & Bunz, 1985; Kay et al. 1987; Kelso, 1984; Kelso & Scholz, 1985; Schöner & Kelso, 1988; see also Kugler & Turvey, 1987, p.258; Turvey, 1990). These methods have been extended to cover the interlimb coordination of discrete movement (Kelso, et al. 1979; Schöner, 1990) as well as a number of other experimental model systems (Kelso, 1990 for review).

Almost without exception, however, phase and frequency synchronization have been modelled in terms of asymptotic solutions of coupled nonlinear differential equations. Little attention has been paid to how a system might enter or exit such mode-locked states, namely what the underlying mechanism might be. In part, this may be because frequency and phase synchronization tend to arise spontaneously: seldom are experiments performed that actually manipulate the degree to which components may interact in this fashion. Here we present experimental results from studies in which a conflict is artificially created between sustaining a constant frequency ratio among the components and an intrinsic tendency on the part of these components to synchronize inphase or antiphase (DeGuzman & Kelso, 1989/in press; Kelso & DeGuzman, 1988; Kelso, DeGuzman & Holroyd, 1991a,b). In such situations, the system solves the problem adaptively be balancing spatial and temporal features of the pattern. We observe, for example, phase slippage between the components, the insertion of additional cycles and hopping in and out of frequency- and phase-locked patterns. Rather than absolute phase and frequency synchronization we find *tendencies* toward certain frequency ration values and *tendencies* toward in-phase or anti-phase attraction. Von Holst (1939/73) coined the terms Magnet or M-effect and *relative coordination* to describe such phenomena.

We establish the connection between less rigid, more flexible forms of coordination and *intermittency* which is a generic feature of dynamical systems near tangent bifurcations. Intermittency refers to a region around a destabilized saddle node which contains both a stable (attractive) and an unstable (repelling) direction. Typically, the system spends some time near the attractive fixed point (in the present case, a frequency and phase synchronized state) and then escapes through the unstable direction before returning via a reinjection process (Bergé, et al. 1984). Intermittency provides a mechanism for entering and exiting phase and frequency synchronized states, thus preventing the biological system from getting stuck. It may be important for vision not to get trapped in resonant, mode-locked states, an argument that applies equally well to neuronal circuits for flexible central pattern generation, coordinated action, and even cognition itself (cf. Mandell, 1983).

2. Multifrequency Coordination: The Intermittency Mechanism Revealed

a) *Attraction only at discrete points.* One of the characteristic features of coordination is that a set of events in one signal is correlated somehow with a set of events in another. Experimentally, the signals themselves may be quite different in nature; however, often they come together at easily recognizable points. For example, it is easy to see in typical records that rather different electrical events in the cat's visual cortex – single unit activities and local field potentials – are tightly coordinated for short periods of time (e.g. Gray et al. 1989; Eckhorn et al. 1988; Bressler, 1990 for review). Similarly, fine wire recordings from individual muscles are phase-locked with each other and with kinematic signals on an entirely different level of description (see e.g. Fig. 1 in Kelso, Schöner, Scholz & Haken, 1987). As a measure of coordination, provided that events such as onsets, peaks or valleys are identifiable, other features of the signals may be ignored. This, along with other evidence (e.g. Beek, 1989) suggests that biological coordination holds only at some points in the signal "trajectories" of the individual components: in between, trajectories may vary spatially (e.g. characteristic amplitudes) and temporally (e.g. characteristic periods and frequency content). In some sense, this attractive tendency to coordinate at certain points may be viewed as a manifestation of motor equivalence.

b) *Multifrequency Coordination Experiments and Results*

That the individual components may be coupled only at certain points also comes out as a dominant feature of experiments in which the frequency relations between rhythmically moving components are experimentally manipulated. In initial experiments (Kelso & DeGuzman, 1988; DeGuzman & Kelso, in press) the frequency and amplitude of one component (Left Hand) were determined passively by a torque motor while the other component (the Right Hand) actively maintained a base rhythm. Six different frequency ratios were studied: f(L):f(R)=4:3, 3:2, 5:3, 2:1, 5:2 and 3:1 over long (90 sec.) time series. More recently, we scanned the frequency ratio in ascending and descending order from just below 1:1 to just above 2:1 and *vice versa* in steps of .1 Hz. In none of the experiments was the initial phase between the components fixed, yet there was still a strong tendency for phase attraction to occur.

For present purposes we draw attention to two major effects. The first is shown in Fig. 1 which plots the relative phase (normalized to [0,1]) of the right versus the left hand for a 2:1 case. Monitoring relative phase in time we observe epochs of locking (Fig. 1a), wandering (Fig. 1b) and then locking again (Fig. 1e), often to one of the phase attractive states. Short term transitions from one mode to the other are clearly present (Fig. 1c,d).

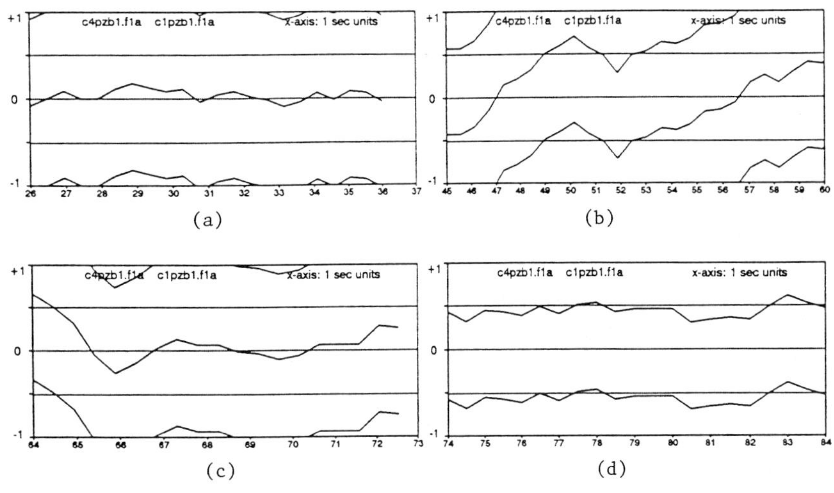

Figure 1: Relative phase of the right vs. the left hand for a 2:1 case normalized to [0.1]. For ease in viewing, a duplicate plot is added in the [-1,0] range. (a) Phase locked mode around $\phi = 0$. (b) Phase wandering. (c) and (d) Phase locking and transition from in-phase to anti-phase mode. The preference for in- phase and anti-phase indicates influence of the intrinsic dynamics.

We want to emphasize the fact that even though subjects are instructed to completely ignore the passive driving of one hand, the *tendency* to phase and frequency synchronization persists. It is clear, however, that the system is not quite stationary (even though every effort has been made to prepare it as such). Absolute coordination, interpreted as pure phase and frequency synchronization, is thus not observed here.

The second major effect occurs when the torque from the driving motor is lowered, enabling a better view of the two-way interaction between the components. Figure 2(a) presents the trajectories of the input signal used to drive the torque motor (top), the actual motion produced by the left hand (middle) and the 'free' hand producing the base frequency (bottom), when the required frequency ratio is again near 2:1. Enhancement of the peaks near inphase regions points again to the discrete nature of coordination, i.e. intermediate portions of the left hand are adjusted to sustain the natural tendency to be inphase with the right hand (indicated by the vertical lines). Occasional slips occur and an additional cycle is injected when the position of the enhanced peak extends beyond the broadened peak of the right hand (3 steps instead of 2). Figure 2(b) displays a similar plot near 2:1 from another time interval, showing the slippage effect on the right hand. This kind of modulation appears rarely and randomly near 1:1 but more frequently near 2:1, where sometimes even trains of alternating low and high amplitudes were seen.

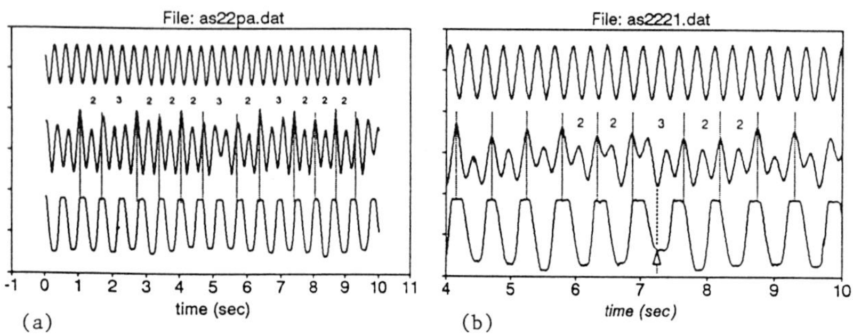

Figure 2: (a) Trajectories of the input signal used to drive the torque motor (top), the actual motion produced by the driven lefft hand (middle) and the "free" hand (bottom) when the required frequency condition is near 2:1. Enhancement of the peaks near inphase regions points to the discrete nature of the coordination, i.e. intermediate portions of the left hand trajectories are adjusted to sustain the natural tendency to be inphase with the right hand (indicated by the vertical lines). Occasional slips occur when the position of the enhanced peak extends beyond the broadened peak of the right hand (3 steps instead of 2). (b) Similar plot near 2:1 from another time interval showing the slippage effect on the right hand.

c) *The Phase Attractive Map.*

To characterize coordination in multifrequency situations in which the components synchronize at only certain event times and may not have a well defined frequency relationship, we need a local measure that characterizes time relationships between events. An often quoted measure of coordination is the relative frequency with which these events occur such as the frequency ratio. But frequency related measures are with respect to events in components taken individually, not between them, and are therefore inadequate. A better measure is the *point estimate of relative phase* calculated experimentally as

$$\phi_n = 2\pi \frac{\tau_n}{T_n} \tag{1}$$

where T_n is the peak-to-peak period of component 1 beginning at time t_o, and τ_n is the interval between that event and the peak onset of component 2.

To study how the components are coordinated in time, we examine the evolution of the phases ϕ_n. The utility of (1) for expressing coordinated behavior in terms of the evolution of ϕ_n at discrete times τ_n depends on the actual dynamics of the system. Phase transition experiments and consequent theoretical modeling show that the relative phase dynamics, with observed fixed point attractors (in-phase and anti-phase), can be derived from nonlinearly coupled autonomous nonlinear oscillators. We can readily extend this continuous form of the phase dynamics to a discrete circle map of order 1 which has the property that in the 1:1 case not only are $\phi = 0$ and $\phi = 1/2$ fixed points but also that either one or both are stable (angle ϕ is now normalized to the interval [0,1]). We put the map in the form

$$\begin{aligned}\phi_{n+1} &= \Omega + f(\phi_n) && (2a)\\ &= \phi_n + \Omega + g(2\pi\phi_n) \bmod 1 && (2b)\end{aligned}$$

where Ω is an added constant term corresponding to the initial frequency ratio and g is a smooth periodic function of period 1 in ϕ (for complete details, see DeGuzman & Kelso, in press).

Performing a Fourier series expansion of g, the lowest order expansion that can satisfy e.g. locally stable fixed points at in phase and antiphase, is

$$g(2\pi\phi) = a_1 \sin(2\pi\phi) + a_2 \sin(4\pi\phi) \tag{3}$$

Transforming (3) to the new parameters (K,A) by letting $a_1 = -K/2\pi, a_2 = -KA/4\pi$ and using (3) in (2b) we obtain the *phase attractive circle map*

$$\phi_{n+1} = \phi_n + \Omega - \frac{K}{2\pi}(1 + A\cos 2\pi\phi_n)\sin 2\pi\phi_n \quad \bmod 1 \tag{4}$$

For the standard circle or sine circle map which characterizes a bewildering array of coupled multifrequency systems in nature (Glazier & Libchaber, 1988 for review) K is a measure of the amplitude strength of an external driving force, or, in general a nonlinear coupling parameter. Also for a general $g(x)$ in (2b), the dominant parameter that scales the overall magnitude of g may be given this interpretation. The "intrinsic parameter" A expresses the bistability of relative phase and behaves as the ratio 4 b/a in the original Haken, Kelso & Bunz (1985) model:

$$\dot{\phi} = -a \sin \phi - 2b \sin 2\phi \tag{5}$$

Since A is the ratio of the coefficients for the sin ϕ and sin 2ϕ terms in the Fourier expansion of g, A is roughly inversely proportional to the basic frequency of oscillation. For a given frequency ratio, either both in-phase and antiphase affect the overall performance, or only the in-phase is important depending on how fast the basic frequency is. Thus the parameter A is a measure of the relative importance of the intrinsic phase attractive states 0 and π.

The relative strength of A, representing the intrinsic phase attractive dynamics and K, the nonlinear coupling term determines many of the observed experimental features of multifrequency behavior mentioned above. The mechanism for pattern *selection*, in fact, may be seen as a *competition* between these terms. For example, it is easy to see why only a few, low-integer frequency lockings are seen in biological systems and why the simple frequency ratios in our experiments are the most stable (least variable). The reason is that the widest mode-locked regions or *Arnold Tongues* (e.g., 1:1, 2:1, 2:3 etc.) corresponding to absolute coordination are the most stable and attractive. If the experimental noise level is low, it is possible to observe other locked states, but the presence of noise can easily kick the system into nearby, more stable attractors (e.g. from 5:2 to 2:1). In addition, theoretical features that are not readily observable in biological experiments, such as chaotic transients and transitions from one chaotic region to another can be found in the map (Kelso, DeGuzman & Holroyd, 1991a). Such random switching back and forth between two chaotic states is deterministic, not due to noise.

The map is invertible if the function $f(\phi)$ of Eq. (2) is monotonic or the slope $f'(\phi)$ is never zero. The boundary in the parameter space separating invertible and non-invertible regions, is called the *critical surface*. Mode-locked regions, i.e. parameter regions of *absolute coordination* in our language, are found below the critical surface of the map. For the sine circle map (A=0 in Eq. (4)) this is the region where the nonlinearity parameter K is below 1. For the phase attractive map, the critical surface is obviously also a function of the intrinsic parameter A. For A>0 the critical surface is depressed toward small K. For A <0 the surface at first shifts up (beyond K=1) and then is depressed again. Representative values of A reveal dramatic effects of the phase attractive (intrinsic) dynamics on the widths of the tongues. The approach to the critical surface (relative to K=1 in the sine circle map) is either delayed or accelerated. For example, at A=1.0 the critical surface is depressed toward small K, the tongues are broader and therefore overlap at smaller values of the driving term. Thus, relative to the sine circle map (Eq. 4 with the phase attraction parameter A=0), it is easier to stay in *some* mode-locked region beyond the critical surface as K is increased. On the other hand, for A=-.5 the tongues are thinner but the critical region is reached later. The drawback in this régime is that a very small amount of noise can easily kick the system out of these narrow stability regions inducing quasiperiodicity and chaos. Representative examples of these tongues for different A values are shown in Figure 3.

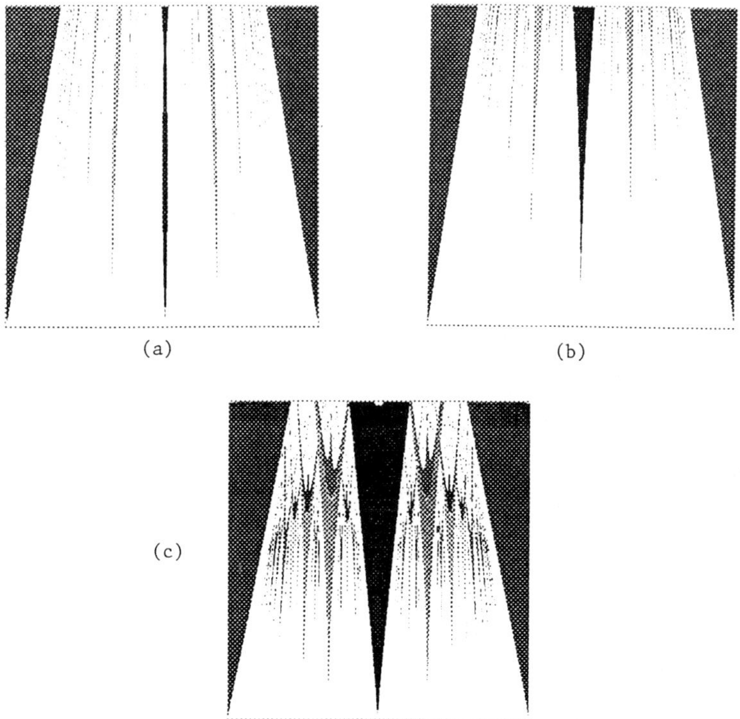

Figure 3: Arnold tongues for various strengths of the intrinsic parameter A relative to K. K, plotted between 0 and 1 is on the Y-axis, Ω between 0 and 1 is on the X-axis (a) A = -.5 shrinks the tongue widths and delays overlapping. (b) A = 0 gives well-known results for the sine circle map. (c) A = 1.0 yields widened tongues and earlier overlappings in the direction of increasing K.

Our experimental observations *cum* theoretical modeling reveal that generic or universal features of a system's ability to generate multi-frequency behavior are governed by the differential stability of mode-locked states as seen through the width of Arnold tongues. In our map, behavioral patterns arise from the competition between extrinsic and intrinsic, phase attractive dynamics. Pattern complexity is related to the hierarchy of the frequency ratios (the so called Farey tree, see also Beek, 1989) and is inversely proportional to tongue width. This rationalizes the degree to which different tasks are "hard" or "easy" to perform, as well as the frequency with which different patterns occur in a large variety of experimental preparations, at many levels of observation (Kelso & DeGuzman, 1988). Phase attraction sits inside these multifrequency patterns acting as an ordering mechanism even when absolute coordination is not easily attained or possible.

d) *The Intermittency Mechanism.*

Our main goal is to show how the phase attractive map can explain relative (not just absolute) coordination. A close look at the trajectories shown in Figure 2 reveals 'slips' and sometimes even 'jumps' in cycles of the LH driven component. For example, when a peak of the LH is just at the edge of a flattened peak of the RH, either the LH jumps over a cycle or shortens the next one. An analogous situation happens in the example of a father walking along with his small child. Since their intrinsic frequencies are different, synchronization is difficult unless either one or both adjust their periods. If the mean frequencies are constant for time scales not too large compared to the larger of the two periods (the father's) a less rigid form of coordination may be observed. Like our data (cf. Fig. 2 and von Holst (1939/73) for many more examples), in order to keep pace with each other, the child sometimes skips a step or the father slows down and we observe *phase slippage*, followed by more or less regular cycles again.

A generic or universal feature of dynamical systems (and, of course, of our map) near a tangent bifurcation is the phenomenon of *intermittency*, i.e. abrupt slips away from a previously stable fixed point. Phase slippage in a circle map occurs because of an unstable phase direction while return to more regular cycles is due to the stable direction. That is, the order parameter relative phase is *hyperbolic*, attraction taking place in one direction and divergence in another. The surface containing convergent trajectories is called the *stable manifold* while the surface containing the divergent trajectories is called the *unstable manifold.* Figure 4 shows how the phenomenon of intermittency occurs in the map. In Figure 4(a) a pair of fixed points are shown, one stable (slope < 1) the other unstable, i.e. there is frequency-locking. When the slope of the function is exactly 1 the graph is just tangent to the diagonal, a single fixed point subsists. When the graph leaves the diagonal, the iterates pass through the channel, go round the circle and enter from the other side. Phase slippage occurs between the two quasiregular oscillatory periods and there is no frequency-locking (Figure 4b) because the fixed points have disappeared. The appearance of phase slippage means that between two channel crossings, one of the oscillators gains a period with respect to the other: exactly the phenomenon of *relative coordination.* Note that close to the tangent bifurcation the phase concentrates (*phase attraction persists*) and slows. The reason, of course, is because the iterations are compressed in the channel. The relative phase, ϕ is plotted as a function of time (x-axis) in Figure 5 as the system approaches a fixed point (1:1 phase- and frequency-locked state). As one proceeds from Figure 5(a) to 5(c), with the frequency ratio, Ω, decreasing, the time spent in the channel (revealed by the flat portion of the curve) get longer and longer. Abrupt slips in the phase occur following these pauses: the phase leaves the channel and reenters after going once around the circle where it visits once more the 'remnant' or 'ghost' of the fixed point. Only the relative frequency of occurrence of phase slippage is affected as the tangent point is approached; the shape of the orbit does not change. Much more exotic, bursting behavior is shown in Figure 5(d) where the map parameters are in the chaotic regime, i.e. above the critical surface where the map is noninvertible. Mixed with slow phases near the fixed point are 'turbulent' bursts of unpredictable duration, rather like the spontaneous firing of neurons.

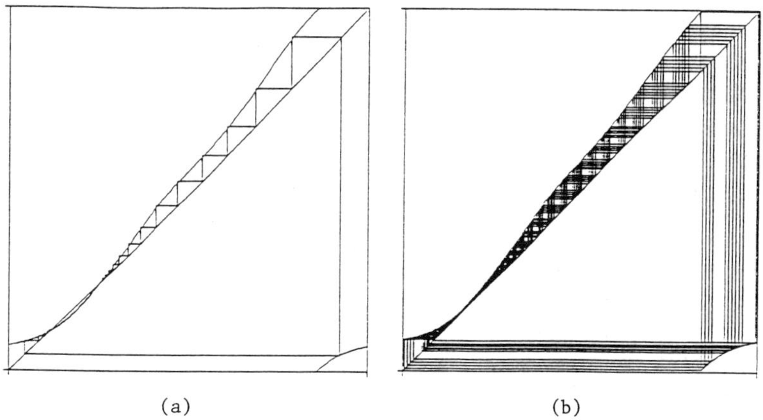

Figure 4: The phenomenon of intermittency in the phase attractive circle map. Note that the dicontinuity of the function (Eq. 11) is not real but due to rectangular coordinates parameterized in the interval [0,1]. (a) Ω=0.07, K=0.4, A=0.9. An initial condition near the unstable fixed point moves up and to the right until it wraps around and falls into the stable fixed point (lower left). (b) Ω=0.085, K=0.4, A=0.9. The stable and unstable fixed points have disappeared, leaving a channel through which iterates can pass causing phase slippage.

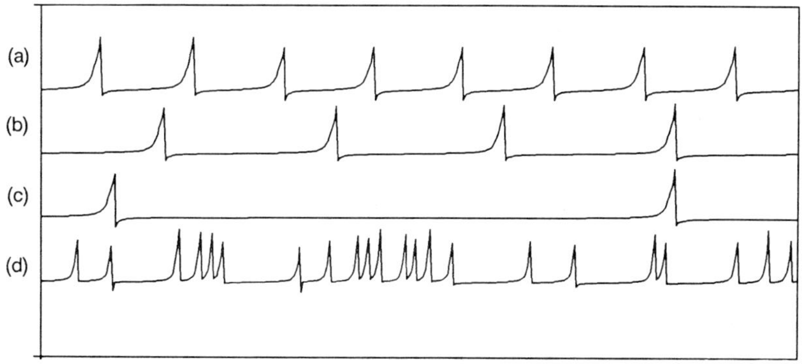

Figure 5: (a)-(c) Plots of the time series ϕ_n for K=0.4, A=0.9 and decreasing values of Ω, showing the slowing down of the bursts. (a) Ω=0.081, (b) Ω=0.08025, (c) Ω=0.08. For fixed K and A, the frequency of the burst depends on how far Ω is from the fixed point. (d) Bursting in the chaotic régime of the map for K=0.9, A=0.9, and Ω=0.1805.

For non-1:1 frequency ratios, one observes slippage of the orbits instead. Intermittency in this case may be formulated in terms of the behavior of an appropriate iterated point, i.e. second iterate in the case of 2:1. In Figure 6 is plotted the orbit near a tangent bifurcation at 2:1 using the first (a) and the second (b) iterate. In Figure 6b, the pattern of jumps between the two regions of concentration is qualitatively very similar to the phase wandering and phase locking found in the experiment (Fig. 1).

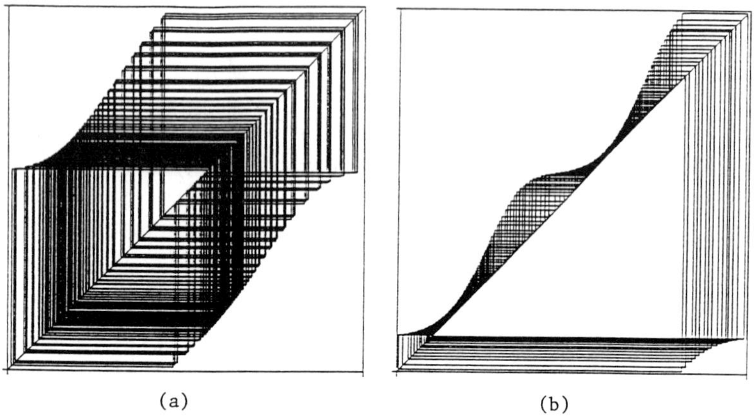

Figure 6: Intermittency in the phase attractive map near 2:1. Return maps are plotted using the first iterate (a) and the second iterate (b). Parameters are Ω=0.55, K=0.4, and A=1.1 in each case.

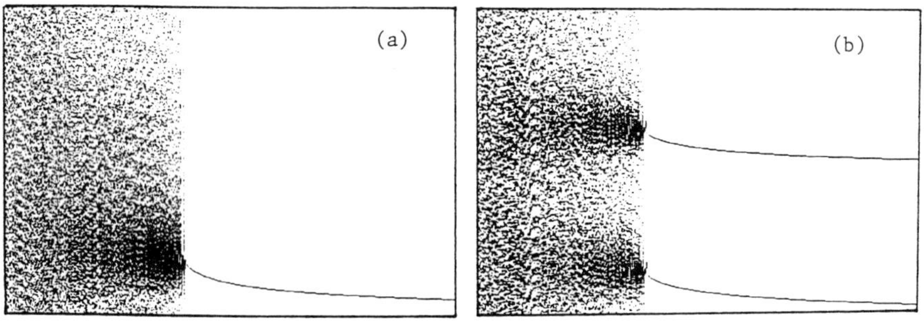

Figure 7: Bifurcation diagram showing the phase behavior (y-axis) when crossing the Arnol'd tongues at 1:1 (a) and 2:1 (b) for fixed A and increasing K (X-axis).

We note that the appearance of phase gathering near mode-locked solutions has an *anticipatory* quality about it. A good way to see this is through the corresponding bifurcation diagram shown in Figure 7(a). In this figure, the fuzzy area reflects quasiperiodic motion because the asymptotic frequency ratio (winding number) between the components is irrational. Notice, however, that the progressive darkening "anticipates" the upcoming stable solution (the single line) which indicates the system is trapped or mode-locked 1:1. The bifurcation diagram for the 2:1 case is plotted in Figure 7(b), showing entirely analogous behavior.

3. Summary and Conclusions

Our main points are: (i) that relative coordination – a ubiquitous, but largely unexplained phenomenon in biological systems – is to be understood as a generic property of dynamical systems (flows or maps) near tangent bifurcations which leads naturally to intermittency. One may speak of a "dwell" time, the average time the system stays near the same point (or the same orbit as in a non 1:1 case) before running away. Because the frequency ratio among the components is not necessarily 1:1, the fixed point states of the intrinsic dynamics need not be realized. An optimal synchronization would then be measured by how close the system gets, overall, to these intrinsic phase points; and (ii) the growth of phase densities and the resulting slowing is *predictive* of upcoming critical points, what one might call an *anticipatory dynamical system* (Kelso, 1991). Anticipatory dynamical systems stay in contact with the future by living *near* but not *in* mode-locked regions, thereby retaining an optimal mixture of flexibility and stability (see also Beek, 1989, for a similar suggestion in the case of juggling).

We suggest that orderly but nonstationary behavior is a general feature of coordination in real biological systems. A casual survey of time-dependent processes on many levels of description in many different experimental systems suggests that absolute phase and frequency synchronization may be the exception rather than the rule. Rigid entrainment (absolute coordination) which reflects asymptotic convergence to a well-defined frequency and phase relation state (a mode-locked attractor) may be more a feature of biological oscillator *models* than of reality. Biological systems clearly exhibit *attraction* in this flexible régime where the individual components adjust spatially and temporally but strictly speaking there are no *attractors*, at least in the sense we have defined the term, i.e. as attractors of the collective variable dynamics. Our studies indicate that intermittency is crucial, on the one hand affording the possibility to phase and frequency synchronize but also providing the necessary mechanism for going in and out of coherent states as well as for exploring the full state space. The mechanism we have identified allows biological systems - on several levels - the vital mix of coherent yet flexible function. An important technical point for understanding complex systems like the brain is that this intermittency mechanism arises from low dimensional, deterministic dynamics.

4. Acknowledgments

The research discussed herein is supported by NIMH (Neuroscience Research Branch) Grant MH 42900, ONR contract N000114-88-J1191 and BRS Grant RR07258. We thank A. Mandell and H. Haken for discussion and encouragement and Tom Holroyd for his help in producing the computer graphics.

5. References

1. Beek, P.J. 1989 *Juggling dynamics.* Free University Press, Amsterdam.

2. Bergé, P., Pomeau, Y. & Vidal, C. (1984). *Order within chaos: Towards a deterministic approach to turbulence.* John Wiley, New York.

3. Bressler, S.L. (1990). The gamma wave: a cortical information carrier? *Trends in Neuroscience, 13*, 161-162.

4. Cohen, A.V., S. Rossignol, & S Grillner (Eds.). (1988). *Neural control of rhythmic movements in vertebrates.* New York: John Wiley.

5. DeGuzman, G.C. & Kelso, J.A.S. (1989/in press). Multifrequency behavioral patterns and the phase attractive circle map. FAU Center for Complex Systems preprint, July 1989; To appear in *Biological Cybernetics.*

6. Eckhorn, R., Bauer, R., Jordan, W., Brosch, M., Kruse, W., Monk, M. & Reitboeck, H.J. (1988). Coherent Oscillations: A mechanism of feature linking in the visual cortex? *Biological Cybernetics, 60*, 121-130.

7. Hamburger, V. (1970). Embryonic mobility in vertebrates. In F.O. Schmidt (Ed.). *The Neurosciences: Second Study Program.* New York: Rockefeller University Press.

8. Glazier, J.A., Libchaber, A. (1988). Quasi-periodicity and dynamical systems, *IEEE Transactions on Circuits and Systems, 35* 790-809.

9. Gray, C.M., Konig, P., Engel, A.K. & Singer, W. (1989). Oscillatory responses in cat visual cortex exhibit inter-columnar synchronization which reflects global stimulus properties. *Nature, 338*, 334-337.

10. Guevara, M.R., Glass, L. & Shrier, A. (1981). Phase locking, period-doubling bifurcations and irregular dynamics in periodically stimulated cardiac cells. *Science, 214*, 1350-1353.

11. Haken, H., Kelso, J.A.S. & Bunz, H. (1985). A theoretical model of phase transitions in human hand movements. *Biological Cybernetics, 39*, 139-156.

12. Kay, B.A., Kelso, J.A.S., Saltzman, E.L., & Schöner, G. 1987. The space-time behavior of single and bimanual movements: data and model. *Journal of Experimental Psychology: Human Perception and Performance, 13*, 178-192.

13. Kay, B.A., Saltzman, E.L. & Kelso, J.A.S. (in press). Steady-state and perturbed rhythmical movements: dynamical models using a variety of analytical tools. *J. Exp. Psych: Human Perc. & Perf.*.

14. Kelso, J.A.S. (1984). Phase transitions and critical behavior in human bimanual coordination. *American Journal of Physiology: Regulatory, Integrative and Comparative Physiology, 15*, R1000-R10004.

15. Kelso, J.A.S. (1990). Phase transitions: Foundations of behavior. In H. Haken & M. Stadler (eds.). *Synergetics of Cognition*, Springer-Verlag, Berlin, pp. 249-268.

16. Kelso, J.A.S. (1991). Anticipatory dynamical systems, intrinsic pattern dynamics and skill learning. *Human Move. Sci.*

17. Kelso, J.A.S. & DeGuzman, G. (1988). Order in time: How cooperation between the hands informs the design of the brain. In H. Haken (ed.), *Neural and synergetic computers*. Berlin: Springer-Verlag, pp. 180-196.

18. Kelso, J.A.S., DeGuzman, G.C. & Holroyd, T. (1991a). The self-organized phase attractive dynamics of coordination. In A. Babloyantz (Ed.) *Self Organization, Emerging Properties and Learning*, Plenum Press, NY.

19. Kelso, J.A.S., DeGuzman, G.C. & Holroyd, T. (1991b). Synergetic dynamics of biological coordination with special reference to phase attraction and intermittency. In H. Haken & H.P. Koepchen (Eds.) *Synergetics of Rhythms*, Springer, Berlin.

20. Kelso, J.A.S. & Scholz, J.P. (1985). Cooperative phenomena in biological motion. In H. Haken (Ed.), *Complex Systems: operational approaches in neurobiology, physical systems and computers*, (pp. 124-149). Berlin: Springer-Verlag.

21. Kelso, J.A.S., Southard, D.L. & Goodman, D. (1979). On the nature of human interlimb coordination. *Science, 203*, 1029-1031.

22. Kugler, P.N. & Turvey, M.T. (1987). Information, natural law and the self assembly of rhythmic movement. Lawrence Erlbaum, Hillsdale, NJ.

23. Mandell, A.J. (1983). From intermittency to transitivity in neuropsychobiological flows. *American J. Physiol., 245*, R484-R494.

24. Schöner, G. (1990). A dynamic theory of coordination of discrete movement. *Biol. Cybern., 63*, 257-270.

25. Schöner, G. & Kelso, J.A.S. (1988). Dynamic pattern generation in behavioral and neural systems. *Science, 239*, 1513-1520. Reprinted in *From Molecules to Models: Advances in the Neurosciences.*

26. Turvey, M.T. (1990). Coordination, *American Psychologist, 45*, 938-953.

27. von Holst, E. (1939/1973). Relative coordination as a phenomenon and as a method of analysis of central nervous function. Reprinted in: *The collected papers of Erich von Holst.* Coral Gables, FL: University of Miami Press.

Tutorials in Motor Behavior II
G.E. Stelmach and J. Requin (Editors)

Learning and transfer as dynamical paradigms for behavioral change[1]

P.G. Zanone and J.A.S. Kelso

Program in Complex Systems and Brain Sciences, Center for Complex Systems, Florida Atlantic University, P.O. Box 3091, Boca Raton, Fla 33431 (USA)

Abstract.

Our window into the topic of learning is bimanual coordination to a visually-specified phase relationship. Previous research reveals that only a few phasing patterns are produced stably, which are mapped onto attractors of the system's *intrinsic dynamics*. Specific task constraints introduce *behavioral information* into the dynamics, attracting the system's behavior toward a required pattern. Learning is the process by which environmental behavioral information which defines the visuomotor pattern to be learned becomes memorized. Once learning is achieved, the memorized pattern constitutes an attractor of the behavioral pattern dynamics. The rationale for the present experiments is to periodically probe the phase diagram (the set of all phasing relations) while a particular phasing pattern is practiced. Such probing allows one to determine the existing stable phasing patterns before learning. As practice proceeds, periodic probing also allows one to observe the evolution of the phase diagram as a new task is learned. The results unveil several processes that are central to understanding learning. Pattern stability depends on whether behavioral information competes or cooperates with the intrinsic dynamics. A behavioral pattern is learned to the extent that the intrinsic dynamics are modified in the direction of the required pattern. A qualitative alteration involves a nonequilibrium phase transition, whereas a parametric change results from the drift of a stable pattern in parameter space. Both kinds of dynamical changes are observed in transfer to an untrained pattern, attesting, in the present case, to the important role played by symmetry in the pattern dynamics.

1. INTRODUCTION

One of the most outstanding feature of living things is their ability to adapt flexibly and durably in response to environmental constraints. Broadly speaking, adaptation may be conceived of as the *emergence of a new form in an already organized ensemble.* The novel form reduces the demands from the milieu in some adequate way and can then be reproduced in similar situations. Actually, several adaptive processes may unfold

[1]This research was funded partly by NIMH grant MH42900, BRSG grant NSS 1-SO7-RR07258-01, and contract N00014-88-J-119 from the U.S. ONR. The first author was supported by the Swiss National Science Foundation, grant 8210-026064.

simultaneously along different time scales and affect the current state of the ensemble. Typically, evolution reflects adaptive changes across generations of a given species and among them. Ontogenesis does so within the lifespan of a single individual, whereas learning, proceeding on the fastest time scale, pertains to more "real-time" and "daily-life" behavioral adaptation. Therefore, any general theory of biological systems has to deal with lawfully describing the processes that relate newly acquired forms to the preexisting ensemble, on any spatial or temporal scale.

In the field of evolutionary theories, the endeavor of identifying the principles of adaptation has motivated intense and controversial debates as to how morphological and functional modifications of the individual are passed on across generations (e.g., Piatelli-Palmarini, 1989). As far as ontogeny is concerned, rather extreme points of view have been defended too. To limit ourselves to the behavioral sciences, traditional behaviorism views adaptation as a mere epigenetic phenomenon (e.g., Watson, 1913; Skinner, 1938) as opposed to preformism, whether in its maturational (e.g., Gesell, 1929) or selectionist (e.g., Chomsky, 1988) versions. Basically, the same picture can be drawn concerning the shorter time scale of learning. In our opinion however, none of the frameworks at hand really affords an answer as to how the individual's current state both undergoes and constrains the adaptive process. Indeed, the perspective adopted by Piaget (1952) conceives of development and learning as being governed by the principle of equilibration, which bears upon the balanced interaction between the mechanisms of scheme accommodation and scheme assimilation. Nonetheless, the experimental foundations for such processes remain quite shallow.

Whatever the level of description and the time scale, fundamental and recurrent problems in understanding adaptive change are: a) to address the mechanisms governing behavior in response to environmental constraints; b) to determine the behavioral repertoire proper to the task at hand, and to assess its adaptive modifications (viz., "structural" change); and c) to identify the principles leading to adaptive change in behavior (viz., "functional" change).

Obviously, these issues are intertwined, to the extent that searching for a solution may seem a circular enterprise. In order to be fully understood, each point requires that the others be already answered. Furthermore, the theoretical models that address these issues often lack operational tools to test their predictions. Likewise, available methods are subverted or flawed by the fuzziness surrounding the theoretical concepts. Such a situation points to the lack of a unifying and coherent framework that could provide both methods and concepts to tackle *operationally* coordinated behavior and change. This is what the present paper is about: Presenting a combination of theory, methods, and results that can offer some insight into understanding adaptive change and foster an operational approach to the topic.

The studies presented in this paper address the topic of adaptive behavioral change through *perceptual-motor learning*. Insofar as skill acquisition, among all adaptive processes, develops on a time scale fairly compatible with experimental investigations, it affords a good paradigm to study. More specifically, our window is a bimanual skill, coordination to a visually-specified phase relationship. The general perspective adopted here is that of *nonlinear dynamical systems*, which aims at providing a theory (i.e., a formal model) of the time course of a phenomenon. Such an approach is rooted in physics and mathematics and has recently pervaded numerous scientific disciplines, importing rather exotic models and concepts to these fields, such as bifurcations, catastrophes, fractals and chaos (see Gleick, 1987, for an easy overview; Glass & MacKey, 1988; Haken, 1985; Haken & Stadler, 1990; Kelso, Mandel & Shlesinger, 1988; Velarde, 1987, for more specialized readings). One of the key ideas is that a system, although determined by simple dynamics (i.e., low-dimensional equations of motion), may exhibit very complex or totally unpredictable behavior (cf. May, 1976, for an elementary but spectacular example). Conversely, complicated and seemingly chaotic behavior does not imply absence of ordering principles. As we shall see, such dynamical principles are also at work during learning, determining behavior and underlying change. Of course, the particular form of the dynamics must be identified in the system under study at a particular level of description.

2. GENERAL FRAMEWORK

Understanding the emergence of new forms or patterns in complex systems (i.e., with many degrees of freedom) is a main challenge facing natural sciences (see Haken, 1983a; Nicolis & Prigogine, 1989; Yates, 1987). According to our definition of adaptation, this issue is all the more important for understanding learning. Basically, our framework draws on physical theories of self-organization in nonequilibrium systems, especially synergetics (see Haken, 1983a, 1983b, 1985). More specifically, it is grounded on an entire body of work on biological systems, so-called "Dynamic Pattern Theory" (see Kelso & Schöner, 1987, 1988; Schöner & Kelso, 1988a, 1988b, 1988c), which tightly articulates experimental findings and theoretical modelling in a coherent fashion (for a stepwise presentation of such theory/experiment link in the case of learning, see Schöner, Zanone & Kelso, in press). The cornerstone of the approach is to understand behavior in terms of pattern formation. The behavior of a system over time is characterized by *stable* collective states, that is, observable and reproducible *behavioral patterns.* The nature of the dynamics describing such behavior is revealed around *phase transitions*, that is, spontaneous changes in the behavioral pattern brought about by parametric influences. Indeed, at critical points, a dramatic reduction of the degrees of freedom occurs (Haken's "slaving principle"): The system's dynamics are characterized by a minimal set of collective variables (or *order parameters*). These low-dimensional dynamics are defined by mapping the behavioral patterns onto *attractors* of the collective variables and by studying their stability. Boundary conditions (e.g., environmental, task, energetic constraints) act as parameters on the dynamics, producing changes in the observed behavioral pattern. If these parameters are quite non-specific to the resulting behavioral pattern, they are coined *control parameters*, and the collective variables dynamics are said to constitute the system's *intrinsic dynamics.* These dynamics exist in absence of any specific requirement and determine the stable collective states toward which behavior spontaneously relaxes. In contrast, if the parameters are specific, they serve as *behavioral information* which attracts behavior toward a *required* behavioral pattern. In particular, environmental requirements, intentional or purposeful needs, and tasks to be learned may act as behavioral information. By definition, behavioral information is expressed by the same type of collective variables that are used to characterize the behavioral patterns (i.e., defined in the same space as the intrinsic dynamics).

The joint concepts of intrinsic dynamics and behavioral information (see Schöner, 1989; Schöner & Kelso, 1988d, 1988e) offer a window into the topic of learning. Intrinsic dynamics define the stable behaviors that the system adopts spontaneously independent of specific environmental constraints. More precisely, the layout of the behavioral attractors (or *phase diagram* of the collective variables dynamics[2]) indicates which stable patterns can be observed in the absence of specific requirements, such as those of the learning task. The learning task itself introduces behavioral information, which attracts the system's behavior to a required pattern. Learning is then the process by which *environmental* behavioral information defining a pattern to be learned becomes *memorized* behavioral information. Thus, a required pattern is learned to the extent that it modifies the intrinsic dynamics in the direction of the to-be-learned pattern. If any dramatic modification of the collective variable dynamics happens in that direction (i.e., the attractor layout turns out to be qualitatively different before and after practice of the required pattern), then *learning involves a phase transition* (or *bifurcation*, to use the term usually preferred by mathematicians). A crucial methodological consequence is that the phase diagram allows one to establish prior to learning which pattern is to be learned "from scratch", and to determine after learning to what extent this pattern has actually been learned. The phase diagram provides a probe of the "structural", qualitative modifications of the behavioral repertoire with learning, beyond mere "functional", quantitative changes in performance.

The concept of intrinsic dynamics offers a way to operationalize an issue that learning theorists have oftentimes emphasized but have not been able to do much about, namely, that organisms acquire new forms of skilled behavior on the background of already existing capacities. The initial state seldom, if ever, corresponds to a disordered random network, but is already ordered in some way. However, it must be stressed that the term intrinsic dynamics is not to be equated with innate biological constraints, but rather reflects capacities that exist at the time when a new task is to be learned. In this, the present approach offers an interesting point of departure with the ethologists (e.g., Tinbergen, 1951/1989), who stressed that learning must be preceded by a study of innate mechanisms, expressions of which, called fixed action patterns, were difficult to measure objectively. Instead, we provide an operational means to identify patterns and their dynamics using phase transitions as an entry-point. A strong point of conceptual agreement, however, is that learning involves a "secondary modification" (ibid. p. 6) of these so-called intrinsic dynamics. Psychology, for the most part, equates for the initial state by adopting as arbitrary a learning task as possible, but avoids a direct confrontation with the issue itself. On other levels of description, evidence for spontaneous movements

[2]The term "phase diagram" derives from thermodynamics. More generally, a phase diagram defines regions in parameter space that do not exhibit qualitative changes of the system's dynamics (hence, similar phases in the thermodynamic framework), as well as the boundaries across which such changes occur. In nonlinear dynamical systems, change can be continuous or qualitative depending on the region in parameter space occupied. We use the image "attractor layout" synonymously with phase diagram in this article. However, it is important to note that a typical attractor layout or phase diagram may contain attractive, repelling, and saddle points that occupy basins and separatrices (e.g., Abraham & Shaw, 1982).

in early embryonic development which coincide with rhythmical activity in spinal cord neurons (Hamburger, 1970), as well as for neuronal circuits for central pattern generation (Grillner, 1975), is consistent with the idea of intrinsic dynamics. Such a definition of the intrinsic dynamics makes the individual the only relevant unit of observation, insofar as each subject may "bring in" different initial pattern dynamics, depending on previous experience, volitional or perceptual factors, and so forth. Therefore, knowing the initial attractor layout is instrumental to the study of learning, in that it takes into account the various boundary conditions affecting the dynamics before any practice.

A first experimental evidence in biological systems for pattern formation following the dynamical principles briefly exposed here was the discovery of nonequilibrium phase transitions in human interlimb coordination. The basic phenomenon was observed in bimanual finger movements by Kelso (1984). Subjects were requested to move homologous fingers rhythmically at a common frequency. Two patterns of coordination proved to be stable at various frequencies, namely, in-phase (simultaneous flexion and extension of both fingers) and anti-phase (the flexion of one finger coincides with the extension of the other). However, with frequency increasing further (a non-specific parameter), a spontaneous switch from the anti-phase to the in-phase pattern was always observed above a critical value (about 2.2 Hz), whereas the in-phase pattern remained stable at all reachable frequencies. Such a switch between behavioral patterns has been modelled as a nonequilibrium phase transition from a bistable to a monostable régime of the collective variable dynamics, relative phase (ϕ)[3] (Haken, Kelso, & Bunz, 1985; Schöner, Haken, & Kelso, 1986). Theoretically predicted features of spontaneous phase transitions, such as enhancement of fluctuations (Kelso & Scholz, 1985; Kelso, Scholz & Schöner, 1986) and critical slowing-down (Scholz, Kelso & Schöner, 1987; Scholz & Kelso, 1989). have been confirmed experimentally. Even though they are not always identified or analyzed as such, numerous evidence for transition-like phenomena has have been reported in human interlimb coordination (e.g., Baldissera, Cavallari & Civaschi, 1982; Cohen, 1971; Tuller & Kelso, 1990, Yamanishi, Kawato & Suzuki, 1979), intralimb coordination (Kelso, Buchanan & Wallace, 1990), perceptual-motor behavior (Kelso, DelColle & Schöner, 1990; Schmidt, Carello & Turvey, 1990) and perception (Hock, Kelso, & Schöner, 1990).

3. COMING TO GRIPS WITH LEARNING

Consider the case where a subject must learn a phasing pattern specified environmentally (e.g., the required pattern, $\psi = 90\,\text{deg}$) that does *not* correspond to the intrinsically stable patterns (i.e., $\phi = 0$ or $\pm 180\,\text{deg}$). As this new relative phase is learned, the influence of the initially bistable dynamics attracting the system to in-phase or anti-phase patterns dwindles, due to the progressively overwhelming attraction by the pattern being memorized. Thus, with the passage from environmental to memorized information, a *phase transition in learning* is predicted. In particular, the least stable of the two in-

[3]Note the different usages of the term "phase". The collective variable relative phase is a relative timing variable expressing the coordination between active components. A phase transition, or bifurcation, is a qualitative change in the system's dynamics, corresponding to the passage across distinct regions of the phase diagram (see previous note).

trinsic patterns, the anti-phase state, should lose stability as the strength of memorized information increases. This should take the form of a definite change in the behavioral pattern observed in the learning task and the emergence of a new behavioral attractor corresponding to the learned pattern. An experiment by Zanone & Kelso (in press) was devised to test the theoretical prediction that learning can involve a phase transition, that is, a qualitative modification of the pattern dynamics. The backbone of this study was to systematically probe the evolving pattern dynamics during the process of learning a required relative phase. For the sake of clarity, the results concerning only two subjects will be reported in the present paper, insofar as they are prototypical of key processes and principles pertaining to learning (for full details, cf. Zanone & Kelso, in press). Let us first describe the learning task.

Subjects' hands are slipped into a bimanual finger apparatus which allows flexion-extension movements of the index fingers to be monitored. In front of subjects, a "visual metronome" displays different relative phases, by controlling the onset of two light-emitting diodes (LED). Subjects are required to flex each finger in temporal coincidence with the onset of the respective left or right LED. No other constraint is imposed on motion but to execute as smooth and regular movements as possible. The metronome frequency is set at 1.75 Hz, below the threshold above which the 180-deg pattern becomes unstable. A required phasing $\psi = 90$ deg (with a right lead) is chosen, because theoretically, 90 deg is an unstable fixed point of the collective variable dynamics, separating the two basins of attraction for $\phi = 0$ deg and $\phi = 180$ deg. Thus, the task is expected to make an unstable fixed point stable through learning, thereby promoting qualitative changes in the theoretical phase diagram. Subjects are administered fifteen learning trials per day, lasting 20 s, on five consecutive days. After every trial subjects receive a complete knowledge of results. One week after the last day of practice, two recall trials are carried out in order to test the persistence of any learning effect. in the recall test, subjects have to produce from memory the relative phase required in the practice sessions for one minute.

3.1. WHAT IS LEARNED?

Figure 1 shows the performance of two selected Subjects TM and MS in the practice trials and the two recall trials (see $\star$ curves). (We neglect for the time being, the $\square$ curves.) On the early trials of Subject TM (left Panel of Figure 1), the mean produced relative phase (top solid curves) indicates that a 180-deg pattern is performed very steadily in spite of the task requirements to produce 90 deg of relative phase. Then, performance tends gradually to 90 deg, until it reaches the required relative phase at the beginning of the second day of practice. In this interval, the produced pattern is very variable (bottom dashed curves), but such fluctuations, within as well as across trials, diminish substantially with practice. In contrast, Subject MS (right Panel of Figure 1) performs the required relative phase in an accurate and fairly stable manner (compared to TM) just after the first trial. Nevertheless, more practice entails a noticeable decrement in the variability of the produced pattern.

What conclusions can be drawn from such a differentiated picture between subjects? In layman's language, Subject TM has acquired the ability to produce a 90-deg pattern, thereby adding to his behavioral repertoire. Subject MS instead seems to have simply

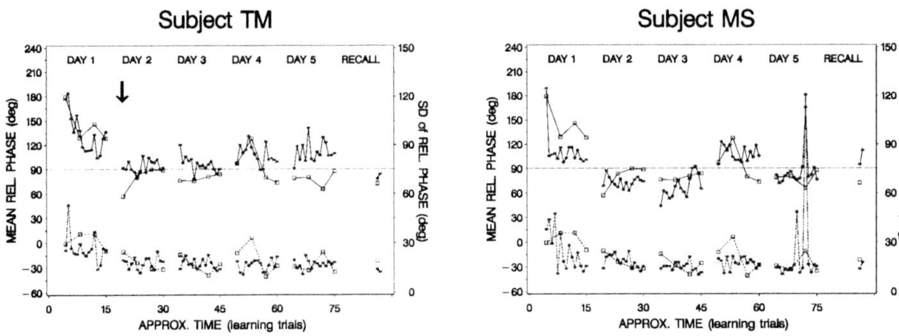

Figure 1: Evolution of performance with practice for Subjects TM and MS when a 90-deg pattern is required in the learning trials ($\star$) and probing scans ($\square$). The top solid curves plot the mean relative phase as a function of the learning trials, while the bottom dashed curves display the corresponding SD (see text for details).

practiced further an already existing phasing pattern. Therefore, subjects' individual repertoires are different initially, before any practice whatsoever. In order to test this assertion, it is necessary to probe the pattern dynamics, that is, to determine the phase diagram. The probing procedure consists in scanning a large set of required phasing patterns. The rationale is that if no intrinsic dynamics come into play, the produced relative phase will precisely match the required relative phase. On the contrary, systematic distortions with respect to the required performance reflect the presence of stable patterns attracting the behavioral pattern elsewhere. By definition, these intrinsic patterns must exhibit the smallest variability. During an actual probe, the relative phase required by the visual metronome is increased from 0 (simultaneous blink of the two LEDs) to 180 deg (alternate blink) by steps of 15 deg (i.e., 13 plateaus), with the right LED leading. Of course, no knowledge of results is given after a probe, which was administered before, after, and twice during each daily practice session, as well as once at the end of the recall session.

The initial, final and recall phase diagrams are presented in Figure 2 for Subjects TM and MS. Let us focus on the initial probes on Day 1 (left part of both Panels). On the top solid curves, DELTA RP is plotted as a function of the required relative phase. DELTA RP is the difference between the produced and the required relative phase, so that when the required phasing is overestimated, DELTA RP has a positive value, and inversely. For Subject TM (left Panel of Figure 2), DELTA RP exhibits a humped curve as a function of the required relative phase, that is, the error is lowest when the required phasing is 0 or 180 deg. Moreover, DELTA RP exhibits a systematic bias below 180 deg: The produced relative phases depart from the required phasing in the direction of the 180-deg pattern, and such discrepancy increases with the difference between the required phasing and 180 deg. Thus, the negative slope of DELTA RP about 180 deg signifies

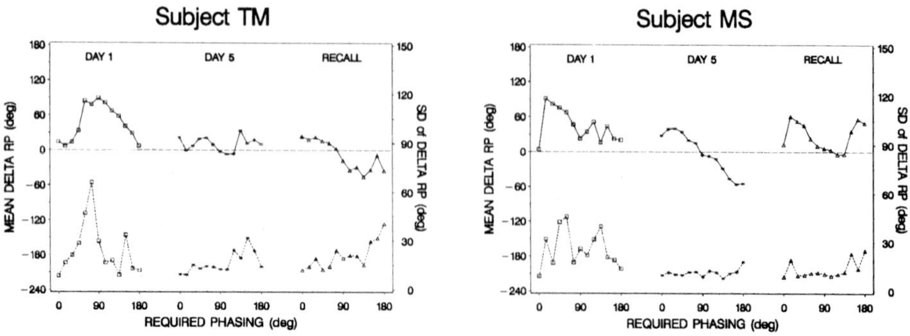

Figure 2: Individual phase diagrams before and after learning, and during the recall session. The upper solid graphs plot mean DELTA RP (produced minus required relative phase) as a function of the required phasing. The bottom dotted graphs present the corresponding SD.

that this pattern is an attractor for the nearby phasing patterns. Some attraction is also noticeable with respect to the 0-deg pattern. In keeping with this interpretation, the bottom dotted curves show that the SD of DELTA RP is lowest at 0 and 180 deg, increasing markedly at intermediate values. The 0 and 180-deg patterns are less variable than the others. Thus, the in-phase and anti-phase patterns are inferred to constitute attractors of the collective variable dynamics.

The effects of the five days of practice on the pattern dynamics are illustrated in the middle graphs of both Panels in Figure 2. For Subject TM (left Panel), the mean intratrial relative phase (top curves) does not show a systematic bias (negative slope) around 180 deg any longer, but around 90 deg instead. In terms of variability, the lower dotted curves indicate that the 90-deg pattern stabilizes with practice (SD reduces sharply for intermediate required RP), while the 180-deg pattern becomes more variable. This ensemble of features is the signature of an attractor at 90 deg, which was not present in the initial phase diagram, accompanied by the destabilization of the 180-deg pattern: Such a phenomenon is a clear *nonequilibrium phase transition* from a bistable to a tristable régime of the pattern dynamics.

For Subject MS, the initial pattern dynamics (left part of the right Panel in Figure 2) exhibit a negative slope of DELTA RP (upper solid curves) for intermediate required phasing, as well as below 180 deg. The pattern variability (lower dotted curves) appears to be smallest at 0 and 180 deg, as well as for several intermediate values, where the produced pattern is about 110-120 deg. These features suggest a tristable layout of attractors before any practice of the 90-deg pattern. After learning, the final dynamics (middle part of the lower Panel in Figure 2) appears to be bistable at 0 and 90 deg. Indeed, DELTA RP (top curves) shows a negative slope all the way across the interval between 45 and 180 deg, intersecting the zero axis at 90 deg. Meanwhile, SD is very low, comparable to that of the 0-deg pattern. Thus, the 90-deg pattern is a strong attractor, which "sucks in" the 180-deg pattern itself[4]. From initially tristable dynamics, in which the 0-, 90-, and 180-deg patterns constitute behavioral attractors, a bistable régime emerges following the destabilization of the 180 deg attractor. Here again, a qualitative change in the phase diagram occurs accompanied by loss of stability on the intrinsically less stable anti-phase pattern.

The two learning-related phase transitions are rendered in a more flowing fashion in Figure 3. The average relative phases within a plateau are coded A to O as the required phasing is increased from 0 to 180 deg during each probe. They are plotted as a function of the moment at which they were administered in the learning procedure (i.e., the time axis is roughly comparable to that of Figure 1). A cubic polynomial interpolation of these average values is drawn, such that the trend may be followed across consecutive probes. If there were no influence of the intrinsic dynamics, the produced relative phase would match each required relative phase in every probe. So, if no change in the dynamics occurred with practice, thirteen equidistant horizontal line would be plotted. On the contrary, the clustering of produced data points indicates an attraction. Changes in the attractor layout may be then observed over the time scale of the experiment, such as drift of a stable pattern (fluctuation of a bunch of curves), broadening or narrowing of its basin (convergence or divergence of curves, respectively).

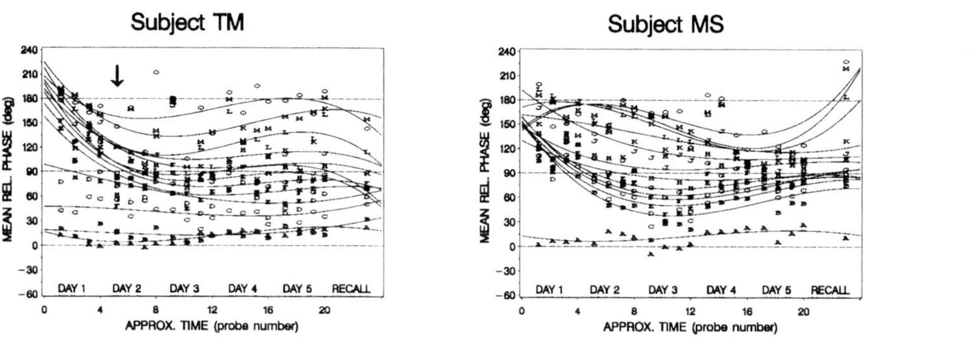

Figure 3: Evolution of the phase diagrams with learning.

In the left Panel of Figure 3 (Subject TM), the salient phenomenon is the convergence of a large number of "iso-requirement" curves toward 90 deg across successive probes. This illustrates very nicely how the attraction of the 90-deg pattern with respect to its neighbors is progressively established. Mostly, curves belonging to the 180-deg basin fall into that centered at 90 deg. The 90-deg stable pattern even "sucks in" the 180-deg pattern itself, as observed at the end of Day 2 and the beginning of Day 3. Afterwards, the

[4]The positive shift in DELTA RP for 0 deg, consistently observed in all subjects, suggests that this intrinsically stable pattern is less attractive than before too. Such drift may be a putative sign of an emerging bifurcation in which the in-phase pattern is eventually absorbed into the basin of attraction of the learned pattern (for details, see Zanone & Kelso, in press).

relative instability of this pattern is still reflected by its very small basin of attraction. For Subject MS (right Panel of Figure 3), the initial tristable dynamics are indicated by the clusters of data points around 0, 115, and 180 deg. With practice, all the iso-requirement curves except 0-deg phasing (coded A) converge gradually to 90 deg, as a huge basin of attraction is built up (cf. again the length of the negative slope in Figure 2 for MS middle). Finally, the 90-deg pattern absorbs the 180-deg pattern itself.

Two arguments have to be discussed proving the coherence of the dynamical approach to the study of learning. The first point is that learning is expected to entail rather permanent changes. As far as performance in the learning task is concerned, the scores in the recall trials are displayed in the right part of both Panels in Figure 1. No statistical difference between the recall performance and that at the end of the fifth day of practice was detected beyond normal fluctuations across trials and days. Thus, the effects of practice are robust over the retention period of one week in both (and in fact for all) subjects. Concerning the recall probe presented in the right graphs of the two Panels in Figure 2, the modifications of the phase diagrams associated with learning still prevail after the retention interval. Indeed, the destabilization of the 180-deg pattern persists in both subjects, and the newly created attractor at 90 deg is still present after one week. Such persistence suggests that the 90-deg pattern has become a durable part of the attractor layout, confirming that environmental behavioral information has become memorized, and hence recallable. Conceptually, the fact that the learned pattern persists attests to the stability of the underlying collective variable dynamics.

The second validation resides in a clear parallel between the modifications of the pattern dynamics, seen through the probe of the phase diagram, and the changes in the behavioral pattern observed during the learning task itself. If both tasks involve the same dynamics, the substantial fluctuations across trials and days of the relative phase produced during the learning trials should correspond to comparable changes in performance when 90-deg RP is required in the probes. Recall that in Figure 1, the learning trials were coded by a $\star$. For the probing scans, coded by a $\Box$, mean and *SD* of the relative phase produced within the 90-deg plateau are plotted for the 21 probes at the same position on the abscissa as the learning trial closest in time. Both Panels of Figure 1 show a very close covariation across trials and days between scores in the learning runs and the probes. In particular, the large jumps in produced RP between days in the learning task coincide with similar variations in the probes. In other words, within-day as well as across-day fluctuations, which unfold on two separate time scales, are captured coherently, suggesting that both tasks are tapping into the same underlying dynamics. Note also that the moment at which Subject TM finally performs the 90-deg pattern in a stable fashion in the practice trials coincides closely with the moment at which the 90-deg attractor appears in the phase diagram, namely, in the middle of the second day (cf. the arrows in the right Panels of Figures 1 and 3). This is an unequivocal demonstration of the intimate linkage between observed behavior and underlying dynamics.

In sum, learning involves the stabilization of the required pattern that theoretically becomes an attractor of the pattern dynamics. Changes in behavior with learning, usually measured as simple improvements in performance in the learning task itself, are then to be viewed as the outcome of modifications of the whole underlying pattern dynamics, including, for instance, stability. Therefore, the basic contention of the dynamic approach that the concepts of stability and attraction are co-implicative stands also for learning: A pattern is an attractor to the extent that it is stable, and a stable pattern act as an attractor for less stable patterns.

3.2. HOW IS IT LEARNED?

Conceptually, the results of the probes bring to light two essential processes pertaining to perceptual-motor behavior which account for the observed differences in pattern stability as a function of the task requirements (see Figure 2). When the required pattern corresponds to one of the intrinsic attractors, the intrinsic dynamics and behavioral information *cooperate* to attract the behavioral pattern to the same relative phase, so that the resulting state is accurate and highly stable. Conversely, when the required pattern does not coincide with an attractor, the intrinsic dynamics and behavioral information *compete*: Not only does the behavior pattern deviate from the requirement toward a nearby intrinsically stable pattern, but also fluctuations occur, and the resulting state is much less stable. In other words, the extent to which behavioral information cooperates or competes with the intrinsic dynamics determines the behavioral patterns observed. For instance, it is little wonder that in the initial trials of practice (cf. right Panel of Figure 1), Subject TM executes highly variable phasing patterns except when a 180-deg relative phase is produced. The same analysis can be done for Subject MS (left Panel) who exhibits a stable pattern about 115 deg instead of 90 deg. Note that when the 90-deg pattern is an intrinsic attractor originally, the variability of performance in the first practice trials is considerably smaller (for data, cf. Zanone & Kelso, in press).

With practice, the required pattern has become an attractor of the pattern dynamics, so that eventually memorized behavioral information (i.e., the newly learned stable pattern) cooperates with environmental information (i.e., the task requirements) to stabilize the produced pattern. Put another way, the initial instability of the behavioral pattern resulting from competition with environmental information diminishes with learning, and finally vanishes when there is cooperation. The interplay between competitive and cooperative mechanisms reflects as well the entire evolution of performance with learning for Subject MS. Following the eventual cooperation between environmental information and memorized information (shift of the middle stable pattern from 115 to 90 deg), the growing strength of memorized information (i.e., 90 deg) with more practice, adding to the congruent environmental information, competes with the initially stable patterns (0 and 180 deg), so that eventually, the 180-deg pattern completely loses stability and disappears from the phase diagram (see right part of right Panel in Figure 3). At the behavioral level in the learning task, such reduction of competition between memorized behavioral information and the intrinsic dynamics may account for the further decrease in the variability of the behavioral pattern with practice.

In sum, all observed behavioral patterns and the evolution of their dynamics with learning ultimately emerge from the interplay between competitive and cooperative processes. Thus, changes in behavior with learning relies fundamentally upon mechanisms that reduce pattern instability, for the same reason that, on another time scale, switching to another stable behavior follows from the pattern destabilization produced through a control parameter. Indeed, stability and loss of stability appear to be the general principles governing behavioral adaptation to specific as well as non-specific constraints on different time scales.

3.3 IS ANYTHING ELSE LEARNED?

The foregoing findings emphasize the pertinence of systematically probing the pattern dynamics and establishing their phase diagram in order to properly address the process of learning. First, the probing procedure presented here affords a coherent and reliable picture of the current pattern dynamics. Indeed, comparable phase diagrams were also shown by Tuller and Kelso (1989) and by Yamanishi, Kawato and Suzuki (1980), although they used different methods to probe the dynamics. Such a offers a means to evaluate the existing "structure" before the exposure to a new task (the initial pattern dynamics) and to identify the intimate effects of learning. Second, similar methods may prove to be powerful at operationalizing the interaction between a limited behavioral repertoire (viz. initial dynamics) and the external constraints (viz. behavioral information) in other domains. Numerous examples can be found in perception, memory, linguistics, and so forth, in which processes such as generalization, categorization, assimilation, discrimination, and many others play a central role. In particular, the topic of *transfer* is closely related to that of learning. Indeed, transfer (i.e., generalization of learning to a non-trained task) is deemed to be an unequivocal sign that the task has actually been learned. In the light of the framework developed above, an operational definition of transfer can be formulated: Transfer involves modifications of the initial pattern dynamics following practice of a required pattern that are *not* in the direction of the to-be-learned pattern.

Obviously, defining the extent to which such dynamical changes are related to the learning task is non-trivial. In the bimanual system studied here, the theory — in keeping with common sense — posits that the intrinsic pattern dynamics are symmetric. Actually, this is a non-issue in the case of bistable dynamics since +0 and +180 deg equal −0 and −180 deg. Such symmetry is broken as soon as behavioral information specifies a "signed" required pattern (i.e., with left or right lead). As well, when tristable dynamics are observed in the 0 to 180-deg range (e.g., there is an attractor at 90 deg), the question arises of the existence of a stable symmetric pattern (i.e., −90/ + 270 deg). Moreover, when learning involves phase transitions, and the required pattern becomes an attractor, a fundamental point of theory bears upon the occurrence of an equivalent phase transition in the other half of parameter space (henceforth, hemispace). That is, do the pattern dynamics remain symmetric? If so, this would be an unmistakable case of (positive) transfer of a learned task to an unpracticed one. If not, the assumption of symmetry of the dynamics would somehow be violated.

On these premises, an experiment was conducted that basically adopts the same methods as the previous study on learning. On the first day, a full-range phase diagram is established between 0 and 360 deg (reminder: the reference for relative phase is the right LED of the metronome or the right finger). The actual procedure scans from 0 to 180 deg and from 0 to −180 deg in two successive scans. Depending on whether the pattern dynamics show an attractor at 90 deg or not, the required pattern is set either at 135 or at 90 deg respectively[5], to ensure that a *novel* pattern has to be learned. Hence, a phase transition may be expected with learning. Twenty practice trials lasting 20 s

[5]Here again, these relative phases are theoretical unstable fixed points of their respective dynamics.

are then administered. On the second day, a half-range probe (from 0 to 180 deg) of the dynamics is carried out in order to trace changes with practice in the attractor layout. Such a limited probe prevents any practice in the other hemispace (i.e., 0 to −180 deg). Thirty more practice trials follow, until a last complete phase diagram is established (i.e., between 0 and 360 deg).

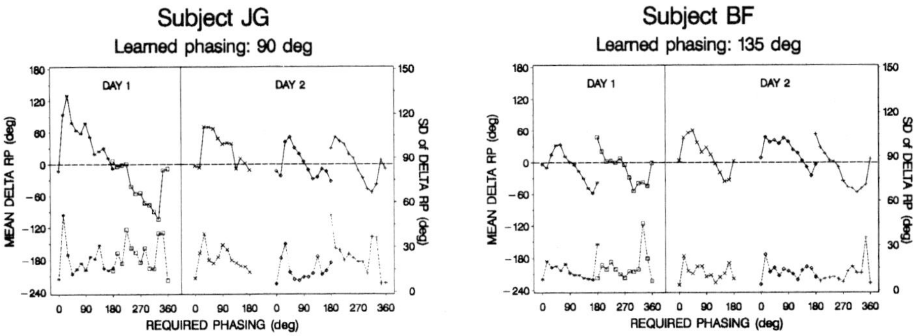

Figure 4: Individual phase diagrams before, during and after learning for Subjects JG and BF. Same legend as in Figure 2.

Preliminary results will be presented here concerning two model subjects. Figure 4 displays the phase diagrams revealed by the three successive probes. The left Panel concerns the attractor layout of Subject JG. Before practice on Day 1, the initial layout (left couple of graphs) exhibits the characteristic features of bistable dynamics. The two attractors at 0 and 180 deg are indicated by the negative slope and the zero crossing of DELTA RP, along with the small variability at these values. Note that the picture is quite symmetric. This subject will be then administered a learning task at 90 deg of relative phase. At the beginning of Day 2 (middle pair of graphs), no qualitative change may be noticed in spite of 20 trials of practice. By the end of the learning procedure (rightmost two graphs), an attractor has clearly emerged at 90 deg, accompanied by a destabilization of the 180 deg pattern. This is a nonequilibrium phase transition in learning, similar to that described in the previous section. More striking is that an attractor appears at 270 deg too, although such a pattern has not be practiced at all. Let us emphasize that not only the 270 deg pattern is produced quite stably when required, but also it strongly attracts nearby phasing patterns. So, a phase transition is also observed in the interval 180–360 deg, resulting from learning the 90-deg pattern. This is a clear instance of transfer. Indeed, there is no doubt that if a 270 deg pattern were required, according to a classical transfer paradigm, Subject JG would be able to perform it readily, since an attractor exists that would stabilize the behavioral pattern through cooperation with behavioral information. To sum up, learning and transfer jointly involved a phase transition from bistable dynamics at 0 and 180 deg to a tristable régime in which the 0-, 90- and 270-deg patterns are behavioral attractors.

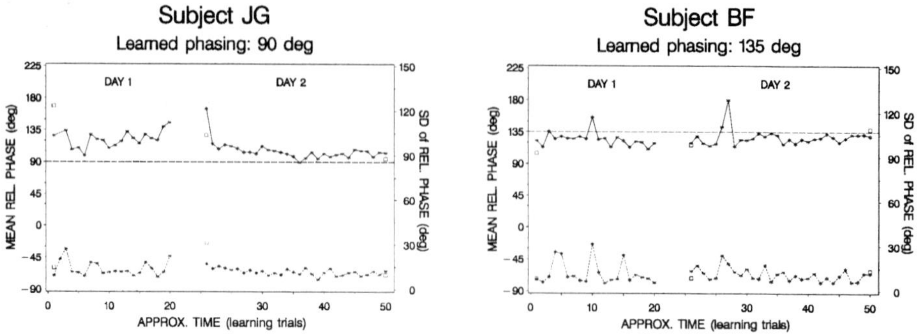

Figure 5: Evolution of performance with practice for Subjects JG and BF. Same legend as Figure 1.

In order to check the consistency between the dynamical modifications and change in performance, the left Panel of Figure 5 displays the learning performance of Subject JG over the 50 practice trials. A marked improvement in performance (cf. ⋆ solid curves) is noticeable in the very first trials of Day 2. This is however quite understandable: Before the first trial on Day 2, the current dynamics which do not show any evidence for an attractor at 90 deg (middle graph in the left Panel of Figure 4) hinder producing this pattern in a stable fashion, since only competition can arise between the current pattern dynamics and the required pattern. Then, the sharp drop of the produced relative phase in the direction of the required pattern and the reduction in across-trial fluctuations may reflect the abrupt phase transition occurring at that moment, leading to cooperation between memorized and environmental information. A consistent evolution of performance is observed in the probe plateau in which a 90-deg pattern is required, as shown by the □ in the left Panel of Figure 4.

The right Panel of Figure 4 displays the phase diagram for Subject BF. Initially, the pattern dynamics turn out to be stable about 0, 90, 180, and 270 deg. So, this subject practiced 135 deg of relative phase as the learning task. At the beginning of Day 2, no qualitative change is detected, the dynamics remaining in the same régime. Nevertheless, a slight drift of the 90-deg attractor is noticeable toward 120 deg. At the end of Day 2, the attractor location is very close to the required pattern around 135 deg. Now, a concomitant drift in the stable pattern initially centered at 270 deg is observed too, reaching the value of 240 deg at the beginning of Day 2 and that of 225 deg at the end of the experiment. Such a symmetric evolution of 270-deg attractor mirroring that of the learned pattern suggests strongly that transfer has occurred, since practice has been actually administered only in one hemispace. A point of theoretical interest is that another route to learning is identified here, involving only parametric, quantitative change in the pattern dynamics, namely, the drift of an existing attractor in parameter space.

Regarding the learning performance of Subject BF, the right Panel of Figure 5 displays the produced pattern as a function of the learning trials. The mean produced relative phase (⋆ solid curve) tends progressively toward the relative phase required across trials, while its intertrial fluctuations diminish markedly, so that the last trials are pretty accurate. Meanwhile, although on the average the intratrial SD (bottom dotted curve) does not decrease that much, its intertrial fluctuations exhibit a substantial decrement, suggesting the stabilization of the 135-deg pattern with practice. Such an evolution parallels the modifications of the pattern dynamics shown above. Put another way, such tight compatibility strongly suggests that the modifications of the pattern dynamics underlie changes in performance. Indeed, performance at 135 deg in the probes, represented by □ in Figure 4, is very much in keeping with that in the learning trials.

To summarize, the first important finding of this preliminary experiment is that the dynamical modifications of the phase diagram in the direction of the to-be-learned pattern with learning appear to be consistently accompanied by changes in the untrained hemispace. This constitutes a first evidence of transfer of learning that would follow a principle of symmetry conservation. The second point is that the forms that the alterations of the pattern dynamics may take with learning (and transfer) are multiple, depending crucially on the interplay between existing intrinsic dynamics and behavioral information. A third point is that behavioral information itself evolves dynamically with learning (Schöner, Zanone, & Kelso, in press, for a discussion).

4. CONCLUSION

The framework and the findings presented in this paper provide some conceptual and operational tools that are instrumental for describing perceptual-motor behavior in a lawful and unequivocal fashion. In turn, the study of coordination between perception and action from this perspective offers a window to capture the basic mechanisms of behavioral adaptation. On the one hand, establishing the system's current phase diagram through probing the pattern dynamics allows one to understand its behavior when confronted with specific task constraints in terms of cooperation and competition between the behavioral information and the intrinsic dynamics. On the other hand, the knowledge of the initial phase diagram allows one to clearly detect learning and transfer as modifications of the current pattern dynamics with practice. A methodological issue, already pointed out, is that the pertinent unit of observation must be the individual. Indeed, not only do the initial dynamics tend to be idiosyncratic, but also their evolution through adaptive mechanisms such as learning may take different forms and unfold along separate time scales.

To sum up the results reported here, the first study captured clear instances of learning according to the admitted criteria, insofar as changes in performance were observed with practice in the direction of the task requirements. Nevertheless, a new understanding of the process is afforded in that behavioral changes with learning pertain to the modifications of the current pattern dynamics toward the to-be-learned pattern. Such alterations stem ultimately from competition between behavioral information and the intrinsic dynamics. The second study shows evidence for transfer to an unpracticed task. The pattern symmetric to that required by the learning task either appears to be performed stably as soon as the latter is actually learned, or it undergoes an evolution that mirrors that of the practiced pattern. Here again, such changes in performance are unambiguously related to the underlying alterations in the pattern dynamics. Thus, two dynamical mechanisms are uncovered leading to learning by practice or transfer: a) a qualitative modification of the pattern dynamics following the destabilization of an initial attractor, namely, a nonequilibrium phase transition; and b) a parametric, non-qualitative change in the pattern dynamics, namely, the drift of an attractor in parameter space.

No doubt that further investigations are needed to answer the numerous questions arising from these findings. In particular, one may wonder what makes learning take one or the other form of dynamical modification. A candidate is the "distance" between the required pattern and the existing attractors in parameter space, while another possibility is a limitation in the number of behavioral attractors. Other learning-related issues are to be dealt with as well, such as the rate of learning as a function of the initial dynamics and the required pattern, the various time scales along which fluctuations occur, forgetting, interference, and so forth. Nevertheless, the methods and the concepts used in the present studies offer a promising way to operationalize these issues.

To conclude, we must emphasize again that the form that learning and transfer take appear to be paradigmatic of other adaptive mechanisms: The principles are valid independent of the level of description (micro- vs. macroscopic) and the time scale on which adaptation unfolds (e.g., learning vs. ontogenesis). Thus, the dynamical principles leading to learning as well as the mechanisms governing behavior during the process may constitute a general theoretical model for adaptive change at several levels of description.

There is presently a great deal of interest in identifying mechanisms in the form of cellular changes, that may be important for learning in very different organisms, for example, in invertebrates such as *Aplysia* (e.g., Kandel, 1979) or mammalian hippocampus (e.g., Stanton & Sejnowski, 1989). A major point of convergence is that during learning, patterns of cooperative activity "reinforce" or stabilize connections within neuronal assemblies (e.g., Barnes, 1986). At the same time, there appears to be elimination of synapses, similar to processes that occur with morphogenesis during development (e.g., Paillard, 1986; Changeux & Dehaene, 1990). These joint effects of stabilization and elimination are quite similar to cooperation and competition in our model system. This similarity between cooperation and competition at the behavioral level and processes such as stabilization and elimination in neuronal ensembles suggests that very general, level-independent mechanisms are at work in self-organizing, pattern forming systems (Grossberg, 1982; Haken, 1983a; von der Malsburg, 1987).

Learning is also of primary interest in the field of artificial neural networks. Neural nets that implement dynamical systems are also being used for adaptive control and motor learning (e.g., Bullock & Grossberg, in press; Jordan, 1990; Kawato, Furukawa & Suzuki, 1987). The modification of the synaptic strengths or coupling constants among the units of the net constitutes the main learning mechanism. Moreover, for a given set of synaptic weights several stable network configurations may emerge. Hence attractors of the network dynamics can be used to model content-addressable memory and so forth. Such theoretical representations are probably powerful enough to model the present results, but they do not predict them. A reason could be that many mathematical network models completely ignore the biological components themselves or the behavioral patterns that they exhibit (Abbott, 1990). In our language, the level of the intrinsic pattern dynamics is not taken into account. To ignore the role of such dynamics may leave an important gap, insofar as they are ultimately responsible for predicted and observed transitions in learning. Indeed, intrinsic dynamics place constraints on what can be learned and how learning occurs. Such limitations and abilities are certainly essential features of biological, if not artificial, systems.

6. REFERENCES

Abbott, L. F. (1990). Learning in neural network memories. *Network, 1*, 105–122.

Abraham, R., & Shaw, C. (1982). *Dynamics – The geometry of behavior. Part 1: Periodic behavior.* Santa Cruz: Aerial.

Baldissera, F., Cavallari, P., & Civaschi, P. (1982). Preferential coupling between voluntary movements of ipsilateral limbs. *Neuroscience Letters, 34*, 95–100.

Barnes, D. M. (1986). Lessons from snails and other models. *Science, 231*, 1046–1049.

Bullock, D., & Grossberg, S. (in press). Adaptive neural networks for control of movement trajectories invariant under speed and force rescaling. *Human Movement Science.*

Changeux, J. P., & Dehaene, S. (1989). Neuronal models of cognitive functions. *Cognition, 33*, 63–109.

Chomsky, N. (1988). *Language and problems of knowledge: The Managua lectures.* Cambridge, Mass: M.I.T. Press.

Cohen, L. (1971). Synchronous bimanual movements performed by homologous and nonhomologous muscles. *Perceptual and Motor Skills, 32*, 639–644.

Gesell, A. (1929). Maturation and infant behavior. *Psychological Review, 36*, 307–319.

Glass, L., & MacKey, M. C. (1988). *From clocks to chaos – The rhythms of life.* Princeton, NJ: Princeton.

Gleick, J. (1987). *Chaos – Making a new science.* New York: Viking Penguin.

Grillner, S. (1975). Locomotion in vertebrates: Central mechanisms and reflex interaction. *Physiological Review, 55*, 247–304.

Grossberg, S. (1982). *Studies of mind and brain.* Dordrecht: Reidel.

Haken, H. (1977/1983a). *Synergetics, an introduction: Non-equilibrium phase transitions and self-organization in physics, chemistry and biology.* Berlin: Springer.

Haken, H. (1983b). *Advanced synergetics: Instability hierarchies of self-organizing systems and devices.* Berlin: Springer.

Haken, H. (1985). *Complex systems: Operational approaches in neurobiology, physical systems and computers.* Berlin: Springer.

Haken, H., Kelso, J. A. S., & Bunz, H. (1985). A theoretical model of phase transitions in human hand movements. *Biological Cybernetics, 51*, 347–356.

Haken, H., & Stadler, M. (1990). *Synergetics of cognition.* Berlin: Springer.

Hamburger, V. (1970). Embryonic mobility in verterbrates. In F. O. Schmidt (Ed.), *The neurosciences: Second study program.* New York: Rockefeller University Press.

Hock, H., Kelso, J. A. S., & Schöner, G. (1990). *Bistability, hysteresis and loss of temporal stability in the perceptual organization of apparent motion.* Manuscript submitted for publication.

Jordan, M. I. (1990). Motor learning and the degrees of freedom problem. In M. Jeannerod (Ed.), *Attention and performance, XIII* (pp. 796–836). Hillsdale, NJ: Erlbaum.

Kandel, E. R. (1979). *Behavioral biology of* Aplysia. San Francisco: Freeman.

Kawato, M., Furukawa, K., & Suzuki, R. (1987). A hierarchical neural-network model for control and learning of voluntary movement. *Biological Cybernetics, 57*, 167–185.

Kelso, J. A. S. (1984). Phase transitions and critical behavior in human bimanual coordination. *American Journal of Physiology: Regulatory, Integrative and Comparative Physiology, 15*, R1000–R1004.

Kelso, J. A. S., Buchanan, J. J., & Wallace, S. A. (1990). *Order parameters for the neural organization of single, multijoint limb movement patterns.* Manuscript submitted for publication.

Kelso, J. A. S., Delcolle, J. D., & Schöner, G. S. (1990). Action-perception as a pattern formation process. In M. Jeannerod (Ed.), *Attention and performance XIII* (pp. 139–169). Hillsdale, NJ: Erlbaum.

Kelso, J. A. S., Mandell, A. J., & Shlesinger, M. S. (1988). *Dynamic patterns in complex systems.* Singapore: World Scientific.

Kelso, J. A. S., & Scholz, J. P. (1985). Cooperative phenomena in biological motion. In H. Haken (Ed.), *Complex systems: Operational approaches in neurobiology, physical systems and computers* (pp. 124–149). Berlin: Springer.

Kelso, J. A. S., Scholz, J. P., & Schöner, G. S. (1986). Non-equilibrium phase transitions in coordinated biological motion: Critical fluctuations. *Physics Letters, A118*, 279–284.

Kelso, J. A. S., & Schöner, G. S. (1987). Toward a physical (synergetic) theory of biological coordination. In R. Graham & A. Wunderlin (Eds.), *Lasers and synergetics* (pp. 224–237). Berlin: Springer.

Kelso, J. A. S., & Schöner, G. S. (1988). Self-organization of coordinative movement patterns. *Human Movement Science, 7*, 27–46.

May, R. (1976). Simple mathematical models with very complicated dynamics. *Nature, 261*, 459–467.

Nicolis, G., & Prigogine, I. (1989). *Exploring complexity: An introduction.* San Francisco: Freeman.

Paillard, J. (1986). Development and acquisition of motor skills: A challenging prospect for neurosciences. In M. Wade & J. Whiting (Eds.), *Motor development in children: Aspects of coordination and control* (pp. 415–441). Dordrecht: Martinus Nijhoff.

Piaget, J. (1952). *The origin of intelligence in the child.* New York: Basic Books.

Piatelli-Palmarini, M. (1989). Evolution, selection, and cognition: From learning to parameter setting in biology and in the study of language. *Cognition, 31*, 1–44.

Schmidt, R. C., Carello, C., & Turvey, M. T. (1990). Phase transitions and critical fluctuations in the visual coordination of rhythmic movements between people. *Journal of Experimental Psychology: Human Perception and Performance, 16*(2), 227–247.

Scholz, J. P., & Kelso, J. A. S. (1989). A quantitative approach to understanding the formation and change of coordinated movements patterns. *Journal of Motor Behavior, 21*(2), 122–144.

Scholz, J. P., Kelso, J. A. S., & Schöner, G. S. (1987). Non-equilibrium phase transitions in coordinated biological motion: Critical slowing down and switching time. *Physics Letters, A123*, 390–394.

Schöner, G. S. (1989). Learning and recall in a dynamic theory of coordination pattern. *Biological Cybernetics, 62*, 39–54.

Schöner, G. S., Haken, H., & Kelso, J. A. S. (1986). A stochastic theory of phase transitions in human hand movement. *Biological Cybernetics, 53*, 442–452.

Schöner, G. S., & Kelso, J. A. S. (1988a). Dynamic pattern generation in behavioral and neural systems. *Science, 239*, 1513–1520.

Schöner, G. S., & Kelso, J. A. S. (1988b). Dynamic patterns in biological coordination: Theoretical strategy and new results. In J. A. S. Kelso, A. J. Mandell, & M. F. Shlesinger (Eds.), *Dynamic patterns in complex systems* (pp. 77–102). Singapore: World Scientific.

Schöner, G. S., & Kelso, J. A. S. (1988c). A dynamic theory of behavioral change. *Journal of Theoretical Biology, 135*, 501–524.

Schöner, G. S., & Kelso, J. A. S. (1988d). A synergetic theory of environmentally-specified and learned patterns of movement coordination. I. Relative phase dynamics. *Biological Cybernetics, 58*, 71–80.

Schöner, G. S., & Kelso, J. A. S. (1988e). A synergetic theory of environmentally-specified and learned patterns of movement coordination. II. Component oscillator dynamics. *Biological Cybernetics, 58*, 81–89.

Schöner, G. S., Zanone, P. G., & Kelso, J. A. S. (in press). Learning coordination patterns as dynamics of dynamics. *Journal of Motor Behavior.*

Skinner, B. F. (1938). *The behavior of organisms.* New York: Appleton-Century.

Stanton, P. K., & Sejnowski, T. J. (1989). Associative long-term depression in the hippocampus induced by Hebbian covariance. *Nature, 338*, 215–218.

Tinbergen, N. (1951). *The study of instinct.* New York: Oxford University Press.

Tuller, B., & Kelso, J. A. S. (1989). Environmentally-specified patterns of movement coordination in normal and split-brain subjects. *Experimental Brain Research, 75*, 306–316.

Tuller, B., & Kelso, J. A. S. (1990). Phase transitions in speech production and their perceptual consequences. In M. Jeannerod (Ed.), *Attention and performance XIII* (pp. 429–452). Hillsdale, NJ: Erlbaum.

Velarde, M. G. (1987). *Synergetics, order, and chaos.* Singapore: World Scientific.

von der Malsburg, C. (1987). Ordered retinotectal projections and brain organization. In E. F. Yates (Ed.), *Self-organizing systems. The emergence of order* (pp. 265–277). New York: Plenum.

Watson, J. B. (1913). Psychology as the behaviorist views it. *Psychological Review, 20*, 158–177.

Yamanishi, T., Kawato, M., & Suzuki, R. (1979). Studies on human finger tapping neural networks by phase transition curves. *Biological Cybernetics, 33*, 199–208.

Yamanishi, T., Kawato, M., & Suzuki, R. (1980). Two coupled oscillators as model for the coordinated finger tapping by both hands. *Biological Cybernetics, 37*, 219–225.

Yates, E. F. (1987). *Self-organizing systems. The emergence of order.* New York: Plenum.

Zanone, P. G., & Kelso, J. A. S. (in press). The evolution of behavioral attractors with learning: Nonequilibrium phase transitions. *Journal of Experimental Psychology: Human Perception and Performance.*

Tutorials in Motor Behavior II
G.E. Stelmach and J. Requin (Editors)

An Exception That Proves the Rule!

H.T.A. WHITING
Department of Psychology
University of York
Heslington, York YO1 5DD
England

G.J.P. SAVELSBERGH
Faculty of Human Movement Sciences
Free University, Amsterdam, Netherlands
and Department of Psychology
University of York, York, England

ABSTRACT. This paper addresses the frequently reported - particularly in the earlier literature - phenomenon of a transfer from visual to kinesthetic control of limb positioning with experience. Evidence is provided, from experiments on one-handed ball catching. The first experiment discussed provides circumstantial evidence suggesting the importance of individual differences in mediating any proposed transfer effects. The second experiment in which comparisons were made between subjects who trained in the dark (with only a luminous ball available in an otherwise completely dark room) for a period of three/four days before transferring on the third/fifth day to a post-test in the light (i.e. both ball and catching limb visible) and subjects who trained for the whole time in the light, provides evidence that questions the idea that movement skill is specific to the feedback conditions present while the skill was being learned. Attention is drawn to an experimental artefact that may lead to misconceptions about putative transfer effects pointing, instead, to the versatility of subjects in being able to make use of whatever environmental information happens to be available.

1. Introduction

If one examines the natural history of motor learning, two predicates will be perceived to have pervaded the literature, namely, that:

1. with suitable experience, there is a transfer from visual to kinesthetic control of limb positioning,
2. skill is specific!

The relation between these two predicates has seldom been signalled or addressed - although, it seems clear, that they are not necessarily mutually exclusive. For example, the first predicate does not deny the possibility that although such transfer may occur, subjects may still be able to operate effectively when the need, or possibility, arises to make use of visual information. From the point of view of the flexibility of system operation, there is much to be said for such an interpretation allowing the system, as it does, to operate effectively under varying informational constraints. In contrast, the second predicate imposes many more limitations on the system which, from an economical point of view, could be very costly.

It is not the intention, here, to trace out such a natural history, or to come down in favour of one position rather than another, but rather to point out that, at particular phases of that history, questions of this nature have been recurrent - albeit, often formulated in novel ways. Thus, the question of transfer from visual to kinesthetic control with experience surfaced in the late seventies/early eighties in the new guise of progress, with learning, from feedback to open-loop control . More recently, interest in mixed control models - implying an interplay between central planning and the processing of feedback - in focusing further on this topic has resurrected, once again, the question of *specificity* of skill learning.

To take a particular example, the latter type of control model has motivated Marteniuk and Proteau (1990) to pose the question:

> ...how do people acquire the ability to use central and feedback processes in a highly skilled way?'.

Or, in the context of *visual aiming movements*, recast as follows:

> ...what feedback sources are most relevant to the learning and performance of this type of skill and, to what extent this movement skill is specific to the feedback conditions present while the skill was being learned?

Their phrasing of the second part of the question in the form:

> ...to what extent does transfer of movement skill occur when the source of feedback for use in control is either eliminated or changed?

can be seen as a variation on the earlier theme of transfer from visual to kinesthetic monitoring. Experimental work of Proteau and his colleagues (Proteau & Cournoyer, 1990; Proteau, Marteniuk, Girouard & Dugas, 1987; Proteau, Marteniuk & Levesque, 1990) led to their adopting a *specificity of skill learning hypothesis* couched in terms of an increasing dependence on particular kinds of feedback with increasing practice.

The Proteau et al. 1987 study had, as its task, the making of 90cm aiming movements to a target in a standard time of 550ms. Amongst the conditions of practice were performing with both *vision of the performing limb and of the target* or of the *target alone* - KR being provided following each trial. The transfer condition provided vision of the target only (with no KR). The group which had received extensive practice with vision of the performing limb available was shown to be particularly vulnerable to the transfer condition - showing (under one of the conditions) a 400% increase in RMSE leading the authors of this study to suggest that the role played by visual information coming from the environment and the *ongoing limb* does not diminish as amount of practice increases - quite the reverse! A more recent study (Marteniuk & Proteau, 1990) confirmed the finding for a task requiring shorter movement times - 250 ms or 400 ms - where it might have been predicted that learning such relatively rapid movements would decrease or eliminate the necessity for the use of visual feedback. Overall, the findings from these two studies led the authors to conclude that:

> ...the earlier proposition suggesting that movement control goes from a reliance on visuo-spatial feedback to either a totally open-loop mode of control, or a kinesthetic type of control should be rejected.

It is not wished, here, to take issue with the experimental findings *per se* that they report, but rather, in what follows, to question the generality of this statement. While it may hold for the kind of task they are studying, there is evidence from more everyday tasks (for example one-handed catching) that suggests the need for some qualification.

2. One-handed Catching

Up until the early '80's studies on catching behaviour tended to be limited to the effect of the *amount* of information available, in the framework of information processing theoretical frameworks (See Savelsbergh, Whiting, & Pijpers, 1991, for an overview). In 1982, a new concern became the *quality* of that information - more particularly with the question:

> ...is viewing of the hand as well as viewing of the ball necessary for efficient one-handed catching?

It was Smyth and Marriott (1982) who first appear to have posed such a question in the context of catching behaviour. Their initial thesis was that as articular proprioception is (normally) considered to provide accurate information about limb position, particularly in ball skills in which the eyes are thought to be occupied with tracking the ball, prevention of sight of the catching hand should, in principle, have no detrimental effect on catching performance. In fact, Smyth and Marriott (1982) produced contrary evidence in showing that more position (spatial) than timing (temporal) errors were made when sight of the catching hand was prevented i.e., that sight of the hand is necessary for optimal catching performance. A finding that, in retrospect, falls nicely into line with the ideas of Proteau et al., namely, a continued reliance - even after extensive experience - on vision of the catching limb for optimal performance.

Subsequent studies, utilising similar paradigms, to that of Smyth and Marriott, produced evidence for and against their proposition (e.g. Fischman & Schneider, 1985; Diggles, Grabiner and Garhammer, 1987; Rosengren, Pick & Von Hofsten, 1988). Two contrasting methodologies for preventing sight of the hand were to be seen in such studies, namely, the use of an occluding screen and the use of a luminous ball in an otherwise dark room. Fischman et al (1985) and Diggles et al (1987) also introduced the topic of individual differences into their studies utilising expert or inexpert games players as their criterion groups. In general, however, the results obtained were equivocal leading Savelsbergh and Whiting in 1988 to address the necessity for viewing the catching hand in a study that not only utilised contrasting groups of (persistently) 'poor' and 'good' catchers - defined in terms of a within-task criterion (i.e., one-handed catching within a laboratory set-up) but also the *two* methods reported in the literature for occluding sight of the catching hand . The importance of using a within-task criterion for classifying subjects in this kind of comparative study was signalled in an earlier study of Whiting, Alderson and Sanderson (1973) where the interpretive problems which can ensue when groups of expert or inexpert games players are used as the criteria for individual differences in performance on laboratory ball catching tasks was demonstrated. Savelsbergh and Whiting (1988) were able to qualify the previous work by demonstrating that it is only 'poor' catchers for whom sight of the hand is necessary. When vision of the hand is prevented such subjects make significantly more spatial errors. In the context of the Proteau et al. studies discussed earlier, this is an interesting finding and one which questions the generality of their position. There are two further concerns about the Proteau et al. (1987) study.

The first of these relates to the transfer condition. In the experiments of Proteau et al. - because of the question they wished to ask - subjects were always transferred from a condition in which they could view the hand (and target) involved in the movement aiming task to a condition in which sight of the acting hand was prevented. What would the prediction be, from their theoretical standpoint, for subjects who trained without vision of the hand and were then transferred to a condition in which vision of the hand was possible? Presumably, if their theoretical position is to be general, they would have to say that subjects would have become dependent on kinesthetic feedback and, therefore, the availability of additional information would not be seen as relevant. Such information would certainly not (at least in the initial stages) be expected to enhance performance.[1]

The second concern has to do with the number of trials allowed on the transfer task and, from which, conclusions were drawn. Subjects, in these studies were trained over shorter (200) or longer (2000) series of trials under conditions in which either the *target* or the *hand and target* were visible, transfer being made to a condition in which the hand could not be seen. However, the number of trials allowed in the transfer task was only 20. Was this a sufficient number to overcome the usual traumatic effects of transferring from one condition to another? Often, in such experiments, where viewing conditions are being manipulated, subjects are allowed a number of acclimatisation trials (20?) before the condition proper is explored.

In summary, there are three issues that lead us to question the generality of the proposition of Proteau et al. - particularly with respect to an 'open' skill such as catching a ball travelling on a relatively unpredictable flight path. The first *two* of these will be addressed in what follows:

1) The differences shown in the catching experiments of Savelsbergh and Whiting (1988) between 'poor' and 'good' catchers - suggesting that individual differences may play an important role i.e., only after really extensive practice would a transfer from visual to kinesthetic monitoring be observed. That such an alternative explanation of the findings of Proteau et al. (1987) is doubtful is apparent from the fact that they showed quite the converse i.e., that the greater the number of trials, the more traumatic the effect of removing vision of the hand/arm!

2) In the Proteau et al studies the transfer was always from a condition in which the hand (and target) could be viewed to a condition in which sight of the acting hand was not possible. What would their theoretical position predict if subjects trained in the dark and were then transferred into performing in full-light? Would such a prediction be empirically upheld?

---

1 It would appear that, in the interim period, this 'reverse' transfer condition has, in fact, been carried out (but not yet published) The results, essentially, supported the theoretical position of Proteau et al (Marteniuk, personal communication).

3) The number of trials given on the *transfer* task. What, for example, would happen if this number were considerably extended and would the theoretical position of Proteau et al., be able to account for such findings?

Here, we will explore the first *two* of these issues only, on the basis of experiments carried out by the present authors.

Experiment 1: Individual Differences:

The nature of individual differences in one-handed ball catching was, as previously stated, a topic that interested Whiting et al., as long ago as 1973. Their study was able to demonstrate the need to base individual difference comparisons on criterion groups established on the basis of a within-task performance rather than on some arbitrarily proposed high correlation between games playing ability and one-handed catching within a laboratory based task. It was for this reason that the 1988 study of the present authors utilised groups of (persistently) 'poor' and 'good' catchers - the criterion for allocation being the number of successful catches made in a *series* of pre-tests in the laboratory situation similar to that used in the experiment proper.

In this study, groups of 'poor' and 'good' catchers were compared under five different catching conditions - Full-light (FL), Transparent screen between head and catching arm (TS), Opaque screen between head and catching arm - thus obscuring sight of the catching hand (BS), Luminous *ball* and *hand* in an otherwise dark room (UVBH) and Luminous *ball* in an otherwise dark room (UVB) - with, as dependent variables, number of catches, number of spatial errors, number of temporal errors. The results of only the first two of these variables are reported in what follows - the temporal errors being less relevant to the question, here, being addressed.

On the dependent variable 'number of catches' both 'good' and 'poor' catchers showed a significant ($p<.025$) negative effect when sight of the viewing hand was prevented (conditions BS and UVB). That this effect was less traumatic for the 'good' catchers is apparent from the analysis of the spatial errors made (Table 1). Only for the 'poor' group of catchers were significantly more spatial errors made when the hand could not be seen (interaction $p=0.056$).

Thus, preventing sight of the hand - for catchers used to being able to view their catching hand - does have an effect on performance but this effect is less traumatic for the 'good' catchers than for the 'poor'. Such a finding questions the generality of the proposal of

Proteau et al (Proteau & Cournoyer, 1990; Proteau , Marteniuk, Girouard & Dugas, 1987; Proteau, Marteniuk & Levesque, 1990) that as learning trials are increased movement control becomes even more dependent on sensory feedback (of the performing limb).

Table 1

Means and S.D's of number of Spatial Errors under the five conditions for *Good* and *Poor* Catchers

SPATIAL ERRORS	Condition	'Good Catchers' (N=15)		'Poor Catchers' (N=14)	
		Mean	S.D.	Mean	S.D.
	FL	0.06	0.25	4.42	3.10
	TS	0.80	0.94	6.21	4.62
	BS	1.20	1.56	8.28	4.14
	UVBH	3.00	3.50	12.57	5.47
	UVB	4.13	3.99	15.50	4.76

Experiment 2 - training under restricted viewing conditions

It is the opinion of the present authors that the results of the previous experiment are more suggestive than conclusive (particularly given the marginal significance of the interaction) and, if it is wished to question the findings of Proteau et al., in a more principled way it is necessary to look at the findings of experiments that - in the same way - have addressed themselves directly to training under restricted viewing conditions and the subsequent effects when subjects are transferred to less restricted viewing conditions.

The experiments reported in the literature by Proteau et al., to date can be characterised as exploring the effects of training under favourable conditions and transferring to less favourable (i.e. from viewing both hand and target to viewing target only). We have, earlier in this paper, pointed to the need - if the generality of the position of Proteau et al. is to be maintained - to explore the alternative transfer condition i.e., from relatively unfavourable to relatively favourable conditions (from viewing the target only to viewing both hand and target). If, as Proteau et al., have suggested, subjects become increasingly dependent on particular kinds of feedback with increasing practice they should not benefit from being transferred into a condition in which additional forms of feedback are available that were not available during the training trials. It is this experimental manipulation that Savelsbergh and Whiting carried out.

Three groups of relatively 'poor' catchers[2] (mean number of catches out of 30 being 12.4, 13.1 and 12.0, respectively, on the *second* of two series of pre-tests) were required to learn to catch, one-handed, a ball projected from a ball machine at a speed of 10.5 m/s at an angle of 20 degrees, from a height of 1.14 m above the floor. The distance from the ball-projection machine to the subject was 5.6 m, resulting in a ball flight time of approximately 535 ms. The three conditions of training were as follows:

- FL (long training in the light): Pre-test (1x30 trials) in the light (i.e. ball and catching hand visible) followed by four days of training in the light (5x30 trials each day) and a post-test on the fifth day in the light (5x30 trials) .
- DL (long training in the dark): Pre-test (1x30 trials) in the light (i.e., ball and catching hand visible) followed by four days of training in the dark - with only a luminous ball visible - (5x30 trials each day) and a post-test (transfer) on the *fifth* day in the light (5x30 trials).
- DS (short training in the dark): Pre-test (1x30 trials) in the light (i.e., ball and catching hand visible) followed by 3 days of training in the dark with only a luminous ball visible - (5x30 trials on days 1 and 2: 2x30 trails on day 3) and a post-test (transfer) on the *third* day in the light (3x30 trials).

Results:

The results, for the dependent variables 'number of catches' and 'number of spatial errors' are presented in Table 2.

Analyses:

Number of catches:

Pre-post test training effects: In order to explore the effects of training over longer or shorter periods, a 3(Group: FLvDLvDS) x 2(Test: pre/post) ANOVA with repeated

---

2 The necessity to use 'poor' catchers in this kind of experiment should be appreciated. Including subjects who have little or nothing to learn (i.e., so-called 'good' catchers) could bias the results considerably.

measures on the last factor was carried out for the dependent variable 'number of catches'. Only the factor Test was significant ($F(1,20)= 46.32$; $p<.001$) indicating a significant pre-post test increase in the number of catches made independent of condition. Comparisons between the three conditions revealed no significant differences in performance on either the pre-tests or the post-tests.

Table 2

Number of **catches** (out of 30) and number of **spatial errors** for Pre-test (light - hand and ball visible), training trials (light/dark) and post-test (transfer - light) for the three conditions of training - Full light (FL), Dark training -long (DL) and Dark training - short (DS).

Dependent Variable		Pre-test	Training				Post-test (transfer)
			day 1	day 2	day 3	day 4	
Number of Catches							day 5
	FL	12.3	17.6	20.4	22.0	23.2	24.2
	DL	13.1	8.6	10.7	12.9	12.6	21.7
							day 3
	DS	12.0	9.3	10.6	11.7		18.3
Spatial Errors							day 5
	FL	5.2	3.8	1.4	0.85	0.6	0.30
	DL	2.85	4.2	4.1	2.1	2.4	0.96
							day 3
	DS	2.62	5.1	2.1	1.6		0.34

Pre-test/training day 1 effects: The apparent increase (Table 2) in performance from *pre-test* to *training Day 1* for the FL group and the decrease in performance for the other two groups was explored by means of a 3(Groups: FLvDLvDS) x 2(pre-test v training Day 1) - with repeated measures on the last factor - ANOVA. There was a significant Groups x Test interaction ($F(2,20)= 4.41$; $p<.026$) reflecting the significant increase in number of catches made under the FL condition and the decrease under the DL and DS conditions. Newman Keuls post-hoc comparison showed significant differences for the first training between FL and DL and between FL and DS ($p< .05$). No differences between conditions were found for the pre-test or between DL and DS on the training Day 1.

Training over days effects: In order to explore whether or not the pre-test/training Day 1 increments/decrements persisted over days, a 2(Groups:FLvDL) x 4(training Days 1-4) - with repeated measures on the last factor - ANOVAS, were carried out. A significant groups effect ($F(1,13)=19.7$; $p<.001$) and a significant Day effect were apparent ($F(3,39)=15.4$; $p<.001$). Post hoc Newman-Keuls tests showed significant differences between all mean comparisions ($p<.05$) except between day 3 and day 4.

A further, repeated measures, ANOVA - 3(Groups: FLvDLvDS) x 3(training Days 1-3) was carried out so as to include the training of the DS group - which only continued until Day 3. A significant groups (F2,20)=9.87; $p<.002$) and a significant Day effect (F2,40=15; $p<.001$)were found. Post-hoc Newman-Keuls tests showed.significant differences between all mean comparisions ($p<.05$).

Putative transfer effects: A putative transfer effect from last training trial to post test was examined by means of a further 3(Groups: FLvDLvDS) x 2(Training Day 3/Day 5 v post-test) ANOVA with repeated measures on the last factor. This revealed significant main effects for Groups ($F(1,20)= 8.35$; $p<.003$) and Test ($F(1,20)= 51.66$; $p<.001$) and a significant Groups x Test interaction ($F(2,20)= 13.57$; $p<.001$). Post-hoc (Newman Keuls) tests demonstrated significant improvements between the last training and the post-test (transfer) for both the DL and the DS conditions ($p< .01$) but no significant improvement for the FL group.

While, in the context of the findings of Proteau et al., this putative positive transfer effect from training in the dark to performing in the light is interesting, care should be taken in attributing it to the effects of training in the dark *per se* (a result which would be the antithesis of that, apparently, found by Proteau and his co-workers. Examination of Table 2 will confirm that by the end of their training in the dark, subjects in both the DL and the DS conditions only reach the level of performance that they were able to demonstrate (in the light, on the pre-test) prior to training in the dark. Furthermore, at the end of their training *and* transfer to full light their performance is no better than the performance of the FL group on training Day 1. Thus, the apparent positive effects of transferring from training in the dark to performing in the light may be artefactual. In order to explore this possibility, a 3 (Groups: FLvDLvDS) x subjects (23) x Test (FL group - pre-test and training Day 1: DL group - pre-test and post-test (Day 5); DS - pre-test and post-test (Day 3)) ANOVA - see Table 3 - was carried out.

Table 3

Scores submitted to ANOVA to explore potential artefact - *number of catches*

Condition	Pre-test score		
		Training Day 1	
FL	12.3	17.6	
		Post-test score	
		Day 3	Day 5
DL	13.1		21.7
DS	12.0	18.3	

Only a significant effect of Tests was found ($F(1,20) = 34.65$; $p<.001$) and no significant interaction i.e., there were no significant, differential, effects of training under any of the three conditions.

Spatial Errors:

As with the dependent variable *number of catches,* six ANOVAS were carried out as follows:

Pre-post test training effects: A 3(Groups: FLvDLvDS) x 2(Test: pre/post) ANOVA with repeated measures on the last factor was carried out for the dependent variable 'spatial errors' (misses). Only the factor Test was significant ($F(1,20)= 13.57$; $p<.002$) - indicating a significant pre-post test decrease in the number of misses made independent of condition.

Pre-test/training Day 1 effects: A 3(Groups: FLvDLvDS) x 2(pre-test v first-training (Day 1)) ANOVA - with repeated measures on the last factor - was carried out. No significant effects were found.

Training over days effects: In order to explore whether or not the pre-test/training Day 1 increments/decrements persisted over days, a 2(Groups:FLvDL) x 4(training Days 1-4) - with repeated measures on the last factor - ANOVA, was carried out. A significant Day effect were apparent ($F(3,39)=3.16$; $p<.036$). Post hoc Newman-Keuls tests showed significant difference between day 1 and day 3, and day1 and day 4 ($p<.01$).

Training over days effects: A further, repeated measures, ANOVA - 3(Groups: FLvDLvDS) x 3(training Days 1-3) was carried out so as to include the training of the DS group - which only continued until Day 3. Only a significant Day effect ($F(2,40)=7.42$; $p<.002$) was found. Post-hoc Newman-Keuls tests showed a significant difference between day 1 and day 3 ($p<.01$).

Putative transfer effects: A 3(Groups: FLvDLvDS) x 2(Last training v post-test) ANOVA - with repeated measures on the last factor - revealed (nearly) significant main effects for Group ($F(1,20)= 3.30$; $p=.058$) and Test ($F(1,20)= 15.67$; $p<.001$). No significant Group x Test interaction was found.

Table 4
Scores submitted to ANOVA to explore potential artefact - *spatial errors*

Condition	Pre-test score		
		Training Day 1	
FL	5.2	3.8	
		Post-test score	
		Day 3	Day 5
DL	2.85		0.96
DS	2.62	0.34	

Potential Artefact: A further 3 (Groups: FLvDLvDS) x Subject (23) x Test (FL group - pre-test and training Day 1: DL group - pre-test and post-test (Day 5); DS - pre-test and post-test (Day 3)) ANOVA - Table 4 - was carried out in order to explore a potential artefact. Only a significant effect of test was found ($F(1,20) = 5.02$; $p<.037$) with no significant interactions i.e., as with the dependent variable *number of catches*, there were no significant differential effects of training under any of the three conditions.

Discussion:

For both dependent variables - number of catches and number of spatial errors - subjects in all three groups showed highly significant pre-post test increases (number of catches)/decreases (number of spatial errors). The fact that moving from performing in the light to training in the dark is different from performing in the light is confirmed by the significant decrease in *number of catches* on Day 1 for subjects in groups DL and DS. Although corresponding increases in spatial errors were also apparent for these two groups, the relatively large number of spatial errors (5.2) for the FL group (brought about by the very poor performance of two of the Ss in this group) meant that the ANOVA results did not reach significance. In contrast, subjects who trained in full light (FL) showed positive training effects up until day 3 for both the dependent variables.

A putative, significant, positive transfer effect for the groups DL and DS (in moving from training in the dark to performing in full light) was apparent for both dependent variables.

That these putative transfer effects may, however, be an artefact, is indicated by the comparison made between the pre-test scores for all groups and the training scores Day 1 for the FL group and the post-test scores for groups DL (Day 5) and DS (Day 3), *i.e., comparisons between first and second performance sessions in full-light for all groups.*

3. General Discussion:

The results of Experiment 1, while not being conclusive, draw attention to the way in which individual differences at the beginning of learning experiments of this kind may bias the results obtained if subjects are not suitably selected on the basis of an appropriate pre-test. Basically, the message is that if subjects have little to learn (having already reached a ceiling on the task in question) their inclusion in an experimental design may bias the results in such a way that interpretation is difficult, if not meaningless.

While the putative positive transfer effects for groups DL and DS - on both dependent variables - could be used to speak against the conclusion of Proteau et al., that movement skill is specific to the feedback conditions pertaining when the skill was learned, such a statement would need to be treated with caution. The finding of no significant differences between the three groups (FL, DL and DS) when their pre-test scores were compared with their performances on training Day 1 (FL) and post-tests (on Day 5 for DL and on Day 3 for DS) - on both dependent variables - suggests another interpretation of the results. It is as if performing in the light and performing in the dark are treated as separate skills. 'Poor' catchers who train in the light show increments in performance at least up to Day.3 while similar, matched, groups of subjects when transferred to training in the dark show, following an initial decrement in performance, increments up until Day.3. When transferred, at the end of a dark training period, into a different environmental condition (full-light) they simply pick up where they left off in their pre-test in full light. It does not seem to matter how much training in the dark takes place between the pre-test and the post-test. (In table 2 DL group carried out 600 trials in the dark, DS 300 trials, and in table 5, the dark group 90 training trials in the dark). This was shown in Experiment 2 for groups DL (4 days) and DS (3 days) and was also shown in a similar, catching, experiment of Savelsbergh and Whiting (Savelsbergh, 1990) - designed to address a different question - when the training in the dark was restricted (on Day 1) to 3 blocks of 30 trials (Table 5).

Table 5

Means and standard deviations (in parentheses) of successful catches (out of 30) for pre-test, training blocks and post-test (Day 1) for the FL (full-light) and D (dark - luminous ball only visible) groups (Savelsbergh, 1990)

	FL N=9	D N=8
Day 1		
Pre-test	**6.66 (4.47)**	**5.25 (5.00)**
Training session 1	8.00	3.37
Training session 2	9.22	4.25
Training session 3	8.33	4.62
Post-test	**8.44 (6.24)**	**8.62 (7.17)**

A similar and, as at that time suggested, probably spurious transfer effect was earlier shown by Whiting (1967) using a continuous ball-throwing and catching task in which subjects (following on a pre-test in full light) trained under a variety of restricted viewing conditions (of ball, hand and target) for a period of six one-minute trials - with half minute rests between trials - all on the same day, before being transferred to a post test in full light.

Together, the results of Experiments 1 and 2 suggest that the contention of Proteau and his co-workers that movement skill is specific to the feedback conditions present while the skill was being learned should be treated with caution. Certainly, the findings do not seem to be generalisable to catching tasks. The results presented here, rather, point to the ability of subjects to be able to switch from operating under one set of environmental information to operating under another without any, apparent, residual effects of the one performance on the other. This gives credence to Bingham's (1988) explanation of goal-directed behaviour as requiring the relating of properties of the environment and properties of the actor and their *temporary* organization into task-specific devices. Substantially changing the environment - as, for example, in moving from the light to the dark conditions in the above experiments - calls for the mobilisation of *a new* task-specific device. In this sense, there *is* a specificity to skill learning but not couched in terms of all or not dependence on some specific set of feedback information.

Acknowledgement: This paper was written while the second author held a fellowship from The Commision of The European Communities for Science, Research and Development.

4. References

Diggles, V.A., Grabiner, M.D. & Garhammer, J. (1987). Skill level and efficacy of effector visual feedback in ball catching. *Perceptual and Motor Skills*, 64, 987-993.

Fischman, M.G. & Schneider, T. (1985). Skill level, vision and proprioception in simple one-handed catching. *Journal of Motor Behavior,* 17, 219-229.

Marteniuk, R.G. & Proteau, L.. (1990). Evidence for feedback control of learned fast movements: Further support for specificity of learning. (submitted).

Proteau, L., Marteniuk, R.G., Girouard, Y. & Dugas, C. (1987). On the type of information used to control and learn an aiming movement after moderate and extensive training. *Human Movement Science,* 6, 181-199.

Proteau, L., Marteniuk, R.G. & Levesque, L. (1990). A sensorimotor basis for motor learning: evidence indicating specificity of practice. (submitted).

Proteau, L. & Cournoyer, J. (1990). Vision of the stylus in a manual aiming task: the effects of practice. *Quarterly Journal of Experimental Psychology,* (in press).

Rosengren, K.S., Pick, H.L. & Hofsten, C. von (1988). Role of visual information in ball catching. *Journal of Motor Behavior*, 20, 150-164.

Savelsbergh, G.J.P. (1990). *Catching behaviour*. Meppel: Krips Repro.

Savelsbergh, G.J.P.& Whiting, H.T.A. (1988). The effect of skill level,external frame of reference and environmental changes on one-handed catching. *Ergonomics*, 31, 1655-1663.

Savelsbergh, G.J.P., Whiting, H.T.A. & Pijpers, J.R. (1991). The control of catching. In J.J. Summers (Ed.), *Approaches to the study of motor control and learning.* Amsterdam: North Holland (in press).

Smyth , M.M. & Marriott, A.M. (1982). Vision and proprioception in simple catching. *Journal of Motor Behavior,* 14, 143-152.

Whiting, H.T.A. (1967). Visuo-motor coordination. Unpublished Ph.D Thesis. Department of Psychology, Leeds.

Whiting, H.T.A., Alderson, G.J.K. & Sanderson, F.H. (1973). Critical time intervals forviewing and individual differences in performance on a ball-catching task. *International Journal of Sport Psychology,* 4, 155-166.

Tutorials in Motor Behavior II
G.E. Stelmach and J. Requin (Editors)

Frequency locking, frequency modulation, and bifurcations in dynamic movement systems

P. J. Beek[ab], C. E. Peper[a] and P. C. W. van Wieringen[a]

[a]Department of Psychology, Faculty of Human Movement Sciences, Amsterdam, The Netherlands

[b]Center for the Ecological Study of Perception and Action, Department of Psychology, University of Connecticut, Storrs CT, U.S.A.

Abstract

This tutorial is concerned with the dynamical study of frequency locking, frequency modulation, and bifurcations between frequency locks in coordinated rhythmic movements, such as breathing and walking, cascade juggling, and polyrhythmic tapping. In modeling these phenomena, concepts and tools are borrowed from classical analytical dynamics (the force balance and the Lagrangian) and modern qualitative dynamics (the circle map and the Farey tree) in order to demonstrate their usefulness for the movement scientist. In so doing, a pragmatic style of inquiry is promoted that has an eye for the continuity between these two branches of dynamics, and that seeks to exploit the strengths of both, depending on the nature of the problem confronted.

1. INTRODUCTION

Rhythmic interlimb coordination is a ubiquitous aspect of biological movement. In many motor skills and activities, the limbs move rhythmically together in often intricate phase and frequency relations. Understanding such rhythmic interlimb coordination is a major goal of movement science and a variety of research strategies have been pursued to achieve it.

Relatively new to movement science is the application of concepts and tools borrowed from the physics of self-organizing systems and the mathematics of nonlinear dynamics [1-3]. Such applications date back, in their modern form, to Poincaré, but build on the discipline of dynamics as a whole. This approach represents an interdisciplinary field of study concerned with pattern formation in complex, non-equilibrium systems [4-10]. In the context of living systems, its significant contribution has been in demonstrating that pattern formation in such open, dissipative systems does not require the existence of independent pattern generators that underlie the observed order, but may be governed by general principles that have no material (symbolic) representation within the system itself. Spatial and temporal patterns may arise spontaneously (i.e., self-organize) when one or a few so-called *control parameters* are changed. They guide the system through its respective collective states in unspecific ways. In contrast to symbolic representations (e.g., schemes, motor programs), these control parameters do not prescribe the resulting patterns in any deterministic way. The strategic power of the approach derives from the possibility it offers for capturing the macroscopic orderly behavior of complex systems in terms of the low-dimensional dynamics of a collective variable (or *order parameter*) characterizing the emergent patterns [6].

Many examples of self-organization have been found in physical, chemical, and biological systems [5, 11]. The analogies between such self-organizing systems are drawn at a high level of abstraction, i.e., at the level of the collective behavior of the system as described by the dynamics of its order parameter(s). When these systems are analyzed in increasing detail in terms of the properties of their subsystems, additional differences may be revealed between them [5]. Quite often, when we ask more local and specific questions, the need for an analytical treatment increases.

The aim of this tutorial is to introduce the movement scientist to the following concepts and tools: the *force balance* (a method for constructing equations of motion), the *Lagrangian* (providing a method for identifying motion invariance based on the principle of least action), the *circle map* (the simplest description of frequency locking, frequency modulation, and chaotic behavior), and the *Farey tree* (a rather abstract tool for the qualitative study of frequency locking in rhythmic activity), and to demonstrate the application of these concepts and tools in the study of frequency locking and frequency modulation in coordinated rhythmic movements. The discussion is set up in such a way that the continuity between classical analytical dynamics and modern qualitative dynamics becomes apparent. Both approaches are useful, depending on the nature of the questions confronted.

The approaches will be discussed in the context of three examples of movement coordination: the adjustment of respiratory to locomotory rhythms, cascade juggling, and polyrhythmic tapping. The appealing feature of these activities is that, apart from the fact that they exhibit some properties that seem to apply to movement systems rather generally, each one of them introduces specific, theoretically significant properties that demand a particular strategy on the part of the scientist. In order to provide the reader with an adequate picture of what can be achieved and what is at issue in this rapidly evolving field of study, these properties and their implications will be discussed.

Before addressing our first example we will briefly introduce some concepts which will be used in describing the time evolution of dynamic systems. Generally speaking, such behavior may be conveniently visualized by means of the *state space* (*phase space*). The coordinates of this space are formed by variables relevant to the description of the system in question. Typically, in a two-dimensional state space, these variables are displacement and velocity. The resulting trajectories in state space are called the *phase portrait*. They often take on a recognizable geometric form or topology, especially when *attractor states* are present, i.e., regions in state space to which the behavior of the system is attracted and where it will eventually settle down. Such attractors may be point attractors (*fixed points*), periodic attractors (*limit cycles*), quasiperiodic attractors, or chaotic attractors.

It was Poincaré who first recognized the potential importance of studying topological characteristics of trajectories in state space, but it took about fifty more years before this insight took firm hold in the field of dynamics [12].

2. FREQUENCY LOCKING BETWEEN BREATHING AND RUNNING

In human and animal running the inspiration-expiration cycle adjusts itself to a comfortable value relative to the step cycle. In order to analyze this phenomenon we first study the motion of the diaphragm in terms of its deflection from rest (s) as a function of the reactive force F(t), which is exerted on the diaphragm by the surface of support as a result of the footfall. The motion of the diaphragm is described, using the notation $\dot{}$ and $\ddot{}$ for the first and second time-derivative respectively, by the following *balance of forces*

$$m\ddot{s} + r'\dot{s} + cs = F(t)$$

or

$$\ddot{s} + r\dot{s} + \omega^2 s = \frac{F(t)}{m} \qquad (1)$$

Eq. (1) is based on Newton's Second Law stating that the sum of all forces acting on an object (in this case the diaphragm) is equal to its mass (m) times its acceleration ($\ddot{s}$). Relevant forces besides F(t), the external force due to running, are: a restoring force with coefficient of elasticity c (proportional to s), and a frictional force with coefficient of resistance r' (proportional to $\dot{s}$). The frequency of the system is $\omega = \sqrt{c/m}$, while $r = r'/m$.

Just as with any second-order differential equation, we can write eq. (1) as two coupled first-order equations. For this we introduce an auxiliary quantity u, such that

$$\dot{s} = u\omega - rs \qquad (2a)$$

and

$$\dot{u} = \frac{F(t)}{m\omega} - \omega s \tag{2b}$$

Let us assume now that the phase plane (s,u) contains a limit cycle that approximates a circle with radius R. Then, for this weakly nonlinear system, it is convenient to replace the variables s and u by the polar coordinates R and θ

$$s = R\cos\theta \quad \text{and} \quad u = R\sin\theta \tag{3a, b}$$

Substitution of these quantities in eqs. (2) produces the following set of differential equations for R (which would be a measure for the total amount of energy stored in the diaphragm) and θ (the phase difference between the motion of the diaphragm and the periodic motion of running)

$$\dot{R} = -rR\cos^2\theta + \frac{F(t)}{m\omega}\sin\theta \tag{4a}$$

and

$$\dot{\theta} = -\omega + r\cos\theta\sin\theta + \frac{F(t)}{m\omega R}\cos\theta \tag{4b}$$

This system of equations is equivalent to eq. (1).

What we have done thus far is to pursue the methods for analyzing weakly nonlinear phenomena involving limit cycles that are nearly circles, i.e., we study nearly harmonic behavior. These methods, which were developed by Andronov [13] and Krylov and Bogoliubov [14], and elaborated later by many others (e.g., Pearson [15]; see also [16]), enable us to identify fixed points, i.e., frequency locks. The description according to eqs. (4) provides a means to calculate the number of breaths per step, that is the ratio $\theta(T)/\omega_1 T$, in which ω_1 is the frequency of running and T the observation time which should be sufficiently large (many steps). Of course, θ(T) is a cyclic function taking a modulo value between 0 and 2π (360°) after any n full cycles. With the symbol θ(T), we mean here θ(T)'s modulo value plus 2πn.

Hoppenstaedt [17] provided a slightly extended version (involving mechanoreceptors and inspiratory and expiratory neurons) of the model presented here, which he used for numerically simulating the ratio between respiratory and locomotory rhythms. The resulting régimes of stable frequency locking compared reasonably well with the empirical measurements of Bramble and Carrier [18] on breathing patterns of running mammals, including humans. These researchers observed that, whereas untrained runners have little synchronization between the frequencies of breathing and stride, trained runners commonly settle down to the ratios 1:1, 1:2, 2:3, 1:3, 2:5, and 1:4 when running on various slopes and at various speeds. Interestingly, when the amplitude of F(t) is large, as in climbing backpackers, mainly the ratios 2:1 and 1:1 are observed (later we will see again how scaling of a control parameter, in this case the magnitude of external forcing, may drive a system through a series of mode-locked states).

Hoppenstaedt's numerical results for the mode locking between running and breathing can be carried one analytical step further by writing eq. (4b) as follows:

$$\lim_{\omega_1 T >> 1} \frac{\theta(t)}{\omega_1 t} = -\frac{\omega}{\omega_1}\left(+ \text{vanishing terms of order } [\frac{\sin \omega_1 T}{\omega_1 T}]\right) \tag{5}$$

in which $\lim \theta(t)/\omega_1 t = 1/W$, where W is the so-called *winding* or *rotation* number, i.e., the mode-locked ratio between the locomotory frequency and the respiratory frequency.

Thus, in case of weak nonlinearity, that is with small values of r and $A/\omega_1 R$ (where A is the amplitude of the diaphragm) relative to ω, it follows that

$$\omega_1 = W\omega \tag{6}$$

This implies that for winding number W = 1 the diaphragm moves in harmony with the gait. For W = 2 a circular limit cycle describes the motion of the diaphragm, in which case its potential and kinetic energy are converted two-harmonically into one another. In case of Integer [W] > 2, the nonlinearities in eqs. (4) create higher harmonics, which drive the representation in the phase plane (s,u) farther and farther away from a circle.

On the basis of this analysis it may also be derived that

$$\dot{R} = -rR \tag{7}$$

(see eq. 4a for $\theta \to 0$) implying that the approach holds better as $r \to 0$ ($r << \omega_1$), but $r \neq 0$ (in order to avoid resonance). This shows the limitation of approaching the problem on the assumption of near-linearity.

The importance of Bramble and Carrier's findings—a series of ratios of relatively prime integers between two frequencies—is that they illustrate the existence of preferred regions of frequency locking in the state space of coordinated movement systems. Moreover, they draw attention to the fact that such frequency locking may not only occur between two limbs, as in walking, flying, and swimming, but between two different subsystems (e.g., the respiratory and locomotory subsystem) as well. Frequency locking is an omnipresent property of biological systems, because it guarantees dynamic stability, often associated with the minimization of some energy cost function (e.g., the reactive force of the ground may be used to relieve the work of the respiratory muscles). The example of frequency locking between breathing and locomotion shows that in some cases an analytical treatment based on the assumption of near-linearity might be feasible. However, when nonlinearities are more prominent another approach is required based on equations for which closed-form solutions are unobtainable. Nowadays, frequency locking phenomena in nonlinear systems are often studied with discrete maps, which has led to a semi-quantitative summary of the behavior of such systems in what is called the Farey tree, which we will discuss later (see section 6).

3. FREQUENCY MODULATION IN RHYTHMIC HAND MOVEMENTS

This section introduces the concept of frequency modulation using a versatile tool for analyzing constrained multi-body movement. The key quantity in this analysis is the *Lagrangian*: the difference between the total kinetic and the total potential energy of the system. Readers who are less interested in this derivation can opt for continuing with eq. (12), which summarizes the analytical result: Constrained movement involving more than one limb segment often leads to modulation.

It is well-known that Newton worked out the laws of dynamics in such a way that this branch of knowledge became a self-contained discipline. During the 18th and 19th century, mechanics achieved, due to the clever work of mathematicians, astronomers, and physicists, a degree of elegance that enabled analysis of systems with many interacting points of mass. Thus, the whole science of mechanics could be based upon a single notion known as the principle of least action. This principle states that the path followed by a dynamic system in passing from one point (A) to another (B) in a state space is such that the total phase change along this path is minimal (technically: stationary) relative to the total phase change along neighboring paths with the same end points (A and B) and transversed in the same time interval [19], i.e.,

$$\frac{d}{dt}\left(\frac{\delta L}{\delta \dot{x}}\right) - \frac{\delta L}{\delta x} = Q \tag{8}$$

where L is the Lagrangian (which is proportional to phase change), x the position, $\dot{x}$ the velocity, and Q all forces not derivable from a potential (i.e., if the system is not preserving energy).

As a case in point consider an oscillator (of mass m), which is driven back to its neutral position (x = 0) by a force –cx. With eq. (8) it is possible to derive the equation of motion for an undamped, harmonic oscillator (again, with $\omega^2 = c/m$)

$$\ddot{x} + \omega^2 x = 0 \tag{9}$$

When frictional forces are proportional (with a factor r) to the velocities of the *m* components of a system, a Rayleigh function (F) for the rate of dissipation can be defined (*mj* spatial dimensions), i.e., for a system of *m* components each free to move in *j* directions

$$F = \frac{1}{2}\sum_i r_i \dot{x}_i^2 \; (i = 1, ..., mj)$$

and Lagrange's principle—not for one, but for *mj* degrees of freedom—is stated as

$$\frac{d}{dt}\left(\frac{\delta L}{\delta \dot{x}_i}\right) - \frac{\delta L}{\delta x_i} = Q = -\frac{\delta F}{\delta \dot{x}_i} \; (i = 1, ..., mj) \tag{10}$$

If eq. (9) is applied to our one-dimensional oscillator, now with friction coefficient r (proportional to $\dot{x}$), it is possible to prove that wherever this damped oscillator starts, it will eventually come to a standstill ($x = 0$; $\dot{x} = 0$). Hence, forcing not derivable from a potential (Q) is needed to sustain its motion. This is usually achieved by injecting discrete squirts of energy into the system. Often this energy is being delivered by an energy relaxation system as in a clock: a harmonic oscillator (a pendulum) supplied by quanta of energy making up for frictional loss by means of a relaxation oscillator (a spring operating against ratchet and pawl, i.e., the escapement).

Lagrange took his analysis of stable motion one step further by considering *n* configuration constraints of the type

$$\Phi_s(x_i, t) = 0 \; (s = 1, ..., n; i = 1, ..., mj) \tag{11a}$$

with the result

$$\frac{d}{dt}\left(\frac{\delta L}{\delta \dot{x}_i}\right) - \frac{\delta L}{\delta x_i} = \sum_{s=1}^{n} \lambda_s(t) \frac{\delta \Phi_s}{\delta x_i} \; (i = 1, ..., mj) \tag{11b}$$

Eq. (11b) constitutes *mj* equations (one for each x_i) and eq. (11a) *n* equations (one for each λ_s). The λ_s are called Lagrange multipliers. They are a priori undetermined: Their physical meaning can only be inferred after eqs. (11) have been solved.

We may now consider the following example of constrained coordination: two symmetric hands (1 and 2) moving harmonically with one degree of freedom, such that the sum of their total potential energies is constant

$$L = \frac{1}{2}m\dot{x}_1^2 - \frac{1}{2}cx_1^2 + \frac{1}{2}m\dot{x}_2^2 - \frac{1}{2}cx_2^2$$

and

$$\Phi = \frac{1}{2}cx_1^2 - \frac{1}{2}cx_2^2 + \text{constant} = 0$$

$$\therefore \; m\ddot{x}_1 + cx_1 = -\lambda(t)cx_1 \quad \text{and} \quad m\ddot{x}_2 + cx_2 = -\lambda(t)cx_2$$

Hence, the two oscillating hands obey what is called the Mathieu-Hill equation

$$\ddot{x} + \omega^2 \{1 + \lambda(t)\}x = 0 \qquad (12)$$

The quintessence of this equation is that it provides an expression for the fact that the movements of the hands are frequency and phase modulated, i.e., they move with an angular frequency that varies in time due to the presence of a time-dependent modulation strength $\lambda(t)$. As long as $\lambda(t) << 1$, the movement will be near or pseudo-harmonic. A special case is the occurrence of "detuning", in which the oscillator's eigenfreqency, due to the influence of another oscillator, is changed with a fixed value (λ = constant).

What this example shows is that the presence of one (or a few) configuration constraint(s) may be sufficient to induce frequency modulation in a Lagrangian system. In human movement systems, of course, such constraints abound—hence, the ubiquity of frequency modulation in such systems. In contrast with frequency locking, frequency modulation guarantees flexibility of operation and adaptability to changing conditions. Let us now elaborate this picture of a pair of frequency-modulated hands for the skill of cascade juggling.

4. FREQUENCY LOCKING AND MODULATION IN CASCADE JUGGLING

Juggling is a complex, cyclic activity that is intrinsically rhythmic. In this particular case, we are able to define precisely what is meant by "intrinsically rhythmic": A pair of coordinated hands ($H = 2$) manipulate N balls such that, on average, N* of them are airborne. The act has to match the flight time (t_f) of the ball such that it comprises N*/H times the cycle time of one hand (t_h). This is a basic law to be satisfied at the macroscale, i.e., from hand loop to hand loop, in order to perform an ongoing act. The law implies that, for cascade juggling to take place, there has to be a locking at the macroscopic level of task execution itself between the frequency of the hand ($1/t_h$) and the frequency of the balls ($1/t_b \equiv 1/(t_l + t_f)$, where t_b is the cycle time of a ball and t_l (time-loaded) is the time that the hand is filled with a ball), so that $t_b/t_h = N/H$ [20, 21]. (Note that, at the macroscale of juggling, the commensurability of the winding number derives from the fact that both N and H are integers (cf. [22]).)

The law can also be derived from Lagrangian analysis ($m = 5$, i.e., 3 balls and 2 hands, $j = 2$, i.e., juggling in a plane, and at least $n = 2$ constraints, i.e., one for the movement of the hands relative to each other and one for the hands relative to the center of mass of the balls). However, such an approach is unnecessarily complicated to achieve a result which can be obtained more easily.

This is not the case for the temporal microstructure of the act, i.e., the partitioning of the hand loop time (t_h) in the time that a hand is filled with a ball (t_l) and the time that the hand is empty (t_u: time-unloaded). The basic structure for the law describing this partitioning has already been identified (see eq. 12)

$$\frac{d^2x}{d(\omega t)^2} + \{1 + A \cos a\omega t\}x = 0,\ 0 < t < t_l$$

where $\omega = 2\pi/t_h$ and $A \cos a\omega t$ is the modulation term. To ensure that the modulated behavior of a hand moving with a ball goes, at ball release, into a harmonic mode (in order to aim steadily), the following rule has to be obeyed

$$a(A)\omega t_l = \frac{\pi}{2} + n\pi$$

or

$$a(A)\frac{t_l}{t_h} = \frac{1}{4} + \frac{n}{2} \tag{13}$$

with $t_l/t_h < 1$.

Eq. (13) reveals that when modulation is restricted, discrete ratios between characteristic time scales have to be adhered to, resulting in frequency locking between the shorter-term dynamic régime underwriting the transport of an object and the longer-term dynamic régime underwriting the rhythmic movement of a hand. To identify frequency locking between the repetitive subtasks of juggling, we first have to assume that the juggling behavior in skilled jugglers is almost harmonic ($A \rightarrow 0$). For a skilled juggler the value of $a(A \rightarrow 0)$ is then, according to Mathieu-Hill theory, 1. So, for n = 1, $t_l/t_h = 3/4$.

The results of experiments reported in detail elsewhere [21, 23] suggested that $k = t_l/t_h = 3/4$ is indeed a "symmetry solution" governing the temporal organization of cascade juggling. In these experiments, eight three-ball jugglers (N/H = 3/2) and eight five-ball jugglers (N/H = 5/2) were required to cascade juggle in three self-selected frequency modes of juggling (low, preferred, and high). In addition, three seven-ball jugglers (N/H = 7/2) juggled at a single frequency (they reported being unable to juggle seven balls at different frequencies). Two-dimensional film recordings (at 40 or 64 frames/s) of three complete juggling cycles were analyzed. The continuous variables of juggling (t_l, t_u, and t_f) and the k-ratio (t_l/t_h) were computed and averaged over the number of observations (N x 2 hands x 3 cycles) for each frequency and ball condition.

The empirical data are collected in Figure 1, which shows the range of attained k–values for each ball condition, and across all frequency modes. Three observations are called for. First, the variation of the data for N/H = 3/2 is much larger than for N/H = 5/2 and N/H = 7/2, reflecting the fact that, in the first case, the need for the juggler to juggle with A close to 0 is less demanding due to the relaxed nature of the task constraints relative to five- and seven-ball juggling. Second, the prediction following from eq. (13) (i.e., k = 3/4 for all ball conditions) holds true for N/H = 5/2 and N/H = 7/2. In fact, the group mean of the averaged k-values for N/H = 5/2 was exactly .75, while the three measurements of k for N/H = 7/2 were all close to this value (.75, .76, and .78). Third, for N/H = 3/2, the group mean of the averaged k-values is significantly lower than 3/4 (mean k = .70, $t(23) = -2.78$, $p < .05$, two-tailed), suggesting that the relaxed temporal constraints on the strength of modulation ($\lambda(t) = A \cos a\omega t$) are exploited by the jugglers to achieve, by means of frequency modulation, richer patterns leading to a range of k-values around the mode-locked value of 3/4.

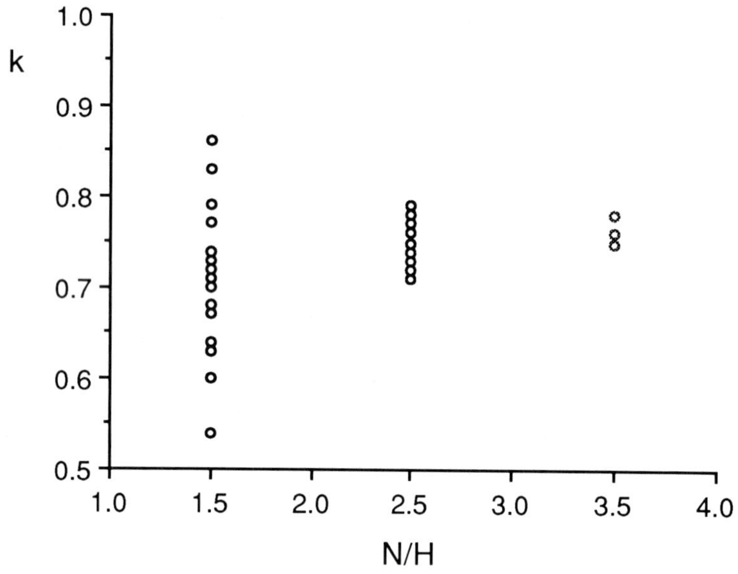

Figure 1. Distribution of k-values for N/H = 3/2, N/H = 5/2, and N/H = 7/2.

What this example teaches us is that frequency locking and frequency modulation are two sides of one coin, and that (nonlinear) dynamics may provide a single, unitary account for both. Although we have not done so, it is possible to study frequency modulation in cascade juggling through an analysis of the values that A and a may take on. Biologically speaking, frequency modulation around a frequency-locked state has the advantage of supplying the system with the best of two worlds: stability and reliability on the one hand (frequency locking) and adaptability and flexibility on the other (frequency modulation) [20, 21, 24].

The example also reveals that a truly complex system, such as a juggling system, may be amenable to an analysis in terms of the principle of least action from classical dynamics. We will now show the continuity between this particular dynamical tool and more modern, topological tools of analysis (as have also been employed in the study of cascade juggling; cf. [20, 21]).

5. THE CONTINUITY BETWEEN CLASSICAL AND MODERN DYNAMICS

It is sometimes argued that classical and modern dynamics are entirely at odds with one another, and that, therefore, classical dynamics and its concern with the kinetic causes of motion, should not be confused with modern nonlinear dynamics and its concern with the topological properties underlying time evolution. Although the latter is of course true, it should not be read to imply that there is no theoretical continuity between the two. Particularly in the study of dynamic systems that only lend themselves to an analytical treatment under some conditions and not under others, it is important to appreciate how such a treatment can be extended into a topological one. Before demonstrating that human movement control systems belong to the class of systems that demand a pluriform approach, we show how modern dynamics is continuous with classical dynamics.

Mathieu-Hill functions have the property that stable, periodic solutions are to be found only if the base frequency (ω) has a value out of a set of discrete values determined by the modulation strength (λ). Permitted values of ω, given λ, are known as frequency or mode locks (that is between modulation frequencies and eigenfrequencies). Before discussing, in the next section, a particular type of discrete dynamical equation that is often used to study the complexities of nonlinear system dynamics, we will show how this equation can be derived from eq. (12). First we rewrite eq. (12) into

$$\frac{d\theta}{d\omega t} = 1 + \frac{1}{2}\sqrt{\lambda(t)}$$

where θ is the phase of the oscillator. From here, we can proceed with the following form

$$\frac{\theta_{n+1} - \theta_n}{\omega T} = 1 + \frac{1}{2}\sqrt{\lambda(t)} = 1 + \frac{g(\theta_n)}{\omega T} \tag{14}$$

where the nonlinear coupling $g(\theta_n)$, which projects θ_n onto θ_{n+1} according to some rule, carries, in fact, all the properties of the modulation term $\lambda(t)$.

Eq. (14) is called a circle map because it maps the circumference of a circle onto itself (i.e., θ_n is mapped onto θ_{n+1}). The study of complex dynamic systems, especially systems of coupled nonlinear oscillators, is often simplified by the use of discrete maps such as the circle map. Not only do these maps capture qualitatively the kinds of behavior found in mathematical systems (be it in eq. 12 or eq. 14), but, in addition, their scaling behavior quantitatively carries over to real systems. Consequently, discrete maps can be used to represent the behavior of complex systems in a simpler fashion. It is much easier to identify periodic, quasiperiodic, and chaotic solutions by iterating the map (mapping it onto itself) than by numerical integration of the underlying differential equations [21, 25, 26].

The crux of eq. (14) is that it approximates an as yet unknown, time-dependent Lagrange multiplier, $\lambda(t)$, by a discrete nonlinear function of the phase, $g(\theta_n)$. This step from time space to phase space sacrifices quantitative rigor in leading to nearly unsolvable equations, but provides a useful qualitative approach—based on educated guesses for $g(\theta_n)$—for studying dynamical behavior globally.

In the next section, we expand on the circle map, because it will be used later in studying polyrhythmic tapping. Here we conclude with the observation that classical and modern dynamics are not at odds, but rather that the modern approach permits a wider application. It is less analytical and more topological in nature.

6. CIRCLE MAP DYNAMICS AND THE FAREY TREE

Circle maps are, in general (and as in Eq. 14), defined through

$$\theta_{n+1} = f_\Omega(\theta_n) = \theta_n + \Omega + g(\theta_n) \tag{15}$$

where

$$g(\theta_n) = g(\theta_{n+1}) \ (\mathrm{mod}\ 1) \tag{16}$$

The variable θ_n represents the phase of the oscillating system measured at periodic time intervals $t_n = 2\pi/\omega_n$, using the frequency of the external oscillator as a clock. A phase shift $\theta_n \rightarrow \theta_n + 2\pi$ represents a full rotation and therefore functions as the periodic property of g (eq. 16). The term Ω represents the ratio between the period of the external forcing and the eigenperiod of the forced oscillator ($\Omega \equiv T_e/T_o$) in the absence of the nonlinear coupling $g(\theta_n)$.

The iteration of the map is conveniently described by its winding number W. The winding number is the time-averaged rate of rotation of the angle θ, i.e., the average frequency of the underlying system, so $W = \Omega$ in the absence of the nonlinear coupling. Under iteration the variable θ_n may converge to a series which is either periodic, with rational winding number $W = P/Q$ (P and Q are integers); quasiperiodic with irrational winding number $W = p/q$ (p and q are not integers); or chaotic, where the series behave irregularly. The winding number depends on the value of the coupling parameter K in the function $g(\theta_n)$, as in, e.g., $g(\theta_n) = -(K/2\pi) \sin 2\pi\theta_n$, and on the value of Ω, and is defined as $W(K,\Omega) = (\theta_n - \theta_0)/n$, taken in the limit as the iteration n approaches infinity. The range of Ω's within which a certain rational winding number is found is given as a function of K in a *régime diagram.* Such a diagram shows how coupled oscillators are mode locked as a function of the control parameter. The régimes where locking occurs are known as Arnol'd tongues (see e.g., [27]). Figure 2 shows an example of such stable entrainment regions. For small values of the nonlinear coupling K (K < 1) there is room for quasiperiodic orbits between the periodic entrainment regions.

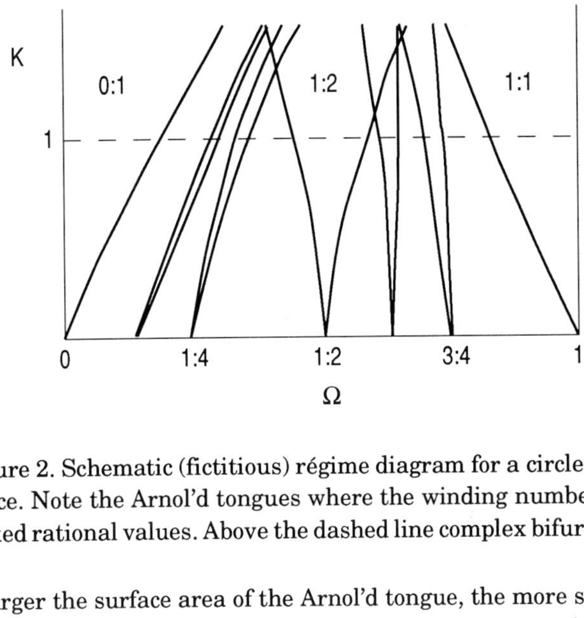

Figure 2. Schematic (fictitious) régime diagram for a circle map in (Ω,K) space. Note the Arnol'd tongues where the winding number W assumes locked rational values. Above the dashed line complex bifurcations occur.

The larger the surface area of the Arnol'd tongue, the more stable is the corresponding winding number W = P/Q for the tongue in question. A régime diagram is structured as follows: Between every two entrainment tongues corresponding to the ratios $P_1:Q_1$ and $P_2:Q_2$ another, smaller, tongue is situated: $(P_1 + P_2):(Q_1 + Q_2)$ [cf. 27-29]. This generally implies that higher order integer ratios are less stable than lower order ones. As a function of the control parameter K, ratios can become more or less stable or stability can completely disappear to give way to another, more stable ratio, depending on the initial conditions and the structure of the régime diagram. Thus, transitions from less stable ratios to more stable ratios can be induced by manipulating coupling strength as a control parameter. If K continues to increase even very stable ratios such as 1:1 and 1:2 bifurcate to chaos (when all the resonance tongues begin to overlap).

The ratio $(P_1 + P_2):(Q_1 + Q_2)$ is the result of the so-called Farey summation of the ratios $P_1:Q_1$ and $P_2:Q_2$:

$$P_1:Q_1 \oplus P_2:Q_2 = (P_1 + P_2):(Q_1 + Q_2) \tag{17}$$

where the symbol $\oplus$ denotes the Farey summation [28-30]. All rational numbers between 0 and 1 (all possible entrainment régimes) can be organized in what is called the *Farey tree* [31] by application of this summation, starting with the parents 0:1 and 1:1. The zero*th* level is defined as $0:1 \oplus 1:1 = 1:2$. Through Farey addition of these ratios the first level of the tree yields $0:1 \oplus 1:2 = 1:3$ and $1:1 \oplus 1:2 = 2:3$. In this way each subsequent level of the tree can be constructed (see Figure 3). At the n*th* level of the tree 2^n elements are present. For stability considerations it is important to distinguish between symmetric ratios and asymmetric ratios. A ratio is symmetric when the sum of numerator and denominator is even and asymmetric when it is odd. The series SAASAA (S = symmetric, A = asymmetric) re-occurs layer after layer, revealing the ordered structure of the tree.

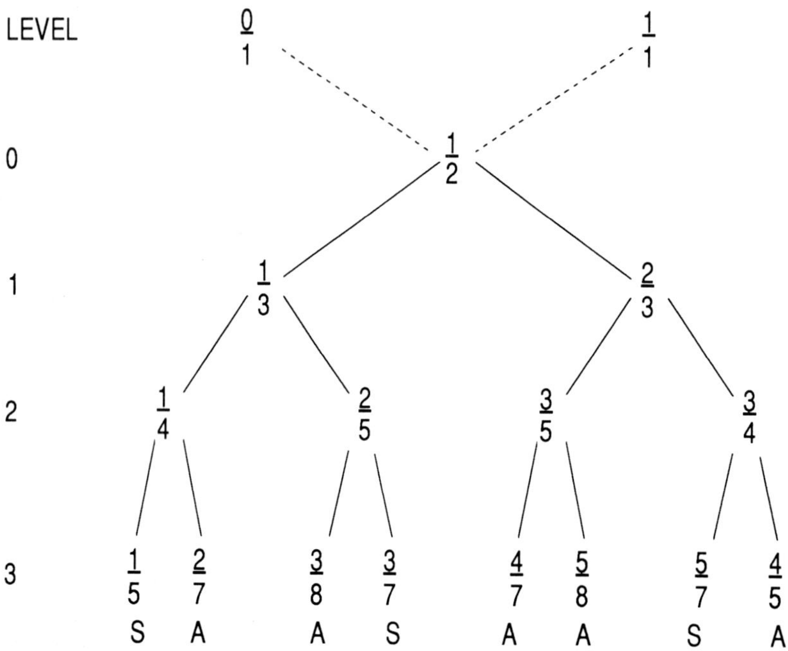

Figure 3. The Farey tree.

The Farey tree is a generic mathematical object that summarizes all the possible mode locks that complex dynamic systems may attain, so it may serve as an inventory for solutions of eqs. such as (12) and (14). It derives its significance in the analysis of such systems from the fact that its branching structure coincides with known bifurcation routes in both mathematical and natural systems.

If the coupling strength (control parameter) increases, transitions occur from higher order ratios to one of their parents. Thus, starting from some higher order ratio bifurcations along the branches of the tree can be induced by increasing the coupling strength [31]. The path 1:1, 1:2, 2:3, 3:5, 5:8 in Figure 3 represents the Fibonacci ratio series, which is based on the Fibonacci series (in which every element equals the sum of the two preceding elements, starting with 0 and 1, i.e., 0, 1, 1, 2, 3, 5, 8, 13, etc. [32]). The Fibonacci ratio series represents a frequently occurring pattern in nature. Speaking generally, the Fibonacci ratio series, the terms of which provide the best rational approximation to the "golden mean" $(\sqrt{5} - 1)/2$, appears to be the most stable path, along which periodic/quasiperiodic behavior is preserved the longest. Experimenters who are able to preset winding numbers therefore often induce this path (e.g., [33-35]).

Some additional remarks are in order to put the Farey tree in perspective. The phenomena we are discussing indeed obey one physical-mathematical description, but, at the same time, they have many possible solutions in principle. They are truly *complex*. Small differences in initial conditions or relatively small variations in a dominant, independently controllable variable (such as the velocity of running in the example treated above) can lead to considerable differences in the end result. Therefore, the Farey tree is more a qualitative than a quantitative aid in determining which mode locks are most likely to occur in systems of coupled oscillators.

In summary, from numerical data obtained with different test functions, such as the $g(\theta_n)$'s in eq. (14), and a still limited, but rapidly increasing body of experimental observations, the following rules may be formulated with regard to the relative stability of adjacent mode locks:

(i) mode locks of a higher order (level) are stable in a smaller area of operation than mode locks of a lower order;

(ii) *symmetric* mode locks bifurcate to adjacent *asymmetric* mode locks of a lower order [29];

(iii) en route to aperiodic behavior and chaos the locked-in frequency ratios P/Q belonging to the Fibonacci sequence (located at the right flank of the tree) are usually the last to remain unaffected as the degree of nonlinear coupling is increased;

(iv) in natural systems there is a tendency to seek the right flank of the tree because the right flank (with the primitive 1:1) culminates in sustained behavior, while the left flank (with the primitive 0:1) culminates in the expiry thereof.

These rules may be used as heuristic guidelines in studies of rhythmic interlimb coordination, as is done in the next section.

7. POLYRHYTHMIC TAPPING

Let us now turn to the activity of polyrhythmic tapping with two hands, which has served in the past as an experimental paradigm to study the operational structure of central time-keeping mechanisms [36-38]. In bimanual tapping, each hand taps a cadence at a certain frequency. Two broad types of rhythms are distinguished in this literature: simple rhythms and polyrhythms. In simple rhythms the frequencies of the tapping hands can be represented as an integer ratio with 1 as numerator (1:1, 1:2, 1:3, etc.). For polyrhythmic tapping this is impossible. Examples of polyrhythmic ratios are 2:3, 3:4, 2:5, 3:5, 4:5, etc. Without exception polyrhythms are more difficult to perform than simple rhythms. Moreover, these polyrhythms themselves differ in difficulty, and it is an open question what principle governs the stability of their production (cf. [36]).

Recently, we investigated the stability of tapping 2:5 and 3:5 polyrhythms using a dynamical paradigm, in which subjects were instructed to sustain the required polyrhythm as long as possible while the frequency of tapping (as prescribed by an auditory stimulus) was gradually increased [39]. We assumed that the tapping frequency would be a control parameter that was related to the coupling parameter K and could, thus, guide the system through the various régimes of the circle map. Following the logic of the régime diagram, we expected consistent bifurcations to occur from the 2:5 and 3:5 mode locks, respectively, to mode locks comprised of smaller integers. We were especially interested whether these bifurcations could be interpreted in the light of known bifurcation routes in the Farey tree. The general rules (i to iv) formulated at the end of section 6 were our guidelines.

We tested both skilled drummers and unskilled subjects. Our expectancy of finding bifurcations to simpler ratios (e.g., 2:3, 1:3, and 1:2) by speeding up the act proved not to be sound for unskilled tappers. Apparently, their lack of experience in producing stable frequency ratios prevented them from finding the entrainment regions corresponding to the simpler (poly)rhythms. One could compare their behavior with attempting to pick up a broadcasting station when running the tuner of a radioset through a series of discrete wavelengths. The next station is easily missed in doing so. Analogously, in the majority of the unskilled subjects, speeding up the tapping act resulted in its complete breakdown (compare this finding to Bramble and Carrier's observations on untrained runners in section 2). The performance of the experienced drummers, however, fitted better our expectancies. They cascaded through a series of simpler polyrhythms along paths which were by and large consistent with those anticipated from nonlinear dynamics.

The bifurcation routes observed in two skilled drummers may exemplify the behavior found in subjects with different learning histories. These routes and their number of occurrences for Subject A are presented in Table 1.

Table 1.
The bifurcation routes observed in Subject A. The complete Farey route corresponding to the starting ratios are displayed at the top of each series.

Ratio 2:5					Ratio 3:5				
route				#	route				#
2:5	1:3	1:2	1:1	0	3:5	2:3	1:2	1:1	0
2:5	1:3			1	3:5	2:3			5
2:5		1:2		60	3:5	3:4			51
2:5		1:2	2:3	10	3:5	3:4	2:3		14
2:5				4	3:5	3:4	2:3	1:1	1
					3:5	3:4		1:1	1
					3:5	1:2	3:4	1:2	1
					3:5	2:5	3:4		1
					3:5				1
			total	75				total	75

The transition routes found in Subject A show that the 2:5 ratio nearly always bifurcated to 1:2, consistent with the expected bifurcation route in the Farey tree. Apparently, the Arnol'd tongue of the 1:3 mode lock was too small to be picked up (in the sense of the radio tuning example). However, in this subject 3:5 bifurcated to 3:4 in the vast majority of cases (67 out of 75), a portion of which (15 out of 67) later bifurcated to 2:3. The transition from 3:5 to 3:4 is not immediately transparent in the light of the Farey principles, although it does meet in some regards the criteria formulated in section 6. First, it is a transition to a mode lock comprised of smaller integers. Second, 3:4 is an asymmetric ratio while 3:5 is symmetric. Third, the transition from 3:5 to 3:4 is in accordance with the postulated tendency of the system to seek the right flank of the tree, a tendency which is also manifest in the fact that the 1:3 mode lock rarely occurs in the observed bifurcation routes originating from the 2:5 ratio.

A possible explanation for the "attractiveness" of the 3:4 ratio in Subject A may be found in his learning history. Being a professional drummer, he had extensive experience with the production of polyrhythms in quadruple time (i.e., 2:4, 3:4, and 4:4), among which the 3:4 rhythm is prevalent. This may be interpreted as evidence that the intrinsic dynamics of biological systems, or, more specifically, the widths of Arnol'd tongues associated with different mode locks, may be changed by learning on the basis of information specifying new behavioral patterns, as, indeed, has been suggested recently by others [8, 9, 40, 41]. This, in turn, implies that learning itself may be conceptualized as a dynamic process in which the system's intrinsic dynamics—given the intention to perform a to-be-learned task—are "perturbed" (or "forced") in a task-specific way until the design of the system (i.e., its attractor landscape) is so modified that the performance of the task can emerge autonomously when the appropriate boundary conditions are set. The observed bifurcations from 1:2 to 2:3 larger integer locks in 10 of the routes originating from 2:5, remind us that the fine structure of bifurcation routes in tapping requires further analysis.

We now turn to Subject B, whose performance is summarized in Table 2.

Table 2.
The bifurcation routes observed in Subject B. The complete Farey route corresponding to the starting ratio is displayed at the top of each series.

Ratio 2:5					Ratio 3:5				
route				#	route				#
2:5	1:3	1:2	1:1	0	3:5	2:3	1:2	1:1	0
2:5	1:3	1:2		1	3:5	2:3		1:1	1
2:5		1:2		52	3:5		1:2		7
2:5				14	3:5	2:3			19
					3:5	2:3	3:4		1
					3:5	1:2	2:3		1
					3:5	3:4			1
					3:5	3:4	2:3		1
					3:5	3:4		1:1	1
					3:5				28
no 2:5 locking				8	no 3:5 locking				15
total				75	total				75

Subject B needed a number of trials to achieve 2:5 and 3:5 frequency locking. When he was able to produce the required rhythms the transition from 3:5 to 3:4 rarely occurred (3 out of 75). All other observed transitions are consistent with the identified Farey principles. It remains unclear, however, why, in this particular subject, transitions between mode locks were absent in a large number of trials.

The two polyrhythms tested form an interesting pair, since both are located at the same Farey level. Being situated at the right hand side of the tree, and being, in addition, a Fibonacci ratio, the 3:5 mode lock was assumed to be relatively stable. The difference in stability (indicated by the critical tapping frequency at which a bifurcation occurred or the performance broke down) was studied in order to get more insight in the way the rules mentioned in section 6 combine.

The difference in stability between 2:5 and 3:5 as a function of practice was investigated. Overall we found in the skilled drummers an initial difference between the stabilities in favor of 2:5. This can be understood if we assume the coupling strength to be strong in the early stages of learning. In this situation the mode locks will have to be realized by external forcing, which will be easier for the 2:5 than for the 3:5 ratio, because 2:5 has a more transparent distribution of taps than 3:5. However, if this coupling is weakened by training, as is suggested by Yamanishi, Kawato, and Suzuki [42, 43], the system will begin to display more autonomous behavior. The general stability rules are supposed to apply to the latter situation.

The difference in stability disappeared as a result of training. After practice the two performed polyrhythms turned out to be equally stable. Additional research is required to obtain more information about the relative contributions to stability by the three rules mentioned previously. In a follow-up experiment we will test the stability of mode locks situated at a higher level in the Farey tree (e.g., 3:8, 3:7, 4:7, and 5:8). Starting from this level the difference in stability between asymmetric and symmetric, Fibonacci and non-Fibonacci, and right flank and left flank ratios can be examined more adequately.

The example of polyrhythmic tapping contains two important lessons about coordinated rhythmic movements. First, it demonstrates that bifurcations in such movements are more common than one might expect from a naive point of view. If the right parameters are manipulated, order-order transitions may be induced from one phase relation to another as well as from one mode locking to another. Second, the interindividual differences in tapping performance suggest that the "attractiveness" of specific frequency locks is determined in part by learning and experience.

8. CONCLUDING REMARKS

Our efforts in this paper have been directed at presenting a number of dynamical tools and concepts, ranging from the more analytical to the more qualitative and topological, as they may be applied in the study of dynamic movement systems. Indeed, we demonstrated their effective use in studying frequency locking, frequency modulation, and bifurcation phenomena in such systems. Three cases of coordination were considered: adjustments of the rhythm of breathing to the rhythm of locomotion, cascade juggling, and polyrhythmic tapping. Each one of them served to illustrate particular problem areas in the dynamical analysis of complex systems and called for a specific analysis.

The adjustments in the frequency of respiration relative to the frequency of locomotion could be captured with a local analysis of the forces acting on the diaphragm, resulting in nearly harmonic limit cycle oscillators with frequency locks corresponding to empirically observed ratios.

The analysis of the temporal organization of cascade juggling showed that the (underlying) invariant value of the ratio (k) between the time a hand is loaded with a ball and the total hand loop time equals 3/4. Whereas in earlier publications [20, 21] this value was derived from global topological considerations, the present analysis was based on the classical principle of least action. These converging results underscore our opinion that no real discontinuity exists between classical analytical dynamics and modern qualitative dynamics when the appropriate transformations between differential equations and difference equations are known (e.g., the Mathieu-Hill equation can be rewritten into the circle map equation). After all, particular topological solutions, such as the partitioning of time in juggling, relate to underlying principles that may be identified analytically. As a case in point one may compare a topological analysis of the 120° angles that are often observed in natural forms (e.g., in leaves, cracks, and crystals) with an analytical treatment of these angles using, for instance, surface tension considerations and some minimization rule of force distributions (see [44]).

In the case of polyrhythmic tapping, the rich and intricate dynamic behavior could be studied qualitatively with the help of heuristic guidelines provided by nonlinear dynamics, i.e., the Farey tree. Even here, however, it might be feasible to treat the matter more analytically by deriving the energy distribution associated with mode locks in the Farey tree. Assuming the general concept of least action, one might then suggest as a working hypothesis that tappers who are sufficiently trained to find Arnol'd tongues will bifurcate, if tapping frequency is increased, to adjacent tongues for which the ratio of the energies for the left and right hand tapping is closest to 1.

We would like to emphasize that both the invariant (frequency locking) and variant (frequency modulation) timing characteristics of movement should be understood as interrelated properties of dynamic systems. The unified conceptualization of these phenomena with iterative maps is at odds with models (e.g., the proportional duration model, [45]) in which the invariant features are represented in motor programs, whereas the temporal variance is attributed to other mechanisms such as closed loop corrections or peripheral noise.

All in all, we implicitly promoted a dynamical approach to movement coordination that employs a mix of analytical and more qualitative tools of analysis. The way we strike a balance between these two complementary sets of tools depends on the nature of the problems confronted. In this regard our style of inquiry is entirely pragmatic. As long as we are not sure about the formative principles at work in the coordination of movement, we see little reason to restrict ourselves to a topological analysis of the relation between trajectories in state space (as exemplified by the majority of studies employing a dynamical approach to movement coordination) and to refrain from more local, analytical considerations. Different analyses reveal different properties of the system under study, and, hence, answer different questions. One of the intriguing aspects of physics, however formal and categorical its models may appear, is that it allows for multiple points of observations of one and the same phenomenon that we are trying to understand.

Authors' notes. The first author's contribution to the writing of this article was supported in part by a grant from the National Science Foundation (BNS-8811510) awarded to M. T. Turvey, University of Connecticut, U.S.A. Further support for this work came from a Fellowship at the Netherlands Institute for Advanced Study (N.I.A.S.) awarded to P. C. W. van Wieringen. The authors gratefully acknowledge the helpful comments of W. J. Beek, J. B. Hopkins, and R. E. A. van Emmerik on earlier drafts. Correspondence concerning this article should be addressed to P. J. Beek, Faculty of Human Movement Sciences, Vrije Universiteit Amsterdam, Van der Boechorststraat 9, 1081 BT Amsterdam.

REFERENCES

1 Kugler, P. N., Kelso, J. A. S., & Turvey, M. T. (1980). On the concept of coordinative structures as dissipative structures: I. Theoretical lines of convergence. In G. E. Stelmach & J. Requin (Eds.), *Tutorials in motor behavior*. Amsterdam: North-Holland.

2 Kugler, P. N., Kelso, J. A. S., & Turvey, M. T. (1982). On control and co-ordination of naturally developing systems. In J. A. S. Kelso & J. E. Clark (Eds.), *The development of movement control and coordination*. New York: Wiley.

3 Haken, H., Kelso, J. A. S., & Bunz, H. (1985). A theoretical model of phase transitions in human hand movements. *Biological Cybernetics*, *51*, 347-356.

4 Haken, H. (1977). *Synergetics: An introduction*. Berlin: Springer.

5 Haken, H. (1983). *Advanced synergetics*. Berlin: Springer.

6 Kelso, J. A. S. (1989). Phase transitions: Foundations of behavior. In H. Haken & M. Stadler (Eds.), *Synergetics of cognition*. Heidelberg: Springer.

7 Kugler, P. N. (1986). A morphological perspective on the origin and evolution of movement patterns. In M. G. Wade & H. T. A. Whiting (Eds.), *Motor development in children: Aspects of coordination and control*. The Hague: Nijhoff.

8 Schöner, G., & Kelso, J. A. S. (1988). A synergetic theory of environmentally-specified and learned patterns of movement coordination. 1. Relative phase

dynamics. *Biological Cybernetics, 58,* 71-80.

9 Schöner, G., & Kelso, J. A. S. (1988). A synergetic theory of environmentally-specified and learned patterns of movement coordination. 2. Component oscillator dynamics. *Biological Cybernetics, 58,* 81-89.

10 Schöner, G., & Kelso, J. A. S. (1988). Dynamic patterns of biological coordination: Theoretical strategy and new results. In J. A. S. Kelso, A. Y. Mandell, & M. F. Shlesinger (Eds.), *Dynamic patterns in complex systems.* Singapore: World Scientific.

11 Beek, W. J. (1990). Synergetics and self-organization: A responese. In H. T. A. Whiting, O. G. Meijer, & P. C. W. van Wieringen (Eds.), *The natural-physical approach to movement control.* Amsterdam: VU University Press.

12 Thompson, J. M. T., & Stewart, H. B. (1986). *Nonlinear dynamics and chaos.* New York: Wiley.

13 Andronov, A. (1930). Sur la théorie des auto-oscillations. *Comptes Rendues Académie des Sciences,* 256.

14 Krylov, N. M., & Bogoliubov, N. N. (1947). *Introduction to nonlinear mechanics.* (Annals of Mathematics Studies, Vol. 11). Princeton, NJ: Princeton University Press.

15 Pearson, C. E. (1976). *Handbook of applied mathematics.* New York: Van Nostrand-Reinhold.

16 Beek, P. J., & Beek, W. J. (1988). Tools for constructing dynamical models of rhythmic movement. *Human Movement Science, 7,* 301-342.

17 Hoppenstaedt, F. C. (1986). *An introduction to the mathematics of neurons* (Cambridge Studies in Mathematical Biology, Vol. 6.). Cambridge: Cambridge University Press.

18 Bramble, D., & Carrier, D. R. (1983). Running and breathing in mammals. *Science, 21,* 251-256.

19 Goldstein, H. (1950). *Classical mechanics.* Reading, Mass.: Addison-Wesley.

20 Beek, P. J. (1989). Timing and phase locking in cascade juggling. *Ecological Psychology, 1,* 55-96.

21 Beek, P. J. (1989). *Juggling dynamics.* Ph.D. Thesis. Amsterdam: VU University Press.

22 Beek, P. J. (1988). Tessellation of time in cascade juggling. *PAW-Review.* A technical report of the Perceiving-Acting Workshop, *III,* 22-25.

23 Beek, P. J., & Turvey, M. T. (submitted). Temporal order in cascade juggling.

24 deGuzman, C. G., Kelso, J. A. S., & T. Holroyd (in press). The self-organized phase attractive dynamics of coordination. In A. Babloyantz (Ed.), *Self-organization, emerging properties and learning.* New York: Plenum.

25 Jensen, M. H., Bak, P., & Bohr, T. (1984). Transitions to chaos by interaction of resonances in dissipative systems: I. Circle maps. *Physical Review A, 30,* 1960-1969.

26 May, R. M. (1976). Simple mathematical models with very complicated dynamics. *Nature, 261*, 459-467.
27 Glass, L., & Mackey, M. C. (1988). *From clocks to chaos: The rhythms of life.* Princeton: University Press.
28 Cvitanovic, P., Shraiman, B., & Söderberg, B. (1985). Scaling laws of mode locks in circle maps. *Physica Scripta, 32*, 263-270.
29 González, D. L., & Piro, O. (1985). Symmetric kicked self-oscillators: Iterated maps, strange attractors, and symmetry of phase-locking Farey hierarchy. *Physical Review Letters, 55*, 17-20.
30 Keener, J. P., & Glass, L. (1984). Global bifurcations of the periodically forced nonlinear oscillator. *Journal of Mathematical Biology, 21*, 175-190.
31 Allen, T. (1983). On the arithmetic of phase-locking: Coupled neurons as a lattice on R^2. *Physica, 6D*, 305-320.
32 West, B. J., & Goldberger, A. L. (1987). Physiology in fractal dimensions. *American Scientist, 75*, 354-365.
33 Feigenbaum, M. J., Kadanoff, L. P., & Shenker, S. J. (1982). Quasiperiodicity in dissipative systems: A renormalization group analysis. *Physica, 5D*, 370-386.
34 Fein, A. P., Heutmaker, M. S., & Gollub, J. P. (1985). Scaling at the transition from quasiperiodicity to chaos in a hydrodynamic system. *Physica Scripta, T9*, 79-84.
35 Stavans, J., Heslot, F., & Libchaber, A. (1985). Fixed winding number and the quasiperiodic route to chaos in a convective fluid. *Physical Review Letters, 55*, 596-599.
36 Deutsch, D. (1983). The generation of two isochronous sequences in parallel. *Perception and Psychophysics, 34*, 331-337.
37 Jagacinski, R. J., Marshburn, E., Klapp, S. T., & Jones, M. R. (1988). Test of parallel versus integrated structure in polyrhythmic tapping. *Journal of Motor Behavior, 20*, 416-442.
38 Klapp, S. T., Hill, M. D., Tyler, J. G., Martin, Z. E., Jagacinski, R. J., & Jones, M. R. (1985). On marching on two different drummers: Perceptual aspects of the difficulties. *Journal of Experimental Psychology: Human Perception and Performance, 11*, 814-827.
39 Peper, C. E., Beek, P. J., & van Wieringen, P. C. W. (1991). Bifurcations in bimanual tapping: In search of Farey principles. In J. Requin & G. E. Stelmach (Eds.), *Tutorials in motor neuroscience.* N.A.T.O. Advanced Study Institute. Dordrecht: Kluwer.
40 Kelso, J. A. S., & deGuzman, G. C. (1988). Order in time: How the cooperation between the hands informs the design of the brain. In H. Haken (Ed.), *Neural and synergetic computers.* Berlin: Springer.
41 Schöner, G. (1989). Learning and recall in a dynamic theory of coordination patterns. *Biological Cybernetics, 62*, 39-54.

42 Yamanishi, J., Kawato, M., & Suzuki, R. (1979). Studies on human finger tapping neural networks by phase transition curves. *Biological Cybernetics*, *33*, 199-208.

43 Yamanishi, J., Kawato, M., & Suzuki, R. (1980). Two coupled oscillators as a model for the coordinated finger tapping by both hands. *Biological Cybernetics*, *37*, 219-225.

44 Stevens, P. S. (1974). *Patterns in nature*. Boston: Little, Brown.

45 Gentner, D. R. (1987). Timing of skilled motor performance: Tests of the proportional duration model. *Psychological Review*, *94*, 255-276.

SECTION 6

BIOELECTRICAL AND BIOMECHANICAL CORRELATES OF MOVEMENT

Tutorials in Motor Behavior II
G.E. Stelmach and J. Requin (Editors)

Bioelectrical and biomechanical correlates of rapid human elbow movement

G. L. Gottlieb[a], D. M. Corcos[b] and G. C. Agarwal[c]

[a]Department of Physiology, Rush Medical College, 1753 W. Congress Parkway, Chicago, IL 60612, USA

[b]College of Kinesiology, University of Illinois at Chicago, Chicago, IL 60680, USA

[c]Department of Electrical Engineering and Computer Sciences, University of Illinois at Chicago, Chicago, IL 60680, USA

Abstract

Relatively fast, single-joint human movements are performed by stereotyped activation pulses of an agonist muscle and slightly delayed, of its antagonist muscle. It is their combined action that first accelerates the limb and then arrests it at a desired position. The control of such movements requires that the intensity and duration of both pulses and their relative timing be specified either explicitly, or that such parameters emerge from the interaction of descending control signals and afferent feedback from the ongoing movement. This work demonstrates how muscle myoelectrical activity can help us interpret the kinetic actions of the muscles and through them, the kinematic behavior of the limb. We will further show that this requires taking account of two patterns of single-joint control. These patterns emerge from two movement strategies that differ in the way that subjects control forces to produce movement. For each strategy, different rules exist to control the degree and timing of activation of the agonist and antagonist muscles. The basis on which a strategy is chosen, the rules that characterize each and supporting data are presented.

1. INTRODUCTION

How do kinematic features of a voluntary movement vary when a single parameter of the movement task is systematically altered? What are the accompanying electromyographic (EMG) changes? What inferences can be made about the motor system's control mechanisms from the relations found in answering the first two questions? These questions have lead to many experimental studies of the consequences of asking subjects to move different distances or at different speeds or with different loads. They have not lead to any consensus however, as to the rules that underlie the control of such tasks (Gottlieb, Corcos, & Agarwal, 1989b).

We will develop an hypothesis for the control of single joint movements which is based upon an alternative to the first question. Regularities should be sought not in kinematics but in kinetics. We should look first, not at the angular trajectories but at the joint torques. From the torques and the laws of mechanics, kinematics emerge. Further, muscle tension and myoelectrical activity both arise from the same neural input to the muscle and therefore will reveal some common features of that control.

Four organizing principles are useful in the study of the control of single joint movements (Gottlieb, et al., 1989b) .

I. A task requires a "strategy" for performing movements to satisfy constraints that are explicitly or implicitly a part of it. Strategies also resolve the problem of how to choose among many possible movements that can accomplish the task.

II. Strategies are operationalized in terms of sets of rules for the amplitude and timing of muscle activation.

III. Rules for muscle activation lead to consistent patterns of both muscle tension and electromyographic (EMG) signals. Because of their common drive, many measures of tension and EMG will be highly correlated.

IV. Muscle forces interact with the dynamic properties of the limb and load to produce movement. Because the same forces will produce different movements for different loads, correlations between task variables and EMG and force measures will be more generally descriptive than those between task variables and any kinematic measures.

A corollary to principle III above is that the same relations between EMG and tension should apply to both agonist and antagonist muscles. Differences in EMG patterns therefore should be explainable in terms of the differences in joint torques produced by muscle actions on different sides of the joint and acting under different biomechanical conditions.

In this paper we will discuss experimental evidence to show that the correlation between myoelectrical and kinetic measures is the most descriptive association that exists between the two physically different expressions of muscle contraction. We will show this under a variety of single-joint movement tasks for both agonist and antagonist muscles. We will also show that the application of the above principles to the observed control patterns suggest that even movements as simple as single-joint flexions need to be partitioned into two qualitatively different sets in order to understand their controlling mechanisms.

2. THE DUAL-STRATEGY HYPOTHESIS

2.1. The excitation pulse

To describe how muscles are controlled during fast movements, many investigators have considered that the EMG bursts seen in each muscle at or near the onsets of their contractions to be the most significant features. We can go beyond this by hypothesizing that the muscles' EMGs can be interpreted, not merely as measures of muscle activity, but as indirect measures of the net excitation of their motoneuron pools. Although the precise relation between excitation taking place in the anterior horn of the spinal cord and the peripherally measured EMG is complex, our understanding of neuron behavior suggests that a useful simplifying approximation to this relationship is a linear, first-order differential equation (eq. 1) (Knox, 1974).

$$\frac{de(t)}{dt} + \frac{1}{a}e(t) = x(t) \tag{1}$$

Here $e(t)$ is the muscle EMG signal, $x(t)$ is the motoneuron pool excitation and a is the characteristic time constant. This is the equation of a low-pass filter and it is the properties of this filtering, rather than the specific form of the equation, that are important.

Let us suppose that for the control of fast movements, the excitation signal, $x(t)$, can be approximated by a rectangular pulse of controllable height (H) and width (W). The assumptions of a rectangular excitation pulse passing through a first-order low-pass filter are not a unique combination for producing signals that have EMG burst-like properties but are the simplest set of assumptions that give us the minimum necessary properties. Such highly simplifying assumptions will not capture all the details of muscle excitation but they can capture the most important ones. This does not imply that pulses are the only waveform that the CNS creates for controlling movements, but it is the simplest and is sufficient for describing some classes of movements (Corcos, Agarwal, Flaherty, & Gottlieb, 1990).

What are the essential features of the EMG bursts that are captured by this model? The transformation of a rectangular pulse $x(t)$ through a filter described by equation 1 leads to smoothly rising and falling pulses for $e(t)$. The myoelectrical waveform $e(t)$ cannot change instantaneously but only at a finite rate that depends upon the ratio H/a. If the excitation pulse is sufficiently long (eg $W > 3a$), then $e(t)$ will approach an equilibrium value before the pulse ends that is proportional to H. However if W is briefer than this, the peak value of $e(t)$ will rise monotonically with W, even though H may be constant. The area of $e(t)$ will be proportional to the product HW which is the area of the excitation pulse.

2.2. Two strategies

The term "strategy" is used to denote a set of rules that specify the parameters of the excitation pulses for agonist and antagonist muscles. Five parameters completely describe a two pulse, agonist-antagonist burst pattern. These are the heights and widths of the pulse for each muscle and the latency or delay of the antagonist pulse relative to the agonist. We have found that two different strategies or sets of rules are necessary to describe how the parameters of the excitation pulses for fast movements vary for different distances, with different inertial loads and at different intended speeds. The two strategies that we have described are called speed-sensitive (SS) (Corcos, Gottlieb, & Agarwal, 1989) and speed-insensitive (SI) (Gottlieb, Corcos, & Agarwal, 1989a). The rules for these are summarized in the Table below:

Table 1
The rules for adjusting the parameters of the excitation pulses for the Speed Sensitive (SS) strategy that is used for intentionally changing movement speed and the Speed-Insensitive (SI) strategy that is used for changing movement distance or adapting to changing loads. H is pulse height, W is pulse width and T_{ant} is the relative latency of the antagonist burst.

	SS	SI
H	covaries with speed	is constant
W	is constant	covaries with distance or load
T_{ant}	covaries inversely with speed	covaries with distance or load

A qualitative distinction between classes of movements has been suggested before (Brown, & Cooke, 1981; Mustard, & Lee, 1987). It is also implicit in the imposition of kinematic boundary constrictions on descriptive rules for movement (Wallace, 1981). Our definition of strategies provides an *a priori* basis for how movements will be performed without requiring that some behavioral feature (such as movement time or speed) be held constant by the mover. The SI rules do not imply constant speed (and in fact are never associated with it). They imply that the features of the control signals that appear to be invariant over task changes are held constant in spite of changes in speed. Movements of different speeds (or movement time) over one distance are performed by an SS strategy (Mustard, et al., 1987; Wallace, & Wright, 1982), as are movements of different distances in the same time (Freund, & Budingen, 1978; Gielen, van den Oosten, & Pull ter Gunne, 1985; Shapiro, & Walter, 1986).

Each strategy implies many kinematic and kinetic correlates that follow from the dynamical laws of motion, as well as similar myoelectrical correlates that follow from the rules for muscle activation. Because both the myoelectrical and mechanical responses are direct consequences of the same excitation pulses, these diverse relations are not independent so that the rules of the strategies predict specific EMG and mechanical correlates. It is these that we will discuss in the experimental section below.

2.3. Distinguishing between strategies

The defining features of the two strategies are to be found in the excitation pulses. In part, the SS strategy is pulse-height modulation while the SI strategy is pulse-width modulation. These are incomplete descriptions of the strategies because they omit timing of the antagonist. These pulses are not accessible to direct measurement. The variables we can measure are myoelectric and kinematic. For freely moving limbs we cannot measure muscle force but can estimate joint torque, at least early in a trajectory, by calculating inertial torque from measurements of the acceleration. Equation 1 shows that the initial rate of change of EMG will be proportional to the height of the excitation pulse. Therefore, the rules for the SS strategy indicate that when subjects intentionally change speed this will be associated with corresponding changes in the slopes of the rising phases of the EMG bursts. The SI rules indicate that for movements of different distances or of different loads over one distance, the rising phases will be insensitive to distance and load because the height of the excitation pulses will be unchanged as long as the subject makes no attempt to adjust movement speed. Note that this does not imply that movement speed will remain constant. On the contrary, it is well known that movement speed increases with distance if the target is of constant size (Fitts, 1954; Hancock, & Newell, 1985) and that it decreases if the load increases (Danoff, 1979; Lestienne, 1979; Wadman, Denier van der Gon, Geuze, & Mol, 1979). However, these changes are not induced by the subjects' deliberate intent or by instruction. Because the contractile process is also a form of low-pass filter, the rates of rise of muscle tension will behave in the same manner described for the EMGs. That is, the initial rate at which joint torque increases should vary when speed is deliberately modified but should be unaffected by distance or load.

3. METHODS

3.1. General features

We will confine our discussion to flexion of the elbow in the horizontal plane. In all the experiments to be considered here, seated subjects faced a computer monitor placed 1.5 m in front of them. The right shoulder was abducted 90° and the forearm pointed forward. A computer tone signalled the subject to make a flexion movement to a target, defined by a horizontal band on the monitor that also provided an indication of the subjects' joint angle. Subjects made 11 movements under each set of task conditions. The first movement was discarded as were any that did not have well defined EMG burst patterns. Measurements were made from each EMG record of areas and latencies. The records were aligned to the onset of the agonist burst and averaged.

All EMGs were measured with surface electrodes (Boston Myoelectrodes) amplified 1600X and bandpass filtered at 60 and 500 Hz before digitization at 1000/s. We also measured joint angle and joint acceleration. Velocity was computed.

3.2. Movement classes

Two different sets of experiments will be discussed in the following section. In the first, subjects performed a set of 16 groups of movements. Four different instructions were given regarding movement speed and for each instruction, movements were made over four distances. The instructions were to move at a subject-selected, "comfortable" speed that was usually quite slow; to move to the target "as accurately as possible" which was faster; to move "fast" and finally to move "as fast as possible". In all four cases accuracy of movement was explicitly requested and blocks of 11 movements with each instruction were made to a 6° target at one of four different distances. Some of the results of analyzing these movements has been presented in (Corcos, et al., 1989). One additional experiment of this type was performed on one subject. Four different speeds of 36° movements were made with a 2.27 kg weight added to the manipulandum, increasing its moment of inertia by 10.7 Nm. This was done to enhance the antagonist EMG signal at slow movement speeds in order to increase the accuracy with which its latency could be measured.

The second set of experiments again asked the subjects to move to targets at one of four different distances. Four different inertial loads were used for every movement distance. Some of the results of analyzing these movements has been presented in (Gottlieb, et al., 1989a).

3.3. Quantification of variables

Quantification of the degree to which muscles were activated was done by integrating the area under the full-wave rectified EMG signal. The area under the agonist burst (Q_{ag}) was integrated from the onset of the burst to the reversal of acceleration (equal to the moment of peak velocity). The area under the antagonist burst (Q_{ant}) was integrated from agonist onset to approximately the time the limb returned to zero velocity. These methods are described in greater detail in (Gottlieb, et al., 1989a).

The mechanical variables that we can directly measure are angle and acceleration and from these, velocity can be computed. Velocity or acceleration have often been used as the mechanical index of performance (Brown, & Cooke, 1990; Marsden, & Rothwell, 1983; Milner, 1986). These we will term "kinematic" indices.

"Kinetic" indices are those that depend upon the torques. One simple mechanical model of the limb is the linear mass-spring-damper system defined by equation 2. It describes the time varying dependence of joint torque (τ) produced by the combined action of all muscles acting about the joint on the angle (θ). The parameter M represents the moment of inertia of the combined limb-manipulandum-load, B is the viscous damping of the manipulandum and the effective viscosity of the muscles and K is the elastic stiffness of the muscles.

$$\tau = M\frac{d^2\theta}{dt^2} + B\frac{d\theta}{dt} + K\theta \qquad (2)$$

Under non-isometric conditions joint torque is not directly measurable in intact human subjects but must be estimated. If we assume that most of the torque for a rapid limb movement in a manipulandum is generated to overcome inertia, then it can be directly computed from acceleration if the constant moment of inertia is estimated. The validity of this assumption will be considered later.

There are many possible kinetic indices that have meaningful physical interpretations. One is peak torque (Gottlieb, et al., 1989a). If we use only the first term of equation 2, this equivalent to peak acceleration as long as the moment of inertia is constant.

Instead of peak torque, Karst and Hasan (Karst, & Hasan, 1987) used average decelerating torque to interpret the EMG of the antagonist muscle. Assuming a symmetrical velocity trajectory, they derived an equation for average torque over the deceleration phase of movement given by equation 3. D is movement distance. Since symmetry was assumed, the average torque during acceleration is also given by this equation but with opposite sign.

$$\tau_{av} = \frac{M}{D}\left\{\frac{d\theta}{dt}\right\}^2_{max} \tag{3}$$

Another kinetic alternative is the work done by the muscles to move the limb. From movement onset to some time T, it is defined by equation 4 where τ is defined by equation 2.

$$\text{Work} = \int_0^T \tau \, d\theta \tag{4}$$

Since work is initially done by the muscles to accelerate the limb and increase its kinetic energy and then on the muscles to dissipate that energy, a reasonable simpler measure is the peak kinetic energy, which occurs at peak velocity as in equation 5 (Bouisset, & Goubel, 1968; Bouisset, & Goubel, 1973). The time of peak velocity corresponds to zero acceleration so in this interval inertial torque is towards the target. All the kinetic energy gained during acceleration will be dissipated during deceleration to halt the movement at the target.

$$KE_{max} = \frac{1}{2} M \left\{\frac{d\theta}{dt}\right\}^2_{max} \tag{5}$$

The final alternative we will consider is mechanical impulse (I), defined by the equation 6.

$$I = \int_0^T \tau \, dt \tag{6}$$

The integration interval is is the same as that for kinetic energy. Using only the inertial term from equation 2 to compute torque, this measure is the equivalent of peak momentum or peak velocity as shown by equation 7.

$$I_M = M \left\{\frac{d\theta}{dt}\right\}_{max} \tag{7}$$

Clearly, the inertial component reflects only a fraction of the torque produced by the muscles and restricting our calculations to use it exclusively is a matter of attempted simplification. A consequence of this is that calculations of peak or average torque or of work or impulse may not be sufficiently accurate representations of the muscles' mechanical output. A better estimate of torque could be obtained by incorporating the dependence of force on velocity (Hill, 1940) and length (Abbott, & Aubert, 1952; Joyce, & Westbury, 1969). We can incorporate velocity dependent or viscous forces by including a second term in the torque equation (2). This inclusion invalidates the simplified indices (equations 3, 5 and 7). A simplified form of the index for impulse, assuming a symmetrical movement, is given by equation 8.

$$I_{MB} = M \left\{\frac{d\theta}{dt}\right\}_{max} + B \frac{\theta_{target}}{2} \tag{8}$$

We will consider this latter form of impulse in the discussion. The increased complexity that would be entailed by also including the last term in equation 2 that is dependent upon joint stiffness is beyond the scope of this work.

4. RESULTS

4.1. Kinematic and kinetic similarity

Similarity between movements depends upon which variables are compared. Figure 1 shows three families of movements, illustrating that by appropriately choosing pairs of movement sets, similarity may be found either between kinematic or between kinetic and electromyographic variables. Figure 1 (left) shows movements of a constant inertial load over four different distances while figure 1 (middle) shows kinetically similar movements of four different inertial loads over a single distance. The lower three frames show the inertial torque and EMG envelopes of a single agonist (biceps) and antagonist (triceps) muscle. There are several features that are noteworthy. These are: 1) rising torques that have similar slopes, independent of distance or load. Movements of smaller distances or loads reach smaller and earlier peak torques because of an earlier decrease in their rate of rise. 2)The agonist EMG bursts all rise at similar rates that are independent of distance or load. The areas of these bursts increase with distance or load. Peak EMG often increases with distance or load but an equally common pattern is a flattening of the tops of the bursts at a level that is similar for different distances and loads. 3) The antagonist EMG shows a small, very early component (latency relative to the onset of the agonist burst is about 25-30 ms), the amplitude of which is independent of distance or load. 4) the principal burst of antagonist activity occurs at a latency that increases with distance or load. Its slope is relatively independent of distance or load. Its area increases with load but behaves inconsistently with distance. On the left, the area of the antagonist burst is smallest for the 72° movement. The most common pattern is for its area toshow a decreasing trend with distance although we will show examples of moderate increase as well.

The upper three panels of the figure demonstrate that kinetic similarity does not imply kinematic similarity. The accelerations on the left differ from the inertial torques only by a multiplicative constant moment of inertia. Moving larger distances is associated with increases in peak accelerations and velocities. These larger peaks occur later and overall movement time increases. In the middle however, increases in the inertial load on the manipulandum lead to reductions in the rates and peaks of acceleration and velocity. While movement distance remains constant, the times of the kinematic peaks and the total movement times increase with load. In both cases, average and peak velocities behave similarly.

A different kind of similarity, kinematic similarity, is to be found in a comparison of the middle and right hand parts of figure 1. All the kinematic features of the middle set that are described in the preceding paragraph are equally true of the right hand set. In the latter case however, different speeds are a result of deliberate changes by the subject in the way the muscles are activated rather than consequences of externally imposed changes in load. This is readily evident from the lower three panels at the right. The different rates of acceleration arise from correspondingly different rates of rise in inertial torque. This difference must follow from different patterns of muscle activation which is implied by the different rates at which the agonist EMG burst rises. Note too that the durations of the agonist bursts are relatively constant while the latencies of the antagonist bursts increase with movement time.

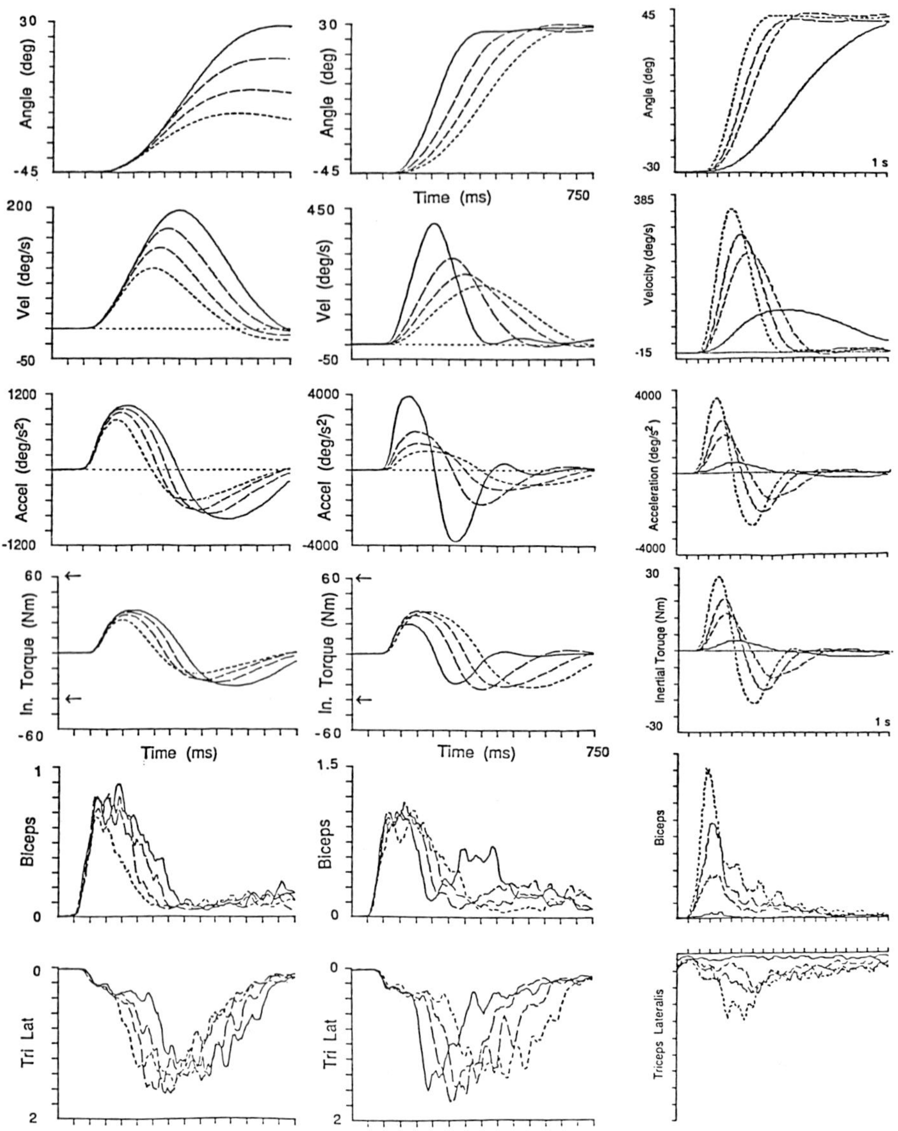

Figure 1. Plotted from top to bottom are averages of joint angle, velocity and acceleration, inertial torque, biceps and triceps EMG (rectified and smoothed with a 30 ms moving average filter). At the left are average movements over four different distances (18°, 36°, 54°, 72°). In the middle are four sets of 72° movements with four different loads. At the right are 72° movements at four different speeds.

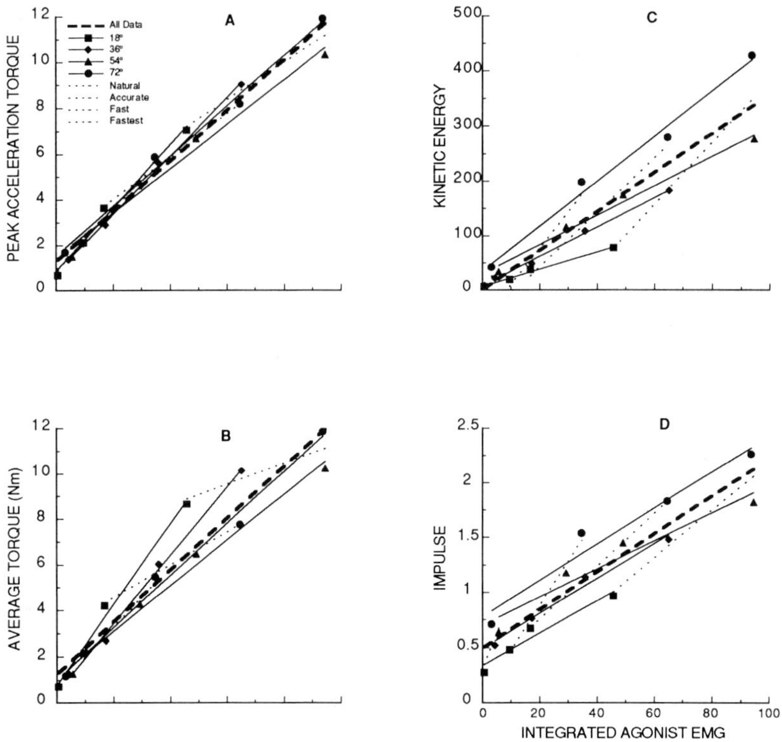

Figure 2 A-D. Kinetic (or kinematic) indices of movement plotted against agonist and antagonist myoelectrical activity for movements of four different distances at four different speeds. Four mechanical indices versus integrated agonist activity Q_{ag}: A-Peak Accelerating Torque (or peak acceleration if divided by the moment of inertia), B-Average Accelerating Torque, C- Peak Kinetic Energy and D-Impulse (or peak velocity if divided by the moment of inertia).

4.2. Mechanical and myoelectrical correlates - distance and speed

The relations between agonist myoelectrical activity (Q_{ag}) and four kinetic indices; peak and average torque (eq 3), kinetic energy (eq 5) and impulse (eq 7) are illustrated in Figure 2A-D. Two kinds of task were asked of the subject. One was to move a specified distance at different speeds. This required that the subject use an SS strategy for controlling the muscles of about the elbow. The thin, solid lines show the regression curves for movements over a single distance at different speeds. Each of the four lines show the results for each of four different distances (18°, 36°, 54° and 72°).

These data can also be partitioned in an alternate way. We can describe the subject as having moved four different distances with a single instruction that influenced movement speed. This would evoke an SI strategy. The dotted lines show the regression curves obtained when the data are regrouped and different distances are traversed with each of four different

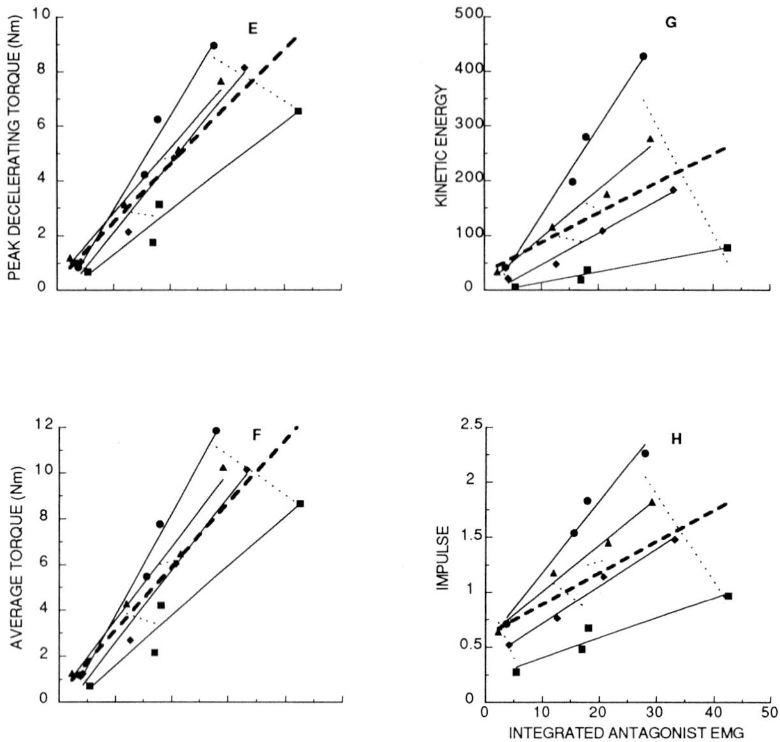

Figure 2 E-F. Kinetic (or kinematic) indices of movement plotted against agonist and antagonist myoelectrical activity for movements of four different distances at four different speeds. Four mechanical indices versus integrated antagonist myoelectrical activity Q_{ant} in parts E-H: E-Peak Decelerating Torque, F-Average Decelerating Torque, G- Peak Kinetic Energy and H-Impulse.

instructions affecting speed (Gottlieb, Corcos, Agarwal, & Latash, 1990a). The thick dashed lines are regression curves computed from all 16 sets of movements. We do not plot kinematic indices separately because peak velocity and acceleration differ from impulse and peak torque by only a constant scale factor proportional to the moment of inertia which was the same for all these movements. All indices have high, positive correlations with Q_{acc} for both tasks. Here, kinematic indices such as peak acceleration are as valid as kinetic ones in correlating the mechanical and electrical consequences of contraction. It is of significance that the regression curves for movements performed with the SS strategy (solid lines) have different slopes than those for movements performed with the SI strategy (dotted lines). The relative steepness of the lines depends upon the kinetic or kinematic measure used.

The same kinetic measures are shown for the antagonist muscle using Q_{ant} in figure 2E-H. Because of the equations used (3 ,5 and 7), the only kinetic measure that differs between agonist and antagonist is peak torque which is directly obtained from the peak of deceleration.

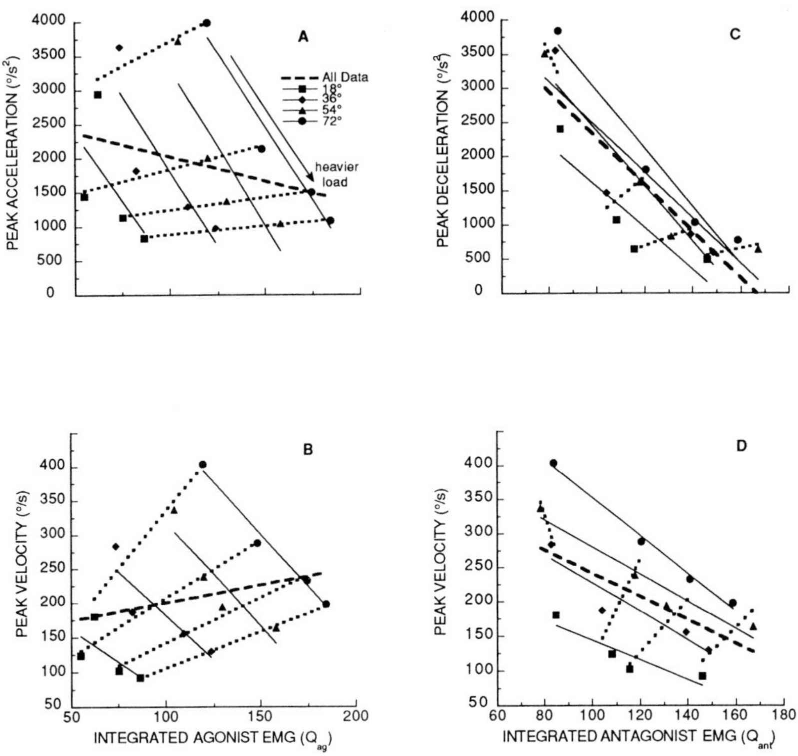

Figure 3. Kinematic indices of movement plotted against myoelectrical activity in the agonist and antagonist muscles. The area of the agonist burst Q_{ag} and antagonist burst Q_{ant} for movements of different distances and loads (A) Q_{ag} vs Peak Acceleration, (B) Q_{ag} vs Peak Velocity, (C) Q_{ant} vs Peak Deceleration and (D) Q_{ant} vs Peak Velocity.

An important feature of all four indices is that for movements over different distances (dotted lines), there is a clear tendency of the antagonist muscle's EMG burst to diminish, in spite of the fact that all kinetic and kinematic indices are increasing. Hence we have an apparent task-specific incompatibility between antagonist myoelectrical and kinetic mechanical indices of performance for these movements under the SI strategy.

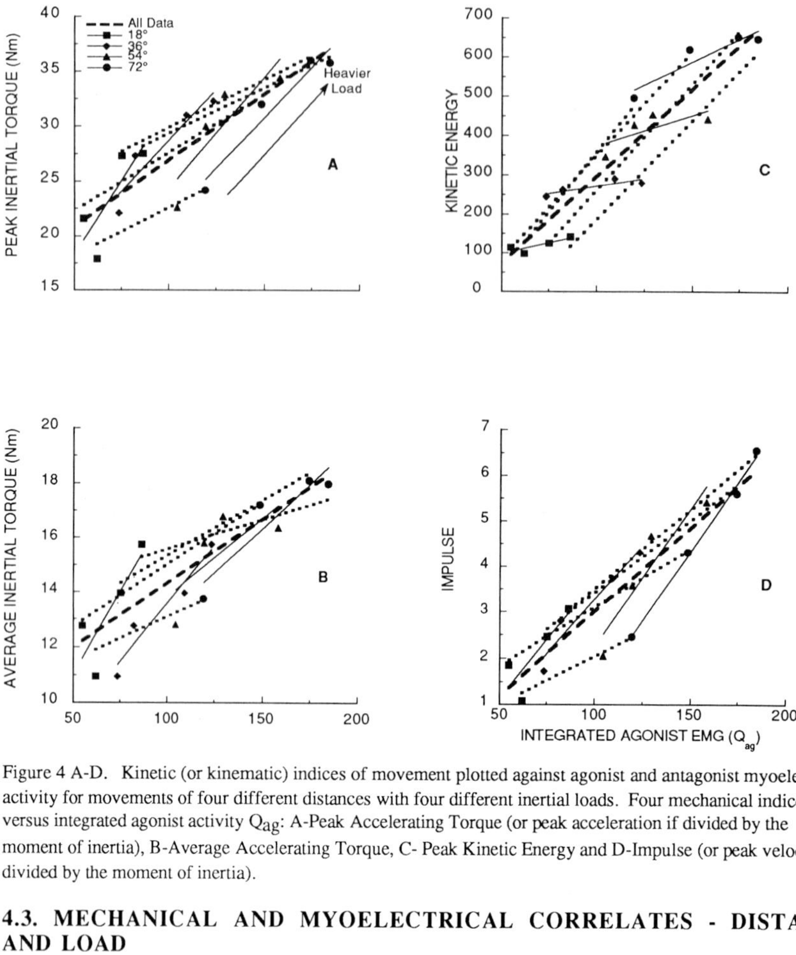

Figure 4 A-D. Kinetic (or kinematic) indices of movement plotted against agonist and antagonist myoelectrical activity for movements of four different distances with four different inertial loads. Four mechanical indices versus integrated agonist activity Q_{ag}: A-Peak Accelerating Torque (or peak acceleration if divided by the moment of inertia), B-Average Accelerating Torque, C- Peak Kinetic Energy and D-Impulse (or peak velocity if divided by the moment of inertia).

4.3. MECHANICAL AND MYOELECTRICAL CORRELATES - DISTANCE AND LOAD

4.3.1 Kinematic and myoelectrical correlates

Kinematic and kinetic indices are equivalent descriptors differing by only a constant scale factor if the load moved is constant. That equivalence is not maintained when the subject moves different inertial loads. Figure 3A,B shows kinematic indices for movements of different loads over four different distances versus the area of the agonist EMG burst. The thin solid lines show the regressions for each distance with the four inertial loads. The dotted lines show the regressions over four distances with the same load. In this experiment, both kinds of tasks are performed by the SI strategy. Q_{ag} increases with both distance and load but load reduces the kinematic peaks while distance increases them. The contrary effects of load and distance are

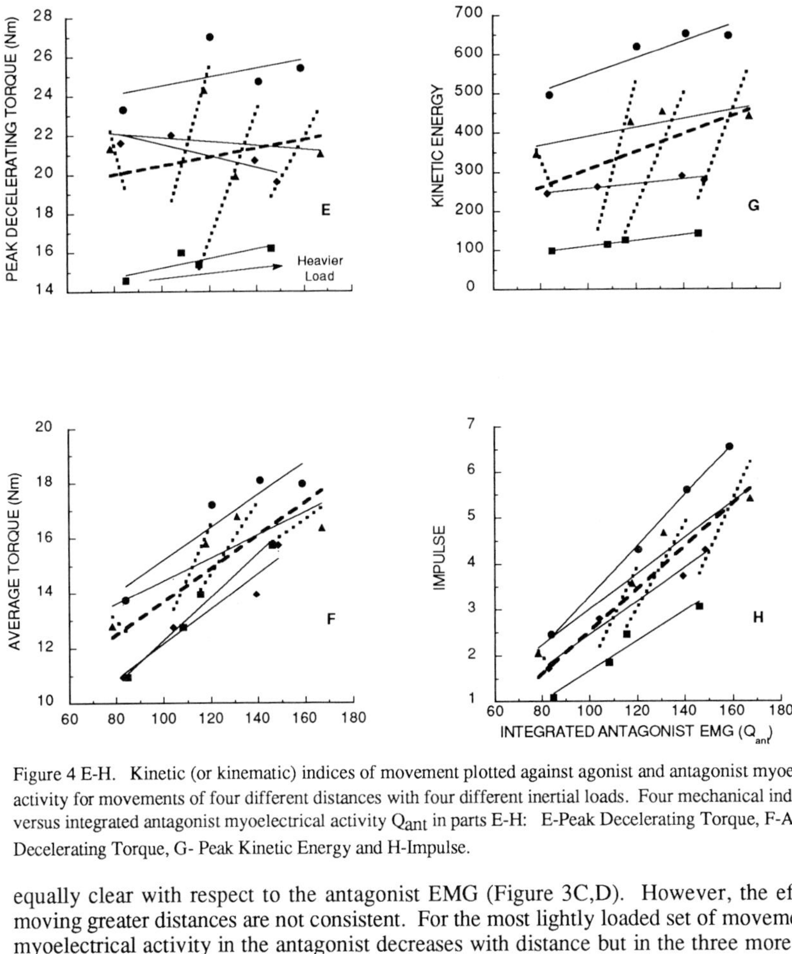

Figure 4 E-H. Kinetic (or kinematic) indices of movement plotted against agonist and antagonist myoelectrical activity for movements of four different distances with four different inertial loads. Four mechanical indices versus integrated antagonist myoelectrical activity Q_{ant} in parts E-H: E-Peak Decelerating Torque, F-Average Decelerating Torque, G- Peak Kinetic Energy and H-Impulse.

equally clear with respect to the antagonist EMG (Figure 3C,D). However, the effects of moving greater distances are not consistent. For the most lightly loaded set of movements, the myoelectrical activity in the antagonist decreases with distance but in the three more heavily loaded movement series it increases slightly. It is clear that in series of movements where both oad and distance vary, the regression curve between integrated EMG of either agonist or antagonist and these kinematic indices (heavy dashed line) accounts for little of the variance.

4.3.2 Kinetic and myoelectrical correlates

The four kinetic indices for these movements, plotted as a function of agonist EMG activity, are shown in figure 4A-D. Figure 4E-H shows the equivalent data for the antagonist.

The SI strategy is likely to be used whether movements of different distances with the same inertial load or of different inertial loads over a single distance are made by a subject. In each case, there is a positive correlation between the kinetic measures and the agonist EMG burst but the slopes of the regression curves vary greatly depending on the task and on the kinetic measure in question. Note that changes in inertial load lead to large changes in the agonist burst for which kinetic energy is a poor indicator.

Looking at the relations between the antagonist EMG and average torque or impulse suggests that the antagonist behaves much like the agonist. Looking at the peak decelerating torque or at the kinetic energy would lead to a different conclusion since these mechanical measures are quite insensitive to changes in load but extremely sensitive to changes in distance. It is also important to note that movements over different distances without weight added to the manipulandum show slight negative correlations between kinetic measures and the antagonist EMG burst. This loading condition is identical to that under which the data of figure 2 were collected.

4.4 Antagonist latency

Accurate movement requires that the muscles contract both to the correct degree and at the correct time. For the simple movements studied here, this implies that the timing of the antagonist muscle's activity must be properly controlled in order to appropriately time the development of the decelerating torque. Figure 1 shows that the antagonist usually has two distinguishable components. The first is small and not always present. When present, it has a constant latency of about 25 ms. The second, larger component with a variable latency is the antagonist "burst" as it is usually defined.

It is informative to look at the latency of the antagonist in the same way we looked at the kinetic measures of performance. Figure 5A plots antagonist latency as a function of the area of the agonist EMG burst for the data set of experiments shown in figure 4. Figure 5B shows another experiment where the subject performed movements of 36° at different speeds. These graphs show that there is a profound difference in this relation that is strategy dependent. For SI tasks (Fig 5A) antagonist latency is directly proportional to the agonist burst while for both SS task (Fig 5B) it is inversely proportional.

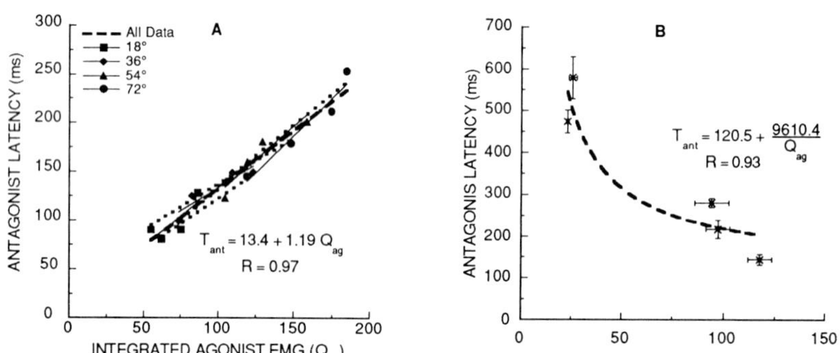

Figure 5. Latency of the antagonist burst (A) for movements of different distances and loads and (B) latencies (with standard error bars) for 36° movements with a constant load at different, subject-chosen speeds .

5. DISCUSSION

The motivation for trying to identify appropriate measures of both the electrical and the mechanical behaviors of contracting muscle is the fact that they are driven by the same neural command. The change from a positively to a negatively correlated correspondence between kinetic and myoelectrical indices of performance for the antagonist muscle in figure 4 (and kinematic and myoelectrical indices for agonist and antagonist in figure 3) seems inconsistent with this premise. In fact, the differences in slopes of the regressions for different tasks that can be seen for the agonist muscle in figure 2 are indicative of the same inconsistency, although it is to a lesser degree. We will consider the degree to which electromechanical correlations are consistent for different movement tasks employing the same strategy. We will also consider their consistency across different strategies.

5.1 The necessity for kinetic measures

Kinematic correlations with the EMG have been extensively used because they appear to provide a rationale for interpreting the EMG patterns associated with movements of different sorts (Brown, et al., 1990; Marsden, et al., 1983; Milner, 1986). The studies that have exploited such correlations have all been performed with constant loading on the limb. Equations 2-8 show that under these conditions, kinematic and kinetic measures differ only by a constant scale factor. Kinematic correlations really reflect the underlying kinetic relations and fail to appear if the mechanical load changes as shown in figure 3.

Mechanical impulse is one of many possible kinetic measures that provide a way to account for muscle performance that can be applied uniformly to both the agonist and antagonist muscles, whether or not the load is constant. With one exception, myolectrical and kinetic measures such as torque, kinetic energy or impulse, all positively covary with changes in the task. This positive covariation brings qualitative consistency between independent measures of the muscles' electrical and mechanical performance.

The fact that kinematic and electromyographic variables change in opposite directions when the inertial load is altered is a reflection both of a choice made by the motor controller and the constraints of Newtonian mechanics. The latter constraint can be considered by examining the implications of Newton's second law of motion embodied in equation 2. Ignoring viscous and elastic forces for the moment, if a constant force is applied to different loads, then the acceleration will vary inversely with the load as will its time integrals over any fixed period. The uniformly rising torques shown in figure 1 for such movements lead to kinematics that vary inversely as shown in figure 3. To this degree mechanics and not physiology is the underlying process leading to changes in behavior.

However, the subject was not obligated to use such a uniform pattern of muscle excitation. That is, the subject could have graded the intensity of the excitation pulse to increase the initial rate of rise of joint torque, in exactly the same way that was done for movements of intentionally different speeds that are shown in figure 1. The failure to do so was neither part of the task description nor due to some upper limit on the motoneurons or other neurons since such uniformity can be found over a wide range of strengths of contraction (Gottlieb, et al., 1990a). It must, therefore, represent a feature of the movement plan.

It is in general only correct to associate electromyographic changes with changes in kinetic measures, not with kinematic ones. The figures show that kinematic measures may be poor indicators of muscle activation. When they are good indicators, as in figure 2 and (Brown, et al., 1990), it is because for those tasks they are interchangeable with some kinetic measure. This raises a question of which kinetic measure should be used.

5.2 Agonist-Antagonist relations

Examining figures 2-4 shows that although kinetic measures have a more consistent, positive correlation with the electromyographic activity in the muscles, the degree of correlation depends strongly on the task. These differences point to an important question that has not been addressed. Why should the relationship between mechanical and myoelectrical indices depend upon the task?

Part of the answer to this question must consider that we have attempted to correlate the electromyographic behavior of one muscle with some mechanical event that is caused by the contraction of more than one muscle. The EMG patterns in figure 1 suggest that there is very little time in which the forces acting about a joint can be attributed to an isolated agonist contraction and none at all in which they can be attributed to an isolated antagonist contraction. The forces of the two muscle groups overlap in time. Therefore, any accurate description must take into account the details of this overlap. Figure 5 shows the surprising result that the latency of the antagonist EMG burst, and therefore the timing of its decelerating torque, is very tightly coupled to the activity of the agonist. Our proposed model of the EMG as a low-pass filtered version of the motoneuron pool excitation pulse implies that the areas of the EMG burst and the pulse will be linearly related. This allows us to write the following equation for the latency T_{ant} of the antagonist EMG burst, based upon the data in figure 5, in terms of the parameters of the agonist excitation pulse (cf Table 1).

$$T_{ant} = a + b\frac{W}{H} \tag{9}$$

where a and b are constants. This equation applies to both strategies since the SI strategy varies only W (figure 5A) while the SS strategy varies only H (figure 5B).

5.3. The Relation between impulse and the electromyogram

Another part of the reason for the discrepancy between myoelectrical and kinetic indices of muscle contraction may be that the method we use to estimate joint torque is not accurate. Equation 2 states that inertial torque captures only part of the mechanical output of the muscle. As a second approximation, we can consider the addition of a linear viscous term in estimating joint torque with equation 2. This would reflect a simplified form of the force-velocity properties of both agonist and antagonist muscles (Hill, 1940).

This term requires us to recalculate all the kinetic measures according to equations (2)-(8). There is no *a priori* reason to prefer any of those measures but recalculating impulse using equation (8) is by far the simplest technique and the one we will consider here.

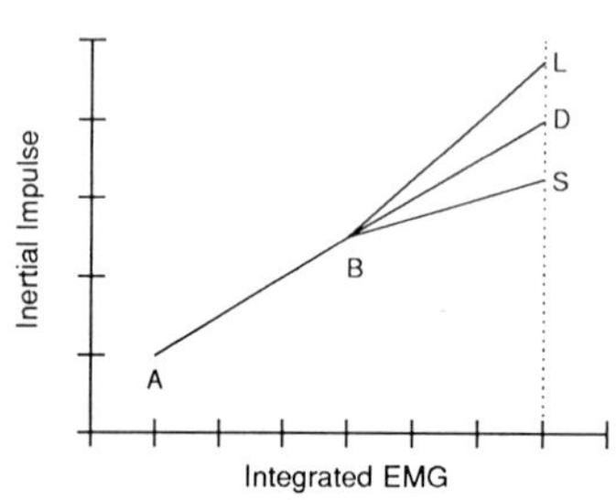

Figure 6. Relative effects of single task manipulations on impulse and the area of the agonist EMG burst.

In figure 6 we have drawn a line from A to B representing the relationship observed between inertial impulse and the agonist burst for movements over different distances with a constant inertial load. We know by observation that in going from A to B, subjects increase activation of the agonist muscle and and reach higher peak velocities thereby increasing inertial impulse; movement time increases and the antagonist burst changes little in area but gets progressively delayed. Further increases in distance would extend the relationship from point B to point D. If the distance at point B is fixed and the subject asked to move a heavier load, the movement slows, movement time increases but inertial impulse increases. The agonist burst would increase to a point L, above the level of D. This can be deduced from figure 4D where the solid regression lines through points of constant distance and different load have steeper slopes than the dotted lines drawn in the figure for constant loads over different distances. If we next ask for a movement over the same distance and load corresponding to point B and ask the subject to move faster, we will again measure an increased inertial impulse. From figure 2D we can deduce that the agonist burst area will increase to a point S that will be below that of D. Unlike kinematic measures, impulse increases for each of the three kinds of task manipulations, although not to the same degree. Let us consider next, the reason for the different slopes.

The first term on the right in equation (8) is due to inertia and the second to viscosity. The increase in EMG from point B to D results from increased activation which also leads to a larger impulse. Changes in task distance lead to increases in both the inertial impulse component (peak velocity will increase) and the viscous impulse component (the task definition will increase the far right term of eq. 8). Giving the subject a larger load only increases the inertial component (in spite of peak velocity decreasing) of the above relation and therefore does not produce as great an increase in impulse or muscle activation. Applying this notion to the data in figure 2D and H and adding a viscous component (assuming B=.06 for all movements) leads to a convergence of the regression lines for both agonist and antagonist muscles as shown in figures 7A and B.

According to the rules of strategies, instructing the subject to change speed leads to a change in the intensity of the excitation pulse. We propose that this has a direct effect on the velocity dependent properties of the muscles. An increase in intended speed leads to an increase in the inertial component of impulse because peak velocity increases. It also leads to an increase in the viscous component because the effective B increases. This can be explicitly introduced by assuming that the viscosity B in equation 8 is proportional to the intensity with which the subject contracts the limb muscles. This implies that impulse (and therefore EMG) could decrease more steeply for deliberate changes in speed than for changes in speed related to changes in distance.

We can show that this manipulation of the data is capable of aligning the separate regression lines by using instruction dependent values of B. This is done for the agonist in figure 7C and for the antagonist in figure 7D. Comparison of the scales of figures 2, 4 and 7 show that viscous and inertial forces must be of comparable magnitudes if this transformation is reasonably correct. The problem in testing this hypothesis is that we lack an independent measure of the viscous forces.

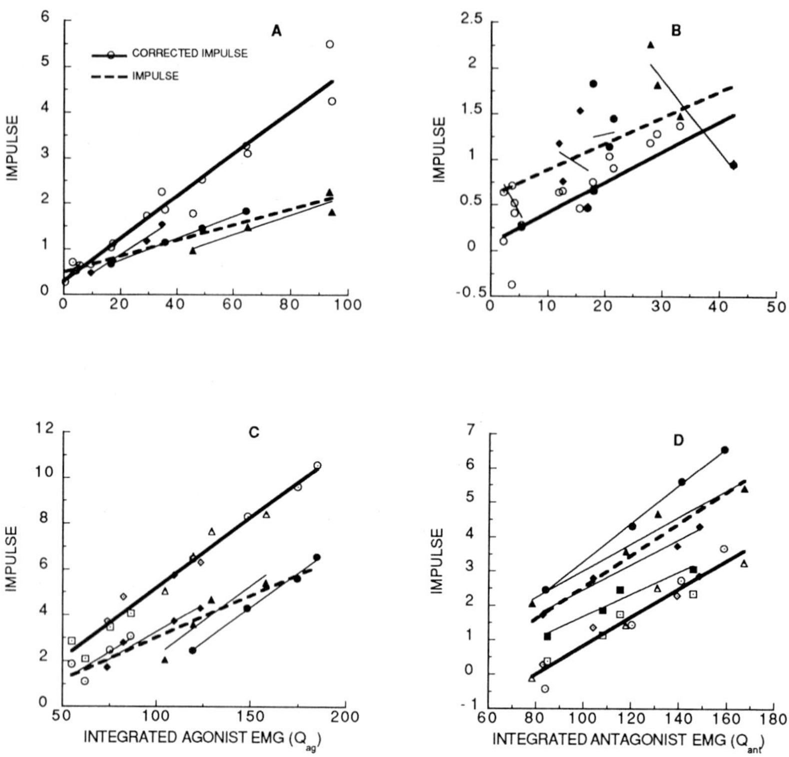

Figure 7. The area of the agonist burst Q_{ag} for movements of different distances at four different speeds (A) Q_{ag} vs impulse and (B) Q_{ant} vs impulse. The open symbols are adjusted values of impulse using an estimate of joint viscosity. Agonist (C) and Antagonist (D) EMG for movements of different distances and loads with impulses computed with an instruction-dependent viscous term.

5.4 The excitation pulse and the equilibrium-point hypotheses

Let us consider one possible way that the CNS might go about "computing" the parameters of agonist and antagonist excitation pulses when asked to move a given distance "as fast and accurately as possible." Fitts' (1954) showed that these two criteria of speed and accuracy are competitive. Therefore, the subject will choose an agonist excitation pulse intensity that is large but usually not the largest possible, in order to satisfy both accuracy and distance constraints. Having chosen so, the net agonist excitation will require correct specification of pulse duration to generate sufficient accelerating forces. This is done based upon prior experience of moving the limb over similar distances with similar loads. It is a guess.

Determining the agonist excitation pulse parameters places rigid constraints upon the allowable parameters of the antagonist pulse. The strength of the antagonist's contraction is not uniquely specified however until the latency of that contraction has been set. This is where the observation of Figure 5 is important because it shows that the latency of the antagonist's excitation pulse in the SI strategy is completely specified by the parameters of the agonist's excitation pulse. The simplest rule for its height and duration is to make the antagonist a scale model of the agonist. This would require the specification of only one additional constant which must take into account the characteristics of the load. This too would be a guess. Of the five parameters needed to specify agonist and antagonist excitation pulses, one would be chosen based on external criteria and the rest are coupled together such that only two of them, agonist width and antagonist scaling parameters need be "tuned" to the specific features of the movement. Precisely how they are adjusted by trial and error to correct for undershoot and overshoot or misjudgments in the dynamics of the load is an area that requires further investigation.

This description of control makes no reference to the influences of sensory feedback from joint and muscle proprioceptors. It is not incompatible with such feedback however. The onsets of the agonist and antagonist bursts seem to be entirely programmed and independent of such feedback. Models that have tried to make this phase of muscle activation sensitive to afferent input (Feldman, Adamovitch, Ostry, & Flanagan, 1990) do not predict the results shown in figure 5. We have discussed the relationship between the two approaches in (Gottlieb, Corcos, Latash, & Agarwal, 1990b).

One approach to incorporating both open-loop and closed-loop control is to consider two phases to the control of fast movements from one stationary position to another. A "transition phase" initiates the movement and launches it towards a target. This phase must deal with the dynamic aspects of the physical system but need not be concerned with accuracy of movement. The transition phase will include a plan for the initial activation of the antagonist muscle because the relatively slow speed of the muscles' contractile mechanism requires antagonist muscle activation after only about half of the distance to the target has been traversed. Its motoneuron pool must be activated even earlier in the trajectory.

The dynamics of limb movement are largely those of moving very lightly damped inertial loads with relatively slow force generating mechanisms. This would seem to make accurate movement difficult unless the control of both agonist and antagonist was extremely precise, both in degree and timing. With relatively little practice, subjects can perform simple movements with a coefficient of variation of end point position that is less than 5% of the distance moved. Such precision does not seem possible if the variance of the EMG or such kinematic measures as peak velocity or acceleration can be taken as its measure of the control signal's inherent variance.

A final "position phase" based on the idea of an equilibrium point between opposing, position dependent forces could solve this problem and be independent of the mechanisms that initiated the transition phase. Coactivation of the muscles about the joint at some steady level (Polit, & Bizzi, 1979), coupled with the activation of length-dependent reflexes (Asatryan, & Feldman, 1965; Feldman, 1986), would accomplish this.

5.5 Conclusions

The first conclusion we wish to draw from the above data is that the theoretical premise that muscle force and the electromyogram do represent independent observations of the same controlling input. A consequence of this fact is that they share qualitative and quantitative features of that signal. This has been experimentally supported for both agonist and antagonist muscles and across three different tasks. This is, to our knowledge, the only successful attempt to describe both muscle groups by a uniform set of rules. However, this conclusion must not be taken too strongly because of the fact that all the kinetic and kinematic measures that have appeared in the literature are ultimately the produces of the action of both agonist and antagonist muscle groups. Relating such measures to the activation of only one of these groups is large simplication that is certainly subject to falsification under appropriately chosen conditions.

The second conclusion is that it is necessary to distinguish at least two strategies for controlling single joint movements that specify the degree and the timing of muscle activation. In the face of different kinematic and kinetic demands by different tasks, the CNS selects either a pulse-height or a pulse-width modulation scheme for the motoneuron pools. This distinction must be invoked to account for the way in which movements may share kinematic but not kinetic similarity or alternatively, share kinetic but not kinematic similarity. The quantitative differences between strategies are most clearly evident in the earliest moments of the myoelectrical signals or in the torque trajectories. They may not be apparent from observations confined to the kinematic trajectories.

The suggestion that movements are controlled by the selection of appropriate patterns for muscle activation does not answer the question of how these patterns are planned in order to move the limb to specific targets and sometimes, along specific trajectories. Most human movements are goal directed and have trajectories that appear well chosen to achieve that goal. To move along a specific trajectory requires a well chosen set of net torques to be applied to each joint. To compute those torques from knowledge of the desired trajectory and the load of the mechanical system being moved is called the inverse kinematic problem. Solving this problem is relatively simple for single joints but becomes rapidly more complex as the number of joints increases. Such complexity has inspired many to speculate that the real-time calculation of such solutions, while potentially a practical approach for some robotic systems, is not likely to be the way the CNS controls movement. If this is true, how can the CNS know what forces to apply and therefore, how can it know what parameters to select for the excitation pulses?

Our answer to this must necessarily be highly speculative. We would suggest that to perform accurate, fast movements, the CNS has a very good idea of the forces necessary to perform such movements based upon prior movement experience. This allows it to make one arbitrary selection; excitation pulse width if the task allows an SI strategy or excitation pulse height if an SS strategy is required. The calculation of the other parameters is a matter of linear approximation from prior movements around the work space. Separating the movement task into transition and position phases separates the problem of speed control from that of position control. For both phases however, this implies that if we lack adequate information to make accurate calculations we will make errors of movement. Alternatively, we will make slower movements to allow visual or proprioceptive corrections to be made as we approach the target. A further implication is that to improve movement accuracy under a variety of conditions and to a variety of endpoints, we must practice. None of these suggestions seem inconsistent with normally observed behavior.

6. ACKNOWLEDGEMENTS

This work was supported in part by NIH grant AR 33189 and NS 23593 and with the technical assistance of Mr. Om Paul.

7. REFERENCES

Abbott, B. C., & Aubert, X. M. (1952). The force exerted by active striated muscle during and after change of length. *Journal of Physiology (London), 117*, 77-86.

Asatryan, D. G., & Feldman, A. G. (1965). Functional tuning of the nervous system with contro of movement or maintenance of a steady posture - I. Mechanographic analysis of the work of the joint or execution of a postural task. *Biofizika, 10*, 837-846 [English translation 925-935].

Bouisset, S., & Goubel, F. (1968). Interdependence of relations between integrated EMG and diverse biomechanical quantities in normal voluntary movements. *Electromyography, 8 (Suppl. 1)*, 151-162.
Bouisset, S., & Goubel, F. (1973). Integrated electromyographical activity and muscle work. *Journal of Applied Physiology, 35*, 696-702.
Brown, S. H., & Cooke, J. D. (1990). Movement-Related Phasic Muscle Activation I. Relations with temporal profile of movement. *Journal of Neurophysiology, 63*(3), 455-464.
Brown, S. H. C., & Cooke, J. D. (1981). Amplitude- and instruction-dependent modulation of movement-related electromyogram activity in humans. *Journal of Physiology (London), 316*, 97-107.
Corcos, D. M., Agarwal, G. C., Flaherty, B., & Gottlieb, G. L. (1990). Organizing principles for single joint movement: IV - Implications for isometric contractions. *Journal of Neurophysiology, 64*(3), 1033-1042.
Corcos, D. M., Gottlieb, G. L., & Agarwal, G. C. (1989). Organizing principles for single joint movements: II - A speed-sensitive strategy. *Journal of Neurophysiology, 62*, 358-368.
Danoff, J. V. (1979). The integrated electromyogram related to angular velocity. *Electromyography and Clinical Neurophysiology, 19*, 165-174.
Feldman, A. G. (1986). Once more on the equilibrium-point hypothesis (λ model) for motor control. *Journal of Motor Behavior, 18*, 17-54.
Feldman, A. G., Adamovitch, S. V., Ostry, D. J., & Flanagan, J. R. (1990). The Origin of Electromyograms - Explanations Based on the Equilibrium Point Hypothesis. In J. Winters, & S. Woo (Ed.), *Multiple Muscle Systems: Biomechanics and Movement Organization* (pp. 195-213). New York, NY: Springer-Verlag New York Inc.
Fitts, P. M. (1954). The information capacity of the human motor system in controlling the amplitude of movement. *Journal of Experimental Psychology, 47*, 381-391.
Freund, H., & Budingen, H. J. (1978). The relationship between speed and amplitude of the fastest voluntary contractions of human arm muscles. *Experimental Brain Research, 31*, 1-12.
Gielen, C. C. A. M., van den Oosten, K., & Pull ter Gunne, F. (1985). Relation between EMG activation patterns and kinematic properties of aimed movements. *Journal of Motor Behavior, 17*, 421-442.
Gottlieb, G. L., Corcos, D. M., & Agarwal, G. C. (1989a). Organizing principles for single joint movements: I - A Speed-Insensitive strategy. *Journal of Neurophysiology, 62*(2), 342-357.
Gottlieb, G. L., Corcos, D. M., & Agarwal, G. C. (1989b). Strategies for the control of single mechanical degree of freedom voluntary movements. *Behavioral and Brain Sciences, 12*(2), 189-210.
Gottlieb, G. L., Corcos, D. M., Agarwal, G. C., & Latash, M. L. (1990a). Organizing principles for single joint movements: III - The Speed-Insensitive strategy as default. *Journal of Neurophysiology, 63*(3), 625-636.
Gottlieb, G. L., Corcos, D. M., Latash, M. L., & Agarwal, G. C. (1990b). Principles underlying single joint movement strategies. In J. Winters, & S. Woo (Ed.), *Multiple Muscle Systems: Biomechanics and Movement Organization* (pp. 1990). New York, NY: Springer-Verlag New York Inc.
Hancock, P. A., & Newell, K. M. (1985). The movement speed-accuracy relationship in space-time. In H. Heuer, U. Kleinbeck, & K. H. Schmidt (Ed.), *Motor Behavior: Programming, Control and Acquisition* (pp. 153-188). New York: Springer-Verlag.
Hill, A. V. (1940). The dynamic constants of human muscle. *Proc. Royal Society London, Series B, 128*, 263-274.

Joyce, G. C., Rack, P. M. H., & Westbury, D. R. (1969). The mechanical properties of cat soleus muscle during controlled lengthening and shortening movements. *Journal of Physiology*, *204*, 461-474.
Karst, G. M., & Hasan, Z. (1987). Antagonist muscle activity during human forearm movements under varying kinematic and loading conditions. *Experimental Brain Research*, *67*, 391-401.
Knox, C. K. (1974). Cross-correlational functions for a neuronal model. *Biophysical Journal*, *14*, 567-582.
Lestienne, F. (1979). Effects of Inertial load and velocity on the braking process of voluntary limb movements. *Experimental Brain Research*, *35*, 407-418.
Marsden, C. D., Obeso, J. A. , & Rothwell, J. C. (1983). The function of the antagonist muscle during fast limb movements in man. *Journal of Physiology*, *335*, 1-13.
Milner, T. E. (1986). Controlling velocity in rapid movements. *Journal of Motor Behavior*, *18*, 147-161.
Mustard, B. E., & Lee, R. G. (1987). Relationship between EMG patterns and kinematic properties for flexion movements at the human wrist. *Experimental Brain Research*, *66*, 247-2256.
Polit, A., & Bizzi, E. (1979). Characteristics of motor programs underlying arm movements in monkeys. *J. Neurophysiol.*, *42*, 183-194.
Shapiro, D. C., & Walter, C. B. (1986). An examination of rapid positioning movements with spatiotemporal constraints. *Journal of Motor Behavior*, *18*, 372-395.
Wadman, W. J., Denier van der Gon, J. J., Geuze, R. H., & Mol, C. R. (1979). Control of fast goal-directed arm movements. *Journal of Human Movement Studies*, *5*, 3-17.
Wallace, S. A. (1981). An impulse-timing theory for reciprocal control of muscular activity in rapid, discrete movements. *Journal of Motor Behavior*, *13*, 144-1160.
Wallace, S. A., & Wright, L. (1982). Distance and movement effects on the timing of agonist and antagonist muscles: a test of the impulse-timing theory. *Journal of Motor Behavior*, *14*, 341-352.

Tutorials in Motor Behavior II
G.E. Stelmach and J. Requin (Editors)

Human jaw movement kinematics and control

D.J. Ostry[a], J.R. Flanagan[a], A.G. Feldman[b] and K.G. Munhall[c]

[a] Department of Psychology, McGill University, Montreal, Canada

[b] Institut de génie biomédical, Université de Montréal and Institut de réadaptation de Montréal, Centre de recherche, Montreal, Canada

[c] Department of Psychology, Queen's University, Kingston, Canada

Abstract

In this paper we describe the kinematics of two-dimensional jaw motion based on X-ray microbeam recordings. We assess the relationship between jaw rotation and translation and compare empirical records with computer simulations based on the equilibrium point hypothesis (λ model). In speech trials, subjects produced consonant-vowel combinations at different rates and volumes. In the mastication trials, the subjects chewed unilaterally on rubber tubing. The rotation of the jaw and its translation along the articular eminence were determined from the motion of X-ray tracking pellets on the jaw. In both mastication and speech, jaw rotation and translation start and end simultaneously and have straight line paths when rotation is plotted against translation. Several manipulations suggest that jaw rotation and translation can be separately controlled. For example, in jaw movements in speech, the slope of the relationship between rotation and translation was dependent on the consonant composition of the utterance but did not depend on the identity of the vowel or upon speech rate. The λ model successfully accounts for the jaw kinematics in mastication and speech. Using the model, we show that separate central commands can be defined for jaw rotation, jaw translation, and muscle co-activation without motion. Commands may be linearly superimposed to give combinations of rotation, translation and muscle co-activation. Jaw movement kinematics in both mastication and speech can be reproduced by the model by simple constant velocity shifts in equilibrium in each phase of the movement.

1. INTRODUCTION

This paper focuses on the two-dimensional kinematics of human jaw motion in a sagittal plane. We describe the relationship between jaw rotation and translation and present evidence that these can be independently controlled. We also describe a computer model of jaw motion based on the equilibrium point hypothesis or λ model (see Flanagan, Ostry & Feldman, 1990, for a detailed description of the model).

According to the hypothesis, central commands control the EP of the system by specifying the muscle lengths (λs) at which motoneuron recruitment begins. In multiple muscle systems such as the jaw, these commands control the λs of many muscles in concert. We have posited three basic central commands for the jaw system which control specific motor functions via various combinations of λs. One command is associated with the level of co-activation of all muscles and the other two commands are associated with motions in specific degrees of freedom, jaw rotation and jaw translation (Flanagan, Ostry & Feldman, 1990). We posit that jaw motions are planned in equilibrium coordinates associated with rotation and translation of the jaw. We demonstrate, using the model, that in each phase of the movement, constant velocity shifts in the equilibrium lengths of all muscles can account for the patterns of jaw motion in both speech and mastication.

To date, human jaw movements have mostly been recorded in one dimension. For example, we have used an linear voltage displacement transducer to measure vertical motion of the jaw in speech and mastication (Ostry & Flanagan, 1989). Unidimensional measurements can provide a gross description of jaw motion. However, the relative contributions of jaw rotation and translation to the transduced motion cannot be uniquely determined since different combinations of rotation and translation yield the "same" transduced movement. In this paper we present jaw movement data obtained with the X-ray microbeam. With the microbeam, the planar motion of a number of pellets attached to the mandible was recorded simultaneously. Thus it was possible to estimate the planar rotation and translation of the jaw.

The recording of jaw motions in two dimensions introduces several issues which have previously been examined in work on multi-joint arm movements. One problem is the identification of the coordinates in which movements are planned and controlled. This problem stems from the fact that multi-joint movements can be described in alternative coordinate frames. For example, multi-joint arm movements can be described in extrinsic coordinates corresponding to the position of the endpoint (e.g., hand) in space or intrinsic coordinates related to joint angles. Thus, the issue arises as to whether one of these coordinate systems is the preferred one for motion planning and control. In the case of jaw movements, the question can be asked whether motions are planned in rotations and translations of the mandible or the position of specific points on the jaw in oral cavity coordinates?

In the case of arm movements, findings from single unit recording and kinematic studies have been used to address the issue of planning coordinates. Reports of unit activity in motor cortex during reaching movements in monkeys indicate that these units collectively code the direction of hand movement relative to the body in extrinsic space (e.g., Georgopoulus, Kettner, & Schwartz, 1988). This suggests that these movements may be planned in endpoint coordinates. Evidence of endpoint planning has also been provided in kinematic studies of reaching movements in humans in which hand paths form straight lines in extrinsic space regardless of movement direction and rate (Morasso, 1981, but cf., Atkeson & Hollerbach, 1986; Flanagan & Ostry, 1990). In contrast, Soechting and colleagues (e.g., Soechting & Flanders, 1989) have shown consistent relationships between joint angles in a number of movement tasks involving straight line and curved hand paths, suggesting joint level planning.

Kinematic findings are difficult to interpret since output trajectories may deviate substantially from centrally planned trajectories. Since we cannot directly record the form of the equilibrium trajectory, computer simulations, based on the λ model, enable us to examine the form of *equilibrium* trajectories underlying actual output trajectories. Our initial work on human reaching movements shows that these movements are planned in equilibrium coordinates corresponding to the position of the hand (see Flanagan, Feldman & Ostry, this volume). In contrast, the work presented in the present paper and work on frog withdrawal movements (Ostry, Feldman, & Flanagan, 1991) suggests that these motions may be coded in equilibrium joint coordinates.

Another central problem is to specify the form of the central control signals subserving movement. In our work on reaching movements to visual targets we have assumed that the equilibrium position of the hand shifts at a constant rate in the direction of the target. In contrast, Flash (1987) has assumed that the equilibrium trajectory is bell-shaped in form. Our studies on human reaching movements to visually displaced targets have shown that if the target position is displaced during movement, the equilibrium position continues - at the same rate - towards the new target. This is consistent with the idea of a constant velocity shift in the equilibrium hand position (Flanagan, Feldman & Ostry, this volume). Furthermore, our initial modelling work to account for jaw movement kinematics in mastication and speech indicates that these movements are also subserved by simple constant velocity shifts in equilibrium (Flanagan, Ostry & Feldman, 1990).

Another problem is how central commands are coordinated in systems with multiple muscles which effect motion in a number of degrees of freedom. Consider, for example, the jaw system in which both jaw rotation and translation involve motion about the temporomandibular joint. In this system, individual jaw muscles contribute to motion in rotation as well as translation. Moreover, the relative contribution of different muscles will vary with jaw position.

In jaw opening movements, the jaw rotates downward and translates forward; during closing, the opposite pattern is observed. Three groups of muscles produce these motions in the sagittal plane. Jaw closers, including masseter and medial pterygoid, serve both to raise and retract the jaw; jaw openers, such as the anterior belly of the digastric, act to lower and retract the jaw; jaw protrusion is produced by the lateral pterygoid. Thus, both jaw closers and openers rotate and translate the jaw. Jaw protruders produce translation and, indirectly, rotation because of changes to the lengths of the other muscles. Because there is no one to one mapping between muscle actions and kinematic degrees of freedom, commands to all three muscle groups must be coordinated in order to produce rotation, translation or co-activation of muscles without motion. Using the model, we have demonstrated that separate central commands can be defined which result in pure rotation, pure translation and pure co-contraction regardless of the jaw position.

The X-ray microbeam system was used to record the kinematics of human tongue and jaw movement (Abbs, Nadler & Fujimura, 1988; Westbury, in press). The system uses a low dosage narrow beam X-ray to track the motions of radio-dense markers (typically, 2-3 mm spherical gold pellets) in 2-dimensions. Jaw rotation and translation are determined from the motion of X-ray tracking pellets.

2. METHODS

The X-ray microbeam system was used to obtain mid-sagittal recordings of pellets attached to the tongue and jaw. Pellet motions were corrected for planar head motion and, in the case of mandibular and maxillary molar pellets, for their distance from the mid-sagittal plane (see Westbury, in press, for details). After completion of the experimental trials, mid-sagittal palate tracings were recorded for all subjects.

Jaw movements were examined in both cartesian oral cavity coordinates and mandibular joint coordinates (Munhall, Ostry & Flanagan, in press). In the oral cavity system one axis corresponds to the occlusal plane; the other axis is perpendicular to the occlusal plane and the origin is at the tip of the maxillary incisors. In the joint coordinate system, movements are described in terms of rotation of the jaw and translation of the condyle along the articular eminence.

In speech trials, consonant-vowel combinations were produced continuously at different rates and volumes. The utterances were composed of the vowels *a* and *e* and the consonants *t* and *k*. The selection of vowels enabled movement amplitude to be varied. The vowel *a* is associated with large amplitude jaw motion whereas the vowel *e* is associated with smaller amplitude motion. In mastication trials, unilateral chewing was tested with rubber tubing. Tracking pellets on the jaw were sampled at various frequencies between 60 and 90 Hz. The data were then low-passed filtered at 8 to 10 Hz. Jaw rotation and translation were derived from the motion of the tracking pellets on the jaw.

3. JAW MOVEMENT KINEMATICS

In this section we describe jaw movements in oral cavity and joint based coordinate frames. We provide experimental data to suggest that jaw rotation and translation can be independently controlled.

The basic patterns of jaw rotation and translation are presented in Figure 1. The upper panel shows rotation and horizontal and vertical jaw translation during a single trial in which a subject chewed unilaterally on hard rubber tubing. The lower panel shows jaw translation and rotation recorded from the same subject during cyclical repetitions of the syllable *ka*. Both chewing and speech trials were recorded at the subject's preferred rate. As can be seen in the figure, the magnitudes of rotation and translation were typically greater in mastication than in speech. In addition, rotation and translation tended to begin and end simultaneously.

The oral cavity motion paths of jaw pellets are shown in Figure 2. The data for mastication (solid line) and speech (dotted line) are presented for all conditions tested. Paths at the right of each panel give the motion of the mandibular incisors. The paths at the left show movements of left and right side mandibular molars. The figure shows the amplitude of jaw movements to be greater in general for mastication than for speech. For subject BH, the jaw is more protruded for speech than for mastication, whereas for subject TB, the jaw appears to be more protruded for mastication.

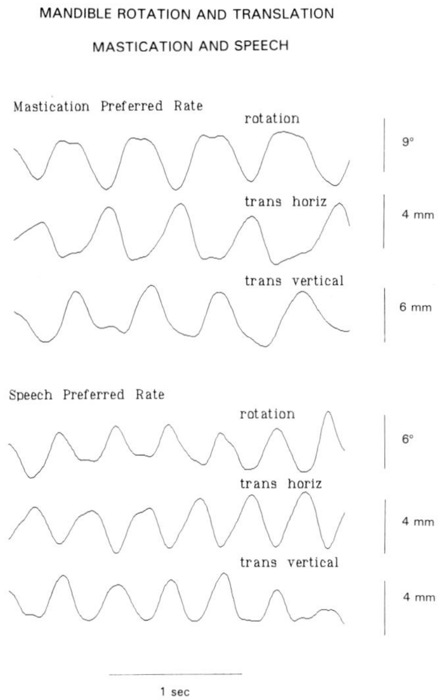

Figure 1. Mandible rotation and translation computed from X-ray microbeam recordings of jaw movement in mastication and speech.

The oral cavity jaw motion paths were most noticeably affected by differences in the consonant composition of speech (Figure 3). The solid lines are for syllables involving the consonant *t* (specifically, *ta* or *te*); the dotted lines are for syllables involving k (*ka* or *ke*). Again, the paths to the right of the figure indicate motion of the mandibular incisors; the paths to the left are for mandibular molars. The remaining manipulations had more subtle effects on jaw motion paths in the oral cavity. Rate differences affected the amplitude of the movement but typically not the shape or position of the path. The compliance of the bolus in mastication and differences in the vowel composition of speech utterances had little effect on the paths in oral cavity coordinates.

Figure 4 shows motion paths of the jaw in joint coordinates. The figure shows for three subjects the jaw rotation plotted as a function of horizontal jaw translation. Although some exceptions are apparent, it is seen that when jaw rotation is plotted against jaw translation straight line paths are observed. This shows that jaw rotation and jaw translation start and stop simultaneously and that the ratio of their displacements is constant throughout the movement.

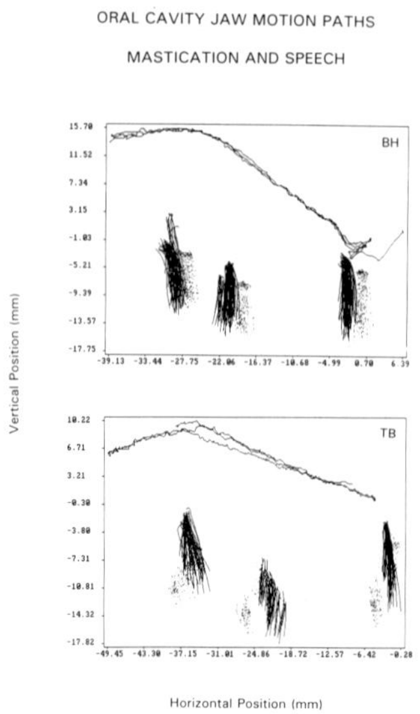

Figure 2. Motion paths of jaw pellets during mastication (solid) and speech (dots). Hard palate tracings have been superimposed. All pellet positions have been projected onto the mid-sagittal plane.

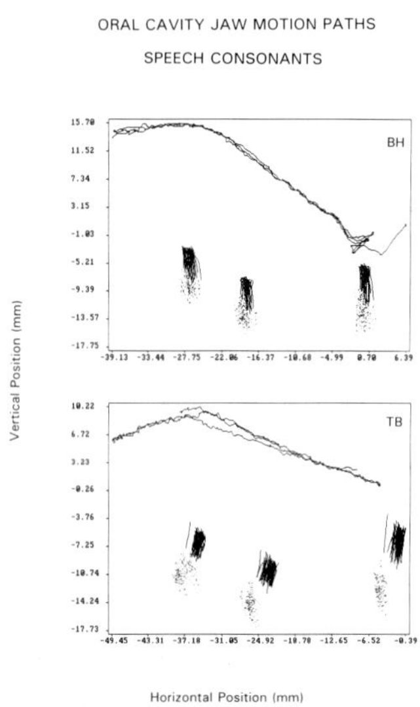

Figure 3. Oral cavity jaw motion paths during cyclical repetitions of *ta* and *te* (solid lines) and *ka* and *ke* (dotted lines).

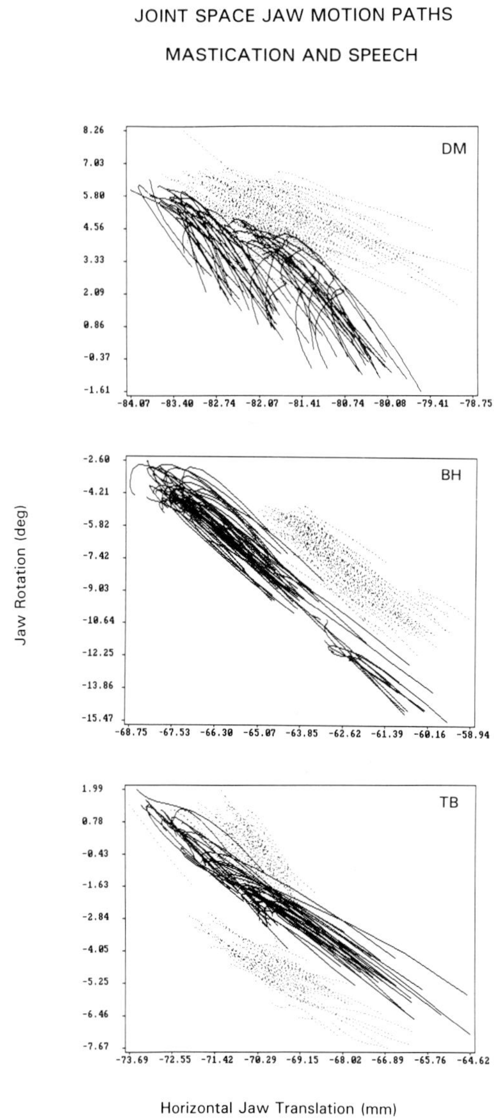

Figure 4. Joint space paths for jaw movements in mastication (solid) and speech (dotted). Rotation is shown as a function of horizontal translation. (The horizontal axis is parallel to the occlusal plane).

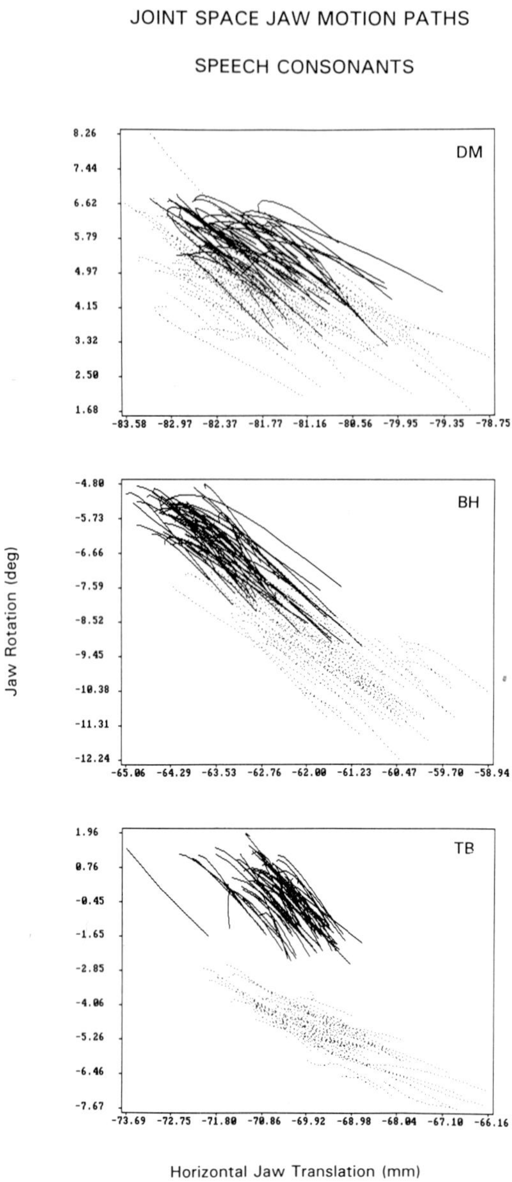

Figure 5. Joint space paths for the speech movements shown above in Figure 3. The solid lines are for *ta* and *te*; the dotted lines are for *ka* and *ke*.

Figure 4 also demonstrates that the relationship between jaw rotation and jaw translation is not fixed. Indeed, the pattern of coordination may be seen to differ for different subjects. For subject DM, the slope of jaw rotation plotted against jaw translation is different in speech and mastication. For subject BH, the slopes are similar for mastication and speech but the two types of movement occupy different areas of the workspace. For TB, the slopes and intercepts differ for mastication and speech; in fact, slopes and intercepts differ for different speech utterances.

Several manipulations suggest that jaw rotation and translation may be separately controlled. When we examined jaw movements in speech, we found that the slope of the relationship between jaw rotation and translation varied with the consonant but was not dependent on speech rate or the vowel composition of the utterance. Figure 5 shows that when jaw rotation was plotted against jaw translation, slopes for subject DM differed for syllables involving the consonants *t* (solid lines) and *k* (dotted lines). For subject BH, slopes for *t* and *k* were similar, but movements for *k* were produced from a position in which the jaw was translated forward and down relative *t* and rotated over a different range. For subject TB, the slope was steeper for *t* than for *k*. Furthermore, *k* was produced with the jaw in a more protruded position.

Other manipulations also support the view that jaw rotation and translation may be separately controlled. When we compared loud and fast speech for the syllables *sa* and *ka*, we found that the slope of the relationship between jaw rotation and jaw translation varied with consonant but not with speech rate or volume (Figure 7). This demonstrates that the relationship between jaw rotation and translation may vary. It can also be seen that translation may occur without altering the slope of the relationship between jaw rotation and translation. For example, in cyclical repetitions of the syllable *sa* the jaw is seen to be translated forward for loud speech but the slope of path for *sa* is not altered. The relationship between rotation and translation was also found to vary in mastication. In fast chewing, we have observed jaw rotation without any translation whereas in slow chewing, rotation and translation were both observed.

4. λ MODEL FOR JAW MOTION

The kinematics patterns of jaw movement are well accounted for by the λ model. In summary, the model proposes that voluntary movements result from shifts in the equilibrium position of the limb which is defined by the interaction of central commands, reflex mechanisms, muscle properties and external loads. This process is under the control of central neural commands which establish, in different combinations, the motoneuron recruitment threshold lengths of multiple jaw muscles (see Flanagan, Ostry & Feldman, 1990, for details).

The λ model for the jaw motion comprises three muscles (closer, opener, protruder), central neural control signals, segmental reflex mechanisms and muscle mechanical properties. The muscle origins and insertions, and the force generating capabilities of the modelled muscles were chosen to approximate those of the superficial masseter, the anterior belly of the digastric and the lateral pterygoid, respectively. The equations of motion for the jaw system were derived by assuming that the jaw could be represented as a moving pendulum that rotates about a suspension point which is itself free to translate linearly along the articular eminence (see Figure 6). Muscle forces bring about motion of the pendulum.

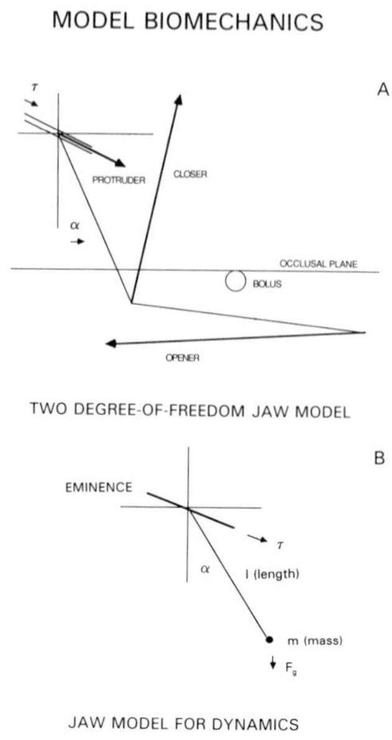

Figure 6. Upper panel: schematic drawing of the jaw showing the approximate lines of action of closer, opener and protruder muscles. In this two-degree of freedom model the jaw may translate along a unidimensional articular eminence and rotate about its instantaneous position. Lower panel: simplified jaw model used to calculate dynamics (see Flanagan, Ostry & Feldman, 1990 for details).

The model demonstrates that separate central commands can be defined for jaw rotation, jaw translation, and co-activation of muscles without motion. Each of these commands affects the motoneuron recruitment threshold lengths (λs) of all three modelled muscles. The co-activation command was derived such that rotation torques and translation forces which result from changes to muscle λs cancel one another and produce neither rotation nor translation of the jaw. Rotation and translation commands are orthogonal to the co-activation command and produce either jaw rotation or jaw translation alone. The rotation and translation commands are not themselves orthogonal. The central commands may be superimposed in order to obtain combinations of rotation, translation and muscle co-activation. We found that the empirical patterns of jaw motion could be accounted for by the model by assuming piecewise constant velocity shifts in the threshold lengths of all muscles simultaneously.

Actual and simulated speech movements are shown in Figure 7. The B panel shows the empirical patterns of jaw rotation and jaw translation during repetitions of *sa* at a loud volume. The C panel shows jaw movement patterns simulated by the λ model. Jaw opening which corresponds to a decreasing value of α is seen to be accompanied by forward translation as indicated by an increasing value of τ. The changes to individual muscle λs associated with this pattern are given in panel D. It can be seen that constant velocity changes to muscle λs result in smooth patterns of jaw rotation and translation. Also note that the rate and duration of λ shifts are different for the simulated opening and closing movements. In simulating jaw movements in speech, λ shifts were produced by combining rotation and translation commands. The co-contraction command was held constant.

Figure 8 shows actual and simulated patterns of jaw movement in mastication. In the upper panel, the simulated patterns of rotation and translation and the predicted bite force during chewing are shown. The changes to muscle λs which produce this movement are given in the middle panel. As was shown in speech movements, constant velocity shifts in muscle λs can produce the smooth patterns of jaw movement observed empirically. The actual patterns of jaw rotation and translation during chewing are presented in the bottom panel. In order to simulate mastication, it was necessary to produce λ shifts through a combination of all three commands. Specifically, the co-contraction command was increased in conjunction with jaw rotation and jaw translation commands during jaw closing. This provides for an increase in the stiffness of the jaw system prior to contact with the bolus.

5. DISCUSSION

The general pattern of jaw rotation and jaw translation has been reported previously (e.g., Edwards & Harris, 1990; Gibbs, Messerman, Reswick & Derda, 1971; Sarnat, 1964). In this paper, we have studied jaw movement kinematics in detail, in both oral cavity and mandibular joint coordinate frames. When jaw movements were examined in the joint coordinate system, several manipulations indicated that jaw rotation and translation can be separately controlled.

We have restricted our attention to jaw motions in the sagittal plane and, in our modelling work, have made the additional simplifying assumption that the mandibular condyle translates linearly along the articular eminence. As a result, only two degrees of freedom were needed to characterize the position of the jaw: the rotation of the mandible and the linear translation of the condyle along the articular eminence.

We have demonstrated that separate central commands can be defined for each kinematic degree of freedom. Thus, there are separate commands for jaw rotation and translation as well as for muscle co-activation without motion. We have also found that central commands do not depend on jaw position. In other words, the same set of shifts in muscle threshold lengths produce the same kinematic outcome regardless of position of the jaw. This was an unexpected but important finding since the muscle moment arms and the forces produced by the jaw opener and closer muscles depend on jaw position. Apparently, biomechanical factors are appropriately balanced so that central commands are invariant for different jaw positions.

According to the equilibrium point hypothesis, movement occurs when the actual and the equilibrium joint angles differ. In general, this difference is signalled by changes in afferent activity in muscle spindle receptors. Jaw closer muscles in humans are known to richly supplied with muscles spindles. In contrast, there are relatively few muscle spindles in the

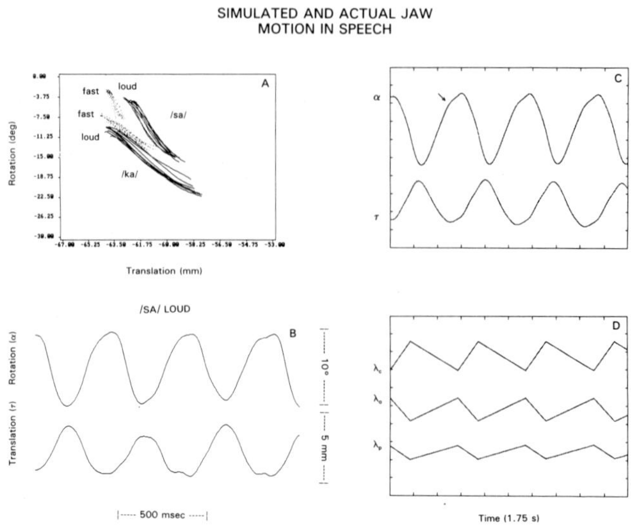

Figure 7. Real and simulated jaw movements in speech. A: jaw motion paths during repetitions of *sa* and *ka*. B: jaw rotation and translation during a single speech trial. C: simulation of jaw rotation and translation based on constant velocity shifts in the equilibrium lengths of the closer, opener and protruder muscles. (From Flanagan, Ostry & Feldman, 1990.)

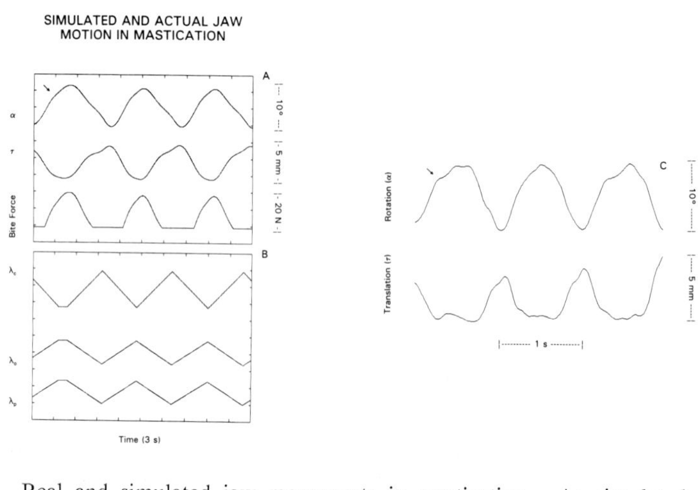

Figure 8. Real and simulated jaw movements in mastication. A: simulated rotation, translation and predicted bite force during bolus contact. B: equilibrium shifts controlling the movement in A. C: jaw rotation and translation during a single mastication trial. (From Flanagan, Ostry & Feldman, 1990.)

jaw openers. Nevertheless, the presence of a tonic stretch response in jaw opening muscles (Neilson, Andrews, Guitar & Quinn, 1979) suggests that the afferent activity used to achieve the equilibrium angle may arise from the jaw opener muscle spindles. The feedback could also arise from sources other than the muscle spindle. For example, mechanoreceptors with autogenic reflex connections may provide this information. This possibility is consistent with the demonstration of a tonic vibration reflex in jaw openers in humans (Hellsing, 1977) and the presence of labelled neurons in the mesencephalic nucleus following horse-radish peroxidase injection into jaw opening muscles (Alvarado-Mallart, Batini, Buisseret-Delmas & Corvisier, 1975). It should be noted, however, that the equilibrium position may be attained in the absence of afferent input. The λ model suggests that a combination of central commands and afferent feedback determine the equilibrium state. Thus, the nervous system can specify desired positions using central commands alone, without the need for afferent feedback.

6. REFERENCES

Abbs, J.H., Nadler, R.D. & Fujimura, O. X-ray microbeams track the shape of speech, *SOMA*, 29-34, 1988.

Alvarado-Mallart, M.R., Batini, C., Buisseret-Delmas, C. & Corvisier, J. Trigeminal representations of the masticatory and extraocular proprioceptors as revealed by horseradish peroxidase retrograde transport. *Exp. Brain Res.*, 23: 167-179, 1975.

Atkeson, C.G. & Hollerbach, J.M. Kinematic features of unrestrained vertical arm movements. *J. Neurosci.*, 5: 2318-2330, 1985.

Edwards, J. & Harris, K.S. Rotation and translation of the jaw during speech. *J. Speech Hear. Res.*, 33: 550-562, 1990.

Feldman, A.G. Composition of central programs subserving horizontal eye movement in man. *Biol. Cybern.*, 42: 107-116, 1980.

Feldman, A.G. Once more for the equilibrium-point hypothesis (λ model) for motor control. *J.Motor Behav.* 18: 17-54, 1986.

Feldman, A.G., Adamovich, S.V., Ostry, D.J. & Flanagan, J.R. The origins of electromyograms - explanations based on the equilibrium point hypothesis. In J. Winters and S. Woo (Eds.), *Multiple muscle systems: Biomechanics and movement organization.* London: Springer-Verlag, 1990.

Flanagan, J.R. & Ostry, D.J. Trajectories of human multi-joint arm movements: Evidence of joint level planning. In V. Hayward and O. Khatib (Eds.), *Experimental Robotics 1*, Lecture Notes in Control and Information Science, Springer-Verlag.

Flanagan, J.R., Ostry, D.J. & Feldman, A.G. Control of human jaw and multi-joint arm movements. In G. Hammond (Ed.), *Cerebral control of speech and limb movements.* London: Springer-Verlag, 1990.

Flanagan, J.R., Feldman, A.G., & Ostry, D.J. Equilibrium trajectories underlying rapid target-directed arm movements. In G.E. Stelmach & J. Requin (Eds)., *Tutorial in Motor Behavior II.* North Holland Publishing, in press.

Flash, T. The control of hand equilibrium trajectories in multi-joint arm movements. *Biol. Cybern.*, 57: 57-74, 1987.

Georgopoulus, A.P., Kettner, R.E., & Schwartz, A.B. Primate motor cortex and free arm movements to visual targets in three-dimensional space. II. Coding of the direction of movement by a neuronal population. *J. Neurosci.*, 8: 2928-2937, 1988.

Gibbs, C.H., Messerman, T., Reswick, J.B., & Derda, H.J. Functional movements of the mandible. *J. Pros. Dent.*, 26: 604-620, 1971

Hellsing, G. A tonic vibration reflex evoked in the jaw opening muscles in man. *Arch. oral Biol.*, 22: 175-180, 1977

Morasso, P. Spatial control of arm movements. *Exp. Brain Res.*, 42: 223-227, 1981.

Munhall, K.G., Ostry, D.J. & Flanagan, J.R. Coordinate spaces in speech planning. *J. Phonetics*, in press.

Neilson, P.D., Andrews, G., Guitar, B.E., & Quinn, P.T. Tonic stretch reflexes in lip, tongue and jaw muscles. *Brain Res.*, 178: 311-327, 1979.

Ostry, D.J., Feldman, A.G. & Flanagan, J.R. Kinematics and control of frog hindlimb movement. *J. Neurophysiol.*, 65: 547-562, 1991.

Ostry, D.J. & Flanagan, J.R. Human jaw movement in mastication and speech. *Arch. oral Biol.* 34: 685-693, 1989.

Sarnat, B.G. *The temporomandibular joint.* Springfield, IL: Thomas, 1964.

Soechting, J.F. & Flanders, M. Errors in pointing are due to approximations in sensorimotor transformations. *J. Neurophysiol.*, 62: 595-608, 1989.

Westbury, J.R. Head position during X-ray microbeam experiments: Its significance and measurement. *J. Acoust. Soc. Am.*, in press.

Tutorials in Motor Behavior II
G.E. Stelmach and J. Requin (Editors)

Equilibrium trajectories underlying rapid target-directed arm movements

J.Randall Flanagan[a], Anatol G. Feldman[b] and David J. Ostry[a]

[a] Department of Psychology, McGill University, 1205 Dr. Penfield Ave., Montréal, Québec, Canada, H3A 1B1

[b] Institut de génie biomédical, Université de Montréal and Institut de réadaptation de Montréal, Centre de recherche, 6300 Darlington Ave., Montréal, Québec, Canada, H3S 2J4

Abstract

The control of rapid target-directed arm movements was examined within the framework of the equilibrium point hypothesis (λ model). Subjects performed rapid arm movements to both single- and double-step targets (LEDs) located in a horizontal plane. The position of targets and the inter-stimulus interval were varied. Experimental trajectories of the hand were compared with simulated trajectories based on the λ model. The findings suggest that horizontal multi-joint reaching movements are planned in equilibrium coordinates corresponding to the position of the hand. Moreover, the results indicate that the equilibrium position of the hand is shifted at a constant velocity, in a straight line, towards the present target. For rapid motions the rate of shift appears to be independent of movement amplitude.

1. INTRODUCTION

A number of recent studies have examined the kinematics of reaching movements to displaced visual targets (Flash, 1990; Georgopoulos, Kalaska & Massey, 1981; Péllison, Prablanc, Goodale & Jeannerod, 1986; Soechting & Lacquaniti, 1983; van Sonderjen, Gielen & Denier van der Gon, 1989) and mathematical models of the control of reaching to displaced targets have been proposed (Flash, 1990; van Sonderjen & Denier van der Gon, 1990). These studies investigate the "on-line" control of visually guided reaching by changing the visual input to the system with target displacements. The results of these experiments indicate that visual information about target position can be used continuously - or at least frequently - during the on-going movement to smoothly modify the motion trajectory.

Péllison et al. (1986) recorded eye and hand movements to both single- and double-step visual targets without vision of the moving arm. In single-step trials, the target was laterally displaced 30-50 cm from the midline to a peripheral position. In double-step trials, the target was shifted again - either in the direction of the initial displacement or in the opposite direction - when the initial saccade reached maximum velocity. (As a result, subjects were unaware of the second shift.) Péllison et al. reported that the hand velocity and acceleration profiles for single- and double-step trials with the same final target were similar. The same result was found for the eye saccade. Thus, the form of the movement trajectory depended only on the final target and was independent of the initial target. This observation is consistent with the findings presented in this paper for double-step trials with small inter-stimulus intervals (ISIs) and co-aligned targets and suggests that visual information about target position is used continuously to control the on-going movement.

Van Sonderjen et al. (1990) examined the kinematic responses to single- and double-step target displacements during fast two-joint horizontal reaching movements. The target was initially displaced from a central position to one of eight positions of equal radius from the centre. The target was subsequently shifted to another of the eight positions on double-step trials (in a different direction from the centre). Following a second target shift, van Sonderjen et al. observed that the direction of hand motion changes gradually from the first target towards the second target. They proposed that hand movements are directed towards an internal representation of the target which, following the actual target shift, is gradually translated from the initial to the displaced target. The observation that the direction of hand movement shifts gradually is consistent with an earlier study by van Sonderjen, Denier van der Gon & Gielen (1988) in which the initial direction of hand movement was found to depend on the delay between the first and the second target presentation. With shorter delays, the initial hand movement was directed more towards the second target.

In a subsequent modelling study, van Sonderjen & Denier van der Gon (1990) introduced an *internal hand* which is shifted towards an internal representation of the target at a constant velocity. At movement onset, agonist torques are specified which accelerate the hand towards the initial target. When the internal hand reaches the internal target (in advance of the actual hand), antagonist torques are computed which decelerate the hand. In the case of a double-step displacement, the internal target is shifted gradually towards the second target and the internal hand continues to move in the direction of the shifting internal target. If the internal hand "catches" the internal target, the internal hand stops moving until the internal target reaches the second actual target.

A disadvantage of this model is that the mechanism of visuomotor control changes over the movement. For example, when the first target appears, the position of the internal and actual targets coincide right away. In contrast, when the second target appears, the internal target shifts gradually to the second target position. Moreover, the rule by which the internal hand is directed towards the internal target must be suspended if the internal hand reaches the internal target before the end of the movement. In the simulations presented in this chapter, a single visuomotor control mechanism is proposed for both single- and double-step trials and for all phases of the movement.

Flash (1990) modelled trajectories to double-step targets as the superposition of two trajectories to single-step targets; the first from the start position to the initial target and the second from the initial target to the final target. Each of the superimposed trajectories was assumed to have straight line hand paths and smooth bell-shaped hand speed profiles. The time at which the second trajectory was superimposed on the first depended on the interval between targets. This kinematic model can account well for the curved hand paths and smooth bi-modal hand speed profiles observed for motions to double-step targets with sufficiently large intervals between target shifts. In the present paper, we offer an alternative view which suggests that curved hand paths and smooth bi-modal hand speed profiles result from movement dynamics as the equilibrium position of the hand is shifted at a constant rate towards the first and then the second target.

In this paper, we describe the kinematics of rapid arm movements to single- and double-step visual targets located in a horizontal plane. The location of targets and the inter-stimulus interval (ISI) between double-step targets were systematically and randomly varied. Movements to both co-aligned and non-aligned double-step targets were examined. We also present simulated trajectories generated from a model of two-joint planar arm movement based on the equilibrium point (EP) hypothesis or λ model. According to the EP hypothesis, motions arise from shifts in the equilibrium state of the motor system. The equilibrium state is associated with the dynamic interaction of supraspinal and segmental neural mechanisms, muscle properties, and loads. Central commands govern this process by regulating muscle threshold lengths (λs) for motoneuron (MN) recruitment. A summary review of the λ model - at the level of a single muscle and at the level of a single joint - is provided.

1.1. Summary of the λ Model

Aspects of the λ model at the level of a single muscle acting against a load (L) are illustrated in Figure 1. For simplicity, the load is assumed to be constant regardless of muscle length and the same level of muscle activity is required to balance the load in different positions. Figure 1A depicts four limb configurations and Figure 1B shows the corresponding levels of depolarization of the motoneurons (MNs) innervating the muscle. The horizontal line represents the depolarization threshold (T_1) at which the first MN is recruited. As the level of depolarization increases beyond this threshold, the number of MNs recruited and the firing rates of recruited MNs increases. The level of depolarization of MNs is assumed to depend on the summation of central facilitation (open box) and afferent facilitation (filled box).

In a, the system is in equilibrium with muscle length x_a. The level of MN depolarization exceeds threshold - with some specific combination of central and afferent facilitation - such that MNs are recruited and muscle force balances the load. Consider, in b, the response of the system to a perturbation which stretches the muscle to length x_b. Due to muscle stretch the level of length dependent afferent facilitation increases, more MNs are recruited, and the resulting flexion torque restores the system's equilibrium position to a. Now consider, in c, the response of the system to a perturbation which shortens the muscle to length x_c. Afferent facilitation decreases, the level of MN depolarization is reduced below threshold, all MNs are de-recruited, and the load restores the system's equilibrium position to a.

Figure 1C shows the effect of perturbing the limb in terms of the muscle force-length curve. As shown in the figure, the parameter λ may be defined as the threshold muscle length at which the first MN is recruited and active force begins to develop. Initially the muscle is at length $x_a > \lambda$ corresponding to a force L1. The muscle is then stretched to length $x_b > x_a$ and the resulting force exceeds the load. Finally, the muscle is shortened to length $x_c < \lambda$ and zero force is produced. Figure 1C illustrates that all possible equilibrium states of the system associated with a constant level of central facilitation can be characterized by an invariant force-length curve which is defined by λ. Thus, the parameter λ provides a measure of central facilitation which is independent of position or load.

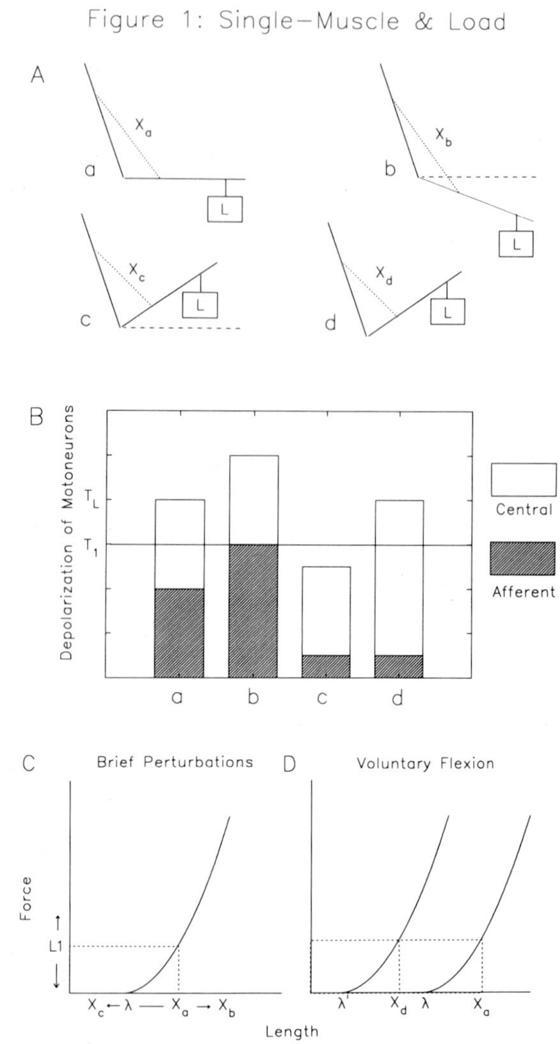

Figure 1. Limb postures (A), levels of depolarization of MNs (B), and force-length curves (C,D) are shown. In a and d, the limb is in equilibrium. Brief perturbations into extension and flexion are depicted in b and c respectively. Following a perturbation, afferent facilitation, MN recruitment, and muscle force increase (b) or decrease (c). A voluntary flexion of the limb (from a to d) is associated with an increase in central facilitation and a shift in the muscle threshold length (λ) for MN recruitment.

In d, consider how a voluntary flexion movement (from a to d) is produced. Central facilitation is augmented so that the level of MN depolarization increases and more MNs are recruited. The muscle actively shortens to length x_d and the length dependent afferent facilitation diminishes. Since the load is assumed to be position independent, when the sum of central and afferent facilitation is restored to the same level as in a, a new equilibrium position is established in which the load is once again balanced. Figure 1D shows the force-length curves corresponding to a and d. The effect of increasing central facilitation is to decrease the recruitment threshold length of the muscle from λ to λ'.

In a and d the same load is supported in two different positions with the same level of MN activity. The sole difference between a and d is the relative amounts of central and afferent facilitation. Clearly, models which suggest that MN recruitment (i.e., muscle activity) is directly controlled by the nervous system fail to explain how the system differentiates between postures a and d.

The λ model attributes an fundamental role to afferent regulation of MN activity in the control of posture and movement. Afferent feedback establishes a unique mapping between external space (i.e., muscle length) and muscle activity for a given level of central facilitation. The level of central facilitation translates the mapping between activation and length such that same load can be balanced in different positions. In the deafferented system, this elegant correspondence is lost and MN activity must be directly (centrally) controlled in order to produce movement.

For a given level of central facilitation, varying the load will change the equilibrium position of the limb. In the case of predictable loads, the motor system presumably compensates at the central planning level. (In contrast, central commands must be adjusted *following* sudden load perturbations). This planned compensation may be achieved by transforming the relationship between central facilitation and desired (equilibrium) positions. Perhaps the most predictable loads that the motor system must handle are gravitational loads which depend on limb position. Note that this position dependence applies to both external loads and internal loads associated with the limb itself. It is plausible that the nervous system deals with external and internal loads in a similar fashion (see Atkeson & Hollerbach, 1986, for a discussion of torque scaling associated with internal and external loads).

Aspects of the λ model at the single-joint level are presented in Figure 2. A simple single-joint system with a flexor and an extensor muscle is shown in Figure 2A. We define a joint angle Θ such that it increases with extension. Figure 2B shows the torque-angle curves for both the flexor and extensor muscles. The system is in static equilibrium where the torque produced by the flexor is equal and opposite to the torque produced by the extensor. The equilibrium joint angle (R) is specified by the combined actions of both muscles and corresponds to the angle at which the net joint torque is zero. The positions of the flexor and extensor torque-angle curves are determined by the threshold lengths for the flexor (λ_f) and extensor (λ_e) respectively. We may consider the effects of briefly perturbing this system. If the limb is perturbed into extension (increasing Θ) then the torques produced by the flexor and extensor muscles will increase and decrease respectively and a net flexion torque will restore the system towards equilibrium. On the other hand, if the system is perturbed in flexion (decreasing Θ) then the extensor torque will increase while the flexor torque decreases and a net extensor torque will result.

Consider, with reference to Figure 2B, two independent ways in which the nervous system can centrally control the system. First, the nervous system can alter the level of co-activation without changing the equilibrium angle by shifting λ_f and λ_e - and the corresponding torque-angle curves - in opposite directions. Second, the nervous system can change the equilibrium angle without altering the level of muscle co-activation by shifting λf and λe in the same direction. Thus, central commands to the motoneuron pools of both muscles can control the equilibrium joint angle and muscle co-activation independently. This figure also illustrates the *static* relationship between the level of muscle co-activation and joint stiffness. The sum of the two muscle torque-angle curves represents the total torque-angle function for the joint as a whole. It can be shown that when the level of co-activation is increased the slope of the torque-angle relationship for the joint also increases. The slope of this relationship represents joint stiffness. Thus, joint stiffness can be controlled independently of joint angle.

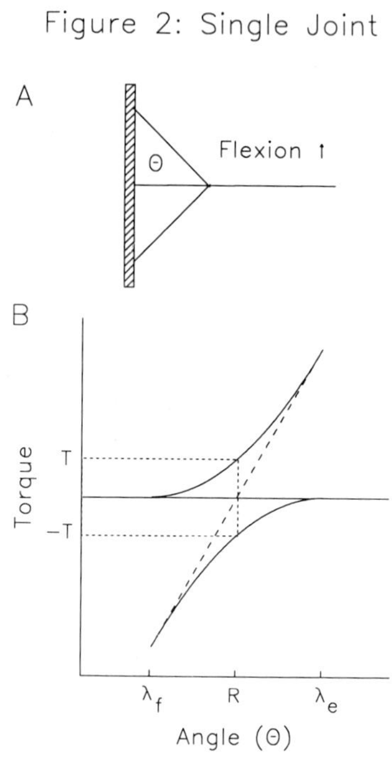

Figure 2. The λs and corresponding torque-angle curves are shown in B for a flexor and an extensor muscle acting at a single joint (A). The equilibrium joint angle, R, is defined when the flexor and extensor torques are balanced. Central commands can change R and the level of co-activation independently by shifting λ_f and λ_e in the same direction or in opposite directions respectively. The sum of muscle torque-angle curves (dashed line) gives the torque-angle curve for the joint. The slope of this function represents joint stiffness.

The two-joint planar arm model that we have used to generate the simulated trajectories presented in this chapter includes three pairs of antagonist muscles; a pair of single-joint antagonists at both the shoulder and elbow and a pair of double-joint antagonists spanning both joints. The two-joint model also includes a full geometric and mechanical description of the planar arm, position and velocity sensitive afferent feedback, and muscle properties (e.g., relaxation). Central commands specify the equilibrium of the system in terms of position of the endpoint (e.g., hand) in extrinsic coordinates. The corresponding equilibrium joint angles and muscle lengths are given by geometry. Central commands also specify the levels of co-activation for the three antagonist muscle pairs. For an overview of the mechanisms underlying the λ model see Feldman (1986). See Feldman, Adamovich, Ostry & Flanagan (1990) and Flanagan, Ostry & Feldman (1990) for a complete description of the two-joint planar model.

2. METHOD

Subjects made rapid arm movements to illuminated targets (LEDs) inlaid in a horizontal surface at a level just below the shoulder and were instructed not to make corrective movements. Both single-step targets and double-step targets with 50, 75, 100, 125, 175, 250, 350 and 700 ms inter-stimulus intervals (ISIs) were presented. Single-step trials and double-step trials with different ISIs were randomly mixed. Target positions were randomly varied such that subjects could not predict the location of single-step or double-step targets.

The positions of infrared emitting diodes (IREDS) attached to the hand, wrist, forearm and upper arm were recorded in 3-D using the Watsmart system at 400 Hz. The experiments were carried out in a darkened room to limit visual feedback of the position of the arm. Position data were numerically filtered using a Butterworth low-pass filter with a cutoff frequency of 20 Hz. The filtered data were numerically differentiated using a second-order least squares method. In order to align hand speed profiles from single trials (see Figure 6), movement onset was selected as the point at which the tangential velocity of the hand reached an absolute threshold of 0.2 m/s.

3. RESULTS AND DISCUSSION

The results are considered in two parts. The first deals with single- and double-step trials to two midline targets of different amplitude (Figure 3, top panel). The proximal target was 30 cm from the start position whereas the distal target was 45 cm from the start position. The second part deals with double-step trials in which the target is shifted, first, to a midline location 30 cm from the start position (i.e., the same position as the proximal target in part 1) and then to a lateral position located either 40 cm to the right of the midline or 30 cm to the left (Figure 3, bottom panel). In all cases, the starting position was located in the midline 5 cm from the subject's torso.

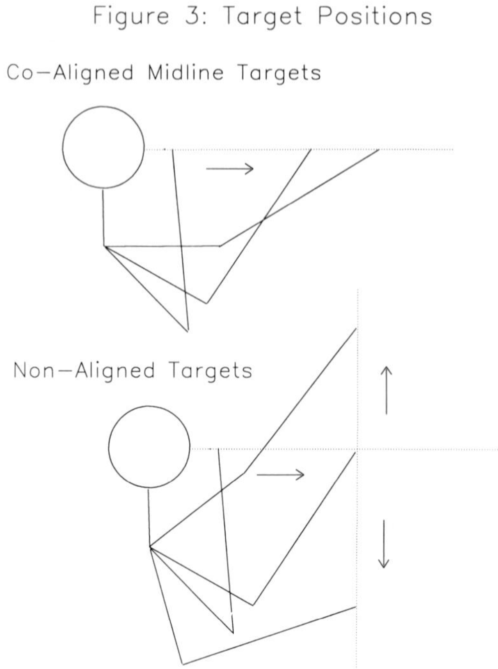

Figure 3. The positions of visual targets in the horizontal plane are shown (top view). Movements to co-aligned midline targets and non-aligned targets were recorded. In double-step trials with non-aligned targets, the second target was displaced laterally either to the left or right.

3.1. Movements to Co-Aligned Midline Targets

Figure 4 shows position and velocity records for a double-step trial with a 700 ms ISI directed initially to the proximal target and then to the distal target (top panels). Two distinct movements can be seen. Corresponding simulated position and velocity records are also illustrated (bottom panels). In this simulation, the equilibrium position of the hand was shifted at a constant rate (6 m/s) in a straight line towards the current target. As can be seen, the model is able to generate trajectories which are consistent with the experimental data.

The predictions of the model for fast movements of two different amplitudes are shown schematically in Figure 5. The equilibrium position of the hand (solid traces) as well as the predicted actual position of the hand (dotted traces) for both a small and a large amplitude movement are shown in the top panel. The corresponding equilibrium velocity records of the hand are presented in the bottom panel. The equilibrium position of the hand is assumed to shift at a constant rate and in a straight line towards the present target. Moreover, in the case of rapid movements, the rate of shift is assumed to be independent of movement amplitude. Thus, amplitude is determined by the duration of the shift. The predicted actual hand position records for the small and large amplitude movements coincide over the initial phase of the movement (up until the equilibrium position of the hand reaches the proximal target) and then diverge as indicated by the arrow in the top panel. An advantage of constant velocity shifts in the equilibrium position of the hand is that, in contrast to the minimum jerk model (Flash, 1987), amplitude need not be specified prior to the initiation of equilibrium shift.

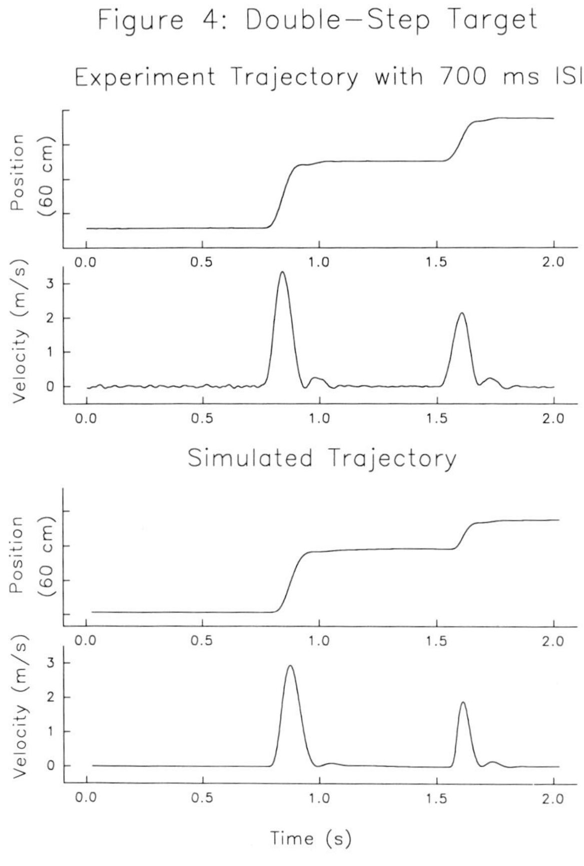

Figure 4. Experimental and simulated trajectories (position and velocity profiles) are shown for a double-step trial in which the target was initially displaced 30 cm from the start position and then an additional 15 cm following a 700 ms delay. The targets were located along the midline axis. The trajectories along the midline are shown.

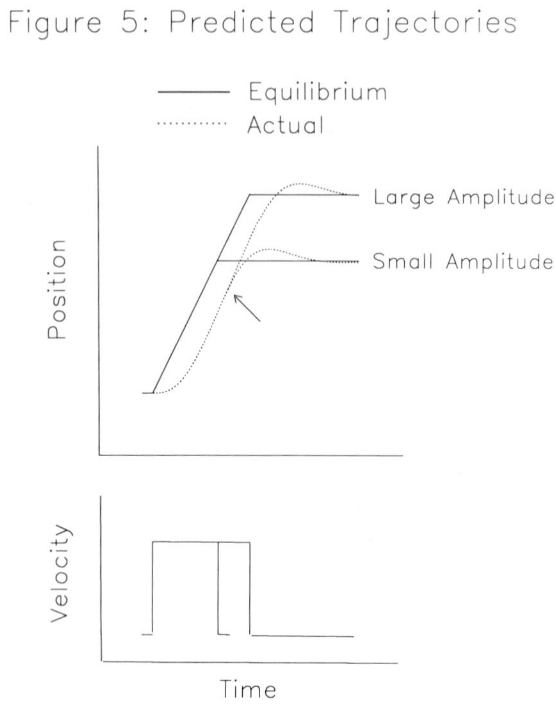

Figure 5. Schematic equilibrium and actual trajectories predicted by the model for different amplitude movements in the same direction. The equilibrium position of the hand shifts at a constant rate independent of amplitude. The predicted actual hand positions of the two movements initially coincide and then diverge. Corresponding equilibrium velocity profiles are shown in the lower panel.

Experimental hand speed (i.e., tangential velocity) profiles for two subjects are presented in Figure 6. The profiles have been aligned so that they start at the same time. Hand speed profiles for single-step trials to the proximal (thick traces) and the distal (light traces) targets are shown in Figure 6A. Consistent with the model prediction, these two sets of profiles are similar over the initial phase of the movement and then diverge. Thus, the data are consistent with the hypothesis that the rate of shift of the equilibrium position of the hand appears to be independent of movement amplitude.

The equilibrium position of the hand is assumed to shift at a constant rate in a straight line towards the presently illuminated target. Thus, if the target shifts, distally, early in the trial, the equilibrium position of the hand simply continues to shift at the same rate towards the second (more distal) target. Therefore the model predicts that double-step trials with short ISIs should be equivalent to single-step movements to the distal target. This prediction was tested by comparing the hand speed profiles of such double-step trials with the profiles of single-step trials to both the proximal and the distal targets.

Figure 6B shows hand speed profiles for single-step trials to the proximal target (thin traces) and double-step trials in which the proximal and then the distal target was presented with a short ISI of 70 ms (thick traces). As predicted, these two sets of profiles are similar over the initial part of the movement and then diverge. The pattern is similar to that shown in Figure 6A. Hand speed profiles for single-step trials to the distal target (thick traces) and the same double-step movements (thin traces) are presented in Figure 6C. With few exceptions, the two sets of profiles are similar as predicted by the model. This suggests that, in the case of the double-step movements, the shift in the equilibrium position of hand is simply continued, at the same rate, towards the second target. These experimental results are consistent with the results of Péllison et al. (1986) in which subjects were asked to look and point quickly and accurately to the present target. Therefore, it appears that, even when

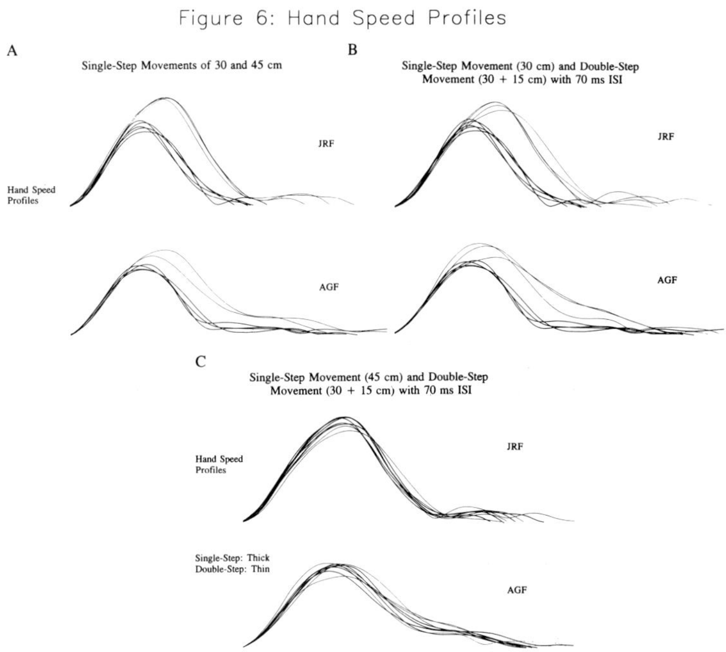

Figure 6. Hand speed profiles recorded for two subjects. Individual trials are aligned with respect to an absolute speed threshold (.2 m/s). Movements to single-step targets of different amplitude are initially similar and then diverge (A). A similar pattern is observed when the large amplitude movement is initially directed towards the small amplitude target (B). Single-step trials and double-step trials with small ISIs and the same final target have similar hand speed profiles (C).

accuracy constraints are imposed, rapid arm movements to double-step targets with short ISIs have trajectories which are similar to the trajectories of rapid movements to single-step targets.

In these fast movements the rate of equilibrium shift was estimated - in simulations - to be about 6 m/s. Therefore, for the small amplitude (30 cm) movements, the equilibrium shift is completed in approximately 50 ms. Not surprising, deflections in the trajectory were frequently observed for double-step trials with ISIs greater than 50 ms and sometimes even for double-step trials with 50 ms ISIs.

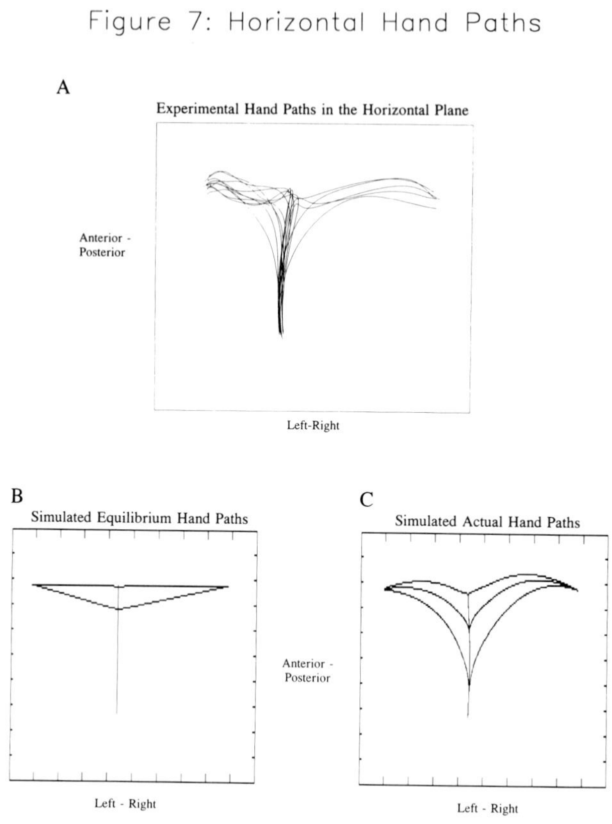

Figure 7. Horizontal (top view) hand paths recorded for double-step trials with different ISIs are shown in A. Movements to two different final targets are presented. Simulated equilibrium and actual hand paths are illustrated in B and C respectively. Straight line (constant rate) shifts of the equilibrium position of the hand generate curved hand paths characteristic of empirical trajectories.

3.2. Movements to Non-aligned Targets

The second part of the results deals with double-step movements in which the position of the second target requires the subject to changes movement direction. The first target was located 30 cm in front of the subject and the second target was positioned either 30 cm to the left or 40 cm to the right of the first target with respect to the subject.

Figure 7A shows measured hand paths in the horizontal plane for double-step trials (with both final targets) with a range of ISIs. With small ISIs the hand begins to curve towards the second target before reaching the first target. Simulated equilibrium and actual hand paths corresponding to these experimental paths are presented in Figures 7B and 7C respectively. The equilibrium position of the hand shifts towards the second target before reaching the first only with the shortest ISIs. In comparison, the actual position of the hand reaches the first target only with the largest ISIs. Figures 7B and 7C show that constant rate shifts in the hand's equilibrium position directed in a straight line towards the illuminated target can account, qualitatively, for the smoothly curved hand paths that are observed experimentally.

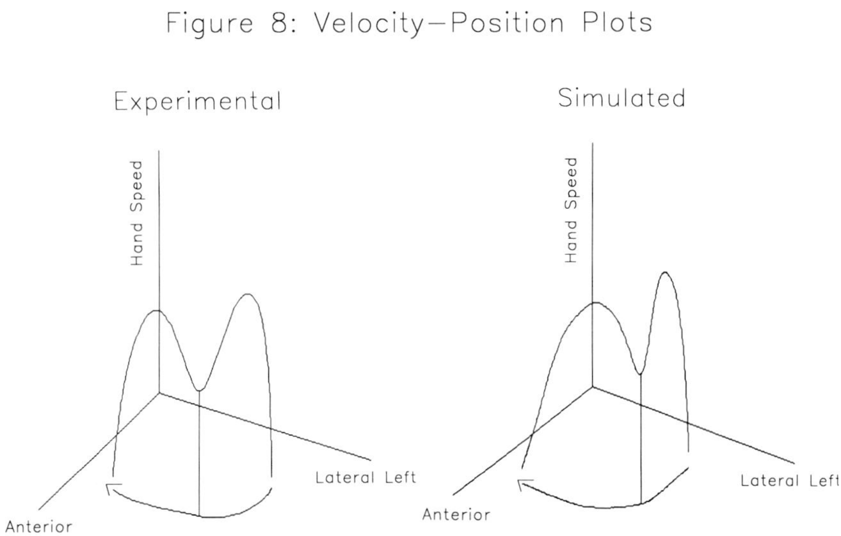

Figure 8. Recorded and simulated velocity-position plots are shown for a movement towards an initial midline target and then a final lateral target. The hand speed profiles are smooth and bi-modal and the hand paths (arrows) are curved.

Experimental and simulated velocity-position plots are presented in Figure 8. Hand speed is represented on the vertical axis and the planar path of the hand (in 2-D) is depicted by the two axes. A single trial with a 100 ms ISI is shown. This figure shows that the model can account well for the smooth bi-modal hand tangential velocity profile in addition to the curved hand path recorded.

4. CONCLUSIONS

Simulated trajectories, generated with a model based on the EP hypothesis (λ model), were compared to empirical trajectories of horizontal reaching movements to visual targets. Simulations in which the equilibrium position of the hand is shifted at a constant rate in a straight line towards the present target provided good agreement with the experimental data. Therefore, the results are consistent with the view that horizontal reaching movements are planned in coordinates which specify the equilibrium position of the hand in extrinsic space (Flash, 1987). The proposal that the equilibrium position of the hand is shifted at a constant velocity towards the present target is an alternative to the minimum-jerk (or maximum smoothness) hypothesis that the equilibrium velocity profile of the hand is bell-shaped (Flash, 1987). An advantage of constant velocity shifts is that movement amplitude need not be planned in advance of the movement.

We suggest that following target displacement the equilibrium position of the hand simply continues to shift (at the same rate) in the direction of the new target. The gradual change in the direction of actual hand movement which is experimentally observed (van Sonderjen et al., 1990; Flash, 1990) is viewed as a consequence of biomechanical and neural dynamics. In addition, the smooth unimodal and bi-modal velocity profiles observed in reaching to single- and double-step targets can also viewed as a response to the dynamic interaction of central commands, afferent reflex mechanisms, muscle properties, and limb mechanics.

In contrast to other models of reaching movements, the λ model predicts electromyographic (EMG) patterns in addition to movement kinematics (see Feldman et al., 1990). Muscle activity is a predicted output of the model rather than a directly controlled parameter. Although the current chapter has focused on movement kinematics, a latter report will deal with experimental and simulated EMG patterns in target-directed reaching.

5. REFERENCES

Atkeson, C.G., Hollerbach, J.M. (1985). Kinematic features of unrestrained vertical arm movements. *Journal of Neuroscience*, 5, 2318-2330.

Feldman, A.G. (1986). Once more on the equilibrium-point hypothesis (λ model) for motor control. *Journal of Motor Behavior*, 18, 17-54.

Feldman, A.G., Adamovich, S.V., Ostry, D.J., Flanagan, J.R. (1990). The origin of electromyograms - explanations based on the equilibrium point hypothesis. In J. Winters,

S. Woo (Eds.), *Multiple muscle systems: biomechanics of movement organization*. Springer-Verlag.

Flanagan, J.R., Ostry, D.J., Feldman, A.G. (1990). Control of human jaw and multi-joint arm movements. In G. Hammond (Ed.), *Cerebral control of speech and limb movements*. Springer-Verlag.

Flash, T. (1987). The control of hand equilibrium trajectories in multi-joint arm movements. *Biological Cybernetics*, 57, 57-74.

Flash, T. (1990). The organization of human arm trajectory control. In J. Winters, S. Woo (Eds.), *Multiple muscle systems: biomechanics of movement organization*, pp. 282-301, Springer-Verlag.

Georgopoulos, G.P., Kalaska, J.F., Massey, J.T. (1981). Spatial trajectories and reaction times of aimed movements: effects of practice, uncertainty, and change in target location. *Journal of Neurophysiology*, 46, 725-743.

Péllison, D., Prablanc C., Goodale, M.A., Jeannerod, M. (1986). Visual control of reaching movements without vision of the limb. II. Evidence of fast unconscious processes correcting the trajectory of the hand to the final position of a double-step stimulus. *Experimental Brain Research*, 62, 303-311.

Soechting, J.F., Lacquaniti, F. (1983). Modification of trajectory of a pointing movement in response to a change in target location. *Journal of Neurophysiology*, 49, 548-564.

Sonderjen, J.F. van, Denier van der Gon, J.J., Gielen, C.C.A.M. (1988). Conditions concerning early modification of motor programmes in response to changes in target location. *Experimental Brain Research*, 71, 320-328.

Sonderjen, J.F. van, Denier van der Gon, J.J. (1990). A simulation study of a programme generator for centrally programmed fast two-joint arm movements: responses to single- and double-step displacements. *Biological Cybernetics*, 63, 35-44.

Sonderjen, J.F. van, Gielen, C.C.A.M., Denier van der Gon, J.J. (1989). Motor programmes for goal-directed movements are continuously adjusted according to changes in target location. *Experimental Brain Research*, 78, 139-146.

Tutorials in Motor Behavior II
G.E. Stelmach and J. Requin (Editors)

Augmented feedback for enhanced skill acquisition

D.E. Young[a] and R.A. Schmidt[b]

[a]Department of Physical Education, California State University, Long Beach, Long Beach, CA 90840, USA

[b]Department of Psychology, University of California, Los Angeles, Los Angeles, CA 90024, USA

Abstract

In this chapter, we discuss some of the more recent research on knowledge of results (KR) and augmented kinematic feedback, and the implications this work has for understanding the role of augmented feedback in skill learning and performance. Whereas early research established that the performance of simple laboratory skills was enhanced when more frequent, precise, and immediate feedback was provided, recent investigations indicate that certain reduced relative frequencies of feedback may be more effective for learning and retention. In addition, our review of research on movement pattern information suggests that this kinematic feedback may influence learning processes in a similar fashion. Overall, effects from both lines of research run counter to many earlier long-held beliefs about how feedback operates in skill acquisition. As one alternative explanation, we elaborate on a guidance hypothesis to account for how these types of feedback function in performance and learning.

1. AUGMENTED FEEDBACK AND SKILL ACQUISITION

Of the many variables that influence the organization and structure of practice, augmented post-response information feedback about goal achievement or outcome success--termed knowledge of results (KR)--has been shown to be essential for the performance and learning in a variety of settings (Bilodeau, Bilodeau, & Schumsky, 1959; Elwell & Grindley, 1938; Newell, 1974; Stelmach, 1970; Trowbridge & Cason, 1932; Young & Schmidt, 1990; but see also Archer, Kent, & Mote, 1956; Magill & Beukers, 1991). Furthermore, KR is considered to be one of the most critical variables for the learning process (e.g., Adams, 1971; Bilodeau, 1966; Newell, 1976), and has been one of the most extensively examined variables in motor learning. Thus, research on KR provides much of the current understanding of information feedback's operation in the acquisition of laboratory skills (refer to Salmoni, Schmidt, & Walter, 1984, for a review of KR and its many variants).

Although the KR research is undeniably essential for understanding the fundamental processes involved in learning skills with and without feedback, it may not provide sufficient information about how feedback functions in the performance and learning of the complex skills that are common in physical education, sport, dance, industry, and other every-day settings. A discrepancy occurs when one considers the multiple-degree-of-freedom tasks that require feedback about the outcome *and* feedback about the pattern of action necessary to achieve it. For example, a skill such as a golf shot requires that a performer coordinate upper- and lower-limb movements effectively to meet environmental demands. Here, the performer generates a tremendously complex action, and relies heavily on some form of movement pattern feedback to alter this action for efficient learning and enhanced performance. Because this movement requires the control of more than a single dimension (or degree of freedom), feedback about at least one aspect of the action pattern would seem necessary to increase learning rates and overall performance (Young, 1988; Young & Schmidt, 1991). Augmented kinematic feedback, or information regarding response pattern characteristics (e.g., limb velocity), has been found to enhance learning and performance in a variety of tasks (see Newell, Morris, & Scully, 1985, and Schmidt & Young, 1991, for reviews). We argue that the study of this form of augmented feedback is essential for understanding the interaction between feedback and the learning of complex tasks, as well as the practical application of this work to every-day movement learning situations.

In this chapter, we highlight some of the more recent KR research, emphasizing this tradition of research as a foundation for our understanding of feedback. The renewed interest in KR research over the last few years has brought to the forefront of motor behavior new, counter-intuitive empirical relationships that challenge many long-standing views about how feedback functions in skill learning. We also review the work examining how augmented kinematic (and kinetic) information functions as feedback, and explain how this research may provide valuable insight about how feedback functions in the acquisition of complex skills. And finally, we present a guidance hypothesis as one explanation about how both of these types of augmented feedback function to influence the learning process.

2. KNOWLEDGE OF RESULTS

Early researchers in motor behavior investigated KR as the main variable for insight about how augmented feedback functions in learning. Here, some variation of KR (e.g., its frequency) was typically manipulated during the practice of a simple motor task to determine the differences in the rate of gain in proficiency, the final performance level, or both. With these general procedures, interpretations were made about the influence of KR variants on skill learning. Findings from these KR experiments have consistently indicated that nearly any variation that made feedback more frequent, immediate, or precise produced benefits for performance during practice. Because gains in performance during practice were viewed as being representative of gains in learning, the general consensus was that these feedback variations enhanced the learning process, and that feedback was a critical variable for learning (Adams, 1971; Schmidt, 1975; Thorndike, 1927).

The problem with this early methodology, and with the subsequent conclusions from this work, is that it ignored the well-known distinction between learning and performance (Guthrie, 1952; Hull, 1942; Tolman, 1929). That is, performance in an acquisition or practice phase is a function of both the relatively permanent capabilities for responding (i.e., learning) and numerous temporary effects (e.g., fatigue, guidance). Therefore, the failure to separate the temporary effects of performance from the more permanent effects attributed to learning limit the interpretations of how any KR variant influences learning. As one solution to this problem, transfer (or retention) designs have been utilized, where subjects perform a test at some time (e.g., 1-day) after the acquisition session (Salmoni et al., 1984), but with practice conditions equated across groups.

When feedback experiments had this learning methodology included, the role of several variations of augmented feedback on learning--as measured by performance in an immediate or delayed retention test--was in some ways surprising and counterintuitive. In general, these studies are consistent with earlier work in that several variations in feedback scheduling, relative to a condition with frequent feedback (e.g., feedback after every practice trial), that provide information less frequently produce decrements in performance during acquisition. But more importantly, these schedules have been shown to produce *benefits* in retention performance, and are in direct contradiction to the perspectives that suggest more frequent feedback is best for learning. We now provide a brief review of the work that has reported these empirical effects of feedback--specifically, experiments that involve relative frequency, fading, and summary KR.

2.1 Relative frequency and fading

An early perspective was that learning increased as a direct function of the absolute feedback frequency (the total number of trials that receive feedback), but that relative frequency (the proportion of the total trials having feedback provided) was irrelevant for learning (Bilodeau & Bilodeau, 1958; Bilodeau et al., 1959). This work showed the addition of no-feedback trials made no significant contribution to performance when the total number of feedback trials (absolute frequency) was held constant, suggesting that the no-feedback trials were "neutral" for the learning process. However, these findings were based on performance differences in acquisition, confounding the relatively permanent and temporary effects of feedback.

Contrary to the previous notions, work with retention designs demonstrate effects that are in direct contrast to the earlier research. Johnson, Wicks, and Ben-Sira (1981) and Ho and Shea (1978) examined the relative frequency of KR in a simple linear-positioning task, by holding the absolute frequency of KR trials constant, and varying the number of no-KR trials between the KR trials (creating KR groups with relative frequencies ranging from 10% to 100%). Analysis of performance accuracy on the trials immediately following the presentation of KR indicated no differences between groups in acquisition. However, in the no-KR retention tests, the group with the lowest relative frequency (i.e., 10%) performed most effectively, while performance for groups with higher frequencies was systematically degraded (although not significantly so). Hence, lower relative frequency tended to aid learning and retention, contrary to the earlier findings that considered only the acquisition phase.

Unfortunately, the experiments by Johnson et al. and Ho and Shea both confounded the amount of original practice with relative frequency. Therefore, one relatively uninteresting interpretation of these effects could simply be that the groups with larger amounts of practice (i.e., lower relative frequency conditions) learned the task more effectively--the well known practice effect. In light of this consideration, Schmidt, Shapiro, Winstein, Young, and Swinnen (1987) varied the relative frequency conditions in the acquisition phase and controlled for the amount of practice. In a series of experiments employing several tasks (e.g., ballistic timing, movement pattern reproduction), decreased relative frequency degraded performance in acquisition, but generally enhanced performance in no-KR retention tests. Thus, relative to an every-trial feedback schedule, it is clear that reduced relative frequency schedules of KR tended to depress performance in acquisition, but enhance performance in retention.

Winstein and Schmidt (1990; Winstein, 1988) also provided compelling evidence against the earlier notions that more frequent feedback was essential for enhanced learning. In this work, the total number of practice trials was held constant for various groups, while the number of feedback trials was varied between groups (with absolute and relative frequency confounded). Their task required subjects to produce a spatial-temporal pattern with a horizontal limb movement in 800 ms; performance was scored as the RMS error between the goal pattern and the subject's movement. On feedback trials, subjects received information after response completion on a computer terminal that showed (a) the subject's movement superimposed over the goal pattern and (b) the computed RMS error for that trial. Two experimental groups were contrasted; one received feedback after each of 196 trials across two days of practice (100% group), and another received feedback on only 50% of the trials. This second group had feedback faded across practice, with high feedback frequencies in early practice and low frequencies later (50%-faded group). This faded schedule was used in an attempt to improve learning by the 50% group, based on the suspicion that frequent feedback would be needed for error reduction in early practice, but that subjects would become "dependent" on it in some way if it were provided too frequently in later practice. In acquisition, the feedback frequency did not have a strong effect on performance, with only a slight tendency for the 50%-faded group to perform with more error than the 100% group. But, in a delayed retention test, the 50%-faded group had approximately 20% less error than the 100% group. Reduced relative (and absolute) frequency facilitated learning relative to every-trial feedback.

Nicholson and Schmidt (1991a) examined this feedback schedule further with the same task, but separated the fading and relative-frequency effects. In their Experiment 1, four conditions were contrasted: a 100% condition, a 50%-faded condition (essentially the same as in the Winstein-Schmidt study), a 50% relative frequency with feedback provided after every other trial, and another 50% relative-frequency condition with feedback provided or not in alternate blocks of 5 trials. As before, there were only small effects of feedback manipulations in the acquisition days, with only a tendency for the 100% group to perform best in acquisition. However, on the 2-day retention test there was a clear effect for the 50% conditions to perform with less error than the 100% conditions, with no differences among the 50% groups. Again, the main effect was that reducing the feedback frequency facilitated learning, but that its scheduling had only minor effects.

In a subsequent experiment by Nicholson and Schmidt (1991a; Experiment 2), a scheduling effect was found with relative frequency held constant at 50%, and the feedback schedule differing among three groups. One had a uniform schedule with feedback after every trial (50%-uniform), another had a faded schedule as before (50%-faded), and a third had a reversed-faded schedule (50%-reverse) that provided a low feedback frequency early in acquisition and gradually increased it to 100% by the end of practice (exactly the reverse of the faded schedule). If the scheduling of feedback was not important for learning, no differences between groups would be expected in a retention test. However, on a 2-day retention test, the 50%-reverse group performed poorest, with the 50%-fade group performing best followed by the 50%-uniform group. This indicates that both the schedule of feedback and the relative frequency does appear to influence learning.

2.2 Summary-KR

A scheduling procedure that provides feedback as a summary has produced effects analogous to those for relative frequency and fading manipulations. Originated by Lavery (1962; Lavery & Suddon, 1962), this schedule provides a learner with KR about each trial in a set of trials (say, 10) after the completion of these trials--usually in graphical form. With this schedule, the subject receives feedback for 100% of the trials, but not until the last trial in the set is completed. In this way, summary feedback is somewhat similar to reduced relative frequency, because of the no-KR trials that are interjected in acquisition, as well as the learner's reduced capability to use information for the next trial.

The pioneering efforts of Lavery's experiments on summary feedback introduced a KR variant that would later have a significant impact on the role of KR's function in learning (Salmoni et al., 1984). Lavery had subjects perform various simple motor tasks on 5 days of practice under three different feedback conditions: an Immediate condition had KR after each trial, a Summary-KR condition had a summary after the last trial in each 20-trial set, and a Both group had feedback after each trial and a summary after each set of 20 trials. After practice with one of these feedback schedules, subjects returned for several retention tests without feedback. The Immediate and Both conditions performed far better than the Summary-KR condition in acquisition, showing a faster rate of improvement and a higher asymptotic level near the last acquisition day. But in the retention tests up to three months later, the order of conditions was reversed; the Summary condition performed best, with the Immediate and Both conditions showing poorer performance, and at about the same level. This result was surprising in that, relative to every-trial feedback, summary feedback degraded performance during practice, but enhanced learning as measured by performance in retention tests. Because the Immediate and Both group, which had the benefits of immediate and summary feedback during acquisition, performed so poorly in retention, it appears that every-trial feedback was detrimental to learning, as this feedback was the common factor in the two groups. Therefore, we argue that it was not the summary feedback that aided retention, but rather the every-trial feedback that interfered with it.

Motivated by Lavery's findings, we investigated further the role of summary KR for learning with a series of related experiments. Specifically, we were interested in examining the possibility of an optimum summary length--the number of trials contained in the summary-feedback reports--based on our suspicion that feedback can have both beneficial and detrimental effects on learning. In one experiment (Schmidt, Young, Swinnen, & Shapiro, 1989), we examined the effectiveness of different summary lengths in search of an optimum schedule for the acquisition of a relatively simple arm movement task, where the goal was to make a movement pattern in 1 s. We studied lengths of 1 (essentially every-trial feedback), 5, 10, and 15 trials in acquisition, and in retention tests without feedback provided after 10 min and 2 days. Results for this experiment are shown in Figure 1 in terms of absolute constant errors. In acquisition, increased summary length degraded performance as indicated by the slowed the rate of improvement and depressed performance for most of the phase. There were no important performance differences in the 10-min retention test. But, in the delayed test, seen at the right of Figure 1, the order of treatment groups was just opposite to that in acquisition--with the 15-trial condition showing best performance and the 1-trial group being worst (Guay, Salmoni, & McIlwain, 1990, have similar findings). Again, summary feedback degraded performance in acquisition, but facilitated learning as measured by performance in retention.

In a subsequent experiment (Schmidt, Lange, & Young, 1990, Experiment 1), we tested the effectiveness of summary KR in a task with a larger number of motor control dimensions required for proficient performance. This task necessitated the control of a two-segment striking movement, similar to the coincident-timing skills found in baseball batting or tennis, and was arguably "more difficult" to produce effectively. Again, summary lengths of 1 (every-trial feedback), 5, 10, and 15 trials were contrasted in acquisition, with no-feedback retention tests similar to those discussed in

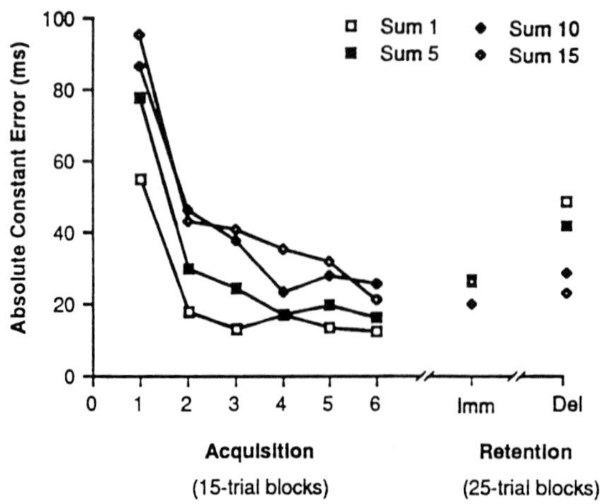

Figure 1. Average absolute constant errors in a timing task for four summary-KR conditions in acquisition, and immediate (10-min) and delayed (2-day) retention tests without feedback (from Schmidt, Young, Swinnen, & Shapiro, 1989).

the preceding experiment. As shown in Figure 2, the 1-trial summary length condition led to enhanced performance in the acquisition phase relative to the higher summary-length conditions. However, in the no-KR retention tests (right of Figure 2), the 5-trial summary-length group performed most effectively, followed by the 1-, 10-, and 15-trial groups, respectively, indicating an inverted-U effect. Thus, similar to previous summary-KR experiments, immediate 1-trial summary information degraded retention performance, at least in comparison to the 5-trial summary length schedule, while summary lengths that spanned a greater number of trials (i.e., 10- and 15-summary lengths) were not beneficial for learning processes in this task.

These findings tend to confirm our suspicion that summary feedback--together with other schedules that provide no-KR trials (e.g., low relative frequencies) in acquisition--can have positive effects on skill acquisition relative to every-trial KR. One final experiment (Schmidt et al., 1990, Experiment 2) was conducted to examine the efficacy of summary KR in a retention test *with* KR. All previous summary KR work had employed no-KR retention tests to index learning and we asked if summary's learning effect was simply due to the similarity of the acquisition- and retention-test conditions, both of which withheld feedback. Accordingly, we examined how 1- and 5-trial summary length conditions performed in retention tests with KR. Using the coincident-timing task described earlier, the conditions were provided with 90 acquisition trials followed by a KR-retention test. Consistent with previous findings, 1-trial summary feedback enhanced performance in acquisition, but there was a tendency for the 5-trial condition to be best for learning, which argued against a training-test specificity view.

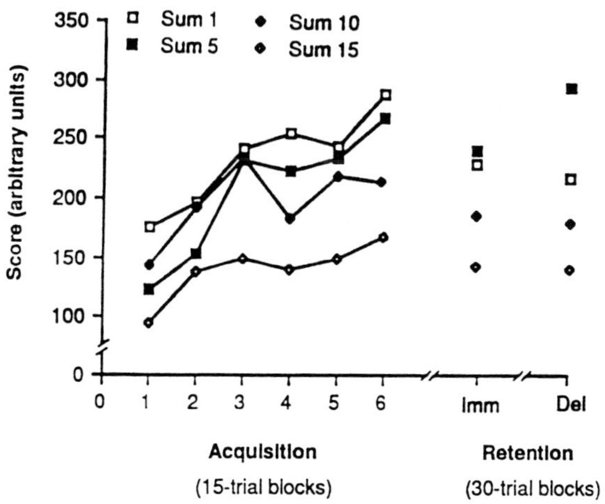

Figure 2. Average scores in a coincident-timing task for four summary-KR conditions in acquisition, and immediate (10-min) and delayed (2-days) retention tests without feedback (from Schmidt, Lange, & Young, 1990).

3. AUGMENTED KINEMATIC FEEDBACK

Although the KR research we have described here is undeniably critical to the understanding of how information feedback enhances the learning of movement skills, it is uncertain if the principles can be generalized to the complex skills found in practical settings, such as in sport, music, industry, physical education, and the military (refer to Schmidt & Young, 1991, for a more thorough examination of this issue). Because KR only informs about the movement's outcome in the environment, it is possible that the principles of KR are not applicable to other types of feedback commonly provided to learners (e.g., movement pattern information), and that learning processes are not affected similarly by the various forms of information feedback. A more appropriate variable for study, as we discuss next, may be augmented information feedback about the pattern of action or what is called *kinematic feedback*.

For complex skills, studies on augmented kinematic information (also termed knowledge of performance; Gentile, 1972; Newell & Walter, 1981) provide another significant contribution to our understanding of the relationship between feedback and learning. This feedback can be fundamentally separate from KR in two important ways. First, against a backdrop of an overwhelming amount of information from sensory receptors, kinematic feedback augments intrinsic feedback by directing a learner's attention to the part(s) of the movement that is critical for performance. Second, kinematic feedback can inform learners directly about what is needed to improve behavior. Whereas KR simply provides information about the outcome of performance, kinematic feedback can provide specific information about which aspects of the movement pattern should be altered to maximize the performance and learning of a skill. In other words, this type of extrinsic, post-response information can help the performer correct a specific aspect(s) of the movement to achieve the desired action and, therefore, the outcome. This type of movement information is typically provided in most complex movement learning settings, but has been examined only on occasion in the laboratory with a number of experimental methods and procedures (refer to Newell, in press, Newell & Walter, 1981, and Newell et al., 1985, for reviews). However, our analysis of this work indicates that augmented kinematic feedback can produce benefits for both performance and learning. To highlight this work, we first discuss some of the typical studies that examine how kinematic feedback alters the performance of different relatively complex tasks. Then, we provide a description of our recent work (Young & Schmidt, 1991; Young, 1988) that examines how kinematic parameters (i.e., aspects of a complex movement pattern) function as feedback for *learning*--based on work that has clearly separated the learning effects from the temporary effects of practice.

3.1 Performance Effects

One of the first indications that kinematic or kinetic information could enhance performance was provided by English (1942), who reported that army recruits made remarkable improvements in shooting performance when provided with information about their trigger pressure relative to that of an expert marksman. Although no data were actually provided, this observation typifies the benefits that kinematic feedback may provide for the performance of skills. A few years later, Lindahl (1945) reported data that indicated similar effects for machine operator trainees. Here, workers made rapid gains in the execution of foot movements with kinematic information, with these gains being far larger than for those who performed without this augmented feedback. More recently, Hatze (1976) demonstrated that kinematic feedback could improve the performance of a kicking skill beyond the level achieved with KR. The task required a subject to perform a simple leg raise action in minimal movement time. The subject performed with KR about movement time and made gains that stabilized by the 120th trial. However, when KR was replaced with kinematic information about hip-knee velocity and coordination, performance was significantly improved.

In contemporary work by Newell and colleagues (Newell & Carlton, 1987; Newell, Carlton, & Antoniou, 1990; Newell, Sparrow, & Quinn, 1985; Newell, Quinn, Sparrow, & Walter, 1983; see Newell, in press, for a review), kinematic (and kinetic) information has been systematically manipulated in a series of related experiments. In most of these studies, the effectiveness of kinematic feedback was contrasted with KR in single degree-of-freedom tasks. An exemplar experiment is provided by Newell and Carlton (1987, Experiment 1). In this study, three groups performed 126 trials of a pre-determined isometric force-time pattern, with either global information regarding movement pattern success provided via an error score (KR), the actual force-time pattern and KR, or a combination of the actual force-time pattern superimposed over the goal criterion. Twenty s after completion of these acquisition trials, all groups were given 25 trials with no augmented feedback. Subjects performed most effectively when they were able to compare the actual movement pattern with the movement goal. This effect was found in the acquisition phase and in the immediate test provided without augmented feedback.

In addition to these experiments reviewed here, there have also been various other investigations indicating similar beneficial performance effects from movement pattern feedback (e.g., Howell, 1956; Lionvale, 1979; Rothstein & Arnold, 1976). Together these and other studies provide separate accounts that illustrate the potential effectiveness of kinematic (and kinetic) information as augmented feedback in vastly different tasks and learning environments.

3.2 Learning effects

One of the major problems that has prevented a thorough understanding of how KR functions in motor learning has also limited the understanding of augmented kinematic feedback. The problem is the general failure to distinguish the difference between learning and performance by using separate acquisition and retention sessions after a significant delay. A number of the kinematic feedback experiments have not had transfer designs that separate the relatively permanent effects from transient effects (e.g., Del Rey, 1971; English, 1942; Hatze, 1976; Howell, 1956; Newell et al., 1983; but see also Wallace & Hagler, 1979). Other investigations have used extremely short time intervals (as little as 20 s) between acquisition and retention (Newell & Carlton, 1987; Newell et al., 1990; Newell et al., 1985). Here, the interval between acquisition and retention phases may not be sufficient to allow the temporary effects to dissipate; as a result, retention performance appears to be heavily influenced by temporary variables that would not normally survive a longer delay.

A second problem with some of the recent work on augmented feedback deals with movement patterns and goal requirements that are isomorphic. In feedback research conducted by Newell and colleagues (Newell & Carlton, 1987; Newell et al., 1990; Newell et al., 1985; Newell et al., 1983), the subjects produce a specific movement pattern (or force-time pattern) to achieve the environmental goal. In this situation, the movement pattern is identical with the goal, and the kinematic feedback becomes analogous to KR. As a result, it becomes nearly impossible to separate the effectiveness of these two types of feedback.

In light of these methodological problems, we (Young & Schmidt, 1991; Young, 1988) reopened the question of the role of kinematic feedback for learning, particularly in light of recent studies of KR reviewed earlier. In our first experiment, we contrasted how different kinematic variables that describe optimal performance (see Schmidt & Young, 1991; Young, 1988) functioned as feedback in skill acquisition, relative to KR. More specifically, we were interested in whether kinematic variables that involved positional or temporal characteristics of the patterns, and which were presented as the performer's average value or as the variability of these values about this mean, would be effective for learning. This experiment contrasted a KR-only control condition, which received only overall performance information, with four kinematic feedback conditions: mean-positional (M-P), variability-positional (V-P), mean-temporal (M-T), or variability-temporal (V-T) information. Subjects practiced 100 trials on two consecutive days and received one of four different types of kinematic information (e.g., spatial, temporal) or only KR. On a third day, subjects returned for a retention test where kinematic feedback was withdrawn. As shown in Figure 3, each of the kinematic feedback variables (M-P, V-P, M-T, and V-T) tended to enhance performance in acquisition, in a more or less similar way to the effects documented in previous experiments on kinematic feedback. However, retention findings, shown on the right of Figure 3, indicate that only the M-P kinematic feedback condition had significantly enhanced performance relative to the KR-control condition. Thus, kinematic feedback variables that improve acquisition performance did not necessarily enhance learning, as the benefits for some of the kinematic feedback conditions (e.g., M-T) in acquisition were not retained in the no-kinematic feedback test. Again, this highlights the importance of a retention (or transfer) test that evaluates learning after the strong temporary effects of practice are allowed to dissipate.

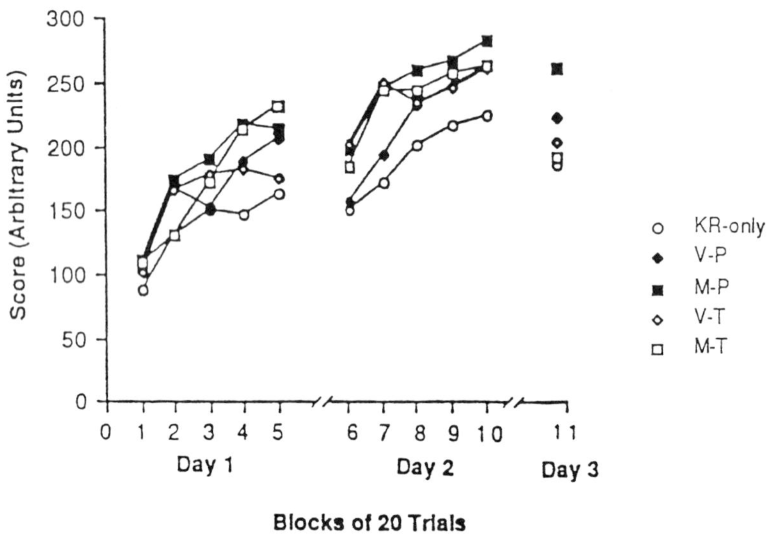

Figure 3. Average scores in a coincident-timing task for four kinematic feedback conditions and a KR-only control condition in two acquisition days, and a 1-day retention test (from Young & Schmidt, 1991).

In a second experiment, we contrasted various scheduling manipulations of kinematic feedback; we were searching for parallel learning effects between KR and kinematic feedback, and therefore potentially common learning principles. Specifically, we were interested in whether kinematic information feedback provided in reduced relative frequencies would be more effective for learning than feedback after every trial, as it has been for KR. This study contrasted different schedules of kinematic feedback using the information most important for learning--mean-positional information--as based on the findings from the first experiment. An Average group received feedback as a mean value for a set of five trials after every fifth trial. This Average feedback provided an overall representation for the set of trials only after the completion of a set (similar to a summary format). An Average-Fade group received this averaged information feedback in a faded format, where the frequency was systematically reduced at the end of acquisition. A final Single-Trial group received kinematic feedback after every trial about that trial. Subjects also received KR after every trial in the 200 trials of practice and in the no-kinematic feedback retention tests given one day and one week later.

As shown in Figure 4, all groups performed almost identically in the initial part of acquisition, but then plateaued at different levels, with the average groups actually performing more effectively by the end of this session. In the retention tests, these trends continued. Both Average feedback groups performed significantly better than the Single-trial group indicating that, like KR, augmented feedback that is given less frequently is more effective for learning than feedback given after every trial. Thus, schedules with relatively frequent feedback--not every-trial feedback--were most effective for learning, suggesting that there may be important similarities between KR and augmented kinematic feedback. Further, the finding that average feedback schedules, in which the amount of feedback was reduced, facilitated learning is clearly contrary to the expectations of many earlier perspectives (e.g., Adams, 1971; Bilodeau, 1966; Schmidt, 1975; Thorndike, 1927) about how feedback functions in learning. However, these effects are consistent with the notion that feedback works in ways more or less similar to guidance, as discussed next.

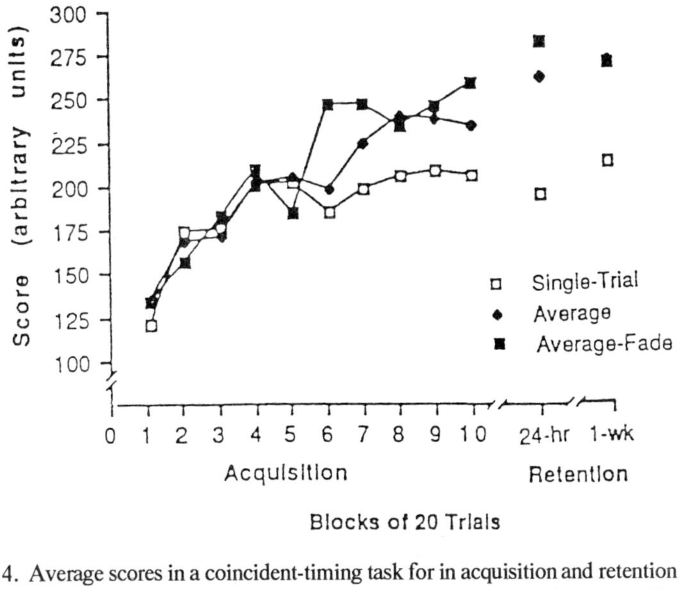

Figure 4. Average scores in a coincident-timing task for in acquisition and retention tests (1-day and 1-wk) for the three conditions with different schedules of augmented kinematic feedback (from Young & Schmidt, 1991).

4. A GUIDANCE HYPOTHESIS

As presented in the previous sections, there is substantial evidence indicating that feedback--either as outcome or movement pattern information--provided after every trial can be detrimental for learning as compared to several schedules that withhold feedback in several ways. Select schedules with reduced relative frequency and summary schedules may serve to retard the adverse influence every-trial feedback has on retention. Thus, there is a strong tendency for trials without feedback, and/or schedules that make it "difficult" for the learner to link the action with its consequences, to enhance learning over every-trial feedback.

Because of frequent feedback's effects to degrade the establishment of long-term retention capabilities, a number of otherwise reasonably well supported theoretical viewpoints that account for feedback's operation for motor learning (Adams, 1971; Bilodeau, 1966; Newell, 1977; Schmidt, 1975) are brought into question. As one alternative to these explanations, we have proposed a guidance hypothesis (Salmoni et al., 1984; Schmidt et al., 1989; Winstein & Schmidt, 1990). In this final section, we elaborate on the guidance notion, providing a framework that describes the various ways in which feedback appears to influence learning (see Schmidt, 1991, for additional insights).

The guidance hypothesis for KR and other forms of augmented feedback, such as kinematic information, was conceived as a possible way to understand how frequent feedback degrades learning. This perspective proposes that there are both positive and negative effects of feedback on learning. The positive effects that contribute to learning have been recognized for decades; these include the tendency for KR to facilitate motivation ("energizing" effects), and to provide information about errors for trial-to-trial correction, performance improvement, and maintenance of goal objectives. We have thought about these effects as guidance, due to their similarity to physical and verbal guidance effects in the skills literature (e.g., Holding, 1976). In addition, we have recently postulated a set of negative effects that detract from learning. One idea is that the learner becomes dependent on frequent feedback, almost as if the feedback became a "part of the task," and performs somewhat ineffectively in retention tests where feedback is removed or altered. A second view is that frequent feedback interferes with or blocks information processing activities that are important for learning, such as the processing of response-produced sensory information that leads to the development of error-detection capabilities. And third, frequent feedback may encourage the learner to make too many corrections during practice, leading to the learner's failure to produce stable and consistent behavior. We elaborate on each of these negative effects next.

4.1 Feedback as part of the task

When feedback is presented frequently, it may be that a learner begins to form a kind of "reliance" on this feedback during acquisition. This reliance may develop because the feedback stimuli become learned as a part of the collection of stimuli that are processed as the task, just as a learner depends on concurrent analog or "on-line" visual feedback to generate an effective rapid limb movement (Proteau, Marteniuk, Girourd, & Dugas, 1987; see also, Annett, 1969). If augmented feedback does become a part of the task, performance will suffer in retention tests where feedback is withdrawn (e.g., no-KR retention tests). To minimize this dependency, providing less frequent feedback in acquisition will encourage the learner to rely on his or her own capabilities, and to develop them, and thus the learner will not suffer performance decrements when the feedback is removed in a retention test.

4.2 Information processing activities

Augmented feedback that provides information about the movement pattern or outcome is important to subjects for performance and, therefore, it attracts attention when it is given. Because of this attraction toward augmented feedback and the processing that it triggers, other information processing activities that would occur after response completion are often interfered with or may be completely blocked. More specifically, frequent feedback may prevent the learner from engaging in an analysis of response-produced feedback that is directed at determining the effectiveness of performance on that trial. In one account of these processes, the learner compares the response-produced feedback from a completed action with a reference of correctness that indicates how the correct action should have felt (or looked, sounded), with discrepancies indicating errors (e.g., Adams, 1971; Schmidt, 1975). With practice, the learner develops a learned capability to detect errors as a basis for recognition memory; that is, the learner develops an error-detection mechanism (Schmidt & White, 1972). Consequently, when augmented feedback is not present, as in a no-feedback retention test, performance is not severely degraded because of a learner's acquired ability to evaluate and correct movements over several test trials. In contrast, frequent feedback tends to block the processing of response-produced information, and produces less proficient performance in retention because of the weaker error-detection capability developed during acquisition.

As a test of this interpretation, Swinnen, Schmidt, Nicholson, and Shapiro (1990; Experiment 2) provided some learners with essentially instantaneous feedback in an attempt to block post-trial evaluation of response-produced feedback. Their rationale was that a learner would not engage in the relatively effortful analysis of response-produced feedback to obtain an estimate of performance proficiency when the experimenter provides this perfectly accurate information immediately with augmented feedback. Therefore, instantaneous feedback should lead to less effective learning because less effective error-detection capabilities are acquired. In contrast to a condition that had KR provided with a 240 ms delay, the instantaneous group showed less learning, with performance being degraded on tests 10 min, 2 days, and 4 months later--in accordance with Swinnen et al.'s prediction.

In a different test of the error-detection capabilities developed through practice with feedback, Schmidt et al. (1990, Experiment 1) asked learners to perform the task in a retention test and to estimate their own performance score after each trial. As discussed earlier, this experiment examined the effectiveness of summary feedback lengths of 1, 5, 10, and 15 trials in a coincident-timing task, where the 5-trial summary length was nearly optimal for learning. In addition, we also gave a final unannounced retention test requiring subjective estimation just after the no-KR test of learning. Evaluation of the error-detection capabilities were measured as the within-subject correlation (over trials) between the estimated and actual performance score. The condition with the largest correlation was the 5-trial condition--the same condition that had the most effective performance--and the estimates of error-detection strength for the other conditions roughly paralleled the levels of performance proficiency as well. One interpretation is that the 5-trial summary condition led to the most proficient error-detection capabilities, which translated into better performances on the retention test when feedback was withdrawn. Although none of the groups in this experiment had correlations that were particularly strong (the largest was .43, suggesting that the error detection capabilities in this task were not particularly well learned) there is some support for the hypothesis that frequent feedback blocks the learning of error detection. This notion deserves additional study to determine the extent to which this is a major mechanism in frequent feedback's operation.

4.3 Maladaptive short-term corrections

When learners receive information about errors, it motivates a change in behavior; conversely, when no information is provided after an action, the learner tends to repeat the previous action rather than to alter it (Bilodeau, 1966). This relatively old notion about feedback has led to the idea that frequent feedback leads to changes in the action on every trial, and may prevent the learner from producing stable behavior during practice. As a consequence, a practice sequence that is very effective for keeping the learner near the target and prevents any tendency to drift off target may also produce detrimental long-term effects because the learner has not acquired a stable representation for producing the action. These frequent trial-to-trial changes are referred to as "maladaptive short-term corrections"--effective in the short term for holding behavior on target, but maladaptive in the long term--with respect to the achievement of the main goal of effective retention performance. In this hypothesis, frequent feedback is detrimental to learning because it produces too many modifications to the action during the acquisition phase.

Another possibility that could account for these maladaptive short-term corrections is related to the sources of error in the neuromuscular,"noise-like" processes associated with force and time variability in muscle contraction (as modeled by Meyer, Smith, Kornblum, Abrams, & Wright, 1990; Schmidt, Zelaznik, Hawkins, Frank, & Quinn, 1979). These processes are thought to be fundamental to the neuromuscular system, and to be beyond the learner's control. However, when feedback is given after any trial, it will contain this "noise" variability as a part of its variance and may direct the learner to attempt to compensate for each deviation from the target. Because the noise component is inherently uncorrectable, any compensations made in attempt to minimize the noise could actually degrade learning.

It is also possible that feedback operates to force compensations that disrupt behavior almost involuntarily. Evidence for this suggestion comes from experiments by Nicholson and Schmidt (1990b), patterned after an experiment by Bilodeau, Sulzer, and Levy (1962). In this experiment, subjects learned a simple task of pressing a lever for exactly 1600 ms. On certain trials during practice, subjects received (or did not) KR about the previous trial, and were then instructed to repeat the action, and *not* to respond to the KR. On these so called repeat trials, when the subject had received feedback prior to the repeat instruction there was far more error in repetition than when the subject did not receive feedback--as if this feedback interfered with the memory of the previous action, and thus prevented the learner from producing it again. If other experiments in this series determine that feedback operates in the same general fashion when the instruction to repeat is given before feedback is received, it will suggest that feedback might be very difficult to ignore, almost as if feedback has invoked involuntary corrections to the action.

5. SUMMARY

Our review of the recent work with both KR and augmented kinematic feedback indicates that skill learning is facilitated with various schedules (e.g., faded, summary, and average schedules) that do not provide feedback after every trial. Conversely, when feedback is provided after every trial, it tends to degrade the establishment of long-term retention performance. These learning effects are clearly counter to earlier ideas about how feedback functions in skill acquisition because trials without feedback had been regarded as "neutral" (Bilodeau, 1966; Newell, 1977; Schmidt, 1975) or even detrimental (Adams, 1971) for learning. Because these theories are not able to account for how these effects and, therefore, how feedback operates for learning, we have sought other explanations for these phenomena. As an alternative solution, we have proposed a guidance hypothesis (Salmoni et al., 1984; Schmidt et al., 1989; Winstein & Schmidt, 1990), in which feedback is argued to have two classes of effects on learning. The positive influences provided by feedback have been known for decades: feedback indicates errors, directs corrections, guides behavior to the target, motivates, "energizes," and generally facilitates performance. In addition to these positive effects, though, we postulate that several negative processes also influence how skills are acquired. Feedback could become a "part of the task" when presented frequently, creating problems in performance when feedback is removed later--as in a retention test. Frequent feedback could also block important between-trial information processing activities, such as the development of error-detection capabilities. Finally, frequent feedback could force the learner to make trial-to-trial corrections that degrade the capability to produce stable behavior on the retention test. These various hypotheses on the way to the formulation of a viable theory of feedback's operation in motor learning are only beginning to be evaluated, and much additional work is needed in this area before we understand feedback's function in learning.

6. REFERENCES

Adams, J.A. (1971). A closed-loop theory of motor learning. *Journal of Motor Behavior, 3,* 111-150.

Archer, E.J., Kent, G.W., & Mote, F.A. (1956). Effect of long-term practice and time-on-target information feedback on a complex tracking task. *Journal of Experimental Psychology, 51,* 103-112.

Bilodeau, E.A., & Bilodeau, I.M. (1958). Variable frequency knowledge of results and the learning of simple skill, *Journal of Experimental Psychology, 55,* 379-383.

Bilodeau, E.A., Bilodeau, I.M., & Schumsky, D.A. (1959). Some effects of introducing and withdrawing knowledge of results early and late in practice, *Journal of Experimental Psychology, 58,* 142-144.

Bilodeau, E.A., Sulzer, J.L., & Levy, C.M. (1962). Theory and data on the interrelationships of three factors of memory, *Psychological Monographs: General and Applied, 76,* 1-19.

Bilodeau, I.M. (1966). Information feedback, in E.A. Bilodeau (ed.), *Acquisition of Skill,* Academic Press, New York, pp. 255-296.

Del Rey, P. (1971). The effects of video-taped feedback on form, accuracy, and latency in an open and closed environment. *Journal of Motor Behavior, 3,* 281-287.

Elwell, J.L. & Grindley, G.S. (1938). The effect of knowledge of results on learning and performance. *British Journal of Psychology,* 29, 39-53.

English, H.B. (1942). How psychology can facilitate military training: A concrete example. *Journal of Applied Psychology, 26,* 3-7.

Guay, M., Salmoni, A.W., & McIlwain, J. (1990). *Summary knowledge of results for skill acquisition: Testing the guidance hypothesis,* Unpublished manuscript, Laurentian University.

Gentile, A.M. (1972). A working model of skill acquisition with application to teaching. *Quest, 17,* 3-23.

Guthrie, E.R. (1952). *The Psychology of Learning,* Harper and Row, New York.

Hatze, H. (1976). Biomechanical aspects of successful motion optimization. In P.V. Komi (Ed.), *Biomechanics V-B,* 7-17. Baltimore: University Park Press.

Ho, L., & Shea, J.B. (1978). Effects of relative frequency of knowledge of results on retention of a motor skill. *Perceptual and Motor Skills, 46*, 859-866.
Holding, D.H. (1976). An approximate transfer surface, *Journal of Motor Behavior, 8*, 1-9.
Howell, M.L. (1956). Use of force-time graphs for performance analysis in facilitating motor learning. *Research Quarterly, 27*, 12-22.
Hull, C.L. (1943). *Principles of behavior.* New York: Appleton-Century-Crofts.
Johnson, R.W., Wicks, G.G., & Ben-Sira. (1981). *Practice in the absence of knowledge of results: Acquisition and transfer.* Unpublished manuscript, University of Minnesota.
Lavery, J.J. (1962). Retention of simple motor skills as a function of type of knowledge of results. *Canadian Journal of Psychology, 15*, 231-237.
Lavery, J.J., & Suddon, F.H. (1962). Retention of simple motor skills as a function of the number of trials by which KR is delayed. *Perceptual and Motor Skills, 15*, 231-237.
Lindahl, L.G. (1945). Movement analysis as an industrial training method. *Journal of Applied Psychology, 29*, 420-436.
Lionvale, J.T. (1979). *The effect of augmented auditory feedback and auditory modelling on learning a complex motor skill.* Unpublished doctoral dissertation, University of Oregon.
Magill, R.A. & Beukers, M. (1991). Unpublished data. Louisana State University.
Meyer, D.E., Smith, J.E.K., Kornblum, S., Abrams, R.A., & Wright, C.E. (1990). Speed-accuracy tradeoffs in aimed movements: Toward a theory of rapid voluntary action, in M. Jeannerod (ed.), *Attention and Performance XIII*, Erlbaum, Hillsdale, NJ, pp. 173-226.
Newell, K.M. (1974). Knowledge of results and motor learning. *Journal of Motor Behavior, 6*, 235-244.
Newell, K.M. (1976). Knowledge of results and motor learning. In J. Keogh & R.S. Hutton (Eds.), *Exercise and Sport Sciences Reviews* (Vol. 4, pp. 195-228). Santa Barbara, CA: Journal Publishing Affiliates.
Newell, K.M. (1977). Knowledge of results and motor learning, *Exercise and Sport Sciences Reviews, 4*, 195-228.
Newell, K.M. (in press). Agumented information and the acquisition of skill. In R. Daugs & K. Blischke (Eds.), *Motor Learning and Training.* Schormdork: Hofmann.
Newell, K.M., & Carlton, M.J. (1987). Augmented information feedback and the acquisition of isometric tasks. *Journal of Motor Behavior, 19*, 4-12.
Newell, K.M., Carlton, M.J., & Antoniou, A. (1990). The interaction of criterion and feedback information in learning a drawing task. *Journal of Motor Behavior, 22*,536-552.
Newell, K.M., Morris, L.R., & Scully, D.M. (1985). Augmented information and the acquisition of skill in physical activity. In R.L. Terjung (Ed.), *Exercise and Sport Sciences Reviews* (Vol. 13, pp. 235-261). Lexington, MA: Collamore Press.
Newell, K.M., Quinn, J.T., Jr., Sparrow, W.A., & Walter, C.B. (1983). Kinematic information feedback for learning a simple rapid response. *Human Movement Science, 2*, 255-270.
Newell, K.M., Sparrow, W.A., & Quinn, J.T. (1985). Kinetic information feedback for learning isometric tasks. *Journal of Human Movement Studies, 7*, 235-254.
Newell, K.M., & Walter, C.B. (1981). Kinematic and kinetic parameters as information feedback in motor skill acquisition. *Journal of Human Movement Studies, 7*, 235-254.
Nicholson, D.E., & Schmidt, R.A. (1991a). *Feedback scheduling effects in skill acquisition*, Unpublished manuscript, Motor Control Laboratory, University of California, Los Angeles.
Nicholson, D.E., & Schmidt, R.A. (1991b). *Effects of feedback on subsequent movements*, Unpublished manuscript, Motor Control Laboratory, University of California, Los Angeles.
Proteau, L., Marteniuk, R.G., Girouard, Y., & Dugas, C. (1987). On the type of information used to control and learn an aiming movement after moderate and extensive training, *Human Movement Science*, *6*, 181-199.
Rothstein, A.L. & Arnold, R.K. (1976). Bridging the gad: Application of research on videotape feedback and bowling. *Motor skills Theory Into Practice, 1*, 35-62.

Salmoni, A.W., Schmidt, R.A., & Walter, C.B. (1984). Knowledge of results and motor learning: A review and critical reappraisal. *Psychological Bulletin, 95*, 355-386.
Schmidt, R.A. (1975). A schema theory of discrete motor skill learning. *Psychological Review, 82*, 225-260.
Schmidt, R.A. (1991). *Feedback for skill acquisition: Preliminaries to a theory of feedback.* Technical Report No. 1/91, Motor Control Laboratory, UCLA. (Contract No. MDA903-85-K-0-225, U.S. Army Research Institute, Basic Research).
Schmidt, R.A., Lange, C., & Young, D.E. (1990). Optimizing summary knowledge of results in motor learning. *Human Movement Science, 9*, 225-248.
Schmidt, R.A., Shapiro, D.C., Winstein, C.J., Young, D.E., & Swinnen, S. (1987). *Feedback and motor skill training: Relative frequency of KR and summary KR.* Technical Report No. 1/87, Motor Control Laboratory, UCLA.
Schmidt, R.A., & White, J.L. (1972). Evidence for an error detection mechanism in motor skills: A test of Adams' closed-loop theory, *Journal of Motor Behavior 4*, 143-153.
Schmidt, R.A., & Young, D.E. (1991). Methodology for motor learning: A paradigm for kinematic feedback. *Journal of Motor Behavior, 23*, 13-24.
Schmidt, R.A., Young, D.E., Shapiro, D.C., & Swinnen, S. (1989). Summary knowledge of results for skill acquisition: Support for the guidance hypothesis. *Journal of Experimental Psychology: Learning, Memory, and Cognition, 15*, 352-259.
Schmidt, R.A., Zelaznik, H.N., Hawkins, B., Frank, J.S., & Quinn, J.T. (1979). Motor output variability: A theory for the accuracy of rapid motor acts. *Psychological Review, 86*, 415-451.
Stelmach, G.E. (1970). Learning and response consistency with augmented feedback. *Ergonomics, 13*, 421-425.
Swinnen, S.P., Schmidt, R.A., Nicholson, D. E., & Shapiro, D.C. (1990). Information feedback for skill acquisition: Instantaneous knowledge of results degrades learning. *Journal of Experimental Psychology: Learning, Memory, and Cognition, 16*, 706-716.
Thorndike, E.L. (1927). The law of effect. *American Journal of Psychology, 39*, 212-222.
Tolman, E.C. (1929). *Purposive Behavior of Animals and Men*, Century, New York.
Wallace, S.A., & Hagler, R.W. (1979). Knowledge of performance and the learning of a closed motor skill. *Research Quarterly, 50*, 265-271.
Winstein, C.J. (1988). *Relative frequency of information feedback in motor performance and learning.* Unpublished doctoral dissertation, University of California, Los Angeles.
Winstein, C.J., & Schmidt, R.A. (1990). Reduced relative frequency of knowledge of results enhances motor learning. *Journal of Experimental Psychology: Learning, Memory, and Cognition, 16*, 677-691.
Young, D.E. (1988). *Knowledge of performance and motor learning.* Unpublished doctoral dissertation, University of California, Los Angeles.
Young, D.E., & Schmidt, R.A. (1991). *Augmented kinematic feedback for skill learning*, Manuscript submitted for publication, Motor Control Laboratory, University of California, Los Angeles.

Tutorials in Motor Behavior II
G.E. Stelmach and J. Requin (Editors)

Coordination of upper-limb movement: a neuro-dynamics account

Stephan P. Swinnen

Motor Control Laboratory, Dept. of Kinantropology, Group Biomedical Sciences, Catholic University of Leuven, Tervuurse Vest 101, 3001 Heverlee, Belgium

Abstract

Human performers are often limited in doing more than one thing at a time. This becomes particularly evident when different movements are to be performed simultaneously. The emerging limitations result from a tendency to synchronize the patterns of motor output, irrespective of whether the movements are of a discrete or continuous nature. However, for differentiated patterns of activity to emerge, mutual synchronization has to be overcome. This paper addresses limitations in discrete dual-task performance and describes dissociation of action with respect to structural and metrical specifications of movement. Moreover, the role of augmented information feedback sources on interlimb dissociation is discussed. Findings are interpreted in view of a neuro-dynamics perspective on motoric dual-task performance.

1. INTRODUCTION

When observing skilled movements as they occur in sports, music performance, and industry, it becomes apparent that limb actions are coordinated with great ease whereby the necessary anticipatory postural adjustments are being made to ensure body equilibrium. The novice, however, experiences difficulties in acquiring these complex patterns of coordination, due to constraints that are, among other things, a consequence of the design of the nervous system and that impose limitations on our capability to do more than one thing at a time. In spite of the evidence for a fine differential recruitment behavior of even subpopulations of motor units in certain human arm muscles in accordance with specific task demands (Jongen, Denier Van Der Gon, & Gielen, 1989), recent research has also shown that large groups of muscles are often constrained to function in a synchronous fashion when multi-limb action is concerned. The latter phenomenon can be interpreted from two different standpoints. On the positive side, it is seen as an expression of the human motor control system's preferential use of larger muscle groups that are constrained to act as a functional unit, thereby reducing the degrees of freedom of the system (Kelso, Southard, & Goodman, 1979a, 1979b; Kelso & Tuller, 1984). This curtails computational complexity and frees the higher levels of the control system for other tasks. On the negative side, synchronization tendencies impose limitations on the differentiation of action patterns, as required for a variety of complex motor skills. Indeed, most skilled manual activities require both hands to play a different role so that the division of labor is asymmetric (Guiard, 1987). Luckily, there is an inherent plasticity in the central nervous system to cope with these natural synchronization tendencies. Thus, an important goal in acquiring complex patterns of coordination is to reduce or eliminate synchronization effects (Swinnen, in press; Swinnen & Walter, 1988).

2. DISSOCIATING THE METRICAL AND STRUCTURAL SPECIFICATIONS OF BIMANUAL MOVEMENTS

Since 1984, we initiated a series of experiments in which the subjects' capability to differentiate (dissociate) action patterns was the primary goal (Swinnen, Walter, & Shapiro, 1988). Subjects performed a unidirectional elbow flexion movement in the nondominant limb together with a flexion-extension-flexion (reversal) movement in the dominant limb, both in the horizontal plane (see Figure 1). They were instructed to perform these movements simultaneously but independent of each other.

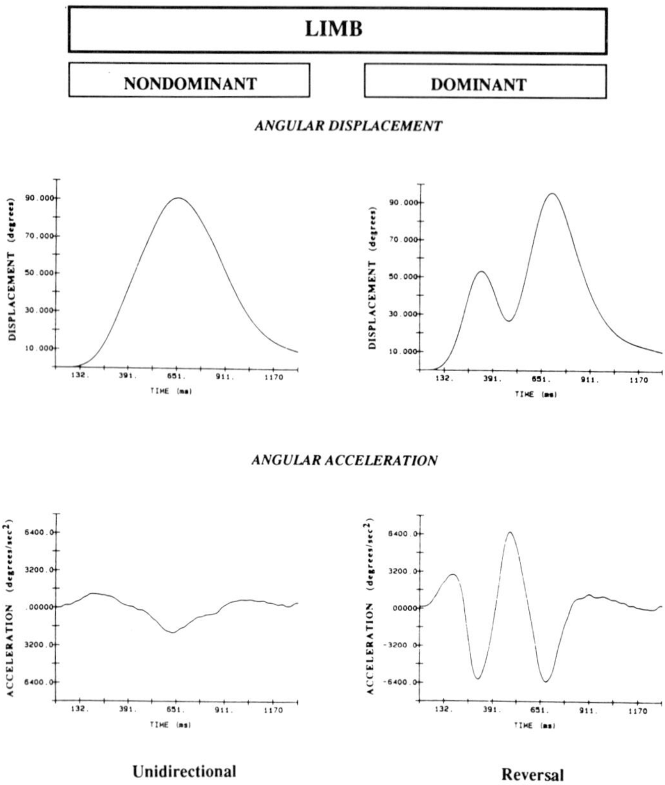

Figure 1. Idealtypical angular displacement-time and acceleration-time traces of the required unidirectional (nondominant limb) and reversal (dominant limb) movement patterns.

To evaluate the degree of success in accomplishing this goal, a distinction was made in subsequent research between metrical and structural dissociation (Swinnen, Walter, Beirinckx, & Meugens, in press). This distinction emanates from a categorization of movement features that has been promoted by action theorists in recent years (Kelso, 1981; Kelso & Tuller, 1984; Kugler, Kelso, & Turvey, 1980; Turvey, Shaw, & Mace, 1978): Qualitative or structural specifications refer to essential aspects of movement whereas quantitative or scalar changes can be imposed on movement while leaving its underlying structure untouched (see also Newell, 1985). In other words, changes in structural prescription refer to modifications of the dynamic topography of a biokinematic chain whereas a change in the metrical prescription refers to the speed (among other things) with which the dynamic topography is realized (Turvey et al., 1978). A similar distinction can be found within the motor programming perspective (Schmidt, 1988a). The capability to perform movements with a different overall size or in a different time or speed while preserving the essential aspects, is called movement parametrization. The essential variables are denoted as invariant features that are supposedly represented in the motor program.

When applying this distinction to bimanual or multi-limb action, a tentative categorization of tasks in reference to their difficulty level can be proposed, consisting of two continua as shown below.

Structural Prescription
Same -------------------------------------- Different

Metrical Prescription
Same -------------------------------------- Different

Motor tasks that are to be performed simultaneously can differ with respect to their metrical prescription, their structural prescription, or both. The easiest tasks (in terms of building the pattern of coordination) appear to be those characterized by the same structural and metrical specifications as in fully symmetrical activities (e.g., weightlifting, rope jumping, arm action in breaststroke). The most difficult tasks are characterized by a differentiation of the structural as well as the metrical specifications of the limb actions (playing musical instruments, vehicle control). Finally, there are those tasks that require the assignment of different metrics or intensity specifications within a common organizational framework and a number of experiments have shown this to be possible (e.g., simultaneously pointing to different locations in space). This type of tasks can be located somewhere in between both aforementioned extremes.

Evidence for the dissociation of both structural and metrical specifications is generally sparse. Some studies have provided initial hints for deviations from perfect synchrony when the spatio-temporal differences of the tasks, to be performed together in the upper limbs, are gradually increased (Corcos, 1984; Marteniuk, MacKenzie, & Baba, 1984). The goal of our experiments was to set up a more stringent test of interlimb dissociation with respect to metrical <u>and</u> structural specifications. Structural dissociation was assessed by cross correlating the acceleration patterns of both limb movements in real time. Squaring this correlation coefficient and multiplying it by 100 % provides an idea of the degree of common variance between both acceleration signals (coefficient of determination). Since the moment of inertia was constant in the present experimental setup, angular acceleration was proportional to the torque produced at the elbow joint which is considered to be an important mechanical characteristic for the central nervous system. On the other hand, metrical dissociation was assessed through division of the total amount of positive relative work required for production of the reversal movement by that required for production of the unidirectional movement (Swinnen, Walter, Beirinckx et al., in press). The resulting ratio provided an indication of the differentiation of the intensity specifications for both limb actions, irrespective of their topological interactions.

Work was calculated from the time integral of the power curve. Power, defined as the rate of doing work, is the product of the net muscle moment and angular velocity (Enoka, 1988). Due to the proportionality between acceleration and force under the present task conditions, the power-time profile associated with the movement was obtained by multiplying angular acceleration and velocity at each instant. Accordingly, the variable so obtained is proportional to power and its time integral is proportional to work. Therefore, we call it relative work. Due to the reciprocity of positive and negative work, only the total amount of positive work (when the muscle moment acts in the same direction as the angular velocity) was computed for each of the limb movements.

3. FEEDBACK AND THE DISSOCIATION OF ACTION PATTERNS

A series of experiments was initiated in which the following goals were put forward: First, the question was asked how bimanual actions with widely different spatiotemporal features (see Figure 1) are coordinated. Secondly, the role of practice with or without the aid of augmented information feedback on action dissociation was determined.

3.1. The effect of overall timing feedback on interlimb dissociation

In a first experiment, subjects practiced each limb movement separately on the first day of practice. On the second day, one group continued to practice the movements in isolation (unimanual group) whereas another group performed them simultaneously (bimanual group). All subjects received information feedback about the overall temporal requirements of both movements (MT's = 600 ms) with a relative frequency schedule of 25 %. Although subjects of the bimanual group were instructed to make the movements independently of each other, findings showed some degree of mutual synchronization between the limbs (Swinnen, Walter, Beirinckx, et al., in press). The cross correlation between the acceleration pattern of the left and right limb movement (structural dissociation coefficient) was in the order of .50 to .60 (common variance = 25 to 36 %) without major changes occurring across bimanual practice. These values were higher than those determined under fully independent performance conditions (< .15). Similarly, the intensity specifications for both limbs interacted with each other under bimanual practice conditions: The metrical dissociation coefficient was lower in the bimanual as compared to the unimanual group and no profound changes occurred across bimanual practice. Additional analyses on the amount of relative work produced by each limb separately, revealed that the inflation of the metrical dissociation coefficient was mainly due to an excess of work generated for production of the unidirectional movement (up to 100 % in comparison to unimanual baseline conditions). Conversely, the amount of relative work with respect to the reversal movement was only slightly changed, i.e., it was decreased by about 10 %. These findings are indicative of an asymmetric mutual synchronization effect: The less complex unidirectional movement was more attracted to the reversal movement than vice versa and I will come back to that issue later in this chapter.

All together, this experiment demonstrated moderate degrees of interlimb synchronization that did not undergo profound changes across practice. However, subjects were only provided knowledge of results about the deviations from the target time for each limb movement without receiving information about the movement patterns they had actually produced. This matter was followed up in subsequent experiments where subjects were provided augmented information feedback about their movement patterns, discussed next.

3.2. The effect of kinematic information feedback on interlimb dissociation

The first experiment on augmented kinematic information feedback (Swinnen & Walter, in press), used three groups, two of which performed the aforementioned movements (see Figure 1) simultaneously from the start. A first group performed both limb movements in isolation at all times (unimanual). A second group received displacement information feedback after every fourth trial (bimanual displacement FB) and a third group was not provided augmented information feedback about the patterns actually produced (bimanual no-displacement FB). Displacement information feedback was shown after every fourth trial via the computer terminal that displayed the left and right limb actions as a function of time, superimposed on each other. In addition, subjects of all three groups were informed of the deviations from the target movement times (MT = 600 ms) with a relative frequency schedule of 25 %. Subjects performed 100 bimanual practice trials across two days. Again, both bimanual groups were instructed to perform both movements simultaneously but independent of each other.

Findings showed variable degrees of success in performing these spatiotemporally different movements simultaneously. On the one hand, there was evidence for structural dissociation, at least within the present dual-task boundaries: The kinematic FB group displayed lower cross correlations than the no-kinematic FB group but values were higher than those of the unimanual group, suggesting that dissociation was not perfect. On the other hand, subjects displayed a capability to differentiate the metrical specifications of movement to a certain degree, a result supported by earlier findings (Kelso et al., 1979a, 1979b; Marteniuk et al., 1984). Nevertheless, both bimanual groups showed lower dissociation scores than the unimanual group which can be interpreted as metrical coupling or the covariation of intensity specifications for both limb actions. This was mainly due to an increase in amount of relative work generated in the left limb (for production of the unidirectional action) which was in the order of 100 % for the kinematic FB group in comparison to unimanual baseline values. These values were lower than those for the no-kinematic FB group which showed increases of over 200 %. This suggests that excess of work in the nondominant limb was more successfully controlled through kinematic information feedback. Such major changes were not apparent in the right limb.

In summary, this experiment showed displacement information feedback to aid subjects in reducing mutual interference through the generation of more independent acceleration patterns, supporting previous work (Swinnen, Walter, Pauwels, Meugens, and Beirinckx, 1990). However, the baseline scores as evident from the unimanual group were not accomplished, neither for structural, nor for metrical dissociation. It cannot be ruled out that additional practice might have led to a further differentiation of both limb actions. Nevertheless, there was evidence of a ceiling effect on the second practice day which appears to suggest that subjects were unable to further decrease the cross correlations under the present circumstances.

One reason why the aforementioned ceiling effect may have occurred is that displacement information feedback falls short of conveying interlimb interactions at more advanced practice stages and that higher derivatives (e.g., velocity) are to be presented to uncover more refined patterns of interference. This matter was addressed in another experiment using the same task in which the effect of velocity information feedback on structural and metrical dissociation was compared against displacement-FB and no-FB (Swinnen, 1990). Findings revealed that kinematic information feedback in comparison to no-kinematic feedback aided subjects in interlimb dissociation. However, subjects receiving velocity information feedback did not differ significantly in their degree of structural dissociation from those receiving displacement feedback. Metrical dissociation was slightly better in the velocity FB group although this effect failed to reach significance.

The following general conclusions can be drawn from the above experiments. First, there is a tendency for differing movements to become synchronized when performed together. The easier and less forceful unidirectional movement is thereby more attracted to the complex reversal movement than vice versa. In other words the mutual synchronization effect is asymmetric in nature and this is evident at the structural as well as the metrical level of movement specification. For example, at the metrical level, an excess of relative work is generated in the nondominant limb for production of the unidirectional movement whereas the amount of positive relative work in the dominant limb for production of the reversal movement is only slightly affected (i.e., decreased). Previous studies using similar tasks have identified this asymmetrical synchronization effect at the neural output level: Increased electrical activity was found in the left elbow flexors and extensors when the unidirectional movement was performed together with the reversal movement whereas muscle activity in the right arm muscles was only slightly decreased. Nevertheless, a significant reduction in superfluous muscle activity was evident as practice continued (Swinnen et al., 1988; Swinnen, Young, Walter, & Serrien, in press). These findings are consistent with the above mentioned significant increases in the metrical dissociation coefficient through a reduction of work generated in the nondominant limb. This reduction was most successfully accomplished with the aid of augmented information feedback.

Second, some information about the produced movement patterns seems to be required to aid interlimb dissociation. The changes in dissociation that can be accomplished without augmented feedback about interlimb coupling/decoupling are rather limited. This may imply that components of a synergy do not lend themselves easily to self-induced error monitoring (Swinnen, Walter, Pauwels, et al., 1990).

Third, inspection of the individual subjects' data across experiments shows marked individual differences in coordination patterns. Even under augmented kinematic feedback conditions, there is a great variety in the degree of success in structural and metrical dissociation. These observations point to fundamentally different modes of bimanual movement organization. In a more general way, they also comply with considerable evidence for differences among people in general time-sharing ability, as documented by experimental psychologists and human factors specialists (Braune & Wickens, 1986; Wickens, 1984, 1989; Wickens & Benel, 1982).

4. STRATEGIES UNDERLYING DISSOCIATION OF ACTION

As mentioned previously, there are marked individual differences in patterns of interlimb coordination and these have become evident under a variety of practice conditions. In order to better characterize success in interlimb dissociation, it was decided to more carefully investigate and compare the performance features of successful and less successful subjects under augmented kinematic (displacement) feedback conditions. This experiment will be reported here in more detail. We will proceed by inferring central interactive processes, mainly through determination and assessment of changes in biomechanical variables, e.g., acceleration and work.

4.1. The experiment

In the present experiment, subjects (N=50) were to put each of both forearms on a horizontal lever and they were instructed to perform the unidirectional and reversal movement (see Figure 1) simultaneously from the start. Position data were registered by means of high-precision shaft encoders, mounted at the basis of the proximal axis of each lever. Displacement information feedback was provided after every fourth trial in addition to movement timing information. In other words: After every fourth trial, the computer terminal was turned to the performer and the displacement patterns made in both limbs were shown as a function of time and superimposed upon each other. This visual display showed patterns of interlimb interference whenever they occurred. One hundred trials were completed in two days. Subjects were informed about the deviations from the target movement time (MT = 600 ms) after every fourth trial during both practice days. A retention test was held 10 minutes after the second acquisition phase, consisting of 10 trials without any information feedback.

4.2. Structural dissociation

To obtain insight into the degree of structural dissociation, the cross correlations between the angular acceleration patterns of both limb movements were computed for all subjects at completion of the experiment. Subsequently, the 10 most successful (lowest cross correlations at retention) and the 10 least successful subjects (highest cross correlations at retention) were extracted from the total sample and were used for further analysis (hereafter referred to as the decoupling and coupling group, respectively). As shown in Figure 2, cross correlations of the coupling group were high across both practice days. Apparently, they were unable to get rid of the common organizational structure governing both limb movements, in spite of the displacement information feedback that confronted them with the emerging patterns of interference. The decoupling group, on the other hand, displayed a high degree of synchronization initially. As practice continued, they became more successful in structural dissociation as shown by lowering cross correlations. Their decrease in common variance between both acceleration patterns was in the order of 60 %.

4.3. Metrical dissociation

Since both groups were classified according to their degree of structural dissociation, the question remained whether any differences in metrical dissociation could be observed. Metrical dissociation was determined by division of the amount of positive relative work for the reversal movement by the relative work generated for production of the unidirectional movement (see Figure 3). In contrast to the structural coefficient, higher scores are reflective of better dissociation. The decoupling group's ratios were found to he higher than those of the coupling group during acquisition, $F(1, 18) = 8.35$, $p < .01$ as well as during retention, $F(1, 18) = 8.28$, $p < 01$, indicative of more successful metrical dissociation in the former group. Metrical dissociation increased with practice, resulting in a significant effect for acquisition phase, $F(1, 18) = 7.02$, $p < .01$.

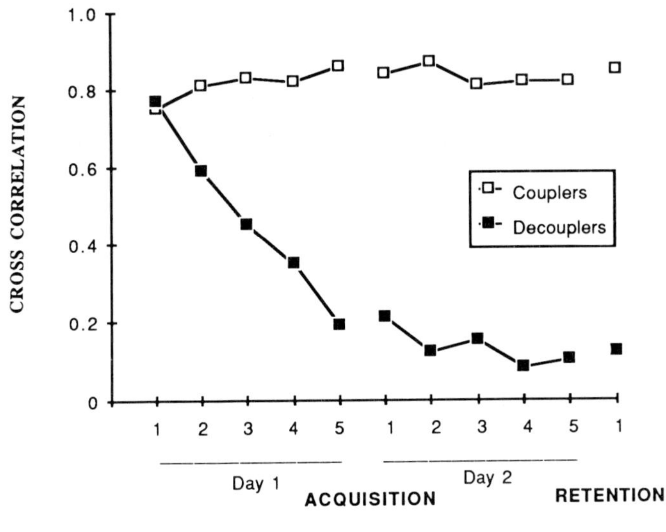

Figure 2. Cross correlations between the angular acceleration patterns of the left and right limb movement for the coupling and decoupling group across acquisition and retention.

Whereas the coupling group only showed a small increase in metrical dissociation across practice, much larger increases were found for the decoupling group. These findings suggest that subjects who were more successful in structural dissociation also reached higher degrees of differentiation of the intensity specifications and this effect became more prominent with increasing practice.

To obtain further insight into the underlying reasons for these changes in the metrical dissociation ratio, the amount of relative work generated in each limb was analyzed separately (see Figure 4). It is apparent that an excess of work was generated for production of the unidirectional movement (Figure 4, bottom). When performed in isolation, the amount of relative work required for this movement (and produced by a similar group of subjects) would be at around or just below 300 units (Swinnen & Walter, in press; Swinnen, Walter,

Beirinckx, et al., in press). Across practice, the decoupling group was able to reduce the excess of work and to approach these baseline values closely whereas this was not the case for the coupling group. The differences between groups almost reached significance during acquisition, $F(1, 18) = 3.78$, $p = .06$, and became significant during retention, $F(1, 18) = 7.3$, $p < 05$. The decrease in work across both phases of acquisition was significant, $F(1, 18) = 6.68$, $p < .05$. This effect was predominantly due to the decoupling groups' scores that decreased steadily across practice.

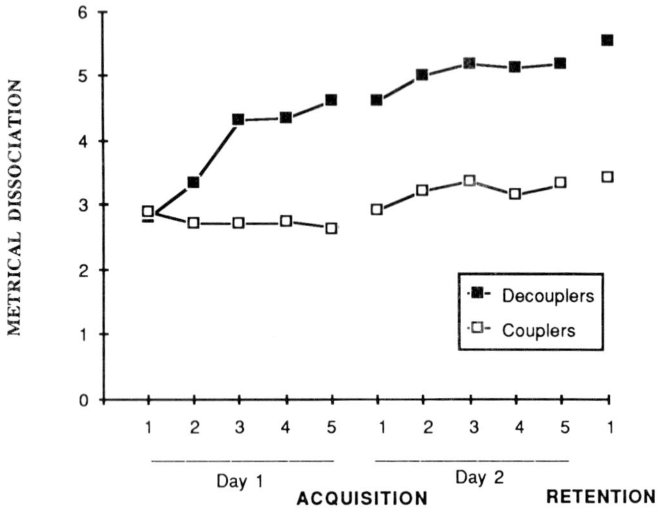

Figure 3. Metrical dissociation ratios of the coupling and decoupling group across acquisition and retention.

With respect to the reversal movement, the decoupling group was found to generate a significantly higher amount of relative work than the coupling group during acquisition, $F(1, 18) = 4.22$, $p = .05$, but the differences faded at retention, $F(1, 18) = .09$, $p > .05$ (see Figure 4, top). Both groups showed increases in relative work at the start of practice (day 1), followed by a small decrease. During the second day, the scores of the decoupling group stabilized whereas those of the coupling group further increased.

Overall, it appears that subjects who were successful in overcoming the common organizational framework governing both limb actions (decouplers) were also more successful in dissociating the required intensity specifications. This was mostly accomplished through a reduction of the amount of excessive work that was generated for production of the unidirectional movement whereas the amount of relative work for the reversal movement was originally increased whereafter it stabilized. On the other hand, subjects not successful in structural dissociation (couplers) showed no such clear decreases in amount of relative work for the unidirectional movement whereas relative work for the reversal movement was increased across both days of practice. In contrast to the decoupling group, they showed a similar trend in the work scores for both limb movements, predominantly during the first practice day: When work for production of the reversal movement was increased, work for the unidirectional movement was increased as well. This observation does not only hold for the group as a whole but for a number of individual subjects as well, as shown in Figure 5.

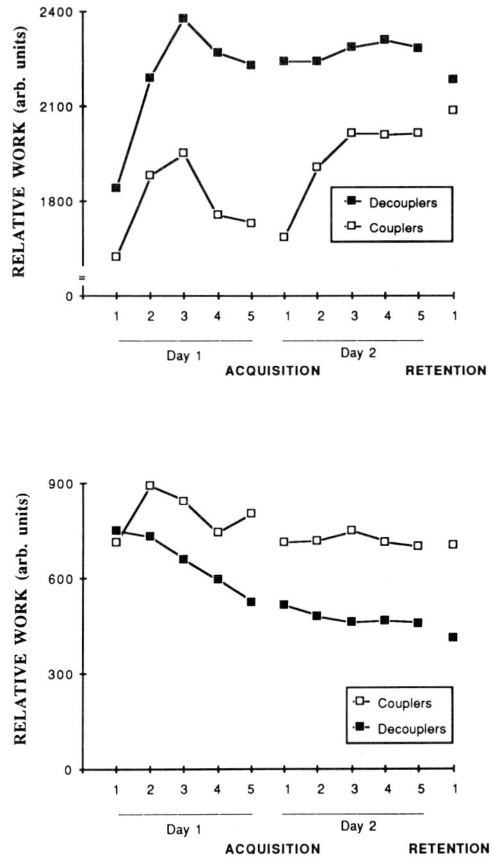

Figure 4. Positive relative work generated by the coupling and decoupling group for production of the unidirectional (bottom) and reversal (top) movement across acquisition and retention.

The two upper examples A and B (representative of the decoupling group), show a differentiation in the pattern of relative work for the unidirectional and reversal movement: An increase is found for the reversal movement whereas values for the unidirectional movement remain at a steady level or gradually decrease. The two examples of couplers (C and D) show less motor output differentiation. In example C, increases in reversal work scores are accompanied with increases in unidirectional scores. In example D, relative work for the reversal movement gradually decreases towards the values obtained for the unidirectional movement.

On the basis of the aforementioned findings, it is proposed that the analysis of work can provide insights into the nature of central processes and their interactions. It is hypothesized that success in interlimb dissociation is (at least partly) dependent on the degree of *neural output differentiation* that can reside within the central nervous system. Apparently, less successful subjects (couplers) have greater difficulty in preventing the 'neural overflow' from the control centers of the right arm to those of the left arm (and vice versa). Consequently, the intensity specifications of both action patterns become more similar to each other. In addition, they experience more difficulties in giving up the common organizational structure that governs both limb movements, e.g., the cross correlations remain very high across practice. Conversely, decouplers are better capable of organizing movements with a different organizational structure in a parallel fashion and they are more successful in reducing interference between the limbs' intensity specifications.

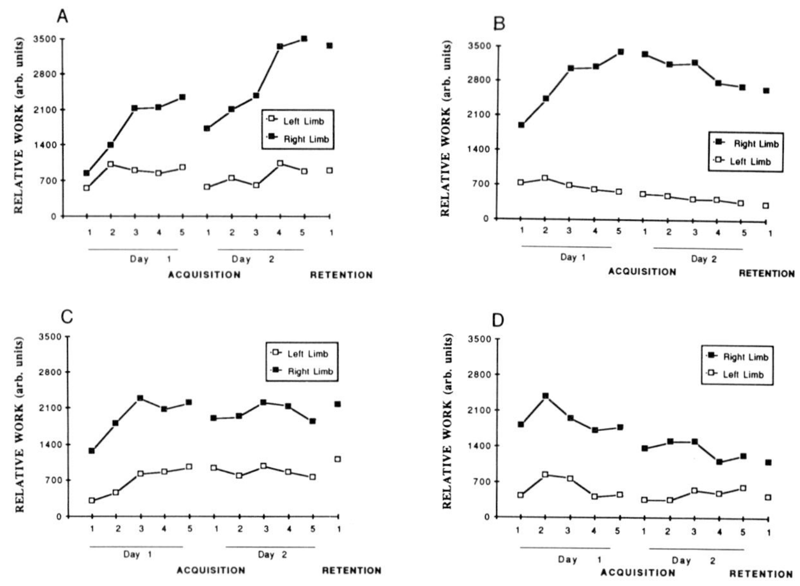

Figure 5. Patterns of relative work with respect to the unidirectional and reversal movement as produced by some typical subjects of the coupling and decoupling group.

4.4. Parallel response organization as revealed through kinematics

It can be instructive to inspect kinematic data patterns of individual subjects to better understand the nature of parallel response organization. The Figures 6 through 8 show some examples of left and right displacement-time and acceleration-time patterns of individual subjects from both groups. The 10 retention trials are plotted consecutively to show the degree of stability in the acquired pattern of coordination. The general forms of these plots are to be compared to those of Figure 1. Structural coupling/decoupling is particularly evident from the degree of synchronization of the acceleration-time traces of both limb movements. Metrical coupling/decoupling can be inferred from the absolute differences between the peak acceleration and deceleration values of both limb movements. Note that the angular displacement and acceleration patterns of the limb movements are plotted against different ordinate scales to enhance qualitative comparisons.

Among the subjects who show a strong degree of structural coupling (Example 1 and 2), a distinction can be made with respect to the degree of metrical or intensity dissociation. Example 1 (see Figure 6) shows both strong structural and metrical coupling. Metrical coupling is so pervasive that the subject even reverses direction with the left limb. Example 2 (see Figure 7) also shows strong structural coupling but the intensity specifications are more differentiated than in Example 1. In fact, they are so finely differentiated that interference can hardly be observed in the unidirectional displacement pattern. The acceleration patterns, however, are very similar in form. Example 3 shows largely successful metrical and structural dissociation (see Figure 8).

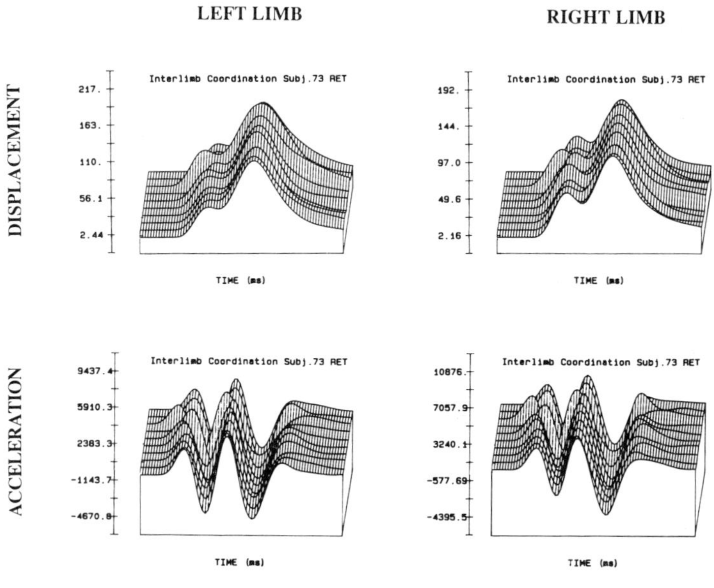

Figure 6. Example 1: Three-dimensional plots of the angular displacement-time and acceleration-time patterns of the left and right limb movement as produced during the retention test (coupler).

Even though certain subjects are successful in dissociation, they often show some signs of interlimb interdependence, mostly at movement initiation. Although they display an essentially correct acceleration pattern for the unidirectional movement (with one peak acceleration and one peak deceleration), it differs from an idealtypical acceleration signal as produced under unimanual (or isolated) performance conditions. More specifically, there is an extension of the decelerative phase, or, a phase of zero acceleration in the middle portion of movement (that can last up to about 100 ms) becomes apparent. This possibly occurs in response to an oversized initial muscle burst that can be accounted for by a synchronization tendency or neural irradiation effect between the right and left limb control centers before the movement has even started. The phase of zero acceleration implies in principle that no major changes in the level of activity of the muscles is occurring. It may be indicative of a "let-the-limb-go" strategy, possibly providing the advantage that attention is not required for this part of the unidirectional action so that it can be fully devoted to the directional shifts of the reversal movement pattern.

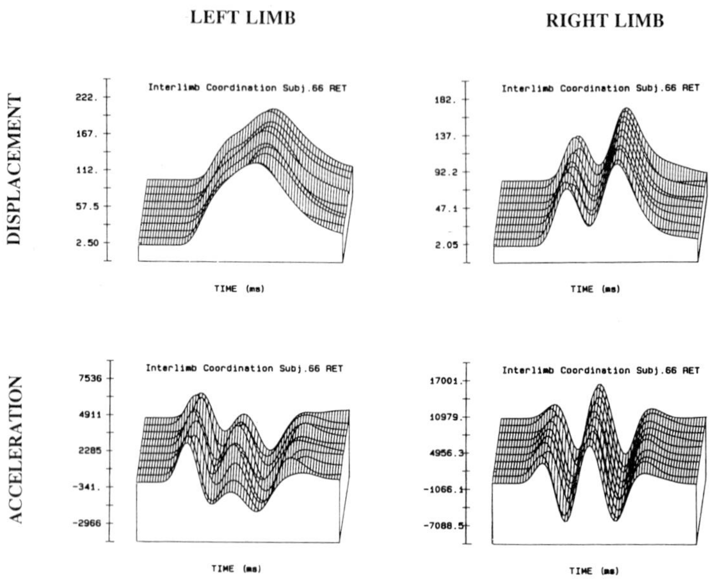

Figure 7. Example 2: Three-dimensional plots of the angular displacement-time and acceleration-time patterns of the left and right limb movement as produced during the retention test (coupler).

5. ON THE RELATIONSHIP BETWEEN METRICAL AND STRUCTURAL DISSOCIATION

Whereas it has been suggested in a number of studies with unimanual skills that reparametrization of movement is possible while leaving the basic organizational invariants untouched (Schmidt, 1988b), there is only limited information available concerning the degree of independence between metrical and structural specifications in bimanual action and how changes in one specification possibly affect the other. Although the above mentioned experiment did not constitute the critical conditions to address this matter, it provides some preliminary insights into this relationship. Across practice, the subjects that were less successful in structural dissociation also reached lower levels of metrical dissociation, indicative of some degree of covariation between both movement specifications. More direct evidence for their link has been provided in other studies in which increasing the speed (Swinnen & Walter, 1991) or torque requirements for production of the reversal movement induced increased structural coupling strength (Walter & Swinnen, 1990a, 1990b).

Nevertheless, there are also indications that structural and metrical specifications can operate independently of each other under certain conditions or that they are possibly specified at different locations within the central nervous system. As mentioned previously, although a number of subjects appeared incapable to desynchronize the movements under the present task constraints, some of them succeeded in differentiating the intensity specifications for both limb movements to such an extent that interference was hardly observable at the level of the produced displacement patterns (see Figure 7). In another study, Walter and Swinnen (1991) reported a correlation of .536 between between metrical and structural dissociation which represents a common variance of approximately 29 %.

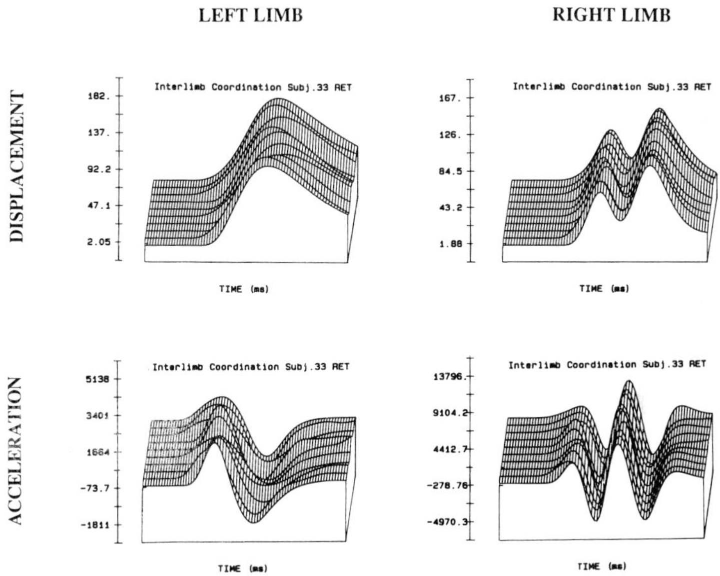

Figure 8. Example 3: Three-dimensional plots of the angular displacement-time and acceleration-time patterns of the left and right limb movement as produced during the retention test (decoupler).

6. A NEURO-DYNAMICS ACCOUNT OF DUAL-TASK PERFORMANCE

The present approach may hold some promise for unraveling the mechanisms involved in time-sharing. Time-sharing performance has received considerable interest in the past decades not only from experimental psychology but also from more applied professions like ergonomics/human factors. Indeed, human operators are often required to monitor more than one thing at a time and their failure to do so may cause serious accidents. Limitations in dual-task performance have been accounted for by a variety of theoretical or pretheoretical concepts, e.g., limited-capacity or (multiple) resources. The present approach differs from these perspectives in that it does not a priori rely on these constructs, but, instead attempts to provide a detailed description of interlimb interactions and the parameters that affect it (Swinnen & Walter, in press). Thereby, use is made of biomechanical variables that are directly or indirectly controlled by the central nervous system and that may open a window to interactions occurring at a central level. The present findings appear to suggest that these interactions can most optimally be revealed at the level of acceleration-time or force-time descriptions of movement. Furthermore, the work measures may provide additional insight into interactions between the limb movements' intensity specifications, possibly as biophysical concomitants of mental work(load) or 'cost' associated with movement.

Because the use of these biophysical variables is believed to be central to understanding dual-task interference, we refer to this as the dynamics (the force-mass-acceleration) approach. Future research issues that need to be addressed to further develop this line of thinking concern the study of the effects of manipulations of particular force-time histories on dual-task performance on the one hand and absolute force levels on the other hand. It should hereby be emphasized that force parameters not only enter into motoric dual- or multi-task performance but also entail upon more cognitive types of activities that involve various sensory modalities. For example, in time-sharing an auditory attention task together with a tracking movement under different degrees of force-loading, Mastroianni and Schopper (1986) found that performing the auditory task was significantly degraded with increased amounts of force exerted on the pursuit rotor manipulandum.

The present findings indicate that the emergent patterns of interference, as revealed through these biophysical measures, can most parsimoniously be explained by 'neural cross-talk' between simultaneously active control centers within a unitary neural medium. This is inferred from the nature of errors that can be observed in one task which clearly reflect the pattern of activity of the concurrent task. In other words, due to neural irradiation, one action becomes dominant for control and imposes its pattern of activity on the other with which it is performed simultaneously, or, both patterns mutually interfere with each other. This has also become evident from the electromyographic patterns of the left and right elbow flexors and extensors during bimanual performance (Swinnen, Young et al., in press). The bursty right biceps-triceps-biceps sequence of activity for the reversal action shows up in the activity pattern of the left limb. Consequently, success in the dissociation of these actions appears to depend on the capability to reduce or eliminate the intrusions. As this synchronization tendency can already be observed in the electrical activity of the muscles prior to the start of any observable displacement, it evidently has a central origin.The pathways responsible for these interactions can possibly be located at various levels within the central nervous system including cortical and subcortical structures (Swinnen, Young, et al., in press).

Cross-talk is not unique to motoric task combinations. In studying typing while shadowing, Shaffer (1975) found that the secretary occasionally typed words that were phonemically or semantically similar to words that she should have shadowed and vice versa. In a dual-task reaction-time experiment, Navon and Miller (1987) had subjects monitor four visual channels: Two of these channels presented the name of boys and girls (Task 1) and two defined the names of either cities or states (Task 2). Two-choice classification responses for each task were made and performance was measured under single-and dual-task conditions. When a target relevant to one channel appeared on the other channel, they found that processing of the first channel was delayed and this was accounted for by so-called outcome conflicts.

If neural spread of activity is the main cause of interference, the hypothesis can be inferred that increased levels of activation, needed for production of one task, will lead to increased neural irradiation, which in turn will result in increased synchronization effects or patterns of interference (when different things are to be done simultaneously). This hypothesis has been supported in previous work (Swinnen & Walter, 1991; Walter & Swinnen, 1990a, 1990b). This line of reasoning can also account for the subjects' tendency to reduce the torque requirements at initiation of practice through slowing down the movement (Swinnen & Walter, in press). In a general way, the present account is consistent with the model of 'functional cerebral space' as developed by Kinsbourne and associates (Kinsbourne, 1982; Kinsbourne & Hicks, 1978; Kinsbourne & Hiscock, 1983).

Given that dual-task performance is subject to interference as a result of neural cross-talk, successful dissociation becomes dependent on the degree of differentiation of patterns of activity within a unitary, continuous medium or neural space. Findings of the present study have provided evidence that neural output differentiation is one distinguishing feature between decouplers and couplers. As shown previously, decouplers can more easily generate different intensity specifications simultaneously that remain to some extent independent of each other. Conversely, couplers show more similar work values for both limb actions (e.g., less metrical dissociation), which may suggest they encounter greater difficulty in confining neural overflow. In a similar way, Hirst (1986) has noted that the difficulty in performing certain tasks concurrently is to keep them insulated from one another and not merely doing them simultaneously. He denotes this capability as "segregation".

The present approach may prove to be a useful complement to more traditional attentional accounts that rely on pretheoretical constructs or metaphors like (a) capacity-consuming executive(s) or resource(s). In essence, it represents a more direct approach to dual-task performance that puts great emphasis on neural cross-talk as a basic framework that accounts for limitations in time-sharing. Its strength lies in a detailed assessment of interlimb interactions at the structural as well as the metrical level of movement specification. It is congruent with other perspectives that have underscored the importance of 'outcome conflict' as a basic source of interference in dual tasks (Navon & Miller, 1987). A provocative research program for the future might consist of sorting out what share of dual-task interference can be accounted for by means of neural cross-talk or response outcome conflict before the need arises to invoke hypothetical constructs or metaphors that remain obscure and difficult to come to grips with. In this respect, Fracker and Wickens (1989) and Wickens (1989) have already argued that confusions, although important, do not give a complete account of task interference. Instead, they propose three mechanisms: resource competition, confusions, and incompatible task proximity between processing stages.

Studies on the concurrent performance of motor tasks may play an important role in elucidating the general nature of time-sharing ability and parallel response organization in humans because, in comparison to many cognitive activities, motor activities lend themselves more easily to careful registration with very small time envelopes.

ACKNOWLEDGEMENTS

Support for the present study was provided through a grant from the Research Council of K.U. Leuven, Belgium (Contract No. OT/89/26). Further support was made available through a Collaborative Research Grant from the NATO Scientific Affairs Division (Contract No. 86/732). I am indebted to Charles B. Walter from the University of Illinois at Chicago with whom I have had many discussions and daily E-mail notes concerning the problem of movement coordination in the past years. Thanks are also extended to Veerle Hermans, Annemie Daelman, and Johan Dupont for their help with data collection.

REFERENCES

Braune, R., & Wickens, C. D. (1986). Time-sharing revisited: test of a componential model for the assessment of individual differences. *Ergonomics, 29,* 1399-1414.

Corcos, D. M. (1984). Two-handed movement control. *Research Quarterly for Exercise and Sport, 55*, 117-122.

Enoka, R. M. (1988). *Neuromechanical basis of kinesiology*. Champaign, IL: Human Kinetics.

Fracker, M. L., & Wickens, C. D. (1989). Resources, confusions, and compatibility in dual-axis tracking: displays, controls, and dynamics. *Journal of Experimental Psychology: Human Perception and Performance, 15*, 80-96.

Guiard, Y. (1987). Asymmetric division of labor in human skilled bimanual action: the kinematic chain as a model. *Journal of Motor Behavior, 19*, 486-517.
Hirst, W. (1986). The psychology of attention. In J. E. LeDoux & W. Hirst (Eds.), *Mind and brain. Dialogues in cognitive neuroscience* (pp. 105-141). Cambridge: Cambridge University Press.
Jongen, H. A. H., Denier Van Der Gon, J. J., & Gielen, C.C.A.M. (1989). Inhomogeneous activation of motoneurone pools as revealed by co-contraction of antagonistic human arm muscles. *Experimental Brain Research, 75*, 555-562.
Kelso, J. A. S. (1981). Contrasting perspectives on order and regulation in movement. In J. Long & A. Baddeley (Eds.), *Attention and performance (Vol 9)*. Hillsdale, N.J.: Erlbaum.
Kelso, J. A. S., Southard, D. L., & Goodman D. (1979 a). On the coordination of two-handed movements. *Journal of Experimental Psychology: Human Perception and Performance, 2*, 229-238.
Kelso, J. A. S., Southard, D. L., & Goodman D. (1979 b). On the nature of human interlimb coordination. *Science, 203*, 1029-1031.
Kelso, J. A. S., & Tuller, B. (1984). A dynamical basis for action systems. In M. S. Gazzaniga (Ed.), *Handbook of cognitive neuroscience* (pp. 321-356). New York: Plenum Press.
Kinsbourne, M. (1982). Hemispheric specialization and the growth of human understanding. *American Psychologist, 37*, 411-420.
Kinsbourne, M., & Hicks, R. E. (1978). Functional cerebral space: a model for overflow, transfer and interference effects in human performance: a tutorial review. In J. Requin (Ed.), *Attention and performance. Vol VII* (pp. 345-362). Hillsdale: Erlbaum.
Kinsbourne, M., & Hiscock, M. (1983). Asymmetries of dual-task performance. In J. B. Hellige (Ed.), *Cerebral hemisphere asymmetry: Method, theory, and application* (pp. 255-334). New York: Praeger.
Kugler, P. N., Kelso, J. A. S., & Turvey, M. T. (1980). On the concept of coordinative structures as dissipative structures: I. Theoretical lines of convergence. In G. E. Stelmach, & J. Requin (Eds.), *Tutorials in motor behavior* (pp. 3-47). Amsterdam: North-Holland.
Marteniuk, R. G., MacKenzie, C. L., & Baba, D. M. (1984). Bimanual movement control: information processing and interaction effects. *The Quarterly Journal of Experimental Psychology, 36A*, 335-365.
Mastroianni, G. R., & Schopper, A. W. (1986). Degradation of force-loaded pursuit tracking performance in a dual-task paradigm, *Ergonomics, 29*, 639-647.
Navon, D., & Miller, J. (1987). Role of outcome conflict in dual-task interference. *Journal of Experimental Psychology: Human Perception and Performance, 13*, 435-448.
Newell, K. M. (1985). Coordination, control and skill. In D. Goodman, R. B. Wilberg, & I. M. Franks (Eds.), *Differing perspectives in motor learning, memory, and control* (pp. 295-317). Amsterdam: North-Holland.
Schmidt, R. A. (1988a). Motor and action perspectives on motor behaviour. In O. G. Meijer & K. Roth (Eds.), *Complex Movement Behaviour: 'The 'motor-action controversy* (pp. 3-44). Amsterdam: North-Holland.
Schmidt, R. A. (1988b). *Motor control and learning. A behavioral emphasis.* Champaign, IL: Human Kinetics.
Shaffer, L. H. (1975). Multiple attention in continuous verbal tasks. In P. Rabbit & S. Dornic (Eds.), Attention and performance Vol V. New York: Academic Press.
Swinnen, S. P. (in press). Motor control. In R. Dulbecco (Ed.), *Encyclopedia of Human Biology*. San Diego: Academic Press.
Swinnen, S. P. (1990). *The effects of various sources of kinematic information feedback on interlimb dissociation.* Technical Report, Motor Control Lab, K.U. Leuven, Belgium.
Swinnen, S. P. , & Walter, C. B. (1988). Constraints in coordinating limb movements. In A. M. Colley & J. R. Beech (Eds.), *Cognition and action in skilled behaviour* (pp. 127-143). Amsterdam: North-Holland.

Swinnen, S. P. , & Walter, C. B. (1991). The effect of movement speed on upper-limb coupling strength. Paper presented at the conference of the North American Society for the Psychology of Sport and Physical Activity, Asilomar, California.
Swinnen, S. P., & Walter, C. B. (in press). Toward a movement dynamics perspective on dual-task performance. *Human Factors*.
Swinnen, S. P., Walter, C. B., Beirinckx, M. B., & Meugens, P. F. (in press). Dissociating the structural and metrical specifications of bimanual movement. *Journal of Motor Behavior*.
Swinnen, S. P., Walter, C. B., Pauwels, J. M., Meugens, P. F., & Beirinckx, M. B. (1990). The dissociation of interlimb constraints. *Human Performance*, *3*, 187-215.
Swinnen, S., Walter, C. B., & Shapiro, D. C. (1988). The coordination of limb movements with different kinematic patterns. *Brain and Cognition*, *8*, 326-347.
Swinnen, S. P., Young, D. E., Walter, C. B., & Serrien, D. J. (in press). Control of bilateral asymmetrical movements. *Experimental Brain Research*.
Turvey, M. T., Shaw, R. E., & Mace, W. (1978). Issues in the theory of action: degrees of freedom, coordinative structures and coalitions. In J. Requin (Ed.), *Attention and performance VII*, Hillsdale, N.J.: Lawrence Erlbaum.
Walter, C. B., & Swinnen, S. P. (1991). *Adaptive tuning of interlimb attraction to facilitate bimanual dissociation*. Manuscript accepted for publication in Journal of Motor Behavior.
Walter, C. B., & Swinnen, S. P. (1990a). Asymmetric interlimb interference during the performance of a dynamic bimanual task. *Brain & Cognition*, *14*, 185-200.
Walter, C. B., & Swinnen, S. P. (1990b). Kinetic attraction during bimanual coordination. *Journal of Motor Behavior*, *22*, 451-473.
Wickens, C. D. (1984). *Engineering psychology and human performance*. Columbus: Merrill.
Wickens, C. D. (1989). Attention and skilled performance. In D. H. Holding (Ed.), *Human skills* (2nd ed.) (pp.71-105). Chichester: John Wiley and Sons.
Wickens, C. D., and Benel, D. C. R. (1982). The development of time-sharing skills. In J. A. S. Kelso, & J. E. Clark (Eds.), *The development of movement control and coordination* (pp. 253-274). Chichester: Wiley.

Tutorials in Motor Behavior II
G.E. Stelmach and J. Requin (Editors)

PLANNING OF MOTOR SEQUENCES IN LANDING FROM A JUMP-DOWN

P.A. McKinley

School of Physical and Occupational Therapy, McGill University, 3654 Rue Drummond Montreal, Canada H3G1Y5

Abstract

Various paradigms used in studying landing from a jump-down are discussed with respect to the inter-relationship of planning take-off and landing aspects of the movement. It is proposed that the take-off and landing sequences are planned independently of one another, that both sequences are adaptable to environmental changes in task requirements and that adjustments for landing may be affected during execution of the takeoff sequence.

1. INTRODUCTION

Landing from a jump-down from a higher to lower surface is a natural, learned movement that is common in many vertebrates and is first attempted at a relatively young age. While seemingly simple, this act requires integration of visual, proprioceptive and vestibular input to accomplish the task successfully, particularly when either the height or location of the landing surface is not known (1-4). While individuals may be able to complete jump-downs successfully when one of these senses is unavailable, it becomes difficult or impossible when two are missing (2).

Successful landing depends on planning ahead. At takeoff, the body must be projected into space so that the center of gravity is projected onto the targeted landing area and positioned within the body's base of support at touchdown. For landing, impact forces must be anticipated so that shock absorption is optimized. The notion that the motor program for landing from a jump is prepared in advance to include takeoff as well as landing has previously been suggested for studies using cat (2,5) and monkey (3) and recently has been suggested to be important in postlanding control as well (6). However, these studies did not address the complex and intriguing questions of how a motor plan might be constructed for such a complex movement that would be *general* enough to satisfy global task requirements, that is to land in a stable position at a given target and *flexible* enough to adapt to variable types of surfaces, impact forces experienced from different heights, or environmental constraints that might alter the reliability or availability of sensory input.

Recently, in our laboratory at McGill, and in Milan, at the Bioengineering Center with A. Pedotti, the act of landing from a jumpdown has been studied in human subjects using various paradigms including: the role of height and vision when planning landing in adults (4); the role of vision in landing from a jump in children (7,8); the effect of similarity or difference in compliance of the takeoff and landing surfaces on jump execution (9); and the role of skill in landing from a jump onto two surfaces of differing compliance (10). While the constraints of these paradigms differ, they all rely on successful completion of 2 similar task goals: to take off from a support stage and land within a targeted area with both feet, maintain balance and reach stability quickly. While the flight trajectory set at takeoff influences the actual landing site of the body, it may also have an effect on muscle activity planned in anticipation for landing. Thus, the question arises as to whether or not takeoff and landing are programmed independently or as a unified motor plan. If they are independently planned, then one might ask whether they are planned together prior to jump initiation, or whether the landing component is planned during the execution of the jump.

To address the question of whether the two goals are planned as one program or are separate, two sets of experiments are compared, where landing parameters are changed by either altering the height of the jump (which examines the effect of changing momentum on landing preparation) or by altering the compliance of the landing surface (which alters the initial impact force experienced at landing). As will be discussed below, prelanding adjustments appear to be specific to the landing impulse characteristics, while takeoff strategies are predominantly subject rather than context dependent. Thus it is postulated that the landing and takeoff aspects of the jump are planned independently. A third study, examining jumpdowns in children supports this hypothesis. The second question is examined briefly by comparing the difference between skilled and unskilled subjects in planning for landing on surfaces of differing compliance in addition to the effect that altering the takeoff surface compliance has on planning landing.

2. METHODS

To analyze the movement we collected surface EMG from 6 leg muscles including the knee extensor Vastus Lateralis (VL), knee extensor/hip flexor Rectus Femoris (RF), the hip extensor/knee flexor Biceps Femoris (BF), the knee flexor/ankle plantarflexor Lateral Gastrocnemious (LG), the ankle plantarflexor soleus (SOL), and the ankle dorsiflexor, Tibialis Anterior (TA). Takeoff and landing were ascertained by pressure sensitive footswitches placed on the toe, midsole and heel. Kinematics for analysis of joint motion at the head, trunk, hip, knee and ankle were collected at 60Hz using a video shutter camera (Panasonic WD5000) and analyzed using Peak Performance Technologies hard and soft ware for all paradigms except that involving skilled and unskilled performers. In that paradigm, kinematic data was collected and analyzed using the ELITE motion analysis system and kinetic data at landing was collected with a Kistler force plate and used to demarcate landing and to determine a performance index that was based on center of pressure information and time to stability at landing.

Briefly, the center of pressure information was used to determine the amount of deviation from the anterior/posterior axis during landing and stabilization, while stability time referred to the time for the vertical force component to oscillate about 1 body weight after impact. These two factors were combined to give a measure of performance that was used to evaluate each jump and overall jumping ability of two groups of young women.

Our skilled population consisted of 4 volleyball players ranging in age from 16-21, 65-70Kg, 1.65-1.73m in height and our untrained subjects were 4 girl scouts of similar age, height, and weight with no specific athletic training. The individuals from each group were reassessed using the Performance Index criteria. All volleyball players fell into the skilled group, while only one girl scout was classified as skilled. Volleyball players rather than gymnasts were used as trained subjects as the subjects were required to hold a ball in their hands at chest level when jumping to minimize arm movement and because they were accustomed to landing on surfaces of differing compliances such as sand and hardwood floors. They are also trained to land with minimal anterior/posterior and lateral sway. For the other paradigms using adults, a group of 10 well-practiced young women (21-26 yrs of age) were used for all the experiments. For the paradigm involving children, well-practiced youngsters between the ages of 7-13 were studied.

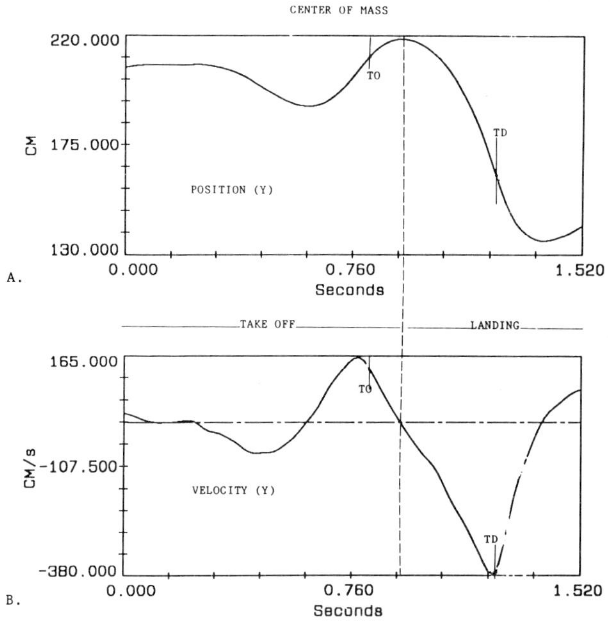

Figure 1: Y component of the center of mass for a jump down. A) trajectory and B) velocity. Dashed line represents peak flight trajectory. Solid lines and abbreviations: TO, takeoff and TD, touchdown.

In order to evaluate these goals across the various paradigms, we divided the jump-down into two phases : takeoff and landing. The takeoff phase includes stance preparation before initiation of the jump, the takeoff motion from the support stage and the ascending part of flight (from toeoff to peak trajectory, when vertical velocity is zero). The landing phase is comprised of the descending limb of flight, impact, shock absorption, and stabilization to a standing position post-landing (Fig 1). Flight itself was not considered independent of takeoff and landing for two reasons. The flight trajectory is a consequence of takeoff, and muscle activity for the landing phase is initiated in the descending limb of the flight period and is thought to be visually triggered in both falls (1,11-13), steps (14) and jumps (2-3).

3. RESULTS

3.1 Independence of Takeoff And Landing Components

Alteration of Takeoff style with a consistent landing style. Takeoff phases were analyzed across all paradigms and it was observed that there were two distinct styles of takeoff that were subject specific, not related to skill, height of the jump, or compliance of the landing surface. That is, a subject preferentially utilized one of the two styles at least 80% of the time. These are described as *Roll off* and *Push off* styles and are illustrated in figure 2 for the hip and knee segments.

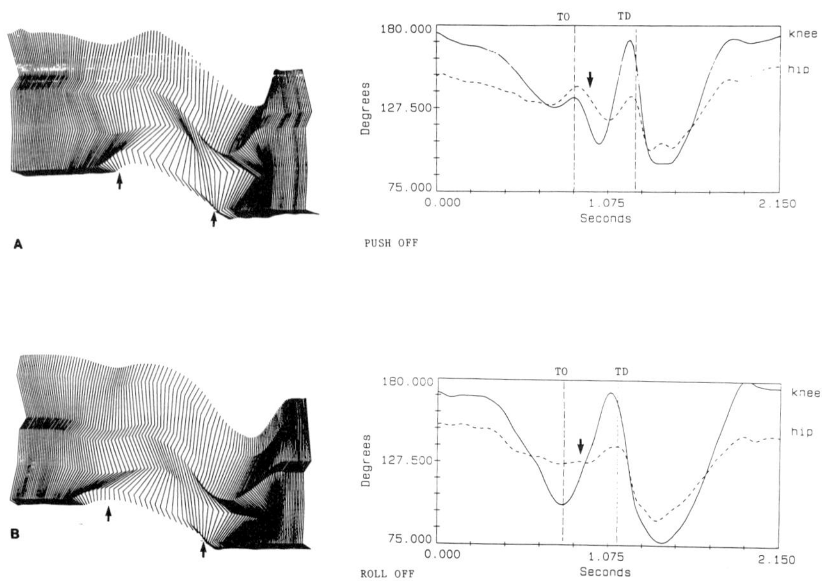

Figure 2: Stick figures (every 16.7ms) and hip (dotted lines) and knee (solid lines) angles during the jumpdown for two strategies: A) Push off; B) Roll off. Flight is between the vertical dashed lines which mark takeoff(TO) and touchdown(TD). Arrows on joint position graphs mark peak trajectory; arrows on stick diagrams mark TO and TD.

It can be seen that when using the *push off* style, the subject bends the lower limb segment in preparation for takeoff and extends the limb in a propulsive motion so that at the instant of takeoff the limb is almost fully extended. Subsequently, during the ascending part of flight, the limb flexes slightly to swing ahead. Peak flexion usually occurs close to the point when peak trajectory is reached (Fig 2a, arrow). The *roll off* style is different in that it lacks a yield and propulsion component during preparation, and the subject appears to flex continuously during the preparation phase and takes off from the platform in a flexed position. The ascending flight period is minimal and is reached shortly after takeoff while the limb segments are beginning to extend (Fig 2b arrow).

EMG during this phase was different for the two styles. When executing a *push off* style, there was considerable activity in the TA prior to propulsion phase and minimal activity prior to and at takeoff. There was cocontraction of the ankle plantarflexors LG and SOL during propulsion and up to takeoff. Activity in the VL and RF alternated with that of the BF so that the VL and RF were coactive not only with each other but with the early plantarflexor activity. At takeoff, however, these muscles were often silent. BF activity began closer to takeoff and ceased shortly after takeoff. During the early part of flight there was a small burst of activity in the RF Fig 3A). When executing the roll off style, activity occurred primarily in the TA prior to and during takeoff. There was little activity in any of the other muscles studied, although there was occasionally small bursts in the SOL and LG which alternated with that of the TA (Fig 3B).

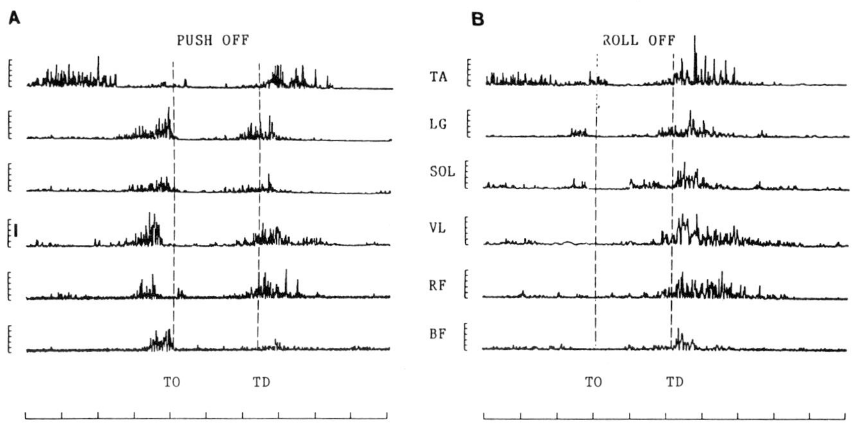

Figure 3: Rectified EMG of the TA, LG SOL, VL, RF, and BF for the two styles Push Off (A) and Roll Off (B)in 2 subjects. Conventions as in Figure 2. Tick marks represent 200 ms and all EMG is scaled to 0.3V.

At landing, the overall joint motion (Fig 2) and onset patterns of EMG (Fig 3) were similar regardless of the takeoff style used. Typically, the joints reached maximum extension prior to landing so that the hip, knee and ankle were already partially flexed at impact (Fig 2a,b). Prelanding EMG was initiated in the ankle plantarflexors LG and SOL first. TA onset was variable, although it usually followed that of the plantarflexors. Knee and hip musculature always followed that of the ankle and was typically characterized by low level tonic activity in the BF during midflight and a burst of activity at landing, while VL and RF bursts began prior to landing. While this overall pattern was seen regardless of whether subjects were landing from jumps of different heights, or whether they were landing on surfaces of differing compliances, adjustments in the amount of joint flexion and timing and amplitude of prelanding EMG were made that were dependent on whether there were changes in compliance of the landing surface or in the height of the jump.

Alteration of landing style with a consistent takeoff style. In contrast to adults, two landing styles are often observed when landing on a stiff surface from a constant height in children between 7 and 13. One style is seen more frequently in motorically less developed children and is one where joint action at the hip and knee is serial or 'uncoupled'. That is, knee flexion or extension during flight and landing precedes that at the hip (Fig 4A). The other is the normal adult pattern where knee and hip flexion or extension occurs in concert, that is, 'coupled' (Fig 4B). In the older child (11-13 yrs), these two landing styles are often used interchangeably but are preceded by a consistent subject-selected takeoff style (8).

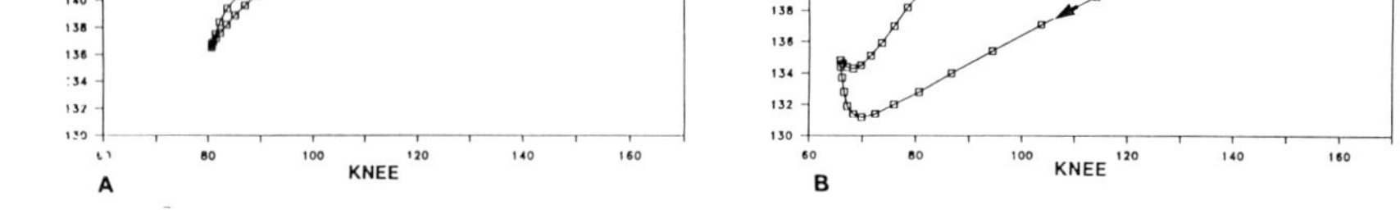

Figure 4: Angle angle diagrams of a 13 yr old subject using 2 landing strategies, uncoupled hip and knee motion (A) and coupled knee and hip motion (B). Arrows point direction of movement from takeoff until stance, postlanding.

3.2 Task Specific Landing Adjustments

Prelanding EMG onset latency adjustments. When jumping onto surfaces of differing compliances from a stiff takeoff surface, muscle onset was dependent on the type of landing surface. When landing on a stiff surface, onsets of the SO, LG and RF occurred significantly earlier than when landing on a compliant surface. This had the effect of changing the onset patterns considerably, so that when landing on a stiff surface, prelanding activity began first in the LG and SOL, followed by the TA,BF and subsequently the RF and VL. On the compliant surface, onsets of the SO,LG,TA and BF occurred together followed by the VL and RF shortly before landing. This was most clearcut in skilled subjects (Fig 5A). Activity in the SOL and LG in the 200ms prior to landing was also significantly damped in the skilled group when landing on the compliant surface (10).

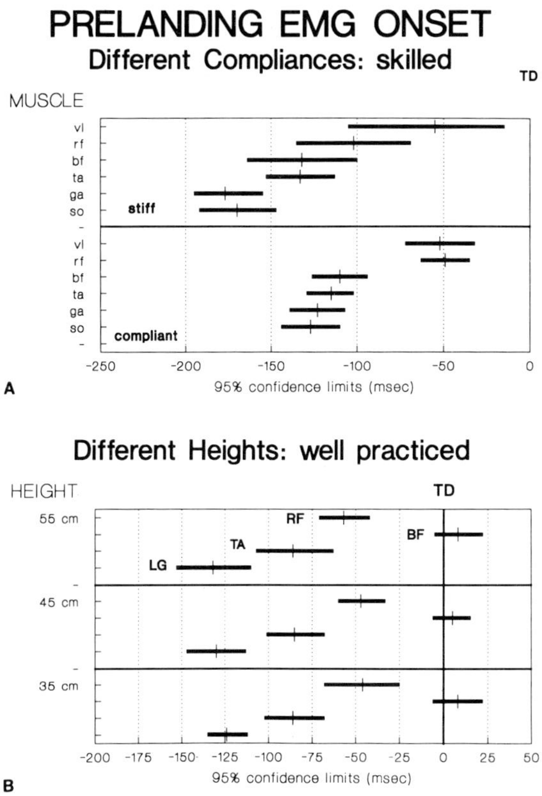

Figure 5: Mean prelanding EMG onsets and 95% confidence intervals for 2 sets of experiments. A) landing on surfaces of different compliance for 5 skilled subjects (pooled data), B) landing at 3 heights (35, 45 and 55cm), pooled data, n=10 subjects.

In contrast, when landing from jumpdowns of 3 different heights (35, 45 and 55cm), well practiced subjects did not alter the onsets of the prelanding bursts of activity (Fig 5B) for the various heights. Rather, the onset of activity began a set time prior to landing. The activity of 4 muscles (RF,BF,TA,LG) in the 200ms prior to landing was also compared across the three heights. and was found to be significantly different only in the RF, where activity increased as a function of jump height (4).

Joint adjustments for landing. When landing from different heights, there was not always a clear cut difference between heights. Often this was because subjects chose to alter the trajectory of the 55cm jump so that the peak trajectories for 45 and 55cm jumps were similar (fig 6A).

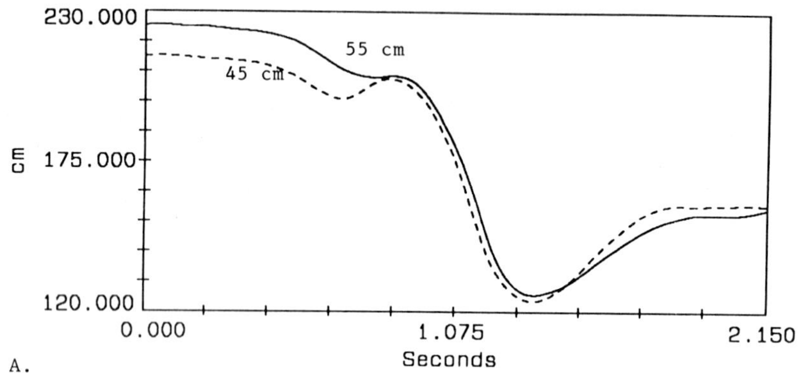

A.

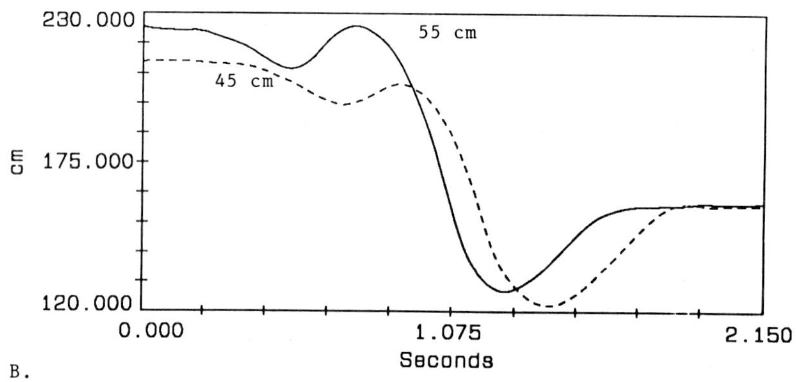

B.

Figure 6: Y component of iliac crest marker for jumps at 55cm (solid line) and 45cm (dashed line) for two different strategies; a) trajectory adjustment for height; b) no adjustment for height. Individual jumps, different subject for a and b.

When no adjustments were made in the jump trajectory (fig 6B), joint adjustments in the lower limb occurred primarily at the knee, and hip, and not at the ankle (Table 1).

TABLE 1
Range of Motion post-landing (1 subject) at different heights

	ANKLE	KNEE	HIP
35cm	49 ±4	59 ±3.8	27 ±4.7
45cm	50 ±1.4	63 ±2.1	31 ±3.1
55cm	48 ±2.2	69 ±3.7	43 ±9.5

When landing onto surfaces of differing compliance, changes were not significant at the hip or knee in the skilled individuals, but were significantly different at the ankle. We found that skilled jumpers made adjustments in ankle position so that the ankle was significantly more plantarflexed (amount of plantarflexion at normal stance being equivalent to 0°) when landing on a stiff surface (27 $\pm 3^o$ PF)than when landing on a compliant one (17 $\pm 3^o$ PF). This had the effect of increasing range of motion during the post-landing flexion when landing on the stiff surface (50 $\pm 3^o$) as compared to the compliant surface (38 ± 2°), and placing the body in a more stable position when landing on foam, as the weight upon impact was distributed more rapidly on the entire plantar surface of the foot by the more dorsiflexed position (10).

Thus it appears from the above comparisons that either takeoff or landing styles can be chosen independently of one another, and further, that modifications in the basic landing style can be made to adjust to varying external conditions. It is with this thought in mind that the question of when the landing component is planned is addressed. We have begun to explore this issue as explained below.

3.3 Planning and Execution of the Landing Component

Comparison of skilled and unskilled subjects. As described above, skilled jumpers made adjustments in the amount of plantarflexion at the ankle to adapt to the stiffness of the landing surface. In contrast, unskilled individuals did not alter the ankle angle or the range of motion for changes in compliance, but adopted an ankle angle for touchdown that was intermediate between the two angles used by the skilled subjects, being 23 $\pm 3^o$ and 21 ± 3° for stiff and compliant surfaces respectively (10). Thus unskilled subjects appeared to be unable to adapt the basic landing style to adjust for minor differences in landing requirements, but instead used an intermediate or 'default' angle that was the same for both surfaces.

Effects of takeoff surface compliance on landing adjustments. Adjustments in landing are presently being studied in well practiced subjects when both the takeoff and landing surfaces are altered. The same low memory foam (C) and metal surfaces (S) are used in four combinations: takeoff and landing surfaces similar (S-S, C-C) or different (S-C, C-S). Preliminary results (Bastien and McKinley, work in progress) indicate that in some individuals, ankle position at landing may be affected in some way by the takeoff surface. This effect was highly variable. For example, when the degree of plantarflexion at landing is expressed as a percent of the plantarflexed position for the S-S condition, the following values were observed for the three other conditions in one individual: S-C, 92%; C-S, 90%; C-C, 85%, while in another individual they were 60%, 42% and 19% respectively. Thus, while the ankle is indeed less plantarflexed when landing on a compliant surface, the diminution is even greater when taking off from a compliant surface (compare S-C to C-C). Also notable is the ankle position at landing under the C-S condition when compared to the other conditions. In the C-S condition, the amount of plantarflexion at landing is similar to the S-C condition rather than to the S-S condition. Thus it appears that the takeoff surface may have an effect on planning adjustments for the landing surface for some individuals.

4. DISCUSSION

Independence of the two landing programs. The comparison of landing from a jump when height is changed to that of landing when surface stiffness is altered yields two points that support the notion that the landing and takeoff phases are planned independently. One is the observation that the takeoff style chosen is independent of skill, compliance or height of the jump. Although comparisons have been made based on different groups of individuals in each paradigm, recently we have had the opportunity to observe the same well-practiced individuals in both changing height and changing compliance paradigms, and the type of takeoff style is subject specific regardless of whether they are jumping from different heights or onto different surfaces (McKinley and Bastien, personal observations). The second is the observation that the landing program, while maintaining an overall style, is adjusted to fit the needs of the task. We have postulated that these adjustments are specifically related to the forces experienced at landing (10). For example, when landing surface compliance is changed, initial impact forces are different, while momentum is similar. In contrast, when landing from jumps of different heights, initial impact forces are similar while momentum is different. Thus the adjustments observed at the ankle for surfaces of differing compliance (changes in range of motion, and EMG onset) as compared to adjustments observed at the knee when landing from different heights (changes in range of motion and RF activity but no change in EMG onset) may reflect this difference. The two different kinematic patterns observed during the descending part of flight in children while holding takeoff kinematics constant, suggests further that these two aspects may be planned independently of one another.

The question arises, given the relative independence of the two phases of the jumps down, as to whether the adjustments for surface compliance are planned in advance of the entire movement, during completion of the takeoff phase, or during execution of the landing phase. Previous observations that onset of prelanding EMG is triggered by visual cues (cf 5 for review) would lend support to the idea that the landing component of the motor program was initiated during the movement rather than prior to its onset. The shift in onset demonstrated with a compliant surface may indicate a different trigger setting based on expected changes in ground reaction forces, stability and plantar proprioceptors at landing. The observations that the takeoff surface may have an effect on planning ankle adjustments for the landing surface may be an indication that the planning of the landing program occurs or at least is affected by execution of the takeoff phase. This carry-over effect of the last surface experienced has also been reported in the planning for grasp of objects of varying roughness (15). Additionally, the default kinematic program demonstrated by unskilled subjects is a strategy that has been attributed to incomplete specification prior to movement onset (16-17). Thus the observation that skilled subjects make adjustments for surface compliance during flight may be indicative of an ability to update or adjust the kinematic and muscle parameters rather than to plan the sequence at this time. This mechanism has been proposed as a way in which subjects improve accuracy in force amplitude during reaction time tasks (15). However, it is not clear when, during the jump, specifications for the landing component are completed. As adjustments for landing surface are influenced by the takeoff surface it may be that specifications are completed during the execution of the takeoff phase.

5. **CONCLUSIONS** In summary, it is suggested that the takeoff and landing components of the jumpdown task are independent programs that are assembled to meet varying requirements of the environment such as surface compliance or height. It is further suggested that the landing component is incompletely specified prior to movement initiation but may be completed during the takeoff phase of the jump.

6. REFERENCES

1 V. Dietz, and J.Noth, Brain Res., 142 (1978) 576-579
2 P.A. McKinley and J.L. Smith, Exp. Brain Res. 52 (1983) 483-495
3 P. Dyre-Poulsen and A.M. Laursen, J. Physiol., 350 (1984) 121-136
4 H. Thompson and P. McKinley, Soc Neurosci. Absts. 14 (1988) 66
5 P.A. McKinley, J.L. Smith and R. Gregor, Exp Brain Res., 49 (1983) 218-228
6 P. Dyre-Poulsen, E.B. Sinonsen and M. Voigt, J. Physiol., (in press)
7 L. Pelland, and P. McKinley, Soc Neurosci Absts. 14 (1988) 65
8 L. Pelland, P.McKinley and A. Beuter in Disorders of Posture and Gait (1990) (Eds T Brandt, W Paulus, W Bles. M. Dieterich, S. Krafczyk, A. Struabe), Georg Thieme, Verlag, New York, 249-252
9 M. Bastien and P. McKinley, Soc Neurosci Absts 14 (1988) 66
10 P. A. McKinley and A. Pedotti, Exp Brain Res (in review)
11 G. Melville-Jones and D.G.D. Watt, J. Physiol., 219 (1971) 729-737
12 R. Greenwood and A. Hopkins, Brain, 99 (1976) 375-386
13 D. Lee, in Tutorials in Motor Behavior (1980) G.E. Stelmach and J. Requin, (eds), North Holland, p281-295
14 R.L. Craik, B.A. Cozzens and W. Freedman, Exp Brain Res., 45 (1982) 399-409
15 G. Westling and R.S. Johannsen, Exp. Brain Res., 53 (1984) 277
16 W. Hening, D. Vicario and C. Ghez, Exp Brain Res., 71 (1988a) 103-115
17 W. Hening, M. Favilla and C. Ghez, Exp Brain Res., 71 (1988b) 116-128

SECTION 7

FEATURE CODING AND SELECTIVE ACTIVATION

Tutorials in Motor Behavior II
G.E. Stelmach and J. Requin (Editors)

Salient-Features Coding in Response Selection

Robert W. Proctor[a], T. Gilmour Reeve[b], and Trisha Van Zandt[a]

[a]Psychology Department, Purdue University, 1364 Psychology Building Room 3150, West Lafayette, IN 47907-1364

[b]Motor Behavior Center, Auburn University, Auburn, AL 36849-5323

Abstract

Salient-features coding has been proposed to account for a wide variety of response-selection phenomena. This chapter discusses the evidence for such coding in choice-reaction tasks. It then provides coding accounts for phenomena that have been attributed to motoric processes or to direct perceptual-motor interactions. Finally, the salient-features perspective is placed within the context of alternative models of response selection. Our general conclusion is that salient-features coding is fundamental to performance in both laboratory settings and "real-world" environments.

There is no doubt that the bee constructs a model of the spatial location of the food source, and is able to transmit the salient features of this model to her fellow workers.

-- P. N. Johnson-Laird, 1983

Communication of information between an organism and its environment requires that relevant environmental stimuli be coded in a manner that allows efficient translation into appropriate responses. This coding may be based on those features of the environment that are perceptually salient -- a possibility acknowledged by many authors. For example, Miller (1982) interpreted choice reactions to visual stimuli as indicating that a hierarchical decision tree is used to select the response to a given stimulus. According to Miller, "the most natural choice for a decision node at the highest level is the most salient stimulus characteristic" (p. 284). Similarly, Gordon (1990) attributed results obtained in a speech-production task to "differences in the perceptual salience of phonetic features" (p. 356). Despite such acknowledgments of the importance of saliency, the concept of salient-features coding has not received much attention in studies of human performance.

What is a salient feature? There is a potential problem of circularity in the definition of such a feature. That is, if certain features are more salient than others, performance should be best when responses are based on these features; if performance is best in the presence of these features, then they are salient. Circularity can be minimized by designing experiments in consideration of known principles. As long as there is independent evidence to indicate that one feature is more salient than another, predictions can be derived for specific stimulus-response (S-R) assignments from the concept of salient-features coding. Even if the concept is used to provide an ad hoc interpretation of results, converging evidence can be generated by testing additional implications of the interpretation. Thus, it is possible to circumvent the problem of circularity.

By adhering to these requirements, we have obtained evidence a fortiori that the relative efficiency of response selection within a variety of choice-reaction tasks can be attributed to salient-features coding of both the stimulus and response sets. The present chapter summarizes this evidence, extends salient-features coding to a variety of phenomena, and compares the account to alternative explanations of response-selection efficiency.

1. SALIENT-FEATURES CODING

Three processing stages are needed to characterize performance in choice-reaction tasks (e.g., Hasbroucq, Guiard, & Ottomani, 1990; Miller, 1982; Proctor, Reeve, & Weeks, 1990). These stages are labeled differently by different researchers, but reflect processes that are influenced by stimulus properties, S-R relations, and response properties, respectively (see Figure 1). The intermediate stage, often called S-R translation or response selection, is presumed to involve mediating processes that determine the response to make to a stimulus. These processes are thought to operate on coded representations of the stimulus and response sets (see, e.g., Proctor & Reeve, 1990). The contribution of the translation stage to reaction time (RT) is greater when a direct physical or conceptual correspondence between stimuli and responses is lacking (e.g., Alluisi & Warm, 1990). In other words, additional processing is needed to determine which response to make to a stimulus when the S-R relations are relatively arbitrary.

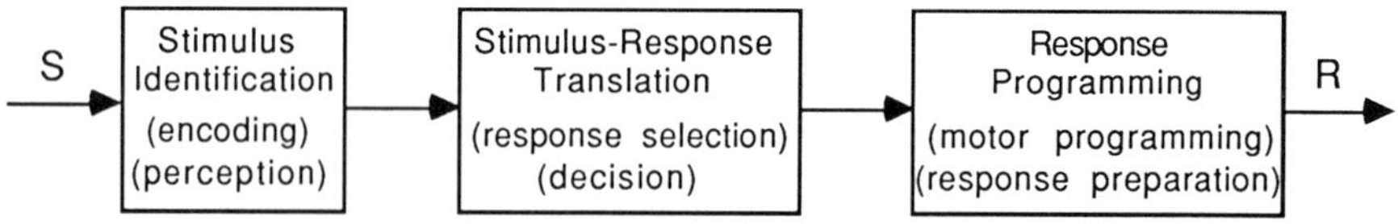

Figure 1. The three-stage model of human information processing in choice-reaction tasks.

Figure 2. Compatible (a) and incompatible (b) mappings of stimuli to responses in the two-choice spatial-compatibility task.

The nature of the codes used in the translation stage has been investigated in studies of S-R compatibility. In such studies, either different combinations of stimulus and response sets (e.g., Fitts & Seeger, 1953) or different assignments of stimuli to responses (e.g., Fitts & Deininger, 1954) are examined. For "spatial-location" stimuli and responses, defined by their respective positions, RTs are fastest when the stimulus locations correspond directly to the response locations, regardless of how the response is effected (e.g., Brebner, Shephard, & Cairney, 1972). For example, in a two-choice task (see Figure 2), responses are faster when left and right responses are made to left and right stimuli, respectively, than when the assignment is reversed. Such performance differences have been interpreted by many authors as indicating that the translation stage operates on spatial codes (e.g., Heister, Schroeder-Heister, & Ehrenstein, 1990; Umilta & Nicoletti, 1990). We have investigated such coding processes in more detail using four-choice spatial-precuing tasks, and have extended coding interpretations to nonspatial stimulus sets in four-choice symbolic-cuing tasks.

In the spatial-precuing task, stimulus displays consist of four stimulus locations assigned to four response locations. For the standard version of the task, both stimuli and responses are arranged in horizontal rows (see Figure 3a). On each trial, a warning signal of stimuli in all four locations is presented, followed by a precue row that most often includes stimuli in only two of the four locations. Following a variable interval, a target occurs in one of the two cued locations, and the subject is to execute the corresponding response as quickly as possible.

This task shows evidence for spatial coding much like that obtained in the two-choice compatibility tasks. With a normal, adjacent-hand placement (see Figure 4a), responses are fastest when the two left or two right locations are cued and slowest when either pair of alternate locations is cued (Miller, 1982; Reeve & Proctor, 1984). Coding based on anatomical features can be ruled out, because the same pattern of RTs is obtained when the specific fingers

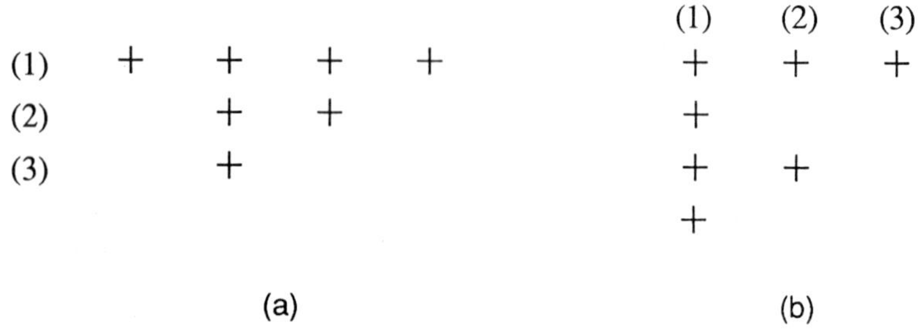

Figure 3. Examples of displays from horizontal (a) and vertical (b) spatial-precuing tasks. The warning (1) indicates all four locations, the precue (2) two locations, and the target (3) a single location.

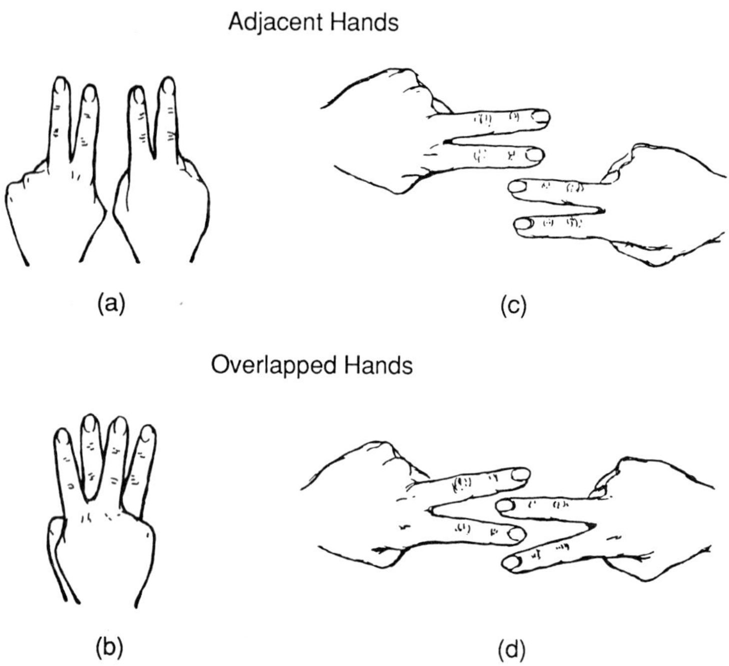

Figure 4. Adjacent (a and c) and overlapped (b and d) hand placements for the horizontal and vertical spatial-precuing tasks.

are dissociated from the response locations by using an overlapped-hand placement (see Figure 4b), for which the fingers from the two hands are alternated (Proctor & Reeve, 1988; Reeve & Proctor, 1984). A similar benefit for precuing either the two top or two bottom locations is obtained when the stimulus and response sets are oriented vertically (see Figures 3b and 4c and 4d; Proctor & Reeve, 1986).

Our interpretation is that the pattern of differential precuing benefits is due to the codes used in the translation stage. Among the findings that implicate a locus in this stage is that the pattern of differential precuing benefits attenuates (e.g., the precuing benefits for all pairs become more equal) as the interval between the precue and target increases (e.g., Reeve & Proctor, 1984). The pattern also attenuates as subjects become practiced (e.g., Proctor & Reeve, 1988). The codes used in the spatial-precuing task appear to be based on positions relative to the centers of the stimulus and response arrangements. With the horizontal arrangements, this coding is in terms of the two locations to the left or right of center. Subjects can translate between the precue stimuli and responses faster when the precue is consistent with the relative-location coding than when it is not. These translations do not depend on similar orientations of the stimulus and response sets. When the sets are oriented orthogonally (e.g., the stimulus display is vertical, as in Figure 3b, and the response arrangement horizontal, as in Figure 4a and b), the same pattern of precuing benefits is obtained (Reeve, Proctor, Weeks, & Dornier, 1991a).

While spatial location can be used to code the stimulus set, so can other stimulus features. For example, in the symbolic-cuing task, four responses at distinct spatial locations are used as in the spatial-precuing task. However, symbolic stimuli constructed from two features, such as letter identity and size, are presented in a central location, and the assignment of the features to responses is manipulated. The important characteristic of the stimuli is that one of the two features is more salient than the other. For example, Proctor and Reeve (1985) provided independent evidence that letter identity was more salient than size for the stimulus set O, o, z, Z, by demonstrating that identity could be discriminated faster than size. Responses in the four-choice task were faster when the assignment of stimuli to responses matched the salient letter-identity feature to the salient left-right spatial feature of the response arrangement (e.g., a left-to-right assignment of O, o, z, Z) than when it did not (e.g., a left-to-right assignment of O, z, o, Z). Thus, performance benefited from a correspondence between the most salient nonspatial feature of the stimulus set with the most salient spatial feature of the response set.

Just as stimulus features can be nonspatial, so can response features. For example, coding based on anatomical distinctions is used in some circumstances. When the hands are overlapped for the symbolic-cuing task (see Figure 4b), RTs for assignments in which letter identity distinguishes the alternate locations (e.g., O, z, o, Z) become equivalent to those in which identity distinguishes the two left and two right locations (e.g., O, o, z, Z; Proctor & Reeve, 1985). This result suggests that subjects code stimuli and responses by the correspondence between letter identity and the hand distinction for the alternate-location assignment. Similar evidence suggesting hand coding is apparent in the vertical version of the spatial-precuing task. The precuing advantage for the two top and two bottom locations is accentuated when the distinction between the left and right hands coincides with the salient spatial distinction (see Figure 4c; Proctor & Reeve, 1986). Apparently, turning the hands inward increases the salience of the hand distinction in the spatial-precuing task.

These and other findings are consistent with what we believe to be a fundamental principle of S-R translation. This principle is that subjects code stimulus and response sets in terms of the salient features of each; translation is faster when the salient features correspond than when they do not. The *salient-features coding principle* emphasizes that compatibility and precuing effects reflect general translation processes and not specific stimulus and response properties. The primary determinants of coding are the structures inherent in the stimulus and response sets, and the extent to which those structures correspond.

2. EXTENSIONS OF SALIENT-FEATURES CODING

Our recent work has taken three approaches. First, we have embedded the salient-features view of translation within a skill-acquisition framework (Proctor et al., 1990). Specifically, we have systematically examined practice effects with the spatial-precuing and symbolic-cuing tasks. These effects are consistent with the phases of skill acquisition originally proposed by Fitts (1964) and extended by Anderson (1983). The differences in RTs between the respective cues and assignments in the two tasks apparently reflect an initial "cognitive" phase of skill acquisition. These differences attenuate as subjects become practiced and enter a second "associative" phase (Proctor & Reeve, 1988; Proctor, Reeve, Weeks, Dornier, & Van Zandt, 1991). This attenuation is consistent with the taxonomy's implication that the role of the translation stage should decrease as performance becomes more proceduralized.

The benefits of practice are retained relatively well for a period of a week. That is, the initial differences in RT do not reappear. However, the benefits of practice do not transfer well to new task variations. We have interpreted such benefits as reflecting a shift from general, translation-based processes to task-specific procedures that directly specify the appropriate response to a stimulus. When some aspect of the stimulus or response set is changed for the new task variation, performance typically reverts to the cognitive phase that relies on codes to translate between the stimuli and responses.

Our second approach has dealt with the flexibility of salience. Perceptual grouping manipulations that affect the salience of various subsets of locations in the spatial-precuing task have been shown to alter systematically the pattern of differential precuing benefits (Reeve, Proctor, Weeks, & Dornier, 1991b). Those subsets congruent with the grouping distinction benefit from this congruence. For example, when pairs of locations are grouped by spatial proximity (see Figure 5), the precuing benefits are greatest for those precues that are consistent with the grouping. It also is possible to increase the salience of the alternate locations by having subjects practice the spatial-precuing task with only the alternate-location precues (Proctor et al., 1991). When transferred to the symbolic-cuing task, subjects appear to code the stimulus and response sets through the relation of the salient letter-identity feature to the alternate locations. That is, responses are no slower with the O, z, o, Z type of assignment

Figure 5. Displays for which proximity groups the two left and two right locations (a) and two inner and two outer locations (b).

than with the usually superior O, o, z, Z type, for which letter identity distinguishes the two left and two right locations. Exposure to only alternate-location precues during practice thus makes those pairs of locations more distinct than they would have been otherwise.

Our third approach has extended the principle of salient-features coding by reinterpreting effects in related tasks that formerly were attributed to processes other than S-R translation (Proctor & Reeve, 1991). In movement-precuing tasks, parameters of arm movements (arm, direction, extent) are precued in advance of a target signal (Rosenbaum, 1983). The effects obtained in such tasks typically have been attributed to the motor system. However, since the work of Goodman and Kelso (1980), it has been known that differential movement-precuing benefits may be due to translation processes, rather than to motor processes, if the relation between stimuli and responses is indirect. Larish and Frekany (1985) assumed that translation processes would not be a factor if stimulus locations were directly assigned to response locations. In such a situation, they found that subjects were faster at responding when direction rather than arm was precued. Based on the assumption that translation was equivalent for the two precue conditions, they attributed the difference in RT to the programming of movement parameters. Specifically, Larish and Frekany argued that direction must be programmed before arm.

Yet, our evidence from the spatial-precuing task indicates that translation processes can be the source of differential precuing benefits even when stimulus locations are directly assigned to response locations (Reeve & Proctor, 1984). In Larish and Frekany's (1985) study, the arm parameter was signaled by stimuli in left or right locations, while the direction parameter was signaled by stimuli in above or below locations. Dornier and Reeve (1990) removed this confound of relative locations, using four response targets aligned in a horizontal row, and found no difference for precuing arm or direction. Thus, the effects that Larish and Frekany observed are probably due to translation processes rather than motor processes.

The motor system has also been implicated for spatial compatibility effects where stimuli and responses are oriented orthogonally. Bauer and Miller (1982) examined two-choice tasks in which the stimuli differed in location along a spatial axis (e.g., vertical) that was orthogonal to the axis along which the response locations differed (e.g., horizontal). They obtained a compatibility effect for the assignment of stimulus locations to response locations, which they interpreted in terms of the motor system. Weeks and Proctor (1990) examined a variety of such situations and found that responses were faster for the above-right/below-left assignment than for the reverse assignment, regardless of whether the stimuli were physical locations or symbolic arrows, and of whether the left-right responses were aimed finger movements, keypresses or vocal utterances. This compatibility effect for orthogonal stimulus dimensions seems to be based on known asymmetries in the coding of above-below and left-right (Chase & Clark, 1971; Olson & Laxar, 1973). When the salient "above" and "right" polar referents of the respective dimensions correspond, translation is faster than when they do not. Thus, the orthogonal effects again seem to be based in translation processes and not motor processes.

Salient-features coding also is the basis for compatibility effects that have been attributed to direct perceptual-motor interactions. Michaels (1988) had subjects respond to the destination of an apparently moving target stimulus. Responses were faster at the destination location than at the opposite location. Michaels attributed this destination compatibility effect to a direct perception of "catchableness" specified by the changing optical pattern. Proctor, Van Zandt, Lu, and Weeks (1991) have demonstrated that the effect is more parsimoniously explained by a coding account in which direction of motion serves as a salient feature that designates location. Because the destination compatibility effect occurs for a variety of display and response situations, in which "left" and "right" are specified through changes other than optical expansion, the catching-affordance notion is too specific. Ad hoc affordances would have to be postulated to explain the range of destination compatibility effects observed, and it is not clear that an affordance interpretation could be extended to other compatibility effects.

Finally, a compatibility effect for speech stimuli reported by Gordon and Meyer (1984) can be explained in a similar manner. They found that responding was faster when a speech stimulus shared a voicing feature with a speech response (e.g., PUH and TUH are both unvoiced) than when it did not (e.g., PUH is unvoiced DUH is voiced). Gordon (1990) interpreted this speech compatibility effect in terms of direct activation of motor features by speech features. However, Proctor, Weeks, and Kelly (1991) have shown that similar results are obtained as a function of the salient-feature relations. Such effects have been observed when the speech stimuli are assigned to keypress responses, when spatial-location stimuli are assigned to the speech responses, and when two-dimensional symbolic stimuli presented visually are assigned to the speech responses. In other words, the speech-compatibility effect does not reflect any special relation between the stimuli and responses. Thus, the effect is consistent with predictions of the salient-features coding account.

3. RELATION TO OTHER VIEWS

A wide range of S-R compatibility and related effects can be attributed to the use of salient-features coding in the translation stage. However, several alternative explanations for S-R compatibility have been proposed. Most contemporary theories can be placed into two categories. One category emphasizes cognitive coding, whereas the other emphasizes automatic orientation of attention or activation of responses. The salient-features view is a member of the first category. Other coding accounts include ones proposed by Umilta and Nicoletti (1990), Heister, Schroeder-Heister, and Ehrenstein (1990), and Ladavas (1990).

Coding theorists have focused primarily on spatial-compatibility effects in two-choice tasks. They have demonstrated that the basis for coding varies systematically with the task environment and is not a function of absolute physical location. For example, both relative location and egocentric location (i.e., position relative to the body midline) of stimuli have been shown to provide bases for spatial coding (Umilta & Liotti, 1987). It also has been demonstrated that in certain situations the response set can be coded in terms of anatomical distinctions (e.g., Ladavas & Moscovitch, 1984). The consistent theme that emerges from these investigations of two-choice tasks is that coding is hierarchical but flexible.

Our work has extended these issues of coding to more complex four-choice tasks and to nonspatial stimulus and response sets. Our findings are in agreement with the view of coding derived from two-choice tasks and indicate more generally the factors involved in S-R compatibility. The crux of the salient-features coding principle is that the specific characteristics of the stimulus and response sets are not important in determining when compatibility effects will occur. Rather, it is the structural relationship between the salient features of the sets that determines performance.

Accounts from the second category, which are distinguished by automatic response tendencies, have been developed primarily to explain the Simon effect. This effect refers to responses being faster if they are executed on the side to which the stimulus is presented and the stimulus location is irrelevant to the task (see Simon, 1990, for a review). Simon initially speculated that this effect arose from an innate tendency to orient in the direction of stimulation. Verfaellie, Bowers, and Heilman (1990) have modified this explanation to account for the finding that the Simon effect occurs when both stimuli are in the same hemispace (Umilta & Nicoletti, 1985); they link the effect to patterns of hemispheric activation induced by response preparation. The automatic-activation hypotheses for the Simon effect have been proposed primarily because there is no obvious reason why the irrelevant dimension of stimulus location would be attended and coded. However, it should be noted that Wallace's (1971, 1972) initial work on spatial coding was conducted with the Simon effect; thus, coding accounts may be applicable to the Simon effect.

Kornblum, Hasbroucq, and Osman (1990) recently proposed a detailed automatic-activation model intended to explain not only the Simon effect but also other S-R compatibility effects. Kornblum et al. suggest that overlap between stimulus and response dimensions determines the degree to which responses will be activated and, hence, the speed with which they can be executed. When the activated response is also appropriate, responding is facilitated relative to when it is not appropriate. The purpose of this assumption is to allow classification of the Simon effect along with other S-R compatibility phenomena. However, the connection between the Simon effect and compatibility effects in general is not well understood. For example, Hasbroucq and Guiard (1991) have reported evidence that the Simon effect is a function of stimulus congruity (i.e., the relation between the relevant and irrelevant stimulus dimensions), rather than of direct translation between stimulus and response locations.

Although the automatic-activation model was proposed as an explanation of all S-R compatibility effects, Hasbroucq, Guiard, and Ottomani (1990) stress that if the Simon effect is removed from consideration, the concept of automatic activation does not seem to be necessary to explain S-R compatibility.

In agreement with the coding types of explanations, Hasbroucq et al. (1990) have proposed instead that translation processes are best characterized as being rule-based. A similar explanation has been developed by Rosenbloom and Newell (1987). According to this view, responding will be faster if a rule for translating stimuli to responses exists than if one does not. The view has its basis in studies by Morin and Grant (1955) and Duncan (1977a, 1977b) showing that responses are fast when a perfect negative correlation exists between linearly arranged stimulus and response locations. The basic idea is that when such a correlation is present, a single rule can be applied to determine the response to a given stimulus. This is in contrast to situations in which no correlation exists, for which multiple rules must be invoked or search through a list of individual mappings performed.

The rule-based view of translation processes complements our emphasis on salient-features coding. Specifically, translation is most efficient when the salient features of the stimulus and response sets are assigned in such a way that some aspect of the stimulus set is preserved in the structure of the response set. This efficiency likely is due to the application of rules based on the features deemed most salient. The emphasis on the relation between features of the stimulus and response sets is similar to the concept of dimensional overlap proposed by Kornblum et al. (1990). According to them, dimensional overlap is determined not only by the extent to which the mapping preserves the structure of the sets, but also by the similarity of the specific dimensions that define the sets.

It is the similarity between dimensions that determines the extent of automatic activation in Kornblum et al.'s (1990) model. If the Simon effect is distinct from S-R compatibility, as Hasbroucq and Guiard (1991) have argued, and, consequently, automatic activation is not involved in compatibility effects, then similarity of dimensions is no longer relevant. With similarity removed, the definition of dimensional overlap now becomes equivalent to our emphasis on structural correspondence based on salient features, independent of the specific dimensions involved. In short, the view of translation processes that emerges from our research treats translation as based on rules derived from the structural relations between the stimulus and response sets.

4. CONCLUSIONS

We are proposing salient-features coding as a general principle that applies to virtually any response-selection task, at least for situations in which the responses to the stimuli are not highly overlearned. Because such situations have been so prevalent in research on human performance and motor control, salient-features coding must be a significant factor in many experimental tasks. Moreover, there is some evidence to suggest that translation-based coding remains an important determinant of RT for practiced subjects on at least some tasks (Gopher,

Karis, & Koenig, 1985), although we have not interpreted our data from the spatial-precuing and symbolic-cuing tasks in this manner. Therefore, in any task where it is presumed that response selection requires a translation to intervene between stimuli and responses, it is necessary to consider the influence of salient features before attributing performance differences to other factors.

There is evidence to suggest that the importance of salient-features coding extends far beyond the laboratory. Lynch's (1960) influential notion concerning the "imageability" of a city was based on two premises (Holahan & Sorensen, 1985). He proposed that high imageability occurs when the city has salient and organized features. Holahan and Sorensen extended Lynch's conception in an experimental study and showed that salience aids imageability when the map of a city is organized but hinders imageability when the map is disorganized. These and related findings have led Gifford (1987) to conclude that, "apparently, salient features can enhance the cognition of settings..." (p. 38). Thus, as reflected in Johnson-Laird's quote with which this chapter began, there is every reason to believe that salient-features coding is fundamental to performance in "real world" environments.

5. REFERENCES

Alluisi, E. A., & Warm, J. S. (1990). Things that go together: A review of stimulus-response compatibility and related effects. In R. W. Proctor & T. G. Reeve (Eds.), *Stimulus-response compatibility: An integrated perspective* (pp. 3-30). Amsterdam: North-Holland.

Anderson, J. R. (1983). *The architecture of cognition.* Cambridge, MA: Harvard University Press.

Bauer, D. W., & Miller, J. (1982). Stimulus-response compatibility and the motor system. *Quarterly Journal of Experimental Psychology, 34A*, 367-380.

Brebner, J., Shephard, M., & Cairney, P. T. (1972). Spatial relationships and S-R compatibility. *Acta Psychologica, 36*, 1-15.

Chase, W. G., & Clark, H. H. (1971). Semantics in the perception of verticality. *British Journal of Psychology, 63*, 311-326.

Dornier, L. A., & Reeve, T. G. (1990). Evaluation of compatibility effects in the precuing of arm and direction parameters. *Research Quarterly for Exercise and Sport, 61*, 37-49.

Duncan, J. (1977a). Response selection errors in spatial choice reaction tasks. *Quarterly Journal of Experimental Psychology, 29*, 415-423.

Duncan, J. (1977b). Response selection rules in spatial choice reaction tasks. In S. Dornic (Ed.), *Attention and performance VI* (pp. 49-61). Hillsdale, NJ: Erlbaum.

Fitts, P. M. (1964). Perceptual-motor skill learning. In A. W. Melton (Ed.), *Categories of human learning* (pp. 243-285). New York: Academic Press.

Fitts, P. M., & Deininger, R. L. (1954). S-R compatibility: Correspondence among paired elements within stimulus and response codes. *Journal of Experimental Psychology, 48*, 483-492.

Fitts, P. M., & Seeger, C. M. (1953). S-R compatibility: Spatial characteristics of stimulus and response codes. *Journal of Experimental Psychology, 46*, 199-210.

Gifford, R. (1987). *Environmental psychology: Principles and practice.* Boston: Allyn and Bacon.

Goodman, D., & Kelso, J. A. S. (1980). Are movements prepared in parts? Not under compatible (nautralized) conditions. *Journal of Experimental Psychology: General, 109*, 475-495.

Gopher, D., Karis, D., & Koenig, W. (1985). The representation of movement schemas in long-term memory: Lessons from the acquisition of a transcription skill. *Acta Psychologica, 60*, 105-134.

Gordon, P. C. (1990). Perceptual-motor processing in speech. In R. W. Proctor & T. G. Reeve (Eds.), *Stimulus-response compatibility: An integrated perspective* (pp. 343-362). Amsterdam: North-Holland.

Gordon, P. C., & Meyer, D. E. (1984). Perceptual-motor processing of phonetic features in speech. *Journal of Experimental Psychology: Human Perception and Performance, 10*, 153-178.

Hasbroucq, T., & Guiard, Y. (1991). Stimulus-response compatibility and the Simon effect: Towards a conceptual clarification. *Journal of Experimental Psychology: Human Perception and Performance, 17*, 246-266.

Hasbroucq, T., Guiard, Y., & Ottomani, L. (1990). Principles of response determination: The list-rule model of S-R compatibility. *Bulletin of the Psychonomic Society, 28*, 327-330.

Heister, G., Schroeder-Heister, P., & Ehrenstein, W. H. (1990). Spatial coding and spatio-anatomical mapping: Evidence for a hierarchical model of spatial stimulus-response compatibility. In R. W. Proctor & T. G. Reeve (Eds.), *Stimulus-response compatibility: An integrated perspective* (pp. 117-143). Amsterdam: North-Holland.

Holahan, C. J., & Sorensen, P. F. (1985). The role of figural organization in city imageability: An information processing analysis. *Journal of Environmental Psychology, 5*, 279-286.

Johnson-Laird, P. N. (1983). *Mental models*. Cambridge, MA: Harvard University Press.

Kornblum, S., Hasbroucq, T., & Osman, A. (1990). Dimensional overlap: Cognitive basis for stimulus-response compatibility. *Psychological Review, 97*, 253-270.

Ladavas, E. (1990). Some aspects of spatial stimulus-response compatibility in adults and normal children. In R. W. Proctor & T. G. Reeve (Eds), *Stimulus-response compatibility: An integrated perspective* (pp. 145-162). Amsterdam: North-Holland.

Ladavas, E., & Moscovitch, M. (1984). Must egocentric and environmental frames of reference be aligned to produce spatial S-R compatibility effects? *Journal of Experimental Psychology: Human Perception and Performance, 10*, 205-215.

Larish, D. D., & Frekany, G. A. (1985). Planning and preparing expected and unexpected movements: Reexamining the relationships of arm, direction, and extent of movement. *Journal of Motor Behavior, 17*, 168-189.

Lynch, R. (1960). *The image of the city*. Cambridge, MA: MIT Press.

Michaels, C. F. (1988). S-R compatibility between response position and destination of apparent motion: Evidence of the detection of affordances. *Journal of Experimental Psychology: Human Perception and Performance, 14*, 231-240.

Miller, J. (1982). Discrete versus continuous stage models of human information processing: In search of partial output. *Journal of Experimental Psychology: Human Perception and Performance, 8*, 273-296.

Morin, R. E., & Grant, D. A. (1955). Learning and performance of a key-pressing task as a function of the degree of spatial stimulus-response correspondence. *Journal of Experimental Psychology, 49*, 39-47.

Olson, G. M., & Laxar, K. (1973). Asymmetries in processing the terms 'right' and 'left'. *Journal of Experimental Psychology, 100*, 284-290.

Proctor, R. W. & Reeve, T. G. (1985). Compatibility effects in the assignment of symbolic stimuli to discrete finger resonses. *Journal of Experimental Psychology: Human Perception and Performance, 11*, 623-639.

Proctor, R. W., & Reeve, T. G. (1986). Salient-feature coding operations in spatial precuing tasks. *Journal of Experimental Psychology: Human Perception and Performance, 12*, 277-285.

Proctor, R. W., & Reeve, T. G. (1988). The acquisition of task-specific productions and modification of declarative representations in spatial-precuing tasks. *Journal of Experimental Psychology: General, 117*, 182-196.

Proctor, R. W., & Reeve, T. G. (Eds.) (1990). *Stimulus-response compatibility: An integrated perspective.* Amsterdam: North-Holland.

Proctor, R. W., & Reeve, T. G. (1991). The prevalence of salient-features coding in choice-reaction tasks. In J. Requin & G. Stelmach (Eds.), *Tutorials in motor neuroscience.* Dortrecht: Kluwer.

Proctor, R. W., Reeve, T. G., & Weeks, D. J. (1990). A triphasic approach to the acquisition of response-selection skill. In G. H. Bower (Ed.), *The psychology of learning and motivation* (Vol. 26, pp. 207-240). San Diego, CA: Academic Press.

Proctor, R. W., Reeve, T. G., Weeks, D. J., Dornier, L. A., & Van Zandt, T. (1991). Acquisition, retention, and transfer of response selection skill in choice-reaction tasks. *Journal of Experimental Psychology: Learning, Memory, and Cognition, 17*, 497-506.

Proctor, R. W., Van Zandt, T., Lu, C.-H., & Weeks, D. J. (1991). *Stimulus-response compatibility for destination of apparent motion: Catching affordances or directional coding?* Manuscript submitted for publication.

Proctor, R. W., Weeks, D. J., & Kelly, P. (1991). *Performance with consonant-vowel and spatial-location stimulus and response sets: A salient-features account.* Manuscript in preparation.

Reeve, T. G., & Proctor, R. W. (1984). On the advance preparation of discrete finger responses. *Journal of Experimental Psychology: Human Perception and Performance, 10*, 541-553.

Reeve, T. G., Proctor, R. W., Weeks, D. J., & Dornier, L. (1991a). *Correspondence between stimulus and response set orientations in spatial-precuing tasks.* Manuscript in preparation.

Reeve, T. G., Proctor, R. W., Weeks, D. J., & Dornier, L. (1991b). *Manipulating the salience of stimulus and response features in choice-reaction tasks.* Manuscript in preparation.

Rosenbaum, D. A. (1983). The movement precuing technique: Assumptions, applications, and extensions. In R. A. Magill (Ed.), *Memory and control of action* (pp. 231-274). Amsterdam: North-Holland.

Rosenbloom, P. S., & Newell, A. (1987). An integraded computational model of stimulus-response compatibility and practice. In G. H. Bower (Ed.), *The psychology of learning and motivation* (Vol. 21, pp. 1-52). San Diego, CA: Academic Press.

Simon, J. R. (1990). The effects of an irrelevant direction cue on human information processing. In R. W. Proctor & T. G. Reeve (Eds.), *Stimulus-response compatibility: An integrated perspective* (pp. 31-86). Amsterdam: North-Holland.

Umilta, C., & Liotti, M. (1987). Egocentric and relative spatial codes in S-R compatibility. *Psychological Research, 49*, 81-90.

Umilta, C., & Nicoletti, R. (1985). Attention and coding effects in S-R compatibility due to irrelevant spatial cues. In M. I. Posner & O. S. M. Marin (Eds.), *Attention and performance XI* (pp. 457-471). Hillsdale, NJ: Erlbaum.

Umilta, C., & Nicoletti, R. (1990). Spatial stimulus-response compatibility. In R. W. Proctor & T. G. Reeve (Eds.), *Stimulus-response compatibility: An integrated perspective* (pp. 89-116). Amsterdam: North-Holland.

Verfaellie, M., Bowers, D., & Heilman, K. M. (1990). Attentional processes in spatial stimulus-response compatibility. In R. W. Proctor & T. G. Reeve (Eds.), *Stimulus-response compatibility: An integrated perspective* (pp. 261-275). Amsterdam: North-Holland.

Wallace, R. J. (1971). S-R compatibility and the idea of the response code. *Journal of Experimental Psychology, 88*, 354-360.

Wallace, R. J. (1972). Spatial S-R compatibility effects involving kinesthetic cues. *Journal of Experimental Psychology, 13*, 163-168.

Weeks, D. J., & Proctor, R. W. (1990). Salient-features coding in the translation between orthogonal stimulus and response dimensions. *Journal of Experimental Psychology: General, 119*, 355-366.

Tutorials in Motor Behavior II
G.E. Stelmach and J. Requin (Editors)
1992 Elsevier Science Publishers B.V.

DIMENSIONAL OVERLAP AND DIMENSIONAL RELEVANCE IN STIMULUS–RESPONSE AND STIMULUS-STIMULUS COMPATIBILITY

Sylvan Kornblum
Mental Health Research Institute
University of Michigan

Abstract. Stimulus response coding is treated in the framework of compatibility. A taxonomy is presented based on the dimensional overlap model (Kornblum et al., 1990) that includes eight different types of S-R ensembles. Some of the literature on human performance with these ensembles is reviewed and new data are presented.

1.0 Introduction

In this chapter the concept of compatibility is used to address some fundamental issues in stimulus-response coding. An attempt is made to show how the concept of compatibility can be used to organize the material on this topic, and how research on compatibility has generated experimental paradigms, theoretical models and data which, if they could all be made to fit together into a coherent whole, would give us a good grasp of what stimulus-response, and stimulus-stimulus coding is, and how it works. I start by considering the common-sense meaning of the term "compatibility".

Consider the three sets of lists shown in Table 1. I have labeled one set "compatible", the next set "compatible/incongruent" or "incompatible", and the third set "non-compatible". Consider the compatible set first. Here, the meaning is clear. The reason we call Lists A and B compatible is that the set of digits in List A, and the set of digit names in List B *correspond*; number is their common referent; they are similar in some sense. It is this commonality, correspondence, or similarity that makes us call these lists compatible. In the model that I will be presenting later, I call this correspondence the dimensional overlap between lists or sets. The lists are also compatible at a

---

This research was supported in part by grants from the National Institute of Mental Health, MH-43287, and the Office of Naval Research N-00014-87-J-1557. I thank Tony Whipple. Huazhong Zhang, Lindsay Oliver, and Eric Lauber for their contributions to various aspects of this work. Portions of this paper have appeared in *Tutorials in Motor Neuroscience*, J. Requin and G.E. Stelmach (eds.) Kluwer Academic Publishers: Dordrecht, The Netherlands, 1991. Portions were presented at the Annual meeting of the Psychonomic Society, November 1990, New Orleans, LA.
Address correspondence to: Sylvan Kornblum, Mental Health Research Institute, 205 Zina Pitcher Place, The University of Michigan, Ann Arbor, MI 48109. Electronic Mail address: Sylvan_Kornblum@um.cc.umich.edu

more detailed level. Suppose that we constructed pairs of items from these two lists by picking the first element from List A, and pairing it with the first element from List B, and so on. We would end up with a collection of four pairs in which digits were paired with their own names. This again would be a highly compatible combination, for the two members of each pair would share a common referent (i.e. the identical number) and have a high degree of correspondence. Thus, considered at the global level of the lists themselves, and at the local level of pairs constructed of elements from these lists, we have a highly compatible situation.

Consider the following set of lists next. These I have called "compatible/incongruent". The reason I call these lists "compatible/--" is that the lists themselves, except for the order of their elements, are identical to those in the previous example; i.e., List A consists of a set of digits and List B consists of a set of digit names. As was the case before, the two lists are compatible by virtue of their global commonality and correspondence. It is at the more detailed, element level that they clash. Suppose that we tried to construct pairs from these two lists in the same way that we did before, by picking the first element from List A and pairing it with the first element from List B. The

COMPATIBLE		COMPATIBLE/INCONGRUENT		NON-COMPATIBLE	
List A	List B	List A	List B	List A	List B
2	two	2	five	2	Steve
4	four	4	two	4	John
5	five	5	eight	5	Paul
8	eight	8	four	8	Frank

Table 1. Three sets of lists illustrating the different levels at which compatibility occurs.

result would be four pairs where one item was a digit and the other item a digit name, but instead of being its own name, it would be the name of another digit. The members of these pairs would, therefore, conflict and be incongruent. Thus, at the level of the lists themselves we have compatibility, but at the level of the individual item pairs we have incompatibility, which is why I have chosen the double label "compatible/incongruent". In the literature where the distinction between levels is often not made, these cases are frequently called "incompatible".

We now come to the third set of lists which I have labeled "non-compatible". Here we have two lists of items: List A consisting of digits, and List B consisting of boys' first names. One would be hard pressed to argue that these lists were similar, or had a common referent. There simply *is* no correspondence between them. Similarly, at the level of item pairs, whether one constructed the pairs by taking the first item from List A and the first item from List B, or whether one randomly chose one item from each list, the items in the resulting pairs would neither match, correspond, nor conflict. Compatibility is, therefore, not an appropriate or applicable attribute of these lists. I have labeled these lists "non-compatible".

A number of interesting properties become clear by these terminological distinctions. First, note that the term "compatibility" is applicable to both the set of lists, and to the individual item pairs. Second, unless compatibility exists at the list level, the issue of compatibility at the item level is moot. Third, whether at the list level, or at the individual item level, compatibility is a relational property that deals with the correspondence, similarity, or match between two or more entities. The consequences of compatibility at any level will, therefore, be observed as interactions between these entities.

In all that I have said so far I have deliberately avoided identifying any of the lists in my examples as either stimuli or responses. It is clear that by labeling them appropriately these examples are easily transformed into specific instances of either Stimulus-Stimulus (S-S), Stimulus-Response (S-R), or Response-Response (R-R) compatibility. In the next section I introduce the problem of S-R compatibility, and show how it fits into the general scheme that I have just outlined.

2.0 S-R Compatibility: The Origins

The problem of stimulus-response compatibility (SRC) was first identified

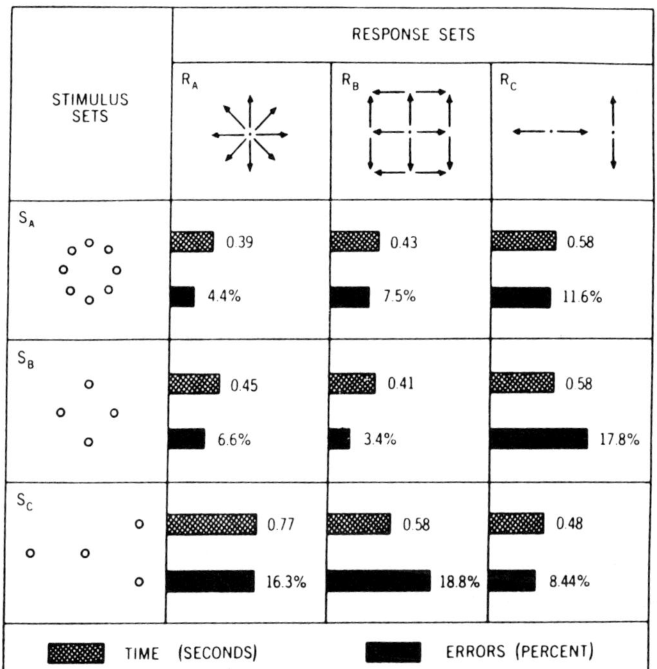

Figure 1. The three stimulus and three response sets, and thier combinations as S-R ensembles, that were used in Fitts and Seeger (1953) (adapted from Fitts and Seeger, 1953, in the public domain).

by Fitts in two classic articles (Fitts & Deininger, 1954, Fitts & Seeger, 1953). In the first (Fitts & Seeger, 1953), Fitts reports the results of an experiment in which he combined three different sets of spatially arranged stimuli with three different sets of spatially arranged responses to form nine different stimulus-response combinations.

The stimuli consisted of neon lights arranged in three different patterns, and the responses consisted of moving a stylus in the manner indicated by the arrows (see Figure 1). Think of these sets of stimuli and responses as the equivalent of the lists in our previous example. The cells in the resulting 3 x 3 matrix represent combinations of particular stimulus and response sets, or S-R ensembles. Note first that for any one stimulus set, the fastest reaction time (RT) and the lowest error rate are obtained with a particular response set, and that this response set differs for different stimulus sets. Let us call the stimulus-response ensemble that yields the best performance "the most compatible ensemble". Clearly, compatibility is not a simple matter of a stimulus or a response effect, it is an interaction - in this case, it is an interaction between stimulus, and response sets. Note also that the most compatible ensembles are those for which the spatial arrangements of the stimuli and responses are most similar. This experiment illustrates the fact that set level (or list level) compatibility plays a significant role in determining performance.

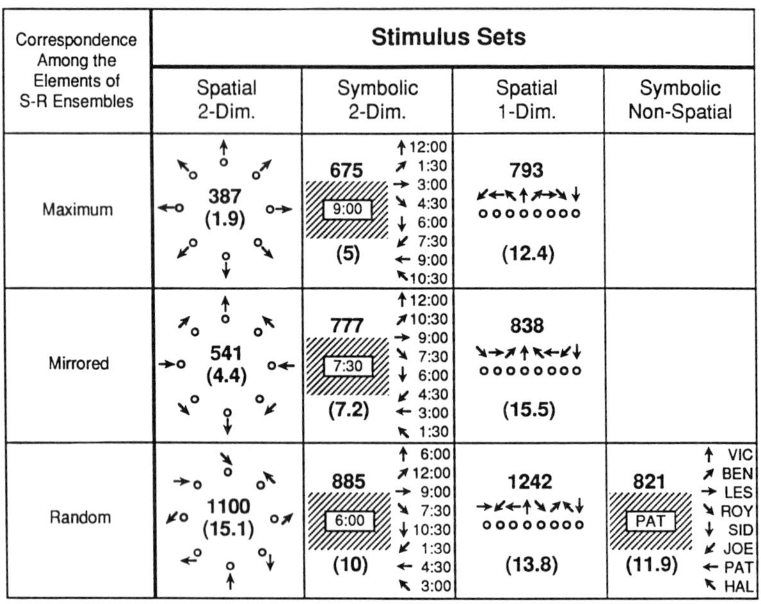

Figure 2. The four S-R ensembles used in Fitts and Deininger (1954). (Adapted from Fitts and Deininger, 1954; in the public domain)

Fitts addressed the question of element level, or pair-wise compatibility, in a second study (Fitts & Deininger 1954). A single set of eight spatially defined responses was combined with four different stimulus sets to form four different stimulus-response ensembles (see Figure 2). Within three of those ensembles

Fitts defined three separate stimulus-response pairings such that the correspondence between the elements in the pairs was either maximal, some systematic rule-based transformation of this maximal correspondence, or random.

As was true of the effects of S-R compatibility at the set level, performance was best, i.e., times were fastest and errors fewest, for those pairings that had greatest correspondence *within* each ensemble. It is also worth noting that the worst performance was obtained with the random pairing, and that performance with the rule-based transformations was in-between. We shall return to this point.

These two studies set the stage for all subsequent studies on SRC. They also identified two separate levels at which compatibility could occur: the global, and the local level. Fitts summarized the SRC problem as follows:

> "Compatibility effects are conceived as resulting from hypothetical information transformation processes (encoding and/or decoding) that intervene between receptor and effector activity"
> (Fitts & Deininger, 1954, p. 483).

The rest of this chapter may be construed as elaborations of this statement.

2.1 The Effect of Irrelevant Dimensions

Do the corresponding aspects of the stimulus and response sets have to be relevant in order for them to affect performance? In the two studies that we have just reviewed they clearly are. Must they always be?

We define aspects of the stimulus or response sets as irrelevant if they are uncorrelated with the required response.

How, one might well ask, could any aspect of a task that is uncorrelated, hence uniformative (in the statistical sense) about the response, have an effect on that response? The "how" portion of this question is taken up in the model presented further on in this chapter. At this point I address the empirical question by briefly presenting the results from two illustrative studies that show that corresponding aspects of the stimulus and response sets need not be relevant in order to affect performance.

Simon (Simon & Small, 1969) asked subjects to press either a left or a right hand key in response to a 400 or 1000 hz tone presented monaurally and randomly in either the left or the right ear. The ear in which the tone was presented was irrelevant to the task (see Figure 3). Nevertheless, when the ear and the side of the responding key were the same, the reaction time was about 60 ms faster than when they conflicted. Simon (1969) had found identical results when he asked subjects to move a lever to the right or to the left in response to a single frequency tone presented either to the right or to the left ear. In one condition the side of the stimulated ear corresponded to the direction of the required response; in another condition they were opposed. When the side of the stimulated ear corresponded to the direction of the responding movement, the RT was about 60 ms faster than when it conflicted.[1]

[1] The similarity between the numbers in the two experiments is probably a coincidence. The important point is that whether the side on which the stimulus is presented was relevant or not, its correspondence with the response had the same qualitative effect on performance.

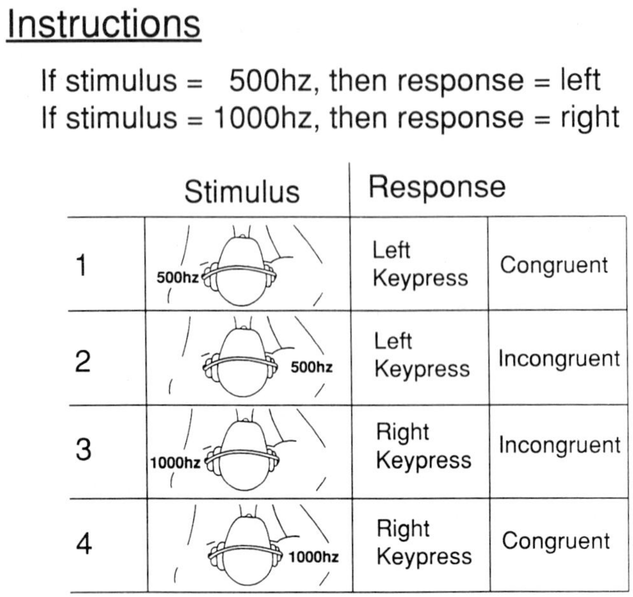

Figure 3 The four types of trials illustrating the essential features of the experimental paradigm (Type 3 ensembles) used by Simon.

Similar results were reported by Wallace (1971) who asked subjects to press either a left or a right key in response to a circle or a square. These geometric stimulus figures were randomly presented on the left, on the right, above or below a central fixation point. When the relative position of the geometric figure corresponded with the side of the response key (left or right), the RT was about 54 ms faster than when it conflicted. When the stimulus was presented above or below the fixation point, so that the question of correspondence with the response was not applicable (i.e., when the stimulus was spatially neutral with respect to the response), the RT was halfway between.

These two studies, by Simon and by Wallace, together with the two studies by Fitts provided the empirical underpinnings for the representational part of a model that we have recently developed (Kornblum, Hasbroucq, & Osman 1990), and on the basis of which we proposed a taxonomy of S-R ensembles in compatibility tasks. I now turn to these issues.

3.0 Dimensional Overlap

Given the list examples used in the introduction to this chapter, and the results of the studies by Fitts, by Simon, and by Wallace, it would appear that there are at least two levels at which entities may be said to be compatible. The first is the global level where lists, collections, or sets of items are perceived as either corresponding or not. The second is the local level where elements from these sets are selected to form pairs whose members may either correspond or conflict. The basis of the correspondence at the set level is what we have called the "dimensional overlap" between sets. We define "dimensional overlap" as the degree to which two sets of items have properties or attributes in common, and the degree to which such attributes are similar to one another. Thus, in Fitts' studies, the sets of stimuli and the sets of responses were arranged in spatially similar or dissimilar patterns, and the degree of similarity determined the degree of dimensional overlap. In the list examples, the set of digits and the set of digit names are not physically similar in the same way that Fitts' spatial ensembles are; however, the mental representations of digits and digit names have more in common than the mental representations of digits and male first names. Dimensional overlap is thus a property of the representation of sets, not of the physical sets themselves. One of the interesting and important properties of sets with dimensional overlap is that isomorphic, or homomorphic mappings may be defined on them (see Kornblum, et al. 1990).

Given that two sets have dimensional overlap, a second level of compatibility can be identified at the element level. That is, pairs may be constructed out of elements from each set, so that the elements in the pair either match and are compatible, or conflict and are incompatible. Note that unless the two sets from which the elements are chosen have dimensional overlap, their pairings are neither compatible nor incompatible. Dimensional overlap is, therefore, a necessary condition for pair-wise compatibility. Proposals that capture some, but not all, aspects of dimensional overlap have variously been made by Alluisi (1961), Greenwald (1970), Proctor and Reeve (1986), Theios (1975), Virzi and Egeth (1985), and Wickens, Sandry, and Vidulich (1983).

3.1 Taxonomy

We have taken these two factors, dimensional overlap[2] and dimensional relevance, and combined them to construct a general taxonomy of ensembles that produce compatibility effects. The taxonomy includes eight classes of ensembles that differ depending on whether the relevant, the irrelevant, neither, or both stimulus, or a stimulus and response dimension overlap (see Table 2).

Type 1 ensembles are characterized by the absence of any dimensional overlap in either the relevant or the irrelevant dimensions.

Examples of Type 1 ensembles that we have encountered in our review thus far include: 1) the last set of lists used in the introduction section of this chapter, in which one list consisted of a set of digits and the other list consisted of boys' first names; 2) the last stimulus-response ensemble in the Fitts and Deininger (1954) study, in which the stimuli consisted of proper names and the responses consisted of spatially defined movements (see Figure 2), and 3) that

[2] For purposes of the taxonomy we are treating dimensional overlap as if it were a discrete, dichotomous variable. In the theory, however, dimensional overlap is viewed as continuous.

condition in the Wallace (1971) study in which the geometrical figures used as stimuli were presented above and below the fixation point, when the responses consisted of left and right key presses.

Ensemble type	Overlapping Ensemble Dimensions		
	Stimulus-response dimensions		Stimulus-Stimulus dimensions
	relevant	irrelevant	
1	no	no	no
2	yes	no	no
3	no	yes	no
4	no	no	yes
5	yes	yes	no
6	yes	no	yes
7	no	yes	yes
8	yes	yes	yes

Table 2. A taxonomy of S-R ensembles illustrating the various combinations of dimensional overlap in the relevant and/or irrelevant stimulus and/or response dimensions. (Some ensembles require extrinsic dimensions to be implemented.)

If compatibility requires dimensional overlap, then it follows that Type 1 ensembles preclude compatibility effects. However, such ensembles may be quite useful in constructing neutral, baseline, control conditions in the study of such effects.

Type 2 ensembles are characterized by the presence of dimensional overlap in the relevant stimulus and response dimensions, and its absence in any irrelevant dimension.

An excellent example of Type 2 ensembles is found in the Fitts & Seeger study, (1953), where any one stimulus set was a member of three different S-R ensembles, and these ensembles differed in terms of the spatial similarity, or dimensional overlap, between the stimulus and the response sets. The majority of the studies on stimulus-response compatibility have used ensembles of Type 2.[3]

Type 3 ensembles are characterized by the presence of dimensional overlap in the irrelevant stimulus and relevant response dimensions, and its absence with the relevant stimulus dimension.

---

[3] The Fitts and Seeger (1953) ensembles also illustrate the continuous nature of dimensional overlap: the degree of dimensional overlap for some of these ensembles is very high, for some very low, and for others in-between. Procedures to determine the degree of dimensional overlap are presently under investigation in our laboratory.

Examples of Type 3 ensembles are found in the Simon and the Wallace studies just reviewed. In both of these studies the responses (left and right key presses) had a correlation of one with stimulus attributes that had no dimensional overlap with the response set (frequency or geometric shape), and a correlation of zero with stimulus attributes that had a high degree of dimensional overlap with the response set (ear or side).

Type 4 ensembles are characterized by the presence of dimensional overlap in the relevant and irrelevant stimulus dimensions. (See figure 15B for illustration.)

Type 5 ensembles are those in which the relevant and irrelevant stimulus and response dimensions overlap, and the stimulus dimensions do not (e.g. Hedge & Marsh, 1975).

Type 6 ensembles are those for which there is overlap in the relevant stimulus and response dimensions as well as in the simulus dimensions, and the S-R and S-S dimensions are different[4].

Type 7 ensembles are those for which there is overlap in the irrelevant stimulus and response dimensions as well as in the stimulus dimensions, and the S-R and S-S dimensions are different.

Type 8 ensembles are those for which there is overlap in the relevant and irrelevant stimulus and response dimensions as well as in the stimulus dimensions (e.g. Stroop, 1935).

The essential features of Ensemble 8, or standard Stroop task, are illustrated for two-choice tasks in Figures 4a and 4b. In 4a, the relevant stimulus dimension consist of the colors red and green; the responses consist of the color names "red" and "green" (shown congruently mapped onto the stimuli, as Stroop and most subsequent investigators have done, although in principle, the mapping could be assigned incongruently [see below]). The irrelevant stimulus dimension consists of the words "red" and "green". By combining the relevant and the irrelevant stimulus dimensions, four types of trials may be constructed: two represent the traditional Stroop conflict (Trials 2 and 4) and two represent no conflict (Trials 1 and 3). Another instance of a Type 8 ensemble is illustrated in Figure 4b in which the experimental conditions used by Simon and Rudell (1967) are displayed. Here, the relevant stimulus dimension consists of the words "left" and "right"; the response consists of pressing the left or right key (shown congruently mapped as in example 4a); the irrelevant dimension consists of the laterality of the stimulus word, which was presented on either the right or on the left ear. Again, by combining the relevant and irrelevant dimensions, four types of trials are constructed that are equivalent to the four types of trials generated by the color/color-word stimuli in 4a. For both of these examples, the relevant dimension (color, or the words

---

[4] In Type 6 and 7 ensembles if the S-S and S-R dimensions are one and the same the ensemble necessarily becomes Type 8.

"left"/"right"), and the irrelevant dimension (color-words, or ear) overlap with each other and with the response (color words or left/right key press). Formally, therefore, these two ensembles are identical.

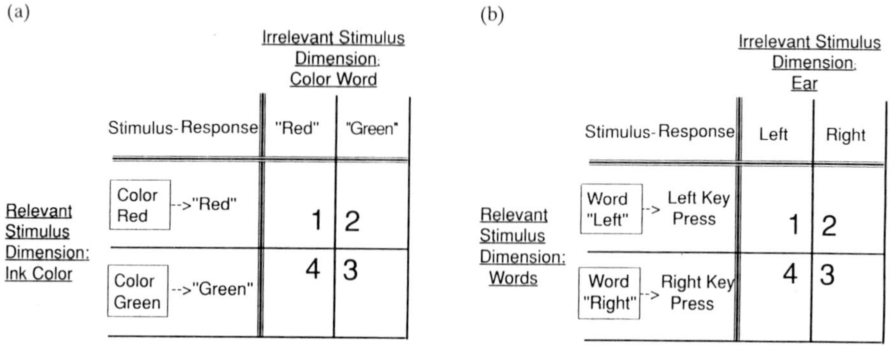

Figure 4. The four types of trials (cells 1, 2, 3, and 4) illustrating the essential features of the experimental paradigm in standard, Stroop-type tasks (ensemble Type 8).
4a: the traditional Stroop task; 4b: a formally identical task used by Simon and Rudell (1967).

This taxonomy will serve as the organizing framework for the remainder of this chapter. Some of the major issues, data, and models, as well as some of the experimental paradigms that have been used with some of these ensemble types will be discussed. I will also summarize some results from our own laboratory.

3.2 A Processing Model

We have developed a processing model for some of these ensembles types. The response production part of the model is illustrated in Figure 5.

Type 2 ensembles

For greater ease of exposition we shall consider ensembles of Type 2 first. The processing path for those ensembles is indicated by the solid lines in Figure 5. Here, the encoded form of the stimulus constitutes the input to the response identification process. Depending on the mapping instruction (where mapping is the assignment of stimuli to responses), the correct response may be identified either by search or by rule. If by rule, it is either the identity rule, or some other rule. The model postulates that identification by search is the slowest, by identity rule the fastest, and by rules other than the identity rule in-between. The response identification process thus constitutes a differential source of delay in response production whose magnitude depends on the mapping instructions.

In parallel with the response identification process, the stimulus automatically activates its corresponding response; this automatic activation is functionally equivalent to response priming. These two responses, the one identified as correct and the automatically activated one, are now compared by the verification process. If, as a result of the mapping instructions, they are the same, then the mapping is said to be congruent and the response is executed rapidly and accurately. If, as a result of the mapping instructions they are different, then the mapping is said to be incongruent and the automatically-activated, preprogrammed response must be eliminated by a time-consuming abort process. This generates a further delay beyond the one already caused by the response identification process.

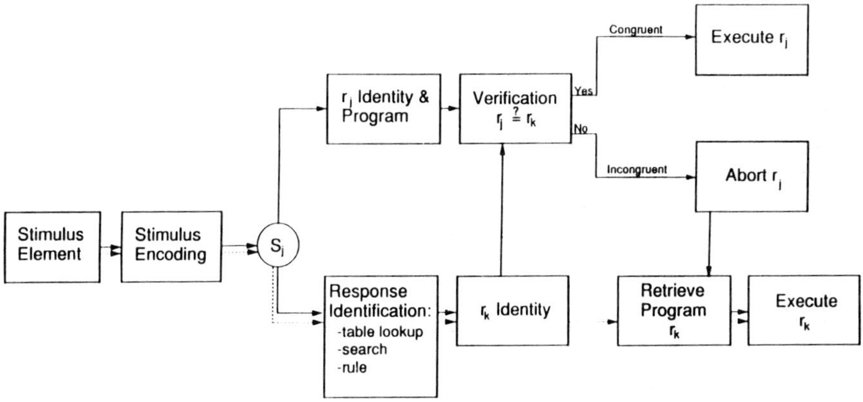

Figure 5. Block diagram of the major operations of the response production stage in stimulus-response (S-R) compatibility tasks *with* (solid lines) and *with no* (dotted lines) dimensional overlap. (The top branch of the solid line path illustrates the operations involved in the automatic activation of the congruent response for S-R ensembles with dimensional overlap. The bottom branch of the solid path illustrates the operations involved in the identification of the correct response.)

Our model thus predicts that for ensembles with overlap on the relevant stimulus and response dimensions, the fastest correct response will be the one produced with congruent mapping assignments, the next fastest will be the incongruent response that can be identified by rule, and the slowest will be the incongruent response whose identity is the result of a search.[5] Recall that the ordering of the data in the Fitts and Deininger study (1954) is consistent with this prediction.

Type 1 ensembles

Consider ensembles of Type 1 next. These are ensembles none of whose dimensions overlap, hence, have no automatically activated responses associated with them. Furthermore, because there is no dimensional overlap, there is no way that the response can be identified by rule. The mapping instructions, therefore, set up an S-R table which is subsequently searched, irrespective of what the mapping instructions may be. Once the correct

[5]It is not possible to distinguish between random and rule-based S-R mappings in tasks with fewer than three choices.

response has been identified there is no need, in this class of ensembles, to verify or to abort it. The process, therefore, proceeds without interruption to retrieve the appropriate program, and to execute the response. According to this argument, ensembles without dimensional overlap can neither benefit from the automatic activation of a response or the potential applicability of a rule, nor do they bear the cost of verifying and aborting erroneous responses. One would, therefore, expect the reaction time for Type 1, non-overlapping ensembles to be longer than for congruent mapping conditions with Type 2 ensembles, shorter than for incongruent random mapping conditions and, depending on the complexity of the rule, either longer or shorter than for incongruent rule-governed mapping conditions. The model thus defines a neutral condition with respect to which it predicts facilitation in the case of congruent mapping and interference in the case of incongruent search - based mapping with Type 2 ensembles.

Type 3 ensembles

The processing path for ensembles of Type 3 combines some of the processing of Type 1 ensembles with some of the processing of Type 2 ensembles. Since the relevant stimulus dimension does not overlap with the response, this dimension is processed as if it were a Type 1 ensemble; i.e. response identification proceeds by search through a table. However, because the irrelevant stimulus dimension does overlap with the response set, its occurrence in a stimulus automatically activates the corresponding response. We assume that if the buffer in the verification process is non-empty, then the correctly identified response is automatically compared to the contents of this buffer. And now we are in familiar territory: if the contents of this buffer are the same, then the irrelevant stimulus is congruent with the required response and this response will be executed rapidly and accurately; if the contents are different, then the automatically activated response will be aborted, the program for the correct response will be retrieved, and the correct response will eventually be executed, but with a cost. Note that in the case of Type 3 ensembles the only source of facilitation or interference is the automatic response activation process. This contrasts sharply with processing in Type 2 ensembles where the response identification process constitutes an additional and variable source of facilitation. One might, therefore, expect the range of facilitation effects of overlapping dimensions to be smaller when they are irrelevant (Type 3) than when they are relevant (Type 2).

Type 4 and Type 8 ensembles

A careful examination of the results with Types 4 and 8 ensembles [see our discussion below of Green and Barber (1983), Hintzman et al. (1972), Keele (1967), Simon and Sudalamaithu (1979)] makes it clear that if the relevant and irrelevant dimensions of the stimulus overlap, then irrespective of the overlap with the response, the consistency or inconsistency of the two stimulus dimensions has a marked effect on performance; this implicates the stimulus identification stage in the processing of Type 4 ensembles.

Consider the case of a one-dimensional stimulus, or a two-dimensional stimulus in which one dimension is relevant and the other irrelevant, and these dimensions do not overlap. In both cases, the stimulus identification process produces a single stimulus identity code that corresponds either to the single dimension or to the relevant dimension; this code is then passed on to the response production stage. Consider next the case of a two-dimensional stimulus in which one dimension is relevant and the other irrelevant, and the two dimensions overlap. In this case, because of the overlap in the two dimensions, the stimulus identification code produces two identity codes, one for the relevant and one for the irrelevant dimension. The existence of these two stimulus codes, just like the existence of two response codes in the response production stage, requires that they be compared. If a comparison shows that the two stimulus codes are the same, this code passes directly to the response production process. If a comparison shows that they are different, an additional step is required in order to identify the relevant one. This is illustrated in Figure 6. The stimulus identification and the response

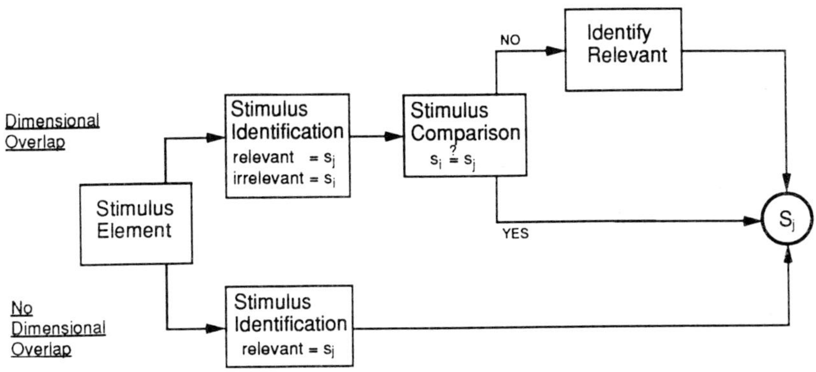

Figure 6. Steps in the stimulus identification process (see text for explanation).

production processes may be thought of as two networks that are linked by what Schweickert, Fisher and Goldstein (1991) have called a cut point, and whose effects are additive.

Type 5 and Type 6 ensembles

(Details of the processing model for these ensembles are being developed.)

Type 7 ensembles

The processing of Type 7 ensembles may be parsed into Type 3 and Type 4 processing. To the extent that these occur on either side of a cut point, we expect these effects to be additive.

In the next section I present an overview of some experimental results in the framework of the dimensional overlap model.

4.0 The Effects of S-R Mapping in Type 1 and Type 2 Ensembles.

The model predicts that in order to obtain a mapping effect, the stimulus and response sets in the experimental ensembles must have dimensional

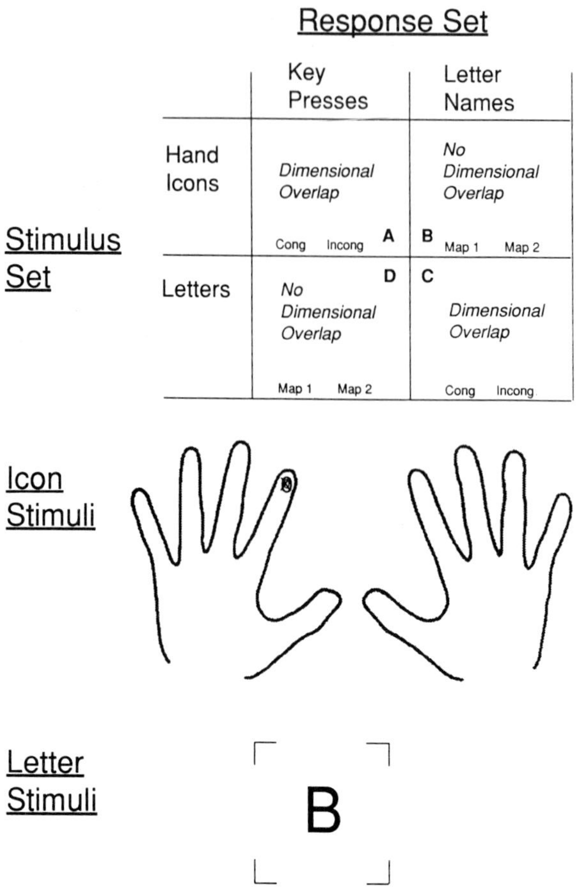

Figure 7. The top panel shows the various combinations of stimulus and response sets that generated the four S-R ensembles (A, B, C, and D). The middle panel illustrates the graphic display that constituted the "hand icons" set, with the left index finger identified as the stimulus finger. The lower panel illustrates the graphic display that constituted the "letters" set , with the letter B as an example.

overlap. The corollary is that for S-R ensemble without dimensional overlap all mappings are equivalent.

The model further asserts that the difference between congruent and incongruent mapping conditions reflects the action of facilitation and interference processes. The RT for congruent mapping should, therefore, be faster than a neutral baseline, and the RT for incongruent mapping slower. These predictions were tested in our laboratory (Kornblum & Lee, 1990).

Two stimulus sets were used: hand icons and visual letters. These were combined with two response sets (key presses and verbal letter names) to form the four S-R ensembles shown in Figure 7. There were six alternatives in each stimulus and response set. We assumed that there was dimensional overlap[6] between the sets of hand icons and key presses (Ensemble A), and the sets of letters and letter names (Ensemble C); and that there was no dimensional overlap between the sets of hand icons and letter names (Ensemble B), and the sets of letters and key presses (Ensemble D). Ensembles A and C thus comprised Type 2 ensembles; B and D comprised Type 1 ensembles. Two S-R mappings were defined for each ensemble. For Ensembles A and C, one of the mappings was congruent and the other incongruent . For Ensembles B and D, since there was no dimensional overlap, we chose two arbitrary S-R mappings. The two S-R mappings for each of four S-R ensembles thus yielded a total of eight experimental conditions on which eight subjects were run for three days.

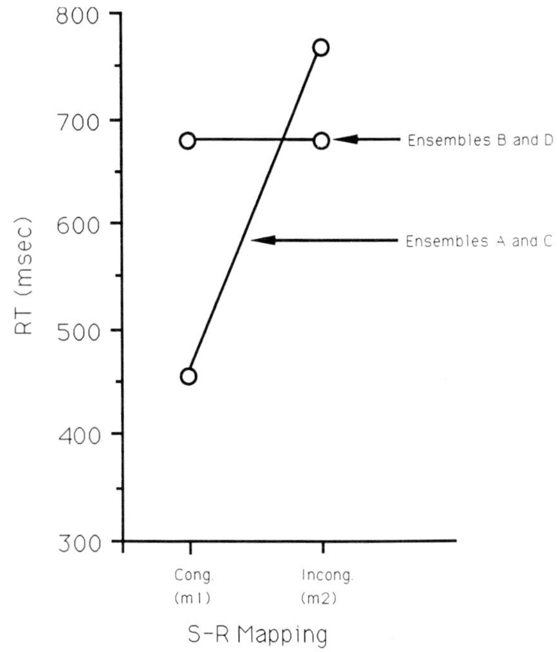

Figure 8. Mean reaction time in a six choice task averaged over Ensembles A and C (with dimensional overlap), and B and D (without dimensional overlap) as a function of two mappings: congruent and incongruent for Ensembles A and C; m_1 and m_2 for Ensembles B and D.

---

6 Our assumption for the presence/absence of dimensional overlap in the ensembles for this experiment, and in our review of the literature, is based on intuition. However, a study is presently underway in which we assess the degree of dimensional overlap independently of its interaction with mapping and population stereotype.

The results are shown on Figure 8. In order to examine the effects of dimensional overlap and mapping without having those effects confounded with either stimulus or response factors, we took the means of the data for each of the two mapping conditions in the two ensembles with dimensional overlap, and compared them with the means of the data for the two mapping conditions without dimensional overlap. The results are in accord with the predictions of the model.

First, a highly significant mapping effect of 315 ms was obtained for the ensembles of Type 2 (A and C). In contrast, mapping had no effect with the ensembles of Type 1 (B and D). Second, according to the model, the effects of congruent and incongruent mappings reflect processes of facilitation and interference respectively. Therefore, when compared to the RT of an appropriate neutral condition, the RT for congruent and incongruent mappings should be faster, and slower, respectively, than this neutral condition. When compared to the mean of the Type 1 Ensembles (B and D), which we are taking as the neutral condition, the RT for the congruent mapping conditions for A and C shows a highly significant facilitation effect of 226 ms, and the RT for the incongruent mapping conditions a highly significant interference effect of 89 ms.

4.1 The Effect of the Number of Alternatives and S-R Compatibility in Type 1 and Type 2 Ensembles

The model that we have developed is quite general, and seems to account well for some aspects of performance with Type 1 and Type 2 ensembles. However, it does not account for all aspects. And now I would like to turn to a set of results that are historically and substantively interesting, that the model accounts for only partially: the effects of the number of alternatives on stimulus-response compatibility.

SRC was originally identified as an important problem with cognitive overtones at a time when information theory was thought to have provided a key to the understanding of human performance, and cognition was an undesirably soft theoretical concept. The paradigmatic data were those of Hick (1952) who demonstrated that the monotonic increase of choice RT with the number of alternatives, which had been known since the work of Merkel in 1885 (cited in Woodworth, 1938), could be expressed as a linear function of the information transmitted from the stimuli to the responses. The implication was that people could be treated as information channels whose transmission capacity was measured by the reciprocal of the slope of this RT function. Ideally, channel capacity measured in this way would remain constant, and thus reflect an important invariant human property. It was, therefore, disconcerting to discover that the slope of this function, hence the capacity of the channel, could be altered by varying what Fitts had labeled, the stimulus - response compatibility of the task. Figure 9 summarizes the data from ten studies that addressed this issue.

For comparable ranges of stimulus information, it can be seen that the slopes of the RT functions range from values close to zero (conditions G, H, I, and J), to values exceeding 0.2. Fitts proposed that the key to understanding these compatibility-caused departures of RT from their information theoretic benchmark lay in understanding the efficiency with which stimulus information was coded, recoded, and transformed or translated into the required-response information. Our model is consistent with this view. The response identification process in our model takes on one of three states depending on the mapping instructions in the task: in State 1 it uses the identity rule, in State 2 it formulates and implements a different rule, and in State 3 it searches through a list.

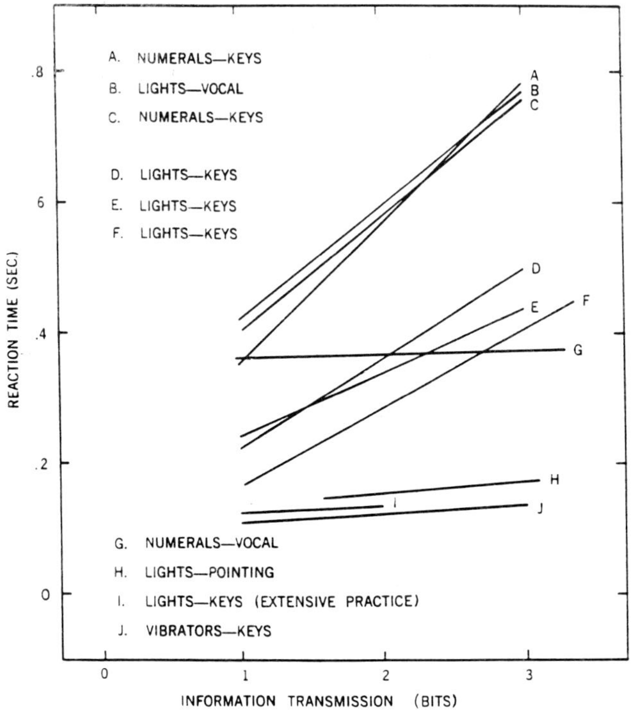

Figure 9. Reaction time as a function of uncertainty ($\log_2$ of the number of alternatives) for a number of different S-R ensembles (reproduced from Fitts and Posner, 1967, in the public domain).

Some of the data in an early study by Schvaneveldt and Staudenmeyer (1970) bear on the question of whether these three states are sufficiently comprehensive to account for the data. They used digits as stimuli and digit names as the responses, to design nine different experimental conditions that varied only in the mapping assignment between stimuli and responses. All nine experimental conditions included two-choice, four-choice and eight-choice subconditions. The results from four of these nine conditions are illustrated in Figure 10a.

The fastest RT was obtained in the condition where subjects had to name the digits. This, of course, is the congruent condition and is expected to be the fastest. The slowest RT was in the random mapping condition, where subjects had to produce a digit name that had been randomly assigned as the correct response for each stimulus digit. The in-between conditions were those in which response identification could be made by means of a rule, either adding one (+1) to, or subtracting one (-1) from the digit that was presented as the stimulus. These results replicate the ordering that was found by Fitts and Deininger (1954), and are in accord with the three states that we postulated for the response identification process. Furthermore, the nature of these states is consistent with the fact that the congruent, and rule-based conditions appear not to show any increase in RT as the number of alternatives increases from four to eight, whereas the RT in the random condition does increase. The

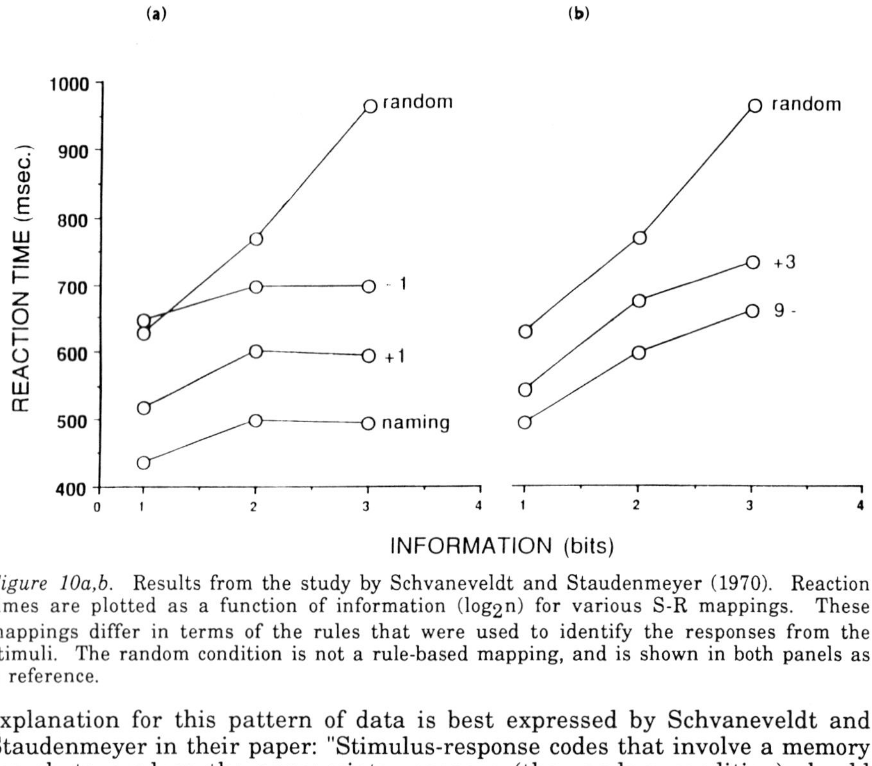

Figure 10a,b. Results from the study by Schvaneveldt and Staudenmeyer (1970). Reaction times are plotted as a function of information ($\log_2 n$) for various S-R mappings. These mappings differ in terms of the rules that were used to identify the responses from the stimuli. The random condition is not a rule-based mapping, and is shown in both panels as a reference.

explanation for this pattern of data is best expressed by Schvaneveldt and Staudenmeyer in their paper: "Stimulus-response codes that involve a memory search to produce the appropriate response (the random condition) should show an effect of uncertainty on RT, while codes that produce the response directly through stimulus identification (i.e. naming) or through a constant operation upon the result of the stimulus identification[(i.e.(+1), (-1)] should not" (p. 115). Thus far, the model does well. However, when the rule gets slightly more complex, the data get more complicated as well.

Figure 10b shows the results of two more conditions in the Schvaneveldt and Staudenmeyer study. Here, instead of adding and subtracting one from the digit presented, subjects either had to add three (+3) or subtract nine (-9). Like the results in Figure 10a, these data also appear to be separated by a constant that may reflect the relative difficulty of these rules. However, the RT for these rule-based conditions, instead of being flat, increases with the number of alternatives. Furthermore, the slope of these functions is less than for the random mapping condition. Similar results were obtained by Smith (1980) in a key pressing task in which he used tactile stimuli to the finger tips. Clearly these data pose a problem for the three-state model of response identification. The continuous nature of the change in slope with rule complexity seems to indicate either: a) that some experimental conditions may be a mixture of these states, b) that one should not think of these three states as being discrete, or c) that the three-state response identification process is an incomplete account.

4.2 Spatially Defined Stimuli and Responses in Type 2 Ensembles

Even though SRC phenomena had been observed with many different types of stimuli and responses, it is relatively recently that the idea has been put

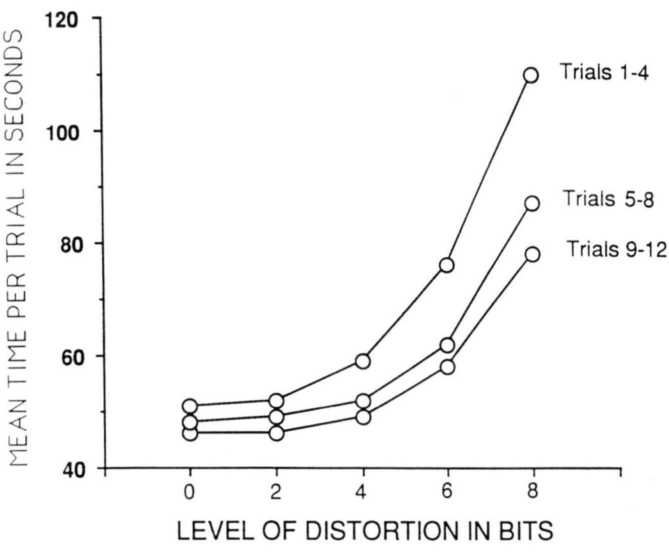

Figure 11. Results of a study by Keele (1967) in which the spatial arrangements of the stimulus and response sets were identical at zero distortion, and increasingly dissimilar with increasing levels of distortion. Practice is the parameter.

forward that in spite of differences in stimulus and/or response modality, SRC phenomena may be a reflection of common, fundamental, cognitive mechanisms. Much of the past work on SRC, therefore, appears fragmented and domain-specific, as is illustrated by the distinction that Welford (1976) drew between "symbolic" and "spatial" compatibility. Some of the work using spatially identified stimuli and/or responses is particularly interesting, not only because it addressed and cleared up a number of important questions, and has come up with generalizable answers and suggestions, but also because spatial variables are ubiquitous, and easily manipulable. Because of this, they continue to be widely used in current experimental paradigms. In one early study, Keele (1967) used a set of eight stimulus lights and a set of eight response buttons that were each randomly and identically arranged in their own 16 x 16 matrices. By gradually and systematically distorting the spatial arrangements of the stimulus lights, while holding the response buttons fixed, Keele obtained a series of S-R ensembles in which the stimulus and response sets were made increasingly dissimilar, as measured by an information metric (see Garner, 1962, for a review). His results, illustrated on Figure 11, showed that RT was an increasing monotonic function of dissimilarity between the stimulus and the response sets. This, of course, is consistent with the idea developed in our model that the degree of facilitation with congruent mapping is proportional to the degree of dimensional overlap in S-R ensembles.

A great deal of the work on "spatial compatibility" was, and continues to be done with two-choice tasks. The early work focused on the question "what spatial property or feature, is the effective stimulus underlying SRC effects?" This question took many different forms. For example, is the effective stimulus (left or right) defined in terms of an egocentric or a geocentric referent? Is functionally effective congruence defined as the correspondence between the stimulus and the effector, or between the stimulus and the manipulandum [The work on these questions is well summarized in the recent book by Proctor & Reeve (1990); see particularly, the chapters by Heister, Schroeder - Heister, & Ehrenstein (1990), Ladavas (1990), Simon (1990), and Umilta & Nicoletti (1990)]. Umilta and his colleagues have shown that it is the relative spatial positions of stimuli and responses that determine how they are coded. Simon (see Simon, Hinrichs, & Craft, 1970) and many others after him have shown that effector location matters little; what matters is the correspondence between the stimulus and the manipulandum. Heister and her colleagues (Heister et al., 1990) on the other hand, have argued that categorical answers to these questions ignore the hierarchical ordering of egocentric, and geocentric frames of reference. That is, egocentric, relative, and anatomical organization can all be shown to function in the coding process; however, they do so in a preferred order. If the most preferred mode is not available, then the next most preferred one will be brought into operation, etc.

A particularly interesting development in the search for "the effective compatibility stimulus" is the work of Proctor and Reeve (see Reeve & Proctor, 1990) whose studies include four-choice tasks in which spatial and non-spatial dimensions are often combined into single S-R ensembles. By identifying, what they call, salient features in both the stimulus and the response sets, they have been able to show that these features function as points of reference in structuring the sets of stimuli and responses. Performance with mapping instructions that preserve this structure is better than with mapping instructions that violate this structure. This structural isomorphism may be viewed as a variant of the dimensional overlap postulated in our model; and mapping instructions that preserve, as against mappings instructions that violate this structure are equivalent to what we have called congruent and incongruent mappings.

4.3 The Effects of Spatial and Other Dimensions in Type 3 Ensembles

In 1969 Simon published the first in a long series of experiments with prototypical Type 3 ensembles. The basic paradigm was described earlier in this chapter and is illustrated in Figure 3. The stimuli usually consisted of elements whose relevant aspects (pitch, in our illustration) were neutral with respect to the response (left/right key presses), but whose irrelevant aspects (left/right ear, in our illustration) either coincided or conflicted in a random, uncorrelated manner with the response. The basic data showed that when the stimulus location matched the response location, RT was faster than when it conflicted. He also showed (see Simon, 1990 for a review) that:

1. This effect was independent of the anatomical laterality of the sensory organ, the sensory field, and/or the responding limb;
2. This effect was independent of the sensory modality, and the quality of the stimulus;
3. This effect is replicated, in attenuated form, when the irrelevant aspect of the stimulus is conveyed by a stimulus event that is physically separate, rather than being an intrinsic part of the stimulus itself;
4. This effect is cross-modal, i.e., if the relevant aspect of the stimulus is visual, an appropriate irrelevant auditory stimulus produces the effect.

Simon's hypothesis throughout these studies has been that there is a basic natural tendency for humans to move toward the source of stimulation, and he has interpreted his results as confirming this hypothesis (Simon, 1990). This finding has been dubbed the "Simon effect"[7] in the literature (Hedge & Marsh, 1975).

I believe that a broader principle than "a natural tendency to respond to the source of stimulation" is involved in the Simon task that we have been describing. The principle derives from the model: When a response dimension overlaps with an irrelevant stimulus dimension (whether this dimension is spatial, or anything else), and does not overlap with the relevant stimulus dimension, automatic processes are triggered that produce facilitation when the response and the irrelevant dimensions are congruent, and produce interference when they are incongruent.

I would like very quickly to present the results of a study that we conducted to test this hypothesis (Kornblum & Lee, 1990). This was a four-choice task using the same four S-R ensembles that were used previously (see Figure 7). Two of the ensembles were assumed to have high dimensional overlap (Ensembles A and C on Figure 7), and two had low dimensional overlap (Ensembles B and D). The one difference between this and the previous

---

[7] This term is particularly unfortunate because of its ambiguity which stems from the fact that a single term is used to denote two distinct phenomena: 1) the effect of an irrelevant spatial dimension when it overlaps with the stimulus and response sets, and is the only overlapping dimension in the ensemble - what we have called Type 3 ensembles; and 2) the effect of an irrelevant spatial dimension when it overlaps not only with the stimulus and the response sets, but with the relevant dimension as well - what we have called Type 8 ensembles. Thus, for example, when the responses consist of a left or right key press, and the irrelevant dimension consists of the left and right ear, it makes a difference whether the relevant stimuli are tones that differ in pitch (Type 3), or whether they are the words "left" and "right" (Type 8). To use the same term to denote both phenomena may lead to confusion.

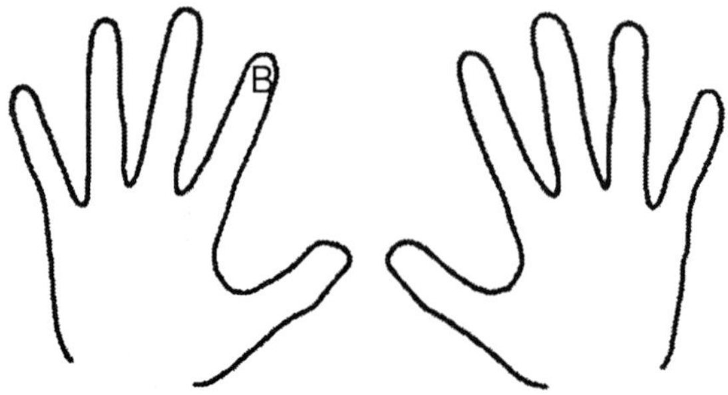

Figure 12. Illustration of the graphic stimulus display used in our experiment with Type 1, Type 2, and Type 3 ensembles. The example shows the left index finger being singled out as the stimulus finger by the letter B appearing in its fingertip. Whether the left index finger, or the letter B is the relevant stimulus depends on the particular ensemble (see text for explanation).

experiment, aside from this being a four-choice task, was the nature of the stimulus. Recall that in the previous experiment the letter stimuli appeared by themselves in the center of the screen, and the finger stimuli consisted of an asterisk appearing in the tip on the finger in the hand icon. In this experiment, regardless of the ensemble, the physical stimuli always consisted of hand icons where, instead of an asterisk, a letter appeared in one of the fingertips. This is illustrated in Figure 12.

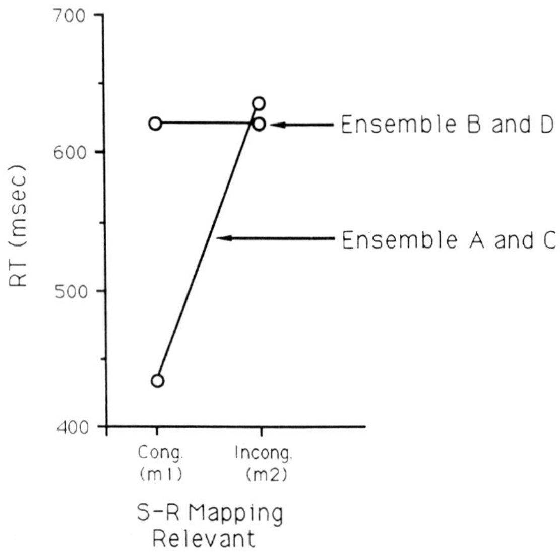

Figure 13. Mean RT, averaged over Ensembles A and C (with dimensional overlap), and B and D (without dimensional overlap) in our four-choice task. The RT are plotted as a function of the S-R mapping of the *relevant* dimensions.

Now consider the situation with Ensemble A. Here, the relevant stimulus is whatever finger the letter appears in, and the response is a key press. The set of finger stimuli has high dimensional overlap with the response set; however, the set of letters that is used to identify the stimulus finger has no dimensional overlap with the response set, and is irrelevant to the task. Consider Ensemble B next. Here the physical stimuli are identical to what they were in Ensemble A, however, instead of responding with a key press to the finger stimulus, the subject is asked to respond with a letter name. The relevant and irrelevant dimensions of the stimulus are identical to what they were in Ensemble A. What has changed is the stimulus dimension that overlaps with the response: in Ensemble A the overlapping dimension was the relevant one, in Ensemble B it is the irrelevant one. According to the model we should expect no effects of the irrelevant dimension in Ensemble A, and an effect of facilitation and interference, depending on the nature of the match, in Ensemble B. And so on for Ensembles C and D. The results for the relevant dimensions, collapsed over the irrelevant dimensions are shown on Figure 13.

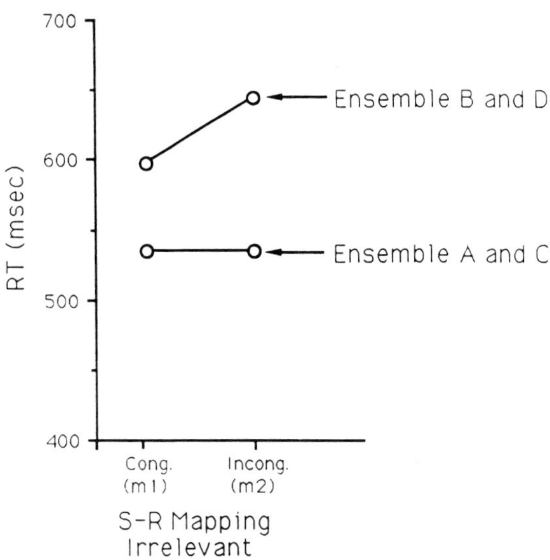

Figure 14. Mean RT, averaged over Ensembles A and C, and B and D in our four-choice task. The data are plotted as a function of the S-R mapping of the *irrelevant* dimension.

As was found previously, there is a large mapping effect (203 ms) for the two ensembles with dimensional overlap (A and C), and no mapping effect for the other two ensembles (B and D) . The results for the irrelevant dimensions are shown on Figure 14. When the irrelevant stimulus dimension does not overlap with the response, i.e., in Ensembles A and C, the RT is identical for all pairings with respect to the irrelevant dimensions. When the irrelevant dimension does overlap with the response, i.e., in Ensemble B and D, the RT is shorter for congruent than for incongruent irrelevant matches.

These results not only support our model, but they permit Simon's conclusions concerning irrelevant spatial dimensions, and the natural tendency to respond to the source of stimulation, to be restated in more general terms. In particular the description of Simon's five, broad findings can now be rephrased and subsumed under the framework of overlapping stimulus and response dimensions, and the automatic processes triggered by them:

> Given Type 3 ensembles, if the value of the overlapping irrelevant stimulus dimension matches the value of the response, RT will be faster than when it conflicts.

4.4 Type 4 and Type 8 Ensembles: Stroop, and Other Similar Tasks

In the standard Stroop task (see Figure 4 and Ensemble Type 8) the relevant stimulus (color), the irrelevant stimulus (color word), and the response (saying the name of the color) all share a common referent, hence overlap on the same dimension: color. This confounding makes it impossible to tell whether the observed interference is the result of conflict between the two aspects of the stimulus (color, and color word), or between an irrelevant aspect of the stimulus (color word) and the response (color name).

This confounding notwithstanding, one of the most common explanations for the interference in the original Stroop task, and all of its variants that include words as one of the stimulus objects, has been that the printed color word is automatically encoded, and thus activates a reading response that conflicts with the required naming response which is different. As has been pointed out by others this explanation, taken at face value, would make ordinary reading impossible because as we tried to read one word, the adjoining words on the same line of text would interfere. Furthermore, if this explanation were correct, the irrelevant word would always interfere with the relevant color, and irrelevant color could never be made to interfere with relevant words. However, the latter has been reported in a number of studies (e.g. Virzi & Egeth, 1985). One of the critical issues raised by this pattern of results is identifying the locus of the interference: Does it arise at the perceptual analysis level, or as a result of response conflict; is it a stimulus effect, or a response effect? In attentional terms: Does the attentional bottleneck occur early, or late?

Clearly, in order to answer this question experimentally, one must first eliminate the confounding between the relevant and the irrelevant stimulus, and the response. There are at least two different approaches to this problem, and these are illustrated on Figure 15 with a two-choice task as the example. In Figure 15a, instead of requiring the subject to respond with the same name as the color of the color patch, the mapping calls for the name of the other color. In Figure 15b, instead of requiring color names as the responses, a completely different response set - key presses - is used. Both procedures have been employed, and the results implicate a stimulus conflict rather than a response conflict as the source of the interference.

Keele (1967) addressed the confounding issue by requiring subjects to make key press, rather than color naming responses to the actual colors in

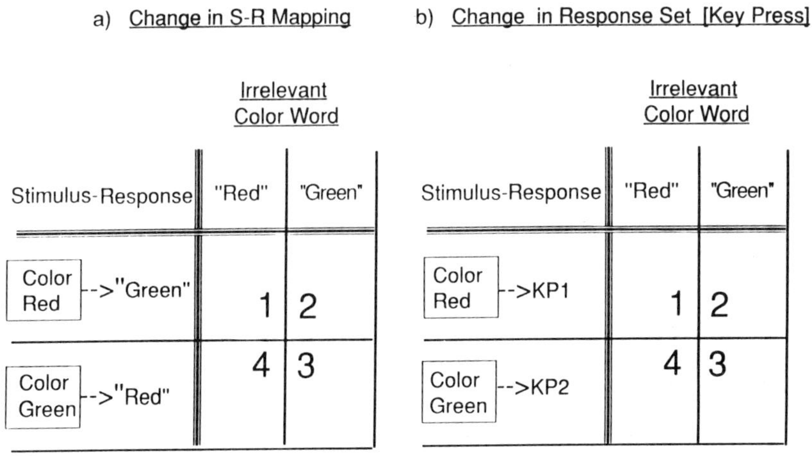

Figure 15. Two ways of unconfounding the effects of the stimulus, the response, and the irrelevant dimension in the Stroop task. The ilustrations are based on two-choice examples. In panel 15a the S-R mapping of color to color-name is made incongruent. In panel 15b, the color response is replaced by a key-press response.

several different kinds of stimuli (see Figure 15b): some of the stimuli consisted of color words[8] that conflicted with the color of the ink that they were printed in,others were non-color words printed in various colors[9] , and still others were nonsense shapes also in different color. Even though the responses were not verbal, the RT for stimuli in which color words conflicted with the color that they were printed in, was about 60 ms longer than to stimuli consisting of non-color words. This suggests that the conflict causing the interference occurs before the response stage. Keele also found that non-color words had the same RT as geometric shapes, both of which were faster than the conflicting color words. This, Keele argues, suggests that the color and non-color words were discriminated from each other, and consequently had to have reached the memory retrieval stage. Hintzman et al.(1972) replicated Keele's results using a task with verbal responses, and showed in addition that congruent color word, were faster than the neutral control words. Together these two sets of results locate the site of the observed conflict after memory retrieval, and prior to response selection .

In an elaborate study, Simon and Sudalamaithu (1979) tackled the confounding issue by using congruent and incongruent S-R mapping assignments in an otherwise standard two-choice Stroop task (see Figure 15a). They reported "...for both compatible (congruent) and incompatible (incongruent) S-R mapping, the stimulus conditions that produced the slowest responses were those characterized by a lack of congruence between the

---

[8] Note that this is a Type 4 ensemble.

[9] These are Type 1 ensembles.

relevant and the irrelevant cue" (p.182). These results are consistent with those of Keele (1967) in identifying the conflict between relevant and irrelevant dimensions of the stimulus as the factor responsible for the interference in the Stroop task.

Finally, Green and Barber (1983) report the results of an experiment in which the stimuli consisted of the words "boy" and "girl," pronounced by a male and a female voice. The subject's task consisted of identifying the speaker's gender. In the congruent mapping condition the response to be given was the speaker's actual gender, in the incongruent mapping condition the response was the opposite. The design of this experiment thus conforms to that illustrated in Figure 15a. As was true of Keele's (1967), and Simon and Sudalamaithu's (1979) experiments, the data show a marked effect of stimulus consistency in addition to the expected S-R mapping effect (see Figure 16). In

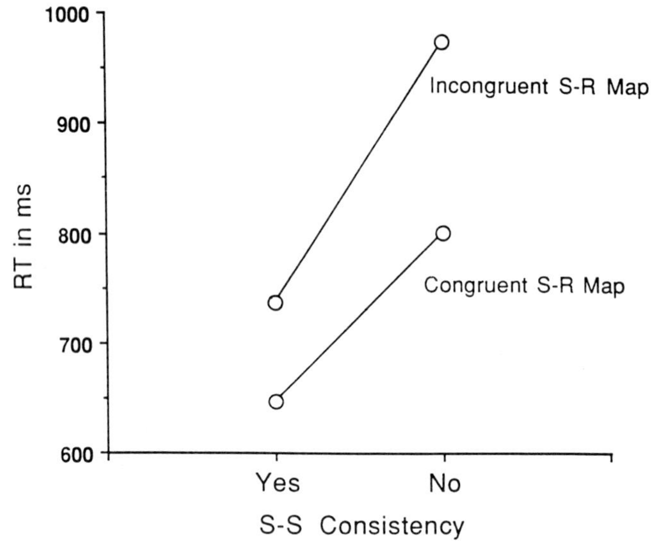

Figure 16 Results of a study by Green and Barber (1981) in which the two stimulus dimensions consisted of the words "boy" and "girl", spoken by a male and female voice. The spoken word and the gender of the speaker were either consistent (yes), or inconsistent (no), and the task either called for identifying the speaker's gender correctly (congruent), or give the opposite gender (incongruent).

neither this, nor in Simon and Sudalamaithu's (1979) case, however, are the data unequivocal so that locating the site of the interference is still an open question.

5.0 Extrinsic Irrelevant Dimensions in Type 3, 7 and Type 8 Ensembles

In order to examine this question more closely we have begun a series of experiments that uses a new experimental procedure in which the irrelevant aspects of the stimulus are extrinsic to the relevant ones. This procedure draws on the work of Ericksen (e.g. Ericksen & Ericksen, 1979), and of Coles and his colleagues (Coles et al., 1985, see also Coles, this volume), and rests on the

Stimuli: 2,8
Responses: "two", "eight"
Noise: 2,8,⏢,⬡

Sample Displays

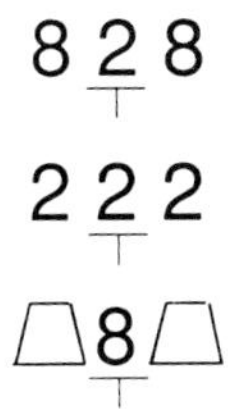

Conditions for the experiment

Condition	Stimuli	Responses	S_R map	Noise
A.	2,8	"two", "eight"	cong	2,8
B.	2,8	"two", "eight"	cong	⏢,⬡
C.	2,8	"two", "eight"	incong	2,8
D.	2,8	"two", "eight"	incong	⏢,⬡

Figure 17. Conditions of our first experiment with extrinsic irrelevant dimensions. Elements of the various ensembles are listed on the top under "stimulus", "response", and "noise". The particular ensembles and S-R mapping assignments are listed under "conditions". The sample displays illustrate some of the stimulus displays used in the experiment; the stimulus is always identified by the "T" shaped pedestal underneath it.

assumption that whether an overlapping dimension or cue is presented as an intrinsic part of the stimulus, or as a physically separate stimulus object, it does not alter the fundamental processes that give rise to the facilitation and interference effects that are observed in performance. There is some evidence in the literature that supports this assumption (e.g. Kahneman & Chajczyk, 1983, Kahneman & Henick, 1981, Kamlet & Egeth, 1969). This, of course, is an issue for our model. That is to the extent that extrinsic stimuli (called "noise" or "flankers" in the Ericksen-related literature) appear to function in a manner equivalent to intrinsically presented, irrelevant aspects of the stimulus, according to our model, it should have differential effects on performance depending on whether it overlaps with the stimulus, the response, neither, or both. If our assumption and the representational aspects of our model are both valid, a new set of experimental conditions becomes available that may enable us to dissect the information processing chain in Type 3, Type 4 and Type 8 ensembles with greater precision than was previously possible.

In the first experiment we used Type 8, or standard Stroop-like ensembles. The conditions of the experiment are illustrated in Figure 17. The stimuli consisted of the digits 2 and 8; the noise, or flankers, consisted either of digits, or of geometrical figures. The responses consisted of the digit names "two" and "eight", which were mapped either congruently (Conditions A and B), or incongruently (Conditions C and D) onto the stimuli. These stimulus, noise and mapping specifications defined the four conditions of the experiment, which were blocked. On each trial, one digit was presented as the stimulus and was flanked on both sides either by itself, by the other digit, or by a pair of identical geometric figures. Taxonomically, the ensemble with geometric, non-overlapping noise (Figure 17, Conditions B and D) corresponds to a Type 2 ensemble in which mapping is expected to generate the normal congruent-incongruent mapping effect, and the noise is not expected to produce any effect at all. The ensemble with digit overlapping noise (Figures 17, Conditions A and C) corresponds to a Type 8, or standard Stroop-like ensemble, in which mapping is again expected to produce a congruent-incongruent mapping effect, and the effect of noise a qualitatively similar effect. Note that the use of the flanking noise procedure in the context of our model permits the construction of a super-Stroop ensemble where the relevant and irrelevant dimensions not only overlap, but are identical. The question now is, does the noise interfere with the

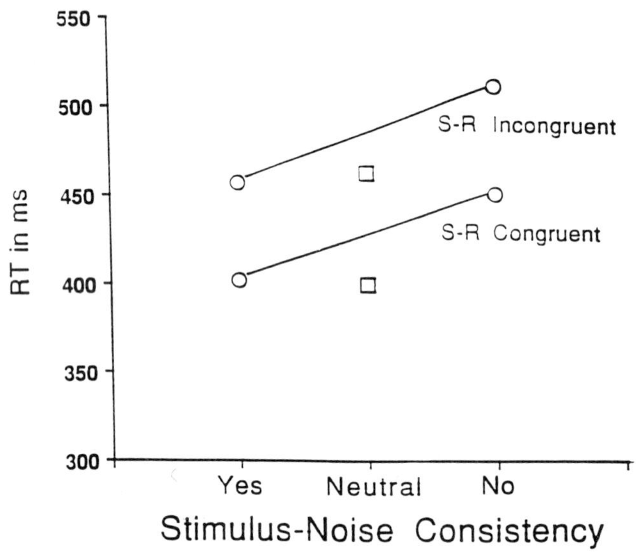

Figure 18 Results of our first experiment with extrinsic, irrelevant dimensions (see text for explanation).

stimulus, the response, neither, or both (see Figures 4). The results are shown on Figure 18. The reaction time for congruent conditions (Figure 17, conditions A and B) is faster than for the incongruent mapping conditions (Figures 17, Conditions C and D). Trials in which the stimulus and the noise were consistent (half the trials in Conditions A and C) were faster than trials on which the stimulus and the noise were inconsistent (the other half of the trials in A and C). Finally, when the noise had no dimensional overlap with either the stimulus or the response sets (geometric noise, Conditions B and D), the RT did not differ significantly from the consistent stimulus-noise trials in either the congruent mapping condition[RT (geometric noise) = 400ms, RT (consistent noise) = 402 ms], or the incongruent mapping condition [RT (geometric noise) = 462 ms, RT (consistent noise) = 458 ms]. The neutral conditions (B and D) disambiguate an important aspect of these results by suggesting that the difference between the consistent and inconsistent conditions may be an absolute and not a relative difference. Note that the additivity in our data of the effects of S-R mapping, and the effects of relevant-irrelevant stimulus consistency, confirms and strengthens the results previously reported by Green and Barber (1983), Hintzman et al. (1972), Keele (1967), and Simon and Sudalamaithu (1979), which placed the locus of interference in the Stroop task before the response selection stage.

In the next experiment we used the same procedure to compare the locus of conflict in Type 3 and Type 4 ensembles. Recall that Type 3 ensembles are those in which there is no dimensional overlap on the relevant dimension, but there is on the irrelevant dimension. The conditions of the experiment are illustrated on Figure 19.

The stimuli were two geometric figures, a trapezoid and a hexagon; the responses were the digit names "two" and "eight" for which the mapping was counterbalanced. There was no dimensional overlap between the stimulus and the response sets, as is required for ensembles of Type 3 and 4. The flanking noise, which the subjects were instructed to ignore, overlapped with different aspects of the stimulus and/or response, and defined the four conditions of the experiment. In Condition A, (cf Figure 19) the noise consisted of the digits 2 and 8 which obviously overlaps with the response set and, according to the model, was expected to produce interference when it conflicted with the response. This corresponds to the standard, intrinsic, Type 3 ensemble used by Simon and others. In Condition B, the noise consisted of the two geometric figures that were identical to those being used as stimuli. This, according to our taxonomic definition is a novel Type 4 ensemble made possible through this new procedure, and is characteristic of the type used by Ericksen, by Coles, and by their colleagues. Here, the noise set overlaps with the stimulus set and, according to the model, might be expected to produce interference when it conflicts with the stimulus. In Condition C, the noise consisted of an asterisk and a plus-sign; this noise set did not overlap with either the stimulus or the response sets (Type 1) and was, therefore, not expected to interact with any of the factors in the experiment. Finally in Condition D, the noise consisted of digits embedded in geometric figures so that it overlapped with both the stimulus and the response set (Type 8). Interference was expected in the case of conflict with either stimulus, response or both. The results are shown on Figure 20.

The three panels show the magnitude of the difference between those trials on which the noise conflicted on the overlapping dimension, and those on which it matched. The square, which is present in all three panels, represents the mean RT for Condition C, in which the noise did not overlap with any of the dimensions in the ensemble. Note that compared to the previous experiments these differences are all very small, but statistically very significant. Thus, when the noise consisted of digits (Figure 19 Condition A) the only significant effect was the interaction of noise with response. When the noise consisted of geometric figures (Figure 19, Condition B) the only significant effect was the interaction of noise with stimulus, and when the noise consisted of digits embedded in geometric figures (Figure 19, Condition D) there was a significant

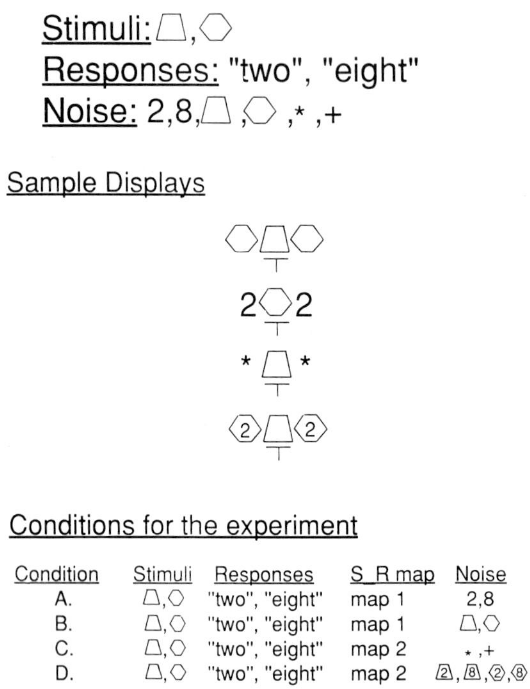

Figure 19 Conditions of our second experiment with extrinsic, irrelevant dimensions. The format of the information is identical to that in Figure 17.

interaction of noise with stimulus, with response, and with both. This pattern of interactions identifies instances of stimulus-stimulus and stimulus-response compatibility, and is consistent with our model. These results suggest that the site of interference in ensembles of Types 3 and 4 depends on the

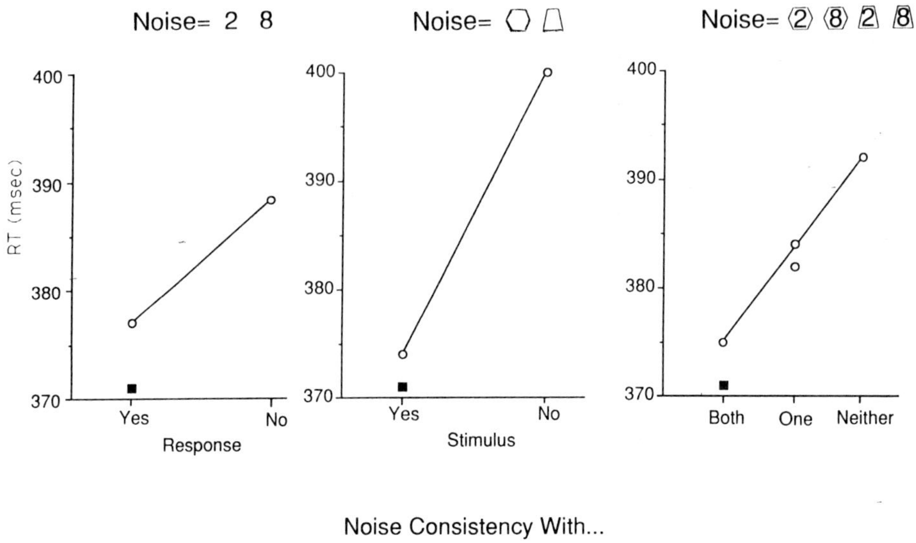

Figure. 20 Results of our second experiment with extrinsic irrelevant dimensions. The abscissa in all three panels represents the consistency status of the noise (flankers) with either the response (left panel -Condition A), the stimulus (middle panel - Condition B), neither/both/or one (right panel - Condition D). The square in each panel represents the RT for the conditions in which the noise is neutral with respect to all aspects of the experiments (Condition C on Figure 19).

particular sets on which the irrelevant dimension overlaps. If it overlaps with the response set, as is true of all Type 3 ensembles with intrinsically presented irrelevant dimensions, the interference is associated with the response. If it overlaps with the stimulus set (Type 4), the interference is associated with the stimulus. If it overlaps with both (Type 8) the interference in associated with both the stimulus and the response. However, as Coles and his colleagues have demonstrated, there appear to be response consequences to the stimulus conflict (see Coles this volume) in Type 4 ensembles.

6.0 Summary

In this chapter I have examined various aspects of the stimulus-response coding problem in the framework of a model that we are developing for stimulus-response and stimulus-stimulus compatibility. This framework includes a taxonomy that identifies five broad classes of stimulus-response combinations, each of which seems to have its own characteristic processing consequences. This taxonomy enabled us to bring under a single roof many different types of studies, compare their properties and characteristics, and examine how they affect or contribute to the stimulus-response coding processes. Together with this taxonomy, which rested on a characterization of the representational aspects of coding, I presented a processing model that appears to work well for some ensembles, less well for others, and remains to be developed for others still. Some of the data that I presented appear to confirm certain aspects of the model; other data appear to identify problems that need to be worked on.

At one time I believed that by being explicit, and by deliberately identifying the representational and the processing aspects of a model I could avoid being deluded by my own theoretical fantasies. That was before I had heard Steve Kosslyn, at another meeting, remind me of the unavoidable trade-off that is inherent in theory construction: "properties of representations," he said, "are only expressed via properties of the processes that operate on them; a given behavioral result always reflects the joint properties of the structure and the process. Hence, a very large range of representations could be used when one performs any given task, with differences in the processes compensating for differences in the representation." (Van Cleek & Kosslyn, in press). The problem is not as hopeless as might appear, for there exists one additional source of constraints for our theorizing, and this comes from studies of the brain itself. And we are fortunate in this section to have at least two chapters that are going to keep our theoretical fantasies in check.

References:

Alluisi, E. A. (1961). Toward optimizing man's tactile communication *Perceptual and Motor Skills, 12*, 235-245.

Coles, M. G. H., Gratton, G., Bashore, T., Ericksen, C. W., & Donchin, E. A. (1985). Psychophysiological investigation of the continuous flow model of human information processing. *Journal of Experimental Psychology: Human Perception and Performance, 11*, 529-553.

Ericksen, B. A., & Ericksen, C.W. (1974). Effects of noise letters upon the identification of a target letter in a nonsearch task. *Perception and Psychophysics, 16*,143-149.

Fitts, P. M., & Deininger, R. L. (1954). S-R compatibility: Correspondence among paired elements within stimulus and response codes. *Journal of Experimental Psychology, 48*, 483-492.

Fitts, P. M., & Posner, M. I. (1967). *Human Performance.* Brooks/Cole: Belmont, California.

Fitts, P. M., & Seeger, C. M. (1953). S-R compatibility: Spatial characteristics of stimulus and response codes. *Journal of Experimental Psychology, 46*, 199-210.

Garner, W. R. (1962). *Uncertainty and structure as psychological concepts.* New York: Wiley.

Green, E. J., & Barber, P. J. (1983). Interference effects in an auditory Stroop task: Congruence and correspondence. *Acta Psychologica, 53*, 183-194.

Greenwald, A. G. (1970). A choice reaction time test of ideomotor theory. *Journal of Experimental Psychology, 86*, 20-25.

Hedge, A., & Marsh, N. W. A. (1975). The effect of irrelevant spatial correspondence on two-choice response-time. *Acta Psychologica, 39*, 427-439.

Heister, G., Schroeder-Heister, P., & Ehrenstein, W. H., (1990). Spatial coding and spatio-anatomical mapping: Evidence for a hierarchical model of spatial stimulus-response compatibility. In R. W. Proctor & T. G. Reeve (Eds.), *Stimulus-Response compatibility: An integrated perspective* (pp. 117-143). Amsterdam, The Netherlands: North Holland, Elsevier Science publisher.

Hick, W. E. (1952). On the rate of gain of information. *Quarterly Journal of Experimental Psychology, 4*, 11-26.

Hintzman, D. L., Carre, F. A., Eskridge, V. L., Owens, A. M., Shaff, S. S., & Sparks, E. (1972). "Stroop" effect: input or output phenomenon? *Journal of Experimental Psychology, 95*, 458-459.

Kahneman, D., and Chajzyk, D. (1983). Tests of automaticity of reading: Dilution of Stroop effects by color-irrelevant stimuli. *Journal of Experimental Psychology: HPP*, (497-509).

Kahneman, D., & Henick, A. (1981). Perceptual organization and attention. in M. Kubovy and J. R. Pomerants (Eds.), *Perceptual Organization* (pp 181-211). Hillsdale, N. J.: Erlbaum.

Kamlet, A.S., and Egeth, H.E. (1969). Note on Construction of Stroop-type stimuli. *Perceptual and Motor Skills, 29*, 914.

Keele, S.W. (1972). Attention demands of memory retrieval. *Journal of Experimental Psychology, 93*, 245-248.
Keele, S. W. (1967). Compatibility and time sharing in serial reaction time. *Journal of Experimental Psychology, 75*, 529-539.
Kornblum, S. (1990 November). S-S & S-R compatibility effects as processing consequences of overlap on relevant and irrelevant dimensions. Paper presented at the meeting of the Psychonomic Society, New Orleans, Louisiana.
Kornblum, S., & Lee, J. W., (1990). Mapping effects for relevant and irrelevant dimensions, with and without dimensional overlap in stimulus-response compatibility tasks. Unpublished manuscript.
Kornblum, S., Hasbroucq, T., and Osman, A. (1990). Dimensional overlap: Cognitive basis for stimulus-response compatibility - A model and taxonomy. *Psychological Review, 97*, 253-270.
Ladavas, E., (1990). Some aspects of spatial stimulus-response compatibility in adults and normal children. In R. W. Proctor & T. G. Reeve, (Eds.), *Stimulus-Response compatibility: An integrated perspective* (pp. 145-162). Amsterdam, The Netherlands: North Holland, Elsevier Science publisher.
MacLeod, C. (1991). Half a century of research on the Stroop effect: An integrative review. Pscyhological Bulletin, *109*, 163-203.
Proctor, R. W., & Reeve, G. T. (1990). *Stimulus-response compatibility: An integrated perspective*. North-Holland: Amsterdam.
Reeve, G.T., & Proctor, R.W., (1990). The Salient-features coding principle for spatial-and symbolic-compatibility effects. In R. W. Proctor, & T. G. Reeve, (Eds.), *Stimulus-Response compatibility: An integrated perspective* (pp. 163-180). Amsterdam, The Netherlands: North Holland, Elsevier Science publisher.
Schvaneveldt, R. W., & Staudenmayer, H. (1970). Mental arithmetic and the uncertainty effect in choice reaction time. *Journal of Experimental Psychology, 85*, 111-117.
Schweickert, R., Fisher, D. L., & Goldstein, W. M. (1991) General latent network theory: Structural and quantitative analysis of networks of cognitive processes. Manuscript.
Simon, J. R. (1969). Reactions toward the source of stimulation. *Journal of Experimental Psychology, 81*, 174-176.
Simon, J. R., & Rudell, A. P. (1967). Auditory S-R compatibility: The effect of an irrelevant cue on information processing. *Journal of Applied Psychology, 51*, 300-304.
Simon, J. R., Hinrichs, J. V., & Craft, J. L. (1970). Auditory S-R compatibility: Reaction time as a function of ear-hand correspondence and ear-response-location correspondence. *Journal of Experimental Psychology, 86*, 97-102.
Simon, J.R. & Small, A. M. (1969). Processing auditory information: Interference from an irrelevant cue. *Journal of Applied Psycholoy, 53*, 433-435.
Simon, J.R., & Sudalaimuthu, P. (1979). Effects of S-R mapping and response modality on performance in a Stroop task. *Journal of Experimental Psychology: Human Perception and Performance, 5*, 176-187.

Simon, R. J., (1990). The Effects of an Irrelevant Directional Cue on Human Information Processing. In R. W. Proctor, & T. G. Reeve, (Eds.), *Stimulus-Response compatibility: An integrated perspective* (pp. 31-86). Amsterdam, The Netherlands: North Holland, Elsevier Science publisher.

Smith, G. A. (1978). Studies of compatibility and investigations of a model of reaction time. Unpublished Ph. D. dissertation. University of Adelaide.

Smith, G. A. (1980). Models of choice reaction time. In A. T. Welford, (Ed.), *Reaction Times* (pp 173-214). London: Academice Press.

Stroop, J. R. (1935). Studies of interference in serial verbal reactions. *Journal of Experimental Psychology, 18*, 643-662.

Theios, J. (1975). The components of response latency in simple human information processing tasks. In P. M. A. Rabbitt & S. Dornic (Eds.), *Attention and Performance V* (pp. 418-440). London: Academic Press.

Umilta, C., & Nicoletti, R., (1990). Spatial stimulus-response compatibility. In R. W. Proctor, , and T. G. Reeve, (Eds.), *Stimulus-Response compatibility: An integrated perspective* (pp 89-116). Amsterdam, The Netherlands: North Holland, Elsevier Science publisher.

Van Cleek, M. N., & Kosslyn, S. (in press). Visual information processing. In D. E. Meyer & S. Kornblum (Eds.). *Attention and Performance XIV: A Silver Jubilee*, MIT Press: Cambridge, MA.

Virzi, R. A., & Egeth, H. E. (1985). Toward a translational model of Stroop interference. *Memory and Cognition, 13*, 304-319.

Wallace, R. J. (1971). S-R compatibility and the idea of a response code. *Journal of Experimental Psychology, 88*, 354-360.

Welford, A. T. (1976). *Skilled performance: Perceptual and motor skills.* Glenview, IL: Foreman.

Wickens, C. D., Sandry, D.L, & Vidulich, M. (1983). Compatibility and resource competition between modalities of input, central processing and output. *Human Factors, 25*, 227-248.

Woodworth, R. S. (1938). *Experimental Psychology*. New York: Henry Holt and Co.

Tutorials in Motor Behavior II
G.E. Stelmach and J. Requin (Editors)
1992 Elsevier Science Publishers B.V.

Response Activation and Verification: A Psychophysiological Analysis[1]

M. G. H. Coles, W. J. Gehring, G. Gratton, and E. Donchin

Cognitive Psychophysiology Laboratory, University of Illinois, 603 E. Daniel, Champaign, Illinois 61820, USA

Abstract

In this chapter, we illustrate how psychophysiological measures can be used to illuminate the processes by which responses are selected and activated. We will focus on studies using stimulus-response compatibility and related paradigms. Our data suggest that, when a stimulus-response mapping is incongruent, incorrect responses are activated - although this activation may be insufficient for the elicitation of an overt behavioral response. These findings provide support for the notion of automatic activation of responses that has been incorporated into the model proposed by Kornblum and his colleagues (Kornblum, Hasbroucq, & Osman, 1990; see also Kornblum, this volume). Furthermore, we have recently identified a brain potential component that appears to be a manifestation of the process associated with the detection of erroneous responses. Such a process is also a critical component of the Kornblum model.

1. THE PSYCHOPHYSIOLOGICAL APPROACH

Traditional approaches to the study of stimulus-response compatibility (and of mental chronometry in general) have relied on measures of the subject's overt behavior (see, for example, Meyer, Osman, Irwin, & Yantis, 1988 and Proctor & Reeve, 1990). The subject is required to respond overtly to particular events (or imperative stimuli), and measures of the speed and accuracy of these responses are used to make inferences about the covert processes engaged by the task. In contrast, the psychophysiological approach relies on measures of **both** speed and accuracy **and** of psychophysiological function (see Coles, 1989; Coles, Gratton, & Fabiani, 1990; Donchin & Coles, 1989). The idea is that the psychophysiological measures are manifestations of some of the covert processes of interest.

[1] Preparation of this chapter was supported in part by grant # MH 41445. This chapter is based on a presentation entitled "Stimulus-response compatibility and psychophysiology" given by the first author at the NATO Advanced Study Institute (Tutorials in Motor Neuroscience), Ajaccio, Corsica, 1990. An abstract of that presentation has appeared in "Tutorials in Motor Neuroscience" (Dordrecht: Kluwer, 1991). Sylvan Kornblum made helpful comments on an earlier version of the chapter.

In our research, we have focussed on measures of the event-related brain potential and of the electromyogram. In a typical experiment, subjects perform a choice-reaction time task (that includes a warning signal on each trial) and they must choose between a response with either their left- or right-hands depending on the imperative stimulus. To register a response, they must squeeze zero-displacement dynamometers, and the force level must exceed a certain criterion, in order for the squeeze is to be registered as a "complete" response. This criterion is usually set at 25% of the maximum force that can be exerted by a subject. Subjects are given extensive training with this procedure. (See Coles, Gratton, Bashore, Eriksen, & Donchin, 1985, for a discussion of this response requirement.)

Along with measures of the subject's squeeze responses, we derive measures of the electroencephalogram (EEG) from various scalp locations. Embedded in these EEG records are the event-related brain potentials (ERPs) that represent neural activity that is time-locked to particular events in the task. The ERPs are generally revealed by averaging the EEG data from many trials. We also record integrated electromyographic activity from the forearm flexors, the agonist muscles involved in executing the squeeze response.

One advantage of using dynamometers is that they can be used to detect responses that do not necessarily reach the criterion for registration as a complete overt response -- that is, we can detect sub-threshold response activation. We have focussed especially on trials where the subjects make **partial** errors. Recall that, in our experiments, subjects are choosing between left- and right-hand responses as a function of an imperative stimulus. Thus, sometimes the left-hand response is correct and the right-hand response is incorrect, and sometimes the opposite is the case. Had we relied strictly on measures of the subjects' overt behavior derived from the usual discrete response manipulandum (i.e., a button or computer key), we could only have identified two kinds of trials in this kind of choice reaction time experiment: **correct** trials, when the subject executes the correct response, and **incorrect** trials when the subject executes the incorrect response. However, our approach allows us to identify trials on which the correct response is executed but the incorrect response is partially activated. This partial activation can be revealed in measures of EMG and of squeeze activity that does not reach the criterion for an overt response. Based on these measures, we have been able to identify two kinds of partial errors: those on which a correct response is executed but incorrect EMG activity is also present without any detectable force being exerted on the dynamometers (partial EMG errors) and those on which a correct response is executed but incorrect EMG and squeeze activity is present (partial squeeze errors).

Measures of partial response activation have enabled us to address a variety of important questions. We will review these shortly. For the time-being, it is important to note that the partial error trials would have been treated as correct response trials, if standard discrete response devices had been used and electromyographic and squeeze activity had not been recorded.

We have also looked at a measure of movement-related brain activity -the *lateralized readiness potential* (LRP) - to evaluate the prevalence of partial response activation in choice reaction time tasks. This measure is sensitive to central response activation processes that do not necessarily reach the level required for peripheral EMG or squeeze activity.

The readiness potential was first described by Kornhuber and Deecke (1965), who observed that a negative potential develops at the scalp prior to the execution of voluntary motor responses. Subsequent research has shown that the potential tends to be larger over the hemisphere contralateral to the responding limb (e.g., Kutas & Donchin, 1980). Furthermore, the scalp distribution of the potential is related to known lateralization in the motor system. This is consistent with our interpretation that the potential can qualify as a measure of motor system activity. This inference is supported by other psychophysiological and neurophysiological research (for review, see Coles, 1989).

One can also observe this lateralized potential in reaction time tasks. Generally speaking, the potential appears to become lateralized when the subject begins to prepare the hand that will be used to execute a response (see Kutas & Donchin, 1980; Rohrbaugh, Syndulko, & Lindsley, 1975). Before subjects execute a left-hand response, the negative potential is larger over the right, than the left, side of the brain: the converse is true for right-hand movements. To focus on preparatory processes associated with specific responses (i.e., hands), we have developed a subtraction and averaging procedure to isolate the lateralized portion of these potentials (see Coles, 1989, for a detailed description of the procedure[2]). The measure yielded by this procedure (the LRP) represents the degree to which the subject has differentially primed one or other of the two responses (hands). In practice, the subtraction is performed separately for trials when a left-hand movement is the correct response and for trials when a right-hand movement is the correct response. The resulting values are then averaged to yield a measure of the degree to which the subject shows lateralization associated with the preparation of the correct or incorrect response. We use the measure, then, to infer whether the subject has preferentially activated the correct or incorrect response, and by what time such preferential activation must have happened.

2. THE PSYCHOPHYSIOLOGICAL APPROACH AND STIMULUS RESPONSE COMPATIBILITY

As we noted earlier, there are two aspects of the Kornblum model for which psychophysiological data are particularly relevant (see Kornblum et al., 1990, and Kornblum, this volume, for an elaboration of the model). First, there is the process associated with automatic activation of responses following stimulus presentation. According to Kornblum, this process occurs as a result of the *dimensional overlap* between stimulus and response sets. The presentation of a stimulus automatically primes the corresponding response. When the activated and required responses are the same, the mapping is said to be "congruent" - when they are different, the mapping is "incongruent".

The second process of interest involves the comparison of a representation of the automatically activated response with a representation of the required response.

---

[2] Note that the procedure used to derive the LRP is equivalent to that described by de Jong, Wierda, Mulder, & Mulder (1988) to derive their measure of the *Corrected Motor Asymmetry*.

According to the model, if these two representations do not match, then the activated response is aborted.

2.1 "Automatic" response activation

2.1.1 The Eriksen Noise Compatibility Paradigm.

In this paradigm (see Eriksen & Eriksen, 1974), subjects must respond with either the left- or right-hand to stimuli that are comprised of attributes some of which may be mapped to the correct response and some to the incorrect response. On any trial, one of four arrays are presented to the subject. The arrays contain a central target letter and four "noise" letters arranged symmetrically to the left and right of the target letter. Subjects are required to respond with, say, their left-hand if the central target letter is an H, and with their right hand, if the central target letter is an S. Note that, for two of the arrays (referred to by us as "incompatible"), the noise letters are those associated with the incorrect response.

This paradigm is not strictly a "Stimulus-Response Compatibility" paradigm, because there is no dimensional overlap between stimulus and response sets. The dimension of the stimulus set (the letters - H or S) has nothing in common with the dimension of the response set (the response hand - left or right). However, because subjects always make a response with the same hand to a given target letter, it is reasonable to propose that the representations of particular letters come to be associated with particular responses without the need for look-up or search processes. Thus, the letters may, in fact, automatically prime particular responses.

This implies that, when arrays contain noise that is associated with the incorrect response, presentation of the array may lead to the activation of the incorrect response, even though the correct response is eventually executed when the central target letter has been identified. In this sense, the S-R mapping for so-called incompatible arrays may lead to an effect that is analogous to that produced by incongruent S-R mappings when there is dimensional overlap.

Recall that, by recording the EMG and squeeze activity associated with both correct and incorrect responses, we can identify two classes of partial errors: those for which incorrect EMG activity is present and those for which both incorrect EMG and incorrect squeeze activity are present. Data from two experiments in which measures of partial errors have been obtained (Coles et al., 1985; Eriksen, Coles, Morris, & O'Hara, 1985) reveal that partial errors occurred more often when the array contained incompatible noise than when the array was compatible. Thus, even though the noise letters that flanked the target letter were irrelevant to the subject's task, they were evidently processed to the extent of activating the responses associated with them. In this regard, our data are consistent with the idea of automatic activation proposed by Kornblum.

The Kornblum model focusses on those incorrect responses that are activated if the stimulus array contains attributes that are associated with the incorrect response. If this were the only mechanism responsible for incorrect responses, then one would not expect subjects to make partial errors (or indeed any errors) under congruent mapping conditions. However, Coles et al. (1985) found that approximately 45% of compatible trials contained partial errors, mostly involving incorrect EMG activation without incorrect squeeze activation. We attribute this phenomenon to an aspecific priming process by which subjects prime responses independently of the information provided by the stimulus. Such a process can be triggered by guessing strategies that involve the development of response biases during the foreperiod as well as by "mere presentation" effects, by which responses are indiscriminately activated following stimulus presentation (Coles et al., 1985; Gratton, Coles, Sirevaag, Eriksen, & Donchin, 1988).[3]

Another interesting aspect of the partial error data concerns the temporal dynamics of correct response execution as a function of the activation of the incorrect response. Regardless of the kind of array (compatible or incompatible), the correct response had a longer latency when the incorrect response was partially activated. In addition, the interval between the first sign of correct EMG activity and the first sign of correct squeeze activity was longer under these partial error conditions. Both these observations suggest that correct response activation processes were disrupted when the incorrect response was also activated. These data suggest that at least part of the delay in correct response execution under incongruent mapping conditions may be attributed to a competition between responses that are activated on the same trial.

We have also examined the behavior of the lateralized readiness potential in the Eriksen task. As we noted earlier, this potential is a manifestation of central response activation processes. Figure 1 shows the brain potential data for the compatible and incompatible conditions. In the upper part of the slide, we see averaged data over all trials, including those on which the subjects executed incorrect responses. Note that when the array was incompatible, there is a dip in the lateralized readiness potential shortly after stimulus presentation. This dip indicates that, on the average, at this point in time, the incorrect response was preferentially activated. In the lower part of the figure, we see data for a subset of trials for which the subject responded relatively slowly - that is, they did not guess -and for which there was no evidence in the EMG of incorrect response activation. Notice that the dip in the lateralization function is still evident for the incompatible condition. This suggests that partial incorrect response activation can occur centrally without resulting in any signs of peripheral response activation.

Taken together, then, these data indicate that incorrect responses can be activated in the Eriksen paradigm by the presence of "irrelevant" noise that is associated with the incorrect response. This incorrect response activation can be seen centrally, in the lateralized readiness potential, and more peripherally, in the electromyogram and small overt responses.

2.1.2 The Go/No-go paradigm.

Strictly speaking, the Eriksen paradigm does not qualify as a "Stimulus-Response Compatibility" paradigm because it does not involve dimensional overlap between stimulus and response sets. Furthermore, the "incompatibility" that arises in the Eriksen paradigm is due to a conflict between an **irrelevant** stimulus attribute (the noise) and

---

[3] Kornblum (1991, personal communication) also believes that there is a random error producing process of the kind described here. In this regard, it should be noted that the model described in Kornblum et al. (1990) was not intended to provide a general account of errors.

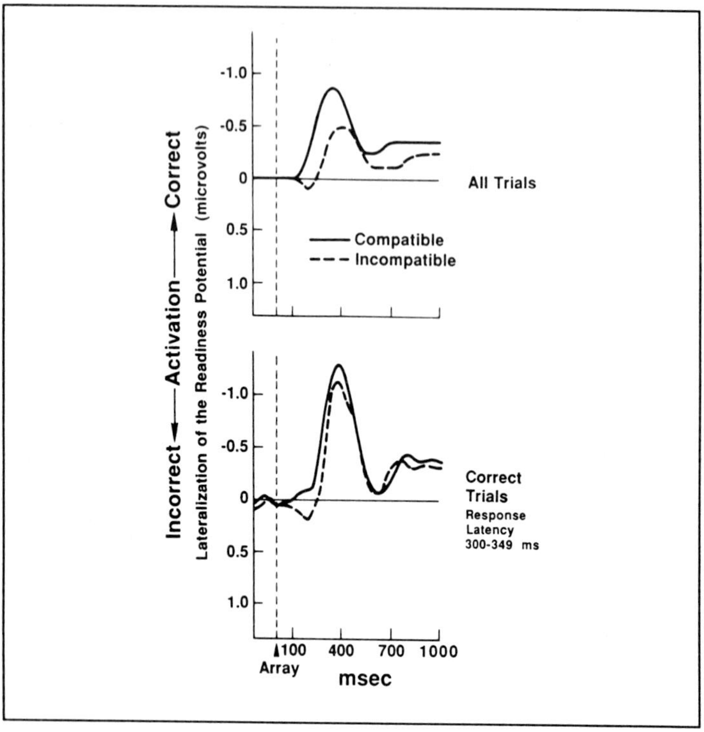

Figure 1. Lateralized readiness potential data for compatible and incompatible trials, from Gratton et al. (1988). Copyright 1988, American Psychological Association, reprinted by permission.

the required response. In a study by Osman and his colleagues (Osman, Bashore, Coles, Donchin, & Meyer, in press) the psychophysiological approach was used to study response processes in a paradigm in which a **relevant** dimension of the stimulus (location on a screen to the left or right of fixation) **did** overlap the response dimension (left or right-hand response). In this task, subjects had to **execute** a response if the stimulus was a letter, but to **withhold** the response if the stimulus was a digit. The stimulus could appear to the left or right of fixation. Under compatible conditions, a stimulus on the left designated a response with the left-hand (if the stimulus was a letter), and a stimulus on the right required a response with the right hand. In incompatible conditions, the mapping was reversed.

For our purposes, the question of interest is whether the incorrect response is automatically activated by the location of the stimulus in the incompatible condition.

Figure 2 shows that there is indeed a dip in the lateralized readiness potential for both go and no-go trials in the incompatible condition.[4]

Thus, as in the Eriksen experiments, psychophysiological data support the proposal that there are conditions under which responses are automatically activated. In the case of the Osman experiment, however, there **was** dimensional overlap between stimulus and response sets and this overlap was between a **relevant** stimulus dimension and the response. Thus, the Osman data perhaps provide even stronger support for the automatic activation process that is an important aspect of the Kornblum model.

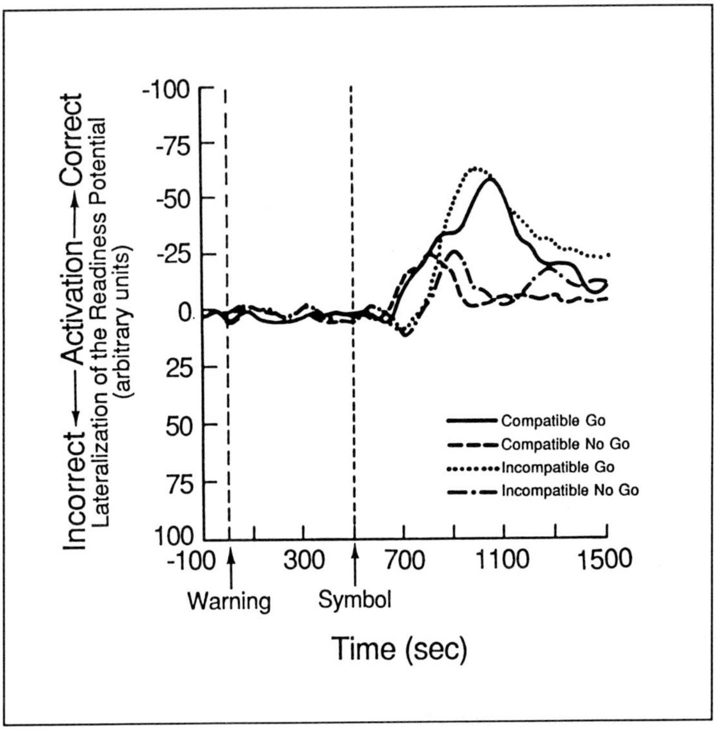

Figure 2. Lateralized readiness potential data for compatible and incompatible go and no-go trials from Osman et al. (in press). Copyright 1992, American Psychological Association, reprinted by permission.

[4] An analysis of the LRP waveforms, averaged across go and no-go trials for the incompatible conditions, revealed that the waveform in the region between 150 and 250 ms after the stimulus was significantly different from zero ($t(5)=2.77$, $p = .039$).

2.1.3 On the automaticity of "automatic" activation.

The experiments reviewed in the previous two sections suggest that certain stimulus attributes are processed to the level of response activation even though this may result in the activation of the incorrect response. Given that this kind of activation is evidently antithetical to the task requirements placed on the subject for fast and accurate performance, it is tempting to infer that the activation is somehow outside the subject's control -- and in this sense, "automatic".

In a recent chapter (Coles, De Jong, Gehring, & Gratton, 1991; see also Coles, Gratton, & Donchin, 1988), we reviewed the results of a variety of reaction time experiments involving stimuli with (at least) two attributes, one of which was easier to discriminate than the other. In all these experiments, the LRP was used to determine whether both attributes were always processed to the level of response activation. While such processing did indeed occur in some experiments, this was not invariably the case. Furthermore, even under those circumstances in which the **same** stimuli were used, but in different task situations, the LRP data revealed that processing of the easier-to-discriminate attribute did not always result in response activation (cf. De Jong et al., 1988; Miller & Hackley, 1990). We interpreted these data as suggesting that the subject can exert control over the degree to which responses are activated following stimulus presentation. To the extent possible, this control will be exercised so as to optimize performance in the context of task goals.

This notion has been examined recently by a series of experiments by Gratton (Gratton, Coles, & Donchin, 1988). The results of these experiments indicate that the effect of noise compatibility in the Eriksen paradigm can be modified when the probability of compatible and incompatible noise is varied. This modification was evident in both overt behavioral and LRP measures and appeared to reflect the actions of a control process that adjusts the degree to which processing of the noise letters leads to response activation. It is clear, then, that the kind of activation observed in the Eriksen paradigm must be "weakly" automatic (cf. Kornblum et al., 1990).

2.2 The Verification Process

A second feature of the Kornblum model is a mechanism by which the accuracy of the automatically activated congruent response is verified and the response is aborted, if necessary.

Psychophysiological evidence for the verification process comes from a comparison of the brain potentials that are temporally related to the initiation of correct and incorrect responses. In contrast to the brain potential data discussed previously, these data are derived by using the subject's response as the event of interest rather than the stimulus. Figure 3 shows such a comparison. These data were derived from the Eriksen noise compatibility paradigm described previously. The Figure shows wave-forms representing brain potential activity for correct and incorrect trials. In this case, the presence and accuracy of a response was defined by the first "complete" overt response detected. Although we only show data for incompatible trials and for the C3 electrode, comparable differences between correct and incorrect compatible trials are found and similar effects are observed at other electrode locations.

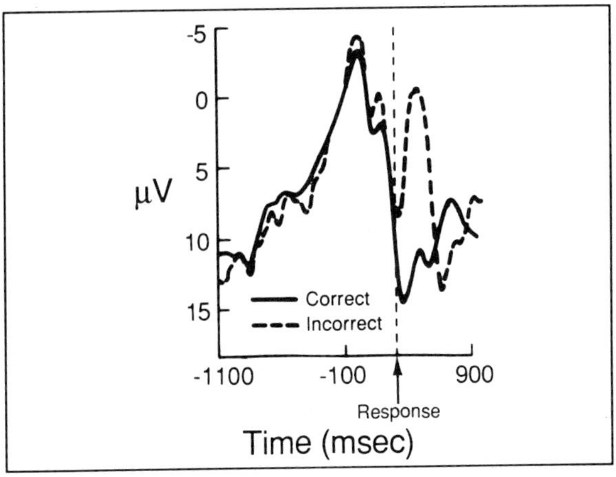

Figure 3. The error-related negativity in the Eriksen task. Response-locked averages (for the Cz electrode) for correct and incorrect trials.

The most striking feature of these data is the negative-going potential that begins at around the time that overt response is recorded. Note that the potential is present in both conditions, on both sides of the scalp, and that it is absent on correct trials. The fact that there is a brain process that distinguishes between correct and incorrect responses at about the time of overt response initiation implies the existence of a mechanism that verifies the accuracy of the response before or during response execution. Thus, the presence of this "error-related negativity" provides support for the existence of the kind of verification process that is integral to the Kornblum model.

We have observed the error-related negativity in a number of different choice-reaction time tasks, including Sternberg memory set tasks, precueing tasks, sentence verification tasks, and speed-accuracy tradeoff tasks (see Gehring, Meyer, Coles, & Donchin, 1990). Thus the phenomenon is not dependent on a particular group of subjects, a particular kind of task, or a particular response device (we have used both dynamometers and response buttons). The data, then, suggest that there is a distinct brain response that occurs at about the time subjects make an incorrect motor response. The existence of this response suggests that some part of the system must have representations both of the response being executed and of the response that *should* be executed. Of course, it is the comparison of these representations that is the essence of the verification process.

Another important finding is that the error-related negativity is not lateralized - that is, the distribution of this brain response across the scalp does not depend on the hand used by the subject in making the incorrect response. (Note that this contrasts with the *lateralized readiness potential.*) This suggests that the brain process does not occur in those cortical areas responsible for ultimate control of the movement - or the implementation of an abort process.

From the foregoing it seems clear that the brain process we have observed on error trials is related to a comparison process of the kind proposed by the Kornblum model.

2.2.1 On the need for a response abortion process.
Kornblum and his colleagues propose that, if the verification process reveals that the incorrect response has been activated, then it must be actively aborted. As we have noted, incorrect responses are activated when the stimulus contains attributes that correspond to the incorrect response. Furthermore, this incorrect response activation can occur at a "subthreshold" level. One interpretation of this finding is that these kinds of partial error trials represent partially successful attempts to abort incorrect responses. Alternatively, they may just represent cases where bias processes and/or the available stimulus information are insufficient to lead to complete response activation -- that is, they are "miscarriage" trials rather than partially successful abortion trials. Two arguments favor the latter explanation. First, as we noted earlier, psychophysiological data support the idea that there can be a close linkage between the system responsible for stimulus analysis and that responsible for the activation of responses. Thus, as evidence about a particular stimulus waxes *and wanes*, so activation of the associated responses will increase *and decrease*. According to this view, then, a decrease in response activation does **not** reflect the operation of an abortion process. Rather, it reflects the fact that evidence in favor of a particular response is declining. Second, in one experiment (Gratton et al., 1988: Figure 6), we found evidence for the mutual inhibition of two concurrently activated responses in two-choice reaction time experiments. As the activation of one response approached the threshold required for overt response execution, so the activation of the other response decreased. This kind of inhibitory coupling is similar to that observed for EMG and squeeze responses (see above) and presumably represents the operation of a local control process rather than a centrally initiated abortion process.

Thus, our data indicate that decrease in response activation can occur **without** there being an active inhibitory process (i.e., abortion) of the kind proposed by Kornblum and his colleagues. This is not to say that such an active process might not be operative. In fact, in a different experimental context, we did find evidence for an active inhibitory mechanism (De Jong, Coles, Logan, & Gratton, 1990). However, this mechanism appeared to function to inhibit **all** activated responses. Such a mechanism would clearly be inappropriate in the kind of two-choice reaction time experiments described earlier in which some response must **always** be executed.

3. CONCLUSIONS

3.1 The locus of the stimulus-response compatibility effect

Our psychophysiological data provide support for the existence of a generic response activation process that is an essential aspect of the explanation of stimulus-response compatibility effects proposed by Kornblum and his colleagues. Both peripheral and central measures suggest that, under some circumstances, responses are activated automatically following stimulus presentation.

These data were derived from two experimental paradigms. In one paradigm (Osman et al., in press), there was dimensional overlap between stimulus and responses sets (location) and the LRP measure revealed that a *relevant* stimulus attribute (location) was associated with response activation under incongruent mapping conditions. In the second paradigm (the Eriksen paradigm), an *irrelevant* stimulus attribute (peripheral noise letter identity) was also associated with response activation. In particular, when relevant (i.e., target letter identity) and irrelevant attributes conflicted, the incorrect response was activated.

In a recent paper, Hasbroucq and Guiard (1990) have argued that the effects of irrelevant S-R incongruity are best understood in terms of stimulus incongruity rather than in terms of S-R incongruity (see also Stoffels & van der Molen, 1988). Thus, delays in reaction time that are occasioned by a conflict between relevant and irrelevant stimulus attributes (as in the Eriksen paradigm) are ascribed to delays in stimulus processing rather than to delays due to the activation of an incorrect response. It is clear that our psychophysiological data are at variance with this ascription -- we have clearly demonstrated that incorrect response activation occurs in the Eriksen paradigm. However, our data also indicate that the delay in reaction time that can be attributed to incorrect response activation and response competition is not sufficient to account for the overall effect of noise-compatibility.

In the experiment by Coles et al. (1985), the effect of noise- compatibility on reaction time was 47 ms. Based on our analysis of the temporal dynamics of correct response execution as a function of incorrect response activation, we were able to determine that response competition effects could account for 22 ms of the noise-compatibility effect. Thus, 25 ms remained to be explained by other mechanisms. In this experiment, we also measured the P300 component of the event-related brain potential. We have argued elsewhere that the latency of this component reflects the duration of stimulus evaluation processes and is relatively independent of response-related processes[5] (Donchin & Coles, 1988). In fact, P300 latency was 27 ms longer when the noise was incompatible, suggesting that stimulus evaluation processes were prolonged by incompatibility. Thus, it appears that **both** S-S incongruity **and** S-R incongruity effects operate in the Eriksen paradigm to delay reaction time (see Coles et al., 1985, for details of these analyses).

---

[5] This claim has been challenged by those who consider that the results of Ragot and his colleagues (Ragot, 1984; Ragot & Renault, 1981) demonstrate that P300 latency is sensitive to response-related processes. Ragot found that P300 latency was longer, when the (irrelevant) spatial position of a light did not correspond with the side of the response hand indicated by the light. In fact, when the data obtained in these experiments are analyzed in terms of the scheme proposed by Hasbroucq and Guiard (1990), the effect on P300 is attributable to S-S incongruity rather than to irrelevant S-R incongruity. Of course, the finding of an effect of S-S incongruity on P300 latency is entirely consistent with the proposal that this measure is sensitive to the duration of stimulus evaluation processes. Note also that in Ragot's work, **relevant** S-R incongruity was not associated with a delay in P300 although it did delay reaction time.

3.2 The Verification Process

Our data support the proposal of Kornblum and his colleagues that "automatically" activated responses are checked against the required response. The presence of a distinctive brain potential component on incorrect trials suggests that a special process is invoked when there is a mismatch between activated and required responses. However, it is presently unclear whether this brain potential component is a manifestation of error detection or whether it is more closely related to the consequences of error detection, among which may be an attempt to abort the incorrect response. There are, of course, other functions that are served by a response verification process. For example, Rabbitt has shown that the detection of an error on a particular trial leads to a change in behavior on subsequent trials (Rabbitt, 1966; see also Donchin, Gratton, Dupree, & Coles, 1988). Thus, an error-detection mechanism is clearly an important component of any model of human information processing, although its *raison d'etre* need not be inextricably linked to an abortion process.

4. REFERENCES

Coles, M. G. H. (1989). Modern mind-brain reading: Psychophysiology, physiology, and cognition. *Psychophysiology*, *26*, 251-269.

Coles, M. G. H., De Jong, R., Gehring, W. J., & Gratton, G. (1991). Continuous versus discrete information processing: Evidence from movement-related potentials. In C. H. M. Brunia et al. (Eds.), *Proceedings of the Ninth International Conference on Evoked Potentials*. Amsterdam: Elsevier.

Coles, M. G. H., Gratton, G., Bashore, T. R., Eriksen, C. W., & Donchin, E. (1985). A psychophysiological investigation of the continuous flow model of human information processing. *Journal of Experimental Psychology: Human Perception and Performance*, *11*, 529-553.

Coles, M.G.H., Gratton, G., & Donchin, E. (1988). Detecting early communication: Using measures of movement-related potentials to illuminate human information processing. *Biological Psychology*, *26*, 69-89.

Coles, M. G. H., Gratton, G., & Fabiani, M. (1990). Event-related potentials. In J. T. Cacioppo & L. G. Tassinary (Eds.), *Principles of Psychophysiology: Physical, Social, and Inferential Elements*. New York: Cambridge University Press, pp. 413-455.

De Jong, R., Coles, M. G. H., Gratton, G., & Logan, G. L. (1990). In search of the point of no return: The control of response processes. *Journal of Experimental Psychology: Human Perception and Performance*, *16*, 164-182.

De Jong, R., Wierda, M., Mulder, G., & Mulder, L.J.M. (1988). Use of partial information in responding. *Journal of Experimental Psychology: Human Perception and Performance*, *14*, 682-692.

Donchin, E., & Coles, M. G. H. (1988). Is the P300 component a manifestation of context updating? *The Behavioral and Brain Sciences*, *11*, 355-372.

Donchin, E., Gratton, G., Dupree, D., & Coles, M. G. H. (1988). After a rash action: Latency and amplitude of the P300 following fast guesses. In G. C. Galbraith,

M. L. Kietzman, & E. Donchin (Eds.), *Neurophysiology and psychophysiology: Basic mechanisms and clinical applications*. New York: Academic Press, pp. 173-188.

Eriksen, B. A., & Eriksen, C. W. (1974). Effects of noise letters upon the identification of target letters in visual search. *Perception and Psychophysics*, *16*, 143-149.

Eriksen, C. W., Coles, M. G. H., Morris, L. R., & O'Hara, W. P. (1985). An electromyo-graphic examination of response competition. *Bulletin of the Psychonomic Society*, *23*, 165-168.

Gehring, W. J., Coles, M. G. H., Meyer, D. E., & Donchin, E. (1990). The error-related negativity: An event-related brain potential accompanying errors. *Psychophysiology*, *27*, S34 (Abstract).

Gratton, G., Coles, M. G. H., & Donchin, E. (1988). Modulation of the noise/compatibility effect. *Psychophysiology*, *26*, 450 (Abstract).

Gratton, G., Coles, M. G. H., Sirevaag, E., Eriksen, C. W., & Donchin, E. (1988). Pre- and post-stimulus activation of response channels: A psychophysiological analysis. *Journal of Experimental Psychology: Human Perception and Performance*, *14*, 331-344.

Hasbroucq, T., & Guiard, Y. (1990). Stimulus-response compatibility and the Simon Effect: Towards a conceptual clarification. *Journal of Experimental Psychology: Human Perception and Performance*, in press.

Kornblum, S., Hasbroucq, T., & Osman, A. (1990). Dimensional overlap: Cognitive basis for stimulus-response compatibility - A model and a taxonomy. *Psychological Review*, *97*, 253-270.

Kornhuber, H. H., & Deecke, L. (1965). Hirnpotentialanderungen bei Wilkurbewegungen und passiven Bewegungen des Menschen: Bereitschaftpotential und reaffarente Potentiale. *Pflugers Archiv*, *284*, 1-17.

Kutas, M., & Donchin, E. (1980). Preparation to respond as manifested by movement-related brain potentials. *Brain Research*, *202*, 95-115.

Meyer, D. E., Osman, A. M., Irwin, D. E., & Yantis, S. (1988). Modern mental chronometry. *Biological Psychology*, *26*, 3-67.

Miller, J., & Hackley, S. A. (1990). *Movement-related brain potentials in the absence of movement: Evidence for temporal overlap among contingent mental processes.* Manuscript submitted for publication.

Osman, A., Bashore, T. R., Coles, M. G. H., Donchin, E., & Meyer, D. E. (in press). On the transmission of partial information: Inferences from movement-related brain potentials. *Journal of Experimental Psychology: Human Perception and Performance.*

Proctor, R. W., & Reeve, T. G. (Eds.) (1990). *Stimulus-response compatibility.* Amsterdam: Elsevier Science Publishers.

Rabbitt, P. M. A. (1966). Errors and error-correction in choice-response tasks. *Journal of Experimental Psychology*, *71*, 264-272.

Ragot, R. (1984). Perceptual and motor space representation: An event-related potential study. *Psychophysiology*, *21*, 159-170.

Ragot, R., & Renault, B. (1981). P300 as a function of S-R compatibility and motor programming. *Biological Psychology*, *13*, 289-294.

Rohrbaugh, J.W., Syndulko, K. & Lindsley, D.B. (1976). Brain wave components of the contingent negative variation in humans. *Science*, *191*, 1055-1057.
Stoffels, E. J., & van der Molen, M. W. (1988). Effects of visual and auditory noise on visual choice reaction time in a continuous flow paradigm. *Perception and Psychophysics*, *44*, 7-14.

Tutorials in Motor Behavior II
G.E. Stelmach and J. Requin (Editors)
1992 Elsevier Science Publishers B.V.

QUANTITATIVE ANALYSIS OF STIMULUS-RESPONSE LINKING IN A SEQUENCE OF CORTICAL STRUCTURES.

J. Seal[1], M. Akamatsu[2], T. Hasbroucq[1], S. Kornblum[3] and I. Mouret[1].

[1]Cognitive Neuroscience Unit, C.N.R.S., chemin J. Aiguier, 13402 Marseille Cedex 9, France

[2]Industrial Products Research Institute, 1-1-4 Higashi, Tsukuba, Ibaraki 305, Japan

[3]Mental Health Research Institute, University of Michigan, Ann Arbor, MI 48109-0720, U.S.A.

Abstract

It is in its passage from the source of sensory input to the motor output that the initial sensory influx evoked by a cue for movement becomes transformed into the motor activity expressed at the level of the muscles. Our aim has been to follow this neuronal activity and describe the transformation mechanism along a sequence of cortical structures. Using descriptive and novel quantitative methods of data analysis we have attempted to characterize the functional properties of the different neuronal populations encountered and to formalize the results into a simple model.

1. GENERAL INTRODUCTION

We have been investigating the neuronal mechanism by which a sensory cue can give rise to movement. If we consider the brain as a processing unit, then the source of input is the sensory receptors and the output is expressed as modifications of muscular activity. Neuro-anatomical studies have described a complex pattern of interconnectivity of neurons going from input to output. It is this intricate network of neurons which forms the substrate for transforming the sensory influx arising at the receptors into a specific pattern of muscle activation and, hence, movement of a body part. If the patterns of interconnectivity between neurons can indicate the *physical pathways* linking inputs with outputs, it is the activity of the neurons within these pathways which reflects *how* the sensory influx is translated into a motor output. Unfortunately, our knowledge of the code or codes used for transmitting information within the central nervous system is poor and mainly concerns the coding of certain physical attributes of the stimulus or the motor act (Evarts, 1981; Mountcastle, 1984). Thus, we are faced with the paradoxical situation where we are doing experiments to reveal the neural correlates of a translation mechanism without really knowing how the code used for this mechanism will reveal itself in the patterns of neuronal discharge we record. We have to use recordings made in primary sensory and motor areas of the cortex to establish the characteristics of the neuronal discharge in these areas which we can consider as being reference points. These reference characteristics can then be used to aid the interpretation of the data obtained in those cortical areas which are considered, on the basis of anatomical and lesion studies, to play a role in the mechanism of sensory to motor translation. To this end, an important part of our work has been to develop exploratory methods of data analysis in the search for the neural codes of information transfer.

1.1. INTRODUCTION

We have attempted to follow the sensory influx initially evoked at the level of the sensory receptors, as it passes through the central nervous system and becomes transformed into the motor activity expressed at the level of the muscles. To do this, we have made single neuron recordings in four cortical areas which can be considered, on the basis of their neuroanatomical connections, to form part of one of the possible pathways linking sensory input to motor output i.e. primary somaesthetic cortex (areas 3, 1 and 2), the superior parietal cortex (area 5), the premotor cortex (area 6) and the primary motor cortex (area 4) (Jones et al. 1978).

Neuronal activity was recorded in these areas whilst the monkey performed a tactile choice reaction task in which the stimulus was a brief vibration applied to the glabrous surface of the tips of either the fingers or the thumb and the motor response was a press with the stimulated digit/s. An advantage of this task was that, given the strict somatotopy of the primary receiving areas, we could precisely localize the digit region of the primary somaesthetic cortex and then make rostro-caudal displacements of the recording electrode to find neurons with task-related changes in neuronal activity in the other cortical areas (Pons et al. 1985). In addition, the four cortical areas of the input/output chain were available for exploration with the same recording chamber. Not only was this experimental task interesting from a neuroanatomical point of view but, also, the physical characteristics of the sensory input (e.g. frequency and intensity of the vibratory stimulus) and the motor output (e.g. effector used, force changes) were clearly defined. This enabled us to identify neurons involved in sensory or motor processes by the strong correlation of any changes in neuronal activity during the task with one or other characteristic of the stimulus or the motor response.

An analytical method we have developed to study sensory to motor translation is based on a measure of the strength of the temporal correlation between a change in neuronal activity and the sensory and motor events of the experimental protocol (Commenges and Seal, 1985). This measure has been called the variance-relation from which we can derive the variance ratio to define a sensory to motor gradient (Commenges et al. 1986). An interesting feature of this ratio is that it enables us to place the different populations of recorded neurons along a sensory to motor gradient going from purely sensory processes to purely motor processes (Seal and Commenges, 1986). In our experiments, these two properties are represented by the characteristics of neurons recorded in the primary somaesthetic cortex and the primary motor cortex, respectively.

The variance ratio, thus, enables us to follow the neuronal activity initially evoked by the sensory input as it passes through the different cortical areas to become transformed into the motor activity observed at the level of the primary motor cortex. This interpretation of the results of the variance ratio is based on the temporal properties of the transmission of action potentials from one neuron to another in a chain of neurons. There is a time delay due to the transmission across the synapse and the conduction of the action potentials along the axon to the next synapse. However, the delay is not fixed but depends on several factors including the level of excitability of the post-synaptic membrane, the number of action potentials arriving at the pre-synaptic membrane and the speed of conduction in each neuron. These factors vary continually and, thus, the delay in transmission of action potentials from one neuron to another varies. When the sensory stimulus is given repeatedly, then the mean and variance of the time interval stimulus onset to change in neuronal activity can be calculated. In a *sequence* of neurons, the time interval stimulus onset to change in neuronal activity is the sum of each of these delays and as one goes along the sequence of neurons so the overall delay and its variance increases. A similar logic can be applied when the reference point is not the stimulus onset but is instead muscle contraction and the onset of the motor response. As the recorded neuron is located more and more synapses away from the motoneuron and the muscle endplate, so the mean and the variance of the time interval change in neuronal activity to onset of motor response will increase. It is an interesting point for reflection that when studying sensory processes, it is the stimulus that is considered to give rise to the change in neuronal activity whereas in the study of motor processes, it is the change in neuronal activity that is considered to give rise to the motor response. However, we can also ask the question of at what moment does a stimulus-evoked change in activity become motor activity? The aim of the present series of experiments was to provide experimental evidence for this key translation process. We have attempted to describe, in both qualitative and quantitative terms, the process of sensory to motor translation within a circumscribed neuronal network consisting of the primary somaesthetic cortex (S1), the superior parietal cortex (A5), the premotor cortex (A6) and the primary motor cortex (A4).

2. METHODS

Single neuron activity was recorded in four different cortical areas of a Rhesus monkey (Macaca mulatta) during the performance of a choice reaction time task. The manipulandum consisted of two oval plates placed at 90 degrees one to the other such that the tip of the thumb rested on one and the tips of the fingers rested on the other. Each plate could be vibrated by an electromagnet. The vibration was in a plane perpendicular to the surface of the plate and changes in force applied on the plate in this plane were measured by force sensors. The monkey was trained to maintain the resting force on each plate within a force window that was either side of the level of force produced when the digits were just resting on the plates. It is interesting to note that the animal adopted a procedure of lightly touching the plates in a similar way to that of a human subject when he is trying to feel a weak tactile stimulus. The task consisted of a brief vibratory tactile stimulus (50 or 100 msec duration, 100 μm amplitude, 75 Hz frequency) applied to either the thumb or the fingers of the right hand and the motor response was an increase in force produced by a press with the stimulated digit/s.

As described in the introduction, one of the aims of this series of experiments was to obtain reference data in the primary sensory and motor areas of the cortex which would serve to aid the interpretation of the data obtained in the cortical areas located between the sensory and motor areas of the proposed processing chain. By recording the activity of neurons in the primary somaesthetic and primary motor cortical areas, the discharge properties of which are well documented, we have been able to "calibrate" the cortical processing going on at the input and output stages during our experimental task (Evarts, 1981; Mountcastle, 1984).

To obtain this reference data, it was of prime importance to record the activity of neurons located within the digit region of the primary somaesthetic cortex and the primary motor cortex. The neurons of the primary somaesthetic cortex can be considered to be the privileged target for the sensory influx evoked at the level of the sensory receptors. The localization of the digit region was greatly aided by the use of magnetic resonance imaging of the monkey's brain prior to implantation of the recording chamber. Images were taken of the brain every 1 mm in the sagittal, frontal and horizontal planes. The resulting images were further treated by computer-assisted analysis and enlarged ten times. The detail of the images so obtained was quite remarkable and enabled us to compare the pattern of sulci in the experimental monkey's brain with that of established maps of the cortex so as to locate the position of the digit region of the primary somaesthetic cortex (Pons et al. 1985). This position was defined with respect to reference points on the skull of the experimental animal so that the recording chamber could be centered over this region during the surgical procedure to prepare the animal for single neuron recordings. With this method, we were able to record task-related changes in neuronal activity with the first electrode penetration into the cortex. Rostral displacements of the recording electrode enabled us to record from the digit region of the primary motor cortex. Although the somatotopic organization was not so rigid in the premotor area and the superior parietal cortex, further rostro-caudal displacements were equally associated with the presence of task-related changes in neuronal activity.

3. RESULTS AND DISCUSSION

The distributions of the variance ratio of neurons recorded in the different cortical areas show that there was an overall sequential order in which the changes in activity most closely related to sensory input were recorded from neurons in S1 (figure 1). At the other extremity, the changes in activity most closely related to motor output were recorded from neurons in the primary motor cortex. However, within the population of neurons recorded in A4, some neurons presented changes in activity that were more strongly related to sensory input than to motor output. Similarly, the frequency histogram of time of change in activity with respect to stimulus onset for neurons in A4 showed two peaks, the first of which occurred at about 100 msec after the onset of the stimulus (figure 2). When the change in activity was analyzed with respect to the onset of change in force, this peak did not appear. This suggests that the changes in activity which made up the first peak were more strongly time-locked to stimulus onset than to the onset of change in force. Other authors have described similar stimulus-related changes in neuronal activity within A4, although the functional significance of these changes is not apparent (Kwan et al. 1981; Lamarre et al. 1983). In our experiments, the sensory cue was a vibration and it may be that the stimulus-related changes in neuronal activity observed in A4 are simply a reflection of the afferent volley that was transmitted from S1 to A4 via a direct cortico-cortical projection (Jones et al. 1978). However, the majority of changes in neuronal activity in S1 occurred at about 40 msec after stimulus onset and it is unlikely that the afferent volley takes a further 60 msec to arrive at A4. There is a second peak in the frequency histogram of S1 which occurred at about 80 to 90 msec after stimulus onset and the time difference between this peak and that of A4 (about 10 msec) is more compatible with the transmission time along a direct cortico-cortical pathway. We are presently investigating whether the two peaks in the frequency histogram of S1 are due to the activation of two different populations of sensory receptors, one of which may have a preferential projection via S1 onto A4.

Analysis of the frequency histograms for changes in neuronal activity of the four different cortical areas shows that there is a complex temporal organization for the time of change in neuronal activity as the sensory influx evoked at the level of the receptors passes through the different cortical areas to arrive at the level of A4. There is overlap in the distribution of time of change in neuronal activity for the four cortical areas, although the distributions for S1 and the premotor cortex show clearcut peaks when the time of change is analyzed with respect to the onset of the stimulus. This suggests that the changes in activity which form these peaks are better related, i.e. more strongly time-locked, to the onset of the stimulus than to the onset of change in force. This is as we would expect for the changes in activity recorded in S1 given that the sensory cue was a tactile stimulus. Furthermore, quantitative analysis of data recorded in S1 supported the interpretation of a purely sensory role for these neurons e.g. change in activity after the stimulus whether or not the motor response was performed, the bursts of action potentials were correlated with each cycle of the vibratory stimulus and the change in activity was specific to stimulation of either the thumb or the fingers. The peak of the stimulus-related changes of neuronal activity in the premotor cortex occurred about 30 msec after that of S1 and these changes were

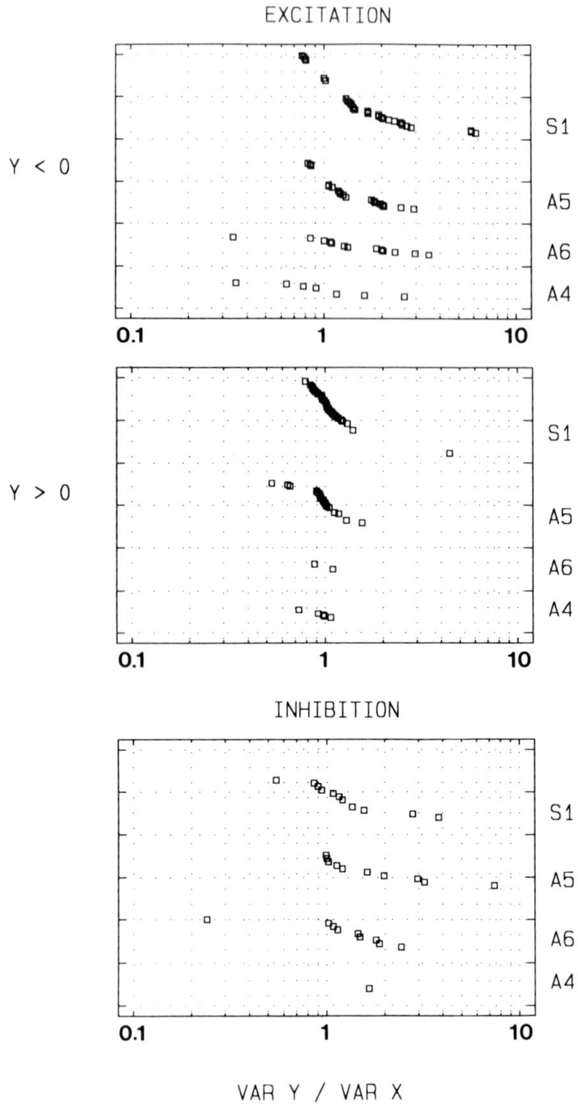

Figure 1. Distribution of the variance ratio for neurons recorded in the primary somaesthetic cortex (S1), the superior parietal cortex (A5), the premotor cortex (A6) and the primary motor cortex (A4). The variance ratio is given for excitatory changes in activity *prior* to (top)and *after* the onset of change in force (middle) and for inhibitory changes in activity which were only observed prior to the force change (bottom). Variance ratios are plotted on a logarithmic scale. Consecutive values were slightly displaced upwards on the ordinate to limit overwriting of points.

qualitatively different to those of S1 e.g. in trials when the stimulus was not followed by the motor response, the amplitude of the stimulus-related change in activity was smaller than when the motor response was performed, changes in activity occurred when either effector was sollicited, no correlation between the burst of action potentials and each cycle of the vibratory stimulus. Thus, these neurons in the premotor cortex do not appear to have purely sensory properties yet their change in activity is time-locked to the onset of the stimulus. On the sensory to motor gradient as defined by the variance ratio, the neurons positioned closest to sensory input were located in S1, followed by a population of premotor neurons which, again suggests that the neural processing going on in these premotor neurons is after that of the purely sensory processes.

The distribution of timing of changes in activity in area 5 extended through and beyond the range of time of change in S1 and area 6. This suggests that area 5 neurons were active throughout the time interval stimulus to motor response, rather than at particular moments in time as was the case for neurons in S1, area 6 and A4. The largest peak in the distribution of time of change in neuronal activity in A4 occurred about 50 msec prior to the onset of change in force. It should be noted that the onset of the motor response in our experiments was the change in force of digit pressure on one or other of the vibrating plates and not the onset of digit displacement, as is more commonly used. We chose to measure force for two reasons. First, the change in the force signal was abrupt and, thus, the moment of onset of change in force could be determined with accuracy. Secondly, force is one of the few parameters of movement for which a coding in the discharge of A4 neurons has been clearly demonstrated. This is important for the interpretation of the variance ratio data. At the input side, it is physical stimulation by the tactile cue which evokes changes in the activity of neurons in S1, thus the purely sensory changes in the activity of S1 neurons depend upon the physical parameters of the stimulus. In contrast, it is the change in activity of neurons in A4 which evokes the motor response. However, we must ask the question of what parameters of the motor response are evoked by the change in activity? Suppose that the change in activity of a population of neurons in A4 codes direction of movement rather than change in force for a given direction of movement, then the change of force will be only an approximation of the true parameter coded. This approximation will add variance to the time interval change in neuronal activity-onset of change in force. This variance will be all the more important as the characteristics of the motor response vary from trial to trial. In an attempt to limit this source of error, we trained the monkey to produce a motor response to within strictly defined limits of amplitude of change in force and within a fixed time limit after the onset of the stimulus.

A further point that we would like to discuss concerning the variance ratio is the observation that the activity of some neurons in S1 and area 5 was modified after the onset of change in force but the measure of the variance ratio suggested that these changes in activity were more strongly related to sensory input than to motor output. The interpretation

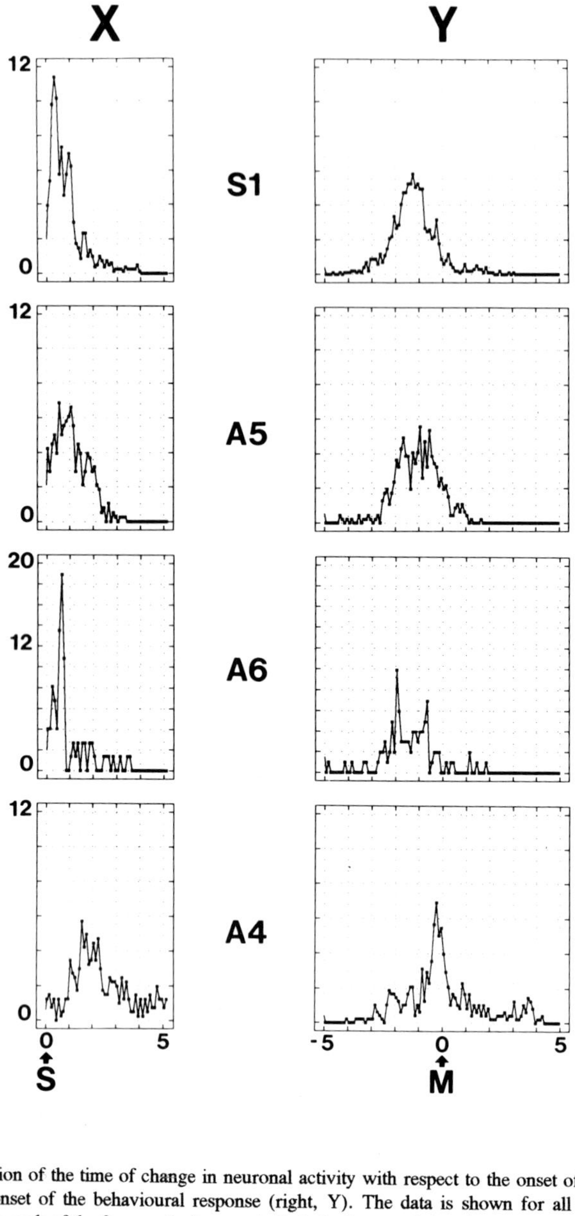

Figure 2. Distribution of the time of change in neuronal activity with respect to the onset of the tactile stimulus (left, X) and the onset of the behavioural response (right, Y). The data is shown for all the trials of all the neurons recorded in each of the four cortical areas studied. Ordinate: relative frequency of occurrence shown as the number of changes in activity per 10 msec bin, normalized for the same number of values in each cortical area. Abscissa: time aligned to the onset of the tactile stimulus (S) or the onset of the behavioural response (M), intervals 100msec. Abbreviations as in figure 1.

of the results of the variance ratio for these neurons is difficult in that changes in activity of neurons in S1 and area 5 occurring after the onset of movement are usually interpreted as being due to sensory feedback from the moving body part. Given that it is the displacement of a body part which gives rise to the sensory feedback, we would expect such changes in activity to be more strongly time-related to the onset of displacement than to the onset of the sensory cue. In our experiments, the motor response was measured as a change in force and not as the displacement of the digits although the two are related. It is possible that these late occurring, stimulus-related changes in activity were, in fact, evoked by the stimulus but that they occurred at a latency such that the motor response had already begun. This could be the case for stimulus-related changes in activity triggered by the end of the tactile stimulus. This observation requires further investigation.

Visual examination of the peri-event histograms of discharge activity revealed that about one third of the neurons in the premotor cortex presented two changes in activity, one time-locked to the onset of the sensory cue and the other prior to and time-locked to the onset of the change in force. However, it was not possible to visualize the two changes in activity in the same peri-event histogram because of the variation in behavioural reaction time from one trial to the next. Thus, from simple visual examination of peri-event histograms, it was impossible to evaluate the relative timing of the different changes in activity of the same neuron or compare the timing of changes in activity of neurons in different cortical areas. However, the transformation of input to output occurs by the interaction of neuronal activity within neural networks and the pattern of interaction can be revealed by following the relative timing of excitatory and inhibitory changes in neuronal activity within the network. To overcome this problem, we have developed a novel method of within-burst analysis based on template matching (Akamatsu et al, in preparation).

From the normalized peri-event histograms, it can be seen that there is a clear temporal organization for the time of change in neuronal activity, whether it be the onset of change or the peak change. The sequence is S1, area 6, area 5 then A4. About one third of the area 6 neurons studied presented two peaks in the burst of activity following the sensory cue and the within-burst analysis enabled us to compare the relative timing of these peaks with respect to the timing of similar peaks in activity in the other cortical areas studied. The general pattern is illustrated by the examples in figure 3. It can be seen that the first important peak in activity of the area 6 neurons follows that of the S1 neurons whereas the second peak appears to occur at the same time as the peak in activity of the A4 neurons. The peak in activity of the area 5 neurons occurs after the first peak but before the second peak of the area 6 neurons. Quantitative analysis showed that the first peak of the area 6 neurons was time-locked to the onset of the stimulus whereas the second peak was time-locked to the onset of change in force. The peak of activity in the A4 neurons was time-locked to the onset of change in force, as was expected.

A tentative interpretation of the pattern of time of change in activity within the cortical network we have studied is as follows. The initial sensory impulse initiated at the receptors triggers a change in activity of the S1 neurons which in turn transmit this impulse to initiate the first peak in activity of the area 6 neurons. We then postulate that it is the

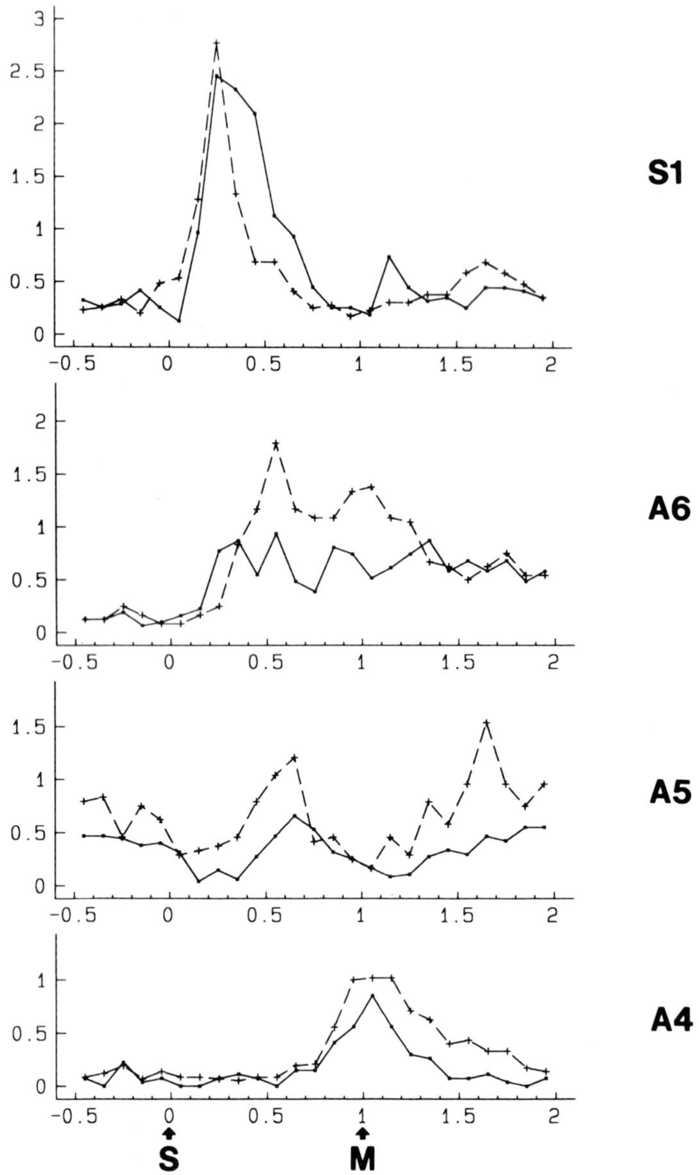

Figure 3. Two examples of normalized histograms for each of the four cortical areas studied. 0: onset of the tactile stimulus, 1: onset of the behavioural response. The ordinate shows the relative amplitude of each histogram. Abbreviations as in figure 1.

increase in activity of the area 5 neurons which maintains the level of activation of the area 6 neurons high until some motor pulse arrives and triggers a "motor" burst in both area 6 and A4. We observed that in those trials where the animal did not respond to the stimulus, the change in activity of area 6 neurons was less intense and the second "motor" peak was absent. Furthermore, there was no apparent change in neuronal activity of area 5 neurons in similar stimulus-no motor response trials. Thus, although the change in activity of the area 5 neurons was time-locked to the onset of the sensory cue, this change was conditional on the execution of the motor response. We can say that these changes were *stimulus- and response-dependent.*

It is also interesting to note that whereas the changes in activity in the other cortical areas occurred at punctual moments in time during the stimulus-response process, the changes in activity in area 5 occurred throughout this time period as if the activity of the area 5 neurons was generally elevated during the stimulus-response process. In the hypothetical sequence of events that we propose, the change in activity of certain area 5 neurons would serve as a modulator of the activity in area 6. The presence or absence of these modulatory influences would govern whether or not the "motor" burst occurs in area 6 neurons. This burst would appear to be necessary for the execution of the motor response. In those trials in which the animal did not respond behaviourally to the sensory cue, we can postulate that for some as yet unknown reason, the area 5 neurons were not activated thus their facilitatory effect on the initial, sensory activation of the area 6 neurons would not be exerted. In this case, any motor pulse arriving at area 6 would find these neurons in a low state of excitation, insufficient to trigger a motor output.

Of course, two major questions arise from this hypothesis, the first is where does the motor pulse come from, the second is what is the reason for the modulation of activity of the area 5 neurons in the stimulus-no behavioural response trials i.e. how do these changes become stimulus- and response-dependent ?

4.CONCLUSION

The results presented here have been interpreted in terms of a cortical network linking sensory input to motor output. Within this network, the primary receiving areas, i.e. S1 in our task, appear to be totally implicated in the sensory processing of the behaviourally-relevant sensory input. However, what was designated as the primary motor area, i.e. A4, appears to have not only a primary motor role but also to be directly influenced by the sensory input. The functional importance of the "sensory" responses in a primary motor area remains unclear. It is proposed that areas 5 and 6 function together in a translation mechanism by which the initial stimulus-related activity becomes transformed into a form of motor output. The fact that the peak of the motor-related changes in activity of areas 5 and 6 occurred at about the same time was interpreted as being due to a common "motor" pulse acting simultaneously on both areas. We may then ask where does this "motor" pulse come from and a likely source is the cortico-cerebellar pathway. The cerebellum has been implicated in the programming of movement and there are well known pathways linking S1 and area 5 with the cerebellum which, in turn, projects back to area 6 and A4 of the cerebral cortex (Brooks, 1979). It is also possible that the motor-related burst in activity in area 6 initiates a similar, almost simultaneous burst in A4, via the direct cortico-cortical connections. Area 6 and A4 both have corticospinal projections to the intermediate and ventral parts of the spinal cord and so the two areas may each have a distinct motor output acting on the motoneurons.

In the mechanism we have described, the activity of area 5 neurons plays an important role in the linking of sensory input and motor output in area 6 neurons. We have proposed that certain area 5 neurons have a modulatory action to facilitate the initial change in activity of the area 6 neurons triggered by the sensory cue. This modulatory action may work by maintaining the level of excitability of the area 6 neurons above a certain threshold until some "motor" pulse triggers the motor-related burst in area 6 and A4. When this facilitatory effect is absent, as in trials where the cue is not followed by the motor response, the initial, stimulus-related burst in activity of area 6 neurons is not maintained at above threshold and, hence, when the "motor" pulse arrives, these neurons are insufficiently excited to produce the motor burst. However, the question arises as to the origin of the stimulus- and movement-related nature of the changes in activity of these area 5 neurons. A possible source of influence is the limbic system which, via the hypothalamus, projects to area 5 (Kievit and Kuypers, 1975). Finally, the ratio variance Y/variance X appears to be a useful measure of the relative position on a sensory to motor gradient of the different neurons recorded and experiments are continuing to study a larger population of neurons.

5.ACKNOWLEDGEMENTS

We would like to thank D. Porcheron (C.H.U. de la Timone, Marseille) and P. Rage (C.N.R.S., Marseille) for the magnetic resonance imaging of the monkey brain. We are also grateful to M. Coulmance, N. Vitton, B. Arnauld and R. Fayolle for their valuable technical assistance. Supported by the Office of Naval Research, U.S.A., grant N00014-89-J1557.

6. REFERENCES

Brooks, V. B. (1979). Control of intended limb movements by the lateral and intermediate cerebellum. In H. A. Wilson, V.J. Asanuma (Editors.), Integration in the Nervous System. Tokyo: Igaku Shoin.

Commenges, D., & Seal J. (1985). The analysis of neuronal discharge sequences : change-point estimation and comparison of variance. Statistics in Medicine, 4, 91-104.

Commenges, D., Pinatel, F., & Seal, J. (1986). A program for analyzing single neuron activity by methods based on estimation of a change-point. Computer Methods and Programs in Biomedicine, 23, 123-132.

Evarts, E. V. (1981). Role of motor cortex in voluntary movements in primates. In V. B. Brooks (Editor.), Handbook of Physiology. Volume II. Motor control (pp. 1083-1120). Bethesda: American Physiological Society.

Jones, E. G., Coulter, J. D., & Hendry, S. H. C. (1978). Intracortical connectivity of architectonic fields in the somatic sensory, motor and parietal cortex of the monkeys. Journal of Comparative Neurology, 181, 291-348.

Kievit, J. & Kuypers, H.G.J.M. (1978). Basal forebrain and hypothalamic connections to frontal and parietal cortex in the Rhesus monkey. Science, 187, 660-662.

Kwan, H.C., MacKay, W.A., Murphy, J.T. & Wong, Y.C. (1981). Distribution of responses to visual cues for movement in precentral cortex of awake primates. Neuroscience Letters, 24,123-128.

Lamarre, Y., Busby, L., & Spidalieri, G. (1983). Fast ballistic movements triggered by visual, auditory, and somesthetic stimuli in the monkey. I. Activity of precentral cortical neurons. Journal of Neurophysiology, 50(6), 1343-1358.

Mountcastle, V. B. (1984). Central nervous mechanisms in mechanoreceptive sensibility. In I. Darian-Smith (Editor.), Handbook of Physiology. Volume III. Sensory Processes (pp. 789-878). Bethesda: American Physiological Society.

Pons, T. P., Garraghty, P. E., Cusik, C. G., & Kaas, J. H. (1985). The somatotopic organization of area 2 in macaque monkey. Journal of Comparative Neurology, 241, 445-466.

Seal, J., & Commenges, D. (1986). Modeling of the stimulus-response process and the determination of function in the central nervous system. Mathematical Modelling, 7, 905-913.

Tutorials in Motor Behavior II
G.E. Stelmach and J. Requin (Editors)

Some Historical Roots of Phenomena and Methods in Motor Behavior Research

Charles J. Worringham

Department of Movement Science, The University of Michigan, 401 Washtenaw Avenue, Ann Arbor, MI 48109-2214 U.S.A.

Abstract

Some pioneering motor behavior studies undertaken in the late nineteenth century by a number of German and two French researchers, as well as one American writing in German, are reviewed. At least nine contemporary issues were either explicitly or indirectly studied in this period, including the preselection effect, the spatial speed-accuracy trade-off, phase transitions in bimanual motions, amplitude-velocity scaling, velocity-curvature relationships, and the range effect. While restricted to relatively simple methods, quite ingenious approaches to motor problems were employed, including detailed kinematic analysis and limb movement perturbation. Three of the studies appear to have been the earliest kinematic analyses of voluntary motion. The significance of these neglected contributions to motor behavior is discussed as is their historical background.

1. INTRODUCTION

Only recently has the study of human motor behavior emerged as an international scientific endeavor with a distinct identity. The publication of the first volume in this series (Stelmach and Requin, 1980) represented a significant landmark in this development. The field has blossomed strikingly in the ten intervening years, as reflected in the diverse contributions in the current volume. With the field of motor behavior burgeoning, it is easy to overlook the fact that its historical roots run deep and wide, especially within philosophy, physiology and psychology. There is, as yet, a mere handful of works which explicitly trace the development of the field and of the theoretical issues which are central to it (see, for example, Adams (1987) for an examination of the history of research in motor learning, Schmidt, 1988 (Chapter 1) for a general historical background to contemporary motor behavior, Scheerer (1987) for a detailed account of early work on "muscle sense"), and parts of Viviani (this volume) on thinking about perceptual-motor interactions in the last 250 years). It is easy, of course, to overstate the importance of a historical perspective in motor behavior research. Ground-breaking studies can indeed be successfully performed with minimal knowledge of work undertaken before the Second World War. A student of early studies of motor behavior can reap several rewards, however, not the least of which are an awareness of the development of theoretical issues, and an appreciation of the ingenuity and diligence often manifest in the work of our predecessors. A more specific reason for drawing attention to these early forays into motor behavior is that they presage some quite contemporary issues. I shall suggest that at least nine phenomena, topics or methods of current or very recent interest were either explicitly studied or foreshadowed during this period. These are: the range effect, the preselection phenomenon, the notions of initial impulse and feedback-based control, phase transitions in bilateral simultaneous movements, the spatial speed-accuracy trade-off, the distance/location dichotomy in motor memory research, amplitude-velocity scaling, the inverse curvature-velocity relationship, and the use of kinematic recording and of experimental perturbations in limb movement studies. With these thoughts in mind I have translated in whole or in part some motor behavior studies undertaken in late nineteenth century, in Germany and France, and prepared from them the following summary.

2. SOME AUTHORS AND THEIR STUDIES

No attempt has been made to give a complete account of the studies which follow, rather, selected results of interest to modern readers were chosen for inclusion. The choice of works for this review was guided by the same principle, but is somewhat eclectic and is biassed towards experimental work, less well-known research, mostly that undertaken by German writers. Thus other works deemed of less interest to a modern readership were excluded, such as those by Leyden (1869), Bernhardt (1872), Mach (1875), Lewinski (1879), Schaefer (1887), Sternberg (1885), Kröner (1887), Cremer (1887), Müller and Schumann (1889) and Falk (1890). The review which follows is arranged by author, and is primarily chronological.

2.1 Wilhelm von Camerer.

To the present author's knowledge, Camerer's dissertation (1866) is the first kinematic study of human voluntary movement, performed at Tübingen in the mid-1860s. This analysis predates the first chronophotographic studies of human and animal motion of Marey (1886) and Muybridge (1888), as well as the more strictly biomechanical work of Fischer (1906), much of which was also undertaken last century. Camerer contrasted the performance of voluntary arm movements with different temporal constraints. His investigations encompassed 256 elbow extension and 227 flexion movements, the subject being Camerer himself. These movements varied in duration between .8 and 20 s, their extent being in the order of 6 cm. Three faster movements were recorded, however, including the .34 s flexion movement shown in Figure 1. Movements were recorded with a device used in studies of the velocity of human circulatory system. In this application, the index and middle fingers of the pronated right hand were lightly rested on two brass rods, mounted so that at the other end a steel tip inscribed the displacement record on the carbon-covered paper attached to the drum of a hand-turned kymograph. A second "channel" indicated the passage of time by recording either pendulum motion or the vibrations of a tuning fork. In this manner, complete kinematic data was recorded in analog form. The apparatus had one limitation, namely the extent of the movements, which could not be much greater than about 6 cm. Camerer was careful to ensure that these movements were terminated voluntarily, rather than by impact with the end of the device.

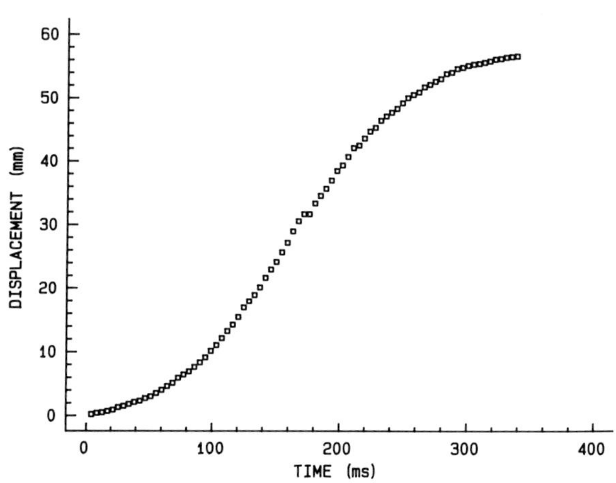

Figure 1. Position-time profile of Camerer's .34 s flexion movement, showing characteristic sigmoidal shape. (Note one aberrant, repeated data point, possibly a misprint, in the original table).

For the three rapid movements, Camerer used a microscope fitted with a micrometer to measure the displacement (on the ordinate) at each millimeter interval on the abscissa. Thus the movement shown in Figure 1 was analyzed at less than 5 ms intervals. The laboriousness of this precision led him to divide movements into ten equal intervals for the analysis of the remaining 483 movements. The studies were part of a larger investigation by Karl Vierordt into the perception of time (Vierordt, 1868), and included uniform, accelerated, and decelerated movements.

The work is of interest not only for its methodological precociousness. Camerer had noted features of movement which might loosely be termed "invariant". Specifically, he observed that even with different movement time goals, the general structure of movements showed some qualitative similarities. Movements showed an initial increase in velocity, a uniform velocity phase (he was no doubt strongly influenced by the preponderance of very slow movements in this study which show such a phase) and a period of deceleration. The movements also showed some scaling of peak velocity with duration for approximately similar amplitude, as shown in Figure 2, in which Camerer's tabulated displacement data for four movements are depicted graphically as velocity profiles. These data make a case for his being

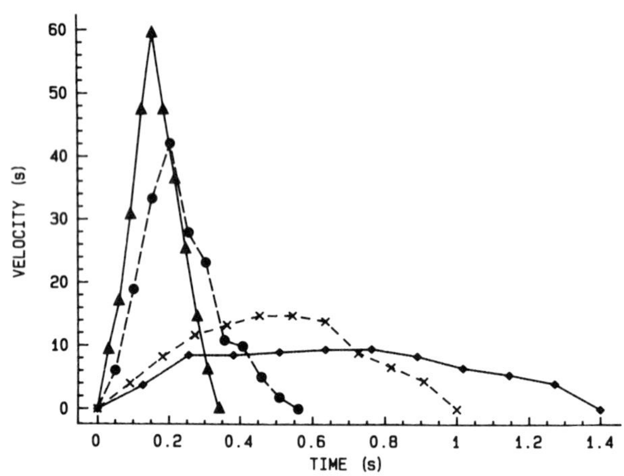

Figure 2. Velocity-time profiles for four flexion movements whose durations vary from .34 to 1.4 s.

considered as the unwitting discoverer of the unimodal velocity profile. In support of this claim, it should be noted that much of his presentation and discussion of data centered not on absolute position/time data but on the relative size of displacements covered in equal intervals of time - analagous to instantaneous estimates of velocity. Camerer noted in particular that movements of different intended and actual speeds but similar extents did not commence with equal velocities, but that scaling occurred, making the general proposition that "the initial velocities produced by the muscles have a proportional relationship to the average velocities actually achieved and, respectively, intended" (p.42). Camerer noted that the deceleration phase was subject to similar scaling.

2.2 Jacques Loeb.

Another early kinematic study (Loeb and von Koranyi, 1890) examined the effects of gravity on vertical arm movements. The apparatus used by Loeb is shown in Figure 3. As in Camerer's study, a kymograph was the instrument used to record data, but a novel method was used for its acquisition. Loeb mounted a set of alternating wood and metal plates on a drawing board, connecting the metal plates to one pole of a power source, the other pole being connected to a metal stylus. In moving the stylus across the drawing board, each contact (and loss of contact) between the stylus and the metal plates closed (and opened) an electrical cicuit and was marked on the kymograph, a second pen recording the oscillations of a tuning fork to provide a temporal record.

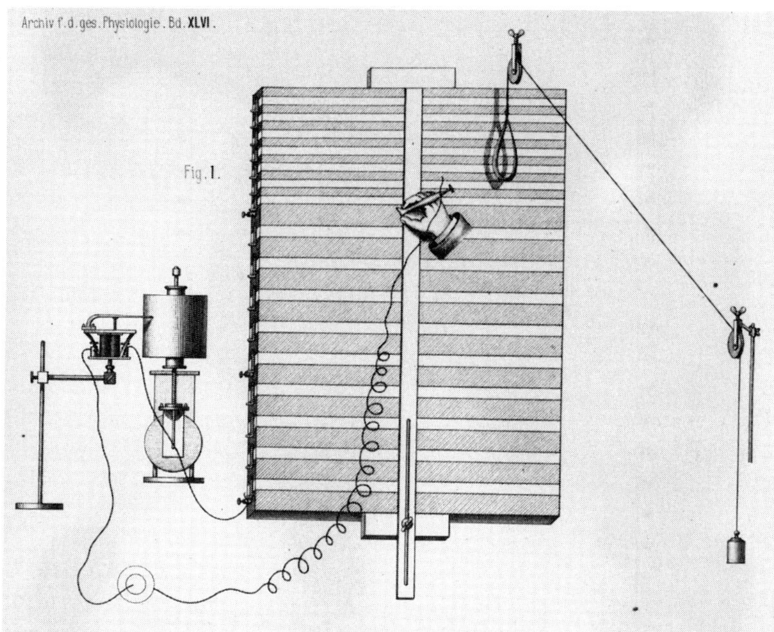

Figure 3. Apparatus used by Loeb (1890) to study vertical arm movements.

Subjects made straight-line movements guided by a ruler clamped to the drawing board. Loeb's major conclusion was that downward, as well as upward arm movements must be under muscular control, and were not the simple consequence of gravity's acceleration of the limb. His reasoning was that the displacement profile of a free-falling limb should be skewed, whereas his recordings showed it to be indistinguishable from an upward movement. In particular, in both types the half-duration of the movement almost exactly coincided with the time to cover half the distance (T/2 and S/2 respectively, in Figure 4). Loeb observed that the discrepancy between these times rarely exceeded 5% of the total duration.

It will be noticed in Figure 3 that Loeb also studied movements experimentally perturbed during their execution by means of a load attached via a pulley and cable to a sling around the subject's wrist. By judiciously arranging the degree of slack in the cable, this load could be made to take effect roughly in the mid-course of the subject's movement. It will be seen in Figure 4 that the displacement profile of the segment of the movement following this perturbation was practically indistinguishable from that of an unperturbed motion, a fact remarked upon by Loeb in his discussion. This study of gravity's effects of planar vertical motions finds a strong echo in a much more recent study of similar phenomena using an infra-red tracking system (Atkeson and Hollerbach, 1985).

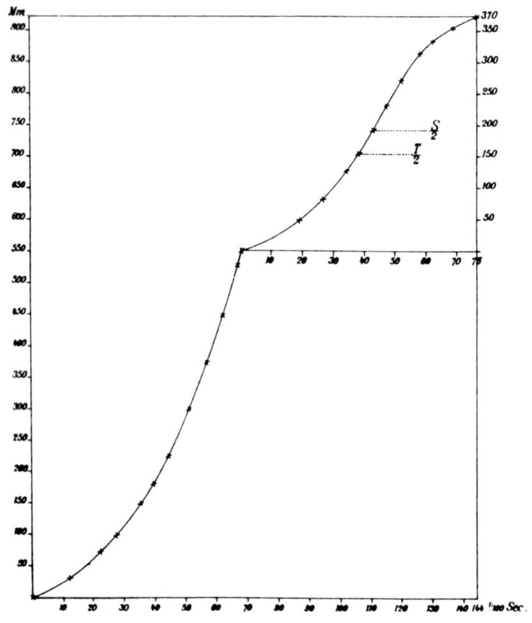

Figure 4. Position-time profile of a perturbed 90 cm movement as recorded by Loeb opposing load encountered during execution.

In a pair of studies, Loeb (1887, 1890) investigated the perception of limb position and motion. As part of these, Loeb described an effect in which simultaneous, vertical linear movements of the hands differed in length by an amount related to the vertical difference in the starting position of each. In this study, the motion of one arm was constrained by the attachment of a string of fixed length, while the other was free. The subject had to move the limbs the same distance upwards, downwards or laterally in the same time, with the vertical distance between left and right arms being the independent variable. These results are shown in Figure 5, in which constant error (constrained limb distance - free limb distance) served as the dependent measure. Constant error was not zero, but nor did it vary with the degree of vertical separation when the movements were made laterally. Note, however, a change from negative to positive constant error as the free limb moved from a starting position above that of the constrained limb to a position below it, and vice versa. This indicates a tendency for the limbs to end closer to each other than they started, travelling unequal distances in equal times as if in an attempt to end at the same position. These results call to mind findings from the "distance vs. location" controversy in motor memory research of the 1970s favoring the latter (e.g. Russell, 1976). In some senses it also hints at the bimanual aiming phenomenon described by Kelso, Southard and Goodman (1979) in which different task demands for simultaneously conducted aiming are met with the limbs moving in a close to synchronous fashion.

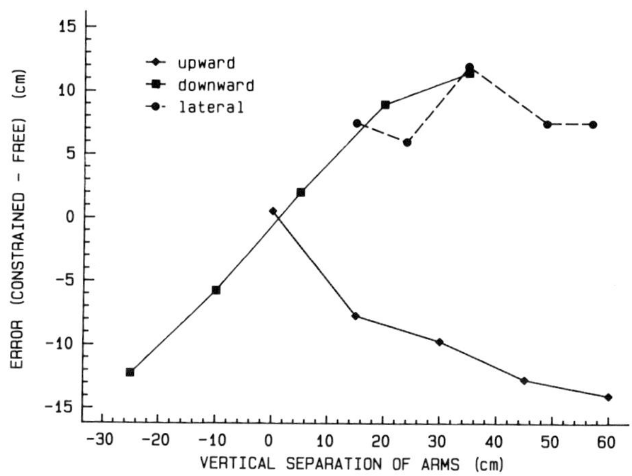

Figure 5. Error for simultaneous bimanual movements in different directions as a function of the degree of vertical separation of the hands, from a study by Loeb (1890).

2.3 Edmund Burke Delabarre.

To Delabarre (1891) we can attribute one of the earliest, and certainly one of the clearest accounts of the 'range effect' in movement reproduction, a phenomenon linked with the name of Poulton (1975), and earlier, Fullerton and Cattell (1892) and Hollingworth (1909, 1910). In a series of motor memory experiments for his dissertation Delabarre used a linear slide (Figure 6) devised by Münsterberg (some of whose work is reviewed in the next section) and later used in one of the three major experimental methods in Woodworth's dissertation (1899). This early linear slide could be oriented horizontally or vertically and the effects of gravity on the limb reduced by a counterweight.

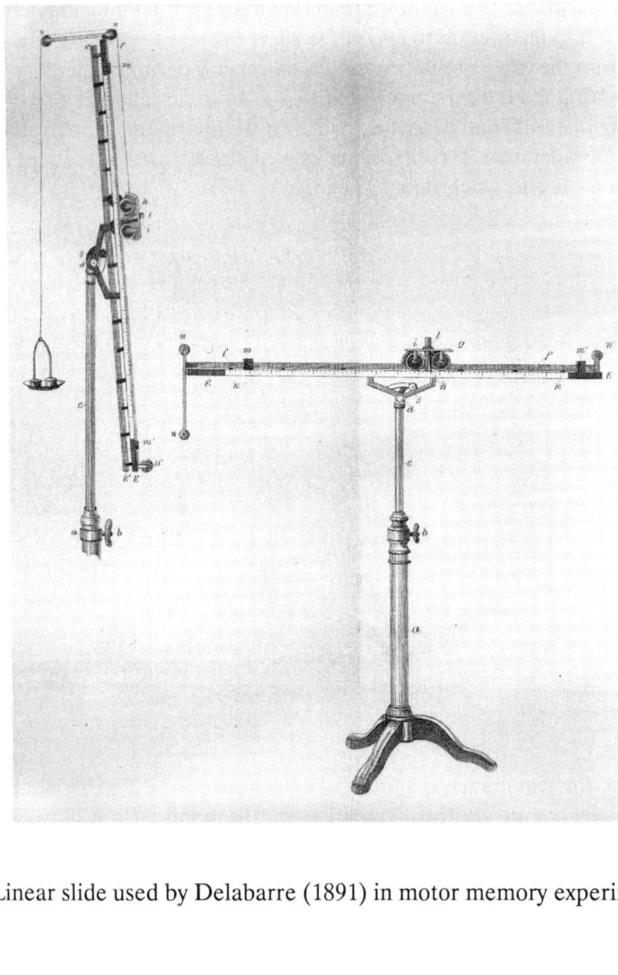

Figure 6. Linear slide used by Delabarre (1891) in motor memory experiments.

In the conduct of his experiments, some unimanual with criterion and reproduction movements, others simultaneous motions using a second slide, Delabarre noted a tendency for longer movements to be undershot, and shorter ones to be overshot. This is evident in both his tabulated data and the text: "A general tendency is evident to reproduce short distances longer. With longer distances this tendency can be reversed". (p. 86). He later acted as a subject himself and replicated these findings, both with eyes open and closed: "these experiments show, how constant is the tendency, ... to underestimate [the reproduction movements of] shorter distances [i.e to overshoot], and to overestimate longer ones [i.e. to undershoot]" (p.103).

A second comparison made in Delabarre's work, but not explicitly discussed, is the comparison between preselected and constrained movements, and between preselected and passively presented criterion motions. These studies used a single limb reproduction paradigm, usually with a four second interval between criterion and reproduction movements. Preselected movements had amplitudes selected voluntarily by the subject, while constrained criterion motions made use of mechanical stops which could be positioned at any point along the slide. Passive criterion movements required the participation of the experimenter. While a formal repeated measures design was not used, there were two subjects who participated in preselected and constrained conditions, with data for both upward and downward vertical movements presented, and three subjects who attempted reproductions of both preselected and passive criterion movements.

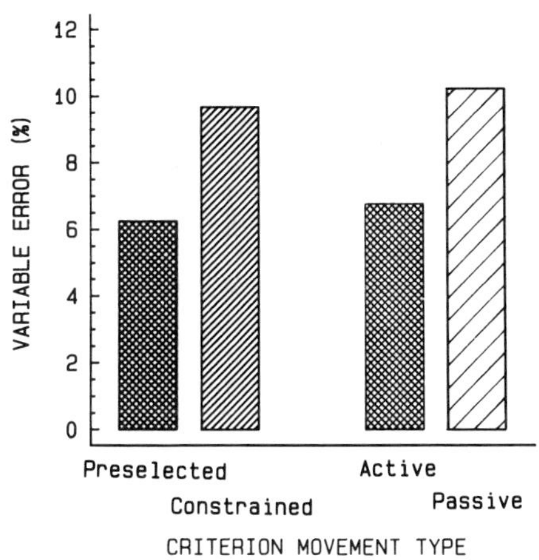

Figure 7. Errors for movement reproduction for preselected as opposed to constrained movements (left two bars), and preselected active as opposed to passive movements (right two bars) from the work of Delabarre (1891).

I have calculated mean values from this subset of the data and present these in Figure 7. Note that the variable error was calculated as the average of the absolute differences between the average signed error across trials (i.e. constant error) and the signed error on each trial for a given subject. These calculations were performed not on errors expressed in distance units, but on errors expressed as percentages of the criterion movements. Briefly, this figure shows that a tendency was present for the superior reproduction of preselected criterion movements over both constrained and passive ones (an early observation of the preselection phenomenon later investigated by Stelmach, Kelso and Wallace, 1975).The superior reproduction of active movements over passive was also observed, preceding by many decades similar observations of, for example, Paillard and Brouchon (1968).

2.4 Hugo von Münsterberg.

In four volumes of his "Contributions on Experimental Psychology", Münsterberg covers many psychological issues that are purely mental phenomena. He had a clear interest in motor behavior, however, and two chapters of the fourth volume deal with "Size Estimation" and "Simultaneous Movements". Some of his observations on phase transitions in bimanual motions will be described below, a phenomenon investigated by Cohen (1970) and, more recently, by Kelso (1984). These experiments involved the production of circles, lines and triangles, the case of circles will be considered here (Münsterberg, 1892). Subjects were required to make bimanual circular motions of the hand, approximately 20 cm in diameter and centered on points equidistant from the mid-sagittal axis. Circles were to be either both clockwise or both counter-clockwise, (i.e. asymmetric and requiring the use of non-homologous muscles), and were typically conducted at a rate of about one revolution each 2/3 or 1 second, paced by a metronome. Subjects held test-tubes, the bottom of which continuously contacted the surface of a smooth horizontal board. Several of Münsterberg's colleagues observed each trial, making graphical sketches of the paths followed and requiring agreement on what had occurred on each trial for this to be reported. In one series, seven subjects were instructed to direct their attention primarily to the right hand. Two of them were reported as being able to conduct such motions without error for over one hundred consecutive revolutions. One fell into a pattern of making circles which were still asymmetrical but out-of-phase after about 15-25 revolutions, and another subject showed a transition from circles to flat ellipses and finally simple horizontal lines. In three subjects there was a transition in which the left hand reversed its direction so as to produce circles for left and right hands which were symmetrical, using homologous muscles. These transitions took place as early as after 5-7 revolutions, or as late as after 20-30 revolutions. Münsterberg noted similarly mixed results for variations on this experiment, using different shapes and directions, as well as in conditions in which a distracting task was used (mentally adding to a given number by sevens). His general conclusion is in the form of a law: "every strong arm movement of one side acts as a stimulus for the release of the arm movement on the other side, which is best suited for offsetting superfluous simultaneous movements of the body and leading to the greatest possible saving of muscular work". This idea not only hints at some constraints on motor control (energy expenditure minimization), a concept which has been the subject of much recent attention (e.g. Nelson, 1985; Sparrow and Irizarry-Lopez, 1987), but also recognizes the mechanical interaction between voluntary movement of the upper extremities and the postural stabilization of the trunk. This line of thought might be seen as an antecedent to the more recent work in postural control during arm movements (e.g. Cordo and Nashner, 1982).

2.5 Alfred Binet and J. Courtier.

A brief, somewhat descriptive but nonetheless insightful kinematic study of hand movements was undertaken by Binet and Courtier (1893), the latter to become known more widely for his later work on human intelligence. This work was known to American psychologists early in the century and was described briefly by Hollingworth (1909, p.6). The study examined simple hand and writing movements made with an "Edison pen" in which a cam-driven needle punctured the paper surface used for drawing at a rate of 11,000 times per minute (approximately 183 Hz). A permanent record of movement trajectories was thus left on the paper. Movements examined include straight-line lateral hand motions, circular motions of different diameters, ellipses, two straight lines separated by an acute angle, and the handwritten word "diapason" shown in Figure 8. The authors present no numerical analyses of results, but instead summarize five major findings:

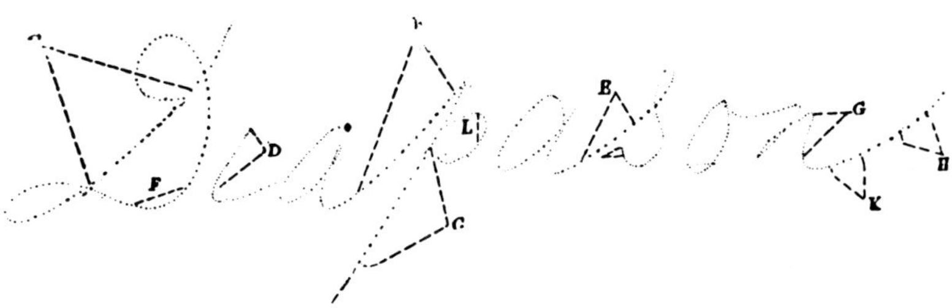

Fig. 5.

Figure 8. Trajectory of the word 'Diapason' written with an Edison electric pen (Binet and Courtier, 1893).

1. "A direct relationship exists between the size of a graphical figure and the speed with which this figure is traced" (p.664). It seems that the authors were referring to peak velocity, since their data gave direct visual information about the distance covered by the pen between sampling intervals. This observation parallels that of Camerer in specifying an amplitude/velocity relationship generally attributed today to Freund and Budingen (1978).

2. "In all of the regular line which is traced by the hand, a straight line or a circular line, the movement is slower at the beginning of the line and the end, than in the middle". Along with Camerer, Binet and Courtier appear to overstate the extent to which the central portion of the movement was of uniform velocity, probably because no differentiation of the displacement data was undertaken.

3. "The speed varies with the direction of the movement." The authors described a greater speed for rightward than for leftward horizontal lines made with the right hand, but also noted that oblique lines made from left to right and away from the body were executed "with a very great speed", anticipating the findings of a very recent report by Gordon and Ghez (1989) in which planar arm movements in exactly that direction are reported as being faster than others.

4. "A movement is above all less rapid if it has to satisfy a larger number of conditions" (p.665). More explicitly, a straight line made "between two reference points is slower than if the length of the line is left to the initiative of the hand" (p.665), an early observation of a spatial speed-accuracy trade-off.

5. "All brisk changes in the direction of a movement lead to a loss of speed" (p.666), a statement made after examination of both acute angle direction changes as well as more continuous curves, and noted to occur even when the subject believed that a uniform velocity movement was being made. This observation is surely the prototype for the later observations of, for example, Viviani and Cenzato (1985), and Wann, Nimmo-Smith and Wing (1988). The illusion of constant velocity despite its variations with curvature anticipates contemporary interest in this phenomenon (see Viviani, this volume).

DISCUSSION

It is of interest to consider some possible reasons why these works have become obscure, since several contributions of this period have certainly not been forgotten. For example, the pioneering role of Gustav Fechner (1860) in psychophysics is clearly acknowledged, as is that of Wilhelm Wundt (1904), who founded his psychological laboratory in Leipzig in the same year as did William James at Harvard (1875). The studies of Donders (1898/1969) in mental chronometry and Goldscheider (1898) in proprioception - the former being 'rediscovered' in 1969 (Sternberg, 1969) have also been amply recognized, as has the contribution of von Helmholtz (1896). American psychologists of the nineteenth and early twentieth centuries who studied movement are also still cited frequently: Woodworth (1899), Fullerton and Cattell (1892), Bryan and Harter (1897) and Hollingworth (1909, 1910) falling into this category. Indeed, many of the studies described here were known to and cited by these early American motor behaviorists. Today, however, these studies of Loeb, Münsterberg, Delabarre, Camerer and Binet and Courtier rest in comparative obscurity. Since several psychological studies of the 19th century as well as other influential work not originally written in English (e.g Bernstein[1] (Whiting, 1984)) are widely known today, it appears that the languages and century in which these authors wrote are not the principal causes of their obscurity. It may be fairly said that none of the studies reviewed above are landmark contributions comparable in caliber to Fechner's pioneering work in psychophysics (1860) or Donders' subtractive logic (1868/1969), and were simply not weighty enough to have had an enduring influence. It is also reasonable to suppose that voluntary movement phenomena were not accorded the same importance as other psychological topics, such as memory and perception.

Indeed, several of these researchers themselves went on to work in different or only loosely associated areas. Loeb crossed the Atlantic to Berkeley in the 1890s and wrote extensively on animal 'tropism' - influential and translated work (1905). Münsterberg moved into what may best be described as organizational psychology at Harvard (Moskowitz, 1977). Binet's contributions to understanding human intelligence need no mention here. Delabarre, the only American of this group, remained in psychology (founding Brown University's Psychology Laboratory), but engaged in such diverse endeavors as the first Brown/Harvard Arctic expedition, studying the mental effects of cannabis use, and writing a comprehensive archaeological account of native American petroglyphs near his summer home in Massachussets ("Dighton Rock", 1928). Movement was not the single or central focus in the careers of these individuals, nor for most of their contemporaries. An exception was the French physiologist Marey who created a movement laboratory in Paris in 1864 and published many works on the subject up to the turn of the century, culminating in Le Mouvement (1894). In the wider context, however, movement phenomena were hardly the most pressing issues in either psychology, philosophy, or physiology at that time. Some of the contributions presented in the previous section, while profoundly psychological in both spirit and conduct, were undertaken in physiological institutes (e.g. Loeb at Würzburg and Strassburg, Schaefer at Jena).

---

[1] Despite renewed interest in Bernstein's work, it should be noted one of his key works ("On the construction of movements", 1947), which won him a State prize, remains unavailable in English).

This was a period in which psychology was emerging as an independent discipline from philosophy and physiology, an evolution necessitated in part by the intractability of mental phenomena to purely physiological or philosophical explanation. At this transitional stage, some of these research endeavors, while psychological in character, predate the establishment of psychological laboratories even at the same institution. For example, Jacques Loeb conducted his studies on movement at Würzburg some ten years before Külpe founded the psychology laboratory there, initiating the the 'Würzburger school' of 'imageless thought'.

It is instructive to consider the interplay between German and American psychology during this period. German influence is abundant, and is just as clear for those who studied movement as for other areas of psychology. Of those whose studies are summarized above, several were part of this German-American exchange: Münsterberg, Loeb and Delabarre in particular. A major point of early contact was between William James and Wilhelm Wundt. James had also been impressed by Wundt's protegé Hugo Münsterberg, who had publicly taken issue with Wundt over the matter of the purported central origins of the 'sense of effort' in voluntary actions. James recruited the young Münsterberg to Harvard to run his laboratory in 1892. (Roback, 1952, pp. 192-206). Münsterberg was on the Harvard faculty when Woodworth was a student, before the latter pursued his doctoral studies at Cornell under Cattell. Cattell, in turn, had been a student of Wundt's in Leipzig. Edmund Burke Delabarre, an American from Massachussetts, ran James' laboratory for a year (1896-1897) while Münsterberg was back in Freiburg, and obtained his doctorate at Freiburg under Münsterberg with the work described above. To a great extent modern motor behavior has been strongly influenced by experimental psychology. We should recognize not only the impetus given to "mainstream" American experimental psychology by German researchers before the turn of the century, but also the central role in this intellectual traffic of those who - albeit for some only in passing - found human motor behavior sufficiently interesting to warrant some ingenious and sometimes exacting and prescient study.

REFERENCES

Adams, J. A. (1987). Historical review and appraisal of research on the learning, retention, and transfer of human motor skills. Psychological Bulletin, 101, 41-74.

Atkeson, C. G., & Hollerbach, J. M. (1985). Kinematic features of unrestrained vertical arm movements. Journal of Neuroscience, 5, 2318-30.

Bernhardt, M. (1872). Zur Lehre vom Muskelsinn [On the study of muscle sense]. Archiv für Psychiatrie, 3, 618-635.

Bernstein, N. A. (1947). O postroenii dvizhenii [On the construction of movements], Moscow: Medgiz.

Binet, A., & Courtier, J. (1893). Sur la vitesse des mouvements graphiques [On the speed of writing movements]. Revue Philosophique, 35, 664-71.

Bryan, W., & Harter, N. (1897). Studies in the physiology and psychology of telegraphic language. Psychological Review, 4, 27-53.

Camerer, von, W. (1866). Versuche über den zeitlichen Verlauf der Willensbewegung [Experiments on the temporal structure of voluntary movement]. Unpublished doctoral dissertation, University of Tübingen.

Cohen, L. (1970). Interaction between limbs during bimanual voluntary activity. Brain, 93, 259-272.

Cordo, P. J., & Nashner, L. M. (1982). Properties of postural adjustments associated with rapid arm movements. Journal of Neurophysiology, 47, 287-302.

Cremer, M. (1887). Ueber das Schätzen von Distanzen [On the estimation of distances]. Doctoral dissertation, University of Würzburg. Würzburg: A. Memminger's Buchdruckerei.

Donders, F.C. (1868/1969). On the speed of mental processes. Translation by W.G. Koster in W.G. Koster (Ed.) Attention and Performance II (pp.412-431). Amsterdam: North-Holland Publishing Co. Originally published in Onderzoekingen gedaan in het Physiologisch Laboratorium der Utrechtsche Hoogeschool, Tweede reeks, 1868-1869, II, 92-120.

Delabarre, E. B. (1891). Über Bewegungsempfindungen [On sensitivity to movement] Doctoral dissertation, Unversity of Freiburg. Freiburg, West Germany: Buchdruckerei Hch. Epstein.

Delabarre, E.B. (1928). Dighton Rock. New York: Walter Neale. Falk, M. (1890). Raumschätzung mit Hülfe von Armbewegungen [Experiments in the estimation of space with the help of arm movements]. Doctoral dissertation, University of Dorpat.

Fechner, G. T. (1860). Elemente der Psychophysik. Leipzig: Breitkopf und Hartel.

Fischer, O. (1906). Theoretische Grundlagen für eine Mechanik der lebenden Körper mit speziellen Anwendungen auf den Menschen, sowie auf einige Bewegungs-Vorgänge an Maschinen [Theoretical foundations for a mechanics of the living body with special applications to the human, as well as to some processes of motion in machines]. Leipzig: Teubner.

Freund, H. J., & Budingen, H. J. (1978). The relationship between speed and amplitude of the fastest voluntary contractions of human arm muscles. Experimental Brain Research, 31, 1-12.

Fullerton, G. S., & Cattell, J. McK. (1892). On the perception of small differences with special reference to the extent, force and time of movement. Philadelphia: University of Pennsylvania Press.

Goldscheider, A. (1898). Gesammelte Abhandlungen, Band II: Physiologie des Muskelsinnes [Collected works, Volume II: Physiology of the muscle sense]. Leipzig: Johann Ambrosius Barth.

Gordon, J., & Ghez, C. (1989). Independence of direction and amplitude errors in planar arm movements. Society for Neuroscience Abstracts, 15, 50.

Helmholtz, von, H. L. F. (1896). Handbuch der physiologischen Optik. Hamburg: L. Voss.

Hollingworth, H. L. (1909). The inaccuracy of movement. Archives of Psychology, 13, 1-87.

Hollingworth, H. L. (1910). The central tendency in judgment. Journal of Philosophy, Psychology and Scientific Methods, 7, 461-69.

Kelso, J. A. S., Southard, D.L., & Goodman, D. (1979). On the nature of human interlimb coordination. Science, 203, 1029-1031.

Kelso, J. A. S. (1984). Phase transitions and critical behaviors in human bimanual coordination. American Journal of Physiology, 246, R1000-1004

Kröner, E. (1887). Das Körperliche Gefühl [Bodily sensation]. Breslau: Verlag von Eduard Trewendt.

Lewinski, L. (1879). Ueber den Kraftsinn [On the sense of force]. Virchow's Archiv, 77, 134-146.

Leyden, E. (1869). Ueber Muskelsinn und Ataxie [On muscle sense and ataxia]. Archiv für Pathologische Anatomie und Physiologie und für Klinische Medicin, 47, 321-351.

Loeb, J. (1887). Untersuchungen uber den Fühlraum der Hand [Investigations into the perceptual space of the hand]. Pflüger's Archiv, 41, 107-27.

Loeb, J. (1890). Untersuchungen uber die Orientirung im Fühlraum der Hand und im Blickraum [Investigations of orientation in the perceptual space of the hand and in visual space]. Pflüger's Archiv, 46, 1-46.

Loeb, J. (1905). Studies in general physiology (M. H. Fisher, trans.). Chicago, University of Chicago Press.

Loeb, J., & von Koranyi, A. (1890). Ueber den Einfluss der Schwerkraft auf den zeitlichen Verlauf der geradlinigen Willkurbewegungen unseres Armes [On the influence of gravity on the kinematic structure of straight-line voluntary movements of our arm]. Pflüger's Archiv, 46, 101-14.

Mach, E. (1875). Grundlinien der Lehre von den Bewegungsempfindungen [Foundations of the study of movement perception]. Leipzig: W. Engelmann.

Marey, E.-J. (1868). Du mouvement dans les fonctions de la vie [Movement in the functions of life]. Paris.

Moskowitz, M. J. (1977). Hugo Münsterberg: A study in the history of applied psychology. American Psychologist, 32, 824-842.

Müller, G.E., & Schumann, F. (1889). Ueber die psychologischen Grundlagen der Vergleichung gehobener Gewichte [On the psychological foundations of the comparison of lifted weights]. Pflüger's Archiv, 45, 37-112.

Münsterberg, H. (1892). Beitrage zur experimentellen Psychologie, Heft 4 [Contributions to experimental psychology, Volume 4]. Freiburg: Akademische Verlagsbuchhandlung von J. C. B. Mohr.

Muybridge, E. (1888). Animal locomotion. The Muybridge work at the University of Pennsylvania. Philadelphia: J. B. Lipincott Company.

Nelson, W. L. (1985). Physical principles for economics of skilled movements. Biological Cybernetics, 46, 135-147.

Paillard, J., & Brouchon, M. (1968). Active and passive movements in the calibration of position sense. In S. J. Freedman, (Ed.), The neuropsychology of spatially oriented behavior. New York: Dorsey.

Poulton, E. C. (1975). Range effects in experiments on people. American Journal of Psychology, 88, 3-32.

Roback, A. A. (1952). History of American psychology. New York: Library Publishers.

Russell, D. G. (1976). Spatial location cues and movement production. In: G. E. Stelmach, (Ed.), Motor control: Issues and trends. New York: Academic Press.

Schaefer, K. (1887). Ueber die Wahrnehmung eigener passiver Bewegungen durch den Muskelsinn [On the perception of some passive movements through the muscle sense]. Pflüger's Archiv, 41, 566-640.

Scheerer, E. (1987). Muscle sense and innervation feelings: A chapter in the history of perception and action. In H. Heuer, & A. F. Sanders (Eds.) Perspectives on perception and action. Hillsdale, N.J.: Lawrence Erlbaum. pp. 171-194.

Schmidt, R. A. (1988). Motor control and learning (2nd. ed.). Champaign: Human Kinetics Publishers. pp. 3-17.

Sparrow, W. A., & Irizarry-Lopez, V. M. (1987). Mechanical efficiency and metabolic cost as measures of learning a novel gross motor task. Journal of Motor Behavior, 19, 240-264.

Stelmach, G. E., Kelso, J. A. S., & Wallace, S. A. (1975). Preselection in short term motor memory. Journal of Experimental Psychology: Human Learning and Memory, 1, 745-755.

Stelmach, G.E., & J. Requin, (Eds.) (1980). Tutorials in motor behavior. Amsterdam: North-Holland.

Sternberg, M. (1885). Zur Lehre von den Vorstellungen uber die Lage unserer Glieder [On the study of the representation of the position of our limbs]. Pflüger's Archiv, 37, 1-6.

Sternberg, S. (1969). The discovery of processing stages: Extensions of Donders' method. In W.G. Koster (Ed.) Attention and Performance II (pp. 276-315). Amsterdam: North-Holland Publishing Co.

Vierordt, K. (1868). Der Zeitsinn [The sense of time]. Tübingen: Verlag der H. Laupp'schen Buchhandlung.

Viviani, P., & Cenzato, M. (1985). Segmentation and coupling in complex movements. Journal of Experimental Psychology: Human Perception and Performance, 11, 828-45.

Wann, J., Nimmo-Smith, I., & Wing, A.M. (1988). Relation between velocity and curvature in movement: Equivalence and divergence between a power law and a minimum-jerk model. Journal of Experimental Psychology: Human Perception and Performance, 14, 622-637.

Whiting, H. T. A. (Ed.) (1984). Human motor actions: Bernstein reassessed. Elsevier: North-Holland.

Woodworth, R. S. (1899). The accuracy of voluntary movement. Psychological Review, 3, 1-114.

Wundt, W. (1904). Principles of physiological psychology (Vol. 1) (E.B. Titchener, Trans.) [Original work published 1904, 5th Ed.) New York: Macmillan.

ACKNOWLEDGEMENTS

I thank Mario Wiesendanger for bringing the work of Etienne-Jules Marey to my attention, Friedemann Müller for obtaining a copy of Camerer's dissertation, and my wife, Maria Miller, for her help with parts of the translations used in the preparation of this paper. The occasional obscurity of nineteenth century scientific German was sometimes problematical, a fact noted by an earlier Englishman working in America and translating German psychology: "there are many and many passages where a half-way literal English rendering would be unintelligible; where one is forced, in translating, to be concrete without losing generality; and in cases like these the translator's lot is not a happy one." (from E.B. Titchener's Translator's preface to the the 5th. edition of Wundt's "Grundzuge" (1904), p.xi).

Correspondence and requests for reprints should be sent to the author at the following address: Department of Movement Science, The University of Michigan, 401 Washtenaw Avenue, Ann Arbor, Michigan 48109-2214.

SECTION 8

ANATOMICAL AND BEHAVIOR CONTRIBUTION TO MOVEMENT

Tutorials in Motor Behavior II
G.E. Stelmach and J. Requin (Editors)

Contribution of the thalamic messages to motor cortex in the learning of motor skills

M. Fabre-Thorpe

Institut des Neurosciences (C.N.R.S.-U.P.M.C.), Département de Neurophysiologie Comparée. 9, Quai Saint Bernard, 75230 Paris Cedex 5. France

Abstract

The brain pathways involved in the performance of a motor skill may differ according to the task level of pratice. In the present paper emphasis is given to the differential role played by the thalamic nucleus ventralis lateralis depending on whether the motor skill is being learnt or is executed after a long period of training that has stabilized the performance. A brief review of the data in favor of an involvement of the thalamic projection to motor cortex in motor learning is presented. To conclude, a duality of the motor system is proposed with a sequential organization, where a cerebral pathway involving a thalamo-cortical step would be essential during motor learning but would be bypassed by a subcortical pathway involving the red nucleus, when learning has been completed.

INTRODUCTION

When learning a new motor skill, movement execution becomes faster, smoother, and more automatic. The importance of attentional constraints linked to the performance decreases progressively whereas the use of sensory feedback becomes more efficient because only the relevant important sensory information is extracted and processed. Hence, with repeated pratice, the sensory-motor strategy used to perform the motor act is progressively modified. Therefore, there have been a number of suggestions that the neuronal substrate for learning motor skills is distinct from the one involved in the selection and execution of a well established motor program [1-4]. Consequently, a structure crucially involved in the "dynamic" motor learning phase of a new skill may progressively lose its importance as learning proceeds until it plays a very minor role (if any) when the skill is well learned. A similar situation occurs in the case of episodic memory, where there is good evidence that such a structure could be the hippocampus; its integrity is necessary to memorize new events but not to recall events that had been well memorized before the lesion. However, hippocampectomy does not affect the ability to learn new motor skills [5]; thus, the cerebral pathway involved in the learning and the retention of motor skills is presumably distinct from that involved in learning and retention of other types of information. The hippocampal analog for motor learning could be the thalamic nucleus ventralis lateralis (VL). VL is the main subcortical relay for messages originating in the basal ganglia and in the cerebellum on their way to the motor cortex [6-11], and the firing of VL neurons has been shown to be tightly linked to motor and sensori-motor activities [12-14]. However, bilateral VL lesions in cats or monkeys have now been reported by many authors to have remarkably little effect on the execution of well learned motor acts [1, 15-17]. If one postulates that well learned movements can be performed using a motor program that has been progressively built during acquisition and stored in the brain, VL could well be a necessary structure for establishing and storing such a program but have little or no role to play when the motor program has been well established and needs just to be triggered. In recent years, data have been obtained that support such an hypothesis. In this paper, my goal is to stress the differential role played by VL, depending on whether the performed movement is well learned or new. I will first present the data that I have obtained with my collaborators [1, 4] that support a crucial role for the VL in the learning or re-learning of a motor skill, and then briefly review the data available in the literature that are consistent with a major role of either the VL itself or its cortical output in motor learning.

1. ON THE ROLE OF VL IN MOTOR LEARNING

The role of VL was investigated during the acquisition phase of a reaching movement performed towards a moving target.

1.1. Methods

We used a task previously described [18] in which cats had to point towards a moving lever. Between trials, the target-lever was hidden from view; it became visible and accessible only during a short period of time (800ms) when crossing, once a trial, an aperture located in front of the animal (Figure 1). When accessible in the aperture, the target moved along a predictable trajectory (arc of a circle), either clockwise or counterclockwise at random, with a constant speed. The evaluation of the cat's visuo-motor performance included measurements of accuracy (number of trials for which the target had been reached) and overall response time (corresponding to reaction time + movement time).

When cats were overtrained to perform this task, a bilateral electrolytic lesion of VL had been shown to have no effect on performance [1]. Thus we investigated whether the same lesion would affect the acquisition period of the task.

The learning procedure included two phases. Cats were first trained to reach an immobile lever when kept immobile (phase 1) until they obtained a success rate of a 100%. In a second phase (phase 2) the lever became mobile crossing the aperture once a trial, its speed was first low and then progressively increased during training to reach 0.25 m/s corresponding to a 800 ms accessibility time of the target. Animals were trained until they reached a criterion of less than 20% unsuccessful trials due to guiding errors. From the large number of cats that had been trained on that task for other studies we knew that, after completion of phase 1, completion of phase 2 normally takes a maximum of 5 weeks, this period being shorter when cats had completed phase 1 quickly. Thus, for this study, five cats were carefully selected on their ability to reach phase 1 criteria (less than 5 daily training sessions corresponding to 200 trials). After completion of phase 1 and before entering phase 2, they underwent either a bilateral VL lesion (3 cats), or a sham operation (2 cats).

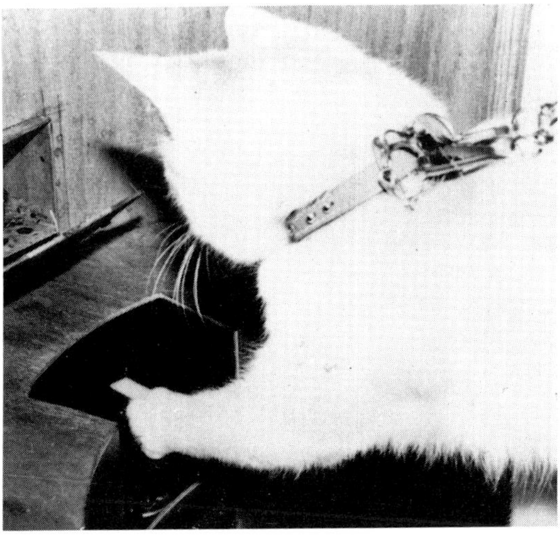

Figure 1: **"Lever Task"**: Accurate reaching movement performed towards the lever (light rectangle under the paw) while crossing the aperture situated in front of the cat. A meat reward is brought to the cat by a retractable tray.

1.2. Results

The bilateral VL lesions only partially destroyed VL, without encroaching on other thalamic nuclei.

After operation, none of the 5 cats displayed any deficit in pointing towards the fixed target and they all entered learning phase 2. After 5 weeks of training their visuo-motor capacities were determined.

Before the end of the 4th week of training, the sham operated cats had reached criterion with the target moving at maximal speed (corresponding to 800ms of accessibility). By contrast, out of the 3 VL lesioned animals only one could reach for the target when moving at the usual maximal testing speed but did not reach criterion even after 6 weeks of training (Figure 2). Its accuracy was severely impaired (46% unsuccessful trials due to guiding errors) compared to the sham operated animals (4 and 7%) and to the global performance reached by the previously trained group of normal cats (15%).

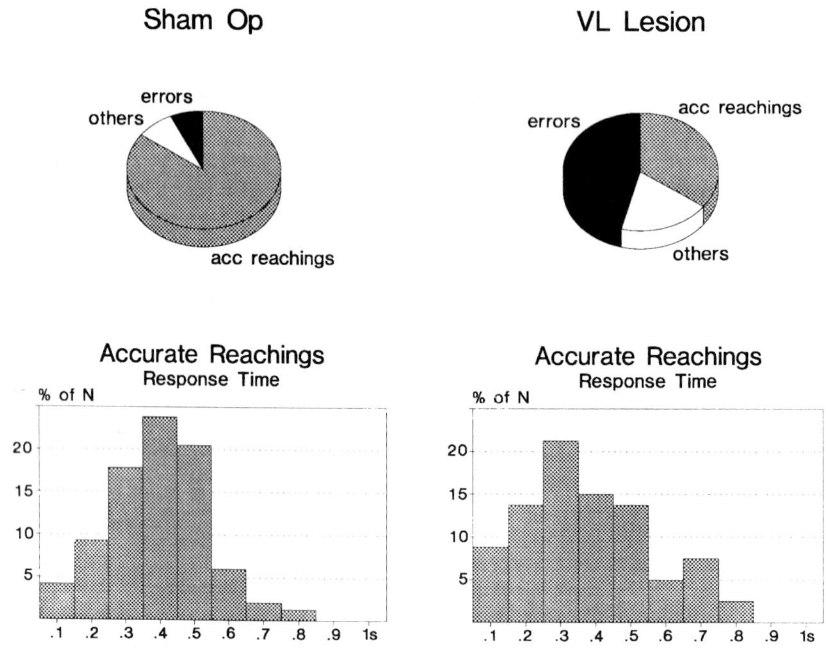

Figure 2: **Effect of a VL lesion on learning to reach towards a moving lever**. The motor performance recorded after 5 weeks of training are shown on the left for one sham operated cat and on the right for a VL operated cat. Displayed as sectors diagrams are the percentages of trials were the reaching was accurate (dots), or missed the target (black). The third sector in white includes all other trials (inattentiveness, holding of the lever without pressing, aborted attempts etc...). Below, and for each cat, are shown the response time histograms of the accurate reachings, each class of 100 msec is expressed in percentage of the total number of trials (N) (Response time values must not be considered as absolute values, they just have a comparative meaning). Note the severely impaired accuracy of the VL lesioned animal shown by the large proportion of pointing errors contrasting with the unimpaired speed of movement.

However, although the accuracy was impaired, the speed at which the movements were performed when they were accurate was not affected (Figure 2).The 2 other VL lesioned cats could not reach criterion, even when the target was moving at lower speeds, a learning failure which was never seen in normal cats able to complete phase 1.

Thus the thalamic nucleus VL, which is not a critical structure for performing over-learned motor actions, appears, on the other hand, to play a crucial role during the learning phase of new visuo-motor skills.

More recently, we have examined whether it is possible to generalize this finding to other types of motor plasticity, such as the period of functional recovery that follows brain damage to another structure. In other words, if the performance of an overlearned movement has been altered by a cerebral lesion, would VL again be found to play a critical role while the visuo-motor system "re-learns" how to perform the appropriate motor act with the remaining intact cerebral pathways.

2. ON THE ROLE OF VL IN MOTOR RECOVERY AFTER BRAIN DAMAGE

In a second series of experiments [4] the role of VL was investigated in the phase of motor recovery that follows the destruction of another thalamic nucleus, the lateroposterior nucleus (LP), which is now considered as the main thalamic relay of the extrageniculate visual system.

2.1. Methods

Another set-up was used in which cats were trained to reach a spot of light (Figure 3) that appeared and moved randomly on a tilted screen in front of them [19]. A trial started with a 500 msec tone in response to which the animal had to stand still with its forepaws resting on a pair of "starting plates" until the target appeared on the screen. They were then allowed 10 sec and three attempts to reach the spot of light. Evaluation of the pointing movement included measurements of (i) the accuracy (proportion of trials on which the first pointing attempt reached the target), (ii) the reaction time (RT), delay between the target's appearance and the lift of the cat's paw from the starting plate, and (iii) the movement time (MT), delay between the paw lift and the contact with the target when the first pointing attempt was correct.

2.2. Results

When cats had been overtrained to reach a stabilized level of performance, they underwent a bilateral lesion of either VL (2 cats), LP (3 cats) or both VL and LP (2 cats). The lesion induced deficits and the functional recovery were analyzed during a postoperative period of up to 3 months.

Figure 3: **"Spot task"**: Ongoing reaching movement performed towards the spot of light moving randomly on the tilted screen. A milk reward is to reward accurate reachings.

Effect of lesioning VL,

The only effect induced by a bilateral thermocoagulation lesion of VL was an increase of RT, whereas MT and accuracy were unimpaired (Figures 4 & 5). Testing could start the second day after lesion, which can explain the large RT increase recorded during the first four post-operative days. Recovery was quick and complete and within a week, cats were able to trigger their movement within their preoperative range. Thus the VL induced deficit was very transient in accordance with our previous data [1].

Effect of lesioning LP,

On the other hand, the bilateral thermocoagulation of the lateroposterior thalamic nucleus (LP), relay of the extrageniculate visual pathway, induced a severe deficit that was relatively long-lasting (4 to 6 weeks). The accuracy was severely impaired (Figure 4), and the movement was delayed whereas MT was unaffected (Figure 5). Although the deficits were severe, postoperative training led eventually to complete recovery after 4 to 6 weeks [20] for both accuracy and RT.

The three LP lesioned animals displayed similar deficits. They all progressively recovered their preoperative level of performance. All animals displayed full functional recovery that was achieved with a similar time course in different animals. Thus, the phase of recovery from a LP lesion was chosen in order to determine how an additional VL lesion would affect the way it was completed and its time course.

Effect of simultaneously lesioning VL and LP,

When VL and LP were lesioned simultaneously, the induced visuo-motor deficit was severe. The accuracy showed a dramatic decrease (Figure 4), the movement onset was more delayed than after any of the individual thalamic lesions, and the movement time was also increased (Figure 5). Thus the immediate effect of the combined lesion was a strengthening of the deficit normally observed after LP lesion alone and the apparition of a new feature, the slowing down of the movement execution itself. The additional VL lesion had clear effects on the recovery phase. First the cats were never able to fully compensate for their deficits, and second, regular training was necessary to maintain the postoperative performance accuracy level.

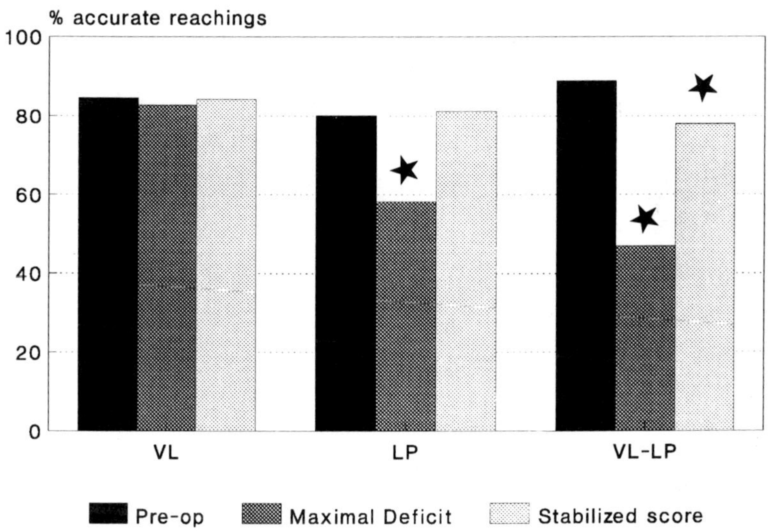

Figure 4: **Effect of VL, LP and VL-LP lesions on the accuracy of a pointing movement**. For each group of lesion (VL, LP and VL-LP), the scores of one subject are shown. The accuracy level is represented for the preoperative period (black), the period of maximal deficit (dark grey) and the period of stabilized score after recovery has been completed (light grey). Accuracy was not affected by VL lesion, whereas it was impaired after LP and combined VL-LP lesions. Note that it is only in the case of the combined VL-LP lesion that the recovery is not complete. Stars indicate statistically significant results.

Unlike the full recovery observed when LP was lesioned on its own, and in spite of a long postoperative training period (up to 3 months) the functional compensation was only partial after combined VL and LP lesion. The permanent deficit included longer RT, and impaired accuracy. Moreover, regarding the movement execution itself, the statistically significant increase in MT recorded immediately after the combined lesion changed progressively into a statistically significant decrease of MT (Figure 5). Therefore, after completion of the recovery phase and stabilization of the postoperative performance, the cat's reaching movement was triggered late, but executed faster and with much less accuracy; all these changes were statistically significant.

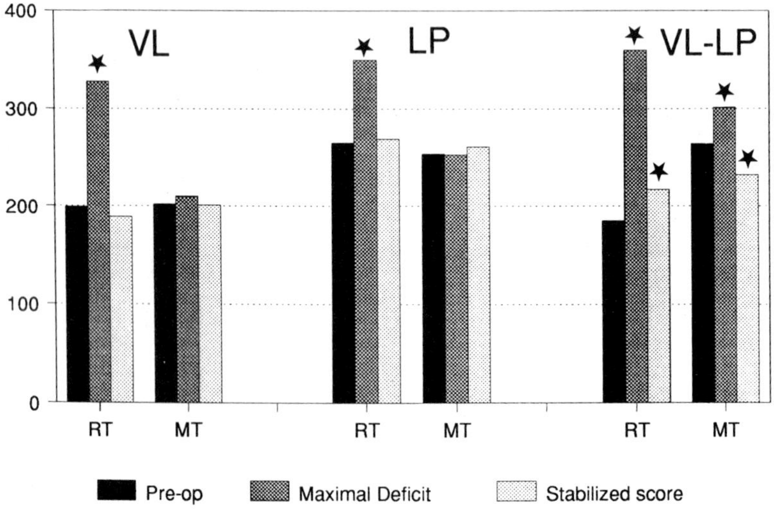

Figure 5: **Effect of VL, LP and VL-LP lesions on the RT and MT of a pointing movement**. For each group of lesion (VL, LP and VL-LP), the scores of one subject are shown. The mean reaction time (RT), and the mean movement time (MT) are represented for the preoperative period (black), the period of maximal deficit (dark grey) and the period of stabilized score after recovery has been completed (light grey). RT was increased for all types of lesion but the phase of maximal deficit lasted only a week in the case of the VL lesion and 4 weeks in case of LP lesion. Note that it is only in the case of the combined VL-LP lesion that the RT recovery is not complete. Note also that the combined lesion is the only lesion affecting MT; the movement being at first performed slower and then when recovery has been completed being executed faster than during the preoperative period. Stars indicate statistically significant results.

It has been reported [21] that shortening MT reduced timing errors, and suggested that this could be due to the greater temporal stability of fast movements relatively to slow ones. When comparing the types of errors performed by the cats either before or after lesion, spatial errors were increased after recovery whereas anticipation and delay (the two classes that included timing errors) were decreased. The strategy used to perform the visuo-motor skill was thus, after recovery from a VL-LP lesion, clearly different from the one used preoperatively or after either thalamic lesion performed on its own.

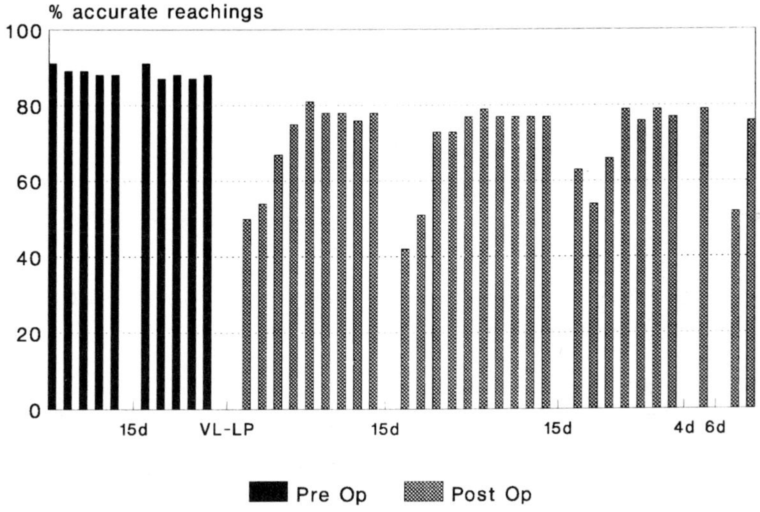

Figure 6: **Effect of combined VL-LP lesions on the accuracy of a pointing movement**. The daily accuracy performance is represented in black for the preoperative period, and in grey for the post operative period. Note that the full compensation of the accuracy deficit is never completed. Also shown is the effect induced, on the accuracy scores, by interruptions of the daily training ranging between 4 to 21 days. Note that a drop of postoperative performance accuracy is obtained when the training is stopped for 6 days or more, whereas accuracy remained unaffected when training had been interrupted during the preoperative period.

Another observation was that *training had to be regular in order to maintain the newly acquired level of accuracy*. When testing was stopped for six days or more, the performance accuracy dropped (Figure 6). However, the severity of the reinduced deficit was not a function of the length of the interruption. Either the length of the training interruption was not long enough to induce the drop of accuracy level or, when it lasted six days or more, the drop was directly maximal as the accuracy deficit re-appeared with all the initial strength observed just after the lesion. Interruption of regular training never induced such a drop in accuracy when performed in normal cats or in lesioned animal with a thalamic destruction of either VL or LP.

Thus VL plays a major role during the recovery phase following LP damage. The recovery which is only partial together with the lack of stability of the accuracy scores may indicate an inability to build a new motor program, or to consolidate a new "motor engram". After combined lesion, the animals would still be able to perform the reaching movement required, using a basic motor program and the postoperative training would allow adaptation and thus improvement of this primary program. This would lead to a motor strategy distinct from the preoperative one, and less efficient. However, these adaptations appear not to be longlasting and need regular training (or reinforcement) to persist, as the improvement in acuracy was found to vanish when training was stopped. In "cognitive memory" it is usual to distinguish a short term memory from a long term memory. That distinction may be also valid in the case of the retention of motor programs. VL could thus be considered as necessary to build a new motor program and to consolidate the trace of the new engram, but not to adapt a preexisting one.

3. CONTRIBUTION OF THE THALAMIC MESSAGES TO MOTOR CORTEX IN LEARNING MOTOR SKILLS.

Considering VL as an essential step of the brain circuit involved in motor skill acquisition, one may speculate about which other brain structures, apart from VL, belong to this cerebral pathway. Regarding first the origin of VL inputs, the two main sources are the cerebellum and the basal ganglia. The relative contribution of both structures can be tackled using the almost total segregation of their projections at the thalamic level. Distinct projection zones with very little overlap have been described both in monkeys [22] and cats [10]. The cerebellum has long been implicated in motor learning by numerous authors and attractive theories have been proposed [2, 23-32]. Regarding more specifically the possible involvement of the cerebello-thalamic messages themselves, it has been reported in cats [33] that lesioning the cerebellar-recipient zone of VL is more effective in inducing a deficit in learning a visually guided activity than lesioning other parts of VL. Moreover, the involvement of VL in relearning how to perform motor actions after brain lesion that has been stressed above, may be at least partly attributed to the cerebellar messages since the interruption of the cerebello-thalamic fibers has been shown to potentiate the deficit induced by red nucleus lesions, to induce new deficits and to alter the postoperative recovery that normally follows the rubral lesion [34]. Thus the cerebellum appears as a likely candidate to be part of the cerebral circuit involved in motor learning. On the other hand, recent data [35] conflict with those obtained by Batuev and his collaborators. These authors reported that, in the monkey, the learning of a conditional associative motor response was more impaired when they lesioned the VL zone that receives messages from the basal ganglia than when the

VL "cerebello-recipient" zone was destroyed. The functional role of the basal ganglia is certainly far from being totally understood, but it has also been suggested that it may be involved in modifying behavioural responses on the basis of recently acquired information [36]. Thus it would be able to modify and adapt preexisting motor programs. The two main VL sources of information can therefore both be considered as possibly involved in motor acquisition. One may even consider that both structures would have an essential role to play in different phases of the learning, the basal ganglia being involved in the cognitive phase of the acquisition, the learning of "what to do"; while the cerebellum would take in charge the motor phase of the acquisition, the learning of "how to do it".

Downstream, the informations originating in the cerebellum or the basal ganglia and processed by VL are forwarded towards motor cortex [37-40]. Recently, many investigators have addressed the question of whether functional modifications could be observed in the motor cortex when this pathway was repeatedly sollicited. In a series of experiments in the monkey, Sasaki and Gemba [41-44] used a correlative approach to analyse the evolution of evoked cortical potentials to a visual stimulus in response to which the animal had to learn to perform a motor response. Whereas during the early stages of learning a bilateral evoked potential could be recorded from the prefrontal cortex, it was only at later stages of learning that a contralateral potential appeared at the level of the motor cortex in response to the visual stimulus suggesting a distinct role of motor cortex according to the level of acquisition of the new motor skill. Since this observed cortical potential was similar to the one they had obtained using stimulation of either VL or cerebellar nuclei [45, 46], they studied the effect of restricted cerebellectomies and reported that when cerebellar messages that were normally forwarded through the dentate and interposate nuclei were suppressed, the evoked motor cortical potential did not develop. Moreover, the learning took longer and the learned motor response remained unstable. This series of experiments stressed the importance of the cerebello-thalamo-cortical pathway in learning motor skills, a role that is also supported by a study by Rispal-Padel et al. [47] showing the plasticity of the cerebellar efferent circuit to motor cortex. Using a classical conditioning paradigm where a conditional stimulus (sub-threshold electric shock to a cerebellar nucleus) was paired with an unconditional stimulus (cutaneous electric stimulation causing reflex forearm flexion), they observed initially a conditioned flexion movement that after few days of conditioning was modified into an extension, this motor adaptation being memorized until extinction was provoked by a normal procedure.

Turning now towards the motor cortex itself we can consider the modifications that have been recorded during or after learning. After Pavlovian conditioning in cats, Brons & Woody [48] reported long-term changes in the excitability of neurons in the motor cortex, and, using the acquisition phase of a flexion arm movement, Burnod et al. [49] have shown, in monkeys, that the firing probability of motor cortical units was progressively increased during learning. Recently, many investigations have been directed towards the possible cellular basis of this increased synapse efficiency in the motor cortex. What kind of mechanisms could be able to induce long-lasting cellular modifications in the motor cortex? Facilitation of synaptic transmission has been now reported in the motor cortex by various authors. Following Hebb's (1949) postulate [50], Baranyi & Fehér have reported [51] an increased effectiveness of VL to excite motor cortex after pairing of presynaptic activity (using VL stimulation) and postsynaptic activity in pyramidal cells (using antidromic activation from the pyramidal tract). Moreover, although this facilitation of synapses could be obtained using pairings between a variety of converging pathways with induced changes lasting up to 30 mn [52, 53], not all pairings resulted in synaptic facilitation. Thus, and this is of considerable interest as far as learning is concerned, this heterosynaptic activation proved selective since the plastic changes seem to be restricted to certain postsynaptic regions. On the other hand, since long-term potentiation (LTP) was shown in the hippocampus [54], it has been considered as a possible mechanism underlying memory, and many authors have investigated whether LTP of synaptic transmission could also be found in other brain structures. As far as the cerebello-thalamo-cortical pathway is concerned it must be noted that LTP has been observed in the cerebellar nuclei [55] and also in the motor cortex [56, 57]. Looking into more detail at the LTP recorded in the cat motor cortex, it has been shown that short tetanic microstimulation of the somatosensory cortex is able to induce LTP in motor cortical neurons [56] whereas tetanization of VL does not. However, LTP of VL thalamic inputs to motor cortical neurons is induced when both sensory cortex and VL are simultaneously stimulated at high frequency [57]. This associative LTP is only induced in the neurons from the superficial layers that receive monosynaptic inputs from both stimulated areas. These neurons could then influence corticofugal cells. This associative LTP may again constitute a basis for motor learning. However, as these authors had also shown that lesioning the sensory cortex (areas 1 and 2) delayed the learning of motor skill but did not alter well-learned performance [3], they suggested that the function of the sensory cortex LTP was to facilitate the learning and the retention of motor skills with the latter function being progressively transferred to VL LTP during learning. The results we obtained with VL lesions are in disagreement with this interpretation since VL, like the sensory cortex in their experiment, can only be considered as crucial during learning whereas its role appears very minimal during the performance of well-learned motor skills.

Thus it seems that both VL and cortical sensory areas have a crucial role to play in motor learning. However, regarding now the involvement of motor cortex, it may not be essential for the retention of learned skills, and in fact, the interruption of the pyramidal tract has been shown to have little influence on motor performance [58, 59]. However, motor cortex is involved in various loops with cerebellum and can influence the red nucleus. In fact, the red nucleus appears in a strategic position to take charge of the motor command after learning. First, it processes the same cerebellar messages as VL since it receives mainly (if not only) collaterals from the cerebello-thalamic neurons and also has access to the motor cortical output as it receives collaterals from the pyramidal tract. Moreover its lesion has been shown, in cats, to produce severe deficits in the performance of well learned acts [34] and its activity is tightly associated with the execution of overlearned movements [60-63]. Repeated practice could induce an association at the rubral level between cerebellar and cerebral messages, and the red nucleus would therefore be in a position to predict motor cortex outputs on the basis of cerebellar outputs. Thus, the cortical participation may be essential when a new motor skill is first performed, then a transfer of the motor command would allow the subcortical cerebello-rubro-spinal pathway to take charge of the performance of a well-learned motor skill as has been suggested previously [2, 4, 64, 65]. However, even with well-learned motor responses, there may be changes in the overall context where the task has to be performed that require the motor cortical pathway to be used again; and it has recently been suggested [66] that this switching from one system to another could depend upon the rubro-olivary pathway. Therefore the cerebral site of the motor engram would have to be considered as not so much distributed in the brain, as Lashley [67] had proposed, but rather as moving from one structure to another depending on the level of acquisition of the motor skill considered. The VL would hold in motor memory a similar position as the hippocampus in episodic memory, it would be essential for laying down the trace but lose its importance when the trace can be selected and executed through other brain pathways.

4. REFERENCES.

1 Fabre, M., & Buser, P. Structures involved in acquisition and performance of visually guided movements in the cat. *Acta Neurobiologica Experimentalis, 40* (1980) 95-116.

2 Ito, M. *The cerebellum and Neural control.* Raven press (New-york) (1984).

3 Sakamoto T., Arissian K., Asanuma H. Functional role of the sensory cortex in learning motor skills in cats. *Brain Research, 503* (1989) 258-264.

4 Fabre-Thorpe, M., & Levesque, F. Visuo-motor relearning after brain damage crucially depends on the integrity of the ventrolateral thalamic nucleus. *Behavioral Neuroscience, 105* (1991) 176-192.

5 Milner B. Amnesia following operation on the temporal lobes. In Whitty C.W.M. & Zangwill O.L. (Eds) *Amnesia*. Butterworths (London) (1966) 109-133.

6 Angaut, P. The ascending projections of the nucleus interpositus posterior of the cat cerebellum: an experimental study using silver impregnation methods. *Brain Research, 24* (1970) 377-394.

7 Angaut, P., & Bowsher, D. Ascending projections of the medial cerebellar (fastigial) nucleus: an experimental study in the cat. *Brain Research, 24* (1970) 49-68.

8 Dormont, JF., & Ohye, C. Entopedoncular projection to the thalamic ventrolateral nucleus of the cat. *Experimental Brain Research, 12* (1971) 254-264.

9 Rispal-Padel, L., Massion, J., & Grangetto, A. Relations between the ventrolateral nucleus and motor cortex and their possible role in the central organization of motor control. *Brain Research, 60* (1973) 1-20.

10 Hendry, S.H.C., Jones, E.G., & Graham, J. Thalamic relay nuclei for cerebellar and certain related fiber systems in the cat. *Journal of Comparative Neurology, 185* (1979) 679-714.

11 Uno, M., Yoshida, M., & Hirota, I. The mode of cerebello-thalamic relay transmission investigated with intracellular recording from cells of the ventrolateral nucleus of cat's thalamus. *Experimental Brain Research, 10* (1979) 121-139.

12 Neafsey, A.J., Hull, C.D., & Buchwald, N.A. Preparation for movement in the cat. II - Unit activity in the basal ganglia and thalamus. *Electroencephalography and Clinical*

Neurophysiology, 44 (1978) 714-723.

13 Schmied, A., Bénita, M., Condé, H., & Dormont, J-F. Activity of ventrolateral thalamic neurons in relation to a simple reaction time task in the cat. *Experimental Brain Research, 36* (1979) 285-300.

14 Macpherson, J.M., Rasmusson, D.D., & Murphy, J.T. Activity of neurons in "motor" thalamus during control of limb movement in the primate. *Journal of Neurophysiology, 44* (1980) 11-28.

15 Moll, L., & Kuypers, H.G.J.M. Role of the premotor cortical areas and VL nucleus in visual guidance of relatively independent hand and finger movement in monkey. *Experimental Brain Research, suppl 23* (1975) 142.

16 Ranish, N. A., & Soechting, J.F. Studies on the control of simple motor tasks. Effects of thalamic and red nuclei lesions. *Brain Research, 102* (1976) 339-345.

17 Bénita, M., Condé, H., Dormont, J-F., & Schmied, A. Effects of cooling the thalamic ventrolateral nucleus of cats on a reaction time task. *Experimental Brain Research, 34* (1979) 435-452.

18 Fabre, M., André, C,. & Buser, P. Testing visually guided forepaw movements in the cat training apparatus and procedure. *Physiology and behaviour, 23* (1979) 263-266.

19 Fabre-Thorpe, M., Viévard, A., André, C., Fuzellier, J., & Buser, P. Visually guided movements in the cat: a test using a randomly moving target. *Behavioural Brain Research, 11* (1984) 11-19.

20 Fabre-Thorpe, M., Viévard, A., & Buser, P. Role of the extra-geniculate pathway in visual guidance: II - Effects of lesioning the pulvinar-lateral posterior thalamic complex in the cat. *Experimental Brain Research, 62* (1986) 596-606.

21 Schmidt, R.A. Movement time as a determiner of timing accuracy. *Journal of Experimental Psychology, 79* (1969) 43-47.

22 Schell, G.R., Strick, P.L. The origin of thalamic inputs to the arcuate premotor and supplementary motor areas. *The Journal of Neuroscience, 4* (1984) 539-560.

23 Marr, D. A theory of the cerebellar cortex. *Journal of Physiology (London), 202* (1969) 437-470.

24 Albus, J.S. A theory of cerebellar function. *Mathematical Biosciences. 10* (1971) 25-61.

25 Gilbert, P.F.C. A theory of memory that explains the function and structure of the cerebellum. *Brain Research, 70* (1974) 1-18.

26 Gilbert, P.F.C. How the cerebellum could memorize movements. *Nature, 254* (1975) 688-689.

27 Gilbert, P.F.C., & Thach, W.T. Purkinje cell activity during motor learning. *Brain Research, 128* (1977) 309-328.

28 Llinas, R. & Walton, K. Place of the cerebellum in motor learning. In Brazier M.A. (Ed) *Brain mechanisms in memory and learning: from the single neuron to man*, Raven Press, New-York, (1979) 17-35.

29 Ito, M. Experimental evidence for cerebellar motor learning. In Pompeiano O; & Ajmone-Marsan C. (Eds) *Brain mechanisms of perceptual awareness and purposeful behavior*, Raven Press, New-York, (1981) 261-267.

30 Lisberger, S.G. Role of the cerebellum during motor learning in the vestibulo-ocular reflex. Different mechanisms in different species? *Trends in Neurosciences, 5* (1982) 437-441.

31 Yeo, C.H., Hardiman, M.J., & Glickstein M. Discrete lesions of the cerebellar cortex abolish the classically conditioned nictitating membrane response of the rabbit. *Behavioural Brain Research, 13* (1984) 261-266.

32 Houk, J.C. An adaptative sensorimotor network inspired by the anatomy and physiology of the cerebellum. In Miller R.S., Sutton, P.J. & Werbos, P.J. (Eds) *Neural networks for control,* MIT Press (1990).

33 Batuev, A.S., Cherenkova, L.V., & Yunatov, Y.U.A. Association brain systems and

visually guided movements in the cat. *Physiology and Behaviour, 31* (1983) 29-38.
34 Levesque, F., & Fabre-Thorpe, M. Motor deficit induced by red nucleus lesion: re-appraisal using kaïnic acid destructions. *Experimental Brain Research, 81* (1990) 191-198.
35 Canavan, A.G.M., Nixon, P.D., & Passingham, R.E. Motor learning in monkeys (Macaca fascicularis) with lesions in motor thalamus. *Experimental Brain Research, 77* (1989) 113-126.
36 Buchwald, N.A., Hull, C.D., & Levine, M.S. Neuronal Activity of the basal ganglia related to the development of "behavioral sets". In Brazier M.A.B. (Ed.), *Brain Mechanisms in memory and learning* (pp 93-103): from the single neuron to man. New-York: Raven Press (1979).
37 Buser, P. Subcortical control of pyramidal activity. In Purpura D.P. & Yahr M.D. (Eds), *The thalamus,* Columbia University Press, New-York, (1966) 323-347.
38 Rispal-Padel, L., & Massion, J. Relations between the ventrolateral nucleus and motor cortex in the cat. *Experimental Brain Research, 10* (1970) 331-399.
39 Strick, P.L. Cortical projections of the feline thalamic nucleus ventralis lateralis. *Brain Research, 20* (1970) 130-134.
40 Strick, P.L. Light microscopic analysis of the cortical projections of the thalamic ventralolateral nucleus in the cat. *Brain Research, 55* (1973) 1-24.
41 Sasaki, K., & Gemba, H. Changes of premovement field potentials in the cerebral cortex during learning processes of visually initiated hand movements in the monkey. *Neuroscience Letters, 27* (1981) 125-130.
42 Sasaki, K., & Gemba, H. Cortical field potential preceeding visually initiated hand movements and cerebellar actions in the monkey. *Experimental Brain Research, 46* (1982) 29-36.
43 Sasaki, K., & Gemba, H. Development and change of cortical field potentials during learning processes of visually initiated hand movements in the monkey. *Experimental Brain Research, 48* (1982) 429-437.
44 Sasaki, K., & Gemba, H. Learning of fast and stable hand movement and cerebro-cerebellar interactions in the monkey. *Brain Research, 277* (1983) 41-46.
45 Sasaki, K., Kawaguchi, S., Oka, H., Sakai, M., & Mizuno N. Electrophysiological studies on the cerebellocerebral projections in monkeys. *Experimental Brain Research, 24* (1976) 495-507.
46 Sasaki, K., Jinnai, K., Gemba, H., Hashimoto, S., & Mizuno N. Projection of the cerebellar dentate nucleus onto the frontal association cortex in monkeys. *Experimental Brain Research, 37* (1979) 193-198.
47 Rispal-Padel, L., Meftah E., Riviere G. The role of the cerebello-thalamo-cortical pathway in motor command adaptation to peripheral disturbances. *European Journal of Neuroscience, Suppl 30* (1988), 11.10.
48 Brons, J.F., & Woody, C.D. Long-term changes in excitability of cortical neurons after pavlovian conditioning and extinction. *Journal of Neurophysiology, 44* (1980) 605-615
49 Burnod, Y., Maton, B., & Calvet, J. Short-term changes in cell activity of area 4 and during operant conditioning. *Experimental Neurology, 78* (1982) 227-240.
50 Hebb, D.O. The organization of behavior. A neuropsychological theory. New-York: Wiley (1949).
51 Baranyi, A., & Fehér, O. Conditioned changes of synaptic transmission in the motor cortex of the cat. *Experimental Brain Research, 33* (1978) 283-298.
52 Baranyi, A., & Fehér, O. Synaptic facilitation requires paired activation of convergent pathways in neocortex. *Nature, 90* (1981) 413-415.
53 Baranyi, A., & Fehér, O. Selective facilitation of synapses in the neocortex by heterosynaptic activation. *Brain Research, 212* (1981) 164-168.
54 Bliss, T.V.P, & Lomo, T. Long-lasting potentiation of synaptic transmission in the dentate area of the anaesthetized rabbit following stimulation of the perforant path.

Journal of Physiology (London) 232 (1973) 331-356.
55 Racine, R.J., Wilson, D.A., Gingell, R. & Sunderland D. Long-term potentiation in the interpositus and vestibular nuclei in the rat. *Experimental Brain Research, 63* (1986) 158-162.
56 Sakamoto T., Porter L.L., Asanuma H. Long-lasting potentiation of synaptic potentials in the motor cortex produced by stimulation of the sensory cortex in the cat: a basis of motor learning. *Brain Research, 413* (1987) 360-364.
57 Iriki, A., Pavlides C., Keller, A., & Asanuma, H. Long-term potentiation in the motor cortex. *Science, 245* (1989) 1385-1387.
58 Kuypers, H.G.J.M. The descending pathways to the spinal cord, their anatomy and function. In Eccles J.C. and Shadé J.P. (Eds), *Progress in Brain Research,* Elsevier (Amsterdam, North-Holland) (1964) 178-202.
59 Paillard, J. The pyramidal tract: two millions fibres in search of a function. *Journal of Physiology (Paris), 74* (1978) 155-162.
60 Otero J.B. Comparison between red nucleus and precentral neurons during learned movements in the monkey. *Brain Research, 101* (1976) 37-46.
61 Ghez, C. & Kubota, K. Activity of red nucleus neurons associated with a skilled forelimb movement in the cat. *Brain Research, 131* (1977) 383-388.
62 Amalric, M;, Condé H., Dormont, J-F., Farin, D. & Schmied, A. Cat red nucleus changes of activity during the motor initiation in a reaction time task. *Experimental Brain Research, 52* (1983) 210-218.
63 Gibson, A.R., Houk, J.C., & Kohlerman, N.J. Magnocellular red nucleus activity during different types of limb movement in the macaque monkey. *Journal of Physiology (London), 358* (1985) 527-549.
64 Paillard, J. Development and acquisition of motor skills: a challenging prospect for neuroscience. In Whiting H.T.A. & Wade M.G. (Eds), *Motor development in children : aspects of coordination and control.* Martinus Nijhoff (La Haye) (1986) pp 1-24.
65 Massion, J. Red nucleus: past and future. *Behavioural Brain Research, 28* (1988) 1-8.
66 Kennedy, P.R. Corticospinal, rubrospinal and rubro-olivary projections: a unifying hypothesis. *Trends in Neurosciences, 13* (1990) 474-479.
67 Lashley K.S. In search of the engram. *Symp. Soc. Exp. Biol. 4* (1950) 454-482.

Tutorials in Motor Behavior II
G.E. Stelmach and J. Requin (Editors)

Behavioral and anatomical correlates of postlesion plasticity of the pyramidal tract during development in the cat

J. Armand and B. Kably

Centre National de la Recherche Scientifique, Laboratoire de Neurobiologie, B.P. 71, 13402 Marseilles Cedex 09, France.

Abstract

Studies have been performed at different ages in newborn and adult cats to correlate the behavioral effects of sensorimotor cortex lesions with the reorganization of corticospinal and corticosubcortical projections originating from the intact hemisphere. Regardless of the age-at-lesion, all animals could achieve simple task-related forelimb movements, but only animals operated on as newborns could accomplish complex tasks. The critical dates for recovery of distal and proximal skills were postnatal day 30 and 60 respectively. Kinematic analysis of target-reaching movements demonstrated that neonatal-operated animals compensated for the motor strategy observed in control animals by a motor equivalent. Anterograde transport of horseradish peroxidase injected into the intact pericruciate cortex of neonatal-operated animals demonstrated the formation of new corticospinal and corticosubcortical projections to numerous structural substrates deprived of their innervation by the cortical lesion. This plasticity is unable to prevent the loss of programming of the whole movement, but allowing recovery of some functions such as motor skills can account for the development of compensatory motor strategies.

1. INTRODUCTION

Behavioral recovery from sensorimotor cortex damage is reportedly better when injury is inflicted in newborns than adults [1-4], and various assumptions were made about its structural substrate [5]. In recent cat studies, attempts were made to correlate behavioral effects of sensorimotor cortex lesions [6-7] or hemispherectomy [8-13] with the reorganized corticospinal and corticosubcortical projections from the intact hemisphere in newborns and adults. These studies confirmed better recovery in newborns, but the correlation with structural reorganization was not convincing for two reasons. First developmental changes in simple reflexes, neurological tests, and locomotor activity patterns may not reflect the specific deficits and recoveries expected after a sensorimotor cortex lesion. Second these studies have only confirmed the well known crossed corticorubral projections [7, 13], and have revealed little reorganization of the corticospinal and corticosubcortical projections at the dorsal column nuclei [11], and thalamus [7, 12] level. In order to correlate functional recovery and anatomical reorganization after cerebral lesion, one must first know the function of the damaged structural substrate and second define the meaning of functional recovery.

The concept of behavioral function has long been considered in the framework of two opposing theories of cerebral organization [for review see 14]. The 'localizationist' theory holds that each discrete cerebral and particularly cortical area is responsible for a specific component of behavior. Conversely the 'functionalist' theory states that several structural substrates are called upon to achieve any one component. Nowadays, taking into account the functional level under study, these two theories are viewed as being more complementary than contradictory. While a particular component of behavior may depend on a well-defined neural substrate, integrated behavior requires several substrates acting in a simultaneous mode of operation [15].

The concept of behavioral recovery has also been variously used. Depending on the lesion inflicted, the resulting behavioral impairments may partially or completely disappear with time. Some authors accept the idea of graded recovery. On the other hand, purists advocate a stricter definition : 'Recovery is a theoretical construct that implies a complete regaining of identical functions that were lost or impaired after brain damage' [16]. In addition to recovery, other approaches have been used to assess postlesion events. For instance, functions are said to be spared if behavioral deficits expected in adult-lesioned animals do not emerge in neonatal ones. Compensation is said to occur when the behavioral program used to achieve an objective in control animals is lost but replaced by new strategies. Like the two concepts linking behavior and brain organization, recovery and compensation could apply to different functional levels. The concept of recovery could account for the performances of a precise component of behavior, whereas compensation would cover the strategy implicated in an integrated behavior. In the present study the effects of the sensorimotor cortex lesions on behavior were analysed with respect to the functional potentials of the damaged structure.

Retrograde and anterograde transport studies showed that in cats the corticospinal tract has a twofold structure consisting of a somatosensory and a motor component [17-21]. The primary and secondary somatosensory cortices, respectively composed of areas 3, 2, 1, and 2 prae-insularis, are at the origin of crossed corticospinal fibers terminating in the dorsal horn. The motor cortex, composed of areas 4 and 6, is at the origin of crossed and uncrossed corticospinal fibers terminating on interneurons of the intermediate zone, but not on motoneuronal cell groups. Some crossed fibers terminate in the dorsolateral part of the intermediate zone at the cervical or lumbosacral enlargement, these fibers controlling distal extremity muscles via short propriospinal neurons. Some crossed and uncrossed fibers also terminate at each spinal enlargement, contralaterally in the dorsolateral part of the intermediate zone and bilaterally in its ventromedial part, these fibers controlling proximal and girdle muscles via intermediate propriospinal neurons. Other crossed and uncrossed fibers terminate in the same bilateral regions of the spinal gray but throughout the spinal cord, these fibers controlling axial muscles via long propriospinal neurons.

Corticospinal fibers can also terminate at supraspinal levels by axonal collaterals as well as specific corticosubcortical projections [22]. The sensorimotor cortex thus projects to the cells of origin of other descending pathways, e.g. the red nucleus, to relay structures of ascending pathways, e.g.

the dorsal column nuclei and the ventrobasal complex of the thalamus, and to groups of cells involved in cortico-cerebello-cortical loops, e.g. the pontine nuclei and the lateral reticular nucleus.

The structural substrate of the pyramidal tract, with its corticospinal and corticosubcortical components thus includes several functional potentials. These are gating of sensory inputs at their different relay stations, control of motor outputs to distal, proximal, and axial muscles through either supraspinal structures or spinal interneurons, and input-output coupling within internal loops. Thus this structural substrate can be considered not only to have control over contralateral distal muscles but also to be involved in the elaboration of motor strategies.

Ablation of the sensorimotor cortical areas containing the cells of origin of the pyramidal tract was chosen because it involved spinal as well as supraspinal components. To evaluate postlesion plasticity at different developmental stages, this cortical lesion was performed at various ages in newborn and adult cats. At adulthood, behavior was analysed both in terms of motor skills and strategies. After behavioral testing, reorganization of the intact pyramidal tract was studied by anterograde transport of horseradish peroxidase (HRP) injected in the intact sensorimotor cortex.

2. MATERIALS AND METHODS

Experiments were carried out on 22 cats. In 17 operations were performed at various times between postnatal days (PND) 1 to 75 and, in 1, operation was performed in adulthood. The other 4 animals were used as controls.

2.1. Cortical lesion

Animals operated on during the first postnatal month were anesthetized with Alfatesine (1.2 ml/Kg, I.M.). Thereafter Pentobarbital (30 mg/Kg, I.P.) was used. Ablation which always involved the left hemisphere consisted in aspiration under a dissection microscope of the precruciate, postcruciate, and lateral pericruciate regions, as well as the cruciate sulcus.

2.2. Behavioral methods

In adult animals the effects of ablation were analysed using operant conditioning tests [23]. The task which consisted in retrieving a piece of raw meat with the forelimb was presented as four tests differing with regard to the posture of the animal and the position of the target. In the two simple tests, the animal in the sitting position had to retrieve the meat placed either on the ground behind vertical bars (test I) or in a rectangular groove placed at mouth level (test II). In two complex tests, the animal had to retrieve the meat either sitting on its hindquarters from the bottom of a horizontal tube placed at shoulder level (test III) or standing in the quadrupedal position with its forelimb placed on a platform from a vertical tube (test IV). In order to alternatively test the left and right forelimbs, a bootee was placed over the inactive paw to prevent its use.

All four task-related movements were subdivided into three phases, i.e. : reaching during which the limb was lifted to the target, grasping during which the meat was seized by combined plantar flexion, claw flexion, and paw adduction, and wrist rotation during which the meat was brought to the mouth by supination and flexion. Experimental sessions consisting of 5 trials for each forelimb were conducted at the rate of 3 per week for 32 weeks.

Forelimb movement was scored at three levels : goal achievement, motor skills and motor strategy. Goal achievement in each of the four tests was defined as the ability to retrieve food in 100% of trials per week. Motor skills were evaluated by different parameters of the movement. These parameters were defined by a selected phase of the movement in the four different tests. Proximal skills, such as the amplitude and precision of the movement, were estimated by the reaching phase in test I and II respectively. Distal skills were evaluated by the wrist rotation and the grasping phases in tests III and IV. If the phase was accomplished on the first attempt, the animal was given a positive mark, if not the trial was discarded. Motor strategy was studied by means of kinematic analysis. The coordinates of each forelimb joint, i.e. the shoulder, elbow, and wrist, and the tip of the paw, were digitized during test III. The positions of the different limb segments could thus be reconstructed, and the acceleration curve of the tip of the paw plotted.

2.3. Anatomical methods

After behavioral testing, a solution of free HRP (30%, Boehringer) was injected into the right pericruciate cortex of operated and control animals. Injections were performed stepwise over a 2-hour period using a glass micropipette. At each step, 0.1μl of HRP was injected below and above cortical layer V, where the cells of origin of the pyramidal tract are located. The total amount of HRP injected was 4-5 μl.

Three days after injection, the animals were deeply anesthetized with Pentobarbital (60 mg/Kg, I.P.) and intracardially perfused with 2 l of washing

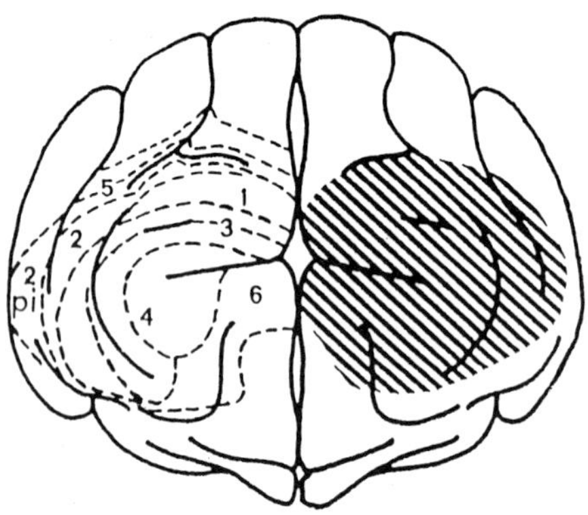

Figure 1. Frontal view showing the sensorimotor cortex lesion (hatched area) in the left hemisphere and the borders (broken lines) of the cytoarchitectonic areas of the motor (4, 6), primary (3, 2, 1) and secondary (2 p. i.) somatosensory cortices in the right hemisphere.

solution (NaCl 0.9%, 4 g procaïne, 4 ml heparine), followed by 4 l of fixative solution (paraformaldehyde 1%, glutaraldehyde 1.25% in 0.2 M phosphate buffer) and 2 l of postperfusion solution (sucrose 30%). The brain and spinal cord were removed.

The lesioned frontal lobe was postfixed in formaline for several weeks, dehydrated, and embedded in paraffin. Parasagittal sections (thickness : 10 μm) were stained with Cresyl violet in order to define the extent of the lesion. The remaining histological blocks were stored overnight in a sucrose buffer (30%). Transverse sections (thickness : 40 μm) were cut on a freezing microtome and submitted to a tetramethylbenzidine histochemical procedure [24].

3. RESULTS

3.1. Cortical lesion

Histological reconstruction of cortical lesions was achieved at adulthood by identifying the spared cytoarchitectonic areas [25]. The damaged region

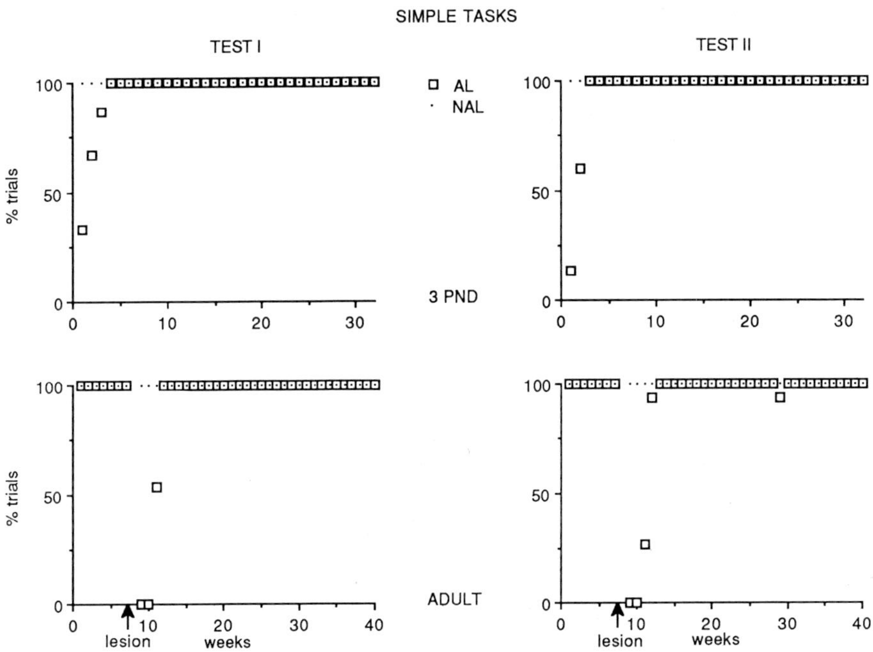

Figure 2. Ability to retrieve food in 100% of trials per week in tests I and II with the affected limb (AL = square) and the non-affected limb (NAL = dot) of animals which underwent surgery on PND 3 and in adulthood. The arrow indicates the date of operation.

included most of areas 4 and 6 in the motor cortex, all of areas 3, 2, and 1 in the primary somatosensory cortex, and part of area 2 prae-insularis in the secondary somatosensory cortex (Figure 1). The periphery within area 2 prae-insularis accounted for most of lesion variability between cases.

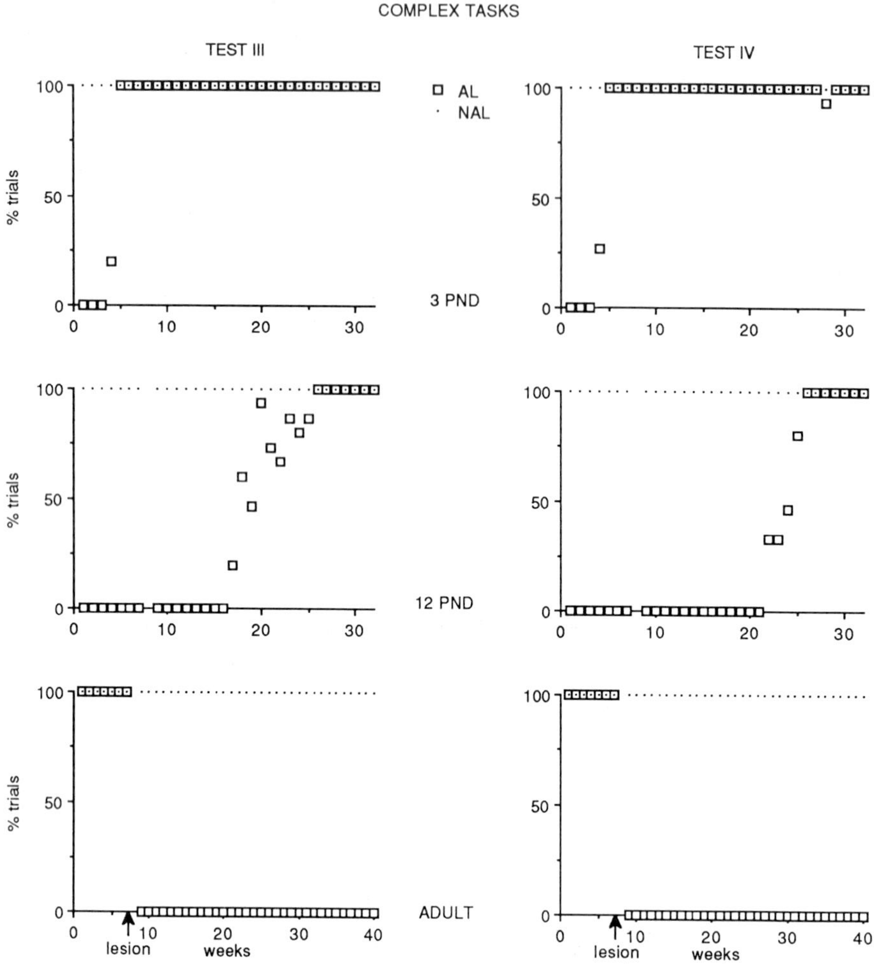

Figure 3. Ability to retrieve food in 100% of trials per week in tests III and IV with the affected limb (AL = square) and the non-affected limb (NAL = dot) in animals which underwent surgery on PND 3, PND 12, and in adulthood. The arrow indicates the date of operation.

3.2. Behavioral results.

In control animals no difference was observed betwen the right and left forelimbs. Comparison of motor behavior in operated and control animals showed no difference between the right forelimbs (i.e. contralateral to the intact hemisphere in operated animals). This limb is referred to as the non-affected limb (NAL). During behavioral tests, the NAL of each operated animal was used as the intra-individual reference for analysis of the forelimb contralateral to the cortical lesion, i.e. the affected limb (AL). Motor behavior of the AL was analysed at three levels : goal achievement, proximal and distal motor skills, and motor strategy.

Goal achievement was scored in all four tests. In simple tasks (tests I and II), all operated animals took 2-3 weeks longer to achieve the task with the AL than the NAL (Figure 2). This short delay did not depend on age at time of lesion.

In complex tasks (tests III and IV), an initial period of complete impairment was always observed (Figure 3). For animals operated on up to PND 10, this period lasted 3 to 4 weeks. For those operated on up to PND 30, it lasted 15 to 25 weeks. For animals operated on as adults, the deficit was permanent. Thus, for complex tasks impairment of the AL was age dependent.

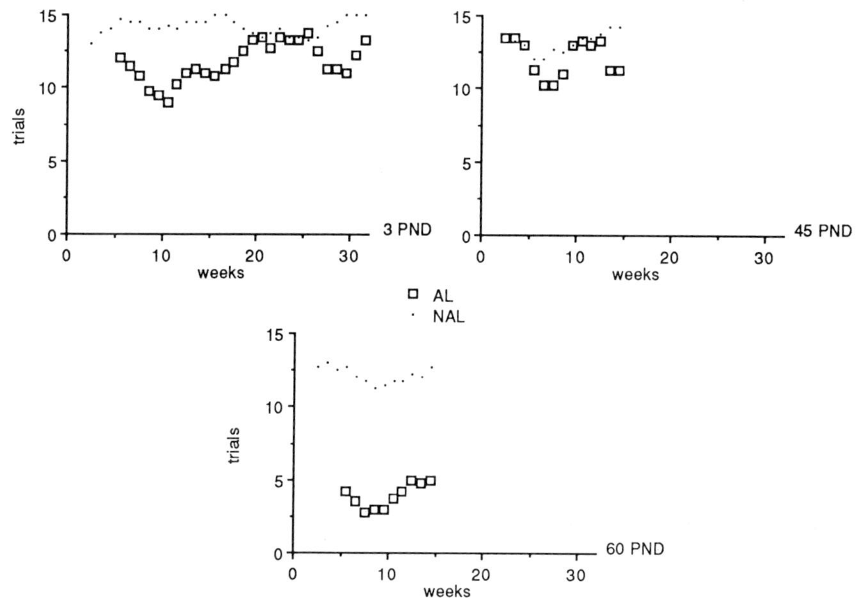

Figure 4. Comparison of the amplitude of the reaching phase of test I in the affected (AL = square) and non-affected (NAL = dot) limbs in animals which underwent surgery on PND 3, PND 45, PND 60.

These task-related movements only indicated if the NAL of operated animals could achieve the goal. To obtain further insight it is necessary to analyse different parameters of the movement itself.

Recovery of proximal skills was assessed on the basis of the amplitude and precision of the reaching phase in tests I and II respectively (Figure 4). Animals operated on before PND 60 recovered proximal skills, while those operated on later remained severely handicapped.

Recovery of distal skills was based on evaluation of wrist rotation and grasping in tests III and IV (Figure 5). Animals operated on up to PND 30 recovered, while those operated on later did not. Thus, the critical dates for the cortical lesion is different for proximal and distal skills : PND 60 and PND 30 respectively.

As shown in Figure 5, grasping in animal which underwent surgery on PND 23 could not be evaluated during the first 28 weeks of tests, because this distal skill was not yet coordinated with the movement. This is the time required by neonatal-operated animals to elaborate a compensatory strategy. This elaboration was a progressive process starting with initially unsuccessful strategies and culminating with a successful strategy.

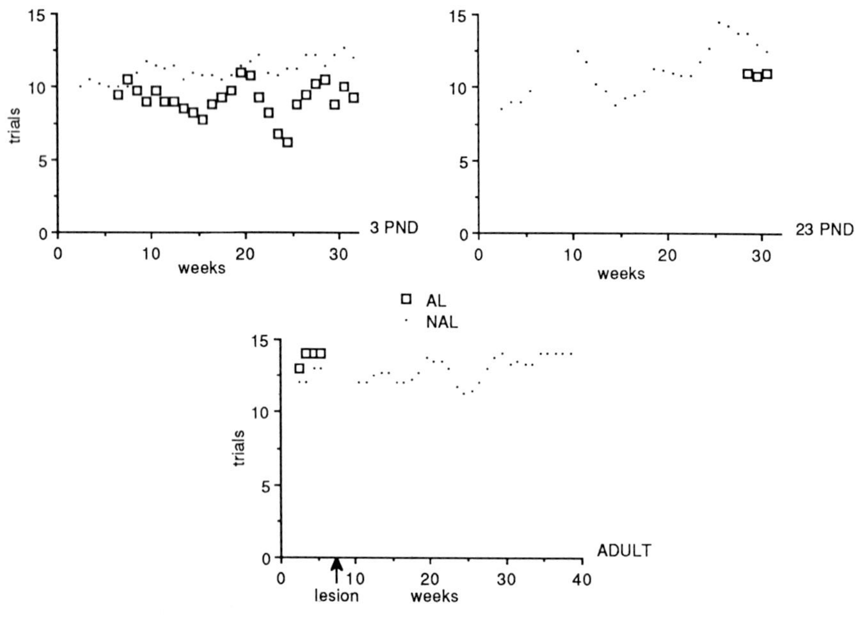

Figure 5. Comparison of the grasping in test III in the affected (AL = square) and non-affected (NAL = dot) limbs of animals which underwent surgery on PND 3, PND 23, and in adulthod. The arrow indicates the date of operation.

Motor strategy was studied by kinematic analysis of forelimb movement in test III (Figure 6). In control animals, the acceleration curve of the tip of the paw was plotted as the forelimb was raised from the ground and placed in the tube. The ballistic portion consisted of a large acceleration and deceleration, and the terminal adjustment consisted of a succession of small accelerations and decelerations. In animals operated on as adults, only the ballistic portion occured, and it was always unsuccessful. In animals operated on as newborns, the reaching movement from the ground to the tube level was composed of consecutive accelerations and decelerations indicating that it was permanently controlled by sensory feedback. This new motor strategy was sometimes successful.

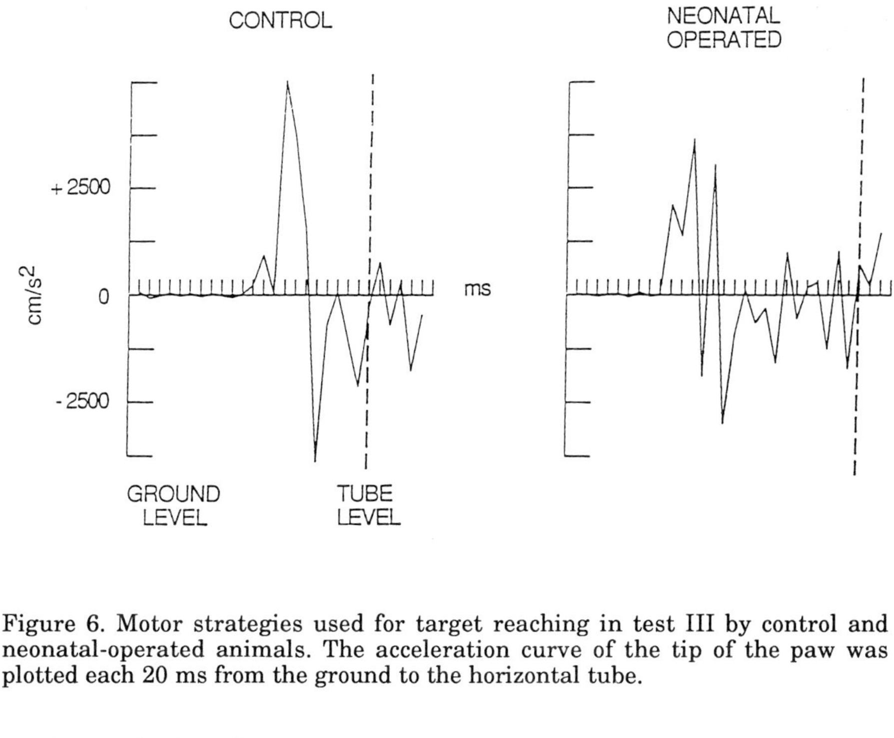

Figure 6. Motor strategies used for target reaching in test III by control and neonatal-operated animals. The acceleration curve of the tip of the paw was plotted each 20 ms from the ground to the horizontal tube.

3.3. Anatomical results

The corticospinal and corticosubcortical projections from the intact pericruciate cortex of operated animals was compared to those of adult controls. In all animals HRP cortical labelling on transverse sections extended to the anterior, posterior, and lateral sigmoid gyri, as well as to the rostral depth of the cruciate sulcus.

In control animals, anterograde-labelled fibers terminated in the gray matter of all spinal segments, but especially in the cervical and lumbosacral enlargements. With the exception of motoneuronal cell groups, these corticospinal terminations were distributed contralaterally in the dorsal horn and the dorsolateral part of the intermediate zone and bilaterally in its ventromedial part. This pattern indicated that a representative sample of the various corticospinal components was labelled (Figure 7).

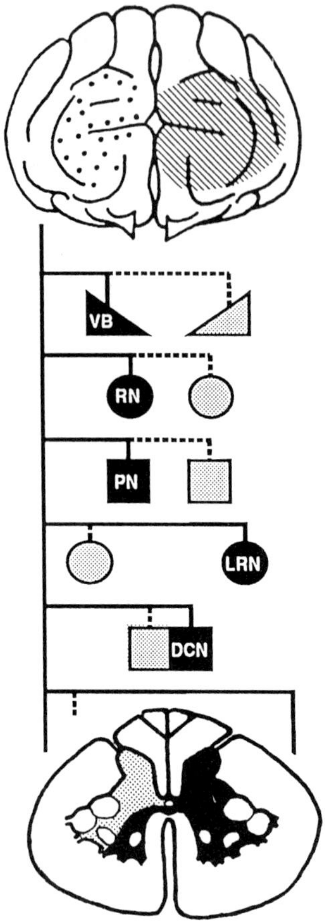

Figure 7. When sensorimotor cortex lesion (hatched area) was inflicted on the day of birth and horseradish peroxidase injection into the pericruciate cortex (dots = penetrations of the micropipette) was performed at adulthood, new corticospinal and corticosubcortical projections (dotted lines and dotted areas) were observed in comparison with the control animal (solid lines and black areas). Abbreviations : DCN : dorsal column nuclei, LRN : lateral reticular nucleus, PN : pontine nuclei, RN : red nucleus, VB: ventrobasal complex of the thalamus.

In an animal which underwent surgery on PND 1, labelled fibers also terminated throughout the spinal cord but bilaterally in the whole gray matter except the motoneuronal cell groups. Thus in addition to the terminations observed in control animal, corticospinal terminations were also found in the ipsilateral dorsal horn and dorsolateral part of the intermediate zone. Conversely, in animal operated on as adult, the corticospinal termination pattern did not differ from that of control ones.

Labelled projections from the intact pericruciate cortex to subcortical targets, which were unilateral in control animals, were bilateral in neonatal-operated animals. Three examples of such corticosubcortical projections were selected in an animal which underwent surgery on PND 1 for comparison with controls, i. e. : projections to the cells of origin of other descending pathways, projections to relay stations of ascending pathways, and projections to cell groups involved in cortico-cerebello-cortical loops.

Corticorubral projections which were mainly ipsilateral in the control animal, were found to be bilateral in animals operated on as newborns. Cortical projections to the dorsal column nuclei and the ventrobasal complex of the thalamus which were contralateral and ipsilateral respectively in the control animal, were found to be bilateral in neonatal-operated animals. In the control animal, cortical projections to the pontine nuclei were mainly ipsilateral and those to the lateral reticular nucleus were exclusively contralateral. In neonatal-operated animals, contralateral corticopontine projections were much more numerous and widely distributed and cortical projections to the ipsilateral lateral reticular nucleus were numerous.

4. DISCUSSION

The behavioral effects of sensorimotor cortex lesions were evaluated at several levels. First in terms of ability to perform task-related movements we found that whatever the age of operation all animals were promptly able to achieve the goal in simple tasks. Conversely only animals operated on as newborns were able to achieved the goal in complex tasks, the duration of the initial deficit increasing with the age-at-lesion. Second in terms of motor skills we found that animals operated on before PND 30 recovered both distal and proximal skills, animals operated on before PND 60 recovered only proximal skills, and animals operated on later recovered neither. Finally, in terms of motor strategy defined as target reaching movement observed in control animals, we found that only animals operated on as newborns were able to elaborate a replacement strategy.

To determine recovery of function, one must insure that the behavioral tests selected reflect the function of the lesioned neural substrate. Some tests are inadequate, while others only detect one functional aspect. Recovery of function has to be analysed at several levels. In the present study, forelimb movement was chosen on the basis of the functional potentials of the pyramidal tract in sensorimotor integration. However simple task-related movements did not detect the effect of age-at-lesion. Animals operated on as newborns were able to perform complex task-related movements successfully even though normal motor strategy was always destroyed. Studies of the effects of hemispherectomy [8-10] or sensorimotor cortex lesion [6] on the development of different limb reflexes and the pattern of locomotor activity have showed that motor behavior was normal as long as control was mediated at the subcortical levels. However, when during development cortical control came into play motor abnormalities were noted. This 'growing-into-a-deficit' exemplified the corticalization process rather than the functional potentials of the pyramidal tract that we wanted to investigate.

Critical dates, i.e. the point after which recovery was no longer possible, were determined by performing the sensorimotor cortex lesion at several postnatal ages. For example, in animals operated on before PND 30 distal skill performances with the AL were as good as with the NAL while animals operated on later never recovered. Such critical dates were assumed to exist from earlier studies [6]. Distal skill performances assessed by a paw attitude-movement test have been compared in animals which underwent hemispherectomy either at a mean age of 8 days (range 5-25) or in adulthood [9]. Neither of the operated groups were ever able to perform as well as controls. Unfortunately some of the animals in the newborn group were operated on as late as PND 25 which is very close to the critical date for distal skills established in the present study.

Several neural substrates are implicated in target reaching including the sensorimotor cortex which gives the final motor command. The motor strategy observed in control animal was always destroyed whatever the age-at-lesion. However neonatal-operated animals were able to develop a compensatory strategy. The development of replacement motor strategy composed of consecutive accelerations and decelerations has been previously reported under different experimental conditions. Discontinuous arm movement during the training period of a step-tracking task in monkeys was interpreted as a characteristic mode of motor control at this stage involving sensory feedback [26]. Afterwards limb movement consisted in a quick and precise ballistic phase followed by terminal adjustment. In another set of experiments, the motor program of deafferented animals shifted from the optimal, feed-forward mode to a much less efficient mode based on peripheral feedback. As a result, overall performance deteriorated [27]. Discontinuous movement during reaching observed after neonatal cortical lesion in the cat appears to last too long to be considered as learning-related. We attribute this finding to a deficit that neonatal animals are able to overcome by a motor strategy that is not as good as the one observed in control animals but nevertheless is successful. Compensatory strategy has been reported after sensorimotor cortex lesion performed in both newborn and adult cats. It consisted in increasing the velocity of flexion during the swing phase to compensate for the time lost due to the increased number of misplacements during conditioned locomotion [6]. In summary, after sensorimotor cortex lesion inflicted in newborns, some functions of the pyramidal tract such as motor skills can be recovered, but its integrated function in the programming of the movement is abolished.

After sensorimotor cortex lesions inflicted in newborn cats, extensive anatomical reorganization of the intact pyramidal tract is observed at both the spinal and supraspinal levels. Corticospinal terminations are distributed bilaterally in the gray matter except the motoneuronal cell groups. Cortical projections to diencephalic, mesencephalic, pontine, and medullary nuclei, which terminate unilaterally in control animals, terminate bilaterally in animals operated on as newborns. Partial and largely conflicting results were reported in previous studies.

Anterograde amino-acid transport studies disclosed ipsilateral corticospinal terminations in the base of the dorsal horn and at the cervical enlargement after neonatal hemispherectomy [11]. In contrast, anterograde WGA-HRP transport showed no change in distribution of the corticospinal tract terminations originating from the intact sensorimotor cortex [7]. Both these results contrast with the bilateral corticospinal terminations presented here. These discrepancies could be due to technical and methodological differences in the experimental conditions. Because of the very short survival and exposure times, the autoradiographic protocol used in the first study could have missed some terminations in controls as well as experimental animals. In the second study the neonatal cortical lesion spared some cytoarchitectonic areas at the origin of the pyramidal tract and thus may have been too limited to induce reorganization of the intact pyramidal tract.

Ipsilateral cortical projections to both dorsal column nuclei in animals operated on at birth have not been mentioned previously. After neonatal hemispherectomy, anterograde transport of labelled amino-acids injected into the intact motor cortex and sparing the somatosensory cortex disclosed ipsilateral corticogracile projections in addition to the contralateral ones observed in control animal [11].

Previous data concerning the contralateral cortical projections to the ventrobasal complex of the thalamus observed in neonatal-operated animals are uninterpretable because the authors did not distinguish the various thalamic nuclei. In one study an overall increase in the number of contralateral thalamic projections from the intact hemisphere was observed after neonatal hemispherectomy but damage of the thalamus during the operation was not ruled out [12]. In another study, a greater increase in contralateral corticothalamic projections was reported in the medial than the ventral nuclei [7], but the medial thalamic nuclei are known to receive bilateral cortical projections in controls.

In the present report the only finding which confirms previous data concerns corticorubral projections. In anatomical [7, 13, 28-29] and electrophysiological [30-31] studies, numerous contralateral corticorubral projections in addition to the ipsilateral ones observed in controls have been identified after neonatal sensorimotor cortex lesion. Retrograde double labelling further suggested that these new contralateral projections were not axonal collaterals of ipsilateral corticorubral fibers [32].

The extensive reorganization of corticospinal and corticosubcortical projections from the intact pericruciate cortex of cat after unilateral neonatal lesions seems to affect functional potentials. This assumption is exemplified by the new ipsilateral corticospinal terminations and the crossed rubrospinal terminations from the red nucleus which receives new cortical projections. These terminations overlap in the dorsolateral part of the spinal intermediate zone which contains propriospinal neurons projecting to motoneurons of distal extremity muscles contralateral to the lesion. These anatomical data are in keeping with the behavioral recovery of distal skills in neonatal-operated animals. Although this intense plasticity did not spare the programming of the whole movement, it may have been necessary to develop the compensatory strategies.

Acknowledgements
The authors whish to sincerely thank Andrew Corsini for revising the English.

5. REFERENCES

1 M.A. Kennard, Am. J. Physiol., 115 (1936) 138-146.
2 M.A. Kennard, J. Neurophysiol., 1 (1938) 477-496.
3 M.A. Kennard, Arch. Neurol. Psychiat. (Chicago), 44 (1940) 377-397.
4 M.A. Kennard, Arch. Neurol. Psychiat. (Chicago), 48 (1942) 227-240.
5 S. Finger and C.R. Almli, in : S. Finger, T.E. LeVere, C.R. Almli and D.G. Stein (eds.), Brain Injury and Recovery. Theoretical and Controversial Issues, Plenum Press, New-York and London, 1988, 117-132.
6 C.T. Leonard and M.E. Goldberger, Dev. Brain Res., 32 (1987) 1-14.
7 C.T. Leonard and M.E. Goldberger, Dev. Brain Res., 32 (1987) 15-30.
8 J.R. Villablanca, J.W. Burgess, and C.E. Olmstead, Behav. Brain Res., 19 (1986) 205-226.
9 J.W. Burgess and J.R. Villablanca, Behav. Brain Res., 20 (1986) 1-18.
10 J.W. Burgess, J.R. Villablanca, and M.S. Levine, Behav. Brain Res., 20 (1986) 217-230.
11 F. Gomez-Pinilla, J.R. Villablanca, B.J. Sonnier, and M.S. Levine, Brain Res., 385 (1986) 343-355.
12 J.R. Villablanca and F. Gomez-Pinilla, Brain Res., 410 (1987) 219-231.
13 J.R. Villablanca, F. Gomez-Pinilla, B.J. Sonnier, and D.A. Hovda, Brain Res., 453 (1988) 17-31.
14 H.L. Teuber, in : E. Eidelberg and D.G. Stein (eds.), Functional Recovery after Lesions of the Nervous System, Neurosci. Res. Progr. Bull., 12 (1974) 197-209.
15 D.G. Stein, in : E. Eidelberg and D.G. Stein (eds.), Functional Recovery after Lesions of the Nervous System, Neurosci. Res. Progr. Bull., 12 (1974) 209-211.
16 C.R. Almli and S. Finger, in : S. Finger, T.E. LeVere, C.R. Almli, and D.G. Stein (eds.), Brain Injury and Recovery. Theoretical and Controversial Issues, Plenum Press, New-York and London, 1988, 1-14.
17 R. Nyberg-Hansen and A. Brodal, J. Comp. Neurol., 120 (1963) 369-391.
18 J. Armand and R. Aurenty, Neurosci. Lett., 6 (1977) 1-7.
19 J. Armand and H.G.J.M. Kuypers, Exp. Brain Res., 40 (1980) 23-34.
20 J. Armand, in : H.G.J.M. Kuypers and G.F. Martin (eds.), Descending Pathways to the Spinal Cord, Progr. Brain Res., 57 (1982) 329-358.
21 J. Armand, G. Holstege, and H.G.J.M. Kuypers, Brain Res., 343 (1985) 351-355.
22 C.G. Phillips and R. Porter (eds.), Corticospinal Neurones. Their Role in Movement, Monographs of the Physiological Society 34, Academic Press, London, New York, San Francisco, 1977.
23 E. Sybirska and T. Gorska, Acta Neurobiol. Exp., 40 (1980) 821-841.
24 M.M. Mesulam, Tracing Neural Connections with Horseradish Peroxidase, I.B.R.O. Handbook Series, Methods in Neurosciences, Wiley and Sons, New York, 1982.
25 R. Hassler and K. Mühs-Clement, J. Hirnforsch., 6 (1964) 377-420.
26 V.B. Brooks and S.L. Watts, J. Mot. Behav., 20 (1988) 17-132.

27 M. Jeannerod, The Neural and Behavioural Organization of Goal-Directed Movements, Oxford Psychology Series 15, Clarendon Press, Oxford,1988.
28 C.C. Naus, B.A. Flumerfelt, and A.W. Hrycyshyn, Exp. Brain Res., 59 (1985) 365-371.
29 F. Murakami and S. Higashi, Brain Res., 447 (1988) 98-108.
30 N. Tsukahara, Y. Fujito, and M. Kubota, Exp. Brain Res., 51 (1983) 45-56.
31 F. Murakami, Y. Oda, and N. Tsukahara, Behav. Brain Res., 28 (1988) 175-179.
32 C.C. Naus, B.A. Flumerfelt, and A.W. Hrycyshyn, Neurosci. Lett., 70 (1986) 52-58.

Tutorials in Motor Behavior II
G.E. Stelmach and J. Requin (Editors)

ANATOMICAL AND BEHAVIORAL PARALLELS IN THE DEVELOPMENT OF THE CORTICOSPINAL TRACT

Emma Hall, Didier Flament, Keree Bennett and Roger Lemon

Department of Anatomy, Cambridge, Downing Street, Cambridge CB2 DY England.

Abstract

The development of the corticospinal tract: its origin, growth and myelination is reviewed. In both cats and monkeys there is a close parallel between the functional maturation of the corticospinal tract and the development of motor skill. In monkeys, direct cortico-motoneuronal (CM) projections do not appear until 6-8 months after birth and it is at this time that skilled independent finger movements are first observed. The development of these connections has been followed using non-invasive brain stimulation to excite the corticospinal projection. Both cross-sectional and longitudinal studies have been carried out, and both indicate appearance of CM mediated responses at around 4 months and maturation 8 months of age.

THE ORIGIN OF THE CORTICOSPINAL TRACT

Although the corticospinal tract is one of the most important descending pathways controlling the hand and arm, and although errors in development give rise to a variety of movement disorders, our knowledge of how this pathway develops is itself very much in its infancy. Animal models are problematic because the rate of development in different species is subject to considerable variation (Passingham, Perry & Wilkinson, 1983; Passingham, 1985). In the cat, the corticospinal projection can be identified as early as 50-55 days after gestation, before there is any clear sign of laminar organisation in the cortex and before other efferent projections can be recognised (Wise, Hendry & Jones, 1977). The full maturation of these neurones is, however, a slow process since Oka, Samejima & Yamamoto (1985) showed that kitten pyramidal tract neurones are still undergoing changes postnatally and do not show a mature form until around 4 weeks after birth.

The density and proportion of synaptic contacts in the developing macaque motor cortex was studied at the EM level by Zecevic, Bourgeois & Rakic (1989). The first synapse was detected at embryonic (E) day E53; at the middle of the gestation period (E89) synapses were present through all cortical layers but at a low density ($5/100\mu m^3$ of neuropil). During the last two months of gestation there was a dramatic 8-fold increase in synaptic density to reach $40/100\mu m^3$ at birth (E165); it reached a maximum of $60/100\mu m^3$ two months postnatally. There then followed a substantial and rapid elimination of synapses, principally of the asymmetric (presumed excitatory) type, until the age of 3 years, after which the density remained at the adult level of around 30/100μm ^{3}. This pattern of development reflects the changes in the influence of cortico-cortical, thalamo-cortical and other inputs upon the corticospinal output neurones, and this can also be expected to result in considerable differences in the susceptibility of these neurones to external electrical or magnetic stimuli (see below).

In the adult primate, the corticospinal tract is derived from at least five different cortical areas: primary motor cortex (area 4), the SMA, the premotor cortex, the primary somatosensory cortex (areas 3,1 and 2) and the inferior bank of the cingulate sulcus (areas 23c and 24c) (Kuypers, 1981; Murray & Coulter, 1981; Hutchins, Martino & Strick, 1988). In developing rodents, the area of origin of the corticospinal tract is substantially larger than in the adult, and even includes the occipital lobe (Stanfield & O'Leary, 1985); whether or not a similar phenomenon occurs in the primate is not yet known.

GROWTH OF THE CORTICOSPINAL TRACT

There are marked species differences in the growth of the tract. In the cat corticospinal fibres have reached the medullary decussation 20 days before birth, and have reached all levels of the spinal cord at birth (Wise et al., 1977; Leonard & Goldberger, 1987; Theriault & Tatton, 1989). In the monkey corticospinal fibres have reached at least to the level of the lower cervical segments at birth (Kuypers, 1962). The development in cat and monkey contrasts strongly with that in rodents, where spinal innervation is not complete until 15 days after birth (Jones, Schreyer & Wise, 1982; Schreyer & Jones, 1983). There would appear to be a 'waiting period' before corticospinal axons invade the spinal grey matter. The earliest terminations to appear are in the dorsal horn; in the monkey, the direct cortico-motoneuronal projections, most of which are derived from area 4, do not appear until 6-8 months of age (Kuypers, 1962, 1981).

Immature corticospinal neurones show an exuberant pattern of branching. Thus in the kitten, axon densities labelled from the pericruciate cortex are widespread throughout the spinal grey matter, from Rexed lamina I to IX, compared to a much more restricted distribution in the adult, and corticospinal branches also cross the midline at all levels (Theriault & Tatton, 1989; Armand, Kably & Jacomy, 1991).

Many studies have been directed towards the substantial remodelling of the corticospinal projection that occurs after neonatal injury in the rat, hamster and kitten. These studies have indicated that, for instance, after unilateral section of the pyramidal tract (Castro, 1978) or hemispherectomy (Castro, 1975; Leong, 1976; Armand et al., 1991) new aberrant pathways develop. In general, the evidence seems to indicate that most of the new projections arise by sprouting of the intact fibres in response to injury (Murakami & Higashi, 1988; Villablanca, Gomez-Pinalla, Sonnier & Hovda, 1988). Armand et al. (1991) have recently shown when sensorimotor lesions are made at birth with subsequent injection of HRP into the intact sensorimotor cortex, widespread aberrant projections are revealed including contralateral projections to the thalamus, red nucleus and pontine nuclei and ipsilateral projections to the dorsal column nuclei and spinal cord. The extent of such sprouting in adult animals is severely curtailed, as is recovery from lesions (Bregman and Goldberger, 1983; Armand et al., 1991).

In the primate, the evidence for exuberant corticospinal projections is scarce. Sloper, Brodal & Powell (1983) could not find any substantial differences in the subcortical projections from the intact sensorimotor cortex in monkeys that had been subjected to ablation of the opposite sensorimotor area at birth. Passingham et al. (1983) have suggested that this relative lack of any compensatory plasticity in motor pathways may be due to the relatively advanced stage of development reached by the monkey at birth. This may also explain why infant monkeys subjected to bilateral pyramidotomy at birth (Lawrence & Hopkins, 1976) fail to develop a normal pattern of relatively independent finger movements (see below).

MYELINATION OF THE CORTICOSPINAL TRACT

According to Jones et al. (1982), all corticospinal axon growth is complete before myelination begins. Myelination, which begins postnatally in all species studied to date, is a protracted process; it takes several years in man (Yakovlev & Lecours, 1967; Müller, Homberg & Lenard, 1991)

In the cat, myelination is still incomplete at 1 month of age and proceeds slowly to completion at 4-5 months after birth. Oka et al., (1985) used the latency of antidromic responses evoked by stimulation of the pyramidal tract to demonstrate a steady increase in the conduction velocity of corticospinal axons during the first month of life. At birth the fastest axons were calculated to conduct at 0.7 $m.s^{-1}$, compared to 15 $m.s^{-1}$ one month later. The entire population of corticospinal fibres showed a continuous decrease in their antidromic latency, although the fastest axons showed a particularly marked reduction around two weeks of age, possibly indicating a wave of myelination in which the largest axons are myelinated first (cf Matthews & Duncan, 1971; Reh & Kalil, 1982). The process of myelination not only increases the conduction velocity of the fibre, but may change it in other ways; the immature, unmyelinated axon cannot support the repetitive firing characteristic of the adult neurone (Huttenlocher, 1970); Sears & McDonald, 1970).

ELECTROPHYSIOLOGICAL AND BEHAVIORAL PARALLELS

Stimulation of the neonatal motor cortex fails to elicit any motor responses comparable to those seen in the adult. When responses do appear, they generally have long latencies and high thresholds. In the kitten, Bruce & Tatton (1980a,b) reported that EMG responses in a variety of facial, upper and lower limb muscles could not be activated by intracortical microstimulation (ICMS) in the motor cortex until around 37-45 days postnatally. Even ICMS trains of long duration and high strength (up to 100μA) were ineffective. At 37-45 days, clear cut short-latency responses were evident, and were indistinguishable from those in adult cats. Bruce & Tatton (1980b) reported that such responses develop synchronously in all muscles investigated. Interestingly, these authors reported that responses to ICMS appeared before neurones in the motor cortex showed responses to peripheral stimulation, which occurred at around 55-65 days. These input-output changes precede changes in motor behaviour, including the maturation of beam-walking and forelimb contact placing (Amassian & Ross, 1978). There is thus a clear sequence of events: appearance of functional outputs, input-output linkage and finally, behavioral maturation.

Until recent studies using non-invasive brain stimulation were carried out (Eyre, Ramesh & Miller, 1991; Flament, Hall & Lemon, 1992) there was only a single, isolated report on the development of corticospinal responses in the primate. In an infant monkey, 7 weeks old, Felix & Wiesendanger (1971) found that stimulation of the motor cortex failed to produce any short latency EMG responses, while a 10 month old animal yielded essentially adult responses.

In a classic study of the development of motor control, Lawrence & Hopkins (1976) made extensive observations on hand and finger movements in infant Rhesus monkeys. They hand-reared infants from birth. Control animals were tested on a variety of tasks, including the retrieval of small food morsels from a test board, similar to that used by Lawrence and Kuypers (1968). The earliest signs of reaching in the control animals was at 3-4 weeks of age. Reaching was inaccurate and grasping of food rewards was part of a rather gross whole arm and hand movement. The retrieval of food was clumsy and, when successful, was achieved by closure of all digits around the reward; release of the food at the mouth was often achieved with difficulty. Smooth reaching occurred in the third month and the first signs of relatively independent finger movements (RIFM) were present in the second to third month. These control animals were judged to have fully mature RIFM at 7-8 months of age. Five other animals underwent bilateral pyramidotomy 5-28 days after birth; RIFM completely failed to develop in these monkeys. Hinde, Rowell & Spencer-Booth (1964) have observed that normal infant monkeys first begin to groom other monkeys at around 6 months of age. RIFM are a quintessential requirement for grooming, when often a single hair or a tiny flea must be isolated and gripped (Tower, 1940).

AN EXPERIMENTAL STUDY OF CORTICO-MOTONEURONAL (CM) DEVELOPMENT IN THE MONKEY USING NON-INVASIVE MAGNETIC STIMULATION OF THE MOTOR CORTEX

Cortico-motoneuronal connections are found almost exclusively in primates, and are a relatively recent feature of mammalian evolution (Phillips, 1971; Heffner & Masterton, 1975). The results presented above suggest that the establishment of direct, cortico-motoneuronal connections is one of the important factors contributing to the development of skilled hand and finger movements. The aim of our experimental study was to obtain a neurophysiological measure of the functional development of the direct CM projections. For this purpose we used non-invasive magnetic stimulation of the cortex which has been shown to elicit short-latency EMG responses in muscles of the hand and forearm (Edgley, Eyre, Lemon & Miller, 1990). These responses strongly resemble those observed in man (Hess, Mills & Murray, 1987; Day, Dressler, Maertens de Noordhout, Marsden, Nakashima, Rothwell & Thompson, 1989). Edgley et al. (1990, 1991) have further demonstrated that magnetic brain stimulation directly excites the neurones

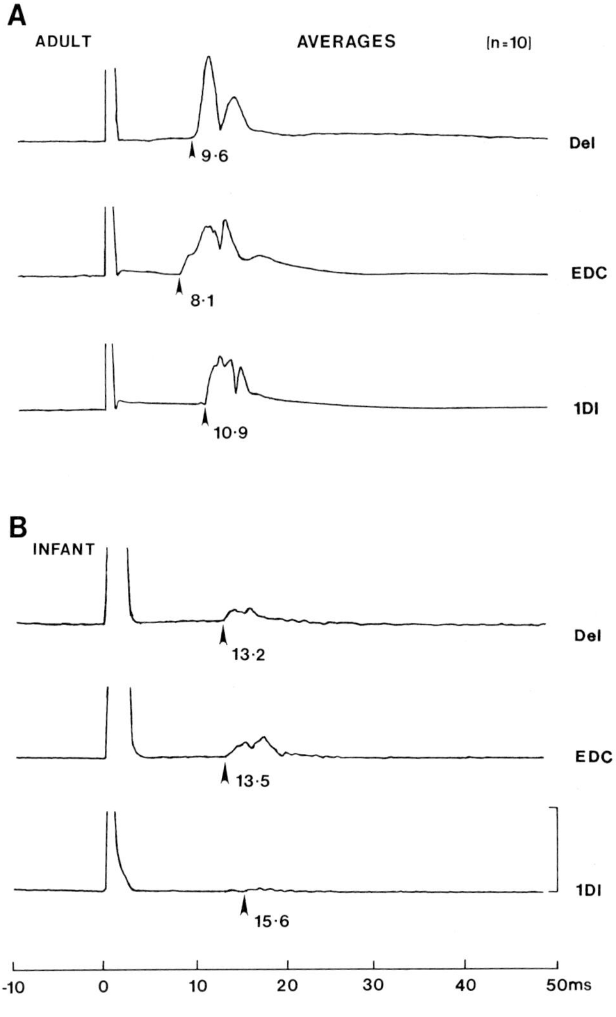

Figure 1. EMG response averages from different muscles to magnetic stimulation in adult (A) and infant (B) monkeys. Stimuli delivered (at time zero) during periods of spontaneous EMG activity. Subjects: adult, monkey KA (10 yr) and infant, JE (2.5 months). Onset latencies (in ms) are arrowed. Del: deltoid; EDC: extensor digitorum communis; 1DI: 1st dorsal interosseous. Calibration: Del 750 µV, EDC 750 µV and 1DI 300 µV.

giving rise to the corticospinal tract at the level of the motor cortex in both conscious and anaesthetized macaque monkeys, and that this is particularly true of the fast-conducting corticospinal neurones; these neurones probably provide the bulk of the direct CM connections (Phillips & Porter, 1977; Kuypers, 1981; Lemon, Bennett & Werner, 1991). Magnetic stimulation is ideally suited for the study of infant monkeys because of its non-invasive and painless nature; it has already been used for a large cross-sectional study of human infant (Eyre et al., 1991).

METHODS Five infant M. mulatta monkeys from the Rhesus colony housed in the Sub-department of Animal Behaviour, Cambridge University and on 6 purpose-bred adult macaques were used in this study. The infants (3 males: LE, HO, TH; 2 females: PU, JE) were aged 4.75, 5.75, 6.5, 10.25 and 12.0 months, respectively, at the time they were investigated for the cross sectional study. Their body weights ranged from 0.85 to 3.07 kg. The adults (2 male M. fascicularis: UG, MA and 4 females: DI, EL (M. nemestrina); KA, JO (M. fascicularis)) were between 1.5-10 years old and weighed 1.3-8.2 kg. We were able to follow two of the infant monkeys (LE, JE) in a longitudinal study over a 15 month period. Monkeys were sedated with ketamine (10 mg/kg i.m.) throughout the experimental procedure and body temperature was maintained at 37-39°C. Infant monkeys were returned to their mothers immediately after the experimental session was over (typically 20-30 min). Surface EMGs were recorded from 1st dorsal interosseous (1DI), abductor pollicis brevis (AbPB), extensor digitorum communis (EDC) and deltoid (Del) on the right side. All data was transferred to a PC computer for off-line analysis.

MAGNETIC BRAIN STIMULATION This was carried out using a Novametrix 200 electromagnetic brain stimulator with a standard 9 cm diameter coil. Stimuli ranging from 30-100% of the maximum stimulator output (1.5 Tesla) were applied in blocks of 5-10, at a rate of 1 shock every 2-4 s. The coil was centred above the vertex and oriented such that the current in the coil was anti-clockwise (A-side up). A comparison was made of responses elicited when the muscles were relaxed (i.e. during periods of EMG silence) and the periods of spontaneous, low-level muscle activity which generally occurred towards the end of the sedation period. Both single sweeps and averages were analysed, and the probability of evoking responses was calculated by determining the number of sweeps generated by a stimulus at a given strength which evoked a clear response. The threshold for evoking these responses was defined as that which yielded clear effects in at least two of the 5-10 sweeps sampled at that strength.

RESPONSES TO MAGNETIC STIMULATION IN ADULT MONKEYS As shown previously (Edgley et al., 1990), magnetic stimulation evoked short-latency EMG responses and overt contractions from deltoid, EDC and 1DI in all of the adult monkeys studied. Averaged EMG records are shown in Figure 1A from a 10 yr old adult (KA). Responses in adults were readily evoked in both relaxed and active muscles. Mean response thresholds were lower in active 1DI (46 ± 4% of stimulator output) than in the relaxed muscle (50 ± 8%), and similar differences were found for both EDC and deltoid..

Examination of the response latencies confirmed that the earliest part of the response in the intrinsic hand muscle (1DI; mean latency 10.5

ms, n=5) and in the forearm muscle (EDC; 7.9 ms, n=5) to magnetic stimulation were indeed cortico-motoneuronal in origin. By comparing, in the same monkey, EMG responses to magnetic stimulation and to electrical stimuli delivered through electrodes implanted in the medullary pyramidal tract, it was found that responses to magnetic stimulation had only slightly longer latencies than the pyramidal evoked effects. The earliest response to pyramidal tract stimulation can be confidently attributed to the CM projection, and the magnetic responses were typically only 0.7 to 1.7 ms longer than pyramidal. This difference can be attributed to the additional conduction delay from cortex to pyramid (see Edgley et al., 1990; Flament et al., 1992).

In four of the five monkeys in which deltoid was recorded, its responses had longer latencies than EDC (see Figure 1A), and this is not be expected given the shorter conduction distance to deltoid. Indeed, short-latency responses in deltoid to magnetic stimulation that would have been compatible with CM conduction (i.e.<5 ms) were not observed.

AGE-DEPENDENCE OF RESPONSES: CROSS-SECTIONAL STUDY The ease with which responses could be evoked in hand and arm muscles was strongly dependent on age. In the monkeys used for the cross-sectional study, it was found that the threshold intensity for evoking an EMG response was highest in the young animals and lowest in the older and adult animals. Figure 1B shows examples of responses recorded from a 2.5 month old infant (JE). These responses were obtained with 100% stimulator output, and were particularly difficult to obtain in hand muscles. In this animal only one small response was recorded from the 1DI, and this response contributed the very small deflection at 15.6 ms in the average shown. One animal (PU, 4.75 months) showed clear responses in deltoid, but none in EDC or 1DI.

Figure 2 plots the changes in response threshold for EDC and 1DI as a function of age in the infant monkeys used for the cross-sectional study. All stimuli were delivered when the muscles were relaxed. For both EDC and 1DI, all the infants under 6 months had thresholds above 60% of the stimulator output. No clear difference was found between thresholds in the active and relaxed states. The mean threshold in the adults was 51% in EDC and 50% in 1DI. In the infants over 5 months of age the lowest thresholds were observed in active muscles. During periods of EMG activity, older infants and adults had thresholds as low as 35%.

Figure 1 shows that response latencies were longer in the infant than in the adult for all three muscles studied. In the 1DI muscle of monkeys younger than 5 months, we rarely observed any sweeps containing responses with latencies less than 14 ms, compared to a mean value of 10.5 ms in the adults.

AGE-DEPENDENCE OF RESPONSES: LONGITUDINAL STUDY Two monkeys were investigated at approximately two month intervals from 2.5 to 10 months of age. The findings were entirely consistent with the cross-sectional data. Figure 3 shows the 1DI threshold data for the two monkeys. At the beginning of the study (2.5 and 3.5 months, respectively) responses were difficult to obtain in 1DI, even at maximum output. Both animals then showed a decline in the threshold until 6.5 and 8 months respectively, after which no further decrease was observed; in fact, a slight increase in threshold was detected. From the earliest observations until about 5

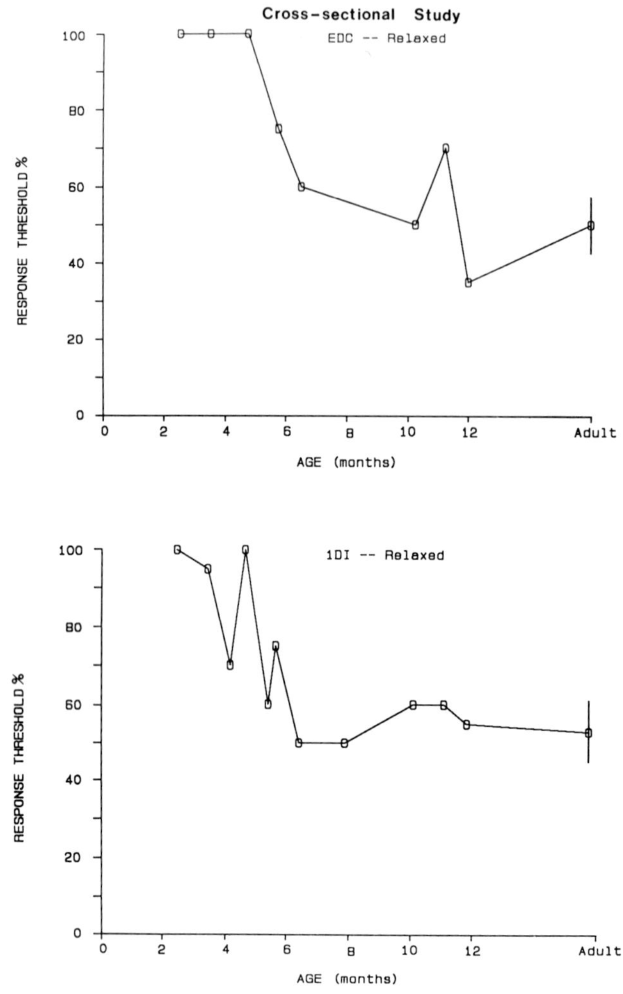

Figure 2. Cross-sectional study. Thresholds (in % max. stimulator output) of EMG responses recorded from EDC (above) and 1DI (below) following magnetic brain stimuli in infant monkeys. Results from 5 adults have been pooled (mean ± SE). Responses were recorded during periods of EMG quiescence.

months of age there was no difference in the response threshold for spontaneously active and relaxed muscles. Thereafter, a clear divergence appeared, with the active thresholds being consistently lower than the

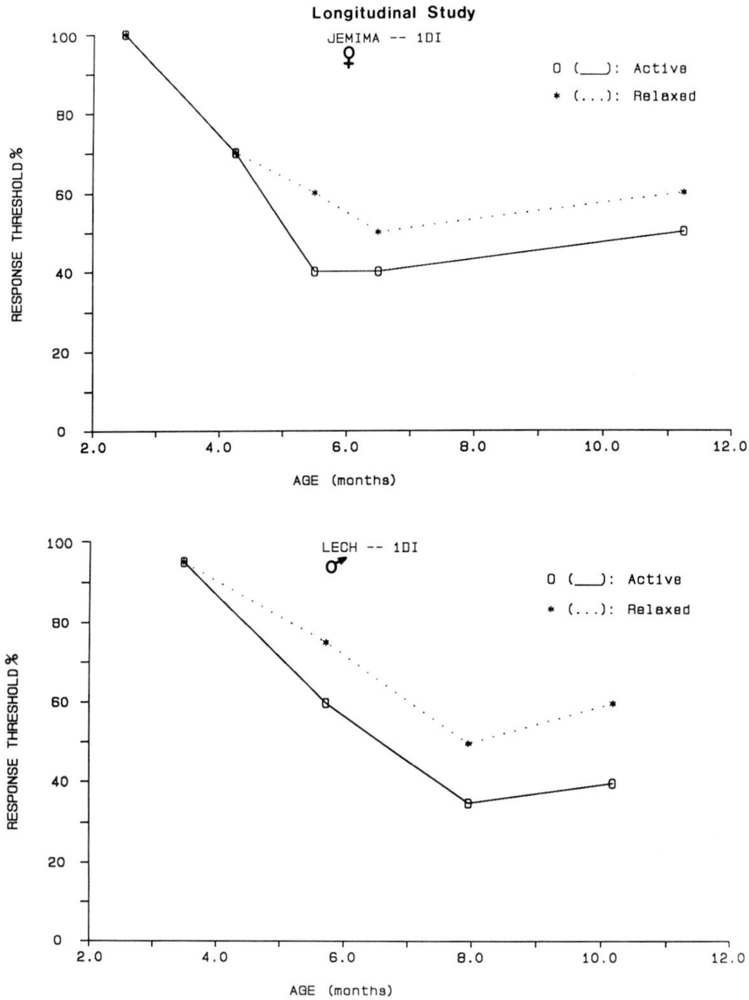

Figure 3. Longitudinal study. Thresholds of EMG responses recorded from 1DI muscle following brain stimuli in 2 infant monkeys (JE, LE) during periods of spontaneous EMG activity (___ active) or during EMG quiescence (.... relaxed).

relaxed values, and differing by 10-20% of stimulator output.

There was again an overall decrease with age in response latency for all muscles tested. At 2.5 months there was little difference in the response latency of deltoid, EDC and 1DI, all responding at latencies around 14-15 ms. As the monkey matured there was a gradual decrease in the latencies of these muscles, but it was particularly marked for deltoid and EDC, falling by around 6 to 7 ms. The reduction in hand muscle latency was less, at only 3 to 4 ms. The most rapid decline in latency was at 4 to 6 months.

BEHAVIORAL OBSERVATIONS Four infants (aged 3-7 months) were observed while interacting freely with their mother and in the presence of other members of their troupe. Monkeys JE and LE (at 3 and 4.5 months old, respectively) spent most of their time in very close proximity, or clinging, to their mother. Their manual dexterity at retrieving small seeds was poor. Movements were slow and clumsy and they tended to grip between the side of the index finger and thumb, in contrast to adults who manipulated small seeds between the tips of the index and thumb. The primary, and apparently most successful, strategy for seed retrieval in these two infants was to use the tongue and lips.

At 5.25 months old, JE had clearly improved her performance. The adult pattern of precision grip was seen but the "side" grip still tended to predominate. Use of the mouth for retrieving seeds was no longer evident. At 6.75 months and 5.5 months respectively, monkeys LE and PU, were competent at the adult precision grip between thumb and index fingertip, although the speed of seed retrieval was clearly slower than in adults. At 7 months, monkey HO could grip small seeds between the tips of the thumb and index finger. Both hands were equally skilled and used in an alternating fashion to bring food to the mouth. This rapid alternation of left and right hand was typical of the adults in the colony and was not seen in any of the younger animals.

CONCLUSIONS

Our study has demonstrated that the short latency EMG responses evoked in a variety of arm and hand muscles by magnetic brain stimulation in adult macaques are not seen in infant monkeys. These responses are first observed in monkeys around 4 months old. The latency, threshold and probability of occurrence of these responses then undergo rapid change and become indistinguishable from those of adult macaques by around 8 months of age. Since there is good evidence that these short-latency EMG responses to brain stimulation reflect the presence of functional cortico-motoneuronal connections, the non-invasive method of magnetic stimulation allows the longitudinal development of these connections in the monkey to be followed.

Why is it difficult to obtain short-latency responses in infant monkeys? The size difference between infant and adult brain is unlikely to be a factor, since the brain of the 2 to 3 month old macaque is almost as large as the adult (Passingham, 1985). However, it is possible, that the magnetic stimulus does not excite the motor cortex (as suggested by the study of Bruce & Tatton, 1980a). The slow myelination of the corticospinal fibres may mean that even if a corticospinal volley is generated by magnetic stimulation, it is not sufficiently large or synchronous to excite the spinal motoneurones.

In our study, we measured peripheral conduction time by recording the responses in the 1DI muscles to stimulation of the ulnar nerve at the elbow. No significant changes in peripheral conduction were found, and therefore it is most likely that the changes in the latency of evoked EMG responses were central in origin. These changes may also reflect the progress of corticospinal myelination.

Finally it is also possible that the slow synaptogenesis of the CM connections does not allow any short-latency excitation of forelimb muscles in the infant monkey. Kuypers' (1962) study suggested that CM connections are not established until around 6 to 8 months, although he did observe corticospinal terminals in the dorsal horn and intermediate zone of new-born macaques. The difference in threshold for relaxed and active muscles, which is so characteristic of the adult, was not observed until 4 to 6 months. This argues against the existence of any functional CM connections in the infant monkey, since in this case even a small descending volley could be expected to excite the target motoneurones, providing there was some background excitatory activity. We suggest, therefore, that the latency shortening observed may be due in part to a progressive change from an oligosynaptic to a monosynaptic linkage between cortex and motoneurone.

Shoulder muscles in the monkey are reported as having a small or absent CM input (Kuypers, 1981; Phillips & Porter, 1964) and in this respect it is interesting that it was relatively easy to excite deltoid in one 4.75 month animal, when responses in EDC and 1DI were absent. We suggest that these responses were conducted over an oligosynaptic pathway that is established at a much earlier stage of development. Short latency responses, compatible with a CM input to deltoid motoneurones, were not observed in this study. At around 4 months of age, the mean latency of EMG responses in EDC and deltoid was rather similar at about 14 ms. Although responses of both muscles subsequently became much shorter, the year-old infant EDC, with the longer peripheral conduction distance, had a shorter latency than deltoid. This difference was also observed in the adults (see Figure 1). This is best explained by the late maturation of fast CM projections to EDC, which thereby overtake the slower, oligosynaptic linkages to deltoid. Interestingly, in apes and in man, there are direct CM projections to deltoid (Schoen, 1964; Kuypers, 1981). This is confirmed by the responses obtained in man to magnetic brain stimulation, where response latency is shortest in deltoid and longest in 1DI. The latency (11.5 ms) of the early component of the deltoid response is certainly compatible with a CM projection (Hall, Flament, Fraser & Lemon, 1990). The smaller latency shift in the responses of hand muscles with age may indicate that they do not receive any substantial oligosynaptic drive from the cortex during infancy, and that slowly conducting CM connections are responsible for their appearance at around 4 months of age.

Our results are comparable with an earlier cross-sectional study of over 300 human subjects aged from 32 weeks gestation to 55 years by Eyre et al. (1991), which revealed similar changes in the threshold and latency of responses to magnetic stimulation over a prolonged time course. Human infants show a rapid decrease in their central motor conduction times until around 2 years of age, which thereafter remain constant at adult values. These authors also reported a rapid decline in the threshold of

EMG responses in hand and arm muscles over the same period, although thresholds continued to fall up to the age of 16 years. These results possibly reflect the protracted period of myelination of the human pyramidal tract (Yakovlev & Lecours, 1967) and the slow maturation of human hand and finger movements (Halverson, 1943; Forssberg, Eliasson, Kinoshita, Johansson & Westling, 1991).

The changes in response of hand muscles to magnetic brain stimulation parallel the maturation of skilled independent finger movements in the same monkeys. Magnetic brain stimulation has therefore proved to be of considerable value in exploring the neurophysiological changes underlying important behavioral developments involving the use of the hand. Although many structural and functional changes must contribute to the lengthy maturation of skilled hand movement in primates, it seems likely that the capacity to perform such movements is dependent upon the establishment of functional CM connections.

Acknowledgements. This work was supported by Action Research and the Medical Research Council. We gratefully acknowledge the extensive help and cooperation of Dr. Michael Simpson and David Rayment of the sub-department of Animal Behaviour, Cambridge University, without which this study would not have been possible. Expert technical assistance was provided by Rosalyn Cummings.

REFERENCES

Amassian, V.E. & Ross, R.J. (1978). Developing role of sensorimotor cortex and pyramidal tract neurons in contact placing in kittens. Journale de Physiologie (Paris) 74, 165-184.

Armand, J., Kably, B. & Jacomy, H. (1991) Lesion-induced plasticity of the pyramidal tract during development in the cat. In Tutorials in Motor Neuroscience ed. J. Requin & G.E. Stelmach pp. 625-640. Kluwer, Dordrecht

Bregman, B.S. & Goldberger, M.E. (1983). Infant lesion effect: III. Anatomical correlates of sparing and recovery of function after spinal cord damage in newborn and adult cats. Developmental Brain Research 9, 137-154.

Bruce, I.C. & Tatton, W.G. (1980a) Sequential output-input maturation of kitten motor cortex. Experimental Brain Research, 39, 411-419.

Bruce, I.C. & Tatton, W.G. (1980b). Synchronous development of motor cortical output to different muscles in the kitten. Experimental Brain Research 40, 349-353.

Castro, A.J. (1975). Ipsilateral corticospinal projections after large lesions of the cerebral hemisphere in neonatal rats. Experimental Neurology 46, 1-8.

Castro, A.J. (1978). Analysis of corticospinal and rubrospinal projections after neonatal pyramidotomy in rats. Brain Research 144, 155-158.

Day, B.L., Dressler, D., Maertens de Noordhout, A., Marsden, C.D., Nakashima, K., Rothwell, J.C. & Thompson, P.D. (1989) Electric and magnetic stimulation of human motor cortex: surface EMG and single motor unit responses. Journal of Physiology 412, 449-473.

Edgley, S.A., Eyre, J.A., Lemon, R.N. & Miller, S. (1990) Excitation of the corticospinal tract by electromagnetic and electrical stimulation of the scalp in the macaque monkey. Journal of Physiology, 425, 301-320.

Edgley, S.A., Eyre, J.A., Lemon, R.N. & Miller, S. (1991) Direct and indirect excitation of corticospinal neurones by electrical and magnetic stimulation in the anaesthetised monkey. Proceedings of the Physiological Society (in press).

Eyre, J.A., Miller, S. & Ramesh, V. (1991) Constancy of central conduction delays during development in man: investigation of sensory and motor pathways. Journal of Physiology, 434, 441-452

Felix, D. & Wiesendanger, M. (1971) Pyramidal and non-pyramidal motor cortical effects on distal forelimb muscles of monkeys. Experimental Brain Research, 12, 81-91.

Flament D., Hall, E.J. & Lemon, R.N. (1992) The development of cortico-motoneuronal projections investigated using magnetic stimulation in the infant macaque. Journal of Physiology (in press).

Forssberg, H., Eliasson, A.C., Kinoshita, H., Johansson, R. & Westling, G. (1991) Experimental Brain Research (in press)

Hall, E.J., Flament, D.A., Fraser, C. & Lemon, R.N. (1990) Non-invasive brain stimulation reveals reorganised cortical outputs in amputees. Neuroscience Letters 116, 379-386

Halverson, H.M. (1943) The development of prehension in infants. In Child Behaviour and Development, ed. Barker, R.G., Konnin, J.S. & Wright, H.F. pp. 49-65 McGraw Hill, New York.

Heffner, R. & Masterton, B. (1975) Variation in the form of the pyramidal tract and its relationship to digital dexterity Brain, Behaviour & Evolution 12, 161-200

Hess, C.W., Mills, K.R. & Murray, N.M.F. (1987) Responses in small hand muscles from magnetic stimulation of the human brain. Journal of Physiology, 388, 397-419.

Hinde, R.A., Rowell, T.E. & Spencer-Booth, Y. (1964) Behaviour of socially living rhesus monkeys in their first six months. Proceedings of the Zoological Society (London), 143, 609-649.

Hutchins, K.D., Martino, A.M. & Strick, P.L. (1988). Corticospinal projections from the medial wall of the hemisphere. Experimental Brain Research 71, 667-672.

Huttenlocher, P.R. (1970). Myelination and the development of function in immature pyramidal tract. Experimental Neurology 29, 405-415.

Huttenlocher, P.R. & Raichelson, R.M. (1989). Effects of neonatal hemispherectomy on location and number of corticospinal neurons in the rat. Developmental Brain Research 47, 59-69.

Kuypers, H.G.J.M. (1962) Corticospinal connections: postnatal development in the rhesus monkey. Science 138, 678-680.

Kuypers, H.G.J.M. (1981) Anatomy of the descending pathways. In Handbook of Physiology, The Nervous System II, ed. Brookhart, J.M. & Mountcastle, V.B. pp 597-666. American Physiological Society, Bethesda.

Lawrence, D.G.& Hopkins, D.A. (1976) The development of motor control in the rhesus monkey: evidence concerning the role of corticomotoneuronal connections. Brain 99, 235-254.

Lawrence, D.G. & Kuypers, H.G.J.M. (1968) The functional organization of the motor system. I. The effects of bilateral pyramidal lesions. Brain 91, 1-14.

Lemon, R.N., Bennett, K.M. & Werner, W. (1991) The cortico-motor substrate for skilled movements of the primate hand. In Tutorials in Motor Neuroscience ed. J. Requin & G.E. Stelmach pp. 477-495. Kluwer, Dordrecht
Leonard, C.T. and Goldberger, M.E. (1987). Consequences of damage to the sensorimotor cortex in neonatal and adult cats. II. Maintenance of exuberant projections. Developmental Brain Research 32, 15-30.
Leong, S.K. (1976). A qualitative electron microscopic investigation of the anomalous corticofugal projections following neonatal lesions in the albino rat. Brain Research 107, 1-8.
McDonald, W.I. & Sears. T.A. (1970) The effects of experimental demyelination on conduction in the central nervous system. Brain, 93, 583-598
Matthews, M.A. & Duncan, D. (1971). A quantitative study of morphological changes accompanying the initiation and progress of myelin production in the dorsal funiculus of the rat spinal cord. Journal of Comparative Neurology 142, 1-22.
Müller, K., Hömberg, V. & Lenard, H.-G. (1991) Magnetic stimulation of motor cortex and nerve roots in children. Maturation of cortico-motoneuronal projections. Electroencephology and Clinical Neurophysiology 81, 63-70.
Murakami, F. & Higashi, S. (1988). Presence of crossed corticorubral fibers and increase of crossed projections after unilateral lesions of the cerebral cortex of the kitten: a demonstration using anterograde transport of Phaseolusvulgaris leucoagglutin. Brain Research 447, 98-108.
Murray, E.A. & Coulter, J.D. (1981). Organization of corticospinal neurons in the monkey. Journal of Comparative Neurology 195, 339-365.
Oka, H., Samejima,A. & Yamamoto, T. (1985) Post-natal development of pyramidal tract neurons in kittens. Journal of Physiology, 363, 481-499.
Passingham, R.E. (1985) Rates of brain development in mammals including man. Brain, Behaviour and Evolution, 26, 167- 175
Passingham, R.E., Perry, V.H. and Wilkinson, F. (1983). The long-term effects of removal of sensorimotor cortex in infant and adult rhesus monkeys. Brain 106, 675-705.
Phillips, C.G. (1971) Evolution of the corticospinal tract in primates with special reference to the hand. Proceedings of the 3rd International Congress of the Primatological Society, Zurich, vol. 2, pp.2-23. Karger, Basel.
Phillips, C.G. & Porter, R. (1964) The pyramidal projection to motoneurones of some muscle groups of the baboon's forelimb. In Physiology of Spinal Cord Neurones, ed. Eccles, J.C. & Schadé, J.P., pp. 222-242. Elsevier, Amsterdam.
Phillips, C.G. & Porter, R. (1977) Corticospinal neurones: their role in movement. Monograph of the Physiological Society no. 34, pp.143-151. Academic Press, London.
Reh, T. & Kalil, K. (1982). Development of the pyramidal tract in the hamster. II. An electron microscopic study. Journal of Comparative Neurology 205, 77-88.
Schoen, J.H.R. (1964) Comparative aspects of the descending fibre systems in the spinal cord. In Physiology of Spinal Cord Neurones, ed. Eccles, J.C. & Schadé, J.P., pp. 203-222. Elsevier, Amsterdam.
Sloper, J.J., Brodal, P. & Powell, T.P.S. (1983). An anatomical study of the effects of unilateral removal of sensorimotor cortex in infant monkeys

on the subcortical projections of the contralateral sensorimotor cortex. Brain 106, 707-716.
Stanfield, B.B. & O'Leary, D.D.M. (1985). The transient corticospinal projection from the occipital cortex during the postnatal development of the rat. Journal of Comparative Neurology 238, 236-248.
Theriault, E. & Tatton, W.G. (1989). Postnatal redistribution of pericruciate motor cortical projections within the kitten spinal cord. Developmental Brain Research 45, 219-237.
Tower, S.S. (1940). Pyramidal lesions in the monkey. Brain 63, 36-90.
Villablanca, J.R., Gomez-Pinilla, F., Sonnier, B.J. & Hovda, D.A. (1988). Bilateral pericruciate cortical innervation of the red nucleus in cats with adult or neonatal cerebral hemispherectomy. Brain Research 453,17-31.
Wise, S.P., Hendry, S.H.C. & Jones, E.G. (1977). Prenatal development of sensorimotor cortical projections in cats. Brain Research 138, 538-544.
Yakovlev, P.I. & Lecours A.R. (1967) Myelogenic cycles of regional maturation in the brain. In Regional Development of the Brain in Early Life, ed. Minkowski, A., pp.3-70. Oxford, Blackwell.
Zecevic, N., Bourgeois, J.-P. & Rakic, P. (1989). Changes in synaptic density in motor cortex of rhesus monkey during fetal and postnatal life. Developmental Brain Research, 50, 11-32.

Tutorials in Motor Behavior II
G.E. Stelmach and J. Requin (Editors)

Brain damage and recovery : the cellular basis of neuroplasticity

A. Nieoullon, L. Kerkerian-Le Goff and A. Daszuta

Neurochemistry Unit, Laboratory of Functional Neuroscience - CNRS 31, chemin Joseph Aiguier - 13402 Marseille cedex 9 (France)

Abstract

Functional recovery subsequent to brain damage in adults is generally thought to primarily result from anatomical rearrangement of neuronal networks. The reactive synaptogenesis hypothesis was indeed the common idea of adaptive brain response to injury. Data from cellular and molecular studies of the CNS have revealed however that neuronal plasticity in response to brain lesion can also be viewed as functional dynamic reactive changes in cellular interactions. Thus, the putative cellular basis of neuroplasticity could actually represent, over post-lesion remodelling of brain architecture, adaptive metabolic responses of the remaining intact systems in the deafferented structures leading to compensate for the loss in neurotransmission for example by reactive change in various neurotransmitter functions. In some cases, adaptive neuronal responses could consist in actual changes in genomic expression leading to apparent changes in neuronal phenotype. Analysis of the more recent data on cellular interactions thus raised the idea that structural, metabolic and genomic responses to brain damage in adults may in fact represent different expressions of common mechanisms, and furthermore that these mechanisms are similar to those contributing to neuronal networks setting during development and to their maintenance in the adult brain.

It is generally thought nowadays that functional recovery subsequent to brain damage may result from a compensatory structural reorganization of the mature central nervous system (CNS) in response to a lesion. Possible interpretations of brain repair after injury in terms of an anatomical restructuring suffer from considerable limitations in adult human neuropathology, however, since no major structural rearrangement has been reported to occur in response to denervation. Indeed, a neoformation of nerve terminals which come to occupy the synaptic sites left vacant will occur mainly in cases of partial lesion involving only a limited part of a given neuronal system. Moreover, in experimental studies, no post-lesion remodelling of the brain has yet been clearly found to accompany functional recovery. Opposing this idea that structural reorganization of the CNS may occur in response to injury, there exists the theoretical concept of the brain as a rigid structure, according to which the limited restructuring capacities of adults can result in only limited post-lesion recovery (KENNARD, 1940). Recent analyse of the cellular mechanisms underlying post-lesion neuroplasticity have suggested however that functional recovery from brain damage may actually be mediated by changes in cellular interactions which are not limited to the injured neuronal systems, and do not involve a simple structural rebuilding of the brain. Cellular and molecular studies on the CNS have now revealed that brain function normally results from dynamic cellular interactions which are able to adapt in response to brain damage being able to bring about functional recovery.

Cellular responses to brain injury : the putative cellular basis of recovery

Since we feel that it is oversimplifying matters to assume that a given behaviour depends on a given neuronal population or neurotransmitter, and since in some cases, quite simple changes of behavioural strategy can compensate efficiently for impairments, we propose to focus here only on the cellular and molecular mechanisms involved in neuroplasticity. Basically, neuroplasticity at cellular level is thought to possibly involve three sets of mechanisms contributing to functional recovery. We will first discuss the axonal sprouting and subsequent "reactive synaptogenesis" hypothesis (see COTMAN and NADLER, 1978) as a possible means of explaining recovery after brain damage in adults on the basis of the anatomical reorganization of neuronal networks. Indeed, whatever the limitations mentioned above, evidence has been obtained that new connections may form in response to brain injury, although their actual contribution to functional recovery is as yet completely unknown. We will then discuss a second type of synaptic mechanism putatively involved in functional recovery consisting of adaptive metabolic changes in the denervated target cells, possibly resulting from alteration of synaptic properties. Lastly, the concept of adaptive genomic expression as applied to neuroplasticity in the mature brain seemed to be worth developing.

1. Post-lesion remodelling of brain architecture in adults (fig. 1)

Neuroplasticity after brain damage is commonly explained by axonal sprouting and subsequent reactive synaptogenesis (see LIU and CHAMBERS, 1958). Neoinnervation can primarily involve **homotypic axonal sprouting** from neuronal elements of the damaged systems. The newly formed nerve terminals can reoccupy the synaptic sites left vacant by the lesion, and establish new connections which are almost as efficient from the functional point of view as the original ones. The density of the newly formed innervation may be regulated by the denervated target cells. Homotypic axonal sprouting can first consist in **regenerative processes** referring to the regrowth of the damaged axons (see BJÖRKLUND and STENEVI, 1979). For example in the rat, axonal transection of central monoaminergic neurons was followed by the disappearance of noradrenergic and serotoninergic fibers within the spinal cord. Interestingly, two to three days after the lesion, the first signs of sprouting were observed from the axotomized axons along the proximal lesion border, and sprouts form very dense fiber patterns as shown using histochemical techniques. The sprouting was found to be maximal at seven days post lesion but continued to develop for two to three weeks. Sprouts can still be observed several months after the lesion. Similar regeneration of serotoninergic fibers with different time-course, have been observed at the level of the inferior olive and spinal cord after selective neurochemical lesion of the raphe nuclei. Homotypic sprouting can also refer to **collateral sprouting** of remaining intact axons. Studies conducted at septal and hippocampal levels have provided several illustrations of axon collateral sprouting from cholinergic and monoaminergic neurons (BJÖRKLUND and STENEVI, 1979 ; GAGE et al., 1983). In fact non myelinated or weakly myelinated systems are thought to have significantly higher regenerative capacities than neurons with myelinated axons. Then, certain type of

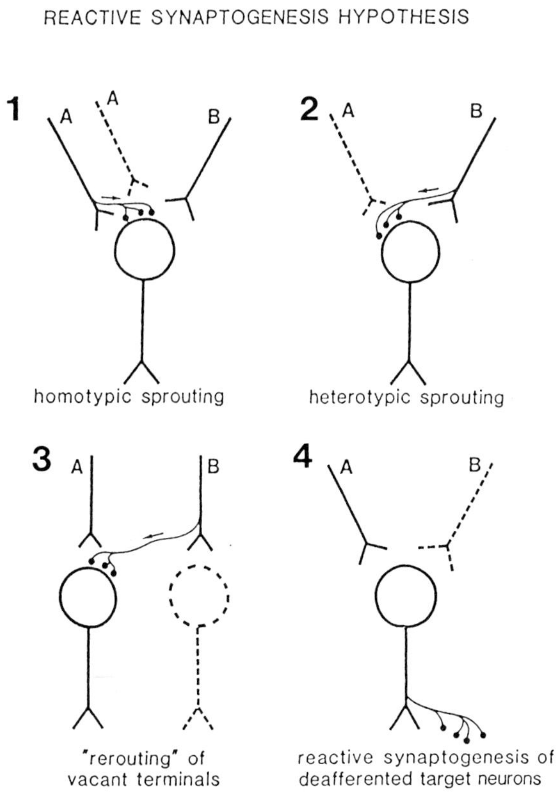

Figure 1. Postlesional remodelling of neuronal circuits : the reactive synaptogenesis hypothesis.

Selective lesion or deafferentation of a particular brain region can induce a sprouting of remaining intact neuronal elements at both presynaptic (1,2,3) and postsynaptic level (4) and subsequently a reactive synaptogenesis in the damaged region.

1. Homotypic sprouting. This process refers to the reorganization of the terminal field of spared axons from a partially damaged pathway A at the target structure level. Those intact axons from the damage of input A terminating in the neighbourhood of the "vacated" synaptic sites can develop sprouts and provide the deafferented target neurons with new connections functionally close to the original ones.

2. Heterotypic sprouting at presynaptic level. This process refers to the reorganization of intact afferent pathways to a structure deprived from one of its natural input. After total elimination of the afferent fibres A, axons of another pathway B which terminal field overlaps that of the destroyed input can develop sprouts and form aberrant connections with the deafferented target neurons.

3. Rerouting of vacant terminals. Lesion of the natural target neurons for an input B can trigger a rerouting of the "vacated" B terminals towards new targets.

4. Heterotypic sprouting at postsynaptic level. In response to the selective elimination of an input B, intrinsic neurons (mostly interneurons) of the target structure can develop sprouts and form additional local connections.

neurons but not exclusively the monoaminergic ones have a high degree of morphological plasticity within the adult CNS. One of the best illustration of this phenomenon was recently provided by a very elegant study on the climbing fiber innervation of Purkinje cells in the rat cerebellar cortex (ROSSI et al., 1989). After partial lesion of the inferior olive using injections of the neurotoxin 3-acetylpyridine, the disappearence of the "point to point" climbing fiber innervation of some Purkinje cells was followed by reinnervation of these cells due to the collateral sprouting of neighbouring climbing fibers. Consequently, some climbing fibers innervated more than one Purkinje cell, which demonstrated that actual structural reorganization could occur in the adult brain.

In the case of larger neuronal deafferentation, however, another frequently suggested possibility is that aberrant connections might develop from axon terminals of another pathway (**"heterotypic sprouting"**) synapsing in the neighbourhood of the deafferented synapses. Although the possibility that newly formed innervation might result from reactive synaptogenesis in a system not actually involved in the lesion was for a long time underestimated in adults, many examples have now been provided which illustrate this type of brain reorganization. It is worth mentioning that these cellular responses involve neuronal systems the terminal fields of which overlap that of the destroyed neurons. This pattern of structural reorganization was first described by RAISMAN (1969) at septum level after selective lesion of fimbria or medial forebrain bundle inputs to this structure, and extensively studied at red nucleus level after lesion of the cerebellar input in the adult cat. TSUKAHARA and co-workers initially provided electrophysiological evidence that disappearance of the interposito-rubral fibers was followed by an increase in the synaptic efficiency of the other major input to the red nucleus neurons, namely the cortico-rubral fibers (see TSUKAHARA, 1981). The increased efficiency of the cortico-rubral transmission was found to be concomitant with the emergence of axo-somatic synapses from the cortico-rubral fibers virtually replacing the degenerating axo-somatic cerebello-rubral ones. Interestingly, it was suggested that this synaptic reorganization of inputs to the red nucleus may involve a "shift" of cortico-rubral synapses from their initial distal axo-dendritic position to a more proximal position on the dendrites and soma of the red nucleus neurons (MURAKAMI et al., 1982). One of the major problems raised by these responses to neuronal deafferentation, which give rise to apparently functional connections, concerns the nature of the neurotransmitter receptors involved in the synaptic activity. Indeed, since the cerebello-rubral and cortico-rubral fibers contain various neurotransmitters, the functionality of the newly formed cortico-rubral synapses may be expected to depend on changes in the rubral targets, leading to emergence of specific post-synaptic receptors sensitive to the neurotransmitter released from the cortico-rubral fibers (NIEOULLON, 1984 ; NIEOULLON et al., 1988). Modifications will therefore occur simultaneously at both pre- and postsynaptic levels. From the above experiments and many others of the same type, it has been concluded that heterotypic sprouting after brain lesion may result in the "rearrangement" of previously existing connections, but that absolutely no new neuronal pathways result from the reorganization.

Interestingly as a postsynaptic consequence of the deafferentation, target neurons are thought to be also able to modify their axonal connections in some cases. Changes of this kind were initially assumed to occur in the rat hippocampus, where GABA containing interneurons have been shown to give off a higher number of nerve terminals after deafferentation (NADLER et al., 1974). We have also reported a sprouting response of GABA interneurons of the red nucleus after cerebellar deafferenation (NIEOULLON et al., 1988 ; VUILLON-CACCIUTTOLO et al., 1986). This type of neuronal response has also been observed for peptidergic neurons, since after lesion of cholinergic basal forebrain afferent to the cerebral cortex in the rat, a large increase in the number of neuropeptide Y and somatostatin containing fibers was detected in the deafferented parietal cortex (GAYKEMA et al., 1989).

Although lesion of a given neuronal system may induce a sprouting response in the remaining intact neurons of the same population, or reactive synaptogenesis in the deafferented neurons, it should also be mentioned that conversely, lesion of the target cells for input fibers can also result in the structural reorganization of the terminal field deprived of its natural target. In this situation, the afferent nerve terminals can be said to have become "vacant". Regenerative axonal cones from such nerve terminals (PESCHANSKI and BESSON, 1987) likely corresponding to "rerouting" of nerve terminals towards new targets is therefore likely to occur, but the loss of neuronal targets may also induce retrograde degeneration of presynaptic nerve terminals, especially if postsynaptic targets normally provide the presynaptic axons with trophic factors such as the nerve growth factor (NGF) the brain-derived neuronotrophic factor (BDNF) or the hippocampus-derived neuronotrophic factor (neuronotrophin 3). Indeed, such factors can actually represent retrograde signals to the presynaptic neuron to promote and maintain synaptic influence during ontogenesis or adapt synaptic transmission during learning. This situation will not be limited to neuronotrophic factors, but may also occur in cases where various other factors are released by the synaptic target acting at presynaptic level. An illustration of this process is provided by arachidonic acid in the case of some central synapses using excitatory amino acids as neurotransmitters (see WILLIAMS et al., 1989). We must however take into consideration the fact that this situation will only occur in cases of retrograde nerve degeneration or when selective degenerating processes are acting on specific neuronal populations. Such a situation is unlikely in human pathology since acute brain damage usually involves ischemia for example, the damaging effects of which can include both the neuronal processes and the somata.

The last aspect of adult brain structural plasticity to be discussed can be illustrated by data showing that induction of synaptic vacancy is not necessary for synaptic remodelling of brain circuitry to occur in a given structure. Indeed, changes in neuronal connections may also indirectly result from polysynaptic activation of neuronal pathways (fig.2). For example, it has been reported that lesion of peripheral nerves led to modifications of the cortical sensory maps (MERZENICH et al., 1983). TSUKAHARA and co-workers have furthermore provided evidence that the patterns of cortical inputs to the red nucleus can be altered by cross-innervation of peripheral nerves (TSUKAHARA et al., 1982). Recent data from ASANUMA and

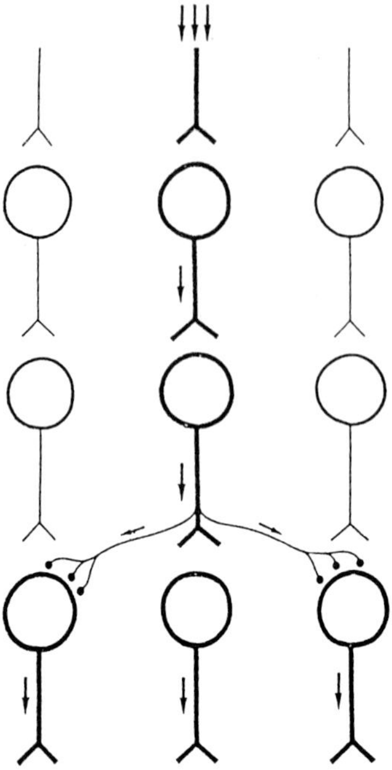

Changing neuronal connections as a putative response to neuronal activation. Neosynaptogenesis or activation of "silent" networks ?

Figure 2. Polysynaptic changes in neuronal activity as possible cause of neuronal circuits remodelling and synaptogeneis in the adult CNS.

Modification of cellular interactions related to change in neuronal activity may result in the development of new connections by means of collateral axonal sprouting in structures that do not present synaptic vacancy. Similar neuronal response can also be related to the activation of preexisting but "silent" networks.

co-workers (KELLER et al., 1990) have shown that these functional changes might be due to an actual generation of new synapses in the adult CNS which was not induced by the elimination of the pre-existing synapses. Indeed, lesion of the deep cerebellar nuclei in the cat that do not directly project to the cerebral cortex resulted in an increase in the density of the synapses within the functionally related cerebral motor cortex concomitant with the gradual disappearance of the motor deficit related to the lesion. It is worth mentioning however that although it has been suggested that synaptic reactivity may be a basic mechanism in learning and memory processes (HEBB, 1949), synaptic restructuring in the brain would not be the only one functional adaptive response to changes in brain circuit activity. Apparent changes in cerebral organization might also result from the activation of the "silent" neurons postulated by WALL many years ago (1976 ; MERRILL and WALL, 1978). For example, after specific unilateral lesion of the nigrostriatal dopaminergic system in the rat the use of the horseradish peroxydase retrograde transport method has helped to show that a small pool of nigrostriatal neurons projects contralaterally to the deafferented striatum (PRITZEL et al., 1983). This crossed nigrostriatal projection was selectively labelled after the lesion, which suggests that under normal conditions these neurons do not take up and carry the retrograde marker to their cell body. It is worth noting that the unilateral sensory deprivation by vibrissectomy leading to behavioural asymmetry, may likewise be concomitant with the putative activation of a crossed nigrostriatal projection of this kind (HUSTON, 1990). Interestingly, similar conclusions have been reached on the basis of other data showing an increase of post-lesion density of biochemically identified neurons using immunocytochemistry or in situ hybridization methods. However, these neurons can be expected to basically express other neurotransmitters, which suggest in addition that expression of colocalisation may be triggered by the lesion.

2 - Adaptive metabolic responses to brain lesions

Functional cellular interactions primarily involve the activatory or depressive effects of neuronal inputs on their target cells, which the electrophysiologists record as excitatory or inhibitory synaptic influences on the membrane potential. Then, suppression of these neuronal inputs will influence the activity of target cells. It is relevant however that changes in the activity of the target neurons do not simply reflect the suppression of excitatory or inhibitory influences, since adaptive mechanisms actually contribute to the functional re-adjustments in brain activity after lesion. From the biochemical point of view, neuronal activity is usually assessed by measuring neurotransmitter biosynthesis, release or inactivation processes at presynaptic level and by studying receptor activation and subsequent metabolic changes at postsynaptic level. Cellular responses to neuronal deafferentation therefore generally seem to involve the alteration of these synaptic mechanisms. For example, lesion of the nigrostriatal dopaminergic system, as in Parkinson's disease, has been shown for a long time to result in a reactive hyperactivity of the striatal cholinergic interneurons (see SCATTON, 1982). This effect contributes to the parkinsonian syndrome since anticholinergic drugs act as potent antiparkinsonian agents. Such expected reactive response by the postsynaptic neurons to deafferentation can be transient, however. Indeed, the experimental lesion of the nigrostriatal dopaminergic neurons also resulted in increase in the activity of the striatal GABA containing neurons, but such activation has been shown to be transitory since it is no longer detectable two to three weeks after the lesion was performed in the rat (see SAMUEL et al., 1988).

Considerable evidence has shown the extremely adaptive functional capacities of nigrostriatal dopaminergic neurons. Progressive loss of this neuronal population in the course of Parkinson's disease, or after partial experimental lesion in animals, triggers an adaptive response in the remaining intact neurons (fig. 3). Parkinsonism does not entail any really severe neurological deficits until the nigrostriatal dopaminergic neuron degeneration is nearly complete, which suggests that extremely powerful adaptive mechanisms have been able, up to then, to compensate for the effects of the degenerative process (ZIGMOND et al., 1990). In the rat, the behavioural syndrome induced by the lesion of the dopaminergic system was quite limited until only 5 to 10% of the striatal dopamine was present. Experimental data have shown that with lesions involving at least about 60% of the dopaminergic neurons, the dopamine turnover from the remaining intact fibres was increased (AGID et al., 1973). This presynaptic homotypic activation may be sufficient to maintain the basal dopaminergic function thus actively compensating for the loss of striatal dopaminergic nerve terminals. It is only under conditions where patients or animals are exposed to stress that the deficits emerge showing the limits of the compensatory process. In the case of more extensive lesions concerning about 90% of the dopaminergic neuronal population, pharmacological experiments in animals have revealed that denervation supersensitivity processes develop at postsynaptic level (UNGERSTEDT et al., 1971). Binding studies have shown that an increase in both the number and the affinity of receptors for dopaminergic ligands occurs within about two to three weeks after the lesion. This postsynaptic adaptive response may help to compensate for the loss of dopaminergic receptor stimulation, and clinical expression of the effects of lesion, or the disease, will occur when these compensatory processes are overwhelmed. Interestingly these adaptive mechanisms are not restricted to the damaged pathway but can affect at pre- and post-synaptic levels the transmission of other neuronal systems. Compensatory presynaptic reactive activation may not be limited to the remaining intact nerve terminals of the degenerating neuronal system but may also affect other neuronal inputs to the denervated target, which means that the presynaptic activation response to deafferentation is probably heterotypic. For example, evidences have obtained that lesion of the nigrostriatal dopaminergic neurons in the rat induces a reactive hyperactivity in the corticostriatal glutamatergic transmission, which is another major input to the striatum (KERKERIAN et al., 1987, LINDEFORS and UNGERSTEDT, 1990). We hypothesized that this reactive activation of the corticostriatal system may contribute to increasing the excitatory processes at work in the striatal area and that overexcitation of the striatal neurons may contribute to some aspects of Parkinson's disease (NIEOULLON et al., 1983). It is likely that the presynaptic adaptive responses to deafferentation are not observed solely after lesion of the dopaminergic system and probably also involve some other brain neuronal systems. It has been shown, for example, that partial lesion of the noradrenergic system using intracisternal 6-hydroxydopamine injections in the rat was concomitant with a dramatic reactive increase in the firing rate of the remaining intact neurons of the locus coeruleus developing 36 h to 21 days after the lesion.

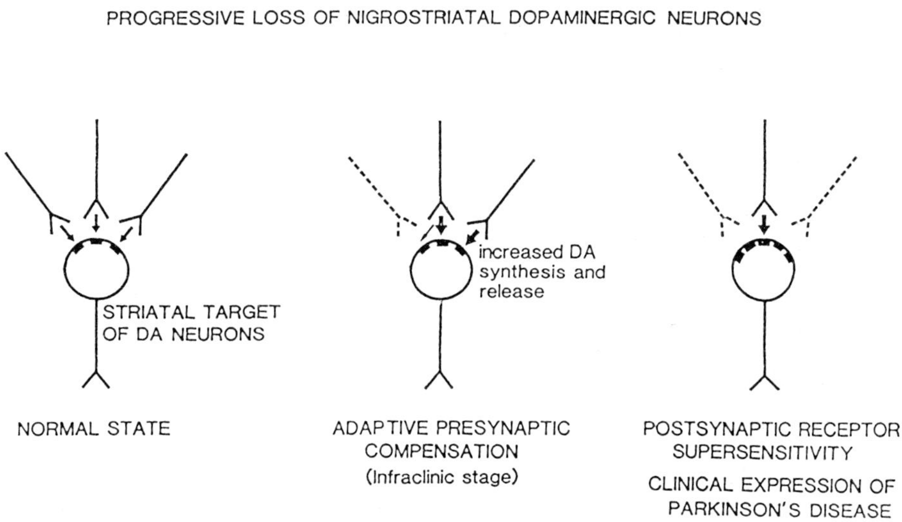

Figure 3. Schematic illustration of the functional adaptive capacities of the nigrostriatal dopaminergic system.

The striatum receives a massive dopaminergic input from the substantia nigra. Progressive loss of nigrostriatal dopaminergic neurons and projections is concomitant of parallel adaptations of striatal dopaminergic elements activity. The initial adaptation occurs at presynaptic level and consists of an increase in the synthesis and release of dopamine (DA) from the spared nigrostriatal afferents. This reactive hyperactivity is considered to fully compensate for lesions reaching up to 80% of nigral dopaminergic neurons. For more extensive lesion, in addition to the presynaptic activation, a supersensitivity response of DA receptors develops at target neurons level, consisting primarily in an increase in the number of these striatal DA receptors.

This postsynaptic response prolongs the compensation of the presynaptic DA deficit by maintaining the efficiency of dopaminergic transmission at striatal level up to 90% decrease in striatal DA concentrations.

Then clinical expression of Parkinson's disease is presumed to only occur for lesions involving more than 90% of the nigrostriatal dopaminergic afferents when such compensatory cellular mechanisms are overwhelmed.

At the postsynaptic level, receptor studies in intact animals have also provided evidences that numerous intracellular receptor-receptor interactions may normally contribute to closely associate neighbouring synapses' activities. Data have been recorded which indicate for example that synaptic activation of the excitatory amino acid receptors of the NMDA subclass in the striatum is followed by a decrease in the activity of the dopaminergic receptors at the level of the phosphorylation of the DARPP-32 protein (NESTLER et al., 1984). Then pharmacological blockade of the NMDA receptors resulted in facilitation of dopamine transmission in the striatum : this suggests that these receptor-receptor interactions of the heterotypic type are functional (GIRAULT et al., 1990). On the other hand, it has been reported that dopaminergic receptor activation putatively decreases the synaptic action of glutamate. In this respect, we found that lesion of the dopaminergic system resulted in increased number of NMDA ligand binding sites (SAMUEL et al., 1990). Concerning the latter mechanism, a decrease in dopaminergic transmission may therefore be indirectly responsible for the decreased dopaminergic activity. Agents which antagonize glutamatergic transmission might thus be putative antiparkinsonian candidates. When these receptor-receptor interactions are disrupted due to brain damage, this will trigger not only adaptive behavioural responses but also the clinical expression of the disease or lesion.

The situation is probably complicated by the frequent coexistence of several neurotransmitters within the same nerve terminals. Indeed, the increased neuronal firing rate of the remaining intact neurons which result from partial brain lesion has been thought in some case to accelerate functional deafferentation by setting up interactions between coexisting neurotransmitters. For example, at hippocampal level some nerve terminals contain both acetylcholine and the neuropeptide galanin. Basically galanin-acetylcholine interactions take the form of an inhibitory influence exerted by galanin on acetylcholine release through the activation of presynaptic receptors. Indeed, increasing the galanin concentration in the extracellular space was found to contribute to a decrease in the acetylcholine release (FISONE et al., 1987). However, acetylcholine and galanin might be differently released from the nerve terminals so that the release of the peptide will occur only when the neuron is overstimulated. Under basal conditions, the main neurotransmitter released in the hippocampus is acetylcholine. It is therefore worth suggesting that if partial lesion of this neuronal pathway contributes to a reactive increase in the firing rate of the remaining intact neurons as was previously found to occur in the case of the monoaminergic neurons, the galanin released due to the increased firing rate is likely to accelerate the impairment of hippocampal acetylcholine function.

Functional adaptive behavioural responses to brain lesion may also involve an interdependence between the various neuronal systems which regulate the same brain function in parallel, on the basis of complex polysynaptic cellular interactions. The dopaminergic system still provides a very good illustration of the changes occuring after focal brain lesion. Many years ago, by using the push-pull cannula method and measuring the dopamine release in vivo in the cat striatum, we observed that unilateral impairment of the nigrostriatal dopaminergic activity resulted in opposite changes in the contralateral striatum (NIEOULLON et al., 1977). Recent experiments have also shown the functional interdependence between the various systems using dopamine as a neurotransmitter in the forebrain. Indeed, a drop in the dopaminergic activity in the amygdala has been found to be concomitant with an activation of dopaminergic transmission in the nucleus accumbens and a decrease in the dopaminergic activity in the cerebral cortex (SIMON et al., 1988). Because of this functional interdependence, which contributes under normal conditions to the coordination of behaviour, selective disruption of dopaminergic transmission at one target structure level will result in complex behavioural changes involving alterations in the activity of the other dopaminergic systems.

3 - Adaptive genomic responses to brain injury (fig. 4)

The first indication that neuronal genomic expression is modified in response to brain lesion was the fact that nerve injury resulted for example within two to three weeks in supersensitivity mechanisms involving the proliferation of postsynaptic receptors. More generally the modifications in gene repression can also concern at both pre- and postsynaptic levels, the neurotransmitter synthesizing enzymes, the peptides precursors and others kinds of proteins. For example, reactive synaptogenesis can be said to reflect an alteration of the genomic program governing the normal cytoskeleton. Recent data have shown more directly that brain lesion can result in profound genomic modifications, involving alteration of the normally expressed gene activities but also activation of early genes, which can lead for example to the expression of neuronal proto-oncogenes. Likewise, various substances produced during development but not in the adult brain can be re-expressed during regeneration processes.

One of the first examples of adaptation in gene expression was obtained by measuring changes in the activity of the catecholamine specific synthesizing enzyme, tyrosine hydroxylase in noradrenergic neurons of the locus coeruleus. For example, increases in the activity of this enzyme have been shown to occur in response to lesion of the locus coeruleus serotoninergic input (see Mc RAE-DEGUEURCE et al., 1982). Western-immunoblot analysis has further indicated that the increase in tyrosine hydroxylase catalytic activity observed in similar models was attributable to an actual increase in the enzyme protein content per neuron (see BLACK et al., 1987). Although the molecular mechanisms of this protein induction are still unknown, protein kinase activations through synaptic receptors may contribute to this cellular response. In fact, the cyclic AMP-dependent protein kinase as well as the calcium-calmodulin-dependent protein kinase II and the protein kinase C have been found to contribute to the neuronal regulation of catecholamine biosynthesis (see MILLER, 1985).

The striatal model further provides an interesting opportunity for studying neuroplasticity at the gene regulation level. Experimental lesions of the nigrostriatal dopaminergic system in the rat were found to durably affect the activity of striatal peptidergic neurons. For example, immunohistochemical studies using antibodies directed against the peptides or their precursors have shown that the striatal enkephalin content increased after the lesion (THAL et al., 1983) whereas the substance P levels decreased after dopaminergic transmission blockade. Since in the case of enkephalins a concomitant increase in the precursor content was observed, it was speculated that the apparent changes in the neuropeptide content did not simply reflect a metabolic alteration of neuronal activity, but rather pointed to modifications in the transcriptional or traductional events affecting the specific genes. Direct evidence that extracellular stimuli may actually control gene expression (which constitute a basic mechanism controlling functional cellular interactions) has been further obtained in the form of showing that the level of

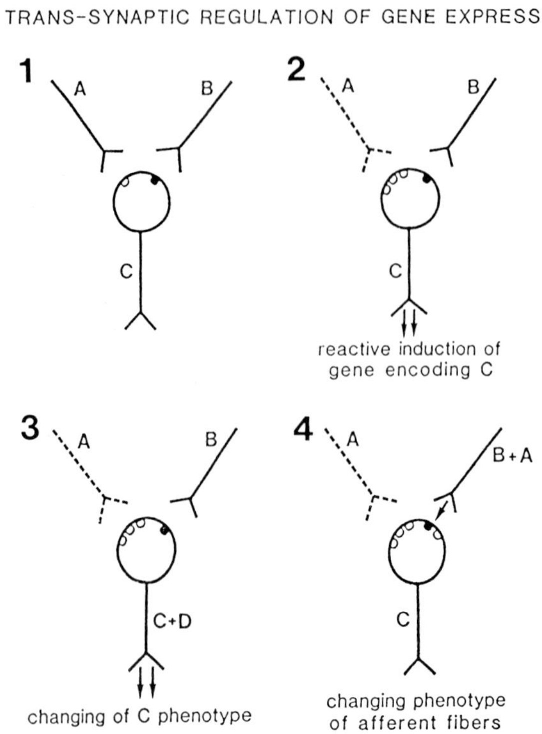

Figure 4. Examples of adaptations in neurotransmitter (i.e. in neuropeptide precursor or in classical neurotransmitter synthetizing enzyme) gene expression in adult CNS.

In this representation (1), a schematic situation of neuronal interactions is considered to occur consisting of 2 distinct afferent pathways A and B using respectively the neurotransmitter A and the neurotransmitter B and innervating a target neuron containing a neurotransmitter C. Selective lesion of the input A can trigger besides a denervation supersensitivity response of the postsynaptic receptor to the neurotransmitter A :

. a postsynaptic increase in the gene expression of the target neuron neurotransmitter C (2) ;

. the postsynaptic activation of the gene expression of a neurotransmitter D in the target neuron normally non expressing D, which reflects an actual change in the target neuron phenotype (3);

. the presynaptic induction in the neuronal afferent input B of the gene expression of another transmitter and in particular of the neurotransmitter A of the damaged pathway, which consists in an actual change in the phenotype of the intact input B (4 ; see text for an illustration).

The possibility can also be considered that neuronal deafferentations may result in a decrease or suppression of the gene expression of neurotransmitters normally expressed by the target neuron or the other afferent to the target structure.

messenger RNA (mRNA) encoding for the transmitter molecule paralleled the cellular content of the neuropeptide. Indeed degeneration of the nigrostriatal dopaminergic system in the rat was found to also induce an increase in the mRNA levels encoding for pre-proenkephalines (NORMAND et al., 1988), while mRNA encoding for substance P was decreased after dopaminergic transmission blockade (BANNON et al., 1986). These data illustrate changes in gene expression of the neurotransmitter normally used by the target neuron. Moreover, actual changes in the target neuron phenotype can occur leading to the activation of normally non expressed neurotransmitter gene. For example, we have observed that the number of striatal neurons containing neuropeptide Y detected by immunocytochemistry markedly increases after nigrostriatal dopaminergic deafferentation. (KERKERIAN et al., 1989). Further in situ hybridization analysis have shown that the dopamine striatal depletion also resulted in an increase in the number of striatal neurons producing mRNA encoding for neuropeptide Y precursor (LINDEFORS et al., 1990). Then, striatal dopaminergic deafferentation appeared to activate expression of neuropeptide Y gene in many neurons normally low- or non-expressing the peptide, which were therefore assimilated to "silent" neuropeptide Y striatal neurons. Similar increases in the number of neurons expressing neuropeptide Y or somatostatin have been observed after cortical lesion (SALIN et al., 1990). It thus emerged that in the mature CNS, gene expression in target cells may actually be regulated by afferent neurotransmitter systems acting at receptor level and providing the cells with the capacity to make long-term adjustments to deafferentation and even more probably to environmental stimuli. As in the case of tyrosine hydroxylase, transduction mechanisms may involve protein kinases inducing the expression of selected genes (see GOODMAN, 1990). Somatostatin mRNA levels have indeed been found to be increased by forskolin in cell cultures, and protein kinase C may also be involved in this activation (see MONTMINY et al., 1986).

In response to a disruption of the brain organization some afferent neurons to the denervated target may also change their neurotransmitter phenotype. One of the most illustrative example of this type of neuronal response was obtained in immunocytochemical studies performed on the autonomic innervation of the rat iris (BJORKLUND et al., 1985). The iris normally contains a dense plexus of neuropeptide Y and tyrosine hydroxylase immunoreactive fibers. After surgical removal of the superior cervical ganglion, almost all of these fibers disappeared, which suggests that these fibers are normally part of the sympathetic system originating in this ganglion. Interestingly, in long-term sympathectomized animals a large number of neuropeptide Y and tyrosine hydroxylase immunodetectable fibers reappeared. Subsequent removal in the same animals of the parasympathetic ciliary ganglion, normally supplying the iris with cholinergic fibers was followed by a re-disappearance of both neuropeptide Y and tyrosine hydroxylase immunopositive fibers. Thus, it seemed likely that adult cholinergic neurons in vivo are able under these experimental conditions to express sympathetic neurotransmitter activities. In that situation, it should be emphasized that the denervated target may have retrogradely influenced the cholinergic parasympathetic neurons by inducing specific gene expression encoding for tyrosine hydroxylase and neuropeptide Y. Phenotypic plasticity has also been observed in vitro in sympathetic neurons which either become noradrenergic or cholinergic depending on the nature of the medium used for the tissue culture. This indicates that external factors can influence genomic expression (see HENDRY, 1985). The neurotransmitter phenotype of neurons actually appears to be determined once and for all in their normal environment, but changes in this environment may induce phenotypic plasticity. It is thus worth suggesting that mature neurons for example may express embryonic properties corresponding to genes which are normally repressed in adults. The question can also be raised as to whether or not these newly expressed potentialities might correspond to pre-existing genomic characteristics which have been repressed in the course of phylogenetic evolution.

It has also been demonstrated that embryonic neuronal properties can be reactivated in adults after nerve crushing and that regeneration processes can be concomitant with production of the protein B 50, of certain forms of tubulin specific to immature neurons or of NGF in areas normally selectively free of this neuronotrophic factor in adults (see WOOD et al., 1990).

The last aspect of genomic plasticity we shall deal with here concerns the putative activation of early gene such as *c-fos* and *c-jun* . Proto-oncogene activation can indeed induce the formation of selective products known to intervene in normal cellular signal transduction processes as "third cellular messengers". The phosphoproteins encoded by *c-fos* and *c-jun* are nowadays thought to form a familly of proteins, which may specifically interact with particular DNA sequences and thus affect specific cell protein production. Proto-oncogene activation products may for example contribute to the secondary activation of gene-encoding for neuropeptides (see GOODMAN, 1990). Although the mechanisms of cellular transduction are far from being fully understood, it is worth mentioning that *c-fos* and *c-jun* induction processes are in turn sensitive to activation of voltage-dependent calcium channels, NGF production and cyclic AMP and protein kinase C-dependant cellular events. Interestingly enough, brain damage in the rat was recently found to induce an activation at cortical level of the *c-fos* proto-oncogene, which is sensitive to administration of NMDA antagonists : these excitatory amino acid receptors are therefore possibly involved in this *c-fos* induction (HERRERA and ROBERTSON, 1990). Moreover, activation of dopamine receptors likewise activated striatal *c-fos* (ROBERTSON et al., 1989).

Neuronal transplants : further evidence pointing to the adaptive capacities of the mature brain

Leaving aside the controversy as to the usefulness of developing brain transplantation techniques with a view to curing neurological disorders in humans, the cell transplant procedure obviously provides neurobiologists with an exceptional opportunity for analyzing the cellular mechanisms underlying brain neuroplasticity (BJÖRKLUND A. and STENEVI, 1979). Intracerebral grafting of embryonic brain tissue into the CNS of immature or adult recipients appeared to be a suitable approach to investigate both the subsequent development of transplanted fetal cells, and the reactivity of mature host elements to the graft. If one focuses on the transplantation of embryonic monoaminergic neurons , which is the model the most largely studied in this context, the data from anatomical, biochemical, electrophysiological and behavioural analysis have all demonstrated a high degree of integration of the grafted neurons by the host tissue (BRUNDIN et al., 1987). Despite their ectopic location in the brain the grafted cells were shown to survive and develop axonal growth in order to establish new synaptic contacts with the neuronal population of the host. These observations have been related to the presence of neuronotrophic molecules that promote CNS neuronal survival and/or neurite extension. Indeed, growth factors, such as NGF can be basically released to maintain the brain structure and in response to CNS injury to inhibit retrograde neuronal death and promote axonal regrowth. In the septo-hippocampal lesion model, which involved injury of cholinergic fibers, growth of transplanted cholinergic neurons was found to be facilitated by local production of NGF-like neuronotrophic factor. In this connection, the role of glial cells as primary sources for some of these factors , and particularly of the astrocytes in guiding development, would constitute a challenging tissue of the transplant studies. Because of the quite limitated development of processes from embryonic neurons transplanted in intact animals without lesion, one has to considere the primary role played by the target cells which could actually produce molecules normally having an inhibitory influence on axonal growth. Then the reinnervation processes observed during homotypic collateral sprouting or following transplantation, may be triggered by similar mechanisms. They also involved reactive synaptogenesis as described above, where target neurons may play an essential role in promoting the reafferentation. However, one of the major differences between these two phenomena is the time-course of the reinnervation processes. In the case of the reactive synaptogenesis normally occurring after partial deafferentation, the occupation of the synaptic sites left vacant can start immediately after the lesion. After complete denervation, transplanted fetal CNS neurons appear to be able to specifically reinnervate the host tissue, even a long time after the lesion, which suggests that the target cells may have preserved their capacity to induce selective synaptic formation. The innate programming of the grafted neurons would also ensure the neosynaptogenesis between the regenerating presynaptic elements and their appropriate targets. Recent data have further showed that the resulting reinnervation can in some cases actually resemble the natural input quite closely. For example, transplantation at hippocampal level of fetal serotoninergic neurons, after destruction of the endogenous innervation, led to extensive reinnervation of the structure, which exhibited near to normal ultrastructural morphological characteristics (DASZUTA et al., 1989). Even their relational features (synaptic incidence, microenvironment) were found to be very similar to those of the normal hippocampus. This suggests that the transplanted embryonic neurons are able to express a genomic program defining the characteristics of serotoninergic innervation within the hippocampus, and that target cells can contribute to regulating the reinnervation. Other data indicate that transplanted neurons can be somewhat reinnervated by the host. On these lines, embryonic dopaminergic neurons transplanted into the rat striatum after destruction of the nigrostriatal dopaminergic system have been found to receive information from the corticostriatal pathway, which actually formed synaptic contacts with the transplanted neurons (DOUCET et al., 1989).

The question as to whether or not intracerebral transplants of fetal tissue can induce some functional recovery has been extensively developed in behavioural experiments. One of the most puzzling questions has been how to explain the quite large degree of functional recovery, or more likely the restoration of extensive cellular interactions, given the generally limited reinnervation area. For example, partial reinnervation of the rat striatum induced by transplanting dopaminergic neurons was associated with changes in the reactivity of striatal peptidergic populations. Indeed, the hyperactivity of enkephalinergic and neuropeptide Y containing systems in response to the dopaminergic denervation was found to be reversed in the grafted striata. The effect was rapidly visible and spread to the entire structure. In addition to the synaptic contacts re-established between the graft-derived fibers and the NPY neurons , these data thus suggest that both dopaminergic synaptic transmission and dopaminergic "diffuse" release may account for functional recovery. It is therefore worth considering the possibility that the functional effects of embryonic neuronal cell transplantations, which are often termed "behavioural recovery", might in fact be due to cellular events extending considerably beyond the limits of actual brain reinnervation.

The adaptive synapse : a challenging issue in brain organization

Recent advances in cellular biology have given rise to the suggestion that the brain organization might be viewed as two types of superimposed neuronal systems which process neuronal information in a complementary manner at synaptic level. According to this dual conception of brain organization, cerebral information may be basically processed in highly organized and efficient neuronal networks termed **processing systems.** In the motor area, these processing systems will consist for example of the corticospinal system, the corticorubrospinal system and the primary sensory afferent pathways. Superimposed neuronal systems characterized by a more diffuse anatomical organization might modulate the basic information processing.These neuronal systems, termed **modulatory systems,** consist typically -but not exclusively- of the central monoaminergic pathways. The latter pathways are known to actually influence the transmission of information in the processing networks by means of presynaptic control mechanisms and postsynaptic interaction processes. It was then suggested that normal adaptation of behaviour to the permanently changing external context may be due to the extremely great adaptability of the synaptic activity resulting from the dynamic interactions between these two different types of neuronal systems.

According to this conception, degeneration of nerve terminals would change these normal synaptic interactions and thus alter the activity of the neuronal populations normally connected with the destroyed systems or indirectly influenced by them, and subsequently modify the functional interactions between these remaining populations. Changes in synaptic activity of this kind may contribute to the complex adaptive postlesional cellular responses described above. Generally speaking, postlesional adaptations may involve changes in cellular interactions that are not restricted to local modulation of neuronal transmission at synaptic level. Recent advances in molecular biology have demonstrated that specific phosphorylation processes triggered by the activation of membrane receptors by neurotransmitters are involved in the control of neuronal gene expression of various proteins, including neurotransmitters and proteins of the cytoskeleton. Alterations of these mechanisms may therefore be partly responsible for changes in neurotransmitter gene expression up to changes in neuron phenotype and for the collateral axonal sprouting observed after brain damage.

On the other hand, glial cells have been thought to also contribute to cellular interactions in the CNS. These cells, which were known to be directly involved in the synaptic metabolism of neurotransmitters such as glutamate, have been recently found to carry neurotransmitter receptors on their membrane. These data suggested that the activity of neuronal and glial elements may be functionally linked. Additional data showing that glial cells constitute one of the main sources of production of neuronotrophic factors have further suggested that brain architecture may indirectly depend on the activity of neuronal elements and that changes in the neuron-glial cell interactions may contribute to the remodelling of neuronal network architecture observed after neuronal degeneration as well as after polysynaptic changes in neuronal activity. All in all, these data show that neither nerve proliferation, synapse formation and stabilization, nor neuronal phenotype determination occur exclusively during ontogenesis, as has been long conjectured, but can also under certain conditions occur in the mature brain.

An interesting hypothesis might be that in the normal adult brain dynamic cellular interactions may limit the expression of these processes and preserve the neuronal network architecture and function by maintaining a functional equilibrium between the activities of the various neuronal systems present in the central structures as well as between the activities of neuronal and glial elements. These interactions would also limit the effects of neuronal loss or dysfunction up to a certain degree, depending on which are damaged, and on the intrinsic properties of the remaining systems, which can vary with age. By contrast, heavy brain damage would lead to marked modifications in cellular interactions which would be reflected in functional and structural reorganizations. For instance, after total lesion of a neuronal pathway, cellular interactions between the remaining neuronal systems liberated from the direct or indirect influence of the damaged systems would induce a shift towards a new functional state and architecture. This may in some cases lead to functional recovery and in other cases reinforce the primary functional deficit triggered by the lesion. One might therefore wonder whether apparently adaptive changes in behavioural strategy after lesions might not reflect changes in the functional organization and activity in neuronal networks.

All these data lead to the view that the mechanisms underlying neuroplasticity do not differ much basically from those involved in neuronal network setting during development and in their maintenance in the adult brain, all of which rely on cellular interactions the expression of which varies continuously.

Brain potentialities and actual functional recovery after brain injury : further considerations on the limits of neuroplasticity functional expression

Although the adaptive capacities of the mature brain at cellular level have turned out to be larger than what was initially expected, one has to take into consideration the rather limited recovery which is usually observed after brain damage in humans. Functional expression of the cellular and molecular mechanisms described as readjusting neuronal activity to brain injury is in fact dependent on genetic and epigenetic factors depending on the patient and the nature of lesion. Referring to KENNARD's principle, ageing for example can be one of the most powerful factors restricting post-lesion functional recovery because adults have only limited restructuring capacities. It is worth mentioning however that limitations of this kind will mainly apply to recovery after lesions sustained at cortical level, whereas recovery after lesion of deep brain structures will not depend so strongly on the degree of brain maturation. In fact, cortical areas can be said to participate in elaborated behaviours if one considers for example the cognitive aspects of brain information, and thus they participate as mentioned above to the permanent adaptation of behaviour to the changing external context ; whereas deep brain structures can be said to act in more stereotyped behaviours showing less flexibility. Moreover, the degree of maturation of each brain structure considered separately is not the same at a given age, since telencephalic areas for example take longer to mature than other brain areas. This concept can of course be extended to senescence, where a differential alteration occurs with time from one brain region to another. In fact these differences in inter-structures maturation also include inter-species differences and even sex differences in a given species. Functional recovery will therefore depend on the actual degree of maturation of the brain structures affected by the lesion.

Besides these maturation factors, actual functional recovery primarily depends on the nature of the brain lesions. As mentioned above, the larger the lesion, the less complete the recovery will be. The functional consequences of brain injury will also depend on the type of lesion. Lesions of cerebral tissue involving loss of cell material will limit the expression of compensatory cellular and molecular mechanisms due for example to the occurence of glial and vascular massive local reactions ; whereas, neurodegenerative processes or even discrete vascular diseases will favour the compensatory reactions, particularly when the development of the disease is progressive. Our feeling is that in cases involving neurodegenerative processes one of the most crucial more critical factors in functional recovery is the actual nature of the neuronal system involved in the lesion. If one views the basic brain organization in terms of processing systems and modulatory /regulatory systems, lesions resulting in impairment of the former neuronal systems will have much more dramatic functional consequences than those affecting the latter. In this connection, monoaminergic systems for example have extremely high adaptive capacities as illustrated and discussed at greater length above, and the recovery observed after brain transplantation strongly reinforces this statement.

The last point to be mentioned is that post-lesion factors can also influence functional recovery. Socio-cultural factors as well as personal motivation have been shown to affect post-lesion recovery, and in cases involving sensorimotor impairment, active rehabilitation has also been found to actually contribute to improving the impaired performances. The pharmacological approach however will be the most appropriate procedure when attempting to promote functional recovery. Direct stimulation of neurotransmission can be performed using compounds acting directly or indirectly as neurotransmitter agonists, in an attempt to restore activity in a deficient neuronal pathway. This has been done for example with L-DOPA or dopaminergic agonists stimulating the dopaminergic transmission in Parkinson's disease or THA acting as anti-cholinesterasic compound in Alzheimer's disease. Gangliosides have been also known for a long time to facilitate post-lesion recovery, and a strategy based on the use of neuronotrophic factor administrations is now frequently proposed for curing or slowing down the development of some neurodegenerative diseases. Indirect promotion of neuronotrophic factor production has also been considered, for example stimulating b-adrenergic receptors in order to increase the synthesis of endogenous gangliosides or performing putative transplantation of transfected fibroblasts expressing NGF. Besides these attempts to counteract the expression of symptomatology, drugs are now being considered as possible means of actually stopping or reducing neuronal death. On these lines, it has been recently proposed to use drugs acting as excitatory amino acid blockers to prevent putative neuro-excitotoxicity, blockers of intracellular calcium increase, potassium conductance modulators to reduce excitability, or substances acting as antioxydants such as vitamine C or a-tocopherol. All these agents will have varying degrees of success in reducing neuronal death and limiting the consequences of brain injury by reinforcing the efficiency of the cellular mechanisms involved in compensating for neuronal loss.

Acknowledgements : The authors are grateful to Katia MATTEI and Nicole DUSTICIER for their excellent preparation of the manuscript. The Neurochemistry Unit was supported by grants from CNRS, Université Aix-Marseille II, INSERM (contrat de recherche externe n° 87 60 16) and DRET (convention n°88 34 049 00 470 75 01).

References

AGID Y., JAVOY F. and GLOWINSKI J. (1973) Hyperactivity of remaining dopaminergic neurons after partial destruction of the nigrostriatal dopaminergic system in the rat. Nature 245, 150-151.

BANNON M.J., LEE J.M., GIRAUD P., YOUNG A., AFFOLTER H.U. and BONNER T.I. (1986) Dopamine antagonist haloperidol decreases substance P, substance K and preprotachykinin mRNAs in rat striatonigral neurons. J.Biol.Chem. 261, 6640-6642.

BJORKLUND A. and STENEVI U. (1979) Regeneration of monaminergic and cholinergic neurons in the mammalian central nervous system. Physiol.Rev. 59, 62-100.

BJORKLUND H., HOKFELT T., GOLDSTEIN M., TERENIUS L. and OLSON L. (1985) Appearance of the noradrenergic markers tyrosine hydroxylase and neuropeptide Y in cholinergic nerves of the iris following sympathectomy. J.Neurosci. 5, 1633-1643.

BLACK I.B., ADLER J.E., DREYFUS C.F., FRIEDMAN W.J., LAGAMMA E.F. and ROACH A.H. (1987) Experience, neurotransmitter plasticity and behavior. in:Psychopharmacology, ed. by H.Y. MELTZER, Raven Press, New York, 463-469.

BRUNDIN P., STRECKER R.E., LINDVALL O., ISACSON O., NILSSON O.G., BARBIN G., PROCHIANTZ A., FORNI C., NIEOULLON A., WIDNER H., GAGE F.H. and BJORKLUND A. (1987) Intracerebral grafting of dopamine neurons. Experimental basis for clinical trials in patients with Parkinson's disease. Ann.New York Acad.Sci., 495, 473-495.

COTMAN C.W. and NADLER J.V. (1978) Reactive synaptogenesis in the hippocampus. in: Neuronal Plasticity, ed. C.W. COTMAN, Raven Press, New York, pp.227-271.

DASZUTA A., BJORKLUND A., BRUNDIN P., CHAZAL G., DESCARRIES L., KALEN P. and STRECKER R. (1989) Morphological and functional analysis of raphe transplants in adult rat hippocampus. Restaur.Neurol.Neurosci. 1, 45-46.

DOUCET G., MURATA Y., BRUNDIN P., BOSLER O., MONS N., GEFFARD M., OUIMET C.C. and BJORKLUND A., (1989) Host afferent into intrastriatal transplants of fetal ventral mesencephalon. Exp.Neurol. 106, 1-19.

FISONE G., WU C.F., CONSOLO S., NORDSTROM O., BRYNNE N., BARTFAI T., MELANDER T. and HOKFELT T. (1987) Galanin inhibits acetylcholine release in the ventral hippocampus of the rat : histochemical, autoradiographic, in vivo and in vitro studies. Proc.Natl.Acad.Sci. USA, 84, 7339-7343.

GAGE F.H., BJORKLUND A. and STENEVI U. (1983) Reinnervation of the partially deafferented hippocampus by compensatory collateral sprouting from spared cholinergic and noradrenergic afferents. Brain Res., 268, 27-37.

GAYKEMA R.P.A., COMPAAN J.C., NYAKAS C., HORVATH E.and LUITEN P.G.M. (1989) Long term effects of cholinergic basal forebrain lesions on neuropeptide Y and somatostatin immunoreactivity in rat neocortex. Brain Res. 489, 392-396.

GIRAULT J.A., HALPAIN S. and GREENGARD P. (1990) Excitatory amino acid antagonists and Parkinson's disease. Trends in Neurosci. 13, 325-326.

GOODMAN R.H. (1990) Regulation of neuropeptide gene expression. Ann.Rev.Neurosci. 13, 111-127.

HEBB D.O. (1949) The organization of behavior : a neurophysiological theory. John Wiley and sons. New York, pp.227-231.

HENDRY I.A. (1985) Phenotypic plasticity of sympathetic adrenergic and cholinergic neurons. Trends in Pharmacol.Sci. 165, 126-129.

HERRERA D.G. and ROBERTSON H.A. (1990) N-methyl-D-aspartate receptors mediate activation of the C-Fos proto oncogene in a model of brain injury. Neuroscience 35, 273-281.

HUSTON J.P. (1990) Neurobehavioral indices of recovery from unilateral sensory deprivation and lesion of the nigrostriatal system. Eur.J.Pharmacol. 183, 32.

KELLER A., ARISSIAN K. and ASANUMA H. (1990) Formation of new synapses in the motor cortex following lesions of the deep cerebellar nuclei. Exp.Brain Res. 80, 23-33.

KENNARD M. (1940) Relation of age to motor impairment in man and in subhuman primates. Arch.Neurol.Psychiatry 44, 377-397.

KERKERIAN L., DUSTICIER N. and NIEOULLON A. (1987) Modulatory effect of dopamine on high affinity glutamate uptake in the rat striatum. J.Neurochem. 48, 1301-1306.

KERKERIAN L., SALIN P. and NIEOULLON A. (1988) Pharmacological characterization of dopaminergic influence on expression of neuropeptide Y immunoreactivity by rat striatal neurons. Neuroscience 26, 809-817.

LINDEFORS N., BRENE S., HERRERA-MARSCHITZ M. and PERSSON H. (1990) Neuropeptide gene expression in brain is differentially regulated by midbrain dopamine neurons. Exp.Brain Res. 80, 489-500.

LINDEFORS N. and UNGERSTEDT U. (1990) Bilateral regulation of glutamate tissue and extracellular levels in caudate-putamen by midbrain dopamine neurons. Neurosci.Lett., 115, 248-252.

LIU C.M. and CHAMBERS W.W. (1958) Intraspinal sprouting of dorsal root axons. Arch.Neurol.Psychiatry 79, 46-61.

Mc RAE-DEGUEURCE A., BEROD A., MERMET A., KELLER A., CHOUVET G., JOH T.H. and PUJOL J.F. (1982) Alterations of tyrosine hydroxylase activity elicited by raphe nuclei lesions in the rat locus coeruleus : evidence for the involvement of serotonin afferents. Brain Res. 235, 285-301.

MERILL E.G. and WALL P.D. (1978) Plasticity of connection in the adult nervous system. in: Neuronal Plasticity, C.W. COTMAN (ed.) Raven Press, New York, pp.97-111.

MERZENICH M.M., KAAS J.H., WALL J., NELSON R.J., SUR M. and FELLEMAN D. (1983) Topographic reorganization of somatosensory cortical areas 3b and 1 in adult monkey following restricted deafferentation. Neuroscience 8, 33-55.

MILLER R.J. (1985) Second messengers, phosphorylation and neurotransmitter release. Trends in Neurosci. 89, 463-465.

MONTMINY M.R., LOW M.J., TAPIA-ARANCIBIA L., REICHLIN S., MANDEL G. and GOODMAN R.H. (1986) Cyclic AMP regulates somatostatin mRNA accumulation in primary diencephalic cultures and in transfected fibroblast cells. J.Neurosci. 6, 1171-1176.

MURAKAMI F., KATSUMARU H., SAITO K. and TSUKAHARA N. (1982) A quantitative study of synaptic reorganization in red nucleus neurons after lesion of the nucleus interpositus of the cat : an electron microscopic study involving intracellular injection of horseradish peroxidase. Brain Res. 242, 41-53.

NADLER J.V., COTMAN C.W. and LYNCH G.S. (1974) Biochemical plasticity of short-axon interneurons : increased glutamate decarboxylase activity in the denervated area of rat dentate gyrus following entorhinal lesion. Exp.Neurol. 45, 403-412.

NESTLER E.J., WALAAS S.I. and GREENGARD P. (1984) Neuronal phosphoproteins : physiological and clinical implications. Science 225, 1357-1364.

NIEOULLON A. (1984) Neuronal plasticity in the red nucleus and the ventrolateral thalamus of the adult cat : a biochemical approach. in: R.G. HASSLER and J.F. CHRIST (eds.) Advances in Neurology 40, Raven Press, New York, pp.107-116.

NIEOULLON A., CHERAMY A. and GLOWINSKI J. (1977) Interdependance of the nigrostriatal dopaminergic systems on the two sides of the brain in the cat. Science 198, 416-418.

NIEOULLON A., KERKERIAN L. and DUSTICIER N. (1983) Presynaptic controls in the neostriatum : reciprocal interactions between the nigrostriatal dopaminergic neurons and the corticostriatal glutamatergic pathways. Exp.Brain Res., suppl.7, 54-65.

NIEOULLON A., VUILLON-CACCIUTTOLO G., DUSTICIER N., KERKERIAN L., ANDRE D. and BOSLER O. (1988) Putative neurotransmitters in the red nucleus and their involvement in postlesion adaptive mechanisms. Beh.Brain Res. 28, 163-174.

NORMAND E., POPOVICI T., ONTENIENTE B., FELLMANN D., PIATIER-TONNEAU D., AUFFRAY C. and BLOCH B. (1988) Dopaminergic neurons of the substantia nigra modulate preproenkephalin A gene expression in rat striatal neurons. Brain Res. 439, 39-46.

PESCHANSKI M. and BESSON J.M. (1987) Structural alteration and possible growth of afferents after kainate lesion in the adult rat thalamus. J.Comp.Neurol., 258, 185-203.

PRITZEL M., HUSTON J.P. and SARTER M. (1983) Behavioral and neuronal reorganization after unilateral substantia nigra lesions : evidence for increased interhemispheric nigro-caudate projections. Neuroscience 9, 879-888.

RAISMAN G. (1969) Neuronal plasticity in the septal nuclei of the adult rat. Brain Res. 14, 25-48.

ROBERTSON H.A., PETERSON M.R., MURPHY K. and ROBERTSON G.S. (1989) D1-dopamine receptor antagonists selectively activate striatal *c-fos* independent of rotational behaviour. Brain Res. 503, 346-349.

ROSSI F., WIKLUND L., VAN DER WANT J.J.L. and STRATA P. (1989) Collateral sprouting of climbing fibres following the subtotal lesion of the inferior olive in the adult rat. Europ.J.Neurosci., suppl.2, Abstr.90.4.

SALIN P., KERKERIAN-LE GOFF L., HEIDET V., EPELBAUM J. and NIEOULLON A. (1990) Somatostatin-immunoreactive neurons in the rat striatum : effects of corticostriatal and nigrostriatal dopaminergic lesions. Brain Res. 521, 23-32.

SAMUEL D., UJENDRA KUMAR and NIEOULLON A. (1988) γ-aminobutyric acid function in the rat striatum is under the double influence of nigrostriatal dopaminergic and thalamostriatal inputs : two modes of regulation ? J.Neurochem. 51, 1704-1710.

SAMUEL D., ERRAMI M. and NIEOULLON A. (1990) Localization of N-methyl-D-aspartate receptors in the rat striatum : effects of specific lesions on the ^{3}H-3-2 carboxypiperazin-4-yl-propyl-1-phosphonic acid binding. J.Neurochem. 54, 1926-1933.

SCATTON B. (1982) Effect of dopamine agonists and neuroleptic agents on striatal acetylcholine transmission in the rat. Evidence against dopamine receptor multiplicity. J.Pharmacol.Exp.Ther. 220, 197-202.

SIMON H., TAGHZOUTI K., GOZLAN H., STUDLER J.M., LOUILOT A., HERVE D., GLOWINSKI J., TASSIN J.P. and LE MOAL M. (1988) Lesion of dopaminergic terminals in the amygdala produces enhanced locomotor response to D-amphetamine and opposite changes in dopaminergic activity in prefrontal cortex and nucleus accumbens. Brain Res. 447, 335-340.

THAL L.J., SHARPLESS N.S., HIRSCHHORN I.D., HOROWITZ S.G. and MAKMAN M.H. (1983) Striatal met-enkephalin concentration increases following nigrostriatal denervation. Biochem.Pharmacol. 32, 3297-3301.

TSUKAHARA N. (1981) Synaptic plasticity in the mammalian central nervous system. Ann.Rev.Neurosci. 4, 351-379.

TSUKAHARA N., FUJITO Y., ODA Y. and MAEDA J. (1982) Formation of functional synapses in the adult cat red nucleus from the cerebrum following cross-innervation of forelimb flexor and extensor nerve. I. Appearance of new synaptic potentials. Exp.Brain Res. 45, 1-12.

UNGERSTEDT U. (1971) Postsynaptic supersensitivity after 6-hydroxydopamine induced degeneration of the nigrostriatal dopamine system. Acta Physiol.Scand. Suppl.367, 69-93.

VUILLON-CACCIUTTOLO G., BOSLER O. and NIEOULLON A. (1986) Immunohistochemical evidence of plasticity of γ-aminobutyric acid neurons in the red nucleus and adjacent reticular formation after contralateral cerebellectomy in the adult cat. Neurosci.Lett. 70, 308-313.

WALL P.D. (1976) Plasticity in the adult mammalian central nervous system. Prog.Brain Res. 45, 359-379.

WILLIAMS J.H., ERRINGTON M. L., LYNESS M.A. and BLISS T.V.P. (1989) Arachidonic acid induces a long term activity-dependent enhancement of synaptic transmission in the hippocampus. Nature 341, 739-742.

WOOD S.J., PRITCHARD J. and SOFRONIEW M.V. (1990) Re-expression of nerve growth factor receptor after axonal injury recapitulates a developmental event in motor neurons : differential regulation when regeneration is allowed or prevented. Eur.J.Neurosci. 2, 650-657.

ZIGMOND M.J., ABERCROMBIE E., BERGER T.W., GRACE A.A. and STRICKER M. (1990) Compensations after lesions of central dopaminergic neurons : some clinical and basic implications. Trends in Neurosci. 13, 290-296.

Tutorials in Motor Behavior II
G.E. Stelmach and J. Requin (Editors)

Eye-head coordination

A. Roucoux

Laboratoire de Neurophysiologie, University of Louvain, B-1200 Brussels, Belgium

Many species orient their gaze by means of combined movements of the eyes in the orbit and of the head about the trunk. In order to achieve the required precision, both movements have to be coordinated. This coordination represents a formidable challenge for the nervous system. Indeed, the static and dynamic properties of the implicated joints are extremely different. For example, the axis of rotation of the eyeball does not coincide with the rotation axis of the head, head movements are rarely pure rotations, the eye is a low inertia object compared to the ponderous head, etc... Some of these coordinating mechanisms have now been discovered and their understanding might reveal profitable to the study of motor coordination in general.

The typical time course of events is illustrated in fig. 1A. The eye saccade is usually triggered first. After a delay of about 30 ms, the head begins to rotate, in the same direction, at a slower velocity. When the gaze attains the target, the eye saccade stops and is immediately followed by a smaller movement of the eye, having the same velocity as the head, but in the opposite direction. During this second phase, gaze is held stable in space. If the head is prevented from moving, the time course and amplitude of gaze are identical. In other words, with head free, the amplitude and velocity of the saccade are reduced so as to keep gaze amplitude accurate. At the end of the movement, the share of the head in the total displacement amounts to about 70%: eye eccentricity at that time is thus 30% of the initial retinal error [1]; this is illustrated in fig. 2. In this sequence of movements, two phases may be distinguished: a period of gaze movement followed by a period of gaze stabilisation. What are the coordinating mechanisms at work during these two periods? Are they identical?

Theoretically, two types of types of coordination mechanisms are possible. The reduction of eye saccade amplitude and velocity, and the compensatory drift back of the eye could be preprogrammed. In this case, the gaze command would be shared out amongst eye and head motor systems. The other possibility is that the eye saccadic command is identical, in head fixed or in head free conditions; the adjustment of the eye saccade parameters and the compensatory phase would be caused by peripheral sensory feedbacks arising from the vestibular system, the neck proprioceptive apparatus or the visual system.

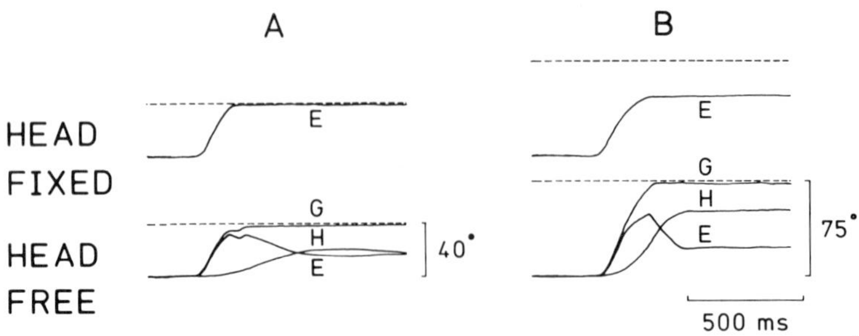

Figure 1. Two type of eye-head coordination. A: within the oculomotor range; B: outside the oculomotor range. The dotted line indicates the target position. E: eye position, H: head, G: gaze. See comments in text. From [42].

1. THE "CLASSICAL OBSERVATIONS"

Bizzi and colleagues [2-3] have tested the two hypotheses. In a first series of experiments, they unexpectedly blocked head movements of monkeys trained to fixate visual targets presented at various horizontal eccentricities (up to 40). A brake was applied at random to a head holder, normally permitting free horizontal rotations, at the very beginning of the head movement. In this condition, though the animal can be assumed to have programmed a head movement, the eye saccade was identical to those of the monkeys whose head was continuously restrained. Moreover, the compensatory eye movement was absent. This observation clearly speaks against the "preprogramming" hypothesis.

The second set of experiments was aimed at identifying which of the possible feedback loops is active. First, the visual component was suppressed by turning off the target light just before the initiation of the eye-head movement. The eye movement was found to be unchanged. Second, monkeys were similarly tested after elimination of the vestibular feedback [4]. The first day after the operation, the animals overshot the target. This was due to the absence of both postsaccadic compensatory eye movement and shortening of saccade amplitude. A few weeks after labyrinthectomy, the compensatory drift-back of the eyes progressively reappeared and reached 90% of compensation after a few months. When tested in the blocking paradigm, a weak compensatory eye movement persisted. They concluded that the process of recovery after labyrinthectomy entails a part of central programming and a part of peripheral feedback, probably of neck origin. Third, the animals underwent a C1 to C6 dorsal rhizotomy. After recovery, a reduction of the eye saccade amplitude was observed together with a shortening of the head movement. In the blocking paradigm, the compensatory eye movement was still present with a gain even higher than in the preceding experiment.

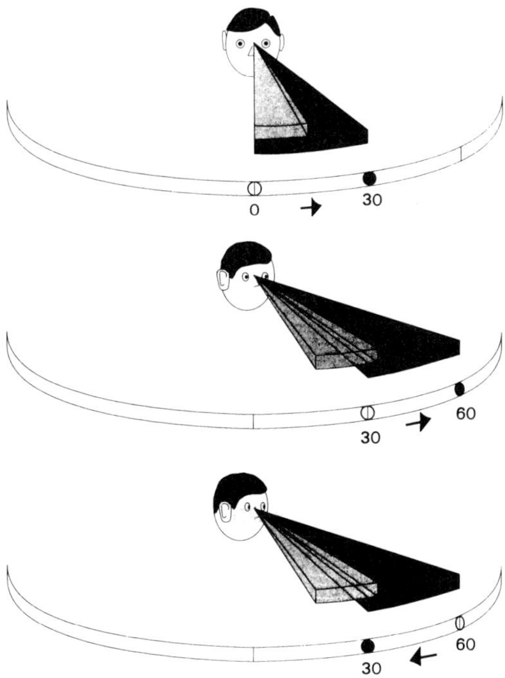

Figure 2. Schematic illustration of three successive gaze fixation movements made by a human subject, without particular instructions, to targets located at 30 and 60° of eccentricity. The final position of the preceding movement is the initial position of the next. In black, gaze movement; in grey, head movement. The proportion of gaze error covered by the head is constant. From [1].

In conclusion to these series of experiments, it appears that eye-head coordination, in the normal monkey trained to fixate visual targets within 40° of eccentricity, exclusively relies on vestibular feedback (the VOR). The vestibular signal (equal to the opposite of head velocity) is continuously fed back into the eye motor circuitry and added to the eye motor command (eye velocity). This mechanism has been referred to as the "addition hypothesis" [5] or "linear summation" [6]. According to this hypothesis, the trajectory of the eye in space (the gaze saccade) is independent of the occurrence and the size of a concomitant head saccade. Gaze saccades that result from the summation of an eye-in-head with a head-in-space movement are indistinguishable from pure eye saccades made with the head stationary. Consequently, the eye-in-head saccade corresponds to a normal eye saccade from which a signal reflecting the concurrent head movement is subtracted; it has a lower velocity and a smaller amplitude than the saccade that would occur without head movement. After completion of the gaze saccade, the eye-in-head position continues to change because a compensatory movement, which is a mirror image of the ongoing head movement, reduces the eye-in-head eccentricity until the head comes to rest, thereby providing for a stable eye-in-space position. By adding the VOR to the intrinsic saccade command the resulting gaze saccade would follow the course specified by the intrinsic command independently of whichever head movement happened to occur concurrently. However, during the recovery period after labyrinthectomy, other mechanisms play a role. The cervico-ocular reflex (COR) increases its gain dramatically (it is very low initially). As demonstrated by the blocking experiments, a partially compensatory eye movement can be preprogrammed. This central rearrangement, though small, even depends on the amount of remaining peripheral feedback, as illustrated by the blocking experiments in the labyrinthectomised, rhizotomised animals. Moreover, a certain recalibration of the eye saccade amplitude, with respect to the retinal input, can occur.

2. THE BEAUTY OF THE ADDITION HYPOTHESIS

The addition hypothesis is particularly attractive due to its elegant mechanism. Eye and head coordination need not to be preprogrammed, what is an obvious advantage. The eye saccade may be programmed without the need to take head movements into account.The feedback automatically compensates for any perturbation in the course of head movement and insures a perfect stabilisation during passive head displacements (provided that the gain of the VOR, i.e. the ratio of eye to head velocity is adequate). Moreover, the same mechanism adequately operates when the head is prevented from moving.

In case of visual target acquisition, the same retinal error is used to elaborate both the eye and the head command. There must however be some adaptation. Indeed, as the eye is mobile in the orbit, there is no fixed relationship between retinal error and the adequate amplitude of the head response. An appropriate head command should take eye position in the orbit into account. Roucoux et al. (1981) [7] and Vidal et al. (1982) [8] demonstrated the existence of an eye position signal in various neck muscles of the cat, when the head is fixed. This signal would be adequate to realize the transformation of the initially retinocentric command into a craniocentric frame of reference. The addition hypothesis is schematised in fig. 3.

3. IS THE ADDITION HYPOTHESIS ALWAYS VALID ?

More recently, a series of observations have accumulated, suggesting that the linear summation hypothesis could be invalidated. The first argument against this hypothesis is related to the extent of the maximum excursion of the eye in the orbit, the oculomotor range (OMR), and how targets can be acquired when their eccentricity lies beyond the limits of this range. The second pertains to how saccades and VOR signals interact. The third is related to the mechanisms of gaze control. Historically, all these objections were raised by the study of Roucoux & Crommelinck (1976) [9]. They were amplified by Roucoux et al. (1980) [10] and Robinson & Zee (1981) [5]. Since then, data have accumulated, disproving the universality of this mechanism.

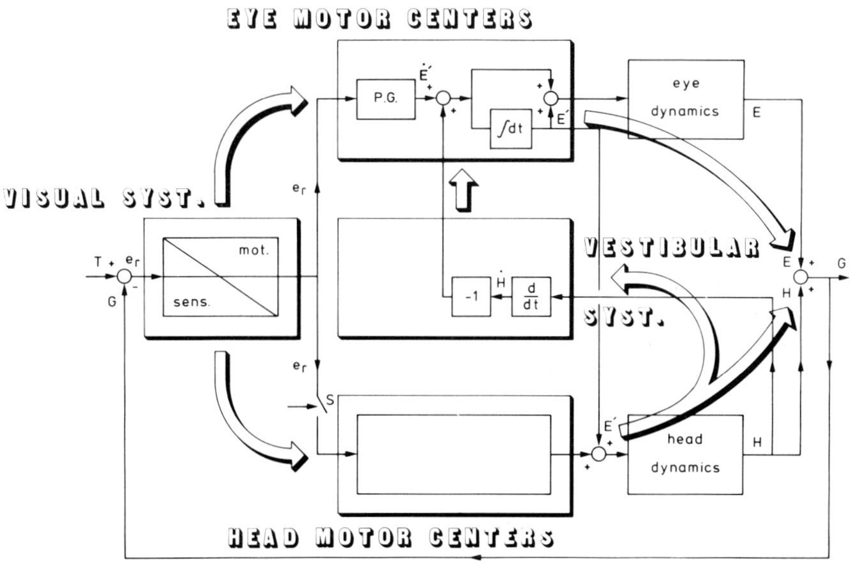

Figure 3. The addition model of eye-head coordination in case of visual target acquisition. Target position in space (T') compared to actual gaze position (G) yields a retinal error (er) which undergoes in the visual system (in particular the Superior Colliculus) a sensory-motor transformation. The motor command signal, retinotopically coded (er) is sent both to eye and head motor centers. For the eye, it triggers a pulse generator (P.G.) creating an eye velocity comand (E') which is transmitted to the eye motoneurons directly and through the integrator loop. Eye dynamics are intercalated between the motoneurons and eye displacement (E). For the head, the pathway is analogous and ends up with a head position signal (H). The functional organisation of head motor centers is presently unknown. The summation of E and H yields G (gaze position), which is externally fed back to the input. The vestibular system detects head acceleration and builds up an internal representation of head velocity (H) which is changed sign and added to the eye velocity command. The output of the head motor centers receives a internal copy of eye position which translates it into head coordinates. It is not known where, in the flow of information through the head motor system, this addition occurs. Finally, a switch S symbolises the possibility of a voluntary diconnection of head movements. This scheme applies to the saccade as well as to the subsequent compensatory drift of the eye. From [42].

3.1. Gaze saccades beyond the limits of the oculomotor range

The OMR extends up to 45 to 50° from the primary position in man and monkey, and up to 25 to 30° in cats. According to the addition hypothesis, the characteristics of a gaze saccade should be identical whether the head moves or is prevented to do so. As a consequence, in order to shift the gaze to targets that lie beyond the OMR with single-step, saccade-like gaze shifts, it would be required that the brain program saccades that are too large to be physically possible. Alternatively, the gaze shifts of amplitude greater than the OMR could only be made by multiple-step smaller gaze shifts. Bizzi et al. (1971) [11] in the monkey, as well as Blakemore & Donaghy (1980) [12] in the cat reported that gaze shifts larger than the OMR are made up of a series of successive smaller saccades. However, though multiple-step gaze saccades may indeed be observed, the most frequent response is a single-step gaze saccade, in cats [13] [14] [7] [15], in monkeys [16], and man [17] [18] [5] [7] [6] [19]. Fig. 1B illustrates a gaze shift to a target lying beyond the OMR. If the head is unexpectedly blocked in human subjects, just before the onset of the movement, the gaze saccade falls short of the target, the eye stopping quite short of the limits of the OMR [7]. The relationships between maximum velocity and amplitude and between duration and amplitude for these saccades were independent of whether they were made with the head fixed voluntarily or unexpectedly prevented from moving by a brake [20]. Cats behave similarly (fig. 4). These data imply that the limit to saccade amplitude is imposed neurally, not mechanically. The fact that the nervous system limits saccade amplitude and yet can program single-step gaze shifts greater than this limit also suggests that the hypotheses underlying the addition strategy are incorrect.

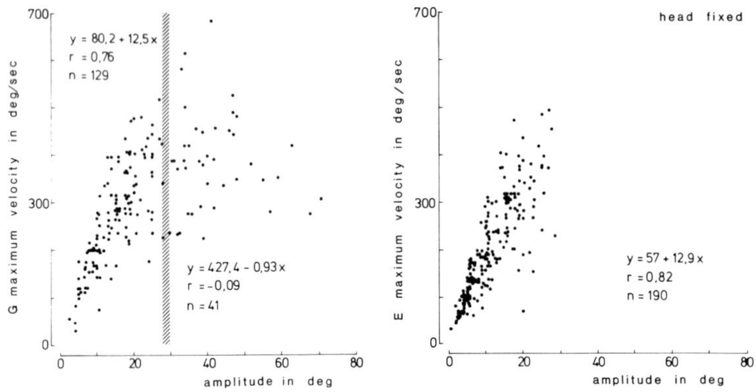

Figure 4. The relation between maximum velocity and amplitude of gaze (eye in space) saccades in an alert cat with his head free (left) and head fixed (right) . The hatched area represents the limit of the oculomotor range (maximum eye deviation in orbit). Equations are linear regressions. In the head-free condition, saccades have been divided into two populations within and outside the oculomotor range. n, number of saccades; r, correlation coefficient. From [7].

3.2. The interaction between saccades and VOR

According to the addition hypothesis, the time course of the gaze shift should be identical, whether the head is immobile or moving, and consequently, the eye saccade would be comparatively slower when the head moves. In man, the velocity of large gaze shifts is, to a large extent, under voluntary control [5]. This is not the case for the eye saccades made while the head is immobile. Head velocity variations, which can be provoked voluntarily, are thus echoed on the gaze trace, contrary to what is predicted by the addition hypothesis. Moreover, it has been repeatedly demonstrated that, in the cat [13] [7] [14] but also in monkeys [16] and man [6] that eye saccades are faster when the head is freely moving than when it is clamped. One way to investigate the problem of saccade-VOR interaction is to brake the head suddenly and unexpectedly during the saccade. In this condition, visual feedback is thought to be too slow to modulate the saccade and neck proprioceptive influences are negligible [11]. Thus, according to the summation hypothesis, this manipulation should suddenly remove the influence of the VOR on the pulse generator, and the saccade should accelerate within 10-20 ms. Such a braking was applied in man, for the first time, by Roucoux et al. (1981) [7]. Their conclusions was that no VOR-saccade interaction could be detected for large shifts of gaze. Fuller et al. (1983) [21] and Guitton et al. (1984) [15] used a brake to interrupt the motion of a cat's head for short periods during eye-head orienting gaze shifts. In the latter study, braking could be timed to occur at different points in the eye trajectory. When the brake was applied early in the eye trajectory, the perturbation caused changes of eye velocity compatible with summation of VOR, when it was applied later, the perturbation was not compensated for, suggesting no saccade-VOR interaction. Tomlinson & Bahra (1986) [16] performed similar experiments in monkeys. A monkey's head was perturbed by a torque motor with the advantage that the head could either be decelerated or accelerated during the saccade. They concluded that there was no saccade-VOR interaction when the gaze shift was approximately larger than 40, but for smaller gaze shifts, particularly smaller than 10°, the VOR and saccade clearly interacted. There was a transition zone between 10 and 40° within which the VOR operated with a gain smaller than unity. Laurutis & Robinson (1986) [6] mechanically perturbed head movements during head fixed and head free gaze shifts in two human subjects. For gaze shifts larger than 40° they concluded that head perturbations did not affect the eye saccade trajectory, but for smaller movements, the results were less clear. Analogous experiments by Guitton & Volle (1987) [19] in four human subjects yielded results in which VOR-saccade interaction was more variable, demonstrating that individual factors do play a role, but also other factors such as the predictability of the task.

3.3. The implications of Superior Colliculus stimulation in cats

The results of electrical focal stimulation of the SC in cats [9] [22] [10] were the first to raise the question of the validity of the addition hypothesis for large shifts of gaze. SC stimulation in cats produces combined eye and head movements. According to the properties of these movements and of their coordination, two main zones may be distinguished in the SC.

Zone 1, the most rostral, receives a retinotopic projection from the central 25 to 30° of the visual field. Stimulation in the intermediate and deep layers of this zone evokes retinocentric saccades. The direction and amplitude of these saccades do not depend on eye position and are mainly determined by the antero-posterior position of the stimulating electrode. A "motor map" can be reconstructed which is in perfect register with the overlying sensory map. This property of evoked saccades has also been described in monkey's SC [23]. When the head of the cat, but also of the monkey, is free to move, these retinocentric saccades are accompanied by a head rotation in the same direction, provided that the eye goes beyond a certain eccentricity. In both species, the whole eye-head pattern is similar, and obeys the addition hypothesis: the eye saccade amplitude and velocity are reduced proportionally to the head movement, by the action of the VOR. This is easy to establish, by comparing the evoked eye saccade parameters, measured respectively when the head is fixed or free, while the electrode is kept at the same site and the stimulation parameters identical (fig. 5). Moreover, the burst of EMG activity evoked in the neck muscles by this stimulation is modulated by eye position. The burst is larger is larger when the eye sits at more eccentric positions towards the side of the recorded muscle [24].

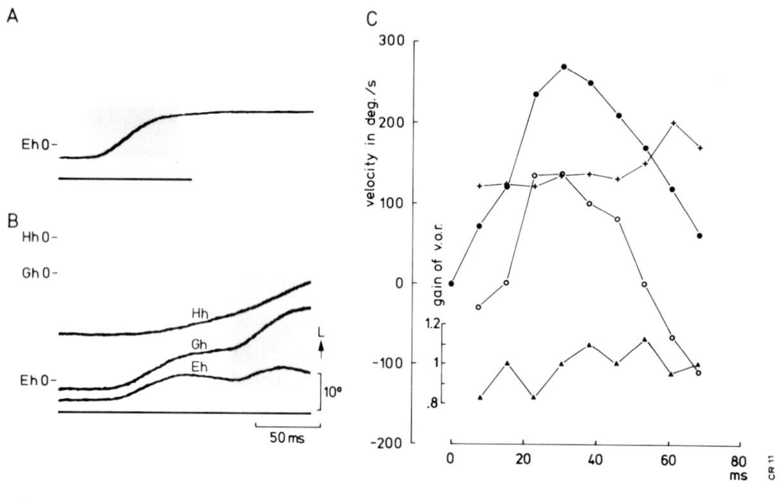

Figure 5. Comparison of the velocity of eye saccades evoked in the anterior zone of the SC with head fixed or free. A: horizontal eye saccade evoked by a 125 ms stimulus train from a site located in the right SC with head fixed. B: at the same stimulation site, horizontal eye (Eh), head (Hh), and gaze (Gh) movements evoked by a 400ms train. C: instantaneous velocity of eye and head analysed during the time delimited by the stippled areas in A and B. The angular velocity of the eye in the orbit during saccade evoked with head fixed is represented by crosses and the gain of the VOR by filled triangles. A negative velocity means a "compensatory" eye movement in the orbit. L: left. From [10].

Zone 2 is more caudal and receives the retinotopic projection from the peripheral retina. Eye saccades evoked there are not retinocentric. Their direction and amplitude depend on initial eye position in such a way that, for a given stimulation site, the eye reaches a rather well defined and constant final position in the orbit (craniocentric saccades). This final position has a rather constant eccentricity (about 15°), but its direction is determined by the antero-posterior position of the electrode. The motor map, also in register with the sensory map, only concerns here the direction of the final position of the eye, not the saccade itself. Each of these saccades is accompanied by a large and saccadic-like head movement. The direction and amplitude of the head saccade is determined by the electrode position on the motor map, which coincides with the sensory retinotopic map. Eye and head movements start almost simultaneously. The saccade, however, does not interact with the VOR, as revealed by the comparison of the saccade parameters in head fixed and head free conditions (fig. 6). The gaze has a much larger amplitude and velocity when the head is allowed to move. The evoked burst of neck muscle discharge corresponding to the accelerating phase of the head saccade is independent of eye position. Thus, the motor map contained in SC zone 2, in the cat, is a head movement map, coded craniocentrically for the eye.

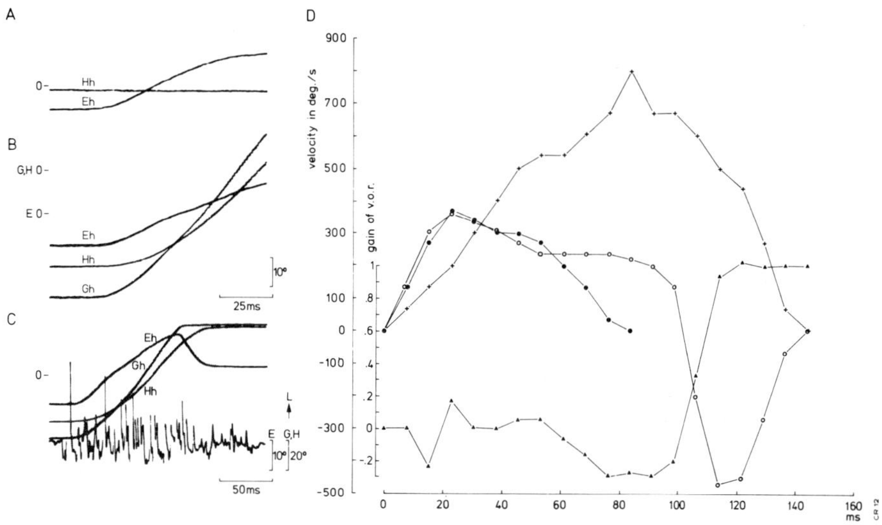

Figure 6. Comparison of the velocity of eye saccades evoked in the intermediate zone of the SC with head fixed or free. A: Horizontal eye saccade evoked by a 400 ms pulse train from a site located in right SC with head fixed. B-C: At the same stimulation site, horizontal eye, head and gaze movements evoked by 400 ms stimulus train represented at two different time scales. C: bottom trace is EMG activity recorded in left Biventer Cervicis muscle. D: Instantaneous velocity of eye and head measured during the time delimited by the stippled area in C. Symbols are identical to Fig. 5. From [10].

To conclude, stimulation of the SC in the cat reveals an organisation that is at least double. Zone 3, which has been described [22], shall not be considered here. This functional subdivision of the structure is based on which part of the visual field is concerned. Moreover, the part of the field projected onto zone 1, almost perfectly corresponds to the oculomotor range. This range, in the cat is limited to about 25° of radius. Zone 2 is concerned with targets lying outside the OMR; fixating these targets requires that the VOR is not added to the saccade.

4. TWO DIFFERENT EYE-HEAD COORDINATION STRATEGIES

The data described above clearly show that the addition hypothesis is not always valid. They also suggest that the addition of the VOR to the saccade would be done when the gaze shift is small (within the OMR), but that larger gaze shifts would require another eye-head coordinating mechanism. There exist other data suggesting an alternative eye-head coordination mechanism, that might coexist with the VOR addition.

Barnes (1979) [18] analysed, in man, gaze shifts made with head free during various fixation tasks: permanently lit target, flashed target, voluntary head rotations in the dark and also passive head rotations in the dark. A striking result was that eye and head movements pattern was very similar in all conditions. This result obviously calls into question the role of retinal error in the elaboration of some of these coordinated movements. Moreover, in the continuous target paradigm, for eccentricities less than 45°, the eye saccade was initiated before head acceleration and errors in gaze displacement were small. For larger eccentricities (e.g. 75°), the head movement almost always preceded the eye saccade and larger errors in initial gaze displacement were made. The author suggests that eye-head control is mediated principally by retinal error information for small target offsets (<45°). Beyond this limit, the control could be achieved by the system responsible for the coordination of eye and head in the dark. In this condition, head acceleration most often precedes eye saccades; therefore, it is possible that the saccade would be activated by a central command collateral of a pathway responsible of neck motor activity. In this case, the saccade could be considered as a "reflex response" to the head turning. This alternative mode of eye-head coordination would be active during voluntary head movements in absence of visual target, or when fixating eccentric objects lying in the peripheral visual field.

The case of "afoveate" saccades is also worth being analysed. Animals without a well developed fovea such as the goldfish, the frog or the rabbit, make eye saccades that are almost exclusively coupled with head movements [25] [13] [26]. Head and eye movements are initiated simultaneously and the whole pattern is similar to that shown in primates. However, when the head is prevented to move, extremely few saccades occur. In these animals, as there is no need to "foveate" the target, the purpose of the saccade is rather to anticipate the head movement, which is aimed at reorienting gaze in another direction. The net result of this process is an acceleration of the process of shifting the gaze. In this respect, the afoveate saccade is similar to a quick phase, the function of which is also to move the eye in the direction of the head turning. However, contrary to quick phases, which appear during passive head movements, afoveate saccades are probably triggered by a central head command. They may be considered as centrally-triggered quick phases.

Some neurological disorders are also of interest in this context. Patients suffering from oculomotor apraxia show abnormal patterns of eye-head coordination during attempted changes of gaze orientation. They usually cannot make normal voluntary horizontal saccades, when their head is immobilised. When the head is free to move, they conspicuously thrust their head [27]. The exact cause of the disorder is unknown. These patients can change effectively their gaze only if they can move their head. It appears that their large, overshooting head movements are a compensatory mechanism to help change gaze direction. As eye and head accelerations are most often synchronous, it seems that the head command is used to trigger or even increase the amplitude of the eye saccade. This strategy can be compared with the afoveate gaze shifting pattern.

A last argument can be derived from the gaze shifting behaviour of human newborns. Roucoux et al. (1982 & 1983) [28-29] have shown that, in the first weeks of life, newborns fixate visual targets by a head rotation accompanied by a series of small eye saccades. The number of these saccades increases with target eccentricity but progressively decreases with age. When the target is more peripheral (e.g. 45°), the head movement is more ample and the accompanying saccade larger and faster. It is postulated that the young infants can only use a foveate mode of fixation for rather central visual objects, for more peripheral objects, they either repeat the process (multiple saccades) or turn to the afoveate mode of fixation. Along with maturation of the central nervous system, the foveate mode develops, to reach a quasi adult performance around one year of age. It has been shown indeed that, after birth, the human fovea is histologically very immature [30] [31]. Like afoveate animals, human newborns rely quasi exclusively on head movements to orient their gaze.

In view of these aguments, we have proposed that eye-head coordination, in higher vertebrates, relies on two distinct but complementary mechanisms [10] [7]. The first calls upon the addition of the VOR to the saccade, the second uses a different mechanism, by which the VOR is temporarily "switched off" during the saccade. It may be called the "switching" hypothesis (fig. 7).

The first eye-head coordination strategy, relying on the addition mechanism, is used to orient gaze towards visual targets lying within the central zone of the visual field. The extent of this central part of the field corresponds more or less to the OMR. Within the OMR, the contribution of the head to the gaze displacement is optional. The advantage of the presence of a head movement is that, at the end of the combined movement, the eye comes back towards a fairly central position in the orbit: this is behaviourly advantageous. The origin of the command sent to the eye, but also to the head, probably resides in the rostral part of the SC. The eye motor map is retinocentric (fig. 3).

When the visual target is situated outside the reach of the eye alone, another strategy is used, calling upon VOR "switch off". In this case, the head movement is "compulsory" and its contribution to the gaze displacement must not be cancelled by the VOR. The caudal part of the SC plays a major role in the elaboration of these gaze shifts. Its output, sent both to the eye and to the head, is craniocentrically organized. This output triggers an eye saccade having properties similar to those of afoveate saccades or quick phases. Like afoveate saccades, it is always synchronous with a central head command and is aimed at redirecting gaze in the direction of the head movement. Like quick phases also, it not added to the slow phase of the VOR [32] [33]. In a sense, the VOR "switches" back and forth between fast and slow phases. Another property of quick phases is that they appear to be coded in craniocentric coordinates [34] (fig. 7).

This double strategy hypothesis fits fairly well with all the available data, reviewed

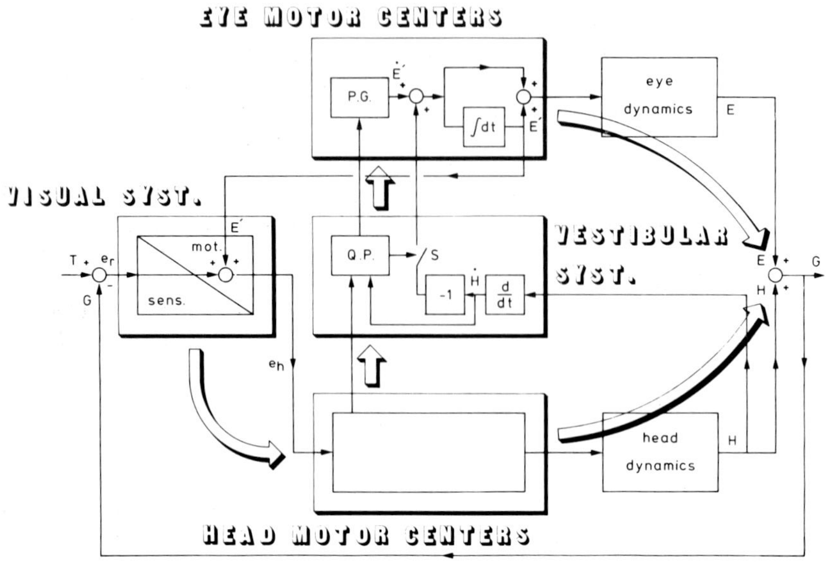

Figure 7. The "switching" model of eye-head coordination in case of visual target acquisition. Unlike schematised in Figure 3 for the addition hypothesis the motor output of the visual system (Superior Colliculus) takes eye position (E') into account and is thus coded in a head frame of reference (e). This command is sent to the head motor centres to generate a head rotation (H). This head motor command triggers the "quick phase" generator (Q.P.) of the vestibular system, which in turns, activates the eye motor centres. In parallel, the Q.P. switches off the slow phase pathway (S). Notice that the input to the quick phase mechanism is coded in head coordinates. This scheme is only valid for the saccadic part of the combined eye and head movement. During the compensation that follows (end of Q.P.) the switch S closes and reestablishes the addition of the vestibular signal. The coordination between eye and head would be realised by the adaptation of the Q.P. parameters to the head motor programme. The latter mechanism is presently not understood. From [42].

above, except one. A "zone 2" has not been discovered yet in the monkey's SC. This fact could however be understood in an evolutionary context. The "switching" strategy may be considered as the most widespread eye-head coordination mechanism among the vertebrates. Afoveate animals would have no other. It can be imagined that, in parallel with the progressive development of the central retina, eye movements became independent of head movements. The reason could be found in a need for an increased precision in gaze positioning: it is mechanically easier to orient the eye alone (what the addition strategy in fact does) than to have to cope with the complex head motor apparatus. In parallel to this behavioural "pressure", SC zone 1 would have evolved to satisfy this new need. The monkey, having a very well developed fovea, an extended OMR, would have a large part of his SC devoted to this "new" orienting mechanism, a "neocolliculus", having relegated the older part of his SC (the "paleocolliculus") to a relatively tiny caudal part, difficult to reach electrophysiologically. The cat has a not so well developed fovea, a narrower OMR, and thus a smaller "neocolliculus" coexisting with a still fairly large "paleocolliculus". The rabbit, the frog, or the goldfish, having quasi no fovea, would only possess a "paleocolliculus".

This attractive hypothesis must however be considered with some caveats. In man [19], there are cases when the choice between one or the other strategy is no clear-cut. It could depend not only on the eccentricity of the target but also on its nature, the behavioural context as well as individual preferences.

The "switching" hypothesis raises also a question, which is of importance: if the VOR is temporarily turned off during the saccade, how are eye and head movements coordinated?

5. THE GAZE FEEDBACK THEORY

In those gaze shifts in which VOR addition is initially absent, there is a time, within the gaze shift, at which the VOR signal is again added and stabilises the visual axis in space. The reactivation of the VOR occurs when gaze position error - the difference between desired and current gaze position- approaches or equals zero, i.e. when gaze is near or on the target. Quite clearly, the control mechanism, that also coordinates eye and head, must rely on a feedback of eye and head position: a gaze feedback. Such an hypothesis has been first proposed by Roucoux et al. (1980) [10] (fig. 8). In this model, an internal copy of actual gaze position is obtained by summing internal copies of eye and head positions. This sum is then subtracted from desired gaze to yield a gaze position error signal, which drives the eye and head motor machineries. The principle that gaze itself is the controlled variable has been reiterated by others [21] [15] [16] [19] [35] and in a more quantitative formulation by Laurutis and Robinson (1986) [6]. Recently, Bottemanne et al. [36] have shown that the reactivation of the VOR, in man, occurs about 30 ms before gaze dynamic error reaches zero, whatever is the velocity of gaze. This suggests that gaze velocity, and not gaze position , is used in the gaze control feedback loop.

On electrophysiological grounds, little is known about the existence of neurons coding gaze position. Munoz & Guitton (1989) [37] have established that output cells of cat's SC (Tecto-reticular neurons -TRNs- and Tecto-reticulo-spinal neurons -TRSNs-) have a phasic discharge preceding a given gaze shift, corresponding to the cell location on the retinotopic map, and coding the velocity and acceleration of the movement. Moreover, cells situated in the rostral part of the SC are maximally active when the cat fixates a target of interest; during gaze shifts, they decrease their discharge. These authors propose that the gaze feedback modulates the activity of these cells at the origin of the eye and head movement . In a very recent study [37], it is suggested that the effect of the gaze feedback would be to shift the zone of activity, along the retinotopic of the SC, during the gaze movement. This movement would stop when this zone of activity reaches the rostral foveal region of the map.

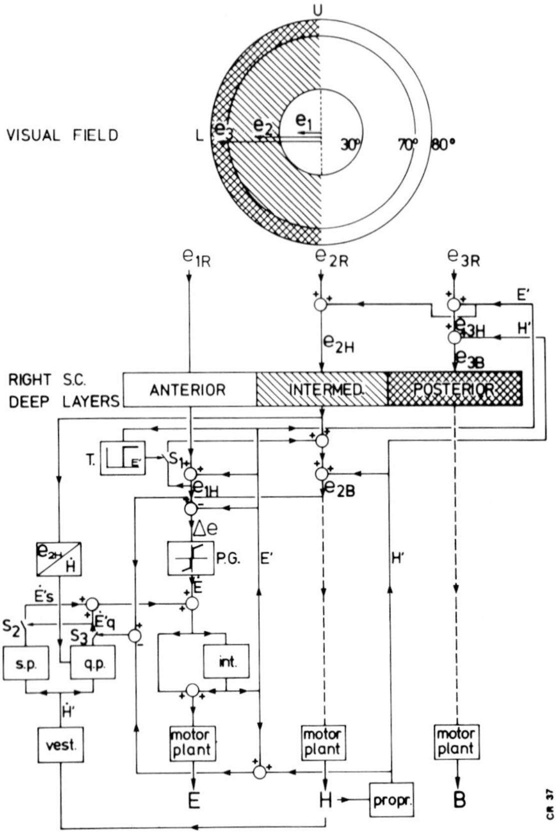

Figure 8. A model of Superior Colliculus control of the fixation reflex of the cat. E: amplitude of eye displacement in orbit. H: amplitude of head rotation. B: amplitude of body rotation. Int: integrator. U: up. L: left. P.G.: pulse generator. S.P.: slow phase. Q.P.: quick phase. From [10].

It has now been clearly established that the addition hypothesis is not the only mechanism responsible for eye-head coordination. The alternate hypothesis, however based on VOR temporary "switch off" and gaze feedback control, has still many fuzzy aspects, most of them at the neuronal level.

On one hand, the neuronal mechanisms responsible for the VOR switching are still largely unknown. One of these mechanisms has however been proposed [38]. The Excitatory Burst Neurons -EBNs-, activated by the TRSNs, project in parallel onto the Inhibitory Burst Neurons -IBNs-, the motoneurons, and onto type II vestibular interneurons. These interneurons, in their turn, inhibit secondary vestibular neurons, resulting in an inhibition of the VOR, as long as the EBNs discharge. On the other hand, the mechanism that generates the quick phase, which has many properties in common with the afoveate saccade, is also poorly understood. It is possible that burst driving neurons (BDNs), found in he prepositus hypoglossi, would be implicated. Their activity show a burst superimposed to a tonic vestibular discharge. They project to the contralateral EBNs and IBNS and could be "triggering" the quick phases.

6. REFERENCES

1 Delreux V., Vanden Abeele S., Lefèvre P. and Roucoux A.; Brain and Space, J. Paillard ed, Oxford Univ. Press, pp 38-48, (1991).
2 Bizzi E., Kalil R. E. and Morasso P.; Brain Res., 40, 45-48, (1972).
3 Morasso P., Bizzi E. and Dichgans J.; Exp. Brain Res., 16, 492-500, (1973).
4 Dichgans J., Bizzi E., Morasso P. and Tagliasco V.; Exp. Brain Res., 18, 548-562, (1973).
5 Robinson D. A. and Zee D. S. Progress in oculomotor research, A. Fuchs and W. Becker eds, Elsevier, pp 3-12, (1981).
6 Laurutis V. P. and Robinson D. A.; J. Physiol., 373, 209-233, (1986).
7 Roucoux A., Crommelinck M., Guérit J. M. and Meulders M.; Progress in oculomotor research, A. Fuchs and W. Becker eds, Elsevier, pp 309-318, (1981).
8 Vidal P. P., Roucoux A. and Berthoz A.; Exp. Brain Res., 46, 448-453, (1982).
9 Roucoux A. and Crommelinck M.; Brain Res., 106, 349-363, (1976).
10 Roucoux A., Guitton D. and Crommelinck M.; Exp. Brain Res., 39, 75-85, (1980).
11 Bizzi E., Kalil R.E. and Tagliasco V.; Science, 173, 452-454, (1971).
12 Blakemore C. and Donaghy M.; J. Physiol. (Lond.), 300, 317-335, (1980).
13 Collewijn H.; J. Physiol. (Lond.), 266, 471-498, (1977).
14 Douglas R., Guitton D. and Volle M.; Physiological and pathological aspects of eye movements, A. Roucoux and M. Crommelinck eds., Junk, pp 411-416, (1982).
15 Guitton D., Douglas R. M. and Volle M.; J. Neurophysiol., 52, 1030-1050, (1984).
16 Tomlinson R. D. and Bahra P. S.; J. Neurophysiol., 56, 1558-1570, (1986).
17 Gresty M.A.; Vision Res., 14, 395-403, (1974).
18 Barnes G. R.; J. Physiol. (Lond.), 287: 127-147, (1979).
19 Guitton D. and Volle M.; J. Neurophysiol., 58, 427-459, (1987).
20 Guitton D.; Control of head movement, B. W. Peterson and F. J. Richmond eds, Oxford University Press, pp 196-207, (1988).
21 Fuller J.H., Maldonado H. and Schlag J.; Brain Res., 271, 241-250, (1983).
22 Guitton D., Crommelinck M. and Roucoux A.; Exp. Brain Res., 39, 63-73, (1980).
23 Robinson D.A.; Vision Res., 12, 1795-1808, (1972).
24 Roucoux A., Vidal P. P., Veraart C., Crommelinck M. and Berthoz A.; Physiological and pathological aspects of eye movements, A. Roucoux and M. Crommelinck eds., Junk, pp 371-378, (1982).
25 Easter S.S., Johns P.R. and Hechenlively D.R.; J. comp. Physiol., 92, 23-35, (1974).
26 Dieringer N., Precht W. and Blight A.R.; Exp. Brain Res., 47, 407-416, (1982).
27 Zee D.S., Yee R.D. and Singer H.S.; Brain, 100, 581-599, (1977).

28 Roucoux A., Culée C. and Roucoux M.; Physiological and pathological aspects of eye movements, A. Roucoux and M. Crommelinck eds., Junk, pp 23-31, (1982).
29 Roucoux A., Culée C. and Roucoux M.; Behavioural Brain Research, 10, 133-139, (1983).
30 Abramov I., Gordon J., Hendrickson A., Hailine L., Dobson V. and La Bossiere E.; Science, 217, 265-267, (1982).
31 Hendrickson A. and Yuodelis C.; Ophthalmology, 91, 603-612, (1984).
32 Guitton D. and Mandl G.; Vision Res., 20, 875-881, (1980).
33 Jürgens R., Becker W., Rieger P. and Widderich A.; Progress in oculomotor research, A. Fuchs and W. Becker eds, Elsevier, pp 11-18, (1981).
34 Chun K.S. and Robinson D.; Biol. Cybernetics, 28, 209-221, (1978).
35 Pélisson D., Prablanc C. and Urquizar C.; J. Neurophysiol., 59, 997-1013, (1988).
36 Bottemanne I., Olivier E., Lefèvre P. and Roucoux A.; Fifth European Conference on Eye Movements, Pavia, (1989).
37 Munoz D. and Guitton D.; Soc. Neurosci. Abstr., 15, 807, (1989). 38 Berthoz A.; Rev. Neurol., 145, 513-526, (1989).
39 Roucoux A. and Crommelinck M.; Control of head movement, B. W. Peterson and F. J. Richmond eds, Oxford University Press, pp 208-223, (1988).
40 Roucoux A., Crommelinck M. and Borel L.; Head-neck symposium vol.2, A. Berthoz, W. Graf and P. P. Vidal eds, Oxford Univ. Press, in press.
41 Roucoux A., Crommelinck M. and Decostre M. F.; Afferent control of posture and lo comotion, J. Allum and M. Hulliger eds, Elsevier, pp 351-362, (1989).
42 Roucoux A. and Crommelinck M.; La coordination oeil-tête. Comportements, 1, 45-62, (1984).

Tutorials in Motor Behavior II
G.E. Stelmach and J. Requin (Editors)
1992 Elsevier Science Publishers B.V.

Posture and elderly persons: evidence for deficits in the central integrative mechanisms

N. Teasdale[a], C. Bard[a], F. Dadouchi[a], M. Fleury[a], J. Larue[a] and G.E. Stelmach[b]

[a]Université Laval, Laboratoire de performance motrice humaine, PEPS, Ste-Foy, Québec, Canada, G1K 7P4

[b]Arizona State University, Exercise and Sport Science Institute, Tempe, AZ 85287, USA

Abstract

Numerous authors have reported that elderly are more affected than young adults when submitted to reduced or conflictual sensory input conditions. These results, however, do not permit to evaluate whether the elderly suffer from a reduced peripheral sensibility or from a deficit in the central integrative mechanisms responsible for configuring the postural set. In this paper, two experiments supporting the hypothesis that elderly have a deficit with the central integrative mechanisms are presented. In the first experiment, young adults adapted rapidly to an augmented sensory condition (i.e, no-vision/vision transition) and reduced their sway dispersion whereas the elderly persons exhibited an increased sway dispersion. This inability to adapt to an augmented sensory condition suggest that the elderly, in addition to a reduced peripheral sensibility, have a deficit in the central integrative mechanisms responsible for reconfiguring the postural set. The second experiment evaluated whether the attentional requirements of maintaining an upright posture were affected by age and whether these attentional demands varied as function of the sensory information available. The attentional demands were greater for the elderly persons than for the young persons and increased with a decreased sensory information suggesting that a decreased attentional capacity and/or a defect in the allocation of the available resources, could be a major determinant of postural stability with increasing age.

Aging yields an increased postural sway (e.g., Era & Heikkinen, 1985; Murray et al., 1975; Sheldon, 1963). Experimenters have often attempted to relate this increased postural sway with observed deteriorations of the peripheral systems involved in posture control (i.e., visual, proprioceptive, and vestibular systems). Another possible cause for the decreased stability with increasing age is a defect or a slowing of the central integrative mechanisms responsible for configuring the postural control system (Stelmach & Worringham, 1985; Stelmach et al., 1989; Straube et al., 1988; Woollacott et al., 1986).

For example, when exposed to repeated perturbations that do not elicit reflex mechanisms, the young adapt rapidly to the perturbations whereas the elderly show an increased range of sway over trials. This increased sway over trials is thought to be an indication that the elderly have difficulty integrating sensory inputs within the central nervous system (Manchester et al., 1989; Stelmach et al., 1989). Another line of evidence for the central hypothesis comes from the work of Woollacott et al. (1986). Elderly and young adults were submitted to various conflicting sensory conditions that were created by rotating the surface platform and/or the visual surround in proportion to the subjects' sway thus making these sources of sensory information inappropriate for the postural task. Results showed that the elderly were much more affected by the combined visual and proprioceptive conflicting conditions than were the young. Similarly, Straube et al. (1988) and Teasdale et al. (1991) have reported that the elderly's balance is more affected than that of young adults when both visual and proprioceptive inputs are altered. Straube et al. (1988) have suggested that these results imply a defect in or slowing of the central integrative mechanisms responsible for configuring the postural control system.

The above experiments have used reduced and/or sensory conflict paradigms to evaluate the integrity of the central integrative mechanisms in the elderly population. The results obtained from such paradigms leave open the possibility that the decreased stability in the elderly persons is the result of a deterioration of the remaining peripheral systems and not of the central integrative mechanisms. Indeed, it has been suggested that the elderly might suffer more from reduced peripheral sensibility than from disruption in central integrative processes (Horak et al., 1989; Manchester et al., 1989; Woollacott et al., 1986). On the other hand, from a cognitive viewpoint there is at least two fondamental problems associated with aging that can affect posture, namely (1) there is a general slowing of the speed at which information can be processed (Cerella et al., 1980; Salthouse, 1985; Stelmach & Worringham, 1985) and, (2) attentional processes (i.e., decreased of the attentional capacities and/or a defective allocation of the ressources available) decline with advancing age (Baron et al., 1988; Craik, 1977). The aim of the two experiments presented in this paper was to evaluate if these cognitive problems associated with aging could be an important limitative factor for the postural control system.

EXPERIMENT 1: POSTURE CONTROL FOLLOWING AUGMENTED VISUAL SENSORY CONDITIONS

To examine the integrity of the central integrative mechanisms, elderly were submitted to successive reduced and augmented visual sensory conditions. The augmented visual sensory conditions addresses more closely the ability to reconfigure the postural set than reduced sensory conditions. If the elderly have problems reorganizing sensory information, then providing visual information after a prolonged period without visual information could disrupt their balance because it requires a reconfiguration of the postural control system.

Methods

Subjects. Seven elderly (4 females and 3 males, mean age = 72.4) and seven young adults (5 females and 2 males, mean age = 21.6) participated in the experiment. The elderly were volunteers obtained from aging coalitions and support groups; the young adults were undergraduate students. The elderly (all caucasians) were selected from a larger pool of elderly persons if they had no musculoskeletal defects, were taking no medication, and were not undergoing treatment for any neurological disease. Subjects with a history of falling were also excluded. This selection procedure is conservative as it serves to minimize any age-related differences. All participants gave informed consent for the procedures used.

Apparatus. A force platform having four load cells (AMTI model 0R6-5-1) measured force and moment components along the x, y, and z axes. The signals from the force platform were amplified (AMTI SGA6-4) prior to being fed to a computer (12 bits A/D conversion). All data signals were sampled at 40 Hz and then filtered with a Butterworth second-order filter (10 Hz lowpass cutoff with dual pass to remove phase shift). Sway behavior in the anterior-posterior and lateral planes was then computed.

Procedures. Participants stood barefoot on the force platform with feet together. They were also asked to fixate a point located in central vision 3 m from the subject. Five trials of 180 s were collected for each subject. All trials had the following temporal sequence: once the subject adopted the proper position and had stabilized their sway behavior, sampling was initiated; ten seconds into the trial, an auditory stimulus directed the subject to close their eyes. Similar stimuli directed the subject to open and close their eyes successively every 30 s (i.e., to open their eyes 40, 100, and 160 s into the trial and to close them 70 and 130 s into the trial). Figure 1 shows the temporal sequencing of a trial.

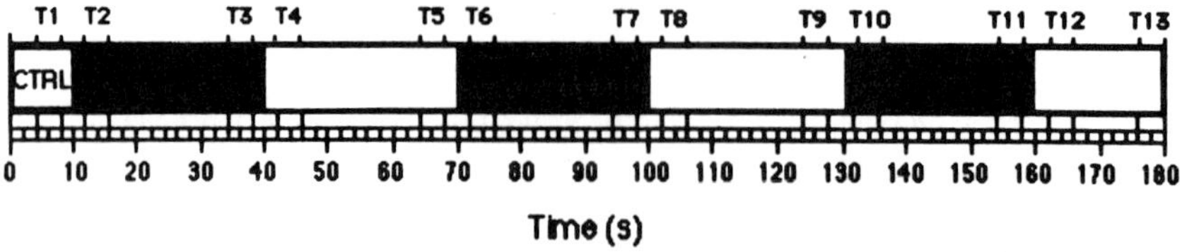

Figure 1. Temporal sequence of a trial and temporal frames used for the different analyses. The dark areas indicate the absence of vision while the white areas indicate the presence of vision. Frame 1 represents the control frame because all trials were initiated with vision.

Data Analysis. The aim of this experiment was to determine the ability of elderly persons to reconfigure the postural set after successive visual transitions. The sway behavior before and after the visual transitions was evaluated according to the pattern illustrated in Figure 1. Each temporal frame represents 4 s of sway behavior. Because, all trials were initiated with sensory conditions that resembled normal upright posture, sway behavior in T_1 was defined as the reference temporal frame. The frames T_2, T_6, T_{10} represent temporal frames immediately after the subjects closed their eyes. The frames T_3, T_7, T_{11} represent temporal frames after vision had been withdrawn for 24 s. The frames T_4, T_8, T_{12} represent temporal frames immediately after the subject open their eyes. The frames T_5, and T_9 represent frames after vision had been available for the last 24 s. Finally, for the frame T_{13}, vision had been available for the last 16 s and it represents the last 4 s of data sampling.

For the different temporal frames, the range and standard deviation of the sway behavior in both planes were evaluated. The range indicated how far the participants' center of foot pressure (COP) deviated from the base of support, while the standard deviation gives the variability of balance reference over the sampled period. The range of the sway behavior, however, can be misleading as it does not provide information about the distribution of the COP within that range. Nevertheless, this experiment analyzed the sway behavior using this common measure as it represents a standard of comparison with other studies. In addition, a measure of sway derived from density histograms of the sway path (Harris et al., 1982) was used to evaluate the dispersion of the COP. To quantify these distributions the average COP of the reference frame was calculated first and the percentage of time the participants spent close to and away from the average COP was determined. From the analysis of the reference frames, it was found that both the elderly and the young adults spent more than 95% of their time within 12 mm of their COP. For this reason, the area within 12 mm of the average COP was defined as "close" while the area beyond 12 mm was defined as "away." Therefore, a wider or spread out sway behavior is indicated by a higher percentage of time spent away from the average COP.

Results

Sway behavior after the no-vision/vision transitions. From a purely sensory organization viewpoint, providing vision after a prolonged period when it has been withheld may be considered a perturbation. The subjects have to reconfigure the postural set to reintegrate visual input with information from vestibular and proprioceptive sources. The sway behavior obtained for the temporal frames T_4, T_8 and T_{12} was compared with that of the reference frame to determine whether elderly persons could rapidly reintegrate visual sensory inputs with vestibular and proprioceptive inputs. The data obtained for the range and the variability of the sway path were submitted to 2 x 4 x 2 (group x temporal frame by direction of sway) ANOVAs with repeated measures on the last two factors. The range obtained for the anterior-posterior and the lateral planes were always similar (ps > .05) and for this reason, the results for the two directions of sway were pooled together.

No group difference were found for the range of sway (F (1,12) = 1.55, p > .05 for the main effect of Group and F (3,36) = 0.63, p > .05 for the interaction of Group by Temporal frame). The main effect of frame was significant (F (3,36) = 4.78, p < .01) and a comparison of the means showed that the sway range obtained for T_4, T_8 and T_{12} were all larger than that obtained for the reference frame: 10.4 vs. 12.8, 12.7, and 13.1 mm for T_1, T_4, T_8 and T_{12}, respectively (F (1,12) = 8.14, 5.26, and 6.27, ps < .05). Similar results were obtained for the variability of the COP (F (1,12) = 1.60, p > .05 for the main effect of Group, and F (3,36) = 0.57, p > .05 for the interaction of Group by Temporal frame). The main effect of frame was significant (F (3,36) = 4.13, p < .01) and the comparison of the means showed that the variability obtained for T_4, T_8 and T_{12} were all larger than that obtained for the reference frame: 2.7 vs. 3.3, 3.2, and 3.3 mm for T_1, T_4, T_8 and T_{12}, respectively (F (1,12) = 7.59, 4.92, and 4.56, ps < .05).

The data obtained for the dispersion of sway (i.e., the percentage of time subjects spent near their COP) were submitted to a 2 x 4 (group by temporal frame) ANOVA. Figure 2 shows the percentages of time spent near the mean COP as a function of the four temporal frames analyzed. When vision became available, the young adults stabilized their sway behavior and rapidly contained it within 12 mm of their initial COP: 95, 97, and 96% of their time within 12 mm of their initial COP for the frames T_4, T_8 and T_{12}, respectively compared to 100% for the reference frame. Such was not the case for the elderly as they spent only 64, 48, and 43% of their time within 12 mm of their initial COP for the frames T_4, T_8 and T_{12}, respectively, compared to 95% for the reference frame. The two-way interaction of Group by Frame was significant (F (3,36) = 5.15, p < .005). A decomposition of the interaction into its orthogonal components showed a significant linear trend (F (1,12) = 9.52, p < .01) suggesting that, following a no-vision/vision transition, the young persons spent a constant amount of time near their COP whereas the elderly showed an increased sway dispersion.

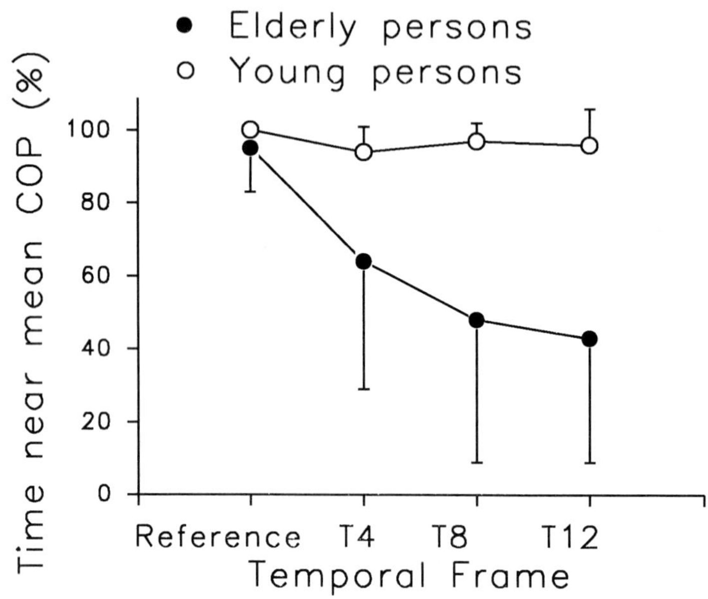

Figure 2. Percentage of time spent near the initial COP immediately following the no-vision/vision transitions.

To determine if, across the different temporal frames, the elderly simply stabilized their sway behavior in a different area, the mean COP (for both direction of sway) for the frames T_4, T_8 and T_{12} were compared with the reference frame. For all analyses, the group by temporal frame interaction not significant (p > .05) suggesting that, over time, the elderly did not simply stabilized their COP in a different area, but rather exhibited a greater sway dispersion. To further illustrate the greater sway dispersion exhibited by the elderly, the sway area was further sub-divided in 10 areas demarcated by 3 mm radiuses from the initial COP. Figure 3 shows the percentage of time spent by the young adults minus the percentage of time spent by the elderly for the ten areas. A positive value shows that the young adults spent more time in the area while a negative value shows the elderly spent more time in the area. Clearly, the elderly exhibited a greater sway dispersion than the young adults; overall, the elderly spent 20% more time than the younger subjects outside 9 mm of their mean COP.

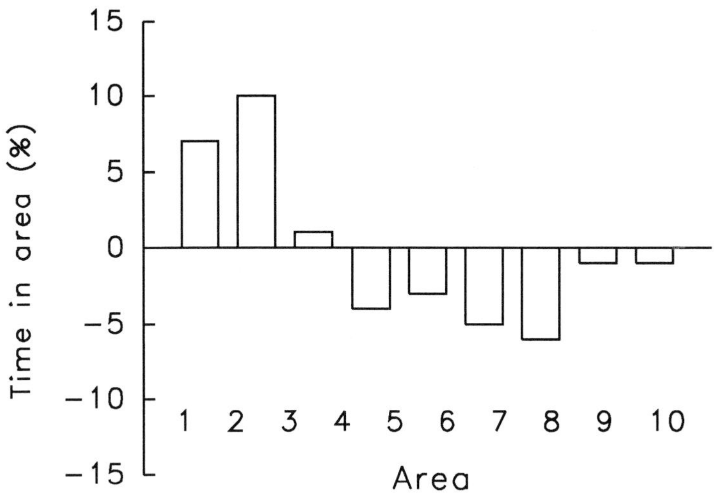

Figure 3. Percentage of time spent in ten different areas, demarcated by radiuses of 3 mm from the COP, immediately following the no-vision/vision transitions. The percentages spent by the young adults in the ten areas was subtracted from the percentages spent by the elderly. Thus, positive values indicate that young adults spent more time in an area than the elderly whereas negative values indicate the reverse.

Vision/no-vision vs. no-vision/vision transitions. The sway behaviors obtained for frames T_2, T_6 and T_{10} were also compared with those obtained for frames T_4, T_8 and T_{12} to determine whether the elderly were as affected by a no-vision/vision transition as by a vision/no-vision transition. The data obtained for the range and the variability of the sway path was submitted to a 2 x 4 x 2 (group x temporal frame x transition) ANOVAs with repeated measures on the last two factors. The main effect of Transition was significant (F (1,12) = 12.05, $p < .005$) but the interaction of Group by Transition was not (F (1,12) = 0.01, $p > .05$). On average, the sway range immediately following a no-vision/vision transition was 12.8 mm while it was 17.3 mm following a vision/no-vision transition. Similar results were obtained for the variability of the sway path (4.4 vs. 3.3 mm, F (1,12) = 12.16, $p < .005$ for the main effect of Transition and F (1,12) = 0.00, $p > .05$ for the two-way interaction of Group by Transition). Thus, the range and variability data suggest that both groups were more affected by a vision/no-vision transition than by a no-vision/vision transition.

The sway dispersion data were submitted to a similar ANOVA. The interaction of Group by Transition was significant (F (1,12) = 7.65, $p < .05$) and is presented in figure 4. The young adults used rapidly vision after a no-vision/vision transition as their percentage of time spent near their COP was 83% for the vision/no-vision transitions and 96% for the no-vision/vision transitions. On the contrary, the elderly showed a greater dispersion after the no-vision/vision transitions than after the vision/no-vision transitions (66% vs. 52%). This result highlights the inability of elderly to rapidly reconfigure the postural set when visual information is suddenly provided after a prolonged period without it.

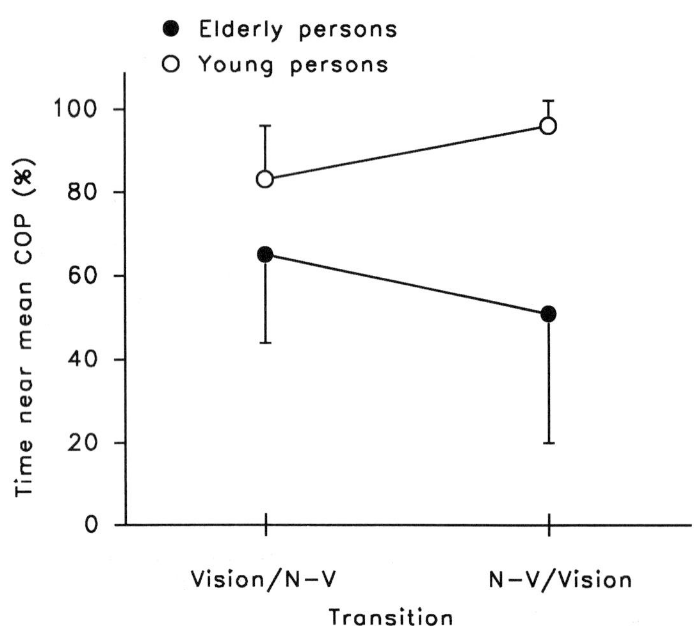

Figure 4. Comparison of the percentage of time spent near the initial COP immediately following the vision/no-vision and the no-vision/vision transitions.

Discussion

The data are consistent with past experiments showing that elderly are more affected than young adults by the withdrawal of vision. When sufficient time was given, both groups reduced their sway range but the older subjects were not able to contain their sway behavior within an area as small as that of the reference frame. On average, the elderly spent only 73% of their time near their COP while the young persons spent more than 87% of their time near their COP. The most striking result, however, is the inability of the elderly persons to reconfigure the postural set following no-vision/vision transitions. Because the no-vision/vision transitions provided greater sensory information as opposed to reduced sensory information as in prior experiments, the decreased stability observed in the elder's balance cannot be explained only by a reduction in the integrity of the peripheral sensory systems. Rather, the increased sway dispersion exhibited by the elderly is a reflection of problems of the central integrative mechanisms responsible for configuring the postural set after changing sensory conditions.

EXPERIMENT 2: ATTENTIONAL REQUIREMENTS FOR MAINTAINING AN UPRIGHT POSTURE

If the locus of the postural deficits observed in the first experiment is central, it is possible to suggest that the micro-postural adjustments necessary for maintaining balance require some cognitive processing. For example, a more eccentric less stable position of the COP could require more attention than a stable position of the COP because when the eccentric position has been identified, a corrective response needs to be subsequently selected, programed, and executed. Within such a cognitive framework, a decreased of the attentional capacities and/or a defect in the allocation of the ressources available could affect the postural stability. From an ecological perspective, maintaining an upright posture is most often a task that subserve an additional task (e.g., reading or talking) and attentional deficits could potentiate the slowness of the corrective postural responses in elderly persons. The aim of the second experiment was to determine if the attentional demands for maintaining an upright posture increased with age and with the nature of the sensory information available.

Methods

Subjects. Nine elderly (6 men, 3 women, mean age= 71.1) and 8 young adults (8 men, mean age = 24.6) participated in the experiment. The selection procedures were similar to that of experiment 1. All subjects were naive as to the purpose of the experiment.

Apparatus and Procedures. The general apparatus was similar to that of the first experiment. In addition to standing feet together on a force platform, the subject's task was to respond as rapidly as possible to an unpredictable auditory stimulus by pressing a handheld button. Each subject's mean COP and range for a condition with vision was initially computed. For each subject, the values obtained served to demarcate regions near and away their mean COP that corresponded to 80% and 130% of their range. Auditory stimulus were then given randomly as a function of the on-line evaluation of the subject's COP position.

Subjects were given auditory stimulus in four conditions of vision/surface that is (a) vision/normal surface, (b) no-vision/normal surface, (c) vision/altered surface, and (d) no-vision/altered surface. The visual and surface conditions were altered to determine if additional attentional ressources need to be allocated to the postural task when there is a reduction of the sensory information available. The four visual/surface conditions were presented randomly (16 trials of 40 s). For each trial, a maximum of 3 randomly presented auditory stimuli separated by at least 1 s could be presented. The position of the COP was displayed on an oscilloscope and a trial was initiated only when the subject was close to their COP.

Finally, before the beginning of the different visual/surface conditions, subjects were submitted to two control conditions in which their RT to an auditory stimulus was evaluated in a seated position and in an upright normal position. For each of these two conditions, 24 randomly presented stimulus were given. The mean RTs obtained for these two conditions were subtracted from the RTs obtained for the visual/surface conditions. This procedure allows to evaluate more precisely the cognitive processing associated with the postural task without the perceptual and velocity conductions differences associated with normal aging.

Results

On average, the RTs for the seated/upright positions were 175 and 219 ms for the young and the elderly persons, respectively. The Vision/Normal surface and Vision/Altered surface conditions yielded no eccentric sway behavior for all subjects and as result prevented the use of a completely balanced ANOVA design. Further, the Altered vision/Normal surface condition yielded eccentric sway behavior in only 4 young and 5 elderly persons. The number of subjects, average number of trials per subject and the average RTs obtained for the different conditions are presented in Table 1.

To examine the attentional demands of the experimental task, the RTs obtained for the seated and the upright conditions were first compared with the RTs for the Vision/Normal surface condition (see figure 5). The RTs for the elderly persons were longer than those of the young persons (on average, 229 vs. 185 ms; $F\ (1,14) = 6.70$, $p < .05$). For both groups, the RTs for the seated and the upright conditions were shorter than for the Vision/Normal surface conditions ($F\ (2,28) = 45.84$, $p < .001$, for the main effect of condition). A post-hoc comparison of means (T-method) showed that the RTs for the vision/normal surface condition were significantly longer than that of the upright and the seated conditions ($Q_{.05,28}$ = 11.65). Therefore, it appears that a smaller support surface (i.e., feet together) stresses the postural system and requires the allocation of additional attentional resources to the postural task.

The modified RTs obtained for the different sensory conditions (Vision/Normal surface, No vision/Normal surface, Vision/Altered surface and No vision/Altered surface) when subjects were near their mean COP (concentric conditions) were compared to examine the variation in attentional demands as function of the sensory information available. Overall, the elderly were slower to respond to the stimulus than the young persons (67 vs. 43 ms; $\underline{F}$ (1,13) = 6.08, $\underline{p}$ < .05). The elderly were also more affected by the withdrawal of vision than the young persons (increase of 28 vs. 8 ms, respectively; $\underline{F}$ (1,13) = 6.74, $\underline{p}$ < .05). This interaction of Group by Vision is lillustrated in figure 6a. The interaction of Vision by Surface was also significant ($\underline{F}$ (1,13) = 5.76, $\underline{p}$ < .05); for both groups, the modified RTs were faster when subjects had vision and stood on a normal surface than in all other conditions. Thus, when subjects were near their mean COP, a decreased of the sensory information available stressed the postural system and required that additional attentional resources be allocated to the postural task.

Table 1. Number of subjects, trials, and RTs obtained for the different visual and surface conditions.

	Vision				No-vision			
	Normal surface		Altered surface		Normal surface		Altered surface	
	Conc	Ecc	Conc	Ecc	Conc	Ecc	Conc	Ecc
Elderly								
N	9	0	9	0	9	5	9	9
n	18(6)		17(8)		13(5)	4(5)	16(3)	11(6)
RT	260(42)		278(57)		296(70)	345(102)	291(63)	307(55)
Young								
N	8	0	8	0	8	4	8	8
n	19(2)		19(3)		17(5)	5(6)	15(3)	15(6)
RT	208(26)		219(36)		222(31)	215(50)	220(33)	222(53)

Conc = Concentric, Ecc = Eccentric. N indicates the number of subjects that exhibited the specific sway behavior; n indicates the average number of trials and its standard deviation; RT indicates the average reaction time and its standard deviation.

To evaluate if the control of posture requires additional attentional ressources when the subjects' COP is in an eccentric area, the transformed RTs obtained for the no-vision/normal surface and the no-vision/altered surface conditions when subjects were near and away from their mean COP were compared using a 2 x 2 x 2 (Group x Surface x Eccentricity) ANOVA with repeated measures on the last two factors. The position of the COP did not affect the young adults' response (48 ms for both the concentric and the eccentric conditions) but greatly affected the elderly's response 83 ms for the concentric conditions vs. 110 ms for the eccentric condition). This interaction of Group by Eccentricity (see figure 6b) was statistically significant ($\underline{F}$ (1,6) = 12.46, $\underline{p}$ < .01).

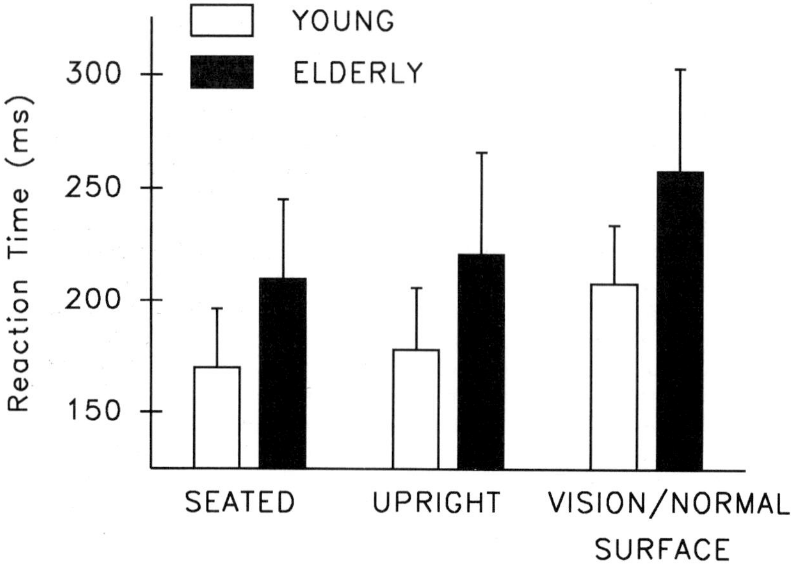

Figure 5. Reaction times for the seated, upright, and vision/normal surface conditions.

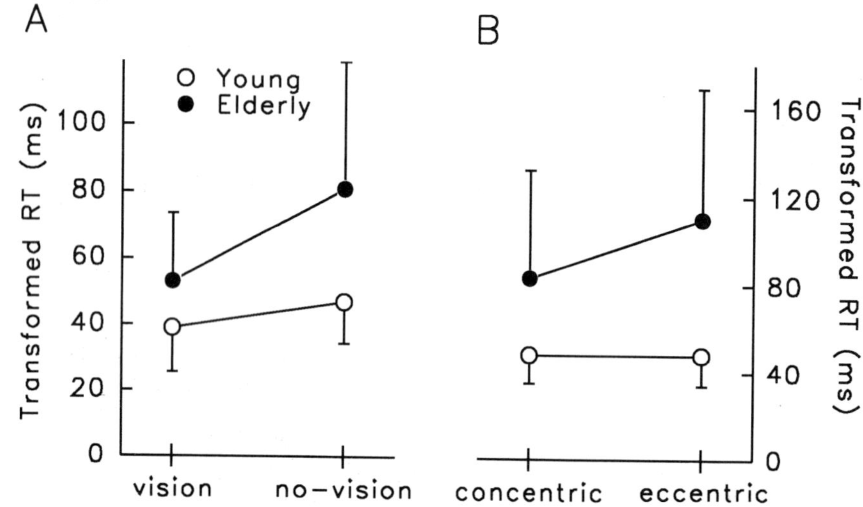

Figure 6. A.Transformed RTs when subjects were near their COP for the vision and no-vision conditions. B.Transformed RTs when subjects had no-vision and were near (concentric) or away (eccentric) from their mean COP.

GENERAL DISCUSSION

The two studies presented in this paper aimed at examining the importance of central deficits for the regulation of upright posture. Both experiments support the hypothesis that central processes are an important determinant of posture control. In the first experiment, the no-vision/vision transitions provided greater sensory information as opposed to reduced sensory information. After a period without vision, the elderly persons were unable to rapidly use the visual information to stabilize their sway. The increased sway dispersion exhibited by the elderly persons imply a defect or a slowing of the central integrative mechanisms responsible for reconfiguring the postural control system after changing sensory conditions (Straube et al., 1988; Teasdale et al., 1991). The results do not trivialize the importance of peripheral sensibility for posture control (Horak et al., 1989; Manchester et al., 1989; Woollacott et al., 1986), rather they suggest an interdependence between the peripheral sensory systems and the central cognitive systems. For example, it is possible that the reconfiguring task increases in difficulty and becomes less accurate with a reduced peripheral sensibility.

The second experiment also suggest an important role for the central integrative mechanisms. As sensory information decreased, the postural task became more and more difficult for the elderly and required more of their attentional capacity (as indexed by the increasingly long RTs). A common observation in the aging cognitive literature is that the amount of slowing in processing information is related to the difficulty or complexity of the task (e.g., Cerella et al., 1980; McDowd & Craik, 1988). There is also evidence that, with increasing age, it is more and more difficult to perform two tasks at once (e.g., Baron et al., 1988; Craik & Byrd, 1982). Thus, the aging literature suggests that aging reduces the processing capacity and impairs the ability to divide attention and to properly allocate the ressources between concurrent tasks. In the present experiment, the reduced peripheral sensibility conditions increased the complexity for the central integrative mechanisms and as a result stressed the attentional system. Because of a reduced peripheral sensibility, the elderly persons had to devote more of the attentional ressources to the postural task.

The results of both experiments highlight the importance of studying more carefully the interactions existing between the central and the peripheral systems and their evolution with age. It is when the quality and quantity of sensory information available decreased (altered surface and/or withdrawal of the visual information) that the attentional demands for the postural task increased the most suggesting that a deterioration of the peripheral sensory systems could potentiate balance problems in the elderly. Recently, many authors stressed the importance of studying the interface between peripheral and more central systems (e.g., Paillard, 1985; Posner & Petersen, 1990; Sperry, 1988). For example, Sperry (1988, p.609) described the interface between mental concepts and the anatomical level common in neuroscience:

> Control from below upward is retained but is claimed to not furnish the whole story. The full explanation requires that one take into account new, previously nonexistent, emergent properties, including the mental, that interact causally at their own higher level and also exert causal control from above downward.

We believe the present experiments provides a basis for further research studying this interface or interdependence between the sensori-motor and the cognitive systems for the control of posture.

REFERENCES

Baron, A., Myerson, J., & Hale, S. (1988). An integrated analysis of the structure and function of behavior: Aging and the cost of dividing attention. In G. Davey & C. Cullen (Eds.), Human operant conditioning and behavior modification (pp. 139-166). New York: John Wiley & Sons.

Cerella, J., Poon, L. W., & Williams, D. M. (1980). Age and the complexity hypothesis. In L. W. Poon (Ed.), Aging in the 1980s (pp. 332-339). Washington (DC): American Psychological Association.

Craik, F. I. M. (1977). Age differences in human memory. In J. E. Birren & K. W. Schaie (Eds.), Handbook of the psychology of aging (pp. 384-420). New York: Van Nostrand Reinhold.

Craik, F. I. M., & Byrd, M. (1982). Aging and cognitive deficits: The role of attentional ressources. In F. I. M. Craik & S. E. Trehub (Eds.), Advances in the study of communication and affect: Aging and cognitive processes (pp. 191-211). New York: Plenum Press.

Era, P., & Heikkinen, E. (1985). Postural sway during standing and unexpected disturbance of balance in random samples of men of different ages. Journal of Gerontology: Medical Sciences, 40, 287-295.

Harris, G. F., Knox, T. A., Larson, S. J., Sances, A., & Millar, E. A. (1982). A method for the display of balance platform center of pressure data. Journal of Biomechanics, 15, 741-745.

Horak, F. B., Diener, H. C., & Nashner, L. M. (1989). Influence of central set on human postural responses. Journal of Neurophysiology, 62, 841-853.

Manchester, D., Woollacott, M., Zederbauer-Hylton, N., & Marin, O. (1989). Visual, vestibular and somatosensory contributions to balance control in the older adult. Journal of Gerontology: Medical Sciences, 44, M118-127.

McDowd, J. M., & Craik, F. I. M. (1988). Effects of aging and task difficulty on divided attention performance. Journal of Experimental Psychology: Human Perception & Performance, 14, 267-280.

Murray, M. P., Seireg, W. A. A., & Sepic, S. B. (1975). Normal postural stability and steadiness: Quantitative assessment. The Journal of Bone and Joint Surgery, 57A, 510-516.

Paillard, J. (1985). Les niveaux sensori-moteur et cognitif du contrôle de l'action. In M. Laurent & P. Therme (Eds.), Recherches en activité physique et sportive 1 (pp. 147-163). Marseille: Publication du centre de recherche de l'U.E.R.E.P.S.
Posner, M. I., & Petersen, S. E. (1990). The attention system of the human brain. Annual Reviews of Neurosciences, 13, 25-42.
Salthouse, T. A. (1985). A theory of cognitive aging . Amsterdam: Elsevier.
Sheldon, J. H. (1963). The effect of age on the controle of sway. Gerontologia Clinica, 5, 129-138.
Sperry, R. L. (1988). Psychology's mentalist paradigm and the religion/science tension. American Psychologist, 43, 607-613.
Stelmach, G. E., & Worringham, C. J. (1985). Sensorimotor deficits related to postural stability: Implications for falling in the elderly. Clinics in Geriatric Medecine, 1, 679-694.
Stelmach, G. E., Teasdale, N., DiFabio, R. P., & Phillips, J. (1989). Age related decline in postural control mecanisms. International Journal on Aging and Human Development, 29, 205-223.
Straube, A., Bötzel, K., Hawken, M., Paulus, W., & Brandt, T. (1988). Postural control in the elderly: Differential effects of visual, vestibular and somatosensory input. In B. Amblard, A. Berthoz, & F. Clarac (Eds.), Posture and gait: Development, adaptation and modulation (pp. 105-114). Amsterdam: Elsevier.
Teasdale, N., Stelmach, G. E., & Breunig, A. (1991). Postural sway characteristics of eldery persons under normal and altered visual and support surface conditions. Journal of Gerontology: Medical Sciences, (in press).
Woollacott, M. H., Shumway-Cook, A., & Nashner, L. M. (1986). Aging and posture control: Changes in sensory organization in muscular coordination. International Journal on Aging and Human Development, 23, 97-114.

ACKNOWLEDGEMENTS

This research was supported by various NSERC, and FCAR grants to Normand Teasdale, Chantal Bard and Michelle Fleury and by a NIA grant to George E. Stelmach. Special thanks to Benoit Genest and Gilles Bouchard for programming and technical expertise and to Ann Brunig and Harry Meewsen for help in collecting data for experiment 1.

AUTHOR INDEX

SUBJECT INDEX